HISTORY OF THE ARABS

HISTORY
OF
THE ARABS

FROM THE EARLIEST TIMES
TO THE PRESENT

PHILIP K. HITTI

FORMERLY
PROFESSOR EMERITUS OF SEMITIC LITERATURE
PRINCETON UNIVERSITY

REVISED TENTH EDITION
NEW PREFACE BY WALID KHALIDI

First edition 1937
Second edition 1940
Third edition 1943
Fourth edition 1949
Fifth edition 1951
Sixth edition 1956
Seventh edition 1960
Eighth edition 1963
Ninth edition 1967
Tenth edition 1970
Revised tenth edition 2002
Published by
PALGRAVE MACMILLAN
Houndmills, Basingstoke, Hampshire RG21 6XS and
175 Fifth Avenue, New York, N. Y. 10010
Companies and representatives throughout the world

PALGRAVE MACMILLAN is the global academic imprint of the Palgrave Macmillan division of St. Martin's Press, LLC and of Palgrave Macmillan Ltd. Macmillan® is a registered trademark in the United States, United Kingdom and other countries. Palgrave is a registered trademark in the European Union and other countries.

ISBN-13: 978-0-333-63141-6 hardback
ISBN-10: 0-333-63141-2 hardback
ISBN-13: 978-0-333-63142-3 paperback
ISBN-10: 0-333-63142-0 paperback

This book is printed on paper suitable for recycling and made from fully managed and sustained forest sources. Logging, pulping and manufacturing processes are expected to conform to the environmental regulations of the country of origin.

A catalogue record for this book is available from the British Library.

Library of Congress Catalog Card Number: 2002026744

9
10 09 08

Printed in China

PREFACE TO THE REVISED TENTH EDITION

This reissue of the tenth (1970) edition of Philip K. Hitti's monumental *History of the Arabs* will be welcomed by all his many admirers and by teachers and students of the Arab and Muslim worlds wherever they may be.

The republication of this great work in the second year of the twenty-first century is also supremely timely for the general English-speaking public in Europe and the United States. With the collapse of the Soviet Union and the end of the cold war Western interest has increasingly focused on Islam. Facile theories of the so-called Clash of Civilizations have abounded. Fundamentalism, in all world religions is on the rise. Muslim minorities and others of Arab origin have grown in number in many European countries and in North America. Western dependence on oil in Arab and Muslim countries continues for the foreseeable future. Regional conflicts in Muslim or Arab countries have brought about in recent years massive Western military intervention in Lebanon, Bosnia, Somalia, Iraq, Kosovo and Afghanistan. Despite peace treaties between Israel and both Jordan and Egypt and the internationally sponsored Madrid peace conference of 1991, the Palestinian–Israeli conflict rages unabated in the Holy Land.

The horrendous events of 11 September in New York and Washington have unleashed a US-led global war against terrorism rightly or wrongly seen by many to have an essentially Muslim or Arab cultural provenance. Concurrently the level of understanding by the general Western public of Arab and Muslim history and civilization remains at a dismally inadequate level. This is manifested on an almost daily basis in the output of the audio-visual media and is often reflected in the glib generalizations of even leading Western pundits and senior officials. In short, never before has there been a greater need in the Western world and particularly in the United States – its paramount leader – for an authoritative and scholarly work on the Arab and Muslim peoples to tell the story as it is without passion or partisanship. Of all the many works that I know, I can think of no one other than Philip K. Hitti's *History of the Arabs* to fulfil this imperative educational purpose.

It was Mr Daniel Macmillan who, in 1927, first commissioned Hitti to write his *History*. The author laboured for ten years to accomplish the task. Already in 1937 the first edition was a *tour de force* of scholarship, the fruit of years of teaching and study at Columbia University, the American University of Beirut and Princeton University. Since 1937 nine editions have appeared, the last in 1970. During this period the *History* was translated into many languages including Arabic, Spanish, Urdu, Italian, Serbo-Croat and Polish.

Each edition elicited tens of review articles by leading experts in their countries of origin. Corrections, suggestions and criticisms came from colleagues and research assistants working under the author. The work was further enriched by ongoing class discussions with generations of students, since it formed the basis of the author's own university course offerings. Simultaneously he kept a watchful eye on new publications in various languages on topics touched upon in his *History* as well as on the latest edited versions of medieval Arabic texts. Meanwhile the author travelled at least once a year, visiting or revisiting at one time or another every Arab country covered in his work and discussing its contents with countless Arab scholars, teachers and students. The *History* was thus essentially a work in progress for more than four decades, incorporating the rich harvest of all this accumulated input – a unique depository of facts and insights about the Arabs and Islam.

A History of the Arabs lays down in some 700 pages a solid infrastructure of knowledge altogether indispensable for understanding developments that followed. It spans more than a millennium of history from pre-Islamic times – pagan, Judaic Christian (the Arabs were Christians before they were Muslim) – until the Ottoman Turkish conquest of the Arab world in the early sixteenth century. Five of the six parts, which constitute the bulk (more than 90 per cent) of the *History* cover this period. Part VI is a bird's-eye view, in broad brush strokes in some 50 pages, of developments political, social and cultural in the Arab world from the Ottoman conquest until the time of publication in 1970. Remarkable and enlightening as Part VI is, the core of the *History* is parts I to V.

In these principal components of the *History* the story is told of the origins of the Arabs, the emergence of Muhammad the Arabian Prophet and the rise of Islam, and the early Righteous Caliphate. The *History* then traces the breathtaking spread of Islam within decades of its foundation across North Africa, into the Iberian Peninsula, across the Pyrenees and up to Poitiers in France in the West, to Byzantine Anatolia in the North and to Western China in the East.

The *History* chronicles the rise and fall of the two central Arab caliphates, the Umayyad (661–750) and the Abbasid (750–1258) based in Damascus and Baghdad respectively – the latter until its capital was overrun and destroyed by the Mongol hordes under Hulagu. It tells the story of the efflorescence of Arab civilization and of its immense contributions to the European Renaissance. It describes the centrifugal forces tearing at imperial unity, the succession of provincial dynasties in Egypt, Spain and elsewhere, and the penetration of the metropolitan Arab elite by non-Arab Muslim elements, Persian, Turkic, Berber and Mamluk, and its resultant fragmentation.

The *History* is mindful of the continuous cultural cross-fertilization process between East and West in philosophy, science, trade, the arts and architecture even during periods of military confrontation, as during the Crusades (1097–1291) and the Christian *Reconquista* in Spain (1085–1492). It is equally mindful of the major contributions to Arab and Muslim civilization by Jews, Christian Arabs, and non-Arab Muslim peoples. The *History* never flinches from a "warts and all" approach and is clear-eyed about sectarian schisms and other internal causes of decline and decay. It never loses sight of the overall picture and brilliantly subsumes an extraordinary mass of details within an easily flowing, often witty, narrative enlivened by direct quotes from scores of original texts: poems, travelogues, speeches and decrees. Political, dynastic and military developments never overshadow social, economic, administrative and intellectual ones: of the fifty-two chapters that make up the entire corpus, fully twenty are exclusively set aside to the latter.

The successive chapters of the *History* are enriched by some 70 illustrations of buildings, coins, portraits of individuals and *objets d'art*; by twenty-one maps and twenty-five dynastic tables. Innumerable subheadings in the margins accompany the text for easier reference. More than 2,000 footnotes cite the primary medieval Arabic sources – a hallmark of this work – as well as the best products of Western orientalism. A voluminous 62-page index of places, personal names and Arabic terms is an invaluable guide to this teasure trove.

Philip K. Hitti, by origin a Maronite Christian from Lebanon, was born in 1886 in the village of Shemlan overlooking Beirut, some five miles away as the crow flies. He received his BA from the American University of Beirut and his Ph.D. from Columbia University, New York. In 1927, when commissioned by Daniel Macmillan to write the *History*, he was assistant professor of Semitic literature at Princeton University, New Jersey, where he became professor of Semitic literature and chairman of the department of oriental languages and literature until his retirement in 1954. He was also visiting professor at the University of Sao Paulo, Brazil and Harvard University. In 1940 his name was inscribed at New York World's Fair among American citizens of foreign birth who made "notable contributions" to American democracy. In 1966, he was awarded a Litt.D. by Princeton Univesity. He died in Princeton in 1978.

It is a great honour and privilege for me to have been asked to write this preface. Let us hope that the reprinting in these difficult times of Philip K. Hitti's *History of the Arabs* will serve the purpose of bridge building between the Western and Arab worlds, which was the lifelong ambition of a foremost historian of the Arab world and a preeminent scholar of the United States.

Walid Khalidi
Former Senior Fellow, Center of
Middle East Studies, Harvard University
Fellow, American Academy of Arts and Sciences,
Cambridge, Massachusetts

PREFACE TO THE TENTH EDITION

THE year 1970 marks the thirty-third anniversary of the publication of *History of the Arabs* and witnesses its tenth edition. The initiative for its writing was taken by Mr. Daniel Macmillan, who, as early as 1927, wrote to the author suggesting a book comparable to Ameer Ali, *A Short History of the Saracens*, first published by Macmillan and Co. in 1900. The occurrence of the word "Saracens" in the title left no doubt about the obsolete character of the work.

In my youthful enthusiasm I signed a contract in 1927 agreeing to deliver the manuscript in three years. (A representative of Macmillan, who was then touring the Arab world, suggested an Arabic version of the book and I thought I could do that in a couple of subsequent years.) When the book at last appeared, in 1937, the New York publisher (before St. Martin's Press) asked my opinion as to the number of copies to be imported and when I offhand suggested a hundred, he shot back, "Who is going to buy that many?"

As a matter of fact the American public, even at its educated level, was then almost illiterate so far as the Arabs and Moslems were concerned. The rare courses in this field were limited to a few graduate schools and offered as subsidiary to Semitic studies and as contributory to philology or linguistics. Nowhere were such courses given for their own sake or as a key to further investigation of Arab history, Islam and Islamic culture. This was substantially the situation until the second World War. It was not until then that the American government and public were awakened to the fact that here are millions of Moslems and tens of thousands of Arabs with whom they had to deal and of whom they should have some understanding.

The demand, subsequent to the appearance of the first English edition, for translation rights—not only into Arabic but into varied Asian and European languages—left no doubt about the timeliness of the work and its capacity to meet the need. It is gratifying to note that since the publication of the ninth edition four years ago new versions have appeared in Italian, Serbo-Croat and Polish.

In this edition, as in earlier ones, an effort was made to take into consideration the results of new researches, to update the material in text and footnote, and to plug that seemingly inexhaustible supply of errors—otherwise called typographical. About sixty sheets, including four maps, have been thus treated.

P. K. H.

January, 1970

PREFACE TO THE FIRST EDITION

THIS is a modest attempt to tell the story of the Arabians and the Arabic-speaking peoples from the earliest times to the Ottoman conquest of the early sixteenth century. It represents many years of study and teaching at Columbia University, the American University of Beirut and Princeton University, and is designed to meet the needs of the student as well as the cultivated layman. The field it covers, however, is so extensive that the author cannot claim to have carried his independent researches into every part of it. He therefore had to appropriate in places the results of the investigation of other scholars in the East and in the West, to whom his indebtedness would have been more apparent had the selected bibliographies appended to each chapter in the manuscript appeared in the printed book.

While in preparation certain chapters of the book were submitted to various scholars for their criticism. Among those who made a distinct contribution were Professor A. T. Olmstead, of the University of Chicago; Dr. Walter L. Wright, Jr., now president of Robert College, Istanbul; Dr. Costi Zurayq, of the American University of Beirūt, Lebanon; and two of my colleagues, Professor Henry L. Savage and Professor Albert Elsasser, of the Department of English.

For several years the manuscript was made the basis of a graduate course, and it benefited considerably from suggestions and criticisms offered by my students. Among these special mention should be made of George C. Miles, now of Rayy, Persia; Buṭrus 'Abd-al-Malik, of Assiut College, Egypt; Edward J. Jurji, of Baghdad; Harold W. Glidden; Richard F. S. Starr; and Nabih A. Faris, of Jerusalem. Dr. Faris rendered further service by collaborating in sketching the maps, reading the proofs and compiling the index.

To all these gentlemen, as well as to my wife, who co-operated in typewriting the manuscript and proposed several improvements, my hearty thanks are due.

P. K. H.

CORLEAR BAY CLUB
LAKE CHAMPLAIN, NEW YORK

CONTENTS

PART I

THE PRE-ISLAMIC AGE

CHAPTER VI

CHAPTER VII

PART II

THE RISE OF ISLAM AND THE CALIPHAL STATE

CHAPTER VIII

CHAPTER IX

CHAPTER X

CHAPTER XI

CHAPTER XII

CHAPTER XIII

CHAPTER XIV

CHAPTER XV

CHAPTER XVI

PART III

THE UMAYYAD AND 'ABBĀSID EMPIRES

CHAPTER XVII

CHAPTER XVIII

CHAPTER XIX

CHAPTER XX

CHAPTER XXI

CHAPTER XXII

CHAPTER XXIII

CHAPTER XXIV

CHAPTER XXV

CHAPTER XXVI

CHAPTER XXVII

CHAPTER XXVIII

CHAPTER XXIX

CHAPTER XXX

CHAPTER XXXI

CHAPTER XXXII

CHAPTER XXXIII

PART IV

THE ARABS IN EUROPE: SPAIN AND SICILY

CHAPTER XXXIV

CHAPTER XXXV

CHAPTER XXXVI

CHAPTER XXXVII

CHAPTER XXXVIII

CHAPTER XXXIX

CHAPTER XL

CHAPTER XLI

CHAPTER XLII

PART V

THE LAST OF THE MEDIEVAL MOSLEM STATES

CHAPTER XLIII

CHAPTER XLIV

CHAPTER XLV

CHAPTER XLVI

CHAPTER XLVII

CHAPTER XLVIII

CHAPTER XLIX

PART VI

OTTOMAN RULE AND INDEPENDENCE

CHAPTER L

CHAPTER LI

CHAPTER LII

LIST OF ILLUSTRATIONS

LIST OF MAPS

PART I

THE PRE-ISLAMIC AGE

CHAPTER I

THE ARABS AS SEMITES

ARABIA THE CRADLE OF THE SEMITIC RACE

Claims on our interest

Of all the lands comparable to Arabia in size, and of all the peoples approaching the Arabs in historical interest and importance, no country and no nationality have perhaps received so little consideration and study in modern times as have Arabia and the Arabs.

Here is a country that is about one-fourth the area of Europe, one-third the size of the United States of America, yet what is known about it is out of all proportion to what is unknown. We are beginning to know more, comparatively speaking, about the Arctic and Antarctic regions than we do about most of Arabia.

As the probable cradle of the Semitic family the Arabian peninsula nursed those peoples who later migrated into the Fertile Crescent and subsequently became the Babylonians, the Assyrians, the Phoenicians and the Hebrews of history. As the plausible fount of pure Semitism, the sandy soil of the peninsula is the place wherein the rudimentary elements of Judaism, and consequently of Christianity—together with the origin of those traits which later developed into the well-delineated Semitic character—should be sought for. In medieval times Arabia gave birth to a people who conquered most of the then civilized world, and to a religion—Islam—which still claims the adherence of some four hundred and fifty millions of people representing nearly all the races and many different climes. Every eighth person in our world today is a follower of Muḥammad, and the Moslem call to prayer rings out through most of the twenty-four hours of the day, encircling the larger portion of the globe in its warm belt.

Around the name of the Arabs gleams that halo which belongs to the world-conquerors. Within a century after their rise this people became the masters of an empire extending from the shores of the Atlantic Ocean to the confines of China, an empire greater than that of Rome at its zenith. In this period of unprecedented expansion they "assimilated to their creed, speech, and even physical type, more aliens than any stock before or since, not excepting the Hellenic, the Roman, the Anglo-Saxon, or the Russian".[1]

It was not only an empire that the Arabs built, but a culture as well. Heirs of the ancient civilization that flourished on the banks of the Tigris and the Euphrates, in the land of the Nile and on the eastern shore of the Mediterranean, they likewise absorbed and assimilated the main features of the Greco-Roman culture, and subsequently acted as a medium for transmitting to medieval Europe many of those intellectual influences which ultimately resulted in the awakening of the Western world and in setting it on the road towards its modern renaissance. No people in the Middle Ages contributed to human progress so much as did the Arabians and the Arabic-speaking peoples.[2]

The religion of the Arabians, after Judaism and Christianity, is the third and latest monotheistic religion. Historically it is an offshoot of these other two, and of all faiths it comes nearest to being their next of kin. All three are the product of one spiritual life, the Semitic life. A faithful Moslem could with but few scruples subscribe to most of the tenets of Christian belief. Islam has been and still is a living force from Morocco to Indonesia and a way of life to millions of the human race.

The Arabic language today is the medium of daily expression for some hundred million people. For many centuries in the Middle Ages it was the language of learning and culture and progressive thought throughout the civilized world. Between the ninth and the twelfth centuries more works, philosophical, medical, historical, religious, astronomical and geographical, were produced through the medium of Arabic than through any other tongue. The languages of Western Europe still bear the impress of its influence in the form of numerous loan-words. Its alphabet, next to the Latin, is the most widely used system in the world. It is the one employed by Persian, Afghan, Urdu, and a number of Turkish, Berber and Malayan languages.

[1] D. G. Hogarth, *The Penetration of Arabia* (New York, 1904), p. 7.

[2] On the distinction between Arabians and Arabs (Arabic-speaking peoples) as used in this book see below, p. 43, n. 3.

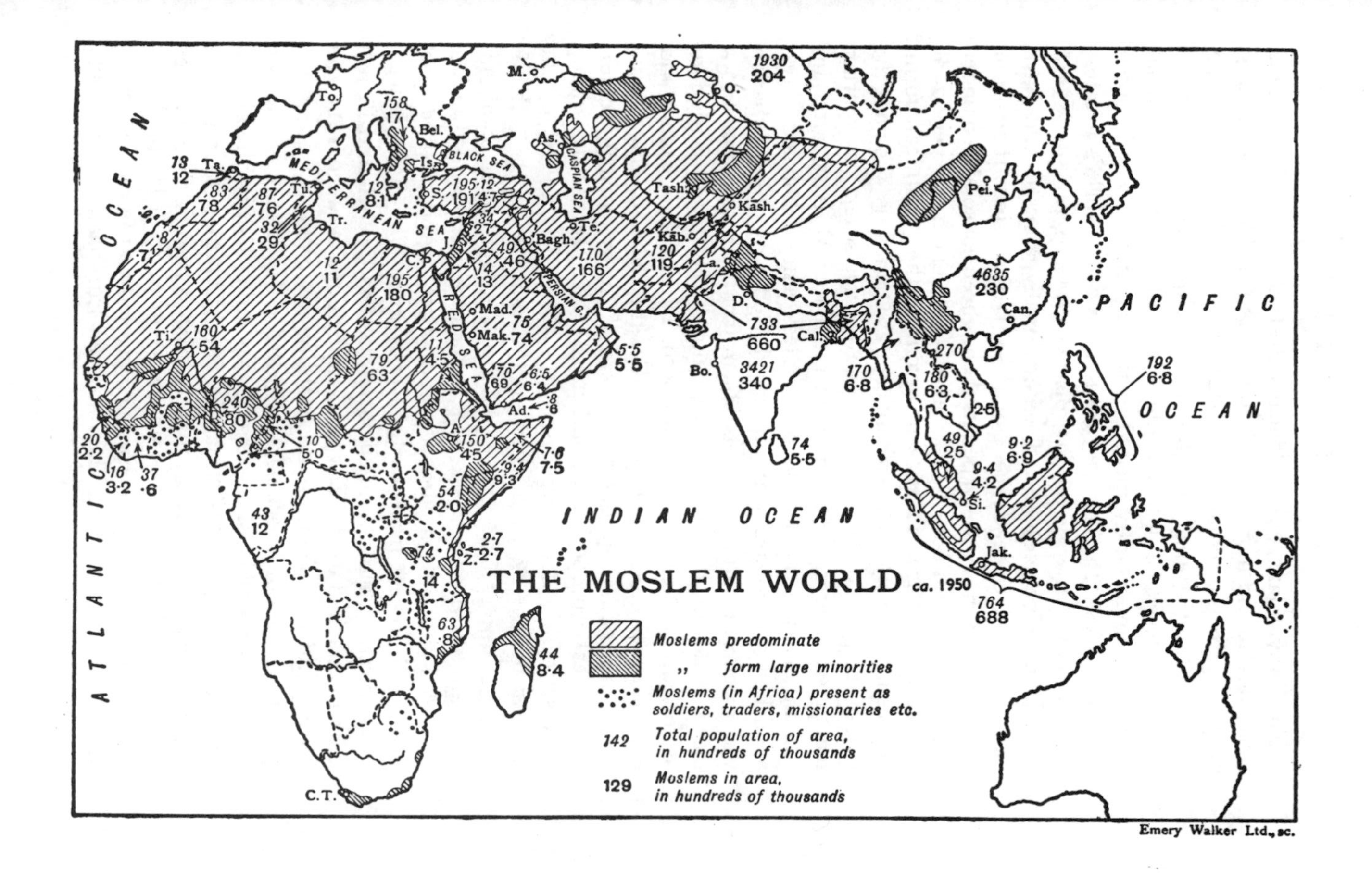
THE MOSLEM WORLD ca. 1950
Moslems predominate
,, form large minorities
Moslems (in Africa) present as soldiers, traders, missionaries etc.
142 Total population of area, in hundreds of thousands
129 Moslems in area, in hundreds of thousands
ATLANTIC OCEAN
INDIAN OCEAN
PACIFIC OCEAN
MEDITERRANEAN SEA
BLACK SEA
CASPIAN SEA
RED SEA
PERSIAN G.
To.
Bel.
M.
O.
As.
Ta.
Tu.
Tr.
Is.
S.
C.
J.
Bagh.
Te.
Tash.
Kāsh.
Kāb.
La.
D.
Mad.
Mak.
Ad.
A.
Z.
Ti.
C.T.
Bo.
Cal.
Pei.
Can.
Si.
Jak.
Emery Walker Ltd., sc.

The Babylonians, the Chaldaeans, the Hittites, the Phoenicians were, but are no more. The Arabians and the Arabic-speaking peoples were and remain. They stand today as they stood in the past in a most strategic geographical position astride one of the greatest arteries of world trade. Currently their international position is importantly medial in the tug of cold war between East and West. In their soil are treasured the world's greatest stores of liquid energy, oil, first discovered in 1932. Since World War I these peoples have been nationally aroused and have achieved full independence. For the first time since the rise of Islam most of the Arabian peninsula has been consolidated under one rule, the Su'ūdi. Egypt, after experiencing a period of monarchy, declared in 1952 in favour of the republican form. In this it followed Syria—whose capital Damascus was once the seat of the glorious Umayyad empire—which seven years earlier had freed itself from the French mandate. Al-'Irāq, after installing a king in Baghdād, kingless since 'Abbāsid days, abolished the monarchy and declared itself a republic. Lebanon was the first to adopt the republican form. Transjordan and a part of Palestine developed in 1949 into the Hāshimite Kingdom of Jordan. In North Africa Morocco, Tunisia, Mauritania and Algeria shook off the French and Libya the Italian tutelage in the 1950s and 1960s. The phœnix, a bird of Araby, is rising again.

Modern explorations

Classical Europe knew southern Arabia: Herodotus, among others, mentions its western coast. The chief interest of the Greeks and the Romans lay in the fact that the South Arabians inhabited the frankincense and spice land and acted as a connecting link with the markets of India and Somaliland. But late medieval and early modern Europe forgot Arabia in great part and had in recent times to discover it anew. The pioneers were adventurers, Christian missionaries, traders, French and British officers attached to the Egyptian expeditions between 1811 and 1836, political emissaries and scientific explorers.

The first modern scholar to describe the land was Carsten Niebuhr, a member of a scientific expedition sent by the king of Denmark in 1761. Al-Yaman in South Arabia, the part best known to classical Europe, was the first to be rediscovered. The north-western part of the peninsula, centring in al-Ḥijāz, though geographically nearer to Europe, was left to the end. Down to the present day no more than a dozen Europeans of those who left records have succeeded in penetrating into this religiously forbidden area.

In 1812 Johann Ludwig Burckhardt, a Swiss, discovered Petra for the learned world, and under the name Ibrāhīm ibn-'Abdullāh visited Makkah and al-Madīnah. His description of the places visited has hardly since been improved upon. Burckhardt's Moslem tomb stands today in the great cemetery of Cairo. The only other European until 1925 who had a chance to study Makkah in its normal life was Professor Snouck Hurgronje of Leyden, who was there in 1885–6. In 1845 a young Finno-Swedish scholar, George Augustus Wallin, paid a visit to Najd for linguistic study. Napoleon III, after withdrawing his troops from Lebanon in 1861, sought a new sphere of influence in central Arabia and thereinto sent, two years later, an Englishman, William Gifford Palgrave, who was a Jew by birth and who at that time, as a member of the Jesuit order, was stationed at Zaḥlah, Lebanon. Palgrave claimed that he covered more ground south of Najd than he actually did. In 1853 Sir Richard F. Burton, famous as the translator of *The Arabian Nights*, visited the holy cities as a pilgrim—al-Ḥājj 'Abdullāh. Lady Anne Blunt, one of two European women to penetrate north Arabia, reached (1879) Najd on several odd missions, including the quest of Arabian horses. In 1875 an Englishman, Charles M. Doughty, traversed northern Arabia as a "Naṣrâny" (Christian) and "Engleysy". His record of the journey, *Travels in Arabia Deserta*, has become a classic of English literature. T. E. Lawrence's *Seven Pillars of Wisdom* has been greeted as a work of special merit in the literature of the first World War. Among the latest explorers may be mentioned a Czechoslovak, Alois Musil, who specialized on the northern territory; and among the recent travellers, the Lebanese-American Ameen Rihani, who interviewed all the kings of the peninsula, and Eldon Rutter, who visited Makkah and al-Madīnah in 1925–6. A special reference should be made to the brave feat of Bertram Thomas, the young English orientalist, who in January 1931 crossed for the first time the great southern desert of Arabia, al-Rab' al Khāli, and bared one of the largest blank spots left on the world's map. His adventure was matched by H. St.J. B. Philby, al-Ḥājj 'Abdullāh, who, starting at al-Hufūf near the Persian Gulf on January 7, 1932, crossed al-Rab' al-Khāli from east to west in ninety days.

The Ḥimyarite inscriptions which afforded us the first opportunity to hear what the South Arabians had to say about themselves were discovered by a Frenchman disguised as a Jewish beggar from Jerusalem, Joseph Halévy, 1869–70, and by an Austrian Jew, Eduard Glaser, between 1882 and 1894 (see below, p. 51). The copious but late and not fully authentic Islamic literature in Arabic, the sporadic Greek and Latin references and the few hieroglyphic and cuneiform statements in the annals of the Pharaohs and the kings of Assyro-Babylonia, supplemented by the recently deciphered Ḥimyarite material and by the reports of the modern travellers and explorers, constitute our chief sources of knowledge of ancient Arabia.

Ethnic relationship: the Semites

Of the two surviving representatives of the Semitic people, the Arabians, in a larger measure than the Jews, have preserved the characteristic physical features and mental traits of the family. Their language, though the youngest among the Semitic group from the point of view of literature, has, nevertheless, conserved more of the peculiarities of the mother Semitic tongue —including the inflection—than the Hebrew and its other sister languages. It therefore affords the best key for the study of the Semitic languages. Islam, too, in its original form is the logical perfection of Semitic religion. In Europe and America the word "Semite" has come to possess a primarily Jewish connotation, and that on account of the wide dispersion of the Jews in these continents. The "Semitic features" often referred to, including the prominent nose, are not Semitic at all. They are exactly the characteristics which differentiate the Jew from the Semitic type and evidently represent an acquisition from early intermarriages between the Hittite-Hurrians and the Hebrews.[1]

The reasons which make the Arabian Arabs, particularly the nomads, the best representatives of the Semitic family biologically, psychologically, socially and linguistically should be sought in their geographical isolation and in the monotonous uniformity of desert life. Ethnic purity is a reward of the most ungrateful and isolated environment, such as central Arabia affords. The Arabians call their habitat *Jazīrat al-ʿArab*, "the Island of the Arabs", and an island it is, surrounded by water on three sides

[1] George A. Barton, *Semitic and Hamitic Origins* (Philadelphia, 1934), pp. 85-7; Ignace J. Gelb, *Hurrians and Subarians* (Chicago, 1944), pp. 69-70.

and by sand on the fourth. This "island" furnishes
unique example of uninterrupted relationship between
and soil. If any immigrations have ever taken place
resulting in successive waves of settlers ousting or sub
one another—as in the case of India, Greece, Italy, England and the United States—history has left us no record thereof. Nor do we know of any invader who succeeded in penetrating the sandy barriers and establishing a permanent foothold in this land. The people of Arabia have remained virtually the same throughout all the recorded ages.[1]

The term Semite comes from Shem in the Old Testament (Gen. 10 : 1) through the Latin of the Vulgate. The traditional explanation that the so-called Semites are descended from the eldest son of Noah, and therefore racially homogeneous, is no longer accepted. Who are the Semites then?

If we consult a linguistic map of Western Asia we find Syria, Palestine, Arabia proper and al-ʿIrāq populated at the present time by Arabic-speaking peoples. If we then review our ancient history we remember that beginning with the middle of the fourth millennium before our era the Babylonians (first called Akkadians after their capital Akkadu, Agade), the Assyrians and later the Chaldaeans occupied the Tigro-Euphrates valley; after 2500 B.C. the Amorites and Canaanites (including the Phoenicians) populated Syria; and about 1500 B.C. the Aramaeans settled in Syria and the Hebrews in Palestine. Down to the nineteenth century the medieval and modern world did not realize that all these peoples were closely related. With the decipherment of the cuneiform writing in the middle of the nineteenth century and the comparative study of the Assyro-Babylonian, Hebrew, Aramaic, Arabic and Ethiopic tongues it was found that those languages had striking points of similarity and were therefore cognates. In the case of each one of these languages the verbal stem is triconsonantal; the tense has only two forms, perfect and imperfect; the conjugation of the verb follows the same model. The elements of the vocabulary, including the personal pronouns, nouns denoting blood-kinship, numbers and certain names of members of the body, are almost alike. A scrutiny of the social institutions and religious beliefs and a comparison of

[1] Cf. Bertram Thomas in *The Near East and India* (London, Nov. 1, 1928), pp. 516-19; C. Rathjens in *Journal asiatique*, ccxv. No. 1 (1929), pp. 141-55.

the physical features of the peoples who spoke these languages have revealed likewise impressive points of resemblance. The linguistic kinship is, therefore, but a manifestation of a well-marked general unity of type. This type was characterized by deep religious instinct, vivid imagination, pronounced individuality and marked ferocity. The inference is inescapable: the ancestors of these various peoples—Babylonians, Assyrians, Chaldaeans, Amorites, Aramaeans, Phoenicians, Hebrews, Arabians and Abyssinians—before they became thus differentiated must have lived at some time in the same place as one people.

Arabia, the cradle of the Semites

Where was the original home of this people? Different hypotheses have been worked out by various scholars. There are those who, considering the broad ethnic relationship between Semites and Hamites, hold that eastern Africa was the original home; others, influenced by Old Testament traditions, maintain that Mesopotamia provided the first abode; but the arguments in favour of the Arabian peninsula, considered in their cumulative effect, seem most plausible. The Mesopotamian theory is vitiated by the fact that it assumes passage of people from an agricultural stage of development on the banks of a river to a nomadic stage, which is the reverse of the sociological law in historic times. The African theory raises more questions than it answers.

The surface of Arabia is mostly desert with a narrow margin of habitable land round the periphery. The sea encircles this periphery. When the population increases beyond the capacity of the land to support it the surplus must seek elbow room. But this surplus cannot expand inward because of the desert, nor outward on account of the sea—a barrier which in those days was well-nigh impassable. The overpopulation would then find one route open before it on the western coast of the peninsula leading northward and forking at the Sinaitic peninsula to the fertile valley of the Nile. Around 3500 B.C. a Semitic migration followed this route, or took the east African route northward, planted itself on top of the earlier Hamitic population of Egypt and the amalgamation produced the Egyptians of history. These are the Egyptians who laid down so many of the basic elements in our civilization. It was they who first built stone structures and developed a solar calendar. At about the same time a parallel migration followed the eastern route northward and struck root in the Tigro-Euphrates valley, already populated by a highly civilized community, the Sumerians.[1] The Semites entered the valley as barbarian nomads, but learned from the Sumerians, the originators of the Euphratean civilization, how to build and live in homes, how to irrigate the land and above all how to write. The Sumerians were a non-Semitic people. The admixture of the two races here gave us the Babylonians, who share with the Egyptians the honour of laying down the fundamentals of our cultural heritage. Among other innovations, the Babylonians bequeathed to us the arch and the vault (probably of Sumerian origin), the wheeled cart and a system of weights and measures.

About the middle of the third millennium before Christ another Semitic migration brought the Amorites into the Fertile Crescent. The component elements of the Amorites included the Canaanites (who occupied western Syria and Palestine after 2500 B.C.) and the coastal people called by the Greeks Phoenicians. These Phoenicians were the first people to popularize an exclusively alphabetic system of writing, comprising twenty-two signs, properly styled the greatest invention of mankind (cf. below, p. 71).

Between 1500 and 1200 B.C. the Hebrews made their way into southern Syria, Palestine, and the Aramaeans (Syrians) into the north, particularly Coele-Syria.[2] The Hebrews, before any other people, revealed to the world the clear idea of one God, and their monotheism became the origin of Christian and Moslem belief.

About 500 B.C. the Nabataeans established themselves north-east of the Sinaitic peninsula. The height to which their civilization later attained under Roman influence may be gauged by the magnificent ruins of their rock-hewn capital, Petra.

The seventh century of our era saw a new and final migration under the banner of Islam, in the course of which the dam broke and not only the lands of the Fertile Crescent, the region forming an arc between the head of the Persian Gulf and the south-east corner of the Mediterranean Sea, but even Egypt, northern Africa, Spain, Persia and parts of central Asia were flooded.[3]

This last migration, which took place within the full light of history, is cited as an historical argument by the supporters of

[1] Cf. C. Leonard Woolley, *The Sumerians* (Oxford, 1929), pp. 5-6.

[2] Hollow Syria, modern al-Biqā', between the two Lebanons.

[3] Hugo Winckler, *The History of Babylonia and Assyria*, tr. James A. Craig (New York, 1907), pp. 18-22.

the theory of Arabia as the Semitic home; they further reinforce their case by the observation that the Arabians have preserved the Semitic traits more purely and have manifested them more distinctly than any other members of that racial group, and that their language is most nearly akin to what scholars believe the primitive form of Semitic speech to have been.

A comparative examination of the dates quoted above suggested to certain Semitists the notion that in recurrent cycles of approximately one thousand years Arabia, like a mighty reservoir, became populated to the point where overflow was inevitable. These same scholars would speak of the migrations in terms of "waves". It is more likely, however, that these Semitic movements partook in their initial stages more of the nature of the European migrations into the New World: a few persons would start moving, others would follow, then many more would go, until a general popular interest was aroused in the idea of going.

This transplantation *en masse* or in bands of human groups from a pastoral desert region to an agricultural territory constitutes a common phenomenon in the Near East and provides an important clue to the understanding of its long and checkered history. The process by which a more or less migratory people imposes itself upon a people which has become rooted in the soil usually results in the invaders assimilating to some degree the main features of the previously existing civilization and in infusing a certain amount of its blood, but hardly ever in the extermination of the indigenous population. This is exactly what happened in the ancient Near East, whose history is to a certain extent a struggle between the sedentary population already domiciled in the Fertile Crescent and the nomadic Arabians trying to dispossess them. For immigration and colonization are, as has been well said, an attenuated form of invasion.

It should be noted in connection with these migrations that in almost every case the Semitic tongue survived. This is a determining factor. If in Mesopotamia, for example, the agglutinative Sumerian language had survived it would have been difficult for us to classify the people of the valley as Semitic. In the case of the ancient Egyptians a Semito-Hamitic language evolved, and we cannot very well include the Egyptians among the Semites. The term "Semite", therefore, has more linguistic than ethnological implication, and the Assyro-Babylonian, Aramaic, Hebrew, Phoenician, South Arabic, Ethiopic and Arabic languages should be viewed as dialects developing out of one common tongue, the *Ursemitisch*. A parallel may be found in the case of the Romance languages in their relation to Latin, with the exception that some form of Latin has survived, in literature at least, to the present day, whereas the Semitic archetype, only a spoken language, has entirely passed away, though its general character may be inferred from whatever points are found common to its surviving daughters.

Accepting Arabia—Najd or al-Yaman—as the homeland and distributing centre of the Semitic peoples does not preclude the possibility of their having once before, at a very early date, constituted with another member of the white race, the Hamites, one community somewhere in eastern Africa; it was from this community that those who were later termed Semites crossed over into the Arabian peninsula, possibly at Bāb al-Mandab.[1] This would make Africa the probable Semito-Hamitic home and Arabia the cradle of the Semitic people and the centre of their distribution. The Fertile Crescent was the scene of the Semitic civilization.

[1] Barton, p. 27

CHAPTER II

THE ARABIAN PENINSULA

The setting of the stage

ARABIA is the south-western peninsula of Asia, the largest peninsula on the map. Its area of 1,027,000 square miles holds an estimated population of only fourteen millions. Su'ūdi Arabia, with an area (exclusive of al-Rab' al-Khāli) of 597,000 square miles, claims some seven millions; al-Yaman five millions; al-Kuwayt, Qaṭar, the trucial shaykhdoms, 'Umān and Masqaṭ, Aden and the Aden protectorate the rest. Geologists tell us that the land once formed the natural continuation of the Sahara (now separated from it by the rift of the Nile valley and the great chasm of the Red Sea) and of the sandy belt which traverses Asia through central Persia and the Gobi Desert. In earlier times the Atlantic westerlies, which now water the highlands of Syria-Palestine, must have reached Arabia undrained, and during a part of the Ice Age these same desert lands must have been pre-eminently habitable grasslands. Since the ice sheet never extended south of the great mountains in Asia Minor, Arabia was never made uninhabitable by glaciation. Its deep, dry wadi beds still bear witness to the erosive powers of the rainwater that once flowed through them. The northern boundary is ill-defined, but may be considered an imaginary line drawn due east from the head of the Gulf of al-'Aqabah in the Red Sea to the Euphrates. Geologically, indeed, the whole Syro-Mesopotamian desert is a part of Arabia.

The peninsula slopes away from the west to the Persian Gulf and the Mesopotamian depression. Its backbone is a range of mountains running parallel to the western coast and rising to a height of over 9000 feet in Midian on the north and 14,000 in al-Yaman on the south.[1] Al-Sarāh in al-Hijāz reaches an elevation of 10,000 feet. From this backbone the eastern fall is gradual and long; the western, towards the Red Sea, is steep and short. The southern sides of the peninsula, where the sea has been

[1] The highest measured point: Carl Rathjens and Hermann v. Wissmann, *Südarabiens-Reise*, vol. iii, *Landeskundliche Ergebnisse* (Hamburg, 1934), p. 2.

receding from the coast at a rate reckoned at seventy-two feet per year, are fringed by lowlands, the Tihāmahs. Najd, the north central plateau, has a mean elevation of 2500 feet. Its mountain range, Shammar, lifts one red granite peak, Aja', 5550 feet above the sea-level. Behind the coastal lowlands rise ranges of various heights on all three sides. In 'Umān, on the eastern coast, the summits of al-Jabal al-Akhḍar soar to a height of 9900 feet, forming one notable exception to the general eastward decline of the surface of the land.

With the exception of the mountains and highlands just discussed the land consists mainly of desert and steppe. The steppes (sing. *dārah*) are circular plains between hills covered with sand and embosoming subterranean waters. The so-called Syrian desert, Bādiyat al-Sha'm, as well as the Mesopotamian desert, are mostly steppeland. The southern part of the Syrian desert is colloquially known as al-Ḥamād. The southern part of the Mesopotamian steppeland is often referred to as Bādiyat al-'Irāq or al-Samāwah.

Of the desert land three varieties may be distinguished:

1. The great Nufūd, a tract of white or reddish sand blown into high banks or dunes and covering a vast area in North Arabia. The classical term is *al-bādiyah*, sometimes *al-dahnā'*. Though dry except for an occasional oasis, al-Nufūd receives in some winters enough rain to cover it with a carpet of verdure and convert it into a paradise for the camels and sheep of the wandering Bedouin. Among the first of the dozen Europeans who have succeeded in traversing the Nufūd are the French Alsatian, Charles Huber (1878); the English diplomatist and poet, Wilfrid S. Blunt (1879); and the Strassburg orientalist, Julius Euting (1883).

2. Al-Dahnā' (the red land), a surface of red sand, extends from the great Nufūd in the north to al-Rab' al-Khāli in the south, describing a great arc to the south-east and stretching a distance of over six hundred miles. Its western part is sometimes distinguished as al-Aḥqāf (dune land). On older maps al-Dahnā' is usually indicated as al-Rab' al-Khāli (the vacant quarter). When al-Dahnā' receives seasonal rains, it abounds in pasturage attractive to the Bedouins and their cattle for several months a year, but in summer-time the region is void of the breath of life. Before Bertram Thomas[1] no European ever ventured to cross

[1] *Arabia Felix: Across the Empty Quarter of Arabia* (New York, 1932).

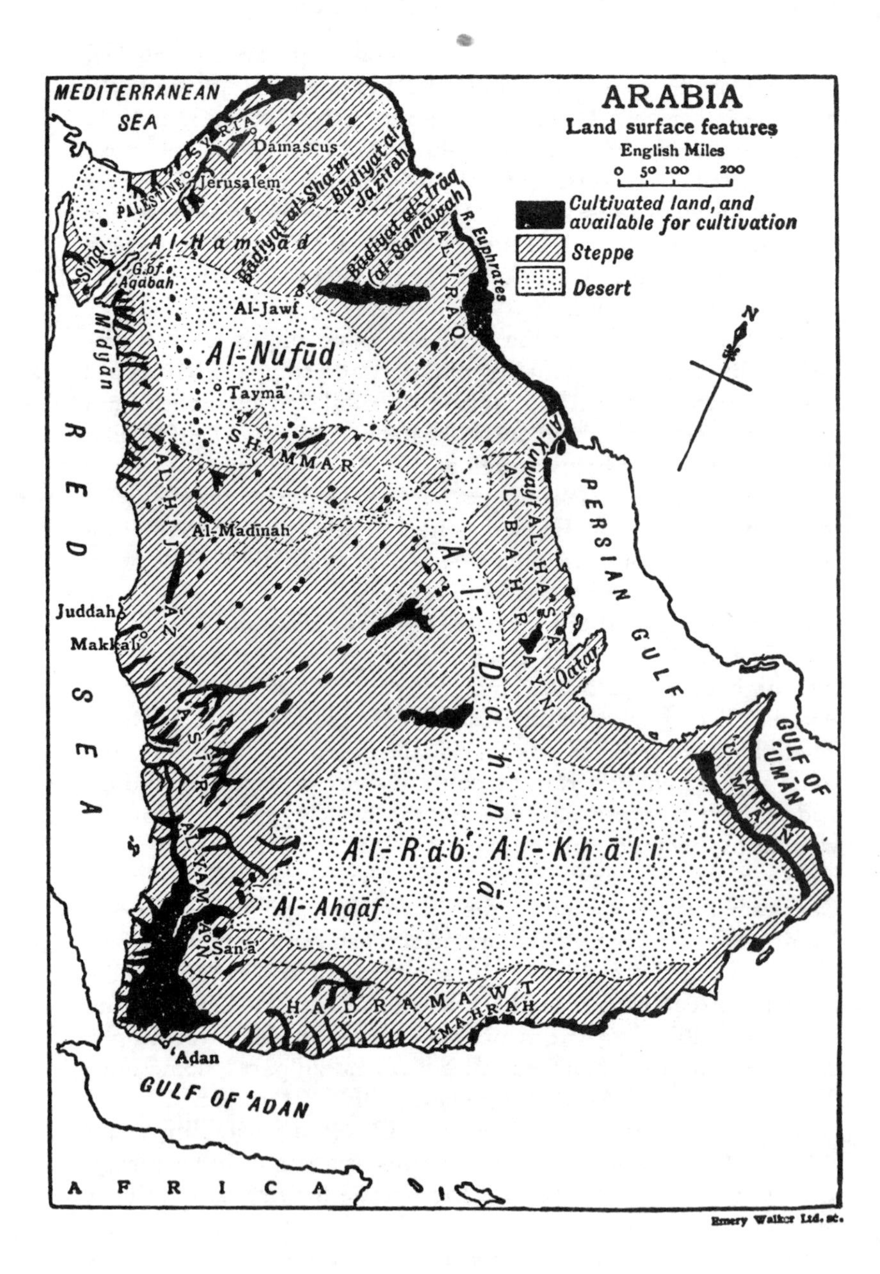

Emery Walker Ltd. sc.

al-Rabʿ al-Khāli, "no man's land" of Arabia. Arabian American Oil Company marked its 250,000 square miles on its maps. Thomas crossed it in fifty-eight days from the Arabian Sea to the Persian Gulf, encountered the phenomenon of singing sands and discovered a "lake of salt water", in reality an arm of the Persian Gulf in the south of Qaṭar. Until then our knowledge of the dreaded and mysterious waste of South Arabia was no more than that of the tenth-century geographers.

3. Al-Ḥarrah, a surface of corrugated and fissured lavas overlying sandstone. Volcanic tracts of this type abound in the western and central regions of the peninsula and extend north as far as eastern Ḥawrān. Yāqūt[1] lists no less than thirty such Ḥarrahs. The last volcanic eruption reported by an Arab historian took place in A.D. 1256.

Within this ring of desert and steppe lies an elevated core, Najd, the Wahhābiland. In Najd the limestone has long been generally exposed; here and there are occasional strips of sand. Mt. Shammar consists of granite and basalt rock.

Climatic conditions

Arabia is one of the driest and hottest of countries. Though sandwiched between seas on the east and west, those bodies of water are too narrow to break the climatic continuity of the Africo-Asian rainless continental masses. The ocean on the south, to be sure, does bring rains, but the simoom (*samūm*) which seasonally lashes the land leaves very little moisture for the interior. The bracing and delightful east wind (*al-ṣaba*) has always provided a favourite theme for Arabian poets.

In al-Ḥijāz, the birthplace of Islam, seasons of drought extending possibly over a period of three or more years are not unknown. Rainstorms of short duration and extraordinary violence may strike Makkah and al-Madīnah and occasionally threaten to overthrow the Kaʿbah; al-Balādhuri[2] devotes a whole chapter to the floods (*suyūl*) of Makkah. Subsequent to these rains the hardy pastoral flora of the desert makes its appearance. In northern al-Ḥijāz the isolated oases, the largest covering an area of some ten square miles, are the only support of settled life. Five-sixths of the population of al-Ḥijāz is nomadic. Certain oases, such as Fadak (now al-Ḥā'iṭ), which figured in early Islam, are

[1] *Muʿjam al-Buldān*, ed. F. Wüstenfeld (Leipzig, 1866–73), index.

[2] *Futūḥ al-Buldān*, ed. de Goeje (Leyden, 1866), pp. 53-5; tr. Philip K. Hitti, *The Origins of the Islamic State* (New York, 1916, reprint Beirūt, 1966), pp. 82-4.

today of no significance. Most of these fertile tracts were cultivated at the time of the Prophet by Jews. The mean annual temperature in the Ḥijāz lowland is nearer 90° than 80° F. Al-Madīnah, with a mean temperature of little over 70° F., is more healthful than its sister to the south, Makkah.

Only in al-Yaman and 'Asīr are there sufficient periodic rains to warrant a systematic cultivation of the soil. Perennial vegetation is here found in favoured valleys to a distance of about two hundred miles from the coast. Ṣan'ā', the modern capital of al-Yaman, is over 7000 feet above the sea and therefore one of the healthiest and most beautiful towns of the peninsula. Other fertile but not continuous tracts are found on the coast. The surface of Ḥaḍramawt is marked by deeply sunk valleys where water is abundant in the subsoil. 'Umān, the easternmost province, receives a fair supply of rain. Especially hot and humid are Juddah (Jedda), al-Ḥudaydah (Hodeida) and Masqaṭ (Muscat).

Arabia cannot boast a single river of significance which flows perennially and reaches the sea. None of its streams are navigable. In place of a system of rivers it has a network of wadis which carry away such floods as occur. These wadis serve another purpose: they determine the routes for the caravans and the pilgrimages. Since the rise of Islam the pilgrimages have formed the principal link between Arabia and the outer world. The chief land routes are from Mesopotamia, by way of Buraydah in Najd, following the Wādi al-Rummah, and from Syria, passing through Wādi al-Sirḥān and skirting the Red Sea coast. The intrapeninsular routes are either coastal, fringing nearly the whole peninsula, or transpeninsular, running from south-west to north-east through the central oases and avoiding the stretch between, namely, the Vacant Quarter.

The tenth-century geographer al-Iṣṭakhri[1] speaks of only one place in al-Ḥijāz, the mountain near al-Ṭā'if, where water freezes. Al-Hamdāni[2] refers to frozen water in Ṣan'ā'. To these places Glaser[3] adds Mt. Ḥaḍūr al-Shaykh, in al-Yaman, where snow falls almost every winter. Frost is more widespread.

Vegetation

The dryness of the atmosphere and the salinity of the soil

[1] *Masālik al-Mamālik*, ed. de Goeje (Leyden, 1870), p. 19, ll. 12-13.

[2] *Al-Iklīl*, Bk. VIII, ed. Nabih A. Faris (Princeton, 1940), p. 7; see also Nazīh M. al-'Aẓm, *Riḥlah fi Bilād al-'Arab al-Sa'īdah* (Cairo, 1937?), pt. 1, p. 118.

[3] In A. Petermann, *Mitteilungen aus Justus Perthes geographischer Anstalt*, vol. 32 (Gotha, 1886), p. 43.

militate against the possibility of any luxuriant growth. Al-Ḥijāz is rich in dates. Wheat grows in al-Yaman and certain oases. Barley is cultivated for horses. Millet (*dhurah*) grows in certain regions, and rice in 'Umān and al-Ḥasa. On the highlands parallel to the southern coast, and particularly in Mahrah, the frankincense tree, which figured prominently in the early commercial life of South Arabia, still flourishes. A characteristic product of 'Asīr is gum-arabic. The coffee plant, for which al-Yaman is now famous, was introduced into South Arabia in the fourteenth century from Abyssinia. The earliest reference to this "wine of Islam" is in the writings of the sixteenth century.[1] The earliest known mention of coffee by a European writer was in 1585.

Of the trees of the desert several species of acacia, including *athl* (tamarisk) and *ghaḍa*, which gives excellent charcoal, are found. Another species, *ṭalḥ*, yields gum-arabic. The desert also produces *samḥ*, the grains of which give a flour used for porridge, and the eagerly sought truffle and senna (*al-sana*).

Among the domestic plants the grape-vine, introduced from Syria after the fourth Christian century, is well represented in al-Ṭā'if, and yields the alcoholic beverage styled *nabīdh al-zabīb*. The wine (*khamr*), however, sung by the Arabic poets, was the brand imported from Ḥawrān and the Lebanon. The olive tree, native in Syria, is unknown in al-Ḥijāz. Other products of the Arabian oases are pomegranates, apples, apricots, almonds, oranges, lemons, sugar-cane, water-melons and bananas. The Nabataeans and Jews were probably the ones responsible for the introduction of such fruit trees from the north.

The date-palm

Among the Arabian flora the date-palm tree is queen. It bears the most common and esteemed fruit: the fruit (*tamr*) par excellence. Together with milk it provides the chief item on the menu of the Bedouin, and, except for camel flesh, is his only solid food.[2] Its fermented beverage is the much-sought *nabīdh*. Its crushed stones furnish the cakes which are the everyday meal of the camel. To possess "the two black ones" (*al-aswadān*), i.e. water and dates, is the dream of every Bedouin. The Prophet is reported to have enjoined, " Honour your aunt, the palm, which was made of the same clay as Adam".[3] Arab authors list

[1] See al-Jazīri in de Sacy, *Chrestomathie arabe*, 2nd ed. (Paris, 1826), vol. i, pp. 138 *seq.*, tr., pp. 412 *seq.*

[2] Consult ibn-Qutaybah, *'Uyūn al-Akhbār* (Cairo, 1930), vol. iii, pp. 209-13.

[3] Al-Suyūṭi, *Ḥusn al-Muḥāḍarah* (Cairo, 1321), vol. ii, p. 255.

a hundred varieties of dates in and around al-Madīnah.

Even this queen of Arabian trees must have been introduced from the north, from Mesopotamia, where the palm tree was the chief object which attracted early man thither. The Arabic vocabulary in Najd and al-Ḥijāz relating to agriculture, e.g. *ba'l* (watered by rain only),[1] *akkār* (ploughman), etc., indicates borrowing from the northern Semites, particularly the Aramaeans.

Fauna

The animal kingdom is represented by panthers (sing. *namir*), leopards (sing. *fahd*), hyenas, wolves, foxes and lizards (especially *al-ḍabb*). The lion, frequently cited by the ancient poets of the peninsula, is now extinct. Monkeys are found in al-Yaman. Among the birds of prey eagles (*'uqāb*), bustards (*ḥubāra*, houbara), falcons, hawks and owls may be counted. Crows are abundant. The most common birds are the hoopoe (*hudhud*), lark, nightingale, pigeon and a species of partridge celebrated in Arabic literature under the name *al-qaṭa*.[2]

Of domestic animals the principal ones are the camel, the ass, the ordinary watch-dog, the greyhound (*salūqi*), the cat, the sheep and the goat. The mule is said to have been introduced from Egypt after the Hijrah by Muḥammad.

The desert yields locusts, which the Bedouin relishes, especially when roasted with salt. Locust plagues are reputed to appear every seventh year. Of reptiles the Nufūd boasts, by all accounts, the horned viper. Lawrence[3] speaks with horror of his experience with the snakes in Wādi al-Sirḥān.

The Arabian horse

Renowned as it has become in Moslem literature, the horse was nevertheless a late importation into ancient Arabia. This animal, for which Najd is famous, was not known to the early Semites. Domesticated in early antiquity somewhere east of the Caspian Sea by nomadic Indo-European herdsmen, it was later imported on a large scale by the Kassites and Hittites and through them made its way, two millenniums before Christ, into Western Asia. From Syria it was introduced before the beginning of our era into Arabia, where it had the best opportunity to keep its blood pure and free from admixture. The Hyksos passed the horse on from Syria into Egypt and the Lydians from Asia Minor into Greece, where it was immortalized by Phidias on the

[1] See below, p. 97.

[2] See R. Meinertzhagen, *The Birds of Arabia* (Edinburgh, 1954).

[3] T. E. Lawrence, *Seven Pillars of Wisdom* (New York, 1936), pp. 269-70.

Parthenon. In the Egyptian, Assyro-Babylonian and early Persian records the Arabian appears as a cameleer, not as a cavalier. The camel, rather than the horse, figured in the tributes exacted by the Assyrian conquerors from the "Urbi".[1] In Xerxes' army, intent upon the conquest of Greece, the Arabs rode camels.[2] Strabo,[3] presumably on the authority of his friend Aelius Gallus, the Roman general who invaded Arabia as late as 24 B.C., denies the existence of the horse in the peninsula.

Renowned for its physical beauty, endurance, intelligence and touching devotion to its master, the Arabian thoroughbred (*kuḥaylān*) is the exemplar from which all Western ideas about the good-breeding of horseflesh have been derived. In the eighth century the Arabs introduced it into Europe through Spain, where it left permanent traces in its Barbary and Andalusian descendants.[4] During the Crusades the English horse received fresh strains of blood through contact with the Arab.

In Arabia the horse is an animal of luxury whose feeding and care constitutes a problem to the man of the desert. Its possession is a presumption of wealth. Its chief value lies in providing the speed necessary for the success of a Bedouin raid (*ghazw*). It is also used for sports: in tournament (*jarīd*), coursing and hunting. In an Arab camp today in case of shortage of water the children might cry for a drink, but the master, unmoved, would pour the last drop into a pail to set before the horse.

The camel

If the horse is the most noble of the conquests of man, the camel is certainly from the nomad's point of view the most useful. Without it the desert could not be conceived of as a habitable place. The camel is the nomad's nourisher, his vehicle of transportation and his medium of exchange. The dowry of the bride, the price of blood, the profit of *maysir* (gambling), the wealth of a sheikh, are all computed in terms of camels. It is the Bedouin's constant companion, his *alter ego*, his foster parent. He drinks its milk instead of water (which he spares for the cattle); he feasts on its flesh; he covers himself with its skin; he makes his tent of its hair. Its dung he uses as fuel, and its urine as a hair tonic and medicine. To him the camel is more than "the ship of the desert"; it is the special gift of Allah (cf.

[1] Below, pp. 39, 41.
[2] Herodotus, *History*, Bk. VII, ch. 86, § 8.
[3] *Geography*, Bk. XVI, ch. 4, §§ 2 & 26.
[4] William R. Brown, *The Horse of the Desert* (New York, 1929), pp. 123 *seq.*

Koran 16 : 5-8). To quote a striking phrase of Sprenger,[1] the Bedouin is "the parasite of the camel". The Bedouins of our day take delight in referring to themselves as *ahl al-baʿīr*, the people of the camel. Musil[2] states that there is hardly a member of the Ruwalah tribe who has not on some occasion drunk water from a camel's paunch. In time of emergency either an old camel is killed or a stick is thrust down its throat to make it vomit water. If the camel has been watered within a day or two, the liquid is tolerably drinkable. The part which the camel has played in the economy of Arabian life is indicated by the fact that the Arabic language is said to include some one thousand names for the camel in its numerous breeds and stages of growth, a number rivalled only by the number of synonyms used for the sword. The Arabian camel can go for about twenty-five days in winter and about five days in summer without water. The camel was a factor in facilitating the early Moslem conquests by assuring its masters more mobility than, and consequent advantage over, the settled peoples. The Caliph ʿUmar is quoted as having said: "The Arab prospers only where the camel prospers". The peninsula remains the chief camel-breeding centre in the world. The horses of Najd, the donkeys of al-Ḥasa and the dromedaries of ʿUmān are world famous. In the past the pearl fisheries of ʿUmān and the Persian Gulf region, the salt mines of certain areas and the camel industry were the main sources of income. But since the beginning of the exploitation of the oil-fields in 1933, the extensive activities connected with the oil industry have become by far the greatest source. The oil-fields of al-Ḥasa are classed among the richest in the world.

From north-western Arabia the camel, like the horse originally an American animal, was introduced into Palestine and Syria on the occasion of the invasion of the Midianites in the eleventh century B.C. (Judges 6 : 5, cf. Gen. 24 : 64), the first record of the widespread use of this animal.[3] It was introduced into Egypt with the Assyrian conquest in the seventh century B.C., and into northern Africa with the Moslem invasion in the seventh century after Christ.

[1] In *Zeitschrift der deutschen morgenländischen Gesellschaft*, xlv (1891), p. 361, l. 13.

[2] *The Manners and Customs of the Rwala Bedouins* (New York, 1928), p. 368. Cf. Bertram Thomas in *The Near East and India*, Nov. 1, 1928, p. 518.

[3] Cf. Carleton S. Coon, *Caravan: the Story of the Middle East* (New York, 1951), p. 61.

CHAPTER III

BEDOUIN LIFE

The nomad

CORRESPONDING to the twofold nature of the land, the inhabitants of Arabia fall into two main groups: nomadic Bedouins and settled folk. The line of demarcation between the wandering and the sedentary elements in the population is not always sharply drawn. There are stages of semi-nomadism and of quasi-urbanity. Certain townsfolk who were at one time Bedouin still betray their nomadic origin, while other Bedouins are townspeople in the making. The blood of the settled population is thus constantly refreshed by a nomadic strain.

The Bedouin is no gypsy roaming aimlessly for the sake of roaming. He represents the best adaptation of human life to desert conditions. Wherever verdant land is found, there he goes seeking pasture. Nomadism is as much a scientific mode of living in the Nufūd as industrialism is in Detroit or Manchester.

Action and reaction between the townsfolk and the desert folk are motivated by the urgent dictates of self-interest and self-preservation. The nomad insists on extracting from his more favourably situated neighbour such resources as he himself lacks, and that either by violence—raids—or by peaceful methods—exchange. He is land-pirate or broker, or both at once. The desert, where the Bedouin plays the part of the pirate, shares certain common characteristics with the sea.

The nomad, as a type, is today what he was yesterday and what he will be tomorrow. His culture pattern has always been the same. Variation, progress, evolution, are not among the laws he readily obeys. Immune to the invasion of exotic ideas and manners, he still lives, as his forbears did, in tents of goats' or camels' hair, "houses of hair", and grazes his sheep and goats in the same fashion and on the same pastures. Sheep- and camel-raising, and to a lesser degree horse-breeding, hunting and raiding, form his staple occupation and are to his mind the only occupations worthy of a man. Agriculture and all varieties of trade and craft are beneath his dignity. If and when he frees himself from his environment he is no more a nomad. In the Fertile Crescent empires have come and gone, but in the barren wastes the Bedouin has remained for ever the same.[1]

Over all the living things of the desert the Bedouin, the camel and the palm are the triumvirate that rules supreme; and together with the sand they constitute the four great actors in the drama of its existence.

To its denizen the desert is more than a habitat: it is the custodian of his sacred tradition, the preserver of the purity of his speech and blood and his first and foremost line of defence against encroachment from the outside world. Its scarcity of water, scorching heat, trackless roads, lack of food-supply—all enemies in normal times—prove staunch allies in time of danger. Little wonder then that the Arabian has rarely bent his neck to a foreign yoke.

The continuity, monotony and aridity of his desert habitat are faithfully reflected in the Bedouin physical and mental make-up. Anatomically he is a bundle of nerves, bones and sinews. The leanness and barrenness of his land show themselves in his physique. His daily food is dates and a mixture of flour, or roasted corn, with water or milk. His raiment is as scanty as his nourishment: a long shirt (*thawb*) with a belt and a flowing upper garment (*'abā'*) which pictures have made familiar. The head is covered by a shawl (*kūfīyah*) held by a cord (*'iqāl*). Trousers are not worn and footwear is rare. Tenacity, endurance (*ṣabr*), seems to be his supreme virtue, enabling him to survive where almost everything else perishes. Passivity is the obverse of this same virtue. Passive endurance is to him preferable to any attempt to change the state in which he finds himself, no matter how hard his lot. Individualism, another characteristic trait, is so deeply ingrained that the Bedouin has never been able to raise himself to the dignity of a social being of the international type, much less to develop ideals of devotion to the common good beyond that which pertains to the tribe. Discipline, respect for order and authority, are no idols in desert life. "O Lord", prayed a Bedouin, "have mercy upon me and upon Muḥammad, but upon no one else besides!"[2] Since the days of Ishmael the

[1] A central feature of ibn-Su'ūd's economic and social reforms is the settlement of nomads on the soil.
[2] Abu-Dāwūd, *Sunan* (Cairo, 1280), vol. i, p. 89.

Arabian's hand has been against every man and every man's hand against him.

Razzia

The *ghazw* (razzia), otherwise considered a form of brigandage, is raised by the economic and social conditions of desert life to the rank of a national institution. It lies at the base of the economic structure of Bedouin pastoral society. In desert land, where the fighting mood is a chronic mental condition, raiding is one of the few manly occupations. Christian tribes, too, such as the banu-Taghlib, practised it without any mental reservations. The poet al-Quṭāmi of the early Umayyad period has given expression to the guiding principle of such life in two verses: "Our business is to make raids on the enemy, on our neighbour and on our own brother, in case we find none to raid but a brother!" [1] In Su'ūdi Arabia raids are now illegal.

According to the rules of the game—and *ghazw* is a sort of national sport—no blood should be shed except in cases of extreme necessity. *Ghazw* does help to a certain extent to keep down the number of mouths to feed, though it does not actually increase the sum-total of available supplies. A weaker tribe or a sedentary settlement on the borderland may buy protection by paying the stronger tribe what is today called *khūwah*. These ideas of *ghazw* and its terminology were carried over by the Arabians into the Islamic conquests.

The principle of hospitality, however, mitigates in some measure the evils of *ghazw*. However dreadful as an enemy he may be, the Bedouin is also within his laws of friendship a loyal and generous friend. Pre-Islamic poets, the journalists of their day, never tired of singing the praises of *ḍiyāfah* (hospitality) which, with *ḥamāsah* (fortitude and enthusiasm) and *murū'ah* (manliness),[2] is considered one of the supreme virtues of the race. The keen competition for water and pasturage, on which the chief causes of conflict centre, splits the desert populace into warring tribes; but the common consciousness of helplessness in the face of a stubborn and malignant nature develops a feeling for the necessity of one sacred duty: that of hospitality. To refuse a guest such a courtesy in a land where no inns or hotels obtain, or to harm him after accepting him as a guest, is an

[1] Abu-Tammām, *Ash'ār al-Ḥamāsah*, ed. Freytag (Bonn, 1828), p. 171.
[2] Cf. Ignaz Goldziher, *Muhammedanische Studien*, pt. 1 (Halle, 1889), p. 13.

offence not only against the established mores and honour but against God Himself, the real protector.

Religiousness The rudiments of Semitic religion developed in the oases, rather than in the sandy land, and centred upon stones and springs, forerunners of the Black Stone and Zamzam in Islam and of Bethel in the Old Testament. In the case of the Bedouin, religion sits very lightly indeed on his heart. In the judgment of the Koran (9 : 98), "the desert Arabians are most confirmed in unbelief and hypocrisy". Up to our present day they never pay much more than lip homage to the prophet.[1]

The clan The clan organization is the basis of Bedouin society. Every tent represents a family; an encampment of tents forms a *ḥayy*; members of one *ḥayy* constitute a clan (*qawm*). A number of kindred clans grouped together make a tribe (*qabīlah*). All members of the same clan consider each other as of one blood, submit to the authority of but one chief—the senior member of the clan—and use one battle-cry. "Banu" (children of) is the title with which they prefix their joint name. The feminine names of certain clans show traces of the earlier matriarchal system. Blood relationship, fictitious or real, furnishes the adhesive element in tribal organization.

The tent and its humble household contents are individual property, but water, pasturage and cultivable land are the common property of the tribe.

If a member of a clan commits murder inside the clan, none will defend him. In case of escape he becomes an outlaw (*tarīd*). If the murder is outside the clan, a vendetta is established, and any fellow clan-member may have to pay for it with his own life.

Blood, according to the primitive law of the desert, calls for blood; no chastisement is recognized other than that of vengeance. The nearest of kin is supposed to assume primary responsibility. A blood feud may last forty years, as in the case of the Basūs War between the banu-Bakr and the banu-Taghlib. In all the *ayyām al-ʿArab*, those intertribal battles of pre-Islamic days, the chroniclers emphasize the blood feud motif, though underlying economic reasons must have motivated many of the events. Sometimes a bloodwite (*diyah*) is accepted.

No worse calamity could befall a Bedouin than to lose his

[1] Ameen Rihani, *Ta'rīkh Najd* (Beirū 928), p. 233.

tribal affiliation. A tribeless man, in a land where stranger and enemy are synonymous, like a landless man in feudal England, is practically helpless. His status is that of an outlaw, one beyond the pale of protection and safety.

Though primarily a matter of birth, clan kinship may be individually acquired by sharing a member's food or sucking a few drops of his blood. Herodotus [1] speaks of this ancient rite of adoption. If a slave is freed he often finds it to his interest to keep some attachment with the family of his former master, thus becoming a client (*mawla*). A stranger may seek such a relationship and is styled a protégé (*dakhīl*). In like manner a whole weaker clan might desire the protection of, and ultimately become absorbed by, a stronger clan or tribe. The Ṭayyi', Ghaṭafān, Taghlib, etc., were confederations of North Arabian tribes which figured prominently in history and whose descendants still survive in Arabic-speaking lands.

An analogous custom in religion made it possible for a stranger to become attached to the service of a sanctuary [2] and thus become a client of the god. To the present day the pilgrims to Makkah are referred to as "the guests of Allah", and the students connected with the mosque of Makkah or any other great mosque are called "[His] neighbours" (sing. *mujāwir*).

'Aṣabīyah

'Aṣabīyah is the spirit of the clan. It implies boundless and unconditional loyalty to fellow clansmen and corresponds in general to patriotism of the passionate, chauvinistic type. "Be loyal to thy tribe," sang a bard, "its claim upon its members is strong enough to make a husband give up his wife." [3] This ineradicable particularism in the clan, which is the individualism of the member of the clan magnified, assumes that the clan or tribe, as the case may be, is a unit by itself, self-sufficient and absolute, and regards every other clan or tribe as its legitimate victim and object of plunder and murder. Islam made full use of the tribal system for its military purposes. It divided the army into units based on tribal lines, settled the colonists in the conquered lands in tribes and treated new converts from among the subjugated peoples as clients. The unsocial features of individualism and *'aṣabīyah* were never outgrown by the Arab character as it developed and unfolded itself after the rise of Islam, and were

[1] Bk. III, ch. 8.
[2] Cf. Ezekiel 44:7.
[3] Al-Mubarrad, *al-Kāmil*, ed. W. Wright (Leipzig, 1864), p. 229, l. 3

among the determining factors that led to the disintegration and ultimate downfall of the various Islamic states.

The sheikh.

The clan is represented by its titular head, the sheikh. Unlike his modern namesake of Hollywood fame, the sheikh (*shaykh*) is the senior member of the tribe whose leadership asserts itself in sober counsel, in generosity and in courage. Seniority in age and personal qualifications determine the choice. In judicial, military and other affairs of common concern the sheikh is not the absolute authority; he must consult with the tribal council composed of the heads of the component families. His tenure of office lasts during the good-will of his constituency.

The Arabian in general and the Bedouin in particular is a born democrat. He meets his sheikh on an equal footing. The society in which he lives levels everything down. The title *malik* (king) the Arabians never used except in referring to foreign rulers and the partially Romanized and Persianized dynasties of Ghassān and al-Ḥīrah. The kings of the banu-Kindah formed the only exception to this rule. But the Arabian is also aristocratic as well as democratic. He looks upon himself as the embodiment of the consummate pattern of creation. To him the Arabian nation is the noblest of all nations (*afkhar al-umam*). The civilized man, from the Bedouin's exalted point of view, is less happy and far inferior. In the purity of his blood, his eloquence and poetry, his sword and horse and above all in his noble ancestry (*nasab*), the Arabian takes infinite pride. He is excessively fond of prodigious genealogies and often traces his lineage back to Adam. No people, other than the Arabians, have ever raised genealogy to the dignity of a science.

The Bedouin woman, whether Islamic or pre-Islamic, enjoyed and still enjoys a measure of freedom denied to her sedentary sister. She lived in a polygamous family and under a baal system of marriage in which the man was the master, nevertheless she was at liberty to choose a husband and leave him if ill-treated.

Ability to assimilate other cultures when the opportunity presents itself is well marked among the children of the desert. Faculties which have remained dormant for ages seem to awake suddenly, under the proper stimuli, and develop into dynamic powers. In the Fertile Crescent lies the field of opportunity. A Hammurabi makes his appearance in Babylon, a Moses in

Sinai, a Zenobia in Palmyra, a Philip the Arab in Rome or a Hārūn al-Rashīd in Baghdād. Monuments are built, like those of Petra, which still arouse the admiration of the world. The phenomenal and almost unparalleled efflorescence of early Islam was due in no small measure to the latent powers of the Bedouins, who, in the words of the Caliph ʿUmar, "furnished Islam with its raw material".[1]

[1] Ibn-Saʿd, *Kitāb al-Ṭabaqāt al-Kabīr*, ed. Eduard Sachau, vol. iii, pt. 1 (Leyden, 1904), p. 246, l. 3.

CHAPTER IV

EARLY INTERNATIONAL RELATIONS

South Arabians

WE have thus far used the term Arabian for all the inhabitants of the peninsula without regard to geographical location. We must now differentiate between the South Arabians and the North Arabians, the latter including the Najdis of Central Arabia. The geographical division of the land by the trackless desert into northern and southern sections has its counterpart in the peoples who inhabit it.

The North Arabians are mostly nomads living in "houses of hair" in al-Ḥijāz and Najd; the South Arabians are in the main sedentary, domiciled in al-Yaman, Ḥaḍramawt and along the neighbouring coast. The Northerners speak the language of the Koran, the Arabic par excellence; the Southerners used an ancient Semitic tongue of their own, Sabaean or Ḥimyarite, with which the Ethiopic of Africa is closely allied. Both are dolichocephalic (long-headed) members of the Mediterranean race. But the Southerners have a considerable coastal element that is brachycephalic (round-headed), with a broad jaw and aquiline nose, flat cheeks and abundant hair, characteristic of the Armenoid (Hittite, Hebrew) type. It is an intrusive element borne to South Arabia perhaps by sea from the north-east.[1] The South Arabians were the first to rise to prominence and develop a civilization of their own. The North Arabians did not step on to the stage of international affairs until the advent of Islam.

The memory and consciousness of this national distinction among the Arabians is reflected in their own traditional genealogies. They divide themselves first into two groups: extinct (*bā'idah*), including Thamūd, 'Ād—both of koranic fame—, Ṭasm and Jadīs, and surviving (*bāqiyah*). The Thamūd were an historical people mentioned in the cuneiform annals of Sargon II[2] and known to classical writers as "Tamudaei".[3] The 'Ādites

[1] Carleton S. Coon, *The Races of Europe* (New York, 1939), pp. 403-4, 408.

[2] D. D. Luckenbill, *Ancient Records of Assyria and Babylonia*, vol. ii (Chicago, 1927), §§ 17, 118.

[3] Pliny, *Natural History*, Bk. VI, ch. 32.

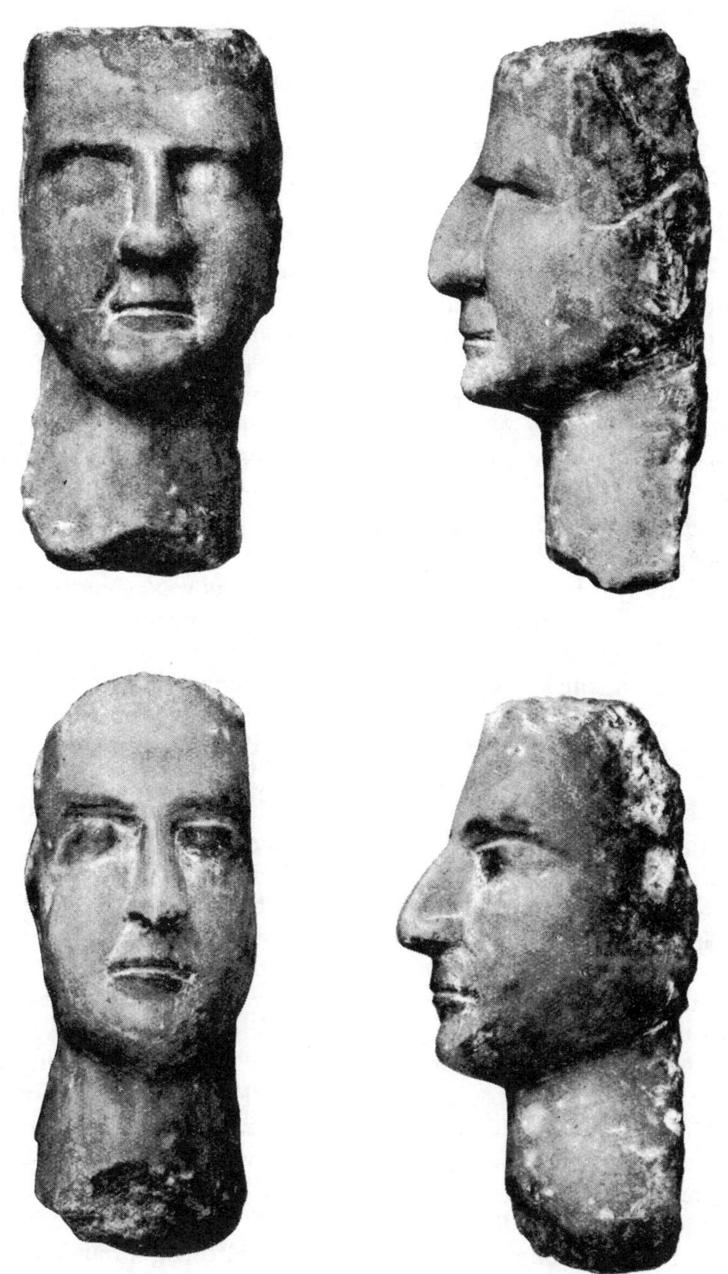

From D. H. Müller, "Südarabische Alterthümer" (Hölder-Pichler-Tempsky, Vienna)

SABAEAN TYPES

are supposed to have flourished in ancient Ḥaḍramawt. Next, the genealogists proceed to subdivide the surviving Arabians into two ethnic stocks: Arabian Arabs (*'āribah*) and Arabicized Arabs (*musta'ribah*). The 'Āribah, according to them, are Yamanites descended from Qaḥṭān (the Joktan of the Old Testament) and constitute the aboriginal stock; the Musta'ribah are the Ḥijāzis, Najdis, Nabataeans and Palmyrenes, all descended from 'Adnān—an offspring of Ishmael—and are "naturalized" in the land. In the traditional Qaḥṭān and 'Adnān is a reminiscence of the differentiation between South Arabians and North Arabians. The Madīnese who rushed to the support of the Prophet at the time of his Hijrah were of Yamanite origin, but his own family, the Quraysh, were Nizāri of the northern stock. The Ghassānids of eastern Syria and the Lakhmids of al-Ḥīrah in al-'Irāq were Southerners domiciled in the north.

This gulf between the two Arabian stocks was never bridged. The age-old division continued to be as prominent as ever, even after Islam had apparently unified the Arabian nation.

I Relations with Egypt

Like a thick wedge the Arabian peninsula thrusts itself between the two earliest seats of culture: Egypt and Babylonia. The Panjāb in India may have been a third cultural focus, and the peninsula lies between it and the West. Although Arabia was not brought within the scope of the river-valley culture of either the land of the one river or the land of the twin rivers, yet it could not entirely have escaped their influence. Its culture, however, was at bottom indigenous. It belonged to the maritime type. Its south-eastern people were possibly the ones who acted as intermediaries between Egypt, Mesopotamia and the Panjāb—the three focal centres of earliest trade—and gave their name to the great intervening sea.

Africa touches Arabia in the north at the Sinaitic peninsula, over which a land route passes, comes close to it in the south at Bāb al-Mandab, only fifteen miles across, and is connected with mid-western Arabia by a third route which follows Wādi al-Ḥammāmāt, opposite the bend of the Nile near Thebes, and connects with the Red Sea at al-Quṣayr. This last route was the chief central connection. During the Twelfth Egyptian Dynasty (*ca.* 2000–1788 B.C.) a canal above Bilbays connected the Nile with the Red Sea. Restored by the Ptolemies, this canal, the antecedent of the Suez Canal, was reopened by the caliphs and used until the discovery (1497) of the route to India round the Cape of Good Hope.

Sinaitic copper

The Egyptian interest in Sinai arose because of its copper and turquoise mines located in Wādi Maghārah in the southern part of the peninsula near the modern town of al-Ṭūr. Even in predynastic days the nomads of Sinai were exporting their valued products to Egypt. Pharaohs of the First Dynasty operated the mines of the peninsula, but the period of great exploitation started with Snefru (*ca.* 2720 B.C.) of the Third Dynasty. The

From G. Elliot Smith, "The Ancient Egyptians and the Origin of Civilisation" (Harper & Bros.)

ANCIENT EGYPTIAN REPRESENTATIONS OF ARABIANS
(*Ca.* 2000 B.C. and 1500 B.C. respectively)

great road connecting Egypt with Syria-Palestine and thence reaching to the rest of the Fertile Crescent and Asia Minor—that first international highway used by man—sent a branch south-east to these copper and turquoise mines of Sinai. In a royal tomb of the First Dynasty at Abydos, Petrie found in 1900 on a piece of ivory a portrait of a typical Armenoid Semite labelled "Asiatic", with a long pointed beard and shaven upper lip, presumably a South Arabian. An earlier relief belonging to the same dynasty shows an emaciated Bedouin chief in a loincloth crouching in submission before his Egyptian captor, who is about to brain the Bedouin with his mace. These are the earliest representations of Arabians extant. The word for Bedouin (Eg. *ʿamu*, nomad, Asiatic) figures prominently in the early Egyptian annals and in some cases refers to nomads around Egypt and outside of Arabia proper.

Frankincense

South Arabia was brought nearer to Egypt when the latter established commercial relationships with Punt and Nubia. Herodotus[1] speaks of Sesostris, probably Senusert I (1980–1935 B.C.) of Dynasty XII, as conquering the nations on the Arabian Gulf, presumably the African side of the Red Sea. The Eighteenth Dynasty maintained a fleet in the Red Sea, but as early as the Fifth Dynasty we find Sahure (2553–2541 B.C.) conducting the first maritime expedition by way of that sea to an incense-producing land, evidently Somaliland on the African shore.

From A. T. Olmstead, "History of Palestine and Syria" (Charles Scribner's Sons)

SEMERKHET, THE SIXTH KING OF THE FIRST DYNASTY, SMITING THE CHIEF OF THE NOMADS

The chief attraction for the Egyptians in South Arabia lay in the frankincense, which they prized highly for temple use and mummification and in which that part of Arabia was particularly rich. When Nubia was subjugated and Punt (modern Somaliland) brought within the commercial sphere of the Egyptian empire many expeditions were conducted to those places to procure "myrrh, fragrant gums, resin and aromatic woods". Such an expedition to Punt was undertaken by Hatshepsut (*ca.* 1500 B.C.), the first famous woman in history. The emissaries of her successor, Thutmose III, the Napoleon of ancient Egypt, brought (1479 B.C.) from the same land the usual cargo of "ivory, ebony, panther-skins and slaves". As these were also the products of al-Yaman in south-western Arabia it is not unlikely that the Egyptians used the term "Punt" for the land on both sides of Bāb al-Mandab. Gold may also have come from Arabia. The incense trade with South Arabia went through Wādi al-Ḥammāmāt, making that central route the most important link with South Arabia.

[1] Bk. II, ch. 102.

From Bertram Thomas, "Arabia Felix" (Charles Scribner's Sons)

A FRANKINCENSE TREE AND A MAHRI COLLECTOR

Ḥaḍramawt,[1] which in ancient times included the coastlands Mahrah and al-Shiḥr,[2] was the celebrated land of frankincense. Ẓafār, formerly a town and now a district on the coast, was its chief centre. The modern name is Dhufar and it is under the nominal rule of the sultan of 'Umān. This Ẓafār, the commercial centre of the frankincense country and situated as it is on the southern coast, should not be confused with the inland Ẓafār in al-Yaman, which was the Ḥimyarite capital.[3] The frankincense (*lubān*, whence "olibanum") tree still flourishes in Ḥaḍramawt and other parts of South Arabia. As of old, Ẓafār is still the chief centre of its trade.

The ancient Egyptians were not the only people who had a commercial interest in Arabia. Their foremost rivals for the trade in spices and minerals were the people of Babylonia.

2. Relations with the Sumerians and Babylonians

Eastern Arabia bordered on Mesopotamia. The early inhabitants of that region, the Sumerians and Akkadians, had already by the fourth millennium before our era become familiar with their neighbours of the Westland (Amurru) and were able to communicate with them both by land and water.

The source of supply of the Sumerian copper, the earliest metal discovered and used in industry, was probably in 'Umān.

On a diorite statue of Narām-Sin (*ca.* 2171 B.C.), a grandson and successor of Sargon (the first great name in Semitic history), we read that he conquered Magan and defeated its lord, Manium.[4] Gudea (*ca.* 2000 B.C.), the Sumerian patesi of Lagash, tells us of his expedition to procure stone and wood for his temple from Magan and Melukhkha. These two Sumerian place-names, Magan and Melukhkha, evidently were first applied to certain regions in east and central Arabia but were later, in the Assyrian period, shifted to more distant localities in the Sinaitic peninsula and eastern Africa. "Magan" is not etymologically identifiable with Arabic "Ma'ān," name of an oasis in northern al-Ḥijāz (now in Transjordan), possibly an ancient Minaean colony on the caravan route. In these cuneiform inscriptions we have the first recorded reference in history to a place in Arabia and to an Arabian people.

[1] Ḥaṣarmāweth of Gen. 10 : 26.

[2] In its later and modern use the name al-Shiḥr has been applied to the whole frankincense coast, including Mahrah and Ẓafār.

[3] Cf. Yāqūt, *Buldān*, vol. iii, pp. 576-7.

[4] Cf. F. Thureau-Dangin, *Les inscriptions de Sumer et d'Akkad* (Paris, 1905), pp. 238, 239.

The "Sealand" of the cuneiform inscriptions was, according to a recent theory, located in Arabia proper and included the western shore of the Persian Gulf as far as the isle of al-Baḥrayn (ancient Dilmun) and possibly al-Nufūd as far west as al-'Aqabah. Nabopolassar was king of the Sealand before he became king of Babylon.

3. Assyrian penetration

The first unmistakable reference to the Arabians as such occurs in an inscription of the Assyrian Shalmaneser III, who led an expedition against the Aramaean king of Damascus and his allies Ahab and Jundub, an Arabian sheikh. The encounter took place in 853 B.C. at Qarqar, north of Ḥamāh. These are the words of Shalmaneser:

> Karkar, his royal city, I destroyed, I devastated, I burned with fire. 1,200 chariots, 1,200 cavalry, 20,000 soldiers of Hadad-ezer, of Aram (? Damascus); . . . 1,000 camels of Gindibu', the Arabian.[1]

It seems very appropriate that the name of the first Arabian in recorded history should be associated with the camel.

Anxious to ensure the safety of the trade highways passing through the far-flung Assyrian empire and converging on the Mediterranean, Tiglath-Pileser III (745–727 B.C.), founder of the second Assyrian empire, conducted a series of campaigns against Syria and its environs. In the third year of his reign he exacted tribute from Zabibi, the queen of "Aribi" land. In the ninth year he conquered another queen of Aribi, Samsi (Shams or Shamsīyah) by name. His annals record that in 728 B.C. the Mas'ai tribe, the city of Temai (Taymā') and the Sab'ai (Sabaeans) sent him tribute of gold, camels and spices. These tribes evidently lived in the Sinai peninsula and the desert to the north-east.[2] Thus was Tiglath-Pileser III the first to fasten the yoke on Arabian necks.

Sargon II (722–705 B.C.), the conqueror of Carchemish and Samaria, reports that in the seventh year of his reign he subjugated among others the tribes of Tamud (Thamūd of the Koran) and Ibādid, "who inhabit the desert, who know neither high nor low official", struck them down and deported the remnant to Samaria.[3] At the same time he received from Samsi,

[1] Luckenbill, vol. i, § 611.

[2] Ditlef Nielsen, *Handbuch der altarabischen Altertumskunde*, vol. i, *Die altarabische Kultur* (Copenhagen, 1927), p. 65.

[3] Luckenbill, vol. ii, § 17.

queen of Arabia, Itʿamara (Yathaʿ-amar), the Sabaean chief, and from other kings of Egypt and the desert "gold, products of the mountain, precious stones, ivory, seed of the maple (?), all kinds of herbs, horses, and camels, as their tribute".[1] This Itʿamara of Saba' was evidently one of the Yathaʿ-amars who bear the royal title *mukarrib* in the South Arabic inscriptions. Likewise his successor Kariba-il of Saba', from whom Sennacherib claims to have received tribute, must have been the south-western Arabian identified with Kariba-il of the inscriptions.[2] If so, the "tribute" claimed by the Assyrians could not have been but freewill presents offered by these South Arabian rulers to the Assyrian kings as equals and probably as allies in the common struggle against the wild nomads of North Arabia.

About 688 B.C. Sennacherib reduced "Adumu, the fortress of Arabia" and carried away to Nineveh the local gods and the queen herself, who was also the priestess. Adumu is the oasis in North Arabia that figured later in the Islamic conquests under the name Dūmat al-Jandal. The queen, Telkhunu (Teʿelkhunu) by name, had allied herself with the rebellious Babylonians against the Assyrian suzerainty, and was assisted by Ḥazāel, the chief of the Qedar (Assyrian Kidri) tribe, whose headquarters were in Palmyrena.

Esarhaddon about 676 suppressed a rebellion headed by Uaiteʿ, the son and successor of Ḥazāel, who, "to save his life, forsook his camp, and, fleeing alone, escaped to distant (parts)".[3] Evidently the Bedouins proved a thorn in the side of the Assyrian empire and were incited to revolt by both Egypt and Babylonia. On his famous march (670) to the conquest of Egypt, the terrible Assyrian was so unnerved by his fearful privations in the North Arabian desert that he saw "two-headed serpents" and other frightful reptiles that "flapped their wings".[4] Isaiah (30 : 6), in his "burden" of the beasts of the south, mentions "the viper and fiery flying serpent". Herodotus[5] assures us that "vipers are found in all parts of the world; but the winged serpents are nowhere seen except in Arabia, where they are all congregated together".

In his ninth campaign, directed against the Arabian tribes,

[1] Luckenbill, vol. ii, § 18.
[2] Nielsen, *Handbuch*, vol. i, pp. 75 *seq.*
[3] Luckenbill, vol. ii, § 946.
[4] Cf. *ibid.* vol. ii, § 558.
[5] Bk. III, ch. 109.

Ashurbanipal (668–626 B.C.) captured Uaiteʿ and his armies after a severe struggle.

Many references are made in the Assyrian annals to Arabian chiefs "kissing the feet" of the kings of Nineveh and offering them among other presents gold, precious stones, eyebrow dyes (kohl, antimony), frankincense, camels and donkeys. In fact we read of no less than nine different campaigns undertaken by Sargon II, Sennacherib, Esarhaddon and Ashurbanipal to chastise the unconquerable Bedouins who were for ever harassing the Assyrian provinces in Syria, interfering with the caravan routes and receiving aid and comfort from Egypt and Babylonia, both hostile to Assyria. The "Urbi" mentioned in these campaigns must have been mainly Bedouins, and their land, "Aribi", must have been the Syro-Mesopotamian desert, the Sinaitic peninsula and North Arabia. In Sinai the Midianites of the Old Testament and not the Nabataeans were those brought under Assyrian control. The Sabaeans proper in south-western Arabia were never subjugated by Nineveh. The Assyrians, though rightly called the Romans of the ancient world, could not have brought under even nominal rule more than the oases and a few tribes in North Arabia.

4. Neo-Babylonian and Persian relations: Taymāʾ

Among the settlements of the north at this period Taymāʾ (Têmâ and Te-ma-a of the Assyro-Babylonian records) won special distinction as the provincial residence of Nabonidus (556–539 B.C.), the last king of the Chaldaeans. The Chaldaeans had fallen heir to the Assyrian empire, which included, since the days of Tiglath-Pileser III (745–727 B.C.), Syria and a portion of North Arabia. In the third year of his reign Nabonidus, in the words of a cuneiform inscription, "slew the prince of Têmâ" and established himself in that oasis.[1]

The most significant reference in cuneiform literature to this Arabian oasis occurs in a chronicle relating to the fall of Babylon (539 B.C.) into the hands of the Persians. The chronicle states that Nabonidus was in "âl Têmâ" in the seventh, ninth, tenth and eleventh years of his reign, while his son (i.e. Belshazzar) and the soldiers were in Babylonia.

In 525 Cambyses, the son and successor of the founder of the Persian empire, passed through northern Arabia and made an alliance with its people while on his way to the conquest of

[1] R. P. Dougherty, *Nabonidus and Belshazzar* (New Haven, 1929), pp. 106-7.

Egypt. Speaking of Darius, Herodotus[1] remarks: "The Arabians were never reduced to the subjection of Persia".

The Taymā' stone, bought by Huber (1883) and now deposited in the Louvre, bears one of the most valuable Semitic inscriptions ever found. Its date goes back to the fifth century B.C. Written in Aramaic, it records how a new deity, Ṣalm of Hajam, was introduced into Taymā' by a certain priest who further provided an endowment for the new temple and established a hereditary priesthood.[2] The new deity is represented in the Assyrian fashion and below him stands his priest who erected the stela.

5. Contacts with the Hebrews

The Jews were geographically next-door neighbours of the Arabians and racially their nearest of kin. Echoes of the desert origin of the Hebrews abound in the Old Testament.[3] Hebrew and Arabic, as we have learned before, are cognate Semitic tongues. Some of the Hebrew Old Testament names are Arabic, e.g. those of almost all of Esau's sons (Gen. 36: 10-14; 1 Ch. 1 : 35-7). A South Arabian would have but little difficulty in understanding the first verse of Hebrew Genesis.[4] The rudiments of the Hebrew religion, modern research shows, point to a beginning in the desert.

On their way to Palestine from Egypt about 1225 B.C. the Hebrew (Rachel) tribes sojourned about forty years in Sinai and the Nufūd. In Midian, the southern part of Sinai and the land east of it, the divine covenant was made. Moses married an Arabian woman, the daughter of a Midianite priest,[5] a worshipper of Jehovah who instructed Moses in the new cult. Yahu (Yahweh, Jehovah) was apparently a Midianite or North Arabian tribal deity. He was a desert god, simple and austere. His abode was a tent and his ritual was by no means elaborate. His worship consisted in desert feasts and sacrifices and burnt offerings from among the herds.[6] The Hebrews entered Palestine as nomads; the heritage of their tribal life from desert ancestors continued to be well marked long after they had settled among, and become civilized by, the native Canaanites.

The Hebrew kingdom in its heyday included the Sinaitic

[1] Bk. III, ch. 88.

[2] G. A. Cooke, *A Text-Book of North-Semitic Inscriptions* (Oxford, 1903), pp. 195-6.

[3] Hos. 9 : 10; Jer. 2 : 2; Deut. 32: 10, etc.

[4] B. Moritz in *Zeitschrift für die Alttestamentliche Wissenschaft*, n. ser., vol. iii (1926), pp. 81 *seq.*; D. S. Margoliouth, *The Relations between Arabs and Israelites* (London, 1924), pp. 8, 15. Consult James A. Montgomery, *Arabia and the Bible* (Philadelphia, 1934), pp. 149 *seq.*

[5] Ex. 3 : 1, 18 : 10-12.

[6] Ex. 3 : 18, 5 : 1; Num. 10 : 35-6.

peninsula. Solomon had his fleet in the Gulf of al-'Aqabah. Ophir, whence the navy of Hiram and Solomon brought gold, algum and precious stones (1 K. 9 : 27-8, 10 : 11; 2 Ch. 9 : 10), was probably Ẓafār in 'Umān. By the time of Job (22 : 24) Ophir had become a synonym for a gold-producing land. Over a century after Solomon, Jehoshaphat (873–849 B.C.) still held sway over Elath (Ezion-geber, modern al-'Aqabah) and the trade routes leading thither and received tribute from the Arabians who "brought him flocks" (2 Ch. 17 : 11). In reporting his third campaign, directed (701) against Syria-Palestine, Sennacherib proclaims: "As for Hezekiah, the terrifying splendor of my majesty overcame him and the Urbi (Arabs) and his mercenary (?) troops which he had brought in to strengthen Jerusalem, his royal city, deserted him".[1] Hezekiah (1 Ch. 4 : 41), and before him Uzziah (2 Ch. 26 : 7), fought against the Minaeans in and around the oasis of Ma'īn (modern Ma'ān). Uzziah (792–740 B.C.) restored Elath to Judah and rebuilt the town (2 K. 14 : 22). The Chronicler (2 Ch. 21 : 16, 17) reports a South Arabian raid against Judah which resulted in the loss of King Jehoram's (848–844 B.C.) sons, wives and treasures, although it is difficult to see how distant Sabaeans, "the Arabians, that were near the Ethiopians", could have carried out such a raid. By the time of Nehemiah,[2] in the middle of the fifth century B.C., the Jews were beginning to look upon their south-eastern neighbours as enemies.

Biblical association: Old Testament references

Etymologically 'Arab is a Semitic word meaning "desert" or the inhabitant thereof with no reference to nationality. In this sense Hebrew 'Ereb is used in Is. 21 : 13, 13 : 20 and Jer. 3 : 2. In the Koran *a'rāb* is used for Bedouins. Second Mac. 12 : 10 makes Arabs and nomads synonymous. The first certain instance of the biblical use of the word as a proper name occurs in Jer. 25 : 24: "kings of Arabia". Jeremiah's prophetic career fell between 626 and 586 B.C. The "kings" referred to were in all probability sheikhs of northern Arabia and the Syrian Desert. By the third century B.C. the term was beginning to be used for any inhabitant of the peninsula, for 2 Ch. 21 : 16 makes mention of "the Arabians, that were near the Ethiopians", leaving no doubt that the people whom the writer had in mind were the Arabians of the south-west, i.e. Sabaeans. Of the four best-

[1] Luckenbill, vol. ii, § 240.

[2] Neh. 2 : 19, 4 : 7.

known kingdoms of ancient Arabia, viz. Saba', Ma'īn, Ḥaḍramawt and Qatabān, the first three—and these were the important ones—are mentioned in the Old Testament. In the commercial chapter of Ezekiel († after 572 B.C.) Arabia is coupled with Kedar, and the articles of merchandise listed are exactly what we would expect in the way of products from Arabia. From verse 21 in this chapter (27), we learn that the Arabians of the sixth century B.C. were engaged, as they are still engaged today, in breeding cattle which they sold to the neighbouring settlers. From Jer. 3 : 2 it is also evident that they were then notorious for highway robbery. Jer. 25 : 23 (American Revised) indicates that they had their heads shaved except for a tuft at the top, a practice similar to that of the Bedouins today.

Dedan (Ar. Daydān), referred to and mentioned repeatedly in the Old Testament (Is. 21 : 13; Jer. 25 : 23; Ezek. 25 : 13), is modern al-'Ula, an oasis in northern al-Ḥijāz. For some time it was the headquarters of the Sabaeans in the northern part of the peninsula. At the height of their commercial power the Sabaeans evidently exercised control over the transport routes leading through al-Ḥijāz northward to the Mediterranean ports and had colonies planted along these routes.

The Kedar (Heb. Qēdār) mentioned by Ezekiel,[1] the "Kidri" of the Assyrian annals[2] and the "Cedrei"[3] of classical literature, held sway over North Arabia. Palmyrena with the region south-east of Damascus was their habitat.

The Shunammite damsel whose beauty is immortalized in the Song ascribed to Solomon (6 : 13, 1 : 5; cf. 1 K. 1 : 3) was probably an Arabian of the Kedar tribe. If historical, the Queen of Sheba (Arabic Bilqīs), who brought to the wise king of Israel gifts of unique value characteristic of South Arabia (1 K. 10 : 10; 2 Ch. 9 : 9), must have had her headquarters neither in al-Yaman nor in Ethiopia, but in one of those Sabaean posts or garrisons in the north on the caravan route. Not until two centuries after the age of Solomon (*ca.* 1000 B.C.) do the Yamanite kings begin to figure in inscriptions.

In Job 6 : 19 the Sheba (Ar. Saba') are associated with Tema (Taymā'). Job, the author of the finest piece of poetry that the ancient Semitic world produced, was an Arab, not a Jew, as the

[1] See also Is. 21 : 16; Gen. 25 : 13. [2] Luckenbill, vol. ii, §§ 820, 869.
[3] Pliny, Bk. V, ch. 12.

form of his name (*Iyyōb*, Ar. *Ayyūb*) and the scene of his book, North Arabia, indicate.[1] The appendix to the Book of Proverbs contains the wise sayings[2] of Agur son of Jakeh (Prov. 30 : 1) and of Lemuel (Prov. 31 : 1), the two kings of Massa, a tribe of Ishmael (Gen. 25 : 14). The names of these two persons occur in some form in certain Minaean and other ancient South Arabic inscriptions. In Baruch 3 : 23 there is a reference to "the Agarenes [sons of Agar = Hagar, i.e. Ishmaelites or North Arabians] that seek wisdom upon earth".

"Qedem" and "Bene Qedem" of the Old Testament, rendered in the English versions (Gen. 29 : 1; Num. 23 : 7; Is. 11 : 14; Jud. 6 : 33; Ezek. 25 : 4; Job 1 : 3) "east", "children of the east", "people of the east", etc., correspond to Arabic *sharq* and *sharqīyūn* (east and easterners). In particular, the terms mean the land and the Bedouins east of Palestine; in general, Arabia and the Arabians. "Saracen" comes from this same Arabic stem and is one of a half-dozen words of Arabic origin which occur in Old English, this word being used as early as the ninth century. It had had a history of its own before the rise of Islam and can be applied to others besides Arabians and Arabs.[3] Job, whose book is considered a masterpiece of wisdom as well as poetry, was a chief of the Bene Qedem (Job 1 : 3). In wisdom Solomon alone excelled this tribe (1 K. 4 : 30). The "wise men from the east" (Matt. 2 : 1), therefore, who followed the star to Jerusalem were possibly Bedouins from the North Arabian desert rather than Magi from Persia.

In the post-exilic literature the word Arab usually signifies Nabataean (2 Mac. 5 : 8; 1 Mac. 5 : 39). First Maccabees 9 : 35 mentions the Nabataeans as such. At the time of Paul the Nabataean kingdom extended as far north as Damascus. The Arabia to which Paul retired (Gal. 1 : 17) was undoubtedly some desert tract in the Nabataean district. The Arabians in Acts 2 : 11 were also in all probability Nabataeans.

[1] Certain technicalities of biblical Hebrew poetry, including parallelism, as illustrated in Job resemble Arabic poetical technique: in both cases the verse is a couplet consisting of two parts which complement each other either appositionally or antithetically. In the Middle Ages Hebrew grammar was modelled after Arabic grammar.

[2] Cf. with those of Luqmān, Koran 31 : 11.

[3] In this book, therefore, such terms as "history of the Saracens", "Saracenic art", "Saracenic architecture", etc., have been avoided. An attempt has been made to use "Arabian" for an inhabitant of the peninsula and "Arab" for any Arabic-speaking person, particularly if a Moslem. To Moslems "Muḥammadan" is objectionable.

6. In classical literature

Arabia and the Arabians were familiar to the Greeks and Romans. The country lay across their path to India and China and produced commodities highly prized in the markets of the west. Its inhabitants were the middlemen of the southern seas, as their kinsmen, the Phoenicians, had been earlier of the Mediterranean.

The classical writers divided the land into Arabia Felix, Arabia Petraea and Arabia Deserta, corresponding to the tripartite political division of the land in the first Christian century, the first being independent, the second subject to Rome and the third nominally controlled in part by Parthia. Arabia Deserta included the Syro-Mesopotamian desert (the Bādiyah). Arabia Petraea (the rocky) centred on Sinai and the Nabataean kingdom, having Petra for its capital. Arabia Felix comprised the rest of the Arabian peninsula, the interior of which was then but little known. Its restriction to the Yaman, the region best known to Europe, was a medieval error. The name itself, meaning "happy", may have been an attempt to translate Ar. *yaman* (to the right hand), confused with *yumn*, happiness. The district was called Yaman because it lay to the right side, i.e. south of al-Ḥijāz, in opposition to al-Sha'm, i.e. Syria, which lay to the left or north.[1] Marcian (*ca.* A.D. 400) of Heraclea[2] uses the term "Saraceni". Before Marcian, Ptolemy,[3] who flourished in the first half of the second century of our era, refers to the Saracens. Ammianus Marcellinus,[4] a native of Antioch who wrote in the latter half of the fourth Christian century, identifies the Saracens with the Scenite Arabs.

The first mention of the Arabians in Greek literature was made by Aeschylus[5] (525–456 B.C.), the reference being to a distinguished Arabian officer in the army of Xerxes. Herodotus[6] (*ca.* 484–425 B.C.) follows with a reference to the Arabians in Xerxes' army, who were evidently from eastern Egypt.

[1] The "Sabaei" (Sabaeans), "Minaei" (Minaeans), "Homeritae" (Ḥimyarites), "Scenitae" (tent-dwellers = Bedouins), "Nabataei" (Nabataeans), "Catabanei" (Qatabānites), "Chatramotitae" (people of Ḥaḍramawt), "Omanitae" ('Umānites), "Sachalitae" (inhabitants of the Sāḥil, i.e. the coast-line, in this case the southern coast-line, medieval al-Shiḥr)—all these figure in Greek and Roman geographies and histories.

[2] *Periplus of the Outer Sea*, tr. Wilfred H. Schoff (Philadelphia, 1927), § 17a.

[3] *Geographia*, ed. Carolus F. A. Nobbe, vol. ii (Leipzig, 1887), Bk. V, ch. 17, § 3.

[4] *Rerum gestarum*, Bk. XXII, ch. 15, § 2; Bk. XXIII, ch. 6, § 13.

[5] *Persians*, l. 320.

[6] Bk. VII, § 69.

To the classical authors from the Greek Eratosthenes († *ca.* 196 B.C.)—the source of Strabo—to the Roman Pliny († A.D. 79) Arabia is a land of fabulous wealth and luxury; it is the country of frankincense and other spices; its people love and enjoy liberty. Indeed, what particularly struck Western writers was the characteristic last mentioned. The independent character of

From Heinrich Kiepert, "Atlas antiquus"

ARABIA OF THE CLASSICAL AUTHORS

the Arabian people has formed a theme of praise and admiration for European authors from the remotest times to the days of Gibbon.[1]

That the Arabians themselves were conscious of those superior advantages which their natural environment afforded may be inferred from the debate with the Persian Chosroes in the presence of the Byzantine, Indian and Chinese deputies, in the

[1] Edward Gibbon, *The Decline and Fall of the Roman Empire*, ed. J. B. Bury (London, 1898), vol. v, p. 319.

course of which the Arab delegation brought out as eloquently and forcefully as possible the points in which their nation excelled.[1] Diodorus Siculus[2] (fl. 2nd half of 1st cent. B.C.) affirms that the Arabians "highly prize and value their liberty". In his *Geography*,[3] Strabo († A.D. 24), on the authority of an earlier Greek, states that the Arabians were the only people who did not send their ambassadors to Alexander, who had planned "to make Arabia the seat of empire".[4]

Roman expedition

Masters of the world, as they were, the Romans failed to fasten the yoke upon Arabian necks. Their famous expedition of 10,000 men conducted from Egypt under the leadership of its prefect Aelius Gallus in 24 B.C., during the reign of Augustus Cæsar, and supported by their Nabataean allies, proved a signal failure. Its object was admittedly to capture those transport routes monopolized by the South Arabians and tap the resources of al-Yaman for the benefit of Rome. After months of southward penetration the decimated army turned back to "Negrana" (Najrān), which it had captured previously, made the coast of the Red Sea and ferried across to the Egyptian shore. The return trip took sixty days. The farthest point in Arabia reached was "Mariaba", which was probably not Ma'rib the Sabaean metropolis but Mariama to the south-east. The celebrated Greek geographer Strabo, historian of the expedition and himself the personal friend of Gallus, blames the many misfortunes on the perfidy of its guide, "Syllaeus the minister of the Nabataeans".[5] Thus ended ignominiously the first, and indeed the last, military campaign of major importance that any European power ever ventured to conduct in inland Arabia.

The aromatic land

To Herodotus[6] "the whole of Arabia exhales a most delicious fragrance", it being "the only country which produces frankincense, myrrh, cassia, cinnamon and ladanum. . . . The trees which bear the frankincense are guarded by winged serpents, small in size and of varied colours, whereof vast numbers hang about every tree."[7] But the geographer Strabo is slightly more judicious than the over-credulous "father of history". To him also South Arabia is "the aromatic country",[8] but its "snakes, a

[1] Ibn-'Abd-Rabbihi, *al-'Iqd al-Farīd* (Cairo, 1302), vol. i, p. 125.
[2] *Bibliotheca historica*, Bk. II, ch. 1, § 5.
[3] Bk. XVI, ch. 1, § 11.
[4] Bk. XVI, ch. 4, § 27.
[5] Bk. XVI, ch. 4, § 23.
[6] Bk. III, ch. 113.
[7] Bk. III, ch. 107.
[8] Bk. XVI, ch. 4, § 25.

span in length, spring up as high as a man's waist".[1] Diodorus Siculus[2] reiterates the same view of Arabia as a spice-producing

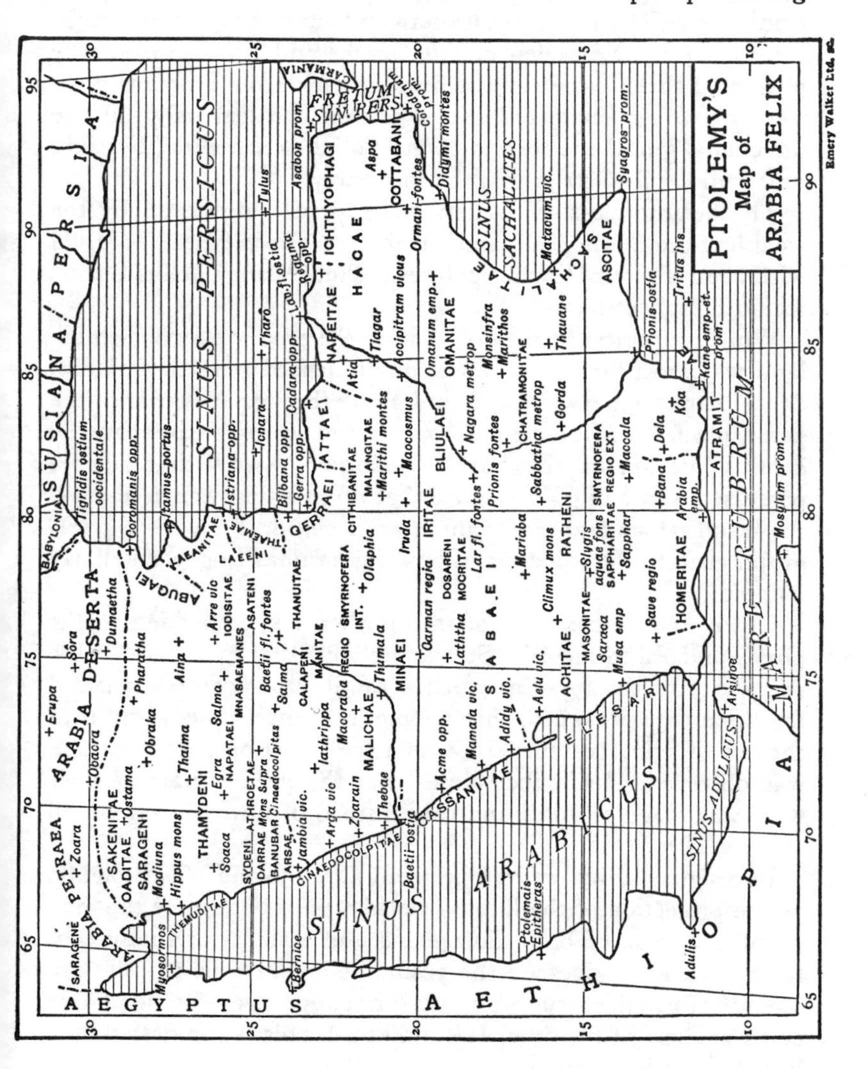

land the very soil of which is redolent. Pliny, who in his *Natural History* (Bk. VI) summarizes the Roman knowledge of the Eastern countries as of A.D. 70, also emphasizes this characteristic

[1] Bk. XVI, ch. 4, § 19. [2] Bk. II, ch. 49, §§ 2-3.

of the land[1] and adds, in another connection, that the Sabaei are "the best known of all the tribes of Arabia on account of their frankincense".[2] Clearly Ḥaḍramawt was in those days the frankincense land par excellence. The Greeks and Romans evidently presumed that all the commodities in which the Arabians dealt were native products of their own land, so jealously did the merchants guard the secrets of their other sources in Abyssinia and India and so strict was the monopoly.

Those same classical writers were greatly impressed by the wealth of the South Arabians. Strabo[3] mentions cities "adorned with beautiful temples and palaces". Pliny,[4] using Aelius Gallus for authority, concurs.

Gold

While frankincense and spices were the products for which the land was most famous, almost equally prized were the mineral deposits, particularly gold, found along the western coast of the peninsula from Midian to al-Yaman and to some extent in the central portion of the land. Diodorus[5] asserts that Arabia possessed mines of gold so pure that no smelting was necessary. Al-Maqdisi[6] and al-Hamdāni[7] (tenth century) devote a paragraph each to the minerals of Arabia, emphasizing particularly its gold.

Other treasured scraps of information are embedded in the Greek and Latin records. Strabo[8] tells us that in South Arabia polyandry of the type in which a number of brothers married the same wife prevailed, that people lived incestuously and that the law of primogeniture, by which the eldest became the chief, was observed. He further states that the greater part of their wine was made of dates and that instead of olive oil sesame oil was used.[9]

In his geography, written between A.D. 150 and 160, Ptolemy, whose projection of the known world was to determine the geographical ideas of both Europeans and Asians for many centuries to come, gives us the result of an attempt to put into scientific form the records and personal impressions of merchants and travellers of his time. His map of Arabia is the first sketch based on such information.

[1] Bk. XII, ch. 30. [2] Bk. VI, ch. 32. [3] Bk. XVI, ch. 4, § 3.
[4] Bk. VI, ch. 32. [5] Bk. II, ch. 50, § 1.
[6] *Aḥsan al-Taqāsīm*, ed. de Goeje (Leyden, 1877), pp. 101-2.
[7] *Ṣifat Jazīrat al-'Arab*, ed. D. H. Müller (Leyden, 1884), pp. 153-4.
[8] Bk. XVI, ch. 4, § 25. [9] *Ibid.* § 26; Pliny, Bk. VI, ch. 32.

CHAPTER V

THE SABAEAN AND OTHER STATES OF SOUTH ARABIA

The South Arabians as merchants

THE Sabaeans were the first Arabians to step within the threshold of civilization. They figure in the late cuneiform inscriptions. The oldest reference to them in Greek literature is in Theophrastus († 288 B.C.), *Historia plantarum*.[1] The south-western corner of the peninsula was the early home of the Sabaeans.

The fertility of that felicitous rain-favoured land, its proximity to the sea and its strategic location on the India route were all determining factors in its development. Here were produced spices, myrrh and other *aromata* for seasoning foods or burning in the ceremonial of the court and the ritual of the church; foremost among these was incense, that most valuable commodity of ancient trade. Thither did rare and highly prized products, such as pearls from the Persian Gulf, condiments, fabrics and swords from India, silk from China, slaves, monkeys, ivory, gold and ostrich feathers from Ethiopia, find their way in transit to Western marts. The author of *The Periplus of the Erythraean Sea*[2] has left us (A.D. 50–60) a bird's-eye view of the market of "Muza", present-day Mukha (Mocha):

> The merchandise imported there consists of purple cloths, both fine and coarse; clothing in the Arabian style, with sleeves; plain, ordinary, embroidered, or interwoven with gold; saffron, sweet rush, muslins, cloaks, blankets (not many), some plain and others made in the local fashion; sashes of different colors, fragrant ointments in moderate quantity, wine and wheat, not much.

The Sabaeans were the Phoenicians of the southern sea. They knew its routes, reefs and harbours, mastered its treacherous monsoons and thus monopolized its trade during the last millennium and a quarter before our era. The circumnavigation of Arabia, stated as a theoretical possibility by Alexander's admiral, Nearchus, was in their case an actuality. To the Greco-Roman

[1] Bk. IX, ch. 4, § 2.

[2] Tr. W. H. Schoff (New York, 1912), § 24.

pilots the frankincense country was "mountainous and forbidding".[1] "Navigation", according to the *Periplus*,[2] "is dangerous along this whole coast of Arabia, which is without harbors, with bad anchorages, foul, inaccessible because of breakers and rocks, and terrible in every way."

Through the Red Sea the main maritime route led from Bāb al-Mandab to Wādi al-Ḥammāmāt on the coast of Middle Egypt. The inherent difficulty of navigating this sea, especially in its northern parts, caused the Sabaeans to develop land routes between al-Yaman and Syria along the western coast of the peninsula, leading through Makkah and Petra and forking at the northern end to Egypt, Syria and Mesopotamia. The Syrian branch strikes the Mediterranean outlet at Ghazzah (Gaza). From Ḥaḍramawt, particularly rich in frankincense, a caravan road led to Ma'rib, the Sabaean capital, where it joined the main commercial artery. Along this south-to-north route a number of Sabaean colonies were planted. From these may have come the Sabaeans who figured in the Assyrian and Hebrew records. An historical snapshot has been preserved for us in Gen. 37 : 25 of a "caravan of Ishmaelites" coming down "from Gilead with their camels bearing spicery and balm and myrrh".

South Arabic inscriptions

The conquests which the South Arabians achieved were in commerce and trade. The kingdoms they built were not military states. The outline of their history can be delineated from such references as those cited above in the ancient Semitic and Greco-Roman writings, from the semi-legendary traditions preserved in early Moslem literature—particularly the works of Wahb ibn-Munabbih († in Ṣan'ā', *ca.* A.D. 728), al-Hamdāni[3] († A.D. 945) and al-Ḥimyari († A.D. 1177)—but above all from the local sources made accessible mainly through the discoveries of Halévy and Glaser. All this native South Arabian literature, however, is epigraphic—on metal and stone. Whatever perishable material was used for recording business transactions, historical narratives, or strictly literary productions has entirely disappeared. The earliest inscriptions found are mostly boustro-

[1] *Erythraean Sea*, § 29.

[2] *Ibid.* § 20; D. H. Müller, *Die Burgen und Schlösser Südarabiens nach dem Iklîl des Hamdânî*, 2 pts. (Vienna, 1879–81).

[3] Bk. VIII, ed. Nabih A. Faris (Princeton, 1940); *The Antiquities of South Arabia* (Princeton, 1938); Bk. X, ed. Muḥibb-al-Dīn al-Khaṭīb (Cairo, 1368).

phedon, dating from the eighth or ninth century B.C. The inscriptions may be classified as follows: (1) votive, engraved on tablets of bronze placed in the temples and dedicated to Almaqah (Ilmuqah), 'Athtar and Shams; (2) architectural, occurring on the walls of the temples and other public edifices to commemorate the name of the builder of or the contributor to the construction; (3) historical, reporting a battle or announcing a victory; (4) police ordinances, inscribed on pillars in the entry; (5) funerary, attached to sepulchres. Of special significance are a few legal documents which reveal a long constitutional development.

Carsten Niebuhr was the first to announce (1772) the existence of South Arabic inscriptions. Joseph Halévy, who since Aelius

From "Journal of the Royal Geographical Society" (1837)

THE RUINS OF NAQAB AL-ḤAJAR AND TWO LINES OF INSCRIPTION WHICH FURNISHED EUROPE WITH ITS FIRST SIGHT OF SOUTH ARABIC INSCRIPTION

Gallus (24 B.C.) was the first European to visit Najrān in al-Yaman (1869–70), brought back copies of 685 inscriptions from thirty-seven different localities. Between 1882 and 1894 Eduard Glaser undertook four scientific expeditions to al-Yaman which yielded some 2000 inscriptions, of which some are still unpublished. In all we possess today about 4000 such inscriptions, extending in date as far back as the seventh century B.C. Th. S. Arnaud, who discovered the ruins of Ma'rib, copied in 1843 at the risk of his life about sixty inscriptions. James R. Wellsted, an English naval officer, published in 1837 a part of the inscription of Naqab al-Ḥajar and this furnished Europe with its second sight of South Arabian writing. The decipherment was accomplished by Emil Rödiger of Halle (1837) and by Gesenius (1841).

As revealed by these inscriptions, the South Arabic or Minaeo-Sabaean language (also called Ḥimyarite) has twenty-nine letters in its alphabet. The characters represent in all probability an early forking from the Sinaitic, which constitutes the connecting link between the Phoenician alphabet and its Egyptian ancestor. These symmetrical rectilinear letters (*al-musnad*) point to a long development.[1] Its alphabet, like other Semitic forms, consists of consonants only. In noun formation, verb conjugation, personal pronouns and vocabulary, South Arabic has certain affinities with Akkadian (Assyro-Babylonian) and Ethiopic (Abyssinian). But it has the broken plural which characterizes North Arabic and Ethiopic. Akkadian, South Arabic and Ethiopic represent in certain respects the older form of Semitic speech. With the decay of the Yamanite culture South Arabic practically disappeared and North Arabic was substituted. The literary fairs of the north, such as the Sūq 'Ukāẓ, the annual heathen pilgrimage to the Ka'bah and the commercial relations with Makkah hastened the process of substitution.

1. The Sabaean kingdom

The first major kingdoms discernible through the mists of South Arabian antiquity were the Sabaean and the Minaean, which during a considerable part of their history were contemporaries. Both kingdoms began as theocracies and ended as secular kinships.

The Sabaeans were the most distinguished branch of the entire South Arabian family. Saba', biblical Sheba, their original homeland, lay south of Najrān in the Yaman district. The Sabaean period, according to the school of Arabists who hold for the low (or short) chronology extended from about 750 B.C. to 115 B.C. with a change in the royal title at about 610 B.C.; the Minaean from about 700 B.C., to the third pre-Christian century.[2] Mukarrib[3] was the title of the priest-king who stood at the head of the state. Two early Sabaean mukarribs, Yatha'-amar and Kariba-il, are cited in the royal Assyrian annals of Sargon II and Sennacherib[4] and must have reigned in the late eighth and

[1] For specimens see *Corpus inscriptionum Semiticarum*, pars iv (Paris, 1889 ff.).

[2] Cf. Nielsen, *Handbuch*, vol. i, pp. 64 *seq.*; F. V. Winnett in *Bulletin, American Schools of Oriental Research*, no. 73 (1939), pp. 3-9; G. Ryckmans in *Bulletin, School of Oriental and African Studies*, vol. xiv (1952), pp. 1 *seq.*; Jacques Ryckmans, *L'Institution monarchique en Arabie méridionale avant l'Islam* (Louvain, 1951), pp. 257 *seq.*

[3] MKRB, vocalization uncertain.

[4] See above, pp. 37-8.

Sinaitic	South Arabic	Phoenician	Ra's al-Shamrah	Later Greek	Latin	Arabic
					A	ا
					B	ب
					CG	ج
					D	د
					E	ه
					FV	و
= (?)					...	ز
					H	ح
...					...	ط
					I	ي
					...	ك
					L	ل
					M	م
					N	ن
					X	...
					O	ع
					P	ف
				...	...	ص
					Q	ق
					R	ر
					S	سش
					T	ت

Constructed with the aid of G. Vinton Duffield

A TABLE OF ALPHABETS, INCLUDING RA'S AL-SHAMRAH CUNEIFORM

early seventh century. In their heyday the kings of Saba' extended their hegemony over all South Arabia reducing their neighbour, the Minaean kingdom, to a state of vassalage. Sirwāḥ, a day's journey west of Ma'rib, was the capital of Saba'. Its principal building was the temple of Almaqah, the moon-god.[1] Its principal ruins, now called al-Kharibah, house a village of a hundred persons. An inscription records that its surrounding wall was built by Yada'-il, an early mukarrib. Another inscription records the victorious campaigns of Kariba-il Watar (*ca.* 450 B.C.), who first assumed the title "MLK [king of] Saba".

Ma'rib dam

In the second period of the Sabaean kingdom (*ca.* 610–115 B.C.) the ruler appears shorn of his priestly character. Ma'rib, some sixty miles east of Ṣan'ā', then became the capital. This city lay 3900 feet above the sea. It has been visited by only a few Europeans, first among whom were Arnaud, Halévy and Glaser. It was the meeting-place of the trade routes connecting the frankincense lands with the Mediterranean ports, particularly Ghazzah. Al-Hamdāni in his *Iklīl*[2] refers to three citadels in Ma'rib, but the construction for which the city was particularly famous was the great dam, Sadd Ma'rib.[3] This remarkable engineering feat, together with the other public works of the Sabaeans, reveal to us a peace-loving society highly advanced not only in commerce but in technical accomplishment as well. The older portions of the dam were constructed in the mid-seventh pre-Christian century. The inscriptions make Sumhu'alay Yanuf and his son Yatha'-amar Bayyin the main builders and cite restorations in the time of Sharaḥbi-Il Ya'fur (A.D. 449–450) and Abraha the Abyssinian (A.D. 543). But al-Hamdāni, and after him al-Mas'ūdi,[4] al-Iṣfahāni[5] and Yāqūt,[6] regard Luqmān ibn-'Ād. a mythical personage, as the builder.

2. The Minaean kingdom

The Minaean kingdom flourished in the Jawf of al-Yaman and in its heyday included most of South Arabia. The original Arabic form Ma'ān (biblical Mā'ōn, Me'ūn, Me'īn as a place

[1] Ahmed Fakhry, *An Archaeological Journey to Yem n*, vol. i (Cairo, 1952), pp. 29-56; Wendell Phillips, *Qataban and Sheba* (New York 1955); Richard L. Bowen and Frank P Albright *Archaeological Discoveries in South Arabia* (Baltimore 1958).

[2] Faris, p. 45 For description of ruins see al- Aẓm, pt. 2, pp. 50 *sey Murūj al-Dhahab*, ed. and tr. de Meynard and de Courteille. vol. iii (Paris, 1864), p. 366.

[5] *Ta'rīkh Sini Mulūk al-Arḍ w-al-Anbiyā'*, ed. Gottwaldt (Leipzig, 1844), p. 126.

[6] *Buldān*, vol. iv, p. 383.

name) was later vocalized Ma'īn, meaning spring-water. The name survives in present-day Ma'ān (south-east of Petra), an important colony on the northern trade route. Minaean inscriptions near al-'Ula[1] and Tabūk attest the existence of several colonies in this region serving as warehouses and relay posts. The Minaean capital Qarnāw, visited by Halévy in 1870, is modern Ma'īn (in southern al-Jawf, north-east of Ṣan'ā'). The religious metropolis, Yathīl, also in southern al-Jawf, is present-day Barāqish, north-west of Ma'rib. The Minaeans spoke the same language as the later Sabaeans, with only dialectal differences. The so-called Minaean inscriptions include the Qatabānian royal inscriptions and few Ḥaḍramawt texts. Carvings in the temple ruins of al-Ḥazm, provincial capital of al-Jawf, represent suspended vessels, probably wine offerings, gazelles and other sacrificial animals, snakes which were divine symbols, dancing girls who were temple servants, and ostriches evidently kept in sacred parks.

3. Qatabān and Ḥaḍramawt

Other than the Minaean and Sabaean kingdoms two other important states arose in this area Qatabān and Ḥaḍramawt. The land of Qatabān lay east of the site of 'Adan, that of Ḥaḍramawt about where it is today. The Qatabān monarchy,[2] whose capital was Tamna' (now Kuḥlān), lasted from about 400–50 B.C.; that of Ḥaḍramawt, whose capital was Shabwah (classical Sabota), lasted from the mid-fifth century before Christ to the end of the first Christian century. At times these kingdoms were under Sabaean and Minaean hegemony. Arab historians knew nothing about all these peoples whose inscriptions extend from North Arabia to Ethiopia, who organized the spice trade and undertook amazing public works.

4. The Ḥimyarite kingdom

From 115 B.C. onwards the entire area falls under new masters who stemmed from the southwestern highlands, the tribe of Ḥimyar. Thence the civilization is referred to as Ḥimyarite, though the royal title remains "king of Saba' and dhu-Raydān". Raydān later became known as Qatabān. This marks the beginning of the first Ḥimyarite kingdom, which lasted till about A.D. 300. The word "Homeritae" occurs first in *The Periplus of the Erythraean Sea* (about A.D. 60) and then in Pliny. The

[1] Liḥyānite capital *ca.* 500–300 B.C. See above, p. 42.

[2] Cf. Phillips, p. 247. For a list of kings see Müller, *Die Burgen*, pt. 2, pp. 60-67; G. Ryckmans, *Les noms propres sud-sémitiques*, vol. i (Louvain, 1934), pp. 36 *seq.*; H. St. J. B. Philby, *The Background of Islam* (Alexandria, 1947), pp. 143-4.

Ḥimyarites were close kinsmen of the Sabaeans and, as the youngest branch of the stock, became the inheritors of the Minaeo-Sabaean culture and trade. Their language was practically the same as that of the Sabaeans and Minaeans before them. Pliny's references to agriculture are confirmed by the wells, dams and cisterns repeatedly mentioned in the inscriptions. The collection of frankincense, considered a religious act, was still the source of greatest income.

Ẓafār (classical Sapphar and Saphar, Sephar of Gen. 10 : 30), the inland town, about one hundred miles north-east of Mukha on the road to Ṣan'ā', was the capital of the Ḥimyarite dynasty. It displaced Ma'rib of the Sabaeans and Qarnāw of the Minaeans.

British Museum

ḤIMYARITE SILVER COIN

Obv. male head with monogram; rev. male head with inscription reading KRB'L WTR (Kariba-ilu Watar)

Ca. A.D. 50

Its ruins can still be seen on the summit of a circular hill near the modern town of Yarim. At the time of the composition of *The Periplus* its king was Kariba-il Watar (Charibael of *The Periplus*).

It was during this Ḥimyarite period that the ill-fated Roman column under Aelius Gallus penetrated as far as Mariama. The "Ilasarus" of Strabo, who was the ruler at that time, is Ilishariḥa Yaḥḍub of the inscriptions.

The Semitic origin of the Abyssinians

Another notable occurrence in the early part of this period was the establishment of Arabian colonists from al-Yaman and Ḥaḍramawt in the "land of Cush", where they laid the basis of the Abyssinian kingdom and civilization and ultimately developed a culture which the native negroes could probably never have achieved. The displacement of South Arabian tribes about the middle of the fifth century of our era (connected by popular tradition with the breaking of the great dam of Ma'rib), which carried some to Syria and al-ʿIrāq, may have resulted in augmenting the earlier South Arabian settlements in Abyssinia. Along the whole coast of East Africa there was an infusion of Arabian blood of far earlier origin than the Moslem invasion. The beginnings of the kingdom of Aksūm (Axum), the original nucleus of later Abyssinia, belong to the first century after Christ.

The castle of Ghumdān

To another Ili-shariḥa (Līsharḥ ibn-Yaḥṣub of Yāqūt[1]), of the first century after Christ, is ascribed the most celebrated castle of "the land of castles", as al-Yaman has been called, Ghumdān in Ṣanʿāʾ. As a measure of protection against Bedouin raids the urban Ḥimyarites found it necessary to erect well-fortified palaces. Al-Hamdāni, and following him Yāqūt, have left us detailed descriptions of Ghumdān, though by their time it was but a gigantic ruin. The citadel, according to these geographers, had twenty stories, each ten cubits high—the first skyscraper in recorded history. It was built of granite, porphyry and marble. The king had his court installed in the uppermost story, the roof of which was covered with one slab of stone so transparent that one could look through it skyward and distinguish between a crow and a kite. The four facades were constructed of stones of various colours. At each corner-stone stood a brazen lion which roared whenever the wind blew. In a poem al-Hamdāni refers to the clouds as the turban of Ghumdān and marble as its belt. The structure survived until the rise of Islam and was apparently destroyed in the course of the struggle which established Moslem supremacy in al-Yaman.

The king of this first Ḥimyarite period appears as a feudal lord, residing in a castle, owning land and issuing coins of gold, silver and copper, with his image on one side and an owl (the Athenian emblem) or a bull's head on the other. Certain older coins bear the head of Athena and show South Arabian dependence on Athenian models as early as the fourth century before our era. Besides coins, bronze figures of Hellenistic and Sāsānid workmanship are occasionally unearthed in al-Yaman. Native art shows no high antiquity. Semitic genius nowhere expressed itself through such a channel.

The social organization of the Sabaeo-Ḥimyarite community as revealed by the inscriptions represents a curious blend of the

[1] *Buldān*, vol. iii, p. 811, l. 8.

old tribal system, caste stratification and feudal aristocracy and monarchy, presenting phenomena many of which may be duplicated elsewhere but which in their aggregate seem unique.

The Romans displace the Arabians in maritime trade

In the course of this first Ḥimyarite period the zenith of the South Arabian power was passed. So long as the Yamanites monopolized the maritime trade of the Red Sea they prospered; but now the control was slipping out of their hands. *The Periplus of the Erythraean Sea* (A.D. 50–60), the first record of organized trading with the East in vessels built and commanded by subjects of a Western power, marks the turning-point of the tide of commerce. The great overland route through the Fertile Crescent and connecting Europe with India, which was a source

British Museum

ḤIMYARITE SILVER COIN

Obv. head of Athena, on her cheek Sabaean letter *nūn*; rev. owl, with olive spray and crescent. Coin belongs to 3rd or 2nd cent. B.C., imitation of the old Attic type of 4th cent. B.C.

of endless friction between the Parthian and Roman empires, had been threatened before this time by Alexander; but the southern maritime route to India remained in the hands of Arabians until almost the first century after Christ. Their task consisted in collecting the products of their own land together with those of East Africa and India and carrying them by camel northward from Ma'rib through Makkah to Syria and Egypt, thus avoiding the hazards of the Red Sea. If, however, transportation by sea seemed preferable the route ran either all the way up the Red Sea to the canal connecting with one of the eastern arms of the Nile or else through the southern part of the Red Sea to Wādi al-Ḥammāmāt and then across the Egyptian desert to Thebes or down the Nile to Memphis. The land route through al-Ḥijāz was dotted with Ḥimyarite stations.[1] Strabo[2] writes that the caravan journey from "Minaea to Aelana" (al-ʿAqabah) takes

[1] See Koran 34:17-18. [2] Bk. XVI, ch. 4, § 4.

seventy days. As the people of the West developed more and more the taste for Oriental cloths, perfumes and spices, the South Arabians raised the price of their own products, especially frankincense and myrrh, and increased the tolls on the foreign goods which passed through their hands. In the meantime they more jealously guarded their control over the routes. Hence their proverbial wealth. Petra and then Palmyra became partners in this commercial system, links in the chain, and consequently shared in the ensuing prosperity. But now the whole situation was beginning to change.

When Egypt under the Ptolemies became once more a world power the first attempt was made to contest the supremacy of the sea with the South Arabians. Ptolemy II (285–246 B.C.) reopened the Nile–Red Sea canal originally dug by Sesostris some seventeen centuries previously. The consequent entry of the Ptolemaic merchant marine into the waters separating Egypt from Arabia proved the beginning of the end for the Ḥimyarite commercial activity. Rome, which captured Egypt from the Ptolemies about the middle of the first century B.C., followed the Ptolemies in the policy of maritime competition against the Arabians and in the desire to free Egypt from commercial dependence upon al-Yaman. In the days of Pliny Roman citizens were already complaining of the high prices exacted by the South Arabian traders for commodities for which Rome had to pay in cash because she had so little to offer by way of goods they desired.[1] The Abyssinians, evidently not content with the share of spoils allotted them by their neighbours to the east, were now courting Roman alliance.

In the early Roman period a Greek or Roman, perhaps in the Abyssinian maritime service, was initiated into the mysteries of the sea routes with their hazards and periodic changes of monsoons, and triumphantly returned to Alexandria with a cargo of the greatly desired and highly priced articles, including cinnamon and pepper produced in India, commodities which the Westerners had believed to be of Arabian origin. This Hippalus, the Columbus of early Roman trade, was followed by others who thus contributed to the final break-up of the Arabian monopoly. But full advantage of the memorable discovery of the periodicity of the monsoons and the direct sea route to India was not taken

[1] Pliny, Bk. XII, ch. 41

till sometime later. The entry of the Roman shipping into the Indian Ocean sounded the knell of South Arabian prosperity.[1] Economic decline brought in its wake, as it always does, political ruin. One by one Petra, Palmyra and north-western Mesopotamia fell under the paws of the Roman wolf.

5. The second Ḥimyarite kingdom

About A.D. 300 the monarchical title in South Arabia becomes "king of Saba', dhu-Raydān, Ḥaḍramawt and Yamanāt". This means that by this time Ḥaḍramawt had lost its independence. To this title a further addition was soon made: "and of their Arabians in the mountains and in the Tihāmah". Yamanāt (Yamānah) might have then embraced the entire southern coastlands; Tihāmah was the Red Sea coast west of Ṣan'ā'.

After an invasion from Abyssinia resulting in a short Abyssinian rule (*ca.* 340–78) the native Ḥimyarite kings resumed their long title and held their position till about A.D. 525. In the Aksūmite inscriptions of the middle of the fourth century the Abyssinian monarch claims to be "king of Aksūm, Ḥimyar, Raydān, Ḥabashah,[2] Salḥ and Tihāmah". This was not the first or only time the Abyssinians invaded Arabia. Once before, in the second and third centuries after Christ, they must have succeeded in establishing temporary authority over parts of South Arabia.

Nine of the Ḥimyarite kings of this period are known to us from inscriptions. Tubba' is the royal title that has survived in Islamic literature. Among the Ḥimyarite kings best known to later Arabic legends was one Shammar Yar'ash, who is represented as having conquered as far as Samarqand, which, according to these legends, takes its name from him. Another was abu-Karib As'ad Kāmil, the Abi-kariba As'ad (*ca.* A.D. 385–420) who is reported to have conquered Persia and who later embraced the Jewish faith. The memory of the latter is still kept alive in the Arabic ballads of adventure. This later Ḥimyarite period was signalized by the introduction of Christianity and Judaism into al-Yaman.

Christianity and Judaism in al-Yaman

The religion of South Arabia was in its essence a planetary astral system in which the cult of the moon-god prevailed. The moon, known in Ḥaḍramawt as Sīn, to the Minaeans as Wadd (love or lover, father), to the Sabaeans as Almaqah (the health-giving god?) and to the Qatabānians as 'Amm (paternal uncle),

[1] Cf. George F. Hourani in *Journal of Near Eastern Studies*, vol. xi (1952), pp. 291-5.

[2] I.e. Ḥaḍramawt. See Nielsen, *Handbuch*, vol. i, p. 104.

stood at the head of the pantheon. He was conceived of as a masculine deity and took precedence over the sun, Shams, who was his consort. ʿAthtar (Venus, corresponding to the Babylonian goddess Ishtar, Phoenician ʿAshtart), their son, was the third member of the triad. From this celestial pair sprang the many other heavenly bodies considered divine. The North Arabian al-Lāt, who figured in the Koran, may have been another name for the sun-goddess.

Christianity of the Monophysite type began to trickle in from the north, particularly Syria, at an early date. Syrian missionaries fleeing persecution may have entered al-Yaman at times unknown to us, but the first Christian embassy to South Arabia that we read of was that sent by the Emperor Constantius in 356 under the leadership of Theophilus Indus, an Arian. The real motive behind the mission lay in the international politics of the day and the rivalry between the Roman and Persian empires for spheres of influence in South Arabia. Theophilus succeeded in building one church at ʿAdan (Aden) and two others in the country of the Ḥimyarites. Najrān, into which Christianity of the Monophysite communion is said to have been introduced by a holy man from Syria named Faymiyūn (Phemion), embraced the new faith about A.D. 500. Ibn-Hishām[1] and al-Ṭabari[2] give us the legend of this ascetic, who was captured by an Arab caravan and brought to Najrān. Yaʿqūb of Sarūj († 521) addressed a comforting letter in Syriac to the Christians of Najrān. The second caliph, ʿUmar, deported (A.D. 635–6) to al-ʿIrāq those of them who had failed to embrace Islam.[3] As late as A.D. 840 we hear of a Mār Petrus, bishop of Ṣanʿāʾ and al-Yaman.

Judaism also became widely spread in al-Yaman under the second Ḥimyarite kingdom. It must have found its way early into North Arabia, perhaps consequent to the conquest of Palestine and the destruction of Jerusalem by Titus in A.D. 70. Judging by the names preserved most of the Jews in Arabia must have been Judaized Aramaeans and Arabians rather than descendants of Abraham. In the early part of the sixth century the Hebrew religion had such a hold upon al-Yaman that the last Ḥimyarite king, dhu-Nuwās (a descendant of the Tubbaʿ Asʿad Kāmil),

[1] *Sīrah*, ed. Wüstenfeld (Göttingen, 1858), pp. 20-22.
[2] *Taʾrīkh al-Rusul*, ed. de Goeje, vol. i (Leyden, 1881–2), pp. 919-25.
[3] Balādhuri, *Futūḥ*, p. 66 = Hitti, *Origins*, pp. 101-2. See below, p. 169.

was a Jew. Virtually all the hundred thousand Jews in al-Yaman have been, after 1948, transferred to Israel.

Rivalry between the South Arabian converts of the two newly introduced monotheistic religions led to active hostility. Evidently dhu-Nuwās, representing the nationalistic spirit, associated the native Christians with the hated rule of the Christian Abyssinians. To this Jewish monarch is ascribed the famous massacre of the Christians of Najrān in October 523 (sūr. 85 : 4).[1] Daws dhu-Tha'labān (or Thu'lubān) survived, according to Arabic tradition, and implored the Emperor Justin I for aid, the Byzantine emperor at that time being regarded as the protector of Christians everywhere. The emperor wrote to the Negus (Najāshi) of Abyssinia (Kaleb Ela Aṣbeḥa in the inscriptions), for he represented the Christian power nearest the scene of trouble. The Negus is said to have sent 70,000 men across the Red Sea to Arabia under a certain Aryāṭ. This campaign therefore falls within the network of the international politics of that age: Byzantium was seeking through Abyssinia to bring the Arabian tribes under her influence and use them against Persia.[2] The Abyssinians were victorious in 523 and again in 525. The leader on the latter occasion was Abrahah (variant of Abraham), originally an officer under Aryāṭ, but who by this time had fallen out with his commander and taken over the supreme command. According to al-Ṭabari,[3] dhu-Nuwās, setting spurs to his steed, "plunged it into the waves of the sea and was never seen again". Thus came to his end the last Ḥimyarite monarch, and with him the period of the independence of al-Yaman was terminated. All that remains of the glorious memory of the ancient Ḥimyarite dynasty is today perpetuated in the name of an obscure tribe, Ḥimyar, east of 'Adan.

The period of Abyssinian rule

The Abyssinians came as helpers, but as often happens remained as conquerors. They turned colonists[4] and remained from 525 to 575 in control of the land whence their ancestors had long before emigrated to the African shore. Abrahah, the acknowledged Aksūmite viceroy, built in Ṣan'ā', now the capital, one of the most magnificent cathedrals of the age, called by the Arabian writers al-Qalīs (al-Qulays, al-Qullays, from Gr.

[1] See Axel Moberg, *The Book of the Himyarites* (Lund, 1924).

[2] Procopius, *History of the Wars*, ed. and tr. H. B. Dewing (London, 1904), Bk. I, ch. 20, §§ 9-12.

[3] Vol. i, pp. 927-8.

[4] Procopius, Bk. I, ch. 20, §§ 2, 6.

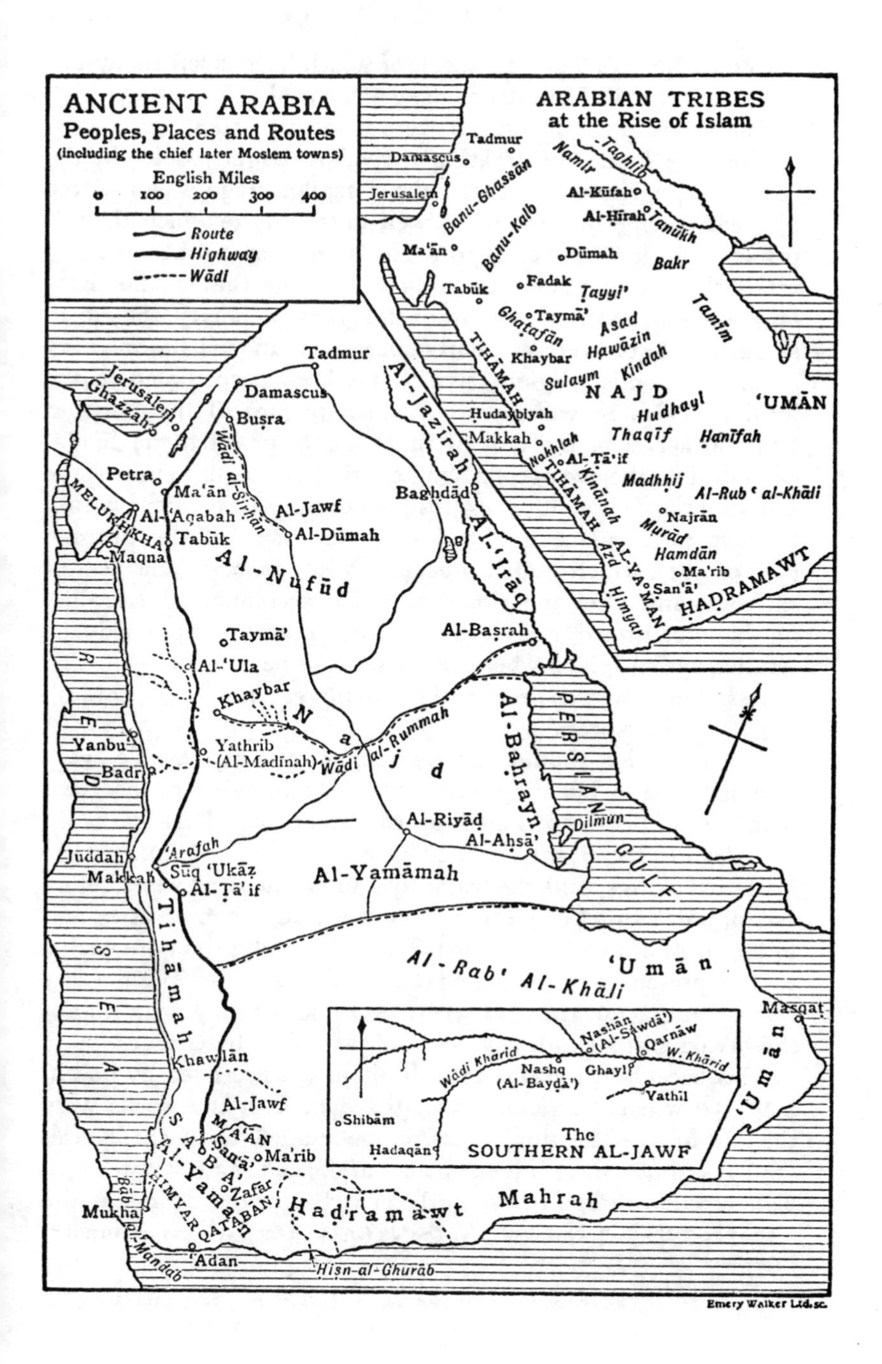
ANCIENT ARABIA
Peoples, Places and Routes
(including the chief later Moslem towns)
English Miles
0 100 200 300 400
Route
Highway
Wādī
ARABIAN TRIBES
at the Rise of Islam
Tadmur
Damascus
Jerusalem
Banu-Ghassān
Namir
Taghlib
Al-Kūfah
Al-Ḥīrah
Tanūkh
Banu-Kalb
Ma'ān
Dūmah
Bakr
Tabūk
Fadak
Ṭayyi'
Tamīm
Ghaṭafān
Taymā'
Asad
Khaybar
Hawāzin
TIHĀMAH
Sulaym
Kindah
NAJD
Hudaybiyah
Hudhayl
'UMĀN
Makkah
Thaqīf
Ḥanīfah
Nakhlah
Al-Ṭā'if
Kinānah
Madhḥij
Al-Rub' al-Khāli
Najrān
Murād
Hamdān
Ma'rib
Azd
AL-YAMAN
San'ā'
Ḥimyar
ḤAḌRAMAWT
Tadmur
Jerusalem
Ghazzah
Damascus
Al-Jazīrah
Buṣra
Wādī al-Sirḥān
Petra
Ma'ān
Baghdād
MELUKHKHA
Al-'Aqabah
Al-Jawf
Tabūk
Al-Dūmah
Al-'Irāq
Maqna
Al-Nufūd
Al-Baṣrah
Taymā'
Al-'Ula
RED SEA
Khaybar
Najd
PERSIAN GULF
Al-Baḥrayn
Wādī al-Rummah
Yanbu'
Yathrib
(Al-Madīnah)
Badr
Dilmun
Al-Riyāḍ
Al-Aḥsā'
'Arafah
Juddah
Sūq 'Ukāẓ
Makkah
Al-Ṭā'if
Al-Yamāmah
Tihāmah
Al-Rab' Al-Khāli
'Umān
Masqaṭ
'Umān
Khawlān
Al-Jawf
MA'ĀN
SABA'
Ṣan'ā'
Ma'rib
Al-Yaman
Ẓafār
QATABĀN
Ḥaḍramawt
Mahrah
Bāb al-Mandab
Mukha
ḤIMYAR
'Adan
Ḥiṣn-al-Ghurāb
Nashān
(Al-Sawdā')
Qarnāw
Wādī Khārid
Nashq
(Al-Bayḍā')
Ghayl
W. Khārid
Yathil
Shibām
Hadaqān
The
SOUTHERN AL-JAWF
Emery Walker Ltd. sc.

ekklēsia, church). The cathedral, of which little is left today but the site, was built from the ruins of ancient Ma'rib.

The Christian Abyssinians were evidently intent upon converting the land and creating a rival to pagan Makkah, the centre of pilgrimage in the north, for pilgrimage was a source of great income to those who dwelt in the city to which the pilgrims travelled or beside the roads leading thither. In the establishment of a southern religious shrine that would draw large crowds, to the detriment of the Ḥijāz sanctuary, the Abyssinian overlords were evidently successful. Indeed the memory of this economic-religious rivalry has been perpetuated in the local tradition in which two Arabian pagans of the Fuqaym tribe, attached to the cult of the Ka'bah, polluted the Ṣan'ā' cathedral on the eve of a festival, causing Abrahah to undertake a disciplinary expedition against Makkah. The incident is said to have taken place in the year of the birth of the Prophet (570 or 571), which year has been dubbed *'ām al-fīl*, the year of the elephant, after the elephant which accompanied Abrahah on his northward march and which greatly impressed the Arabians of al-Ḥijāz, where elephants had never been seen. The Abyssinian army was destroyed by smallpox, "the small pebbles" (*sijjīl*) of the Koran.[1]

The breaking of Ma'rib dam

To this period should also be assigned the memorable event immortalized in Islamic literature as "the bursting of the great dam" of Ma'rib occasioned by the great flood.[2] Al-Iṣfahāni,[3] who devotes the eighth book of his annals (finished A.D. 961) to Ḥimyarite kings, puts the tragic event four hundred years before Islam, but Yāqūt[4] comes nearer to the truth when he assigns it to the reign of the Abyssinians. The ruins of this dam are visible to the present day. A dated South Arabic inscription (date corresponding to A.D. 542–3) by Abrahah dealing with one of the breaks has been discovered and published by Glaser.[5]

This breach in the time of Abrahah was preceded by one in A.D. 450 when the water broke the dam. But the works were then restored. The final catastrophe alluded to in the Koran (34 : 15) must have taken place after 542 and before 570. Connected with one of the early breaches in the dyke was the

[1] 105 : 1-3. See al-Ṭabari, *Tafsīr al-Qur'ān* (Būlāq, 1329), vol. xxx, p. 193; ibn-Hishām, *Sīrah*, p. 36.

[2] Koran 34 : 15. [3] *Op. cit.* p. 126. [4] *Buldān*, vol. iv, p. 383.

[5] In *Mitteilungen der vorderasiatischen Gesellschaft* (Berlin, 1897), pp. 360-488.

migration of the banu-Ghassān to the Ḥawrān region in Syria, where they became the bulwark of Roman rule, and of the banu-Lakhm to the Ḥīrah region, where a number of South Arabic inscriptions have recently been unearthed. The banu-Ghassān chose the year of the breaking of the dam as the starting-point for an era of their own.[1] Besides the Ghassān and Tanūkh of Syria and al-ʿIrāq, the banu-Ṭayyi', Kindah and other large and powerful tribes of North and Central Arabia claim South Arabian origin. There are today families in Syria which trace their entry into the country back to this same event.

Later Arab imagination seized upon this spectacular episode of the great flood and bursting of the dam to explain the whole age-long process of decline and decay in South Arabian trade, agriculture,[2] prosperity and national life; a decline due, as we have already learned, to the entry of Roman shipping into the Red Sea, the introduction of the divisive influence of new religions and the subsequent submission to foreign rule. The legend of "the bursting of the dam"—for so it became in later annals—is perhaps to be analysed as a concentrated and dramatic re-telling of a long history of economic and sociological causes that led to the disintegration and final downfall of South Arabian society and as the crystallization of the results of a long period of decay into one single event. And, with what appears to be a subtle appreciation of the intangible quality of the true causes leading up to this tragedy, the chroniclers[3] report that a rat turned over a stone which fifty men could not have budged, and thus brought about the collapse of the entire dam. Muzayqiyā' ('Amr ibn-ʿĀmir Mā'-al-Samā') was according to tradition the ruler during whose reign this rat did its momentous and epoch-making work.

Then Persia period

The national movement to free al-Yaman from Abyssinian rule found its hero, so the tradition goes, in a scion of the old Ḥimyar royal line, Sayf ibn-dhi-Yazan. The successful struggle (*sīrah*) of Sayf in his romance found a place in the Arabic saga and, revised and embellished in Egypt in the course of the fourteenth century, is still recited by Arab story-tellers in the cafés of

[1] Al-Masʿūdi, *Kitāb al-Tanbīh*, ed. de Goeje (Leyden, 1893), p. 202.

[2] For the theory of climatic desiccation there is no sufficient evidence in historic times; Alois Musil, *Northern Neǧd* (New York, 1928), pp. 304-19.

[3] Masʿūdi, *Murūj*, vol. iii, p. 383; Yāqūt, *Buldān*, vol. iv, p. 384; cf. Masʿūdi, pp. 370-71.

Cairo, Beirūt and Baghdād. Sayf, according to tradition, sought, but naturally failed to receive, Constantinople's aid against Abyssinia, for the latter power was Christian and therefore friendly to Byzantium. He was then presented by the Arab king of al-Ḥīrah to the Persian sovereign, Kisra Anūsharwān, at the Sāsānid court in al-Madā'in (Seleucia-Ctesiphon). The destinies of the world were then chiefly in the hands of the Christian Byzantines and Mazdean Persians, Aksūm acting as the unofficial agent of Byzantium. The Christian Arabians were pro-Byzantine and looked to Constantinople for protection and countenance; the Jewish and pagan Arabians were pro-Persian and expected aid from Ctesiphon. In response to Sayf's prayers the Persian emperor in 575 sent eight hundred men under Wahraz (or Wahriz), who routed the Abyssinian garrison in al-Yaman and freed the country from the hated African rule. At first a system of joint administration was instituted with Sayf as titular head. Sayf took up his residence in the ancient castle of Ghumdān, which was evidently in ruins during the Abyssinian rule. But soon al-Yaman was converted into a Persian satrapy and the South Arabians found they had only changed one master for another.

In this tradition we have preserved for us a clear recollection of the rivalry between the two powers on either side of Arabia —Zoroastrian Persia and Christian Abyssinia (backed by Byzantium)—to inherit their neighbour, the defunct South Arabian kingdom. The native Christian Arabian sympathy with Byzantium served as a wedge for Abyssinian intervention, while Jewish and pagan leanings toward Persia gave the latter its opportunity. With the Syro-Arabian desert in the north barring the penetration of world powers South Arabia thus acted as the gateway through which these powers found their way into the peninsula.

In 628, the sixth year after the Hijrah, Bādhān, the fifth Persian satrap of al-Yaman, embraced Islam. With the birth of this new religion the centre of interest in the peninsula shifted to the north. Henceforth the stream of Arabian history flowed in northern channels, with al-Ḥijāz replacing al-Yaman in public consideration.

CHAPTER VI

THE NABATAEAN AND OTHER PETTY KINGDOMS OF NORTH AND CENTRAL ARABIA

1. The Nabataeans

ASIDE from the South Arabian kingdoms a few petty states evolved during the pre-Islamic period in the northern and central parts of the peninsula. These North Arabian states, like those of the south, drew their strength mainly from commerce and were in no sense militaristic either in their inception or in their development. The earliest among them was the Nabataean kingdom.

We read of no Assyrian campaign directed against the Nabataeans, because they were not then on the main route to the west. In the early part of the sixth century B.C. the Nabataeans (al-Anbāṭ, classical Nabataei)[1] came as nomadic tribes from what is today called Transjordan and occupied the land of the Edomites (Idumaeans, the descendants of Esau), from whom they later wrested Petra. The predecessors of the Edomites in this "land of Seir" were the Horites (Hurris).[2] The Nabataeans, from their metropolis Petra, came into possession of the neighbouring territory. Petra, a Greek word meaning rock, is a translation of the Hebrew Sela' mentioned in Isaiah 16 : 1, 42 : 11 and 2 Kings 14 : 7.[3] Al-Raqīm[4] is the Arabic correspondent and the modern name is Wādi Mūsa (the valley of Moses). The ancient city, located on an arid plateau three thousand feet high, presents today the spectacle of a vast glowing necropolis hewn in a rock (Umm al-Biyārah) whose sandstone strata exhibit almost all the colours of the rainbow.

For upwards of four hundred years, beginning toward the end of the fourth century B.C., Petra was a key city on the caravan route between Saba' and the Mediterranean.

Our first detailed account of the early history of the Naba-

[1] Heb. Nĕbāyōth, Assyr. Nabaitai, Nabaitu, are apparently not the Nabataeans.
[2] Gen. 14 : 6, 36 : 20.
[3] Cf. 2 Ch. 25 : 12; Jer. 49 : 16; Ob. 3-4.
[4] See Josephus, *Antiquities*, Bk. IV, ch. 4, § 7, ch. 7, § 1.

taeans comes from Diodorus Siculus († after 57 B.C.). About 312 B.C. they were strong enough to resist two expeditions sent against them by Antigonus, Alexander's successor as king of Syria, and return victoriously to "the rock".[1] They were then within the Ptolemaic sphere of influence. Later they became the allies of Rome and nominally co-operated in the famous invasion of Arabia in 24 B.C. by Gallus. In the reign of Ḥārithath (al-Ḥārith, Aretas III, *ca.* 87–62 B.C.) the Nabataeans first came into close contact with the Romans. It was then that the royal coins were first struck. Julius Cæsar in 47 B.C. called on Māliku (Mālik, Malchus I) to provide him with cavalry for the Alexandrian war. His successor, 'Obīdath ('Ubaydah, Obodas III, *ca.* 28–9 B.C.), was the ruler under whom the Roman expedition to Arabia took place. Arabia Petraea, whose capital was Petra, reached its height under Ḥārithath IV (9 B.C. to A.D. 40). At the time of Christ the Nabataean kingdom extended north as far as Damascus, which together with Coele-Syria was wrested from Seleucid hands by Ḥārithath III (*ca.* 87 B.C.). It was an ethnarch of Ḥārithath IV who endeavoured to arrest Paul in Damascus.[2] Al-Ḥijr (Madā'in Ṣāliḥ) in northern al-Ḥijāz must have also in the first century of our era been included in the Nabataean kingdom, as the inscriptions there attest. The names of all the Nabataean monarchs from Ḥārithath I (169 B.C.) to the last independent ruler, Rabbīl II (A.D. 70–106), are known to us.[3] In A.D. 105 the Emperor Trajan put an end to the Nabataean autonomy and in the following year their territory became a regular Roman province.

After Diodorus, Josephus († *ca.* A.D. 95) is our chief source of information about the Nabataeans, but Josephus was interested in them only as they crossed wires with the Hebrews. To him Arabia meant the Nabataean state reaching eastward as far as the Euphrates. Malchus or Malichus (Ar. Mālik), mentioned by Josephus[4] as the "king of Arabia" whom Herod and his father had befriended, and the Malchus[5] (Malchus II, A.D. 40–70) who about A.D. 67 sent 1000 horse and 5000 foot to the assistance of Titus in his attack on Jerusalem, were both Nabataeans. In 1 Mac. 5 : 25 and 2 Mac. 5 : 8 the Nabataeans are identified

[1] Diodorus, Bk. XIX, §§ 94-7.
[2] 2 Cor. 11 : 32.
[3] See the list in Cooke, *North-Semitic Inscriptions*, p. 216.
[4] *Antiquities*, Bk. XIV, ch. 14, § 1; *The Jewish War*, Bk. I, ch. 14, § 1.
[5] *Jewish War*, Bk. III, ch. 4, § 2.

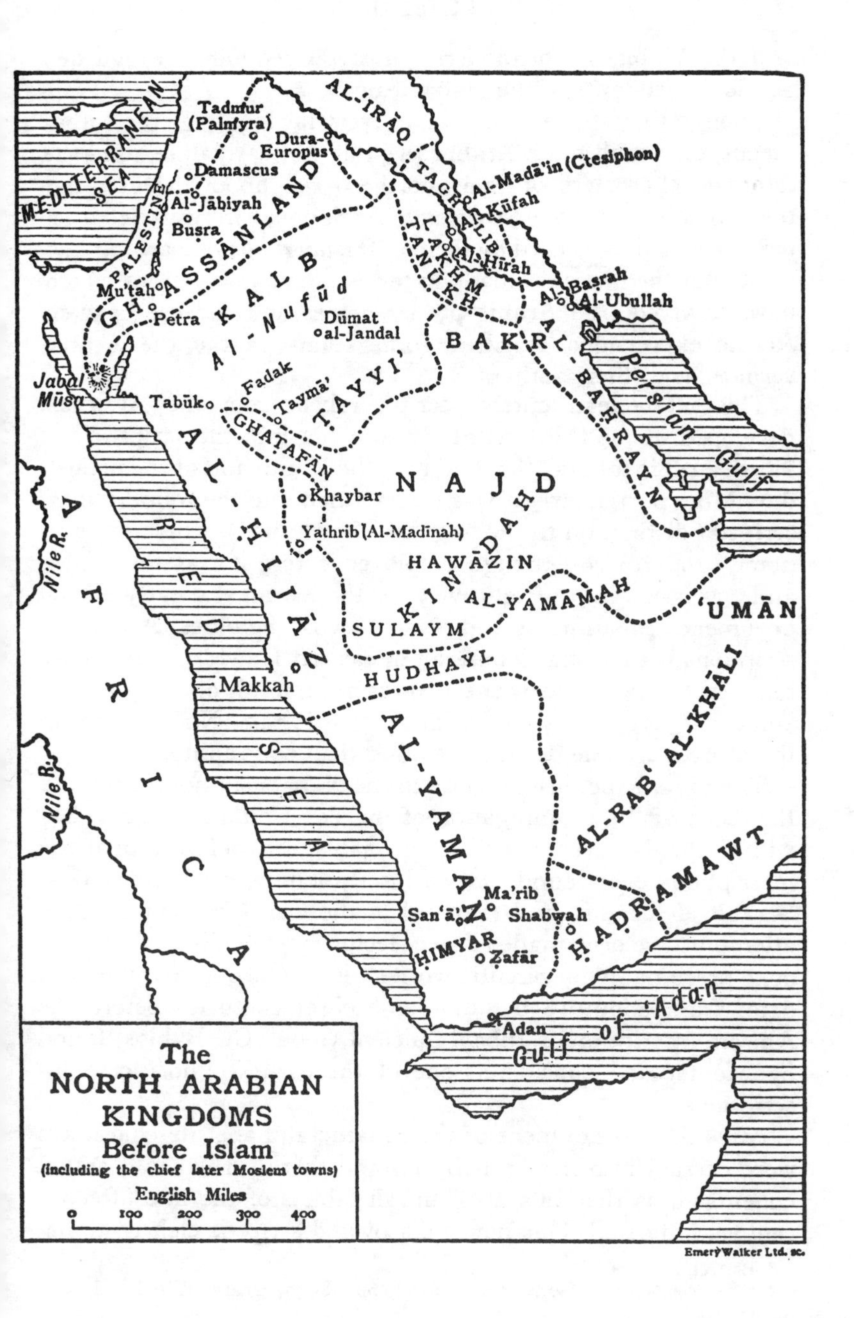
The
NORTH ARABIAN
KINGDOMS
Before Islam
(including the chief later Moslem towns)
English Miles
0 100 200 300 400
MEDITERRANEAN SEA
AL-'IRĀQ
Tadmur (Palmyra)
Dura-Europus
Damascus
Al-Madā'in (Ctesiphon)
Al-Jābiyah
Al-Kūfah
Buṣra
GHASSĀNLAND
PALESTINE
TAGHLIB
LAKHM
TANŪKH
Al-Ḥīrah
Al-Baṣrah
Al-Ubullah
Mu'tah
Petra
KALB
Al-Nufūd
Dūmat al-Jandal
BAKR
AL-BAḤRAYN
Persian Gulf
Jabal Mūsa
Fadak
Taymā'
Tabūk
TAYYI'
GHATAFĀN
NAJD
AL-ḤIJĀZ
Khaybar
KINDAH
Yathrib (Al-Madīnah)
HAWĀZIN
AL-YAMĀMAH
'UMĀN
SULAYM
HUDHAYL
Makkah
AFRICA
Nile R.
RED SEA
AL-YAMAN
AL-RAB' AL-KHĀLI
ḤAḌRAMAWT
Ma'rib
Ṣan'ā'
Shabwah
ḤIMYAR
Ẓafār
'Adan
Gulf of 'Adan
Emery Walker Ltd. sc.

with the Arabians. The modern Ḥuwayṭāt Bedouins are regarded as the descendants of the Nabataeans.

Though they spoke Arabic as an everyday language the Nabataeans, in default of an Arabic script at that early date, used the Aramaic characters of their northern neighbours. Diodorus[1] refers to a letter of theirs written to Antigonus "in Syriac characters". Aramaic was used by them as the language of learning and trade, but the mistakes made in the Aramaic inscriptions which have survived, the Arabic proper names and the use of such Arabic expressions as *ghayr* (other than) betray the Arabic vernacular of their authors.

This Nabataean cursive script, taken from the Aramaic, developed in the third century of our era into the script of the North Arabic tongue, the Arabic of the Koran and of the present day. More particularly it was transformed into the round *naskhi* script in distinction to the angular *Kūfi* (Kufic), which owes its name to al-Kūfah—though employed before it was founded—and was used almost exclusively for the Koran and early official documents, monuments and coins. One of the oldest Arabic inscriptions is that of al-Namārah in eastern Ḥawrān, which goes back to A.D. 328 and was set up as an epitaph on the tomb of Imru'-al-Qays, a Lakhmid king of al-Ḥirah. No Nabataean literature has come down to us other than epigraphic.

The Sinaitic origin of the alphabet

The Sinaitic peninsula, close to the Nabataean homeland and the scene of the promulgation of the Ten Commandments, has within the last years yielded probably the oldest alphabetic inscriptions ever found. These inscriptions were discovered at Sarābīṭ al-Khādim and removed to the Cairo Museum. Many attempts have been made at their decipherment. The writing was done presumably by Sinaitic workers in the turquoise mines and dates from about 1850 B.C.—some eight centuries before the Aḥīrām inscription of Jubayl (ancient Gebal, Gr. Byblos) found by Montet and considered one of the earliest Phoenician inscriptions.

After the development of the Sinaitic alphabet its characters were carried into northern Syria, and there turned into actual cuneiform, as the Ra's al-Shamrah tablets of the late fifteenth century indicate.[2] This newly discovered script is clearly alpha-

[1] Bk. XIX, ch. 96.

[2] F.-A. Schaeffer in *Syria*, vol. x (1929), pp. 285-97; Charles Virolleaud, *ibid.* pp. 304-10.

betic and Semitic, and although written with a stylus on clay tablets its letters were not borrowed from the earlier Sumero-Akkadian characters. In it the Sinaitic alphabet was conventionalized into wedge-shaped signs.

For a long time it has been recognized by modern scholars that the Phoenicians, who were the first to use an exclusively alphabetic system of writing, must have originally received the basis for their system from Egyptian hieroglyphic sources, but the gap always seemed wide between the two systems. The Sinaitic writing now comes in to bridge that gap. The Sinaitic Semite took, for instance, from the hieroglyphics the sign for ox-head (not caring what "ox-head" was in the Egyptian language) and called this sign by the name of the ox-head in his own language, *aleph*. Then according to the principle of acrophony he used this sign for the sound *a*. The same treatment he accorded to the sign for "house", calling it *beth* and using it for the sound *b* and so on.

This Sinaitic origin of the alphabet explains how it could have been transmitted on the one hand to South Arabia, where it underwent an independent development and was employed by the Minaeans perhaps as early as 1200 B.C., and how on the other hand it was carried northward to the Phoenician coast. With the trade in turquoise, which the Arabs sold to the Phoenicians, went the alphabet, just as it later went with the trade from the Phoenicians to the Greeks to become the mother of all European alphabets.

The inscriptions, discovered in the volcanic Ṣafa region of Ḥawrān, which date from about A.D. 100 or later,[1] as well as the Dedanite and Liḥyānite inscriptions of al-'Ula in northern al-Ḥijāz (the so-called proto-Arabic) of the seventh to the third century B.C., and the Thamūdic writings of the same region, particularly of al-Ḥijr and Taymā' (of the fifth century B.C. to the fourth Christian century), represent in their epigraphy by-forms of the South Arabic alphabet;[2] but the language of all these inscriptions is North Arabic differing but little from the well-known classical Arabic. The Thamūdic graffiti are a development of the Liḥyānite script, another development of which is seen in the Ṣafa graffiti. The Ṣafa inscriptions are the northernmost South

[1] Cf. F. V. Winnett, *A Study of the Lihyanite and Thamudic Inscriptions* (Toronto, 1937), p. 53.

[2] René Dussaud, *Les Arabes en Syrie avant l'Islam* (Paris, 1907), pp. 57-73; Dussaud and F. Macler, *Voyage archéologique au Ṣafa et dans le Djebel ed-Drûz* (Paris, 1901), pp. 3-14.

Arabian writings found. The South Arabic script has also survived in Ethiopic.

The historical relations of the three northern peoples who used these similar scripts, Ṣafaitic, Liḥyānite and Thamūdic, have not been completely determined. The Liḥyānites, whom Pliny[1] mentions under the name Lechieni, were an ancient people, probably a section of the Thamūd, and their capital Daydān was once a Minaean colony on the great trade route which carried the merchandise of al-Yaman and India to the Mediterranean ports. After the fall of Petra (A.D. 105) the Liḥyānites seem also to have held the important Nabataean centre al-Ḥijr (modern Madā'in Ṣāliḥ), once a Thamūdic town. The Minaean as well as the Nabataean civilization greatly influenced the later Liḥyānite culture. The ruins of al-'Ula, which include tombs decorated with sculptures in high relief, indicate an advanced pre-Islamic civilization of which very little is known.[2]

Petra

Petra reached its greatest wealth and prosperity in the first century of our era under the patronage of the Romans, who treated it as a buffer state against Parthia. On three sides, east, west and south, the city was impregnable. Carved out of the solid rock, it was surrounded on all sides by precipitous and almost impassable cliffs and was entered through a narrow winding defile. The city provided the only spot between the Jordan and Central Arabia where water was not only abundant but invitingly pure. Here the South Arabians obtained on their northward caravan march fresh relays of camels and drivers. Thus the Nabataeans formed an important link in the commercial chain by which South Arabia flourished. The spectacular ruins of Petra still attract many tourists and constitute an important source of income to the modern state of Transjordan.

Petra had a kind of Ka'bah with Dūshara (Dusares), worshipped under the form of a black rectangular stone, at the head of the pantheon; Allāt, identified by Herodotus[3] with Aphrodite Urania, was the chief female deity. Dūshara (dhu-Shara, i.e. the lord of Shara) was later associated with the vine, introduced to the land of Nabataeans in the Hellenistic period, and

[1] Bk. VI, ch. 32.

[2] Consult Eduard Glaser, *Skizze der Geschichte und Geographie Arabiens* (Berlin, 1890), vol. ii, pp. 98-127; Jaussen and Savignac, *Mission archéologique en Arabie* (Paris, 1909), pp. 250-91.

[3] Bk. III, ch. 8.

as the god of wine borrowed some of the traits of Dionysus-Bacchus.

From Alexander Kennedy, "Petra: Its History and Monuments" ("*Country Life*")

PETRA: THE PALACE

From Alexander Kennedy, "Petra: Its History and Monuments" ("*Country Life*")

PETRA: THE DAYR

In the first two centuries after Christ, as the sea route to India became more and more familiar to the Roman sailors, as the caravan route from east to west was gradually diverted to a more northerly region centring at Palmyra, and as the north-to-south trade took a course farther east corresponding to the later pilgrimage route and the present Ḥijāz Railway, Petra lost its advantageous position and the Nabataean state began to decline. After the reduction of the city in A.D. 105 through the cupidity and short-sightedness of Trajan, Arabia Petraea was incorporated (106) into the Roman empire under the name Provincia Arabia, and henceforth the history of Petra remained almost a blank for many centuries.[1]

2. Palmyrena

The new conditions created in Western Asia by the Parthian conquest of Mesopotamia and the new routes which began to be used on a large scale after the first century of our era gave prominence to a city situated in an oasis in the middle of the Syrian desert and whose fame has since become world wide. This is the city of Palmyra (Ar. Tadmur), whose present ruins are among the most magnificent and least-studied remains of antiquity. Located between the two rival empires of Parthia and Rome, Palmyra depended for its security upon the maintenance of a balance between the two and in profiting by its neutrality.[2] Its geographic position, with its plentiful supply of fresh and mineral waters, afforded a rendezvous not only for the eastern and western trade but for the south-to-north commerce starting in South Arabia. The "chief of the caravan" and the "chief of the market" figure in inscriptions as leading citizens.[3] In the course of the second and third centuries of our era this desert metropolis became one of the richest cities of the Near East.

Tadmor (the early Semitic name of Palmyra) must have been a very ancient settlement, for it was cited under the name Tadmar of Amurru[4] in an inscription of Tiglath-Pileser I (*ca.* 1100 B.C.). So impressed by its ruins were the Arab story-tellers that they ascribed its origin to the jinn who, they believed, had built it for King Solomon.

Exactly when the Arabs came into possession of Palmyra local tradition does not seem to remember. The first authentic mention of the town is when Mark Antony in 42–41 B.C. made a vain

[1] A recently identified Nabataean site, 'RM, twenty-five miles east of al-'Aqabah, is koranic Iram (sūr. 89 : 6).

[2] Pliny, Bk. V, ch. 21.

[3] Cooke, pp. 274, 279.

[4] Luckenbill, vol. i, §§ 287, 308. The Hebrew chronicler (2 Ch. 8 : 4) and the Greek translator of 1 K. 9 : 18 confused it with Tamar in Idumaea built by Solomon. Cf. Ezek. 47 : 19, 48 : 28.

attempt to possess himself of its riches. Its earliest native inscription goes back to 9 B.C., at which time Palmyra was already an important trade centre between the Roman and Parthian states.

The city must have come within the Roman political orbit early in the imperial period, for we find decrees relative to its customs duties issued in A.D. 17. In the time of Hadrian (A.D. 117–38) Palmyra and its dependent cities became vassals of Rome. As a consequence of Hadrian's visit in 130, the city received the name Hadriana Palmyra. Septimius Severus (A.D. 193–211) transformed Palmyra and its towns into provincial cities of the empire. At the beginning of the third century Palmyra assumed the status of a colony, but even then it must have enjoyed administrative independence with only a nominal recognition of Roman suzerainty. Palmyrenes then began to add to their names Roman ones. The Romans recognized the city's military importance, for their road from Damascus to the Euphrates passed through it.

Palmyra reached its period of splendour between A.D. 130 and 270. To this period most of its inscribed monuments belong. Its international trade extended as far east as China, and as a city created by the caravan trade it became the true heir of Petra.

Odaynath and Zenobia

The Palmyrenes did not distinguish themselves as warriors until their chieftain Odaynath (Odenathus, Ar. Udhaynah) drove out of Syria Shāpūr I, who in A.D. 260 had captured the Emperor Valerian and conquered a large portion of Syria. Odaynath pursued Shāpūr to the very walls of his capital, Ctesiphon (al-Madā'in). In the protracted struggle between the Romans and the Sāsānidṣ, who succeeded (226) the Parthians, the Palmyrene chief sided with the former and was appointed in 262 *dux Orientis*, vice-emperor over the Orient. The Emperor Gallienus bestowed on him the honorific title of Imperator and acknowledged him master of the Roman legions in the East. This meant that over Asia Minor and Egypt the supreme authority was nominally in his hand; over Syria, North Arabia and possibly Armenia it was virtually so. Thus did Palmyra become mistress of Western Asia. Four years later (266–7) Odaynath and his eldest son were treacherously assassinated at Ḥimṣ (Emesa), possibly at the instigation of Rome, which had suspected him of disloyalty.

Odaynath's beautiful and ambitious wife Zenobia (Aramaic

Bath-Zabbay, Ar. al-Zabbā', also Zaynab) proved a worthy successor. Ruling on behalf of her young son Wahb-Allāth (the gift of al-Lāt, Greek Athenodorus) she arrogated to herself the title of Queen of the East and for a time defied the Roman empire. With masculine energy she pushed forward the frontiers of her kingdom so as to include Egypt and a large part of Asia Minor, where the Roman garrisons in 270 were thrust back as far as Ankara (Ancyra). Even in Chalcedon opposite Byzantium a military attempt was made to establish her rule. Her victorious troops in the same year occupied Alexandria, the second city of the empire, and her minor son, who was then proclaimed King of Egypt, issued coins from which the head of Aurelian was omitted. Her success on the battlefield was due in the main to her two Palmyrene generals, Zabbay and Zabda.

Aurelian at last bestirred himself. In a battle at Antioch followed by another near Ḥimṣ he defeated Zabda, and in the spring of 272 he entered Palmyra. The proud Arab queen fled in despair on a swift dromedary into the desert, but was finally taken captive and led in golden chains before the chariot of the victor to grace his triumphal entry into Rome. En route to his capital Aurelian was informed of an uprising in Palmyra and thereupon speedily returned to the city, completely destroyed its walls and dissolved its commonwealth. The ornaments of the glorious Temple of the Sun (Bel) he transferred to the new temple he erected in Rome to the sun-god of the East in memory of his notable victory. The city was left in ruins, in practically the same state as at present. Thus did the brilliant and meteoric glory of Palmyra come to an end.

The Palmyrene civilization was an interesting blend of Greek, Syrian and Parthian (Iranian) elements. It is significant not only in itself but, as in the case of the Nabataean civilization which we have already studied, as an illustration of the cultural heights which the Arabians of the desert are capable of attaining when the proper opportunities present themselves. That the Palmyrenes were of Arabian stock is evidenced from the proper names and the frequent occurrence of Arabic words in their Aramaic inscriptions. The language they spoke was a dialect of Western Aramaic not unlike the Nabataean and Egyptian Aramaic. Their religion had the prominent solar features that characterized the religion of North Arabians. Bel, of Babylonian

PALMYRA: THE COLONNADE AND TRIUMPHAL ARCH

origin, stood at the head of the pantheon; Baal Shamin (the lord of the heavens) figured in votive inscriptions and no less than twenty other names of deities occur in Palmyrene.

With the fall of the ephemeral kingdom of Palmyrena land traffic sought and found other paths. Buṣra (Bostra) in Ḥawrān and other Ghassānid towns became beneficiaries of the desert city as that city had itself once been the beneficiary of Petra.

3 The Ghassānids

The Ghassānids claim descent from an ancient South Arabian tribe, headed formerly by ʻAmr Muzayqiyā' ibn-ʻĀmir Mā'-al-Samā', which is supposed to have fled to Ḥawrān[1] and al-Balqā' from al-Yaman towards the end of the third Christian century at the destruction of the Ma'rib dam. Jafnah, a son of ʻAmr, is regarded as the founder of the dynasty, for which abu-al-Fidā'[2] claims thirty-one sovereigns, Ḥamzah al-Iṣfahāni[3] thirty-two, and al-Masʻūdi[4] and ibn-Qutaybah[5] only eleven. These figures show how obscure Jafnid history has remained to Arab chroniclers.

This Yamani tribe displaced the Salīḥ, the first Arabians to found a kingdom in Syria, and established itself in the region south-east of Damascus at the northern end of the great transport route that bound Ma'rib with Damascus. In course of time the banu-Ghassān were Christianized and Syrianized, adopting the Aramaic language of Syria without, however, abandoning their native Arabic tongue. Like other Arabian tribes in the Fertile Crescent they thus became bilingual. About the end of the fifth century they were brought within the sphere of Byzantine political influence and used as a buffer state to stay the overflow of Bedouin hordes, serving a purpose not unlike that of Transjordan under the British today. Facing the Byzantine empire as they did, the Ghassānids adopted a form of Christianity which, though of the local Monophysite variety, still coincided with their political interests. Their capital was at first a movable camp; later it may have become fixed at al-Jābiyah in the Jawlān (Gaulanitis) and for some time was located at Jilliq.[6]

The Syro-Arab kingdom at its height

The Ghassānid kingdom, like its rival and relative at al-

[1] Assyrian Ḫaurānu (cf. Luckenbill, vol. i, §§ 672, 821), biblical Bashan, classical Auranitis.

[2] *Ta'rīkh* (Constantinople, 1286), vol. i, pp. 76-7.

[3] *Op. cit.* pp. 115-22.

[4] *Murūj*, vol. iii, pp. 217-21.

[5] *Al-Maʻārif*, ed. F. Wüstenfeld (Göttingen, 1850), pp. 314-16.

[6] Consult Leone Caetani, *Annali dell'Islām* (Milan, 1910), vol. iii, p. 928.

Ḥīrah, the kingdom of the Lakhmids, attained its greatest importance during the sixth century after Christ. In this century al-Ḥārith II ibn-Jabalah of Ghassān (*ca.* 529–69) and al-Mundhir III ibn-Mā'-al-Samā' of al-Ḥīrah (Alamundarus of Byzantine histories, † 554) dominate Arab history. This al-Ḥārith (nicknamed al-A'raj, the lame, by Arab chroniclers) is the first authentic name and by far the greatest in Jafnid annals. His history can be checked with the Greek sources.[1] As a reward for defeating his formidable Lakhmid rival, al-Mundhir III, the Byzantine Emperor Justinian appointed him (529) lord over all the Arab tribes of Syria and created him patricius and phylarch —the highest rank next to that of the emperor himself. In Arabic the title was rendered simply *malik*, king.

The greater part of al-Ḥārith's long reign was occupied with wars in the service of the Byzantine interests. About 544, in a battle with al-Mundhir III, the latter captured a son of al-Ḥārith and offered him as a sacrifice to al-'Uzza, the counterpart of the Greek Aphrodite.[2] But ten years later al-Ḥārith took his revenge and slew his Lakhmid enemy in a battle in the district of Qinnasrīn. This battle is perhaps the "Day of Ḥalīmah" of Arabic tradition, Ḥalīmah being the daughter of al-Ḥārith who, before the battle, perfumed with her own hands the hundred Ghassānid champions ready for death and clad them in shrouds of white linen in addition to coats of mail.[3]

In 563 al-Ḥārith paid a visit to the court of Justinian I at Constantinople.[4] The appearance of this Bedouin phylarch left a deep impression on the emperor's entourage. During al-Ḥārith's stay in Constantinople he secured the appointment of the Monophysite bishop Jacob Baradaeus (Ya'qūb al-Barda'i) of Edessa as prelate of the Syrian Arabs. So zealous was this Jacob in the propagation of the faith that the Syrian Monophysite church became known after him as Jacobite.

Al-Mundhir, son of al-Ḥārith

Al-Ḥārith's successor was his son al-Mundhir, also Alamundarus in Byzantine chronicles. Like his father, al-Mundhir proved an ardent protector of Monophysitism,[5] and this temporarily

[1] Procopius, Bk. I, ch. 17, §§ 47-8; Joannes Malalas, *Chronographia*, ed. L. Dindorf (Bonn, 1831), pp. 435, 461 *seq.*

[2] Procopius, Bk. II, ch. 28, § 13.

[3] Ibn-Qutaybah, pp. 314-15; cf. abu-al-Fidā', vol. i, p. 84.

[4] Theophanes, *Chronographia*, ed. C. de Boor (Leipzig, 1883), p. 240.

[5] John of Ephesus, *Ecclesiastical History*, ed. William Cureton (Oxford, 1853), pp. 251-2; tr. R. Payne Smith (Oxford, 1860), pp. 284-5.

alienated the sympathy of Byzantium and resulted in an open rebellion on the part of the Ghassānids. In 580 he visited Constantinople with his two sons and was received with great honour by Tiberius II, who replaced the precious diadem on his head with a still more precious crown. In the same year he successfully raided and burned al-Ḥīrah,[1] the capital of his Lakhmid foes. But this was not enough to remove the suspicion of treachery to the imperial cause with which his father before him had been charged. At the dedication of a church in Ḥūwārīn, between Damascus and Palmyra, he was apprehended and taken prisoner to Constantinople, later to be incarcerated in Sicily. Likewise his son and successor, al-Nuʿmān, who ventured to raid and devastate Byzantine territory, was carried away to Constantinople.

Fall of the banu-Ghassān

After al-Mundhir and al-Nuʿmān anarchy seems to have prevailed in Ghassānland. The various tribes in the Syrian desert chose their own chieftains. The capture of Jerusalem and Damascus (613-14) by the Sāsānid Khusraw Parwīz dealt the last blow to the Jafnid dynasty. Whether Heraclius on his reconquest of Syria in 629 restored the Syro-Arab phylarchate is uncertain. Arab chroniclers make Jabalah ibn-al-Ayham the last king of the house of Ghassān. On the memorable battlefield of Yarmūk (636) this monarch fought on the Byzantine side against the Arabians, but later adopted Islam. As he was circumambulating the Kaʿbah in the course of his first pilgrimage, so the story goes, a Bedouin stepped on his cloak and the ex-king slapped him on the face. The Caliph ʿUmar decreed that Jabalah should either submit to a similar blow from the hand of the Bedouin or pay a fine, upon which Jabalah renounced Islam and retired to Constantinople.[2]

The degree of culture attained by the Ghassānids, neighbours of the Byzantines, was undoubtedly higher than that to which their rivals on the Persian borderland, the Lakhmids, ever attained. Under their régime and during the earlier Roman period a peculiar civilization seems to have developed along the entire eastern fringe of Syria from a mixture of Arabic, Syrian and Greek elements. Houses of basalt, palaces, triumphal arches, public baths, aqueducts, theatres and churches stood where today there is nothing but utter desolation. The eastern and southern

[1] John of Ephesus, p. 415 (text), = p. 385 (tr.).
[2] Ibn-ʿAbd-Rabbihi, *ʿIqd*, vol. i, pp. 140-41.

slopes of Ḥawrān have preserved the ruins of almost three hundred towns and villages where only a few exist at the present day.

A number of the pre-Islamic poets of Arabia found in the Ghassānid phylarchs munificent patrons. Labīd, the youngest of the seven poets who composed the famous "Muʿallaqāt", fought on the Ghassānid side in the battle of Ḥalīmah. When al-Nābighah al-Dhubyāni fell out with the Lakhmid king he found in the court of the sons of al-Ḥārith a haven of refuge. The Madīnese poet Ḥassān ibn-Thābit (b. *ca.* 563), who claimed kinship with the banu-Ghassān, visited their court in his youth before he became the poet laureate of Muḥammad and made a number of references to it in his *dīwān* (anthology). In an apocryphal passage ascribed to him[1] we have a glowing account of the luxury and magnificence of Jabalah's court with its Makkan and Babylonian and Greek singers and musicians of both sexes and its free use of wine.[2]

4. The Lakhmids

From time immemorial streams of Arabian wanderers have been wont to trickle along the eastern coast of their peninsula to the Tigro-Euphrates valley and settle therein. About the beginning of the third century of our era a number of such tribes, calling themselves Tanūkh and said to have been of Yamanite origin, found an abode in the fertile region west of the Euphrates. Their advent may have coincided with the disturbances consequent to the fall of the Arsacid Parthian and the establishment of the Sāsānid dynasty (A.D. 226).

The Tanūkh lived first in tents. Their temporary camp developed in course of time into permanent al-Ḥīrah (from Syriac *ḥerta*, camp), which lay about three miles south of al-Kūfah, not far from ancient Babylon. This al-Ḥīrah became the capital of Persian Arabia.

The native population was Christian belonging to the East Syrian (later Nestorian) Church and was referred to by Arab authors as *ʿibād*, i.e. worshippers (of Christ).[3] Some of the Tanūkh were subsequently Christianized and domiciled in northern Syria. The Tanūkhs who later came to southern Lebanon and professed the secret Druze religion trace their origin to the Lakhmid kings of al-Ḥīrah.[4]

[1] Abu-al-Faraj al-Iṣbahāni, *al-Aghāni* (Būlāq, 1284-5), vol. xvi, p. 15.

[2] Among the Christian families living today in southern Lebanon are some which trace their descent to Ghassānid origin.

[3] Cf. Ṭabari, vol. i, p. 770.

[4] Cf. Hitti, *The Origins of the Druze People and Religion* (New York, 1928, reprint, 1966), p. 21.

Tradition names Mālik ibn-Fahm al-Azdi[1] as the first chieftain of this Arab settlement in al-'Irāq and makes his son Jadhīmah al-Abrash a vassal of Ardashīr. But the real founder of the Lakhmid kingdom was 'Amr ibn-'Adi ibn-Naṣr ibn-Rabī'ah ibn-Lakhm, a son of Jadhīmah's sister, who had married a servant of Jadhīmah. 'Amr established himself in al-Ḥīrah, which he made his capital.

With the establishment of the Naṣrid or Lakhmid dynasty in the latter part of the third century of our era we begin to tread on firm historical ground. The names of some twenty Lakhmid kings have been handed down to us, but the first clearly delineated personage is Imru'-al-Qays I († A.D. 328), whose epitaph is the oldest proto-Arabic inscription yet discovered. The script is a variation of the Nabataean character and shows many signs of transition towards the later North Arabic script, particularly in the matter of joining the letters.[2]

A descendant of Imru'-al-Qays was al-Nu'mān I al-A'war (the one-eyed, *ca.* 400–418), celebrated in poetry and legend. He is credited with having built al-Khawarnaq, a famous castle near al-Ḥīrah, as a residence for Bahrām Gōr, the son of Yazdagird I (399–420), who was anxious to have his son brought up in the salubrious air of the desert. Al-Khawarnaq was declared a miracle of art and was ascribed by later historians to a Byzantine architect who suffered the fate common to many legendary architects in being put to death on the completion of his work —a favourite motif in such stories—so that the construction might never be duplicated. Al-Nu'mān remained a pagan throughout his life and at one time persecuted his own Christian subjects and prevented the Arabs from visiting St. Simeon Stylites, though in the latter part of his life he felt more kindly disposed towards Christianity. Simeon was himself an Arab and the crowds of the desert flocked to see the wonderful sight of this ascetic living on a pillar-top. The erection of al-Sadīr, a castle associated in poetry with al-Khawarnaq and lying "in the midst of the desert between al-Ḥīrah and Syria",[3] is also attributed to al-Nu'mān. Al-Sadīr and other Lakhmid *ḥīrahs* are today but names. None are identified except al-Khawarnaq.

Al-Ḥīrah at the height of its power

Under al-Nu'mān's son and successor, al-Mundhir I (*ca.*

[1] The Azd and the Tanūkh were confederated into one tribe in al-'Irāq.

[2] Dussaud, *Les Arabes en Syrie*, pp. 34-5.

[3] Yāqūt, vol. ii, p. 375.

A.D. 418–62), al-Ḥīrah began to play its important rôle in the events of the day. So great was al-Mundhir's influence that he could force the Persian priests to crown Bahrām, once the protégé of his father, over the claims of a powerful pretender to the throne. In 421 he fought beside his Sāsānid suzerain against the Byzantines.

In the first half of the sixth century al-Ḥīrah was ruled by another Mundhir, al-Mundhir III (*ca.* 505–54), whom the Arabs call ibn-Mā'-al-Samā', Mā'-al-Samā' (the water of heaven) being a sobriquet of his mother Māriyah or Māwīyah. His was the most illustrious rule in Lakhmid annals. He proved a thorn in the side of Roman Syria. His raids devastated the land as far as Antioch until he found more than a match in the Ghassānid al-Ḥārith.[1] About this al-Mundhir, *al-Aghāni*[2] relates the curious story of the two boon-companions whom he is said to have buried alive in the course of a carousal.

His son and successor, 'Amr, surnamed ibn-Hind (A.D. 554–69), though tyrannical was a munificent patron of poets. The greatest bards of Arabia then living, such as Ṭarafah ibn-al-'Abd, al-Ḥārith ibn-Ḥillizah and 'Amr ibn-Kulthūm (three of the seven reputed authors of "Golden Odes", *Mu'allaqāt*), flocked to his court. 'Amr, like other Lakhmid and Jafnid monarchs, recognized in the contemporary poets leaders of public opinion and potential publicity agents. Hence the lavish bounties which he and other patrons, with the hope of seeing their influence extended among the Bedouins, bestowed on the poets who frequented their courts. 'Amr met his death at the hand of his protégé ibn-Kulthūm, who thus avenged an insult to his mother by the king.

The royal family Christianized

Hind, the mother of 'Amr, was a Christian princess of Ghassān; others say of Kindah. She founded in the capital a convent which survived into the second century of Islam;[3] Yāqūt[4] has preserved for us its dedicatory inscription. In this inscription Hind calls herself "the maid of Christ and the mother of His slave ['Amr] and the daughter of His slaves". That there were Christians among the populace professing the East Syrian creed is indicated by the many references to the bishops of al-Ḥīrah, one of whom lived as early as A.D. 410.

[1] Procopius, Bk. I, ch. 17, §§ 45-8; Malalas, pp. 434-5, 445, 460 *seq.*
[2] Vol. xix, pp. 86-8. Cf. ibn-Qutaybah, p. 319; Iṣfahāni, *Ta'rīkh*, p. 111.
[3] Ṭabari, vol. ii, pp. 1882, 1903.
[4] Vol. ii, p. 709.

The Lakhmid dynasty came to an end with al-Nu'mān III abu-Qābūs (*ca.* 580–602), son of al-Mundhir IV. He was a patron of the famous poet al-Nābighah al-Dhubyāni before the latter was driven from al-Ḥīrah as a result of a false accusation. Having been brought up in a Christian home, al-Nu'mān was converted to Christianity and became the first and only Christian Lakhmid king. That no member of the Lakhmid house saw fit before this time to adopt Christianity, the faith of the Byzantines, may be explained on the ground that the Ḥīrah kings found it to their political interest to remain friendly with Persia. Al-Nu'mān was baptized into the East Syrian (Nestorian) communion, the one least objectionable to Persia.

The Arab civilization of al-Ḥīrah, which faced Persia, did not attain the high degree reached by the Arab civilizations of Petra, Palmyra and Ghassānland under Syro-Byzantine influence. The Arabs of al-Ḥīrah spoke Arabic as a daily language but used Syriac in writing, just as the Nabataeans and Palmyrenes spoke Arabic and wrote in Aramaic. The Christians in the lower valley of the Euphrates acted as the teachers of the heathen Arabs in reading, writing and religion. From al-Ḥīrah the beneficent influences spread into Arabia proper. There are those who hold that it was the Syrian church of al-Ḥīrah which was responsible for the introduction of Christianity into Najrān. According to traditions preserved in ibn-Rustah[1] it was from al-Ḥīrah that the Quraysh acquired the art of writing and the system of false belief.[2] From this it is clear that Persian cultural influences likewise found their way into the peninsula through the Lakhmid kingdom.

After al-Nu'mān Iyās ibn-Qabīṣah of the Ṭayyi' ruled (602–11), but beside him stood a Persian resident in control of the government. The Persian kings thus incautiously abolished the system of Arab vassalage and appointed Persian governors to whom the Arab chieftains were subordinate. Such was still the arrangement in 633 when Khālid ibn-al-Walīd at the head of the Moslem army received the submission of al-Ḥīrah.[3]

5. Kindah

As the Ghassānids stood in relation to the Byzantines and the Lakhmids to the Persians so did the Kindite kings of Central

[1] *Al-A'lāq al-Nafīsah*, ed. de Goeje (Leyden, 1892), p. 192, ll. 2-3, and p. 217, ll. 9-10. Cf. ibn-Qutaybah, pp. 273-4.

[2] Ar. *zandaqah*, from Pers. *zandīk* = Magian, fire-worshipper; Manichaean, heretic.

[3] Today where al-Ḥīrah once stood lie a few low mounds.

Arabia stand in relation to the last Tubba's of al-Yaman. Within the peninsula they were the only rulers to receive the title of *malik* (king), usually reserved by the Arabians for foreign potentates.

Though of South Arabian origin and, at the time preceding the rise of Islam, settled in the region to the west of Ḥaḍramawt, the powerful Kindah tribe is not mentioned in early South Arabian inscriptions; the first mention in history is in the fourth century of the Christian era. The reputed founder of the dynasty, Ḥujr, surnamed Ākil al-Murār, was according to tradition a stepbrother of the Ḥimyarite Ḥassān ibn-Tubba' and was appointed by the latter about A.D. 480 ruler of certain tribes whom the Tubba' had conquered in Central Arabia.[1] In this position Ḥujr was succeeded by his son 'Amr. 'Amr's son al-Ḥārith, the most valiant king of Kindah, was the one who for a short time after the death of the Persian Emperor Qubādh, rendered himself master of al-Ḥīrah, only to lose it (about 529) to the Lakhmid al-Mundhir III. Al-Mundhir put al-Ḥārith to death in 529 together with about fifty other members of the royal family, a fatal blow to the power of Kindah. Al-Ḥārith may have resided at al-Anbār, a city on the Euphrates about forty miles north-west of Baghdād.

The discord among the sons of al-Ḥārith, each heading a tribe, led to the dissolution of the confederacy and the final downfall of the ephemeral kingdom. The remnant of Kindah were forced back to their settlements in Ḥaḍramawt. This brought to an end one of the two rivals of al-Ḥīrah in the three-cornered fight for supremacy among the North Arabians, the other rival being the Ghassānids. The celebrated poet Imru'-al-Qays, composer of one of the greatest of the Golden Odes,[2] was a descendant of the royal Kindah line and made many vain attempts to regain a part of his heritage. His poems are bitter with rancour against the Lakhmids. In quest of aid he went as far as Constantinople, hoping to win the sympathy of Justinian, the enemy of al-Ḥīrah. On his way back, so the tradition goes, he was poisoned (about 540) at Ankara by an emissary of the emperor.[3]

[1] Iṣfahāni, *Ta'rīkh*, p. 140; ibn-Qutaybah, p. 308; Gunnar Olinder, *The Kings of Kinda* (Lund, 1927), pp. 38-9.

[2] See below, p. 94.

[3] Al-Ya'qūbi, *Ta'rīkh*, ed. M. Th. Houtsma (Leyden, 1883), vol. i, p. 251; Olinder, pp. 117-18.

In early Islam a number of Kindites came into prominence. Chief among these was al-Ash'ath ibn-Qays, the Ḥaḍramawt chieftain who distinguished himself in the conquest of Syria and al-'Irāq and was rewarded by the governship of a Persian province. The descendants of al-Ash'ath held important posts under the Umayyad caliphs in Syria. Al-Muqanna',[1] the veiled prophet of Khurāsān who posed as an incarnation of the deity and for years defied the forces of the 'Abbāsid Caliph al-Mahdi, was probably a Persian, not a Kindite. The earliest philosopher of Arabian blood was Ya'qūb ibn-Isḥāq al-Kindi,[2] whose millennium Baghdād celebrated in 1962.

Kindah's rise is interesting not only in itself but as the first attempt in inner Arabia to unite a number of tribes around the central authority of one common chief. As such the experiment established a precedent for al-Ḥijāz and Muḥammad.

A hero of Thomas Moore's *Lalla Rookh*. See below, p. 370.

British Museum

NABATAEAN BRONZE COIN

Obv. Trajan's head; rev. city-goddess of Petra, to be identified with Allāt-Manātu

CHAPTER VII

AL-ḤIJĀZ ON THE EVE OF THE RISE OF ISLAM

IN its broad outline Arabian history comprises three main eras:

1. The Sabaeo-Ḥimyarite period, ending at the beginning of the sixth century after Christ;
2. The Jāhilīyah period, which in a sense extends from "the creation of Adam" down to the mission of Muḥammad, but more particularly, as used here, covers the century immediately preceding the rise of Islam;
3. The Islamic period, extending to the present day.

The Jāhilīyah days

The term *jāhilīyah*, usually rendered "time of ignorance" or "barbarism", in reality means the period in which Arabia had no dispensation, no inspired prophet, no revealed book; for ignorance and barbarism can hardly be applied to such a cultured and lettered society as that developed by the South Arabians. The word occurs several times in the Koran (3 : 148, 5 : 55, 33 : 33, 48 : 26). In his anxiety to wean his people from pre-Islamic religious ideas, particularly from idolatry, the intensely monotheistic Muḥammad declared that the new religion was to obliterate all that had gone before it. This was later interpreted as constituting a ban on all pre-Islamic ideas and ideals. But ideas are hard to kill, and no one person's veto is strong enough to cancel the past.

Unlike the South Arabians the vast majority of the population of North Arabia, including al-Ḥijāz and Najd, is nomadic. The history of the Bedouins is in the main a record of guerilla wars called *ayyām al-'Arab* (the days of the Arabians), in which there was a great deal of raiding and plundering but little bloodshed. The sedentary population of al-Ḥijāz and Najd developed no ancient culture of its own. In this they were unlike their neighbours and kindred, the Nabataeans, Palmyrenes, Ghassānids and Lakhmids. The Nabataeans, and to a larger extent the

Palmyrenes, were partially Aramaicized; the Ghassānids and Lakhmids were South Arabian colonists amidst Syro-Byzantine and Syro-Persian cultures. Our study of the Jāhilīyah period therefore limits itself to a survey of the battles between the northern Bedouin tribes in the century preceding the Hijrah and to an account of the outside cultural influences operating among the settled inhabitants of al-Ḥijāz preparatory to the rise of Islam.

The light of authentic record illumines but faintly the Jāhilīyah age. Our sources for this period, in which the North Arabians had no system of writing, are limited to traditions, legends, proverbs, and above all to poems, none of which, however, were committed to writing before the second and third centuries after the Hijrah, two to four hundred years after the events which they were supposed to commemorate. Though traditional and legendary this data is none the less valuable; for what a people believe, even if untrue, has the same influence over their lives as if it were true. The North Arabians developed no system of writing until almost the time of Muḥammad. The only three pre-Islamic Arabic inscriptions thus far found (besides the proto-Arabic inscription of Imru'-al-Qays in al-Namārah, 328) are those of Zabad south-east of Aleppo (512), of Ḥarrān in al-Laja (568) and umm-al-Jimāl (same century).

The term Arabians, as already explained, includes in its broad sense all the inhabitants of the peninsula. In its narrow sense it implies the North Arabians, who did not figure in international affairs until the unfolding of the Islamic power. Likewise the term Arabic signifies the Ḥimyarite-Sabaean as well as the northern dialect of al-Ḥijāz, but since the latter became the sacred language of Islam and utterly superseded the southern dialects of al-Yaman it became the Arabic par excellence. Therefore, when we speak after this of the Arabians and of Arabic we have particularly in mind the North Arabian people and the language of the Koran.

The "days of the Arabians"

The Ayyām al-'Arab were intertribal hostilities generally arising from disputes over cattle, pasture-lands or springs. They afforded ample opportunity for plundering and raiding, for the manifestation of single-handed deeds of heroism by the champions of the contending tribes and for the exchange of vitriolic satires on the part of the poets, the spokesmen of the warring parties. Though always ready for a fight the Bedouin was not necessarily eager to be killed. His encounters, therefore, were not as sanguinary as their accounts would lead one to believe. Nevertheless these Ayyām provided a safety valve for a possible overpopulation in Bedouin land, whose inhabitants were normally in a condition of semi-starvation and to whom the fighting mood was a chronic state of mind. Through them vendetta became one of the strongest religio-social institutions in Bedouin life.

The course of events on each of these "days", as reported to us, follows somewhat the same pattern. At first only a few men come to blows with one another in consequence of some border dispute or personal insult. The quarrel of the few then becomes the business of the whole. Peace is finally restored by the intervention of some neutral party. The tribe with the fewer casualties pays its adversary blood money for the surplus of dead. Popular memory keeps the recollection of the heroes alive for centuries to come.

Such was the case of the Day of Buʿāth,[1] fought between the two related tribes of al-Madīnah, the Aws and the Khazraj, some years before the migration of the Prophet and his followers to that town. The Days of al-Fijār (transgression), so called because they fell in the holy months during which fighting was prohibited, were fought between the Prophet's family, the Quraysh, and their allies the Kinānah on one side, and the Hawāzin on the other. Muḥammad as a young man is said to have participated in one of the four combats.[2]

The Basūs War

One of the earliest and most famous of these Bedouin wars was the Ḥarb al-Basūs, fought toward the end of the fifth century of our era between the banu-Bakr[3] and their kinsmen the banu-Taghlib in north-eastern Arabia. Both tribes were Christianized and considered themselves descendants of Wā'il. The conflict arose over nothing more than a she-camel, the property of an old woman of Bakr named Basūs, which had been wounded by a Taghlib chief.[4] According to the legendary history of the Ayyām this war was carried on for forty years with reciprocal raiding and plundering, while its flames were fanned by poetical

[1] *Aghāni*, vol. ii, p. 162.
[2] Ibn-Hishām, pp. 117-19; quoted by Yāqūt, vol. iii, p. 579.
[3] The city of Diyār-Bakr (Diarbekr) still bears the name of this tribe.
[4] *Aghāni*, vol. iv, pp. 140-52; abu-Tammām, *Ḥamāsah*, pp. 420-23; *ʿIqd*, vol. iii, p. 95.

exhortations. The fratricidal struggle was brought to an end about 525 through the intercession of al-Mundhir III of al-Ḥīrah, but only after the exhaustion of both sides. The names of the leaders on the Taghlib side, Kulayb ibn-Rabī'ah and his brother, the hero-poet Muhalhil († *ca.* A.D. 531), as well as the name of Jassās ibn-Murrah on the Bakr side, are still household words in all Arabic-speaking lands. This Muhalhil became the Zīr of the still popular romance *Qiṣṣat al-Zīr.*

The Day of Dāḥis

Hardly less famous is the Day of Dāḥis and al-Ghabrā', the best known event of the pagan period. This war was fought between the 'Abs and its sister tribe Dhubyān in Central Arabia. Ghaṭafān was the traditional ancestor of both. The occasion was the unfair conduct of the Dhubyānites in a race between a horse called Dāḥis belonging to the chieftain of 'Abs and a mare named al-Ghabrā' owned by the sheikh of Dhubyān. The struggle broke out in the second half of the sixth century, not long after the conclusion of the Basūs peace, and persisted at intervals for several decades into Islamic times.[1] It was in this war that 'Antarah (or 'Antar) ibn-Shaddād al-'Absi (*ca.* A.D. 525–615), the Achilles of the Arabian heroic age, distinguished himself as a poet and warrior.

North Arabic in its influence as a language

No people in the world, perhaps, manifest such enthusiastic admiration for literary expression and are so moved by the word, spoken or written, as the Arabs. Hardly any language seems capable of exercising over the minds of its users such irresistible influence as Arabic. Modern audiences in Baghdād, Damascus and Cairo can be stirred to the highest degree by the recital of poems, only vaguely comprehended, and by the delivery of orations in the classical tongue, though it be only partially understood. The rhythm, the rhyme, the music, produce on them the effect of what they call "lawful magic" (*siḥr ḥalāl*).

Typical Semites, the Arabians created or developed no great art of their own. Their artistic nature found expression through one medium: speech. If the Greek gloried primarily in his statues and architecture, the Arabian found in his ode (*qaṣīdah*) and the Hebrew in his psalm, a finer mode of self-expression. "The beauty of man", declares an Arabic adage, "lies in the eloquence of his tongue." "Wisdom", in a late saying, "has alighted on three things: the brain of the Franks, the hands of the Chinese and the

[1] *Aghāni,* vol. ix, p. 150, vol. vii, p. 150.

tongue of the Arabs." [1] Eloquence, i.e. ability to express one's self forcefully and elegantly in both prose and poetry, together with archery and horsemanship were considered in the Jāhilīyah period the three basic attributes of "the perfect man" (*al-kāmil*). By virtue of its peculiar structure Arabic lent itself admirably to a terse, trenchant, epigrammatic manner of speech. Islam made full use of this feature of the language and of this psychological peculiarity of its people. Hence the "miraculous character" (*i'jāz*) of the style and composition of the Koran, adduced by Moslems as the strongest argument in favour of the genuineness of their faith. The triumph of Islam was to a certain extent the triumph of a language, more particularly of a book.

The heroic age

From the heroic age of Arabic literature, covering the Jāhilīyah period and extending from about A.D. 525 to 622, we have preserved for us a few proverbs, certain legends and in particular a fairly abundant amount of poetry—all compiled and edited in later Islamic days. No scientific literature existed beyond a few magical, meteorological and medicinal formulas. Proverbs constitute a fair index of folk mentality and experience. Luqmān the Sage (*al-ḥakīm*), in whose mouth many of the ancient words of wisdom were put, was either an Abyssinian or a Hebrew. Tradition has handed down the names of a number of wise men and women of the Jāhilīyah, e.g. Aktham ibn-Ṣayfi, Ḥājib ibn-Zurārah and Hind the daughter of al-Khuṣṣ. In the *Majma' al-Amthāl* by al-Maydāni [2] († 1124) and in the *Amthāl al-'Arab* of al-Mufaḍḍal al-Ḍabbi [3] († 786) we have many specimens of this pre-Islamic wisdom literature.

Prose could not have been well represented in the Jāhilīyah literature since no system of writing had then been fully developed. Yet we have a few pieces, mainly legends and traditions, composed in Islamic days, which purport to have come from earlier times. These stories deal mostly with genealogies (*ansāb*) and the intertribal combats, the above-discussed Days of the Arabians. The Arabian genealogist, like his brother the Arabian historian, had a *horror vacui* and his fancy had no difficulty in bridging gaps and filling vacancies; in this way he has succeeded in giving us in most instances a continuous record

[1] Cf. al-Jāḥiẓ, *Majmū'at Rasā'il* (Cairo, 1324), pp. 41-3; *'Iqd*, vol. i, p. 125.

[2] 2 vols. (Cairo, 1310); G. Freytag, *Arabum proverbia* (Bonn, 1838-43).

[3] 2 vols. (Constantinople, 1300); al-Mufaḍḍal ibn-Salamah († *ca.* 920), *al-Fākhir*, ed. C. A. Storey (Leyden, 1915).

from Adam or, in more modest compass, from Ishmael and Abraham. Ibn-Durayd's *Kitāb al-Ishtiqāq* [1] and the encyclopædic work of abu-al-Faraj al-Iṣbahāni (or Iṣfahāni, † A.D. 967) entitled *Kitāb al-Aghāni* (the book of songs) comprise most valuable data on the subject of genealogies. Specimens of rhymed prose attributed to pre-Islamic oracles have likewise survived.

Poetry

It was only in the field of poetical expression that the pre-Islamic Arabian excelled. Herein his finest talents found a field. The Bedouin's love of poetry was his one cultural asset.

Arabic literature, like most literatures, sprang into existence with an outburst of poetry; but, unlike many others, its poetry seems to have issued forth full grown. The oldest pieces of poetry extant seem to have been composed some one hundred and thirty years before the Hijrah in connection with the War of al-Basūs, but these odes, with their rigid conventions, presuppose a long period of development in the cultivation of the art of expression and the innate capacities of the language. The poets of the middle part of the sixth century have never been surpassed. The early Moslem poets as well as the later and present-day versifiers regarded and still do regard the ancient productions as models of unapproachable excellence. These early poems were committed to memory, transmitted by oral tradition and finally recorded in writing during the second and third centuries of the Hijrah. Modern critical research makes it evident that numerous revisions, editions and modifications were made to bring them into accord with the spirit of Islam [2]

The rhymed prose used by the oracles and soothsayers (*kuhhān*) may be considered the first stage in the development of the poetical form. The Koran exhibits such a style. The song of the camel-driver (*ḥudā'*) may have been the second. Native Arabic tradition which tries to explain the origin of poetry in the attempt of the cameleer to sing in time with the rhythmic movements of the camel's pace may after all contain a germ of truth The word *ḥādi*, singer, is synonymous with *sā'iq*, camel-driver.

Rajaz, consisting of four or six feet to the line, evolved out of rhymed prose and constitutes the oldest and simplest metre. "It is the first-born child of poetry", so runs the Arabic definition, "with rhymed prose [*saj'*] for a father and song for a mother."

[1] Ed. F. Wüstenfeld (Göttingen, 1854).
[2] Cf. Ṭāha Ḥusayn, *al-Adab al-Jāhili* (Cairo, 1927).

The ode in the classical period

In this heroic age of literature poetry was the only means of literary expression. The *qaṣīdah* (ode) represented the only, as well as a most finished, type of poetical composition. Muhalhil († *ca.* 531), the Taghlib hero of the Basūs War, is credited with being the first to compose these long poems. It is very likely that the ode developed in connection with the Days of the Arabians, particularly among the Taghlib or Kindah tribes. Imru'-al-Qays († *ca.* 540), originally a Qaḥṭāni from South Arabia, belonged to Kindah. Though one of the most ancient of bards, he is generally esteemed the greatest, the *amīr* (prince) of poets. ʿAmr ibn-Kulthūm († *ca.* 600), on the other hand, was a Taghlibite of the Rabīʿah from North Arabia. Though speaking different dialects these poets produced odes which exhibit the same literary form.

Appearing with Homeric suddenness the *qaṣīdah* surpasses even the Iliad and the Odyssey in metrical complexity and elaborateness. And when it makes its first appearance on the pages of history the *qaṣīdah* seems governed by a fixed set of conventions: stereotyped beginning, common epithets, stock figures of speech and same choice of themes—all of which point to a long period of development. Rich in animated passion, expressed in forceful and compact language, the ode is poor in original ideas, in thought-provoking imagery, and is consequently lacking in universal appeal. The poet and not the poetry is more often the thing to be admired. Translated into a foreign language it loses its value. The personal, subjective element prevails. The theme is realistic, the horizon limited, the point of view local. No national epic was ever developed by the Arabians and no dramatic work of first-class importance.

The Muʿallaqāt

Among the ancient odes the so-called "Seven Muʿallaqāt" (suspended) hold first place. They are still honoured throughout the Arabic-speaking world as masterpieces of poetical composition. Legend has it that each of these odes was awarded the annual prize at the fair of ʿUkāẓ and was inscribed in golden letters and suspended on the walls of the Kaʿbah.[1] Their genesis is explained in this way: at ʿUkāẓ, between Nakhlah and al-Ṭā'if in al-Ḥijāz, was held an annual fair, a sort of literary congress whither hero-poets resorted to celebrate their exploits and contend for the coveted first honour. A poet made a name

[1] Al-Suyūṭi, *al-Muzhir* (Cairo, 1282), vol. ii, p. 240.

for himself here or nowhere. The Fair (*sūq*) of 'Ukāẓ stood in pre-Islamic days for a kind of *Académie française* of Arabia.

The annual fair, we are told, was held during the sacred months when fighting was taboo. The pagan Arabian calendar was like the later Moslem one, lunar; the first three months of its spring season, i.e. dhu-al-Qa'dah, dhu-al-Ḥijjah and Muḥarram, coincided with the period of peace. The fair provided ample opportunity for the exhibition of native wares, and for trade and exchange of commodities. We can easily visualize the sons of the desert flocking to these annual peaceful gatherings, lingering around the booths, sipping date wine and enjoying to the full the tunes of the singing girls.

Though the first ode said to have won the favour of the judges of 'Ukāẓ was that of Imru'-al-Qays († *ca.* 540), no collection of the Mu'allaqāt was attempted until the latter Umayyad period. Ḥammād al-Rāwiyah, the famous rhapsodist who flourished in the middle of the eighth century, chose the Seven Golden Odes, undoubtedly from among many others, and compiled them into a separate group. This collection has been translated into most European languages.[1]

The pre-Islamic poet

Aside from the famous Seven Odes we have from pre-Islamic poetry a collection named, after its compiler, al-Mufaḍḍal al-Ḍabbi († *ca.* 785), *al-Mufaḍḍalīyāt*,[2] containing one hundred and twenty odes composed by lesser lights, a number of *dīwāns* (anthologies) and a large number of fragments and excerpts in the *Dīwān al-Ḥamāsah*, edited by abu-Tammām († *ca.* 845) and in the *Kitāb al-Aghāni* of al-Iṣbahāni († 967).

The Arabian poet (*shā'ir*), as the name indicates, was originally one endowed with knowledge hidden from the common man, which knowledge he received from a demon, his special *shayṭān* (satan). As a poet he was in league with the unseen powers and could by his curses bring evil upon the enemy. Satire (*hijā'*) was therefore a very early form of Arabic poetry.[3]

As his office developed the poet acquired a variety of functions. In battle his tongue was as effective as his people's bravery. In peace he might prove a menace to public order by his fiery harangues. His poems might arouse a tribe to action in

[1] See William Jones, *Works* (London, 1799), vol. iv, pp. 245-335; Anne and Wilfrid S. Blunt, *The Seven Golden Odes of Pagan Arabia* (London, 1903).

[2] Ed. C. J. Lyall, 3 vols. (Oxford & Leyden, 1921–4).

[3] Balaam was a type of primitive Arabian satirist (Num. 23 : 7).

the same manner as the tirade of a demagogue in a modern political campaign. As the press agent, the journalist, of his day his favour was sought by princely gifts, as the records of the courts of al-Ḥīrah and Ghassān show. His poems, committed to memory and transmitted from one tongue to another, offered an invaluable means of publicity. He was both moulder and agent of public opinion. *Qaṭʻ al-lisān* (cutting off the tongue) was the formula used for subsidizing him and avoiding his satires.

Besides being oracle, guide, orator and spokesman of his community the poet was its historian and scientist, in so far as it had a scientist. Bedouins measured intelligence by poetry. "Who dares dispute my tribe . . . its pre-eminence in horsemen, poets and numbers?" exclaims a bard in *al-Aghāni*.[1] In these three elements, military power, intelligence and numbers, lay the superiority of a tribe. As the historian and scientist of the tribe the poet was well versed in its genealogy and folklore, cognizant of the attainments and past achievements of its members, familiar with their rights, pasture-lands and border-lines. Furthermore, as a student of the psychological weaknesses and historical failures of the rival tribes it was his business to expose these shortcomings and hold them up to ridicule.

Aside from its poetic interest and the worth of its grace and elegance, the ancient poetry, therefore, has historical importance as source material for the study of the period in which it was composed. In fact it is our only quasi-contemporaneous data. It throws light on all phases of pre-Islamic life. Hence the adage, "Poetry is the public register [*dīwān*] of the Arabians".[2]

Bedouin character as manifested in poetry

The ideal of Arab virtue as revealed by this ancient pagan poetry was expressed in the terms *murū'ah*, manliness (later *virtus*), and *ʻirḍ* (honour).[3] The component elements of *murū'ah* were courage, loyalty and generosity. Courage was measured by the number of raids (sing. *ghazw*) undertaken. Generosity manifested itself in his readiness to sacrifice his camel at the coming of a guest or on behalf of the poor and the helpless.

The name of Ḥātim al-Ṭā'i († *ca.* A.D. 605) has been handed down to the present day as the personification of the Bedouin ideal of hospitality. As a lad in charge of his father's camels he

[1] Vol. viii, p. 77.
[2] *Muzhir*, vol. ii, p. 235.
[3] On *murū'ah* and *ʻirḍ*, see articles by Bishr Farès in *Encyclopædia of Islām, Supp.*

once slaughtered three of the animals to feed passing strangers and distributed the rest among them, which caused his father to expel him from home.[1]

The name of ʿAntarah ibn-Shaddād al-ʿAbsi (*ca.* 525–615), evidently a Christian, has lived through the ages as the paragon of Bedouin heroism and chivalry. Knight, poet, warrior and lover, ʿAntarah exemplified in his life those traits greatly esteemed by the sons of the desert. His deeds of valour as well as his love episodes with his lady, ʿAblah, whose name he immortalized in his famous Muʿallaqah, have become a part of the literary heritage of the Arabic-speaking world. But ʿAntarah was born a slave, the son of a black maid. He was, however, freed by his father on the occasion of an encounter with an enemy tribe in which the young man refused to take active part, saying, "A slave knows not how to fight; milking camels is his job". "Charge!" shouted his father, "thou art free."[2]

Bedouin heathenism

Judged by his poetry the pagan Bedouin of the Jāhilīyah age had little if any religion. To spiritual impulses he was lukewarm, even indifferent. His conformity to religious practice followed tribal inertia and was dictated by his conservative respect for tradition. Nowhere do we find an illustration of genuine devotion to a heathen deity. A story told about Imru'-al-Qays illustrates this point. Having set out to avenge the murder of his father he stopped at the temple of dhu-al-Khalaṣah[3] to consult the oracle by means of drawing arrows.[4] Upon drawing "abandon" thrice he hurled the broken arrows at the idol exclaiming, "Accursed one! had it been thy father who was murdered thou wouldst not have forbidden my avenging him".[5]

Other than the poetical references, our chief sources of information about pre-Islamic heathenism are to be found in the remains of paganism in Islam, in the few anecdotes and traditions embedded in the late Islamic literature and in al-Kalbi's († 819–20) *al-Aṣnām* (the idols). The pagan Arabian developed no mythology, no involved theology and no cosmogony comparable to that of the Babylonians.

[1] Ibn-Qutaybah, *al-Shiʿr w-al-Shuʿarā'*, ed. de Goeje (Leyden, 1904), p. 124.

[2] *Aghāni*, vol. vii, pp. 149-50; ibn-Qutaybah, p. 130.

[3] The temple stood seven days' journey south of Makkah; its deity was a white stone; al-Kalbi, *al-Aṣnām*, ed. Aḥmad Zaki (Cairo, 1914), p. 34.

[4] See below, p. 100. Divining by arrows forbidden in Koran 5 : 4, 92.

[5] *Aghāni*, vol. viii, p. 70.

The Bedouin religion represents the earliest and most primitive form of Semitic belief. The South Arabian cults with their astral features, ornate temples, elaborate ritual and sacrifices represent a higher and later stage of development, a stage reached by sedentary society. The emphasis on sun-worship in the cultured communities of Petra and Palmyra implies an agricultural state where the association has already been made between the life-giving rays of the sun and the growth of vegetation.

The Bedouin's religion, like other forms of primitive belief, is basically animistic. The striking contrast between oasis and desert gave him perhaps his earliest definite conception of the specialized deity. The spirit of the arable land became the beneficent deity to be catered to; that of the arid land the maleficent, the demon, to be feared.[1]

Even after the conception of a deity was formed, natural objects such as trees, wells, caves, stones, remained sacred objects, since they formed the media through which the worshipper could come into direct contact with the deity. The well in the desert with its cleansing, healing, life-giving water very early became an object of worship. Zamzam's holiness, according to Arabian authors, was pre-Islamic and went back to the time when it supplied water to Hagar and Ishmael.[2] Yāqūt,[3] and after him al-Qazwīni,[4] speak of travellers carrying away water from the Well of ʿUrwah and offering it as a special present to their relatives and friends. Caves became holy through association with underground deities and forces. Such was originally Ghabghab in Nakhlah, where the Arabians sacrificed to al-ʿUzza.[5] *Baʿl* represented the spirit of springs and underground water and must have been introduced into Arabia at the same time as the palm tree. The word left an interesting survival in the Moslem system of taxation, where a distinction is drawn between what *Baʿl* waters (i.e. land that needs no irrigation) and what the sky waters.

Solar aspects

The Bedouin's astral beliefs centred upon the moon, in whose light he grazed his flocks. Moon-worship implies a pastoral society, whereas sun-worship represents a later agricultural stage. In our own day the Moslem Ruwalah Bedouins imagine

[1] Ar. *taqwa*, piety, is from a stem meaning "to be on one's guard, to fear".
[2] Ibn-Hishām, *Sīrah*, p. 71.
[3] Vol. i, p. 434.
[4] *ʿAjāʾib al-Makhlūqāt*, ed. F. Wüstenfeld (Göttingen, 1849), p. 200.
[5] Kalbi, pp. 18, 20; Yāqūt, vol. iii, pp. 772-3.

that their life is regulated by the moon, which condenses the water vapours, distils the beneficent dew on the pasture and makes possible the growth of plants. On the other hand the sun, as they believe, would like to destroy the Bedouins as well as all animal and plant life.

One characteristic feature of all elements of religious belief is their tendency to persist in some form when a higher stage of development has been attained. The survival represents a compromise between these two stages of religious development. Hence Wadd (Koran 71 : 22), the moon-god who stood at the head of the Minaean pantheon. Ibn-Hishām[1] and al-Ṭabari[2] speak of a sacred palm tree in Najrān. Gifts were offered to the tree in the form of weapons, garments and rags which were suspended from it. Dhāt-Anwāṭ[3] (that on which things are hung), to which the Makkans resorted annually, was perhaps identical with the tree of al-'Uzza at Nakhlah.[4] Al-Lāt in al-Ṭā'if was represented by a square stone,[5] and dhu-al-Shara in Petra by a quadrangular block of unhewn black stone four feet high and two feet wide. Most of these deities owned each a reserved grazing-land (*ḥima*).

Jinn

The Bedouin peopled the desert with living things of beastly nature called jinn or demons. These jinn differ from the gods not so much in their nature as in their relation to man. The gods are on the whole friendly; the jinn, hostile. The latter are, of course, personifications of the fantastic notions of the terrors of the desert and its wild animal life. To the gods belong the regions frequented by man; to the jinn belong the unknown and untrodden parts of the wilderness. A madman (*majnūn*) is but one possessed by the jinn. With Islam the number of jinn was increased, since the heathen deities were then degraded into such beings.[6]

The daughters of Allah

Among the urban population of al-Ḥijāz, and only about seventeen per cent. of the population was such, the astral stage of paganism was reached early. Al-'Uzza, al-Lāt and Manāh, the three daughters of Allah, had their sanctuaries in the land which later became the cradle of Islam. In a weak moment the monotheistic Muḥammad was tempted[7] to recognize these power-

[1] *Sīrah*, p. 22. [2] Vol. i, p. 922. [3] *Sīrah*, p. 844.
[4] Kalbi, pp. 24-7 [5] *Ibid.* p. 16. [6] Koran 37 : 158, 6 : 100.
[7] Cf. Koran 22 : 51-2, 17 : 74-6.

ful deities of Makkah and al-Madīnah and make a compromise in their favour, but afterwards he retracted and the revelation is said to have received the form now found in sūrah 53 : 19-20.[1] Later theologians explained the case according to the principle of *nāsikh* and *mansūkh*, abrogating and abrogated verses, by means of which God revokes and alters the announcements of His will; this results in the cancellation of a verse and the substitution of another for it (Koran 2 : 100). Al-Lāt (from al-Ilāhah, the goddess) had her sacred tracts (*ḥima* and *ḥaram*) near al-Ṭā'if, whither the Makkans and others flocked for pilgrimage and sacrifice. Within such an enclosure no trees could be felled, no game hunted and no human blood shed. Animal and plant life therein partook of the inviolability of the deity there honoured. Of similar origin were the cities of refuge in Israel. Herodotus[2] mentions this goddess under the name Alilat among the Nabataean deities.

Al-'Uzza (the most mighty, Venus, the morning star) had her cult in Nakhlah east of Makkah. According to al-Kalbi,[3] hers was the most venerated idol among the Quraysh, and Muḥammad as a young man offered her a sacrifice. Her sanctuary consisted of three trees. Human sacrifice characterized her cult. She was the Lady 'Uzzay-an to whom a South Arabian offered a golden image on behalf of his sick daughter, Amat-'Uzzay-an[4] (the maid of al-'Uzza). 'Abd-al-'Uzza was a favourite proper name at the rise of Islam.

Manāh (from *manīyah*, allotted fate) was the goddess of destiny[5] and as such represented an earlier phase of religious life.[6] Her main sanctuary consisted of a black stone in Qudayd on the road between Makkah and Yathrib (later al-Madīnah) and she was especially popular with the Aws and the Khazraj, who rallied to the support of the Prophet on his fateful Hijrah from Makkah. As an independent deity her name, associated with dhu-al-Shara, appears in the Nabataean inscriptions of al-Ḥijr.[7] To the present day Arabic versifiers blame all misfortunes on *al-manāya* or *al-dahr* (time).

[1] Al-Bayḍāwi, *Anwār al-Tanzīl*, ed. H. O. Fleischer, vol. i (Leipzig, 1846), pp. 636-7; Ṭabari, *Tafsīr al-Qur'ān*, vol. xxvii, pp. 34 *seq.*, vol. xvii, p. 131.
[2] Bk. III, ch. 8. [3] Pp. 18-19. [4] Nielsen, *Handbuch*, vol. i, p. 236.
[5] Cf. Heb. Mĕni, Is. 65 : 11. [6] Kalbi, p. 13.
[7] Cooke, pp. 217, 219; cf. Lidzbarski, *Ephemeris*, vol. iii, 1909-15 (Giessen, 1915), p. 85.

Since the mother's blood rather than the father's formed the original bond of kinship among the Semites and because the family organization was first matriarchal, the Arabian goddess preceded the god as an object of worship.

The Makkan Ka'bah

Hubal (from Aram. for vapour, spirit), evidently the chief deity of al-Ka'bah, was represented in human form. Beside him stood ritual arrows used for divination by the soothsayer (*kāhin*, from Aramaic) who drew lots by means of them. The tradition in ibn-Hishām,[1] which makes 'Amr ibn-Luḥayy the importer of this idol from Moab or Mesopotamia, may have a kernel of truth in so far as it retains a memory of the Aramaic origin of the deity.[2] At the conquest of Makkah by Muḥammad Hubal shared the lot of the other idols and was destroyed.

The pagan Ka'bah, which became the Palladium of Islam, was an unpretentious cube-like (hence the name) building of primitive simplicity, originally roofless, serving as a shelter for a black meteorite which was venerated as a fetish. At the birth of Islam the structure was that rebuilt in 608 probably by an Abyssinian from the wreckage of a Byzantine or Abyssinian ship destroyed on the shore of the Red Sea.[3] The usual sacred territory (*ḥaram*) spread around it. Annual pilgrimages were made thither and special sacrifices offered.

Moslem tradition maintains that the Ka'bah was originally built by Adam according to a celestial prototype and after the Deluge rebuilt by Abraham and Ishmael.[4] Its custody remained in the hands of the descendants of Ishmael until the proud banu-Jurhum, and later the banu-Khuzā'ah, who introduced idol worship, took possession of it. Then came the Quraysh, who continued the ancient Ishmaelite line. While engaged in the rebuilding Ishmael received from Gabriel the Black Stone, still set in the south-east corner of the structure, and was instructed in the ceremonies of the pilgrimage (*ḥajj*).

Allah

Allah (*allāh*, *al-ilāh*, the god) was the principal, though not the only, deity of Makkah. The name is an ancient one. It occurs in two South Arabic inscriptions, one a Minaean found at al-'Ula and the other a Sabaean, but abounds in the form HLH in the Liḥyānite inscriptions of the fifth century B.C.[5] Liḥyān, which

[1] *Sīrah*, pp. 50 *seq.*

[2] The Arabic word for idol, *ṣanam*, is clearly an adaptation of Aramaic *ṣělěm*.

[3] Cf. al-Azraqi, *Akhbār Makkah*, ed. Wüstenfeld (Leipzig, 1858), pp. 104-7; Ya'qūbi, *Ta'rīkh*, vol. ii, pp. 17-18.

[4] Koran 2 : 118-21.

[5] Winnett, p. 30.

evidently got the god from Syria, was the first centre of the worship of this deity in Arabia. The name occurs as Hallāh in the Ṣafa inscriptions five centuries before Islam [1] and also in a pre-Islamic Christian Arabic inscription found in umm-al-Jimāl, Syria, and ascribed to the sixth century.[2] The name of Muḥammad's father was 'Abd-Allāh ('Abdullāh, the slave or worshipper of Allah). The esteem in which Allah was held by the

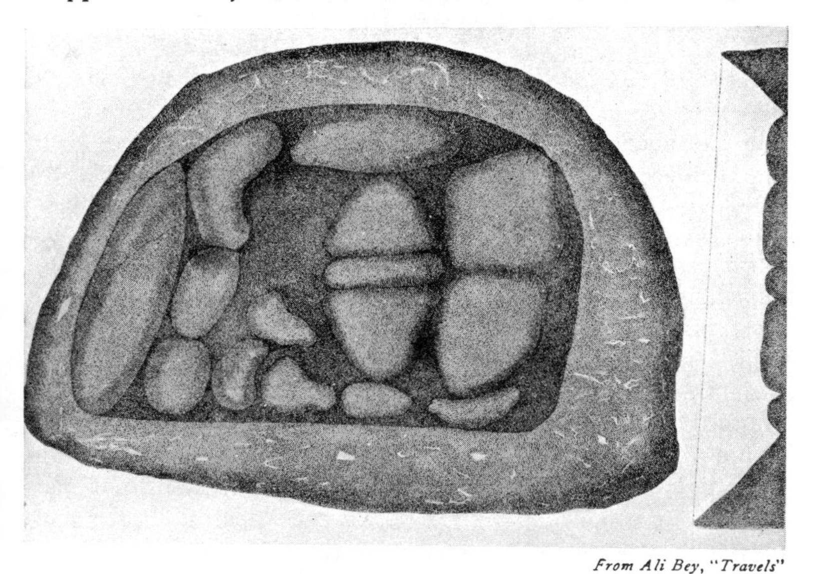

From Ali Bey, "Travels"

THE BLACK STONE OF AL-KA'BAH

pre-Islamic Makkans as the creator and supreme provider and the one to be invoked in time of special peril may be inferred from such koranic passages as 31 : 24, 31; 6 : 137, 109; 10 : 23. Evidently he was the tribal deity of the Quraysh.

Though in an inhospitable and barren valley with an inclement and unhealthy climate this sanctuary at Makkah made al-Ḥijāz the most important religious centre in North Arabia.

Other pagan deities such as Nasr[3] (vulture), 'Awf (the great bird) bear animal names and suggest totemic origin. As for future life, nowhere in the authenticated ancient literature do we find expressed a clear and precise idea of it. The few vague

[1] Dussaud, *Les Arabes en Syrie*, pp. 141-2.

[2] Enno Littmann, *Zeitschrift für Semitistik und verwandte Gebiete*, vol. vii (1929), pp. 197-204.

[3] Koran 71 : 23.

references may be explained as an echo of Christian dogma. The hedonistic Arabian character was too much absorbed in the immediate issues of life to devote much thought to the hereafter. In the words of an old bard:

> We spin about and whirl our way through life,
> Then, rich and poor alike, at last seek rest
> Below the ground in hollow pits slate-covered;
> And there we do abide.[1]

As the Bedouins frequented the settled towns of al-Ḥijāz for the exchange of their commodities, and particularly during the four months of "holy truce", they became inoculated with some of the more advanced urban beliefs and were initiated into ritualistic practices of the Ka'bah and the offering of sacrifices. Camels and sheep were offered at Makkah and at various stones (*anṣāb*) elsewhere which were regarded as idols or altars. In the pilgrimage to some great shrine of the urban Arabians lay the most important religious practice of the nomad. The "holy truce" included what became in the Moslem calendar the eleventh, twelfth and first months of each year (dhu-al-Qa'dah, dhu-al-Ḥijjah and Muḥarram) together with a fourth month in the middle (Rajab). The first three were especially set aside for religious observance, and the fourth for trade. Al-Ḥijāz, through its somewhat central position, its accessibility and its location on the main caravan route running north and south, offered an unexcelled opportunity for both religious and commercial activity. Thus arose its 'Ukāẓ fair and its Ka'bah.

The three cities of al-Ḥijāz: al-Ṭā'if

Al-Ḥijāz, the barren country standing like a barrier (*ḥijāz*) between the uplands of Najd and the low coastal region called Tihāmah (netherland), could boast only three cities: al-Ṭā'if and the two sister cities Makkah and al-Madīnah.

Al-Ṭā'if, nestling among shady trees at an altitude of about 6000 feet and described as "a bit of Syrian earth", was, as it still is, the summer resort of the Makkan aristocracy. Burckhardt, who visited the town in August 1814, declared the scenery en route the most picturesque and delightful he had seen since his departure from Lebanon.[2] Its products included honey, water-melons, bananas, figs, grapes, almonds, peaches

[1] Abu-Tammām, p. 562; cf. Lyall, *Translations*, p. xxvii.
[2] John L. Burckhardt, *Travels in Arabia* (London, 1829), vol. i, p. 122.

and pomegranates.[1] Its roses were famous for the attar which provided Makkah with its perfumery. Its vines, according to a tradition handed down in *al-Aghāni*,[2] were introduced by a Jewess who offered the first slips as a present to a local chief. Its wine, though in great demand, was less expensive than the foreign

From Ibrāhīm Rif'at, "Mir'āt al-Ḥaramayn"

MAKKAH FROM THE MOUNTAIN OF ABU-QUBAYS, WITH MOUNT ḤIRĀ' IN THE BACKGROUND, 1908

brand celebrated in Arabic poetry. Of all places in the peninsula al-Ṭā'if came nearest to the koranic description of Paradise in sūrah 47 : 16–17.

Makkah

The name Makkah, the Macoraba of Ptolemy,[3] comes from Sabaean Makuraba, meaning sanctuary, which indicates that it owes its foundation to some religious association and therefore must have been a religious centre long before Muḥammad was born. It lies in the Tihāmah of southern al-Ḥijāz, about forty-eight miles from the Red Sea, in a barren, rocky valley described in the Koran (14 : 40) as "unfit for cultivation". The thermo-

[1] Cf. ibn-Baṭṭūṭah, *Tuḥfat al-Nuẓẓār*, ed. and tr. C. Defrémery and B. R. Sanguinetti, 3rd impression, vol. i (Paris, 1893), pp. 304-5.

[2] Vol. iv, p. 75, ll. 9-10.

[3] *Geographia*, ed. Nobbe, Bk. VI, ch. 7, § 32.

meter in Makkah can register almost unbearable heat. When the famous Arab traveller ibn-Baṭṭūṭah[1] of Tangier attempted the circumambulation of the Kaʿbah barefooted, he failed because of the "flames" reflected by the stones.

Older still than the south-to-north "spice road" which passes through it, the city early became a midway station between Ma'rib and Ghazzah. The commercially minded and progressive Makkans soon rendered their city a centre of wealth. A Makkan caravan which was involved in the Badr skirmish (Mar. 16, 624) while returning from Ghazzah consisted of a thousand camels, according to al-Wāqidi,[2] and carried merchandise worth 50,000 dinars (about £20,000). Under the leadership of the Quraysh, the custodians of the Kaʿbah, who were evidently responsible for making that sanctuary a national shrine and the ʿUkāẓ fair a commercial and intellectual rendezvous, Makkah's pre-eminence became secure.

Al-Madīnah

Yathrib (YTHRB of the Sabaean inscriptions, Jathrippa of Ptolemy),[3] lay some 300 miles north of Makkah and was much more favoured by nature than its southern sister. Besides lying on the "spice road", which connected al-Yaman with Syria, the city was a veritable oasis, especially adapted for the cultivation of date-palms. In the hands of its Jewish inhabitants, the banu-Naḍīr and banu-Qurayẓah, the town became a leading agricultural centre. Judging by their proper names and the Aramaean vocabulary used in their agricultural life these Jews must have been mostly Judaized clans of Arabian[4] and Aramaean stock, though the nucleus may have been Israelites who fled from Palestine at the time of its conquest by the Romans in the first century after Christ. It was possibly these Aramaic-speaking Jews who changed the name Yathrib into Aramaic Medīnta, the explanation of the name al-Madīnah (Medina) as "the town" (of the Prophet) being a comparatively late one. The two leading non-Jewish tribes were the Aws and the Khazraj, who came originally from al-Yaman.

Cultural influences in al-Ḥijāz: 1. Saba'

Though not in the main stream of world events, pre-Islamic al-Ḥijāz could hardly be said to have been in a backwater. Its exclusiveness is post-Muḥammadan and dates from the eighth

[1] Vol. i, p. 281.
[2] *Al-Maghāzi*, ed. Alfred von Kremer (Calcutta, 1855-6), p. 198.
[3] Bk. VI, ch. 7, § 31; variant Lathrippa.
[4] Yaʿqūbi, vol. ii, p. 49, designates the Arabian tribes from which they descended.

year of the Hijrah, when Makkah was captured and the twenty-eighth verse of sūrah nine revealed.[1] In the first century after Muḥammad, however, there flourished in his birthplace a number of Christian and Jewish physicians, musicians and merchants.

The earlier South Arabian civilization could not have altogether passed away without leaving some trace in its northern successor. The inscription (542–3) of Abrahah dealing with the break of the Ma'rib Dam begins with the following words: "In the power and grace and mercy of the Merciful [*Raḥman-an*] and His Messiah and of the Holy Spirit".[2] The word *Raḥman-an* is especially significant because its northern equivalent, *al-Raḥmān*, became later a prominent attribute of Allah and one of His names in the Koran and in Islamic theology. Sūrah nineteen is dominated by *al-Raḥmān*.[3] Though used in the inscription for the Christian God, yet the word is evidently borrowed from the name of one of the older South Arabian deities. *Al-Raḥīm* (the compassionate) also occurs as the name of a deity (RḤM) in pre-Islamic and Sabaean inscriptions.[4] Another South Arabic inscription uses *shirk*, association in the sense of polytheism, the kind of *shirk* against which Muḥammad vehemently and fervently preached and which consisted of the worship of one supreme being with whom other minor deities were associated. In the same inscription occurs the technical term denoting unbelief, *KFR*, as in North Arabic.[5]

2. Abyssinia

The Semitic population of the south-western coast of the Red Sea found its way thither, as we have learned, by gradual infiltration from south-western Arabia. These Abyssinians, as they were later called, formed an important part of the great international commercial "trust", which under Sabaeo-Ḥimyarite leadership monopolized the ancient spice trade, the main artery of which passed through al-Ḥijāz. For about fifty years prior to the birth of the Prophet, the Abyssinians had their rule established in al-Yaman, and in the year of his birth we find them at the gates of Makkah threatening its precious Ka'bah with

[1] See below, p. 118; cf. Bayḍāwi, vol. i, p. 383; Ṭabari, *Tafsīr*, vol. x, p. 74.

[2] E. Glaser, *Mitteilungen der vorderasiatischen Gesellschaft* (Berlin, 1897), pp. 390, 401; cf. *Corpus inscriptionum Semiticarum*, pars iv, t. i, pp. 15-19.

[3] *Raḥmanān* appears as title of the Christian God in a fifth-century South Arabic inscription.

[4] Dussaud and Macler, *Voyage archéologique*, p. 95, l. 10; Dussaud, *Arabes*, pp. 152-3.

[5] J. H. Mordtmann and D. H. Müller in *Wiener Zeitschrift für die Kunde des Morgenlandes*, vol. x (1896), pp. 285-92.

destruction. Makkah itself was the abode of an Abyssinian, presumably Christian, colony. Bilāl,[1] whose stentorian voice won him the unique distinction of becoming the Prophet's muezzin, was an Abyssinian negro. The koranic references to the sea and its tempests (sūrahs 16 : 14, 10 : 23–4, 24 : 40), which are characterized by unusual clarity and vividness, are an echo of the active maritime intercourse between al-Ḥijāz and Abyssinia. When the infant Moslem community was hard pressed by the pagan Quraysh it was to Abyssinia of all lands that they turned for refuge.[2]

3. Persia

In the century preceding the establishment of Islam, Zoroastrian Persia was contesting with Abyssinia for supremacy over al-Yaman. Knowledge of the military art of Persia was passing into Arabian possession from the south and also from the north through Persian Arabia, with its capital al-Ḥīrah. Tradition relates that it was Salmān the Persian who taught the Prophet how to dig a trench for the defence of al-Madīnah.[3]

Al-Ḥīrah, the Arab satellite of Persia, was the main channel through which not only Persian cultural influences but, later, Aramaean Nestorian influences percolated into the Arabia of pre-Muḥammadan days. As these Nestorians formed later the main link between Hellenism and nascent Islam, so now they acted as a medium for transmitting northern cultural ideas, Aramaic, Persian and Hellenic, into the heart of pagan Arabia.

4. Ghassānland

Just such an influence as the Nestorians of al-Ḥīrah had on the Arabs of the Persian border was exerted by the Monophysites of Ghassānland upon the people of al-Ḥijāz. For four centuries prior to Islam these Syrianized Arabs had been bringing the Arab world into touch not only with Syria but also with Byzantium. Such personal names as Dāwūd (David), Sulaymān (Solomon), 'Īsa (Jesus), were not uncommon among the pre-Islamic Arabians.

[1] His tomb is still standing in Damascus.

[2] Such Ar. words of Ethiopic origin as *burhān* (proof), *ḥawārīyūn* (Christ's disciples), *jahannam* (hell, originally Heb.), *mā'idah* (table), *malak* (angel, originally Heb.), *miḥrāb* (niche), *minbar* (pulpit), *muṣḥaf* (holy book), *shayṭān* (Satan), point to Christian Abyssinian influence over Moslem Ḥijāz. Al-Suyūṭi cites in ch. 38 of his *al-Itqān* (Cairo, 1925), vol. i, pp. 135-41, 118 foreign words in the Koran.

[3] See below, p. 117. Ar. *firind* (sword), *firdaws* (Paradise, sūr. 18 : 107; 23 : 11), *sijjīl* (stone, sūr. 105 : 4), *barzakh* (obstacle, sūr. 23 : 102; 55 : 20; 25 : 55), *zanjabīl* (ginger, sūr. 76 : 17, see below, p. 667), etc., are of Persian derivation.

This northern influence, however, should not be over-estimated, for neither the Monophysite nor the Nestorian church had enough vitality to make its religious ideas contagious. The material collected by Père Cheikho[1] does not suffice to show that Christianity had struck deep root anywhere in North Arabia, yet it reveals many pre-Islamic poets as familiar with certain floating Christian ideas and Christian terms. A considerable number of Aramaic words passed into the ancient Arabic vocabulary.[2]

5. The Jews

The monotheism affecting Arabia was not entirely of the Christian type. Jewish colonies flourished in al-Madīnah and various oases of northern al-Ḥijāz.[3] Al-Jumaḥi († 845) devotes a section of his biographies[4] to the Jewish poets of al-Madīnah and its environs. *Al-Aghāni* cites a number of Jewish poets of Arabia. But the only supposedly Jewish poet who left us a *dīwān* was al-Samaw'al (Samuel),[5] of al-Ablaq near Taymā', a contemporary of Imru'-al-Qays. His poetry, however, has nothing to differentiate it from the current heathen type, and therefore al-Samaw'al's Judaism has been rightly suspected. In al-Yaman Judaism is supposed to have attained the dignity of a state religion under the aegis of dhu-Nuwās.

In summing up it may be safely stated that al-Ḥijāz in the century preceding the mission of Muḥammad was ringed about with influences, intellectual, religious and material, radiating from Byzantine, Syrian (Aramaean), Persian and Abyssinian centres and conducted mainly through Ghassānid, Lakhmid and Yamanite channels; but it cannot be asserted that al-Ḥijāz was in such vital contact with the higher civilization of the north as to transform its native cultural aspect. Then too, although Christianity did find a footing in Najrān, and Judaism in al-Yaman and al-Ḥijāz, neither seems to have left much of an impression on the North Arabian mind. Nevertheless the anti-

[1] *Al-Naṣrānīyah wa-Ādābuha*, 2 pts. (Beirūt, 1912, 1919, 1923); *Shu'arā' al-Naṣrānīyah*, 2 vols. (Beirūt, 1890).

[2] *Kanīsah* and *bī'ah* (church), *dumyah* and *ṣūrah* (image, picture), *qissīs* (monk), *ṣadaqah* (alms), *nāṭūr* (watchman), *nīr* (yoke), *faddān* (acre), *qindīl* (lamp, originally Latin *candela*) are illustrations. Latin *castrum* gave Syriac *qasṭra* and Western Aramaic *qaṣra* from which Arabic *qaṣr* (castle, palace) came and was re-introduced into Europe in the form of Italian *cassero*, Spanish *alcázar*.

[3] *Jibrīl* (Gabriel), *sūrah* (revelation, chapter), *jabbār* (most powerful), illustrate Hebrew words in the Arabic vocabulary.

[4] *Ṭabaqāt al-Shu'arā'*, ed. J. Hell (Leyden, 1916), pp. 70-74.

[5] *Dīwān al-Samaw'al*, 2nd ed., ed. Cheikho (Beirūt, 1920).

quated paganism of the peninsula seems to have reached the point where it failed any longer to meet the spiritual demands of the people and was outgrown by a dissatisfied group who developed vague monotheistic ideas and went by the name of Ḥanīfs.[1] Umayyah ibn-abi-al-Ṣalt († 624), through his mother a second cousin of the Prophet, and Waraqah ibn-Nawfal, a cousin of Khadījah, were such Ḥanīfs, though several sources make Waraqah a Christian. On the political side the organized national life developed in early South Arabia was now utterly disrupted. Anarchy prevailed in the political realm as it did in the religious. The stage was set, the moment was psychological, for the rise of a great religious and national leader.

[1] Loan-word from Aramaic through Nabataean; N. A. Faris and H. W. Glidden, *Journal of the Palestine Oriental Society*, vol. xix (1939), pp. 1-13; cf. Arthur Jeffery, *The Foreign Vocabulary of the Qur'ān* (Baroda, 1938), pp. 112-15. Further archæological and linguistic research will probably confirm the importance of the influence of Nabataean culture not only on Islam but also on early Christianity.

PART II

THE RISE OF ISLAM AND THE CALIPHAL STATE

CHAPTER VIII

MUḤAMMAD THE PROPHET OF ALLAH

IN or about A.D. 571 a child was born to the Quraysh at Makkah and was given by his mother a name which may remain for ever uncertain. His tribe called him al-Amīn[1] (the faithful), apparently an honorific title. The form which his name takes in the Koran (3 : 138, 33 : 40, 48 : 29, 47 : 2) is Muḥammad[2] and once (61 : 6) Aḥmad. In popular usage he is Muḥammad (highly praised)—a name borne by more male children than any other. The baby's father, 'Abdullāh, died before his birth; the mother, Āminah, when he was about six years old. It therefore fell to the lot of his grandfather, 'Abd-al-Muṭṭalib, to bring up the boy, and after the grandfather's death the duty devolved upon his paternal uncle abu-Ṭālib.

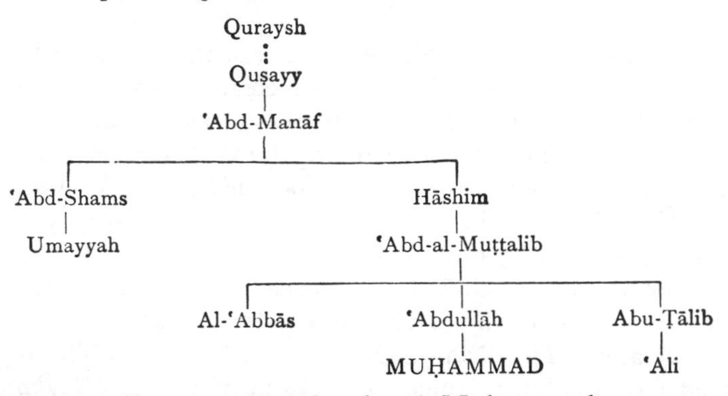

When twelve years old, it is related, Muḥammad accompanied his uncle and patron abu-Ṭālib on a caravan journey to Syria, in the course of which he met a Christian monk to whom legend has given the name Baḥīra.

Though the only one of the world prophets to be born within the full light of history, Muḥammad is but little known to us in

[1] Ibn-Hishām, *Sīrah*, p. 125; Ya'qūbi, vol. ii, p. 18; Mas'ūdi, vol. iv, p. 127.

[2] Name occurs in a South Arabic inscription, *Corpus inscriptionum Semiticarum*, pars iv, t. ii, p. 104.

his early life: of his struggle for a livelihood, his efforts towards self-fulfilment and his gradual and painful realization of the great task awaiting him we have but few reliable reports. The first record of his life was undertaken by ibn-Isḥāq, who died in Baghdād about A.H. 150 (767) and whose biography of the Prophet has been preserved only in the later recension of ibn-Hishām, who died in Egypt about A.H. 218 (833). Other than Arabic sources for the life of the Prophet and the early period of nascent Islam we have none. The first Byzantine chronicler to record some facts about "the ruler of the Saracens and the pseudo-prophet" was Theophanis[1] in the early part of the ninth century. The first reference to Muḥammad in Syriac occurs in a seventh century work.[2]

With his marriage at the age of twenty-five to the wealthy and high-minded widow Khadījah, fifteen years his senior, Muḥammad steps upon the threshold of clear history. Khadījah was a Qurayshite and, as a well-to-do merchant's widow, was conducting business independently and had taken young Muḥammad into her employ. As long as this lady with her strong personality and noble character lived, Muḥammad would have none other for a wife.

The competence which now entered into the economic life of Muḥammad, and to which there is a clear koranic[3] reference, gave him leisure and enabled him to pursue his own inclinations. He was then often noticed secluding himself and engaging in meditation within a little cave (*ghār*) on a hill outside of Makkah called Ḥirā'.[4] It was in the course of one of these periods of distraction caused by doubts and yearning after the truth that Muḥammad heard in Ghār Ḥirā' a voice[5] commanding: "Recite thou in the name of thy Lord who created", etc.[6] This was his first revelation. The Prophet had received his call. The night of that day was later named "the Night of Power" (*laylat al-qadr*)[7] and fixed towards the end of Ramaḍān (610). When after a brief interval (*fatrah*), following his call to the prophetic office, the second vision came, Muḥammad, under the stress of great

[1] *Chronographia*, ed. Carolus de Boor (Leipzig, 1885), p. 333.
[2] A. Mingana, *Sources syriaques*. vol. i. *Bar-Penkayé* (Leipzig, 1908), p. 146 (text) = p. 175 (tr.).
[3] Sūrah 93 : 6-9
[4] See Ibrāhīm Rif'at, *Mir'āt al-Ḥaramayn* (Cairo, 1925), vol. i. pp. 56-60
[5] Al-Bukhāri, *Ṣaḥīḥ* (Būlāq, 1296), vol. i, p. 3.
[6] Koran 96 : 1-5.
[7] Koran 97 : 1.

emotion, rushed home in alarm and asked his wife to put some covers on him, whereupon these words "descended": "O thou, enwrapped in thy mantle! Arise and warn".[1] The voices varied and sometimes came like the "reverberating of bells" (*ṣalṣalat al-jaras*),[2] but later, in the Madīnese sūrahs, became one voice, identified as that of Jibrīl (Gabriel).

In his call and message the Arabian Muḥammad was as truly prophetic as any of the Hebrew prophets of the Old Testament. God is one. He is all-powerful. He is the creator of the universe. There is a judgment day. Splendid rewards in Paradise await those who carry out God's commands, and terrible punishment in hell for those who disregard them. Such was the gist of his early message.

Consecrated and fired by the new task which he felt called upon to perform as the messenger (*rasūl*) of Allah, Muḥammad now went among his own people teaching, preaching, delivering the new message. They laughed him to scorn. He turned *nadhīr* (Koran 67 : 26; 51 : 50, 51), warner, prophet of doom, seeking to effect his purpose by vivid and thrilling description of the joys of Paradise and the terrors of hell, even threatening his hearers with imminent doom. Short, crisp, expressive and impressive were his early revelations, the Makkan sūrahs.

As glorifier of his Lord, admonisher to his people, messenger and prophet (*nabi*) of Allah, Muḥammad was gaining few converts. Khadījah, his wife, predisposed through the influence of her Ḥanīf[3] cousin Waraqah ibn-Nawfal, was the first of the few who responded to his call. Muḥammad's cousin ʿAli and his kinsman abu-Bakr followed. But abu-Sufyān, representing the aristocratic and influential Umayyad branch of Quraysh, stood adamant. What they considered a heresy seemed to run counter to the best economic interests of the Quraysh as custodians of al-Kaʿbah, the pantheon of multitudinous deities and centre of a pan-Arabian pilgrimage.

As new recruits, mainly from among the slave and lower classes, began to swell the ranks of the believers, the ridicule and sarcasm which had hitherto been used unsparingly on the part of the Quraysh were no longer deemed effective as weapons;

[1] Koran 74 : 1 *seq*.

[2] Bukhāri, vol. i, p. 2, l. 11. Compare the call of Isaiah 6 : 1 *seq*. See Tor Andrae, *Mohammed: sein Leben und sein Glaube* (Göttingen, 1932), pp. 39 *seq*.

[3] Cf. ibn-Hishām, pp. 121, 143.

it became necessary to resort to active persecution. These new measures resulted in the migration to Abyssinia of eleven Makkan families followed in 615 by some eighty-three others, chief among whom was that of 'Uthmān ibn-'Affān. The émigrés found asylum in the domain of the Christian Negus, who was unbending in his refusal to deliver them into the hands of their oppressors.[1] Undaunted through these dark days of persecution by the temporary loss of so many followers, Muḥammad fearlessly continued to preach and by persuasion convert men from the worship of the many and false gods to that of the one and true God, Allah. The revelations did not cease to "descend". He who had marvelled at the Jews and Christians having a "scripture" was determined that his people, too, should have one.

Soon 'Umar ibn-al-Khaṭṭāb, destined to play a leading rôle in the establishment of the Islamic state, was enrolled in the service of Allah. About three years before the Hijrah the faithful Khadījah died, and a little later died abu-Ṭālib, who, though he never professed Islam, stood firm to the end in defence of his brother's son, his protégé. Within this pre-Hijrah period there also falls the dramatic *isrā'*,[2] that nocturnal journey in which the Prophet is said to have been instantly transported from al-Ka'bah to Jerusalem preliminary to his ascent (*mi'rāj*) to the seventh heaven. Since it thus served as the terrestrial station on this memorable journey, Jerusalem, already sacred to the Jews and Christians, has become and remained the third holiest city after Makkah and al-Madīnah in the Moslem world. Embellished by later accretions this miraculous trip still forms a favourite theme in mystic circles in Persia and Turkey, and a Spanish scholar[3] considers it the original source of Dante's *Divine Comedy*. That the memory of al-Isrā' is still a living, moving force in Islam is illustrated by the serious disturbance of August 1929, in Palestine, centring on the Wailing Wall of the Jews in Jerusalem, which the Moslems consider the halting-place of the Burāq,[4]

[1] Ibn-Hishām, pp. 217-20; cf. ibn-Sa'd, vol. i, pt. 1, pp. 136-9.

[2] Koran 17 : 1; Bukhāri, vol. iv, pp. 156, 230; al-Baghawi, *Maṣābīḥ al-Sunnah* (Cairo, 1318), vol. ii, pp. 169-72; al-Khaṭīb, *Mishkāt al-Maṣābīḥ* (St. Petersburg, 1898–9), vol. ii, pp. 124-9.

[3] Miguel Asín, *Islam and the Divine Comedy*, tr. H. Sunderland (London, 1926).

[4] Probably from Ar. *barq*, lightning. Modern Palestinians call the wailing place "al-Burāq".

British Museum

MUḤAMMAD'S JOURNEY THROUGH THE CELESTIAL SPHERES

Original in Jāmi, *Yūsuf u Zulaykha*, fifteenth century. British Museum, Or. 4535.

the winged horse with a woman's face and peacock's tail on which Muḥammad journeyed heavenward.

About 620 some Yathribites, mainly of the Khazraj tribe, met Muḥammad at the 'Ukāẓ fair and grew interested in what he had to say. Two years later a deputation of about seventy-five men invited him to make Yathrib (al-Madīnah) his home, hoping thereby to secure a means for reconciling the hostile Aws and Khazraj. In al-Madīnah the Jews, who were looking forward to a Messiah, had evidently predisposed their heathen compatriots in favour of such a claimant as Muḥammad. Having paid a futile propagandist visit to al-Ṭā'if and believing his cause lost in his native town, Muḥammad allowed two hundred followers to elude the vigilance of the Quraysh and slip quietly into al-Madīnah, with which his mother had some uncertain connection; he himself followed and arrived there on September 24, 622. Such was the famous hegira (*hijrah*)—not entirely a "flight" but a scheme of migration carefully considered for some two years. Seventeen years later the Caliph 'Umar designated that lunar year (beginning July 16) in which the Hijrah took place as the official starting-point of the Moslem era.[1]

The Hijrah, with which the Makkan period ended and the Madīnese period began, proved a turning-point in the life of Muḥammad. Leaving the city of his birth as a despised prophet, he entered the city of his adoption as an honoured chief. The seer in him now recedes into the background and the practical man of politics comes to the fore. The prophet is gradually overshadowed by the statesman.

Taking advantage of the periods of "holy truce" and anxious to offer sustenance to the Emigrants (*muhājirūn*) the Madīnese Moslems, now termed *Anṣār* (Supporters), under the leadership of the new chief intercepted a summer caravan on its return from Syria to Makkah, thus striking at the most vital point in the life of that commercial metropolis. The caravan leader abu-Sufyān had got wind of the scheme and sent to Makkah for reinforcement. The encounter between the reinforcement and the Madīnese, mostly Emigrants, took place at Badr, eighty-five miles south-west of al-Madīnah, in Ramaḍān, A.D. 624, and, thanks to the inspiring leadership of the Prophet, resulted in the complete victory of three hundred Moslems over a thousand Mak-

[1] Ṭabari, vol. 1, pp. 1256, 2480; Mas'ūdi, vol. ix, p. 53.

kans. However unimportant in itself as a military engagement,[1] this Ghazwat Badr laid the foundation of Muḥammad's temporal power. Islam had won its first and decisive military victory. The victory itself was interpreted as a divine sanction of the new faith.[2] The spirit of discipline and contempt of death manifested at this first armed encounter of Islam proved characteristic of it in all its later and greater conquests. It is true that in the following year (625) the Makkans under abu-Sufyān avenged at Uḥud their defeat and even wounded the Prophet, but their triumph was not to endure. Islam recovered and passed on gradually from the defensive to the offensive, and its propagation seemed always assured. Hitherto it had been a religion within a state; in al-Madīnah, after Badr, it passed into something more than a state religion—it itself became the state. Then and there Islam came to be what the world has ever since recognized it to be—a militant polity.

In 627 the "confederates" (*al-aḥzāb*), consisting of Makkans with Bedouin and Abyssinian mercenaries, were again measuring swords with the Madīnese. Heathenism was once more arrayed against Allah. On the advice of a Persian follower, Salmān,[3] as we are told, Muḥammad had a trench[4] dug round al-Madīnah. Disgusted with this innovation in warfare, which struck the Bedouin miscellany as the most unsportsmanlike thing they had ever seen, the besiegers withdrew at the end of a month after the loss of some twenty men on both sides.[5] After the siege had been raised Muḥammad conducted a campaign against the Jews for "siding with the confederates", which resulted in the killing of six hundred able-bodied men of their leading tribe, the banu-Qurayẓah, and the expulsion of the rest. The Emigrants were then established on the date plantations thus made ownerless.[6] The banu-Qurayẓah were the first but not the last body of Islam's foes to be offered the alternative of apostasy or death. The year before, Muḥammad had sent into exile the banu-al-Naḍīr,[7] another Jewish tribe of al-Madīnah. The Jews of Khaybar, a strongly fortified oasis north of al-Madīnah, surrendered in 628 and paid tribute.

[1] Al-Wāqidi († 207/822-3) devotes more than a third of his *Maghāzi*, pp. 11-75 to Badr and its heroes.
[2] Koran 3 : 119, 8 : 42-3.
[3] Cf. Josef Horovitz in *Der Islam*, vol. xii (1922), pp. 178-83.
[4] Ar. *khandaq*, from Pers. *kandan* (to dig) through Aramaic.
[5] Koran 33 : 9-25 discusses this battle.
[6] Koran 33 : 26-7.
[7] Balādhuri. *Futūḥ*, pp 17-18=Hitti, pp. 34-5; Wāqidi, pp. 353-6

In this Madīnese period the Arabianization, the nationalization, of Islam was effected. The new prophet broke off with both Judaism and Christianity; Friday was substituted for Sabbath, the *adhān* (call from the minaret) was decreed in place of trumpets and gongs, Ramaḍān was fixed as a month of fasting, the *qiblah* (the direction to be observed during the ritual prayer) was changed from Jerusalem[1] to Makkah, the pilgrimage to al-Ka'bah was authorized and the kissing of the Black Stone—a pre-Islamic fetish—sanctioned.

In 628 Muḥammad led a band of believers to a settlement, al-Ḥudaybiyah, nine miles from Makkah and exacted a pact in which Makkans and Moslems were treated on equal terms.[2] This treaty practically ended the war with his people, the Quraysh. Among other members of this tribe, Khālid ibn-al-Walīd and 'Amr ibn-al-'Āṣ ('Āṣi), destined to become the two mighty swords of militant Islam, were about this time received as recruits to the great cause. Two years later, towards the end of January 630 (A.H. 8), the conquest of Makkah was complete. Entering its great sanctuary Muḥammad smashed the many idols, said to have numbered three hundred and sixty, exclaiming: "Truth hath come, and falsehood hath vanished!"[3] The people themselves, however, were treated with special magnanimity.[4] Hardly a triumphal entry in ancient annals is comparable to this.

It was probably about this time[5] that the territory around the Ka'bah was declared by Muḥammad *ḥaram* (forbidden, sacred), and the passage in sūrah 9 : 28 was revealed which was later interpreted as prohibiting all non-Moslems from approaching it This verse was evidently intended to forbid only the polytheists from drawing nigh to the Ka'bah at the time of the annual pilgrimage The injunction as interpreted is still effective.[6] No more than fifteen Christian-born Europeans have thus far succeeded in seeing the two Holy Cities and escaping with their lives. The first to leave record was Ludovico di Varthema of Bologna[7]

[1] Cf. 1 Kings 8 : 29-30; Dan. 6 : 10.
[2] Balādhuri, pp. 35-6 = Hitti, pp. 60-61.
[3] *Ibid.* p. 40 = Hitti, p. 66; cf. Koran 17 : 83.
[4] Wāqidi, p. 416.
[5] Ibn-Sa'd, vol. ii, pt. 1, p. 99; cf. Bayḍāwi, *Anwār*, vol. i, p. 383, l. 10.
[6] Muḥammad Labīb al-Batanūni, *al-Riḥlah al-Ḥijāzīyah* (Cairo, 1329), p. 47.
[7] He declared false the widely spread European legend that Muḥammad's body lay suspended in the air somewhere above Makkah. See *The Travels of Ludovico di Varthema in Egypt, Syria, Arabia Deserta and Arabia Felix*, tr. J. W. Jones (Hakluyt Society, vol. xxxii, London, 1863), pp. 25 *seq.*

in 1503, and among the latest were an Englishman, Eldon Rutter,[1] and a Hungarian, Julius Germanus.[2] The most interesting was undoubtedly Sir Richard Burton (1853).[3]

In A.H. 9 Muḥammad stationed a garrison at Tabūk, on the frontier of Ghassānland, and without a single engagement concluded treaties of peace with the Christian chief of Aylah (al-ʿAqabah) and the Jewish tribes in the oases of Maqna, Adhruḥ and al-Jarbā' to the south.[4] The native Jews and Christians were taken under the protection of the newly arising Islamic community in consideration of a payment later called *jizyah*. This act set a precedent far-reaching in its consequences.

This year 9 (630–31) is called the "year of delegations" (*sanat al-wufūd*). During it delegations flocked from near and far to offer allegiance to the prince-prophet. Tribes joined out of convenience if not conviction, and Islam contented itself with exacting a verbal profession of faith and a payment of *zakāh* (poor tax). The large number of Bedouins who joined the new order may be surmised from a saying attributed to ʿUmar, "The Bedouins are the raw material of Islam". Tribes and districts which had sent no representatives before sent them now. They came from distant ʿUmān, Ḥaḍramawt and al-Yaman. The Ṭayyi' sent deputies and so did the Hamdān and Kindah. Arabia, which had hitherto never bowed to the will of one man, seemed now inclined to be dominated by Muḥammad and be incorporated into his new scheme. Its heathenism was yielding to a nobler faith and a higher morality.

In the tenth Moslem year Muḥammad entered peacefully at the head of the annual pilgrimage into his new religious capital. Makkah. This proved his last visit and was therefore styled "the farewell pilgrimage". Three months after his return to al-Madīnah, he unexpectedly took ill and died complaining of severe headache on June 8, 632.

To the Madīnese period in the life of the Prophet belong the lengthy and more verbose sūrahs of the Koran which contain, in addition to the religious laws governing fasting and alms-giving and prayer, social and political ordinances dealing with marriage and divorce and the treatment of slaves, prisoners of war and enemies. On behalf of the slave, the orphan, the weak

[1] *The Holy Cities of Arabia*, 2 vols. (London, 1928). [2] *Allah Akbar* (Berlin, 1938).
[3] *Personal Narrative of a Pilgrimage to el-Medinah and Meccah*, 3 vols. (London, 1855–6). [4] Balādhuri, pp. 59 *seq.* = Hitti, pp. 92 *seq.*

and the oppressed we find the legislation of him who was himself once a poor orphan especially benevolent.[1]

Even in the height of his glory Muḥammad led, as in his days of obscurity, an unpretentious life in one of those clay houses consisting, as do all old-fashioned houses of present-day Arabia and Syria, of a few rooms opening into a courtyard and accessible only therefrom. He was often seen mending his own clothes and was at all times within the reach of his people. The little he left he regarded as state property. Some for love, others for political reasons, he took about a dozen wives, among whom his favourite was 'Ā'ishah, the young daughter of abu-Bakr. By Khadījah he had a number of children, none of whom survived him except Fāṭimah, the famous spouse of 'Ali. Muḥammad mourned bitterly the loss of his infant son Ibrāhīm, born to him by Mary, a Christian Copt. "Serious or trivial, his daily behaviour has instituted a canon which millions observe at this day with conscious mimicry. No one regarded by any section of the human race as Perfect Man has been imitated so minutely."[2]

Out of the religious community of al-Madīnah the later and larger state of Islam arose. This new community of Emigrants and Supporters was established on the basis of religion as the Ummat (congregation of) Allah. This was the first attempt in the history of Arabia at a social organization with religion, rather than blood, as its basis. Allah was the personification of state supremacy. His Prophet, as long as he lived, was His legitimate vicegerent and supreme ruler on earth. As such, Muḥammad, in addition to his spiritual function, exercised the same temporal authority that any chief of a state might exercise. All within this community, regardless of tribal affiliation and older loyalties, were now brethren at least in principle. These are the words of the Prophet in his noble sermon at the "farewell pilgrimage":

> O ye men! harken unto my words and take ye them to heart! Know ye that every Moslem is a brother unto every other Moslem, and that ye are now one brotherhood. It is not legitimate for any one of you, therefore, to appropriate unto himself anything that belongs to his brother unless it is willingly given him by that brother.[3]

Thus by one stroke the most vital bond of Arab relationship,

[1] Koran 2 : 172, 218-19; 4 : 40; 9 : 60; 24 : 33; 93 : 9. Consult Robert Roberts, *The Social Laws of the Qorân* (London, 1925).

[2] D. G. Hogarth, *Arabia* (Oxford, 1922), p. 52.

[3] Ibn-Hishām, p. 969; cf. Wāqidi, pp. 433-4.

that of tribal kinship, was replaced by a new bond, that of faith; a sort of Pax Islamica was instituted for Arabia. The new community was to have no priesthood, no hierarchy, no central see. Its mosque was its public forum and military drill ground as well as its place of common worship. The leader in prayer, the *imām*, was also to be commander in chief of the army of the faithful, who were enjoined to protect one another against the entire world. All Arabians who remained heathen were outside the pale, almost outlaws. Islam cancelled the past. Wine (*khamr*, from Aramaic) and gambling—next to women the two indulgences dearest to the Arabian heart—were abolished in one verse.[1] Singing, almost equally attractive, was frowned upon. This contrast between the old order and the new was vividly drawn by the apocryphal words put in the mouth of Ja'far ibn-abi-Ṭālib, the spokesman of the Moslem emigrants to Abyssinia. Said Ja'far to the Negus:

> Jāhilīyah people were we, worshipping idols, feeding on dead animals [*maytah*][2], practising immorality, deserting our families and violating the covenant terms of mutual protection, with the strong among us devouring the weak. Such was our state until Allah sent unto us a messenger from amongst ourselves whose ancestry we know and whose veracity, fidelity and purity we recognize. He it was who summoned us to Allah in order to profess Him as one and worship Him alone, discarding whatever stones and idols we and our forbears before us worshipped in His stead. He moreover commanded us to be truthful in our talk, to render to others what is due them, to stand by our families and to refrain from doing wrong and shedding blood. He forbade committing fornication, bearing false witness, depriving the orphan of his legitimate right and speaking ill of chaste women. He enjoined on us the worship of Allah alone, associating with Him no other. He also ordered us to observe prayer, pay zakāh [alms] and practise fasting.[3]

From al-Madīnah the Islamic theocracy spread all over Arabia and later encompassed the larger part of Western Asia and North Africa. The community of al-Madīnah was in miniature the subsequent community of Islam.

Within a brief span of mortal life Muḥammad called forth out of unpromising material a nation never united before, in a

[1] Koran 5 : 92. The Nabataeans had an anti-bacchic deity.
[2] Cf. Koran 2 : 168.
[3] Fasting was ordained in the Madīnese period, long after the Abyssinian migration; Koran 2 : 179, 183. Ibn-Hishām, p. 219.

country that was hitherto but a geographical expression; established a religion which in vast areas superseded Christianity and Judaism and still claims the adherence of a goodly portion of the human race; and laid the basis of an empire that was soon to embrace within its far-flung boundaries the fairest provinces of the then civilized world. Himself an unschooled man,[1] Muḥammad was nevertheless responsible for a book still considered by one-eighth of mankind as the embodiment of all science, wisdom and theology.

[1] Koranic *ummi* (3 : 19), which Sunni (orthodox) Moslems interpret "illiterate", is explained by Ṭabari, *Tafsīr*, vol. iii, p. 143, as one among the Arabian polytheists, who have no revelation. Critical scholars point out that in the Koran (7 : 156; 3 : 68-9; 62 : 2) the term is used as if in opposition to *ahl al-kitāb* (the people of the Book) and should therefore be taken to mean one unable to read the holy scriptures of the earlier revealed religions; sūrah 25 : 6 is quoted as suggesting Muḥammad's ability to write Arabic.

CHAPTER IX

THE KORAN THE BOOK OF ALLAH

THE year following the death of Muḥammad, according to the orthodox view, abu-Bakr, on the recommendation of 'Umar, who had observed that the Koran memorizers (*ḥuffāẓ*) were becoming extinct, ordered that the scattered portions of the Koran be collected. Zayd ibn-Thābit of al-Madīnah, formerly Muḥammad's secretary, was entrusted with the task. Fragments from "ribs of palm-leaves and tablets of white stone and from the breasts of men" [1] were brought together and a text was constructed. In the caliphate of 'Uthmān (644–56) various readings in the current copies arose, due mainly to the defective nature of Kufic script; 'Uthmān accordingly appointed in 651 the same Zayd as chairman of the committee on revision. Abu-Bakr's copy, then in the custody of Ḥafṣah, daughter of 'Umar and one of Muḥammad's widows, was used as a basis. The original codex of the fresh version was kept in al-Madīnah; [2] three copies of this text were made and forwarded to the three military camps in Damascus, al-Baṣrah and al-Kūfah, and all others were destroyed.

The modern scholarly view, however, doubts whether abu-Bakr ever made an official recension and maintains that 'Uthmān found several metropolitan codices in Arabia, Syria and al-'Irāq with divergent readings. 'Uthmān canonized the Madīnah codex and ordered all others destroyed. The text was finally fixed by the two vizirs ibn-Muqlah and ibn-'Īsa in 933 with the help of the learned ibn-Mujāhid. Ibn-Mujāhid admitted seven readings, which had developed because of lack of vowel and diacritical marks, as canonical.[3]

The Moslem view is that the Koran is the word of Allah

[1] Khaṭīb, *Mishkāh*, vol. i, p. 343.

[2] This copy is said to have been presented by the Turkish authorities to Emperor William II. See Versailles Treaty, Pt. VIII, Sec. II, art. 246.

[3] Arthur Jeffery, *Materials for the History of the Text of the Koran* (Leyden, 1937), pp. 1-10; cf. Hartwig Hirschfeld, *New Researches into the Composition and Exegesis of the Koran* (London, 1902), pp. 138 *seq.*

dictated through Gabriel to Muḥammad from an archetype preserved in the seventh heaven (sūrs. 43:3, 56:76-9, 85:21-2).[1] Not only is the meaning therefore inspired but every word, every letter.

The arrangement of the sūrahs (koranic chapters) is mechanical, in the order of their length. The Makkan sūrahs, about ninety in number and belonging to the period of struggle, are mostly short, incisive, fiery, impassioned in style and replete with prophetic feeling. In them the oneness of Allah, His attributes, the ethical duties of man and the coming retribution constitute the favourite themes. The Madīnese sūrahs, the remaining twenty-four (about one-third of the contents of the Koran) which "were sent down" (*unzilat*) in the period of victory, are mostly long, verbose and rich in legislative material. In them theological dogmas and ceremonial regulations relating to the institution of public prayer, fasting, pilgrimage and the sacred months are laid down. They moreover contain laws prohibiting wine, pork and gambling; fiscal and military ordinances relating to alms-giving (*zakāh*) and holy war (*jihād*); civil and criminal laws regarding homicide, retaliation, theft, usury, marriage and divorce, adultery, inheritance and the freeing of slaves. Sūrahs 2, 4 and 5 contain most of this legislative material. The often-quoted prescription for marriage (sūr. 4:3)[2] limit rather than introduce the practice of polygamy. Critics consider the statutes relating to divorce (4:24, 33:48, 2:229) the most objectionable, and those about the treatment of slaves, orphans and strangers (4:2, 3, 40; 16:73; 24:33) the most humane portions of Islamic legislation. The manumission of slaves is inculcated as something most pleasing to God and regarded as an expiation for many a sin. Flashes of the old eloquence and prophetic spark appear here and there in the Madīnese sūrahs, as in sūrah 24.[3] Among the noblest verses of the Koran are sūrah 2:172, 256.

Almost all the historical narratives of the Koran have their biblical parallels with the exception of a few purely Arabian stories relating to ʿĀd and Thamūd, Luqmān, the "owners of the elephant", and two others alluding to Alexander the Great (*Iskandar dhu-al-Qarnayn*)[4] and to the "Seven Sleepers"—all

[1] Consult Bayḍāwi, vol. ii, pp. 235, 309-10, 396.
[2] Cf. sūr. 70:29-30.
[3] The verses in this sūrah dealing with light betray Zoroastrian influence.
[4] Sūr. 18:82 *seq.*, where he seems to be invested with a divine commission. Dan. 8:5, 21, has a clear reference to Alexander.

of which receive but very brief mention. Among the Old Testament characters, Adam, Noah, Abraham[1] (mentioned about seventy times in twenty-five different sūrahs and having his name as a title for sūrah 14), Ishmael, Lot, Joseph (to whom sūrah 12 is dedicated), Moses (whose name occurs in thirty-four different sūrahs), Saul, David, Solomon, Elijah, Job and Jonah (whose name sūrah 10 bears) figure prominently. The story of the creation and fall of Adam is cited five times, the flood eight and Sodom eight. In fact the Koran shows more parallelism to the Pentateuch than to any other part of the Bible.

All these narratives are used didactically, not for the object of telling a story but to preach a moral, to teach that God in former times has always rewarded the righteous and punished the wicked. The story of Joseph is told in a most interesting and realistic way. The variations in this and in such other instances as the story of Abraham's response to the call of the one true God (sūr. 21 : 52 *seq.*) have their parallels in the midrash, Talmud and other non-canonical Jewish works.[2]

Of the New Testament characters Zachariah, John the Baptist, Jesus (ʿĪsa) and Mary are the only ones emphasized. The last two names are generally associated. Mary the mother of Jesus is also the daughter of ʿImrān and a sister of Aaron.[3] Haman (Hāmān), the favourite of Ahasuerus,[4] is himself the minister of Pharaoh.[5] It is worthy of note that the Arabic forms of the names of the Old Testament characters seem to have come mainly through Syriac (e.g. Nūḥ, Noah) and Greek (e.g. Ilyās, Elias; Yūnus, Jonah) rather than directly from Hebrew.

A comparative study of the above koranic and biblical narratives and such parallel passages as those that follow reveals no verbal dependence: sūr. 2 : 44-58 and Acts 7 : 36-53; sūr. 2 : 273 and Matt. 6 : 3, 4; sūr. 10 : 72 and 2 Pet. 2 : 5; sūrs. 10 : 73, 24 : 50 and Deut. 26 : 14, 17; sūr. 17 : 23-40 and Ex. 20 : 2-17, Deut. 5 : 6-21; sūr. 21 : 20 and Rev. 4 : 8; sūr. 23 : 3 and Matt.

[1] In the Madīnese sūrahs Abraham becomes a Ḥanīf, a Moslem (sūr. 3 : 60). He is held as Muḥammad's ideal predecessor, the spiritual ancestor of Islam (sūrs. 4 : 124; 3 : 61) and the founder of al-Kaʿbah (2 : 118 *seq.*). As the "friend" of God he is cited in the Old Testament (Is. 41 : 8, 2 Ch. 20 : 7), the New Testament (Jas. 2 : 23) and the Koran (4 : 124).

[2] Consult *The Legacy of Israel*, ed. E. R. Bevan and C. Singer (Oxford, 1928), pp. 129-71.

[3] Sūrs. 19 : 16-29; 3 : 31-40.

[4] Esther 3 : 1.

[5] Sūrs. 28 : 38; 40 : 38.

6 : 7; sūr. 36 : 53 and 1 Th. 4 : 16; sūr. 39 : 30 and Matt. 6 : 24; sūr. 42 : 19 and Gal. 6 : 7-9; sūr. 48 : 29 and Mk. 4 : 28; and sūr. 92 : 18 and Lk. 11 : 41. The only quotation is sūr. 21 : 105 (cf. Ps. 37 : 9) where the Koran cites the Psalms as the source. Others which bear striking resemblance are sūr. 21 : 104 and Is. 34 : 4; sūr. 53 : 39-42 and Ezek. 18 : 20; sūr. 53 : 45 and 1 Sam. 2 : 6; and sūr. 53 : 49 and 1 Sam. 2 : 7. Such verses as those dealing with an "eye for an eye" (sūr. 5 : 49 and Ex. 21 : 23-7), the "camel and the needle" (sūr. 7 : 38 and Matt. 19 : 24), the "house built upon the sand" (sūr. 9 : 110 and Matt. 7 : 24-7) and the "taste of death for every man" (sūrs. 21 : 36, 29 : 57, 3 : 182 and Heb. 9 : 27, 2 : 9, Matt. 16 : 28) evidently represent old Semitic proverbs and sayings common to both Hebrew and Arabic. The parallels between Matthew and the Makkan sūrahs seem particularly copious. Certain miraculous acts attributed to Jesus the child, such as speaking in the cradle (sūr. 3 : 41) and creating birds out of clay (sūr. 3 : 43), recall similar acts recorded in the Apocryphal Gospels, including the *Injīl al-Ṭufūlīyah*. The only conspicuous parallel with any of the contents of the sacred books of Persia occurs in the picture of heaven and hell, sketched with a brush dipped in materialistic colours (sūr. 56 : 8-56), which has a counterpart in the late writings of the Parsis. The picture itself may have been inspired by Christian miniatures or mosaics representing the gardens of Paradise with figures of angels which were interpreted as being those of young men and young women.

Though the youngest of the epoch-making books, the Koran is the most widely read book ever written, for besides its use in worship, it is the text-book from which practically every Moslem learns to read Arabic. Other than the official translation into Turkish no authorized Moslem translation into a foreign language exists; but there are unauthorized interlinear free translations by Moslems into several languages, including Persian, Bengali, Urdu, Marathi, Javanese and Chinese. In all, the Koran has been done into some forty languages.[1] The words (77,934), the

[1] The first translation into a foreign language was that into Latin sponsored (1143) by Peter the Venerable, abbot of Cluny, who secured the services of three Christian scholars and an Arab, in an attempt to refute the beliefs of Islam. In English the first translation appeared in 1649 (London), "*The Alcoran of Mahomet*, translated out of Arabique into French; by the Sieur Du Ryer. . . . And newly Englished, for the satisfaction of all that desire to look into the Turkish vanities". Sale's translation (1734) from the original Arabic is a paraphrase influenced by the

verses (6236) and even the letters (323,621) [1] have been painstakingly counted. This unbounded reverence for The Book reached its climax in the later dogma that it is "the uncreated word" of God, an echo of the "Logos" theory.[2] "Let none touch it but the purified." [3] In our own day the sight of a Moslem picking up a piece of paper from the street and tucking it carefully into a hole in a wall—lest the name of Allah be on it—is not rare.

The word Qur'ān itself means recitation, lecture, discourse. This book, a strong, living voice, is meant for oral recitation and should be heard in the original to be appreciated. No small measure of its force lies in its rhyme and rhetoric and in the cadence and sweep, which cannot be reproduced in translation without loss. Its length is four-fifths of that of the Arabic New Testament. The religious influence it exercises as the basis of Islam and the final authority in matters spiritual and ethical is only one side of the story. Theology, jurisprudence and science being considered by Moslems as different aspects of one and the same thing, the Koran becomes the scientific manual, the textbook, for acquiring a liberal education. In such a school as al-Azhar, the largest Moslem university in the world, this book still holds its own as the basis of the whole curriculum. Its literary influence may be appreciated when we realize that it was due to it alone that the various dialects of the Arabic-speaking peoples have not fallen apart into distinct languages, as have the Romance languages. While today an 'Irāqi may find it a little difficult fully to understand the speech of a Moroccan, yet he would have no difficulty in understanding his written language, since in both al-'Irāq and Morocco—as well as in Syria, Arabia, Egypt—the classical language modelled by the Koran is followed closely everywhere. At the time of Muḥammad there was no work of the first order in Arabic prose. The Koran was therefore the earliest, and has ever since remained the model, prose work. Its language is rhythmical and rhetorical, but not poetical. Its rhymed prose has set the standard which almost every conservative Arabic writer of today consciously strives to imitate.

Latin version of Marracci's *Refutatio Alcorani* (1698); Rodwell's (1861) arranges the sūrahs chronologically; Palmer's (1880) tries to reproduce the Oriental flavour; Marmaduke Pickthall's (1930) is especially successful. Richard Bell (1937–9) attempts a critical rearrangement of the verses. The earliest Arabic printing of the Koran was done between 1485 and 1499 in Venice by Alessandro de Paganini.

[1] There are other enumerations. [2] Cf. John 1: 1; Prov. 22-30. [3] Sūr. 56: 78.8:

CHAPTER X

ISLAM THE RELIGION OF SUBMISSION TO THE WILL OF ALLAH

OF the three monotheistic religions developed by the Semites, the Islam of the Koran is the most characteristic and comes nearer the Judaism of the Old Testament than does the Christianity of the New Testament. It has such close affinities with both, however, that in the conception of many medieval European and Oriental Christians it stood as a heretic Christian sect rather than a distinct religion. In his *Divine Comedy* Dante consigns Muḥammad to one of the lower hells with all those "sowers of scandals and schism". Gradually Islam developed into an independent and distinct system of belief. The Ka'bah and Quraysh were the determining factors in this new orientation.

In dealing with the fundamentals of their religion Moslem theologians distinguish between *īmān* (religious belief), *'ibādāt* (acts of worship, religious duty) and *iḥsān* (right-doing), all of which are included in the term *dīn* (religion).[1] "Verily *the* religion [*dīn*] with God is Islam."[2]

Dogmas and beliefs

Īmān involves belief in God and in His angels, His "books" and His messengers and in the last day. Its first and greatest dogma is: *la ilāha illa-l-Lāh*, no god whatsoever but Allah. In *īmān* the conception of God stands supreme. In fact, over ninety per cent. of Moslem theology has to do with Allah. He is the one true God. The profession of His unity receives its most poignant expression in sūrah 112. God is the supreme reality, the pre-existent, the creator (sūrs. 16 : 3-17; 2 : 27-8), the omniscient, omnipotent (13 : 9-17; 6 : 59-62; 2 : 100-101; 3 : 25-7), the self-subsistent (2 : 256; 3 : 1). He has ninety-nine excellent names (*al-asmā' al-ḥusna*,[3] sūr. 7 : 179) and as many attributes. The full Moslem rosary has ninety-nine beads corresponding to His

[1] Cf. al-Shahrastāni, *al-Milal w-al-Niḥal*, ed. Cureton (London, 1842–6), p. 27.
[2] Koran 3 : 17.
[3] Al-Ghazzāli, *al-Maqṣad al-Asna*, 2nd ed. (Cairo, 1324), pp. 12 *seq.*; Baghawi, *Maṣābīḥ*, vol. i, pp. 96-7.

names. His attributes (*ṣifāt*) of love are overshadowed by those of might and majesty (sūr. 59 : 23-4). Islam (sūrs. 5 : 5, 6 : 125, 49 : 14) is the religion of "submission", "surrender", to the will of Allah. The submission of Abraham and his son in the supreme test, the attempted sacrifice by the father, expressed in the verb *aslamā* (sūr. 37 : 103), was evidently the act that provided Muḥammad with the name for the new faith.[1] In this uncompromising monotheism, with its simple, enthusiastic faith in the supreme rule of a transcendent being, lies the chief strength of Islam. Its adherents enjoy a consciousness of contentment and resignation unknown among followers of most creeds. Suicide is rare in Moslem lands.

The second dogma in *īmān* treats of Muḥammad as the messenger (*rasūl*) of Allah (sūrs. 7 : 157; 48 : 29), His prophet (7 : 156, 158), the admonisher (35 : 22) of his people, the last of a long line of prophets of whom he is the "seal" (33 : 40), and therefore the greatest. In the koranic system of theology Muḥammad is but a human being whose only miracle is the *iʿjāz* of the Koran;[2] but in tradition, folklore and popular belief he is invested with a divine aura. His religion is pre-eminently a practical one, reflecting the practical and efficient mind of its originator. It offers no unattainable ideal, few theological complications and perplexities, no mystical sacraments and no priestly hierarchy involving ordination, consecration and "apostolic succession".

The Koran is the word (*kalām*, sūrs. 9 : 6; 48 : 15, cf. 6 : 114-15) of Allah. It contains the final revelation (sūrs. 17 : 107-8; 97 : 1; 44 : 2; 28 : 51; 46 : 11) and is "uncreated". A koranic quotation is always introduced with "saith Allah". In its phonetic and graphic reproduction and in its linguistic form the Koran is identical and co-eternal with a heavenly archetype (sūrs. 56 : 76-9; 85 : 21-2). Of all miracles it is the greatest: all men and jinn in collaboration could not produce its like (17 : 90).

In its angelology Islam gives the foremost place to Gabriel (Jibrīl), the bearer of revelation (2 : 91),[3] who is also "the spirit

[1] C. C. Torrey, *The Jewish Foundation of Islam* (New York, 1933), pp. 90, 102 *seq.*

[2] The elegance of its composition, which constitutes its miraculous character; Koran 13 : 27-30; 17 : 87-96. See ibn-Ḥazm, *al-Faṣl fi al-Milal w-al-Ahwā' w-al-Niḥal*, vol. iii (Cairo, 1347), pp. 10-14; al-Suyūṭi, *al-Itqān fi 'Ulūm al-Qur'ān* (Cairo, 1925), vol. ii, pp. 116-25.

[3] This sūrah contains the only distinct assertion of Gabriel's being the medium of revelation; cf. sūrs. 81 : 19-20; 53 : 5-7.

of holiness" (16 : 104; 2 : 81) and "the faithful spirit" (26 : 193). As a messenger of the supreme deity he corresponds to the Hermes of Greek mythology.

Sin can be either moral or ceremonial. The worst and only unpardonable sin is *shirk*, joining or associating of other gods with the one true God (4 : 51, 116). Ascribing plurality to the Deity seemed most detestable to Muḥammad, and in the Madīnese sūrahs the polytheists are continually threatened with the last judgment (28 : 62 *seq.*, 21 : 98 *seq.*). In Muḥammad's mind "the people of the book", the Scripturaries,[1] i.e. the Christians and Jews, were probably not included among the polytheists, though some commentators on sūr. 98 : 5 would hold a different view.

The most impressive parts of the Koran deal with eschatology. One whole sūrah (75) is entitled The Resurrection (*al-qiyāmah*). The reality of future life is emphasized by the recurrent references to "the day of judgment" (15 : 35-6; 82 : 17-18), "the day of resurrection" (22 : 5; 30 : 56), "the day" (24 : 24-5; 31 : 32), "the hour" (15 : 85; 18 : 20) and "the indubitable" (69 : 1-2). Future life as depicted in the Koran, with its bodily pains and physical pleasures, implies the resurrection of the body.

The five pillars:

The religious duties (*'ibādāt*) of the Moslem centre on the so-called five pillars (*arkān*) of Islam.

1. Profession of faith

The profession of faith (*shahādah*), the first pillar, is summed up in the Koranic double formula *la ilāha illa-l-Lāh; Muḥammadun rasūlu-l-Lāh* (no god whatsoever but Allah; Muḥammad is the messenger of Allah). These are the first words to strike the ear of the new-born Moslem babe; they are the last to be uttered at the grave. Between these two episodes no other words are more often repeated. They also occur in the muezzin's call to prayer chanted many times daily from the tops of minarets. Islam has generally satisfied itself with a verbal profession; once the formula is accepted and reproduced the person is nominally a Moslem.

2. Prayer

Five times a day[2] is the faithful Moslem supposed to turn his face towards Makkah and recite his prescribed prayer. Prayer is the second pillar of faith. A bird's-eye view of the Moslem world at the hour of prayer (ignoring the difference caused by longitude and latitude) would present the spectacle of a series of concentric

[1] H. Lammens, *L'Islam: croyances et institutions* (Beirūt, 1926), p. 62, l. 17, and p. 219, l. 7.

[2] Dawn, midday, mid-afternoon, sunset and nightfall.

circles of worshippers radiating from the Ka'bah at Makkah and covering an ever-widening area from Sierra Leone to Malaysia and from Tobolsk to Capetown.

The word for ritual prayer, *ṣalāh*, is an Aramaic loan-word, as its Arabic orthography (with a *wāw*) suggests. If prayer existed before Islam it must have been unorganized and informal. Though it is encouraged in an early sūrah (87 : 15) and its requirements are set forth in certain Makkan revelations (11 : 116; 17 : 80-81; 30 : 16-17), ritual prayer, with its prescribed number of five separate and distinct orisons per day and the prerequisite state of legal purity or ceremonial cleanliness (2 : 239, 24 : 57,[1] 4 : 46, 5 : 8-9), was not instituted until the Madīnese period. The middle prayer (2 : 239) was the last enjoined. The number five, according to al-Bukhāri,[2] was a compromise reached after Allah had asked for fifty on the occasion of Muḥammad's visit to the seventh heaven on his nocturnal journey (sūr. 17 : 1). Sūr. 4 : 46 seems to suggest that the limitation and later interdiction of the use of wine may have owed its origin to the necessity of keeping the divine service free from undue disturbance.

The ritual prayer is a legally defined act performed by all with the same general bodily postures and genuflections and with the same proper orientation. The worshipper should be in a state of legal purity (*ṭahārah*), and the use of Arabic as a medium of expression is absolutely incumbent upon him, no matter what his native tongue may be. In its stereotyped form prayer is not so much petition or supplication[3] as it is the mention of Allah's name (62 : 9-10; 8 : 47). The simple and meaningful *fātiḥah*, often likened to the Lord's Prayer, is reiterated by the faithful Moslem about twenty times a day. This makes it one of the most often repeated formulas ever devised. Doubly meritorious is the voluntary ritual prayer performed at night (*tahajjud*, 17 : 81; 50 : 38-9), for it is a work of supererogation (*nāfilah*).

The Friday noon prayer is the only public one (62 : 9; 5 : 63) and is obligatory for all adult males. Certain mosques have places reserved for women. One feature of the Friday service is the *khuṭbah* (address) delivered by the leader (*imām*), in which intercessory prayer is offered on behalf of the ruling head of the

[1] Cf. Ps. 55 : 17.

[2] *Ṣaḥīḥ*, vol. i, pp. 85 *seq.*; cf. Gen. 18 : 23-33.

[3] This is *du'ā'*, unregulated and private or individual prayer, not to be confused with the formal *ṣalāh*.

state. This congregational assembly had for its prototype the Jewish synagogue worship, but was influenced in its later development by the Christian Sunday service. In dignity, simplicity and orderliness it is unsurpassed as a manner of collective worship. Standing erect in self-arranged rows in the mosque and following the leadership of the *imām* with precision and reverence, the worshippers present a sight that is always impressive. As a disciplinary measure this congregational prayer must have had great value for the proud, individualistic sons of the desert. It developed in them the sense of social equality and the consciousness of solidarity. It promoted that brotherhood of community of believers which the religion of Muḥammad had theoretically substituted for blood relationship. The prayer ground thus became "the first drill ground of Islam".

3. Alms-giving

Prescribed originally as a voluntary act of love and considered almost identical with piety, *zakāh* (legal alms, sūrs. 2 : 40, 77, 192, 263-9, 273-5, 280) evolved into an obligatory tax on property, including money, cattle, corn, fruit and merchandise. In the Koran (9 : 5; 2 : 40, 77, etc.) zakāh is often associated with the *ṣalāh*. The young Islamic state collected zakāh through regular officials and administered it from a central treasury to support the poor among the community, build mosques and defray government expenses (sūr. 9 : 60). The word *zakāh* is of Aramaic origin and is more specific than *ṣadaqah*, which is voluntary and implies alms-giving in general. Zakāh is a purely denominational institution, involving alms raised and distributed among Moslems alone. Its underlying principle tallies with the tithe, which, according to Pliny,[1] the South Arabian merchants had to pay to their god before they were allowed to sell their spices. Its exact amount varied and has been determined in the various cases by the *fiqh* (religious law), but generally it averaged two and a half per cent. Even soldiers' pensions were not exempt. Later, with the disintegration of the purely Islamic state, zakāh was again left to the Moslem's conscience. Zakāh constitutes the third pillar of the faith.

4. Fasting

Though penitential fasts are prescribed a number of times in the Madīnese sūrahs (58 : 5; 19 : 27; 4 : 94; 2 : 192), Ramaḍān as a fasting month is mentioned only once (2 : 179-81). That particular month, which may have been sacred in pre-Islamic days, was chosen because in it the Koran was first revealed

[1] Bk. XII, ch. 32.

(sūr. 2 : 181) and the victory of Badr won. Abstinence from all food and drink is enjoined from dawn till sunset (sūr. 2 : 183). Instances in which violence has been used in modern times by the government or by the populace against a non-fasting believer in Moslem lands are not unknown.

We have no evidence of any practice of fasting in pre-Islamic pagan Arabia, but the institution was, of course, well established among both Christians and Jews (Matt. 4 : 2; Deut. 9 : 9). Ibn-Hishām [1] states that the Quraysh in the Jāhilīyah days were wont to spend one month a year on Mt. Ḥirā' practising penance (*taḥannuth*). In al-Madīnah and before instituting Ramaḍān, Muḥammad evidently observed the tenth of Muḥarram (*'āshūrā'*) as a fast day; this he had adopted from the Jews.[2] In the Makkan sūrahs the word for fasting (*ṣawm*) occurs only once (19 : 27), and there apparently in the sense of "silence".

5. Pilgrimage

Pilgrimage (*ḥajj*, sūrs. 3 : 91; 2 : 192-6; 5 : 1-2, 96) is the fifth and last pillar of Islam. Once in a lifetime every Moslem of either sex who can afford it is supposed to undertake at a stated time of the year a holy visit to Makkah. *'Umrah* is the lesser pilgrimage to Makkah and may be made individually and at any time.

The pilgrim (*ḥājj*) makes his entry into the holy precincts as a *muḥrim* (wearing a seamless garment) and performs the seven-fold circumambulation of the Ka'bah (*ṭawāf*) and the seven-fold course (*sa'y*) between the adjacent al-Ṣafa mound and the Marwah eminence lying opposite.[3] The ḥajj proper begins with the march to 'Arafah,[4] which lasts from the seventh to the eighth of dhu-al-Ḥijjah. The halts (*wuqūf*) take place at the outlying sanctuaries of 'Arafah, namely, al-Muzdalifah and Mina. The stone-throwing ceremony takes place on the way to the valley of Mina at Jamrat al-'Aqabah. With the sacrifice at Mina of a camel or of a sheep or other horned domestic animal (Koran 22 : 34-7), which always takes place on the tenth of dhu-al-Ḥijjah and is celebrated throughout the Moslem world as 'Īd al-Aḍḥa (the festival of sacrifice), the whole ceremony

[1] *Sīrah*, pp. 151-2.

[2] Bukhāri, vol. ii, p. 208; Lev. 16 : 29.

[3] Moslems, according to their tradition, perform the *sa'y* in commemoration of the fact that Hagar ran back and forth seven times between these two eminences looking for a spring for her thirsty son.

[4] 'Arafah is the valley and 'Arafāt the mountain, according to Rif'at, *Mir'āt*, vol. i, p. 44, but the two words are often used interchangeably.

formally ends. After the shaving of the head the garment (*iḥrām*) is discarded and the *iḥlāl* (secular condition) resumed. As long as he is *muḥrim*, in a sanctified state, the pilgrim must observe, in addition to the abstinences imposed in connection with the fasting of Ramaḍān, such as sexual intercourse, those special regulations forbidding the shedding of blood, hunting and the uprooting of plants. Fasting, however, is not required.

Pilgrimage to holy places was an ancient Semitic institution.[1] Echoes of it survived to Old Testament days (Ex. 23 : 14, 17; 34 : 22-3; 1 Sam. 1 : 3). Originally it may have been a feature of solar cult, the ceremonies of which coincided with the autumnal equinox and constituted a kind of farewell to the harsh rule of the burning sun and a welcoming to Quzaḥ, the thunder-god of fertility. In pre-Islamic days the annual fairs of North Arabia were followed by a pilgrimage in dhu-al-Ḥijjah to the Kaʿbah and ʿArafah. In the seventh year of the Hijrah Muḥammad adopted and Islamized the ancient pilgrim rites centring on the Kaʿbah and ʿArafah. In these rites Islam entered upon its largest share of heritage from pre-Islamic Arabia. Rifʿat[2] relates that when a Bedouin nowadays makes his ritual walk round the Kaʿbah he repeats in colloquial Arabic: "O Lord of this House! I testify that I have come. Say not that I have not come. Forgive me and forgive my father, if you will. Otherwise forgive me in spite of your unwillingness, for I have performed my pilgrimage, as you see."[3]

A constant trek of pilgrims across Central Africa, from Senegal, Liberia, Nigeria, is ever on the move eastward and increasing in numbers as it goes along. Some are on foot, others on camel-back. The majority are men, but a few are women and children. They trade, they beg, they work their way into the Highly Honoured Makkah (al-Mukarramah) and the Greatly Illuminated City (al-Madīnah al-Munawwarah). Many fall by the wayside and are martyrs; those who survive finally strike

[1] W. Robertson Smith, *Lectures on the Religion of the Semites*, 3rd ed. by S. A. Cook (London, 1927), pp. 80, 276.

[2] Vol. i, p. 35.

[3] The same authority (vol. i, p. 35) overheard a Bedouin woman addressing herself to al-Kaʿbah thus: "O Lady Laylah! if you bring rain to our region so that plenty [*khayr*] may follow, I shall fetch you a bottle of ghee so that you may anoint your hair". Hearing this another Bedouin woman asked the speaker, "Do you really mean to fetch her one as you say?" to which the former replied, "Hush, I am fooling her. Once she brings the rain I shall fetch nothing!"

a western Red Sea port whence they are transported across by dhows. But the four major caravans are those from al-Yaman, al-ʿIrāq, Syria and Egypt. Each of these countries used to send annually at the head of its caravan a *maḥmil* symbolic of its dignity. The Maḥmil, a splendidly decorated litter, is carried on a camel that is led and not ridden. Beginning with the thir-

From Ibrāhīm Rifʿat, "Mirʾāt al-Ḥaramayn"

THE EGYPTIAN AND SYRIAN MAḤMILS ON THEIR DEPARTURE FROM AL-MUZDALIFAH TO MINA, 1904

teenth century such Maḥmils were sent by Moslem princes anxious to display their independence and assert their claim as protectors of the Holy Places. Current tradition holds that Shajar-al-Durr, wife of one of the last Ayyūbid sultans, originated the idea of Maḥmil in the middle of the thirteenth century. But in several early works[1] the claim is made that the Umayyad viceroy in al-ʿIrāq, the famous al-Ḥajjāj († 714), was the one who initiated the practice. Whichever of the two stories be correct it was quite

[1] Ibn-Qutaybah, *Maʿārif*, p. 274; Yāqūt, *Buldān*, vol. iv, p. 886, l. 6; ibn Rustah, p. 192; al-Suyūṭi, *al-Kanz al-Madfūn* (Būlāq, 1288), p. 68.

evidently the Mamlūk Baybars (1260–77) who celebrated the occasion with such special festivities that the custom was established on a firm basis.[1] In recent years the Syrian and Egyptian caravans had been distinguished in splendour. The average number of pilgrims annually between the first and second World Wars had been about 172,000. Since then it has been on the increase, reaching in the mid-1960s the million mark with Egypt and Pakistan sending the largest numbers. Puritanical ibn-Su'ūd abolished the Maḥmil, a relic of heathenism. In the pilgrim age Ḥijāz had its main source of income until the discovery of oil.

Down through the ages this institution has continued to serve as the major unifying influence in Islam and the most effective common bond among the diverse believers. It rendered almost every capable Moslem perforce a traveller for once in his lifetime. The socializing influence of such a gathering of the brotherhood of believers from the four quarters of the earth is hard to over-estimate. It afforded opportunity for negroes, Berbers, Chinese, Persians, Syrians, Turks, Arabs—rich and poor, high and low—to fraternize and meet together on the common ground of faith. Of all world religions Islam seems to have attained the largest measure of success in demolishing the barriers of race, colour and nationality—at least within the confines of its own community. The line is drawn only between believers and the rest of mankind. These ḥajj gatherings have undoubtedly contributed their share towards the achievement of that result. They have further provided excellent opportunities for the propagation of sectarian ideas among peoples coming from lands not bound together by the modern means of communication and where the voice of the press is not yet a living voice. Such a movement as the Sanūsi in northern Africa owes its inception and early propagation to the intercourse provided by the pilgrimage to Makkah.

Holy War

The duty of *jihād*, holy war[2] (sūr. 2 : 186-90), has been raised to the dignity of a sixth pillar by at least one Moslem sect, the Khārijites. To it Islam owes its unparalleled expansion as a worldly power. It is one of the principal duties of the caliph to

[1] Suyūṭi, *Ḥusn*, vol. ii, p. 74; cf. al-Maqrīzi, *al-Mawā'iẓ w-al-I'tibār*, ed. Gaston Wiet (Cairo, 1922), vol. iii, p. 300; *al-Sulūk fi Ma'rifat Duwal al-Mulūk*, tr. M. Quatremère, *Histoire des sultans mamlouks de l'Égypte* (Paris, 1845), vol. i (pt. 1), pp. 149-50. The Maḥmil, the *markab* (litter) of the Ruwalah and the Ark of the Covenant may go back to the same ancient Semitic origin.

[2] Theoretically there is no secular war in Islam.

From Ibrāhīm Rif'at, "Mir'āt al-Ḥaramayn"

PILGRIMS AROUND THE KA'BAH PERFORMING THE FRIDAY PRAYER, 1908

From Ibrāhīm Rif'at, "Mir'āt Ḥal-aramayn"

NORTH-EASTERN VIEW OF THE KA'BAH, 1908

keep pushing back the geographical wall separating the *dār al-Islām* (the land of Islam) from the *dār al-ḥarb* (the war territory). This bipartite division of the world into an abode of peace and an abode of war finds a parallel in the communistic theory of Soviet Russia. Of more recent years, however, *jihād* has found less support in the Moslem world, chiefly because of the fragmentation and lingering of many parts under the control of various alien governments considered too strong or too benevolent to be overthrown. The last such call to a universal uprising against non-Moslems, made as late as the autumn of 1914 by the Ottoman Sultan-Caliph Muḥammad Rashād, proved an utter failure.

Another important article of faith is the belief in the divine decree of good and evil (sūr. 9 : 51; 3 : 139; 35 : 2), a dominant factor in Moslem thought and conduct throughout the ages.

The religious obligations (*'ibādāt*) discussed above constitute the fundamentals of Islam. But they are not the only ones instituted by koranic prescription. Right-doing (*iḥsān*) has the same authority behind it. The sanctions of private as well as public morality in the Moslem world are all of a religious character. Basically the will of Allah, as revealed through Muḥammad, determines what is right (*ḥalāl* = permitted, legitimate) and what is wrong (*ḥarām* = forbidden). In the historical evolution of religion in Arabia, Islam was the first to demand personal belief and personal morality (sūrs. 53 : 39-42, 31 : 32). In the realm of ethical conduct it substituted the moral fellowship of religion for the tribal fellowship of blood kinship. Of the human virtues it insists on beneficence, in the form of zakāh, most urgently. In such passages as 2 : 172; 3 : 100, 106, 109-11; 4 : 40; 7 : 31, which stand in favourable comparison with the best in the Old Testament (e.g. Amos 5 : 23-4; Hos. 6 : 6; Mic. 6 : 6-8), its ethical ideals are clearly set forth.

CHAPTER XI

PERIOD OF CONQUEST, EXPANSION AND COLONIZATION
A.D. 632–61

Orthodox Caliphs

1. Abu-Bakr	. .	632–34
2. 'Umar .	. .	634–44
3. 'Uthmān	. .	644–56
4. 'Ali .	. .	656–61

As long as Muḥammad lived he performed the functions of prophet, lawgiver, religious leader, chief judge, commander of the army and civil head of the state—all in one. But now Muḥammad was dead. Who was to be his successor, his *khalīfah* (caliph), in all except the spiritual function? In his rôle as the last and greatest prophet, who had delivered the final dispensation to mankind, Muḥammad evidently could have no one to succeed him.

The Prophet left no male children. Only one daughter, Fāṭimah, the wife of 'Ali, survived him. But the Arabian chiefdom or sheikhdom was not exactly hereditary; it was more electoral, following the line of tribal seniority. So even if his sons had not predeceased him, the problem would not have been solved. Nor did Muḥammad clearly designate a successor. The caliphate is therefore the first problem Islam had to face. It is still a living issue. In March 1924, sixteen months after cancelling the sultanate, the Kemālist Turks abolished the Ottoman caliphate in Constantinople held by 'Abd-al-Majīd II, and since then a number of pan-Islamic congresses have met in Cairo and Makkah to determine the rightful successor to the Prophet, but all to no avail. In the words of the distinguished historian of religions, al-Shahrastāni (†1153):[1] "Never was there an Islamic issue which brought about more bloodshed than the caliphate [*imāmah*]".

As always happens when a serious question is thrown open for popular decision, a number of conflicting parties arose

[1] P. 12.

subsequent to the death of Muḥammad. These were on one side the Emigrants (*muhājirūn*), who based their claim on having belonged to the tribe of the Prophet and on having been the first to accept his mission. On the other stood the Madīnese Supporters (*Anṣār*), who asserted that had they not given Muḥammad and nascent Islam asylum both would have perished. Later these two parties coalesced to form the Companions (*ṣaḥābah*). Then came the Legitimists (*aṣḥāb al-naṣṣ w-al-ta'yīn*), who reasoned that Allah and Muḥammad could not have left the community of believers to the chances and whims of an electorate, and therefore must have made clear provision for its leadership by designating some particular person to succeed Muḥammad. 'Ali, the paternal cousin of the Prophet, the husband of his only surviving daughter and one of the first two or three believers, was the one thus designated and the only legitimate successor. As against the elective principle, this last party held to the divine right of rule. And last but not least came the aristocracy of Quraysh, the Umayyads, who held the reins of authority, power and wealth in the pre-Islamic days (but who were the last to profess Islam) and who later asserted their right to the successorship. It was abu-Sufyān, their head, who had led the opposition to the Prophet until the fall of Makkah.

The orthodox caliphate: A patriarchal age

The first party triumphed. The aged and pious abu-Bakr, a father-in-law of the Prophet and one of the first three or four to believe in him, received the oath of allegiance (*bay'ah*) from the assembled chiefs, probably in accordance with a previously arranged scheme between himself, 'Umar ibn-al-Khaṭṭāb and abu-'Ubaydah ibn-al-Jarrāḥ—the triumvirate who presided over the destinies of infant Islam.

Abu-Bakr headed the list of the four orthodox (*rāshidūn*) caliphs, including 'Umar, 'Uthmān and 'Ali. This was a period in which the lustre of the Prophet's life had not ceased to shed its light and influence over the thoughts and acts of the caliphs. All four were close associates and relatives of the Prophet. They lived in al-Madīnah, the scene of his last ministry, with the exception of the last, 'Ali, who chose al-Kūfah in al-'Irāq for his capital.

Arabia conquers itself

The short caliphate of abu-Bakr (632–4) was mostly occupied with the so-called *riddah* (secession, apostasy) wars. As represented by Arab chroniclers all Arabia outside of al-Ḥijāz, which is alleged to have accepted Islam and acknowledged the temporal authority of the Prophet, upon his death broke off from the newly organized state and followed a number of local and false prophets. The fact is that with the lack of communication, the utter absence of organized methods of missionary activity and the short time involved, not more than one-third of the peninsula could actually have professed Islam during the life of the Prophet or recognized his rule. Even al-Ḥijāz, the immediate scene of his activity, was not Islamized until a year or two before his death. The delegates (*wufūd*) reported to have come to pay him homage could not have represented all Arabia, and for a tribe to become Moslem in those days simply meant that its chiefs so became.

Many such tribes in al-Yaman, al-Yamāmah and 'Umān felt reluctant to pay the zakāh to al-Madīnah. The death of the Prophet provided the excuse for active refusal. Jealousy against the rising hegemony of the Ḥijāz capital was one of the underlying motives. The old centrifugal forces characteristic of Arabian life were once more in full operation.

Abu-Bakr, however, was adamant in his insistence on unconditional surrender from "the seceders" or war unto destruction.[1] Khālid ibn-al-Walīd was the hero of these wars. Within some six months his generalship had reduced the tribes of Central Arabia to submission. First he subjugated the Ṭayyi'; then the Asad and Ghaṭafān, whose prophet, Ṭalḥah, the Moslems scoffingly styled Ṭulayḥah; and finally the banu-Ḥanīfah in al-Yamāmah, who had gathered under the banner of a prophet whose name, Musaylimah, appears derisively in the Arabic annals in this diminutive form. It was this Musaylimah who offered the most stubborn resistance. He unified his religious and worldly interests with Sajāḥ, possibly a Christian, who was the prophetess and soothsayer of the banu-Tamīm and whom he married; with 40,000 men at his command, so we are told, he crushed two Moslem armies before Khālid arrived with a third. Even from among this victorious third Khālid lost enough Koran reciters to endanger the perpetuation of the knowledge of the sacred book. Other campaigns were conducted by various Moslem generals and with varying measures of success[2] in al-Baḥrayn,

[1] Balādhuri, p. 94, l. 14 = Hitti, p. 143, l. 23.
[2] Consult Balādhuri, pp. 94-107 = Hitti, pp. 143-62.

'Umān, Ḥaḍramawt and al-Yaman, where al-Aswad had been acknowledged prophet. Thus most of the *riddah* wars were directed not so much toward holding secessionists by force—which is the view of Arab historians—as toward bringing over to Islam many who had until that time been outside the fold.

The peninsula was now united under abu-Bakr by the sword of Khālid. Arabia had to conquer itself before it could conquer the world. The momentum acquired in these internal campaigns, which transformed Arabia for a number of months after the death of the Prophet into an armed camp, had to seek new outlets, and the newly acquired technique of organized warfare had to be applied somewhere. The warlike spirit of the tribes, now brought together into a nominally common fraternity, had to find new channels for asserting itself.

The two cardinal events of late ancient times are the Teutonic migrations resulting in the disruption of the venerable Roman empire, and the Arab conquests which demolished the Persian empire and shook the Byzantine power to its very foundation. Of these two, the Arab conquests culminating in the occupation of Spain marked the beginning of the Middle Ages.[1] If someone in the first third of the seventh Christian century had had the audacity to prophesy that within a decade some unheralded, unforeseen power from the hitherto barbarous and little-known land of Arabia was to make its appearance, hurl itself against the only two world powers of the age, fall heir to the one—the Sāsānid—and strip the other—the Byzantine—of its fairest provinces, he would undoubtedly have been declared a lunatic. Yet that was exactly what happened. After the death of the Prophet sterile Arabia seems to have been converted as if by magic into a nursery of heroes the like of whom both in number and quality is hard to find anywhere. The military campaigns of Khālid ibn-al-Walīd and 'Amr ibn-al-'Āṣ which ensued in al-'Irāq, Persia, Syria and Egypt are among the most brilliantly executed in the history of warfare and bear favourable comparison with those of Napoleon, Hannibal or Alexander.

The enfeebled condition of the rival Byzantines and Sāsānids who had conducted internecine wars against each other for many generations; the heavy taxes, consequent upon these wars, imposed on the citizens of both empires and undermining their

[1] Henri Pirenne, *Mahomet et Charlemagne*, 7th ed. (Brussels, 1935).

sense of loyalty; the previous domestication of Arabian tribes in Syria and Mesopotamia, and particularly along the borders; the existence of schisms in the Christian church resulting in the establishment of Monophysite communities in Syria and Egypt and Nestorian congregations in al-'Irāq and Persia, together with the persecution by the orthodox church—all these paved the way for the surprisingly rapid progress of Arabian arms. The Byzantines had neglected the frontier forts. After their victory of Mu'tah, in the land of ancient Moab, over the column sent by the Prophet (Sept. 629), Heraclius stopped the subsidies which the Syro-Arab tribes south of the Dead Sea and on the Madīnah-Ghazzah route had regularly received.[1] The native Semites of Syria and Palestine as well as the Hamites of Egypt looked upon the Arabian newcomers as nearer of kin than their hated and oppressive alien overlords. In fact the Moslem conquests may be looked upon as the recovery by the ancient Near East of its early domain. Under the stimulus of Islam the East now awoke and reasserted itself after a millennium of Western domination. Moreover, the tribute exacted by the new conquerors was even less than that exacted by the old, and the conquered could now pursue their religious practices with more freedom and less interference. As for the Arabians themselves, they represented a fresh and vigorous stock fired with new enthusiasm, imbued with the will to conquer and emboldened by the utter contempt of death inculcated by their new faith. But no small share of their seemingly miraculous success was due to their application of a military technique adapted to the open steppes of Western Asia and North Africa—the use of cavalry and camelry—which the Romans never mastered.

The economic causes of the expansion

The "clerical" interpretation of the Islamic movement, emphasized in Arabic sources, makes it entirely or primarily a religious movement and lays no stress on the underlying economic causes. The corresponding and equally discredited hypothesis held by many Christians represents the Arabian Moslems as offering the Koran with the one hand and the sword with the other. Outside of the Arabian peninsula and especially in the instance of the *ahl al-kitāb* (Christians and Jews) there was a third and, from the standpoint of the conquerors, more desirable choice besides the Koran and the sword—tribute.

[1] Theophanes, pp. 335-6.

"Make war . . . upon such of those to whom the Book has been given until they pay tribute offered on the back of their hands, in a state of humiliation."[1] This third choice was later by the necessity of circumstances offered to Zoroastrians and heathen Berbers and Turks; in the case of all of these theory gave way to expediency. Islam did provide a new battle-cry, a convenient rallying-point and a party watchword. It undoubtedly acted as a cohesive and cementing agency for the heterogeneous masses never before united and furnished a large part of the driving force. But it is hardly in itself enough to explain the conquests. Not fanaticism but economic necessity drove the Bedouin hordes, and most of the armies of conquest were recruited from the Bedouins, beyond the confines of their arid abode to the fair lands of the north. The passion to go to heaven in the next life may have been operative with some, but the desire for the comforts and luxuries of the civilized regions of the Fertile Crescent was just as strong in the case of many.

This economic aspect of the interpretation of the conquests, worked out by Caetani,[2] Becker[3] and other modern critical scholars, was not entirely ignored by the Arab chroniclers of old. Al-Balādhuri, the most judicious of the historians of the conquest, declares that in recruiting for the Syrian campaign abu-Bakr "wrote to the people of Makkah, al-Ṭā'if, al-Yaman and all the Arabs in Najd and al-Ḥijāz summoning them to a 'holy war' and arousing their desire for it and for the booty to be got from the Greeks".[4] Rustam, the Persian general who defended his country against the Arab invasion, made the following remark to the Moslem envoy: "I have learned that ye were forced to what ye are doing by nothing but the narrow means of livelihood and by poverty".[5] A verse in the *Ḥamāsah* of abu-Tammām[6] has put the case tersely:

> No, not for Paradise didst thou the nomad life forsake;
> Rather, I believe, it was thy yearning after bread and dates.

Envisaged in its proper setting, the Islamic expansion marks the final stage in the age-long process of gradual infiltration from

[1] Sūr. 9 : 29.
[2] *Annali*, vol. ii, pp. 831-61.
[3] In *Cambridge Medieval History* (New York, 1913), vol. ii, ch. xi.
[4] *Futūḥ*, p. 107 = Hitti, p. 165.
[5] Balādhuri, pp. 256-7 = Hitti, pp. 411-12.
[6] P. 795.

the barren desert to the adjacent Fertile Crescent, the last great Semitic migration.

The chroniclers, all of whom viewed the events of the conquest in the light of their subsequent developments, would also have us believe that these campaigns were conducted through the sagacity of the first caliphs, particularly abu-Bakr and 'Umar, in accordance with carefully prearranged plans. History shows but very few cases in which the course of great events was foreseen by those who launched them. Far from being entirely the result of deliberate and cool calculation, the campaigns seem to have started as raids to provide new outlets for the warring spirit of the tribes now forbidden to engage in fratricidal combats, the objective in most cases being booty and not the gaining of a permanent foothold. But the machine so built soon got beyond the control of those who built it. The movement acquired momentum as the warriors passed from victory to victory. It was then that the systematic campaigns began, and the creation of the Arab empire followed inevitably. Its creation was therefore due less to early design than to the logic of immediate circumstances.

The clerical or theological view favouring a providential interpretation of Islamic expansion, corresponding to the Old Testament interpretation of the Hebrew history and to the medieval philosophy of Christian history, has a faulty philological basis. The term Islam may be used in three senses: originally a religion, Islam later became a state, and finally a culture. Unlike Judaism and the old Buddhism, the religion of Islam proved as much of an aggressive and missionary religion as Christianity. Subsequently it built up a state. The Islam that conquered the northern regions was not the Islamic religion but the Islamic state. The Arabians burst forth upon an unsuspecting world as members of a national theocracy. It was Arabianism and not Muḥammadanism that triumphed first. Not until the second and third centuries of the Moslem era did the bulk of the people in Syria, Mesopotamia and Persia profess the religion of Muḥammad. Between the military conquest of these regions and their religious conversion a long period intervened. And when they were converted the people turned primarily because of self-interest—to escape tribute and seek identification with the ruling class. As for Islam as a culture, it developed slowly after the military conquests on a substratum composed of the core and heritage of the Syro-Aramaean, Persian and Hellenistic civilizations which had preceded it. With Islam the Near Orient not only recaptured the whole of its former political domain but regained in the realm of culture its ancient intellectual pre-eminence.

CHAPTER XII

THE CONQUEST OF SYRIA

ABOUT the same time that Heraclius, newly hailed deliverer of Christendom and restorer of the unity of the Eastern Empire, was in Jerusalem reinstalling the true Cross,[1] which had just been recovered from the Persians, his troops beyond the Jordan reported an attack by an Arabian band which was repelled with little difficulty. Mu'tah, on the frontier of al-Balqā' to the east of the southern extremity of the Dead Sea, was the scene of the encounter. Zayd ibn-Ḥārithah, the adopted son of Muḥammad, was the leader; under him were 3000 men.[2] Zayd lost his life in the raid and the newly converted Khālid ibn-al-Walīd succeeded in leading the remnant of the shattered army back to al-Madīnah. The ostensible object of the raid was to avenge the martyrdom of the Prophet's emissary sent to the Ghassānid prince of Buṣra; the real one was to secure the coveted Mash-rafīyah[3] swords manufactured at Mu'tah and neighbouring towns with a view to using them in the impending attack on Makkah. The event was naturally interpreted as one of the ordinary raids to which the settled peoples of the borderland had long been accustomed; but actually it was the first gun in a struggle that was not to cease until the proud Byzantine capital had fallen (1453) to the latest champions of Islam and the name of Muḥammad substituted for that of Christ on the walls of the most magnificent cathedral of Christendom, St. Sophia.

The Mu'tah engagement was the only campaign against Syria in the lifetime of the Prophet. The Tabūk[4] expedition in the following year (A.H. 9/630) led by him in person was bloodless, though it netted a few Jewish and Christian oases.

At the conclusion of the Riddah wars in the autumn of 633,

[1] Sept. 14, 629, still celebrated with bonfire in the Lebanon.
[2] Ṭabari, vol. i, p. 1610. Cf. Theophanes, p. 336.
[3] From *Mashārif al-Sha'm*, i.e. the highlands overlooking Syria. M. J. de Goeje, *Mémoire sur la conquête de la Syrie* (Leyden, 1900), p. 5.
[4] Wāqidi, pp. 425 *seq.*; Balādhuri, p. 59 = Hitti, p. 92.

three detachments of about 3000 men each, led respectively by 'Amr ibn-al-'Āṣ, Yazīd ibn-abi-Sufyān and Shuraḥbīl ibn-Ḥasanah,[1] marched northward and began operations in southern and south-eastern Syria. Yazīd had as standard bearer his brother Mu'āwiyah, the future distinguished founder of the Umayyad dynasty. Yazīd and Shuraḥbīl took the direct Tabūk-Ma'ān route, whereas 'Amr, who in case of unified action was to be commander in chief, took the coast route via Aylah. The numbers of each detachment were later augmented to some 7500 men. Abu-'Ubaydah ibn-al-Jarrāḥ, soon to become generalissimo, probably headed one of the reinforcements and took the famous pilgrims' route which followed the older transport route from al-Madīnah to Damascus.

In the first encounter, at Wādi al-'Arabah, the great depression south of the Dead Sea, Yazīd triumphed over Sergius the patrician of Palestine, whose headquarters were at Cæsarea (Qaysārīyah). On their retreat towards Ghazzah the remnant of the several thousand Byzantine troops under Sergius were overtaken at Dāthin and almost annihilated (February 4, 634). In other places, however, the natural advantages of the Byzantines were telling and the Moslem invaders were being harassed. Heraclius, whose ancestral home was Edessa (al-Ruhā') and whose six years' campaigning had cleared the Persians from Syria and Egypt, hastened from Emesa (Ḥimṣ) to organize and dispatch to the south a fresh army under his brother Theodorus.

In the meantime Khālid ibn-al-Walīd, "the sword of Allah",[2] who was operating in al-'Irāq at the head of some five hundred Riddah veterans in co-operation with the banu-Shaybān, a subtribe of the Bakr ibn-Wā'il domiciled on the Persian border, was ordered by abu-Bakr to rush to the relief of his fellow generals on the Syrian front. Though a minor affair in itself and undertaken possibly without the knowledge of the caliph, chronologically the raid on al-'Irāq stands at the commencement of the Moslem military enterprises. But from the standpoint of al-Madīnah and al-Ḥijāz neighbouring Syria was the place of chief concern. Before abu-Bakr issued his orders al-Ḥīrah in al-'Irāq had capitulated to Khālid and his ally al-Muthanna ibn-

[1] Cf. al-Baṣri, *Futūḥ al-Sha'm*, ed. W. N. Lees (Calcutta, 1853–4), pp. 8-11, 40-42.
[2] Wāqidi, p. 402; ibn-'Asākir, *al-Ta'rīkh al-Kabīr*, ed. 'Abd-al-Qādir Badrān, vol. v (Damascus, 1332), pp. 92, 102.

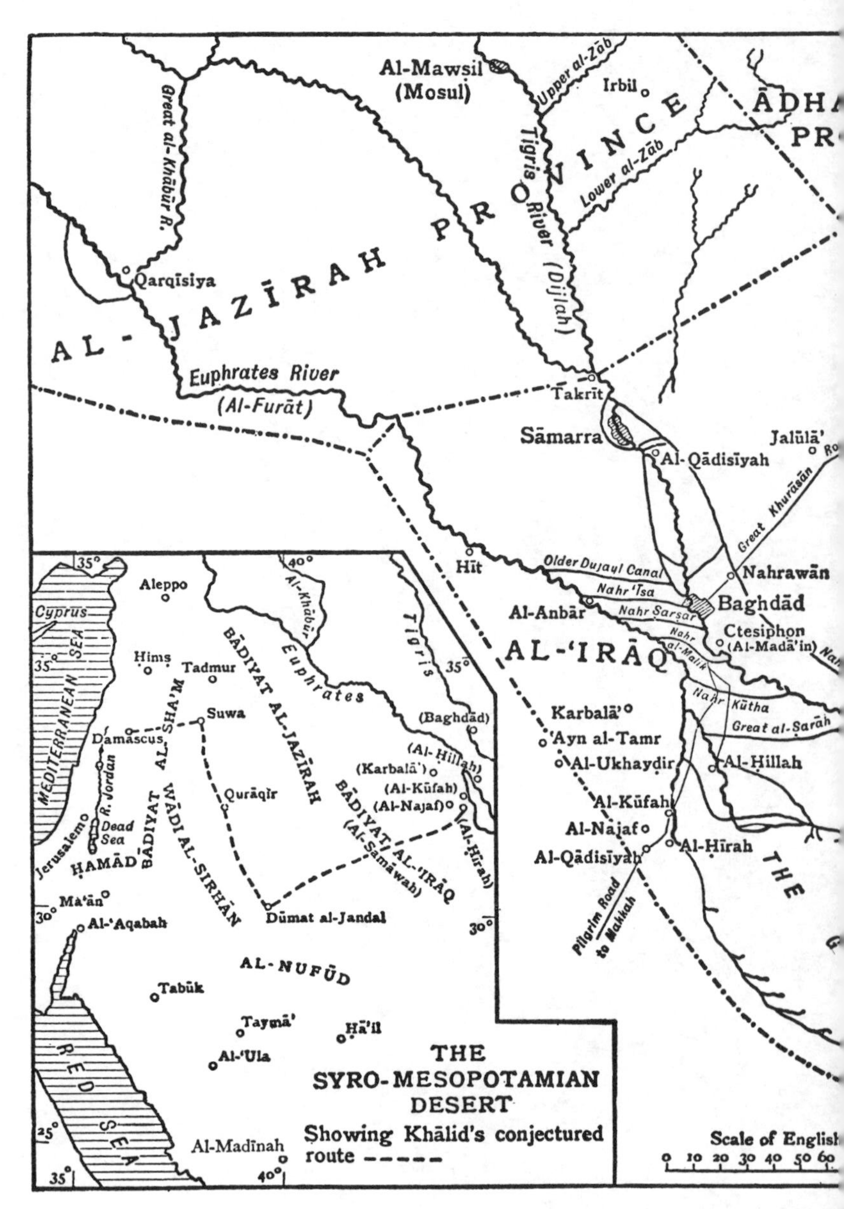

AL-'IRĀQ, KHŪZIS

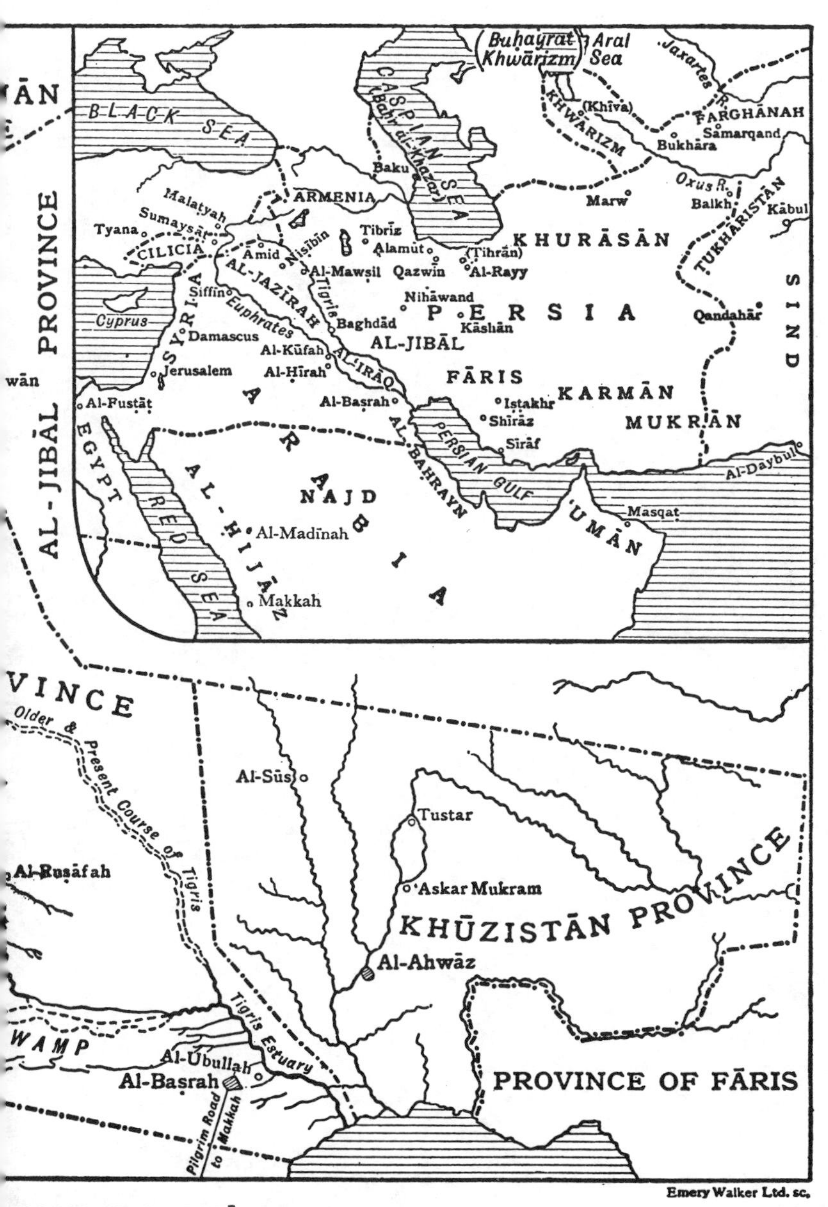

PART OF AL-JAZĪRAH

[Between pages 148 and 149

Ḥārithah, the chief of the Shaybān Bedouins, for a consideration of 60,000 dirhams. This town with its Arab Christian kinglet was the earliest acquisition of Islam outside the peninsula and the first apple to fall from the Persian tree. 'Ayn al-Tamr, a fortified place in the desert north-west of al-Kūfah, had also been captured just before the famous march on Syria.

Khālid's perilcus march

Khālid's itinerary through the desert presents many historical and geographical problems, for different authors have given us different routes and conflicting dates.[1] As reconstructed from a critical examination of all the sources[2] his march probably started from al-Ḥīrah (March 634) and led westward through the desert to the oasis of Dūmat[3] al-Jandal (modern al-Jawf), situated midway between al-'Irāq and Syria on the easiest route. Once in Dūmah he could have continued through Wādi al-Sirḥān (ancient Baṭn al-Sirr) to Buṣra, the first gateway of Syria; but forts lay on the way. Therefore Khālid took the north-western route from Dūmah to Qurāqir[4] on the eastern boundary of Wādi Sirḥān and thence pushed due northward to Suwa,[5] the second gateway of Syria, a journey of five days in an almost waterless desert. A certain Rāfi' ibn-'Umayr of the Ṭayyi' tribe acted as guide. Water for the troops was carried in bags; but for the horses the paunches of the old camels, later to be slaughtered for food, served as reservoirs.[6] The troops, five to eight hundred in all, rode camels; the few horses to be used at the time of the encounter were led alongside. At one spot Rāfi', with eyes so dazzled by the rays of the sun reflected from the sand that he could not see the expected sign for water, besought the men to look for a box-thorn (*'awsaj*). As they dug near it they struck damp sand whence water trickled forth, to the relief of the distressed army.

With dramatic suddenness Khālid appeared in the neighbourhood of Damascus (Dimashq) and directly in the rear of the Byzantine army after only eighteen days' journey. Here he

[1] Cf. Balādhuri, pp. 110-12; Ya'qūbi, *Ta'rīkh*, vol. ii, pp. 150-51; Ṭabari, vol. i, pp. 2111-13, 2121-4; ibn-'Asākir, vol. i, p. 130; ibn-al-Athīr, *al-Kāmil fi al-Ta'rīkh*, ed. C. J. Tornberg, vol. ii (Leyden, 1867), pp. 312-13.

[2] Alois Musil, *Arabia Deserta* (New York, 1927), pp. 553-73.

[3] Mentioned in Gen. 25 : 14, Is. 21 : 11.

[4] Modern Qulbān Qarāqir.

[5] Near modern Sab' Biyār (seven wells) north-east of Damascus.

[6] Ashurbanipal refers to enemy Arabs who "ripped open their riding-camels" to quench their thirst; Luckenbill, vol. ii, § 827; Musil, *Arabia Deserta*, p 570.

began his marauding expeditions in the course of one of which he encountered and defeated the Christian forces of the Ghassānids at Marj Rāhiṭ[1] on their Easter Sunday. Thence Khālid continued his triumphal march against Buṣra (Eski-Shām or Old Damascus). Here he evidently succeeded in effecting a junction with the other Arabian forces, resulting in the bloody victory at Ajnādayn[2] on July 30, 634, which laid open before them practically all Palestine. With the junction of the forces Khālid assumed supreme command of the united army. Systematic campaigning now began. Buṣra, one of the Ghassānid capitals, fell without much resistance. Fiḥl (or Faḥl, Gr. Pella), east of the Jordan and commanding its crossing, followed suit on January 23, 635. The road towards the Syrian metropolis of Damascus was cleared by the rout of the enemy at Marj al-Ṣuffar[3] on February 25, 635. Two weeks later Khālid stood before the gate of the city reputed by tradition to be the oldest in the world and from whose walls Paul was let down in a basket on that memorable night of his flight. Damascus, soon to become the capital of the Islamic empire, surrendered in September 635, after six months' siege, through treachery on the part of the civil and ecclesiastical authorities, who included the father of the celebrated St. John, of whom we shall later hear under the Umayyads. Abandoned by the Byzantine garrison, the civilian population of Damascus capitulated. The terms served as a model for future arrangements with the remaining Syro-Palestinian cities·

> In the name of Allah, the compassionate, the merciful. This is what Khālid ibn-al-Walīd would grant to the inhabitants of Damascus if he enters therein: he promises to give them security for their lives, property and churches. Their city wall shall not be demolished, neither shall any Moslem be quartered in their houses. Thereunto we give to them the pact of Allah and the protection of His Prophet, the caliphs and the believers. So long as they pay the poll tax, nothing but good shall befall them.[4]

The poll tax was evidently one dinar and one *jarīb* (measure of wheat) on every head, which sum 'Umar ibn-al-Khaṭṭāb later increased. Ba'labakk, Ḥimṣ, Ḥamāh (Epiphania) and other towns fell one after the other like ninepins. Nothing stood in

[1] A Ghassānid camp about 15 miles from Damascus, near 'Adhrā'.

[2] Not Jannābatayn; see S. D. Goitein in *Journal, American Oriental Society*, vol. lxx (1950), p. 106.

[3] A plain 20 miles south of Damascus.

[4] Balādhuri, p. 121 = Hitti, p. 187.

Tarsus
Edessa
Dābiq
AL-'AWĀṢIM
Quwayq R.
Aleppo
Antioch
Al-Raqqah
Qinnasrīn
QINNASRĪN
Ṣiffīn
Al-Ruṣāfah
CYPRUS
Al-Lādhiqiyah
Orontes R.
Shayzar
Hamāh
HIMṢ
Hims
Palmyra
Tripoli
Ba'labakk
Marj Rāhiṭ
Beirut
Suwa
Sidon
DIMASHQ
Damascus
Tyre
Al-Jābiyah
Marj al-Ṣuffar
Ṭabarīyah
Al-Ruqqād
HAWRĀN
AL-URDUNN
Yarmūk
Busrā
Baysān
Qaysāriyah
Nābulus
Al-Fiḥl
Al-Ludd
Al-Ramlah
Amwās
Jerusalem
'Asqalān
Ajnādayn
Ghazzah
Bayt Jibrīn
Rafah
FILASṬĪN
Al-'Arīsh
Mu'tah
SYRIA
showing
The Junds or Military Districts
English Miles
0 20 40 60 80 100
Emery Walker Ltd. sc.

the way of the advancing conqueror. "The people of Shayzar [Larissa] went out to meet him accompanied by players on the tambourines and singers and bowed down before him."[1]

The decisive battle of Yarmūk

In the meantime Heraclius had mustered an army of some 50,000 again under his brother Theodorus, and was prepared for a decisive stand. Khālid relinquished for the time being Ḥimṣ, even Damascus and other strategic towns, and concentrated some 25,000 men[2] at the valley of Yarmūk,[3] the eastern tributary of the Jordan. Months of skirmishing came to a climax on August 20, 636, a hot day clouded by the wind-blown dust[4] of one of the most torrid spots on earth and undoubtedly fixed upon by Arabian generalship. Before the terrific onslaught of the sons of the desert the efforts of the Byzantine troops, aided by the chants and prayers of their priests and the presence of their crosses,[5] proved of no avail. Those of the Byzantines and their Armenian and Arab mercenaries who were not slaughtered on the spot were relentlessly driven into the steep bed of the river and the Ruqqād valley; the few who managed to escape across it were almost annihilated on the other side. Theodorus himself fell and the imperial army was converted into a fleeing, panic-stricken mob. The fate of Syria was decided. One of the fairest provinces was for ever lost to the Eastern Empire. "Farewell, O Syria, and what an excellent country this is for the enemy!"[6] were Heraclius' words of adieu.

The turn of the administrator, the pacifier, now came. Abu-'Ubaydah, one of the most esteemed Companions and members of the Madīnese theocracy and hitherto a contingent leader on the Syrian front, was appointed by 'Umar governor-general and caliphal vice-regent to replace Khālid, against whom 'Umar seems to have harboured some personal feeling. Abu-'Ubaydah accompanied Khālid northward. No further serious resistance stood in the way of the Arabian arms until the natural limits of Syria, the Taurus Mountains, were reached, and no difficulty was experienced in reclaiming the cities previously conquered. A

[1] Balādhuri, p. 131 = Hitti, pp. 201-2.

[2] Arab estimates of the Byzantine army at 100,000 to 240,000 and of the Moslem army at 40,000 are as unreliable as the Greek. Cf. Michel le Syrien, *Chronique*, ed. J.-B. Chabot, vol. iv (Paris, 1910), p. 416; tr. Chabot, vol. ii (Paris, 1901), p. 421.

[3] Near the junction of the Yarmūk and al-Ruqqād. Not to be confused with Jarmuth of Josh. 10 : 3, modern Khirbat Yarmūk, near Ajnādayn.

[4] See H. R. P. Dickson, *The Arab of the Desert* (London, 1949), pp. 258-62.

[5] Baṣri, p. 197; ibn-'Asākir, vol. i, p. 163.

[6] Balādhuri, p. 137 = Hitti, p. 210.

statement attributed to the people of Ḥimṣ is representative of the sentiment cherished by the native Syrians towards the new conquerors: "We like your rule and justice far better than the state of oppression and tyranny under which we have been living".[1] Antioch, Aleppo and other northern towns were soon added to the list. Qinnasrīn (Chalcis) was the only city that was not easily dealt with. In the south only Jerusalem and Cæsarea, which was strictly Hellenized, held their gates stubbornly closed in the face of the invaders, the former till 638 and the latter till October 640. Cæsarea received help by sea which the Arabians had no means of intercepting, but after seven years of intermittent raids and siege it succumbed before the attack of Mu'āwiyah, aided by the treachery of a Jew within the walls. Between 633 and 640 all Syria from south to north was subdued.

This "easy conquest" [2] of the land had its own special causes. The Hellenistic culture imposed on the land since its conquest by Alexander (332 B.C.) was only skin-deep and limited to the urban population. The rural people remained ever conscious of cultural and racial differences between themselves and their masters. This racial antipathy between the Semitic population of Syria and the Greek rulers was augmented by sectarian differences. The Monophysite church of Syria insisted that Christ had but one nature instead of the two (divine and human) formulated by the Synod of Chalcedon (451) and accepted by the Greek church of Byzantium. The christological compromise of Heraclius, promulgated in 638 on the basis of a formula devised by Sergius[3] the patriarch of Constantinople, aimed at ignoring the question of the nature or natures in the person of Christ and emphasizing his one will (*thélēma*). Hence the name Monothelite for a Christian who accepted the new formula. Like other religious compromises this one neither pleased the orthodox nor satisfied the dissenters. Instead it resulted in the creation of a third problem and a new party. But the bulk of the population of Syria remained Monophysite. Behind their development and maintenance of a separate Syrian church there undoubtedly lay a submerged, semi-articulate feeling of nationality.

The administration of the new territory

Just before the fall of Jerusalem the Caliph 'Umar came to the

[1] Balādhuri, p. 137, l. 13 = Hitti, p. 211.
[2] Balādhuri, p. 116, l. 18, p. 126, ll. 13, 19 = Hitti, p. 179, l. 17, p. 193, l. 22, p. 194, l. 7.
[3] A Syrian of Jacobite lineage.

military camp of al-Jābiyah, which lay north of the Yarmūk battlefield and whose name is still borne by the western gate of Damascus; his purpose was to solemnize the conquest, fix the status of the conquered, consult with his generalissimo, abu-'Ubaydah, whom he had substituted for Khālid after the Yarmūk battle, and lay down necessary regulations for the administration of the newly acquired territory. When Jerusalem fell it too was visited by 'Umar. As the patriarch of Jerusalem, Sophronius, styled the "honey-tongued defender of the church", was showing the aged caliph round the holy places he was so impressed by the uncouth mien and shabby raiment of his Arabian visitor that he is said to have turned to an attendant and remarked in Greek, "Truly this is the abomination of desolation spoken of by Daniel the Prophet as standing in the holy place".[1]

Soon abu-'Ubaydah fell victim at 'Amwās (or 'Amawās) to an epidemic which is said to have carried off 20,000 of his troops, and after the death of his successor, Yazīd, the power passed to the hands of the shrewd Mu'āwiyah.

Syria was now divided into four military districts (sing. *jund*) corresponding to the Roman and Byzantine provinces found at the time of the conquest. These were: Dimashq, Ḥimṣ, al-Urdunn (Jordan) comprising Galilee to the Syrian desert, and Filasṭīn (Palestine), the land south of the great plain of Esdraelon (Marj ibn-'Āmir). The northern district, Qinnasrīn, was added later by the Umayyad Caliph Yazīd I.

So swift and easy an acquisition of so strategic a territory from the first potentate of the age gave the newly rising power of Islam prestige in the eyes of the world and, what is more important, confidence in its own destiny. From Syria the hordes swept into Egypt and thence made their triumphant way through the rest of northern Africa. With Syria as a base the onward push to Armenia, northern Mesopotamia, Georgia and Ādharbayjān became possible, as did the raids and attacks which for many years to come were to be carried on against Asia Minor. With the help of Syrian troops Spain in far-off Europe was in less than a hundred years from the death of the Prophet brought within the ever widening circle of Islam.

[1] Theophanes, p. 339; Constantine Porphyrogenitus, "De administrando imperio", in J.-P. Migne, *Patrologia Græca*, vol. cxiii (Paris, 1864), col. 109; Dan. 11 : 31. Sophronius was probably of Maronite origin.

CHAPTER XIII

AL-'IRĀQ AND PERSIA CONQUERED

WHEN Khālid in 634 made his memorable dash westward from al-Ḥīrah he left the 'Irāq front in the hands of his Bedouin ally al-Muthanna ibn-Ḥārithah, sheikh of the banu-Shaybān. In the meantime the Persians were preparing a counter-attack and succeeded in almost annihilating the Arabian bands at the Battle of the Bridge[1] near al-Ḥīrah, November 26, 634. Undaunted, al-Muthanna undertook a new raid and in October or November of the following year scored over the Persian general Mihrān a victory at al-Buwayb on the Euphrates. But al-Muthanna was no more than a Bedouin chief, with no Madīnese or Makkan connections, and had not heard of or accepted Islam until after the death of the Prophet. The Caliph 'Umar therefore chose Sa'd ibn-abi-Waqqāṣ, one of those Companions promised Paradise by Muḥammad at the conclusion of the Battle of Badr, as commander in chief and sent him at the head of new reinforcements to al-'Irāq. By that time the victory of Yarmūk had been won and the fate of Syria sealed. Sa'd with his 10,000 men measured his strength for the first time with the Persian Rustam, the administrator of the empire, at al-Qādisīyah, not far from al-Ḥīrah. The day (the last of May or first of June 637) was extremely hot and was rendered dark by the wind-blown dust, a day not unlike that on which the battle of Yarmūk was fought. The same tactics were used with the same results. Rustam was killed, the large Sāsānid army dissolved in panic and all the fertile lowlands of al-'Irāq[2] west of the Tigris (Dijlah) lay open to the invaders. The welcome on the part of the Aramaean peasants was no less cordial than that tendered by the Syrian peasants, and for much the same reasons. The Semitic 'Irāqis

[1] Across the Euphrates. Balādhuri, pp. 251-2; Ṭabari, vol. i, pp. 2194-2201.

[2] *'Irāq*, probably a loan-word from Pahlawi meaning "lowland", corresponds to Ar. *Sawād*, black land, used to bring out the contrast with the Arabian desert Yāqūt, vol. iii, p. 174; cf A. T. Olmstead, *History of Assyria* (New York, 1927), p. 60.

looked upon the Iranian masters as aliens and felt closer kinship with the newcomers. As Christians they had not been especially favoured by the followers of Zoroaster. For centuries before Islam petty Arab chieftains and kinglets had flourished on the 'Irāq-Arabian border. The Arab control of the valley of the two rivers was anticipated by intimate relations with its peoples dating to the early Babylonian era, by growing acquaintance with its culture and by the admixture of border Bedouins with its inhabitants. As in the case of Syria after Yarmūk an influx of fresh Arabian tribes, attracted by the new economic advantages, took place into the newly conquered territory.

The Persian capital, Ctesiphon,[1] was Sa'd's next objective. With characteristic dash and energy he pushed ahead and at a convenient ford effected the crossing of the Tigris, much swollen by the spring floods. The feat was accomplished without loss of life to the army and was hailed as a miracle by Moslem chroniclers. In June 637 Sa'd made his triumphal entry into the capital whose garrison together with the emperor had deserted it. Arab chroniclers outdo themselves in their extravagant description of the booty and treasures captured therein. Their estimate is nine billion dirhams.[2]

The occupation of the greatest royal city in hither Asia brought the sons of barren Arabia into direct contact with the luxuries and comforts of the then modern high life. The *Īwān Kisra*, the royal palace with its spacious audience chamber, graceful arches and sumptuous furnishings and decorations—all celebrated in later Arabic poetry—was now at the disposal of Sa'd. Amusing as well as instructive are some of the anecdotes embedded in the Arabic chronicles which throw light upon the comparative culture of the two peoples. Camphor, never seen before, was naturally taken for salt and used as such in cooking.[3] "The yellow" (*al-ṣafrā'*, i.e. gold), something unfamiliar in Arabia, was offered by many in exchange for "the white" (*al-bayḍā'*, silver).[4] When an Arabian warrior at al-Ḥīrah was blamed for

[1] Arabic al-Madā'in, literally the cities, which included Seleucia and Ctesiphon on either side of the Tigris some 20 miles south-east of Baghdād.

[2] Ṭabari, vol. i, p. 2436; cf. ibn-al-Athīr, vol. ii, p. 400; Caetani, *Annali*, vol. iii, pp. 742-6.

[3] Ibn-al-Ṭiqṭaqa, *al-Fakhri*, ed. H. Derenbourg (Paris, 1895), p. 114.

[4] *Fakhri*, p. 115; tr. C. E. J. Whitting (London, 1947), p. 79. Cf. al-Dīnawari, *al-Akhbār al-Ṭiwāl*, ed. V. Guirgass (Leyden, 1888), p. 134.

selling a nobleman's daughter who fell as his share of booty for only 1000 dirhams, his reply was that he "never thought there was a number above ten hundred".[1]

After al-Qādisīyah and al-Madā'in the systematic conquest of the empire began from the newly founded military base at al-Baṣrah. By express command of the caliph the military camp of al-Kūfah, near older al-Ḥīrah, was to be the capital in preference to Ctesiphon, where Sa'd had built one of the first Moslem places of worship in al-'Irāq.

In the meantime the Sāsānid Yazdagird III and his imperial court were fleeing northward. Another futile stand (end of 637) at Jalūlā' on the fringe of the Persian highlands and all of al-'Irāq lay prostrate at the feet of the conquerors. In 641 al-Mawṣil (Mosul), near the site of ancient Nineveh, was reached and captured. This brought to a successful culmination the expedition which was started from northern Syria by 'Iyāḍ ibn-Ghanm. In the same year the last great battle, that of Nihāwand (near ancient Ecbatana), was fought, with a nephew of Sa'd leading the Arabian forces, and resulted in a disastrous defeat of the last remnant of Yazdagird's army. Khūzistān (ancient Elam, later Susiana, modern 'Arabistān) was occupied in 640 from al-Baṣrah and al-Kūfah. In the meantime an attempt was made on the adjoining province of Pārs (Fāris, Persia proper),[2] on the eastern shore of the Persian Gulf, from al-Baḥrayn, which with al-Baṣrah and al-Kūfah formed now a third military base of operation against Iran. The stiffening resistance of the non-Semitic population was finally broken by 'Abdullāh ibn-'Āmir, the governor of al-Baṣrah, who occupied Iṣṭakhr (Persepolis), the chief city of Fāris, in 649–50.[3] After Fāris the turn of the great and distant province of Khurāsān, in the north-east, came; the path then lay open to the Oxus. The subjection of Mukrān, the coastal region of Baluchistan, shortly after 643 brought the Arabs to the very borders of India.

As early as 640 an attempt was made on Byzantine Armenia by 'Iyāḍ. About four years later an expedition set out from Syria

[1] Balādhuri, p. 244 = Hitti, p. 392; cf. *Fakhri*, pp. 114-15.

[2] The Persians called their country Īrān, of which Pārs (the home of its two greatest dynasties, the Achaemenid and the Sāsānid) was but the southern province. The Greeks corrupted old Pers. *Pārsa* to *Persis* and used it for the whole kingdom.

[3] See Ṭabari, vol. i, pp. 2545-51; Caetani, vol. iv, pp. 151-3, vol. v, pp. 19-27, vol. vii, pp. 219-20, 248-56.

under the leadership of Ḥabīb ibn-Maslamah, but the district was not completely reduced till about 652.[1]

The military camp al-Kūfah became the capital of the newly conquered territories. Heedless of 'Umar's insistence on the old-fashioned simplicity characteristic of al-Ḥijāz, Sa'd erected here a residence modelled on the royal palace of Ctesiphon. The gates of the old capital were transported to the new, a symbolic custom practised repeatedly in the Arab East. Built first of reeds as barracks to house the soldiers and their families, the camp exchanged its huts for unbaked brick houses and soon grew into an important metropolis. Along with its sister camp al-Baṣrah, al-Kūfah became the political and intellectual centre of Arab Mesopotamia until the 'Abbāsid al-Manṣūr built his world-famous city, Baghdād.

In 651 the young and ill-starred Yazdagird, fleeing with his crown, treasures and a few followers, fell victim to the greed of one of his own people in a miller's hut near Marw (Pers. Marv).[2] With his death there came to an ignoble end the last ruler of an empire that had flourished with one interruption for some twelve centuries, an empire that was not fully to rise again for eight hundred years or more.

This initial and inconclusive conquest of Persia took about a decade to achieve; the Moslem arms met with much more stubborn resistance than in Syria. In the campaign some 35,000–40,000 Arabians, inclusive of women, children and slaves, must have taken part. The Persians were Aryans, not Semites; they had enjoyed a national existence of their own for centuries and represented a well-organized military power that had been measuring swords with the Romans for over four hundred years. In the course of the following three centuries of Arab rule Arabic became the official language as well as the speech of cultured society and, to a limited extent, of ordinary parlance. But the old spirit of the subject nation was to rise again and restore its neglected tongue. Persia contributed a large share of the Qarmaṭian (Carmathian) movement which for many years shook the caliphate to its foundation; it also had much to do with the development of the Shī'ite sect and with the founding of the Fāṭimid dynasty which ruled Egypt for over two centuries. Its

[1] Consult Balādhuri, pp. 193-212; Caetani, vol. iv, pp. 50-53, vol. vii, pp. 453-4.

[2] Cf. Michel le Syrien, vol. iv, p. 418=vol. ii, p. 424.

art, its literature, its philosophy, its medicine, became the common property of the Arab world and conquered the conquerors. Some of the most brilliant stars in the intellectual firmament of Islam during its first three centuries were Islamized Iranians.

While this column of Arabian troops was operating eastward under Sa'd another under the more illustrious 'Amr ibn-al-'Āṣ was operating to the west. The latter was bringing within the horns of the rising crescent the people of the valley of the Nile and the Berbers of North Africa. Ostensibly religious, but mainly political and economic, this unparalleled Arabian expansion had now grown into an empire as far flung as that of Alexander, with the caliph at al-Madīnah trying to regulate the flow of a torrent whose tributaries, ever increasing in number and size, were swelling the stream beyond all control.

CHAPTER XIV

EGYPT, TRIPOLIS AND BARQAH ACQUIRED

THE strategic position of Egypt, lying so dangerously near to both Syria and al-Ḥijāz, the richness of its grain-producing soil, which made the land the granary of Constantinople, the fact that its capital Alexandria was the base of the Byzantine navy and that the country was the door to the rest of the North African corridor—all these considerations caused Arabian eyes to turn covetously towards the valley of the Nile quite early in the era of expansion.

The conquest of Egypt falls within the period of systematic campaigning rather than casual raiding. Seeking new fields in which to outshine his illustrious rival Khālid, ʻAmr ibn-al-ʻĀṣ, who in the Jāhilīyah days had made many a caravan trip to Egypt and was familiar with its cities and roads,[1] took advantage of the presence of ʻUmar in Jerusalem to secure his half-hearted authorization for a campaign against the ancient land of the Pharaohs. But when ʻUmar had returned to al-Madīnah and consulted with ʻUthmān and others who pointed out the risks and perils involved, he dispatched a messenger to halt the advance of the column. The caliphal message, we are told, overtook ʻAmr just before crossing the Egypt-Palestine border, but, scenting the unfavourable contents thereof and having in mind ʻUmar's previous instructions: "If my letter ordering thee to turn back from Egypt overtakes thee before entering any part of it then turn back; but if thou enter the land before the receipt of my letter, then proceed and solicit Allah's aid",[2] ʻAmr did not open the letter until he got to al-ʻArīsh (December 639). This ʻAmr was a Qurayshite, forty-five years old, warlike, fiery, eloquent and shrewd. He had already to his credit the conquest of Palestine west of the Jordan. The part he was later to play

[1] Ibn-ʻAbd-al-Ḥakam, *Futūḥ Miṣr*, ed. C. C. Torrey (New Haven, 1922), p. 53.

[2] Yaʻqūbi, vol. ii, pp. 168-9; cf. ibn-ʻAbd-al-Ḥakam, pp. 56-7; J. Wellhausen, *Skizzen und Vorarbeiten*, vol. vi, *Prolegomena zur ältesten Geschichte des Islams* (Berlin, 1899), p. 93.

in the capture of the caliphate for his bosom friend Mu'āwiyah won him the epithet "one of the four Arabian 'political geniuses' [*duhāt*] of Islam".[1] The route he took with his 4000 riders was the same beaten track along the coast trod by Abraham, Cambyses, Alexander, Antiochus, the Holy Family, Napoleon and Djemāl Pasha. It was the international highway of the ancient world connecting its most important centres of civilization.[2]

The first fortified place which the Arabian column struck—and that in the middle of January 640[3]—was al-Faramā' (Pelusium), the key to eastern Egypt. After about a month of resistance the city fell and its defences, probably not repaired since the recent Persian invasion (616) and occupation, were razed. Bilbays (variants Bilbīs, Balbīs) north-east of Cairo came next, and others followed suit. At last the strong castle of Babylon[4] (Bābalyūn), across from the isle of al-Rawḍah in the Nile, stood in the way of further progress. Cyrus (Ar. al-Muqawqis), who since the reoccupation of the country in 631 by Heraclius had been acting as patriarch of Alexandria and imperial representative in civil administration, hurried to Babylon with his commander in chief the Augustalis Theodorus and the troops. 'Amr pitched camp outside Babylon, biding his time and awaiting reinforcements. Soon they came, headed by al-Zubayr ibn-al-'Awwām, the celebrated Companion of the Prophet, thus augmenting the Arabian column to about 10,000 men who were to oppose the 20,000 or so of the Byzantine army exclusive of the fortress garrison numbering about 5000. While besieging Babylon, 'Amr attacked 'Ayn Shams[5] in July 640. The Byzantine army was utterly routed. Theodorus fled to Alexandria and Cyrus was shut up in Babylon. The siege was pressed by the Arabians, who had no engineering or mechanical devices for reducing the fort. The treacherous Cyrus secretly sought to buy off the besiegers, but to no avail. The usual three choices were offered: Islam, tribute or the sword.

1 Ibn-Ḥajar, *al-Iṣābah fi Tamyīz al-Ṣaḥābah*, vol. v (Cairo, 1907), p. 3.
2 See Olmstead, *History of Palestine*, pp. 44-8.
3 This as well as the other dates of the conquest of Egypt are not certain. Ṭabari, vol. i, p. 2592, l. 16, chooses Rabī' I, 16 (Ap. 637) as the date of the conquest of Egypt; cf. ibn-'Abd-al-Ḥakam, pp. 53, 58.
4 See A. J. Butler, *The Arab Conquest of Egypt* (Oxford, 1902), pp. 245-7.
5 Lit. "the spring of the sun", ancient Heliopolis, On (Ōn) of the Old Testament and the hieroglyphic inscriptions.

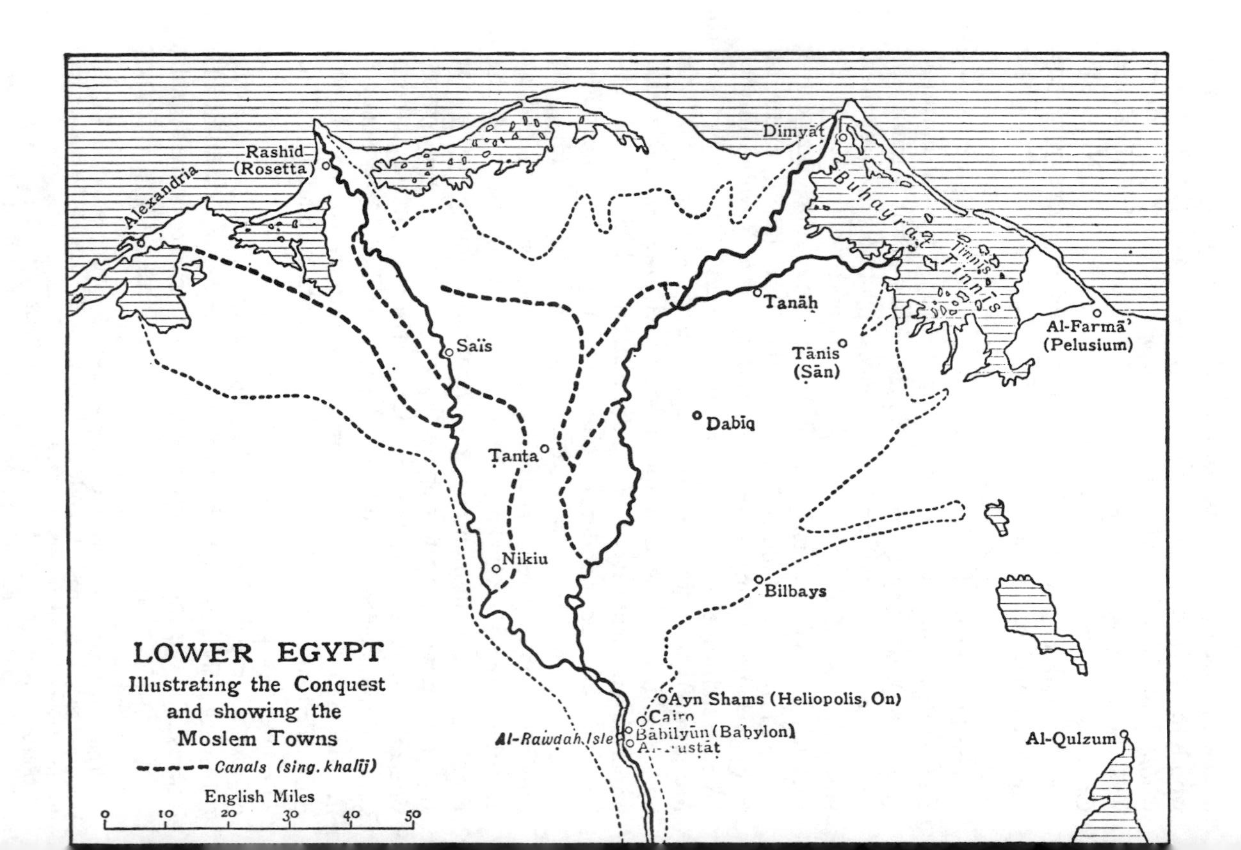

LOWER EGYPT
Illustrating the Conquest
and showing the
Moslem Towns
Canals (sing. khalīj)
English Miles
0
10
20
30
40
50
Alexandria
Rashīd
(Rosetta)
Dimyāt
Buhayrat Tinnīs
Al-Farmā'
(Pelusium)
Tanāh
Tānis
(Sān)
Saïs
Dabīq
Tanta
Nikiu
Bilbays
Ayn Shams (Heliopolis, On)
Cairo
Bābilyūn (Babylon)
Al-Rawdah Isle
Al-Qulzum

The following words put in the mouth of Cyrus' envoys purport to sum up the impression created by the Arabians:

We have witnessed a people to each and every one of whom death is preferable to life, and humility to prominence, and to none of whom this world has the least attraction. They sit not except on the ground, and eat naught but on their knees. Their leader [*amīr*] is like unto one of them: the low cannot be distinguished from the high, nor the master from the slave. And when the time of prayer comes none of them absents himself, all wash their extremities and humbly observe their prayer.[1]

Asking for a delegation to meet him at al-Rawḍah to negotiate peace, Cyrus was shocked to receive one headed by a negro, ʿUbādah ibn-al-Ṣāmit. The three alternatives were reiterated. Cyrus agreed to pay tribute and hastened to Alexandria to forward the terms to the emperor. They were not pleasing to Heraclius, who charged his episcopal viceroy with treason and sent him into exile.

In the meantime the siege of Babylon was being carried on without intermission. At the end of seven months al-Zubayr with his comrades succeeded in filling a part of the moat, scaling the wall on a ladder and overpowering the guard as well as the garrison. The battle-cry of Islam, *Allāhu akbar* (God is most great), echoed victoriously in the halls of the fortress on April 6, 641.[2]

After reducing the eastern border of the Delta the iron grip of ʿAmr began to fasten itself on the apex. Nikiu (Ar. Naqyūs, modern Shabshīr) fell on May 13 and a bloody slaughter ensued. But Alexandria (al-Iskandarīyah), after Constantinople the finest and strongest city in the world, was still ahead.

With fresh recruits from Arabia swelling his army to about 20,000 ʿAmr found himself one morning gazing at the seemingly impregnable line of walls and towers guarding Egypt's capital and leading port. On one side rose the lofty Serapeum,[3] which once housed the temple of Serapis and the great library of Alexandria; on the other loomed the beautiful cathedral of St. Mark, once the Cæsarion[4] temple begun by Cleopatra in

[1] Ibn-ʿAbd-al-Ḥakam, p. 65.
[2] Balādhuri, p. 213 = Hitti, p. 336; ibn-ʿAbd-al-Ḥakam, pp. 61 *seq.*
[3] Called later by the Arabs ʿAmūd al-Sawāri, from Diocletian's pillar which still marks the spot. Maqrīzi, *Mawāʿiẓ*, ed. Wiet, vol. iii, pp. 128 *seq.*
[4] The Qaysārīyah of the Arabs. Ibn-ʿAbd-al-Ḥakam, pp. 41, 42.

honour of Julius Cæsar and finished by Augustus; farther west stood the two red Uswan(Aswān)-granite needles ascribed to Cleopatra, but in reality the work of Thutmose III (*ca.* 1450 B.C.), the same two which now adorn the Thames Embankment in London and Central Park in New York; and in the background towered the Pharos, flashing the sun's rays by day and its own fire by night and rightly considered one of the seven wonders of the world.[1] No doubt to the desert Arabs the impression of such a sight must have been not unlike that which the skyline of modern New York, with its towering skyscrapers, makes upon the immigrant.

Alexandria boasted a garrison some 50,000 strong. Behind it lay the whole strength of the Byzantine navy, of which the city was the base. The invaders, far inferior in number and in equipment, had not a single ship, no siege machines and no immediate source of supply for their man-power.

John of Nikiu, a contemporary authority, describes the first repulse the helpless Arabians suffered under the pounding of catapults from the high walls.[2] Leaving a contingent behind, 'Amr fought his way back to Babylon and later engaged in a few marauding expeditions to Upper Egypt. After the death of Heraclius (February 641) his grandson Constans II (Qusṭanṭīn, 641–68) succeeded. Cyrus, restored to favour, returned to Alexandria in order to conclude peace. Hoping to administer the country for the Arabians independently of Constantinople, the bishop signed with 'Amr in Babylon on November 8, 641, a treaty which may be termed the Treaty of Alexandria, accepting the payment of a fixed tribute of two dinars per adult head and a land tax payable in kind and agreeing not to allow a Byzantine army to return or attempt to recover the land. The city was evacuated in September 642. The Emperor Constans, weak and young, ratified the treaty which meant the transference of one of the fairest provinces of the empire to Arabian hands.

The glad tidings were sent to 'Umar in al-Madīnah in the following words: "I have captured a city from the description of which I shall refrain. Suffice it to say that I have seized therein 4000 villas with 4000 baths, 40,000 poll-tax-paying Jews and

[1] See Maqrīzi, vol. iii, pp. 113-43; Suyūṭi, *Ḥusn*, vol. i, pp. 43-5.

[2] H. Zotenberg, *Chronique de Jean, évêque de Nikiou. Texte éthiopien*, with translation (Paris, 1883), p. 450.

four hundred places of entertainment for the royalty."[1] The caliph entertained his general's messenger with bread and dates and held in the Prophet's Mosque a simple but dignified service of thanksgiving.

The native Copts of Egypt, we are informed by ibn-'Abd-al-Ḥakam[2] († ?257=871), who gives us the earliest surviving account of the conquest of Egypt, were instructed from the very beginning by their bishop in Alexandria to offer no resistance to the invaders. This is not surprising in view of the religious persecution to which they as Monophysites had been subjected by the official Melkite (royal) church. For years Heraclius had tried, through his agent Cyrus, to forbid the Egyptian (Coptic) form of worship and to force his new Monothelite doctrine on a reluctant church. On account of his relentless persecution of the priesthood of the Coptic church Cyrus was regarded as the Antichrist by the later native tradition.

In accordance with 'Umar's policy the site on which 'Amr pitched his camp outside Babylon became the new capital, receiving the name al-Fusṭāṭ[3] and corresponding to the military camps of al-Jābiyah in Syria, al-Baṣrah and al-Kūfah in al-'Irāq. There 'Amr erected a simple mosque, the first to rise in Egypt (641–2), which has survived in name until today and whose present form is the result of repeated rebuildings and additions. Al-Fusṭāṭ (Old Cairo, Miṣr al-'Atīqah) continued to be the capital until the Fāṭimids in 969 built their Cairo (al-Qāhirah). In order to open a direct waterway to the holy cities of Arabia 'Amr now cleared the ancient Pharaonic canal which under the name Khalīj (canal of) Amīr al-Mu'minīn passed through Heliopolis and connected the Nile north of Babylon with al-Qulzum[4] on the Red Sea.[5] Trajan had cleared the canal, but through neglect it had silted up since his reign. After a few months of forced labour, and before the death of 'Umar in 644, twenty ships laden with Egyptian products were unloading their cargoes in Arabian ports.[6] This canal was later known as al-Khalīj al-Ḥākimi, after the Fāṭimid Caliph al-Ḥākim († 1021), and under many other names continued to exist in some parts till the end of the nineteenth century.

[1] Ibn-'Abd-al-Ḥakam, p. 82; cf. Zotenberg, p. 463. [2] Pp. 58-9.
[3] Latin *fossatum* = camp, through Byz. Gr. *phossatun*.
[4] The Klysma of antiquity, modern Suez.
[5] Cf. Mas'ūdi, vol. iv, p. 99. [6] Ya'qūbi, vol. ii, p. 177.

The old machinery of Byzantine administration, including the financial system, was—as one might expect—adopted by the new rulers with certain amendments in the line of centralization. The time-honoured policy of exploiting the fertile valley of the Nile and using it as a "milch cow" was maintained to the utmost, judging by the evidence furnished by newly discovered Egyptian papyri. Shortly before his death 'Umar, feeling that 'Amr was not securing enough revenue, put 'Abdullāh ibn-Sa'd ibn-abi-Sarḥ in charge of Upper Egypt. The new caliph, 'Uthmān, recalled 'Amr from the country and appointed (*ca.* 645) 'Abdullāh, who was his own foster brother, over all Egypt.

Toward the end of 645 the Alexandrians, restive under the new yoke, appealed to the Emperor Constans, who dispatched some 300 ships under Manuel, an Armenian, to reclaim the city.[1] The Arabian garrison of 1000 men was slaughtered and Alexandria was once more in Byzantine hands and a base for new attacks on Arab Egypt. 'Amr was immediately reinstated. He met the enemy near Nikiu, where the Byzantines suffered a heavy slaughter. Early in 646 the second capture of Alexandria took place. The impregnable walls of the city were demolished and the ancient Egyptian capital has ever since remained in Moslem hands.

The library of Alexandria

The story that by the caliph's order 'Amr for six long months fed the numerous bath furnaces of the city with the volumes of the Alexandrian library is one of those tales that make good fiction but bad history. The great Ptolemaic Library was burnt as early as 48 B.C. by Julius Cæsar. A later one, referred to as the Daughter Library, was destroyed about A.D. 389 as a result of an edict by the Emperor Theodosius. At the time of the Arab conquest, therefore, no library of importance existed in Alexandria and no contemporary writer ever brought the charge against 'Amr or 'Umar. 'Abd-al-Laṭīf al-Baghdādi,[2] who died as late as A.H. 629 (1231), seems to have been the first to relate the tale. Why he did it we do not know; however, his version was copied and amplified by later authors.[3]

[1] Balādhuri, p. 221 = Hitti, pp. 347-8.

[2] *Al-Ifādah w-al-I'tibār*, ed. and tr. (Latin) J. White (Oxford, 1800), p. 114.

[3] Al-Qifṭi, *Ta'rīkh al-Ḥukamā'*, ed. J. Lippert (Leipzig, 1903), pp. 355-6; abu-al-Faraj ibn-al-'Ibri, *Ta'rīkh Mukhtaṣar al-Duwal*, ed. A. Ṣāliḥāni (Beirūt, 1890), pp. 175-6; Maqrīzi, vol. iii, pp. 129-30. Consult Butler, pp. 401-26; Gibbon, *Decline*, ed. Bury, vol. v, pp. 452-5.

After the conquest 'Uthmān wanted 'Amr to remain at the head of the army with 'Abdullāh as the financial administrator. The suggestion elicited from 'Amr the famous reply: "My position will then be that of one who holds the cow by its two horns while another milks it".[1] 'Abdullāh was thereupon reinstalled as caliphal vicegerent.

Less a soldier than a financier, 'Abdullāh now proceeded to carry on campaigns to the west and south mainly for booty. He succeeded in extending the boundaries in both directions. But his greatest performance was his part in the establishment of the first Moslem fleet, an honour which he shares with Mu'āwiyah, the governor of Syria. Alexandria was naturally the main dockyard for the Egyptian fleet. The maritime operations, whether from Egypt under 'Abdullāh or from Syria under Mu'āwiyah, were directed against the Byzantines. In 649 Mu'āwiyah seized Cyprus (Qubrus), another important Byzantine naval base too dangerously close to the Syrian coast for comfort. The first maritime victory was thus won for Islam and the first island was added to the Moslem state. Arwād (Aradus), close by the Syrian coast, was captured the following year. In 652 'Abdullāh repulsed the superior Greek fleet off Alexandria. Two years later Rhodes was pillaged by one of Mu'āwiyah's captains.[2] In 655[3] the Syro-Egyptian fleet of Mu'āwiyah and 'Abdullāh destroyed the Byzantine navy of about 500 ships off the Lycian coast near Phœnix. The Emperor Constans II, who led the fight in person, barely escaped with his life. This battle, known in Arabic as dhu-al-Ṣawāri[4] (that of the masts), threatened but did not destroy Byzantine naval supremacy.[5] Because of internal disorders the Moslems failed to press their victory and advance against Constantinople, the chief objective. In 668 or 669 a navy of 200 ships from Alexandria ventured as far as Sicily (Siqilliyah, Ṣiqillīyah) and pillaged it. The island had been sacked at least once before (652) under Mu'āwiyah.[6] In Mu'āwiyah and 'Abdullāh Islam developed its first two admirals.[7]

That these naval expeditions were carried on almost in spite

[1] Ibn-'Abd-al-Ḥakam, p. 178; cf. Balādhuri, p. 223 = Hitti, p. 351.

[2] A later expedition in A.H. 52 (672) is cited in Balādhuri, pp. 235-6 = Hitti, pp. 375-6. [3] Cf. C. H. Becker, art. "'Abd Allāh B. Sa'd", *Encyclopædia of Islām*.

[4] Ibn-'Abd-al-Ḥakam, pp. 189-91. [5] Cf. below, p. 602.

[6] Balādhuri, p. 235 = Hitti, p. 375.

[7] The details about the naval operations of the period, however, are lamentably meagre in Arabic sources.

of, rather than in co-operation with, the Madīnese caliphs is indicated by significant passages in the early sources. 'Umar wrote instructing 'Amr in Egypt: "Let no water intervene between me and thee, and do not camp in any place which I cannot reach riding on my mount".[1] 'Uthmān authorized Mu'āwiyah's expedition to Cyprus, after the latter had repeatedly emphasized the proximity of the island, only on condition that he take his wife along.[2]

The fall of Egypt left the Byzantine provinces bordering on its west defenceless; at the same time the continued occupation of Alexandria necessitated the conquest of those provinces. After the first fall of Alexandria and in order to protect his rear, 'Amr, with characteristic swiftness, pushed (642–3) at the head of his cavalry westward to the neighbouring Pentapolis and occupied Barqah without any resistance. He also received the submission of the Berber tribes of Tripolis, including the Lawātah.[3] His successor, 'Abdullāh, advanced through Tripolis and subjugated a part of Ifrīqiyah whose capital Carthage (Qarṭājannah) paid tribute.[4] 'Uthmān extended even to the pagan Berbers, not within the category of Scripturaries, the same privileges as those of the Dhimmah. Attempts were also made on Nubia (al-Nūbah) in the south, which with its pasturage was more like Arabia and better adapted than Egypt to a nomadic mode of life. For centuries before Islam a more or less continual Arabian infiltration into Egypt and even into the Sudan had been going on. In 652 'Abdullāh entered into treaty relations with the Nubians,[5] who were then far from being subdued. For centuries to come the Christian kingdom of Nubia, with Dongola as its capital and with a mixed population of Libyans and negroes, stood as a barrier against the farther southward onrush of Islam.

[1] Ya'qūbi, vol. ii, p. 180. *Fakhri*, p. 114, reports that 'Umar wrote to Sa'd ibn-abi-Waqqāṣ in al-'Irāq asking him to let no sea intervene between the caliph and the Moslems.

[2] Balādhuri, pp. 152-3 = Hitti, pp. 235-6.

[3] Ya'qūbi, vol. ii, p. 179.

[4] Ibn-'Abd-al-Ḥakam, p. 183.

[5] Balādhuri, pp. 237-8 = Hitti, pp. 379-81.

CHAPTER XV

THE ADMINISTRATION OF THE NEW POSSESSIONS

HOW to administer such vast territories newly acquired and how to adapt the uncodified ordinances of a primitive Arabian society to the needs of a huge cosmopolitan conglomerate living under a multitude of conditions uncontemplated by the original lawgiver was the great task now confronting Islam. 'Umar was the first to address himself to this problem. He is represented by tradition as the one who solved it and therefore as the founder of the second theocracy of Islam—a sort of Islamic Utopia—which, however, was not destined to last long.

'Umar's constitution

'Umar made his starting-point the theory that in the peninsula itself none but the Moslem religion should ever be tolerated. To this end and in utter disregard of earlier treaties[1] he expelled, A.H. 14–15 (635–6), among others, the Jews of Khaybar,[2] who found abode in Jericho and other places, as well as the Christians of Najrān, who fled to Syria and al-'Irāq.[3] The second cardinal point in 'Umar's policy was to organize the Arabians, now all Moslems, into a complete religio-military commonwealth with its members keeping themselves pure and unmixed—a sort of martial aristocracy—and denying the privilege of citizenship to all non-Arabians. With this in view the Arabian Moslems were not to hold or cultivate landed property outside the peninsula. In the peninsula itself the native who owned land paid a kind of a tithe (*'ushr*) thereon. Accordingly the Arabian conquerors in Syria first lived in camps: al-Jābiyah, Ḥimṣ, 'Amwās, Ṭabarīyah[4] (for the Jordan district), and al-Ludd (Lydda) and later al-Ramlah for the Filasṭīn (Palestine) district. In Egypt they settled in al-Fusṭāṭ and the Alexandria camp. In al-'Irāq the newly built

[1] See Wāqidi, *Maghāzi*, pp. 391-2, and abu-Yūsuf, *Kitāb al-Kharāj* (Cairo, 1346), pp. 85-6, for the terms the Prophet gave.

[2] An oasis about 100 miles north of al-Madīnah on the road to Syria.

[3] Balādhuri, p. 66 = Hitti, pp. 101-2.

[4] Modern Ṭabarayyah = Tiberias. 'Amwās or 'Amawās, ancient Emmaus, Lk. 24 : 13.

al-Kūfah and al-Baṣrah served as headquarters.[1] In the conquered territories the subject peoples were left in their professions and the cultivation of the soil, occupying an inferior status and regarded as a kind of reserve for the benefit of the Moslems (*māddat al-Muslimīn*).[2] Even when converted to Islam a non-Arab was to occupy a position subsidiary to that of the Moslem Arabian.

As Dhimmis,[3] the subject peoples would enjoy the protection of the Moslems and have no military duty to perform, since they were barred by religion from service in the Moslem army; but they would have a heavy tribute to pay. Being outside the pale of Moslem law they were allowed the jurisdiction of their own canon laws as administered by the respective heads of their religious communities. This state of partial autonomy, recognized later by the sultans of Turkey, has been retained by the Arab successor states.

When a subject was converted to Islam he was freed, according to this primitive system ascribed by tradition to ʿUmar, from all tributary obligations, including what was later termed poll tax. The land tax inhered in the land whenever the land was considered *fay'*, *waqf*, i.e. for the whole Moslem community, and the Moslem continued to pay it. The only exception to the *fay'* lands was constituted by those districts whose inhabitants according to tradition, voluntarily surrendered to the Arab conquerors on condition that they be allowed to retain their lands. Such districts were called *dār al-ṣulḥ* (the territory of capitulation). Instead of the poll tax the convert incurred a new obligation, that of the zakāh (poor rate); but on the other hand he shared in the pensions and other benefits accruing to him as a Moslem.

Later developments, the result of many years of practice, were attributed by this tradition to the initiative of ʿUmar. The fact is that the original part which the first caliphs and the early Moslem governors played in the imposition of taxes and the administration of finances could not have been great. The frame-

[1] In the first Moslem century a number of such military cantonment arose, including ʿAskar Mukram in Khūzistān, Shīrāz in Fāris, and Barqah asd al-Qayrawān in North Africa.

[2] Yaḥya ibn-Ādam, *Kitāb al-Kharāj*, ed. Juynboll (Leyden, 1896), p. 27.

[3] Or *Ahl al-Dhimmah* (people of the covenant or obligation), a term first applied only to *Ahl al-Kitāb*, i.e. the Jews, Christians and Ṣābians (not to be confused with Sabaeans) and later interpreted to include Zoroastrians and others.

work of the Byzantine provincial government in Syria and Egypt was continued in Allah's name, and no radical changes were introduced into the machinery of local administration in the former Persian domains. From the very beginning taxation varied according to the nature of the soil and the system that had prevailed in that locality under the old rule, whether Byzantine or Persian; it did not necessarily depend upon the acquisition of land by capitulation (*ṣulḥan*) or by force (*'anwatan*) nor upon any legislative act on the part of 'Umar.[1] Conquest by capitulation and conquest by force as used to explain the variation in taxation was often a late legal fiction rather than the real cause. Likewise the distinction between *jizyah* as poll tax and *kharāj* (from Gr. *chorēgia* or Aram. *keraggā*) as land tax had not arisen at the time of the second caliph (634–44). The two words in this early period were used interchangeably; both meant tribute in general. In the Koran the only occurrence of the word *jizyah* is in sūr. 9 : 29, where it has in no sense a legal meaning. *Kharāj* occurs also only once in the Koran (23 : 74), and then in the sense of remuneration rather than land tax. Evidently the original terms made with the conquered people were well-nigh forgotten by the time the historians began to record those events, which they interpreted in the light of later conditions and developments.

The differentiation between the two forms of taxation implied in jizyah and kharāj was not made until the time of the late Umayyads. The land tax was paid in instalments and in kind from the produce of the land and from cattle, but never in the form of wine, pigs and dead animals. The poll tax was paid in a lump sum and as an index of lower status. The latter was generally four dinars[2] for the well-to-do, two for the middle class and one for the poor. In addition the subject people were liable to other exactions for the maintenance of Moslem troops. These taxes applied only to the able-bodied; women, children, beggars, monks, the aged, insane and incurably sick being exempt except when any of them had an independent income.

The third principle said to have been enunciated by 'Umar in consonance with the view of his advisers among the Com-

[1] Cf. Daniel C. Dennett, Jr., *Conversion and the Poll Tax in Early Islam* (Cambridge, Mass., 1950), p. 12.

[2] From Greek-Latin *denarius*; the unit of gold currency in the caliphate, weighing about 4 grams. In 'Umar's time the *dīnār* was the equivalent of 10 dirhams, later 12.

panions[1] was that only movable property and prisoners won as booty constituted *ghanīmah*[2] and belonged to the warriors as hitherto, but not the land. The land as well as all moneys received from subjects constituted *fay'*[3] and belonged to the Moslem community as a whole. Cultivators of *fay'* estates continued to be bound to pay land tax even if they adopted Islam. All such revenues were deposited in the public treasury, and whatever remained after the payment of the common expenses of administration and warfare had to be divided among the Moslems. In order to accomplish the distribution a census became necessary, the first census recorded in history for the distribution of state revenue. 'Ā'ishah headed the list with a pension of 12,000 dirhams[4] a year. After the *Ahl al-Bayt* (the Prophet's family) came the Emigrants and Supporters, each with a subsidy according to his precedence in the profession of the new faith. About 5000 or 4000 dirhams per annum was the average allotment to each person in this category.[5] At the bottom came the mass of Arabian tribes arranged in the register according to military service and knowledge of the Koran. The minimum for an ordinary warrior was 500–600 dirhams; even women, children and clients[6] were included in the register and received annuities ranging from 200 to 600 dirhams. This institution of the *dīwān* (whence Fr. *douane*, for customhouse), or public registers of receipts and expenditures, with which 'Umar was credited was evidently borrowed from the Persian system, as ibn-al-Ṭiqṭaqa [7] asserts and as the word itself (from Pers. *dīwān*) indicates.

'Umar's military communistic constitution set up an ascendancy of Arabism and secured for the non-Arabian believer a status superior to that of the unbeliever. But it was too artificial to stand the test of time. Under 'Umar's immediate successor,

[1] Ibn-Sa'd, vol. iii, pt. 1, p. 212.

[2] For a discussion of *ghanīmah* and *fay'* see al-Māwardi, *al-Aḥkām al-Sulṭānīyah*, ed. M. Enger (Bonn, 1853), pp. 217-45; abu-Yūsuf, pp. 21-32.

[3] According to sūr. 8 : 42, only one-fifth of the booty was the share of Allah and the Prophet, i.e. the state's, the remaining four-fifths belonged to the warriors who secured it.

[4] Ar. *dirham* (Pers. *diram*, from Gr. *drachmē*), the unit of silver coinage in the Arab monetary system, had the nominal value of a pre-war French franc, about 10d. (19 cents in U.S. money), but naturally its real value varied a great deal.

[5] Ibn-Sa'd, vol. iii, pt. 1, pp. 213-14; Māwardi, pp. 347-8; abu-Yūsuf, pp. 50-54; Balādhuri, pp. 450-51.

[6] *Mawāli*, sing. *mawla*, a non-Arab embracing Islam and affiliating himself with an Arabian tribe. His ill-defined rank placed him below the Moslem Arabians.

[7] *Fakhri*, p. 116; cf. Māwardi, pp. 343-4.

'Uthmān, permission was given to the sons of Arabia to hold landed property in the newly conquered territories. With the lapse of years the aristocracy of the Arabians was submerged by the rising tide of the Mawāli.

The army

The army was the *ummah*, the whole nation, in action. Its *amīr* or commander in chief was the caliph in al-Madīnah, who delegated the authority to his lieutenants or generals. In the early stages the general who conquered a certain territory would also act as leader in prayer and as judge. Al-Balādhuri[1] tells us that 'Umar appointed a *qāḍi* (judge) for Damascus and the Jordan and another for Ḥimṣ and Qinnasrīn. If so he was the caliph who established the institution of judgeship.[2]

The division of the army into centre, two wings, vanguard and rear guard was already known at Muḥammad's time and betrays Byzantine and Sāsānid influence. The *khamīs* (five) was the term used for this military unit. The cavalry covered the wings. In the division the tribal unit was preserved. Each tribe had its own standard, a cloth attached to a lance, borne by one of the bravest. The Prophet's banner is said to have been the *'uqāb* (eagle). The infantry used bow and arrow, sling, and sometimes shield and sword; the sword was carried in a scabbard flung over the right shoulder. The *ḥarbah* (javelin) was introduced later from Abyssinia. The chief weapon of the cavalry was the *rumḥ* (lance), the shafts of which, famous in Arabic literature as *khaṭṭi*, were so named after al-Khaṭṭ, the coast of al-Baḥrayn, where the bamboo was first grown and whither it was later imported from India. This, together with the bow and arrow, formed the two national weapons. The best swords were also made in India, whence the name *hindi*. The defensive armour was the coat of mail and the shield. The Arab armour was lighter than the Byzantine.[3]

The order of battle was primitive, in lines or rows and in compact array. Hostilities began with individual combats of distinguished champions who stepped forward out of the ranks and delivered a challenge. The Arabian warrior received higher remuneration than his Persian or Byzantine rival and was sure of a portion of the booty. Soldiering was not only the noblest and most pleasing profession in the sight of Allah but also the most

[1] P. 141 = Hitti, p. 217. [2] Ibn-Sa'd, vol. iii, pt. 1, p. 202, ll. 27-8.
[3] On Arab weapons see ibn-Qutaybah, *'Uyūn*, vol. i, pp. 128-32.

profitable. The strength of the Moslem Arabian army lay neither in the superiority of its arms nor in the excellence of its organization but in its higher morale, to which religion undoubtedly contributed its share; in its powers of endurance, which the desert breeding fostered; and in its remarkable mobility, due mainly to camel transport.[1]

The so-called Arab civilization

By the conquest of the Fertile Crescent and the lands of Persia and Egypt the Arabians came into possession not only of geographical areas but of the earliest seats of civilization in the whole world. Thus the sons of the desert fell heir to these hoary cultures with their long traditions going back to Greco-Roman, Iranian, Pharaonic and Assyro-Babylonian times. In art and architecture, in philosophy, in medicine, in science and literature, in government, the original Arabians had nothing to teach and everything to learn. And what voracious appetites they proved to have! With an ever sharp sense of curiosity and with latent potentialities never aroused before, these Moslem Arabians in collaboration with and by the help of their subject peoples began now to assimilate, adapt and reproduce their intellectual and esthetic heritage. In Ctesiphon, Edessa, Nisibis, Damascus, Jerusalem and Alexandria they viewed, admired and copied the work of the architect, the artisan, the jeweller and the manufacturer. To all these centres of ancient culture they came, they saw and were conquered. Theirs was another instance in which the victor was made captive by the vanquished.

What we therefore call "Arab civilization" was Arabian neither in its origins and fundamental structure nor in its principal ethnic aspects. The purely Arabian contribution in it was in the linguistic and to a certain extent in the religious fields. Throughout the whole period of the caliphate the Syrians, the Persians, the Egyptians and others, as Moslem converts or as Christians and Jews, were the foremost bearers of the torch of enlightenment and learning just as the subjugated Greeks were in their relation to the victorious Romans. The Arab Islamic civilization was at bottom the Hellenized Aramaic and the Iranian civilizations as developed under the ægis of the caliphate and expressed through the medium of the Arabic tongue. In another sense it was the logical continuation of the early Semitic

[1] For a comparison with the Byzantine army consult Charles Oman, *A History of the Art of War in the Middle Ages*, 2nd ed. (London, 1924), vol. i, pp. 208 *seq.*

civilization of the Fertile Crescent originated and developed by the Assyro-Babylonians, Phoenicians, Aramaeans and Hebrews. In it the unity of the Mediterranean civilization of Western Asia found its culmination.

Character and achievements of the orthodox caliphs

The conquest of the world receiving its impulse under abu-Bakr reached its high-water mark under 'Umar and came to a temporary standstill under 'Ali, whose caliphate was too clouded with internal disturbances to admit of further expansion. At the end of a single generation after the Prophet the Moslem empire had extended from the Oxus to Syrtis Minor in northern Africa. Starting with nothing the Moslem Arabian caliphate had now grown to be the strongest power of the world.

Abu-Bakr (632–4), the conqueror and pacifier of Arabia, lived in patriarchal simplicity. In the first six months of his short reign he travelled back and forth daily from al-Sunḥ (where he lived in a modest household with his wife, Ḥabībah) to his capital al-Madīnah, and received no stipend since the state had at that time hardly any income.[1] All state business he transacted in the courtyard of the Prophet's Mosque. His personal qualities and unshaken faith in his son-in-law Muḥammad, who was three years his senior, make him one of the most attractive characters in nascent Islam and have won him the title of *al-Ṣiddīq* (the believer).[2] In character he was endowed with much more strength and forcefulness than current tradition credits to him. Physically he is represented as of fair complexion, slender build and thin countenance; he dyed his beard and walked with a stoop.[3]

Simple and frugal in manner, his energetic and talented successor, 'Umar (634–44), who was of towering height, strong physique and bald-headed,[4] continued at least for some time after becoming caliph to support himself by trade and lived throughout his life in a style as unostentatious as that of a Bedouin sheikh. In fact 'Umar, whose name according to Moslem tradition is the greatest in early Islam after that of Muḥammad, has been idolized by Moslem writers for his piety, justice and patriarchal simplicity and treated as the personification of all the virtues a caliph ought to possess. His irreproach-

[1] Ibn-Sa'd, vol. iii, pt. 1, pp. 131-2; ibn-al-Athīr, *Usd al-Ghābah fi Ma'rifat al-Ṣaḥābah* (Cairo, 1286), vol. iii, p. 219.

[2] Usually translated "the veracious". But see ibn-Sa'd, vol. iii, pt. 1, pp. 120-21.

[3] Ya'qūbi, vol. ii, p. 157.

[4] *Ibid.* p. 185.

able character became an exemplar for all conscientious successors to follow. He owned, we are told, one shirt and one mantle only, both conspicuous for their patchwork,[1] slept on a bed of palm leaves and had no concern other than the maintenance of the purity of the faith, the upholding of justice and the ascendancy and security of Islam and the Arabians. Arabic literature is replete with anecdotes extolling 'Umar's stern character. He is said to have scourged his own son to death[2] for drunkenness and immorality. Having in a fit of anger inflicted a number of stripes on a Bedouin who came seeking his succour against an oppressor, the caliph soon repented and asked the Bedouin to inflict the same number on him. But the latter refused. So 'Umar retired to his home with the following soliloquy:

> O son of al-Khaṭṭāb! humble thou wert and Allah hath elevated thee; astray, and Allah hath guided thee; weak, and Allah hath strengthened thee. Then He caused thee to rule over the necks of thy people, and when one of them came seeking thy aid, thou didst strike him! What wilt thou have to say to thy Lord when thou presentest thyself before Him?[3]

The one who fixed the Hijrah as the commencement of the Moslem era, presided over the conquest of large portions of the then known world, instituted the state register and organized the government of the new empire met a tragic and sudden death at the very zenith of his life when he was struck down (November 3, 644) by the poisoned dagger of a Christian Persian slave[4] in the midst of his own congregation.

'Uthmān, who committed the words of Allah to an unalterable form and whose reign saw the complete conquest of Iran, Ādharbayjān and parts of Armenia, was also a pious and well-meaning old man, but too weak to resist the importunities of his greedy kinsfolk. His foster brother, 'Abdullāh, formerly the Prophet's amanuensis, who had tampered with the words of revelation[5] and who was one of the ten proscribed by Muḥammad at the capture of Makkah, he appointed over Egypt; his half-brother, al-Walīd ibn-'Uqbah, who had spat in Muḥam-

[1] Ibn-Sa'd, vol. iii, pt. 1, pp. 237-9.

[2] Diyārbakri, *Ta'rīkh al-Khamīs* (Cairo, 1302), vol. ii, p. 281 ll. 3-4; al-Nuwayri, *Nihāyat al-Arab*, vol. iv (Cairo, 1925), pp. 89-90.

[3] Ibn-al-Athīr, *op. cit.* vol. iv, p. 61.

[4] Ṭabari, vol. i, pp. 2722-3; Ya'qūbi, vol. ii, p. 183.

[5] Koran 6 : 93; Bayḍāwi, vol. i, p. 300.

mad's face and had been condemned by the latter, he made governor of al-Kūfah; his cousin Marwān ibn-al-Ḥakam, a future Umayyad caliph, he put in charge of the dīwān. Many important offices were filled by Umayyads, the caliph's family.[1] The caliph himself accepted presents from his governors or their partisans, including a beautiful maid offered by the governor of al-Baṣrah. Charges of nepotism became widespread. The feeling of discontent aroused by his unpopular administration was fanned by the three Qurayshite aspirants to the caliphate: 'Ali, Ṭalḥah and al-Zubayr. The uprising started in al-Kūfah among 'Ali's followers and proved particularly strong in Egypt, which in April 656 sent some five hundred rebels to al-Madīnah. The insurgents shut the venerable octogenarian in his residence, and whilst he read the copy of the Koran[2] which he had canonized the house was stormed; Muḥammad, son of abu-Bakr his friend and predecessor, broke in and laid the first violent hand upon him.[3] Thus fell the first caliph whose blood was shed by Moslem hands (June 17, 656). The patriarchal epoch of Islam, during which the awe inspired by the Prophet and the hallowed association connected with al-Madīnah were still an active living force in the lives of the successors of Muḥammad, ended in a stream of blood let loose by the struggle for the now vacant throne, first between 'Ali and his close rivals, Ṭalḥah and al-Zubayr, and then between 'Ali and a new aspirant, Mu'āwiyah, the champion of the Umayyad cause of which the murdered 'Uthmān was a representative.

[1] Ibn-Ḥajar, vol. iv, pp. 223-4; ibn-Sa'd, vol. iii, pt. 1, p. 44; Mas'ūdi, vol. iv, pp. 257 *seq.*

[2] Ibn-Baṭṭūṭah († 1377), vol. ii, pp. 10-11, claims that when he visited al-Baṣrah its mosque still preserved 'Uthmān's copy of the Koran with his blood staining the page on which occurs sūr. 2 : 131, where according to ibn-Sa'd, vol. iii, pt. 1, p. 52, the flowing blood of the wounded caliph stopped. See Quatremère in *Journal asiatique*, ser. 3, vol. vi (1838), pp. 41-5.

[3] Ibn-Sa'd, vol. iii, pt. 1, p. 51.

CHAPTER XVI

THE STRUGGLE BETWEEN 'ALI AND MU ĀWIYAH FOR THE CALIPHATE

The elective caliphate

ABU-BAKR, one of the earliest supporters and staunchest friends of Muḥammad, whose *alter ego* he was and who had conducted the public prayers during the last illness of the Prophet, was designated (June 8, 632) Muḥammad's successor by some form of election in which those leaders present at the capital, al-Madīnah, took part. He was to assume all those duties and privileges of the Prophet with the exception of such as related to his prophetic office—which had ceased with Muḥammad's death.

The designation *khalīfat Rasūl Allāh* (the successor of the Messenger of Allah), applied in this case to abu-Bakr, may not have been used by him as a title. The term *khalīfah* occurs only twice in the Koran (2 : 28, 38 : 25); in neither case does it seem to have any technical significance or to carry any indication that it was intended to be applied to the successor of Muḥammad.

'Umar, the logical candidate after abu-Bakr, was designated by the latter as his successor and is said at first to have used the title with the designation *khalīfat khalīfat* (the caliph of the caliph of) *Rasūl Allāh*, which proved too long and was consequently abbreviated.[1] The second caliph (634–44) is credited with being the first to bear in his capacity as commander in chief of the Moslem armies the distinctive title *amīr al-mu'minīn* (commander of the believers), the "Miramolin" of Christian medieval writers. Before his death 'Umar is represented as having nominated a board of six electors: 'Ali ibn-abi-Ṭālib, 'Uthmān ibn-'Affān, al-Zubayr ibn-al-'Awwām, Ṭalḥah ibn-'Abdullāh, Sa'd ibn-abi-Waqqāṣ and 'Abd-al-Raḥmān ibn-'Awf,[2] with the stipulation that his own son be not elected to succeed him. The constitution of this board called al-Shūra (consultation), including the oldest and most distinguished

[1] Ibn-Sa'd, vol. iii, pt. 1, p. 202. [2] *Ibid.* vol. iii, pt. 1, pp. 245 *seq.*

Companions surviving, showed that the ancient Arabian idea of a tribal chief had triumphed over that of the hereditary monarch.

In the case of the third caliph, 'Uthmān (644), seniority again determined his election over 'Ali. 'Uthmān represented the Umayyad aristocracy as against his two predecessors who represented the Emigrants. None of these caliphs founded a dynasty.

Subsequent to the murder of 'Uthmān, 'Ali was proclaimed the fourth caliph at the Prophet's Mosque in al-Madīnah on June 24, 656. Practically the whole Moslem world acknowledged his succession. The new caliph was the first cousin of Muḥammad, the husband of his favourite daughter, Fāṭimah, the father of his only two surviving male descendants, al-Ḥasan and al-Ḥusayn, and either the second or third to believe in his prophethood. He was affable, pious and valiant. The party he represented, *ahl al-naṣṣ w-al-ta'yīn*[1] (people of divine ordinance and designation = the legitimists), had stoutly averred that from the beginning Allah and His Prophet had clearly designated 'Ali as the only legitimate successor but that the first three caliphs had cheated him out of his rightful office.

The caliphate of 'Ali

'Ali's first problem was to dispose of his two rivals to the high office he had just assumed, Ṭalḥah and al-Zubayr, who represented the Makkan party. Both Ṭalḥah and al-Zubayr[2] had followers in al-Ḥijāz and al-'Irāq who refused to acknowledge 'Ali's successorship. 'Ā'ishah, the most beloved wife of the Prophet and now "the mother of the believers", who had connived at the insurrection against 'Uthmān, now joined the ranks of the insurgents against 'Ali at al-Baṣrah. The youthful 'Ā'ishah, who had married so young[3] that she brought toys with her from her father's (abu-Bakr's) home, hated 'Ali with all the bitterness of a wounded pride; for once, when she loitered behind the caravan of her husband, he had suspected her fidelity until Allah intervened in her favour through a revelation (sūr. 24 : 11-20). Outside of al-Baṣrah on December 9, 656, 'Ali met and defeated the coalition in a battle styled "the battle of the camel", after the camel on which 'Ā'ishah rode, which was the

[1] Shahrastāni, p. 15.
[2] Al-Zubayr's mother was a sister of the Prophet's father.
[3] At the age of nine or ten, according to ibn-Hishām, p. 1001.

rallying-point for the rebel warriors. Both rivals of 'Ali fell; he magnanimously mourned the fallen and had them honourably buried.[1] 'Ā'ishah was captured and treated most considerately and in a manner befitting her dignity as the "first lady" of the land. She was sent back to al-Madīnah. Thus came to an end the first, but by no means the last, encounter in which Moslem stood against Moslem in battle array. The dynastic wars that were to convulse Islam from time to time and occasionally shake it to its very foundation had just begun.

Ostensibly secure on his throne, 'Ali from his new capital al-Kūfah inaugurated his régime by dismissing most of the provincial governors appointed by his predecessor and exacting the oath of fealty from the others. With one of them, Mu'āwiyah ibn-abi-Sufyān, governor of Syria and kinsman of 'Uthmān, he did not reckon. Mu'āwiyah now came out as the avenger of the martyred caliph. He exhibited in the Damascus mosque the blood-stained shirt of the murdered ruler and the fingers cut from the hand of his wife Nā'ilah as she tried to defend him.[2] With the tactics and eloquence of an Antony he endeavoured to play on Moslem emotions. Withholding his homage from 'Ali, Mu'āwiyah tried to corner him with this dilemma: Produce the assassins of the duly appointed successor of the Prophet or accept the position of an accomplice who is thereby disqualified from the caliphate. The issue, however, was more than a personal one, it transcended individual and even family affairs. The real question was whether al-Kūfah or Damascus, al-'Irāq or Syria, should be supreme in Islamic affairs. Al-Madīnah, which 'Ali had left soon after his installation in 656 never to revisit, was already out of the way. The weight of the far-flung conquests had shifted the centre of gravity to the north.

On the plain of Ṣiffīn south of al-Raqqah, on the west bank of the Euphrates, the two armies finally stood face to face: 'Ali with an army reported to have comprised 50,000 'Irāqis and Mu'āwiyah with his Syrians. In a half-hearted manner, for neither side was anxious to precipitate a final decision, the skirmishes dragged on for weeks. The final encounter took place on July 28, 657. Under the leadership of Mālik al-Ashtar, 'Ali's forces were on the point of victory when the shrewd, wily 'Amr

[1] A town bearing his name has grown around the tomb of al-Zubayr.

[2] *Fakhri*, pp. 125, 137.

ibn-al-'Āṣ, Mu'āwiyah's leader, resorted to a ruse. Copies of the Koran fastened to lances were suddenly seen thrust in the air—a gesture interpreted to mean an appeal from the decision of arms to the decision of the Koran. Hostilities ceased. Urged by his followers, the simple-hearted 'Ali accepted Mu'āwiyah's proposal to arbitrate the case and thus spare Moslem blood. The arbitration was, of course, to be "according to the word of Allah"[1]—whatever that may have meant.

Against his better judgment the caliph appointed as his personal representative abu-Mūsa al-Ash'ari, a man of undoubted piety but of lukewarm loyalty to the 'Alid cause. Mu'āwiyah matched him with 'Amr ibn-al-'Āṣ, who has been dubbed a political genius of the Arabs.[2] Armed each with a written document giving him full authorization to act and accompanied by four hundred witnesses each, the two arbiters (sing. *ḥakam*) held their public session in January 659 at Adhruḥ on the main caravan route between al-Madīnah and Damascus and half-way between Ma'ān and Petra.

Exactly what transpired at this historical conference is difficult to ascertain. Various versions appear in different sources.[3] The current tradition is that the two umpires agreed to depose both principals, thus clearing the way for a "dark horse"; but after the elder of the two, abu-Mūsa, had stood up and declared the caliphate of his master null and void, 'Amr betrayed his colleague and confirmed Mu'āwiyah. But the critical studies of Père Lammens,[4] preceded by those of Wellhausen,[5] tend to show that this tradition reflects the view of the 'Irāqi school, to which most of our extant sources belong, which flourished under the 'Abbāsids—the Umayyads' mortal enemies. What probably happened was that both referees deposed both principals, which left 'Ali the loser. Mu'āwiyah had no caliphate to be deposed from. He was but a governor of a province. The very fact of the arbitration itself had raised him to a level equivalent to that of 'Ali, whose position was thereby lowered to that of a mere pretender. The sentence of the judges deprived 'Ali of a real

[1] For the arbitration document see Dīnawari, pp. 206-8.

[2] Mas'ūdi, vol. iv, p. 391. See below, p. 196. Cf. above, p. 161.

[3] Cf. Ṭabari, vol. i, pp. 3340-60; Mas'ūdi, vol. iv, pp. 392-402; Ya'qūbi, vol. ii, pp. 220-22; *Fakhri*, pp. 127-30.

[4] *Études sur le règne du calife omaiyade Mo'âwia Ier* (Beirūt, 1907), ch. vii.

[5] *Das arabische Reich und sein Sturz* (Berlin, 1902), ch. ii = *The Arab Kingdom and its Fall*, tr. Margaret G. Weir (Calcutta 1927), ch. ii.

office, and Muʿāwiyah of a fictitious claim which he had not yet dared publicly to assert. Not until ʿAli's death in 661, two years after the curtain had been lowered on the arbitration farce, did Muʿāwiyah's caliphate receive general recognition

The acceptance of the principle of arbitration proved disastrous to ʿAli in more than one way: it alienated the sympathy of a large body of his own followers. These Khārijites[1] (seceders), as they were called, the earliest sect of Islam, proved his deadly foes. Adopting as a slogan *la ḥukma illa li-l-Lāh*[2] (arbitration belongs to Allah alone), they rose in arms to the number of 4000[3] under the leadership of ʿAbdullāh ibn-Wahb al-Rāsibi. On the bank of the Nahrawān canal ʿAli attacked their camp (659) and almost annihilated them, but they rose again under various names and remained a thorn in the side of the caliphate till the ʿAbbāsid period.

Early on January 24, 661, as ʿAli was on his way to the mosque at al-Kūfah he was struck on the forehead with a poisoned sabre. The weapon, which penetrated to the brain, was wielded by a Khārijite, ʿAbd-al-Raḥmān ibn-Muljam, who was actuated by the desire to avenge certain relatives of a lady, a friend of his, who were slaughtered at Nahrawān. Tradition makes ibn-Muljam one of three accomplices who under oath at al-Kaʿbah had concocted a plan to rid the Moslem community on the same day of its three disturbing elements: ʿAli, Muʿāwiyah and ʿAmr ibn-al-ʿAṣ[4]—all of which sounds too dramatic to be true. The lonely spot near al-Kūfah where ʿAli was interred,[5] the present Mashhad ʿAli in al-Najaf, has developed into one of the great centres of pilgrimage in Islam.

To his Shīʿite partisans the fourth caliph soon became pre-eminently the saint of the sect, the Wali (friend and vicegerent) of Allah, just as Muḥammad had been the Prophet of Islam and the Messenger of Allah. ʿAli dead proved more effective than ʿAli living. As a canonized martyr he retrieved at once more

[1] Also called Ḥarūrīyah, from Ḥarūrā' (Ḥarawrā' in Yāqūt, vol. ii, p. 246).

[2] *Fakhri*, p. 130. Cf. Koran, 12 : 70. [3] 12,000 in Shahrastāni, p. 86.

[4] Cf. Dīnawari, p. 227; Ṭabari, vol. i, pp. 3456 *seq.*; H. Zotenberg, *Chronique de Tabari*, vol. iii (Paris, 1871), pp. 706 *seq.*

[5] The site, as the Shīʿite tradition asserts, was chosen in accordance with the dying wish of ʿAli, who ordered that his corpse be put on a loose camel and buried wherever the camel knelt. The place was kept secret until Hārūn al-Rashīd in 791 fell upon it by chance. For the first detailed account of the tomb see ibn-Ḥawqal, *al-Masālik w-al-Mamālik*, ed. de Goeje (Leyden, 1872), p. 163.

than he had lost in a lifetime. Though lacking in those traits that constitute a leader and a politician, viz. alertness, foresight, resolution, expediency, he still possessed the qualities of an ideal Arabian. Valiant in battle, wise in counsel, eloquent in speech, true to his friends, magnanimous to his foes, he became both the paragon of Moslem nobility and chivalry (*futūwah*) and the Solomon of Arabic tradition, around whose name poems, proverbs, sermonettes and anecdotes innumerable have clustered. He had a swarthy complexion, large black eyes, bald head, thick and long white beard, and was corpulent and of medium stature.[1] His sabre dhu-al-Faqār (the cleaver of vertebræ), wielded by the Prophet on the memorable battlefield of Badr, has been immortalized in the words of the verse found engraved on many medieval Arab swords: *La sayfa illa dhu-al-Faqāri wa-la fata illa 'Ali* = "No sword can match dhu-al-Faqār, and no young warrior can compare with 'Ali!" The later *Fityān* movement, which developed ceremonies and insignia savouring of medieval European chivalry and the modern Scout movements, took 'Ali for its first *Fata* and model. Regarded as wise and brave by all the Islamic world, as idealistic and exemplary by many Fityān and dervish fraternities, as sinless and infallible by his partisans and even held to be the incarnation of the deity by the Ghulāh (extremists) among them, he whose worldly career was practically a failure has continued to exert a posthumous influence second only to that of the Prophet himself. The throngs of pilgrims that still stream to his *mashhad* at al-Najaf and to that of his son al-Ḥusayn, the Shī'ah arch-saint and martyr at near-by Karbalā', and the passion play enacted annually on the tenth of Muḥarram throughout the Shī'ah world testify to the possibility that death may avail a Messiah more than life.

Periods of the great caliphates

With the death of 'Ali (661) what may be termed the republican period of the caliphate, which began with abu-Bakr (632), came to an end. The four caliphs of this era are known to Arab historians as *al-Rāshidūn* (orthodox). The founder of the second caliphate, Mu'āwiyah the Umayyad, a man of the world, nominated his own son Yazīd as his successor and thus became the founder of a dynasty. The hereditary principle was thereby introduced into the caliphal succession never thereafter to be entirely

[1] Mas'ūdi, *Tanbīh*, p. 297.

abandoned. The Umayyad caliphate was the first dynasty (*mulk*) in the history of Islam. The fiction of election was preserved in the *bay'ah*[1] (literally "sale"), the ceremony by which the leaders of the people literally or figuratively took the hand of the new caliph as a sign of homage. The Umayyad caliphate (661–750) with its capital at Damascus was followed by the 'Abbāsid (750–1258) at Baghdād. The Fāṭimid caliphate (909–1171), whose main seat was Cairo, was the only Shī'ite one of primary importance. Another Umayyad caliphate at Cordova (Qurṭubah) in Spain lasted from 929 to 1031. The last great caliphate of Islam was non-Arab, that of the Ottoman Turks in Constantinople (*ca.* 1517–1924). In November 1922 the Grand National Assembly at Ankara declared Turkey a republic, deposed the Sultan-Caliph Muḥammad VI and made his cousin 'Abd-al-Majīd caliph, denying him the sultanate. In March 1924 the caliphate itself was abolished.[2]

[1] Ibn-Khaldūn, *Muqaddamah*, i.e. vol. i of *Kitāb al-'Ibar wa-Dīwān al-Mubtada' w-al-Khabar* (Cairo, 1284), pp. 174-5 = pp. 376-7 of Quatremère's ed., in *Notices et extraits* etc., vol. xvi (Paris, 1858), and pp. 424-6 of de Slane's tr., vol. xix (Paris, 1862).

[2] The subjoined tree shows the connection of the lines of caliphs:

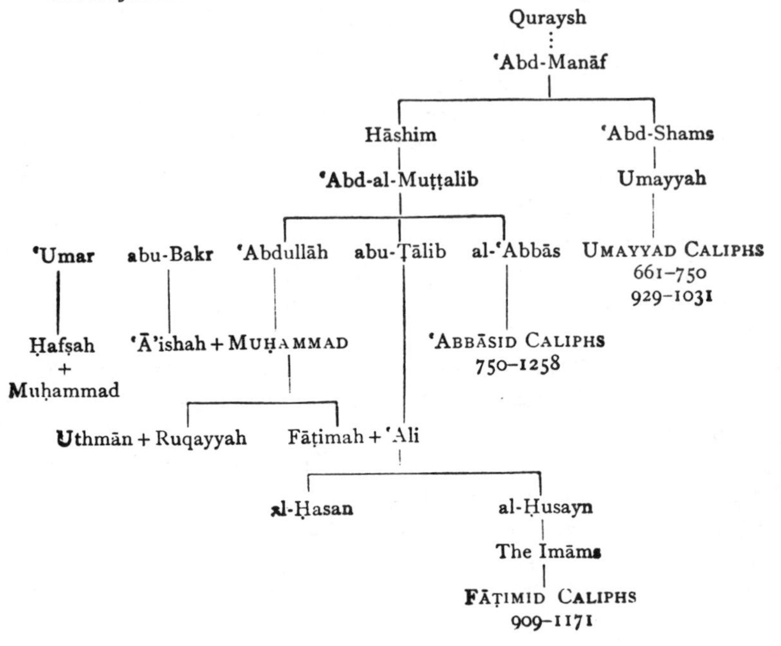

The caliphate, a pre-eminently political office

We should here guard against the common fallacy that the caliphate was a religious office. In this regard analogies drawn from the headship of the Holy Roman Empire and from the modern Christian distinction between the spheres of temporal and religious powers are misleading. As *amīr al-mu'minīn*, commander of the believers, the military office of the caliph was emphasized. As *imām* (leader in public prayer) the caliph could and did lead the religious service and pronounce the Friday *khuṭbah* (sermon); but this was a function which the humblest of Moslems could perform. Succession to Muḥammad (*khilāfah*) meant succession to the sovereignty of the state. Muḥammad as a prophet, as an instrument of revelation, as a messenger (*rasūl*) of Allah, could have no successor. The caliph's relation to religion was merely that of a guardian. He defended the faith just as any European emperor was supposed to do, suppressed heresies, warred against unbelievers and extended the boundaries of the Dār al-Islām (the abode of Islam), in the performance of all of which he employed the power of his secular arm.[1]

Later theoretical legists, flourishing mostly in Makkah, al-Madīnah and other centres, and out of touch with the course of events in the Islamic capitals of Damascus, Baghdād and Cairo, worked out nicely-drawn qualifications, privileges and functions said to pertain to the caliph. Al-Māwardi[2] († 1058) in his utopian treatise on politics, al-Nasafi († 1310), ibn-Khaldūn († 1406) in his famous critical prolegomena[3] and later writers representing the Sunnite (orthodox) theory list the following caliphal qualifications: membership in the Quraysh family; being male and adult; soundness of body and mind; courage, energy and other traits of character necessary for the defence of the realm; and the winning of the allegiance of the community by an act of *bay'ah*. The Shī'ah, on the other hand, who make less of the caliphate and more of the imāmate, confine the office to the family of 'Ali, who they hold was nominated by Muḥammad as his successor on the basis of a divine ordinance (*naṣṣ*) and whose qualifications passed on to his descendants pre-ordained for the high office by Allah.[4] Among the caliphal functions according to the Sunnite school are: protection and main-

[1] Consult Thomas W. Arnold, *The Caliphate* (Oxford, 1924), pp 9-41.
[2] Pp. 5-10.
[3] *Muqaddamah*, p. 161.
[4] Shahrastāni, pp. 108-9; ibn-Khaldūn, pp. 164-5.

tenance of the faith and the territory of Islam (particularly the two sacred places—*al-ḥaramayn*—of Makkah and al-Madīnah) and in case of necessity the declaration of a holy war (*jihād*); appointment of state officials; collection of taxes and administration of public funds; punishment of wrongdoing and the execution of justice.[1] The privileges include the mention of the caliph's name in the Friday *khuṭbah* and on the coinage; the wearing of the *burdah* (the Prophet's mantle) on important state occasions; the custody of such holy relics as the staff, seal, shoe, tooth and hair that are said to have been Muḥammad's.[2]

Not until the latter part of the eighteenth century did the notion prevail in Europe that the Moslem caliph was a kind of pope with spiritual jurisdiction over the followers of Muḥammad throughout the world. In his *Tableau général de l'empire othoman* (Paris, 1788),[3] d'Ohsson, a Constantinople Armenian, was one of the first to give currency to this fallacy. The shrewd ʿAbd-al-Ḥamīd II made capital of the idea to strengthen his prestige in the eyes of the European powers who had by this time come to dominate most of the Moslems in Asia and Africa. An ill-defined movement had its inception in the latter part of the last century and under the name pan-Islamism (*al-Jāmiʿah al-Islāmīyah*) exerted special effort to bring about some unity of action to oppose the Christian powers. With Turkey as its rallying-point it unduly stressed the ecumenical character of the caliphate.

[1] Māwardi, pp. 23-4; al-Nasafi, *ʿUmdat ʿAqīdat Ahl al-Sunnah*, ed. W. Cureton (London, 1843), pp. 28-9.

[2] As the last Moslem caliphs the Ottoman sultans had charge of these Prophetic treasures (*dhakhā'ir Nabawīyah*), which Sultan Salīm in 1517 brought to Constantinople upon his return from the conquest of Egypt. The relics have ever since been enshrined in a special pavilion within the stronghold of the Grand Seraglio and cherished as the priceless insignia of the exalted office of the caliphate.

[3] Vol. i, pp. 213 *seq*.

PART III

THE UMAYYAD AND ʻABBĀSID EMPIRES

CHAPTER XVII

THE UMAYYAD CALIPHATE: MU'ĀWIYAH ESTABLISHES A DYNASTY

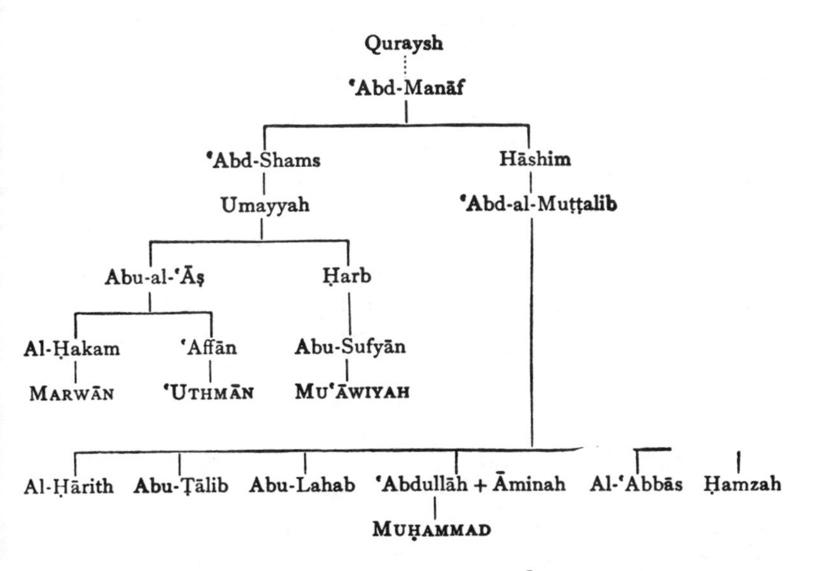

The claimants to the caliphate disposed of

MU'ĀWIYAH was proclaimed caliph at Īliyā' (Jerusalem) in A.H. 40 (660).[1] With his accession the seat of the provincial government, Damascus, became the capital of the Moslem empire, though that empire was somewhat circumscribed. During the arbitration 'Amr ibn-al-'Āṣ, Mu'āwiyah's right-hand man, had wrested Egypt from 'Alids, but al-'Irāq now declared al-Ḥasan, eldest son of 'Ali and Fāṭimah, the legitimate successor of 'Ali, and Makkah and al-Madīnah were lukewarm in their loyalty to the representations of the Sufyānids, who had failed to acknowledge Muḥammad until the fall of Makkah and whose Islam was therefore considered of convenience rather than

[1] Ṭabari, vol. ii, p. 4; cf. Mas'ūdi, vol. v, p. 14.

conviction. The interests of al-Ḥasan, who was more at home in the harem than on the throne, lay in fields other than those of imperial administration. It was not long before he abdicated in favour of his more able rival and retired to al-Madīnah to a life of ease and pleasure, a step which he was induced to take by Mu'āwiyah's guarantee of a magnificent subsidy and pension[1] which he himself had fixed and which included five million dirhams from the Kūfah treasury[2] plus the revenue of a district in Persia for the duration of his lifetime. Though he died at the age of forty-five (*ca.* 669), possibly poisoned[3] because of some harem intrigue, al-Ḥasan is said to have made and unmade no less than a hundred marriages, which earned him the title of *miṭlāq*[4] (great divorcer). The Shī'ah laid the fatal act at Mu'āwiyah's door and thus made al-Ḥasan a *shahīd* (martyr), in fact the "*sayyid* [lord] of all martyrs".

His younger brother al-Ḥusayn, who had also lived in retirement at al-Madīnah throughout the rule of Mu'āwiyah, in 680 refused to acknowledge Mu'āwiyah's son and successor Yazīd, and in response to the urgent and reiterated appeals of the 'Irāqis, who had declared him the legitimate caliph after al-Ḥasan and 'Ali, started at the head of a weak escort of relatives (including his harem and devoted followers) for al-Kūfah. 'Ubaydullāh, whose father Ziyād had been conveniently acknowledged by Mu'āwiyah as his brother, was now the Umayyad governor of al-'Irāq and had established outposts on all the roads leading from al-Ḥijāz to al-'Irāq. On the tenth of Muḥarram, A.H. 61 (October 10, 680), 'Umar, son of the distinguished general Sa'd ibn-abi-Waqqāṣ, in command of 4000 troops surrounded al-Ḥusayn with his insignificant band of some two hundred souls at Karbalā', about twenty-five miles north-west of al-Kūfah, and upon their refusal to surrender cut them down. The grandson of the Prophet fell dead with many wounds and his head was sent to Yazīd in Damascus. The head was given back to al-Ḥusayn's sister and son, who had gone with it to Damascus,[5] and was buried with the body in Karbalā'. In commemoration of al-Ḥusayn's "martyrdom" the Shī'ah Moslems have established the practice of annually observing the

[1] See ibn-Ḥajar, vol. ii, p. 13; Dīnawari, p. 231. [2] Ṭabari, vol. ii, p. 3.
[3] Ya'qūbi, vol. ii, p. 266. [4] Ibn-'Asākir, vol. iv, p. 216, l. 21.
[5] Ibn-Ḥajar, vol. ii, p. 17.

first ten days of Muḥarram as days of lamentation, and have developed a passion play stressing his "heroic" struggle and suffering. This annual passion play is enacted in two parts, one called *'Āshūrā'* (the tenth day) in al-Kāẓimayn (close by Baghdād) in memory of the battle, and the other forty days after the tenth of Muḥarram in Karbalā' entitled "the Return of the Head".

The blood of al-Ḥusayn, even more than that of his father, proved to be the seed of the Shī'ite "church". Shī'ism was born on the tenth of Muḥarram. From now on the imāmship in 'Ali's progeny became as much of a dogma in the Shī'ite creed as that of the prophethood of Muḥammad in Islam. *Yawm* (the day of) *Karbalā'* gave the Shī'ah a battle-cry summed up in the formula "vengeance for al-Ḥusayn", which ultimately proved one of the factors that undermined the Umayyad dynasty. In the other camp the Sunnites argued that Yazīd was *de facto* ruler and that to question his authority constituted a treason punishable with death. They insisted that the Shī'ites should not view the facts otherwise. But how a people actually do view an event is usually more important as a moving force in history than how they should view it. The great schism was made in Islam and the breach has never since been filled.

Although the Umayyads were for some time secure in the caliphate in so far as the 'Alids were concerned, the struggle was in reality three-cornered, for the third party was not yet eliminated. As long as the powerful Mu'āwiyah lived 'Abdullāh, a nephew of 'Ā'ishah and son of al-Zubayr who had fruitlessly disputed the caliphate with 'Ali, kept his peace in al-Madīnah. When Yazīd, well known for his frivolity and dissipation, succeeded to the throne 'Abdullāh declared openly against the new caliph and encouraged al-Ḥusayn to undertake the perilous step which cost him his life and left 'Abdullāh the sole claimant. All al-Ḥijāz proclaimed 'Abdullāh. Yazīd was quick to dispatch against the malcontents of al-Madīnah a disciplinary force which included many Christian Syrians, and was headed by the one-eyed Muslim ibn-'Uqbah, whose old age and infirmity necessitated his carriage all the way in a litter. The punitive expedition encamped on the volcanic plain of al-Ḥarrah east of al-Madīnah, gave battle on August 26, 683, and was victorious. The story of the three days in which the unchecked Damascene soldiery sacked the city of the Prophet is apocryphal. The army then proceeded to Makkah. On the way Muslim died and was succeeded in the chief command by al-Ḥuṣayn ibn-Numayr al-Sakūni,[1] who had his catapults rain stones upon the Ḥaram (holy mosque) of Makkah on whose inviolable soil ibn-al-Zubayr had taken refuge. In the course of the siege the Ka'bah itself caught fire and was burned to the ground. The Black Stone was split in three pieces and the house of Allah looked "like the torn bosoms of mourning women".[2] While these operations were proceeding Yazīd had died and ibn-Numayr, fearing consequent disorders in Syria, suspended on November 27, 683, the operations which had begun on September 24. The second civil war of Islam, which like the first between 'Ali and Mu'āwiyah was also a dynastic war, came to a temporary halt.

Subsequent to the death of his rival and the consequent withdrawal of enemy troops from Arabian soil ibn-al-Zubayr was proclaimed caliph not only in al-Ḥijāz, where he had his seat, and in al-'Irāq, where his brother Muṣ'ab was made his representative, but in South Arabia, Egypt and parts of Syria. Over Damascus, however, al-Ḍaḥḥāk ibn-Qays al-Fihri, leader of the Qaysite (North Arabian) party which had favoured ibn-al-Zubayr, had been appointed by this caliph provisional regent. Al-Ḍaḥḥāk was finally crushed in July 684, at Marj Rāhiṭ[3] —a second Ṣiffīn for the Umayyads—by his Kalbite (including the Yamanite or South Arabian) opponents, who supported the aged[4] Umayyad Marwān ibn-al-Ḥakam. The Kalbites were Syro-Arabs domiciled in Syria before the Hijrah and mostly Christianized. Marwān (684–5), the cousin of 'Uthmān and formerly his secretary of state, then became the founder of the Marwānid branch of the Umayyad dynasty. He followed Mu'āwiyah II (683–4), Yazīd's weak and sickly son, who had ruled

[1] Ṭabari, vol. i, p. 2220; Ya'qūbi, vol. ii, p. 299.

[2] Ṭabari, vol. ii, p. 427; al-Fākihi, *al-Muntaqa fi Akhbār umm-al-Qura*, ed. F. Wüstenfeld (Leipzig, 1859), pp. 18 *seq.*; Azraqi, *Akhbār Makkah*, p. 32. The Ka'bah was rebuilt by ibn-al-Zubayr on the withdrawal of the Umayyad army.

[3] A plain east of the village Marj 'Adhrā' not far from Damascus. See *'Iqd*, vol. ii, pp. 320-21; Mas'ūdi, vol. v, p. 201. These internal feuds between the Qays, representing the new emigrants from North Arabia, and the Kalb, who were ever the staunch supporters of the Umayyad cause, were among the events which precipitated the fall of the Umayyad dynasty. The Qaysi and Yamani parties figured even in the modern politics of Lebanon and Syria. See below, p. 281.

[4] Ya'qūbi, vol. ii, p. 304, l. 19.

only three months and left no successor.[1] But the defection of al-Ḥijāz under the rival caliph continued until Marwān's son and successor, ʿAbd-al-Malik, sent his iron-handed general al-Ḥajjāj, formerly a schoolmaster in al-Ṭā'if, at the head of a Syrian army which gave the *coup de grâce* to the anti-caliphate. Beginning March 25, 692, al-Ḥajjāj pressed the siege against Makkah for six and a half months and used his catapults effectively.[2] Inspired by the heroic exhortation of his mother, Asmā',[3] daughter of abu-Bakr and sister of ʿĀ'ishah, ibn-al-Zubayr fought valiantly but hopelessly until he was slain. His head was sent to Damascus [4] and his body, after hanging for some time on the gibbet, was delivered to his aged mother. With the death of ibn-al-Zubayr the last champion of the old faith passed away. ʿUthmān was fully avenged, if not by Muslim certainly by al-Ḥajjāj. The Anṣār's (Supporters') power was for ever broken. After this debacle a number of them began to leave Makkah and al-Madīnah to join the armies operating in North Africa, Spain and other theatres of war. Henceforth the history of Arabia begins to deal more with the effect of the outer world on the peninsula and less with the effect of the peninsula on the outer world. The vigour of the mother "island" had spent itself.

Muʿāwiyah the model Arab sovereign

After gaining supremacy over the opposing parties Muʿāwiyah (661–80) was free to direct his efforts against the great enemy of Islam to the north-west, the Byzantines. In ʿAkka (Acre) he found soon after the conquest of Syria well-equipped Byzantine shipyards (sing. *dār al-ṣināʿah*, whence Eng. arsenal) which he utilized for building the Moslem navy. These dockyards were

[1] The subjoined tree shows the Sufyānid branch of the Umayyad dynasty in its relation to the founder of the Marwānid branch:

Umayyah
- Abu-al-ʿĀṣ
  - Al-Ḥakam
    - 4. MARWĀN I (684–5)
- Ḥarb
  - Abu-Sufyān
    - 1. MUʿĀWIYAH (661–80)
      - 2. YAZĪD I (680–83)
        - 3. MUʿĀWIYAH II (683–4)

[2] Dīnawari, p. 320; ibn-ʿAsākir, vol. iv, p. 50.
[3] Ṭabari, vol. ii, pp. 845-8.
[4] Ṭabari, vol. ii, p. 852.

probably the second after those of Egypt in Islamic maritime history. The Syrian yards, according to al-Balādhuri,[1] were transferred by later Umayyads to Ṣūr (Tyre),[2] where they remained until the 'Abbāsid period. This fleet must undoubtedly have been manned by Greco-Syrians accustomed to seafaring. The Arabians of al-Ḥijāz, the mainstay of Islam, had only little acquaintance with the sea, for it was a principle of 'Umar's policy to let no body of water intervene between him and his lieutenants. Such a policy explains, for instance, why 'Umar would not authorize the proposed invasion of Cyprus (Qubrus) by Mu'āwiyah. It was 'Umar's successor, 'Uthmān, who was finally persuaded to yield a half-hearted assent to the invasion of the island; and it was in compliance with the caliph's order that Mu'āwiyah had his wife accompany him (649).[3] Her presence was proof positive of the proximity of Cyprus and of the contemplated ease with which it could be subdued.

Mu'āwiyah's reign witnessed not only the consolidation but the extension of the territories of the caliphate. To this period belongs the expansion in North Africa for which 'Uqbah ibn-Nāfi' was in the main responsible. In the east the complete conquest of Khurāsān was undertaken (663–71) from al-Baṣrah,[4] the Oxus was crossed and Bukhāra in far-away Turkestan raided (674). Thus Mu'āwiyah became not only the father of a dynasty but the second founder of the caliphate after 'Umar.

In securing his throne and extending the limits of Islamic dominion, Mu'āwiyah relied mainly upon Syrians, who were still chiefly Christian, and upon the Syro-Arabs, who were mainly Yamanites, to the exclusion of the new Moslem immigrants from al-Ḥijāz. Arabic chronicles dwell upon the sense of loyalty which the people of Syria cherished towards their new chief.[5] Though as a soldier he was certainly inferior to 'Ali, as a military organizer Mu'āwiyah was second to none of his contemporaries. He whipped the raw material which constituted his Syrian army into the first ordered and disciplined force known in Islamic warfare. He rid the military machine of its archaic tribal organization, a relic of the ancient patriarchal days. He abolished many

[1] P. 118 = Hitti, p. 181.
[2] Consult Guy Le Strange, *Palestine under the Moslems* (Boston, 1890), p. 342; cf. ibn-Jubayr, *Riḥlah* (Leyden, 1907), p. 305.
[3] Above, p. 168.
[4] Ya'qūbi, vol. ii, p. 258; Balādhuri, p. 410; Ṭabari, vol. ii, pp. 166 *seq.*
[5] Ṭabari, vol. i, pp. 3409-10; Mas'ūdi, vol. v, pp. 80, 104; cf. '*Iqd*, vol. i, p. 207, l. 31.

traditional features of the government and on the earlier Byzantine framework built a stable, well-organized state. Out of seeming chaos he developed an orderly Moslem society. Historians credit him with being the first in Islam to institute the bureau of registry and the first to interest himself in postal service, *al-barīd*,[1] which developed under 'Abd-al-Malik into a well-organized system knitting together the various parts of the far-flung empire. From among many other wives he chose as his favourite a Syro-Arab Kalbite of the banu-Baḥdal, Maysūn by name, who scorned court life at Damascus and yearned for the freedom of the desert. The verses attributed to her, though she may never have composed them, express the feeling of homesickness which many Bedouins who were now passing into an urban state must have experienced.[2]

Maysūn was a Jacobite Christian like her predecessor Nā'ilah, 'Uthmān's wife, who also belonged to the Kalb tribe. She often took her son Yazīd, subsequently the successor of Mu'āwiyah, to the *bādiyah* (Syrian desert), particularly to Palmyrena, in which her Bedouin tribe roamed and where the youthful crown prince became habituated to the chase, hard-riding, wine-bibbing and verse-making. Al-Bādiyah from this time on became the school of the Umayyad princes, where they acquired the pure Arabic[3] unadulterated with Aramaicisms and where they also escaped the recurrent city plagues. Later Umayyad caliphs, including 'Abd-al-Malik and al-Walīd II, continuing the tradition, built country residences on the border of the Syrian desert and called them "al-Bādiyahs".

Manṣūr ibn-Sarjūn (Gr. Sergius),[4] who figured in the treacherous surrender of Damascus at the time of the Arab invasion, was the scion of a prominent Christian family some of whose members had occupied the position of financial controller of the state in the last Byzantine period. Next to the supreme command of the army this office became the most important in the Arab government. The grandson of this Manṣūr was the illustrious St. John (Yūḥanna) the Damascene, who in his

[1] *Fakhri*, p. 148. See below, p. 322.
[2] Abu-al-Fidā', vol. i, p. 203; Nicholson, *Literary History*, p. 195.
[3] *'Iqd*, vol. i, p. 293, l. 30.
[4] For the confusion in the Arabic chronicles between the name of this man and his son Sarjūn ibn-Manṣūr, consult Ṭabari, vol. ii, pp. 205, 228, 239; Mas'ūdi, *Tanbīh*, pp. 302, 306, 307, 312; cf. Theophanes, p. 365.

youth was a boon companion of Yazīd. The caliph's physician, ibn-Uthāl, was likewise a Christian, whom Mu'āwiyah made financial administrator of the province of Ḥimṣ[1]—an unprecedented appointment for a Christian in Moslem annals.[2] The Umayyad poet laureate, al-Akhṭal, another boon companion of Yazīd, belonged to the Taghlib Christian Arabs of al-Ḥīrah and was a friend of St. John. This poet of the court would enter the caliphal palace with a cross dangling from his neck and recite his poems to the delight of the Moslem caliph and his entourage. Jacobites and Maronites brought their religious disputes before the caliph,[3] who is reported by Theophanis[4] to have even rebuilt a Christian church in Edessa which had been demolished by an earthquake.

When in 679 Mu'āwiyah nominated his son Yazīd as his successor[5] and caused deputations to come from the provinces and take the oath of allegiance, he introduced into the caliphate the hereditary principle followed thereafter by the leading Moslem dynasties, including the 'Abbāsids. Following this precedent the reigning caliph would proclaim as his successor the one among his sons or kinsmen whom he considered most competent and would exact for him an anticipatory oath of fealty, first from the capital and then from the other principal towns of the empire.

No small measure of the success of the Caliph Mu'āwiyah should be attributed to the circle of collaborators with whom he surrounded himself, particularly 'Amr ibn-al-'Āṣ, the vicegerent over fertile Egypt, al-Mughīrah ibn-Shu'bah, the governor of turbulent al-Kūfah, and Ziyād ibn-Abīh, the ruler of malcontent al-Baṣrah. These three with their chief, Mu'āwiyah, constituted the four political geniuses (*duhāt*) of the Arab Moslems. Ziyād was at first styled ibn-Abīh because of the doubt which clouded the identity of his father. His mother was a slave and prostitute in al-Ṭā'if whom abu-Sufyān, Mu'āwiyah's father, had known. Ziyād was pro-'Alid. In a critical moment Mu'āwiyah acknowledged Ziyād as his legitimate brother.[6] Ziyād proved a great

[1] Ibn-'Asākir, vol. v, p. 80.
[2] Ya'qūbi, vol. ii, p. 265 Wellhausen, *Reich*, p. 85, considers the report of this appointment fictitious.
[3] Wellhausen, *Reich*, p. 84.
[4] P. 356.
[5] Mas'ūdi, vol. v, pp. 69-73; cf. Ṭabari, vol. ii, pp. 174-7.
[6] Dīnawari, pp. 232-3; Ṭabari, vol. ii, pp. 69-70; ibn-'Asākir, vol. v, p. 397.

asset to his caliph brother. His unrelenting hand weighed heavily over al-Baṣrah, a centre of Shīʿism. After the death of al-Mughīrah he was elevated to the governorship of al-Kūfah, a position which made him the absolute ruler of the eastern part of the empire, including Arabia and Persia. With a trained bodyguard 4000 strong who acted also as spies and police, he ruled tyrannically and tracked down mercilessly anyone who dared show favour to ʿAli's descendants or revile Muʿāwiyah.

In Muʿāwiyah the sense of *finesse politique* was developed to a degree probably higher than in any other caliph. To his Arab biographers his supreme virtue was his *ḥilm*,[1] that unusual ability to resort to force only when force was absolutely necessary and to use peaceful measures in all other instances. His prudent mildness by which he tried to disarm the enemy and shame the opposition, his slowness to anger and his absolute self-control left him under all circumstances master of the situation. "I apply not my sword", he is reported to have declared, "where my lash suffices, nor my lash where my tongue is enough. And even if there be one hair binding me to my fellowmen, I do not let it break: when they pull I loosen, and if they loosen I pull."[2] The following is a copy of a letter he is supposed to have forwarded to al-Ḥasan on the occasion of the latter's abdication: "I admit that because of thy blood relationship thou art more entitled to this high office than I. And if I were sure of thy greater ability to fulfil the duties involved I would unhesitatingly swear allegiance to thee. Now then, ask what thou wilt." Enclosed was a blank for al-Ḥasan to fill in, already signed by Muʿāwiyah.[3]

Despite many excellences Muʿāwiyah was no favourite with several of the historians whose works have come down to us. They regarded him as the first *malik* (king) in Islam; and to the true Arab the title was so abhorrent that it was applied almost exclusively to non-Arab potentates. The historians' attitude was a reflection of that of the puritans, who accused him of having secularized Islam and changed the *khilāfat al-nubūʾah* (the prophetic, i.e. theocratic, caliphate) to a *mulk*[4]—a temporal sovereignty. Among his profane creations, they point out, was

[1] *Fakhri*, p. 145; *ʿIqd*, vol. ii, p. 304; Masʿūdi, vol. v, p. 410.
[2] Yaʿqūbi, vol. ii, p. 283; *ʿIqd*, vol. i, p. 10.
[3] Ṭabari, vol. ii, p. 5.
[4] Ibn-Khaldūn, *Muqaddamah*, pp. 169 *seq*. Yaʿqūbi, vol. ii, p. 257.

the *maqṣūrah*,[1] a sort of bower inside the mosque reserved for the exclusive use of the caliph. The Friday noon sermon (*khuṭbah*) he read while seated.[2] He was the first to institute a royal throne (*sarīr al-mulk*).[3] The Arabic annals, mostly composed in the 'Abbāsid period or under Shī'ite influence, impugn his piety. The Syrian tradition, however, preserved in ibn-'Asākir, reveals him as a good Moslem. To his Umayyad successors he bequeathed a precedent of clemency, energy, astuteness and statesmanship which many tried to emulate,[4] though few succeeded. He was not only the first but also one of the best of Arab kings.

[1] Ya'qūbi, vol. ii, p. 265; Dīnawari, p. 229; Ṭabari, vol. ii, p. 70, l. 20.

[2] Ibn-al-'Ibri, p. 188.

[3] Ibn-Khaldūn, *Muqaddamah*, p. 217; al-Qalqashandi, *Ṣubḥ al-A'sha*, vol. iv (Cairo, 1914), p. 6.

[4] Mas'ūdi, vol. v, p. 78. Mu'āwiyah's tomb in the cemetery of [al-]Bāb al-Ṣaghīr at Damascus is still visited.

CHAPTER XVIII

HOSTILE RELATIONS WITH THE BYZANTINES

WHILE Mu'āwiyah was still insecure in his new position and had his hands full with domestic affairs he found it expedient to purchase (658 or 659) a truce from the Emperor Constans II (641–68) at the price of a yearly tribute mentioned by Theophanis[1] and referred to in passing by al-Balādhuri.[2] But soon afterward the tribute was repudiated and hostilities against the Byzantine possessions both by land and sea were pressed more zealously and persistently than by any of Mu'āwiyah's immediate successors. Twice did Mu'āwiyah stretch out his mighty arm against the enemy capital itself. The main object of these raids into *Bilād al-Rūm* (the territory of the Romans, Asia Minor) was of course the acquisition of booty, though the dim spectacle of Constantinople may have beckoned beyond in the distant background. Gradually the razzias became annual summer affairs and served the purpose of keeping the army physically fit and well trained. Yet the Arabs never succeeded in establishing a permanent foothold in Asia Minor. Their main energy was directed eastward and westward along the lines of least resistance. Otherwise the story of Arab-Byzantine relations in Asia Minor and even across the Hellespont might have been different. On the north the lofty ranges of the Taurus and Anti-Taurus seem to have been eternally fixed by nature as the boundary line, and the Arabic language appears to have frozen upon their southern slopes. Though brought later by Saljūq and by Ottoman Turks within the political orbit of Islam, no part of Asia Minor ever became Arabic speaking. Its basic population from earliest antiquity, beginning with Hittite days, has always been non-Semitic, and its climate has proved too rigorous for Arab civilization to strike deep root in its soil.

The long cordon of Moslem fortifications stretching from Malaṭyah (or Malaṭīyah, Melitene) by the upper Euphrates to

[1] P. 347.

[2] P. 159, l. 1 = Hitti, p. 245.

Ṭarsūs near the Mediterranean coast and including Adhanah, al-Maṣṣīṣah (Mopsuestia) and Mar'ash (Germanicia) had its units all strategically situated at the intersections of military roads or at the entrances of narrow mountain passes. These strongholds with their environs were called *'awāṣim*. But *'awāṣim* in the narrower sense meant the inner, the southern, line of fortresses within the military marches in contradistinction to the outer, northern, strip of land called *thughūr*,[1] which shrank under the 'Abbāsids, reaching only from Awlās on the Mediterranean past Ṭarsūs to Sumaysāṭ (Samosata) on the Euphrates.[2] The line guarding Mesopotamia to the north-east was styled *al-thughūr al-Jazarīyah*; that guarding Syria, *al-thughūr al-Sha'mīyah*.[3] Ṭarsūs, which commanded the southern entrance of the celebrated pass across the Taurus known as the Cilician Gates and served as a military base for Arab attacks on the land of the Greeks, was no less than four hundred and fifty miles in a direct line from the Bosporus. The other pass by which the mountain range of the Taurus could be traversed lay to the north-east and was called Darb al-Ḥadath. It led from Mar'ash north to Abulustayn[4] and was less frequented. These Arab marches formed a "no man's land" and their strongholds changed hands again and again as the tide of war ebbed or flowed. Under the Umayyads and 'Abbāsids almost every foot was fought over repeatedly and bitterly; scarcely any land in Asia is more soaked in blood.

As early as A.H. 34 (655), while Mu'āwiyah was still governor of Syria under 'Uthmān, his fleet under Busr ibn-abi-Arṭāh[5] in co-operation with the Egyptian fleet under 'Abdullāh ibn-abi-Sarḥ met the Greek navy led by the Emperor Constans II, son of Heraclius, at Phoenix (modern Finike) on the Lycian coast and scored the first great naval victory of Islam. This maritime engagement is referred to in Arabic chronicles as dhu (or dhāt) -al-Ṣawāri (that of the masts).[6] The Arabs transformed

[1] Cf. Guy Le Strange, *The Lands of the Eastern Caliphate* (Cambridge, 1905), p. 128.

[2] Iṣṭakhri, pp. 67-8.

[3] Balādhuri, pp. 183 *seq*., 163 *seq*.

[4] Yāqūt, vol. i, pp. 93-4; cf. Le Strange, *Eastern Caliphate*, p. 133. The Byzantine name was Ablastha, the Greek Arabissus, late Arabic al-Bustān.

[5] Ibn-'Abd-al-Ḥakam, pp. 189-90; ibn-Ḥajar, vol. i, 153.

[6] Either after the name of the place itself, which is said to have been rich in cypress trees from which masts (*ṣawāri*) could be fashioned, or because of the number of masts of the many ships engaged.

the sea fight into a hand-to-hand encounter by tying each Arab ship to a Byzantine vessel.[1] The battle proved a second Yarmūk; the Byzantine forces were completely destroyed.[2] Al-Ṭabari[3] describes the water of the sea as saturated with blood. The Arabs, however, did not take advantage of the victory and push on to Constantinople, probably because of the murder of 'Uthmān, which occurred about this time, and other concomitant civil disturbances.

Three times was Constantinople attacked by Umayyad forces, the only occasions on which Syro-Arabs ever succeeded in reaching the high triple wall of the mighty capital. The first was in A.H. 49 (669) under the leadership of the crown prince Yazīd, whose warriors were the first ever to set eyes on Byzantium.[4] Yazīd was sent by his father to support the land campaign of Faḍālah ibn-'Ubayd al-Anṣāri, who had wintered (668–9) in Chalcedon (the Asiatic suburb of Byzantium), and as a response to those puritans who might look askance at Yazīd's intended nomination as successor to the reigning caliph. The siege laid by Yazīd and Faḍālah in the spring of 669 was raised in the summer of the same year; Byzantium had a new and energetic emperor, Constantine IV (668–85).

In legend Yazīd distinguished himself for bravery and fortitude below the walls of Constantinople and earned the title *fata al-'Arab* (the young champion or hero of the Arabs). The *Aghāni*[5] relates that alternate shouts of jubilation were heard from two separate tents as the Arabs or the Byzantines made headway in the battle. On learning that one tent was occupied by the daughter of the king of the Rūm and the other by the daughter of Jabalah ibn-al-Ayham, Yazīd was spurred to extraordinary activity in order to seize the Ghassānid king's daughter. But the real legendary hero of the campaign was the aged abu-Ayyūb al-Anṣāri, the standard-bearer of the Prophet, who had harboured Muḥammad in al-Madīnah on the occasion of the Hijrah[6] and whose presence in Yazīd's contingent was desired more for the blessing it might bring. Tradition asserts that in the course of the siege abu-Ayyūb died of dysentery and was buried before the walls of Constantinople. His legendary tomb soon

[1] Ibn-'Abd-al-Ḥakam, p. 190, ll. 18-19.
[2] Theophanes, pp. 332, 345-6.
[3] Vol. i, p. 2868.
[4] Ṭabari, vol. ii, p. 86; cf. p. 27.
[5] Vol. xvi, p. 33.
[6] Balādhuri, p. 5 = Hitti, p. 19.

became a shrine even for the Christian Greeks, who made pilgrimages to it in time of drought to pray for rain.[1] During the siege of Constantinople in 1453 by the Turks, the tomb was miraculously discovered by rays of light—an episode comparable to the discovery of the holy lance at Antioch by the early Crusaders—and a mosque was built on the site. Thus did the Madīnese gentleman become a saint for three nations.

The second attack on Constantinople was made in the so-called seven years' war[2] (54–60/674–80), which was waged mainly between the two fleets before Constantinople. The Arabs had secured a naval base in the Sea of Marmara on the peninsula of Cyzicus,[3] mistaken for "the isle of Arwād"[4] in the Arab chronicles. This served as winter headquarters for the invading army, whence hostilities were resumed every spring. The Arab accounts of these campaigns are badly confused. The use of Greek fire is supposed to have saved the city. This highly combustible compound, which would burn even on water, was invented by a Syrian refugee from Damascus named Callinicus. The Greek accounts dilate on the disastrous effect of this fire on the enemy ships. Agapius of Manbij,[5] who follows Theophanes, emphasizes the habitual use of Greek fire by the Byzantines, who were the first to employ it in warfare.

To this period also belongs the temporary occupation of Rhodes (Rūdis,[6] 672) and Crete (Iqrīṭish, 674). Rhodes was again temporarily occupied in 717–18. On a previous occasion (654) it had been pillaged by the Arabs, and two years later the remains of its once famous colossus were sold for old metal to a dealer who is said to have employed nine hundred camels to carry them away. Later it was again conquered by Arab adventurers from Spain.

On the death of Muʻāwiyah (680) the Arab fleet withdrew from the Bosporus and Aegean waters, but attacks against "the territory of the Romans" were by no means relinquished.

[1] Ibn-Sa'd, vol. iii, pt. 2, p. 50; followed by Ṭabari, vol. iii, p. 2324. Both authorities fix A.H. 52 as the year of his death.

[2] See J. B. Bury, *A History of the Later Roman Empire* (London, 1899), vol. ii, p. 310, n. 4.

[3] Theophanis, pp. 353-4.

[4] Ṭabari, vol. ii, p. 163; Balādhuri, p. 236 = Hitti, p. 376.

[5] "Kitāb al-'Unwān," pt. 2, ed. A. Vasiliev, in *Patrologia Orientalis* (Paris, 1912), vol. viii, p. 492.

[6] Balādhuri, p. 236 = Hitti, p. 375.

We read of almost yearly summer incursions (*ṣā'ifah*), though none assumed importance until the caliphate of Sulaymān (715–17). Sulaymān considered himself the person referred to by the current *ḥadīth* that a caliph bearing a prophet's name was to conquer Constantinople. The second and last great siege of Constantinople was conducted (August 716–September 717 [1]) under his reign by the stubborn Maslamah, the caliph's brother. This remarkable siege, the most threatening of the Arab attacks, is the one best known because of the many descriptions extant. The besiegers were reinforced both by sea and by land and received aid from Egyptian ships. They were provided with naphtha and special siege artillery.[2] The chief of Maslamah's guard, 'Abdullāh al-Baṭṭāl, particularly distinguished himself and won the title of champion of Islam. In the course of a later campaign (740 [3]) he was killed. In later tradition, as Sayyid Ghāzi, al-Baṭṭāl became one of the Turkish national heroes. His grave, at which a Baktāshi *takīyah* (monastery) with a mosque has risen, is still shown near Eski-Shahr (medieval Dorylæum). His was another instance of "an illustrious Moslem for whom Christians have raised a statue in one of their churches".[4]

At last Emperor Leo the Isaurian (717–41), a soldier of humble Syrian origin from Mar'ash who knew Arabic as perfectly as Greek,[5] outwitted Maslamah and saved the capital. In connection with this siege we have the first historical reference to the chain which barred the way of the attacking fleet into the Golden Horn. The famous Greek fire and the attacks of the Bulgars wrought havoc in the ranks of the invaders. Famine, pestilence and the rigours of an unusually severe winter also did their share. But Maslamah persisted. The death of the caliph in Syria did not deter him from pushing the siege. But the order of the new caliph, 'Umar ibn-'Abd-al-'Azīz (717–20), he had to heed. On the way back a tempest finished the work begun by the Byzantines; out of the 1800 vessels, if we are to believe Theophanis,[6] only five were spared to reach port in Syria. The Arab armada was gone. The Syrian founder of the Isaurian dynasty was hailed the saviour of Europe from the Arab Moslems as Heraclius, the Armenian founder of the Heraclean dynasty, had

[1] Ṭabari, vol. ii, p. 1346; cf. Bury, vol. ii, p. 401, n. 2.
[2] *Kitāb al-'Uyūn w-al-Ḥadā'iq*, ed. de Goeje (Leyden, 1871), pt. 3, p. 24.
[3] Ṭabari, vol. ii, p. 1716.
[4] Mas'ūdi, vol. viii, p. 74.
[5] *Kitāb al-'Uyūn*, pt. 3, p. 25.
[6] Pp. 395, 399.

before him been declared the deliverer of Christendom from heathen Persia. Only on one other occasion after this did an Arab host venture to make its appearance within sight of Constantinople, and that when Hārūn, son of the Caliph al-Mahdi, encamped at Scutari (Chrysopolis) in 782 and the Empress Irene hastened to make peace by agreeing to pay tribute. The "city of Constantine" was not again to see a Moslem army beneath its walls until some seven centuries had passed and a new racial element, the Mongoloid Turks, had become the standard-bearers of the religion of Muḥammad.

Though ending in failure, this determined and energetic expedition by Maslamah, like the one preceding it, has left many a legendary souvenir, including tales of the building of a mosque by the caliph's brother in Constantinople,[1] of the erection by him of a fountain[2] and a mosque[3] at Abydos (Abdus) and of his entrance on horseback into St. Sophia. Writing in 985, al-Maqdisi[4] has this to say: "When Maslamah ibn-'Abd-al-Malik invaded the country of the Romans and penetrated into their territory he stipulated that the Byzantine dog should erect by his own palace in the Hippodrome (*maydān*) a special building to be occupied by the [Moslem] notables and noblemen when taken captive".[5]

The Mardaites

One factor in the check of the Arab policy of northward penetration was the activity of the Christian Mardaites (rebels) in the service of the Byzantine cause. A people of undetermined origin leading a semi-independent national life in the fastnesses of al-Lukkām (Amanus), these Jarājimah (less correctly Jurājimah), as they were also styled by the Arabs, furnished irregular troops and proved a thorn in the side of the Arab caliphate in Syria. On the Arab–Byzantine border they formed "a brass wall"[6] in

[1] Ibn-Taghri-Birdi, *al-Nujūm al-Zāhirah fi Mulūk Miṣr w-al-Qāhirah*, ed. W. Popper (Berkeley, 1909–12), vol. ii, pt. 2, p. 40, ll. 12-13, refers to a Fāṭimid *khuṭbah* pronounced in this mosque. See ibn-al-Qalānisi, *Dhayl Ta'rīkh Dimashq*, ed. H. F. Amedroz (Beirūt, 1908), p. 68, ll. 27-8. The mosque survived in tradition in the Mamlūk period.

[2] Ibn-Khurdādhbih, *al-Masālik w-al-Mamālik*, ed. de Goeje (Leyden, 1889), p. 104, l. 1; Mas'ūdi, vol. ii, p. 317, calls the place *Andalus*.

[3] Ibn-al-Faqīh (al-Hamadhāni), *Kitāb al-Buldān*, ed. de Goeje (Leyden, 1885), p. 145, l. 15; Yāqūt, vol. i, p. 374, refers to the town under the name *Andus*, a mistake for Abdus.

[4] P. 147.

[5] This building, al-Balāṭ, is referred to in Yāqūt, vol. i, p. 709, as being in use at the time of Sayf-al-Dawlah al-Ḥamdāni (944–67). For etymology of *balāṭ* see below, p. 501, n. 1.

[6] Theophanes, p. 364.

defence of Asia Minor. About 666 their bands penetrated into the heart of Lebanon and became the nucleus around which many fugitives and malcontents, among whom were the Maronites, grouped themselves. Muʿāwiyah agreed to the payment of a heavy annual tribute to the Byzantine emperor in consideration of his withdrawal of support from this internal enemy, to whom he also agreed to pay a tribute. About 689 Justinian II once more loosed the Mardaite highlanders on Syria, and ʿAbd-al-Malik, following "the precedent of Muʿāwiyah",[1] accepted the new conditions laid down by the emperor and agreed to pay a thousand dinars weekly to the Jarājimah. Finally the majority of the invaders evacuated Syria and settled in the inner provinces or on the coast of Asia Minor, where they became seafarers; others remained and constituted one of the elements that entered into the composition of the Maronite community that still flourishes in the northern Lebanon.

[1] Balādhuri, p. 160, l. 8 = Hitti, p. 247, l. 28.

CHAPTER XIX

THE ZENITH OF UMAYYAD POWER

MARWĀN (683–5), the founder of the Marwānid branch of the Umayyad dynasty, was succeeded by his son ʿAbd-al-Malik (685–705), the "father of kings". Under ʿAbd-al-Malik's rule and that of the four sons who succeeded him[1] the dynasty at Damascus reached the meridian of its power and glory. During the reigns of al-Walīd and Hishām the Islamic empire reached its greatest expansion, stretching from the shores of the Atlantic Ocean and the Pyrenees to the Indus and the confines of China —an extent hardly rivalled in ancient times and surpassed in modern times only by the British and Russian empires. To this glorious period belong the subjugation of Transoxiana, the reconquest and pacification of North Africa and the acquisition of the largest European country ever held by Arabs—Spain.

This era witnessed the nationalizing, or Arabicizing, of the administration, the introduction of the first purely Arab coinage, the development of the postal service and the erection of such monuments as the Dome of the Rock in Jerusalem—the third holiest sanctuary in Islam.

At his accession and during his first decade as caliph ʿAbd-al-Malik was hemmed in by many foes, and like his great predecessor, Muʿāwiyah, whose counterpart he was, had to face enemies on various fronts. Yet when he died at the close of a second decade he passed on to his son al-Walīd a consolidated and pacified empire that included not only the whole world of Islam but also new conquests of his own. Al-Walīd proved a worthy successor of a capable father.

The acquisition of Syria, al-ʿIrāq, Persia and Egypt under ʿUmar and ʿUthmān having brought to an end the first stage in the history of Moslem conquest, the second now begins under ʿAbd-al-Malik and al-Walīd.

[1] Al-Walīd (705–15), Sulaymān (715–17), Yazīd II (720–24) and Hishām (724–743). ʿUmar (717–20), who interrupted the filial succession, was a son of ʿAbd-al-Malik's brother ʿAbd-al-ʿAzīz.

An energetic viceroy: al-Ḥajjāj

The brilliant military achievements of these two reigns centre on the names of al-Ḥajjāj ibn-Yūsuf al-Thaqafi in the east and Mūsa ibn-Nuṣayr in the west.

Al-Ḥajjāj, the young schoolmaster of al-Ṭā'if[1] in al-Ḥijāz who had laid down the pen and taken up the sword in support of the tottering Umayyad throne, was appointed governor of Arabia after having crushed (692) at the age of thirty-one the formidable pretender 'Abdullāh ibn-al-Zubayr, who for nine years had held the title and power of caliph. In two years al-Ḥajjāj pacified al-Ḥijāz and with it al-Yaman and even al-Yamāmah to the east, and was in December 694 summoned by 'Abd-al-Malik to perform a similar task in turbulent and dissatisfied al-'Irāq, whose people were "men of schism and hypocrisy".[2] Here the 'Alids and the Khārijites had continually made trouble for the Umayyads. The unexpected arrival of al-Ḥajjāj at the famous mosque of al-Kūfah, in disguise and accompanied only by twelve cameleers, his brusque mounting of the pulpit and removal of the heavy turban which veiled his face, and his fiery oration, are among the most dramatic and popular episodes recounted in Arabic literature. The proclamation of his policy in unequivocal terms showed the 'Irāqis from the very start that his would be no kid-glove methods of dealing with a disloyal populace. Introducing his oration with a verse quoted from an ancient poet:

> "I am he who scattereth darkness and climbeth lofty summits.
> As I lift the turban from my face ye will know me",

the speaker continued, "O people of al-Kūfah! Certain am I that I see heads ripe for cutting, and verily I am the man to do it. Methinks I see blood between the turbans and the beards. . . ."[3]

In fact no head proved too mighty for the relentless Umayyad viceroy to crush, no neck too high for him to reach. Even Anas ibn-Mālik, the prolific traditionist and highly respected Companion of the Prophet, accused of sympathy with the opposition, had to wear around his neck a collar bearing the viceroy's seal.[4] Human lives to the number of 120,000[5] are said to have been

[1] Ibn-Rustah, p. 216; ibn-Durayd, *Ishtiqāq*, p. 187.
[2] Ya'qūbi, vol. ii, p. 326; Mas'ūdi, vol. v, p. 295.
[3] Mubarrad, *Kāmil*, pp. 215-16; cf. Ya'qūbi, vol. ii, p. 326; Mas'ūdi, vol. v, p. 294.
[4] Ṭabari, vol. ii, pp. 854-5.
[5] Ibn-al-'Ibri, p. 195; cf. Mas'ūdi, vol. v, p. 382; *Tanbīh*, p. 318; Ṭabari, vol. ii, p. 1123.

sacrificed by this governor of al-ʿIrāq, who is represented by the Arab historians, most of whom, it should be noted, were Shīʿites or Sunnites writing during the ʿAbbāsid régime, as a bloodthirsty tyrant, a veritable Nero. In addition to his bloodthirstiness, his gluttony and impiety are favourite themes with the historians.[1]

Justifiable or not, the drastic measures of al-Ḥajjāj did not fail to restore order both among the rebellious Baṣrans and Kūfans and throughout his vast viceroyalty, which included al-ʿIrāq and Persia. His lieutenants, led by al-Muhallab ibn-abi-Ṣufrah, practically exterminated (698 or 699) the Azraqis,[2] the most dangerous to Moslem unity of all the Khārijites, who under the leadership of Qaṭari ibn-al-Fujā'ah had acquired control of Karmān,[3] Fāris and other eastern provinces. On the opposite coast of the Persian Gulf, ʿUmān, which in the days of the Prophet and ʿAmr ibn-al-ʿĀṣ had been nominally brought under Islam, was now fully incorporated with the Umayyad realm. From his newly built capital on the west bank of the Tigris, Wāsiṭ (medial), so called from its half-way position between the two key cities of al-ʿIrāq—al-Baṣrah and al-Kūfah[4]—the Syrian garrison of al-Ḥajjāj held all these territories in submission. His blind faith in his Syrian troops, like his untainted loyalty to the Umayyad cause, knew no bounds.

With his domain pacified and well rounded out, the energetic viceroy now felt free to authorize his lieutenants to penetrate further east. One of them, ʿAbd-al-Raḥmān ibn-Muḥammad ibn-al-Ashʿath, a scion of the ancient royal line of Kindah and governor of Sijistān, who later led a frightful revolt against the authority of al-Ḥajjāj, was sent (699–700) against the Zunbīl (less correctly Rutbīl),[5] Turkish king of Kābul (in modern Afghanistan), who had refused to pay the customary tribute.[6]

[1] Dīnawari, *Akhbār*, pp. 320-22; Masʿūdi, vol. vii, p. 218; Ṭabari, vol. ii, pp. 1122-3; ibn-ʿAsākir, vol. iv, p. 81.

[2] So called from their first leader, Nāfiʿ ibn-al-Azraq, who taught that all followers of other than Khārijite doctrine were without exception infidels and doomed to death with their wives and children; Shahrastāni, pp. 89-90.

[3] Or Kirmān; Yāqūt, vol. iv, p. 263.

[4] Yāqūt, vol. iv, pp. 881-2; cf. Ṭabari, vol. ii, pp. 1125-6. The town is but a mound of ruins.

[5] Wellhausen, *Reich*, p. 144, n. 3. "Zunbīl" was a title. These kings may have been Persian.

[6] Almost all the subjects of this and other kings in Central Asia were Iranian; the dynasties and armies were mostly Turkish.

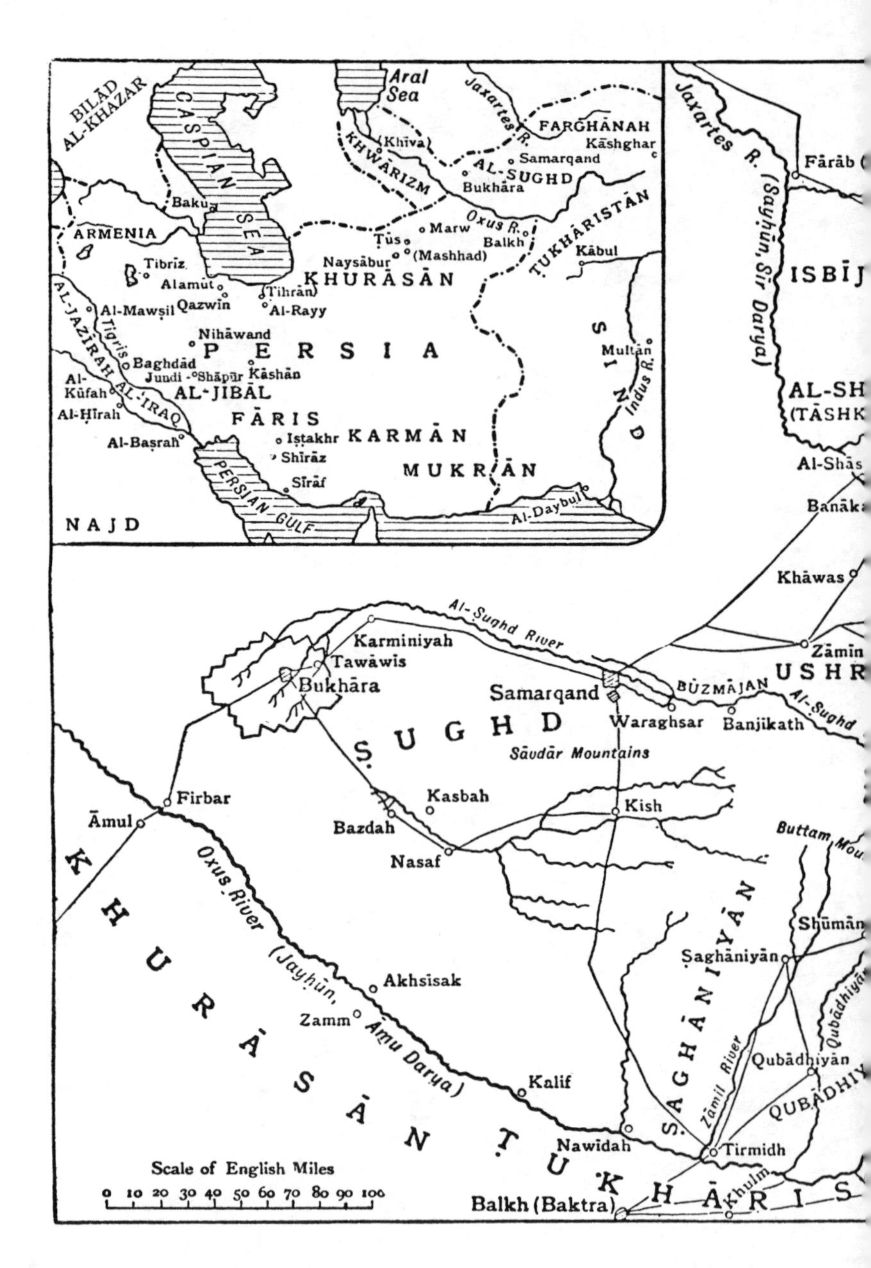

PROVINCES OF

S AND JAXARTES

Between pages 208 *and* 209

'Abd-al-Raḥmān's campaign at the head of such a magnificently equipped army that it was styled "the army of peacocks" [1] was entirely successful, but his exploits paled before those of Qutaybah ibn-Muslim and Muḥammad ibn-al-Qāsim al-Thaqafi, a son-in-law of al-Ḥajjāj. On the recommendation of al-Ḥajjāj, Qutaybah was in 704 appointed governor over Khurāsān with his capital at Marw; according to al-Balādhuri [2] and al-Ṭabari [3] he had under his command in Khurāsān, which he held as a subordinate of al-Ḥajjāj, 40,000 Arab troops from al-Baṣrah, 7000 from al-Kūfah and 7000 clients.

Conquests "beyond the river"

The Oxus,[4] which until now had formed the traditional, though not historical, boundary-line between "Īrān and Tūrān", i.e. between the Persian-speaking and the Turkish-speaking peoples, was now under al-Walīd crossed and a permanent Moslem foothold established beyond it. In a series of brilliant campaigns Qutaybah recovered (705) lower Ṭukhāristān with its capital, Balkh (the Baktra of the Greeks), conquered (706–9) Bukhāra in al-Ṣughd (Sogdiana) and the territory around it and reduced (710–12) Samarqand (also in al-Ṣughd) and Khwārizm (modern Khīwa) to the west. In 713–15 he led an expedition into the Jaxartes provinces, particularly Farghānah, thus establishing nominal Moslem rule in what were until recent times known as the Central Asian khānates. The Jaxartes rather than the Oxus formed the natural political and racial frontier between Iranians and Turks, and its crossing constituted the first direct challenge by Islam to the Mongoloid peoples and the Buddhist religion. Bukhāra, Balkh and Samarqand had Buddhist monasteries. In Samarqand Qutaybah fell upon a number of idols whose devotees expected instant destruction to overtake him who dared outrage them. Undeterred, the Moslem general set fire to the images with his own hand, an act which resulted in a number of conversions to Islam.[5] But no large numbers accepted the new faith until the pious caliphate of 'Umar II (717–20), when they were accorded the concession as Moslems of paying no tribute. Likewise the fire-temple of Bukhāra with its sanctuary was demolished. Thus Bukhāra with Samarqand and the province of Khwārizm were soon to become centres of Arabic

[1] Mas'ūdi, *Tanbīh*, p. 314. [2] P. 423. [3] Vol. ii, pp. 1290-91.

[4] Modern Āmu Darya, Ar. and Pers. Jayḥūn. Jayḥūn for the Oxus and Sayḥūn for its sister river, the Jaxartes (Sīr Darya), are adaptations of Gihon and Pison of Gen. 2 : 13, 11. [5] Balādhuri, p. 421.

culture, nurseries of Islam in Central Asia, corresponding to Marw and Naysābūr (Pers. Nīshāpūr) in Khurāsān. Qutaybah is said by al-Ṭabari[1] and others to have conquered (715) Kāshghar in Chinese Turkestan and even to have reached China proper, but this tradition is evidently an anticipation of the later conquest by Naṣr ibn-Sayyār and his successors.[2] This Naṣr was appointed by the Caliph Hishām (724–43) as the first governor of Transoxiana and had to reconquer, between 738 and 740, most of the territory overrun earlier by Qutaybah. The Arab agents established by Qutaybah were merely military overseers and tax-collectors functioning side by side with the native rulers, who retained the civil administration. An attempt in 737 on al-Khazar, Huns beyond the Caucasus who were later Judaized, failed. In 751 the Arabs occupied al-Shāsh (Tāshkand), thus definitely establishing the supremacy of Islam in Central Asia so firmly that it was not further disputed by Chinese.[3]

Thus was Transoxiana (*ma warā' al-nahr*, what lies beyond the river) at last incorporated with the rising empire of the caliphs. The world of Islam was thereby brought into vital contact with a new racial element and a new culture in itself old—the Mongolian. We shall later deal at length with the significant part played by these fresh recruits to Islam.

Conquests in India

The other column in the eastern theatre of war was in the meantime moving southward under Muḥammad ibn-al-Qāsim. Advancing in 710 at the head of a considerable army, of which 6000 were Syrians, this son-in-law of al-Ḥajjāj subdued Mukrān, pushed on through what is now termed Baluchistan and in 711–12 reduced Sind, the lower valley and delta of the Indus (Sindhu). Among the cities captured here were the seaport al-Daybul, which had a statue of the Buddha (Ar. Budd) "rising to a height of forty cubits",[4] and al-Nīrūn (modern Ḥaydarābād). The conquest was extended (713) as far north as Multān in

[1] Vol. ii, p. 1275.

[2] H. A. R. Gibb in *Bulletin of the School of Oriental Studies, London Institution*, vol. ii (1921), pp. 467-74.

[3] The native rulers of Samarqand, Khwārizm and Shāsh were perhaps related by marriage to the khān, or khāqān, of the Western Turks, though they appear in Arab histories with such Persian titles as *khudāh*, *shāh* and *dihqān*. The ruler of Sogdiana residing at Samarqand, also bore the Persian title *ikhshīd*, as did the king of Farghānah. See ibn-Khurdādhbih, pp. 39-40; Ya'qūbi, vol. ii, p. 479. The Arabs applied the term "Turk" to any non-Persian people north-east of the Oxus

[4] Ya'qūbi, vol. ii, p. 346.

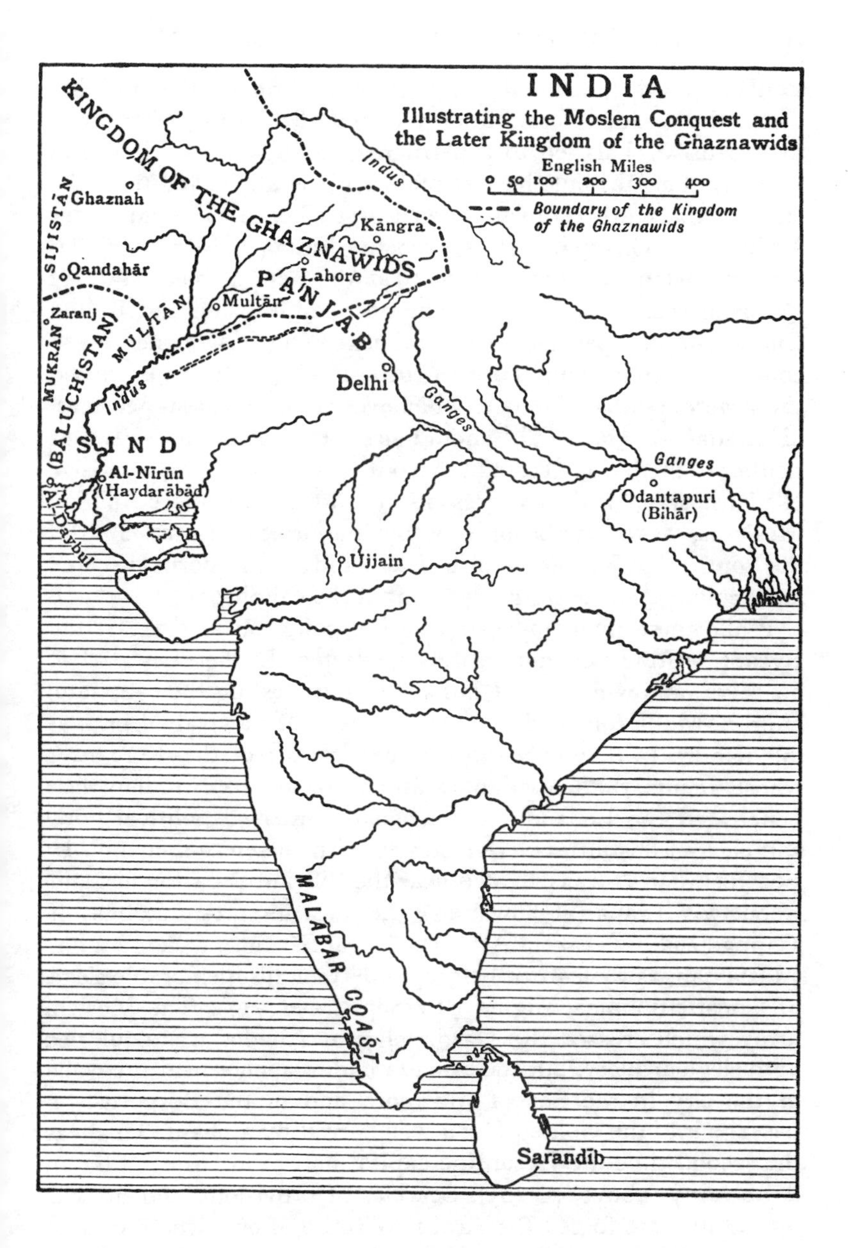
INDIA
Illustrating the Moslem Conquest and the Later Kingdom of the Ghaznawids
English Miles
0 50 100 200 300 400
Boundary of the Kingdom of the Ghaznawids
KINGDOM OF THE GHAZNAWIDS
SIJISTĀN
Ghaznah
Qandahār
Zaranj
MUKRĀN
(BALUCHISTAN)
MULTĀN
Multān
Lahore
Kāngra
PANJAB
Indus
Delhi
Ganges
SIND
Al-Nīrūn
(Ḥaydarābād)
Al-Daybul
Ujjain
Odantapuri
(Bihār)
MALABAR COAST
Sarandīb

southern Panjāb, the seat of a renowned shrine of the Buddha, where the invaders found a large crowd of pilgrims, whom they took captive. This led to a permanent occupation of Sind and southern Panjāb, but the rest of India was unaffected until the close of the tenth century, when a fresh invasion began under Maḥmūd of Ghaznah. Thus were the Indian border provinces for ever Islamized. As late as 1947 the new Moslem state of Pakistan was born. Contact between Semitic Islam and Indian Buddhism was permanently established, just as farther north contact was made with Turkish culture. Al-Ḥajjāj had promised the governorship of China to whichever of his two great generals, al-Thaqafi or Qutaybah, should first set foot on its soil. But neither of them ever crossed the frontier. China proper, exclusive of Turkestan, with its present-day fifteen or more million Moslems, was never brought within the orbit of Islam. Sind in the south, like Kāshghar and Tāshkand in the north, became and remained the easternmost limit of the caliphate.

Against the Byzantines

While these major operations were going on in the east the Byzantine front was not entirely neglected. In the early part of his reign, and while ibn-al-Zubayr was contesting the caliphate, 'Abd-al-Malik followed "the precedent of Mu'āwiyah"[1] in paying tribute (A.H. 70/689–90) to the "tyrant of the Romans", whose agents, the Christian Jarājimah of al-Lukkām, had then penetrated the Lebanon. But when the internal political horizon cleared hostilities were resumed with the eternal enemy. In 692 Justinian II was defeated near the Cilician Sebastopolis, and about 707 Tyana (al-Ṭuwānah), the most important fortress of Cappadocia, was taken. After capturing Sardis and Pergamum, Maslamah, as we learned before, undertook his memorable siege of Constantinople (August 716–September 717). The Moslem army which crossed the Dardanelles at Abydos was equipped with siege artillery, but the armada had to anchor near the walls of the city in the Sea of Marmora and in the Bosporus, as passage into the Golden Horn was barred by a chain. This was the second time the Byzantine capital had been besieged by an Arab army (above, p. 203). Scarcity of provisions and attacks by the Bulgars forced the Arabs to retire after a whole year of beleaguering.[2] Armenia, which had been conquered for Mu'āwi-

[1] See above, p. 205. Balādhuri, p. 160.

[2] Consult Theophanes, pp. 386-99; Ṭabari, vol ii, pp 1314-17; ibn-al-Athīr, vol. v, pp. 17-19.

yah by Ḥabīb ibn-Maslamah al-Fihri as early as 644–5, had later taken advantage of the ibn-al-Zubayr debacle to revolt, but was now again reduced.[1]

Conquests in northern Africa and southwestern Europe

The conquests on the western front under Mūsa ibn-Nuṣayr and his lieutenants were no less brilliant and spectacular than those on the east by al-Ḥajjāj and his generals. Soon after the subjugation of Egypt (640-43) raids were carried westward into Ifrīqiyah,[2] but a thorough conquest of that territory was not undertaken until the foundation of al-Qayrawān[3] in 670 by ʿUqbah ibn-Nāfiʿ, an agent of Muʿāwiyah, who used it as a base for operations against the Berber tribes. ʿUqbah, who is said by tradition to have advanced until the waves of the Atlantic stopped his horse, suffered a martyr's death (683) near Biskra in modern Algeria, where his tomb has become a national shrine. Even then the Arab hold on Ifrīqiyah was so precarious that soon after ʿUqbah's death his successor had to evacuate the territory. Not until the governorship of Ḥassān ibn-al-Nuʿmān al-Ghassāni (*ca.* 693–700) was an end put to Byzantine authority and Berber resistance. With the co-operation of a Moslem fleet, Ḥassān drove the Byzantines from Carthage (698) and other coast towns. He was then free to take the field against the Berbers, now led by a prophetess (Ar. *kāhinah*)[4] who exercised a mysterious influence over her followers. The heroine was at last defeated by treachery and killed near a well that still bears her name, Bīr al-Kāhinah.

Ḥassān, the reconqueror and pacifier of Ifrīqiyah, was followed by the famous Mūsa ibn-Nuṣayr, under whom the government of the region, administered from al-Qayrawān, was made independent of Egypt and held directly from the caliph in Damascus. Mūsa, whose father (together with the grandfather of ibn-Isḥāq, the Prophet's biographer) was one of the Christian captives who fell into the hands of Khālid ibn-al-Walīd while they were studying the Gospels in the church at ʿAyn al-Tamr,[5] extended

[1] Balādhuri, pp. 205 *seq.* = Hitti, pp. 322 *seq.*

[2] More exact than "Ifrīqīyah"; name borrowed by Arabs from Romans and given to the eastern part of Barbary, the word Maghrib being reserved for the western part. Today the term Ifrīqiyah includes the whole continent of Africa.

[3] From Pers. *kārwān*, whence Eng. caravan.

[4] Balādhuri, p. 229; ibn-Khaldūn, vol. vii, pp. 8-9; ibn-ʿIdhāri, *al-Bayān al-Mughrib fi Akhbār al-Maghrib*, ed. R. Dozy (Leyden, 1848), vol. i, pp. 20-24. That she belonged to a Jewish tribe is doubtful.

[5] Others claim he was a Lakhmid or Yamanite. Cf. Balādhuri, p. 230; ibn-ʿIdhāri, vol. i, p. 24.

the boundaries of his province as far as Tangier. This brought Islam definitely and permanently into contact with another racial group, the Berbers. The latter belonged to the Hamitic branch of the white family, and in prehistoric times probably formed one stock with the Semites.[1] At the time of the Moslem conquest most of the Berbers on the strip of fertile land bordering on the sea had become Christians. In this region Tertullian, St. Cyprian and above all St. Augustine became princes among early Christian fathers. Otherwise the population was not deeply touched by Roman civilization, for the Romans and Byzantines lived mainly in towns on the coast and represented a culture that was quite alien to the mentality of these nomadic and semi-nomadic North Africans. On the other hand Islam had a special attraction for people in such a cultural stage as that of the Berbers; moreover, the Semitic Arabs, akin to the early Phoenicians who had colonized parts of northern Africa and developed in Carthage a formidable rival to Rome, readily established intimate relations with their Hamitic cousins. Punic survived in country places until shortly before the Moslem conquest. This explains the seemingly inexplicable miracle of Islam in Arabicizing the language and Islamizing the religion of these semi-barbarous hordes and using them as fresh relays in the race toward further conquests. Thus did the blood of the conquerors find fresh ethnic strains for its enrichment, the Arabic tongue a vast field for conquest and rising Islam a new foothold in its climb toward world supremacy.

After the subjugation of the North African coast as far as the Atlantic by Mūsa,[2] the way was open for the conquest of the neighbouring south-western part of Europe. In 711 Ṭāriq, a Berber freedman and lieutenant of Mūsa, took the momentous step of crossing into Spain on a marauding expedition. The raid developed into a conquest of the Iberian Peninsula (al-Andalus) (below, pp. 493 *seq.*). This constituted the last and most sensational of the major campaigns of the Arabs and resulted in the addition to the Moslem world of the largest European territory ever held by them. After the capture of several towns in southern Gaul the advance of the Arab-Berber army was checked in 732 between

[1] Eng. "Berber", generally considered as coming ultimately from Ar. *Barbar*, may have come, together with the Arabic form, from L. *barbari* (originally Gr.), barbarians, applied in current usage by the Latinized cities of Roman Africa to all natives who did not adopt the Latin tongue.

[2] Ibn-'Abd-al-Ḥakam, pp. 203-5.

Tours and Poitiers by Charles Martel. This point marks the north-western limit of Arab penetration.

The year 732 marked the first centennial of the Prophet's death. From this vantage point in history and geography let us pause to view the general situation. One hundred years after the death of the founder of Islam his followers were the masters of an empire greater than that of Rome at its zenith, an empire extending from the Bay of Biscay to the Indus and the confines of China and from the Aral Sea to the lower cataracts of the Nile, and the name of the prophet-son of Arabia, joined with the name of almighty Allah, was being called five times a day from thousands of minarets scattered over south-western Europe, northern Africa and western and central Asia. Damascus, which young Muḥammad according to tradition hesitated to enter because he wished to enter paradise only once, had become the capital of this huge empire.[1] In the heart of the city, set like a pearl in the emerald girdle of its gardens, stood the glittering palace of the Umayyads, commanding a view of flourishing plain which extended south-westward to Mount Hermon[2] with its turban of perpetual snow. Al-Khaḍrā'[3] (the green one) was its name. Its builder was none other than Muʿāwiyah, founder of the dynasty, and it stood beside the Umayyad Mosque which al-Walīd had newly adorned and made into that jewel of architecture which still attracts lovers of beauty. In the audience chamber a square seat covered with richly embroidered cushions formed the caliphal throne, on which during formal audiences the caliph, in gorgeous flowing robes, sat cross-legged. On the right stood his paternal relatives in a row according to seniority, on the left his maternal relatives.[4] Courtiers, poets and petitioners stood behind. The more formal audiences were held in the glorious Umayyad Mosque, even today one of the most magnificent places of worship in the world. In some such setting must al-Walīd (others say Sulaymān, who had just ascended the throne) have received Mūsa ibn-Nuṣayr and Ṭāriq, the conquerors of Spain, with their vast train of prisoners[5] including members of

[1] For other traditions extolling Damascus see ibn-ʿAsākir, vol. i, pp. 46 *seq.*

[2] *Al-Jabal al-Shaykh*, the greyheaded mountain.

[3] Ibn-Jubayr, p. 269, l. 3; "al-Qubbah al-Khaḍrā", the green dome, in *Aghāni* vol. vi, p. 159.

[4] *Aghāni*, vol. iv, p. 80.

[5] 30,000 according to al-Maqqari, *Nafḥ al-Ṭīb min Ghuṣn al-Andalus al-Raṭīb*, ed. Dozy, Wright *et al.* (Leyden, 1855), vol. i, p. 144; cf. ibn-al-Athīr, vol. iv, p. 448.

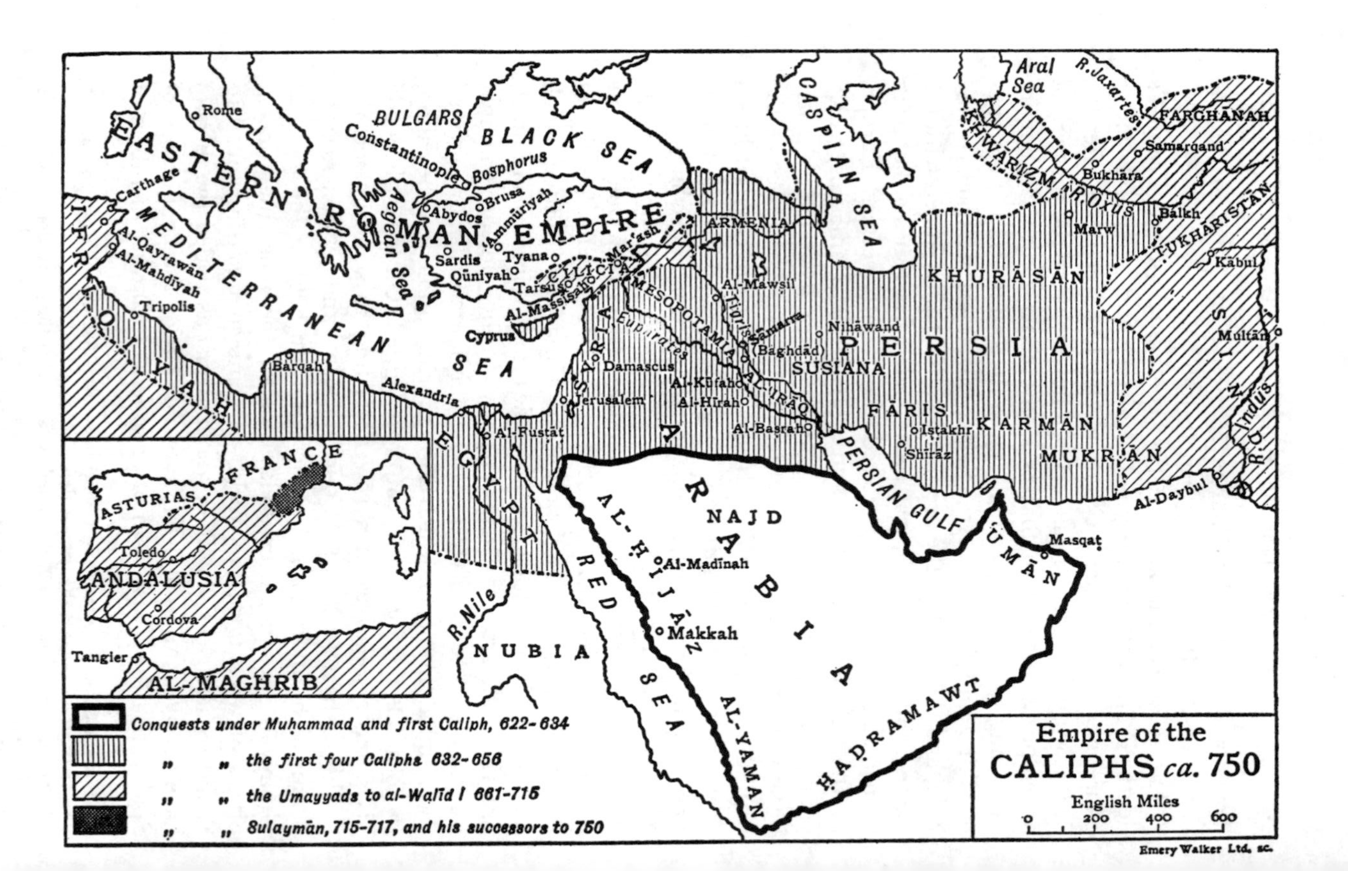
Empire of the
CALIPHS ca. 750
English Miles
0 200 400 600
Conquests under Muḥammad and first Caliph, 622-634
" " the first four Caliphs 632-656
" " the Umayyads to al-Walīd I 661-715
" " Sulaymān, 715-717, and his successors to 750
EASTERN ROMAN EMPIRE
BULGARS
Constantinople
Bosphorus
BLACK SEA
Rome
Carthage
Al-Qayrawān
Al-Mahdīyah
Tripolis
IFRIQIYAH
Barqah
MEDITERRANEAN SEA
Aegean Sea
Abydos
Brusa
Ammūriyah
Sardis
Tyana
Qūniyah
Tarsus
CILICIA
Mar'ash
Al-Maṣṣīṣah
Cyprus
Alexandria
Al-Fusṭāṭ
EGYPT
R. Nile
NUBIA
SYRIA
Damascus
Jerusalem
Euphrates
MESOPOTAMIA
ARMENIA
Al-Mawṣil
Tigris
Sāmarrā
(Baghdād)
Al-Kūfah
Al-Ḥīrah
AL-'IRĀQ
Al-Baṣrah
SUSIANA
Nihāwand
PERSIA
FĀRIS
Iṣṭakhr
Shīrāz
KARMĀN
MUKRĀN
KHURĀSĀN
CASPIAN SEA
Aral Sea
R. Jaxartes
FARGHĀNAH
Samarqand
Bukhāra
KHWĀRIZM
R. Oxus
Marw
Balkh
TUKHĀRISTĀN
Kābul
Multān
SIND
R. Indus
Al-Daybul
PERSIAN GULF
'UMĀN
Masqaṭ
ARABIA
NAJD
AL-ḤIJĀZ
Al-Madīnah
Makkah
RED SEA
AL-YAMAN
ḤAḌRAMAWT
FRANCE
ASTURIAS
Toledo
ANDALUSIA
Cordova
Tangier
AL-MAGHRIB
Emery Walker Ltd. sc.

the fair-haired Gothic royalty and undreamt-of treasures. If any single episode can exemplify the zenith of Umayyad glory it is this.

Nationalizing the state

The Arabicization of the state under ʿAbd-al-Malik and al-Walīd consisted in changing the language of the public registers (*dīwān*) from Greek to Arabic in Damascus and from Pahlawi to Arabic in al-ʿIrāq and the eastern provinces and in the creation of an Arabic coinage. With the change of language a change in personnel naturally took place. The early conquerors, fresh from the desert and ignorant of book-keeping and finance, had to retain in the exchequer the Greek-writing officials in Syria and the Persian-writing officials in al-ʿIrāq and Persia who were familiar with the work. But now the situation had changed. Undoubtedly certain non-Arab officials who by this time had mastered the Arabic language were retained, as was the old system itself. The transition must have been slow, beginning under ʿAbd-al-Malik and continuing during the reign of his successor. This is probably the reason why some authorities ascribe the change to the father and others to the son.[1] The step was part of a well-planned policy and not due to any such trivial cause as that put forth by al-Balādhuri—the urination of a Greek clerk in an inkwell.[2] In al-ʿIrāq and its eastern dependencies it was evidently the famous al-Ḥajjāj who initiated the change.

In pre-Islamic days Roman and Persian money was current in al-Ḥijāz, together with a few Ḥimyarite silver coins bearing the Attic owl. ʿUmar, Muʿāwiyah and the other early caliphs contented themselves with this foreign coinage already in circulation[3] and perhaps in some cases stamped on it certain koranic superscriptions. A number of gold and silver pieces were struck before the time of ʿAbd-al-Malik, but those were imitations of Byzantine and Persian types. ʿAbd-al-Malik struck at Damascus, in 695, the first gold dinars and silver dirhams which were purely Arabic.[4] His viceroy in al-ʿIrāq, al-Ḥajjāj, minted silver in al-Kūfah in the following year.[5]

Besides instituting a purely Islamic coinage and Arabicizing the administration of the empire, ʿAbd-al-Malik developed a

[1] Balādhuri, pp. 193, 300-301; Māwardi, pp. 349-50; *ʿIqd*, vol. ii, p. 322.

[2] P. 193 = Hitti, p. 301.

[3] Balādhuri, pp. 465-6.

[4] Ṭabari, vol. ii, p. 939; Balādhuri, p. 240.

[5] Cf. Yāqūt, *Buldān*, vol. iv, p. 886.

regular postal service,[1] using relays of horses for the conveyance of travellers and dispatches between Damascus and the provincial capitals. The service was designed primarily to meet the needs of government officials and their correspondence, and the postmasters were charged among other duties with the task of keeping the caliph posted on all important happenings in their respective territories.

From "Katalog der orientalischen Münzen, Königliche Museen zu Berlin" (Walter de Gruyter & Co., Berlin)

AN IMITATION IN GOLD OF A BYZANTINE COIN WITH ARABIC INSCRIPTION

Retaining on the obverse the figures of Heraclius, Heraclius Constantine, and Heracleonas, and on the reverse a modified Byzantine cross. No mint name is given.

Fiscal and other reforms

In connection with the monetary changes it may be well to note the fiscal and administrative reforms that took place at this time. In principle no Moslem, whatever his nationality might be, was under obligation to pay any tax other than the zakāh or poor rate, though in practice the privilege was often limited to Arabian Moslems. Taking advantage of this theory many new converts to Islam, particularly from al-'Irāq and Khurāsān, now began to leave the villages where they had worked as agriculturists and flock to the cities, hoping thereby to join the army as *mawāli* (clients).[2] This constituted a double loss to the treasury, for at conversion their taxes were greatly reduced and upon becoming soldiers they were entitled to a special subsidy. Al-Ḥajjāj took the necessary measures to restore such men to their farms[3] and reimposed on them the high tribute they had paid before conversion,

From "Katalog der orientalischen Münzen in Berliner Museen" (Walter de Gruyter & Co., Berlin)

COPPER COIN OF 'ABD-AL-MALIK

Bearing on the obverse his image and his name and on the reverse ȸ on four steps together with the *shahādah* and the mint name, Ba'labakk. An imitation of a Byzantine coin.

[1] Al-'Umari, *al-Ta'rīf bi-al-Muṣṭalaḥ al-Sharīf* (Cairo, 1312), p. 185.
[2] This word, used later for freedmen, had at this time no connotation of inferiority.
[3] Mubarrad, p. 286.

which included the equivalent of kharāj (land tax) and jizyah (poll tax). He even made Arabs who acquired property in a kharāj territory pay the usual land tax.

The Caliph 'Umar II (717–20) tried to remedy the resultant dissatisfaction among the Neo-Moslems by re-establishing the old principle of his earlier namesake that a Moslem, whether Arab or *mawla*, need pay no tribute whatsoever, but he insisted that the kharāj land was the joint property of the Moslem community.[1] He thus prohibited after the year A.H. 100 (718–19) the sale of kharāj lands to Arabs and Moslems and declared that if the owner of such land be converted his property should revert to the village community and he might continue to use it as a leaseholder.

Though inspired by the best of intentions, 'Umar's policy was not successful. It diminished the revenues of the state and increased the number of clients in the cities.[2] Many Berbers and Persians embraced Islam to enjoy the pecuniary privileges thus accorded them. Later practice reverted to the system of al-Ḥajjāj, with minor modifications. It was not until then that the distinction was drawn between jizyah, a burden which "falls off with the acceptance of Islam", and kharāj, which does not. Since the jizyah was a comparatively small item, the treasury continued to receive its main income from the kharāj and did not in the long run appreciably suffer.

Other cultural and agricultural reforms are attributed to the versatility and energy of al-Ḥajjāj. He dug a number of new canals and restored the large one between the Tigris and the Euphrates. He drained and tilled submerged or uncultivated lands. He contributed to the development of diacritical marks in Arabic orthography to distinguish such similarly written letters as *bā'*, *tā'* and *thā'*, *dāl* and *dhāl*, and to the adaptation from Syriac of vowel signs, *ḍammah* (*u*), *fatḥah* (*a*) and *kasrah* (*i*), inserted above and below the consonants.[3] In this orthographic reform he was prompted by the desire to prevent errors in the

[1] Ibn-Sa'd, vol. v, pp. 262, 277; ibn-'Asākir, vol. iv, p. 80; Ya'qūbi, vol. ii, p. 362; ibn-al-Jawzi, *Sīrat 'Umar ibn-'Abd-al-'Azīz* (Cairo, 1331), pp. 88-9.

[2] Ibn-al-Jawzi, pp. 99-100.

[3] Ibn-Khallikān, *Wafayāt al-A'yān* (Cairo, 1299), vol. i, pp. 220 21 = de Slane, *Ibn Khallikān's Biographical Dictionary* (Paris, 1843), vol. i, pp. 359-60; cf. Suyūṭi, *Itqān*, vol. ii, p. 171; Theodor Nöldeke, *Geschichte des Qorâns* (Göttingen, 1860), pp. 305-9; cf. G. C. Miles, *Journal, Near East Studies*, vol. viii (1948), pp. 236-42.

recitation of the sacred text, of which he evidently prepared a critical revision. He who started life as a schoolmaster never lost interest in literature and oratory. His patronage of poetry and science was notable. The Bedouin satirist Jarīr, who with his rivals al-Farazdaq and al-Akhṭal formed the poetical triumvirate of the Umayyad period, was his panegyrist as well as poet laureate of the Caliph 'Umar. His physician was a Christian named Tayādhūq.[1] The "slave of Thaqīf", as he was dubbed by his 'Irāqi enemies, died in Wāsiṭ, June 714, at the age of fifty-three, leaving a name that is undoubtedly one of the greatest in the annals of Islam.

Architectural monuments

Among the outstanding achievements of the period were the many architectural monuments, some of which have survived to the present day.

In Palestine the Caliph Sulaymān built on the ruins of a more ancient town the city of al-Ramlah,[2] which he made his residence. Traces of his palace could be seen there until the time of the first World War, and the minaret of his White Mosque (which after the Umayyad Mosque of Damascus and the Dome of the Rock in Jerusalem became the third leading sanctuary of Syria) as rebuilt by the Mamlūks in the early part of the fourteenth century is still standing. With Sulaymān the imperial capital ceased to be the home of the caliphs. Hishām resided in al-Ruṣāfah, a Roman settlement near al-Raqqah.[3] In 691 'Abd-al-Malik erected in Jerusalem the magnificent Dome of the Rock (Qubbat al-Ṣakhrah), wrongly styled by Europeans "the Mosque of 'Umar", in order to divert thither the pilgrimage from Makkah which was held by his rival ibn-al-Zubayr. That 'Abd-al-Malik was the builder is attested by the Kufic inscription still preserved round the dome. Over a century later the structure underwent restoration by the 'Abbāsid Caliph al-Ma'mūn (813–33), who unscrupulously substituted his own name for that of 'Abd-al-Malik but inadvertently forgot to change the date.[4] The 'Abbāsid architect set close together the letters of the new name, crowding them into the narrow space originally occupied by the name of

[1] Or Tiyādhūq, Gr. Theodocus. Ibn-al-'Ibri, p. 194.

[2] Balādhuri, p. 143 = Hitti, p. 220.

[3] Identified by others with al-Ḥayr al-Sharqi, east of Palmyra.

[4] The inscription in its present form runs as follows: HATH BUILT THIS DOME THE SERVANT OF GOD 'ABD[ULLAH AL-IMĀM AL-MA'MŪN CO]MMANDER OF THE BELIEVERS IN THE YEAR TWO AND SEVENTY.—MAY GOD ACCEPT OF HIM AND FAVOUR HIM! AMEN.

'Abd-al-Malik.[1] Close by the Dome and in the southern section of the sacred area 'Abd-al-Malik erected another mosque, possibly on the site of an earlier church. Local usage designates this mosque al-Masjid al-Aqṣa (the farther mosque[2]), but the term is also used in a more general sense to include the whole collection of sacred buildings on that area. Al-Ḥaram al-Sharīf (the noble sanctuary) is another name for this group, only less sacred than the two Ḥarams of Makkah and al-Madīnah.

The greatest Umayyad builder, however, was al-Walīd, son of 'Abd-al-Malik, whose rule was one of comparative peace and opulence. So great was this caliph's penchant for building that during his reign whenever people in Damascus met together fine buildings formed the chief topic of conversation, as cookery and the fair sex did under Sulaymān, and religion and the Koran under 'Umar ibn-'Abd-al-'Azīz.[3] This al-Walīd, who lived only forty years, enlarged and beautified the great mosque of Makkah,[4] rebuilt that of al-Madīnah, erected in Syria a number of schools and places of worship and endowed institutions for the lepers, the lame and the blind.[5] He was perhaps the first ruler in medieval times to build hospitals for persons with chronic diseases, and the many lazar houses which later grew up in the West followed the Moslem precedent.[6] From a church in Ba'labakk al-Walīd removed a dome of gilded brass which he set over the dome of his father's mosque in Jerusalem. But his greatest accomplishment was the conversion in Damascus of the site of the Cathedral of St. John the Baptist, which he seized from his Christian subjects, into one of the sublimest places of worship in the world. This Umayyad Mosque is still considered the fourth holiest sanctuary of Islam, after the three Ḥarams of Makkah, al-Madīnah and Jerusalem. Before al-Walīd the Moslems shared a part of the sacred enclosure with its Christian owners. To justify the seizure later tradition claimed that the eastern half of the city was captured by force and the western by capitulation and that the two Moslem contingents, each

[1] De Vogüé, *Le temple de Jérusalem* (Paris, 1864), pp. 85-6, was the first to discover the falsification.

[2] From a reference to the site in Koran 17 : 1. Al-Burāq made a stop there. *Fakhri*, p. 173, makes al-Walīd the builder of al-Aqṣa.

[3] *Fakhri*, p. 173; Ṭabari, vol. ii, pp. 1272-3.

[4] Balādhuri, p. 47 = Hitti, p. 76.

[5] Ṭabari, vol. ii, p. 1271; ibn-al-Faqīh, pp. 106-7.

[6] Consult Hitti, art. "Chivalry: Arabic", *Encyclopædia of the Social Sciences*.

without knowing what the other had done, met in the metropolitan cathedral. The cathedral stood on the site of an earlier Roman temple almost in the centre of the town. Over the lintel of the southern portal of the enclosure, long since walled up, an ancient inscription in Greek can still be read: "Thy kingdom, O Christ, is an everlasting kingdom, and Thy dominion endureth throughout all generations".[1]

Of the remaining caliphs in this period of Umayyad glory there is little to be said save of 'Umar II (717–20) and Hishām. 'Umar was entirely under the influence of the theologians and has enjoyed through the ages a reputation for piety and asceticism that stands in glaring contrast with the alleged impiety of the Umayyad régime. He was, in fact, the Umayyad saint. To the later tradition, which expected a *mab'ūth* (one sent) to appear every hundred years to renovate Islam, he became the one sent "at the head" of the second century (A.H. 100), just as al-Shāfi'i stood "at the head" of the third. His biographer[2] tells us that 'Umar wore clothes with so many patches and mingled with his subjects on such free terms that when a stranger came to petition him he would find it difficult to recognize the caliph. When one of his agents wrote that his fiscal reforms in favour of new converts would deplete the treasury 'Umar replied, "Glad would I be, by Allah, to see everybody become Moslem, so that thou and I would have to till the soil with our own hands to earn a living."[3] 'Umar discontinued the practice established in the time of Mu'āwiyah of cursing 'Ali from the pulpit at the Friday prayers.[4] The piety of 'Umar, who died at the age of thirty-nine, saved his grave from the desecration which was visited by the 'Abbāsids upon the other tombs of the preceding dynasty.

With Hishām (724–43), the fourth son of 'Abd-al-Malik, the Umayyad golden age came to a close. After Mu'āwiyah and 'Abd-al-Malik, Hishām was rightly considered by Arab authorities the third and last statesman of the house of Umayyah.[5] When his young son Mu'āwiyah, ancestor of the Spanish Umayyads, fell from his horse while hunting and was killed, the

[1] Cf. Ps. 145 : 13; Heb. 1 : 8.

[2] Ibn-al-Jawzi, pp. 173-4, 145 *seq.*

[3] *Ibid.* pp. 99-100. *Kitāb al-'Uyūn w-al-Ḥadā'iq fi Akhbār al-Ḥaqā'iq*, ed. de Goeje (Leyden, 1865), p. 4.

[4] *Fakhri*, p. 176.

[5] Mas'ūdi, vol. v, p. 479; cf. Ya'qūbi, vol. ii, p. 393; ibn-Qutaybah, *Ma'ārif*, p. 185; abu-al-Fidā', vol. i, p. 216; *Kitāb al-'Uyūn*, p. 69.

father's comment was, "I brought him up for the caliphate and he pursues a fox!" [1] His governor of al-'Irāq, Khālid ibn-'Abdullāh al-Qasri, under whom the region prospered especially through the engineering and drainage works of Ḥassān al-Nabaṭi, appropriated for himself a surplus of 13,000,000 dirhams after squandering revenue to nearly three times that sum.[2] Subsequently Khālid met the same fate that befell others like him—he was apprehended in 738, jailed, tortured and required to give an account of the state moneys and make repayments. His case is only one illustration of that maladministration and corruption in the body politic which helped to undermine the Umayyad throne and render its occupants an easy prey for their 'Abbāsid rivals.

[1] Ṭabari, vol. ii, pp. 1738-9.
[2] Ṭabari, vol. ii, p. 1642; Ya'qūbi, vol. ii, p. 387.

By courtesy of E. T. Newell
From "Numismatic Notes and Monographs," No. 87 (*New York*, 1939).

A BYZANTINE WEIGHT VALIDATED BY AL-WALĪD (†715)

Bearing on the obverse a cross with the inscription ΓΒ, i.e. two ounces, and on the reverse a Kufic inscription stating that the caliph has recognized this as equivalent to two *wuqīyahs*. Probably the earliest inscribed Moslem weight thus far found.

CHAPTER XX

POLITICAL ADMINISTRATION AND SOCIAL CONDITIONS UNDER THE UMAYYADS

THE administrative divisions of the empire in Umayyad and even 'Abbāsid times corresponded in general to the provinces of the preceding Byzantine and Persian empires. They comprised: (1) Syria-Palestine; (2) al-Kūfah, including al-'Irāq; (3) al-Baṣrah with Persia, Sijistān, Khurāsān, al-Baḥrayn, 'Umān and probably Najd and al-Yamāmah; (4) Armenia; (5) al-Ḥijāz; (6) Karmān and the frontier districts of India; (7) Egypt; (8) Ifrīqiyah; (9) al-Yaman and the rest of South Arabia.[1] Gradually combinations were made and five viceroyalties resulted. Mu'āwiyah combined al-Baṣrah and al-Kūfah into one viceroyalty,[2] that of al-'Irāq, which included most of Persia and eastern Arabia and had al-Kūfah for its capital. Later the viceroy of al-'Irāq was to have a deputy governor for Khurāsān and Transoxiana, usually residing at Marw, and another for Sind and Panjāb. Likewise al-Ḥijāz, al-Yaman and Central Arabia were combined into another viceroyalty. Al-Jazīrah (the northern part of the land between the Tigris and Euphrates) with Armenia, Ādharbayjān and parts of eastern Asia Minor formed the third. Lower and Upper Egypt constituted the fourth. Ifrīqiyah, which embraced northern Africa west of Egypt, Spain, Sicily and other adjacent islands formed the fifth viceroyalty with al-Qayrawān as its seat of government.

The threefold governmental function of political administration, tax collection and religious leadership was now directed as a rule by three different officials. The viceroy (*amīr*, *ṣāḥib*) would appoint his own *'āmil* (agent, prefect) over any particular district and simply forward the name to the caliph. Under Hishām (724–43) we find the newly appointed governor of Armenia and

[1] Cf. ibn-Khaldūn, vol. iii, pp. 4, 10, 15, 17, 134-41; Alfred von Kremer, *Culturgeschichte des Orients unter den Chalifen*, vol. i (Vienna, 1875), pp. 162-3.

[2] Ya'qūbi, vol ii, p. 272.

Ādharbayjān remaining in Damascus and sending a *nā'ib* (accredited deputy) in his stead. The viceroy had full charge of political and military administration in his province, but quite often the revenues were under a special officer, *ṣāḥib al-kharāj*, responsible directly to the caliph. Mu'āwiyah was apparently the first to appoint such an officer, whom he sent to al-Kūfah.[1] Previously the government of a province in the Moslem empire had meant chiefly its financial administration.

The revenue of the state was derived from the same sources as under the orthodox caliphate, chief among which was tribute from subject peoples. In the provinces all expenses of local administration, state annuities, soldiers' stipends and miscellaneous services were met from the local income, and only the balance went to the caliphal treasury. Mu'āwiyah's measure of deducting the zakāh, about 2½ per cent., from the fixed annuities of the Moslems,[2] bears a close resemblance to the income tax of a modern state.

The judiciary had to do with Moslems only, all non-Moslems being allowed autonomy under their own religious heads. This explains why there were judges only in large cities. The Prophet and the early caliphs administered justice in person, as did their generals and prefects in the provinces, for the various functions of government were as yet undifferentiated. The first purely judicial officials in the provinces received their appointment from the governors. Under the 'Abbāsids appointment by the caliphs became more common. Tradition, however, credits 'Umar with having appointed a judge (*qāḍi*) over Egypt as early as A.H. 23 (643).[3] After 661 we find in that country a regular series of judges succeeding one another. They were always recruited from the *faqīh* class, whose members were scholars learned in the Koran and Moslem tradition. Besides deciding cases they administered pious foundations (*waqf*) and the estates of orphans and imbeciles.

Discovering that some of his signed correspondence was being forged, Mu'āwiyah created a bureau of registry,[4] a kind of state chancery, whose duty it was to make and preserve one copy of

[1] Ibn-Khaldūn, vol. iii, p. 4, l. 24. [2] Ya'qūbi, vol. ii, p. 276, l. 10.

[3] Al-Kindi, *Kitāb al-Wulāh*, ed. R. Guest (Beirūt, 1908), pp. 300-301. See also ibn-Qutaybah, *'Uyūn al-Akhbār*, vol. i, p. 61.

[4] *Dīwān al-khātim*, "bureau of the signet". Ṭabari, vol. ii, pp. 205-6; *Fakhri*, p. 149.

each official document before sealing and dispatching the original. By the time of 'Abd-al-Malik the Umayyads had developed a state archive in Damascus.[1]

Military organization

The Umayyad army was modelled in its general organization after that of the Byzantines. The division was into five corps: centre, two wings, vanguard and rearguard. The formation as of old was in lines. This general plan continued until the time of the last caliph, Marwān II (744–50), who abandoned the old division and introduced the small compact body of troops called *kurdūs* (cohort).[2] In outfit and armour the Arab warrior was hard to distinguish from the Greek. The weapons were essentially the same. The cavalry used plain and rounded saddles not unlike those of the Byzantines and precisely like the ones still in fashion in the Near East. The heavy artillery was represented by the ballista (*'arrādah*), the mangonel (*manjanīq*) and the battering-ram (*dabbābah*, *kabsh*). Such heavy engines and siege machines together with the baggage were carried on camels behind the army.

The forces kept at Damascus were chiefly Syrians and Syrianized Arabians. Al-Baṣrah and al-Kūfah were the main recruiting grounds for the army of all the eastern provinces. Under the Sufyānids the standing army numbered 60,000, entailing a yearly expenditure of 60,000,000 dirhams, including family stipends.[3] Yazīd III (744) reduced all annuities by 10 per cent. and thereby won the sobriquet *nāqiṣ* (diminisher, also deficient).[4] Under the last Umayyad the army is said to have reached 120,000,[5] a figure which is probably a mistake for 12,000.

The arab navy was likewise an imitation of the Byzantine model. The fighting unit was a galley with a minimum of twenty-five seats on each of the two lower decks. Each seat held two men, and the hundred or more rowers in each ship were armed. But those who specialized in fighting took up their positions on the upper deck.

Royal life

The evenings of the caliphs were set apart for entertainment and social intercourse. Mu'āwiyah was particularly fond of

[1] Mas'ūdi, vol. v, p. 239.

[2] Ṭabari, vol. ii, p. 1944; ibn-Khaldūn, vol. iii, p. 165, l. 16 (cf. p. 195, ll. 25-7); ibn-al-Athīr, vol. v, p 267, ll. 7-8.

[3] Mas'ūdi, vol. v, p. 195.

[4] Ibn-al-Athīr, vol. v, p. 220; Ya'qūbi, vol. ii, p. 401.

[5] *Fakhri*, p. 197; abu-al-Fidā', vol. i, p. 222. See below, p. 285.

listening to historical narratives and anecdotes, preferably South Arabian, and poetical recitations. To satisfy this desire he imported from al-Yaman a story-teller, ʻAbīd ibn-Sharyah, who entertained the caliph through many long nights with tales of the heroes of the past. The favourite drink was rose sherbet, celebrated in Arabic song[1] and still enjoyed in Damascus and other Eastern towns. It was relished particularly by the women.

Muʻāwiyah's son Yazīd was the first confirmed drunkard among the caliphs and won the title *Yazīd al-khumūr*, the Yazīd of wines.[2] One of his pranks was the training of a pet monkey, abu-Qays, to participate in his drinking bouts.[3] Yazīd, we are told, drank daily, whereas al-Walīd I contented himself with drinking every other day; Hishām, once every Friday after the divine service, and ʻAbd-al-Malik only once a month, but then so heavily that he perforce disburdened himself by the use of emetics.[4] Yazīd II felt such attachment to two of his singing girls, Sallāmah and Ḥabābah, that when the latter was choked on a grape which he playfully threw into her mouth the passionate young caliph fretted himself to death.[5] But the palm for drinking should be handed to his son al-Walīd II (743–4), an incorrigible libertine, who is said to have gone swimming habitually in a pool of wine of which he would gulp enough to lower the surface appreciably.[6] Al-Walīd is reported to have opened the Koran one day, and as his eye fell upon the verse "And every froward potentate was brought to naught",[7] he shot the sacred book to pieces with his bow and arrow, meanwhile repeating in defiance two verses of his own composition.[8]

This caliph spent his time in his desert castles, one of which stood by al-Qaryatayn, midway between Damascus and Palmyra. The *Aghāni*[9] has preserved for us an eye-witness's report of one of his debauched drinking parties. As always, dancing, singing and music served as the handmaids of drinking. When the caliph

[1] *Aghāni*, vol. xv, p. 48, l. 12.
[2] *ʻIqd*, vol. iii, p. 403; Nuwayri, *Nihāyah*, vol. iv, p. 91.
[3] Masʻūdi, vol. v, p. 157.
[4] Most of our information about the lighter side of the caliphs' lives comes from *Aghāni*, primarily a literary work, and similar books, which should not be taken too literally. *Aghāni*, vol. i, p. 3, gives this criterion for the choice of data: "elegance that pleases the onlooker and entertains the hearer".
[5] *Kitāb al-ʻUyūn* (1865), pp. 40-41; cf. *Aghāni*, vol. xiii, p. 165.
[6] Al-Nawāji, *Ḥalbat al-Kumayt* (Cairo, 1299), p. 98.
[7] Sūr. 14:18.
[8] *Aghāni*, vol. vi, p. 125.
[9] Vol. ii, p. 72.

was one of those who maintained reasonable self-respect he screened himself behind curtains which separated him from the entertainers. Otherwise, as in the case of al-Walīd, he joined the party on a footing of equality.[1]

Such festivities as these were nevertheless not entirely lacking in cultural value. They undoubtedly encouraged the development of poetry, music and the esthetic side of life in general and were not always mere orgies.

Among the more innocent and fashionable pastimes which engaged the interest of the caliphs and their courtiers were hunting, horse-racing and dicing. Polo, which became a favourite sport under the 'Abbāsids, was probably introduced from Persia towards the end of the Umayyad period, and cock-fights at the time were not infrequent. The chase was a sport early developed in Arabia, where the saluki (*salūqi*, from Salūq in al-Yaman) dog was at first exclusively used. The cheetah (*fahd*) came on the scene later. Legend makes Kulayb ibn-Rabī'ah, hero of the War of Basūs, the first Arabian to use it in hunting. The Persians and Indians had trained this animal long before the Arabians. Yazīd I, son of Mu'āwiyah, was the first great hunter in Islam and the first who trained the cheetah to ride on the croup of a horse. He adorned his hunting dogs with gold anklets and assigned to each a special slave.[2] Horse-racing was extremely popular among the Umayyads. Al-Walīd, son of 'Abd-al-Malik, was one of the first caliphs to institute and patronize public races.[3] His brother and successor, Sulaymān, had just completed arrangements for a national competition in horse-racing when death overtook him.[4] In one of the courses organized by their brother Hishām the number of racers from the royal and other stables reached 4000, "which finds no parallel in pre-Islamic or Islamic annals".[5] A favourite daughter of this caliph kept horses for racing.[6]

The ladies of the royal household seem to have enjoyed a relatively high degree of freedom. A Makkan poet, abu-Dahbal al-Jumaḥi, did not hesitate to address love poems to 'Ātikah, the beautiful daughter of Mu'āwiyah, of whom he had caught a glimpse through the lifted veils and curtains as she was on a pil-

[1] Al-Jāḥiẓ, *al-Tāj fi Akhlāq al-Mulūk*, ed. Aḥmad Zaki (Cairo, 1914), p. 32.
[2] *Fakhri*, p. 76.
[3] Mas'ūdi, vol. vi, pp. 13-17.
[4] Ibn-al-Jawzi, *Sīrat 'Umar*, p. 56.
[5] Mas'ūdi, vol. v, p. 466.
[6] *Kitāb al-'Uyūn* (1865), p. 69, l. 12.

grimage and whom he later followed to her father's capital. The caliph had at last to "cut off the tongue of the poet" by offering him a subsidy and finding him a suitable wife.[1] Another poet, the handsome Waḍḍāḥ al-Yaman, ventured to make love to one of the wives of al-Walīd I in Damascus in spite of the threats of the caliph, and finally paid for his audacity with his life.[2] The influence exercised by the shrewd and pretty 'Ātikah, granddaughter of Mu'āwiyah, over her husband-caliph, 'Abd-al-Malik, may be illustrated by the story which tells how she locked her door when angry with the caliph and refused to open it until a favourite courtier came weeping and falsely said that one of his two sons had killed the other and that the caliph was intent on executing the fratricide.[3] The harem system, with its concomitant auxiliary of eunuchs, was not, it seems, fully instituted until the time of al-Walīd II.[4] The first eunuchs were mostly Greeks and were evidently introduced into the Arab world following the Byzantine precedent.[5]

The capital

It is safe to assume that Damascus has not much changed its general tone of life and character since its days as the Umayyad capital. Then, as now, in the narrow, covered streets the Damascene with his wide trousers, red pointed shoes and huge turban could be seen rubbing shoulders with the sun-tanned Bedouin in his loose gown surmounted by *kūfīyah* (head shawl) and *'iqāl* (head band) and occasionally meeting a European-dressed *Ifranji*.[6] Here and there the aristocrat, the well-to-do Damascene, might be seen on horseback cloaked in a white silk *'abā'* and armed with a sword or lance. A few women, and those all veiled, cross the streets; others stealthily peep through the latticed windows of their homes overlooking the bazaars and public squares. Sherbet sellers and sweetmeat vendors raise their voices to the highest pitch in competition with the incessant tramp of the passers-by and the multitude of donkeys and camels laden with the varied products of the desert and the sown. The city atmosphere is charged with every kind of smell which the olfactory sense is capable of perceiving.

[1] *Aghāni*, vol. vi, pp. 158-61.
[2] *Ibid.* pp. 36 *seq.*, vol. xi, p. 49.
[3] Mas'ūdi, vol. v, pp. 273-5.
[4] *Aghāni*, vol. iv, pp. 78-9.
[5] J. B. Bury, *The Imperial Administrative System in the Ninth Century* (London, 1911), pp. 120 *seq.*; Charles Diehl, *Byzance: grandeur et décadence* (Paris, 1919), p. 154.
[6] A Frank, a word used for all Europeans; especially common during the Crusades

Photo *Bonfils*

DAMASCUS TODAY, AS SEEN FROM AL-ṢĀLIḤĪYAH

As in other cities the Arabians lived in separate quarters of their own according to their tribal affiliation. In Damascus, Ḥimṣ, Aleppo (Ḥalab) and other towns these *ḥārahs* (quarters) are still well marked. The doorway of each house opened from the street into a courtyard in the centre of which usually stood a large water-basin with a flowing jet emitting from time to time a veil-like spray. An orange or citron tree grew by the basin. The rooms surrounded the courtyard, which in larger houses was provided with a cloister. It is to the eternal glory of the banu-Umayyah that they supplied Damascus with a water system which was unexcelled in the contemporary Orient and still continues to function. Yazīd's name is borne today by a canal, Nahr Yazīd, which this son of Mu'āwiyah dug from the Barada, or more probably widened,[1] in order to perfect the irrigation of the Ghūṭah. This rich oasis outside Damascus with its luxurious gardens owes its very existence to the Barada. Besides the Nahr Yazīd, the Barada sends off four other arms or channels which spread fertility and freshness throughout the town.

Society

The population throughout the empire was divided into four social classes. The highest consisted naturally of the ruling Moslems headed by the caliphal household and the aristocracy of Arabian conquerors. Exactly how numerous was this class cannot be ascertained. Under al-Walīd I the number of annuities apportioned to Arabian Moslems in Damascus and its district (*jund*) reached 45,000.[2] Under Marwān I, Ḥimṣ and its district registered 20,000 pensions. The number of converted Moslems could not have been great before the restrictions imposed by 'Umar II. Although the capital of the caliphate may have presented by the end of the Umayyad period the aspect of a Moslem town, Syria as a whole remained largely Christian until the third Moslem century. The small towns and villages and especially the mountainous regions—always the home of the lost cause—preserved their native features and ancient cultural patterns. In fact the Lebanon remained Christian in faith and Syriac in speech for centuries after the conquest. Only the physical conflict had ended with the conquest; the religious, the racial,

[1] Consult Iṣṭakhri, p. 59; cf. H. Sauvaire, "Description de Damas: 'Oyoûn et-Tawârîkh, par Mohammad ebn Châker", *Journal asiatique*, ser. 9, vol. vii (1896), p. 400.

[2] Consult H. Lammens, *La Syrie: précis historique* (Beirūt, 1921), vol. i, pp. 119-20.

the social and above all the linguistic conflicts were just beginning.

Clients

Next below the Arabian Moslems came the Neo-Moslems, who by force or persuasion had professed Islam and were thereby admitted in theory, though not in practice, to the full rights of Islamic citizenship. Here Arabian chauvinism, pitted against theoretical claims, proved too strong for those claims to be realized. There is no doubt that throughout practically all the period of the Umayyads, holders of land, whether believers or unbelievers, were made to pay kharāj (land tax). There is no evidence of mass conversion to Islam in the provinces until after such stringent regulations as those of 'Umar II and the 'Abbāsid al-Mutawakkil (847–61). In Egypt resistance to the new religion was always least obstinate. The revenue of that country was reduced from fourteen million dinars in the time of 'Amr ibn-al-'Āṣ to five in the time of Mu'āwiyah and later to four under the 'Abbāsid Hārūn al-Rashīd (786–809).[1] In al-'Irāq it fell from a hundred million under 'Umar ibn-al-Khaṭṭāb to forty million in the days of 'Abd-al-Malik.[2] One of the causes for the decline of state revenue was undoubtedly conversion to Islam. Under the early 'Abbāsids, the Egyptians, Persians and Aramaeans who had accepted Islam began to outnumber the Moslems of Arabian origin.

Reduced to the position of clients (*mawāli*), these neophyte Moslems formed the lowest stratum of Moslem society, a status which they bitterly resented. This explains our finding them in many cases espousing such causes as the Shī'ite in al-'Irāq or the Khārijite in Persia. Some of them, however, as often happens, proved religiously "more royal than the king", and their zeal for the new faith, bordering on fanaticism, made them persecute non-Moslems. Among the most intolerant early Moslems were some of these converts from Christianity and Judaism.

Within the Moslem society these clients were naturally the first to devote themselves to learned studies and fine arts, for they represented the longer tradition of culture. As they outshone the Moslem Arabians in the intellectual field they began to contest with them the political leadership. Through their intermarriages

[1] Al-Ya'qūbi, *Kitāb al-Buldān*, ed. de Goeje (Leyden, 1892), p. 339.

[2] Cf. Ya'qūbi, vol. ii, p. 277; T. W. Arnold, *The Preaching of Islam*, 2nd ed. (London, 1913), p. 81.

with the conquering stock they served to dilute the Arabian blood and ultimately make that element inconspicuous amidst the mixture of varied racial strains.

Dhimmis

The third class was made up of members of tolerated sects, professors of revealed religions, the so-called *ahl al-dhimmah*, i.e. the Christians, Jews and Ṣābians with whom the Moslems had made covenant. The Ṣābians, who were identical with the Mandeans, the so-called Christians of St. John who still survive in the marshy district at the mouth of the Euphrates, are mentioned thrice in the Koran (2 : 59, 5 : 73, 22 : 17). From this it would appear that Muḥammad regarded them as believers in the true God. This recognition of tolerated religions, whose devotees were to be disarmed and compelled to pay tribute in return for Moslem protection, was the chief political innovation of Muḥammad and was largely due to the esteem in which the Prophet held the Bible and partly to the aristocratic connections of the banu-Ghassān, Bakr, Taghlib and other Christian tribes.

In this status the dhimmis enjoyed, against the payment of land and capitation taxes, a wide measure of toleration. Even in matters of civil and criminal judicial procedure, except where a Moslem was involved, these people were practically under their own spiritual heads. Moslem law was too sacred to be applicable to them. Essential parts of this system were still in force as late as the Ottoman period and the mandatory regimes of 'Irāq, Syria and Palestine.

Originally confined to the *ahl al-kitāb* (Scripturaries) of the Koran[1] who came under the rule of Islam, the tolerated status was later extended by the Moslems to include the fire-worshipping Zoroastrians (*Majūs*), the heathen of Ḥarrān and the pagan Berbers. Though not devotees of a revealed religion and thus technically outside the pale of protection, the Persian Zoroastrians and the North African Berbers were offered by the Moslem invaders the three choices: Islam, the sword or tribute, rather than the first two only. Here, where the sword of Islam was not long enough to reach all the necks involved, technicality gave way to expediency. In such inaccessible regions as the Lebanon the Christians remained always in the ascendant and defied even 'Abd-al-Malik at the height of the Umayyad caliphate.[2] Throughout all Syria the Christians were well treated under the

[1] Sūrs. 9 : 29; 2 : 99, 103; 3 : 62-65, etc. [2] See above, p. 205.

banu-Umayyah until the reign of the pious 'Umar II. As we have already learned, Mu'āwiyah's wife was a Christian, as were his poet, physician and secretary of finance. We read of only one conspicuous exception, that of al-Walīd I, who put to death the chief of the Christian Arab tribe of the banu-Taghlib for refusing to profess Islam.[1] Even in Egypt Copts rose several times against their Moslem overlords before they finally succumbed in the days of the 'Abbāsid al-Ma'mūn (813–33).[2]

"The Covenant of 'Umar"

The fame of 'Umar II does not rest solely on his piety or on his remission of taxes imposed on neophyte Moslems. 'Umar was the first caliph and the only Umayyad to impose humiliating restrictions on Christian subjects—measures wrongly ascribed to his earlier namesake and maternal great-grandfather, 'Umar I. This so-called "covenant of 'Umar", implying 'Umar I, is recorded in several forms,[3] mostly in later sources; and the provisions presuppose closer intercourse between Moslems and Christians than was possible in the early days of the conquest. The most striking regulations issued by this Umayyad caliph were the excluding of Christians from public offices, prohibiting their wearing turbans, requiring them to cut their forelocks, to don distinctive clothes with girdles of leather, to ride without saddles or only on pack saddles, to erect no places of worship and not to lift their voices in time of prayer. According to his decree if a Moslem killed a Christian his penalty was only a fine and no Christian's testimony against a Moslem in courts could be accepted. The Jews were evidently also included under some of these restrictions and excluded from governmental positions.[4] That many of these enactments were not long in force is indicated by the fact that Khālid ibn-'Abdullāh al-Qasri, governor of al-'Irāq under Hishām, built a church in al-Kūfah to please his Christian mother,[5] granted Christians and Jews the privilege of building places of worship and even appointed Zoroastrians to posts in the government.

[1] *Aghāni*, vol. x, p. 99. H. Lammens in *Journal asiatique*, ser. 9, vol. iv (1894), pp. 438-9.

[2] Kindi, pp. 73, 81, 96, 116, 117; Maqrīzi, *Khiṭaṭ* (Būlāq, 1270), vol. ii, p. 497.

[3] Ibn-'Abd-al-Ḥakam, pp. 151-2; ibn-'Asākir, vol. i, pp. 178-80; al-Ibshīhi, *al-Mustaṭraf* (Cairo, 1314), vol. i, pp. 100-101.

[4] Abu-Yūsuf, *Kharāj*, pp. 152-3; ibn-al-Jawzi, *Sīrat 'Umar*, p. 100; *'Iqd*, vol. ii, pp. 339-40; ibn-al-Athīr, vol. v, p. 49; A. S. Tritton, *The Caliphs and their non-Muslim Subjects* (Oxford, 1930), pp. 5-35.

[5] Ibn-Khallikān, vol. i, p. 302 = de Slane, vol. i, p. 485.

At the bottom of society stood the slaves.[1] Islam preserved the ancient Semitic institution of slavery, the legality of which the Old Testament admitted, but it appreciably ameliorated the condition of the slave. Canon law forbade the Moslem to enslave his co-religionist, but promised no liberty to an alien slave who adopted Islam. Slaves in early Islam were recruited from prisoners of war, including women and children, unless ransomed, and by purchase or raiding. Soon the slave trade became very brisk and lucrative in all Moslem lands. Some slaves from East or Central Africa were black; others from Farghānah or Chinese Turkestan were yellow; still others from the Near East or from eastern and southern Europe were white. The Spanish slaves, called *Ṣaqālibah*,[2] from Spanish *esclavo*, fetched about a thousand dinars each, while Turkish slaves fetched only six hundred apiece. According to Islamic law the offspring of a female slave by another slave, by any man other than her master, or by her master in case he does not acknowledge the fatherhood of the child, is likewise a slave; but the offspring of a male slave by a freewoman is free.

Slaves

An idea of the number of slaves flooding the Moslem empire as a result of conquest may be gained from such exaggerated figures, as the following: Mūsa ibn-Nuṣayr took 300,000 captives from Ifrīqiyah, one-fifth of whom he forwarded to al-Walīd,[3] and from the Gothic nobility in Spain he captured 30,000 virgins;[4] Qutaybah's captives from Sogdiana alone numbered 100,000;[5] al-Zubayr ibn-al-ʿAwwām bequeathed among other chattels one thousand male and female slaves.[6] The famous Makkan poet of love, ʿUmar ibn-abi-Rabīʿah († *ca.* 719), had many more than seventy slaves.[7] For an Umayyad prince to maintain a retinue of about a thousand slaves was nothing extraordinary. Even the private in the Syrian army at the battle of Ṣiffīn had from one to ten servants waiting on him.[8]

Between the master and the female slave concubinage, but not legal marriage, was permissible. The children of such a union

[1] Ar. *ʿabd* (pl. *ʿabīd*), especially if black; otherwise *mamlūk* (pl. *mamālīk*), possessed.

[2] Same term used by the Arabs for the Slavs. See below, p. 525.

[3] Maqqari, vol. i, p. 148.

[4] Ibn-al-Athīr, vol. iv, p. 448.

[5] *Ibid.* vol. iv, p. 454.

[6] Masʿūdi, vol. iv, p. 254.

[7] *Aghāni*, vol. i, p. 37.

[8] Masʿūdi, vol. iv, p. 387. Consult Jurji Zaydān, *Taʾrīkh al-Tamaddun al-Islāmi*, 3rd ed. (Cairo, 1922), vol. v, pp. 22 *seq.*

belonged to the master and were therefore free; but the status of the concubine was thereby raised only to that of *umm-walad* (mother of children), who could neither be sold by her husband-master nor given away and who at his death was declared free. In the melting-pot process which resulted in the amalgamation of Arabians and foreigners, the slave trade undoubtedly played an extremely important rôle.

The liberation of slaves was always looked upon as a good work (*qurbah*) entitling the master to a special reward in the next world. When liberated the slave enjoyed the status of a client to his former master, now his patron. In case the patron died without heirs the client inherited his estate.

Al-Madīnah and Makkah

The quiet life of al-Madīnah, rendered venerable by its early Moslem association, attracted thither would-be scholars devoted to the study of the mementos of its sacred past and to the collecting of legal and ritual enactments. The city containing the burial-place of the Prophet thus became the first centre of Islamic tradition, which under such men as Anas ibn-Mālik († between 709 and 711) and 'Abdullāh ibn-'Umar ibn-al-Khaṭṭāb[1] († 693) developed into a science of the first order.

The school of Makkah owes its reputation to 'Abdullāh ibn-al-'Abbās, surnamed abu-al-'Abbās († *ca.* 688), a cousin of the Prophet and ancestor of the 'Abbāsid caliphs, a man who was so universally admired for his knowledge of profane and sacred tradition and jurisprudence and for his skill in commenting on the Koran that he won the enviable title of *ḥibr al-ummah* (the sage of the community). Modern criticism, however, has exposed him as a fabricator of several ḥadīths.

Under the Umayyads the two cities of al-Ḥijāz entirely changed their aspect. To al-Madīnah, the forsaken capital of Arabia, now retired many of those anxious to keep aloof from the turmoil of political activity or desirous of enjoying undisturbed the great fortunes which the wars of conquest had gained for them. Following al-Ḥasan and al-Ḥusayn, a large number of *nouveaux riches* flocked there. Inside the city arose palaces and outside it villas, all swarming with servants and slaves and providing their occupants with every variety of luxury.[2] Makkah shared with its

[1] Eldest son of the second caliph. As a traditionist he is considered more reliable than ibn-Mālik, whose collection has been preserved in the *Musnad* of Aḥmad ibn-Ḥanbal.

[2] Mas'ūdi, vol. iv, pp. 254-5.

sister city this attractiveness for lovers of pleasure. As life in the two cities became more luxurious its excesses became more notorious.[1] Pilgrims from all over the Moslem world brought every year vast fresh supplies of money. What a contrast to the primitive times when the Caliph ʻUmar's agent arrived from al-Baḥrayn claiming to be the bearer of tribute amounting to 500,000 dirhams! The caliph questioned the possibility of such a figure, and when doubly assured that it was "a hundred thousand five times", he summoned the people and proclaimed, "O ye men, we have just received an enormous sum. If ye wish we shall give each his share by measure, otherwise by count."[2]

With this increased flow of wealth the two Holy Cities became less holy. They developed into a centre of worldly pleasure and gaiety and a home of secular Arab music and song. In Makkah was established a kind of clubhouse patronized by guests who, we are told, had facilities for hanging their outer garments on pegs—apparently an innovation for al-Ḥijāz—before indulging in chess, backgammon, dice or reading.[3] To al-Madīnah Persian and Byzantine slave songstresses (*qiyān*) flocked in increasing numbers. Amorous poetry kept pace with other new developments. Houses of ill repute (*buyūt al-qiyān*) flourished in al-Madīnah and were patronized by no less a poet than al-Farazdaq of national fame.[4] As these female slaves sang and played soft melodies for the entertainment of their wealthy masters and guests, the latter, attired in colourful robes, reclined on square mattresses or cushions while they inhaled the perfume of burning spices and sipped from silver goblets the ruddy wines of Syria.

Al-Madīnah boasted under the early Marwānids the proud and beautiful Sayyidah[5] Sukaynah († 735), daughter of the martyred al-Ḥusayn and granddaughter of ʻAli, one of the most remarkable women of the age.

Sukaynah's rank and learning combined with her fondness for song and poetry and her charm, good taste and quick-wittedness to make her the arbiter of fashion, beauty and literature in the region of the sacred cities. Sukaynah was noted for her jests and hoaxes.[6] The crude humour appreciated even in the high society of the time is illustrated by the occasion when she

[1] *Aghāni*, vol. xxi, p. 197.
[2] Ibn-Saʻd, vol. iii, pt. 1, p. 216.
[3] *Aghāni*, vol. iv, p. 52; cf. below, p. 339.
[4] *Ibid.* vol. xxi, p. 197.
[5] "Lady", a title originally reserved for the descendants of ʻAli and Fāṭimah.
[6] *Aghāni*, vol. xiv, pp. 164-5; vol. xvii, pp. 97, 101-2.

made an old Persian sheikh sit on a basket of eggs and cluck like a hen, to the merriment of her incoming guests. On another she sent word to the chief of police that a Syrian had broken into her apartment; when the chief himself and his aide arrived in haste they found her maid holding a flea.[1] Then as now Syria was evidently noted for its fleas. The brilliant assemblies of poets and jurists held in her residence, a sort of salon, never failed to be enlivened by her sallies of repartee. Special pride she took in her ancestry, in her daughter, whom she liked to bedeck with jewels, and in her own hair, which she had her own peculiar way of dressing. This coiffure *à la* Sukaynah (*ṭurrah Sukaynīyah*)[2] became popular among men and was at a later date strictly prohibited by the puritan Caliph 'Umar II,[3] one of whose brothers had married Sukaynah without consummating the union. As for the successive husbands whom the charms of this lady captivated for a longer or shorter period, they could hardly be counted on the fingers of two hands.[4] In more than one instance she made complete freedom of action a condition precedent to marriage.

Sukaynah had a rival in al-Ṭā'if, the famous summer resort of Makkah and al-Madīnah, whose patricians witnessed a number of striking scenes and episodes centring on young 'Ā'ishah bint-Ṭalḥah. 'Ā'ishah's father was a distinguished Companion of the Prophet; her mother was a daughter of abu-Bakr and sister of 'Ā'ishah, Muḥammad's favourite wife. This daughter of Ṭalḥah combined with noble descent a rare beauty and a proud and lofty spirit—the three qualities most highly prized in a woman by the Arabs. No favour she requested could very well be refused. Her appearance in public was even more impressive than that of Sukaynah.[5] Once when she was on a pilgrimage to Makkah she asked the master of ceremonies, who was also the governor of the town, to defer the public religious service until she had completed the last of the seven prescribed processions around the Ka'bah. This the gallant governor of course did, which resulted in his dismissal from office by the Caliph 'Abd-al-Malik.[6] 'Ā'ishah's record of marriages included

[1] *Aghāni*, vol. xiv, p. 166; vol. xvii, p. 94.
[2] Ibn-Khallikān, vol. i, p. 377.
[3] *Aghāni*, vol. xiv, p. 165.
[4] Compare their lists in ibn-Sa'd, vol. viii, p. 349; ibn-Qutaybah, *Ma'ārif*, pp. 101, 109-10, 113, 122, 289-90; ibn-Khallikān, vol. i, p. 377; *Aghāni*, vol. xiv, pp. 168-72.
[5] *Aghāni*, vol. x, p. 60.
[6] *Ibid.* vol. iii, p. 103.

only three.[1] When her second husband, Muṣʿab ibn-al-Zubayr, who had also married Sukaynah and is said to have given each a million dirhams as dowry,[2] took her to task for never veiling her face her characteristic reply was, "Since God, may He remain blessed and exalted, hath put upon me the stamp of beauty, it is my wish that the public should view that beauty and thereby recognize His grace unto them. Under no conditions, therefore, will I veil myself."[3]

[1] Ibn-Saʿd, vol. viii, p. 342. [2] *Aghāni*, vol. iii, p. 122.
[3] *Ibid* vol. x, p. 54.

CHAPTER XXI

INTELLECTUAL ASPECTS OF LIFE UNDER THE UMAYYADS

THE invaders from the desert brought with them no tradition of learning, no heritage of culture, to the lands they conquered. In Syria, in Egypt, in al-ʿIrāq, in Persia, they sat as pupils at the feet of the peoples they subdued. And what acquisitive pupils they proved to be!

The closeness of the Umayyad period to the Jāhilīyah age, its many wars, civil and foreign, and the unsettled social and economic conditions of the Moslem world—all these militated against the possibility of intellectual development in that early epoch. But the seed was then sown and the tree of knowledge which came into full bloom under the early ʿAbbāsids in Baghdād certainly had its roots in this preceding period of Greek, Syrian and Persian culture. The Umayyad age, therefore, was in general one of incubation.

As Persians, Syrians, Copts, Berbers and others flocked within the fold of Islam and intermarried with the Arabians the original high wall raised earlier between Arabians and non-Arabians tumbled down. The nationality of the Moslem receded into the background. No matter what his nationality may originally have been, the follower of Muḥammad now passed for an Arab. An Arab henceforth became one who professed Islam and spoke and wrote the Arabic tongue, regardless of his racial affiliation. This is one of the most significant facts in the history of Islamic civilization. When we therefore speak of "Arab medicine" or "Arab philosophy" or "Arab mathematics" we do not mean the medical science, philosophy or mathematics that are necessarily the product of the Arabian mind or developed by people living in the Arabian peninsula, but that body of knowledge enshrined in books written in the Arabic language by men who flourished chiefly during the caliphate and were themselves Persians, Syrians, Egyptians or Arabians, Christian, Jewish or Moslem, and who may have drawn some of their material from Greek, Aramaean, Indo-Persian or other sources.

Al-Baṣrah and al-Kūfah

As the two sister cities of al-Ḥijāz, Makkah and al-Madīnah, became under the Umayyads the home of music and song, love and poetry, so did the twin cities of al-'Irāq, al-Baṣrah[1] and al-Kūfah, develop during this period into centres of the most animated intellectual activity in the Moslem world.

Arabic grammar

These two capitals of al-'Irāq, as we have learned before, were originally military camps built by order of the Caliph 'Umar in the Moslem year 17 (638).[2] Al-Kūfah, the former capital of 'Ali, arose not far from the ruins of ancient Babylon and in a sense fell heir to its neighbour, al-Ḥīrah, the Lakhmid capital. Through favoured location, commerce and immigration the sister towns soon grew into wealthy and populous cities of over a hundred thousand inhabitants. Al-Baṣrah, from which Khurāsān was governed under the Umayyads, is said to have reached as early as the year 50 (670) a total population of 300,000 and to have had at a later date 120,000 (!) canals.[3] Here on the borderland of Persia the scientific study of the Arabic language and grammar was begun and carried on mainly for foreign converts and partly by them. The first impulse came from the desire to supply the linguistic needs of Neo-Moslems who wanted to study the Koran, hold government positions and converse with the conquerors. In addition, the ever-widening gap between the classical language of the Koran and the everyday vernacular corrupted by Syriac, Persian and other tongues and dialects was partly responsible for evoking such linguistic interest.

It was by no mere chance, therefore, that the legendary founder of Arabic grammar, abu-al-Aswad al-Du'ali († 688), should have flourished in al-Baṣrah. According to the famous biographer ibn-Khallikān[4] it was "'Ali who laid down for al-Du'ali this principle: The parts of speech are three—noun, verb and particle, and told him to found a complete treatise thereon". This he successfully did. Arabic grammar, however, shows slow and long

[1] Eng. Bassora. Present-day al-Baṣrah lies six miles to the north-east of the ancient city.

[2] Al-Kūfah may have been built one or two years after al-Baṣrah; Yāqūt, vol. iv, pp. 322-3.

[3] Iṣṭakhri, p. 80; ibn-Ḥawqal, p. 159.

[4] Vol. i, pp. 429-30 = de Slane, vol. i, p. 663.

development and bears striking marks of the influence of Greek logic. Al-Du'ali was followed by al-Khalīl ibn-Aḥmad, another Baṣrite scholar, who died about 786. To al-Khalīl, who was the first to compile an Arabic dictionary, the *Kitāb al-'Ayn*, biographers attribute the discovery of Arabic prosody and its rules, which still hold sway today. His pupil the Persian Sībawayh († *ca.* 793) composed the first systematic textbook on Arabic grammar, known by the honorific title *al-Kitāb* (the book), which has ever since been the basis of all native studies of the subject.

Religious tradition and canon law

The study of the Koran and the necessity of expounding it gave rise to the twin sciences of philology and lexicography as well as to that most characteristically Moslem literary activity —the science of tradition (*ḥadīth*, literally "narrative"). In its technical sense a tradition is an act or saying attributed to the Prophet or to one of his Companions. The Koran and tradition provided the foundation upon which theology and *fiqh* (law), the obverse and reverse of sacred law, were raised. Law in Islam is more intimately related to religion than to jurisprudence as modern lawyers understand it. Roman law, directly or through the Talmud and other media, did undoubtedly affect Umayyad legislation, but to what extent has not been fully ascertained. In fact, of this period, from which hardly any literature has come down to us, we know only a few of the traditionists and jurists, the most renowned of whom were al-Ḥasan al-Baṣri and ibn-Shihāb al-Zuhri († 742). The latter, who traced his descent to the Prophet's tribe, was always so deeply absorbed in his studies to the neglect of all worldly concerns that his wife once remarked, "By Allah, these books of yours are worse to me than three rival wives possibly could be!"[1] Al-Baṣri was highly esteemed as a transmitter of tradition, since he was believed to have known personally seventy of those who took part in the battle of Badr. Most of the religious movements within Islam trace their origin back to al-Baṣri. The Sufis felt throughout the ages the lasting influence of his ascetic piety, the orthodox Sunnis[2] never tire of quoting his devout sayings and even the Mu'tazilites reckon him as one of themselves. No wonder the populace of al-Baṣrah turned out in a body to follow his funeral on Friday the tenth of October 728, and none was left to attend or conduct the afternoon prayer in

[1] Ibn-Khallikān, vol. ii, p. 223; abu-al-Fidā', vol. i, pp. 215-16.
[2] See below, p. 393, n. 2.

the mosque that day—"an unprecedented happening in the history of Islam".[1]

The contributions of the fickle and unorthodox Kūfans, many of whom were Shī'ites or 'Alids, to Arabic philology and Moslem learning were almost, but not quite, as brilliant as those of their neighbours the Baṣrites. Rivalry between the scholars of the two camps developed two well-recognized schools of Arabic grammar and literature. Among the celebrated Companions, regarded as authorities on Moslem tradition, who settled in al-Kūfah during the caliphates of 'Umar and 'Uthmān was the red-haired, thin-legged 'Abdullāh ibn-Mas'ūd (*ca.* 653), who is said to have been responsible for eight hundred and forty-eight traditions.[2] It was a peculiar feature of ibn-Mas'ūd, when giving information about the Prophet, to tremble, exude sweat from his forehead and express himself with deliberate and hesitant caution, lest he transmit something inexact.[3] Equally distinguished among the Kūfan traditionists was 'Āmir ibn-Sharāḥīl al-Sha'bi († *ca.* 728), one of the many South Arabians who gained eminence in the early days of Islam, who is said to have heard traditions from some hundred and fifty Companions[4] which he related from memory without putting down a single line in black and white. Withal, the general judgment of modern critics is quite favourable in regard to his trustworthiness. The most eminent of al-Sha'bi's pupils was the great abu-Ḥanīfah. We have it on the authority of al-Sha'bi that he himself was sent by the Caliph 'Abd-al-Malik on an important mission to the Byzantine emperor in Constantinople.

It was under the 'Abbāsids, as we shall see later, that these twin cities of al-'Irāq reached their highest level of intellectual endeavour and achievement. In their later development the 'Irāq schools of tradition and jurisprudence were not swayed by the old conservative traditions as were the schools of al-Ḥijāz.

History-writing

Arabic historiography, which also began at this time, started in the form of tradition (*ḥadīth*). It was therefore one of the earliest disciplines cultivated by the Arab Moslems. The desire of the early caliphs to scan the proceedings of kings and rulers

[1] Ibn-Khallikān, vol. i, p. 228.
[2] Al-Nawawi, *Tahdhīb al-Asmā'*, ed. F. Wüstenfeld (Göttingen, 1842–7), p. 370.
[3] Ibn-Sa'd, vol. iii, pt. i, pp. 110-11.
[4] Al-Sam'āni, *al-Ansāb*, ed. Margoliouth (Leyden, 1912), fol. 334 recto; cf. ibn-Khallikān, vol. i, p. 436.

before their time, the interest of the believers in collecting the old stories about the Prophet and his Companions—which stories became the bases of later books on biography (*sīrah*) and conquests (*maghāzi*)—the necessity of ascertaining the genealogical relationship of each Moslem Arabian in order to determine the amount of stipend he received from the public treasury, the elucidation of passages in Arabic poetry and the identification of persons and places cited in religious works, the anxiety of the subject peoples to record the past achievements of their races as a counterpoise to Arab chauvinism—all these provided the stimulus for historical research. Among the early distinguished story-tellers was the semi-legendary South Arabian 'Abīd ('Ubayd) ibn-Sharyah, who on the invitation of Mu'āwiyah went to Damascus to inform the caliph about "the early kings of the Arabians and their races".[1] 'Abīd composed for his royal patron a number of works on his specialty, one of which, the *Kitāb al-Mulūk wa-Akhbār al-Māḍīn* (the book of kings and the history of the ancients), was in wide circulation at the time of the historian al-Mas'ūdi[2] († 956). Another of those versed in the "science of origins" (*'ilm al-awā'il*) was Wahb ibn-Munabbih († in Ṣan'ā', *ca.* 728), a Yamanite Jew of Persian origin who probably professed Islam and one of whose works has recently been published.[3] Wahb, whose trustworthiness is open to grave question, became one of the chief sources of information, or rather misinformation, about pre-Islamic South Arabia and foreign lands.[4] Still another was Ka'b al-Aḥbār (Ka'b of the rabbis, † 652 or 654 in Ḥimṣ), also a Yamanite Jew, who accepted Islam under one of the first two caliphs and acted as teacher and counsellor to the court of Mu'āwiyah when the latter was still governor of Syria.[5] Thus did Ka'b become the earliest authority for the Jewish-Moslem traditions. Through Ka'b, ibn-Munabbih and other Jewish converts a number of talmudic stories ultimately found their way into Moslem tradition and were incorporated with Arabic historical lore.

[1] Al-Nadīm, *al-Fihrist*, ed. G. Flügel (Leipzig, 1872), p. 89, l. 26; cf. ibn-Khallikān, vol. ii, p. 365.

[2] Vol. iv, p. 89.

[3] *Al-Tījān fi Mulūk Ḥimyar* (Ḥaydarābād, 1347), with a supplement (pp. 311-489) entitled "Akhbār 'Abīd", by 'Abīd.

[4] Ibn-Khallikān, vol. iii, pp. 106-7; Ṭabari, vol. iii, pp. 2493-4; Nawawi, p. 619.

[5] Consult Nawawi, p. 523; ibn-Sa'd, vol. vii, pt. 2, p. 156; ibn-Qutaybah, *Ma'ārif*, p. 219.

In the Umayyad period we can also detect the rudiments of many of those religio-philosophical movements which were later to shake Islam to its very foundation. In the first half of the eighth century there flourished in al-Baṣrah a certain Wāṣil ibn-'Aṭā' († 748), the founder of the famous school of rationalism termed Mu'tazilah. The Mu'tazilites (seceders, schismatics) were so called because of their major doctrine that he who commits a mortal sin (*kabīrah*) secedes from the ranks of the believers but does not become an unbeliever; he occupies a medial position between the two.[1] Wāṣil was a pupil of al-Ḥasan al-Baṣri, who inclined for a time to the doctrine of free will, which doctrine became another cardinal point in Mu'tazilite belief. This doctrine of free will was at the time held by a group called Qadarites (from *qadar* = power) as opposed to the Jabrites (from *jabr* = compulsion).[2] The Qadarites represent a reaction against the harsh predestinarianism of Islam, a corollary of God's almightiness so strongly emphasized in the Koran,[3] and betray Christian Greek influence. The Qadarites were the earliest school of philosophy in Islam, and how widely spread their ideas were may be inferred from the fact that two of the Umayyad caliphs, Mu'āwiyah II and Yazīd III, were Qadarites.[4]

To the cardinal doctrine of free will the Mu'tazilites added another: the denial of the coexistence with God of the divine attributes, such as power, wisdom and life, on the ground that such conceptions would destroy the unity of God. Hence the Mu'tazilites' favourite appellation for themselves: "the partisans of justice and unity". This rationalistic movement attained significant importance under the 'Abbāsids, especially al-Ma'mūn (813–33), as we shall see later. Intellectually, Baghdād began where al-Baṣrah and al-Kūfah ended.

St. John of Damascus

One of the principal agents through whom Christian lore and Greek thought at this time found their way into Islam was St. John of Damascus (Joannes Damascenus), surnamed Chrysorrhoas (golden-tongued), as his earlier Antiochene namesake was surnamed Chrysostom. Although he wrote in Greek, John was

[1] Mas'ūdi, vol. vi, p. 22, vii, p. 234. Cf. Shahrastāni, p. 33; al-Baghdādi, *Uṣūl al-Dīn* (Istanbul, 1928), vol. i, p. 335; do., *Mukhtaṣar al-Farq bayn al-Firaq*, ed. Hitti (Cairo, 1924), p. 98; al-Nawbakhti, *Firaq al-Shī'ah*, ed. H. Ritter (Istanbul, 1931), p. 5.

[2] Cf. al-Īji, *Kitāb al-Mawāqif*, ed. Th. Soerensen (Leipzig, 1848), pp. 334, 362.

[3] Sūrs. 3 : 25-26, 15 : 21, 42 : 26, 43 : 10, 54 : 49, etc.; cf. ibn-Ḥazm, vol. iii, p. 31.

[4] Ibn-al-'Ibri, p. 190; Ya'qūbi, vol. ii, p. 402.

not a Greek but a Syrian who spoke Aramaic at home and knew, in addition to both of these languages, Arabic. His grandfather Manṣūr ibn-Sarjūn was the financial administrator of Damascus at the time of its Arab conquest and connived with its bishop in surrendering the town. He kept his position under the Moslems and John's father succeeded to the office. As a young man John attended drinking bouts of al-Akhṭal and Mu'āwiyah's son Yazīd and succeeded his father in that most important office in the Arab government. In his early thirties he gave it all up in favour of a life of asceticism and devotion in the monastery of St. Sāba near Jerusalem. Here he died about 748. Among St. John's works is a dialogue with a "Saracen" on the divinity of Christ and the freedom of human will which is intended to be an apology for Christianity, a manual for the guidance of Christians in their arguments with the Moslems. John himself probably held many such debates in the presence of the caliph. His influence is not hard to detect in the formation of the Qadarite school. To St. John tradition ascribes the story of the ascetic Barlaam and the Hindu prince Josaphat, perhaps the most famous religious romance of the Middle Ages. Modern critics recognize the story as a Christian version of an episode in the life of the Buddha, who under the name Josaphat (or Ioasaph) was, strange as it may seem, canonized by both the Latin and the Greek Churches. Thus did the Buddha twice become a Christian saint. The medieval story of Barlaam and Josaphat goes back through Latin, Greek and Georgian into Arabic, itself evidently a translation from Pahlawi done after St. John's days.[1] Mention is made in the *Fihrist*[2] of a *Kitāb al-Budd* (the book of Buddha) and of a *Kitāb Būdāsaf*. John Damascene is considered the greatest and last theologian of the Oriental Greek Church. In ecclesiastical literature the hymns he composed (some of which are still used in Protestant hymnals) mark the highest attainment of beauty by Christian Church poets. As hymnologist, theologian, orator, polemic writer, father of Byzantine music and codifier of Byzantine art he stands out as an ornament to the body of the Church under the caliphate.

Khārijites The Qadarite was the earliest philosophical school of thought in Islam, but the Khārijites formed the earliest religio-political

[1] Paulus Peetrus in *Annalecta Bollandiana*, vol. xlix (Brussels, 1931), pp. 276-312.
[2] P. 305.

sect. These deadly opponents of 'Ali, once his supporters, repeatedly arose in armed opposition to the prerogative conferred on the Quraysh that the caliph should be one of their number.[1] In endeavouring to maintain the primitive, democratic principles of Islam the puritanical Khārijites caused rivers of blood to flow in the first three Moslem centuries. In course of time they forbade the cult of saints with the attendant local pilgrimages and prohibited Sufi fraternities. Today they survive in the form of a subdivision called Ibāḍite (commonly Abāḍite), after ibn-Ibāḍ[2] (second half of first Moslem century), the most tolerant of the Khārijite founders of sub-sects, and are scattered in Algeria, Tripolitania and 'Umān, whence they later crossed to Zanzibar.

Murji'ites

Another sect, but of minor importance, which arose in the Umayyad age was the Murji'ite, whose fundamental article of faith consisted in the suspension (*irjā'*) of judgment against believers who commit sins and in not declaring them infidels.[3] More specifically, the Murji'ites refused to see in the suppression of religious law by the Umayyad caliphs a justifiable cause for denying that house the homage due them as the *de facto* political leaders of Islam. To the followers of this doctrine the fact that the Umayyads were nominally Moslems sufficed. 'Uthmān and 'Ali as well as Mu'āwiyah were all servants of God, and by God alone must they be judged. In general, Murji'ite influence was on the side of tolerance. The most illustrious representative of the moderate wing of this school was the great divine abu-Ḥanīfah († 767), who founded the first of the four orthodox schools of jurisprudence in Islam.

The Shī'ah

The Shī'ah, one of the two hostile camps into which early Islam split on the issue of the caliphate, took definite form during the Umayyad period. The imāmship then became, and has since continued to be, the differentiating element between Sunnites (orthodox) and Shī'ites. The persistence with which the Shī'ah clings to its basic belief in 'Ali and 'Ali's sons as the true imāms, not unlike the persistence of the Roman Catholic Church in the dogma of its relation to Peter and his successors, has ever remained its distinguishing feature. The founder of Islam made a revelation, the Koran, the intermediary between God and man;

[1] Ibn-al-Jawzi, *Naqd al-'Ilm w-al-'Ulamā'* (Cairo, 1340), p. 102.
[2] Shahrastāni, p. 100; Baghdādi, ed. Hitti, pp. 87-8; Īji, p. 356.
[3] Cf. Baghdādi, *op cit.* pp. 122-3; ibn-Ḥazm, vol. ii, p. 89.

the Shī'ah made the intermediary a person, the imām.[1] To "I believe in Allah the one God" and "I believe in the revelation of the Koran, which is uncreated from eternity", the Shī'ites now added a new article of faith: "I believe that the imām especially chosen by Allah as the bearer of a part of the divine being is the leader to salvation".

The institution of the imāmate was a product of theocratic opposition to the profane conception of might. According to its theory, as opposed to the Sunnite view,[2] the imām is the sole legitimate head of the Moslem community, divinely designated for the supreme office. He is a lineal descendant of Muḥammad through Fāṭimah and 'Ali. He is a spiritual and religious leader as well as a secular one, endowed with a mysterious power transmitted to him from his predecessor.[3] As such he stands far superior to any other human being and enjoys impeccability (*'iṣmah*).[4] Extremists among the Shī'ah went so far as to consider the imām, on account of this divine and luminous essence, the incarnation of God himself.[5] To them 'Ali and his descendent imāms constitute a continuous divine revelation in human form. A later ultra-Shī'ite sect even held that Gabriel mistook Muḥammad for 'Ali,[6] who was originally intended for the reception of the revelation. In all this the Shī'ite stands in opposition to the Sunnite creed.

How much Shī'ah in its birth and evolution owed to Persian notions and how much to Judaeo-Christian ideas is hard to ascertain. The Mahdi hypothesis which developed later and involved the expectation of a saviour-leader who will usher in a new era of liberty and prosperity was undoubtedly a reflex of Messianic and allied ideas. The enigmatic 'Abdullāh ibn-Saba', who was converted to Islam during the caliphate of 'Uthmān and embarrassed 'Ali with his excessive veneration, thus be-

[1] From an Arabic stem meaning to precede, to lead. The term, which occurs in the Koran (2:118, 15:79, 25:74, 36:11) in no technical sense, is ordinarily applied to the person who in the canonical services indicates the ritual movements. Originally the Prophet, and after him the caliphs or their delegates, filled this office. Ibn-Khaldūn, *Muqaddamah*, pp. 159-60.

[2] For this view consult Īji, pp. 296 *seq.*

[3] Shahrastāni, pp. 108-9; Mas'ūdi, vol. i, p. 70.

[4] Immunity from error and sin is ascribed in varying degrees by Sunnites to the prophets only, especially to Muḥammad. Ibn-Ḥazm, vol. iv, pp. 2-25; I. Goldziher in *Der Islam*, vol. iii (1912), pp. 238-45; Īji, pp. 218 *seq.*

[5] See below, pp. 440 *seq.*

[6] Baghdādi, ed. Hitti, p. 157; ibn-al-Jawzi, *Naqd*, pp. 103-4.

coming the founder of extreme Shī'ism,[1] was a Yamanite Jew. Gnosticism also undoubtedly contributed its share to the development of the imāmate conception. Of all the lands of Islam, al-'Irāq proved the most fertile soil for the germination of 'Alid doctrines, and to the present day Persia with its fifteen millions is the bulwark of the Shī'ah.[2] Within the Shī'ite community itself an almost unlimited number of minor sects arose. Different members of "the house of the Prophet" (*ahl al-bayt*, i.e. 'Ali and his descendants) became the natural centre of attraction for all sorts of non-conformists and malcontents, economic, social, political and religious. Many of the heterodoxies which arose in the first century of Islam and were in themselves a veiled protest against the victorious religion of the Arabians, gradually gravitated to the bosom of Shī'ah as the representative of opposition to the established order. The Ismā'īlites, the Qarmaṭians, the Druzes, the Nuṣayris and the like, with whom we shall deal later, were all offshoots from the Shī'ite sect.

Oratory

Public speaking in its several forms was cultivated during the Umayyad epoch as never before and attained a height unsurpassed in later times. The ***khaṭīb*** used it as an instrument of religion in his Friday noon sermons, the general resorted to it as a means of arousing military enthusiasm among his troops and the provincial governor depended upon it for instilling patriotic feeling in his subjects. In an age with no special facilities for propaganda, oratory provided an excellent channel for spreading ideas and kindling emotions. The highly ethical orations of 'Ali, with their rhymes and wise sayings, the sermonettes of the ascetic al-Ḥasan al-Baṣri († 728) delivered in the presence of the Caliph 'Umar ibn-'Abd-al-'Azīz and preserved by the latter's biographer,[3] the military and patriotic speeches of Ziyād ibn-Abīh and the fiery al-Ḥajjāj—all these are among the most valuable literary treasures handed down to us from that early age.[4]

[1] Īji, p. 343.

[2] In all there are today some 50,000,000 Shī'ites, of whom about eighteen millions live in Iran, seven in India, three in al-'Irāq, four in al-Yaman, where they are known by the name of Zaydis, 350,000 in Lebanon and Syria, where they go by the name of Matāwilah (i.e. partisans [of 'Ali]). Ultra-Shī'ite sects, including the Ismā'īlites, Druzes, Nuṣayris, Yazīdis and 'Ali-Ilāhis, swell the total to approximately 60,000,000, about 14 per cent. of the whole Moslem body. Cf. above, p. 3; below, p. 449.

[3] Ibn-al-Jawzi, *Sīrah*, pp. 121-6.

[4] Consult ibn-Qutaybah, '*Uyūn al-Akhbār*, vol. ii, pp. 231-52; al-Jāḥiẓ, *al-Bayān*, vol. i (Cairo, 1926), pp. 177 *seq.*, vol. ii, pp. 47 *seq.*; '*Iqd*, vol. ii, pp. 172 *seq.*

Corre-spondence

Political correspondence under the orthodox caliphs was so brief and to the point that we hardly have an official note more than a few lines in length.[1] To 'Abd-al-Ḥamīd al-Kātib (i.e. the scribe, † 750), secretary of the last Umayyad caliphs, is ascribed by ibn-Khallikān[2] the introduction of the flowery, long-drawn-out style with its conventional, polite phraseology betraying Persian influence. This affected style became a model for future generations of writers. A favourite Arabic saying had it that "the art of epistolary composition [*inshā'*] began with 'Abd-al-Ḥamīd and ended with ibn-al-'Amīd".[3] Persian literary influence can also be detected in the many wise sayings and proverbs attributed to 'Ali, to his lieutenant al-Aḥnaf (the bandy-legged)[4] ibn-Qays († after 687) and even to Aktham ibn-Ṣayfi of pre-Islamic reputation, one of whose titles was "the sage [*ḥakīm*] of the Arabians".[5]

Poetry

The greatest intellectual measure of progress achieved under the Umayyads, however, was undoubtedly in the field of poetical composition. That the birth of Islam was not favourable to the chief of the Muses is evinced by the fact that the glorious period of conquest and expansion inspired no poet in a "nation of poets". With the accession of the worldly Umayyads the old connections with the goddesses of wine, song and poetry were re-established. For the first time the poet of love makes his full appearance in Arabic. While many pre-Islamic bards did preface their long pieces (*qaṣīdahs*) with a few verses of erotic character, yet none of them could be said to have specialized in love poetry (*ghazal*). From this amatory prelude (*nasīb*) of the early *qaṣīdahs* Arabic lyric poetry arose under the influence of Persian singers and after their example.

The peninsular school has 'Umar ibn-abi-Rabī'ah[6] († *ca.* 719) as its chief exponent. This prince of erotic poetry, "the Ovid of Arabia", was an impious Qurayshite of independent means,[7] who made it his business to make love to the beautiful damsels

[1] For specimens consult Qalqashandi, *Ṣubḥ*, vol. vi, pp. 388-91.

[2] Vol. i, p. 550; cf. Mas'ūdi, vol. vi, p. 81.

[3] A vizir of Rukn-al-Dawlah the Buwayhid.

[4] Jāḥiẓ, *Bayān*, vol. i, p. 58. See ibn-Qutaybah, *Ma'ārif*, p. 216; Ṭabari, vol. ii, pp. 438-9.

[5] Ibn-Qutaybah, *Ma'ārif*, p. 153; cf. *Aghāni*, vol. xv, p. 73, l. 28. See Jāḥiẓ, *Bayān*, vol. ii, p. 63.

[6] His *Dīwān*, ed. Paul Schwarz, 2 vols. (Leipzig, 1901–9).

[7] *Aghāni*, vol. i, p. 32. On his life and works, see Jibrā'īl Jabbūr, *'Umar ibn-abi-Rabī'ah*, 2 vols. (Beirūt, 1935–9).

pilgrimaging in Makkah and al-Madīnah as well as to such charming residents as the famous Sukaynah.[1] In language of intense passion and exquisite felicity he immortalized his feeling towards the fair sex. The freshness and chivalry of his verse stand in marked contrast to the primitive passion of Imru'-al-Qays on the one hand and to the stereotyped sentiment of a later age on the other.[2]

If 'Umar represented free love in poetry, his contemporary Jamīl († 701) of the banu-'Udhrah, a Christian tribe of Yamanite origin settled in al-Ḥijāz, stood for pure and innocent love of the platonic type. Jamīl's verses, all addressed to his sweetheart Buthaynah, who belonged to the same tribe,[3] breathe a spirit of tenderness unparalleled in that age. Because of their esthetic value and simple unaffected language they have since been set to music by many Arabic singers. Like Jamīl al-'Udhri, the semi-mythical Majnūn Layla,[4] whose original name is said to have been Qays ibn-al-Mulawwaḥ,[5] represents the lyric type of poetical composition. Qays, according to legend, became infatuated to the point of madness (whence his surname *majnūn*) with a woman of the same tribe named Layla, who reciprocated his love but was obliged to marry another to satisfy her father. Crazed with despair, Qays passes the rest of his life wandering half-naked among the hills and valleys of his native Najd singing the beauty of his beloved and yearning for a sight of her. Only when her name was mentioned would he return to his normal self.[6] Thus did Majnūn Layla become the hero of numberless Arabic, Persian and Turkish romances extolling the power of undying love. Undoubtedly many of the poems attached to the names of Jamīl and Majnūn were not actually composed by them but were originally ballads and folk-songs.

Besides love poetry, political poetry made its appearance under Umayyad auspices. The first occasion was the request made of Miskīn al-Dārimi to compose and sing publicly verses commemorating the nomination of Yazīd to the caliphate.[7] To this

[1] Ibn-Qutaybah, *Shi'r*, p. 349.
[2] See W. G. Palgrave, *Essays on Eastern Questions* (London, 1872), p. 279.
[3] Consult ibn-Qutaybah, *Shi'r*, pp. 260-68; *Aghāni*, vol. vii, pp. 77-110.
[4] *Aghāni*, vol. i, p. 169, quoted by ibn-Khallikān, vol. i, p. 148.
[5] Al-Kutubi, *Fawāt al-Wafayāt* (Būlāq, 1283), vol. ii, p. 172, makes the date of his death about A.H. 80 = 699.
[6] Ibn-Qutaybah, *Shi'r*, pp. 358-62.
[7] *Aghāni*, vol. xviii, pp. 71-2; cf. ibn-Qutaybah, *Shi'r*, p. 347.

period also belongs the first attempt to compile ancient pre-Islamic poetry, which attempt was undertaken by Ḥammād al-Rāwiyah (i.e. the transmitter, *ca.* 713–72).[1] Ḥammād was born in al-Kūfah of a Daylami (Persian) prisoner of war[2] and spoke Arabic with an accent, but he was one of those famed in Arabic annals for possessing phenomenal memories. In answer to a question by al-Walīd II he offered to recite of the *jāhilīyah* poems alone, rhyming in each of the letters of the alphabet, at least one hundred different odes for each letter. After listening in person and by proxy to 2900 *qaṣīdahs*, as we are told, al-Walīd felt satisfied and ordered 100,000 dirhams for the reciter.[3] Ḥammād's great merit, no doubt, was his collection of the famous Golden Odes, otherwise called Mu'allaqāt.

The provincial school of poetry in the Umayyad period was headed by al-Farazdaq (*ca.* 640–728) and Jarīr († *ca.* 729), that of the capital by al-Akhṭal (*ca.* 640–*ca.* 710). All three were born and brought up in al-'Irāq. They were satirists as well as panegyrists. As poets the trio stand in the very front rank among those with whom Arab criticism has found nothing to compare since their time. Al-Akhṭal, the Christian, was the champion of the Umayyad cause against the theocratic party;[4] al-Farazdaq, the dissolute, was the poet laureate of 'Abd-al-Malik and his sons al-Walīd, Sulaymān[5] and Yazīd; Jarīr, the greatest satirist of the age, was the court poet of al-Ḥajjāj.[6] In their panegyrics, on which they lived rather than on their lampoons, these poets performed the same function as the party press today. Al-Farazdaq[7] and Jarīr often attacked each other in the most virulent and abusive language, and al-Akhṭal as a rule sided with the former. How lightly Christianity sat on the heart of the profane, wine-bibbing Akhṭal is illustrated by the words of consolation he addressed to his pregnant wife as she rushed to touch

[1] *Fihrist*, p. 91; ibn-Khallikān, vol. i, p. 294.
[2] Ibn-Qutaybah, *Ma'ārif*, p. 268.
[3] Ibn-Khallikān, vol. i, p. 292; *Aghāni*, vol. v, pp. 164-5. See *'Iqd*, vol. iii, pp. 137-8.
[4] Ibn-Qutaybah, *Shi'r*, pp. 301-4.
[5] *Ibid.* pp. 297-8. For Farazdaq's eulogies of his patron caliphs see his *Dīwān*, ed. R. Boucher (Paris, 1875), *passim*.
[6] Ibn-Qutaybah, p. 287. For samples of his encomiums see his *Dīwān* (Cairo, 1313), vol. i.
[7] On him see *Aghāni*, vol. viii, pp. 186-97, vol. xix, pp. 2-52; ibn-Khallikān, vol. iii, pp. 136-46 = de Slane, vol. iii, pp. 612-28; Joseph Hell, *Das Leben des Farazdak* (Leipzig, 1903).

the garment of a passing bishop and succeeded only in reaching the tail of the donkey he was riding: "He and the tail of his ass—there is no difference!"[1]

Education of the formal type was not common in those days. To the early Umayyad princes the *bādiyah*, Syrian desert, acted as a sort of school to which they sent their young sons to acquire the pure Arabic tongue and become well versed in poetry. It was thither that Mu'āwiyah sent his son and future successor Yazīd. The public considered him educated who could read and write his native language, use the bow and arrow and swim. Such a person was styled *al-kāmil*, the perfect one.[2] The value of swimming was enhanced by life on the Mediterranean coast The ethical ideals of education as gleaned from the literature bearing on the subject were courage, endurance in time of trouble (*ṣabr*), observance of the rights and obligations of neighbourliness (*jiwār*), manliness (*murū'ah*), generosity and hospitality, regard for women and fulfilment of solemn promises. Many of these will be recognized as the virtues highly prized in Bedouin life.

Education

After the time of 'Abd-al-Malik the tutor or preceptor (*mu'addib*), usually a client or a Christian, became a standing figure in the court. The tutor of this caliph's sons received the following injunction from their father: "Teach them to swim and accustom them to little sleep".[3] 'Umar II took his children so severely to task for violating the rules of Arabic grammar that he was inclined to use corporal punishment.[4] Significant are the instructions he communicated officially to their tutor: "Let the first moral lesson impressed upon them be hatred of means of amusement, whose initiative is from the devil and whose consequence is the wrath of God".[5]

The public desiring to secure an education, as education went in those days, patronized the mosques where classes centring on the Koran and ḥadīth were given. The earliest teachers in Islam were therefore the Koran readers (*qurrā'*). As early as the year 17 (638) the Caliph 'Umar sent such teachers in all

[1] *Aghāni*, vol. vii, p. 183, where the anecdote is reported to illustrate his devotion to religion.

[2] Ibn-Sa'd, vol. iii, pt. 2, p. 91, ll. 10-11, cf. vol. v, p. 309, ll. 7 *seq.*; *Aghāni*, vol. vi, p. 165, l. 9.

[3] Mubarrad, p. 77, ll. 6-7.

[4] Yāqūt, *Mu'jam al-Udabā'*, ed. Margoliouth, vol. i (Leyden, 1907), pp. 25-6.

[5] Ibn-al-Jawzi, *Sīrah*, pp. 257-8. Consult Jāḥiẓ, *Bayān*, vol. ii, pp. 138-43.

directions and ordered the people to meet with them on Fridays in the mosques. 'Umar II sent as chief judge to Egypt Yazīd ibn-abi-Ḥabīb († 746), who is said to have been the first to distinguish himself as teacher there.[1] In al-Kūfah we read of a certain al-Ḍaḥḥāk ibn-Muzāḥim[2] († 723), who kept an elementary school (*kuttāb*) and made no charges for instruction.[3] In the second Moslem century we even hear of a Bedouin settling in al-Baṣrah and conducting a school where fees were charged.[4]

Science

"Science," the Arabs say, ascribing the words to the Prophet, "is twofold: that which relates to religion and that which relates to the body [i.e. medicine]."

The peninsular medicine was very primitive indeed. Legitimate remedies mingled with magical practices and talismans against the evil eye. A few prescriptions limiting treatment to the use of honey, cupping and bleeding embedded in traditions termed "the Prophet's medicine" have been preserved and handed down to posterity. The critical ibn-Khaldūn in his famous *Muqaddamah*[5] speaks slightingly of this type of medicine, declaring that the Prophet was sent to teach religious laws and principles rather than medication.

Scientific Arab medicine springs from sources mainly Greek and partly Persian. Persian medicine itself was influenced by Greek tradition. The list of Arabian physicians in the first century of Islam is headed by al-Ḥārith ibn-Kaladah († *ca.* 634) of al-Ṭā'if, who studied in Persia.[6] Al-Ḥārith was the first scientifically trained man in the peninsula and won the honorary title of "the doctor of the Arabians".[7] In the art of healing he was succeeded, as was customary, by his son al-Naḍr, whose mother was the Prophet's maternal aunt.[8]

By the time of the Arab conquest of Western Asia, Greek science was no more a living force. It was rather a tradition in the hands of Greek- or Syriac-writing commentators and practitioners. The court doctors of the Umayyads belonged to this group. Outstanding among them were ibn-Uthāl, the Christian

[1] Suyūṭi, *Ḥusn*, vol. i, p. 134; cf. Kindi, *Wulāh*, p. 89.
[2] Mentioned by Jāḥiẓ, *Bayān*, vol. i, p. 175, as a tutor to 'Abd-al-Malik's sons.
[3] Ibn-Sa'd, vol. vi, p. 210. [4] Yāqūt, *Udabā'*, vol. ii, p. 239. [5] P. 412.
[6] Ibn-abi-Uṣaybi'ah, *'Uyūn al-Anbā' fi Ṭabaqāt al-Aṭibbā'*, ed. A. Müller (Cairo, 1882), vol. i, p. 109; ibn-al-'Ibri, p. 156.
[7] Ibn-al-'Ibri, pp. 156-7; Qifṭi, *Ḥukamā'*, p. 161.
[8] Ibn-abi-Uṣaybi'ah, vol. i, p. 113; cf. Nawawi *Tahdhīb*, p. 593.

physician of Mu'āwiyah,[1] and Tayādhūq, the evidently Greek physician of al-Ḥajjāj.[2] Some of Tayādhūq's aphorisms have been preserved, but none of the three or four books ascribed to him. A Jewish physician of Persian origin, Māsarjawayh of al-Baṣrah, who flourished in the first days of Marwān ibn-al-Ḥakam, translated (683) into Arabic a Syriac treatise on medicine originally composed in Greek by a Christian priest in Alexandria, Ahrūn by name,[3] and was thus responsible for the earliest scientific book in the language of Islam. The Caliph al-Walīd is credited with having segregated persons afflicted with leprosy and with having made special provision for their treatment.[4] 'Umar II is said to have transferred the schools of medicine from Alexandria, where the Greek tradition flourished, to Antioch and Ḥarrān.[5]

Alchemy

Alchemy, like medicine, one of the few sciences in which the Arabs later made a distinct contribution, was one of the disciplines early developed. Khālid († 704 or 708), the son of the second Umayyad caliph and the "philosopher [*ḥakīm*] of the Marwānids", was according to the *Fihrist*[6] (our oldest and best source of information) the first in Islam to have translations made from Greek and Coptic books on alchemy, medicine and astrology. Though proved legendary,[7] the ascription of this activity to Khālid is significant, since it points out the truth that the Arabs drew their scientific knowledge from the older Greek sources and received their first impulse therefrom. With the name of this Umayyad prince legend associates the name of the famous Jābir ibn-Ḥayyān (Latinized Geber); but Jābir flourished later, about 776, and will be dealt with under the 'Abbāsids. Likewise the astrological and alchemical treatises ascribed to Ja'far al-Ṣādiq (700–765),[8] a descendant of 'Ali and one of the twelve imāms of the Shī'ah, have been discredited by critical modern scholarship.[9] The most unfortunate fact about the intellectual

[1] Ibn-abi-Uṣaybi'ah, vol. i, p. 116. [2] *Ibid.* p. 121; see above, p. 220.
[3] Ibn-al-'Ibri, p. 192. [4] *Ibid.* p. 195; Ṭabari, vol. ii, p. 1196.
[5] Ibn-abi-Uṣaybi'ah, vol. i, p. 116, ll. 25-6. [6] Pp. 242, 354.
[7] Julius Ruska, *Arabische Alchemisten*, I. *Chālid Ibn Jazīd Ibn Mu'āwija* (Heidelberg, 1924), pp. 8 *seq.*
[8] *Fihrist*, p. 317, l. 25; ibn-Khallikān, vol. i, p. 185 = de Slane, vol. i, p. 300; Ḥājji Khalfah, *Kashf al-Ẓunūn 'an Asāmi al-Kutub w-al-Funūn*, ed. Fluegel, vol. ii (Leipzig, 1837), pp. 581, 604, vol. iii (London, 1842), pp. 53, 128.
[9] J. Ruska, *Arabische Alchemisten*, II. *Ǵa'far Alṣādiq, der Sechste Imām* (Heidelberg, 1924), pp. 49-59.

life under the Umayyads is that it left no extant traces in the form of documents from which we can properly evaluate it.

Architecture

If there ever was an indigenous Arabian architecture it could have existed only in al-Yaman, concerning which our present state of investigation and exploration is as yet unable to afford sufficient data. Even then South Arabian art could not have played much of a part in the northern life of the peninsula. Here the tent was the ordinary dwelling, the open air the temple and the desert sands the tomb. The inhabitant of the rare oasis had, as he still has today, a rude architecture represented by buildings of sun-dried brick covered with flat roofs of palm wood and clay, devoid of decoration and ornament and suited only to the simplest needs. Even the Ḥijāz national shrine, al-Kaʿbah, was nothing but a primitive cube-like structure with no roof. As the structure stood at the time of Muḥammad it was the work of a Coptic Christian carpenter who used wood salvaged from the wreck of some Byzantine ships cast ashore at Juddah. The rock-cut tombs of Madāʾin Ṣāliḥ (ancient al-Ḥijr), the picturesque chambers carved in the multi-coloured sand cliffs of Petra, the colonnaded and arched palaces and sanctuaries of Palmyra, such churches as the magnificent one rebuilt by the Ghassānid phylarch al-Mundhir ibn-al-Ḥārith on the grave of the martyred St. Sergius at al-Ruṣāfah—all these indeed reveal a high order of artistic technique, but it is a technique borrowed from Hellenized Egypt and Syria and is not characteristically Arabian.

Architecture, as the first and most permanent of the arts, has in its religious variety always been the principal representative of the building art. The place of worship, literally the home of the deity, is the first structure on which the newly awakened soul strives to impress a loftier character than that required to satisfy the material needs of a human habitation. In the case of the Moslem Arabs art found its supreme expression in religious architecture. The Moslem architects, or the men they employed, evolved a scheme of building, simple and dignified, based on earlier patterns but singularly expressive of the spirit of the new religion. Thus we have in the mosque (from Ar. *masjid*, a place to prostrate oneself) an epitome of the history of the development of Islamic civilization in its interracial and international relationships. Perhaps no clearer example could be cited to illustrate

Photo *Bonfils*

INTERIOR OF THE DOME OF THE ROCK

the cultural interplay between Islam and its neighbours than the mosque.

The Mosque of al-Madīnah

The simple mosque of Muḥammad at al-Madīnah rather than the Makkan sanctuary fortuitously became the general prototype of the congregational mosque in the first century of Islam. This mosque consisted of a courtyard open to the sky enclosed by walls of sun-baked clay.[1] As a protection from the sun the Prophet later extended the flat roof from the adjacent buildings

From Ibrāhīm Rif'at, "Mir'āt al-Ḥaramayn"

THE MOSQUE OF MAKKAH SEEN FROM THE EAST

to cover the whole open court. The roof consisted of palm trunks used as columns to support a cover of palm fronds and mud.[2] A palm trunk fixed in the ground served first as a pulpit (*minbar*)[3] for the Prophet to stand on while addressing the congregation.[4] This was later replaced by a small platform of tamarisk wood with three steps copied from those seen in Christian churches in Syria.

[1] Ibn-Hishām, pp. 336-7.

[2] Balādhuri, p. 6; Bukhāri, vol. i, pp. 106-7.

[3] In *Orientalische Studien. Theodor Nöldeke*, ed. C. Bezold (Giessen, 1906), vol. i, pp. 331 *seq.*, C. H. Becker has shown that the *minbar* was originally a raised seat or throne used by the ruler and not associated with worship.

[4] Ibn-Sa'd, vol. i, pt. 2, p. 9; F. Wüstenfeld, *Geschichte der Stadt Medina* (Göttingen, 1860), p. 63; cf. Bukhāri, vol. i, p. 107.

Whether the Prophet found it necessary to erect an indicator (*miḥrāb*) of the direction of prayer (*qiblah*) in his mosque is not certain. In reciting their prayers the worshippers arranged themselves in ranks parallel to and facing the wall, originally toward Jerusalem and later toward Makkah.[1] From the top of the flat roof the Abyssinian Bilāl with his stentorian voice called the believers to prayer.[2] Here, then, we have in their simplest forms almost all the rudiments of a congregational mosque—a court, some cover to shelter the worshipper and a pulpit.

The subsequent advance of the Arabians fanwise through Western Asia and North Africa brought them into possession

From Ibrāhīm Rif'at, "Mir'āt al-Ḥaramayn"

THE INTERIOR OF THE MOSQUE OF AL-MADĪNAH

of numberless standing and ruined structures representing a high artistic development and, what is more essential, it put them in control of the living technical knowledge and skill inherited by members of the conquered races from ages past. This technique, applied to the religious needs of the Moslem community as indicated by the Madīnah Mosque and modified by local conditions in different regions, produced in course of time what has been variously designated Saracenic, Arabian, Moslem and Mohammedan[3] art. The structural material, whether stone, brick

[1] Ibn-Sa'd, vol. i, pt. 2, pp. 3-5.

[2] One or two years after his arrival in al-Madīnah the Prophet decided on the *adhān* as the formal call to prayer after considering the possibility of using the *nāqūs* (wooden gong) as in the Christian churches. Ibn-Sa'd, vol. i, pt. 2, p. 7.

[3] Modern Moslems object to the use of this term because of its parallelism to the term "Christian" applied to the worshippers of Christ, while they, as they maintain, are not worshippers of Muḥammad.

or clay, was in each case determined by what had prevailed in the particular locality. In Syria Moslem architecture was influenced by the pre-existent Christian Syro-Byzantine style with its native and Roman antecedents. In Mesopotamia and Persia it was affected by the Nestorian and Sāsānid forms based on an earlier native tradition. In Egypt many decorative motifs were supplied by the local Copts. Thus there gradually developed a number of distinct schools of Arab art: (1) Syro-Egyptian, following the Greco-Roman and native precedents; (2) 'Irāqo-Persian, based on Sāsānid and ancient Chaldaean and Assyrian styles; (3) Spanish and North African, showing native Christian and Visigothic influence and often called Moorish or Maghribi; and (4) Indian, bearing clear marks of the Hindu style. In China the mosque is almost a replica of the Buddhist temple.

Early mosques in the provinces

The first mosque erected in a conquered land was that of al-Baṣrah built by 'Utbah ibn-Ghazwān (637 or 638), who also founded the city itself as a winter camp for the army. This place of prayer was at first an open space fenced round with reeds. The edifice was later rebuilt of clay and sun-dried bricks (*libn*) by abu-Mūsa al-Ash'ari, 'Umar's governor, who covered the roof with grass.[1] In 638 or 639 the invading general, Sa'd ibn-abi-Waqqāṣ, established the other military camp, al-Kūfah, with a simple mosque as its centre. Close by the mosque stood the governor's residence (*dār al-imārah*). As in al-Baṣrah, the mosque was originally an open square with walls of reed and later of clay and sun-dried bricks.[2] Ziyād, the viceroy of Mu'āwiyah, rebuilt this mosque with a colonnade following the Sāsānid model. In other respects the mosque conformed to the type fortuitously formulated by Muḥammad in al-Madīnah. No trace is left of this structure or of the Baṣrah mosque. Of the 'Ali mosque in al-Kūfah, erected about 656 and visited in 1184 by the famous Andalusian traveller ibn-Jubayr,[3] little is known.

The third important camp in Islam was that of 'Amr ibn-al-'Āṣ in al-Fusṭāṭ (Old Cairo). Here in 642 'Amr laid out the first Moslem place of prayer in Africa. In its original form 'Amr's mosque, of which there is likewise no trace,[4] was like the others a simple quadrangle with no niche (*miḥrāb*) to indicate the direc-

[1] Balādhuri, pp. 346-7, 350; Yāqūt, *Buldān*, vol. i, p. 642.
[2] Ṭabari, vol. i, p. 2489; Yāqūt, vol. iv, pp. 323-4.
[3] Pp. 211-12.
[4] For the many early rebuildings it underwent see Yāqūt, vol. iii, pp. 899-900.

tion of prayer and with no minaret (*mi'dhanah*). 'Amr equipped it later with a pulpit built and presented by the Christian king of Nubia.[1] The next important mosque was that of 'Uqbah ibn-Nāfi' in al-Qayrawān (670–75) which, like al-Fusṭāṭ, was a military camp. 'Uqbah started with the mosque and government house as a centre and grouped the people's dwellings around them.[2] The mosque was rebuilt several times by his successors and finally by the Aghlabid Ziyādat-Allāh I (817–38), since whose days it has stood as one of the greatest sanctuaries in Islam.

In those cases where Moslems established themselves in towns already standing, use was made of older structures. In al-Madā'in, Sa'd ibn-abi-Waqqāṣ used the *Īwān* (arched hall) of the Persian emperor as a place of worship.[3] In Damascus the Cathedral of St. John was rebuilt into a mosque by al-Walīd I.[4] But in Ḥimṣ the same building is said to have been used in common as a mosque and as a church.[5]

The *miḥrāb*, a recess or niche in the wall of the mosque indicating the direction of prayer, was a later addition into the equipment of the mosque taken over from the church. Al-Walīd and his governor, 'Umar ibn-'Abd-al-'Azīz, are usually credited with its introduction,[6] though some credit Mu'āwiyah.[7] The Madīnah Mosque was evidently the first to get a *miḥrāb*. The *miḥrāb* rapidly became a common feature of all mosques and like the Christian altar appropriated for itself the largest measure of sacredness. As such it became the recipient of the varied forms of decoration lavished on it by the believers and may therefore be considered the standard for determining the quality of the continually changing styles of Islamic decorative art.

A profane innovation in the mosque for which Mu'āwiyah[8] is generally blamed is the *maqṣūrah*, a fenced-off part in the interior of the mosque reserved for the use of the caliph. Different

[1] Maqrīzi (Būlāq), vol. ii, p. 248, l. 30. [2] Yāqūt, vol. iv, p. 213.
[3] Ṭabari, vol. i, pp. 2443, 2451.
[4] Balādhuri, p. 125; Yāqūt, vol. ii, p. 591; ibn-Jubayr, p. 262.
[5] Iṣṭakhri, p. 61; ibn-Ḥawqal, p. 117; Maqdisi, p. 156.
[6] Maqrīzi, vol. ii, p. 247, ll. 16-17; Maqdisi, p. 80, l. 17; ibn-Baṭṭūṭah, vol. i, pp. 271, 272; ibn-Duqmāq, *al-Intiṣār li-Wāsiṭat 'Iqd al-Amṣār*, ed. Vollers (Būlāq, 1893), pt. iv, p. 62, l. 12; Suyūṭi, *Ḥusn*, vol. ii, p. 149.
[7] Ibn-al-Faqīh, p. 109, l. 2.
[8] Ya'qūbi, vol. ii, p. 571. Others ascribe it to Marwān ibn-al-Ḥakam (Balādhuri, p. 6, l. 16 = Hitti, p. 20) or to 'Uthmān (Maqrīzi, vol. ii, p. 247, l. 32).

reasons have been assigned for its introduction, the chief being protection for the person of the caliph after the Khārijite attempt upon his life.[1] The *maqṣūrah* was evidently used by the caliphs for retirement and rest or for deliberation.[2]

Like the *miḥrāb*, the minaret was introduced by the Umayyads. Syria was therefore the original home of the minaret. Here the minaret took the form of the native watch-tower or of its successor the church tower, which was square.[3]

One of the earliest authorities[4] to mention a minaret on the Umayyad Mosque in Damascus explicitly states that it had been a watch-tower (*nāṭūr*) belonging to the Cathedral of St. John. In Egypt the minaret is said to have been introduced by a governor of Mu'āwiyah who provided each of the four corners of the Mosque of 'Amr in al-Fusṭāṭ with one.[5] In al-'Irāq the Baṣrah Mosque was provided by Mu'āwiyah's governor, Ziyād, with a stone minaret.[6] But it was again the famous Umayyad builder, al-Walīd, who was probably responsible for many minarets in Syria and al-Ḥijāz. Al-Walīd's governor, 'Umar, introduced the new feature into the Madīnah Mosque.[7] After his time minarets became more and more numerous.

While the square stone minaret of Syria was the oldest in Islam and served as prototype for others, especially in North Africa and Spain, it was not the only type developed. Moslem minarets followed the traditional shape of the towers of the country in which they arose. In Egypt minarets for many centuries were built only of brick and the famous lighthouse of Alexandria, the Pharos, is said by some to have exercised some architectural influence. In al-'Irāq a ninth-century Moslem tower-minaret at Sāmarra on the Tigris reflects the ancient Assyrian *ziggurat* (high place) with its seven stories representing the sun, the moon and the five planets then known.[8]

The Dome of the Rock

Because of its biblical association and as the first *qiblah* of Islam[9] and the traditional stopping-place of Muḥammad on

[1] Dīnawari, p. 229; ibn-Khaldūn, *Muqaddamah*, pp. 224-6; cf. Ṭabari, vol. i, p. 3465, ll. 8-9.
[2] Cf. *Aghāni*, vol. xvii, p. 116, l. 6.
[3] Maqdisi, p. 182, ll. 8-9.
[4] Ibn-al-Faqīh, p. 108; cf. ibn-Baṭṭūṭah, vol. i, p. 203.
[5] Maqrīzi, vol. ii, p. 248.
[6] Balādhuri, p. 348.
[7] Wüstenfeld, *Stadt*, p. 75; ibn-Baṭṭūṭah, vol. i, p. 272.
[8] Morris Jastrow, Jr., *The Civilization of Babylonia and Assyria* (Philadelphia, 1915), pp 376-7. See below, pp. 418-19.
[9] Ibn-Sa'd, vol. i, pt. 2, p. 3; see Koran 2 : 136, 138.

From Karl Gröber, "Palästina, Arabien und Syrien" (Atlantis-Verlag, Berlin)

THE DOME OF THE ROCK AND THE DOME OF THE CHAIN

his famous nocturnal journey heavenward, Jerusalem very early acquired special sanctity in the eyes of all Moslems.[1] In 638 when the Caliph 'Umar visited the city he possibly erected a simple place of worship of timber or brick on the Moriah hill, where once stood the Temple of Solomon and later a heathen sanctuary and a Christian church. When 'Abd-al-Malik felt the need for a centre of worship that should outshine the Church of the Holy Sepulchre,[2] rival the Mosque of Makkah then in the hands of the anti-caliph 'Abdullāh ibn-al-Zubayr and deviate therefrom the current of pilgrimage,[3] he built in 691 on the same site in Jerusalem the Dome of the Rock, wrongly called the "Mosque of 'Umar". The Dome therefore stands on one of the most sacred spots on earth, a spot hallowed by Jewish, heathen, Christian and Moslem associations and considered by tradition the place where Abraham intended to sacrifice his son Isaac. The Kufic inscription round its dome, a part of which was later falsified by the Caliph al-Ma'mūn,[4] is one of the oldest Islamic writings extant.[5] 'Abd-al-Malik used materials derived from the Christian buildings that had stood there before they were destroyed or damaged by Chosroes II in 614 and employed native craftsmen, some of whom may have been of Byzantine origin. Here was a radical change from the old pattern, involving the introduction of mosaic and other decorative motifs and a dome intended to surpass the beautiful cupola of the Church of the Holy Sepulchre.[6] The result was an architectural monument of such noble beauty that it has scarcely been surpassed anywhere. To the Moslems the Dome of the Rock is more than a place of archæological interest and artistic value—it is a living symbol of their faith. Although it has gone through a few changes and repairs, particularly as a result of the terrific earthquake of 1016,[7] the Dome has preserved in general its original form and is therefore the earliest Moslem monument surviving. The oldest description of it is that of ibn-al-Faqīh,[8] written about 903, followed by that of al-Maqdisi[9] written about 985.

[1] For Jerusalem as the scene of judgment day see Nuwayri, vol. i, pp. 334 *seq.*

[2] Maqdisi, p. 159. [3] Ya'qūbi, vol. ii, p. 311. [4] See above, p. 220.

[5] In the Arab Museum at Cairo is a tombstone found in the cemetery of Old Cairo bearing a Kufic inscription dated A.H. 31/651–2. See Ḥasan Muḥammad al-Hawāri in *al-Hilāl*, vol. xxxviii (1930), pp. 1179-91.

[6] Maqdisi, p. 159. The Dome was modelled after the cathedral of Buṣra. Cf. M. S. Briggs, *Muhammadan Architecture in Egypt and Palestine* (Oxford, 1924), p. 37.

[7] Ibn-al-Athīr, vol. ix, p. 209. [8] Pp. 100-101. [9] Pp. 169-71.

The Aqṣa Mosque

The Dome is the shrine of which the Aqṣa Mosque is the sanctuary. The term al-Masjid al-Aqṣa, as we have learned before, is used in Arabic literature in a general sense to include the whole collection of sacred buildings comprising the Dome itself, the tombs, dervish monasteries (sing. *takīyah* or *zāwiyah*) and public fountains (sing. *sabīl*) erected by many caliphs from 'Abd-al-Malik to the Ottoman Sultan Sulaymān the Magnificent which cover an area of some thirty-four acres. Strictly, the word Aqṣa is applied to the mosque built by 'Abd-al-Malik not far from the Dome. In its construction use was made of the ruins of St. Mary's Church of Justinian, which stood on that site until demolished by Chosroes. The Aqṣa was rebuilt about 771 by the 'Abbāsid al-Manṣūr following an earthquake, and was later modified by the Crusaders. Ṣalāḥ-al-Dīn (Saladin) restored it (1187) to Islam. As in the case of the Dome our earliest description of it dates from ibn-al-Faqīh [1] and al-Maqdisi.[2]

The Umayyad Mosque

In 705 'Abd-al-Malik's son al-Walīd took over the site of the basilica of Damascus dedicated to St. John, originally a temple of Jupiter, and built there the grand mosque named after the Umayyads.[3] How much of the Christian construction was preserved in al-Walīd's mosque is difficult to ascertain. The two southern minarets stand on ancient church towers which belonged to the old basilica,[4] but the northern minaret, used as a beacon tower, was certainly constructed by al-Walīd and became the model for similar structures in Syria, North Africa and Spain. It is the oldest purely Moslem minaret surviving. The three naves and a transept, above which rises the great dome, with their mosaics, are also the work of this caliph who, we are told, employed Persian and Indian craftsmen as well as Greek artisans provided by the emperor of Constantinople.[5] Papyri recently discovered show that material and skilled workmen were imported from Egypt.[6] The walls were sumptuously decorated with marbles and mosaics. The geographer al-Maqdisi,[7] who visited the mosque in the latter part of the tenth century, speaks

[1] P. 100.
[2] Pp. 168-9.
[3] Among the present leading mosques of Aleppo, Ḥimṣ and Beirūt are some which were churches in the past.
[4] Cf. Yāqūt, vol. ii, p. 593.
[5] Maqdisi, p. 158; ibn-'Asākir, vol. i, p. 202; ibn-Jubayr, p. 261; cf. Ṭabari, vol. ii, p. 1194.
[6] H. I. Bell in *Der Islam*, vol. ii (1911), pp. 274, 374.
[7] P. 157; see also Iṣṭakhri, p. 57; ibn-Rustah, p. 326.

Photo *Bonfils*

UMAYYAD MOSQUE OF DAMASCUS: THE COLONNADE AND NORTHERN MINARET

of its mosaics of gold and precious stones representing trees and cities and bearing beautiful inscriptions. These same representations, covered later by some pious caliph, were rediscovered in 1928.[1] In this mosque we find the first appearance of the semicircular niche for prayer (*miḥrāb*). Here the horseshoe arch is also apparent. The vignette decorations served as a model for those of the great Qayrawān Mosque as remodelled by the Aghlabids in the ninth century. Though it was burned in 1069, again in 1400 by Tamerlane and for the last time in 1893, the Umayyad Mosque has always held its place in Moslem imagination as the fourth wonder of the world.[2] It is also considered the fourth sanctuary in Islam (above, p. 221).

In the period between the first primitive place of worship of al-Madīnah and the two sumptuous mosques of Jerusalem and Damascus the evolution of the Moslem congregational (*jamā'ah*) mosque was rendered complete. The congregational mosque, be it noted, has always been more than a building for devotion; it serves as a general assembly hall and as a political and educational forum.[3] The physical needs of the congregation are now amply provided for by a sheltered sanctuary and a covered approach; the ritual needs are met by the minarets, niches, pulpits and outside fountains for ablution; and the political needs by a majesty of plan and splendour of ornament that help to serve notice on the world that the followers of the new faith are in nowise behind those who worship in the grand cathedrals of Christendom.

Palaces: Quṣayr 'Amrah

In architectural fields other than the religious the Umayyads left but few monuments. Chief among these are the desert palaces erected by princes of the caliphal family. Most of the caliphs themselves, like the Ghassānid rulers before them, had country seats, and apart from Mu'āwiyah and 'Abd-al-Malik hardly any of them lived in Damascus. In the capital itself nothing is left of the Khaḍrā',[4] the imperial residence adjoining the great mosque, nor are any traces left of al-Ḥajjāj's residence of the same name, al-Qubbah al-Khaḍrā',[5] in Wāsiṭ. But the

[1] E. de Lorey and M. van Berchem, *Les mosaïques de la mosquée des Omayyades à Damas* (Paris, 1930). K. A. C. Creswell, *Early Muslim Architecture*, pt. 1 (Oxford, 1932), pp. 119-20.

[2] Ibn-al-Faqīh, p. 106; ibn-'Asākir, vol. i, p. 198; Yāqūt, vol. ii, p. 591.

[3] In recent years the principal outbreaks against European authority in Syria and Egypt have had their inception in the Friday mosque meetings.

[4] See above, p. 215. Ibn-al-Athīr, vol. v, p. 224.

[5] Balādhuri, p. 290; Mas'ūdi, *Tanbīh*, p. 360; Ya'qūbi, p. 322

From B. Moritz, "Bilder aus Palästina, Nord-Arabien und dem Sinai" (Dietrich Reimer Verlag, Berlin)

FAÇADE OF AL-MUSHATTA

fringes of the Syrian desert are strewn with the remains of palaces which were originally either Roman fortresses on the *limes* repaired and remodelled by Umayyad architects or which were erected by those architects on Byzantine and Persian patterns. The ruins of a palace known by the modern name of al-Ukhayḍir lie not far from 'Ayn al-Tamr on the eastern side of the Syrian desert, but it is not certain whether they belong to a late Umayyad or an early 'Abbāsid structure.[1] On the south-western edge of the desert the remains are more numerous. Here Yazīd, son of 'Abd-al-Malik, either built or restored a palace called Muwaqqar,[2] of which few remains are left. His son al-Walīd II, who was addicted to the chase and less innocent pastimes, occupied the neighbouring Qasṭal[3] and al-Azraq,[4] both Roman posts in Transjordan. To this same Caliph al-Walīd II is ascribed the building of another palace in this region known by the modern name al-Mushatta (al-Mashta),[5] which was the first in this region to be visited by archæologists The structure was left unfinished at the death of its caliph-builder. The magnificently carved façade of this beautiful château is now in the Kaiser Friedrich Museum, Berlin.[6] The best known structure in this group is, however, Quṣayr (the little palace of) 'Amrah, lying east of the Jordan in a direct line from the northern edge of the Dead Sea. This castle, built between 712 and 715 probably by al-Walīd I, was discovered for the learned world by Alois Musil[7] in 1898. The name is presumably modern, since we see no trace of it in Arabic literature. What makes this building especially remarkable is the extraordinary mural paintings to be discussed in the next section.

Painting

Most theologians of Islam maintained that the representation of men and animals was the prerogative of God alone and

[1] Gertrude L. Bell, *Palace and Mosque at Ukhaiḍir* (Oxford, 1914), p. 167.

[2] Yāqūt, vol. iv, p. 687. Al-Balqā', where the palace stood, was the southern region of the eastern Jordan district and comprised ancient Moab.

[3] From Latin *castellum*, castle. Yāqūt, vol. iv, p. 95.

[4] Ṭabari, vol. ii, p. 1743.

[5] Bedouin pronunciation Mshatta, winter resort.

[6] Consult R. E. Brünnow and A. v. Domaszewski, *Die Provincia Arabia*, vol. ii (Strassburg, 1905), pp. 105-70; B. Schulz and J. Strzygowski, "Mschatta", *Jahrbuch der königlich-preuszischen Kunstsammlungen*, vol. xxv (1904), pp. 205-373.

[7] *Ḳuṣejr 'Amra und andere Schlösser östlich von Moab*, pt. 1 (Vienna, 1902), pp. 5 *seq.*; Musil, *Ḳuṣejr 'Amra*, I. *Textband* (Vienna, 1907). Musil considered al-Walīd II the builder.

From B. Moritz, "Bilder aus Palästina, Nord-Arabien und dem Sinai" (Dietrich Reimer Verlag, Berlin)

QUSAYR 'AMRAH FROM THE SOUTH-EAST

considered him who intruded on this domain a blasphemer. This hostile attitude toward representational art, a corollary of the uncompromising monotheism of the Koran and its prohibition of idolatry, derives its direct sanction from a *ḥadīth* in which the Prophet is reported to have declared that those to be most severely punished on the day of judgment are the painters.[1] The term used, *muṣawwirūn* (portrayers), would apply to sculptors as well. No representation of human beings therefore occurs anywhere on mosques, though in a few cases we find it on palaces and in books. Almost all decorative motifs in Moslem art are derived from the vegetable kingdom or from geometrical figures. The success achieved in later ages in this field is evinced by the term "arabesque" applied to this style of decoration in most of the European languages. But the Arabians themselves had no developed feeling for either plastic or pictorial art, as their remains in the peninsula and the literary descriptions of their sanctuaries clearly indicate. What we call Moslem art was eclectic in its origin, motifs and execution, mostly the product of the artistic genius of the subjugated peoples, but developed under Moslem auspices and peculiarly adapted to the demands of the Moslem religion.

The earliest illustrations of Moslem pictorial art are the frescoes of Quṣayr ʿAmrah, which suggest workmanship of Christian painters. On the walls of this Transjordanian pleasure-house and bath of al-Walīd I are pictures of six royal personages, including Roderick, the last Visigothic king of Spain. "*Qayṣar*" (Caesar) and "*Najāshi*" (Negus) are inscribed above two of the figures and "Chosroes" (in Greek) above the third. Sāsānīd influence is manifest in the painting. Other symbolic figures represent Victory, Philosophy, History and Poetry. A hunting-scene depicts a lion attacking a wild ass. A number of nude pictures represent dancers, musicians and merrymakers. The ornament consists of draperies, foliage growing out of vases, vines, palm trees with clusters of fruit, laurel and birds of the desert. The inscriptions are mostly Arabic with a few names in Greek.

Music

In pre-Islamic time the Arabians had various types of song: caravan, martial, religious and amorous. Traces of the primitive religious hymns are still preserved in the *talbiyah*[2] of the

[1] Bukhāri, vol. vii, p. 61.

[2] The recitation of the hymn beginning with "*Labbayka*" (here I am); Bukhāri, vol. ii, p. 135.

By courtesy of the Akademie der Wissenschaften, Vienna

PICTURES ON WEST WALL OF THE MAIN HALL OF THE QUSAYR 'AMRAH

pilgrimage ceremony. The *inshād*, or chanting of poetry, is maintained in the cantillation (*tajwīd*) of the Koran. But the caravan song, *ḥudā'*, was their favourite and, in their estimation, the first form of singing. The *ḥudā'*—so goes the legend in al-Mas'ūdi [1]—originated when one of the founders of the race, Muḍar ibn-Ma'add,[2] fell from his camel, fractured his hand and in his beautiful voice began to cry, "Yā-yadāh! Yā-yadāh!" (O, my hand! O, my hand!), which synchronized with the steps of the camel and kept it moving. It was this cry that created the metre of *rajaz* used in caravan songs and the simplest of all poetical metres.

The South Arabians undoubtedly had their own types of song and musical instruments [3] about which very little is known, but it is doubtful whether that tradition formed a part of the heritage of the Northern, and consequently the Moslem, Arabians. The pre-Islamic inhabitants of al-Ḥijāz used as their principal instruments the square tambourine (*duff*), the flute (*qaṣabah*, *qaṣṣābah*) and the reed pipe or oboe (*zamr*, *mizmār*).[4] They also knew the skin-bellied lute (*mizhar*).[5] At about the time of the Prophet foreign musical influences were beginning to tell. The Ghassānid princes kept choruses of Greek girl singers. The Lakhmids of al-Ḥīrah had the Persian wooden-bellied lute (*'ūd*, whence Eng. "lute"), which the Ḥijāzis borrowed. One tradition makes al-Naḍr ibn-al-Ḥārith ibn-Kaladah, the physician and poet-minstrel whose pagan recitals competed with the revelations of Muḥammad in winning the favour of the people,[6] responsible for the introduction of this instrument into Makkah from al-Ḥīrah.[7] Another tradition credits ibn-Surayj († *ca.* 726) with introducing this Persian lute. He is said to have seen it for the first time in the hands of Persian workers brought to Arabia in 684 by 'Abdullāh ibn-al-Zubayr to rebuild the Ka'bah.[8] Later the wood-wind instrument called in Persian *nāy* (vertical flute) was likewise borrowed, together with the name, as the researches of Henry G. Farmer [9] indicate. Evidently

[1] Vol. viii, p. 92.
[2] Cf. "Almodad" in 1 Ch. 1 : 20.
[3] Mas'ūdi, vol. viii, p. 93.
[4] *Aghāni*, vol. ii, p. 175.
[5] *'Iqd*, vol. iii, p. 237; Mas'ūdi, vol. viii, p. 93.
[6] He is supposed to be the one referred to in sūr. 31 : 5-6.
[7] Mas'ūdi, vol. viii, pp. 93-4.
[8] *Aghāni*, vol. i, p. 98.
[9] In *Journal Royal Asiatic Society* (1929), pp. 119 *seq.*, pp. 489 *seq.*; *A History of Arabian Music to the XIIIth Century* (London, 1929), p. 7.

most of the Jāhilīyah professional singers were female, and the *Aghāni*,[1] itself a book of songs, has handed down to us the names of a few of them. Some of the elegies mourning the famous hero Ṣakhr by his sister al-Khansā', a contemporary of the Prophet and celebrated as the greatest poetess of the Arabs, were evidently composed as songs.[2] Most of the pre-Islamic poets evidently sang their compositions to music.

Muḥammad's denunciation of poets[3] was not directed against them as such but merely as the mouthpieces of heathenism. The Prophet may have looked with disfavour upon music also because of its association with pagan religious rites. According to a *ḥadīth* he is said to have declared the musical instrument to be the devil's muezzin, serving to call men to his worship.[4] Most Moslem legists and theologians frowned on music; some condemned it in all its aspects; a few looked upon it as religiously unpraiseworthy (*makrūh*), though not actually sinful (*ḥarām*); but the view of the masses was better expressed in the adage, "Wine is as the body, music as the soul, and joy is their offspring".[5]

Soon after the first awe inspired by Islam had worn off the tendency of social change in al-Ḥijāz veered toward the esthetic side, especially under 'Uthmān, the first caliph with a taste for wealth and display. Harmony between voice and instrument was then learned. What the Arabic authors style *al-ghinā' al-mutqan* or *al-raqīq*, artistic or elegant singing, that highly developed type in which there is application of rhythm (*īqā'*) to the melody of song, became well established in al-Ḥijāz. Male professional musicians appear for the first time under the sobriquet *mukhannathūn*, i.e. effeminate, men who dyed their hands and affected the manners of women. Such a man was Ṭuways (the little peacock, 632–710) of al-Madīnah, considered the father of song in Islam. Ṭuways is supposed to have introduced rhythm into Arabic music and to have been the first to sing in that language to the accompaniment of an instrument, the tambourine.[6]

[1] Vol. viii, p. 3, vol. x, p. 48. [2] *Aghāni*, vol. xiii, p. 140. [3] Sūr. 26 : 224-6.

[4] Consult Nuwayri, *Nihāyah*, vol. iv, pp. 132-5; Farmer, *Arabian Music*, pp. 24-5; A. J. Wensinck, *A Handbook of Early Muhammadan Tradition* (Leyden, 1927), p. 173.

[5] Nawāji, p. 178. Consult Nuwayri, vol. iv, pp. 136 *seq.*

[6] *Aghāni*, vol. ii, pp. 170, 171, 173.

The first generation of Moslem singers, headed by Ṭuways, consisted of foreign libertines. Ṭuways left a progeny of students, chief among whom was ibn-Surayj (*ca.* 634–726), regarded as one of the four great singers of Islam.[1] Besides crediting him with the introduction of the Persian lute tradition ascribes to him the use of the baton for directing musical performances. Ibn-Surayj was a freedman, the son of a Turk, and enjoyed the patronage of the famous beauty Sukaynah, daughter of al-Ḥusayn. He counted among his teachers the Makkan negro client Sa'īd ibn-Misjaḥ (or Musajjaḥ, † *ca.* 714). Sa'īd, the first Makkan musician and perhaps the greatest of the Umayyad period, is said to have travelled in Syria and Persia and to have been the first to put Byzantine and Persian songs into Arabic.[2] He is evidently the one who systematized Arabian musical theory and practice of classical times. Another student of his was al-Gharīḍ,[3] a half-breed Berber who, as a slave of Sukaynah, was also trained by ibn-Surayj[4] and, after his second master, attained the enviable rank of one of the four singers of Islam. The other two were ibn-Muḥriz († *ca.* 715), of Persian origin, popularly dubbed "the cymbalist [*ṣannāj*] of the Arabs",[5] and Ma'bad († 743), a Madīnese mulatto who was a special favourite at the courts of al-Walīd I, Yazīd II and al-Walīd II.[6] Before settling in the capital Ma'bad had wandered as a minstrel all over Arabia. Among the songstresses (*qiyān*) Jamīlah († *ca.* 720), a Madīnese freedwoman, was the artistic queen of the first generation.[7] Her residence proved a centre of attraction for the leading musicians and singers of Makkah and al-Madīnah, many of whom were her pupils; conspicuous among the frequent auditors at her concerts was the poet of love, 'Umar ibn-abi-Rabī'ah. Among her pupils she counted Ḥabābah and Sallāmah, the favourites of Yazīd II. The crowning event of Jamīlah's picturesque career was her imposing pilgrimage to Makkah at the head of a gorgeous procession of singers and songstresses, poets and musicians, admirers and friends, all in gala dress and on richly caparisoned mounts.[8]

Occasional concerts and brilliant musical events held in the

[1] *Aghāni*, vol. i, p. 98.
[2] *Ibid.* vol. iii, p. 84.
[3] His first name was 'Abd-al-Malik. *Gharīḍ* means "the good singer".
[4] *Aghāni*, vol. i, pp. 99-100.
[5] *Ibid.* vol. i, p. 151.
[6] *Ibid.* pp. 19 *seq.*
[7] *Ibid.* vol. vii, pp. 124 *seq.*
[8] *Ibid.* vol. vii, p. 135.

homes of aristocratic ladies attracted throngs of dilettanti. The wood-bellied lute introduced from Persia through al-Ḥīrah had by this time partly superseded the native skin-bellied lute. Another favourite stringed instrument was the *mi'zafah*, a kind of psaltery. The wind instruments included the flute (*qaṣabah*) and reed pipe (*mizmār*) as well as the horn (*būq*). The percussion instruments were represented by the square tambourine, especially favoured by the women, and by the drum (*ṭabl*) and cymbals or castanets (*ṣunūj*). Notes, when known, were transmitted by word of mouth from one generation to another and have consequently been entirely lost. The *Aghāni* is replete with verses set to music under the Umayyads, yet it has preserved not a solitary note for us. On the occasion of a visit to al-Ḥijāz by the Christian Ḥunayn al-Ḥīri, dean of the 'Irāq singers, such a crowd gathered at the residence of Sukaynah to hear him that the porch on which they met collapsed, resulting in the death of the distinguished visiting artist.[1] The holy pilgrimage, with all the celebrities it brought from different parts of the Moslem world, afforded the Ḥijāz musicians and singers an annual opportunity for the display of their talent. It was customary for them on special occasions to meet the caravan and perform en route. The *Aghāni* has left us a description of a pilgrimage-parade in which 'Umar ibn-abi-Rabī'ah, the representative of the poetical spirit of the age, clad in his finest attire and flirting with female wayfarers, took the leading part. In his company was ibn-Surayj, whose singing of 'Umar's verses distracted the pilgrims from the observance of their ritualistic ceremonies.[2]

Thus did Makkah, and more particularly al-Madīnah, become in the Umayyad period a nursery of song and a conservatory for music.[3] As such they supplied the court of Damascus with an ever-increasing stream of talent. In vain did the conservatives and ulema press their objections, linking music and song with wine-bibbing and gaming as forbidden pleasures (*malāhi*) and quoting Prophetic *ḥadīths* which place such diversions among the most powerful means by which the devil seduces men. The tide could not be stemmed; the Muses stood too high in public favour to suffer from such verbal attacks. Their devotees could quote equally striking sayings ascribed to the Prophet[4] and

[1] *Aghāni*, vol. ii, p. 127. [2] *Ibid.* vol. i, p. 102. [3] *'Iqd*, vol. iii, p. 237.
[4] Ghazzāli, *Iḥyā' 'Ulūm al-Dīn* (Cairo, 1334), vol. ii, pp. 238 *seq.*

THE ḤARAM AREA FROM THE NORTH-WEST WITH THE AQṢA MOSQUE IN THE BACKGROUND

might very well argue that poetry, music and song did not always tend to debase, that they contributed their share to the refinement of social intercourse and to the sublimation of the relationships between the sexes.[1] It was the second Umayyad caliph, Yazīd I, himself a composer, who introduced singing and musical instruments into the Damascus court.[2] He initiated the practice of holding grand festivities in the palace which featured wine and song, hereafter inseparable in royal festivals. 'Abd-al-Malik patronized ibn-Misjaḥ of the Ḥijāz school. His son al-Walīd, the patron of arts, summoned ibn-Surayj and Ma'bad to the capital, where they were received with great honour. Yazīd II, successor of the austere and puritanical 'Umar, reinstated poetry and music in public favour through his Ḥabābah and Sallāmah.[3] Hishām bestowed his patronage on Ḥunayn of al-Ḥīrah. The pleasure-loving Walīd II, himself a player on the lute and composer of songs, welcomed to his court a host of musician-singers, including the noted Ma'bad.[4] His reign coincided with the blossoming of music in the twin cities of al-Ḥijāz. So widely spread was the cultivation of the musical art under the last Umayyads that it provided their enemies, the 'Abbāsid faction, with an effective argument in their propaganda to undermine the house of "ungodly usurpers".

[1] *'Iqd*, vol. iii, pp. 225-6; Nawāji, pp. 177-9.
[2] *Aghāni*, vol. xvi, p. 70; cf. Mas'ūdi, vol. v, pp. 156-7.
[3] Mas'ūdi, vol. v, pp. 446 *seq.* [4] *Ibid.* vol. vi, p. 4.

CHAPTER XXII

DECLINE AND FALL OF THE UMAYYAD DYNASTY

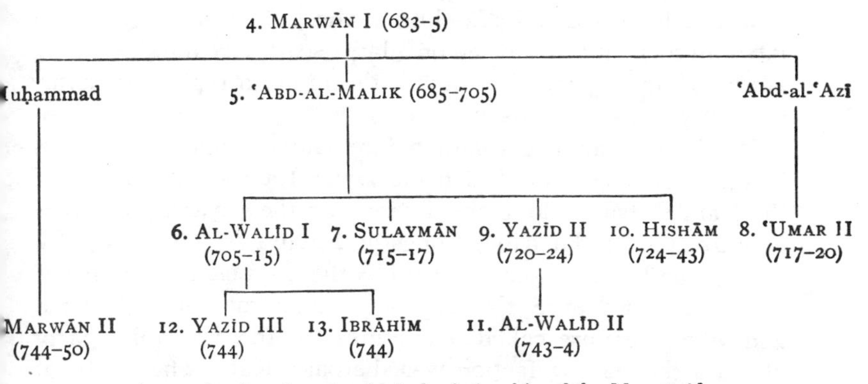

A tree showing the genealogical relationship of the Marwānid caliphs of the Umayyad dynasty

ARAB authorities highly esteem Hishām and, as we learned before, rightly rank him after Mu'āwiyah and 'Abd-al-Malik as the third and last true statesman of the banu-Umayyah. His four successors, with the exception of Marwān II, who ended the dynasty, proved incapable if not dissolute or degenerate. Even before the time of Hishām it became the fashion for the caliph, as exemplified by Yazīd II, to pass his time in the chase and over his wine cup and to be absorbed more in music and poetry than in the Koran and state affairs. The eunuch system, which made the harem institution possible, was now fully developed. Indulgence in luxury due to increased wealth and a superabundance of slaves was rife. Even the reigning family could no longer boast pure Arabian blood. Yazīd III (744) was the first caliph in Islam born of a slave mother.[1] His two successors were also sons of such freed women.[2] Such evils among

Ṭabari, vol. ii, p. 1874; Ya'qūbi, vol. ii, p. 401; Mas'ūdi, vol. vi, pp. 31-2. See below, p. 332.

[2] Ya'qūbi, vol. ii, pp. 403, 404.

the ruling class were only too symptomatic of general moral turpitude. The characteristic vices of civilization, especially those involving wine, women and song, had seized upon the sons of the desert and were beginning to sap the vitality of the youthful Arab society.

Qays *versus* Yaman

The ancient and typical weakness of Arabian social life, with its over-emphasis on individualism, tribal spirit (*'aṣabīyah*) and feuds, was again reasserting itself. Such bonds as Islam had temporarily provided for holding in check the centrifugal forces latent in social life organized on a large scale were now becoming loose. Beginning with 'Uthmān, the hitherto repressed family spirit began to assert itself.

North Arabian tribes had before Islam emigrated into al-'Irāq, where they established the Diyār Rabī'ah (the abode of the Rabī'ah tribe) along the Tigris, and the Diyār Muḍar (the abode of the Muḍar tribe) along the Euphrates. The first place among the banu-Muḍar was held by the Qays clan. Other tribes who had settled in Syria originally came from South Arabia and were therefore called Yamanites. In the Yamanite party of Syria the leading faction was the banu-Kalb. The Arabs of Khurāsān, the north-eastern province of Persia, were mainly colonists from al-Baṣrah and were therefore mostly North Arabians; the leading tribe there was Tamīm, corresponding to Qays in the Euphrates region. In Khurāsān the Yamanite party went by the appellation of Azdite, after the name of the leading family. In other regions the Qaysites were called Nizārites or Ma'addites.[1] But no matter what name these tribes went by the alignment was usually that of North Arabian against South Arabian tribes. Conscious of some deep-rooted national distinction, the North Arabians, who traced their descent to Ishmael and styled themselves 'Adnāni, were never fully amalgamated with the South Arabians, who carried their pedigree back to Qaḥṭān, the Joktan of Genesis 10 : 25 *seq*. The Qaysites became in course of time the nucleus of one political party, and the Yamanites of another.

Mu'āwiyah, the founder of the Umayyad dynasty, raised his Syrian throne on Yamanite shoulders. His son and successor,

On Arab tribes consult ibn-Durayd, *Ishtiqāq*; F. Wüstenfeld, *Genealogische Tabellen der arabischen Stämme* (Göttingen, 1852); and *Register zu den genealogischen Tabellen der arabischen Stämme* (Göttingen, 1853).

Yazīd, whose mother, Maysūn, belonged to the Kalbites of the Yamanite party, contracted a marriage with a Kalbite woman. The jealous Qaysites refused to recognize his successor, Muʿāwiyah II, and declared for the pseudo-caliph ibn-al-Zubayr. The decisive victory of the Kalbites over the Qaysites at Marj Rāhiṭ (684) secured the throne for Marwān, the father of the Marwānid branch of the Umayyad house. Under al-Walīd I Qaysite power reached its culmination in al-Ḥajjāj and his cousin Muḥammad, the conqueror of India, and in Qutaybah, the subduer of Central Asia. Al-Walīd's brother Sulaymān favoured the Yamanites. Yazīd II, however, under the influence of his Muḍari mother patronized the Qaysite party, as did al-Walīd II; Yazīd III relied upon Yamani arms in wresting the sceptre from the hands of his predecessor, al-Walīd II. Thus did the caliph in the latter part of the Umayyad period appear to be rather the head of a particular party than the sovereign of a united empire.

The polarization of the Moslem world by this Arab dualism of Qays and Yaman, who also appear under other names, became now complete. It precipitated the downfall of the dynasty and its ill effects were manifest in years to come and in widely separated places. The district of Damascus itself was once the scene of relentless warfare for two years all because, as we are told,[1] a Maʿaddite had filched a water-melon from a Yamanite's garden. In distant Murcia in Spain blood is said to have flowed for several years because a Muḍarite picked a vine leaf from the yard of a Yamanite.[2] Everywhere, in the capital as well as in the provinces, on the banks of the Indus, the shores of Sicily and the borders of the Sahara, the ancestral feud, transformed into an alignment of two political parties, one against the other, made itself felt. It proved a potent factor in ultimately arresting the progress of Moslem arms in France and in the decline of the Andalusian caliphate. In Lebanon and Palestine the issue seems to have remained a living one until modern times, for we know of pitched battles fought between the two parties as late as the early part of the eighteenth century.

The problem of succession

The lack of any definite and fixed rule of hereditary succession to the caliphal throne caused no small measure of national disturbance. Muʿāwiyah initiated the wise and far-sighted policy

[1] Abu-al-Fidā', vol. ii, p. 14.
[2] Ibn-ʿIdhāri, *Bayān*, vol. ii, p. 84.

of nominating his son as his successor, but the antiquated Arabian tribal principle of seniority in succession stood in constant conflict with the natural ambition of the ruling father to pass the sovereignty on to his son. Homage by the people became the only sure title to the throne. Of the fourteen Umayyad caliphs only four—Mu'āwiyah I, Yazīd I, Marwān I and 'Abd-al-Malik—had their sons as immediate successors. The already complicated problem was rendered more complicated by the precedent established when the founder of the Marwānid branch designated his son 'Abd-al-Malik as his successor, to be followed by his other son 'Abd-al-'Azīz.[1] Once in power, 'Abd-al-Malik did the natural thing: he tried to divert the succession from his brother 'Abd-al-'Azīz to his own son al-Walīd, in the meantime designating his other son, Sulaymān, as the second nominee.[2] Al-Walīd in his turn made an unsuccessful effort to deprive his brother Sulaymān of his right in favour of his own son. All these manœuvres were, of course, far from being conducive to the stability and continuity of the régime.

The partisans of 'Ali

The dissentient Shī'ites, who never acquiesced in the rule of the "Umayyad usurpers" and never forgave them the wrong they perpetrated against 'Ali and al-Ḥusayn, became now more active than ever. Their whole-hearted devotion to the descendants of the Prophet made them the focus of popular sympathy. To their camp rallied many of those who were dissatisfied politically, economically or socially with the rule of the banu-Umayyah. In al-'Irāq, where the majority of the population had by now become Shī'ah, opposition to Syrian rule, which arose originally out of the feeling that it deprived their country of its national independence, now took on a religious colour. In the Sunnite ranks themselves, the pietists charged the caliphs with worldliness and neglect of koranic and traditional law and were everywhere ready to give religious sanction to any opposition that might be raised.

'Abbāsid claimants

Still another destructive force was in operation. The 'Abbāsids, descendants of an uncle of the Prophet, al-'Abbās ibn-'Abd-al-Muṭṭalib ibn-Hāshim, began to press their claim to the throne. Cleverly they made common cause with the 'Alids by emphasizing the rights of the house of Hāshim. The Shī'ah regarded this family as consisting primarily of the descendants of 'Ali, but

[1] Ya'qūbi, vol. ii, p. 306. [2] *Ibid.* pp. 334-5.

the ʿAbbāsids included themselves as members of the Hāshimite branch of the Quraysh and therefore closer to the Prophet than the banu-Umayyah.[1]

Taking advantage of the widespread discontent and posing as defenders of the true faith, the descendants of al-ʿAbbās soon became the champions and leaders of the anti-Umayyad movement. For their headquarters and seat of propaganda they chose a little village south of the Dead Sea, al-Ḥumaymah[2] by name, seemingly harmless and aloof from the rest of the world but in reality strategically close to the caravan route and the junction of the pilgrim roads. Here the stage was set for the earliest and most subtle propagandist movement in political Islam.

The Khurāsānians

Non-Arabian Moslems in general and Persian Moslems in particular had good reason for dissatisfaction. Far from being granted the expected economic and social equality with Arabian Moslems, they were instead generally reduced to the position of clients and were not always exempted from the capitation tax paid by non-Moslems. What made them more discontented was the consciousness that they represented a higher and more ancient culture, a fact acknowledged even by the Arabians themselves. It was among such discontented neophytes that the Shīʿite-ʿAbbāsid seed found fertile soil. From al-ʿIrāq, always loyal to the ʿAlid cause, the Shīʿah doctrine spread into Persia and struck root especially in the north-eastern province, Khurāsān, which was then much larger than now. In Persia the way had been somewhat prepared by the Azd-Muḍar feud perpetuated by the Arabs. But deeper forces were at work. Under the guise of Shīʿah Islam, Iranianism was revivifying itself.

The zero hour in the life of the Umayyad dynasty approached when a coalition was effected between the Shīʿite, Khurāsānian and ʿAbbāsid forces which was utilized by the last for their own

[1]
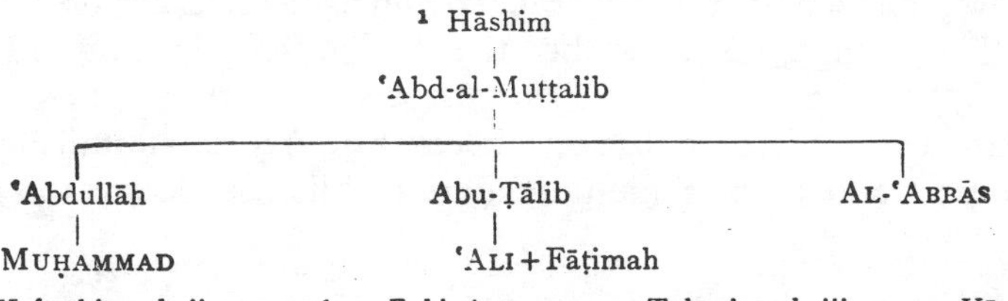

[2] Yaʿqūbi, vol. ii, pp. 356-7; *Fakhri*, pp. 192-3; Ṭabari, vol. iii, p. 34; Yāqūt, vol. ii, p. 342; Musil, *Northern Heǧâz* (New York, 1926), pp. 56-61 and map in pocket.

advantage. This coalition was headed by abu-al-'Abbās, a great-great-grandson of al-'Abbās, the uncle of the Prophet. Under his leadership revolutionary Islam opposed the existing order with a feigned ideal of theocracy and a promise of return to orthodoxy. On June 9, 747, the long-meditated revolt broke out when the 'Abbāsid agent in Khurāsān, abu-Muslim, a Persian freedman of obscure origin,[1] unfurled the black banner, originally the standard of Muḥammad but now the 'Abbāsid emblem. At the head of the Azd (Yamani) tribe he entered the capital, Marw, but the majority of his adherents were Iranian peasants and clients rather than Arabs.[2] In vain did Naṣr ibn-Sayyār, the Umayyad governor of Khurāsān, appeal to Marwān II for aid. In a pathetic letter he had recourse to poetry.[3] But Marwān, though in personal energy and capacity superior to his immediate predecessors, made no response, for his hands were full with an uprising at home which had spread from Palestine to Ḥimṣ. It was the same old trouble between Qaysites and Yamanites which, exploited by ambitious aspirants to the caliphate, had assumed the proportions of civil war under his two predecessors Yazīd III and Ibrāhīm. Yazīd had made matters worse by espousing the Qadarite doctrine. Ibrāhīm headed the Yamanite party. Marwān II, favoured by the Qaysites, had committed the fatal mistake of transferring not only his residence but also the state bureaux to Ḥarrān in Mesopotamia, thus alienating the sympathies of all Syrians. Besides the Syrians, the mainstay of Umayyad power, the Khārijites of al-'Irāq—ever the deadly enemy of established order—were now in open rebellion.[4] In Spain the ancestral feuds were rending in pieces that westernmost province of Islam. For three years the sexagenarian caliph, who previous to his accession had won the sobriquet Marwān al-Ḥimār (the ass) for his unfailing perseverance in warfare,[5] held the field against the Syrian and Khārijite insurgents and proved himself an able general. To him as the military organizer of these campaigns is ascribed the change from fighting in lines (*ṣufūf*), a practice hallowed by association with the Prophet's method of warfare, to that of cohorts (*karādīs*), small units more compact and at the same time more mobile. But it was too late

[1] Cf. *Fakhri*, p. 186. [2] Ṭabari, vol. ii, pp. 1953 *seq.*; Dīnawari, pp. 359 *seq.*
[3] *Fakhri*, p. 194; Nicholson, *Literary History*, p. 251.
[4] Ṭabari, vol ii pp. 1943-9. [5] *Fakhri*, p. 184.

for him to redeem the general situation. The sun of the banu-Umayyah was fast approaching its setting.

The final blow

The fall of the capital of Khurāsān, Marw, was followed in 749 by the fall of the leading city of al-'Irāq, al-Kūfah, the hiding-place of abu-al-'Abbās, which surrendered to the insurgents without much opposition. Here on Thursday, October 30, 749, public homage was paid in the chief mosque to abu-al-'Abbās as caliph.[1] The first 'Abbāsid caliph was thus enthroned. Everywhere the white banner of the Umayyads was in retreat before the black banner of the 'Abbāsids and their confederates. Marwān resolved on a last, desperate stand. With 12,000[2] men he advanced from Ḥarrān and was met (January 750) on the left bank of the Greater Zāb, a tributary of the Tigris, by the enemy forces headed by 'Abdullāh ibn-'Ali, an uncle of the new caliph. The will to win and the expectation of victory were no longer on the side of the Syrian army and its defeat was decisive. After the battle of the Zāb Syria lay at the feet of the 'Abbāsid victors. Its leading towns, one after the other, opened their gates to 'Abdullāh and his Khurāsāni troops. Only at Damascus was it found necessary to lay siege, but the proud capital surrendered on April 26, 750, after a few days. From Palestine 'Abdullāh sent a detachment in pursuit of the fugitive caliph, who was caught and killed (August 5, 750) outside a church in which he had sought refuge at Būṣīr[3] (Busiris) in Egypt, where his tomb is still pointed out. His head and, according to al-Mas'ūdi,[4] the insignia of the caliphate were sent to abu-al-'Abbās.

The 'Abbāsids now embarked upon a policy of exterminating the Umayyad house. Their general 'Abdullāh shrank from no measure necessary for wiping out the kindred enemy root and branch. On June 25, 750, he invited eighty of them to a banquet at abu-Fuṭrus, ancient Antipatris on the 'Awjā' River near Jaffa, and in the course of the feast had them all cut down. After spreading leathern covers over the dead and dying he and his lieutenants continued their repast to the accompaniment of

[1] Ya'qūbi, vol. ii, pp. 417-18; Ṭabari, vol. iii, pp. 27-33; Mas'ūdi, vol. vi, pp. 87, 98.

[2] Ṭabari, vol. iii, p. 47 (cf. p. 45). See above, p. 226.

[3] Also Abūṣīr, probably Būṣīr al-Malaq in the Fayyūm. Consult Sāwīrus ibn-al-Muqaffa', *Siyar al-Baṭārikah al-Iskandarānīyīn*, ed. C. F. Seybold (Hamburg, 1912), pp. 181 *seq.*; Ṭabari, vol. iii, pp. 49-50.

[4] Vol. vi, p. 77.

human groans.[1] Agents and spies were sent all over the Moslem world to hunt down fugitive scions of the fallen family, some of whom "sought refuge in the bowels of the earth".[2] The dramatic escape of the youthful 'Abd-al-Raḥmān ibn-Mu'āwiyah ibn-Hishām to Spain, where he succeeded in establishing a new and brilliant Umayyad dynasty, belongs to a later chapter. Even the dead were not to escape the ruthless chastisement meted out by the 'Abbāsids. The remains of the caliphs in Damascus, Qinnasrīn and other places were exhumed by 'Abdullāh and desecrated. The corpse of Sulaymān was dug out from Dābiq. That of Hishām was disentombed from al-Ruṣāfah, where it was found embalmed, and after being scourged eighty times was burned to ashes.[3] Only the tomb of the pious 'Umar II escaped violation.

With the fall of the Umayyads the glory of Syria passed away, its hegemony ended. The Syrians awoke too late to the realization that the centre of gravity in Islam had left their land and shifted eastward, and though they made several armed attempts to regain their former importance all proved futile. At last they set their hopes on an expected Sufyāni,[4] a sort of Messiah, to come and deliver them from the yoke of their 'Irāqi oppressors. To the present day one hears Moslems in Syria referring to a forthcoming descendant of Mu'āwiyah. But the Umayyad fall meant more than this. The truly Arab period in the history of Islam had now passed and the first purely Arab phase of the Islamic empire began to move rapidly toward its close. The 'Abbāsid government called itself *dawlah*,[5] new era, and a new era it was. The 'Irāqis felt freed from Syrian tutelage. The Shī'ites considered themselves avenged. The clients became emancipated. Al-Kūfah, on the border of Persia, was made the new capital. Khurāsānians formed the caliphal bodyguard and

[1] Ya'qūbi, vol. ii, pp. 425-6; Mas'ūdi, vol. vi, p. 76; ibn-al-Athīr, vol. v, pp. 329-30; Mubarrad, p. 707; *Aghāni*, vol. iv, p. 161; cf. *ibid.* pp. 92-6; *Fakhri*, pp. 203-4; Theophanes, p. 427. Compare the story of Jehu's extermination of Ahab's house (2 K. 9 : 14-34) and the destruction of the Mamlūks of Egypt by Muḥammad 'Ali (Jurji Zaydān, *Ta'rīkh Miṣr al-Ḥadīth*, 3rd ed., Cairo, 1925, vol. ii, pp. 160-62).

[2] Ibn-Khaldūn, vol. iv, p. 120.

[3] Mas'ūdi, vol. v, p. 471; cf. Ya'qūbi, vol. ii, pp. 427-8. See *Fakhri*, p. 204.

[4] Ṭabari, vol. iii, p. 1320; ibn-Miskawayh, *Tajārib al-Umam wa-Ta'āqub al-Himam*, ed. de Goeje and de Jong, vol. ii (Leyden, 1871), p. 526; Yāqūt, vol. iv, p. 1000; *Aghāni*, vol. xvi, p. 88; H. Lammens, *Études sur le siècle des Omayyades* (Beirūt, 1930), pp. 391-408.

[5] Ṭabari, vol. iii, p. 85, ll. 16, 17, p. 115, l. 9.

Persians occupied the chief posts in the government. The original Arabian aristocracy was replaced by a hierarchy of officers drawn from the whole gamut of nationalities under the caliphate. The old Arabian Moslems and the new foreign converts were beginning to coalesce and shade off into each other. Arabianism fell, but Islam continued, and under the guise of international Islam Iranianism marched triumphantly on.

CHAPTER XXIII

THE ESTABLISHMENT OF THE 'ABBĀSID DYNASTY

THE third act in the great political drama of Islam opens with the Caliph abu-al-'Abbās (750–54) playing the chief rôle. Al-'Irāq is the stage. In his inaugural *khuṭbah*, delivered the preceding year in the mosque of al-Kūfah, the first 'Abbāsid caliph referred to himself as *al-saffāḥ*,[1] the bloodshedder, which became his sobriquet. This was ominous, since the incoming dynasty, much more than the outgoing, depended upon force in the execution of its policies. For the first time in the history of Islam the leathern spread beside the caliph's seat, which served as a carpet for the use of the executioner, became a necessary adjunct of the imperial throne. This al-Saffāḥ became the founder of the most celebrated and longest-lived Arab dynasty in Islam, the third, after the Orthodox (Rāshidūn) and the Umayyad. From 750 to 1258 the successors of abu-al-'Abbās reigned, though they did not always rule.

At the time of its achievement the 'Abbāsid victory was generally hailed as representing the substitution of the true conception of the caliphate, the idea of a theocratic state, for the purely secular state (*mulk*) of the Umayyads. As a mark of the religious character of his exalted office, the caliph now donned on such ceremonial occasions as the day of his accession and the time of the Friday prayer the mantle (*burdah*) once worn by his distant cousin, the Prophet.[2] He surrounded himself with men versed in canon law whom he patronized and whose advice on matters of state affairs he sought. The highly organized machinery for propaganda which helped to undermine public confidence in the Umayyad régime was now cleverly directed toward permanently entrenching the 'Abbāsids in public favour. From the very beginning the idea was cultivated that authority should

[1] Ṭabari, vol. iii, p. 30, l. 20; ibn-al-Athīr, vol. v, p. 316.

[2] The genealogical tree on the following page makes clear the relationship between the 'Abbāsids and Muḥammad.

remain forever in 'Abbāsid hands, to be finally delivered to Jesus (*'Īsa*), the Messiah.[1] Later the theory was promulgated that if this caliphate were destroyed the whole universe would be disorganized.[2] As a matter of fact the religious change was more apparent than real; although unlike his Umayyad predecessor he assumed piety and feigned religiosity, the Baghdād caliph proved as worldly-minded as he of Damascus whom he had displaced. In one respect there was a fundamental difference: the Umayyad empire was Arab, the 'Abbāsid was more inter-

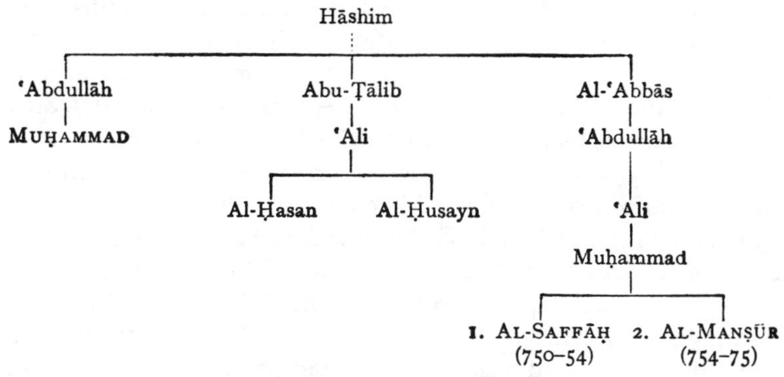

Tree showing the relationship between the 'Abbāsids and Muḥammad

national. The 'Abbāsid was an empire of Neo-Moslems in which the Arabs formed only one of the many component races.

There were also other differences. For the first time in its history the caliphate was not coterminous with Islam. Spain and North Africa, 'Umān, Sind and even Khurāsān[3] did not fully acknowledge the new caliph. Egypt's acknowledgment was more nominal than real. Wāsiṭ, the Umayyad capital of al-'Irāq, held out for eleven months.[4] Syria was in constant turmoil, chiefly as a result of the outrages perpetrated against its royal house. The 'Abbāsid 'Alid alliance cemented solely by a feeling of common hatred toward a mighty foe could not long survive the overthrow of that foe. Those 'Alids who had naïvely thought the 'Abbāsids were fighting the battle for them were soon to be disillusioned.

Feeling insecure in the fickle and pro-'Alid Kūfah, al-Saffāḥ built a courtly residence, al-Hāshimīyah[5] (after Hāshim, an early

[1] Ṭabari, vol. iii, p. 33; ibn-al-Athīr, vol. v, p. 318.
[2] See below, p. 487.
[3] Dīnawari, p. 373.
[4] Dīnawari, pp. 367-72; Ṭabari, vol. iii, pp. 61-6; ibn-al-Athīr, vol. v, p. 338.
[5] Ya'qūbi, vol. ii, p. 429; Dīnawari, pp. 372-3.

ancestor of the family), in al-Anbār.[1] Al-Kūfah's sister city, al-Baṣrah, was avoided for the same reason, also because of its southern situation, which made it unsuitable for a centre of a kingdom. In his newly erected capital al-Saffāḥ died (754) of smallpox in his early thirties.[2]

Al-Manṣūr, the real founder of the dynasty

His brother and successor, abu-Ja'far (754–75), who now assumed the honorific title al-Manṣūr (rendered victorious [by God]), proved one of the greatest, though most unscrupulous, of the 'Abbāsids. He, rather than al-Saffāḥ, was the one who firmly established the new dynasty. All the thirty-five caliphs who succeeded were his lineal descendants. His uncle 'Abdullāh, the hero of the Zāb and under al-Saffāḥ the governor of Syria, now disputed the caliphate with his nephew, but was defeated (November 754) by abu-Muslim at Naṣībīn (Nisibis). After seven years' imprisonment he was ceremoniously conducted into a house the foundations of which had been purposely laid on salt surrounded by water, which buried him under its ruins.[3] Immediately after the victory of Naṣībīn the turn of abu-Muslim himself came. On his way back to his province, Khurāsān, which he ruled almost independently, abu-Muslim was induced to turn aside from his march and visit the caliphal court. The Khurāsāni leader, to whose sword after that of 'Abdullāh the 'Abbāsids owed their throne, was attacked while having an audience with the caliph and treacherously put to death.[4] A curious new sect of Persian extremists, the Rāwandīyah, who tried to identify the caliph with God, were mercilessly put down (758).[5] The revolt of the disgruntled Shī'ah, headed by Ibrāhīm and by his brother Muḥammad, surnamed al-Nafs al-Zakīyah (the pure soul), the great-grandsons of al-Ḥasan,[6] was ruthlessly crushed. Muḥammad was killed and gibbeted (December 6, 762) in al-Madīnah; Ibrāhīm was decapitated (February 14, 763) near the unruly Kūfah and his head dispatched to the caliph.[7] To the irreconcilable 'Alids the 'Abbāsid caliphs were usurpers, the rightful caliphs, imāms, being the descendants of 'Ali and Fāṭimah.

[1] On the left bank of the Euphrates, in the north of al-'Irāq. The site is today quite waste.

[2] Ya'qūbi, vol. ii, p. 434; Ṭabari, vol. iii, pp. 87-8.

[3] Ṭabari, vol. iii, p. 330.

[4] *Ibid.* pp. 105-17; Dīnawari, pp. 376-8.

[5] Ṭabari, vol. iii, pp. 129-33; Mas'ūdi, vol. vi, pp. 26, 54 *seq.*; Baghdādi, ed. Hitti, p. 37. Rāwand was a town near Iṣbahān.

[6] See genealogical tree on following page.

[7] Ṭabari, vol. iii, pp. 245-65, 315-16; Mas'ūdi, vol. vi, pp. 189-203; Dīnawari, p. 381.

The 'Alids never ceased to exercise a disruptive influence on the body politic of Islam, and persisted in claiming for their imāms a measure of hereditary wisdom derived from the Prophet, as well as a sort of special divine illumination. In Khurāsān the insurrection of Sunbād (Sinbādh) the Magian (755), who came out as the avenger of abu-Muslim, and that of Ustādhsīs (767–8), were quenched;[1] Persia, where strong national sentiments were interwoven with ancient Zoroastrian and Mazdakian religious ideas, was at least temporarily pacified. Thus was the greater part of the Islamic empire once more consolidated, with the

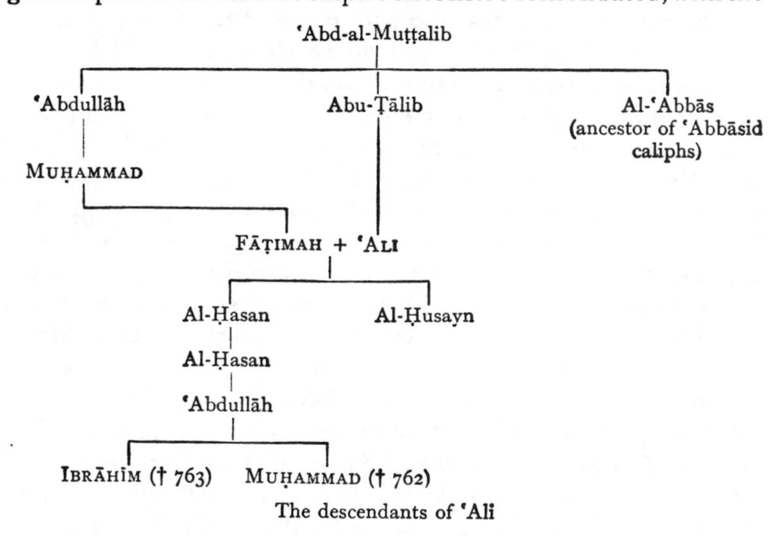

The descendants of 'Ali

exception of North Africa, where the caliph's authority did not extend much beyond al-Qayrawān, and of Spain, where the 'Abbāsid caliph found in the Umayyad 'Abd-al-Raḥmān (whose mother, like al-Manṣūr's,[2] was a Berber slave) more than his match.

With the domestic situation well in hand the baneful frontier wars with the eternal enemy to the west, the Byzantines, which had been carried on intermittently for over a century, were resumed in the nature of raids on neighbouring strongholds. The ruined border fortresses (*thughūr*) of Malaṭyah (Melitene) in Lesser Armenia and al-Maṣṣīṣah in Cilicia were restored.[3] Even

[1] Ṭabari, vol. iii, pp. 119-20, 354-8; Ya'qūbi, vol. ii, pp. 441-2; ibn-al-Athīr, vol. v, pp. 368-9.
[2] Ya'qūbi, vol. ii, p. 436; ibn-Qutaybah, *Ma'ārif*, p. 191.
[3] Ya'qūbi, *Buldān*, p. 238, l. 5.

the naphtha springs of Baku[1] were reached and a tax levied on them. Mountainous Ṭabaristān, south of the Caspian (Baḥr al-Khazar), where a family of high functionaries of the defunct Sāsānid empire had maintained a virtually independent rule, was now temporarily annexed.[2] On the Indian frontier Qandahār (al-Qunduhār), among other places, was reduced, and a statue of the Buddha found in it was demolished.[3] In fact, al-Manṣūr's lieutenants carried their raids as far as Kashmīr (Ar. Qashmīr), the rich and extensive valley of the north-west Himalaya. A fleet was dispatched (770) from al-Baṣrah to the delta of the Indus to chastise pirates who had ventured to plunder Juddah.

Madīnat al-Salām

In 762 al-Manṣūr, who had his residence at al-Hāshimīyah between al-Kūfah and al-Ḥīrah,[4] laid the foundation stone of his new capital, Baghdād, scene of the legendary adventures so brilliantly commemorated by Shahrazād in *The Thousand and One Nights*. The site was an ancient one occupied by a Sāsānid village of the same name,[5] meaning "given by God". Al-Manṣūr fixed on the site after canvassing a number of others "because", said he, "it is excellent as a military camp. Besides, here is the Tigris to put us in touch with lands as far as China and bring us all that the seas yield as well as the food products of Mesopotamia, Armenia and their environs. Then there is the Euphrates to carry for us all that Syria, al-Raqqah and adjacent lands have to offer."[6] In the construction of his city, completed in four years, al-Manṣūr spent some 4,883,000 dirhams[7] and employed about a hundred thousand architects, craftsmen and labourers drawn from Syria, Mesopotamia and other parts of the empire.[8]

Madīnat al-Salām (city of peace), which was the official name given by al-Manṣūr to his city, lay on the west bank of the Tigris in that same valley which had furnished sites for some of the mightiest capitals of the ancient world. It was circular in form, whence the name the Round City (*al-mudawwarah*), with double brick walls, a deep moat and a third innermost wall rising

[1] Mas'ūdi, vol. ii, p. 25; Yāqūt, vol. i, p. 477.
[2] Ya'qūbi, vol. ii, pp. 446-7.
[3] Balādhuri, p. 445; Yāqūt, vol. iv, pp. 183-4; Ya'qūbi, vol. ii, p. 449.
[4] Ya'qūbi, *Buldān*, p. 237.
[5] *Ibid.* p. 235; Balādhuri, p. 294 = Hitti, p. 457.
[6] Ṭabari, vol. iii, p. 272.
[7] Al-Khaṭīb (al-Baghdādi), *Ta'rīkh Baghdād*, vol. i (Cairo, 1931), pp. 69-70; Ṭabari, vol. iii, p. 326; Yāqūt, vol. i, p. 683.
[8] Ṭabari, vol. iii, p. 276; Ya'qūbi, *Buldān*, p. 238; Khaṭīb, vol. i, pp. 66-7.

ninety feet and surrounding the central area. The walls had four equidistant gates from which four highways, starting from the centre of the circle, radiated like the spokes of a wheel to the four corners of the empire. The whole thus formed concentric circles with the caliphal palace, styled the Golden Gate (*bāb al-dhahab*) on account of its gilded entrance, or the Green Dome (*al-qubbah al-khaḍrā'*), as the hub. Beside the palace stood the great mosque. The dome of the audience chamber, after which the imperial palace was named, rose to a height of one hundred and thirty feet. Later tradition topped it by the figure of a mounted man holding a lance which in time of danger pointed the direction from which the enemy might be expected.[1] But Yāqūt, quick to detect the fallacy, remarks that the figure necessarily pointed always in some direction, which would mean the existence of a constant enemy threatening the city, and declares the Moslems "too intelligent to believe such fabrications".[2] The adjacent ruins of the Sāsānid capital, Ctesiphon, served as the main quarry for the new city and furnished the necessary building material, while brick was also made on the spot. Before his death al-Manṣūr built on the bank of the Tigris outside the walls another palace, Qaṣr al-Khuld (palace of eternity), so called because its gardens were supposed to rival those of Paradise (Koran 25 : 16-17), and farther north a third palace called al-Ruṣāfah (causeway), which was intended for the crown prince, the caliph's son al-Mahdi.

The horoscope under which al-Manṣūr started the building of this military post for himself, his family and his Khurāsānian bodyguard certainly proved fully as auspicious as predicted by the court astrologer.[3] In a few years the town grew into an emporium of trade and commerce and a political centre of the greatest international importance. As if called into existence by a magician's wand this city of al-Manṣūr fell heir to the power and prestige of Ctesiphon, Babylon, Nineveh, Ur and other capitals of the ancient Orient, attained a degree of prestige and splendour unrivalled in the Middle Ages, except perhaps by Constantinople, and after many vicissitudes was recently resuscitated as the capital of the new 'Irāqi kingdom under a truly Arabian king, Fayṣal.

[1] Khaṭīb, vol. i, p. 73. [2] Vol. i p 683.
[3] Yāqūt, vol. i, pp. 684-5; Khaṭīb, vol. i, pp. 67-8

The new location opened the way for ideas from the East. Here the caliphs built up a government modelled on Sāsānid Chosroism. Arab Islam succumbed to Persian influence; the caliphate became more of a revival of Iranian despotism and less of an Arabian sheikhdom. Gradually Persian titles, Persian wines and wives, Persian mistresses, Persian songs, as well as Persian ideas and thoughts, won the day. Al-Manṣūr, we are told, was the first to adopt the characteristic Persian head-gear (pl. *qalānis*), in which he was naturally followed by his subjects.[1] Persian influence, it should be noted, softened the rough edges of the primitive Arabian life and paved the way for a new era distinguished by the cultivation of science and scholarly pursuits. In two fields only did the Arabian hold his own: Islam remained the religion of the state and Arabic continued to be the official language of the state registers.

A Persian vizirial family

Under al-Manṣūr the vizirate, a Persian office, appears for the first time in Islamic government. Khālid ibn-Barmak was the first incumbent of that high office.[2] Khālid's mother was a prisoner whom Qutaybah ibn-Muslim captured (705) in Balkh; his father was a *barmak*, i.e. chief priest, in a Buddhist monastery in the same place.[3] Khālid was on such intimate terms with al-Saffāḥ that his daughter was nursed by the wife of the former caliph, whose daughter was likewise nursed by Khālid's wife.[4] Early under the 'Abbāsid régime Khālid rose to the headship of the department of finance (*dīwān al-kharāj*). In 765 he received the governorship of Ṭabaristān, where he crushed a dangerous uprising.[5] In his old age he distinguished himself at the capture of a Byzantine fortress.[6] Though not actually a vizir,[7] a minister in the later sense of the term, this official of Persian origin seems to have acted on various occasions as counsellor for the caliph and became the founder of an illustrious family of vizirs.

On October 7, 775, al-Manṣūr died near Makkah while on a pilgrimage. He was over sixty years of age. One hundred graves were dug for him near the Holy City, but he was secretly interred in another which no enemy might find and desecrate.[8] He was a

[1] Ṭabari, vol. iii, p. 371.

[2] Cf. ibn-Khallikān, vol. i, p. 290. where *wazīr* for al-Hamdāni is probably used in same sense as in *sūr*. 20 : 30.

[3] Ibn-al-Faqīh, pp. 322-4; Ṭabari, vol. ii, p. 1181; Yāqūt, vol. iv, p. 818.

[4] Ṭabari, vol. ii, p. 840.

[5] Ibn-al-Faqih, p. 314.

[6] Ṭabari, vol. iii, p. 497.

[7] Cf. *Fakhri*, pp. 206, 211: Mas'ūdi, *Tanbīh*, p. 340.

[8] Ibn-al-Athīr, vol. vi, p. 13.

slender, tall man, dark of complexion and thin-bearded.[1] Austere in nature and stern in manner, he stands in marked contrast to the type represented by his successors. But his policies continued for many generations to guide those who came after him just as those of Mu'āwiyah had guided the Umayyads.

To Khālid's son Yaḥya, al-Manṣūr's successor, al-Mahdi (775–85), entrusted the education of his son Hārūn. When Hārūn, following the brief reign of his brother al-Hādi (785–6), became caliph he appointed the Barmakid, whom he still respectfully called "father", as vizir with unrestricted power. Yaḥya, who died in 805, and his two sons al-Faḍl and Ja'far practically ruled the empire from 786 to 803.[2]

These Barmakids had their palaces in eastern Baghdād, where they lived in grand style. Here Ja'far's palace, al-Ja'fari, became the nucleus of a large group of magnificent residences later occupied by al-Ma'mūn and transformed into the Caliphal Palace (*dār al-khilāfah*). The buildings stood by the Tigris with spacious gardens behind enclosing many minor structures within their precincts. Fabulous fortunes were amassed by the members of the Barmakid family. Even what they saw fit to bestow on their clients, panegyrists and partisans was enough to make such protégés wealthy. Their generosity was proverbial. Even today in all the Arabic-speaking lands the word *barmaki* is used as a synonym of generous, and "as munificent as Ja'far"[3] is a simile that is everywhere well understood.

A number of canals,[4] mosques and other public works owe their existence to the initiative and munificence of the Barmakids. Al-Faḍl is credited with being the first in Islam to introduce the use of lamps in the mosques during the month of Ramaḍān. Ja'far acquired great fame for eloquence, literary ability and penmanship.[5] Chiefly because of him Arab historians regard the Barmakids as the founders of the class designated "people of the pen" (*ahl al-qalam*). But he was more than a man of letters. He was a leader of fashion, and the long neck which he possessed is said to have been responsible for the introduction of the custom of wearing high collars.[6] Ja'far's intimacy with the

[1] Ṭabari, vol. iii, p. 391; ibn-al-Athīr, vol. vi, p. 14; Mas'ūdi, *Tanbīh*, p. 341.
[2] Ya'qūbi, vol. ii, p. 520. [3] Consult ibn-Khallikān, vol. i, pp. 185 *seq.*
[4] See Ṭabari, vol. iii, p. 645, ll. 18-19; Balādhuri. p. 363.
[5] Ṭabari, vol. ii, p. 843; Mas'ūdi, vol. vi, p. 361.
[6] Jāḥiz, *Bayān*, vol. iii, p. 201.

Caliph Hārūn was not pleasing to his father, Yaḥya, as it was suspiciously immoral.[1]

The time at last came for the caliph to rid himself of this Persian tutelage. The Shī'ite Barmakids were getting too powerful for the strong-willed Hārūn (786–809), in whose caliphal firmament there could not be two suns. First the thirty-seven-year-old Ja'far was slain in 803; his severed head was impaled on one bridge of Baghdād and the two halves of his body on the other two bridges.[2] The usual reason given by historians is that the caliph had allowed him, as a boon companion, to marry in name only his favourite sister, al-'Abbāsah, but discovered later while on a holy pilgrimage that she had secretly given birth to a son whom she had concealed in Makkah.[3] The aged Yaḥya, together with his distinguished son al-Faḍl and his other two sons, were all apprehended and cast into prison. Both Yaḥya and al-Faḍl died in confinement. All the property of the family, said to have amounted to 30,676,000 (dinars) in cash exclusive of farms, palaces and furniture, was confiscated.[4] Thus the celebrated house founded by Khālid al-Barmaki fell, never to rise again.

[1] Ṭabari, vol. iii, pp. 674-6.
[2] '*Iqd*, vol. iii, p. 28; Ṭabari, vol. iii, p. 680.
[3] Ṭabari, vol. iii, pp. 676-7; Mas'ūdi, vol. vi, pp. 387-94; *Fakhri*, p. 288. Cf. ibn-Khaldūn, vol. iii, pp. 223-4; *Kitāb al-'Uyūn*, pt. 3, pp. 306-8.
[4] '*Iqd*, vol. iii, p. 28.

CHAPTER XXIV

THE GOLDEN PRIME OF THE 'ABBĀSIDS

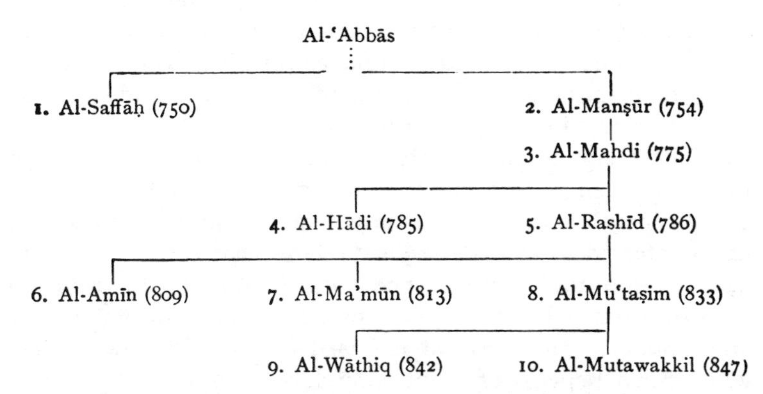

THE 'Abbāsid dynasty, like others in Moslem history, attained its most brilliant period of political and intellectual life soon after its establishment. The Baghdād caliphate founded by al-Saffāḥ and al-Manṣūr reached its prime in the period between the reigns of the third caliph, al-Mahdi, and the ninth, al-Wāthiq, more particularly in the days of Hārūn al-Rashīd and his son al-Ma'mūn. It was chiefly because of these two luminous caliphs that the 'Abbāsid dynasty acquired a halo in popular imagination and became the most celebrated in the history of Islam. The dictum quoted by the anthologist al-Tha'ālibi[1] († 1038) that of the 'Abbāsid caliphs "the opener" was al-Manṣūr, "the middler" was al-Ma'mūn and "the closer" was al-Mu'taḍid (892–902) is therefore not far from the historical truth. After al-Wāthiq the state starts on its downward course until under the Caliph al-Musta'ṣim, the thirty-seventh of the line, it meets its final destruction at the hands of the Mongols in 1258. An idea of the degree of power and glory and progress attained by the 'Abbāsid caliphate at its highest and best may be gained from a scrutiny of its foreign relations, a study of court and aristocratic life in

[1] *Laṭā'if al-Ma'ārif*, ed. P. de Jong (Leyden, 1867), p. 71.

its capital, Baghdād, and a survey of the unparalleled intellectual awakening that culminated under the patronage of al-Ma'mūn.

Relations with the Franks

The ninth century opened with two imperial names standing supreme in world affairs: Charlemagne in the West and Hārūn al-Rashīd in the East. Of the two Hārūn was undoubtedly the more powerful and represented the higher culture. The mutual friendly relations into which these two contemporaries entered were, of course, prompted by self-interest; Charlemagne cultivated Hārūn as a possible ally against hostile Byzantium and Hārūn desired to use Charlemagne against his rivals and deadly foes, the neighbouring Umayyads of Spain, who had succeeded in establishing a mighty and prosperous state. This reciprocity of cordial feelings found expression, according to Western writers, in the exchange of a number of embassies and presents. A Frankish author who knew Charlemagne personally and is sometimes referred to as his secretary relates that the envoys of the great king of the West returned home with rich gifts from "the king of Persia, Aaron", which included fabrics, aromatics and an elephant.[1] This account is based on the *Annales royales*,[2] which further speaks of an intricate clock as among the gifts from Baghdād. But the account of the pipe organ sent to Charlemagne by Hārūn, like many other charming bits of history, is fictitious. Its story is apparently based on a mistranslation of the term *clepsydra* in the sources, which in reality meant a device for measuring time by water and referred to the clock presented. Likewise the assertion that the keys of the Church of the Holy Sepulchre were delivered by Hārūn's consent to Charlemagne has been discredited.[3]

The strange thing about this exchange of embassies and gifts, said to have taken place between 797 and 806, is the utter silence of Moslem authors regarding it. While reference is made to various other diplomatic exchanges and courtesies, none is made to this. The *'Iqd*[4] cites several cases of correspondence between Umayyad caliphs and Byzantine emperors and speaks of a delegation from "the king of India" which brought Hārūn

[1] Éginhard, *Vie de Charlemagne*, ed. and tr. L. Halphen (Paris, 1923), p. 47.
[2] "Annales regni Francorum", ed. G. H. Pertzii and F. Kurze in *Scriptores rerum Germanicarum*, vol. 43 (Hanover, 1895), pp. 114, 123-4.
[3] See below, pp. 507, 635-6. Cf. Louis Bréhier in *Chambre de Commerce de Marseille. Congrès français de Syrie. Séances et travaux*, fasc. 2 (1919), pp. 15-39.
[4] Vol. i, pp. 197-8.

valuable presents and was received with great pomp. Another source[1] states that Hārūn's son al-Ma'mūn received an especially rich gift from his contemporary "the king of the Romans", possibly Michael II.

With the Byzantines

The more-than-century-old struggle between the caliphate and the Byzantine empire was resumed by the third caliph, al-Mahdi (775–85), but the engagements were of less frequency and success. The internal conflicts that convulsed the Arab state and resulted in the transference of the capital to distant Baghdād had made it possible for Constantine V (741–75) to push the imperial border farther east along the entire boundary of Asia Minor and Armenia.[2] The Moslem line of frontier fortifications (*thughūr*) extending from Syria to Armenia retreated as the Byzantine line opposite advanced.

Al-Mahdi, the first 'Abbāsid caliph to resume the "holy war" against the Byzantines, initiated a brilliant and successful attack against the enemy capital itself. Hārūn, his young son and future successor, commanded the expedition. In 782[3] the Arab forces reached the Bosporus,[4] if not Constantinople itself; and Irene, who held the regency in the name of her son Constantine VI, was forced to sue for peace and conclude a singularly humiliating treaty involving the payment of a tribute of 70,000 to 90,000 dinars in semi-annual instalments.[5] It was in the course of this campaign that Hārūn so distinguished himself that his father gave him the honorific title al-Rashīd (follower of the right path) and designated him the second heir apparent to the throne, after his elder brother Mūsa al-Hādi.

This proved the last time that a hostile Arab army stood before the walls of the proud capital. In all there were four distinct expeditions which reached Byzantium; the first three were sent under the Umayyads by Mu'āwiyah and by Sulaymān.[6] Of the four only two involved real sieges of the city: one by Yazīd (49/669) and the other by Maslamah (98/716). Turkish tradition,

[1] Kutubi, *Fawāt*, vol. i, p. 307, ll. 12-13.

[2] A. A. Vasiliev, *History of the Byzantine Empire*, tr. S. Ragozin, vol. i (Madison, 1928), p. 291; Charles Diehl, *History of the Byzantine Empire*, tr. G. B. Ives (Princeton, 1925), p. 55.

[3] *Kitāb al-'Uyūn*, pt. 3, p. 278, dates the expedition 163 (A.D. 780), Ya'qūbi (vol. ii, pp. 478, 486) 164 and Ṭabari (vol. iii, pp. 503-4) 165.

[4] Theophanis, who wrote in 813, says (p. 456) that Hārūn advanced as far as Chrysopolis, on the site of modern Scutari.

[5] Ṭabari, vol. iii, p. 504.

[6] See above, pp. 200 *seq.*

however, makes the sieges seven to nine in number, of which two are ascribed to Hārūn. In the *Arabian Nights* and other Arabic romances of chivalry the Moslem expeditions against Constantinople form the subject of themes highly coloured and developed during the period of the Crusades.

Irene (797–802), who had seized the throne and become "the first instance in Byzantine history of a woman who ruled with full authority of supreme power",[1] was succeeded by Nicephorus I[2] (802–11), who repudiated the terms of the treaty contracted by the empress and even demanded from the caliph, now al-Rashīd, the return of the tribute already paid. Inflamed with rage, al-Rashīd called for pen and ink and wrote on the back of the scornful epistle:

> In the name of God, the merciful, the compassionate.
>
> From Hārūn, the commander of the believers, to Nicephorus, the dog of a Roman.
>
> Verily I have read thy letter, O son of an infidel mother. As for the answer it shall be for thine eye to see, not for thine ear to hear. Salam.[3]

True to his word, Hārūn started at once a series of campaigns directed from his favourite town of residence, al-Raqqah, situated beside the Euphrates and commanding the Syrian frontier. These expeditions ravaged Asia Minor and culminated in the capture of Heraclea (Ar. Hiraqlah) and Tyana (al-Ṭuwānah) in 806 and the imposition, in addition to the tribute, of an ignominious tax on the emperor himself and on each member of his household.[4] This event and date in the reign of Hārūn al-Rashīd may be taken as marking the topmost point ever reached by 'Abbāsid power.

After 806 there was only one serious attempt at securing a footing beyond the Taurus, and that by al-Mu'taṣim in 838. Though al-Mu'taṣim's huge army, "equipped as no caliph's army before had ever been equipped",[5] penetrated into the heart

[1] Vasiliev, vol. i, p. 287.

[2] Niqfūr of Arabic sources. He was of Arab origin; possibly a descendant of Jabalah the Ghassānid; Ṭabari, vol. iii, p. 695; Michel le Syrien, *Chronicle*, ed. J.-B. Chabot, vol. iii (Paris, 1905), p. 15. Irene, whom he dethroned, was the last of the Isaurian or Syrian dynasty (717–802) founded by Leo III (717–41), who with his successors headed the iconoclastic movement which bears traces of Moslem influence. Theophanis, p. 405, calls Leo "the Saracen-minded".

[3] Ṭabari, vol. iii, p. 696.

[4] *Ibid.* pp. 696, 709-10; Ya'qūbi, vol. ii, p. 519, l. 14, p. 523, l. 2; Dīnawari, pp. 386-7; Mas'ūdi, vol. ii, pp. 337-52.

[5] Ṭabari, vol. iii, p. 1236.

of "the land of the Romans" and temporarily occupied Amorium (Amorion, Ar. ʿAmmūriyah), the birthplace of the founder of the then ruling dynasty,[1] the attempt on the whole was unsuccessful. The Arab forces expected to march upon Constantinople but returned on the receipt of alarming reports of a military conspiracy at home. The reigning emperor, Theophilus (829–42), so feared the loss of his capital that he dispatched envoys to Venice, to the Frankish king and to the Umayyad court in Spain soliciting aid. Theophilus had once before been threatened from the east when al-Ma'mūn, son of Hārūn, took the field in person but met his death (833) near Tarsus. After al-Muʿtaṣim no serious offensive on the Arab side was ever undertaken. Those of his successors who sent armies across the border aimed at plunder rather than conquest. In no case did the collision assume significance or occur deep in the land. Yet throughout the ninth century the hostile contacts, though of minor importance, occurred with almost annual regularity on the eastern border-line. One Arab geographer[2] informs us that it was the practice then to make three raids each year: one in winter covering the end of February and the beginning of March, another in spring lasting thirty days from May 10, and a third in summer extending over a period of sixty days from July 10. Such raids served to keep the military forces in good trim and netted profitable spoils. But the original Arabian national motive, and to a large extent the religious impulse which figured in the early campaigns of Islam, had now become far less important factors. The internal weakening of the Moslem state was beginning to tell in its foreign relations. One of the petty dynasties, the Ḥamdānid in Aleppo, which arose about the middle of the tenth century at the expense of the caliphate, did take up the cudgels against Byzantium. But of that we shall hear later.

The glory that was Baghdād

History and legend unite in placing the most brilliant period of Baghdād during the caliphate of Hārūn al-Rashīd (786–809). Though less than half a century old, Baghdād had by that time grown from nothingness to a world centre of prodigious wealth and international significance, standing alone as the rival of Byzantium. Its splendour kept pace with the prosperity of the empire of which it was the capital. It was then

[1] Michel le Syrien, vol. iii, p. 72.
[2] Qudāmah, *Kitāb al-Kharāj*, ed. de Goeje (Leyden, 1889), p. 259.

that Baghdād became "a city with no peer throughout the whole world".[1]

The royal palace with its many annexes for harems, eunuchs and special functionaries occupied one-third of the Round City. Particularly impressive was its audience chamber with its rugs, curtains and cushions, the best the Orient could produce. The caliph's cousin-wife, Zubaydah, who in tradition shares with her husband the halo of glory and distinction bestowed by later generations, would tolerate at her table no vessels not made of gold or silver and studded with gems. She set the fashion for the smart set and was the first to ornament her shoes with precious stones.[2] In one holy pilgrimage she is reported to have spent three million dinars, which included the expense of supplying Makkah with water from a spring twenty-five miles away.[3]

Zubaydah had a rival in the beauteous 'Ulayyah, daughter of al-Mahdi and half-sister of Hārūn, who to cover a blemish on her forehead devised a fillet set with jewels which, as the fillet *à la* 'Ulayyah, was soon adopted by the world of fashion as the ornament of the day.[4]

Especially on ceremonial occasions, such as the installation of the caliph, weddings, pilgrimages and receptions for foreign envoys, did the courtly wealth and magnificence find its fullest display. The marriage ceremony of the Caliph al-Ma'mūn to the eighteen-year-old Būrān,[5] daughter of his vizir, al-Ḥasan ibn-Sahl, was celebrated in 825 with such fabulous expenditure of money that it has lived in Arabic literature as one of the unforgettable extravaganzas of the age. At the nuptials a thousand pearls of unique size, we are told, were showered from a gold tray upon the couple who sat on a golden mat studded with pearls and sapphires. A two-hundred-rotl candle of ambergris turned the night into day. Balls of musk, each containing a ticket naming an estate or a slave or some such gift, were showered on the royal princes and dignitaries.[6] In 917 the Caliph al-Muqtadir received in his palace with great ceremony and pomp the envoys of the young Constantine VII, whose mission evidently

[1] Khaṭīb, vol. i, p. 119.
[2] Mas'ūdi, vol. viii, pp. 298-9.
[3] Cf. ibn-Khallikān, vol. i, p. 337; Burckhardt, *Travels*, vol. i, p. 196.
[4] *Aghāni*, vol. ix, p. 83.
[5] She was ten years old when betrothed to al-Ma'mūn; ibn-Khallikān, vol. i, p. 166.
[6] Ṭabari, vol. iii, pp. 1081-4; Mas'ūdi, vol. vii, pp. 65-6; ibn-al-Athīr, vol. vi, p. 279; Tha'ālibi, *Laṭā'if*, pp. 73-4; ibn-Khaldūn, *Muqaddamah*, pp. 144-5.

involved the exchange and ransom of prisoners.[1] The caliphal array included 160,000 cavalry and footmen, 7000 black and white eunuchs and 700 chamberlains. In the parade a hundred lions marched, and in the caliphal palace hung 38,000 curtains, of which 12,500 were gilded, besides 22,000 rugs. The envoys were so struck with awe and admiration that they first mistook the chamberlain's office and then the vizir's for the royal audience chamber. Especially impressed were they with the Hall of the Tree (*dār al-shajarah*) which housed an artificial tree of gold and silver weighing 500,000 drams, in the branches of which were lodged birds of the same precious metals so constructed that they chirped by automatic devices. In the garden they marvelled at the artificially dwarfed palm trees which by skilled cultivation yielded dates of rare varieties.[2]

Like a magnet the princely munificence of Hārūn, the *beau idéal* of Islamic kingship, and of his immediate successors attracted to the capital poets, wits, musicians, singers, dancers, trainers of fighting dogs and cocks and others who could amuse, interest or entertain.[3] Ibrāhīm al-Mawṣili, Siyāṭ and ibn-Jāmi' led the roster of musician-singers. The libertine poet abu-Nuwās, the boon companion of al-Rashīd and his comrade on many a nocturnal adventure, has depicted for us in unforgettable terms the colourful court life of this period of glory. The pages of *al-Aghānī* abound with illustrative anecdotes whose nucleus of truth is not hard to discern. According to one story the Caliph al-Amīn (809–13) one evening bestowed on his uncle Ibrāhīm ibn-al-Mahdi, a professional singer, the sum of 300,000 dinars for chanting a few verses of abu-Nuwās'. This raised the gratuities thus far received by Ibrāhīm from the caliph to 20,000,000 dirhams.[4] Al-Amīn, of whom ibn-al-Athīr[5] found nothing praiseworthy to record, had a number of special barges shaped like animals built for his parties on the Tigris. One of these vessels looked like a dolphin, another like a lion, a third like an eagle; the cost of one was 3,000,000 dirhams.[6] We read in the *Aghānī*[7] of a picturesque all-night ballet conducted under the Caliph al-Amīn's personal direction in which a large number of

[1] Mas'ūdi, *Tanbīh*, p. 193.
[2] Khaṭīb, vol. i, pp. 100-105; abu-al-Fidā', vol. ii, p. 73; Yāqūt, vol. ii, pp. 520-21.
[3] Balādhuri, *Ansāb al-Ashrāf*, ed. Max Achloessinger, vol. iv B (Jerusalem, 1938), p. 1.
[4] *Aghānī*, vol. ix, p. 71. See below, p. 321.
[5] Vol. vi, p. 207.
[6] *Ibid.* p. 206; Ṭabari, vol. iii, pp. 951-3.
[7] Vol. xvi, pp. 138-9.

beautiful girl dancers performed in rhythmic unison to the soft harmony of music and were joined in their singing by all those who attended. Al-Mas'ūdi[1] relates that on the occasion of a dinner given by Ibrāhīm in honour of his brother al-Rashīd, the caliph was served with a dish of fish in which the slices looked exceedingly small. In explanation the host remarked that the slices were fishes' tongues, and the waiter added that the cost of the hundred and fifty tongues in the dish was over a thousand dirhams. Even when stripped of the adventitious glow cast by Oriental romance and fancy, enough of the splendour of court life in Baghdād remains to arouse our astonishment.

Next to the royal master in high and luxurious living came the members of the 'Abbāsid family, the vizirs, officials, functionaries and other satellites of the imperial household. Members of the Hāshimite tribe, to which the 'Abbāsids belonged, received large regular stipends from the state treasury until the practice was discontinued by al-Mu'taṣim (833–42).[2] Al-Rashīd's mother, al-Khayzurān, is said to have had an income of 160,000,000 dirhams.[3] A certain Muḥammad ibn-Sulaymān, whose property was confiscated on his death by al-Rashīd, left 50,000,000 dirhams in cash and a daily income of 100,000 dirhams from his real estate.[4] The scale on which the Barmakids lived could not have been much lower than that of the caliphal household itself. As for the humdrum life of the ordinary citizen in Baghdād and the feelings that surged in the breast of the common man, we find little in the sources with the possible exception of the poetical works of the ascetic abu-al-'Atāhiyah.

When al-Ma'mūn in 819, after several years of civil war with his elder brother al-Amīn (who had been designated to the successorship by their father) and with his uncle Ibrāhīm ibn-al-Mahdi, who also claimed the throne, made his victorious entry into Baghdād a large part of the city lay in ruins. We hear no more of the Round City. As caliph, al-Ma'mūn took up his abode in the Ja'fari palace, originally built for Ja'far al-Barmaki on the east side of the river. But it was not long before the town rose again to eminence as a commercial and intellectual centre. The natural successor to a long line of distinguished metropolitan towns which flourished in the Tigris-Euphrates valley beginning with

[1] Vol. vi, pp. 349-50.
[2] Cf. Tha'ālibi, *Laṭā'if*, p. 16.
[3] Mas'ūdi, vol. vi, p. 289.
[4] *Ibid.*

Ur and Babylon and ending with Ctesiphon, the 'Abbāsid capital could not be easily suppressed. Its advantageous position as a shipping centre made all parts of the then charted world accessible to it. Along its miles of wharves lay hundreds of vessels, including ships of war and pleasure craft and varying from Chinese junks to native rafts of inflated sheepskins, not unlike those of our present day, which were floated down from al-Mawṣil. Into the bazaars of the city came porcelain, silk and musk from China; spices, minerals and dyes from India and the Malay Archipelago; rubies, lapis lazuli, fabrics and slaves from the lands of the Turks in Central Asia; honey, wax, furs and white slaves from Scandinavia and Russia; ivory, gold dust and black slaves from eastern Africa. Chinese wares had a special bazaar devoted to their sale. The provinces of the empire itself sent by caravan or sea their domestic products: rice, grain and linen from Egypt; glass, metal ware and fruits from Syria; brocade, pearls and weapons from Arabia; silks, perfumes and vegetables from Persia.[1] Communication between the east and west sides of the city was assured by three main pontoon bridges like the Baghdād bridges of today. Al-Khaṭīb[2] devotes a section of his history to the bridges of Baghdād and another to its canals (*anhār*). From Baghdād and other export centres Arab merchants shipped to the Far East, Europe and Africa fabrics, jewellery, metal mirrors, glass beads, spices, etc.[3] The hoards of Arab coins recently found in places as far north as Russia, Finland,[4] Sweden and Germany testify to the world-wide commercial activity of the Moslems of this and the later period. The adventures of Sindbād the Sailor, which form one of the best-known tales in *The Thousand and One Nights*, have long been recognized as based upon actual reports of voyages made by Moslem merchants.

Merchants played a leading part in the Baghdād community. Members of each craft and trade had their shops in the same market (*sūq*),[5] as in the present day. The monotony of street life was interrupted from time to time by the occasional passage of a wedding or circumcision procession. Professional men—physicians, lawyers, teachers, writers and the like—began to occupy a conspicuous place under the patronage of al-Ma'mūn.

[1] Consult Le Strange, *Eastern Caliphate, passim*. See below, pp. 343, 351.
[2] Vol. i, pp. 111-17.
[3] See below, pp. 345 *seq*.
[4] The museum at Helsinki contains many such coins.
[5] Ya'qūbi, *Buldān*, p. 246.

By the time al-Nadīm composed (988) his monumental *al-Fihrist*, a sort of catalogue of existing Arabic works, there were abundant manuscripts dealing even with such subjects as hypnotism, jugglery, sword-swallowing and glass-chewing.[1] Ibn-Khallikān[2] has fortunately left us a cross section of the daily routine of a member of the learned fraternity, Ḥunayn ibn-Isḥāq, which indicates that scholarship had a considerable market value in those days. We are first shown Ḥunayn, after his daily ride, at the public bath, where attendants poured water over him. On emerging he put on a lounging-robe, sipped a drink, ate a biscuit and lay down, sometimes falling asleep. The siesta over, he burned perfume to fumigate his person and ordered a dinner which generally consisted of soup, fattened chicken and bread. Then he resumed his sleep and on waking drank four rotls of old wine, to which he added quinces and Syrian apples if he felt the desire for fresh fruits.

Intellectual awakening

The victory of Moslem arms under al-Mahdi and al-Rashīd over the inveterate Byzantine enemy undoubtedly shed its lustre on this period, the luxurious scale of living made this period popular in history and in fiction, but what has rendered this age especially illustrious in world annals is the fact that it witnessed the most momentous intellectual awakening in the history of Islam and one of the most significant in the whole history of thought and culture. The awakening was due in a large measure to foreign influences, partly Indo-Persian and Syrian but mainly Hellenic, and was marked by translations into Arabic from Persian, Sanskrit, Syriac and Greek. Starting with very little science, philosophy or literature of his own, the Arabian Moslem, who brought with him from the desert a keen sense of intellectual curiosity, a voracious appetite for learning and many latent faculties, soon became, as we have learned before, the beneficiary and heir of the older and more cultured peoples whom he conquered or encountered. As in Syria he adopted the already existing Aramaic civilization, itself influenced by the later Greek, so did he in al-'Irāq adopt the same civilization influenced by the Persian. In three-quarters of a century after the establishment of Baghdād the Arabic-reading world was in possession of the chief philosophical works of Aristotle, of the leading Neo-Platonic commentators, and of most of the medical writings of Galen, as well

[1] P. 312. [2] Vol. i, p. 298.

as of Persian and Indian scientific works.[1] In only a few decades Arab scholars assimilated what had taken the Greeks centuries to develop. In absorbing the main features of both Hellenic and Persian cultures Islam, to be sure, lost most of its own original character, which breathed the spirit of the desert and bore the stamp of Arabian nationalism, but it thereby took an important place in the medieval cultural unit which linked southern Europe with the Near East. This culture, it should be remembered, was fed by a single stream, a stream with sources in ancient Egypt, Babylonia, Phoenicia and Judaea, all flowing to Greece and now returning to the East in the form of Hellenism. We shall later see how this same stream was re-diverted into Europe by the Arabs in Spain and Sicily, whence it helped create the Renaissance of Europe.

India

India acted as an early source of inspiration, especially in wisdom literature and mathematics. About A.H. 154 (771) an Indian traveller introduced into Baghdād a treatise on astronomy, a *Siddhānta* (Ar. *Sindhind*), which by order of al-Manṣūr was translated by Muḥammad ibn-Ibrāhīm al-Fazāri († between 796 and 806), who subsequently became the first astronomer in Islam.[2] The stars had of course interested the Arabians since desert days, but no scientific study of them was undertaken until this time. Islam added its impetus to the study of astronomy as a means for fixing the direction in which prayer should be conducted Kaʿbah-ward. The famous al-Khwārizmi († *ca.* 850) based his widely known astronomical tables (*zīj*) on al-Fazāri's work and syncretized the Indian and Greek systems of astronomy, at the same time adding his own contribution. Among other translations of astronomical works at this period were those from Persian into Arabic by al-Faḍl ibn-Nawbakht[3] († *ca.* 815), the chief librarian of al-Rashīd.[4]

This same Indian traveller had also brought a treatise on mathematics by means of which the numerals called in Europe

[1] Since the latter part of the nineteenth century the modern Arab Orient has been passing through a similar period of translation, mainly from French and English.

[2] Ṣāʿid ibn-Aḥmad (al-Qāḍi al-Andalusi), *Ṭabaqāt al-Umam*, ed. L. Cheikho (Beirūt, 1912), pp. 49-50; Yāqūt, *Udabāʾ*, vol. vi, p. 268; Masʿūdi, vol. viii, pp. 290-91.

[3] Pers. *nawbakht*, good luck. Many members of this family distinguished themselves in the science of the stars. Ṭabari, vol. iii, pp. 317, 318 (where the name occurs as Nībakht or Naybakht), 1364.

[4] *Fihrist*, p 274.

Arabic and by the Arabs Indian (*Hindi*) entered the Moslem world.[1] Later, in the ninth century, the Indians made another important contribution to Arabic mathematical science, the decimal system.

Persia

Except in the arts and *belles-lettres* Persia did not have much that was original to contribute. The esthetic temperament of its Iranian population was a sorely needed element in the cultural life of the Semitic Arabians. Next to the artistic, the literary—rather than the scientific or philosophical—was the influence most clearly felt from Persia. The earliest literary work in Arabic that has come down to us is *Kalīlah wa-Dimnah* (fables of Bidpai), a translation from Pahlawi (Middle Persian) which was itself a rendition from Sanskrit. The original work was brought to Persia from India, together with the game of chess, in the reign of Anūsharwān (531–78). What gives the Arabic version special significance is the fact that the Persian was lost, as was the Sanskrit original, though the material in an expanded form can still be found in the *Panchatantra*. The Arabic version therefore became the basis of all existing translations into some forty languages, including, besides European tongues, Hebrew, Turkish, Ethiopic and Malay. Even Icelandic has a translation. This book, intended to instruct princes in the laws of polity by means of animal fables, was done into Arabic by ibn-al-Muqaffa',[2] a Zoroastrian convert to Islam whose suspect orthodoxy brought about his death by fire *ca.* 757.

Ibn-al-Muqaffa''s translation was in itself a stylistic work of art, and ever since the 'Abbāsid age Arabic prose has borne the impress of Persian style in its extravagant elegance, colourful imagery and flowery expression. The ancient Arabic style with its virile, pointed and terse form of expression was replaced to a large extent by the polished and affected diction of the Sāsānid period. Such Arabic literary works as *al-Aghāni*, *al-'Iqd al-Farīd* and al-Ṭurṭūshi's *Sirāj al-Mulūk*[3] teem with references to earlier Indo-Persian sources, especially when dealing with etiquette, wisdom, polity and history. Arabic historiography, as we shall see, was modelled after Persian patterns.

[1] See below, pp. 573 *seq.*

[2] For printed editions of *Kalīlah wa-Dimnah* see Sylvester de Sacy's (Paris, 1816), reprinted in Būlāq, 1249; Khalīl al-Yāziji's 2nd ed. (Beirūt, 1888); L. Cheikho's (Beirūt, 1905). On ibn-al-Muqaffa' consult *Fihrist*, p. 118; ibn-Khallikān, vol. i, pp. 266-9.

[3] Published in Cairo, 1289, 1306, etc.

In 765 the Caliph al-Manṣūr, afflicted with a stomach disease which had baffled his physicians, summoned from Jundi-Shāpūr[1] the dean of its hospital, the Nestorian Jūrjīs[2] (George) ibn-Bakhtīshū' († *ca.* 771). Jundi-Shāpūr was noted for its academy of medicine and philosophy founded about 555 by the great Anūsharwān. The science of the institution was based on the ancient Greek tradition, but the language of instruction was Aramaic. Jūrjīs soon won the confidence of the caliph and became the court physician, though he retained his Christian faith. Invited by the caliph to embrace Islam his retort was that he preferred the company of his fathers, be they in heaven or in hell.[3] Ibn-Bakhtīshū' became in Baghdād the founder of a brilliant family which for six or seven generations, covering a period of two centuries and a half, with many ups and downs, exercised an almost continuous monopoly over the court medical practice. Scientific lore in those days, like jewellery-making and other forms of craftsmanship, was considered an exclusive family affair and transmitted from father to son. Jūrjīs' son Bakhtīshū' († 801) was chief physician of the Baghdād hospital under al-Rashīd. Bakhtīshū''s son Jibrīl (Gabriel), who successfully treated a favourite slave of al-Rashīd for hysterical paralysis by pretending to disrobe her in public, was appointed the caliph's private physician in 805.[4]

Hellenism

At the time of the Arab conquest of the Fertile Crescent the intellectual legacy of Greece was unquestionably the most precious treasure at hand. Hellenism consequently became the most vital of all foreign influences in Arab life. Edessa (al-Ruhā'), the principal centre of Christian Syrians; Ḥarrān, the headquarters of the heathen Syrians who in and after the ninth century claimed to be Ṣābians (Ar. Ṣābi'ah or Ṣābi'ūn);[5] Antioch, one of the many ancient Greek colonies; Alexandria, the meeting-place of Occidental and Oriental philosophy; and the numberless cloisters of Syria and Mesopotamia where not only ecclesiastical

[1] Ar. Jundaysābūr. The city, founded by the Sāsānid Shāpūr I, whence the name, which may mean "camp of Shāpūr", stood on the site of the modern village Shāhābād in Khūzistān, south-western Persia.

[2] Cf. *Fihrist*, p. 296; ibn-al-'Ibri, pp. 213-15. "Bakht", which ibn-abi-Uṣaybi'ah (vol. i, p. 125) takes for a Syriac word meaning "servant", is for Pahlawi *bōkht*, "hath delivered", making the family name mean "Jesus hath delivered".

[3] Ibn-al-'Ibri, p. 215, copied by ibn-abi-Uṣaybi'ah, vol. i, p. 125.

[4] Ibn-al-'Ibri, pp. 226-7; Qifṭi, pp. 134-5.

[5] See below, p. 357.

but scientific and philosophic studies were cultivated, all served as centres radiating Hellenistic stimuli. The various raids into "the land of the Romans", particularly under Hārūn, resulted in the introduction, among other objects of booty, of Greek manuscripts, chiefly from Amorium and Ancyra[1] (Ankara). Al-Ma'mūn is credited with the dispatch of emissaries as far as Constantinople, to the Emperor Leo the Armenian himself, in quest of Greek works. Even al-Manṣūr is said to have received in response to his request from the Byzantine emperor a number of books, including Euclid.[2] But the Arabians knew no Greek and had at first to depend upon translations made by their subjects, Jewish, heathen and more particularly Nestorian Christian. These Syrian Nestorians, who translated first into Syriac and then from Syriac into Arabic, thus became the strongest link between Hellenism and Islam and consequently the earliest Oriental purveyors of Greek culture to the world at large. Before Hellenism could find access to the Arab mind it had to pass through a Syriac version.

The apogee of Greek influence was reached under al-Ma'mūn. The rationalistic tendencies of this caliph and his espousal of the Mu'tazilite cause, which maintained that religious texts should agree with the judgments of reason, led him to seek justification for his position in the philosophical works of the Greeks. The way the *Fihrist*[3] expresses it is that Aristotle appeared to him in a dream and assured him that there was no real difference between reason and religious law. In pursuance of his policy al-Ma'mūn in 830 established in Baghdād his famous Bayt al-Ḥikmah (house of wisdom), a combination library, academy and translation bureau which in many respects proved the most important educational institution since the foundation of the Alexandrian Museum in the first half of the third century B.C. Down to this time sporadic translation work had been done independently by Christians, Jews and recent converts to Islam. Beginning with al-Ma'mūn and continuing under his immediate successors the work was centred mainly in the newly founded academy. The 'Abbāsid era of translation lasted about a century after 750. Since most of the translators were Aramaic-speaking many of the Greek works were first done into Aramaic (Syriac)

[1] Ar. Anqirah; Ya'qūbi, vol. i, p. 486.
[2] Ibn-Khaldūn, *Muqaddamah*, p. 401 [3] P. 243.

before their rendition into Arabic. In the case of many difficult passages in the original the translation was made word by word, and where no Arabic equivalent was found or known the Greek term was simply transliterated with some adaptation.[1]

The translators into Arabic did not interest themselves in Greek productions of the literary type. No close contact was therefore established between the Arab mind and Greek drama, Greek poetry and Greek history. In that field Persian influence remained paramount. Homer's Iliad was partially translated into Syriac by Thāwafīl (Theophilus) ibn-Tūma of al-Ruhā' († 785),[2] the Maronite astrologer of al-Mahdi, but evidently it was not carried through the second step into Arabic as in other cases. It was first Greek medicine as represented by Galen († *ca.* A.D. 200) and Paul of Aegina (fl. *ca.* A.D. 650),[3] Greek mathematics and allied sciences for which Euclid (fl. *ca.* 300 B.C.) and Ptolemy (fl. first half of second Christian century) stood, Greek philosophy as originated by Plato and Aristotle and expounded by later Neo-Platonists, that served as the starting-point of this voyage of intellectual discovery.

Translators

One of the pioneer translators from Greek was abu-Yaḥya ibn-al-Baṭrīq († between 796 and 806), who is credited with having translated for al-Manṣūr the major works of Galen and Hippocrates (fl. *ca.* 436 B.C.) and for another patron Ptolemy's *Quadripartitum.*[4] The *Elements* of Euclid and the *Almagest*, Arabic *al-Majisṭi* or *al-Mijisṭi* (originally from Gr. *megistē*, greatest), the great astronomical work of Ptolemy,[5] may have also been translated about the same time if a report in al-Mas'ūdi[6] is correct. But evidently all these early translations were not properly done and had to be revised or remade under al-Rashīd and al-Ma'mūn. Another early translator was the Syrian Christian Yūḥanna (Yaḥya) ibn-Māsawayh[7] († 857), a pupil of Jibrīl

[1] Hence such Arabic words as *arithmāṭīqi* (arithmetic), *jūmaṭrīya* (geometry), *jighrāfīyah* (geography), *mūsīqi* (music), *falsafah* (philosophy), *asṭurlāb* (astrolabe), *athīr* (ether), *iksīr* (elixir), *ibrīz* (pure gold), *maghnaṭīs* (magnet), *urghun* (organ). Consult abu-'Abdullāh al-Khwārizmi, *Mafātīḥ al-'Ulūm*, ed. G. van Vloten (Leyden, 1895), index; *Fihrist*, *passim; Rasā'il Ikhwān al-Ṣafā'*, ed. Khayr-al-Dīn al-Zirikli (Cairo, 1928), *passim*.

[2] Ibn-al-'Ibri, pp. 41, 220.

[3] *Ibid.* p. 176.

[4] *Fihrist*, p. 273.

[5] Ya'qūbi, vol. i, pp. 150-51.

[6] Vol. viii, p. 291. Cf. below, pp. 314-15.

[7] Latin Mesuë (Mesua), or Mesuë Major (the Elder) to distinguish him from Mesuë the Younger (Māsawayh al-Māridīni), the Jacobite physician who flourished at the court of the Fāṭimid Caliph al-Ḥākim in Cairo and died in 1015.

ibn-Bakhtīshū' and a teacher of Ḥunayn ibn-Isḥāq, who is said to have translated for al-Rashīd certain manuscripts, mainly medical, which the caliph had brought back from Ancyra and Amorium.[1] Yūḥanna served also under the successors of al-Rashīd. Once when offended by a court favourite his retort was, "If the folly wherewith thou art afflicted were converted into intelligence and divided amongst a hundred beetles, each would then become more intelligent than Aristotle!"[2]

Ḥunayn ibn-Isḥāq

The sheikh of the translators, as the Arabs express it, was Ḥunayn ibn-Isḥāq (Joannitius, 809–73), one of the greatest scholars and noblest characters of the age. Ḥunayn was an 'Ibādi, i.e. a Nestorian Christian from al-Ḥīrah, and as a youth acted as dispenser to the physician ibn-Māsawayh. Taking as a challenge a chiding remark by the master that the people of al-Ḥīrah had no business with medicine and that he had better go and change money in the bazaar,[3] the lad left the service of ibn-Māsawayh in tears, but intent upon the study of Greek. He was then sent by the three scholarly sons of Mūsa ibn-Shākir, who were carrying on independent research work, into various Greek-speaking lands in quest of manuscripts, and later entered the service of Jibrīl ibn-Bakhtīshū', physician-in-ordinary to al-Ma'mūn. Subsequently this caliph appointed Ḥunayn superintendent of his library-academy, and in this capacity Ḥunayn had charge of all the scientific translation work, in which he enjoyed the collaboration of his son Isḥāq[4] and his nephew Ḥubaysh ibn-al-Ḥasan,[5] whom he trained. Of the numerous works ascribed to him some should undoubtedly be credited to these two assistants and to other students and members of his school, such as 'Īsa ibn-Yaḥya[6] and Mūsa ibn-Khālid.[7] In many cases Ḥunayn evidently did the initial translation from Greek into Syriac and his colleagues took the second step and translated from Syriac into Arabic.[8] Aristotle's *Hermeneutica*, for instance, was first done from Greek into Syriac by the father

[1] Ibn-al-'Ibri, p. 227; ibn-abi-Uṣaybi'ah, vol. i, pp. 175 *seq.*; Qifṭi, p. 380.
[2] *Fihrist*, p. 295.
[3] Ibn-al-'Ibri, p 250; ibn-abi-Uṣaybi'ah, vol. i, p. 185.
[4] Ibn-Khallikān, vol. i, p. 116 = de Slane, vol. i, pp. 187-8.
[5] Nicknamed al-A'sam, because of a lame hand. Ibn-abi-Uṣaybi'ah, vol. i, pp. 187, 203; *Fihrist*, p. 297; ibn-al-'Ibri, p. 252.
[6] *Fihrist*, p. 297.
[7] He also translated from Persian into Arabic, *ibid.* p. 244, l. 28.
[8] *Fihrist*, p. 249

and then from Syriac into Arabic by the son Isḥāq, who was the better Arabist[1] and who became the greatest translator of Aristotle's works. Among other books in Arabic Ḥunayn is supposed to have prepared translations of Galen, Hippocrates and Dioscorides (fl. *ca.* A.D. 50) as well as of Plato's *Republic* (*Siyāsah*)[2] and Aristotle's *Categories* (*Maqūlāt*),[3] *Physics* (*Ṭabī'īyāt*) and *Magna Moralia* (*Khulqīyāt*).[4] Among these his chief work was the rendition into Syriac and Arabic of almost all of Galen's scientific output.[5] Seven books of Galen's anatomy, lost in the original Greek, have luckily been preserved in Arabic.[6] Ḥunayn's Arabic version of the Old Testament from the Greek Septuagint[7] did not survive.

Ḥunayn's ability as a translator may be attested by the report that when in the service of the sons of ibn-Shākir he and other translators received about 500 dinars (about £250) per month and that al-Ma'mūn paid him in gold the weight of the books he translated. But he reached the summit of his glory not only as a translator but as a practitioner when he was appointed by al-Mutawakkil (847–61) as his private physician. His patron, however, once committed him to jail for a year for refusing the offer of rich rewards to concoct a poison for an enemy. When brought again before the caliph and threatened with death his reply was, "I have skill only in what is beneficial, and have studied naught else".[8] Asked by the caliph, who then claimed that he was simply testing his physician's integrity, as to what prevented him from preparing the deadly poison, Ḥunayn replied:

> Two things: my religion and my profession. My religion decrees that we should do good even to our enemies, how much more to our friends. And my profession is instituted for the benefit of humanity and limited to their relief and cure. Besides, every physician is under oath never to give anyone a deadly medicine.[9]

Ḥunayn ibn-Isḥāq al-'Ibādi was judged by ibn-al-'Ibri and al-Qifṭi "a source of science and a mine of virtue", and by

[1] *Fihrist*, p. 298, copied by Qifṭi, p. 80.
[2] *Ibid.* p. 246, l. 5.
[3] *Ibid.* p. 248.
[4] Qifṭi, pp. 38, 42.
[5] Ibn-abi-Uṣaybi'ah, vol. i, pp. 188-9; Qifṭi, pp. 94-5.
[6] For a MS. of another work, *al-Ṣinā'ah al-Ṣaghīrah*, comprising ten of the sixteen canonical works of Galen and dated 572 (A.D. 1176), see Hitti, Faris and 'Abd-al-Malik, *Catalog of the Garrett Collection of Arabic Manuscripts* (Princeton, 1938), no. 1075.
[7] Qifṭi, p. 99.
[8] Ibn-abi-Uṣaybi'ah, vol. i, pp. 187-8; ibn-al-'Ibri, p. 251.
[9] Ibn-al-'Ibri, pp. 251-2.

Leclerc "la plus grande figure du IXe siècle", and even "une des plus belles intelligences et un des plus beaux caractères que l'on rencontre dans l'histoire".[1]

Thābit ibn-Qurrah

Just as Ḥunayn stood at the head of the Nestorian group of translators, so did Thābit ibn-Qurrah[2] (*ca.* 836–901) lead another group, recruited from among the heathen Ṣābians[3] of Ḥarrān (ancient Carrhae). These Ṣābians were star-worshippers and as such had interested themselves in astronomy and mathematics from time immemorial. During the reign of al-Mutawakkil their native town became the seat of a school of philosophy and medicine which had been previously transferred from Alexandria to Antioch. In this milieu Thābit and his disciples flourished. They are credited with having translated the bulk of the Greek mathematical and astronomical works, including those of Archimedes († 212 B.C.) and of Apollonius of Perga (b. *ca.* 262 B.C.).[4] They also improved on earlier translations. The translation of Euclid by Ḥunayn, for example, was revised by Thābit.[5] Thābit found a patron in the Caliph al-Mu'taḍid (892–902), whose personal friend and table companion he soon became.[6]

In his great work Thābit was succeeded by his son Sinān († 943), his two grandsons Thābit († 973)[7] and Ibrāhīm († 946)[8] and one great-grandson, abu-al-Faraj,[9] all of whom distinguished themselves as translators and scientists. But the greatest Ṣābian name after Thābit's was that of al-Battāni († 929, the Albategnius or Albatenius of Latin authors), whose first name, abu-'Abdullāh Muḥammad (ibn-Jābir ibn-Sinān), indicates his conversion to Islam. Al-Battāni's fame, however, rests on his original work as an astronomer, as he was not a translator.

The Ḥarrānian school of mathematical and astronomical translators had as its forerunner al-Ḥajjāj ibn-Yūsuf ibn-Maṭar (fl. between 786 and 833), generally credited with making the first translation of Euclid's *Elements* and one of the first of Ptolemy's *Almagest*. Of the former work he evidently prepared two versions, one for al-Rashīd and the other for al-Ma'mūn,[10]

[1] L. Leclerc, *Histoire de la médecine arabe* (Paris, 1876), vol. i, p. 139.
[2] His *al-Dhakhīrah fi 'Ilm al-Ṭibb* was edited by G. Sobhy (Cairo, 1928).
[3] In reality pseudo-Ṣābians. See below, p. 358.
[4] *Fihrist*, p. 267.
[5] Ibn-Khallikān, vol. i, pp. 177, 298.
[6] Ibn-abi-Uṣaybi'ah, vol. i, p. 216.
[7] *Ibid.* pp. 224-6.
[8] *Ibid.* p. 226; Qifṭi, pp. 57-9; *Fihrist*, p. 272.
[9] Qifṭi, p. 428.
[10] *Fihrist*, p. 265.

before Ḥunayn prepared his. Al-Ḥajjāj's version of the notable astronomical work *Almagest* was made in 827–8 from an earlier Syriac version. The first attempt at the *Almagest* had been made as early as the days of Yaḥya ibn-Khālid ibn-Barmak,[1] al-Rashīd's vizir, but the result was not satisfactory. A later adaptation of this work was undertaken by abu-al-Wafā' Muḥammad al-Būzjāni al-Ḥāsib[2] (940–97 or 998), one of the greatest Moslem astronomers and mathematicians. Another late translator of mathematical and philosophical works was Qusṭa ibn-Lūqa († *ca.* 922), a Christian of Baʿlabakk, whose list of original works in the *Fihrist*[3] numbers thirty-four.

The latter part of the tenth century saw the rise of Jacobite, or Monophysite, translators represented by Yaḥya ibn-ʿAdi, who was born in Takrīt in 893 and died in Baghdād in 974, and abu-ʿAli ʿĪsa ibn-Zurʿah of Baghdād († 1008).[4] Yaḥya, who became the archbishop of his church, declared once to the author of the *Fihrist*[5] that he copied in a day and a night an average of a hundred leaves. The Jacobite authors busied themselves with the revision of existing editions of Aristotelian works or the preparation of fresh translations thereof. They were, moreover, the chief influence in introducing Neo-Platonic speculations and mysticism into the Arabic world.

Before the age of translation was brought to an end practically all the extant works of Aristotle, many of which were of course spurious, had become accessible to the Arabic reader. Ibn-abi-Uṣaybiʿah,[6] and after him al-Qifṭi,[7] cite no less than a hundred works attributed to "the philosopher of the Greeks". All this took place while Europe was almost totally ignorant of Greek thought and science. For while al-Rashīd and al-Ma'mūn were delving into Greek and Persian philosophy their contemporaries in the West, Charlemagne and his lords, were reportedly dabbling in the art of writing their names. Aristotle's logical *Organon*, which in Arabic included Aristotle's *Rhetoric* and *Poetics* as well as Porphyry's *Isagoge*, soon took its place side by side with Arabic grammar as the basis of humanistic studies in Islam. This position it has maintained to the present day.

[1] *Fihrist*, pp. 267-8. Cf. above, p. 311.
[2] Būzjān in Qūhistān was his birthplace; *ḥāsib* means "mathematician".
[3] P. 295. Cf. Qifṭi, pp. 262-3.
[4] *Fihrist*, p. 264; ibn-abi-Uṣaybiʿah, vol. i, pp. 235-6; Qifṭi, pp. 245-6.
[5] P. 264. [6] Vol. i, pp. 57 *seq.* [7] Pp. 34 *seq.*

Moslems accepted the idea of Neo-Platonic commentators that the teachings of Aristotle and Plato (Aflāṭūn) were substantially the same. Especially in Sufism, Moslem mysticism, did the influence of Neo-Platonism manifest itself. Through Avicenna (ibn-Sīna) and Averroës (ibn-Rushd), as we shall later see, Platonism and Aristotelianism found their way into Latin and exercised a determining influence upon medieval European scholasticism.

This long and fruitful age of translation under the early 'Abbāsids was followed by one of original contribution which we shall discuss in a later chapter. By the tenth century Arabic, which in pre-Islamic days was only a language of poetry and after Muḥammad mainly a language of revelation and religion, had become metamorphosed in a remarkable and unprecedented way into a pliant medium for expressing scientific thought and conveying philosophic ideas of the highest order. In the meantime it had established itself as the language of diplomacy and polite intercourse from Central Asia, through the whole length of Northern Africa, to Spain. Ever since that time the peoples of al-'Irāq, Syria and Palestine as well as of Egypt, Tunisia, Algeria and Morocco have expressed their best thought in the tongue of the Arabians.

British Museum

From H. W. C. Davis, "Mediæval England" (Clarendon Press)

ANGLO-SAXON GOLD COIN IMITATING AN ARAB DINAR OF THE YEAR 774

It bears on the obverse the *shahādah* and on the reverse OFFA REX inscribed upside down

CHAPTER XXV

THE 'ABBĀSID STATE

The 'Abbāsid caliph

AT the head of the state stood the caliph, who was, in theory at least, the fountainhead of all power. He could and did delegate the exercise of his civil authority to a vizir (*wazīr*), of his judicial power to a judge (*qāḍi*), of his military function to a general (*amīr*), but the caliph himself ever remained the final arbiter of all governmental affairs. In their imperial conduct and function the early caliphs of Baghdād followed the older Persian pattern. Taking advantage of the popular reaction against the ungodliness of the later Umayyads, the 'Abbāsids made their début with emphasis on the religious character and dignity of their office as an imāmate, an emphasis which in later years increased in inverse proportion to their actual power. With the eighth caliph, al-Mu'taṣim bi-Allāh (833–42), and continuing till the end of the dynasty, they began to assume honorific titles compounded with *Allāh*. In the period of decline their subjects started to shower on them such extravagant titles as *khalīfat Allāh* (God's caliph) and later *ẓill Allāh 'ala al-arḍ* (God's shadow on earth). These were evidently first bestowed on al-Mutawakkil (847–61),[1] and persisted until the last days of the Ottoman caliphate.

The ill-defined hereditary principle of succession instituted by the Umayyad caliphs was followed throughout the 'Abbāsid régime with the same evil results. The reigning caliph would designate as his successor that one of his sons whom he favoured or considered competent, or any of his kinsmen whom he regarded as best qualified. Al-Saffāḥ nominated his brother al-Manṣūr, who was succeeded by his son al-Mahdi.[2] Al-Mahdi was succeeded by his eldest son, al-Hādi, who was followed by his brother Hārūn al-Rashīd.[3] Hārūn designated his oldest son, al-Amīn, as his first successor, and his younger but more talented

[1] Mas'ūdi, vol. vii, p. 278.

[2] See Ya'qūbi, vol. ii, pp. 437 *seq.*, 472 *seq.*; *Fakhri*, p. 236.

[3] *Fakhri*, pp. 261-2; Ṭabari, vol. iii, p. 523.

son, al-Ma'mūn, as his second successor. He divided the empire between the two, reserving for al-Ma'mūn the government of Khurāsān with Marw (Marv) for his capital.[1] After a bitter struggle which ended in the assassination of al-Amīn (September 813), al-Ma'mūn usurped the caliphate. Four years later, when he donned the green of the Shī'ah in preference to the black of the 'Abbāsids and designated an 'Alid, 'Ali al-Riḍa, as heir apparent, the enraged Baghdādis elected (July 817) al-Ma'mūn's uncle Ibrāhīm ibn-al-Mahdi as caliph. Not until 819, six years after the death of his predecessor, did al-Ma'mūn succeed in effecting an entry into the capital of the empire. Shortly before his death al-Ma'mūn, ignoring his son al-'Abbās, designated his brother al-Mu'taṣim as his successor, thus almost precipitating a revolt on the part of the army, with whom the son was a special favourite. Al-Mu'taṣim was followed by his son al-Wāthiq († 847), with whom the period of 'Abbāsid glory ended. Of the first twenty-four caliphs, whose reign covered almost two centuries and a half (750–991), only six were immediately succeeded by a son.

Attached to the person of the caliph was the chamberlain (*ḥājib*), whose duty consisted in introducing accredited envoys and dignitaries into the caliphal presence and whose influence naturally became great. There was also the executioner, an outstanding figure in the Baghdād court. Vaulted underground chambers used for torture appear for the first time in Arab history. The court astrologer, like the executioner an importation from Persia, became an adjunct of the 'Abbāsid throne.

Vizir

Next to the caliph stood the vizir (*wazīr*), whose office was influenced by the Persian tradition.[2] The vizir acted as the caliph's *alter ego* and grew in power as his chief indulged increasingly in the pleasures of the harem. In the diploma appointing his vizir the Caliph al-Nāṣir (1180–1225) has given a perfect expression to the theory of "divine right" of kingship working by proxy:

> Muḥammad ibn-Barz al-Qummi is our representative throughout the land and amongst our subjects. Therefore he who obeys him obeys us; and he who obeys us obeys God, and God shall cause him who obeys Him to enter Paradise. As for one who, on the other hand,

[1] Ya'qūbi, vol. ii, pp. 500 *seq.*; *Fakhri*, p. 292; Mas'ūdi, *Tanbīh*, p. 345.

[2] Cf. ibn-al-'Abbās, *Āthār al-Uwal fi Tartīb al-Duwal* (Cairo, 1295), p. 62, S. D. Goitein in *Islamic Culture*, vol. xvi (1942), pp. 255-63, 380-92.

disobeys our vizir, he disobeys us; and he who disobeys us disobeys God, and God shall cause him who disobeys Him to enter hell-fire.[1]

As in the case of the Barmakids the vizir was often all-powerful, appointing and deposing governors and judges, theoretically, of course, with the consent of the caliph, and even transmitting his own office according to the hereditary principle. It was customary for the vizir to confiscate the property of the governor who fell from grace, as it was customary for the governor himself to appropriate the estates of inferior officials and private citizens and for the caliph in his turn to mete out the same penalty to the deposed vizir.[2] Indeed, the forfeiture of possessions was often accompanied by loss of life. Finally a special "bureau of confiscation"[3] was instituted as a regular governmental department. In the days of the Caliph al-Muʿtaḍid the vizir received a monthly salary of a thousand dinars. Al-Māwardi[4] and other legal theorists distinguish between two varieties of vizirate: a *tafwīḍ* (with full authority, unlimited) and a *tanfīdh* (with executive power only, limited). The unlimited vizir exercised all the powers of sovereignty with the exception of the appointment of his successor; the limited vizir took no initiative but confined his duties to the execution of the caliph's orders and the following of his instructions. After the time of al-Muqtadir (908–32) the vizir was supplanted by the *amīr al-umarā'*, commander of the commanders, an office which was subsequently held by the Buwayhids.

Bureau of taxes

The vizir, in reality grand vizir, presided over the council, whose membership included the various heads of the departments of state. Sometimes those heads were also designated vizirs, but their rank was always subordinate to that of the real vizir. Under the ʿAbbāsids the governmental machinery became much more complicated than heretofore, though greater order was brought into state affairs, especially in the system of taxation and the administration of justice. Since finances constituted the main concern of the government the bureau of taxes (*dīwān al-kharāj*), or department of finance (*bayt al-māl*), remained, as under the Umayyads, the most important unit; its chief, often

[1] *Fakhri*, p. 205.
[2] Ibn-al-Athīr, vol. vi, pp. 19-20.
[3] Cf. Hilāl al-Ṣābi', *Tuḥfat al-Umarā' fi Ta'rīkh al-Wuzarā'*, ed. H. F. Amedroz (Beirūt, 1904), p. 306.
[4] Pp. 33-47.

referred to as "master of taxes", continued to be an outstanding figure in the government of the caliph.

The sources of revenue for the state included zakāh, the only legal tax obligatory on every Moslem. Zakāh was imposed on arable lands, herds, gold and silver, commercial wares and other forms of property capable of augmentation through natural increase or by investment. Moslems, as we learned before, paid no poll tax. The official tax-gatherer looked after lands, herds and the like, but personal effects, including gold and silver, were left to the individual's private conscience. All money collected from believers was disbursed from the central treasury for the benefit of believers: the poor, the orphan, the stranger, volunteers for the holy war and slaves and captives to be ransomed. The other main sources of public income were tribute from foreign enemies, truce money, capitation tax from non-Moslem subjects (*jizyah*), land tax (*kharāj*)[1] and tithes levied upon merchandise owned by non-Moslems and imported into Moslem territory. Of these items the land tax was always the largest and constituted the main source of income from unbelievers. All this revenue was at this time referred to as *fay'* (cf. Koran 59 : 7) and applied by the caliph to the payment of the troops, the maintenance of mosques, roads and bridges and for the general good of the Moslem community.[2]

The varying reports of the state revenue that have come down to us from the 'Abbāsid period testify to great prosperity during the first century of the régime, which made it possible for the caliphs to live on the grand scale described above, and to a steady decline in revenue during each succeeding century. Three such reports have been preserved for us: the oldest, in ibn-Khaldūn, showing the income under al-Ma'mūn; the second, in Qudāmah, for the revenue a few years later, possibly under al-Mu'taṣim; and the third, in ibn-Khurdādhbih, indicating the proceeds in the first half of the third Moslem century. According to ibn-Khaldūn[3] the

[1] By this time the differentiation between *jizyah* and *kharāj* had been clearly made. See above, p. 171. In later times the *jizyah* corresponded to *al-badal al-'askari* (scutage), which the Ottomans exacted from their non-Moslem subjects for exemption from military service.

[2] Māwardi, pp. 366 *seq.*

[3] *Muqaddamah*, pp. 150-51. Cf. Huart, *Histoire des Arabes*, vol. i, p. 376; Alfred von Kremer, *Culturgeschichte des Orients unter den Chalifen*, vol. i (Vienna, 1875), pp. 356 *seq.* It is obvious that ibn-Khaldūn's list, like the other two, is neither clear nor accurate.

annual land tax paid by al-Sawād (lower ʿIrāq, ancient Babylonia) in cash, other than what was paid in kind, amounted in the days of al-Ma'mūn to 27,800,000 dirhams; by Khurāsān, 28,000,000; by Egypt, 23,040,000; by Syria-Palestine,[1] 14,724,000; and by all the provinces of the empire, 331,929,008 dirhams exclusive of taxes in kind. From Qudāmah's[2] balance-sheet it may be gathered that the income in both cash and kind from al-Sawād was equivalent to 130,200,000 dirhams;[3] from Khurāsān, 37,000,000; from Egypt, including Alexandria, 37,500,000; from Syria-Palestine, including Ḥimṣ, 15,860,000; and from the whole empire, 388,291,350 dirhams, which includes taxes in kind. Ibn-Khurdādhbih[4] lists a number of items from which we may calculate that the tax of al-Sawād in cash and kind was the equivalent of 78,319,340 dirhams;[5] of Khurāsān and dependencies, 44,846,000; of Syria-Palestine,[6] 29,850,000; and of the whole empire, 299,265,340.[7] As for the expenditures, we have no sufficient data in the scattered references to warrant definite conclusions. But we are told that when al-Manṣūr died the central treasury contained 600,000,000 dirhams and 14,000,000 dinars;[8] when al-Rashīd died it had over 900,000,000,[9] and at the death of al-Muktafi (908) the public treasures including jewellery, furniture and real estate amounted to 100,000,000 dinars.[10]

Other governmental bureaux

Besides the bureau of taxes the ʿAbbāsid government had an audit or accounts office (*dīwān al-zimām*) introduced by al-Mahdi; a board of correspondence or chancery office (*dīwān al-tawqīʿ*) which handled all official letters, political documents and imperial mandates and diplomas; a board for the inspection of grievances; a police department and a postal department.

The board for the inspection of grievances (*dīwān al-naẓar fi al-maẓālim*) was a kind of court of appeal or supreme court intended to set aright cases of miscarriage of justice in the

[1] Qinnasrīn, Damascus, the Jordan and Palestine, the taxes of which are given as 1,227,000 dinars.
[2] *Kharāj*, pp. 237-52.
[3] In cash alone 8,095,800 dirhams; Qudāmah, pp. 249, 239. As a matter of fact he gives different figures in different places and on his lists the totals do not tally with the itemized statements.
[4] *Passim*.
[5] In cash alone about 8,456,840 dirhams; ibn-Khurdādhbih, pp. 5 *seq*.
[6] Qinnasrīn and other frontier towns, Ḥimṣ, Damascus, the Jordan and Palestine.
[7] Zaydān, *Tamaddun*, vol. ii, p. 61. Cf. Huart, vol. i, p. 376.
[8] Masʿūdi, vol. vi, p. 233.
[9] Ṭabari, vol. iii, p. 764.
[10] Thaʿālibi, *Laṭā'if*, p. 72.

administrative and political departments. Its origin goes back to the Umayyad days, for al-Māwardi[1] tells us that 'Abd-al-Malik was the first caliph to devote a special day for the direct hearing by himself of appeals and complaints made by his subjects. 'Umar II zealously followed the precedent.[2] This practice was evidently introduced by al-Mahdi into the 'Abbāsid régime. His successors al-Hādi, Hārūn, al-Ma'mūn and those who followed received such complaints in public audience; al-Muhtadi (869–70) was the last to keep up the custom. The Norman king Roger II (1130–54) introduced this institution into Sicily, where it struck root in European soil.[3]

The police department (*dīwān al-shurṭah*) was headed by a high official designated *ṣāḥib al-shurṭah*, who acted as chief of police and the royal bodyguard and in later times occasionally held the rank of vizir. Each large city had its own special police who also held military rank and were as a rule well paid. The chief of municipal police was called *muḥtasib*, for he acted as overseer of markets and morals. It was his duty to see that proper weights and measures were used in trade, that legitimate debts were paid (though he had no judicial power), that approved morals were maintained and that acts forbidden by law, such as gambling, usury and public sale of wine, were not committed. Al-Māwardi[4] enumerates, among other interesting duties of this prefect of police, the maintenance of the recognized standards of public morality between the two sexes and the chastisement of those who dyed their grey beards black with a view to gaining the favour of the ladies.

A significant feature of the 'Abbāsid government was the postal department,[5] of which the chief was called *ṣāḥib al-barīd*. Among the Umayyads Mu'āwiyah, as we have already learned, was the first to interest himself in the postal service, 'Abd-al-Malik extended it throughout the empire and al-Walīd made use of it for his building operations. Historians credit Hārūn with

[1] P. 131. Cf. ibn-al-Athīr, vol. i, p. 46.

[2] Māwardi, p. 131. Cf. Ya'qūbi, vol. ii, p. 367. Consult al-Bayhaqi, *al-Maḥāsin w-al-Masāwi'*, ed. F. Schwally (Giessen, 1902), pp. 525 *seq*.

[3] M. Amari, *Storia dei Musulmani di Sicilia*, ed. Nallino, vol. iii (Catania, 1937–9), p. 452; von Kremer, *Culturgeschichte*, vol. i, p. 420.

[4] Pp. 417-18, 431.

[5] *Dīwān al-barīd*, bureau of post. Ar. *barīd* is probably a Semitic word, not related to Latin *veredus*, Pers. *birdan*, a swift horse, Ar. *birdhawn*, horse of burden. Cf. Esth. 8 : 10; Iṣfahāni, *Ta'rīkh*, p. 39.

having organized the service on a new basis through his Barmakid counsellor Yaḥya. Though primarily designed to serve the interests of the state, the postal institution did in a limited way handle private correspondence.[1] Each provincial capital was provided with a post office. Routes connected the imperial capital with the leading centres of the empire[2] and systems of relays covered these routes. In all there must have been hundreds of such relay routes. In Persia the relays consisted of mules and horses; in Syria and Arabia camels were used.[3] The *barīd* was also employed for the conveyance of newly appointed governors to their respective provinces and for the transportation of troops with their baggage.[4] The public could make use of it on the payment of a substantial sum.

Pigeons were trained and used as letter-carriers. The first recorded instance relates to the news of the capture of the rebel Bābik (Bābak), chief of the Khurrami[5] sect, carried to al-Muʿtaṣim by this method in 837.[6]

The postal headquarters in Baghdād had itineraries of the whole empire indicating the various stations and the intervening distances. These itineraries assisted travellers, merchants and pilgrims and laid the basis of later geographical research. Early Arab students of geography made use of such postal directories in the composition of their works. One of the leaders among them, ibn-Khurdādhbih († *ca.* 912), whose *al-Masālik w-al-Mamālik*, based on material in the state archives, proved an important source for historical topography, was himself *ṣāḥib al-barīd* for the Caliph al-Muʿtamid in al-Jibāl (ancient Media). This elaborate road system which radiated from the imperial capital was an inheritance from the earlier Persian empire. In it the most famous of the trunk roads was the Khurāsān highway, which stretched north-east through Hamadhān, al-Rayy, Naysābūr, Ṭūs, Marw, Bukhāra, Samarqand, and connected Baghdād with the frontier towns of the Jaxartes and the borders of China. From the principal cities along this highway cross-roads branched off north and south. To the present day the Persian post roads

[1] Masʿūdi, vol. vi, p. 93, ll. 5-6.
[2] Ibn-Khurdādhbih, *passim*.
[3] Cf. ibn-al-Athīr, vol. vi, p. 49, ll. 11-12.
[4] *Ibid.* vol. iv, pp. 373-4.
[5] So called from a district in Persia where the sect evidently arose as a result of the execution of the famous abu-Muslim al-Khurāsāni. Some of them denied that abu-Muslim was dead and foretold his return to spread justice in the world. Masʿūdi, vol. vi, p. 186; Baghdādi, ed. Hitti, pp. 162 *seq.*; *Fihrist*, p. 342.
[6] Masʿūdi, vol. vii, pp. 126-7.

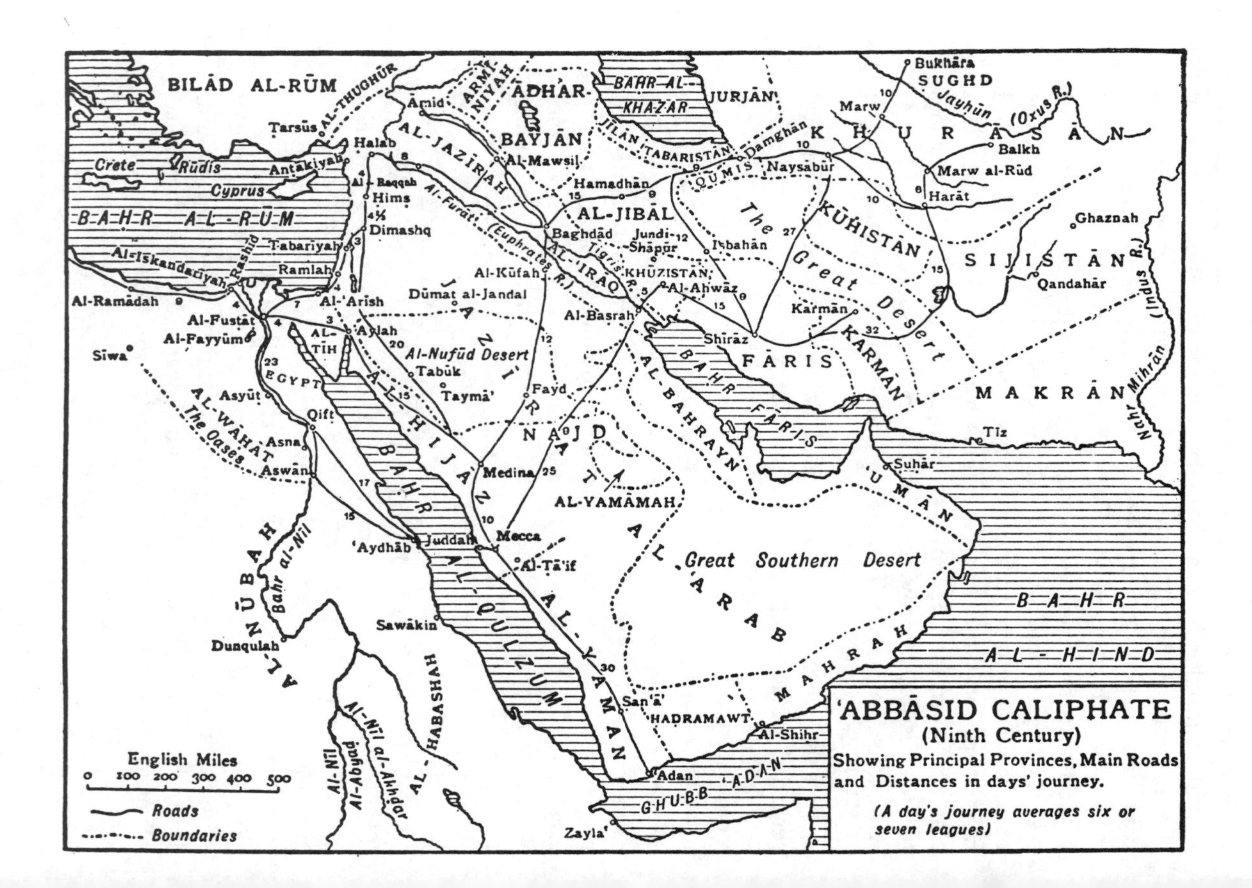
BILĀD AL-RŪM
AL-THUGHŪR
ARMINIYAH
ĀDHARBAYJĀN
BAḤR AL-KHAZAR
JURJĀN
JĪLĀN
ṬABARISTĀN
QŪMIS
KHURĀSĀN
SUGHD
Jayḥūn (Oxus R.)
Bukhāra
Marw
Balkh
Marw al-Rūd
Harāt
Naysabūr
Dāmghān
Tarsūs
Ḥalab
Āmid
AL-JAZĪRAH
Al-Mawṣil
Hamadhān
AL-JIBĀL
Baghdād
Jundi-Shāpūr
Iṣbahān
The Great Desert
KŪHISTĀN
SIJISTĀN
Ghaznah
Qandahār
Crete
Rūdis
Cyprus
Antākiyah
Al-Bāqqah
Ḥimṣ
Dimashq
BAḤR AL-RŪM
Ṭabarīyah
Ramlah
Rashīd
Al-Iskandarīyah
Al-Ramādah
Al-'Arīsh
Al-Furāt (Euphrates R.)
AL-'IRĀQ
Tigris R.
KHŪZISTĀN
Al-Ahwāz
Al-Kūfah
Dūmat al-Jandal
Al-Baṣrah
Karmān
KARMĀN
Shīrāz
FĀRIS
Al-Fusṭāṭ
Al-Fayyūm
Aylah
AL-TĪH
Al-Nufūd Desert
Tabūk
Taymā'
Fayd
JAZĪRAT
NAJD
BAḤR FĀRIS
AL-BAḤRAYN
MAKRĀN
Nahr Mihrān (Indus R.)
Tīz
Ṣuḥār
'UMĀN
Sīwa
EGYPT
Asyūṭ
Qifṭ
Asna
Aswān
AL-WĀḤĀT The Oases
AL-ḤIJĀZ
BAḤR AL-QULZUM
Medina
Mecca
Al-Ṭā'if
AL-YAMĀMAH
AL-'ARAB
Great Southern Desert
Juddah
'Aydhāb
AL-NŪBAH
Baḥr al-Nīl
Dunqulah
Sawākin
AL-ḤABASHAH
Al-Nīl al-Akhḍar
Al-Nīl al-Abyaḍ
AL-YAMAN
Ṣan'ā'
ḤAḌRAMAWT
Al-Shiḥr
MAHRAH
'Adan
GHUBB 'ADAN
Zayla'
BAḤR AL-HIND
English Miles
0 100 200 300 400 500
Roads
Boundaries
'ABBĀSID CALIPHATE
(Ninth Century)
Showing Principal Provinces, Main Roads and Distances in days' journey.
(A day's journey averages six or seven leagues)

centring in Ṭihrān (Teheran), near ancient al-Rayy, follow the same old tracks. Another main road led from Baghdād down the Tigris through Wāsiṭ and al-Baṣrah to al-Ahwāz in Khūzistān and thence to Shīrāz in Fāris. Likewise this road sent off east and west branches which connected its towns with other centres of population and ultimately with the Khurāsān trunk. These roads were frequented by pilgrims, who from Baghdād could take the pilgrim route to Makkah through al-Kūfah or al-Baṣrah. For the benefit of pilgrims and travellers caravanserais, hospices and cisterns dotted the main roads. Such khāns along the Khurāsān road were built as early as the days of 'Umar II.[1] A third highway linked Baghdād with al-Mawṣil, Āmid (Diyār Bakr) and the frontier fortresses. On the north-west Baghdād was connected with Damascus and other Syrian towns through al-Anbār and al-Raqqah.

The postmaster-general had another important function besides looking after the imperial mail and supervising the various postal establishments; he was the chief of an espionage system to which the whole postal service was subordinated. As such his full title was *ṣāḥib al-barīd w-al-akhbār*,[2] controller of the post and intelligence service. In this capacity he acted as an inspector-general and direct confidential agent of the central government. The provincial postmaster reported to him or to the caliph directly on the conduct and activities of the government officials in his province, not excluding the governor himself. Such a report, submitted to al-Mutawakkil against a governor of Baghdād who brought back with him from a pilgrimage to Makkah a beautiful slave girl "with whom he amuses himself from noon till night to the neglect of the affairs of the state", has come down to us in a late source.[3] Al-Manṣūr employed in his espionage system merchants, pedlars and travellers who acted as detectives; al-Rashīd and other caliphs did the same.[4] Al-Ma'mūn is said to have had in his intelligence service in Baghdād some 1700 aged women. Especially was "the land of the Romans" covered with 'Abbāsid spies of both sexes disguised as traders, travellers and physicians.

[1] Ibn-al-Athīr, vol. v, p. 44; Nawawi, *Tahdhīb*, p. 468, l. 16.

[2] Qudāmah, p. 184.

[3] Atlīdi, *I'lām al-Nās* (Cairo, 1297), p. 161.

[4] Cf. *Aghāni*, vol. xv, p. 36, l. 14; Miskawayh, ed. de Goeje and de Jong, pp. 234, 466, 498, 512, 514, 567.

Judicial administration

The dispensing of justice, always considered in Moslem communities a religious duty, was entrusted by the 'Abbāsid caliph or his vizir to a member of the *faqīh* (theologian) class, who thus became a *qāḍi*,[1] or if in Baghdād a *qāḍi al-quḍāh* (chief judge). The first to receive the title of *qāḍi al-quḍāh* was the famous abu-Yūsuf († *ca.* 798), who served under al-Mahdi and his two sons al-Hādi and Hārūn.[2] The judge, according to the theory of Moslem law, had to be male, adult, in full possession of his mental faculties, a free citizen, Moslem in faith, irreproachable in character, sound of sight and hearing and well versed in the prescriptions of law,[3] all of which was of course canon law. Non-Moslems, as noted before, were in matters of civil right under the jurisdiction of their own ecclesiastical heads or magistrates. Al-Māwardi [4] distinguishes between two types of judgeship: one in which the authority is general and absolute (*'āmmah muṭlaqah*) and the other in which the authority is special and limited (*khāṣṣah*). The chief duties of the qāḍi of the first class consisted in deciding cases, acting as guardian for orphans, lunatics and minors, administering pious foundations, imposing punishments on violators of the religious law, appointing judicial deputies (sing. *nā'ib*) in the various provinces and presiding under certain conditions at the Friday congregational prayers. In the early history of the institution the provincial judges held their appointment from the governors, but in the fourth Moslem century those judges were usually deputies of the chief qāḍi in Baghdād. Under al-Ma'mūn the pay of the judge of Egypt is said by a late authority [5] to have reached 4000 dirhams a month. The judge of the second class, one with special and limited authority, had his power restricted in accordance with the diploma of appointment from the caliph, vizir or governor.[6]

Military organization

The Arab caliphate never maintained a large standing army in the strict sense of the term, well organized, under strict discipline and subject to regular instruction and drill. The caliphal bodyguard (*ḥaras*) were almost the only regular troops and formed the nucleus around which clustered bands under

[1] Transliterated in at least thirteen different ways, six of which occur in official British documents: *qadi, qazi, kazi, cadi, al-kali, kathi.*

[2] Ibn-Khallikān, vol. iii, p. 334 = de Slane, vol. iv, p. 273.

[3] Māwardi, pp. 107-11.

[4] Pp. 117-25.

[5] Suyūṭi, *Ḥusn*, vol. ii, p. 100, l. 4.

[6] Consult Richard Gottheil in *Revue des études ethnographiques* (1908), pp. 385-93.

their own chiefs, besides mercenaries and adventurers, and general levies of which the units were tribes or districts. The regulars (*jund*) who were permanently on active service were referred to as *murtaziqah* (regularly paid), for they were in the pay of the government. Others were designated *mutaṭawwiʿah*[1] (volunteers) and received rations only while on duty. The volunteer ranks were recruited from among the Bedouins as well as from the peasants and townspeople. Members of the bodyguard received higher pay and were equipped with better armour and uniforms. In the reign of the first 'Abbāsid caliph the average pay of the foot soldier was, besides the usual rations and allowances, about 960 dirhams a year,[2] the horseman receiving double that amount. Under al-Ma'mūn, when the empire reached its height, the 'Irāq army is said to have numbered 125,000, of whom the infantry received only 240 dirhams a year[3] and the cavalry twice as much. And when it is remembered that al-Manṣūr paid his master builder at the founding of Baghdād the equivalent of about a dirham a day and the ordinary labourer about a third of a dirham,[4] it becomes clear how comparatively well paid the military career was.

The regulars under the early 'Abbāsids were composed of infantry (*ḥarbīyah*)[5] armed with spears, swords and shields, of archers (*rāmiyah*) and of cavalry (*fursān*) wearing helmets and breast-plates and equipped with long lances and battle-axes. Al-Mutawakkil introduced the practice of wearing the sword in the Persian fashion round the waist in preference to the old Arabian way of carrying it over the shoulder.[6] Each corps of archers had attached to it a body of naphtha-throwers (*naffāṭūn*) who wore fireproof suits and hurled incendiary material at the enemy.[7] Engineers in charge of the siege machinery, including catapults, mangonels and battering-rams, accompanied the army. One such engineer, ibn-Ṣābir al-Manjanīqi, who flourished

[1] Or *muṭṭawwiʿah*, Ṭabari, vol. iii, pp. 1008 *seq.*; ibn-Khaldūn, vol. iii, p. 260.

[2] Ṭabari, vol. iii, p. 41, ll. 17-18, copied by ibn-al-Athīr, vol. v, p. 322, ll. 14-15.

[3] When al-Ma'mūn was fighting his brother he had to restore the standard 960 dirhams, which sum was likewise paid by his brother. Ṭabari, vol. iii, p. 830, ll. 7-8, p. 867, l. 14.

[4] Khaṭīb, vol. i, p. 70; Ṭabari, vol. iii, p. 326.

[5] Mentioned by Ṭabari, vol. iii, pp. 998 *seq.*; ibn-Khaldūn, vol. iii, p. 238, l 17 p. 245, ll. 23, 26.

[6] Ibn-Khaldūn, vol. iii, p. 275.

[7] *Aghāni*, vol. xvii, p. 45; ibn-Khaldūn, vol. iii, p. 260, l. 20.

later under al-Nāṣir (1180–1225), left an unfinished book which treats of the art of warfare in all its details.[1] Field hospitals and ambulances in the shape of litters carried by camels accompanied the army when in the field. As usual, Hārūn is the caliph credited with introducing these features and pressing science into the service of warfare.

During the 'Abbāsid régime, which, as we have seen before, owed its rise to Persian rather than Arab arms, the Arabian element lost its military, as it did its political, predominance. Under the first caliphs the bodyguard, the strong arm of the military machine, was largely composed of Khurāsāni troops. The Arab soldiery formed two divisions: one of North Arabians, Muḍarite, and the other of South Arabians, Yamanite. New converts to Islam attached themselves to some Arabian tribe as clients and thus formed a part of the military organization of that tribe. Al-Mu'taṣim added a new division made up of Turks, originally his slaves, from Farghānah and other regions of Central Asia.[2] This new imperial bodyguard soon became the terror of the whole capital, and in 836 the caliph had to build a new town, Sāmarra, to which he transferred his seat of government. After the death of al-Muntaṣir (861–2) these Turks began to play the part of a prætorian guard and exercise a determining influence on affairs of the state.

In Roman-Byzantine fashion every ten men of the army under al-Ma'mūn, al-Musta'īn and other 'Abbāsid caliphs were commanded by an *'arīf* (corresponding to the decurion), every fifty by a *khalīfah*, and every hundred by a *qā'id* (corresponding to the centurion).[3] At the head of a corps of 10,000, comprising ten battalions, stood the *amīr* (general). A body of a hundred men formed a company or squadron and several such companies constituted a cohort (*kurdūs*). Von Kremer[4] has reconstructed for us a realistic picture of an Arab army of those days on the march.

Throughout its first century the 'Abbāsid caliphate depended for its very existence on a strong and contented soldiery, which was used not only for suppressing revolts in Syria, Persia and

[1] Ibn-Khallikān, vol. iii, p. 397.
[2] Mas'ūdi, vol. vii, p. 118.
[3] Ibn-Khaldūn, vol. iii, p. 299, l. 7. Cf. Mas'ūdi, vol. vi, p. 452; Ṭabari, vol. iii, p. 1799.
[4] *Culturgeschichte*, vol. i, pp. 227-9 = S. Khuda Bukhsh, *The Orient under the Caliphs* (Calcutta 1920), pp. 333-5.

Central Asia but for waging aggressive war against the Byzantines. "Two things", in the opinion of a modern scholar,[1] "rendered the Saracens of the tenth century dangerous foes,—their numbers and their extraordinary powers of locomotion." But that was not all. In the treatise on military tactics attributed to the Emperor Leo VI the Wise[2] (886–912) we are told: "Of all the [barbarous] nations they [the Saracens] are the best advised and most prudent in their military operations". The following passage from the Emperor Constantine Porphyrogenitus[3] (913–59) describes the impression left by the Arabs on their Byzantine foes: "They are powerful and warlike, so that if only a thousand of them occupy a camp it is impossible to dislodge them. They do not ride horses but camels." From statements in these and other Byzantine sources such as the work on military tactics composed by the Emperor Nicephorus Phocas (963–9) it is evident that cold and rainy weather was distasteful to the Arab warriors, that once their line was broken in action they usually lacked the necessary discipline to restore it and that their foot was in general a mere rabble of plunderers ineffective as a fighting machine. Yet it is evident that the Byzantines looked upon the Arabs, whom they called infidels and barbarous, as their most formidable enemy. In the course of the tenth century, however, this enemy grew less and less dangerous until by its end the Byzantines were habitually taking the offensive and threatening even Damascus and Baghdād.

The decline of the 'Abbāsid military power began with the introduction by al-Mutawakkil of the foreign units, which contributed to the destruction of the necessary conditions for the upkeep of the morale and *esprit de corps*. Later on al-Muqtadir (908–32) initiated the policy of farming out provinces to governors or military commanders who were to pay their troops from local state funds and not from the depleted imperial treasury. Under the Buwayhid régime soldiers received grants in the form of lands instead of pay in cash. This sowed the seeds of a feudal military system which was further developed under the Saljūqs. It then became customary for governors and generals to receive as grants towns or districts over which they

[1] Oman, *Art of War*, 2nd ed., vol. i, p. 209.
[2] "Tactica", Constitutio xviii, § 123, in Migne, *Patrologia Græca*, vol. cvii.
[3] "De administrando imperio", caput xv, in Migne, *Patrologia Græca*, vol. cxiii.

ruled with absolute power, paying the Saljūq sultan a yearly tribute and, in time of war, marching under his banner with a fixed number of troops equipped and supported by themselves.

The governor

The Umayyad partition of the empire into provinces under governors (sing. *amīr* or *'āmil*), a division based on earlier Byzantine and Persian models, was not radically changed under the 'Abbāsids. The 'Abbāsid list of provinces varied from time to time and the political classification may not always have tallied with the geographical as preserved in al-Iṣṭakhri, ibn-Ḥawqal, ibn-al-Faqīh and similar works; but the following seem to have been the chief provinces under the early caliphs of Baghdād: (1) Africa west of the Libyan Desert together with Sicily; (2) Egypt; (3) Syria and Palestine, which were sometimes separated; (4) al-Ḥijāz and al-Yamāmah (Central Arabia); (5) al-Yaman or Southern Arabia;[1] (6) al-Baḥrayn and 'Umān, with al-Baṣrah in al-'Irāq for its capital; (7) al-Sawād, or al-'Irāq (Lower Mesopotamia), whose leading cities after Baghdād were al-Kūfah and Wāsiṭ; (8) al-Jazīrah (i.e. the island, rather the peninsula, ancient Assyria), whose capital was al-Mawṣil (Mosul); (9) Ādharbayjān, of which Ardabīl, Tibrīz and Marāghah were the leading towns; (10) al-Jibāl (the mountains, ancient Media), later called al-'Irāq al-'Ajami (the Persian 'Irāq),[2] of which the principal cities were Hamadhān (ancient Ecbatana), al-Rayy and Iṣbahān (Iṣfahān, Ispahān); (11) Khūzistān, with al-Ahwāz and Tustar[3] as chief towns; (12) Fāris, of which Shīrāz was the capital; (13) Karmān, whose present capital bears the same name; (14) Mukrān, which included modern Baluchistan and extended to the highlands overlooking the Indus valley; (15) Sijistān or Sīstān, whose capital was Zaranj; (16-20) Qūhistān, Qūmis, Ṭabaristān, Jurjān and Armenia; (21) Khurāsān, which included what has now become the north-western part of Afghanistan and whose leading cities were Naysābūr, Marw, Harāt (Herat) and Balkh; (22) Khwārizm, whose early capital was Kāth; (23) al-Ṣughd (ancient Sogdiana) between the Oxus and Jaxartes, having two famous cities, Bukhāra and Samarqand; (24, etc.) Farghānah, al-Shāsh

[1] These five provinces were often referred to as *aqālīm al-maghrib*, the occidental provinces, in contradistinction to the rest referred to as *aqālīm al-mashriq*, the oriental provinces.

[2] In contrast to al-'Irāq al-'Arabi (the Arabian 'Irāq), i.e. Lower Mesopotamia.

[3] Called Shustar or Shushtar by the Persians.

(modern Tāshkand) and other Turkish lands.[1] The Ottoman Turkish vilayets in Western Asia, it may be noticed, correspond geographically to the old Arab provinces.

In spite of all efforts on the part of the imperial capital, decentralization was the unavoidable consequence of such a far-flung domain with difficult means of intercommunication. In all local affairs the governor's authority tended to become supreme and his office hereditary. In theory he held his position during the pleasure of the vizir, who recommended his appointment to the caliph, and went out of office when that vizir was removed. As in the case of the vizirate al-Māwardi[2] distinguishes between two varieties of governorship: one, *imārah ʿāmmah* (general amīrate), in which the incumbent held supreme direction of military affairs, right of nomination and control of the judiciary, levying of taxes, maintenance of public security, safeguarding the state religion against innovation, administration of police and presiding at public prayers on Friday; and the other of the more restricted type (*khāṣṣah*, special), in which the governor had no jurisdiction over judges and taxes. But all this classification was largely theoretical, as the authority of the provincial governor increased in direct proportion to the personal ability of the governor, the weakness of the caliph and the distance from the federal capital. The local income from each province was in almost every case applied to meet the governmental expenses of that province. If the expenses were less than the local income the governor remitted the balance to the caliphal treasury. The administration of justice was in the hands of a provincial qāḍi assisted by a number of deputies stationed in the various sub-divisions of the provinces.

[1] Compare list of provinces as given here with lists in Le Strange, *Eastern Caliphate*, pp. 1-9; Zaydān, *Tamaddun*, vol. ii, pp. 37-44; von Kremer, *Culturgeschichte*, vol. i, p. 184.

[2] Pp. 47-54.

CHAPTER XXVI

'ABBĀSID SOCIETY

THE primitive tribal system, the basic pattern of Arabian social organization, entirely broke down under the 'Abbāsids, who owed their throne to foreign elements. Even the caliphs in such matters as the choice of wives and mothers for their children set no value on Arabian blood. Among the 'Abbāsids only three caliphs were sons of free mothers: abu-al-'Abbās, al-Mahdi and al-Amīn,[1] of whom the last enjoyed the unique distinction of having both parents from the Prophet's family.[2] Among the Umayyads the twelfth caliph, Yazīd III, was the first whose mother was a non-Arab. But she was at least supposedly a descendant of the last Persian emperor, Yazdagird, and was captured by Qutaybah in Sogdiana and presented by al-Ḥajjāj to the Caliph al-Walīd. Among the 'Abbāsids al-Manṣūr's mother was a Berber slave; al-Ma'mūn's a Persian slave; al-Wāthiq's and al-Muhtadi's were Greek; al-Muntaṣir's was a Greco-Abyssinian; al-Musta'īn's a Slav (*ṣaqlabīyah*); al-Muktafi's as well as al-Muqtadir's were Turkish slaves; and al-Mustaḍī''s Armenian.[3] Hārūn's mother, another foreign slave, was the famous al-Khayzurān—the first woman to exercise any appreciable influence in 'Abbāsid caliphal affairs.[4]

In bringing about this fusion of the Arabians with their subject peoples polygamy, concubinage and the slave trade proved effective methods. As the pure Arabian element receded into the background non-Arabs, half-breeds and sons of freed women began to take their place. Soon the Arabian aristocracy was superseded by a hierarchy of officials representing diverse nationalities, at first preponderantly Persian and later Turkish.

[1] Tha'ālibi, *Laṭā'if*, p. 75.
[2] Ṭabari, vol. iii, p. 937, ll. 12-13.
[3] See Tha'ālibi, pp. 75-7; Mas'ūdi, *passim*.
[4] For the part she was suspected of having played in the death of her son, the Caliph al-Hādi, and the succession of her other and favourite son, al-Rashīd, consult Ṭabari, vol. iii, pp. 569 *seq.*, copied by ibn-al-Athīr, vol. vi, pp. 67 *seq.* Cf. Mas'ūdi, vol. vi, pp. 282-3.

A bard gave expression to the proud Arabian sentiment when he sang:

> Sons of concubines have become
> So numerous amongst us;
> Lead me, O God, to a land
> Where I shall see no bastards.[1]

Unfortunately Arab historians had their interest too much centred in the caliph's affairs and political happenings to leave us an adequate picture of the social and economic life of the common people in those days. But from sporadic, incidental passages in their works, from mainly literary sources and from ordinary life in the conservative Moslem Orient of today, it is not impossible to reconstruct an outline of that picture.

Home life

The early 'Abbāsid woman enjoyed the same measure of liberty as her Umayyad sister; but toward the end of the tenth century, under the Buwayhids, the system of strict seclusion and absolute segregation of the sexes had become general. Not only do we read of women in the high circles of that early period achieving distinction and exercising influence in state affairs—such as al-Khayzurān, al-Mahdi's wife and al-Rashīd's mother; 'Ulayyah, daughter of al-Mahdi; Zubaydah, al-Rashīd's wife and al-Amīn's mother; and Būrān, al-Ma'mūn's wife—but of Arab maidens going to war and commanding troops, composing poetry and competing with men in literary pursuits or enlivening society with their wit, musical talent and vocal accomplishments. Such was 'Ubaydah al-Ṭunbūrīyah (i.e. the pandore-lady), who won national fame in the days of al-Mu'taṣim as a beauty, a singer and a musician.[2]

In the period of decline, characterized by excessive concubinage, laxity of sex morality and indulgence in luxury, the position of woman sank to the low level we find in the *Arabian Nights*. There woman is represented as the personification of cunning and intrigue and as the repository of all base sentiments and unworthy thoughts. In an extraordinary letter of condolence to a friend who had lost his daughter, abu-Bakr al-Khwārizmi († *ca.* 993 or 1002), the first author to leave a collection of literary correspondence, asserts: "We are in an age in which if one of us . . . should marry his daughter to a grave he would acquire thereby the best of sons-in-law".[3]

[1] Mubarrad, p. 302. [2] *Aghāni*, vol. xix, pp. 134-7.
[3] *Rasā'il* (Constantinople, 1297), p. 20.

Marriage has been regarded almost universally in Islam as a positive duty, the neglect of which is subject to severe reproach, and the gift of children, especially if sons, a boon from God. A wife's first duty consisted in the service of her husband, the care of the children and the management of household affairs; any spare time would be occupied with spinning and weaving. The fashionable head-dress for women, introduced by 'Ulayyah, half-sister of al-Rashīd, was evidently a dome-shaped cap, round the bottom of which was a circlet that could be adorned with jewels. Among other objects of feminine adornment were anklets (sing. *khalkhāl*) and bracelets (*asāwir*).

Men's clothing has varied but little since those days. The common head-gear was the black high-peaked hat, *qalansuwah*, made of felt or wool and introduced by al-Manṣūr.[1] Wide trousers (*sarāwīl*) of Persian origin,[2] shirt, vest and jacket (*quftān*),[3] with outer mantle (*'abā'* or *jubbah*[4]), completed the wardrobe of a gentleman.[5] The theologians, following the instructions of abu-Yūsuf, al-Rashīd's distinguished judge, wore distinctive black turbans and mantles (sing. *ṭaylasān*).[6]

Judging by the erotic expressions of the poets of the age the early Arabian ideals of feminine beauty seem not to have suffered much change. Al-Nuwayri devotes a goodly portion of a volume[7] to quotations descriptive of such physical charms. The woman's stature should be like the bamboo (*khayzurān*) among plants, her face as round as the full moon, her hair darker than the night, her cheeks white and rosy with a mole not unlike a drop of ambergris upon a plate of alabaster, her eyes intensely black without any adventitious antimony (*kuḥl*) and large like those of a wild deer, her eyelids drowsy or languid (*saqīm*), her

[1] Above, p. 294. The red fez, *ṭarbūsh*, still worn in Moslem lands, is a modern article.

[2] Jāḥiẓ, *Bayān*, vol. iii, p. 9; R. P. A. Dozy, *Dictionnaire détaillé des noms des vêtements* (Amsterdam, 1845), pp. 203-4.

[3] Dozy, pp. 162-3.

[4] This Arabic word has worked its way from Spanish, where we find it in a late tenth-century dictionary, into the rest of the Romance languages and thence into English and the other Germanic languages as well as the Slavonic. In English it has left an interesting survival in the word "gibbet", meaning "gallows".

[5] This style of dress is still followed by the older generation in Lebanon and Syria.

[6] Ibn-Khallikān, vol. iii, p. 334 = de Slane, vol. iv, p. 273; *Aghānī*, vol. v, p. 109, ll. 23-4, vol. vi, p. 69, l. 23; ibn-abi-Uṣaybi'ah, vol. ii, p. 4, l. 23.

[7] *Nihāyah*, vol. ii, pp. 18 *seq.* For an illustration of the wealth of the Arabic language in terms describing women see ibn-Qayyim al-Jawzīyah, *Akhbār al-Nisā'* (Cairo, 1319), pp. 119 *seq.*

mouth small with teeth like pearls set in coral, her bosom pomegranate-like, her hips wide and her fingers tapering, with the extremities dyed with vermilion henna (*ḥinnā'*).

The most conspicuous piece of furniture now came to be the *dīwān*, a sofa extending along three sides of the room. Raised seats in the form of chairs were introduced under the earlier dynasty, but cushions laid on small square mattresses (from Ar. *maṭraḥ*) on the floor where one could comfortably squat remained popular. Hand-woven carpets covered the floor. Food was served on large round trays of brass set on a low table in front of the *dīwān* or the floor cushions. In the homes of the well-to-do the trays were of silver and the table of wood inlaid with ebony, mother-of-pearl or tortoise-shell—not unlike those still manufactured in Damascus. Those same people who had once enjoyed scorpions, beetles and weasels as a luxury,[1] who thought rice a venomous food[2] and used flattened bread for writing material,[3] by this time had their gastronomic tastes whetted for the delicacies of the civilized world, including such Persian dishes as the greatly desired stew, *sikbāj*, and the rich sweets, *fālūdhaj*. Their chickens were now fed on shelled nuts, almonds and milk. In summer, houses were cooled by ice.[4] Non-alcoholic drinks in the form of sherbet,[5] consisting of water sweetened with sugar and flavoured with extracts of violets, bananas, roses or mulberries, were served, but of course not exclusively. Coffee did not attain vogue until the fifteenth century and tobacco was unknown before the discovery of the New World.[6] A ninth- to tenth-century author[7] has left us a work intended to give an exposition of the sentiments and manners of a man or culture (*ẓarīf*), a gentleman, in that period. He is one in possession of polite behaviour (*adab*), manly virtue (*murū'ah*) and elegant manners

[1] Ibn-Khaldūn, *Muqaddamah*, p. 170. [2] Ibn-al-Faqīh, pp. 187-8.
[3] Ibn-Khaldūn, p. 144. Cf. above, p. 156.
[4] Ibn-abi-Uṣaybi'ah, vol. 1, pp. 139-40. Pp. 82-3 quote from an earlier source a prescription which "can solidify water even in June or July".
[5] From Ar. *sharbah*, drink. Eng. "syrup" comes from a cognate word *sharāb*.
[6] Introduced into South Arabia in the fourteenth century, coffee became domesticated in Makkah early in the fifteenth, and in the first decade of the sixteenth century was first known in Cairo through Sufis from al-Yaman, who used it at the Azhar Mosque to produce the necessary wakefulness for nightly devotions. See above, p. 19. Inhaling of smoke from burning herbs for medical purposes or perhaps for pleasure had been practised before America's discovery.
[7] Al-Washshā', *Kitāb al-Muwashsha*, ed. R. Brünnow (Leyden, 1886), pp. 1, 12, 33, 37, 124, 125, 129-31, 142.

By courtesy of Fahim Kouchakji

A NINTH-CENTURY VASE FROM AL-RAQQAH, PART-TIME CAPITAL OF HĀRŪN AL-RASHĪD

It is of turquoise greenish-blue colour, forty-nine centimetres high

(*ẓarf*), who abstains from joking, holds fellowship with the right comrades, has high standards of veracity, is scrupulous in the fulfilment of his promises, keeps a secret, wears unsoiled and unpatched clothes, and at the table takes small mouthfuls, converses or laughs but little, chews his food slowly, licks not his fingers, avoids garlic and onions and refrains from using the toothpick in toilet rooms, baths, public meetings and on the streets.

Alcoholic drinks were often indulged in both in company and in private. Judging by the countless stories of revelry in such works as the *Aghāni* and the *Arabian Nights* and by the numerous songs and poems in praise of wine (*khamrīyāt*) by the debauched abu-Nuwās († *ca.* 810), the one-day caliph, ibn-al-Mu'tazz († 908), and similar bards, prohibition, one of the distinctive features of Moslem religion, did no more prohibit then than did the eighteenth amendment to the Constitution of the United States. Even caliphs, vizirs, princes and judges paid no heed to the religious injunction.[1] Scholars, poets, singers and musicians were especially desired as boon companions. This practice, which was of Persian origin,[2] became an established institution under the early 'Abbāsids and developed professionals under al-Rashīd. Other than this caliph, al-Hādi, al-Amīn, al-Ma'mūn, al-Mu'taṣim, al-Wāthiq and al-Mutawakkil were given to drink; al-Manṣūr and al-Muhtadi were opposed to it. Indeed al-Nawāji[3] despairs of finding room in his book for all the caliphs, vizirs and secretaries addicted to the use of the forbidden beverage. *Khamr*, made of dates, was the favourite. Ibn-Khaldūn argues that such personages as al-Rashīd and al-Ma'mūn used only *nabīdh*,[4] prepared by soaking grapes, raisins or dates in water and allowing the juice to ferment slightly. Such drink was judged legal under certain conditions by at least one school of Moslem jurisprudence, the Ḥanafite. Muḥammad himself drank it, especially before it was three days old.[5]

[1] See Nuwayri, *Nihāyah*, vol. iv, pp. 92 *seq.*

[2] Jāḥiẓ, *Tāj*, pp. 23, 72; Nawāji, *Ḥalbah*, p. 26.

[3] P. 99, ll. 24-7.

[4] *Muqaddamah*, p. 16. *Khamr* is the term used in the Koran (5 : 92-3) for the prohibited drink. What provides opportunity for the exercise of ingenuity on the part of interpreters is firstly the fact that at the time of the Prophet there was not in al-Madīnah any *khamr* of grapes, the beverage of its inhabitants being prepared from dates; and secondly that these juices do not ferment until a certain time lapses unless they are treated by special methods. Consult *'Iqd*, vol. iii, pp. 405-14.

[5] *Mishkāh*, vol. ii, pp. 172-3; ibn-Ḥanbal, *Musnad* (Cairo, 1313), vol. i, pp. 240, 287, 320; Bukhāri, vol. vi, p. 232.

Convivial parties featuring "the daughter of the vine" and song were not uncommon. At these drinking-bouts (sing. *majlis al-shirāb*[1]) the host and guests perfumed their beards with civet or rose-water and wore special garments of bright colours (*thiyāb al-munādamah*). The room was made fragrant by ambergris or aloes-wood burning in a censer. The songstresses who participated in such gatherings were mostly slaves of loose character, as illustrated by many stories,[2] who constituted the gravest menace to the morals of the youth of the age.[3] The description of a certain home in al-Kūfah during the reign of al-Manṣūr sounds more like that of a *café chantant*, with Sallāmah al-Zarqā' (the blue-eyed) as its prima donna.[4] The laity had access to wine in the Christian monasteries and the special bars conducted mainly by Jews. Christians and Jews were the "bootleggers" of the time.

Baths

"Cleanliness is a part of faith"—so runs a Prophetic tradition that is still on every lip in Moslem lands. Arabia had no baths that we hear of before Muḥammad. He himself is represented as prejudiced against them and as having permitted men to enter them for purposes of cleanliness only, each wearing a cloth. In the time we are studying, however, public baths (sing. *ḥammām*) had become popular not only for ceremonial ablutions and for their salutary effects, but also as resorts of amusement and mere luxury. Women were allowed their use on specially reserved days. Baghdād, according to al-Khaṭīb,[5] boasted in the days of al-Muqtadir (908–32) some 27,000 public baths, and in other times even 60,000,[6] all of which—like most figures in Arabic sources—seem highly exaggerated. Al-Ya'qūbi[7] makes the number 10,000 not long after the foundation of Baghdād. The Moorish traveller ibn-Baṭṭūṭah,[8] who visited Baghdād in 1327, found in each of the thirteen quarters composing its west side two or three baths of the most elaborate kind, each supplied with hot and cold running water.

Then as now the bath-house comprised several chambers with mosaic pavements and marble-lined inner walls clustering round a large central chamber. This innermost chamber, crowned by

[1] Nawāji, p. 38.
[2] *Aghāni*, vol. xi, pp. 98-9, vol. xviii, pp. 182-9.
[3] Washshā', pp. 92 *seq*.
[4] *Aghāni*, vol. xiii, pp. 128 *seq*. Cf. Nuwayri, vol. v, pp. 72 *seq*.
[5] *Ta'rīkh*, vol. i, pp. 118-19.
[6] *Ibid*. p. 117.
[7] *Buldān*, p. 250, ll. 9-10, cf. p. 254, ll. 8-9.
[8] Vol. ii, pp. 105-7.

a dome studded with small round glazed apertures for the admission of light, was heated by steam rising from a central jet of water in the middle of a basin. The outer rooms were used for lounging and for enjoying drinks and refreshments.

Pastimes

Sports, like the fine arts, have throughout history been an appendage more of Indo-European than Semitic civilization. Engaging in them involves physical exertion for its own sake, which could not very well become a desideratum for the son of Arabia with his utilitarian temperament and the warmness of the climate.

Under the caliphate certain indoor games became popular. Reference has already been made to a sort of club-house in Makkah under the Umayyads provided with facilities for playing chess, backgammon and dice. As with several other innovations, al-Rashīd is credited with being the first 'Abbāsid caliph to have played and encouraged chess.[1] Chess (Ar. *shiṭranj*, ultimately from Sanskrit), originally an Indian game,[2] soon became the favourite indoor pastime of the aristocracy, displacing dice. This caliph is supposed to have included among his presents to Charlemagne a chess-board, just as in the Crusading period the Old Man of the Mountain presented another to St. Louis. Among other games played with a board was backgammon (*nard*, trick-track), also of Indian origin.[3]

Notable in the list of outdoor sports were archery, polo (*jūkān*, from Pers. *chawgān*,[4] bent stick), ball and mallets (*ṣawlajān*, pall-mall, a sort of croquet or hockey), fencing, javelin-throwing (*jarīd*), horse-racing and above all hunting. Among the qualifications of a prospective boon companion al-Jāḥiẓ[5] lists ability in archery, hunting, playing ball and chess—in all of which the companion may equal his royal master with no fear of affronting him. Among the caliphs particularly fond of polo was al-Mu'taṣim, whose Turkish general, al-Afshīn, once refused to play against him because he did not want to be against the commander of the believers even in a game.[6] References are made to a ball game in which a broad piece of wood (*ṭabṭāb*) was used.[7] Could

[1] Mas'ūdi, vol. viii, p. 296. [2] *Ibid.* vol. i, pp. 159-61. [3] *Ibid.* pp. 157-8.

[4] Cf. "chicane", name given to an old game in Languedoc and elsewhere played on foot with a mallet and a ball of hard wood.

[5] *Tāj*, p. 72. For other qualifications consult Nawāji, pp. 25 *seq.*

[6] Ibn-al-'Abbās, *Āthār al-Uwal*, p. 130.

[7] Mas'ūdi, vol. viii, p. 296, l. 2. Cf. *Āthār*, p. 129, ll. 3-4.

this be tennis in its rudimentary form?[1] Al-Mas'ūdi[2] has preserved for us the description of a horse-race at al-Raqqah in which a courser of al-Rashīd's won first place, to the enthusiastic delight of the caliph, who witnessed the event. In the *'Iqd*[3] we find a number of poems in description and honour of prize-winning horses. Betting, as we learn from this same source, enlivened such races.

In the 'Abbāsid period, as in the earlier one, hunting was the favourite outdoor pastime of caliphs and princes. Al-Amīn was particularly fond of hunting lions,[4] and a brother of his met his death pursuing wild boars.[5] Both abu-Muslim al-Khurāsāni and al-Mu'taṣim were fond of hunting with the cheetah. The number of early Arabic books dealing with hunting, trapping and falconry testify to the keen interest in these sports.

Falconry and hawking were introduced into Arabia from Persia, as the Arabic vocabulary relating to these sports indicates. They became particularly favoured in the later period of the caliphate[6] and in that of the Crusades.[7] Hunting with the falcon (*bāz*) or sparrow-hawk (*bāshiq*) is still practised in Persia, al-'Irāq, Dayr al-Zūr and the 'Alawite region of Syria in practically the same manner as described in the *Arabian Nights*. For gazelles or antelopes, hares, partridges, wild geese, ducks and *qaṭa* (a species of grouse), hawks and falcons were employed and assisted in the case of big game by dogs. The first thing for a Moslem hunter to do after seizing his prey would be to cut its throat; otherwise its flesh would be unlawful.[8] Under certain conditions the hunting-party would form a circuit (*ḥalqah*) surrounding and closing in on the spot in which the game happened to abound. Al-Mu'taṣim built a horseshoe-shaped wall touching the Tigris at its two extremities and used his

[1] The word "tennis", generally supposed to have come from the French verb *tenez* = take heed, is probably from "Tinnīs", the Arabic name of an Egyptian city in the Delta noted in the Middle Ages for its linen fabrics, which may have been used for making tennis balls. See Malcolm D. Whitman, *Tennis: Origins and Mysteries* (New York, 1932), pp. 24-32.

[2] Vol. vi, pp. 348-9.

[3] Vol. i, pp. 63-5.

[4] Mas'ūdi, vol. vi, pp. 432-3.

[5] *Aghāni*, vol. ix, p. 97, ll. 27-9.

[6] *Fihrist*, p. 315, and ibn-Khallikān, vol. ii, p. 172, vol. iii, p. 209, mention a number of Arabic books on hunting and falconry.

[7] For one of the earliest treatments of this subject in Arabic see Usāmah ibn-Munqidh, *Kitāb al-I'tibār*, ed. Hitti (Princeton, 1930), pp. 191-226; tr. Hitti, *An Arab-Syrian Gentleman and Warrior* (New York, 1929, reprint Beirūt, 1964 pp. 221-54.

[8] Koran 2 : 168, 5 : 4, 16 : 116.

circuit of men to drive the game inside, thus shutting it in between the wall and the river.[1] Al-Musta'ṣim also used the circuit technique in his chase, as did the Saljūqs.[2] Among other late caliphs al-Mustanjid (1160–70) organized a number of regular hunting-parties. Certain caliphs and rulers kept wild beasts such as lions and tigers for striking awe into the hearts of their subjects and visitors;[3] others had dogs and monkeys for pets. A son of al-Muqtadir's vizir, who resided in Cairo and held a high position in its government, had for a hobby the collecting of serpents, scorpions and other venomous animals, which he kept under good care in a special building near his palace.[4]

Slaves

At the head of the social register stood the caliph and his family, the government officials, the scions of the Hāshimite clan and the satellites of all these groups. In this last class we may include the soldiers and bodyguards, the favoured friends and boon companions, as well as the clients and servants.

The servants were almost all slaves recruited from non-Moslem peoples and captured by force, taken prisoner in time of war or purchased in time of peace. Some were negroes, others were Turks and still others were white. The white slaves (*mamālīk*) were mainly Greeks and Slavs, Armenians and Berbers. Certain slaves were eunuchs (*khiṣyān*) attached to the service of the harem. Others, termed *ghilmān*, who might also be eunuchs, were the recipients of special favours from their masters, wore rich and attractive uniforms and often beautified and perfumed their bodies in effeminate fashion. We read of *ghilmān* in the reign of al-Rashīd;[5] but it was evidently al-Amīn who, following Persian precedent, established in the Arabic world the *ghilmān* institution for the practice of unnatural sexual relations.[6] A judge under al-Ma'mūn used four hundred such youths.[7] Poets like abu-Nuwās did not disdain to give public expression to their perverted passions and to address amorous pieces of their composition to "beardless young boys".

The maidens (*jawārī*) among slaves were also used as singers, dancers and concubines, and some of them exerted appreciable influence over their caliph masters. Such was dhāt-al-Khāl (she

[1] *Fakhri*, pp. 73-4.
[2] *Āthār al-Uwal*, p. 135.
[3] *Fakhri*, p. 30; *'Iqd*, vol. i, p. 198, ll. 4 *seq.*
[4] Kutubi, vol. i, pp. 134-5.
[5] Ṭabari, vol. iii, p. 669; same in ibn-al-Athīr, vol. vi, p. 120.
[6] Ṭabari, vol. iii, p. 950, copied by ibn-al-Athīr, vol. vi, p. 205.
[7] Mas'ūdi, vol. vii, p. 47.

of the mole), whom al-Rashīd had bought for 70,000 dirhams and in a fit of jealousy bestowed on one of his male servants. Having taken an oath to grant her request on a certain day, no matter what the request might be, al-Rashīd is said to have appointed her husband governor over Fāris for seven years.[1] In order to wean him from another singing-girl to whom he became attached, al-Rashīd's wife Zubaydah presented her husband with ten maidens, one of whom became the mother of al-Ma'mūn and another of al-Mu'taṣim.[2] The legendary story of Tawaddud, the beautiful and talented slave girl in *The Thousand and One Nights* (nights 437–62) whom al-Rashīd was willing to purchase for 100,000 dinars after she had passed with flying colours a searching test before his savants in medicine, law, astronomy, philosophy, music and mathematics—to say nothing of rhetoric, grammar, poetry, history and the Koran—illustrates how highly cultured some of these maids must have been. Al-Amīn's contribution consisted in promoting a corps of female pages, the members of which bobbed their hair, dressed like boys and wore silk turbans. The innovation soon became popular with both the higher and the lower classes of society.[3] An eye-witness reports that when on a Palm Sunday he called on al-Ma'mūn he found in his presence twenty Greek maidens, all bedecked and adorned, dancing with gold crosses on their necks and olive branches and palm leaves in their hands. The distribution of 3000 dinars among the dancers brought the affair to a grand finale.[4]

An idea of the prevalence of slavery may be obtained from the high figures used in enumerating those in the caliphal household. The palace of al-Muqtadir (908–32), we are told, housed 11,000 Greek and Sudanese eunuchs.[5] Al-Mutawakkil, according to a report, had 4000 concubines, all of whom shared his nuptial bed.[6] On one occasion this caliph received as a present two hundred slaves from one of his generals.[7] It was customary for governors and generals to send presents, including girls received or exacted from among their subjects, to the caliph or vizir;[8]

[1] *Aghānī*, vol. xv, p. 80, quoted by Nuwayri, vol. v, pp. 889.
[2] *Aghānī*, vol. xvi, p. 137.
[3] Mas'ūdi, vol. viii, p. 299.
[4] *Aghānī*, vol. xix, pp. 138-9.
[5] *Fakhri*, p. 352.
[6] Mas'ūdi, vol. vii, p. 276.
[7] *Ibid.* vol. vii, p. 281.
[8] Ibn-al-Athīr, vol. vii, pp. 211-12; Ṭabari, vol. iii, p. 627, copied by ibn-al-Athīr, vol. vi, p. 86.

failure to do so was interpreted as a sign of rebellion. Al-Ma'mūn devised the scheme of sending some of his trusted slaves as presents, expecting them to act as spies on the suspect recipients or to do away with them in case of necessity.[1]

Economic life: commerce

The commonalty was composed of an upper class bordering on the aristocracy and comprised littérateurs and belletrists, learned men, artists, merchants, craftsmen and professionals, and of a lower class forming the majority of the nation and made up of farmers, herdsmen and country folk who represented the native population and now enjoyed the status of dhimmis. In the following chapter we shall treat of the intellectual class at some length. Suffice it to note here that the general stage of culture in the period of 'Abbāsid primacy was by no means low.

The wide extent of the empire and the high level which civilization attained involved extensive international trade. The early merchants were Christians, Jews[2] and Zoroastrians, but these were later largely superseded by Moslems and Arabs, who did not disdain trade as they did agriculture. Such ports as Baghdād, al-Baṣrah, Sīrāf,[3] Cairo and Alexandria soon developed into centres of active land and maritime commerce.

Eastward, Moslem traders ventured as far as China, which according to Arab tradition was reached from al-Baṣrah as early as the days of the second 'Abbāsid caliph, al-Manṣūr.[4] The earliest Arabic source treating of the subject of Arab and Persian maritime communication with India and China is a report of voyages by Sulaymān al-Tājir (the merchant) and other Moslem traders in the third Moslem century.[5] This trade was based on silk, the earliest of China's magnificent gifts to the West, and usually followed what has been styled "the great silk way"[6] going through Samarqand and Chinese Turkestan, a region less traversed today by civilized man than almost any other part of the habitable world. Goods were generally transported by relays; few caravans went the whole distance. But diplomatic relations were certainly established before the time of Arab traders.

[1] *'Iqd*, vol. i, p. 196.
[2] Consult ibn-Khurdādhbih, pp. 153-4.
[3] A town in Persia on the Persian Gulf. The people of Sīrāf and 'Umān (Mas'ūdi, vol. i, pp. 281-2) were among the best-known mariners of the early 'Abbāsid period.
[4] Cf. Marshall Broomhall, *Islam in China* (London, 1910), pp. 5-36.
[5] *Silsilat al-Tawārīkh* [*sic*], ed. Langlès (Paris, 1811); tr. G. Ferrand, *Voyage du marchand arabe Sulaymân en Inde et en Chine* (Paris, 1922).
[6] Thomas F. Carter, *The Invention of Printing in China and its Spread Westward* (New York, 1925), pp. 85 *seq.*

Legend makes Sa'd ibn-abi-Waqqāṣ, the conqueror of Persia, the envoy sent by the Prophet to China. Sa'd's "grave" is still revered in Canton. Certain inscriptions on the old Chinese monuments relating to Islam in China are clearly forgeries prompted by religious pride.[1] By the mid-eighth century several embassies had been exchanged. In the Chinese records of that century the *amīr al-mu'minīn* is called *hanmi-mo-mo-ni*; abu-al-'Abbās, the first 'Abbāsid caliph, *A-bo-lo-ba*; and Hārūn, *A-lun*. In the time of these caliphs a number of Moslems settled in China. At first such Moslems appear under the name *Ta-shih* [2] and later under the title *Hui-Hui* (Muḥammadans).[3] The first European mention of Saracens in China appears to be that of Marco Polo.[4] It was also Moslem traders who carried Islam into the islands that in 1949 formed the United States of Indonesia.

Westward, Moslem merchants reached Morocco and Spain. A thousand years before de Lesseps an Arab caliph, Hārūn, entertained the idea of digging a canal through the Isthmus of Suez.[5] Arab Mediterranean trade, however, never rose to great prominence. The Black Sea was likewise inhospitable to it, though in the tenth century brisk land trade is noticed with the peoples of the Volga regions to the north. But the Caspian Sea, because of its proximity to the Persian centres and the prosperous cities of Samarqand and Bukhāra with their hinterland, was the scene of some commercial intercourse. Moslem merchants carried with them dates, sugar, cotton and woollen fabrics, steel tools and glassware; they imported, among other commodities, spices, camphor and silk from farther Asia, and ivory, ebony and negro slaves from Africa.

An idea of the fortunes amassed by the Rothschilds and Rockefellers of the age may be gained from the case of the Baghdād jeweller ibn-al-Jaṣṣāṣ, who remained wealthy after al-Muqtadir had confiscated 16,000,000 dinars of his property, and became the first of a family of distinguished jewel merchants.[6] Certain Baṣrah merchants whose ships carried goods to distant parts of the world had an annual income of more than a

[1] See Paul Pelliot in *Journal asiatique* (1913), vol. ii, pp. 177-91.

[2] From Pahlawi *Tājik*, modern *Tāzi*, Arab. The term is evidently a Persianized form of Ṭayyi', an Arab tribe.

[3] Consult Isaac Mason in *Journal of the North-China Branch of the Royal Asiatic Society*, vol. lx (1929), pp. 42-78.

[4] For Moslem settlements in Korea (al-Shīla) see ibn-Khurdādhbih, pp. 70, 170.

[5] Mas'ūdi, vol. iv, pp. 98-9.

[6] Kutubi, vol. i, p. 177.

million dirhams each. An uneducated miller of al-Baṣrah and Baghdād could afford to distribute as daily alms among the poor a hundred dinars, and was later appointed by al-Mu'taṣim as his vizir.[1] In Sīrāf the home of the average merchant cost over ten thousand dinars, some over thirty thousand dinars; and many maritime traders were worth 4,000,000 dinars each.[2] Some of these Sīrāf merchants "spent their lives on the water", and al-Iṣṭakhri[3] heard of one who had spent forty years on board ship.

Industry

No commercial activity could have reached such dimensions had it not rested on extensive home industry and agriculture. Hand industry flourished in various parts of the empire. In Western Asia it centred chiefly in the manufacture of rugs, tapestry, silk, cotton and woollen fabrics, satin, brocade (*dībāj*), sofa (from Ar. *ṣuffah*) and cushion covers, as well as other articles of furniture and kitchen utensils. The many looms of Persia and al-'Irāq turned out carpets and textiles maintained at a high standard by distinctive marks. Al-Musta'īn's mother had a rug specially ordered for her at a cost of 130,000,000 dirhams, bearing figures of all sorts of birds in gold which had rubies and other precious stones for eyes.[4] A quarter in Baghdād named after 'Attāb, an Umayyad prince who was its most distinguished resident, gave its name to a striped fabric, *'attābi*,[5] first manufactured there in the twelfth century. The fabric was imitated by the Arabs in Spain and under the trade name *tabi* became popular in France, Italy and other lands of Europe. The term survives in "tabby", applied to streaked or marked cats. Al-Kūfah produced the silk and partly silk kerchiefs for the head that are still worn under the name *kūfīyah*. Tawwaj, Fasa and other towns of Fāris boasted a number of high-class factories where carpets, embroideries, brocades and robes of honour—a mark of distinction in the East—were manufactured first for the use of the royalty.[6] Such products were known as *ṭirāz* (from Pers.) and bore the name or cipher of the sultan or caliph embroidered on them. In Tustar and al-Sūs in Khūzistān[7] (ancient Susiana) were a number of factories famous for the

[1] *Fakhri*, pp. 321-2.
[2] Iṣṭakhri, pp. 127, 139; ibn-Ḥawqal, p. 198; Maqdisi, p. 426.
[3] P. 138.
[4] Ibshīhi, vol. i, p. 144.
[5] Mentioned in Maqdisi, p. 323, l. 20; ibn-Ḥawqal, p. 261, l. 13; Yāqūt, *Buldān*, vol. i, p. 822, l. 22 (where it is misspelt).
[6] Iṣṭakhri, p. 153 Cf. Maqdisi, pp. 442-3.
[7] Maqdisi, pp. 402, 407-9.

embroidery of damask[1] figured with gold and for curtains made of spun silk (*khazz*). Their camel- and goat-hair fabrics as well as their spun-silk cloaks were widely known. Shīrāz yielded striped woollen cloaks, also gauzes and brocades. Under the name of "taffeta" European ladies of the Middle Ages bought in their native shops the Persian silken cloth *tāftah*. Khurāsān and Armenia were famous for their spreads, hangings and sofa and cushion covers. In Central Asia, that great emporium of the early Middle Ages, Bukhāra was especially noted for its prayer-rugs. A complete conception of the development of industry and trade in Transoxiana may be gained from the list of exports from the various towns given by al-Maqdisi:[2] soap, carpets, copper lamps, pewter ware, felt cloaks, furs, amber, honey, falcons, scissors, needles, knives, swords, bows, meats, Slavonic and Turkish slaves, etc. Tables, sofas, lamps, chandeliers, vases, earthenware and kitchen utensils were also made in Syria and Egypt. The Egyptian fabrics termed *dimyāṭi* (after Dimyāṭ), *dabīqi* (after Dabīq) and *tinnīsi* (after Tinnīs)[3] were world-renowned and imitated in Persia. The ancient industrial arts of Pharaonic days survived in an attenuated form in the manufactures of the Copts.

The glass of Sidon, Tyre and other Syrian towns, a survival of the ancient Phoenician industry which after the Egyptian was the oldest glass industry in history, was proverbial for its clarity and thinness.[4] In its enamelled and variegated varieties Syrian glass as a result of the Crusades became the forerunner of the stained glass in the cathedrals of Europe. Glass and metal vases of Syrian workmanship were in great demand as articles of utility and luxury. Sconces of glass bearing enamelled inscriptions in various colours hung in mosques and palaces. Damascus was the centre of an extensive mosaic and *qāshāni* industry. *Qāshāni*[5] (colloquial *qīshāni*, *qāshi*), a name derived from Kāshān[6] in Media, was given to square or hexagonal glazed tiles, sometimes figured with conventional flowers and used in exterior and

[1] This fabric was originally made in Damascus, whence the name.

[2] Pp. 323-6.

[3] Yāqūt, vol. ii, pp. 603, 548, vol. i, p. 882; Maqdisi, pp. 201, 433, ll. 16-17, 443, l. 5. See below, p. 631.

[4] Tha'ālibi, *Laṭā'if*, p. 95.

[5] Mentioned in ibn-Baṭṭūṭah, vol. i, p. 415, vol. ii, pp. 46, 130, 225, 297, vol. iii, p. 79.

[6] Ar. Qāshān; Yāqūt, *Buldān*, vol. iv, p. 15.

interior decoration of buildings. The predominant colours were indigo blue, turquoise blue, green and less often red and yellow. The art, as ancient as the Elamites and Assyrians, survived in Damascus until the latter part of the eighteenth century.

Worthy of special note is the manufacture of writing-paper, introduced in the middle of the eighth century into Samarqand from China.[1] The paper of Samarqand, which was captured by the Moslems in 704, was considered matchless.[2] Before the close of that century Baghdād saw its first paper-mill. Gradually others for making paper followed: Egypt had its factory about 900 or earlier, Morocco about 1100, Spain about 1150; and various kinds of paper, white and coloured, were produced. Al-Mu'taṣim, credited with opening new soap and glass factories in Baghdād, Sāmarra and other towns, is said to have encouraged the paper industry. The oldest Arabic paper manuscript that has come down to us is one on tradition entitled *Gharīb al-Ḥadīth*, by abu-'Ubayd al-Qāsim ibn-Sallām († 837), dated dhu-al-Qa'dah, A.H. 252 (November 13–December 12, 866) and preserved in the Leyden University Library.[3] The oldest by a Christian author is a theological treatise by abu-Qurrah[4] († *ca.* 820) dated Rabī' I, A.H. 264 (Nov. 11–Dec. 10, 877) and preserved in the British Museum. From Moslem Spain and from Italy, in the twelfth and thirteenth centuries, the manufacture of paper finally worked its way into Christian Europe, where with the later discovery of printing from movable type (1450–55) it made possible the measure of popular education which Europe and America now enjoy.

The jeweller's art also had its day. Pearls, sapphires, rubies, emeralds and diamonds were favourites with the royalty; turquoise, carnelian and onyx with the lower classes. One of the best-known gems in Arab history is the big ruby, once owned by several Persian monarchs, on which Hārūn inscribed his name after acquiring it for 40,000 dinars.[5] The ruby was so large and brilliant that " if it were put in the night-time in a dark room it would shine like a lamp". Hārūn's sister, as we learned

[1] Consult Friedrich Hirth, *Chinesische Studien* (Munich and Leipzig, 1890), vol. i, pp. 259-71. See below, p. 414. Paper money, also of Chinese origin, was printed (1294) in Chinese and Arabic at Tibrīz, one of the earliest places in the Moslem world with a record of block printing. [2] Thal'ālibi, p. 126; Maqdisi, p. 326, ll. 3-4.

[3] William Wright, *The Palæographical Society, Oriental Series* (London, 1875–83), pl. vi.

[4] Theodorus abu Ḳurra, *De Cultu Imaginum*, ed. and tr. I. Arendzen (Bonn, 1897).

[5] Mas'ūdi, vol. vii, p. 376. Cf. *Fakhri*, pp. 352-3; Ṭabari, vol. iii, p. 602, l. 12.

before, wore jewels on her head-dress and his wife had them on her shoes. Yaḥya ibn-Khālid the Barmakid once offered 7,000,000 dirhams to a Baghdād merchant for a jewel-box made of precious stones, but the offer was refused.[1] Al-Muktafi is said to have left 20,000,000 dinars' worth of jewels and perfumes.[2] At a gorgeous royal banquet given by al-Mutawakkil, and considered together with al-Ma'mūn's wedding "two occasions that have no third in Islam",[3] tables and trays of gold studded with gems were used. Even ibn-Khaldūn, who claims that the 'Abbāsids could not have indulged in luxurious modes of living, accepts the extraordinary display of gold and jewellery at al-Ma'mūn's marriage ceremony.[4] According to al-Mas'ūdi,[5] al-Mu'tazz (866–9), the thirteenth 'Abbāsid caliph, was the first to appear on horseback in gilded armour on a golden saddle, all caliphs before him having used silver decorations. One of the last caliphs to possess much jewellery was al-Muqtadir (908–32), who confiscated the property of the founder of the richest jewellery house in Baghdād[6] and came into possession of the famous red ruby of Hārūn, as well as the equally famous "unique pearl" weighing three *mithqāls* (miskal) and other gems, all of which he squandered.[7]

The leading mineral resources of the empire which made the jeweller's industry possible included gold and silver from Khurāsān, which also yielded marble and mercury;[8] rubies, lapis lazuli and azurite from Transoxiana;[9] lead and silver from Karmān;[10] pearls from al-Baḥrayn;[11] turquoise from Naysābūr, whose mine in the latter half of the tenth century was farmed out for 758,720 dirhams a year;[12] carnelian from Ṣan'ā';[13] and iron from Mt. Lebanon.[14] Other mineral resources included kaolin and marble from Tibrīz, antimony from the vicinity of Iṣbahān,[15] bitumen and naphtha from Georgia, marble and sulphur from

[1] Ṭabari, vol. iii, p. 703. [2] Tha'ālibi, p. 72. [3] *Ibid.* pp. 72-3.
[4] *Muqaddamah*, p. 15, ll. 20 *seq.*, pp. 144-5.
[5] Vol. vii, pp. 401-2, quoted by ibn-Khaldūn, *Muqaddamah*, p. 15.
[6] Above, p. 344.
[7] *Fakhri*, p. 353. The "unique pearl" is also mentioned by ibn-Ḥawqal, p. 38, l. 7. Cf. Maqdisi, p. 101, l. 16. [8] Maqdisi, p. 326.
[9] *Ibid.* p. 303. "Lazuli", as well as "azure", comes through Latin from Ar. *lāzaward* and ultimately from Pers. *lāzhuward*.
[10] Ibn-al-Faqīh, p. 206. [11] Maqdisi, p. 101. [12] *Ibid.* p. 341, n.
[13] *Ibid.* p. 101. [14] *Ibid.* p. 184, l. 3.
[15] Iṣṭakhri, p. 203; Tha'ālibi, *Laṭā'if*, p. 110. Ar. *kuḥl*, perhaps "galena", consult H. E. Stapleton *et al.* in *Memoirs of the Asiatic Society of Bengal*, vol. viii (1927), p. 352.

Syria-Palestine,[1] asbestos from Transoxiana[2] and mercury, pitch and tar from Farghānah.[3]

Agriculture received great impetus under the early 'Abbāsids because their capital itself lay in a most favoured spot, the alluvial plain commonly known under the name of al-Sawād; because they realized that farming was the chief source of the state income; and because the tilling of the land was almost wholly in the hands of the native inhabitants, whose status was somewhat improved under the new régime. Deserted farms and ruined villages in different parts of the empire were gradually rehabilitated and restored. The lower region of the Tigris-Euphrates valley, the richest in the whole empire after Egypt and the traditional site of the garden of Eden, was the object of special attention on the part of the central government. Canals from the Euphrates, either old and now re-opened or else entirely new, formed a "veritable network".[4] The first great canal, called Nahr 'Īsa after a relative of al-Manṣūr who had re-excavated it, connected the Euphrates at al-Anbār in the north-west with the Tigris at Baghdād. One of the main branches of the Nahr 'Īsa was the Ṣarāh. The second great transverse canal was the Nahr Ṣarṣar, which entered the Tigris above al-Madā'in. The third was the Nahr al-Malik ("river of the king"), which flowed into the Tigris below al-Madā'in.[5] Lower down the two rivers came the Nahr Kūtha and the Great Ṣarāh,[6] which threw off a number of irrigation channels. Another canal, the Dujayl (diminutive of Dijlah, the Tigris), which originally connected the Tigris with the Euphrates, had become silted up by the tenth century, and the name was given to a new channel, a loop canal, which started from the Tigris below al-Qādisīyah and rejoined it farther south after sending off a number of branches.[7] Other less important canals included the Nahr al-Ṣilah dug in Wāsiṭ by al-Mahdi.[8] Arab geographers speak of caliphs "digging" or "opening" "rivers", when in most cases the process involved was one of re-digging or re-opening canals that had existed since

Agriculture

1 Maqdisi, p. 184. 2 *Ibid.* p. 303, ll. 13-15. 3 Ibn-Ḥawqal, p. 362.

4 Iṣṭakhri, p. 85, l. 3; ibn-Ḥawqal, p. 166, l. 2.

5 For these canals see Iṣṭakhri, pp. 84-5; same in ibn-Ḥawqal, pp. 165-6; Maqdisi, p. 124; Khaṭīb, *Ta'rīkh*, vol. i, pp. 91, 111 *seq.*; Guy Le Strange, "Description of Mesopotamia and Baghdād, written about the year 900 A.D. by Ibn-Serapion" (Suhrāb), *Journal, Royal Asiatic Society* (1895), pp. 255-315.

6 Yāqūt, vol. iii, pp. 377-8. 7 Iṣṭakhri, pp. 77-8; Yāqūt, vol. ii, p. 555.

8 Balādhuri, p. 291 = Hitti, p. 451; Qudāmah, p. 241.

Babylonian days. In al-'Irāq as well as Egypt the task consisted mainly in keeping the ancient systems in order. Even before the first World War, when the Ottoman government commissioned Sir William Willcocks to study the irrigation problem of al-'Irāq, his report stressed the necessity of clearing the old watercourses rather than constructing new ones.[1] It should be noted, however, that the face of the alluvial Sawād has greatly changed since 'Abbāsid days and that both the Tigris and the Euphrates have considerably shifted their courses in historical times.

The staple crops of al-'Irāq consisted of barley and wheat, rice, dates, sesame, cotton and flax. Especially fertile was the alluvial plain to the south, al-Sawād, where quantities of fruit and vegetables, both of the cold and the hot regions, were grown. Nuts, oranges, egg-plants, sugar-cane, lupines and such flowers as roses and violets were produced in abundance.

Khurāsān vied with al-'Irāq and Egypt as a rich agricultural country. A review of the revenue sheets discussed above[2] would indicate that it yielded one of the largest kharājs of the empire. Politically it embraced, at least for some time, Transoxiana and Sijistān, and was therefore a great source of man-power as well. No wonder, then, that we hear it referred to in the presence of al-Ma'mūn as "the whole empire".[3]

The land round Bukhāra, in the judgment of Arab geographers, was, especially under the Sāmānids in the 900's, a veritable garden.[4] Here, between Samarqand and Bukhāra, lay the Wādi al-Ṣughd (the valley of Sogdiana), one of the "four earthly paradises", the other three being the Shi'b Bawwān (gap of Bavvān in Fāris), the gardens of the Ubullah Canal, extending from al-Baṣrah to the south-east,[5] and the orchards (*ghūṭah*) of Damascus.[6] In these gardens flourished several varieties of fruits, vegetables and flowers, such as dates, apples, apricots,[7] peaches, plums, lemons, oranges, figs, grapes, olives, almonds, pomegranates, egg-plants, radishes, cucumbers, roses and basil (*rayḥān*). Water-melons were exported from Khwārizm to the

[1] William Willcocks, *Irrigation of Mesopotamia* (London, 1917), pp. xvii *seq.*, 11 *seq.*

[2] P. 321.

[3] Ya'qūbi, vol. ii, p. 555, l. 4.

[4] Iṣṭakhri, pp. 305 *seq.*, copied by ibn-Ḥawqal, pp. 355 *seq.*

[5] Iṣṭakhri, p. 81; same in ibn-Ḥawqal, p. 160; Maqdisi, pp. 117-18.

[6] Yāqūt, vol. i, p. 751, vol. iii, p. 394; cf. vol. i, p. 97, ll. 15-16.

[7] For etymology see below, p. 528, n. 6. The plant itself was a native of China.

courts of al-Ma'mūn and al-Wāthiq in lead moulds packed with ice; such fruit would sell in Baghdād for seven hundred dirhams each.[1] In fact most of the fruit trees and vegetables grown at present in Western Asia were known at the time, with the exception of mangoes, potatoes, tomatoes and similar plants introduced in recent times from the New World and distant European colonies. The orange tree, allied to the citron and lemon, had its native habitat in India or Malay, whence it spread at this time into Western Asia, the adjoining lands of the Mediterranean basin and eventually through the Arabs in Spain into Europe.[2] The sugar-cane plantations of Fāris and al-Ahwāz,[3] with their noted refineries, were about this time followed by similar ones on the Syrian coast, from which place the Crusaders later introduced the cane and the sugar[4] into Europe. Thus did this sweet commodity, probably of Bengalese origin, which has since become an indispensable ingredient in the daily food of civilized man, work its way westward.

Horticulture was not limited to fruits and vegetables. The cultivation of flowers was also promoted, not only in small home gardens round fountains musical with jetting, splashing water, but on a large scale for commercial purposes. The preparation of perfumes or essences from roses, water-lilies, oranges, violets and the like flourished in Damascus, Shīrāz, Jūr and other towns. The whole district of Jūr, or Fīrūzābād, in Fāris was noted for its attar (Ar. *'iṭr*) of red roses.[5] Rose-water from Jūr was exported as far as China eastward and al-Maghrib westward.[6] Fāris included in its kharāj 30,000 bottles of the essence of red roses, which were sent annually to the caliph in Baghdād.[7] Sābūr (Pers. Shāpūr) and its valley produced ten world-famous varieties of perfumed oils, or unguents, extracted from the violet, water-lily, narcissus, palm flower, iris, white lily, myrtle, sweet marjoram, lemon and orange flowers.[8] Among

[1] Tha'ālibi, p. 129.

[2] This is the bitter variety, Ar. *abu-ṣufayr*. Eng. "orange" comes through Sp. from Ar. *nāranj*, from Pers. *nārang*. "Lemon" is Ar. *laymūn*, Pers. *līmūn* (see below, p. 665).

[3] Tha'ālibi, p. 107.

[4] Ar. *sukkar*; "candy" comes from Ar. *qandah*, *qandi*, which is Pers. *qand*. "Cane" is also of Semitic origin corresponding to Ar. *qanāh*, reed, but was separately introduced into European languages.

[5] In Syria red roses are still called *ward jūri*.

[6] Ibn-Ḥawqal, p. 213; Iṣṭakhri, pp. 152-3.

[7] Tha'ālibi, pp. 109-10.

[8] Maqdisi, p. 443.

these the violet extract was the most popular in the Moslem world, as the following words put in the mouth of the Prophet would indicate: "The excellence of the extract of violets above all other extracts is as the excellence of me above all the rest of creation".[1]

Among flowers the rose seems to have been the favourite. In the opinion of the cultured slave girl Tawaddud, whose ideas may be taken as an index of popular opinion between the tenth and twelfth centuries, roses and violets are the best scents; pomegranate and citron the best fruits; and endive the best vegetable.[2] The popular esteem in which the rose is held found expression in a tradition ascribed to Muḥammad: "The white rose was created from my sweat on the night of the nocturnal journey [*mi'rāj*], the red rose from the sweat of Gabriel and the yellow rose from that of al-Burāq".[3] With the words "I am the king of sultans and the rose is the king of the sweet-scented flowers; each of us therefore is worthy of the other", al-Mutawakkil is said to have so monopolized the cultivation of roses for his own enjoyment that in his time that flower could be seen nowhere except in his palace.[4]

The rose and the violet had a rival in the myrtle. "Adam was hurled down from Paradise with three things", claims a Prophetic tradition: "a myrtle tree, which is the chief of sweet-scented plants in the world; an ear of wheat, which is the chief food of the world; and a date, which is the chief of the fruits of this world."[5] Other highly desired flowers were the narcissus, gillyflower, jasmine, poppy and safflower.

As an index of interest in agriculture mention might be made of the several books on plants, including translations from Greek, listed in the *Fihrist*,[6] the few books on attar[7] and the spurious work of ibn-Waḥshīyah entitled *al-Filāḥah al-Nabaṭīyah*.

Dhimmis: Christians

The agricultural class, who constituted the bulk of the population of the empire and its chief source of revenue, were the original inhabitants of the land, now reduced to the position of

[1] Suyūṭi, *Ḥusn*, vol. ii, p. 242.
[2] *Alf Laylah wa-Laylah* (*Thousand and One Nights*), no. 453. Cf. nos. 864, 865.
[3] Suyūṭi, *Ḥusn*, vol. ii, p. 236.
[4] Nawāji, p. 235; Suyūṭi, vol. ii, p. 236.
[5] Suyūṭi, vol. ii, p. 245. Consult Edward W. Lane, *The Thousand and One Nights*, vol. i (London, 1839), pp. 219 *seq.* (in n. 22 to ch. iii).
[6] P. 78, ll. 12, 23, p. 79, l. 3, p. 83, l. 16, p. 252, ll. 9-10.
[7] *Fihrist*, p. 317.

dhimmis. The Arab considered it below his dignity to engage in agricultural pursuits. Originally Scripturaries, viz. Christians, Jews and Ṣābians, the dhimmis had their status widened, as we learned before, to include Zoroastrians, Manichaeans, Ḥarrān Ṣābians and others—all of whom were now treated on a par with those with whom a compact for religious tolerance had been made. In country places and on their farms these dhimmis clung to their ancient cultural patterns and preserved their native languages: Aramaic and Syriac in Syria and al-'Irāq, Iranian in Persia and Coptic in Egypt. Many of those who embraced Islam moved to the cities.

Even in cities Christians and Jews often held important financial, clerical and professional positions. This often led to open jealousy on the part of the Moslem populace and found expression in official enactments. But most of this discriminating legislation remained "ink on paper" and was not consistently enforced.

The first caliph, as we have seen, to order Christians and Jews to don distinctive dress and to exclude them from public offices was the pious Umayyad, 'Umar II, whose pact has often been erroneously ascribed to 'Umar I. Among the 'Abbāsids Hārūn was evidently the first to re-enact some of the old measures. In 807 he ordered all churches in border-lands, together with those erected subsequent to the Moslem conquest, demolished and commanded members of the tolerated sects to wear the prescribed garb.[1] The stringent regulations against dhimmis culminated in the time of al-Mutawakkil, who in 850 and 854 decreed that Christians and Jews should affix wooden images of devils to their houses, level their graves even with the ground, wear outer garments of honey-colour, i.e. yellow, put two honey-coloured patches on the wear of their slaves, one sewn on the back and the other on the front, and ride only on mules and asses with wooden saddles marked by two pomegranate-like balls on the cantle.[2] It was on account of this distinctive dress that the dhimmi acquired the epithet "spotted".[3] One other grave disability under which the dhimmis laboured was a ruling of the Moslem jurists of the period that the testimony of a

[1] Ṭabari, vol. iii, pp. 712-13; ibn-al-Athīr, vol. vi, p. 141.
[2] Ṭabari, vol. iii, pp. 1389-93, 1419.
[3] Cf. Jāḥiẓ, *Bayān*, vol. i. p. 79, ll. 27-8.

Christian or a Jew could not be accepted against a Moslem; for the Jews and Christians had once corrupted the text of their scripture, as the Koran charges,[1] and therefore could no more be trusted. The last caliph to renew in an aggravated form the hostile measures against dhimmis was the Fāṭimid al-Ḥākim (996–1021).

That in spite of these restrictions the Christians under the caliphs enjoyed on the whole a large measure of toleration may be inferred from several episodes. A number of religious debates similar to those staged in the presence of Mu'āwiyah and 'Abd-al-Malik were held in the presence of the 'Abbāsids. The text of an apology for Christianity delivered in 781 by Timothy, patriarch of the Nestorians, before al-Mahdi has come down to us,[2] as has also the famous treatise by al-Kindi[3] professing to be a contemporary account of a controversy held about 819 before al-Ma'mūn on the comparative merits of Islam and Christianity. The religious discussions of 'Ali al-Ṭabari († *ca.* 854) in his *Kitāb al-Dīn w-al-Dawlah*,[4] a semi-official defence and exposition of Islam written at the court with the assistance of al-Mutawakkil, is temperate, singularly free from heat and passion and abounds in references to the Bible, evidently the Syriac version or its early Arabic translation. At the time al-Nadīm wrote his *Fihrist* (988) both the Old and New Testaments were already in existence in Arabic in more than one version.[5] In fact we are told that a certain Aḥmad ibn-'Abdullāh ibn-Salām had translated the Bible into Arabic as early as the days of Hārūn.[6] There is evidence to show that even in the latter part of the seventh century parts of the Bible had been rendered into Arabic either from Syriac or from the Greek Septuagint. Al-Ṭabari[7] notes under A.H. 61 that 'Abdullāh, son of the conqueror of Egypt, had read the Book of Daniel. But the first important Arabic translation of the Old Testament was that of Sa'īd al-Fayyūmi (Saadia Gaon, 882–942) of Egypt, which has remained to this day the version for all Arabic-speaking Jews. These translations aroused the interest of Moslems in the controversial points, and we find al-Jāḥiẓ († 869) among the many

[1] Sūrs. 2 : 70, 5 : 16-18.

[2] A. Mingana in *Bulletin of the John Rylands Library*, vol. 12 (Manchester, 1928), pp. 137-298.

[3] *Risālat 'Abd-al-Masīḥ* (London, 1870), 2nd ed. (London, 1885).

[4] Ed. A. Mingana (Cairo, 1923); tr. Mingana, *The Book of Religion and Empire* (Manchester, 1922).

[5] *Fihrist*, p. 23.

[6] *Ibid.* p. 22. This may have been a partial translation.

[7] Vol. ii, p. 399.

who penned answers to Christians. We even read of Christian vizirs in the latter half of the ninth century, such as 'Abdūn ibn-Ṣā'id, in whose honour a judge in Baghdād rose up in public, thus receiving the disapproval of the spectators.[1] Al-Muttaqi (940–44) had a Christian vizir,[2] as did one of the Buwayhids.[3] Al-Mu'taḍid (892–902) had a Christian as head of the war office.[4] Such Christian high officials received the usual marks of honour, for we find certain Moslems objecting to kissing their hands. Most of the personal physicians of the caliphs, as will be remembered, were members of the Nestorian church. A recently published charter of protection granted to the Nestorians in 1138 by al-Muktafi[5] throws fresh light on the cordial relations between official Islam and official Christianity in that period.

Nestorians

The Christian subjects of the 'Abbāsid caliphs belonged for the most part to the two Syrian churches considered heterodox and commonly called Jacobite and Nestorian, with the Nestorians predominant in al-'Irāq. The Nestorian patriarch or catholicos (corrupted into Ar. *jāthilīq*, *jāthalīq*) had the right of residence in Baghdād, a privilege which the Jacobites had always sought in vain. Round the patriarchate styled Dayr al-Rūm[6] (the monastery of the Romans, i.e. Christians) there grew in Baghdād a Christian quarter called Dār (abode of) al-Rūm. Under the catholicos' jurisdiction there flourished seven metropolitans, including those of al-Baṣrah, al-Mawṣil and Naṣībīn (Nisibis), each with two or three bishops under him. The patriarch-elect received his investiture from the caliph, by whom he was recognized as the official head of all Christians in the empire. In 912–13 the catholicos succeeded in making the caliph prevent the Jacobite patriarch, whose seat was Antioch, from transferring his residence to Baghdād.[7] The main political charge against the Jacobites was that they sympathized with the Byzantines. But the Jacobites had a monastery in Baghdād[8] and a metro-

[1] Yāqūt, *Udabā'*, vol. ii, p. 259.
[2] Al-Tanūkhi, *al-Faraj ba'd al-Shiddah* (Cairo, 1904), vol. ii, p. 149.
[3] Naṣr ibn-Hārūn was the Buwayhid vizir. See Miskawayh, *Tajārib al-Umam*, ed. Margoliouth, vol. ii (Cairo and Oxford, 1915), pp. 408, 412.
[4] Ṣābi', *Wuzarā'*, p. 95.
[5] A. Mingana in *Bulletin John Rylands Library*, vol. 10 (1926), pp. 127-33.
[6] Yāqūt, *Buldān*, vol. ii, p. 662.
[7] On the Monophysite and Jacobite patriarchs see Assemani (al-Sam'āni), *Bibliotheca Orientalis*, vol. ii (Rome, 1721).
[8] Yāqūt, vol. ii, p. 662, l. 18.

politan seat in Takrīt, not far from the capital. In all, Yāqūt[1] lists half a dozen monasteries in east Baghdād, apart from those on the west side.

The Copts of Egypt, as we have noted before, belonged to the Jacobite communion. The Nubian church was likewise Jacobite and acknowledged the primacy of the patriarch of Alexandria. Along the narrow coast west of Egypt, Christianity had a following among the Berbers, but the majority of the inland population had their local cults corresponding to their tribal divisions.

One of the most remarkable features of Christianity under the caliphs was its possession of enough vitality to make it an aggressive church, sending its missionaries as far as India and China. Al-Nadīm[2] reports an interesting interview which he himself held with one such missionary returned from China, whom he met in the Christian quarter[3] of Baghdād. The famous stela at Sian Fu, China, erected in 781 to commemorate the names and labours of sixty-seven Nestorian missionaries,[4] together with the affiliation of the Christian church in India, that of the "Christians of St. Thomas" in Malabar on the south-west coast, with the patriarchate in Baghdād, bear witness to the evangelistic zeal of the East Syrian Church under the Moslems. It is also recognized that the existing characters of Mongol and Manchu are lineal descendants of the original Uighurian forms, which were certainly derived from the Syriac alphabet as used by the Nestorians.

Jews

As one of the "protected" peoples the Jews fared on the whole even better than the Christians, and that in spite of several unfavourable references in the Koran.[5] They were fewer and did not therefore present such a problem. In 985 al-Maqdisi[6] found most of the money-changers and bankers in Syria to be Jews, and most of the clerks and physicians Christians. Under several caliphs, particularly al-Muʿtaḍid (892–902), we read of more than one Jew in the capital and the provinces assuming responsible state positions. In Baghdād itself the Jews maintained a

[1] Under *dayr*. [2] P. 349.

[3] *Dār al-Rūm*, which Flügel, the editor, in his notes erroneously makes Constantinople.

[4] Consult P. Y. Saeki, *The Nestorian Documents and Relics in China* (Tokyo, 1937), pp. 10 *seq*.

[5] Sūrs. 2 : 70-73; 5 : 16, 66-9. [6] P. 183.

good-sized colony[1] which continued to flourish until the fall of the city. Benjamin of Tudela,[2] who visited the colony about 1169, found it in possession of ten rabbinical schools and twenty-three[3] synagogues; the principal one, adorned with variegated marble, was richly ornamented with gold and silver. Benjamin depicts in glowing colours the high esteem in which the head of the Babylonian Jews was held as a descendant of David and head of the community (Aram. *rēsh gālūtha*, prince of captivity[4] or exilarch), in fact as chief of all Jews owing allegiance to the Baghdād caliphate. Just as the catholicos exercised a certain measure of jurisdiction over all Christians in the empire, so did the exilarch over his co-religionists. The "prince of captivity" seems to have lived in affluence and owned gardens, houses and rich plantations. On his way to an audience with the caliph he appeared dressed in embroidered silk, wore a white turban gleaming with gems and was accompanied by a retinue of horsemen. Ahead of him marched a herald calling out: "Make way before our lord the son of David!"

Ṣābians

The Mandeans,[5] the genuine Ṣābians[6] of Arabic writers, were a Judaeo-Christian sect who also called themselves *Naṣoraiē d'Yaḥya*, the Naṣoreans[7] (i.e. the observants) of St. John, and therefore became erroneously known to the modern world as the Christians of St. John (the Baptist). The Mandeans practised the rite of baptism after birth, before marriage and on various other occasions. They inhabited the lower plains of Babylonia, and as a sect they go back to the first century after Christ. Palestine was perhaps the original home of this and other baptist communities. Their language, Mandaic, is a dialect of Aramaic and its script bears close resemblance to the Nabataean and Palmyrene. Mentioned thrice in the Koran, these Babylonian Ṣābians acquired a dhimmi status and were classified by

[1] Yāqūt, vol. iv, p. 1045.

[2] *The Itinerary of Rabbi Benjamin of Tudela*, tr. and ed. A. Asher, vol. i (London and Berlin, 1840), pp. 100-105.

[3] Other contemporaneous travellers make the number only three, which is more credible.

[4] Some of the Baghdād Jews might well have been the descendants of those carried into exile by Nebuchadnezzar in 597 and 586 B.C.

[5] This word is derived from Aramaic *yada'*, to know; the sect was Gnostic.

[6] Ar. *Ṣābi'ah*, or *Ṣābi'ūn*, sing. *Ṣābi'* from Mandaic (Aram.) *Ṣābī'*, immerser; no etymological connection with *Saba'*, the name of the great people in south-western Arabia.

[7] Wrongly rendered Nazarenes, i.e. Christians.

Moslems as a "protected" sect. According to the *Fihrist*[1] they included the *mughtasilah* (those who wash themselves), who occupied the marshes of lower al-'Irāq. The community still survives to the number of five thousand in the swampy lands near al-Baṣrah. Living in the neighbourhood of rivers is necessitated by the fact that immersion in flowing water is an essential, and certainly the most characteristic, feature of their religious practice. In modern Baghdād the Ṣābians are represented by the so-called 'Amārah silversmiths, makers of the *mīnā'* [2] work.

Quite distinct from these Babylonian Ṣābians were the pseudo-Ṣābians of Ḥarrān.[3] Arab writers confuse the two. The Ḥarrān Ṣābians were in reality star-worshippers who under the Moslems adopted the name "Ṣābians" to secure the advantages of toleration accorded by the Koran. This name has stuck to them ever since, and the curious sect continued to flourish close to the headquarters of the caliphate until the middle of the thirteenth century, when the Mongols destroyed their last temple. Undoubtedly the intellectual merits and scientific services of some of its illustrious men helped to gain Moslem protection.[4] Reference has already been made to Thābit ibn-Qurrah and other great Ḥarrānian astronomers. Thābit's son Sinān was forced by the Caliph al-Qāhir to embrace Islam.[5] Among other Ṣābian luminaries were abu-Isḥāq ibn-Hilāl al-Ṣābi', secretary of both al-Muṭī' (946–74) and al-Ṭā'i' (974–91); al-Battāni, the astronomer; ibn-Waḥshīyah (fl. *ca.* 900), pseudo-author of the book on Nabataean agriculture; and possibly Jābir ibn-Ḥayyān, the alchemist. The last three professed Islam.[6]

Magians and other dualists

The Zoroastrians (*Majūs*), mentioned only once in the Koran (22 : 17), could not have been included among the Scripturaries in Muḥammad's mind. But in the ḥadīth and by Moslem legists they are treated as such; the term "Ṣābians" was interpreted to cover them. Practical politics and expediency, as we learned before, made it necessary that the dhimmi status be accorded such a large body of population as that which occupied Iran. After the conquest Zoroastrianism, which was the state religion,

[1] P. 340, l. 26; Mas'ūdi, vol. ii, p. 112. [2] From Pers. *mīno*, heavenly.
[3] Mas'ūdi, vol. iv, pp. 61-71, devotes a section to them.
[4] *Fihrist*, p. 272, l. 11.
[5] *Ibid.* p. 302, quoted by ibn-abi-Uṣaybi'ah, vol. i, pp. 220-21.
[6] For more on the Ṣābians consult D. Chwolsohn, *Die Ssabier und der Ssabismus*, 2 vols. (St. Petersburg, 1856).

continued to exist and its fire-temples remained standing not only in all the Iranian provinces but in al-'Irāq, India and places east of Persia.[1] The Zoroastrians in India are still represented by the Parsis,[2] whose ancestors emigrated from Persia early in the eighth century. Zoroastrianism yielded a number of distinguished converts to Islam, the earliest among whom was ibn-al-Muqaffa'. Certain phases of early Islamic theology were either a reaction against dualism or an imitation of its attitudes.

The Manichaeans, at first mistaken by the Moslems for Christians or Zoroastrians, obtained later the status of a tolerated community. The Persian Mani († A.D. 273 or 274) and his teaching seem to have held a special fascination for the followers of Muḥammad, for we see that both al-Mahdi and al-Hādi issued strict measures against the tendency in that direction. Even the last Umayyad caliph, whose tutor was put to death as a *zindīq*, was suspected of Manichaeism.[3] In 780 al-Mahdi crucified a number of crypto-Manichaeans in Aleppo,[4] and during the last two years of his reign instituted an inquisition against them in Baghdād.[5] Al-Hādi continued the persecution begun by his predecessor.[6] Al-Rashīd likewise appointed a special officer to conduct an inquisition against such dualists.[7] But many Manichaeans and even communistic Mazdakites[8] seem to have survived. And although the Koran[9] entitles idol worshippers to no consideration, practical Islam connived at minor communities in Northern Africa and Central Asia which were too insignificant to attract public attention, and found it impossible to exterminate paganism in India.

The Islamization of the empire

The so-called "Moslem conquests" which were effected mainly under the orthodox caliphs were in reality, as noted

[1] Mas'ūdi, vol. iv, p. 86.

[2] Name derived from Pārs (Fārs), modern Fāris. See above, p. 157, n. 2.

[3] *Fihrist*, pp. 337-8. Early Arab writers applied the term *zindīq* (from Pahlawi *zandīk*) to any Moslem whose religious ideas partook of the dogmatic conceptions of the Persians in general and the Manichaeans in particular. In later usage *zindīq* came to mean any person with liberal views, a free-thinker. Cf. E. G. Browne, *A Literary History of Persia*, vol. i (New York, 1902), pp. 159-60. Cf. above, p. 84, n. 2.

[4] Ṭabari, vol. iii, p. 499.

[5] *Ibid.* pp. 519-20, 588.

[6] *Ibid.* pp. 548-51.

[7] Arabic sources including *Fihrist*, pp. 327 *seq.*, Shahrastāni, pp. 188 *seq.*, and Ya'qūbi, vol. i, pp. 180-82, are among the oldest and best we have on Manichaeism. For a modern treatment consult A. V. Williams Jackson, *Researches in Manichaeism* (New York, 1932).

[8] See Ṭabari, vol. i, pp. 885-6, 897; Shahrastāni, pp. 192 *seq.*; Browne, vol. i, pp. 166-72.

[9] Sūrs. 4 : 116-20, 21 : 98-100, 66 : 9.

before, the conquest of Arab arms and Arab nationals. They netted the military and political subjugation of Persia, the Fertile Crescent and north-eastern Africa. During the first century of 'Abbāsid rule the conquests entered upon their second stage, the victory of Islam as a religion. It was in the course of this stage that the bulk of the population of the empire was converted to the new religion. Many conversions were, to be sure, concurrent with the early military conquests, but such a country as Syria continued to present the aspect of a Christian land throughout the whole Umayyad period. The situation now, however, began perceptibly to change. The intolerant legislation of al-Rashīd and al-Mutawakkil undoubtedly contributed its quota of fresh converts. Cases of individual and collective forcible conversion added to their numbers; five thousand of the Christian banu-Tanūkh whom al-Mahdi saw near Aleppo responded to his orders and embraced Islam.[1] But the process of conversion in its normal working was more gradual and peaceful, though also inescapable. Self-interest dictated it. To escape the payment of the humiliating tribute and other disabilities, to secure social prestige or political influence, to enjoy a larger measure of freedom and security, these were the strong motives in operation.

Persia remained unconverted to Islam until well into the third century after its inclusion in the Arab empire. It counts among its population today some 9000 Zoroastrians. The population of northern al-'Irāq early in the tenth century was still, in the opinion of ibn-al-Faqīh,[2] "Moslem in name but Christian in character". Mt. Lebanon has maintained until the present day a Christian majority. Egypt, which had embraced Christianity but very lightly in the fourth century, proved one of the easiest countries to Islamize. Its Copts today form but a small minority. The Nubian kingdom, which had been Christianized in the middle of the sixth century, was still Christian in the twelfth century[3] and even in the latter part of the fourteenth.[4] The conversion to Islam of the Berbers and North Africans, whose

[1] Ibn-al-'Ibri, *Chronicon Syriacum*, ed. and tr. P. J. Bruns and G. G. Kirsch (Leipzig, 1789), vol. ii (text), p. 133=vol. i, pp. 134-5.

[2] *Buldān*, p. 315, l. 9.

[3] Al-Idrīsi, *Ṣifat al-Maghrib*, ed. and tr. R. Dozy and M. J. de Goeje (Leyden, 1864–66), p. 27 (text) = p. 32 (tr.).

[4] Ibn-Baṭṭūṭah, vol.i v, pp. 396.

church, as we have before noted, had produced several illustrious champions of Christian orthodoxy, was begun with no marked success by 'Uqbah after the founding of al-Qayrawān in 670 as a permanent base of military operation and centre of Islamic influence. It was carried out in the following century according to a new plan of enlisting the Berbers in the Moslem army and thus winning them over by the new prospects of booty. The Berbers formed the nucleus of the armed forces which completed the conquest of West Africa and effected the subjugation of Spain. But even in their case we find three centuries after the Arab conquest some forty bishoprics left[1] of the church which once comprised five hundred. Here the final triumph of Islam was not achieved till the twelfth century, though certain Kabyls (from Ar. *qabā'il*, tribes) of Algeria had the Andalusian Moors, driven out after the fall of Granada in 1492, to thank for their conversion.

The conquest of Arabic

The third stage in the series of conquests was the linguistic one: the victory of the Arabic tongue over the native languages of the subjugated peoples. This was the latest and slowest. It was in this field of struggle that the subject races presented the greatest measure of resistance. They proved, as is often the case, more ready to give up their political and even religious loyalties than their linguistic ones. The complete victory of Arabic as the language of common usage was not assured until the latter part of the 'Abbāsid period. In Persia Arabic became for some time after the military conquest the language of learning and society, but it never succeeded in displacing permanently the Iranian speech. In al-'Irāq and Syria the transition from one Semitic tongue, the Aramaic, to another, the Arabic, was of course easier. In the out-of-the-way places, however, such as the Lebanons with their preponderant Christian population, the native Syriac put up a desperate fight and has lingered until modern times. Indeed Syriac is still spoken in Ma'lūla and two other villages in Anti-Lebanon. With its disappearance Aramaic has left in the colloquial Arabic unmistakable traces noticeable in vocabulary, accent and grammatical structure.[2]

Arabic as the language of learning, it should be noted, won

[1] De Mas Latrie, *Relations et commerce de l'Afrique septentrionale* (Paris, 1886), pp. 27-8; Arnold, *Preaching*, pp. 126 *seq.*

[2] Hitti, *al-Lughāt al-Sāmīyah* (Beirūt, 1922), pp. 30-46.

its day before Arabic as the vernacular. In the preceding chapter we have seen how fresh streams of thought from Byzantium, Persia and India resulted in a new concentration of culture in the 800's in Baghdād, al-Baṣrah and al-Kūfah, comparable only to that of Alexandria in earlier times, and rendered Arabic, never used before for scientific purposes, the vehicle of the Moslem civilization. We shall now proceed to trace that cultural movement.

CHAPTER XXVII

SCIENTIFIC AND LITERARY PROGRESS

THE epoch of translation (*ca.* 750–850), discussed in a previous chapter (XXIV), was followed by one of creative activity; for the Arabs not only assimilated the ancient lore of Persia and the classical heritage of Greece but adapted both to their own peculiar needs and ways of thinking. In medicine and philosophy their independent work was less conspicuous than in alchemy, astronomy, mathematics and geography. In law, theology, philology and linguistics as Arabs and Moslems they carried on original thinking and research. Their translations, transmuted in no small degree by the Arab mind during the course of several centuries, were transmitted, together with many new contributions, to Europe through Syria, Spain and Sicily and laid the basis of that canon of knowledge which dominated medieval European thought. And transmission, from the standpoint of the history of culture, is no less essential than origination, for had the researches of Aristotle, Galen and Ptolemy been lost to posterity the world would have been as poor as if they had never been produced.

Medicine

The line of demarcation between translated and original work is not always clearly drawn. Many of the translators were also contributors. Such was the case with Yūḥanna ibn-Māsawayh (777–857) and Ḥunayn ibn-Isḥāq (809–73). The former, a Christian physician and pupil of Jibrīl ibn-Bakhtīshū‘, failing to obtain human subjects for dissection, a practice which was never encouraged by Islam, had recourse to apes, one of which came from Nubia in 836 as a present to al-Mu‘taṣim.[1] Under these conditions little progress was made in the science of anatomy, except possibly in studying the anatomical structure of the eye. The prevalence of eye diseases in the sunny climate of al-‘Irāq and other Moslem lands concentrated early medical attention on this subject. From the pen of ibn-Māsawayh we

[1] Ibn-abi-Uṣaybi‘ah, vol. i, p. 178.

have the oldest systematic treatise on ophthalmology extant in Arabic.[1] A book entitled *al-'Ashr Maqālāt fi al-'Ayn* (the ten treatises on the eye) and ascribed to his pupil Ḥunayn ibn-Isḥāq has recently been published with an English translation[2] as the earliest existing text-book of ophthalmology.

Arab interest in the curative science found expression in the Prophetic tradition that made science twofold: theology and medicine The physician was at the same time metaphysician, philosopher and sage, and the title *ḥakīm* was indifferently applied to him in all these capacities. The case of the Nestorian Jibrīl ibn-Bakhtīshū' († *ca.* 830), who was court physician of al-Rashīd, al-Ma'mūn and the Barmakids and is said to have amassed a fortune of 88,800,000 dirhams,[3] shows that the medical profession was a paying one. As private physician of al-Rashīd Jibrīl received, we are told, 100,000 dirhams for bleeding the caliph twice a year and an equal sum for administering a semi-annual purgative draught. The Bakhtīshū' family produced six or seven generations of distinguished physicians, the last of whom flourished in the second half of the eleventh century.

In the curative use of drugs some remarkable advances were made at this time by the Arabs. It was they who established the first apothecary shops, founded the earliest school of pharmacy and produced the first pharmacopœia. Several pharmacological treatises were composed, beginning with those of the world-famed Jābir ibn-Ḥayyān, the father of Arabic alchemy, who flourished about 776. As early as the days of al-Ma'mūn and al-Mu'taṣim pharmacists had to pass some kind of examination.[4] Like druggists, physicians also were required to submit to a test. Following a case of malpractice Sinān ibn-Thābit ibn-Qurrah was ordered by al-Muqtadir in 931 to examine all practising physicians and grant certificates (sing. *ijāzah*) only to those who satisfied him. Over eight hundred and sixty such men in Baghdād passed the test and the capital rid itself of its quacks.[5] On the orders of al-Muqtadir's virtuous vizir 'Ali ibn-'Īsa, Sinān organized a staff of physicians who would go from place to

[1] *Daghal al-'Ayn* (the disorder of the eye), MS.; one copy is in Taymūr Pasha's library, Cairo, another in Leningrad.

[2] By Max Meyerhof (Cairo, 1928).

[3] Qifṭi, p. 143.

[4] *Ibid.* pp. 188-9.

[5] Ibn-abi-Uṣaybi'ah, vol. i, p. 222; Qifṭi, p. 191.

place carrying drugs and administering relief to ailing people. Other physicians made daily visits to jails.[1] Such facts show an intelligent interest in public hygiene unknown to the rest of the world at that time. In his efforts to raise the scientific standard of the medical profession and in his efficient administration of the Baghdād hospital lay Sinān's chief title to fame. This hospital, the first in Islam, was created by Hārūn al-Rashīd at the beginning of the ninth century, following the Persian model, as the Arabic name *bīmāristān*[2] indicates. Not long afterwards other hospitals to the number of thirty-four grew up throughout the Moslem world. Cairo saw its first hospital under ibn-Ṭūlūn[3] about 872, an institution which survived until the fifteenth century. Travelling clinics made their appearance in the eleventh century. Moslem hospitals had special wards for women and each had its own dispensary. Some were equipped with medical libraries and offered courses in medicine.

'Ali al-Ṭabari

The most notable medical authors who followed the epoch of the great translators were Persian in nationality but Arab in language: 'Ali al-Ṭabari, al-Rāzi, 'Ali ibn-al-'Abbās al-Majūsi and ibn-Sīna. The portraits of two of these, al-Rāzi and ibn-Sīna, adorn the great hall of the School of Medicine at the University of Paris.

'Ali ibn-Sahl Rabban al-Ṭabari, who flourished in the middle of the ninth century, was originally a Christian from Ṭabaristān, as he tells us in his *Kitāb al-Dīn* and as his father's name indicates.[4] In the reign of al-Mutawakkil he turned Moslem and became a physician to the caliph himself, under whom he produced in 850 his *Firdaws al-Ḥikmah* (paradise of wisdom), one of the oldest Arabic compendiums of medicine. This work includes to some extent philosophy and astronomy and is based on Greek and Hindu sources. After 'Ali the distinguished theologian-philosopher and physician al-Rāzi flourished.

Al-Rāzi

Abu-Bakr Muḥammad ibn-Zakarīyā' al-Rāzi (Rhazes, 865–925), so called after the place of his birth, al-Rayy, not far from Ṭihrān, the capital of modern Persia, was probably "the greatest

[1] Ibn-abi-Uṣaybi'ah, vol. i, p. 221; Qifṭi, pp. 193-4.

[2] Pers. *bīmār*, sick + *stān*, place of.

[3] Ibn-Duqmāq, pt. iv, p. 99.

[4] Pp. 124-5 = *Book of Religion*, p. 147. See also *Fihrist*, p. 296; cf. ibn-Khallikān, vol. ii, p. 503, l. 25. "Rabban" in his father's name, which made scholars think that he was of Jewish origin, is obviously Syriac for "our master", as 'Ali explains in his introduction to *Firdaws al-Ḥikmah fi al-Ṭibb*, ed. Muḥammad Z. Ṣiddīqi (Berlin, 1928).

and most original of all the Muslim physicians, and one of the most prolific as an author".[1] In selecting a new site for the great hospital[2] at Baghdād, of which he was chief physician, he is said to have hung up shreds of meat in different places, choosing the spot where they showed the least signs of putrefaction.[3] He is also considered the inventor of the seton in surgery. The *Fihrist*[4] lists one hundred and thirteen major and twenty-eight minor works by al-Rāzi, of which twelve deal with alchemy. One of his principal works on alchemy, the *Kitāb al-Asrār* (the book of secrets), after having passed through numerous editorial hands was rendered into Latin by the eminent translator Gerard of Cremona († 1187) and became a chief source of chemical knowledge until superseded in the fourteenth century by Jābir's (Geber's) works. Under the title *De spiritibus et corporibus* it was quoted by Roger Bacon. While still in Persia al-Rāzi wrote for Manṣūr ibn-Isḥāq al-Sāmāni of Sijistān a monumental work in ten volumes, named after his patron *Kitāb al-Ṭibb al-Manṣūri*, of which a Latin translation (*Liber Almansoris*) was first published in Milan in the eighties of the fifteenth century. Parts of it have been recently done into French and German. Of his monographs one of the best known is a treatise on smallpox and measles (*al-Judari w-al-Ḥaṣbah*), the earliest of its kind and rightly considered an ornament to the medical literature of the Arabs. In it we find the first clinical account of smallpox.[5]

Translated into Latin in Venice (1565) and later into several modern languages, this treatise served to establish al-Rāzi's reputation as one of the keenest original thinkers and greatest clinicians not only of Islam but of the Middle Ages. His most important work, however, was *al-Ḥāwi* (the comprehensive book), first translated into Latin under the auspices of Charles I of Anjou by the Sicilian Jewish physician Faraj ben-Sālim in 1279. Under the title *Continens* it was repeatedly printed from 1486 onwards, a fifth edition appearing in Venice in 1542. As the name indicates, this book was meant to be encyclopædic in its range of medical information. It sums up the knowledge the

[1] Edward G. Browne, *Arabian Medicine* (Cambridge, 1921), p. 44.

[2] Wrongly referred to by later writers as "al-'Aḍudi", after the Buwayhid ruler 'Aḍud-al-Dawlah, who established on its site his own hospital.

[3] Ibn-abi-Uṣaybi'ah, vol. i, pp. 309-10.

[4] Pp. 299-302.

[5] Ed. Cornelius Van Dyck (London, 1866, and Beirūt, 1872); tr. W. A. Greenhill, *A Treatise on the Small-Pox and Measles* (London, 1848).

Arabs possessed at that time of Greek, Persian and Hindu medicine and adds some fresh contributions. Printed when printing was still in its infancy, these medical works of al-Rāzi exercised for centuries a remarkable influence over the minds of the Latin West.

Al-Majūsi

'Ali ibn-al-'Abbās (Haly Abbas, † 994), originally a Zoroastrian as his last name, al-Majūsi (the Magian), indicates, distinguished himself as the author of *al-Kitāb al-Maliki* (the royal book, *Liber regius*), which he composed for the great Buwayhid 'Aḍud-al-Dawlah Fanna Khusraw, who reigned 949–83.[1] This work, also called *Kāmil al-Ṣinā'ah al-Ṭibbīyah*, a "noble thesaurus comprehending the science and practice of Medicine",[2] was more concise than *al-Ḥāwi* and was diligently studied until superseded by ibn-Sīna's *al-Qānūn*. The best parts of *al-Maliki* are devoted to dietetics and materia medica. Among its original contributions are a rudimentary conception of the capillary system and a proof that in the act of parturition the child does not come out by itself but is pushed out by the muscular contractions of the womb.

Ibn-Sīna

The most illustrious name in Arabic medical annals after al-Rāzi's is that of ibn-Sīna (Latin Avicenna, through Heb. Aven Sīna, 980–1037), called by the Arabs *al-shaykh al-ra'īs*, "the sheikh" (of the learned) and "prince" (of the courtiers).[3] Al-Rāzi was more of a physician than ibn-Sīna, but ibn-Sīna was more of a philosopher. In this physician, philosopher and poet Arab science culminates and is, one might say, incarnated.

Abu-'Ali al-Ḥusayn, to use his first name, was the son of an Ismā'īli, 'Abdullāh. Born near Bukhāra, he spent all his life in the eastern part of the Moslem world and was buried in Hamadhān, where his grave is still shown. As a young man he had the good fortune to cure the Sāmānid sultan of Bukhāra, Nūḥ ibn-Manṣūr (reigned 976–97), and was therefore given the privilege of using the ruler's remarkable library. Endowed with extraordinary powers of absorbing and retaining knowledge, this Moslem Persian scholar devoured the contents of the royal library and at the early age of twenty-one was in a position to embark on his career of writing. This included the systematizing

[1] Ibn-abi-Uṣaybi'ah, vol. i, pp. 236-7; Qifṭi, p. 232.

[2] Qifṭi, p. 232. For a complete MS. copy dated 586 (A.D. 1190) see Hitti, Faris and 'Abd-al-Malik, *Catalog of Arabic Manuscripts*, supp. no. 1.

[3] Also called *al-mu'allim al-thāni*, the second teacher (after Aristotle).

of the knowledge of his time. Al-Qifṭi[1] lists only forty-five works of ibn-Sīna; but a modern bibliographer lists under his name over two hundred titles, dealing with philosophy, medicine, geometry, astronomy, theology, philology and art. Of these his best-known poetical production is a lengthy ode describing "the descent of the soul into the body from the higher sphere" and is still memorized by young students in the Arabic East. Among his scientific works the leading two are the *Kitāb al-Shifā'* (book of healing), a philosophical encyclopædia based upon the Aristotelian tradition as modified by Neo-Platonic influences and Moslem theology, and *al-Qānūn fi al-Ṭibb*, which represents the final codification of Greco-Arabic medical thought. The Arabic text of the *Qānūn* was published in Rome in 1593 and was therefore one of the earliest Arabic books to see print.[2] Translated into Latin by Gerard of Cremona in the twelfth century, this *Canon*, with its encyclopædic contents, its systematic arrangement and philosophic plan, soon worked its way into a position of pre-eminence in the medical literature of the age, displacing the works of Galen, al-Rāzi and al-Majūsi and becoming the text-book for medical education in the schools of Europe. In the last thirty years of the fifteenth century it passed through fifteen Latin editions and one Hebrew. In recent years a partial translation into English was made.[3] The book distinguishes mediastinitis from pleurisy and recognizes the contagious nature of phthisis and the spreading of diseases by water and soil. It gives a scientific diagnosis of ankylostomiasis and attributes it to an intestinal worm. Its materia medica considers some seven hundred and sixty drugs. From the twelfth to the seventeenth centuries this work served as the chief guide to medical science in the West and it is still in occasional use in the Moslem East. In the words of Dr. Osler[4] it has remained "a medical bible for a longer period than any other work".

Among the lesser lights in the medical firmament mention may be made of 'Ali ibn-'Īsa (Jesu Haly), the most famous

[1] P. 418. Cf. ibn-abi-Uṣaybi'ah, vol. ii, pp. 18-20; ibn-Khallikān, vol. i, pp. 273-4; Carl Brockelmann, *Geschichte der arabischen Litteratur*, vol. i (Weimar, 1898), pp. 453-8.

[2] The first edition of a compendium of *al-Shifā'* appeared as a supplement to this work.

[3] O. Cameron Gruner, *A Treatise on the Canon of Medicine of Avicenna* (London, 1930).

[4] William Osler, *The Evolution of Modern Medicine* (New Haven, 1922), p. 98.

oculist (*kaḥḥāl*) of the Arabs. 'Ali, a Christian, flourished in Baghdād in the first half of the eleventh century, a century and a half after the court physician of al-Mu'tamid, whose name, 'Īsa ibn-'Ali,[1] is often confused with his. Of the thirty-two medieval Arabic works on ophthalmology his *Tadhkirat al-Kaḥḥālīn*[2] (a note for oculists), which has survived in its complete and original form, is one of the oldest and worthiest. Only the two treatises by ibn-Māsawayh and Ḥunayn ibn-Isḥāq antedate it. The *Tadhkirah* carefully describes one hundred and thirty eye diseases. It was done once into Hebrew and twice into Latin and is still in use in the East.

Another physician of the second class was ibn-Jazlah (Bengesla, Byngezla, † 1100), originally a Christian,[3] who wrote a medical synopsis entitled *Taqwīm al-Abdān fi Tadbīr al-Insān* (tables of the body with regard to the physical management of man) modelled on the *Taqwīm al-Ṣiḥḥah* by another Christian physician, ibn-Buṭlān,[4] who died in Antioch about 1063. In a *Taqwīm* diseases are arranged as are the stars in astronomical tables. Ibn-Jazlah's work was translated into Latin at Strassburg in 1532. The last physician to be mentioned in this series is Ya'qūb ibn-akhi-Ḥizām, the stable-master of al-Mu'taḍid (892–902), who composed a treatise on horsemanship (*al-Furūsīyah wa-Shiyāt al-Khayl*) which is the first Arabic work of its kind. It contains some rudiments of the veterinary art and has survived in a manuscript now preserved in the British Museum.[5]

Philosophy

To the Arabs philosophy (*falsafah*) was a knowledge of the true cause of things as they really are, in so far as it is possible to ascertain them by human faculties. In essence their philosophy was Greek, modified by the thought of the conquered peoples and by other Eastern influences, adapted to the mental proclivities of Islam and expressed through the medium of Arabic. These Arabs believed Aristotle's works to have represented a complete codification of Greek philosophical lore, as Galen's represented Greek medical lore. Greek philosophy and medicine meant then,

[1] *Fihrist*, p. 297; ibn-abi-Uṣaybi'ah, vol. i, p. 203.

[2] Ibn-abi-Uṣaybi'ah, vol. i, p. 247. Translated, not from the original Arabic, by Casey A. Wood, *The Tadhkirat of Ali ibn Isa* (Chicago, 1936).

[3] *Ibid.* vol. i, p. 255; Qifṭi, p. 365; ibn-Khallikān, vol. iii, p. 255.

[4] Hitti, *Arab-Syrian Gentleman*, pp. 214-16; ibn-abi-Uṣaybi'ah, vol. i, pp. 241 *seq.*; Qifṭi, pp. 294 *seq.*

[5] *Fihrist*, p. 315, mentions an ibn-akhi-Ḥizām, perhaps a son of Ya'qūb.

of course, all that the West possessed. As Moslems the Arabs believed that the Koran and Islamic theology were the summation of religious law and experience. Their original contribution, therefore, was made in the borderland between philosophy and religion on one hand and philosophy and medicine on the other. In course of time Arab authors came to apply the word *falāsifah* or *ḥukamā'* (philosophers or sages) to those philosophers among them whose speculations were not limited by religion, reserving the term *mutakallimūn* or *ahl al-kalām* (speech-makers, dialecticians) for those whose system was conditioned by subordination to revealed religion. The *mutakallimūn*, who corresponded to the scholastic writers of Christian Europe, set forth their theories in the form of propositions and were therefore called by that title. *Kalām* came slowly to mean theology and *mutakallim* became a synonym for theologian. Al-Ghazzāli was primarily a theologian and will be dealt with later. The greatest names in the field of early Arab philosophy were those of al-Kindi, al-Fārābi and ibn-Sīna.

Al-Kindi

Al-Kindi, abu-Yūsuf Ya'qūb ibn-Isḥāq, was born probably in al-Kūfah about 801 and flourished in Baghdād, where he died about 873. His pure Arabian descent earned him the title "the philosopher of the Arabs", and indeed he was the first and last example of an Aristotelian student in the Eastern caliphate who sprang from Arabian stock. Eclectic in his system, al-Kindi endeavoured in Neo-Platonic fashion to combine the views of Plato and Aristotle and regarded the Neo-Pythagorean mathematics as the basis of all science. Al-Kindi was more than a philosopher. He was astrologer, alchemist, optician and music theorist. No less than three hundred and sixty-one works are ascribed to him, but most of them unhappily have been lost. His principal work on geometrical and physiological optics, based on the *Optics* of Euclid in Theon's recension, was widely used in both East and West until superseded by the greater work of ibn-al-Haytham. In its Latin translation, *De aspectibus*, it influenced Roger Bacon. Al-Kindi's three or four treatises on the theory of music are the earliest extant works in Arabic showing the influence of Greek writers on that subject. In one of these treatises al-Kindi describes rhythm (*īqā'*) as a constituent part of Arabic music. Measured song, or mensural music, must therefore have been known to the Moslems centuries before it was introduced into Christian

Europe.[1] Of al-Kindi's writings more have survived in Latin translations, including those of Gerard of Cremona, than in the Arabic original.

Al-Fārābi

The harmonization of Greek philosophy with Islam begun by al-Kindi, an Arab, was continued by al-Fārābi, a Turk, and completed in the East by ibn-Sīna, a Persian.

Muḥammad ibn-Muḥammad ibn-Ṭarkhān abu-Naṣr al-Fārābi[2] (Alpharabius) was born in Transoxiana, educated under a Christian physician and a Christian translator in Baghdād and flourished as a Sufi at Aleppo in the brilliant court of Sayf-al-Dawlah al-Ḥamdāni. He died at Damascus in 950 at the age of about eighty. His system of philosophy, as revealed by his several treatises on Plato and Aristotle, was a syncretism of Platonism, Aristotelianism and Sufism and won him the enviable title of "the second teacher" (*al-muʿallim al-thāni*), after the great Stagirite. Besides a number of commentaries on Aristotle and other Greek philosophers, al-Fārābi composed various psychological, political and metaphysical works, of which the best-known are the *Risālat Fuṣūṣ al-Ḥikam*[3] (epistle containing bezels of wisdom) and the *Risālah fi Ārā' Ahl al-Madīnah al-Fāḍilah* (epistle on the opinions of the people of the superior city).[4] In the latter and in his *al-Siyāsah* (*Siyāsāt*) *al-Madanīyah* (political regime), al-Fārābi, inspired by Plato's *Republic* and Aristotle's *Politics*, presents his conception of a model city, which he conceives as a hierarchical organism analogous to the human body. The sovereign, who corresponds to the heart, is served by functionaries who are themselves served by others still lower. In his ideal city the object of association is the happiness of its citizens, and the sovereign is perfect morally and intellectually.

Al-Fārābi's other writings reveal him as a fair physician and mathematician, an occult scientist and an excellent musician. In fact he is considered the greatest of all Arabic music theorists. Besides his treatment of music in two of his compendiums of the sciences, he devotes three major works to the subject, of which

[1] See below, p. 600.

[2] From Fārāb in Turkestan. Ibn-abi-Uṣaybiʿah, vol. ii, p. 134; Qifṭi, p. 277.

[3] Published by Friedrich Dieterici in his *Die Philosophie der Araber im IX. und X. Jahrhundert n. Chr.*, vol. xiv (Leyden, 1890), pp. 66-83.

[4] Published at Cairo, 1323, and also by Dieterici, *Philosophie der Araber*, vol. xvi (Leyden, 1895), who also translated it as *Der Musterstaat von Alfārābī* (Leyden, 1900).

the leading is the *Kitāb al-Mūsīqi al-Kabīr* (the great book of music).[1] In the presence of his patron Sayf-al-Dawlah he is said to have been able to play his lute so as to cast his hearers into a fit of laughter, draw tears from their eyes or set them all asleep, including even the doorkeepers.[2] Ancient chants attributed to him are still sung by the Mawlawi dervishes.

After al-Fārābi it was ibn-Sīna († 1037) who contributed the most important works in Arabic on the theory of music. Ibn-Sīna, already treated with the medical men, was indebted to al-Fārābi in his philosophical views. In the judgment of ibn-Khallikān[3] "no Moslem ever reached in the philosophical sciences the same rank as al-Fārābi; and it was by the study of his writings and by the imitation of his style that ibn-Sīna attained proficiency and rendered his own work so useful". It was ibn-Sīna, however, who placed the sum-total of Greek wisdom, codified by his own ingenuity, at the disposal of the educated Moslem world in an intelligible form. Through him the Greek system, particularly that of Philo, was rendered capable of incorporation with Islam.

The Brethren of Sincerity

About the middle of the fourth Moslem century (*ca.* 970) there flourished in al-Baṣrah an interesting eclectic school of popular philosophy, with leanings toward Pythagorean speculations, known as Ikhwān al-Ṣafā' (the brethren of sincerity). The appellation is presumably taken from the story of the ringdove in *Kalīlah wa-Dimnah* in which it is related that a group of animals by acting as faithful friends (*ikhwān al-ṣafā'*[4]) to one another escaped the snares of the hunter.[5]

The Ikhwān, who had a branch in Baghdād, formed not only a philosophical but also a religio-political association with ultra-Shī'ite, probably Ismā'īlite, views and were opposed to the existing political order, which they evidently aimed to overthrow by undermining the popular intellectual system and religious beliefs. Hence arises the obscurity surrounding their activities and

[1] Extracts by J. P. N. Land appeared in *Actes du sixième congrès international des orientalistes*, pt. 2, sec. 1 (Leyden, 1885), pp. 100-168. Fr. tr. by Rodolphe d'Erlanger, *La musique arabe*, vols. i, ii, *al-Fārābī* (Paris, 1930–35). Hitti, Faris and 'Abd-al-Malik, *Catalog of Arabic Manuscripts*, no. 1984.

[2] Ibn-Khallikān, vol. ii, p. 501.

[3] Vol. ii, p. 499 = de Slane, vol. iii, p. 307.

[4] From this it would appear that the usual rendition, "the brethren of purity", "les frères de la pureté", "die lauteren Brüder", is not exact.

[5] I. Goldziher in *Der Islam*, vol. i (1910), pp. 22-6.

membership. A collection of their epistles, *Rasā'il,*[1] arranged in encyclopædic fashion survives, bearing some obscure names as collaborators. The epistles number fifty-two and treat of mathematics, astronomy, geography, music, ethics, philosophy, embodying the sum-total of knowledge that a cultured man of that age was supposed to acquire. The first fifty-one epistles lead up to the last, which is a summation of all sciences. The language of the epistles shows that Arabic had by that time become an adequate instrument for expressing scientific thought in all its various aspects. Al-Ghazzāli was influenced by the Ikhwān's writings,[2] and Rāshid-al-Dīn Sinān ibn-Sulaymān, the chief of the Assassins in Syria, used them diligently.[3] When in Baghdād abu-al-'Alā' al-Ma'arri, the great Syrian poet-philosopher, attended the association's Friday meetings.[4] Abu-Ḥayyān al-Tawḥīdi († 1023[5]), the famous Mu'tazilite who with al-Rāwandi († 915) and al-Ma'arri († 1057) formed the trinity of arch-heretics in Islam,[6] was a pupil if not an active member of the fraternity.

Astronomy and mathematics

The scientific study of astronomy in Islam was begun, as we have already learned, under the influence of an Indian work, the *Siddhānta* (Ar. *Sindhind*), brought to Baghdād (771), translated by Muḥammad ibn-Ibrāhīm al-Fazāri and used as a model by later scholars. Pahlawi tables *(zīk)* compiled in the Sāsānid period were soon added in translated form *(zīj)*. Greek elements, last in order of time, were first in importance. An early translation of Ptolemy's *Almagest* was followed by two superior ones: the one by al-Ḥajjāj ibn-Maṭar completed in A.H. 212 (827–8) and the other by Ḥunayn ibn-Isḥāq revised by Thābit ibn-Qurrah († 901). Early in the ninth century the first regular observations *(raṣd)* with fairly accurate instruments were made in Jundaysābūr (south-west Persia). In connection with his Bayt al-Ḥikmah, al-Ma'mūn erected at Baghdād near the Shammāsīyah gate an astronomical observatory under the directorship

[1] Dieterici issued and translated a great part of the text in his *Die Philosophie der Araber*, 16 vols. (Leipzig and Leyden, 1858–1895). The last Oriental edition is that of Khayr-al-Dīn al-Zirikli, 4 vols. (Cairo, 1928).

[2] Cf. *Iḥyā'*, vol. ii, p. 254, ll. 8-12, p. 262, ll. 18-20, with *Rasā'il*, vol. i, p. 180.

[3] M. C. Defrémery in *Journal asiatique*, ser. 5, vol. v (1855), pp. 5-6.

[4] Consult his *Dīwān: Siqṭ al-Zand*, ed. Shākir Shuqayr (Beirūt, 1884), p. 112, l. 15, p. 104, ll. 4-5.

[5] Cf. ibn-Khallikān, vol. ii, p. 470; Yāqūt, *Udabā'*, vol. v, p. 381.

[6] Al-Subki, *Ṭabaqāt al-Shāfi'īyah al-Kubra* (Cairo, 1906), vol. iv, p. 3.

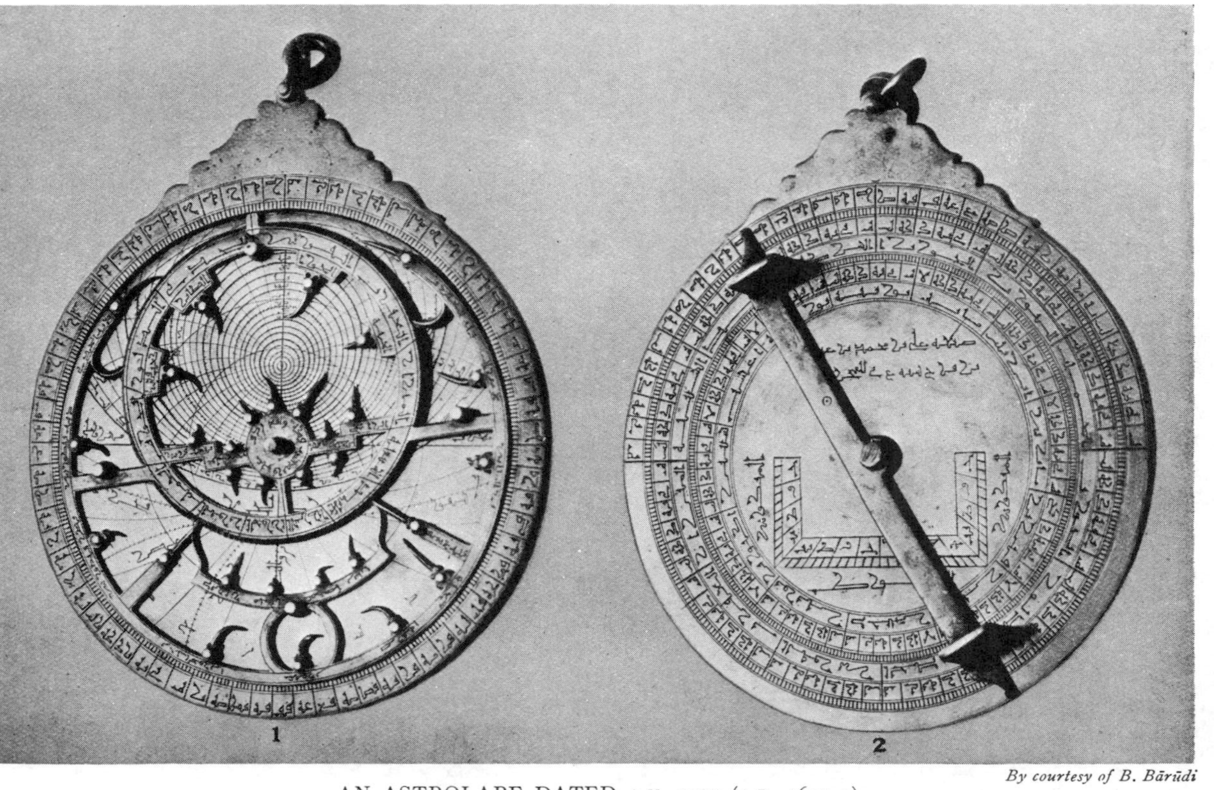

By courtesy of B. Bārūdi

AN ASTROLABE DATED A.H. 1010 (A.D. 1601–2)

of a converted Jew, Sind ibn-'Ali, and Yaḥya ibn-abi-Manṣūr († 830 or 831).[1] Here the caliph's astronomers "not only made systematic observation of the celestial movements, but also verified with remarkably precise results all the fundamental elements of the *Almagest*: the obliquity of the ecliptic, the precession of the equinoxes, the length of the solar year, etc."[2] To this observatory al-Ma'mūn soon added another on Mt. Qāsiyūn outside of Damascus.[3] The equipment in those days consisted of quadrant, astrolabe, dial and globes. Ibrāhīm al-Fazāri († *ca.* 777) was the first Moslem to construct an astrolabe,[4] undoubtedly on the Greek model, as the Arabic name (*asṭurlāb*) indicates. One of the earliest Arabic treatises on this instrument was written by 'Ali ibn-'Īsa al-Asṭurlābi (maker of astrolabes), who flourished in Baghdād and Damascus before 830.

Al-Ma'mūn's astronomers performed one of the most delicate geodetic operations—the measuring of the length of a terrestrial degree. The object was to determine the size of the earth and its circumference on the assumption that the earth was round. The measurement, carried out on the plain of Sinjār north of the Euphrates and also near Palmyra, yielded $56\frac{2}{3}$ Arabic miles as the length of a degree of the meridian—a remarkably accurate result, exceeding the real length of the degree at that place by about 2877 feet.[5] This would make the circumference of the earth 20,400 miles and its diameter 6500. Among those who took part in this operation were the sons of Mūsa ibn-Shākir and perhaps al-Khwārizmi, whose tables (*zīj*), revised a century and a half later by the Spanish astronomer Maslamah al-Majrīṭi († *ca.* 1007) and translated into Latin in 1126 by Adelard of Bath, became the bases for other works both in the East and the West. Such Arab astronomical tables replaced all their Greek and Indian predecessors and came to be used even in China.

Another eminent astronomer of the period was abu-al-'Abbās Aḥmad[6] al-Farghāni (Alfraganus), of Farghānah in Transoxiana, who in 861 superintended for al-Mutawakkil the erection of a Nilometer at al-Fusṭāṭ.[7] Al-Farghāni's principal work, *al-Mud-*

[1] *Fihrist*, p. 275.
[2] C. A. Nallino, art. "Astronomy", *Encyclopædia of Islām*. Cf. Ṣā'id, *Ṭabaqāt*, pp. 50-51. [3] Ibn-al-'Ibri, p. 237. [4] *Fihrist*, p. 273.
[5] Nallino, *'Ilm al-Falak* (Cairo, 1911), pp. 281 *seq.* Ar. *falak* (celestial sphere) may be Babylonian, pp. 105-6.
[6] "Muḥammad" in *Fihrist*, p. 279; followed by Qifṭi, p. 286.
[7] Ibn-abi-Uṣaybi'ah, vol. i, p. 207.

khil ila 'Ilm Ha'yat al-Aflāk,[1] was done into Latin in 1135 by John of Seville and Gerard of Cremona, and also into Hebrew. In Arabic it has survived under different titles.[2]

Besides the Ma'mūni observatory, one was operated by the three sons of Mūsa ibn-Shākir (850–70) in their house at Baghdād. The Buwayhid Sultan Sharaf-al-Dawlah (982–9) instituted another in his Baghdād palace, where 'Abd-al-Raḥmān al-Ṣūfi († 986), whose *al-Kawākib al-Thābitah* (fixed stars) is a masterpiece of observational astronomy, Aḥmad al-Ṣāghāni († 990) and abu-al-Wafā' († 997) [3] worked. In the court of another Buwayhid, Rukn-al-Dawlah (932–76) of al-Rayy, flourished abu-Ja'far al-Khāzin of Khurāsān,[4] who ascertained the obliquity of the eclipitic and solved a problem in Archimedes which leads to a cubic equation. Other astronomers made a systematic study of the heavens in Shīrāz, Naysābūr and Samarqand.

Al-Battāni

Between 877 and 918 abu-'Abdullāh Muḥammad ibn-Jābir al-Battāni[1] (Albategnius), originally a Ṣābian from Ḥarrān and unquestionably the greatest astronomer of his nationality and time and one of the greatest in Islam, made his observations and studies in al-Raqqah. Al-Battāni was an original research worker. He made several emendations to Ptolemy and rectified the calculations for the orbits of the moon and certain planets. He proved the possibility of annular eclipses of the sun, determined with greater accuracy the obliquity of the ecliptic and presented original theories on the determination of the visibility of the new moon.[6]

Al-Bīrūni

At Ghaznah, Afghanistan, lived abu-al-Rayḥān Muḥammad ibn-Aḥmad al-Bīrūni [7] (973–1050), considered the most original and profound scholar Islam produced in the domain of natural science. Here this Arabic author of Persian origin, who spoke Turkish and knew besides Persian Sanskrit, Hebrew and Syriac, produced in 1030 for his patron Mas'ūd, son of the famous Maḥmūd, an account of the science of astronomy entitled *al-*

[1] Ibn-al-'Ibri, p. 236; Qifṭi, p. 78.

[2] See Hitti, Faris and 'Abd-al-Malik, *Catalog of Arabic Manuscripts*, no. 967.

[3] *Fihrist*, p. 283; ibn-al-Athīr, vol. ix, p. 97; ibn-Khallikān, vol. ii, pp. 508-9.

[4] Qifṭi, p. 396; *Fihrist*, pp. 266, 282.

[5] *Fihrist*, p. 279.

[6] His astronomical work *al-Zīj al-Ṣābi'* was edited by C. A. Nallino (Rome, 1899).

[7] Ibn-abi-Uṣaybi'ah, vol. ii, pp. 20-21; ibn-al-'Ibri, pp. 324-5. His surname is derived from Bīrūn (Pers. for outside), a suburb of Kāth, capital of Khwārizm, though an autograph on a manuscript title-page reproduced in *Islamic Culture*, vol. vi (1932), facing p. 534, spells "al-Bayrūni".

Qānūn al-Mas'ūdi fi al-Hay'ah w-al-Nujūm. In the same year he composed a short catechism of geometry, arithmetic, astronomy and astrology entitled *al-Tafhīm li-Awā'il Ṣinā'at al-Tanjīm*. His first work was *al-Āthār al-Bāqiyah 'an al-Qurūn al-Khāliyah*,[1] dealing chiefly with the calendars and eras of ancient peoples. In these works al-Bīrūni discusses intelligently the then debatable theory of the earth's rotation on its axis and makes accurate determination of latitudes and longitudes. Al-Bīrūni, who was a Shī'ite with agnostic leanings, sojourned in India[2] and was charmed by Hindu philosophy. Among his scientific contributions are an explanation of the working of natural springs by the hydrostatic principle, the suggestion that the Indus valley must have been an ancient sea basin filled up with alluvium, and the description of several monstrosities, including what we call Siamese twins.[3]

'Umar al-Khayyām

Of the Saljūq sultans, Jalāl-al-Dīn Malikshāh patronized astronomical studies. He established in 467 (1074–5) at al-Rayy or at Naysābūr an observatory where there was introduced into the civil calendar an important reform based on an accurate determination of the length of the tropical year. To this task of reforming the old Persian calendar he called to his new observatory the celebrated 'Umar al-Khayyām.[4] Born between 1038 and 1048 at Naysābūr, where he died in 1123–4, 'Umar is known to the world primarily as a Persian poet[5] and free-thinker; very few realize that he was a first-class mathematician and astronomer as well. The researches of al-Khayyām and his collaborators resulted in the production of the calendar named after his patron *al-Ta'rīkh al-Jalāli*, which is even more accurate than the Gregorian calendar. The latter leads to an error of one day in 3330 years, whereas al-Khayyām's apparently leads to an error of one day in about 5000 years.

One year after he had destroyed Baghdād, Hūlāgu commenced (1259) the construction near Lake Urmiyah of the great

[1] Ed. E. Sachau (Leipzig, 1878); tr. Sachau (London, 1879).

[2] See his account *Taḥqīq Ma li-al-Hind*, ed. E. Sachau (London, 1887); tr. Sachau (London, 1888), 2 vols. (reprinted London, 1910).

[3] In a still unpublished work of his the first reference to tea in other than Chinese works occurs; F. Krenkow in *Majallat al-Majma'*, vol. xiii (1935), p. 388.

[4] Full Arabic name abu-al-Fatḥ 'Umar ibn-Ibrāhīm al-Khayyāmi (the tent-maker). On his life see Qifṭi, pp. 243-4; Qazwīni, *Āthār*, p. 318.

[5] His *Rubā'īyāt* (quatrains), done first into English by FitzGerald (London, 1859), have since appeared in French, German, Italian, Danish and Arabic translations.

Marāghah observatory, whose first director was the illustrious Naṣīr-al-Dīn al-Ṭūsi[1] († 1274), the last of 'Abbāsid astronomer-philosophers. The instruments at this observatory were much admired and included an armillary sphere, a mural quadrant and a solstitial armil. In this observatory Naṣīr-al-Dīn compiled new astronomical tables called *al-Zīj al-Īl-Khāni* in honour of Hūlāgu, the first Īl-Khān.[2] The tables became popular throughout Asia, even in China. The foundations of this short-lived observatory are still extant. Close by it stood a library, also built by Hūlāgu, and said to have contained 400,000 volumes (?). Most of these books were pillaged by the Mongol armies from Syria, al-'Irāq and Persia.

Astrology

In astrology, a handmaid of astronomy, abu-Ma'shar († 886), a native of Balkh in Khurāsān who flourished at Baghdād, was the most distinguished figure.[3] He is the one most frequently cited as an authority in the Christian Middle Ages and under the name Albumasar figured as a prophet in the iconography. Four of his works were translated into Latin in the twelfth century by John of Seville and Adelard of Bath. Apart from his fantastic belief in astral influence as the cause of the birth, events of life and death of everything, abu-Ma'shar communicated to Europe the laws of the tides, which in a treatise he explained on the basis of the relation to the moon's rising and setting.

Several of the Moslem works on astronomy were translated in course of time into Latin, especially in Spain, and exercised a determining influence on the development of the science in Christian Europe.

The Arabic numerals

The same Hindu scholar who brought to the court of al-Manṣūr the astronomical work *Sindhind* is credited with having also introduced Hindu arithmetical lore with its numeral system (called in Arabic *Hindi*) and the zero.[4] Al-Fazāri's translation of

[1] Ibn-al-'Ibri, p. 500; Rashīd-al-Dīn Faḍl-Allāh, *Jāmi' al-Tawārīkh*, ed. and tr. by Quatremère as *Histoire des Mongols de la Perse*, vol. i (Paris, 1836), pp. 324 *seq.* (where the name occurs as Naṣīr-al-Dīn).

[2] See below, p. 488, n. 1. [3] *Fihrist*, p. 277; ibn-Khallikān, vol. i, pp. 198-9.

[4] G. Cœdès in *Bulletin School of Oriental Studies*, vol. vi (1931), pp. 323-8, notes the appearance of the Arabic figures and the zero early in the seventh Christian century in Indo-China, long before its appearance in India proper. Both "zero", which came to English from an Italian form, and "cipher", which appeared in English about 200 years earlier, come from Ar. *ṣifr*, which is a translation of a Sanskrit word meaning "empty". According to a Syriac source cited by F. Nau in *Journal asiatique*, ser. 10, vol. xvi (1910), pp. 225 *seq.*, the numerals were known to a Syrian at the monastery of Qinnasrīn in 662.

the Hindu works was therefore responsible for making the numerals known to Islam. The tables of al-Khwārizmi and Ḥabash al-Ḥāsib († between 867 and 874) probably spread the use of them throughout the Arabic world. But the Arab mathematicians and astronomers were slow to adopt the ingenious Hindu invention. As late as the eleventh century we find abu-Bakr Muḥammad al-Karaji (wrongly Karkhi, † between 1019 and 1029) still writing out in his *al-Kāfi fi al-Ḥisāb* (the sufficient in arithmetic) all numbers in words. Others, following the old Semitic and Greek practice, used the letters of the alphabet, *ḥisāb al-jummal*. Aḥmad al-Nasawi[1] († *ca.* 1040), whose *al-Muqni' fi al-Ḥisāb al-Hindi* (the convincer on Hindu calculation) explains the division of fractions and the extraction of the square and cubic roots in an almost modern manner, used the Indian numerals as had al-Khwārizmi before him.

Al-Khwārizmi

This al-Khwārizmi,[2] Muḥammad ibn-Mūsa (780–*ca.* 850), was the principal figure in the early history of Arabic mathematics. One of the greatest scientific minds of Islam, he influenced mathematical thought to a greater extent than any other medieval writer. Apart from compiling the oldest astronomical tables,[3] al-Khwārizmi composed the oldest work on arithmetic, known only in a translation, and the oldest work on algebra. The last, *Ḥisāb al-Jabr w-al-Muqābalah* (the calculation of integration and equation), presented through over eight hundred examples, some of which were anticipated by Neo-Babylonians, was his chief work, still surviving in Arabic. Translated in the twelfth century into Latin by Gerard of Cremona, this work of al-Khwārizmi was used until the sixteenth century as the principal mathematical text-book of European universities and served to introduce into Europe the science of algebra, and with it the name. Al-Khwārizmi's works were also responsible for the introduction into the West of the Arabic numerals called algorisms after him.[4] Among later mathematicians influenced by al-Khwārizmi are 'Umar al-Khayyām, Leonardo Fibonacci of Pisa († after 1240) and Master Jacob of Florence, whose Italian treatise

[1] From Nasa in Khurāsān.

[2] Khwārizm, whose name he bears, is modern Khīwa, a country on the lower course of the Āmu Darya (ancient Oxus). Ṭabari, vol. iii, p. 1364, calls him al-Majūsi, i.e. the descendant of a Magian.

[3] Consult *Fihrist*, p. 274, copied by Qifṭi, p. 286. Cf. ibn-al-'Ibri, p. 237.

[4] "Augrim", "augrym", in Chaucer, *A Treatise on the Astrolabe*, pt. i, § 7 and § 8.

on mathematics, dated 1307, contains, as does one of Leonardo's works, the six types of quadratic equations given by the Moslem mathematician. Al-Khayyām's algebra,[1] which marks a considerable advance on that of al-Khwārizmi, contains geometric and algebraic solutions of equations of the second degree and an admirable classification of equations.

Alchemy

After materia medica, astronomy and mathematics the Arabs made their greatest scientific contribution in chemistry. In the study of chemistry and other physical sciences the Arabs introduced the objective experiment, a decided improvement over the hazy speculation of the Greeks. Accurate in the observation of phenomena and diligent in the accumulation of facts, the Arabs nevertheless found it difficult to project proper hypotheses. To draw truly scientific conclusions and elaborate a final system was the weakest point in their intellectual armour.

The father of Arabic alchemy[2] was Jābir ibn-Ḥayyān[3] (Geber), who flourished in al-Kūfah about 776. His name, after that of al-Rāzi († 925), is the greatest in the field of medieval chemical science. Legend makes the Umayyad prince Khālid ibn-Yazīd ibn-Mu'āwiyah († 704) and the sixth imām, Ja'far al-Ṣādiq of al-Madīnah († 765), his teachers. Like his Egyptian and Greek forerunners Jābir acted on the assumption that base metals such as tin, lead, iron and copper could be transmuted into gold or silver by means of a mysterious substance, to the search for which he devoted his energy. He more clearly recognized and stated the importance of experimentation than any other early alchemist and made noteworthy advance in both the theory and practice of chemistry. Some two centuries after his death, as a street was being rebuilt in al-Kūfah, his laboratory was found and in it a mortar and a large piece of gold were unearthed. Western tradition credits him with the discovery of several chemical compounds not mentioned in the twenty-two surviving Arabic works that bear his name.[4] Five of these works ascribed to Jābir, including *Kitāb al-Raḥmah* (the book of mercy), *Kitāb al-Tajmī'* (of concentration) and *al-Zi'baq al-Sharqi* (of

[1] Tr. Daoud S. Kasir, *The Algebra of Omar Khayyam* (New York, 1932).

[2] This word is Ar. *al-kīmiyā'*, which goes back through Gr. to an ancient Egyptian word meaning "black".

[3] Said to have been a Ṣābian converted to Shī'ah; according to others, descended from the South Arabian tribe al-Azd. *Fihrist*, pp. 354-5; Qifṭi, pp. 160-61.

[4] Ḥājji Khalfah, *passim*, cites twenty-seven works. See Paul Kraus, *Jābir Ibn Ḥayyān*, vol. i (Cairo, 1943), pp. 3-170.

Eastern mercury) have been published. It is evident that the vast majority of the hundred extant alchemical works in Arabic and in Latin which pass under his name are spurious. Nevertheless, the works to which his name was attached were after the fourteenth century the most influential chemical treatises in both Europe and Asia. Of a few contributions we are certain. Jābir described scientifically the two principal operations of chemistry: calcination and reduction. He improved on the methods for evaporation, sublimation, melting and crystallization. But the claim that he knew how to prepare crude sulphuric and nitric acids and mix them supposedly with salt so as to produce aqua regia is unsubstantiated. In general Jābir modified the Aristotelian theory of the constituents of metal in a way that survived, with slight alterations, until the beginning of modern chemistry in the eighteenth century.

Later Moslem chemists acclaim ibn-Ḥayyān as their master. Even the best among them, e.g. the Arabic-writing Persian poet-statesman al-Ṭughrā'i[1] († *ca.* 1121) and abu-al-Qāsim al-'Irāqi, who flourished in the second half of the thirteenth century,[2] made very little improvement on his methods. They continued the quest for the two alchemical will-o'-the-wisps: the philosopher's stone[3] and the elixir[4] of life. In fact in no branch of pure or physical science was any appreciable advance made after 'Abbāsid days. The Moslems of today, if dependent on their own books, would have even less than their distant ancestors in the eleventh century. In medicine, philosophy, mathematics, botany and other disciplines a certain point was reached; and then followed a standstill. Reverence for the past with its traditions, both religious and scientific, has bound the Arab intellect with fetters which it is only now beginning to shake off. It should, however, be noted to the eternal glory of medieval Islam that it succeeded for the first time in the history of human thought in harmonizing and reconciling monotheism, the greatest contri-

[1] Famous for his *Lāmīyat al-'Ajam*, the ode rhyming in *l* for the non-Arabs. *Ṭughrā'i* means "chancellor", the one who writes at the top of state papers the elegant flourish containing name and title of the ruler issuing the document. Ibn-Khallikān, vol. i, pp. 284 *seq.*

[2] See Ḥājji Khalfah, vol. iii, p. 218, vol. v, p. 47, vol. vi, p. 304. His *al-'Ilm al-Muktasab fi Zirā'at al-Dhahab* (knowledge acquired concerning the cultivation of gold) was edited and Englished by E. J. Holmyard (Paris, 1923).

[3] *Al-kibrīt al-aḥmar*, literally "the red sulphur"

[4] From Ar. *al-iksīr*, originally Gr.

bution of the ancient Semitic world, with Greek philosophy, the greatest contribution of the ancient Indo-European world, thus leading Christian Europe towards the modern point of view.[1]

In the field of natural history the Arabs' least striking success was in zoology, whereas the Spanish Moslems made a distinct contribution in botany, as we shall later see. Arabic writers on the animal kingdom were primarily literary men whose works consisted of collections of names and epithets given by the Arabs to animals and illustrated by quotations from the poets. The study of the horse formed one conspicuous exception and was developed almost to the rank of a science. A number of special monographs were composed on this animal, enumerating its varieties, naming the parts of its body, describing its colours and designating its desirable and undesirable qualities.[2]

Al-Jāḥiẓ

An early representative of the zoological and anthropological sciences was abu-'Uthmān 'Amr ibn-Baḥr al-Jāḥiẓ (the goggle-eyed, † 868–9), who flourished in al-Baṣrah and whose *Kitāb al-Ḥayawān* (book of animals) is more theological and folkloric than biological. This work, in which the author quotes Aristotle, contains germs of later theories of evolution, adaptation and animal psychology. Al-Jāḥiẓ knew how to obtain ammonia from animal offal by dry distillation. His influence over later zoologists, e.g. the Arabic-writing Persian cosmographer al-Qazwīni[3] († 1283) and the Egyptian al-Damīri († 1405)—both of whom treated zoology as a branch of philology and literature—is manifest. Al-Damīri is the greatest Arab zoologist.[4] But the influence of al-Jāḥiẓ as a radical theologian and man of letters is greater. He founded a Mu'tazilite sect bearing his name[5] and was one of the most productive and frequently quoted scholars in Arabic literature.[6] His originality, wit, satire and learning made him widely known, but his repulsive ugliness made the Caliph al-

[1] See below, p. 580.

[2] Consult al-Aṣma'i, *Kitāb al-Khayl*, ed. August Haffner (Vienna, 1895); ibn-Durayd in William Wright, *Opuscula Arabica* (Leyden, 1859); al-Kalbi, *Nasab al-Khayl fi al-Jāhilīyah w-al-Islām* and al-A'rābi, *Asmā' Khayl al-'Arab wa-Fursāniha*, ed. G. Levi della Vida (Leyden, 1928).

[3] His leading work is *'Ajā'ib al-Makhlūqāt wa-Gharā'ib al-Mawjūdāt* (the wonders of creation and the oddities of existence), ed. Wüstenfeld (Göttingen, 1849).

[4] His *Ḥayāt al-Ḥayawān* (animal life) was printed in Cairo several times; tr. into English by A. S. G. Jayakar (London, 1906, 1908), vol. i and vol. ii, pt. 1.

[5] Baghdādi, ed. Hitti, pp. 117-18.

[6] Yāqūt, vol. vi, pp. 75-8, lists over 120 books from his pen.

Mutawakkil change his mind about appointing him tutor to his sons.[1]

Lapidaries

In mineralogy, which stood in close relation to alchemy, the Arabs made little progress. Their fondness for precious stones and their interest in the occult qualities of minerals explains the many lapidaries, over fifty, composed by Arabic authors. Of these the oldest extant is that of 'Uṭārid ibn-Muḥammad al-Ḥāsib (possibly al-Kātib[2]) of the ninth century, but the best known is *Azhār al-Afkār fi Jawāhir al-Aḥjār* (the flowers of thought on precious stones) by Shihāb-al-Dīn al-Tīfāshi,[3] who died in Cairo, 1253. Al-Tīfāshi discusses twenty-four precious stones: their origin, geography, purity, price, medicinal and magical values and, except for Pliny and the spurious Aristotelian lapidary, quotes only Arabic sources. The famous al-Bīrūni with almost complete accuracy determined the specific gravity of eighteen precious stones and metals.

Geography

The institution of the holy pilgrimage, the orientation of the mosques towards Makkah and the need for determining the direction of the Ka'bah at the time of prayer gave religious impetus to the Moslem study of geography. Astrology, which necessitated the determining of the latitudes and longitudes of all places throughout the world, added its scientific influence. Moslem traders between the seventh and ninth centuries reached China on the east both by sea and by land, attained the island of Zanzibar and the farthest coasts of Africa on the south, penetrated Russia on the north and were checked in their advance westward only by the dreaded waters of the "Sea of Darkness" (Atlantic). The reports of returning merchants naturally aroused popular interest in distant lands and alien peoples. Sulaymān al-Tājir (the merchant) of Sīrāf on the Persian Gulf, the account of whose journeys into the Far East was written by an anonymous author in 851, gives us the first Arabic description of China and the coast-lands of India. Sulaymān reports the use of finger-prints as signatures by the Chinese.[4] From this and similar narratives there gradually

[1] Ibn-Khallikān, vol. ii, pp. 108-9.

[2] *Fihrist*, p. 278. His work *Manāfi' al-Aḥjār* (the uses of precious stones) is preserved in manuscript form in the Bibliothèque Nationale, Paris; de Slane, *Catalogue des manuscrits arabes* (Paris, 1893-5), no. 2775[3].

[3] Ed. and tr. (Italian) Antonio Raineri (Biscia) (Florence, 1818).

[4] *Silsilat al-Tawārīkh*, ed. Langlès, p. 44. Cf. tr. by E. Renaudot (London, 1733), p. 26; *Aḥbār aṣ-Ṣīn wa-l-Hind*, ed. and tr. J. Sauvaget (Paris, 1948), p. 19.

evolved the stories that have clustered round the name of Sindbād the Sailor. The earliest reliable account of Russia is that of Aḥmad ibn-Faḍlān ibn-Ḥammād, sent in 921 by al-Muqtadir to the king of the Bulgars, who resided along the Volga. Most of his account is reproduced in Yāqūt's monumental geographical dictionary, *Mu'jam al-Buldān*. Al-Mas'ūdi[1] refers to Moslem traders among al-Dīr, Slavic tribes perhaps near the Pripet, a tributary of the Dnieper.

Greek antecedents

Ptolemy's *Geography*, which had a list of places located by latitude and longitude, was translated into Arabic either directly or through Syriac several times, notably by Thābit ibn-Qurrah († 901). With this as a model the celebrated Khwārizmi had composed his *Ṣūrat al-Arḍ*[2] (image of the earth), which served as a basis for later works and stimulated geographical studies and the composition of original treatises. Al-Khwārizmi's work was accompanied by an "image of the earth", a map executed by him and sixty-nine other scholars at the instigation of al-Ma'mūn—the first map of the heavens and the world in Islam. Al-Mas'ūdi,[3] who flourished in the first half of the tenth century, consulted this map. Al-Khwārizmi's geography continued to influence Moslem authors down to the fourteenth century, as is illustrated by abu-al-Fidā'.

"World cupola"

In the meantime the early Arab geographers had gained from India the notion that there was a world centre which they styled *arīn*,[4] a corruption of the name of the Indian town Ujjayinī (Ozēnē in Ptolemy's *Geography*), where there had been an astronomical observatory and on the meridian of which the "world cupola"[5] or "summit" was supposed to lie. This *arīn* they located on the equator between the extremes of east and west. The western prime meridian was thought by them to be 90° from this mythical place. Moslem geographers in general measured longitude from the prime meridian used by Ptolemy, that of the islands now called the Canaries.

The first independent geographical treatises in Arabic took the form of road books in which itineraries occupied a prominent place. Ibn-Khurdādhbih († *ca.* 912), of Persian descent, director

[1] Vol. iii, p. 64. [2] Ed. Hans v. Mžik (Leipzig, 1926). [3] Vol. ii, p. 308.

[4] Variants *Ujjain, Uzayn, Udhayn*, etc. Ibn-Rustah, p. 22, l. 17; Mas'ūdi, *Tanbīh*, p. 225, l. 2; abu-al-Fidā', ed. Reinaud and de Slane, p. 376, ll. 8, 12.

[5] *Qubbat al-arḍ*, abu-al-Fidā', pp. 375, 376; ibn-Rustah, p. 22, ll. 17 *seq.*; Bīrūni, *Taḥqīq*, p. 158.

of the post and intelligence service in al-Jibāl (Media), initiated the series with his *al-Masālik w-al-Mamālik*,[1] the first edition of which appeared about 846. This work, especially valuable for its historical topography, was used by ibn-al-Faqīh, ibn-Ḥawqal, al-Maqdisi and later geographical writers. In 891–2 the Shīʻite ibn-Wāḍiḥ al-Yaʻqūbi,[2] who flourished in Armenia and Khurāsān, produced his *Kitāb al-Buldān*[3] (book of countries), which struck a new note in emphasizing topographical and economical detail. Soon after 928 Qudāmah, who was born a Christian but adopted Islam and held office as revenue accountant in the central administration at Baghdād, completed his *al-Kharāj*, which discusses the division of the caliphate into provinces, the organization of the postal service and the taxation for each district. Another Arab geographer of Persian origin, ibn-Rustah, compiled about 903 his *al-Aʻlāq al-Nafīsah*[4] (precious bags of travelling provisions). In that same year ibn-al-Faqīh al-Hamadhāni, so called from his birthplace, completed his *Kitāb al-Buldān*,[5] a comprehensive geography often quoted by al-Maqdisi and Yāqūt.

Literary geographers

The great systematic geographers of the Arabs do not make their appearance until the advent of al-Iṣṭakhri, ibn-Ḥawqal and al-Maqdisi in the middle of the fourth Moslem century. Born in Iṣṭakhr (Persepolis), al-Iṣṭakhri flourished about 950 and produced his *Masālik al-Mamālik*[6] with coloured maps for each country. This work was an elaboration of the geographical system established by abu-Zayd al-Balkhi († 934), who flourished at the Sāmānid court and whose work has not been preserved. The system initiated by al-Balkhi and al-Iṣṭakhri paid little attention to countries outside Islam and made the text largely a description of the accompanying maps. Its representatives were travellers themselves. Al-Iṣṭakhri is the second writer to mention windmills (in Sijistān), the first reference to them having been made by al-Masʻūdi.[7] At al-Iṣṭakhri's request ibn-Ḥawqal (fl. 943–77), who travelled as far as Spain, revised the maps and text of his geography. Ibn-Ḥawqal later rewrote the whole book

[1] Ed. de Goeje (Leyden, 1889).
[2] Al-ʻAbbāsi; Yāqūt, vol. ii, pp. 156-7.
[3] Ed. de Goeje (Leyden, 1892).
[4] Ed. de Goeje (Leyden, 1891–2).
[5] Ed. de Goeje (Leyden, 1885).
[6] Ed. de Goeje (Leyden, 1870).
[7] Vol. ii, p. 80. For an illustration see Dimashqi, *Nukhbat al-Dahr fi ʻAjā'ib al-Barr w-al-Baḥr* (St. Petersburg, 1866), p. 182.

and issued it under his own name as *al-Masālik w-al-Mamālik*.[1] To this same school belongs the more original work of al-Maqdisi (or al-Muqaddasi), so called because he was born in Jerusalem (*Bayt al-Maqdis*). This geographer visited all the Moslem lands except Spain, Sijistān and India and in 985–6 embodied an account of his twenty years of travel in a delightful work, *Aḥsan al-Taqāsīm fi Ma'rifat al-Aqālīm*[2] (the best of classification for the knowledge of regions), which contains much valuable and fresh information.

In this same period flourished the Yamanite geographer and archæologist al-Ḥasan ibn-Aḥmad al-Hamdāni, who died (945) in a prison at Ṣan'ā' and whose two works *al-Iklīl*[3] and *Ṣifat Jazīrat al-'Arab*[4] constitute an important contribution to our knowledge of pre-Islamic and Islamic Arabia. The globe-trotter al-Mas'ūdi, who flourished in this period, we shall treat of with the historians. In the mineralogical part of their epistles[5] the Ikhwān al-Ṣafā', who also belong to this time, elaborated a theory of cosmic cycles by which cultivated lands become desert, desert lands become cultivated, steppes change into seas and seas change into steppes or mountains.

Yāqūt

Before the close of the 'Abbāsid age lived the greatest of the Eastern Moslem geographers, Yāqūt[6] ibn-'Abdullāh al-Ḥamawi (1179–1229), author of the geographical dictionary *Mu'jam al-Buldān*,[7] often cited in the foregoing pages, and of the equally important dictionary of literati *Mu'jam al-Udabā'*. Born in Asia Minor of Greek parents, young Yāqūt was bought in Baghdād by a merchant from Ḥamāh (hence his surname al-Ḥamawi) who, after giving him a good education and employing him for several years as a travelling clerk, enfranchised him. To support himself Yāqūt roamed from place to place copying and selling manuscripts. In 1219–20 he had to flee before the Tartar invasion of Khwārizm "as naked as he shall be when raised from the dust of the grave on the day of the resurrection".[8] The first

[1] Ed. de Goeje (Leyden, 1873); another version, *Ṣūrat al-Arḍ*, ed. J. H. Kramers, 2 vols. (Leyden, 1938-9).

[2] Ed. de Goeje (Leyden, 1877).

[3] See above, p. 50, n. 2.

[4] Ed. D. H. Müller, 2 vols. (Leyden, 1884–91).

[5] Ed. Zirikli, vol. ii, pp. 80 *seq*. Cf. Mas'ūdi, *Tanbīh*, p. 3.

[6] The word means "ruby". Slaves were often given names of precious things, e.g. Lu'lu' (pearl), Jawhar (gem).

[7] Ed. F. Wüstenfeld, 6 vols. (Leipzig, 1866–73).

[8] Ibn-Khallikān, vol. iii, p. 162 = de Slane, vol. iv, p. 10.

draft of his geographical dictionary was drawn at al-Mawṣil in 1224 and the final redaction was completed in 1228 at Aleppo, where he died. This *Mu'jam*, in which names of places are alphabetically arranged, is a veritable encyclopædia, containing, in addition to the whole fund of geographical knowledge of the age, valuable information on history, ethnography and natural science.

Literary Islamic geography left no direct impression on European medieval thought, as the works of these geographers found no translators into Latin. Certain aspects of astronomical geography, including an approximately correct theory of the causation of tides, worked out by abu-Ma'shar, and of the length of the terrestrial degree, did find their way into the West, the latter through a translation of al-Farghāni's work on astronomy. Likewise fragments of the geographical lore of the Greeks as exemplified by Aristotle and Ptolemy were reintroduced to the West through the Arabs. But most of the contribution of the Arab geographers failed to pass on. This contribution included descriptive geography of the Far East, East and Sudanese Africa and the steppe land of Russia; more accurate cartography, especially in the form of world maps; and provincial geography, where one country is taken as a unit and the relation between the lives of the people and the physical environment is shown. The primary interest of the Latin Occident in Arabic books had for its object the preparation of calendars, star tables and horoscopes and the interpretation of the hidden meaning in the words of the Scriptures through commentaries on Aristotle. The bulk of this scientific material, whether astronomical, astrological or geographical, penetrated the West through Spanish and Sicilian channels. The contributions of al-Biṭrūji of Cordova, al-Zarqāli of Toledo and al-Idrīsi of Palermo will be discussed under Spain and Sicily.

Historiography

The majority of the earliest historical writings surviving in Arabic date from the 'Abbāsid period. Few of those composed under the Umayyads have been preserved. The first subject-matter came, as we have learned before, from the oral legends and anecdotes relating to pre-Islamic days and from the religious traditions which clustered round the name and life of the Prophet. In the pre-Islamic field Hishām al-Kalbi of al-Kūfah († 819) particularly distinguished himself. Of the one hundred and twenty-nine works listed in *al-Fihrist*[1] as his, only three have survived;[2] but extracts from others can be found quoted by al-Ṭabari, Yāqūt and other historical writers.

The first work based upon religious traditions was the *Sīrat Rasūl Allāh*, the biography of the Prophet by Muḥammad ibn-Isḥāq of al-Madīnah, whose grandfather Yasār was among the Christian children captured in 633 by Khālid ibn-al-Walīd at 'Ayn al-Tamr in al-'Irāq.[3] This biography by ibn-Isḥāq, who died in Baghdād about 767, has come down to us only in the later recension of ibn-Hishām,[4] who died in 834 at Cairo.[5] Then came works dealing with the early wars and conquests of Islam, the *Maghāzi* by Mūsa ibn-'Uqbah[6] († 758), by al-Wāqidi[7] († 822/3), both of al-Madīnah, and by others. From the pen of ibn-Sa'd, who died in Baghdād in 845 and is known as the secretary of al-Wāqidi,[8] we have the first great book of classified biographies[9] containing sketches of the lives of the Prophet, the Companions and their Successors (*al-tābi'ūn*) down to his own time. Two of the leading historians of the Moslem conquests were the Egyptian ibn-'Abd-al-Ḥakam († 870–71), whose *Futūḥ Miṣr wa-Akhbāruha*[10] is the earliest extant document on the conquest of Egypt, North Africa and Spain, and the Arabic-writing Persian Aḥmad ibn-Yaḥya al-Balādhuri († 892), whose main works were the *Futūḥ al-Buldān*[11] and the *Ansāb al-Ashrāf*[12] (book of the lineages of nobles). Al-Balādhuri was one of the first to integrate the many stories of the conquests of various cities and lands into one comprehensive whole, thus ending the era in which the monograph was the typical form of historical composition.

Early formal historians

The time was now ripe for formal historical composition based on these legends, traditions, biographies, genealogies and

[1] Pp. 95-8.
[2] Of these the best-known is the *Kitāb al-Aṣnām*, ed. Aḥmad Zaki (Cairo, 1914).
[3] Ibn-Khallikān, vol. ii, p. 282.
[4] Ed. Wüstenfeld, 2 vols. (Göttingen, 1858–60).
[5] Ibn-Khallikān, vol. i, p. 520.
[6] Compiled by ibn-Qāḍi Shuhbah in 1387.
[7] Ed. von Kremer (Calcutta, 1856). See ibn-Khallikān, vol. ii, pp. 324-6.
[8] Ibn-Khallikān, vol. ii, p. 326.
[9] Ed. Sachau *et al.*, 9 vols. (Leyden and Berlin, 1904–28).
[10] Ed. Charles C. Torrey (New Haven, 1922).
[11] Ed. de Goeje (Leyden, 1866); tr. Hitti, *The Origins of the Islamic State* (New York, 1916), first part; second part, F. C. Murgotten (New York, 1924).
[12] Ed. W. Ahlwardt, vol. xi (Greifswald, 1883); S. D. F. Goitein, vol. v (Jerusalem, 1936); Max Schloessinger, vol. iv B (Jerusalem, 1938).

narratives. The model was evidently Persian and was provided by such works as the Pahlawi *Khudhāy-nāmah* (the book of kings), which had been turned into Arabic by ibn-al-Muqaffa' († 757) under the title *Siyar Mulūk al-'Ajam.* The concept of a world history in which early events are but a prelude to the history of Islam goes back to Jewish-Christian tradition. The form of presentation, however, continued to be that of the stereotyped Islamic tradition.[1] Each event is related in the words of eye-witnesses or contemporaries and transmitted to the final narrator, the author, through a chain of intermediary reporters. This technique served to develop exactitude, as did also the insistence on dating occurrences even to the month and day. But the authenticity of the reported fact generally depended upon the continuity of this chain (*isnād*) and the confidence in the integrity of each reporter rather than upon a critical examination of the fact itself. Apart from the use of personal judgment in the choice of the series of authorities and in the arrangement of the data, the historian exercised very little power of analysis, criticism, comparison or inference.

Among the first formal historians was ibn-Qutaybah, properly Muḥammad ibn-Muslim al-Dīnawari.[2] Ibn-Qutaybah died at Baghdād in 889 after producing his *Kitāb al-Ma'ārif*[3] (book of knowledge), a manual of history. Another was his contemporary abu-Ḥanīfah Aḥmad ibn-Dāwūd al-Dīnawari[4] († 895), who flourished in Iṣbahān (Iṣfahān) and Dīnawar (in the Persian 'Irāq). His principal work was *al-Akhbār al-Ṭiwāl*[5] (long narratives), a universal history from the Persian point of view. Both were of Iranian extraction and produced several literary and philological works besides histories. At the same time flourished the geographer and historian ibn-Wāḍiḥ al-Ya'qūbi, whose compendium of universal history[6] ending in A.H. 258 (872) preserves the ancient and unfalsified Shī'ite tradition. To this group belongs Ḥamzah al-Iṣfahāni, who worked in Iṣbahān, where he died *ca.* 961, and whose rather critical annals[7] became

[1] See below, p. 394.
[2] See *Fihrist*, pp. 77-8; Nawawi, *Tahdhīb*, p. 771; Sam'āni, *Ansāb*, fol. 443a.
[3] Ed. Wüstenfeld (Göttingen, 1850).
[4] See *Fihrist*, p. 78; Yāqūt, *Udabā'*, vol. i, pp. 123-7.
[5] Ed. Vladimir Guirgass (Leyden, 1888).
[6] *Ta'rīkh*, ed. Th. Houtsma, 2 vols. (Leyden, 1883).
[7] *Ta'rīkh Sini Mulūk al-Arḍ w-al-Anbiyā'*, ed. I. M. E. Gottwaldt (Leipzig, 1844); tr. into Latin by Gottwaldt (Leipzig, 1848).

known comparatively early in modern Europe. Another great historian of Persian stock was Miskawayh[1] († 1030), who held a high office in the court of the Buwayhid 'Aḍud-al-Dawlah and compiled a universal history[2] reaching down to A.H. 369 (979–80). Miskawayh, who was also a philosopher and physician, ranks among the leading Moslem historians, of whom the two greatest were undoubtedly al-Ṭabari and al Mas'ūdi.

Al-Ṭabari

The fame of abu-Ja'far Muḥammad ibn-Jarīr al-Ṭabari (838–923), who was born in Ṭabaristān, that mountainous district of Persia along the south coast of the Caspian Sea, rests on his remarkably elaborate and accurate history *Ta'rīkh al-Rusul w-al-Mulūk*[3] (annals of the apostles and kings), as well as on his commentary on the Koran.[4] In his commentary, originally composed on a far larger scale, he made not only the earliest but the largest collection of exegetical traditions. This became a standard work upon which later koranic commentators drew. His monumental work on universal history, the first complete one in the Arabic tongue, likewise served as a source for later historians such as Miskawayh, ibn-al-Athīr and abu-al-Fidā'. Like most Moslem historians, al-Ṭabari arranges the events chronologically, tabulating them under the successive years of the Hijrah. In fact his history begins with the creation of the world and goes down to A.H. 302 (915). The same annalistic method was used by al-Wāqidi and others before him as well as by Miskawayh, ibn-al-Athīr, abu-al-Fidā'[5] (1273–1331) and al-Dhahabi[6] (1274–1348) after him. The original edition of al-Ṭabari's history is said to have been ten times as long as the surviving edition. His favourite method of presenting the narrative is that of the religious tradition, by *isnād*. Besides making use of the literary sources extant in his day, such as the works of ibn-Isḥāq, al-Kalbi, al-Wāqidi, ibn-Sa'd and ibn-al-Muqaffa' and of several historical translations from Persian, al-Ṭabari procured data for his history from oral traditions collected during his travels and from the lectures of the sheikhs under whom he studied in

[1] Less correctly "ibn-Miskawayh"; Yāqūt, vol. ii, p. 88; Qifṭi, p. 331.

[2] *Tajārib al-Umam*, ed. A. F. Amedroz, 2 vols. (Oxford, 1914–21); tr. D. S. Margoliouth, *The Experiences of the Nations*, 2 vols. (Oxford, 1921).

[3] Ed. de Goeje *et al.*, 15 vols. (Leyden, 1879–1901).

[4] *Jāmi' al-Bayān fi Tafsīr al-Qur'ān*, 30 vols. (Būlāq, 1323–9).

[5] See his *Ta'rīkh*, also called *al-Mukhtaṣar fi Akhbār al-Bashar*, 4 vols. (Constantinople, 1286).

[6] See his *Duwal al-Islām*, 2 vols. (Ḥaydarābād, 1337).

Baghdād and other intellectual centres. His journeys in quest of learning covered Persia, al-'Irāq, Syria and Egypt.[1] On one occasion he was forced to sell the sleeves of his shirt to buy bread for sustenance. An idea of his industry and enthusiasm for learning may be gained from the popular tradition that during forty years al-Ṭabari wrote forty sheets every day.[2]

Al-Mas'ūdi

Abu-al-Ḥasan 'Ali al-Mas'ūdi,[3] styled the "Herodotus of the Arabs", inaugurated among the Arabs the topical method of writing history. Instead of grouping his events around years he grouped them around dynasties, kings and peoples, a treatment followed by ibn-Khaldūn and minor historians. He was also one of the first to make good use of the historical anecdote. Young al-Mas'ūdi, who belonged to the rationalistic school of Mu'tazilites, undertook the usual scholar's "journey in quest of learning" which carried him from his native Baghdād[4] into almost every country of Asia and even into Zanzibar. The last decade of his life he spent in Syria and Egypt compiling the material into a thirty-volume work, surviving in an epitome, *Murūj al-Dhahab wa-Ma'ādin al-Jawhar*[5] (meadows of gold and mines of gems). In this encyclopaedic historico-geographical work the author, with catholicity and scientific curiosity, carried his researches beyond the typically Moslem subjects into Indo-Persian, Roman and Jewish history. At its beginning he states that what is now dry land had been sea, and what is sea had been dry land—all as a result of physical forces. Before his death at al-Fusṭāṭ in 957 al-Mas'ūdi summarized his philosophy of history and nature and the current philosophers' views on the gradation between minerals, plants and animals[6] in *al-Tanbīh w-al-Ishrāf*,[7] comparable to Pliny's.

Arabic historical composition reached its highest point in al-Ṭabari and al-Mas'ūdi, and after Miskawayh († 1030) started on a rapid decline. 'Izz-al-Dīn ibn-al-Athīr[8] (1160–1234) abridged in his *al-Kāmil fi al-Ta'rīkh*[9] (the complete book

[1] *Fihrist*, p. 234.
[2] Yāqūt, vol. vi, p. 424.
[3] A descendant of 'Abdullāh ibn-Mas'ūd.
[4] *Fihrist*, p. 154, wrongly makes him a native of al-Maghrib. Cf. Yāqūt, vol. v, p. 148.
[5] Ed. and tr. de Meynard and de Courteille, 9 vols. (Paris, 1861–77).
[6] Cf. Ikhwān, *Rasā'il*, vol. i, pp. 247-8.
[7] Ed. de Goeje (Leyden, 1893–4).
[8] Born in Jazīrat ibn-'Umar on the Tigris, flourished in al-Mawṣil. Ibn-Khallikān, vol. ii, pp. 35-6.
[9] Ed. C. J. Tornberg, 13 vols. (Leyden, 1867–74).

of chronicles) al-Ṭabari's work and continued the narrative to 1231. The period dealing with the Crusades is an original contribution. Ibn-al-Athīr produced another important work, *Usd al-Ghābah*[1] (the lions of the thicket), a collection of 7500 biographies of the Companions. His contemporary Sibṭ ibn-al-Jawzi[2] (1186–1257), who was born in Baghdād and whose father was a Turkish slave, wrote among other works the *Mir'āt al-Zamān fi Ta'rīkh al-Ayyām*, a universal history from Creation to 1256.[3] To this late 'Abbāsid period belongs the chief judge of Syria, ibn-Khallikān († 1282), the first Moslem to compose what we might term a dictionary of national biography. Before him Yāqūt had issued his dictionary of literati and ibn-'Asākir († 1177) had sketched in eighty volumes the biographies of distinguished men connected with his native town, Damascus.[4]

Like most other treasures of historical and geographical lore written in a foreign tongue the works of al-Ṭabari, al-Mas'ūdi, ibn-al-Athīr and their confrères remained inaccessible to medieval Occidental readers. In modern times many have been translated in part or in full into modern European tongues. This, however, does not mean that the Arabic authors made no contribution to the social sciences. In appreciating their work in this and other disciplines Sarton[5] enthusiastically declares: "The main task of mankind was accomplished by Muslims. The greatest philosopher, al-Fārābī, was a Muslim; the greatest mathematicians, Abū Kāmil[6] and Ibrāhīm ibn Sinān,[7] were Muslims; the greatest geographer and encyclopædist, al-Mas'ūdī, was a Muslim; the greatest historian, al-Ṭabarī, was still a Muslim".

Theology

We now come to those intellectual activities evoked by the predilections of the Arabs as Arabs and Moslems. Foremost among the sciences thus developed were theology, tradition,

[1] 5 vols. (Cairo, 1280).

[2] This surname he owes to his famous maternal grandfather, ibn-al-Jawzi († 1201).

[3] Extracts ed. and tr. in *Recueil des historiens des croisades: historiens orientaux*, vol. iii (Paris, 1884). Pt. 8 was reproduced in facsimile by James R. Jewett (Chicago, 1907).

[4] *Al-Ta'rīkh al-Kabīr*, ed. 'Abd-al-Qādir Badrān and Aḥmad 'Ubayd (Damascus, 1329–51), first seven volumes.

[5] *Introduction to the History of Science*, vol. i (Baltimore, 1927), p. 624.

[6] Shujā' ibn-Aslam of Egypt, who at the beginning of the tenth century perfected al-Khwārizmi's algebra.

[7] Grandson of Thābit ibn-Qurrah, lived 908–46. His quadrature of the parabola was the simplest ever made before the invention of integral calculus.

jurisprudence, philology and linguistics. Most of the scholars in this field were of Arab descent, in contrast to the physicians, astronomers, mathematicians and alchemists cited above, who were of Syrian, Jewish or Persian origin.

The attention and interest of the Moslem Arabs were drawn quite early to those branches of learning motivated by the religious impulse. The necessity of comprehending and explaining the Koran soon became the basis of intensive theologic as well as linguistic study. Contact with Christendom provoked in the first century at Damascus theological speculation leading to the rise of the Murji'ite and Qadarite schools of thought.[1]

Next to the holy Koran, the sunnah,[2] i.e. the deeds, utterances and silent approval (*taqrīr*) of the Prophet, stood as the most important doctrinal source. Transmitted at first orally, this sunnah of Muḥammad was fixed during the second century in the form of written ḥadīths. A ḥadīth, therefore, is a record of an action or saying of the Prophet. In a more general sense it may be used also for a record of an action or saying of any of his Companions or their Successors.[3] Though not equally canonical with the Koran, the Prophetic ḥadīth nevertheless exerted an equally great influence over the development of Islamic thought. In the ḥadīth Muḥammad speaks; in the Koran Allah speaks. In the ḥadīth the meaning only is inspired; in the Koran the meaning and the word are inspired. The bases of jurisprudence (*fiqh*) as well as of theology are firstly in the Koran, secondly in the ḥadīth. Among all peoples Moslems stand unique in having developed a science (*'ilm*) out of their mass of religious traditions (*ḥadīths*).

The science of ḥadīth

To the pious Moslem the science of ḥadīth soon became the science par excellence.[4] It was primarily in its quest that the would-be scholar, in response to the famous Prophetic tradition, "Seek ye learning though it be in China", undertook long and tiresome journeys throughout the extensive domains of the caliphate. Such journeys (*al-riḥlah fi ṭalab al-'ilm*)[5]

[1] Other Moslem sects will be treated in the following chapter.

[2] Etymologically meaning "custom," "use", the word has developed several technical meanings. In opposition to Shī'ah, it is used for the theory and practice of the catholic Moslem community.

[3] See above, p. 242.

[4] Consult the chapter on *'ilm* in Bukhāri, vol. i, pp. 19 *seq*.

[5] Consult ibn-Khaldūn, *Muqaddamah*, p. 476; Alfred Guillaume, *The Traditions of Islam* (Oxford, 1924), pp. 68-9.

were elevated into acts of consummate piety; he who lost his life through their perils was likened to him who lost it in the holy war.

In the course of the first two and a half centuries after Muḥammad the records of his sayings and doings increased in number and copiousness. Whenever an issue—religious, political or sociological—arose each party sought to find authority for its views in some word or decision of the Prophet, be it real or fictitious. The political rivalry between 'Ali and abu-Bakr, the struggle between Mu'āwiyah and 'Ali, the enmity between the 'Abbāsids and Umayyads, the burning question of superiority between Arabs and non-Arabs—these and similar exigencies provided ample opportunity for the fabrication of ḥadīths and motivated their dissemination. Moreover, the manufacture of ḥadīths had commercial value and many teachers thrived on it. Before his execution at al-Kūfah in 772, ibn-abi-al-'Awjā' confessed to having circulated 4000 traditions of his own invention.[1] In general more weight is attached to the Madīnese than to the Kūfan school of traditions, yet here again not all transmitters are above suspicion. Abu-Hurayrah, for instance, a Companion of the Prophet and a most zealous propagator of his words and deeds, reputedly transmitted some 5374 ḥadīths,[2] many of which were unquestionably foisted on him after his death. 'Ā'ishah transmitted 2210 traditions, Anas ibn-Mālik 2286 and 'Abdullāh ibn-'Umar ibn-al-Khaṭṭāb 1630.[3]

Every perfect ḥadīth consists of two parts: a chain of authorities (*isnād*) and a text (*matn*). The text follows the chain and should be in direct address: A related (*ḥaddatha*) to me that B related to him, on the authority of C, on the authority of D, on the authority of E, who said . . . . The same formula was used in historiography and in wisdom literature. In all these fields criticism was usually external, being limited to a consideration of the reputation of the transmitters, who are at the same time guarantors, and to the possibility of their forming an uninterrupted chain leading back to the Prophet. On the basis of such criticism ḥadīths are classified as genuine (*ṣaḥīḥ*), fair (*ḥasan*)

[1] Ṭabari, vol. iii, p. 376, copied by ibn-al-Athīr, vol. vi, p. 3. Cf. Baghdādi, ed. Hitti, p. 164.

[2] Ibn-Ḥajar, *Iṣābah*, vol. vii, p. 201. His title "abu-Hurayrah", "father of the kitten", was due to his fondness for cats; ibn-Qutaybah, *Ma'ārif*, p. 141; ibn-Sa'd, vol. iv, pt. 2, p. 55.

[3] Nawawi, pp. 165, 358.

and weak (*ḍaʿīf*).[1] The ludicrous extreme to which this external criticism may lead is illustrated in the story of a traditionist who accepted a large cup of wine offered him by a Christian, and when reminded that this was a prohibited drink bought by the Christian's slave from a Jew his excuse was: "We traditionists consider as authority such men as Sufyān ibn-ʿUyaynah and Yazīd ibn-Hārūn. Are we then to believe a Christian, on the authority of his slave, on the authority of a Jew? By Allah, I drank it only because of its weak *isnād*!"[2]

The six canonical books

The third Moslem century saw the compilation of the various collections of ḥadīths into six books which have since become standard. Of "the six books" the first and most authoritative is that of Muḥammad ibn-Ismāʿīl al-Bukhāri (810–70).[3] Al-Bukhāri, who was a Persian, selected out of the 600,000 traditions he collected from 1000 sheikhs in the course of sixteen years of travel and labour in Persia, al-ʿIrāq, Syria, al-Ḥijāz and Egypt some 7397 traditions[4] which he classified according to subject-matter, such as prayer, pilgrimage and holy war. Before committing a tradition to writing it was al-Bukhāri's wont to perform the ceremonial ablution and prayer.[5] His collection has acquired a quasi-sacred character. An oath taken on it is valid, as if taken on the Koran itself. Next to the Koran this is the book that has exerted the greatest influence over the Moslem mind. Its author's tomb outside of Samarqand is still visited by pilgrims who accord him the next rank in Islam after Muḥammad.

Al-Bukhāri's corpus of traditions came near finding a rival in the collection of Muslim ibn-al-Ḥajjāj († 875) of Naysābūr, a work on which Islam has conferred the same title, *al-Ṣaḥīḥ*, the genuine collection. The contents of Muslim's *Ṣaḥīḥ* are almost identical with al-Bukhāri's, though the *isnād* may vary. Next to these "two genuine books" come four others which Moslems have elevated to canonical rank. These are the *Sunan* of abu-Dāwūd of al-Baṣrah († 888), the *Jāmiʿ* of al-Tirmidhi († *ca.* 892), the *Sunan* of ibn-Mājah of Qazwīn († 886) and the *Sunan* of al-Nasā'i, who died at Makkah in 915.[6]

[1] Consult ibn-ʿAsākir, *Ta'rīkh*, vol. ii, pp. 18 *seq.*; ibn-Khaldūn, *Muqaddamah*, pp. 370 *seq.*

[2] Nawāji, *Ḥalbah*, p. 17.

[3] *Al-Jāmiʿ al-Ṣaḥīḥ*, 8 vols. (Būlāq, 1296).

[4] Nawawi, pp. 93, 95-6.

[5] Ibn-Khallikān, vol. ii, p. 231.

[6] Various editions of these works, but none critical, have been printed or lithographed in Egypt and India.

Besides clarifying and supplementing the Koran, the ḥadīth literature provided the Moslem community with apostolic precept and example covering the whole range of man's duty. Even such trivial questions as the proper way of cutting a watermelon before eating it or cleaning the teeth with a toothpick—"proper" from the standpoint of the Prophetic practice—did not escape the traditionists' researches. The nocturnal journey vaguely reported in one solitary koranic verse (17:1) developed in the ḥadīth an extensive and colourful crop of elaborate traditions with which the Occident has long been familiar as reflected in the pages of Dante. The ḥadīth literature further served as a vehicle for transmitting wise sayings, anecdotes, parables and miracles—all ascribed to Muḥammad—from various secular and religious sources, including the New Testament. In abu-Dāwūd[1] a version of the Lord's Prayer is put in Muḥammad's mouth. In al-Bukhāri[2] and Muslim,[3] Muḥammad, on the authority of abu-Hurayrah, upon whom many such pious and edifying sayings are fathered, once commended "him who gives alms only in secret, so that his left hand knows not what his right hand does". Nothing could better illustrate the general receptivity and hospitality of Islam as a system. In the ḥadīth lore the Moslem home found its fireside literature and the Moslem community its Talmud.

Juris-prudence

After the Romans the Arabs were the only medieval people who cultivated the science of jurisprudence and evolved therefrom an independent system. Their system, *fiqh*[4] as they called it, was primarily based on the Koran and the sunnah (i.e. ḥadīth), styled *uṣūl* (roots, fundamental principles) and influenced by the Greco-Roman system. *Fiqh* was the science through which the canon law of Islam (*sharī'ah*[5]), the totality of Allah's commandments as revealed in the Koran and elaborated in the ḥadīth, was communicated to later generations. These commandments embrace regulations relative to ritual and worship (*'ibādāt*), civil and legal obligations (*mu'āmalāt*) and punishments (*'uqūbāt*).

Of the six thousand verses or thereabouts in the Koran only about two hundred, most of which occur in the Madīnese portion,

[1] (Cairo, 1280), vol. ii, p. 101.
[2] Vol. ii, p. 105.
[3] (Delhi, 1319), vol. i, p. 331.
[4] Literally "knowledge", "wisdom"
[5] Literally "road to the watering-place", "clear path to be followed".

especially sūrahs two and four, may be classed as strictly legislative. It soon became evident that these statutes were not sufficient to cover all cases—civil, criminal, political, financial—which might and did arise under the new conditions and varied situations encountered in Syria, al-ʿIrāq and other conquered territories. Hence the necessity for speculation. Speculation gave rise to two new fundamental principles: *qiyās*, i.e. analogical deduction, and *ijmāʿ*, i.e. catholic consent. Thus did Moslem jurisprudence come to have two new roots in addition to the Koran and tradition: analogy and consensus of opinion. As for *ra'y*, i.e. private judgment, though often resorted to, it was never quite elevated to the rank of a fifth fundamental principle. A traditional discourse between the Prophet and his appointee as qāḍi over al-Yaman, Muʿādh ibn-Jabal, sums up the Magna Charta of Islamic legal fundamentals:

Muḥammad: "How wilt thou decide when a question arises?"
Muʿādh: "According to the Book of Allah".
Muḥammad: "And if thou findest naught therein?"
Muʿādh: "According to the sunnah of the Messenger of Allah".
Muḥammad: "And if thou findest naught therein?"
Muʿādh: "Then shall I apply my own reasoning".[1]

The four orthodox schools

The leader of the ʿIrāq school, which insisted on the right of juridical speculation in contrast to the Madīnah school, which attached special importance to ḥadīth,[2] was abu-Ḥanīfah, properly al-Nuʿmān ibn-Thābit. Abu-Ḥanīfah was the grandson of a Persian slave,[3] flourished in al-Kūfah and Baghdād and died in 767. A merchant by profession, abu-Ḥanīfah became the first and most influential jurist in Islam. His teachings he imparted orally to his disciples, one of whom, abu-Yūsuf († 798), has preserved for us in his *Kitāb al-Kharāj*[4] the chief views of the master. Abu-Ḥanīfah did not actually introduce, though he emphasized strongly, the principle of analogical deduction leading to what we call legal fiction. He also insisted upon the right of "preference" (*istiḥsān*),[5] departure from analogy on grounds of equity. Like his competitor Mālik of al-Madīnah he had no idea of forming a juridical school (*madhhab*, rite), yet abu-Ḥanīfah became the founder of the earliest, largest and most

[1] Shahrastāni, p. 155. [2] *Ibid.* pp. 160-61; ibn-Khaldūn, *Muqaddamah*, p. 372.
[3] *Fihrist*, p. 201; ibn-Khallikān, vol. iii, p. 74. [4] (Cairo, 1346.)
[5] The *istiḥsān* of the Ḥanafite school, the *istiṣlāḥ* (principle of public advantage) of the Mālikite school, and the *ra'y* are often treated as synonyms of *qiyās* (analogy).

tolerant school of Islam. To his rite almost one half of the world of Sunnite Islam adheres. It was officially recognized in the territories of the defunct Ottoman empire as well as in India and Central Asia. As a system of religio-juridical thought von Kremer considers it "the highest and loftiest achievement of which Islam was capable".[1]

The leader of the Madīnah school, supposedly better acquainted with the Prophet's life and frame of mind, was Mālik ibn-Anas (*ca.* 715–95[2]), whose *al-Muwaṭṭa'*[3] (the levelled path), next to the compendium of Zayd ibn-'Ali[4] († 743), is the oldest surviving corpus of Moslem law. This monumental work, with its 1700 juridical traditions, codified the sunnah, outlined the first formula of the *ijmā'* (consensus of opinion) as prevalent in al-Madīnah and became the canon for the Mālikite rite. This rite drove from the Maghrib and Andalusia the two minor systems of al-Awzā'i († 774) and of al-Ẓāhiri[5] (815–83) and to the present day prevails throughout northern Africa, with the exception of Lower Egypt, and in eastern Arabia. After abu-Ḥanīfah and Mālik juridico-theological studies so developed as to become the most extensively cultivated branch of Arabic learning.

Between the liberal 'Irāq and the conservative Madīnah schools there arose one which professed to have found the golden mean by accepting speculation with certain reservations. This is the Shāfi'ite school, whose founder was Muḥammad ibn-Idrīs al-Shāfi'i. Born in Ghazzah (767), al-Shāfi'i, who belonged to the Quraysh family, studied under Mālik in al-Madīnah, but the main scenes of his activity were Baghdād and Cairo.[6] He died in 820 at Cairo, where his tomb at the foot of al-Muqaṭṭam is still the object of pilgrimage. The Shāfi'i rite still dominates Lower Egypt, eastern Africa, Palestine, western and southern Arabia, the coastal regions of India and the East Indies. Its adherents number about 105,000,000 as against 180,000,000 Ḥanafites, 50,000,000 Mālikites and 5,000,000 Ḥanbalites.

[1] *Culturgeschichte*, vol. i, p. 497. [2] Cf. ibn-Khallikān, vol. ii, p. 201.

[3] Delhi, 1302. See also his *al-Mudawwanah al-Kubra* (Cairo, 1323), 16 vols.

[4] *Majmū' al-Fiqh*, ed. E. Griffini (Milan, 1919).

[5] Dāwūd ibn-Khalaf al-Iṣbahāni (ibn-Khallikān, vol. i, p. 312), surnamed al-Ẓāhiri because he regarded only the literal (*ẓāhir*) meaning of the Koran and ḥadīth as authoritative. Though his teachings found a most gifted protagonist in ibn-Ḥazm of Cordova (994–1064), yet they did not survive.

[6] Yāqūt, *Udabā'*, vol. vi, pp. 367 *seq.*; ibn-Khallikān, vol. ii, pp. 215-16.

The last of the four rites into which the whole Moslem community, exclusive of the Shīʿah, has divided itself is the Ḥanbalite, which takes its name from Aḥmad ibn-Ḥanbal, a student of al-Shāfiʿi and a representative of uncompromising adherence to the letter of the ḥadīth. Ibn-Ḥanbal's conservatism served as the bulwark of orthodoxy in Baghdād against the Muʿtazilite innovations. Though subjected to the inquisition (*miḥnah*) and put in chains under al-Ma'mūn, scourged and imprisoned by al-Muʿtaṣim, ibn-Ḥanbal stubbornly refused to recant and allowed no modification in the traditional form of confession.[1] The 800,000 men and 60,000 women who are estimated to have attended his funeral in 855 at Baghdād[2] testify to the hold this stalwart champion of orthodoxy had on public imagination. Posterity venerated his tomb as that of a saint and honoured him with the same title, imām, bestowed upon abu-Ḥanīfah, Mālik and al-Shāfiʿi. For a long time the collection of over 28,000 traditions, *Musnad*,[3] ascribed to him, enjoyed special renown. Today, however, the Ḥanbalite rite claims no considerable following outside of the Wahhābis.

In the principle of *ijmāʿ*, elaborated by al-Shāfiʿi, the Moslem community hit upon a most useful theological expedient which has enabled its members to adapt their institutions and beliefs to varied and novel situations in a changing world. In a community where no church, no clergy and no central authority are recognized, deference to public opinion naturally assumes an important rôle. It was through this principle that the vulgate text of the Koran was canonized, the six canonical books of ḥadīths were approved, the miracles of the Prophet were accepted, lithographic reproductions of the Koran were authorized and the necessity of belonging to the Quraysh was dispensed with in favour of the Ottoman caliphs. The Shīʿites, it should be remembered, have their own rite and do not accept *ijmāʿ*. To it they oppose the absolute authority and judgment of the infallible imāms, all descendants of ʿAli. With the above four rites, which crystallized traditional dogma and everything necessary for doctrinal and juridical development, the door of *ijtihād*, the right of further interpreting the Koran and the sunnah or of forming a new opinion by applying analogy, was for ever closed to the

[1] Ibn-ʿAsākir, *Ta'rīkh*, vol. ii, pp. 41 *seq*.

[2] Ibn-Khallikān, vol. i, p. 28.

[3] 6 vols. (Cairo, 1313).

Sunnite community; but the Shīʿites still have their *mujtahids*, learned men who are qualified to act as spokesmen for the sublime and hidden imām and to interpret his ideas.

The indebtedness of the Islamic juridical system to the Roman-Byzantine laws, which had been for centuries naturalized in Syria, Palestine and Egypt, has not yet been made the object of the study it deserves by competent scholarship. Certain orientalists see Roman influence not only in particular regulations but also, and what is more important, in questions of principle and methodology. The Justinian Code recognized the method of analogical deduction and private judgment. Certain Byzantine regulations may have left their impress upon the Islamic statutes of purchase, sale and other commercial relationships; others relating to guardianship and will, letting and hiring may have passed through Judaic, rabbinical or talmudic, channels. But it is surprising that the Roman influence is not better marked in the system of the Syrian al-Awzāʿi († 774), who laboured in Beirūt,[1] as late as the sixth century still the seat of a flourishing school of Roman law, and came very near establishing a fifth rite.

Ethics

The prescriptions of the canon law (*sharīʿah*) discussed above regulate for the Moslem his entire life in its religious, political and social aspects. They govern his marital and civic relations as well as his relations with non-Moslems. Accordingly ethical conduct derives its sanctions and inhibitions from the sacred law. All man's acts are classified under five legal categories: (1) what is considered absolute duty (*farḍ*), embracing actions the commission of which is rewarded and the omission punished by law; (2) commendable or meritorious actions (*mustaḥabb*), the performance of which is rewarded but the omission not punished; (3) permissible actions (*jāʾiz*, *mubāḥ*), which are legally indifferent; (4) reprehensible actions (*makrūh*), which are disapproved but not punishable; (5) forbidden actions (*ḥarām*), the doing of which calls for punishment.

Ethical works based on the Koran and tradition, though numerous, do not exhaust all the material in Arabic literature dealing with morals (*akhlāq*).[2] There are at least three other types. Several works deal with good morals and refinement of spirit and deportment (*adab*). These are based mainly on Indo-

[1] Ibn-Khallikān, vol. i, p. 493.

[2] See Ḥājji Khalfah, vol. i, pp. 200-205.

Persian anecdotes, proverbs and wise sayings. *Al-Durrah al-Yatīmah*[1] by ibn-al-Muqaffaʻ (executed *ca.* 757), which eulogizes temperance, courage, liberality and proficiency in discourse and business, may be taken as a specimen of this type. A similarly popular philosophy of morality is found in the fables and proverbs of Luqmān, the Æsop of the Arabs. An ethical treatise by the celebrated constitutional theorist of Baghdād, al-Māwardi († 1058),[2] rich in wise sayings of the Prophet and the Companions, is still popular as a text-book in Egyptian and Syrian schools. Another type of work is philosophical, ultimately going back to Aristotle through Neo-Platonic and Neo-Pythagorean sources. These Greek works, headed by Aristotle's *Nichomachean Ethics* translated as *Kitāb al-Akhlāq* by Ḥunayn or his son Isḥāq,[3] laid the foundation of Arabic moral philosophy (*ʻilm al-akhlāq*), whose aim, like that of Aristotle and Plato, was to facilitate the attainment of earthly felicity. Of this school the most notable representative was the historian Miskawayh, whose *Tahdhīb al-Akhlāq*[4] is the best ethical work of the strictly philosophical or Neo-Platonic type composed by a Moslem. We also have in the epistles of the Brethren of Sincerity, of which the ninth is devoted to *akhlāq*, a characteristic deposit of Greek ethics pervaded by astrological and metaphysico-psychological speculation. The Brethren show special enthusiasm for Christ and Socrates as examples of the moral man, though to the Sunnites Muḥammad and to the Shīʻites ʻAli are the perfect men. The third type of ethics may be styled the mystico-psychological. Its exponents were al-Ghazzāli and various Sufi authors whom we shall consider in a forthcoming chapter. In all these Moslem moral philosophies certain virtues such as resignation, contentment and endurance are admired; vices are treated as maladies of the soul with the moral philosopher as the physician; and the classification is founded on the analysis of the faculties of the soul, each faculty having its own virtue and its own vice.

Literature

In the early centuries of the ʻAbbāsid power an interesting movement developed among the subjected races, particularly the Persians, whose object it was to combat the feeling of

[1] Ed. Shakīb Arislān (Cairo).
[2] *Adab al-Dunya w-al-Dīn*, 16th ed. (Cairo, 1925).
[3] Cf. *Fihrist*, p. 252.
[4] Several Cairo editions, none of them critical.

superiority which those Moslems of Arabian descent, real or claimed, had long manifested. The movement took its name Shu'ūbīyah (belonging to the peoples, non-Arabs) from a koranic verse (49 : 13) the purport of which was to inculcate the brotherhood and equality of all Moslems. Whilst among the Khārijites and the Shī'ites it took dynastic and political aspects, and among some Persians it took religious aspects involving heresy and *zindīqism*, yet the form which al-Shu'ūbīyah assumed in general was that of literary controversy. It derided the Arab pretensions to intellectual superiority and claimed for non-Arabs superiority in poetry and literature. The non-Arab cause was championed by such leaders as al-Bīrūni and Ḥamzah al-Iṣfahāni, whilst the Arab side was represented by several of Arabian as well as others of Persian extraction, including al-Jāḥiẓ,[1] ibn-Durayd,[2] ibn-Qutaybah and al-Balādhuri. It was in connection with such controversial questions that some of the earliest original pieces of Arabic literature were composed.

What we call "Arabic literature" was no more Arabian than the Latin literature of the Middle Ages was Italian. Its producers were men of the most varied ethnic origins[3] and in its totality it represents the enduring monument of a civilization rather than of a people. Even such disciplines as philology, linguistics, lexicography and grammar, which were primarily Arabian in origin and spirit and in which the Arabs made their chief original contribution, recruited some of their most distinguished scholars from the non-Arab stock. Al-Jawhari († *ca.* 1008), whose lexicon,[4] arranged in the alphabetical order of the final radical letters of the words, served as a model for later lexicographers, was a Turk from Fārāb.[5] His contemporary ibn-Jinni († 1002), who adorned the Ḥamdānid court at Aleppo and whose chief merit was a philosophical treatment of philology, was the son of a Greek slave.[6]

Belles-lettres

Arabic literature in the narrow sense of *adab* (belles-lettres) began with al-Jāḥiẓ († 868–9), the sheikh of the Baṣrah littérateurs, and reached its culmination in the fourth and fifth

[1] *Bayān*, vol. iii, pp. 9 *seq.*

[2] A lexicographer, died at Baghdād, 933. He wrote against the Shu'ūbīyah *Kitāb al-Ishtiqāq*, ed. Wüstenfeld (Göttingen, 1854).

[3] In his *Muqaddamah*, pp. 477-9, ibn-Khaldūn has a chapter headed "Most of the learned men in Islam were non-Arabians".

[4] *Ṣiḥāḥ*, 2 vols. (Būlāq, 1292). [5] Yāqūt, *Udabā'*, vol. ii, p. 266.

[6] *Ibid.* vol. v, p. 15.

Moslem centuries in the works of Badīʿ al-Zamān al-Hamadhāni (969–1008), al-Thaʿālibi[1] of Naysābūr (961–1038) and al-Ḥarīri (1054–1122). One characteristic feature of prose-writing in this period was the tendency, in response to Persian influence, to be affected and ornate. The terse, incisive and simple expression of early days had gone for ever. It was supplanted by polished and elegant style, rich in elaborate similes and replete with rhymes. The whole period was marked by a predominance of humanistic over scientific studies. Intellectually it was a period of decline. It supported a literary proletariat, many of whose members, with no independent means of livelihood, roamed from place to place ready to give battle over linguistic issues and grammatical technicalities or to measure poetical swords over trivial matters with a view to winning favours from wealthy patrons. This period also saw the rise of a new form of literary expression, the *maqāmah*.

Badīʿ al-Zamān (wonder of the age) al-Hamadhāni is credited with the creation of the *maqāmah* (assembly), a kind of dramatic anecdote in the telling of which the author subordinates substance to form and does his utmost to display his poetical ability, learning and eloquence. In reality such a form of composition as the *maqāmah* could not have been the creation of any one man; it was a natural development of rhymed prose and flowery diction as represented by ibn-Durayd and earlier stylists. Al-Hamadhāni's work[2] served as a model for al-Ḥarīri of al-Baṣrah,[3] whose *Maqāmāt*[4] for more than seven centuries were esteemed as the chief treasure, next to the Koran, of the literary Arabic tongue. In these *maqāmāt* of al-Ḥarīri and other writers there is much more than the elegant form and rhetorical anecdote which most readers consider the only significant feature. The anecdote itself is often used as a subtle and indirect way of criticizing the existing social order and drawing a wholesome moral. Since the days of al-Hamadhāni and al-Ḥarīri the *maqāmah* has become the most perfect form of literary and dramatic presentation in Arabic, a language which has never

[1] The name means furrier; ibn-Khallikān, vol. i, p. 522. His best-known work is *Yatīmat al-Dahr*, 4 vols. (Damascus, 1302), an anthology of contemporary poets.

[2] *Maqāmāt*, ed. Muḥammad ʿAbduh (Beirūt, 1889).

[3] Ibn-Khallikān, vol. i, p. 68.

[4] Ed. de Sacy, 2 vols. (Paris, 1847–53); tr. into English by Thomas Chenery and F. Steingass, 2 vols. (London, 1867–98).

produced real drama. Early Spanish and Italian tales of the realistic or picaresque type display clear affinities with the Arabic *maqāmah*.

Before the *maqāmah* was developed Arabic literature saw the rise of its greatest literary historian, abu-al-Faraj al-Iṣbahāni, or al-Iṣfahāni (*ca.* 897–967), a lineal descendant of Marwān, the last Umayyad caliph. Abu-al-Faraj flourished in Aleppo, where he produced his *Kitāb al-Aghāni*[1] (book of songs), a veritable treasury of poetry and literature and an indispensable source for the study of Moslem civilization. In his *Muqaddamah*[2] ibn-Khaldūn rightly calls it "the register of the Arabs" and "the final resource of the student of belles-lettres". His Aleppine patron Sayf-al-Dawlah al-Ḥamdāni bestowed on the author a thousand gold pieces as a reward for this work,[3] and the Andalusian al-Ḥakam II sent him a like sum. A Buwayhid vizir, al-Ṣāḥib ibn-'Abbād († 995), who is said to have been wont to take with him on his journeys thirty camel-loads of books, dispensed with them all on receiving a copy of *al-Aghāni*, which he thereafter carried about alone.[4]

The Arabian Nights

In this period, shortly before the middle of the tenth century, the first draft of what later became *Alf Laylah wa-Laylah*[5] (a thousand and one nights) was made in al-'Irāq. The basis of this draft, prepared by al-Jahshiyāri[6] († 942), was an old Persian work, *Hazār Afsāna* (thousand tales), containing several stories of Indian origin. Al-Jahshiyāri added other tales from local story-tellers.[7] The *Afsāna* provided the general plot and framework as well as the nomenclature for the leading heroes and heroines, including Shahrazād. As time went on additions were made from numberless sources: Indian, Greek, Hebrew, Egyptian and the like. Oriental folk-tales of every description were absorbed in the course of centuries. The court of Hārūn al-Rashīd provided a large quota of humorous anecdotes and love romances. The final form was not taken by the *Nights* until the later Mamlūk period in Egypt. Its heterogeneous character has inspired the

[1] 20 vols. (Būlāq, 1285); Brünnow edited vol. 21 (Leyden, 1888) and Guidi issued index (Leyden, 1900).

[2] P. 487.

[3] Yāqūt, vol. v, p. 150; ibn-Khallikān, vol. ii, p. 11.

[4] Ibn-Khallikān, vol. ii, p. 11, cf. vol. i, p. 133.

[5] Būlāq editions A. H. 1251 (1835) and 1279 fixed the vulgate Arabic text.

[6] Better known for his *Kitāb al-Wuzarā' w-al-Kuttāb*, ed. Hans v. Mžik (Leipzig, 1926).

[7] *Fihrist*, p. 304. Cf. Mas'ūdi, vol. iv, p. 90.

facetious words of a modern critic who has described the *Arabian Nights* as Persian tales told after the manner of Buddha by Queen Esther[1] to "Haroun Alraschid" in Cairo during the fourteenth century of the Christian era. First translated into French by Galland,[2] the *Nights* have worked their way into all the principal languages of modern Europe and Asia and have taken their place as the most popular piece of Arabic literature in the West, vastly more popular than in the Moslem East itself. In English the first important translation, incomplete but accurate, is that of Edward William Lane.[3] It has a valuable and full commentary and has gone through several editions. John Payne's translation,[4] the best in English, is complete but has no commentary. In his rendition Sir Richard F. Burton[5] follows Payne's except in the poetical part and endeavours to improve on it by attempting to reproduce the Oriental flavour of the original.

Poetry

The pre-Islamic poetry of the heroic age of the jāhilīyah provided models for the Umayyad bards, whose imitations of the antique odes were treated as classical by the ʿAbbāsid poets. The pietistic spirit fostered by the new régime of the banu-al-ʿAbbās, the foreign cultural and religious influences streaming mainly from Persia, and the patronage of the caliphs under whom the poets flourished and whom they were expected to laud and glorify, tended to produce deviation from the old trodden paths of classicism and develop new forms of poetical expression. Nevertheless poesy proved the most conservative of all Arab arts. Throughout the ages it never ceased to breathe the spirit of the desert. Even modern Arabic versifiers of Cairo, Damascus and Baghdād feel no incongruity in introducing their odes by apostrophizing the deserted encampments (*aṭlāl*) of the beloved, whose eyes they still liken to those of wild cows (*maha*). Other than poetry, law—particularly in its marital ordinances—is perhaps the only field in which the old desert elements have succeeded in perpetuating themselves.

The earliest exponent of the new style in poetry was the blind Persian Bashshār ibn-Burd, who was put to death in 783 under al-Mahdi, according to some for satirizing his vizir but more

[1] Cf. *Fihrist*, p. 304, l. 16, with Ṭabari, vol. i, p. 688, ll. 1, 12-13, and p. 689, l. 1.
[2] 12 vols. (Paris, 1704–17).
[3] 3 vols. (London, 1839–41). Ed. with illustrations by E. S. Poole, 3 vols. (London, 1859). Rev. by E. S. Poole, 3 vols. (London, 1883). Several later reprints.
[4] 9 vols. (London, 1882–4).
[5] 16 vols. (London and "Benares", 1885–8).

probably on account of his *zindīqism*, Zoroastrian or Manichaean secret views. Bashshār, who once thanked Allah for having made him blind "so that I need not see that which I hate",[1] was a rebel against the archaic formulas of ancient poetry.[2] Another early representative of the new school was the half-Persian abu-Nuwās[3] († *ca.* 810), the boon companion of Hārūn and al-Amīn and the poet in whose songs love and wine found their best expression. The name of abu-Nuwās has lived to the present day in the Arabic world as a synonym for clown; in reality he has few rivals in amorous sentiment, erotic expression and elegant diction. He is the lyric and bacchic poet par excellence of the Moslem world. The many songs on the beauty of boys attributed to this dissolute favourite of the 'Abbāsid court, as well as his poems in praise of wine (*khamrīyāt*), which have not ceased to enchant those who read and drink, throw interesting light upon contemporaneous aristocratic life.[4] The *ghazal* of abu-Nuwās, short poems of love ranging from five to fifteen verses, follow the model of Persian bards, who developed this verse form long before the Arabs.

Just as the witty and licentious abu-Nuwās represented the lighter side of court life, so did his ascetic contemporary abu-al-'Atāhiyah[5] (748–*ca.* 828), a potter by profession, give expression to pessimistic meditations on mortality which the common man of religious mentality entertained. The soul of this scion of the Bedouin tribe of 'Anazah rebelled against the frivolous high life of Baghdād, where he lived, and although Hārūn assigned to him a yearly stipend of 50,000 dirhams, he adopted the garb of a dervish and produced those ascetic and religious poems (*zuhdīyāt*) which entitle him to the position of father of Arabic sacred poetry.[6]

The provinces, particularly Syria, reared during the 'Abbāsid period a number of first-class poets, among whom the most renowned were abu-Tammām († *ca.* 845) and abu-al-'Alā'.

[1] *Aghāni*, vol. iii, p. 22.

[2] Consult the collection edited by Aḥmad H. al-Qirni as *Bashshār ibn-Burd: Shi'ruhu wa-Akhbāruhu* (Cairo, 1925); *Aghāni*, vol. iii, pp. 19-73, vol. vi, pp. 47-53; ibn-Khallikān, vol. i, p. 157; ibn-Qutaybah, *Shi'r*, pp. 476-9.

[3] Al-Ḥasan ibn-Hāni'; ibn-Khallikān, vol. i, p. 240.

[4] Consult his *Dīwān*, ed. Maḥmūd Wāṣif (Cairo, 1898); *Aghāni*, vol. xviii, pp. 2-8; ibn-Qutaybah, *Shi'r*, pp. 501-25.

[5] Ismā'īl ibn-al-Qāsim. On his life see *Aghāni*, vol. iii, pp. 126-83; Mas'ūdi, vol. vi., pp. 240-50, 333-40, vol. vii, pp. 81-7; ibn-Khallikān, vol. i, pp. 125-30.

[6] Consult his *Dīwān* (Beirūt, 1887).

Abu-Tammām's father, who kept a wine shop in Damascus, was a Christian by the name of Thādus (Thaddaios), which the son changed to Aws when he embraced Islam.[1] Abu-Tammām was a court poet in Baghdād. His title to fame rests as much on his *Dīwān*[2] as on his compilation of *Dīwān al-Ḥamāsah*,[3] poems celebrating valour in battle. This *Dīwān* embraces gems of Arabic poetry. The collection of *Ḥamāsah*[4] poems of the same description by the other court poet, al-Buḥturi (820–97), is inferior to that of abu-Tammām, after which it was modelled.

The patronage accorded by the ʿAbbāsid caliphs, vizirs and governors to poets, whom they employed as encomiasts, not only made the panegyric (*madīḥ*) an especially favourite form of poetical composition but led poets to prostitute their art, and resulted in that false glitter and empty bombast often said to be characteristic of Arabic poetry. ʿAbbāsid poetry, not unlike Arabic poetry of other periods, was moreover mainly subjective and provincial in character, full of local colour but unable to soar above time and place to gain a position among the timeless and landless offspring of the Muses.

[1] See *Aghāni*, vol. xv, pp. 99-108; Masʿūdi, vol. vii, pp. 147-67; ibn-Khallikān, vol. i, pp. 214-18.

[2] Ed. Shāhīn ʿAṭīyah, (Beirut, 1889).

[3] Ed. as *Ashʿār al-Ḥamāsah* by Freytag (Bonn, 1828), supplemented by a commentary in 2 vols. (Bonn, 1847–51).

[4] Photographic reproduction with indexes by Geyer and Margoliouth (Leyden, 1909).

THE OLDEST REPRESENTATION OF THE CAESAREAN SECTION

From al-Bīrūni, *al-Āthār al-Bāqiyah*, MS. dated A.H. 707 (1307–8), in the Library of the University of Edinburgh

CHAPTER XXVIII

EDUCATION

THE child's education began at home. As soon as he could speak it was the father's duty to teach him "the word" (*al-kalimah*): *La ilāha illa-l-Lāh* (no god whatsoever but Allah). When six years old the child was held responsible for the ritual prayer. It was then that his formal education began.[1]

Elementary

The elementary school (*kuttāb*) was an adjunct of the mosque, if not the mosque itself. Its curriculum centred upon the Koran as a reading text-book. With reading went writing. On visiting Damascus in 1184 ibn-Jubayr[2] noticed that the writing exercises by the pupils were not from the Koran but from secular poetry, for the act of erasing the word of Allah might discredit it. Together with reading and penmanship the students were taught Arabic grammar, stories about the prophets—particularly ḥadīths relating to Muḥammad—the elementary principles of arithmetic, and poems, but not of erotic character. Throughout the whole curriculum memory work was especially emphasized. Deserving pupils in the elementary schools of Baghdād were often rewarded by being paraded through the streets on camels whilst almonds were thrown at them. In one instance the shower had tragic results by destroying the eye of a young scholar.[3] Similar scenes enacted in honour of young pupils who have memorized the Koran are not infrequent today in Moslem lands. In certain cases the scholars were granted a whole or partial holiday whenever one of them had finally mastered a section of the Koran.

Girls were welcome to all the religious instruction in the lower grades of which their minds were capable, but there was no special desire to guide them further along the flowery and thorny path of knowledge. For after all was not the centre of a woman's sphere the spindle?[4] The children of the wealthy had private

[1] Cf. Ghazzāli, *Iḥyā'*, vol. i, p. 83.
[2] P. 272.
[3] *Aghāni*, vol. xviii, p. 101.
[4] Cf. Mubarrad, p. 150, l. 3.

tutors (sing. *mu'addib*) who instructed them in religion, polite literature and the art of versification. Very commonly these tutors were of foreign extraction. The ideals of aristocratic education may be ascertained from the instructions given by al-Rashīd to the tutor of his son al-Amīn:

> Be not strict to the extent of stifling his faculties or lenient to the point of making him enjoy idleness and accustom himself thereto. Straighten him as much as thou canst through kindness and gentleness, but fail not to resort to force and severity should he not respond.[1]

The rod was considered a necessary part of a teacher's equipment and, as is evident from the above, had the caliph's approval for use on his children. In his chapter on the parental management of children in *Risālat al-Siyāsah*,[2] ibn-Sīna speaks of "seeking the aid of the hand" as a valuable auxiliary of the educator's art.

The teacher in the elementary school, called *mu'allim*, sometimes *faqīh* on account of his theological training, came to occupy a rather low status socially. "Seek no advice from teachers, shepherds and those who sit much among women",[3] admonished a favourite adage. A judge under al-Ma'mūn went so far as to refuse to admit teachers' testimonies as satisfactory evidence in court. A whole body of anecdotes in Arabic literature developed round the teacher as a dunce. "More foolish than a teacher of an elementary school"[4] acquired proverbial usage. But the higher grade of teachers were on the whole highly respected. They evidently were organized into a sort of a guild, and the master would grant a recognized certificate (*ijāzah*) to those students who satisfactorily passed the prescribed course of study under him. In his treatise on pedagogy al-Zarnūji,[5] who wrote in 1203, devotes a section to the high regard in which a student should hold the profession of teaching, quoting the adage attributed to 'Ali: "I am the slave of him who hath taught me even one letter". Al-Zarnūji's is the best known of some two score Arabic treatises on education, most of which have survived in manuscript form.[6]

[1] Mas'ūdi, vol. vi, pp. 321-2; ibn-Khaldūn, *Muqaddamah*, pp. 475-6.
[2] Ed. Luwīs Ma'lūf in *al-Mashriq*, vol. ix (1906), p. 1074.
[3] Jāḥiẓ, *Bayān*, vol. i, p. 173.
[4] *Loc. cit.*
[5] *Ta'līm al-Muta'allim Ṭarīq al-Ta'allum*, ed. C. Caspari (Leipzig, 1838), pp. 14-19. See also Ghazzāli, vol. i, pp. 8-11.
[6] For a list see Khalīl A. Totah, *The Contribution of the Arabs to Education* (New York, 1926), pp. 67-76.

Institutions of higher education

The first prominent institution for higher learning in Islam was the Bayt al-Ḥikmah (the house of wisdom) founded by al-Ma'mūn (830) in his capital. Besides serving as a translation bureau this institute functioned as an academy and public library and had an observatory connected with it. The observatories, which sprang up at this time, it should be remembered, were also schools for teaching astronomy, just as the hospitals, which also made their first appearance at this period, served as centres for medical studies. But the first real academy in Islam[1] which made provision for the physical needs of its students and became a model for later institutions of higher learning was the Niẓāmīyah, founded in 1065–7 by the enlightened Niẓām-al-Mulk, the Persian vizir of the Saljūq Sultans Alp Arslān and Malikshāh and the patron of ʿUmar al-Khayyām. The Saljūqs, like the Buwayhids and other non-Arab sultans who usurped the sovereign power in Islam, vied with each other in patronizing the arts and higher education, evidently as a means of ingratiating themselves with the populace. The Niẓāmīyah was consecrated as a theological seminary (*madrasah*), particularly for the study of the Shāfiʿi rite and the orthodox Ashʿari system. In it the Koran and old poetry formed the backbone of the study of the humanities (*ʿilm al-adab*), precisely as the classics did later in the European universities. The students boarded in this academy and many of them held endowed scholarships. It is claimed that certain details of its organization appear to have been copied by the early universities of Europe.[2] That the students cherished a measure of *esprit de corps* is evidenced by the rough treatment accorded a representative of the court who came to seal the door of a room formerly occupied by a scholar who died in 1187 leaving no heirs.[3]

The Niẓāmīyah was a theological institution recognized by the state. Ibn-al-Athīr[4] cites the incident of a lecturer (*mudarris*) who received his appointment but could not perform his duty pending confirmation from the caliph. Evidently one lecturer was appointed at a time.[5] The lecturer had under him two or more *répétiteurs* (sing. *muʿīd*, repeater)[6] whose duty consisted in reading over the lecture after class and explaining it to

[1] Consult Suyūṭi, *Ḥusn*, vol. ii, pp. 156-7. Cf. Qazwīni, *Āthār*, p. 276.
[2] Reuben Levy, *A Baghdād Chronicle* (Cambridge, 1929), p. 193.
[3] Ibn-al-Athīr, vol. xi, p. 115.
[4] Vol. xi, p. 100.
[5] Ibn-al-Athīr, vol. x, p. 123.
[6] See ibn-Khallikān, vol. iii, p. 430.

the less-gifted students. Ibn-Jubayr[1] once attended a lecture delivered after the mid-afternoon prayers by the ranking professor. The lecturer stood on a platform while the students sat on stools and plied him with written and oral questions till evening prayer. It was in this Niẓāmīyah that al-Ghazzāli lectured for four years (1091–5).[2] In the chapter on learning with which he introduced his *Iḥyā'*[3] al-Ghazzāli combated the idea that the imparting of knowledge was the object of education and emphasized the necessity of stimulating the moral consciousness of the student, thus becoming the first author in Islam to bring the problem of education into organic relation with a profound ethical system. Among the later eminent teachers of the Niẓāmīyah was Bahā'-al-Dīn, Ṣalāḥ-al-Dīn's (Saladin's) biographer, who tells us in his reminiscences, as reported in ibn-Khallikān,[4] that to sharpen their memories a group of students once drank such a heavy dose of an infusion of anacardia[5] kernels that one of them lost his wits entirely and came naked to the class. When amidst the laughter of the class he was asked for an explanation, he gravely replied that he and his companions had tried the anacardia infusion, which made them all insane with the exception of himself, who had happily kept his senses.

Al-Niẓāmīyah survived the catastrophe that befell the capital at its capture by Hūlāgu in 1258, as it survived the later invasions by the Tartars, and was finally merged with its younger sister, al-Mustanṣirīyah, about two years after Tīmūr Lang (Tamerlane) captured Baghdād in 1393. Al-Mustanṣirīyah derived its name from the next-to-last caliph, al-Mustanṣir,[6] who built it in 1234 as a seminary for the four orthodox rites. The building had a clock (doubtless of the clepsydra type) at the entrance, was equipped with baths and kitchens and included a hospital and a library. Ibn-Baṭṭūṭah,[7] who visited Baghdād in 1327, gives us a detailed description of the building. Renovated as a school in 1961 this structure and al-*Qaṣr* (palace) *al-'Abbāsi*, now a museum, are the only ones surviving from 'Abbāsid days.

[1] Pp. 219-20.

[2] Ibn-Khallikān, vol. ii, p. 246; *al-Munqidh min al-Ḍalāl* (Cairo, 1329), pp. 29-30.

[3] Vol. i, pp. 43-9; *Ayyuha al-Walad*, ed. and tr. Hammer-Purgstall (Vienna, 1838); tr. (Eng.) G. H. Scherer (Beirūt, 1933).

[4] Vol. iii, pp. 435 *seq.*

[5] Ar. *balādhur*, from Pers. *balādur*. The celebrated historian al-Balādhuri is said to have died as a result of drinking the juice of the anacardia (cashew nut). Hence his surname.

[6] Abu-al-Fidā', vol. iii, p. 179.

[7] Vol. ii, pp. 108-9.

Besides the Niẓāmīyah of Baghdād the Saljūq vizir is credited with establishing several other seminaries in Naysābūr and other towns of the empire. Prior to Ṣalāḥ-al-Dīn he was the greatest patron of higher education in Islam. The Niẓāmīyah type of *madrasah* spread over Khurāsān, al-'Irāq and Syria. Founding a *madrasah* was always considered a meritorious act in Islam. This explains the large number of such institutions reported by travellers. Ibn-Jubayr[1] counted in Baghdād about thirty schools; in Damascus, which then enjoyed its golden age under Ṣalāḥ-al-Dīn, about twenty; in al-Mawṣil, six or more; and in Ḥimṣ only one.

In all these higher institutions of theology the science of tradition lay at the basis of the curriculum, and memory work was especially stressed. In those days of no diaries and no memoranda the retentive faculties must have been developed to phenomenal limits, if we are to believe the sources. Al-Ghazzāli earned his title *ḥujjat al-Islām* (the authority of Islam) by memorizing 300,000 traditions. Aḥmad ibn-Ḥanbal, it is said, knew by heart 1,000,000.[2] Al-Bukhāri was tested by one hundred traditions in which the chain of authorities (*isnād*) of the one was affixed to the text (*matn*) of the other—all of which he straightened out nicely from memory.[3] Poets vied with traditionists in memory work. Having read a copy of a book loaned him by a bookseller, al-Mutanabbi' saw no more reason for buying the book, for its contents were already stored in his mind. Anecdotes of a similar nature are told to prove the prodigious memories of abu-Tammām and al-Ma'arri.

Adult education

Adult education was nowhere carried on in a systematic way, but the mosques in almost all Moslem towns served as important educational centres. When a visitor came to a new city he could make his way to the congregational mosque confident that he could attend lectures on ḥadīth. This is what al-Maqdisi[4] tells us he did on visiting distant al-Sūs. This travelling geographer of the tenth century found in his native Palestine and in Syria, Egypt and Fāris many circles (sing. *ḥalqah*) or assemblies (sing. *majlis*) centring upon *faqīhs*, Koran readers and littérateurs in the mosques.[5] The Imām al-Shāfi'i presided at such a *halqah*

[1] P. 229, l. 10, p. 283, l. 8, p. 236, ll. 1-2, p. 258, l. 20.
[2] Ibn-Khallikān, vol. i, p. 28.
[3] Ibn-Khallikān, vol. ii, pp. 230-31.
[4] P. 415.
[5] Maqdisi, pp. 182, 179, l. 20, pp. 205, 439, l. 11.

at the Mosque of 'Amr at al-Fusṭāṭ, where he taught various subjects every morning till his death in 820.[1] Ibn-Ḥawqal[2] mentions similar assemblies in Sijistān. Not only religious but linguistic and poetical subjects were treated in these assemblies.[3] Every Moslem had free admission to such lectures in the mosques, which remained until the eleventh century the extension school of Islam.

These mosque circles bring to mind another type of coterie, chiefly literary, which met in the homes of the aristocracy and cultured society under the name of *majālis al-adab*,[4] literary salons. These gatherings begin to appear early under the 'Abbāsids. In the presence of several early caliphs poetical contests, religious debates and literary conferences were often held. We owe a few surviving works to such debates.[5]

Libraries

Mosques also functioned as repositories for books. Through gifts and bequests mosque libraries became especially rich in religious literature. Among others the historian al-Khaṭīb al-Baghdādi (1002–71) willed his books "as a *waqf* [mortmain] for the Moslems", but they were housed in the home of a friend of his.[6] Other libraries established by dignitaries or men of wealth as semi-public institutions housed collections bearing on logic, philosophy, astronomy and other sciences.[7] Scholars and men of standing had no difficulty in finding access even to private collections. Al-Mawṣil had before the middle of the tenth century a library, built by one of its citizens, where students were even supplied with free paper.[8] The library (*khizānat al-kutub*) founded in Shīrāz by the Buwayhid 'Aḍud-al-Dawlah (977–82) had its books arranged in cases and listed in catalogues and was administered by a regular staff.[9] In the same century al-Baṣrah had a library whose founder granted stipends for scholars working in it.[10] In al-Rayy there flourished at the same time a "home of books" with over four hundred camel-loads of manuscripts listed in a ten-volume catalogue.[11] Libraries were used as meeting-places for scientific discussion and debate. Yāqūt spent three years collecting material for his geographical dictionary from the

[1] Yāqūt, *Udabā'*, vol. vi, p. 383; Suyūṭi, *Ḥusn*, vol. i, p. 136.
[2] P. 317.
[3] Yāqūt, vol. iv, p. 135, ll. 14-16, vol. vi, p. 432, ll. 14-16.
[4] *Aghāni*, vol. xviii, p. 101.
[5] See above, p. 354.
[6] Yāqūt, vol. i, p. 252, vol. iv, p. 287.
[7] For an illustration see *ibid.* vol. v, p. 467.
[8] Yāqūt, vol. ii, p. 420.
[9] Maqdisi, p. 449. See also Yāqūt, vol. v, p. 446.
[10] Maqdisi, p. 413.
[11] Yāqūt, vol. ii, p. 315.

libraries of Marw and Khwārizm, whence he fled in 1220 at the approach of the Mongol hordes of Chingīz Khān, who committed all these libraries to the flames.

Bookshops

The bookshop as a commercial and educational agency also makes its appearance early under the 'Abbāsids. Al-Ya'qūbi[1] asserts that in his time (891) the capital boasted over a hundred book-dealers congregated in one street. Many of these shops, like their modern successors in Cairo and Damascus, were but small booths by the mosques, but some were undoubtedly large enough to act as centres for connoisseurs and bibliophiles. The booksellers themselves were often calligraphers, copyists and literati who used their shops not only as stores and ateliers but as centres for literary discussion. They occupied a not inconspicuous place in society. Yāqūt started on his career as a book-dealer's clerk. Al-Nadīm († 995), also called al-Warrāq (stationer), was evidently himself a librarian or book-dealer to whose catalogue we possibly owe that scholarly and remarkable work *al-Fihrist*. In this work[2] we read of an 'Irāqi bibliophile whose large trunk housed treasures of manuscripts which included parchments, Egyptian papyri, Chinese paper and leather scrolls, each bearing the name of the scribe attested by the notes of from five to six generations of learned men.

Paper

The common writing-material was parchment or papyrus down to the beginning of the third Moslem century. Certain official documents written on parchment and looted in the civil war between al-Amīn and al-Ma'mūn were later washed clean and sold again.[3] After the beginning of the third century some Chinese paper was imported into al-'Irāq, but soon the paper industry became indigenous. It was first into Samarquand, as we have already pointed out, that certain Chinese prisoners introduced in 751 the art of manufacturing paper from flax, linen or hemp rags.[4] The ancient Arabic word for paper, *kāghad*, is probably of Chinese origin through Persian. From Samarquand the industry soon passed to al-'Irāq. At the instance of the Barmakid al-Faḍl ibn-Yaḥya, who had been governor of Khurāsān in 794, the first paper-mill was established in Baghdād.[5] His brother Ja'far, Hārūn's vizir, had parchment replaced by paper in the

[1] P. 245. [2] P. 40. [3] *Fihrist*, p. 21.

[4] W. Barthold, *Turkestan down to the Mongol Invasion*, 2nd ed. (Oxford, 1928), pp. 236-7. Cf. *Fihrist*, p. 21.

[5] Ibn-Khaldūn, *Muqaddamah*, p. 352.

government offices.[1] Other Moslem towns erected mills on the plan of those in Samarqand. A native factory arose in Tihāmah for the manufacture of paper from vegetable fibre.[2] At the time of al-Maqdisi[3] the Samarqand product was still considered the finest. But in the following century, the eleventh, even better paper was manufactured in such Syrian towns as Tripoli.[4] From Western Asia the industry made its way at the end of the ninth century into the Delta of Egypt, where several towns had been for a long time exporting to the Greek-speaking lands papyrus for writing-material under the name *qarāṭīs*.[5] By the end of the tenth century paper had succeeded in entirely displacing papyrus and parchment throughout the Moslem world.

General level of culture

That there was an élite of highly educated men under the first 'Abbāsids is fully recognized, but how high the general level of culture was among the masses is not so easy to determine. A story about a starving scholar of Baghdād who hesitated to sell his books even when his daughter was taken ill has been preserved in Yāqūt.[6] The answers submitted by the educated slave girl Tawaddud to the questions of the savants as reported in *The Thousand and One Nights* (nos. 438-61) may be taken as an index of the degree of knowledge attained by the cultured person after Hārūn and down to the twelfth century. According to Tawaddud intellect is of two kinds: one innate and the other acquired. Its seat is the heart, where God deposits it and whence it ascends to the brain. Man has three hundred and sixty veins, two hundred and forty bones and five senses. He is compounded of four elements: water, earth, fire and air. The stomach lies in front of the heart, to which the lungs are ventilators. The liver is the seat of compassion; the spleen, of laughter; and the two kidneys, of cunning. The head has five faculties: sensation, imagination, will, fancy and retention. The stomach is the home of all disease, and diet is the source of all healing. The planets are seven: the sun, the moon, Mercury, Venus, Mars, Jupiter and Saturn.[7]

[1] Maqrīzi, *Khiṭaṭ*, ed. Wiet, vol. ii, p. 34. Cf. Qalqashandi, vol. ii, pp. 475-6.

[2] See *Fihrist*, p. 40, l. 23.

[3] P. 326.

[4] Nāsir-i-Khusraw, *Sefer Nāmeh*, ed. and tr. Charles Schefer (Paris, 1881), text p. 12, tr. p. 41.

[5] Sing. *qirṭās*, from Gr. *chartēs*. See Ya'qūbi, p. 338, ll. 8, 13; Qalqashandi, vol. ii, p. 474. See above, p. 347.

[6] Vol. i, pp. 38-9.

[7] The very same planets of the Ptolemaic system. The last five were those known to the Assyrians and Babylonians; Jastrow, *Civilization of Babylonia*, p. 261.

From T. W. Arnold and A. Grohmann, "The Islamic Book," by permission of the Pegasus Press, Paris

A SILVER PORTRAIT COIN OF AL-MUTAWAKKIL (OF THE YEAR 855) WITH A TWO-POINTED BEARD, WEARING A LOW CAP OF THE SĀSĀNID TYPE

(Original in Kunsthistorisches Museum, Vienna)

CHAPTER XXIX

THE DEVELOPMENT OF FINE ARTS

IN his art as in his poetry the Arab, a Semite, revealed himself with a keen appreciation of the particular and the subjective and with a delicate sense for detail, but with no particular capacity for harmonizing and unifying the various parts into a great and united whole. However, in architecture and painting particularly, he did not so early attain a certain degree of progress, and stand still for ever after, as he did in his sciences after the tenth century.

Architecture

Of the architectural monuments which once adorned the city of al-Manṣūr and al-Rashīd no trace has been left, whereas two of the noblest surviving structures of Islam, the Umayyad Mosque at Damascus and the Dome of the Rock at Jerusalem, date from the earlier Umayyad period. The caliphal palace called the Golden Gate (*bāb al-dhahab*) or Green Dome (*al-qubbah al-khaḍrā'*) erected by the founder of Baghdād, as well as his Palace of Eternity (*qaṣr al-khuld*) and the Ruṣāfah palace, built for the crown prince al-Mahdi;[1] the palaces of the Barmakids at al-Shammāsīyah;[2] the palace of the Pleiades (*al-thurayya*), on which al-Mu'taḍid (892–902), who restored Baghdād as capital after Sāmarra, spent 400,000 dinars,[3] and his adjoining palace styled the Crown (*al-tāj*),[4] completed by his son al-Muktafi (902–8); the unique mansion of al-Muqtadir (908–32) designated the Hall of the Tree (*dār al-shajarah*) on account of the gold and silver tree that stood in its pond; the Buwayhid mansion known by the name al-Mu'izzīyah after Mu'izz-al-Dawlah (932–67), which cost 1,000,000 dinars[5]—all these and many others like them left no remains to give us an inkling of the splendour that was theirs. So complete was the destruction wrought by the civil war between al-Amīn and al-Ma'mūn, by the final devastation of the capital by Hūlāgu in 1258 and by natural causes that even the sites of most of these palaces cannot today be identified.

Outside of the capital no 'Abbāsid ruin can be dated with any degree of probability prior to the reigns of al-Mu'taṣim (833–42), founder of Sāmarra, and of his son al-Mutawakkil (847–861), the builder of its great mosque.[6] This congregational mosque, which cost 700,000 dinars,[7] was rectangular and the multifoil arches of its windows suggest Indian influence. Neither here nor in the mosque at abu-Dulaf (also of the mid-ninth century) near Sāmarra has any trace been found of the *miḥrāb* (prayer niche) in the *qiblah* wall. The wall *miḥrāb* seems to have been a Syrian invention, suggested in all likelihood by the apse in the Christian church.[8] Outside, against the wall of the great mosque of Sāmarra, rose a tower which is analogous to the ancient Babylonian *ziggurat*.[9] This tower was copied by ibn-Ṭūlūn for the minaret of his mosque (876–9), in which the pointed arch appears for the third time in Egypt, after the repaired mosque of 'Amr (827) and the Nilometer (861). Such 'Abbāsid remains as have survived at al-Raqqah, of the late

[1] Al-Khaṭīb (al-Baghdādi), vol. i, pp. 82-3.
[2] One of the eastern quarters of Baghdād.
[3] Mas'ūdi, vol. viii, p. 116. This palace was destroyed two centuries later.
[4] Khaṭīb, vol. i, pp. 99 *seq.*
[5] Ibn-al-Athīr, vol. ix, p. 256.
[6] Ya'qūbi, p. 260; Maqdisi, p. 122.
[7] Yāqūt, *Buldān*, vol. iii, p. 17.
[8] Ernest T. Richmond, *Moslem Architecture, 623 to 1516* (London, 1926), p. 54; cf. Ernst Herzfeld, *Erster vorläufiger Bericht über die Ausgrabungen von Samarra* (Berlin, 1912), p. 10. See above, p. 261.
[9] Above, p. 262. This ancient minaret with its spiral outside stairway still exists under the name Malwīyah (the bent one).

From Ernst Herzfeld, "*Erster Vorläufiger Bericht über die Ausgrabungen von Samarra*" (*Dietrich Reimer Verlag, Berlin*)

THE MALWĪYAH TOWER OF THE GREAT MOSQUE AT SĀMARRA, NINTH CHRISTIAN CENTURY

eighth century, and at Sāmarra carry on the tradition of Asiatic, more particularly Persian, architecture in contrast to the Umayyad structures which bear clear traces of Byzantine-Syrian art. Under the Sāsānid dynasty (A.D. 226–641) a distinctive type of Persian architecture was developed, with ovoid or elliptical domes, semicircular arches, spiral towers, indented

From Andrae. "Der Anu-Adad-Tempel" (Hinrichs, Leipzig)

STAGE TOWERS, *ZIGGURAT*, OF THE ANU-ADAD TEMPLE AT ASHUR (A RECONSTRUCTION)

battlements, glazed wall-tiles and metal-covered roofs. This type became one of the most powerful factors in the formation of ʿAbbāsid art.

Painting

The theologians' hostility to all forms of representational art[1] did no more stop its development along Islamic lines than did the more explicit koranic injunction against wine enforce prohibition in Moslem society. We have already noticed that al-Manṣūr set upon the dome of his palace the figure of a horseman which might have served as a weathercock, that al-Amīn had his pleasure boats on the Tigris fashioned like lions, eagles and dolphins and that al-Muqtadir had a gold and silver tree with eighteen branches planted in a huge tank in his palace.

[1] See above, pp. 269-71.

On either side of the tank stood the statues of fifteen horsemen, dressed in brocade and armed with lances, constantly moving as though in combat.

The builder of Sāmarra (836), the Caliph al-Mu'taṣim, had the walls of his palace there ornamented like those of Quṣayr 'Amrah with frescoes of nude female figures and hunting-scenes, probably the work of Christian artists. His second successor, al-Mutawakkil, under whom this temporary capital reached its zenith,[1] employed for the mural decoration of his palace Byzantine painters who had no scruples against including among the many pictures a church with monks.[2]

In Islam painting was pressed into the service of religion at a rather late date and never became its handmaid as it did in Buddhism and Christianity. The earliest record of any pictorial representation of the Prophet was noted by an Arabian traveller of the late ninth century who saw it in the Chinese court,[3] but it may well have been produced by Nestorians. The many representations of the Burāq seem to have taken for their prototype, through Persian channels, Greek centaurs or the human-headed, winged beasts of the earlier Assyrians. Moslem religious painting, however, does not make its full appearance until the beginning of the fourteenth century. Its derivation was evidently from the art of the Oriental Christian churches, particularly the Jacobite and the Nestorian, as the researches of Arnold have shown,[4] and developed from book-decoration. In miniature illustration the Manichaean influence is sometimes apparent.[5] Of the few Arabic works dealing with the history of Islamic painters unfortunately none have survived—so little has been the interest in the subject.

The oldest illustrated Arabic manuscript extant is al-Ṣūfi's astronomy dated 1005 (now in Leningrad). In belles-lettres we have no work before the thirteenth and twelfth Christian centuries, as represented by *Kalīlah wa-Dimnah*, al-Ḥarīri's *Maqāmāt*, and *al-Aghāni*.[6] These miniatures reveal artists who worked under

[1] His buildings are discussed by Ya'qūbi, pp. 266-7, and by Yāqūt, vol. iii, pp. 17-18, who estimates that they cost al-Mutawakkil 294,000,000 dirhams.

[2] Ernst Herzfeld, *Die Malereien von Samarra* (Berlin, 1927), pls. lxi, lxiii.

[3] Mas'ūdi, vol. i, pp. 315-18.

[4] *Painting in Islam* (Oxford, 1928), ch. iii.

[5] Cf. Thomas W. Arnold and Adolf Grohmann, *The Islamic Book* (London, 1929), p. 2.

[6] For a 1217/18 miniature of the Prophet consult *Bulletin de l'Institut d'Égypte*, vol, xxviii (Cairo, 1946), pp. 1-5.

By courtesy of Edinburgh University Library

THE MONK BAḤĪRA RECOGNIZING THE PROPHETIC MISSION OF MUḤAMMAD

Original in Rashīd-al-Dīn, *Jāmiʿ al-Tawārīkh*, MS. dated A.H. 710 (1310–11), Edinburgh University Library, Arabic No. 20

the influence of traditions derived from a Christian source or were Christians themselves. Such Moslems as cared to ignore the teaching of their theologians had first to employ Jacobite or Nestorian painters until the Moslems themselves had time to develop their independent artists. Persia with its old Indo-Iranian instincts and traditions was particularly fertile in the

From Arnold and Grohmann, "The Islamic Book" (The Pegasus Press)

A SCENE FROM AL-ḤARĪRI, *MAQĀMAH* 19

A sick man, with his son behind his head, is visited by his friends

MS., dated A.H. 734 (1334), in the National Library, Vienna

early production of such independent painters. But the prevailing idea that this production was due to non-conformist Shīʿite tendencies cannot be sound in view of the fact that Shīʿism did not prevail in Persia to the extent of becoming the state religion until the establishment of the Ṣafawid dynasty in 1502.

Industrial arts

Since early antiquity the Persians have proved themselves masters of decorative design and colour. Through their efforts the industrial arts of Islam attained a high degree of excellence. Carpet-weaving, as old as Pharaonic Egypt, was especially developed. Hunting and garden scenes were favoured in rug designs, and alum was used in the dye to render the many colours fast. Decorated silk fabrics, the product of Moslem hand-looms in Egypt and Syria, were so highly prized in Europe that they were chosen by Crusaders and other Westerners, above all textiles, as wrappings for relics of saints.

In ceramics, another art as ancient as Egypt and Susa, the reproduction of the human form and of animals and plants, as well as geometric and epigraphic figures, attained a beauty of decorative style unsurpassed in any other Moslem art.[1] In spite of the prejudicial attitude of legists, which crystallized in the second and third Moslem centuries against plastic as well as pictorial art, pottery and metal-work continued to produce distinctive pieces second to none in the Middle Ages. Qāshāni tile, decorated with conventional flowers, which was introduced from Persia to Damascus, found great vogue, together with mosaic work, in exterior and interior decoration of buildings. Better than any others, Arabic characters lent themselves to decorative designs and became a powerful motif in Islamic art. They even became religious symbols. Particularly in Antioch, Aleppo, Damascus and such ancient Phoenician towns as Tyre were the processes of enamelling and gilding glass perfected. Among the treasures of the Louvre, the British Museum and the Arab Museum of Cairo are exquisite pieces from Sāmarra and al-Fusṭāṭ, including plates, cups, vases, ewers and lamps for home and mosque use, painted with brilliant radiant lustres and acquiring through the ages metallic glazes of changing rainbow hue.

Calligraphy

The art of calligraphy, which drew its prestige from its object to perpetuate the word of God, and enjoyed the approval of the Koran (68 : 1, 96 : 4), arose in the second or third Moslem century and soon became the most highly prized art.[2] It was entirely Islamic and its influence on painting was appreciable. Through it the Moslem sought a channel for his esthetic nature, which could not express itself through the representation of animate objects. The calligrapher held a position of dignity and honour far above the painter. Even rulers sought to win religious merit by copying the Koran. Arabic books of history and literature have preserved for us with honourable mention the names of several calligraphers, but kept their silence in the case of architects, painters and metal-workers. Among the founders of Arabic

[1] Gaston Migeon, *Les arts musulmans* (Paris, 1926), pp. 36-7.
[2] See Qalqashandi, vol. iii, pp. 5 *seq.*, vol. ii, pp. 430 *seq.*

calligraphy were al-Rayḥāni[1] (Rīḥāni, † 834), who flourished under al-Ma'mūn and perfected the style named after him; ibn-Muqlah (886–940), the 'Abbāsid vizir whose hand was cut off by the Caliph al-Rāḍi and who could still write elegantly with his left hand and even by attaching a pen to the stump of his right one;[2] and ibn-al-Bawwāb[3] († 1022 or 1032), the son of a porter of the audience chamber of Baghdād and inventor of the *muḥaqqaq* style. The last penman of the 'Abbāsid period to achieve distinction was Yāqūt al-Musta'ṣimi, the court calligraphist of the last 'Abbāsid caliph, from whose name the Yāqūti style derives its designation. Judging by the surviving specimens of the penmanship of Yāqūt[4] and other renowned calligraphers of yore the artistic merits cannot be placed high. Calligraphy is perhaps the only Arab art which today has Christian and Moslem representatives in Constantinople, Cairo, Beirūt and Damascus whose productions excel in elegance and beauty any masterpieces that the ancients ever produced.

Not only calligraphy but its associate arts, colour decoration, illumination, and the whole craft of bookbinding, owed their genesis and bloom to their relation to the sacred book. Under the late 'Abbāsids began the art of book-decoration and Koran illumination which reached its highest development in the Saljūq and Mamlūk periods. Here again the pictorial art of the Nestorians and Jacobites was evidently the main influencing factor. The Moslem gilder (*mudhahhib*), who thus arose after the calligrapher, ranked second to him in importance. After the Koran the art was extended to include profane manuscripts.

Music

The legists' disapproval of music was no more effective in Baghdād than it had been before in Damascus. The 'Abbāsid al-Mahdi began where the last Umayyads ended. He invited and patronized Siyāṭ[5] of Makkah (739–85), "whose song warmed the chilled more than a hot bath",[6] and his pupil Ibrāhīm al-Mawṣili (742–804), who after his master became the patriarch of classical music. When young, Ibrāhīm, a descendant of a noble Persian family,[7] was kidnapped outside al-Mawṣil and during

[1] *Fihrist*, p. 119; Yāqūt, *Udabā'*, vol. v, pp. 268 *seq.*

[2] Ibn-Khallikān, vol. ii, p. 472; *Fakhri*, pp. 368, 370-71; Yāqūt, vol. iii, p. 150. ll. 8-10.

[3] Ibn-Khallikān, vol. ii, pp. 31 *seq.*; Nuwayri, vol. vii, pp. 3-4,

[4] See B. Moritz, *Arabic Palæography* (Cairo, 1905), pl. 89.

[5] 'Abdullāh ibn-Wahb, a freedman of Khuzā'ah; *Aghāni*, vol. vi, p. 7.

[6] *Aghāni*, vol. vi, p. 8, ll. 4-5, quoted by Nuwayri, vol. iv, p. 289.

[7] *Fihrist*, p. 140; ibn-Khallikān, vol. i, p. 14; Nuwayri, vol. iv, p. 320.

his detention learned some of the brigands' songs. He was the first to beat the rhythm with a wand[1] and could detect one girl among thirty lute-players and ask her to tighten the second string of her ill-tuned instrument.[2] Later, al-Rashīd took Ibrāhīm into his service as boon companion, bestowed on him 150,000 dirhams and assigned him a monthly salary of 10,000 dirhams. From his patron the artist received occasional presents, one of which is said to have amounted to 100,000 dirhams for a single song. Ibrāhīm had an inferior rival in ibn-Jāmi', a Qurayshite and stepson of Siyāṭ. In the judgment of the *'Iqd* "Ibrāhīm was the greatest of the musicians in versatility, but ibn-Jāmi' had the sweetest note".[3] When a favoured court minstrel was asked by Hārūn for his opinion of ibn-Jāmi', his reply was: "How can I describe honey, which is sweet however you taste it?"[4]

The refined and dazzling court of al-Rashīd patronized music and singing, as it did science and art, to the extent of becoming the centre of a galaxy of musical stars.[5] Salaried musicians accompanied by men and women slave singers thrived in it and furnished the theme for numberless fantastic anecdotes immortalized in the pages of the *Aghāni*,[6] *'Iqd*, *Fihrist*, *Nihāyah*, and, above all, the *Arabian Nights*. Two thousand such singers took part in a musical festival under the caliph's patronage. His son al-Amīn held a similar night entertainment in which the personnel of the palace, both male and female, danced till dawn.[7] While the army of al-Ma'mūn was investing Baghdād al-Amīn sat pathetically in his palace on the bank of the Tigris listening to his favourite singing girls.[8]

Another protégé of al-Rashīd was Mukhāriq († *ca.* 845), a pupil of Ibrāhīm. When young, Mukhāriq was bought by a woman singer who heard him in his father's butcher shop crying in his beautiful and powerful voice his father's meats. He later passed into the possession of Hārūn, who freed him, rewarded him with 100,000 dinars[9] and honoured him with a seat by the caliph's side. One evening he went out on the Tigris and

[1] *'Iqd*, vol. iii, p. 240, l. 4. Cf. above, p. 275.
[2] *Aghāni*, vol. v, p. 41.
[3] Vol. iii, p. 239.
[4] *Loc. cit.* Cf. *Aghāni*, vol. vi, p. 12.
[5] *'Iqd*, vol. iii, pp. 239 *seq.*
[6] Besides being a treasure-house of information on almost every phase of Arab social life, this "book of songs" is also a history of music from pre-Islamic days to the time of the author, al-Iṣfahāni (897–967), the greatest music historian the Arabs produced.
[7] Above, p. 303.
[8] Mas'ūdi, vol. vi, pp. 426-30.
[9] *Aghāni* vol. xxi, p. 226, vol. viii, p. 20.

started to sing. Immediately torches began to move to and fro in the streets of Baghdād in the hands of people anxious to hear the master-singer.[1]

Al-Ma'mūn and al-Mutawakkil had as a cup companion Isḥāq ibn-Ibrāhīm al-Mawṣili (767–850), dean of the musicians of his age.[2] After his father, Isḥāq personified the spirit of classical Arabic music. As an all-round musician he was "the greatest that Islām had produced".[3] He claimed, as did also his father and Ziryāb, that it was the *jinn* who prompted his melodies.

These and other *virtuosi* of the halcyon days who won undying fame as companions to the caliphs were more than musicians; they were endowed with keen wits and retentive memories well stocked with choice verses of poetry and delightful anecdotes. They were singers, composers, poets and scholars well versed in the scientific lore of the day. Under them stood the instrumentalists (sing. *ḍārib*), among whom the lute was generally most favoured; the viol (*rabāb*) was used by inferior performers. Then came the singing girls (sing. *qaynah*), who as a rule performed while concealed behind curtains. Such girls came to be a necessary adornment of the harem and their keeping and training developed into an important industry. For one educated by Isḥāq, a messenger of the governor of Egypt offered 30,000 dinars, which sum was matched by an envoy of the Byzantine emperor and increased to 40,000 by a messenger of the ruler of Khurāsān. Isḥāq solved the problem by freeing the girl and marrying her.[4]

The caliphal house in Baghdād, more than that of Damascus, developed several distinguished lutanists, singers and composers. Of all the 'Abbāsids Ibrāhīm ibn-al-Mahdi, brother of Hārūn and in 817 rival caliph of al-Ma'mūn, acquired the greatest fame as musician-singer.[5] Al-Wāthiq (842–7), who performed on the lute and composed a hundred melodies,[6] was the first caliph musician. After him both al-Muntaṣir (861–2) and al-Mu'tazz (866–9) showed some poetical and musical talent.[7] But the only real caliph musician was al-Mu'tamid (870–92), in whose

[1] *Aghāni*, vol. xxi, pp. 237-8. Cf. Nuwayri, *Nihāyah*, vol. iv, p. 307.
[2] See ibn-Khallikān, vol. i, pp. 114 *seq.*; *Fihrist*, pp. 140-41; *Aghāni*, vol. v, pp. 52 *seq.*; Nuwayri, vol. v, pp. 1 *seq.*
[3] Farmer, *Arabian Music*, p. 125.
[4] *Fakhri*, pp. 276-9.
[5] Ibn-Khallikān, vol. i, pp. 12 *seq.*; Ṭabari, vol. iii, pp. 1030 *seq.*
[6] *Aghāni*, vol. viii, p. 163, quoted by Nuwayri, vol. iv, p. 198.
[7] Nuwayri, vol. iv, p. 199.

presence the geographer ibn-Khurdādhbih delivered his oration on music and dance, a notable contribution to our knowledge of their state at that time.[1]

Musical theorists

Among the many Greek works translated in the golden age of the ʿAbbāsids were a few dealing with the speculative theory of music. Two such Aristotelian works were done into Arabic under the titles *Kitāb al-Masāʾil* (*Problemata*) and *Kitāb fi al-Nafs* (*De anima*)[2] by the famous Nestorian physician Ḥunayn ibn-Isḥāq (809–73), who also translated a work by Galen under the title *Kitāb al-Ṣawt* (*De voce*). Euclid had two titles ascribed to him in Arabic, *Kitāb al-Nagham* (book of melody), a pseudo-Euclidian work, and *Kitāb al-Qānūn* (canon).[3] Aristoxenus, of the fourth century B.C., was known chiefly by his *Kitāb al-Īqāʿ* (rhythm)[4] and Nicomachus, Aristotle's son, through *Kitāb al-Mūsīqi al-Kabīr* (opus major on music).[5] The Brethren of Sincerity (tenth century), some of whom were evidently musical theorists, classified music as a branch of mathematics and venerated Pythagoras as the founder of its theory.[6] It was from these and other Greek works that the Arab authors acquired their first scientific ideas on music and became schooled in the physical and physiological aspects of the theory of sound. The scientific-mathematical side of Arab music was therefore derived from the Greek, but the practical side, as the researches of Farmer[7] have shown, had purely Arabian models. About this time the word *mūsīqi*, later *mūsīqa* (music), was borrowed from the Greek and applied to the theoretical aspects of the science, leaving the older Arabic term *ghināʾ*, used hitherto for both song and music, to the practical art. *Qītār* (guitar) and *urghun* (organ), as names of instruments, and other technical terms of Greek origin now appear in Arabic. The organ was clearly an importation from the Byzantines. Two organ constructors flourished in the twelfth century, abu-al-Majd ibn-abi-al-Ḥakam († 1180) of Damascus and abu-Zakarīyāʾ Yaḥya al-Bayāsi, who was attached to the service of Ṣalāḥ-al-Dīn.[8]

[1] Masʿūdi, vol. viii, pp. 88-103.
[2] Possibly translated by Ḥunayn's son Isḥāq († 910).
[3] *Fihrist*, p. 266; Qifṭi, p. 65.
[4] *Fihrist*, p. 270. [5] *Ibid*. p. 269. [6] *Rasāʾil*, vol. i, p. 153.
[7] *Arabian Music*, pp. 200-201; "Music" in *The Legacy of Islam*, ed. Thomas Arnold and Alfred Guillaume (Oxford, 1931), pp. 356 *seq*.
[8] Ibn-abi-Uṣaybiʿah, vol. ii, pp. 155, 163.

Musical writers after the Greek school were led by the philosopher al-Kindi, who flourished in the second half of the ninth century and whose works, as noted before, bear the earliest traces of Greek influence. Al-Kindi is credited with six works, in one of which we find the first definite use of notation among the Arabs. Not only al-Kindi but several of the leading Moslem philosophers and physicians were musical theorists as well. Al-Rāzi (865–925) composed at least one such work, cited by ibn-abi-Uṣaybi'ah.[1] Al-Fārābi († 950), himself an accomplished lute performer, was the greatest writer on the theory of music during the Middle Ages. Besides writing commentaries on various lost works of Euclid he produced three original works. Of these *Kitāb al-Mūsīqi al-Kabīr*[2] was the most authoritative in the East. In the West his compendium of sciences, *Iḥṣā' al-'Ulūm*[3] (*De scientiis*), being the earliest and best known of the works dealing with music to be rendered into Latin, exerted powerful influence. Besides the writings of al-Fārābi those of ibn-Sīna († 1037), who abridged earlier works and included in his *al-Shifā'* a study of music, and of ibn-Rushd († 1198) were translated into Latin and became text-books in Western Europe. As for al-Ghazzāli († 1111), it was his defence of *al-samā'* (music and song)[4] that caused music to play such an important part in the ritual of the Sufi fraternities.

Most of these technical treatises unhappily have been lost in the original. Arabic music, with its notation and its two constituent elements of *nagham* (melodic modes) and *īqā'* (rhythmic modes), has been therefore transmitted by word of mouth only and has been finally lost. Arabic chants today are scant in melody but strong in rhythm, and no modern person can interpret properly the few surviving works on classical music or understand fully the meaning of their ancient designations of rhythm and their scientific terminology. Many such terms may be traced to Persian and Indian origins.

[1] Vol. i, p. 320, l. 26. [2] See above, p. 372, n. 1.
[3] Ed. 'Uthmān Muḥammad Amīn (Cairo, 1931).
[4] *Iḥyā'*, vol. ii, pp. 238 *seq*.

CHAPTER XXX

MOSLEM SECTS

We have dwelt at some length on the first two and a half centuries of the ʿAbbāsid period (750–1000) because this was a formative period during which Moslem civilization received that distinctive stamp which it has retained down to our time. In theology and law, in science and philosophy, in literature and the humanities, Islam is today virtually what it was nine centuries ago. Its schools of thought, developed then, have persisted in some form to the present day. Among those schools the sects are the most important.

Rationalism *versus* orthodoxy

The Muʿtazilah started as a rigid puritanical movement asserting that the doctrine that the Koran was the uncreated word of God and eternal would compromise His unity, but developed later a rationalist wing which accorded the products of human reason an absolute value above the Koran. Prompted by his Muʿtazilite judge ibn-abi-Duwād,[1] al-Ma'mūn, whose philosophical interests raised the new creed to a state religion, issued in 827 a momentous proclamation declaring the dogma of "the creation [*khalq*] of the Koran", in opposition to the orthodox view that in its actual form, in its Arabic language, the Koran is the identical reproduction of a celestial original.[2] This new dogma of "the creation of the Koran" soon became the touchstone of Moslem belief. Even judges had to pass its test. In 833 the caliph issued his infamous edict that no qāḍi who did not subscribe to the view of the creation of the Koran could hold his office or be appointed to one. At the same time he instituted the *miḥnah*, an inquisitorial tribunal for the trial and conviction of those who denied his dogma.[3] Thus by a strange irony of fate did the movement which had a party standing for free-thought become a deadly instrument for suppressing thought.

[1] See ibn-Khallikān, vol. i, pp. 38-45; Ṭabari, vol. iii, pp. 1139 *seq.*
[2] See above, pp. 123-4.
[3] A copy of his orders is preserved in Ṭabari, vol. iii, pp. 1112-16.

Moslem inquisition

This was not the first time Islam persecuted heresy. The Umayyad Hishām (724–43) had ordered the execution of al-Ja'd ibn-Dirham for teaching that the Koran was created[1] and had put to death Ghaylān al-Dimashqi (the Damascene) for maintaining the doctrine of free will;[2] and both al-Mahdi and al-Hādi had crucified a number of *zindīqs*.[3] But this *miḥnah* of al-Ma'mūn was the first systematic inquisition into heresy and the earliest formal attempt to stamp it out.

The leading victim of the *miḥnah* was Aḥmad ibn-Ḥanbal,[4] whose bold and stubborn championship of the cause of conservative orthodoxy constitutes one of the glamorous pages in its history. The persecution of the orthodox continued under al-Ma'mūn's two successors. But in the second year of his reign, 848, al-Mutawakkil turned the tables on the Mu'tazilites and restored the old dogma.

Among the leaders of the Mu'tazilite school of this period was al-Naẓẓām († *ca.* 845). This "sheikh of the Mu'tazilites" endeavoured to check the Persian dualistic tendencies in Islam and proclaimed that doubt was the first absolute requirement of knowledge.[5] His system recalls in the main Anaxagoras. Al-Naẓẓām counted among his pupils the encyclopædist al-Jāḥiẓ of al-Baṣrah († 868–9).[6] Another early leader was Mu'ammar ibn-'Abbād al-Sulami[7] († *ca.* 835), a Qadarite who entertained Indian ideas.

The Ash'arite system prevails

On the theological side the man credited with exploding the Mu'tazilite theories and re-establishing the orthodox creed which has since become the heritage of Sunni Islam was abu-al-Ḥasan 'Ali al-Ash'ari of Baghdād († 935–6),[8] a descendant of the arbitrator abu-Mūsa. "Al-Mu'tazilah", in the words of a pious Moslem, "carried their heads high, but their dominion ended when God sent al-Ash'ari." Starting as a pupil of the Mu'tazilite theologian al-Jubbā'i[9] († 915–16), al-Ash'ari later in life changed

[1] Ibn-al-Athīr, vol. v, pp. 196-7.
[2] *Ibid.* p. 197; Ṭabari, vol. ii, p. 1733.
[3] See above, p. 359.
[4] Ṭabari, vol. iii, pp. 1131 *seq.*
[5] For his "heresies" see Shahrastāni, pp. 37-42; Baghdādi, ed. Hitti, pp. 102-9.
[6] Ibn-Ḥazm, vol. iv, p. 148; al-Khayyāṭ, *Kitāb-al Intiṣār*, ed. H. S. Nyberg (Cairo, 1925), index.
[7] Consult Shahrastāni, pp. 46-8; Baghdādi, pp. 109-10.
[8] See his *Maqālāt al-Islāmīyīn*, ed. H. Ritter (Constantinople, 1929), pp. 155-278; Shahrastāni, pp. 65-75.
[9] See Shahrastāni, pp. 54 *seq.*; Baghdādi, p. 121.

fronts[1] and used in his polemics against his former masters the same weapons of logical and philosophical argumentation which they had introduced and developed. Thus he became, in addition to his other achievements, the founder of scholastic theology in Islam (*kalām*). After him the scholastic attempt to reconcile religious doctrine with Greek thought became the supreme feature of Moslem intellectual life as it was of medieval Christian life. To al-Ash'ari is also attributed the introduction of the formula *bila kayf* (without modality), according to which one is expected to accept the anthropomorphic expressions in the Koran without any explanation demanded or given. This new principle served as a damper on free-thought and research. It was with a view to propagating the Ash'ari system of theology that the famous Niẓāmīyah seminary was established by the Saljūq vizir.

Al-Ghazzāli

Al-Ash'ari was followed by al-Ghazzāli[2] (L. Algazel), unquestionably the greatest theologian of Islam and one of its noblest and most original thinkers. It was al-Ghazzāli who fixed the ultimate form of the Ash'arīyah and established its dicta as the universal creed of Islam. This "father of the church in Islam" has since become the final authority for Sunnite orthodoxy. Moslems say that if there could have been a prophet after Muḥammad, al-Ghazzāli would have been the man.

Abu-Ḥāmid al-Ghazzāli was born in 1058 at Ṭūs, Khurāsān, where he died in 1111. He reproduced in his religious experience all the spiritual phases developed by Islam. Here are his own words:

Ever since I was under twenty (now I am over fifty) . . . I have not ceased to investigate every dogma or belief. No Bāṭinite did I come across without desiring to investigate his esotericism; no Ẓāhirite, without wishing to acquire the gist of his literalism; no philosopher,[3] without wanting to learn the essence of his philosophy; no dialectical theologian [*mutakallim*], without striving to ascertain the object of his dialectics and theology; no Sufi, without coveting to probe the secret of his Sufism; no ascetic, without trying to delve into the origin of his asceticism; no atheistic *zindīq*, without groping for the causes of his bold atheism and *zindīqism*. Such was the unquenchable thirst of my soul for investigation from the early days of my youth, an

[1] *Fihrist*, p. 181.

[2] From *ghazzāl* (spinner), less correctly al-Ghazāli; Muḥammad ibn-abi-Shanab in *Majallat al-Majma'*, vol. vii (1927), pp. 224-6. Cf. Duncan B. Macdonald in *Journal Royal Asiatic Society* (1902), pp. 18-22.

[3] Neo-Platonist.

instinct and a temperament implanted in me by God through no choice of mine.[1]

Starting his religious life as orthodox, al-Ghazzāli soon turned Sufi, and when still under twenty he had broken with all the past. In 1091 he was appointed lecturer at the Niẓāmīyah in Baghdād, where he became a sceptic. Four years later he returned to Sufism after a terrific spiritual struggle that left him a physical and moral wreck. Intellectualism had failed him. As a dervish he roamed from place to place enjoying peace of soul and acquiescence of mind. After about twelve years of retirement in various places, including two years of retreat in Syria and a holy pilgrimage, he returned to Baghdād to preach and teach. There he composed his masterpiece *Iḥyāʾ ʿUlūm al-Dīn*[2] (the revivification of the sciences of religion). The mysticism of this work vitalized the law, its orthodoxy leavened the doctrine of Islam. In it and in such other works of his as *Fātiḥat al-ʿUlūm*,[3] *Tahāfut al-Falāsifah*,[4] *al-Iqtiṣād fi al-Iʿtiqād*,[5] orthodox speculation reached its culminating point. These works deposed fiqh from the high rank it had usurped, employed Greek dialectic to found a pragmatic system and made philosophy palatable to the orthodox school of theologians. Partly translated into Latin before 1150, they exerted marked influence on Jewish and Christian scholasticism. Thomas Aquinas, one of the greatest theologians of Christianity, and later Pascal were indirectly affected by the ideas of al-Ghazzāli, who of all Moslem thinkers came nearest to subscribing to Christian views. The scholastic shell constructed by al-Ashʿari and al-Ghazzāli has held Islam to the present day, but Christendom succeeded in breaking through its scholasticism, particularly at the time of the Protestant Revolt. Since then the West and the East have parted company, the former progressing while the latter stood still.

Sufism

Sufism[6] is the form which mysticism has taken in Islam. It is

[1] *Al-Munqidh min al-Ḍalāl*, ed. A. Schmölders (Paris, 1842), pp. 4-5; cf. C. Field, *The Confessions of Al Ghazzali* (London, 1909), pp. 12-13. The autobiographical part of this work runs almost parallel with the experience of St. Augustine

[2] 4 vols. (Cairo, 1334). There are several other editions.

[3] (Cairo, 1322.) [4] Ed. M. Bouyges (Beirūt, 1927). [5] 2nd ed. (Cairo, 1327).

[6] From Ar. *ṣūf*, wool, to denote the practice of assuming a woollen robe on entering the mystic life. Theodor Nöldeke in *Zeitschrift der deutschen morgenländischen Gesellschaft*, vol. 48 (1894), pp. 45-8.

not so much a set of doctrines as it is a mode of thinking and feeling in the religious domain. Moslem mysticism represents a reaction against the intellectualism of Islam and the Koran and the formalism which developed as a consequence. Psychologically its basis should be sought in the human aspiration to a personal, direct approach to, and a more intense experience of, the deity and religious truth. Like other Islamic movements Sufism traces its origin to the Koran and the ḥadīth. Such verses as 4 : 96; 9 : 113; 33 : 47, condemning "greed after the chance good things of this present life", commending "those who turn to God" and emphasizing "trust in God, for God is a sufficient guardian", are not lacking in the Koran. Muḥammad's own relation to God had a mystical aspect, namely, a direct consciousness of divine presence, and the Sufis came to consider themselves the true interpreters of the esoteric teaching of the Prophet as preserved in the ḥadīth.

Beginning simply as an ascetic life, mainly contemplative, such as was commonly practised by Christian monks, Sufism during and after the second Islamic century developed into a syncretic movement, absorbing many elements from Christianity, Neo-Platonism, Gnosticism and Buddhism, and passing through mystical, theosophical and pantheistic stages. Wool (*ṣūf*) was adopted as a dress in imitation of Christian monks, from whom was also borrowed the ideal of celibacy which orthodox Islam never encouraged. The practice of solitary meditations and prolonged vigils likewise show Syrian monastic influence. The Sufi fraternity (*ṭarīqah*,[1] right way), which developed in the thirteenth century, with its master (*shaykh*) and novice (*murīd*), corresponding to the Christian relation of clergy and beginner, approaches the monastic orders, notwithstanding the apocryphal tradition "no monasticism [*rahbānīyah*] in Islam". The fraternity's religious service called *dhikr*[2] is the only elaborate ritual in Islam and betrays Christian litanies as a source.[3] The Sufi eschatological traditions with their Antichrist[4] suggest that the fraternities found many recruits among those newly converted to Islam from the older forms of monotheism.

Asceticism

The term Sufi appears first in Arabic literature in the middle of the ninth century applied to a certain class of ascetics.[5] The

[1] Sūr. 46 : 29 *seq.* [2] Remembrance and mention of God's name; sūr. 33 : 41.
[3] Reynold A. Nicholson, *The Mystics of Islam* (London, 1914), p. 10.
[4] *Al-Masīḥ al-Dajjāl*, from Aramaic *Meshīḥa Daggāla*. Cf. Matt. 24 : 24; Rev. 13 : 1-18; Dan. 11 : 36. [5] Jāḥiẓ, *Bayān*, vol. i, p. 233.

first individual on whom the name Sufi was bestowed, and that by later tradition, was the famous occultist Jābir ibn-Ḥayyān (fl. *ca.* 776), who professed an ascetic doctrine of his own. His contemporary Ibrāhīm ibn-Adham of Balkh († *ca.* 777) may be taken as a type of this early quietist asceticism (*zuhd*). In the Sufi legend of his conversion, evidently modelled upon the story of Buddha,[1] Ibrāhīm appears as a king's son who, while hunting, heard some mysterious voice warning him that he was not created for such a purpose. Thereupon the princely sportsman dismounted and for ever abandoned the path of worldly pomp for that of asceticism and piety. According to another legend his conversion came as a result of having observed from the window of his palace a beggar contentedly enjoying a meal of stale bread soaked in water and seasoned with coarse salt. When assured by the beggar that he was fully satisfied, Ibrāhīm put on haircloth and took to a wandering life.[2] After his Sufi conversion, Ibrāhīm migrated to Syria, where Sufism had its earliest organization, and lived by his own labour.

Mysticism

Under the stimulus of Christian as well as Hellenistic ideas Moslem asceticism became mystical in the second Moslem century; that is, it began to be regarded by its devotees as an emotional means of purifying the human soul, so that it may know and love God and be united with Him, rather than as a means for winning His reward in a future world. This Sufi knowledge (*ma'rifah*) of God is a form of gnosis achieved by the inner light of the individual soul, in contrast to the knowledge (*'ilm*) of Him by the intellect or through acquiescence in the accepted tradition. The doctrine of gnosis was developed by abu-Sulaymān al-Dārāni († 849–50), whose tomb in Dārayya near Damascus was still an object of pilgrimage in the days of Yāqūt.[3] But the first Sufi of the mystic, as opposed to the ascetic, school was Ma'rūf al-Karkhi, of the Baghdād school, who died in 815. Originally a Christian, or possibly a Ṣābian,[4] Ma'rūf was described as a God-intoxicated man and venerated as a saint. His tomb at Baghdād on the west bank of the Tigris is still a great resort for pilgrims and at the time of al-Qushayri[5] († 1074)

[1] T. Duka in *Journal Royal Asiatic Society* (1904), pp. 132 *seq.*

[2] See ibn-'Asākir, vol. ii, pp. 167-96; Kutubi, vol. i, pp. 3-5; al-Qushayri, *al-Risālah* (Cairo, 1284), pp. 9-10.

[3] *Buldān*, vol. ii, p. 536.

[4] Cf. al-Hujwīri, *Kashf al-Maḥjūb*, tr. R. A. Nicholson (Leyden, 1911), p. 114.

[5] *Risālah*, p. 12.

prayer at it was considered a sure remedy for the sick. According to the mystic principle nothing really exists but God, God is eternal beauty, and the path leading to Him is love. Love thus becomes the essence of mysticism.

Theosophy

From speculative mysticism, Sufism advanced to theosophy. In effecting this transition, which took place during the period of translation from Greek, Hellenistic influence was paramount. The exponent of Sufi theosophy was dhu-al-Nūn [1] al-Miṣri (i.e. the Egyptian), of Nubian parents,[2] who died at al-Jīzah (Gizeh) in 860. Sufis in general consider this ascetic the originator of their doctrine. They number him among their first *quṭbs* (pivots of the universe) and follow the mention of his name by the invocation "May God sanctify his inmost soul [*sirr*]!" It was dhu-al-Nūn who gave Sufism its permanent shape. He introduced the idea that the true knowledge of God is attained by one means only, ecstasy (*wajd*). Al-Masʿūdi[3] tells us that dhu-al-Nūn was wont to wander amid the ruined monuments of his native Egypt endeavouring to decipher their mysterious figures as a key to the lost sciences of antiquity.

Pantheism

The step from theosophy to pantheism was not difficult and was made chiefly under Indo-Iranian influences. The *Aghāni*[4] has preserved for us at least one portrayal of an unmistakable Buddhistic view of life, and the *zindīq* monks described by al-Jāḥiẓ[5] were either Indian sadhus, Buddhist monks or their imitators.[6] A Persian, Bāyazīd[7] al-Bisṭāmi († *ca.* 875), whose grandfather was a Magian, probably introduced the doctrine of *fanā'*, self-annihilation, possibly a reflection of Buddhist Nirvana. Another Persian, al-Ḥallāj (the carder), was in 922 flogged, exposed on a gibbet, then decapitated and burned by the ʿAbbāsid inquisition for having declared, "I am the Truth" (i.e. God). His "crucifixion" made him the great Sufi martyr. His mystic theory is made clear in these verses:

[1] "The man of the fish", applied to Jonah in Koran 21 : 87. Dhu-al-Nūn's real name was Thawbān abu-al-Fayḍ ibn-Ibrāhīm.

[2] Qushayri, p. 10; Hujwīri, p. 100.

[3] Vol. ii, pp. 401-2.

[4] Vol. iii, p. 24, ll. 27-8.

[5] *Ḥayawān*, vol. iv, pp. 146-7.

[6] Ignaz Goldziher, *Vorlesungen über den Islam*, ed. F. Babinger (Heidelberg, 1925), p. 160.

[7] Tur. pronunciation of Ar. abu-Yazīd. See Qushayri, pp. 17-18; ibn-Khallikān, vol. i, p. 429.

I am He whom I love, and He whom I love is I.
We are two souls dwelling in one body.
When thou seest me, thou seest Him:
And when thou seest Him, thou seest us both.[1]

Al-Ḥallāj's tomb in west Baghdād stands till now as that of a saint. But the greatest monist and pantheist Sufi was Muḥyi-al-Dīn ibn-'Arabi (1165–1240) of Spain, whose tomb at the foot of Mt. Qāsiyūn in Damascus is today enclosed in a large mosque bearing his name. Unlike such orthodox Sufis as al-Ghazzāli and al-Junayd of Baghdād († 910),[2] ibn-'Arabi endeavoured to reduce Sufism to a science which he intended to have reserved for circles of initiates. The development of the pantheistic idea that all is God was due to him.

Mystic poetry and philosophy

In the field of mystic poetry the Arabs produced only one great name, that of the Egyptian ibn-al-Fāriḍ, 1181–1235, whose masterpiece is a long ode (rhyming in *t*)[3] forming an exquisite hymn of divine love. On the other hand, almost all Persian poets of the first order, e.g. Sa'di, Ḥāfiẓ and al-Rūmi, were mystics. But in the field of philosophic Sufism the Arabic-writing world can claim two of the greatest intellects Islam ever produced, al-Fārābi and al-Ghazzāli. It was the latter who reconciled Sufism, with its many unorthodox practices, with Islam and grafted mysticism upon its intellectualism.

Fraternal orders

For the first five Islamic centuries, that form of religious experience termed Sufism stood almost entirely on an individual basis. Small circles of disciples and followers did cluster round the personality or memory of some inspiring teacher, as in the case of al-Ḥallāj, but such organized bodies were local in provenience and not of permanent character. Before the close of the twelfth Christian century self-perpetuating corporations began to appear. The first fraternity (*ṭarīqah*) established on such a principle was the Qādirite, so named after the Persian 'Abd-al-Qādir al-Jīlāni or al-Jīli (1077–1166),[4] who flourished in

[1] Ibn-Khallikān, vol. i, p. 261. Cf. R. A. Nicholson, *Studies in Islamic Mysticism* (Cambridge, 1921), p. 80; Louis Massignon, *La Passion d'al-Ḥallāj: martyr mystique de l'Islam* (Paris, 1922), vol. ii, p. 518.

[2] Qushayri, pp. 24-5; Hujwīri, pp. 128-30.

[3] *Dīwān*, ed. Amīn Khūri, 3rd ed. (Beirūt, 1894), pp. 65-132; tr. almost entirely by Nicholson, *Studies*, pp. 199-266.

[4] The best extant biography is in al-Dhahabi, "Ta'rīkh al-Islām", D. S. Margoliouth in *Journal Royal Asiatic Society* (1907), pp. 267-310. On his miracles see Shaṭṭanawfi, *Bahjat al-Asrār* (Cairo, 1304), which has on its margin 78 sermons of al-Jīlāni entitled *Futūḥ al-Ghayb*.

Baghdād. The order, one of the most tolerant and charitable, now claims followers throughout the whole Moslem world, including Algeria, Java and Guinea. The second fraternity in order of antiquity was the Rifā'ite, founded by an 'Irāqi, Aḥmad al-Rifā'i († 1183), whose members, like those of other fraternities, can perform strange feats, such as swallowing glowing embers, live serpents and glass, or passing needles and knives through their bodies. The Mawlawite order, commonly known as the whirling dervishes, centres upon the great Persian poet Jalāl-al-Dīn al-Rūmi, who died in Qūniyah (Konieh, classical Iconium) in 1273. In opposition to the general Moslem practice al-Rūmi gave an important place to music in the ceremonies of his order. The order has always had as its superior one of his descendants who lived in Qūniyah. The superior enjoyed the privilege of girding the new sultan-caliph of Turkey with his sword.

Various other independent fraternities developed in various countries at different times, ranging in their Sufism from ascetic quietism to pantheistic antinomianism. In most instances the founder of the order became himself the centre of a cult, invested with divine or quasi-divine powers, and the headquarters of his order developed into a foyer of saint-worship. In Africa the strongest religious brotherhood is the Shādhilite,[1] founded by 'Ali al-Shādhili († 1258), which is especially strong in Morocco and Tunisia and has sub-orders under special names. Islam in Morocco is characterized by saint-worship to a greater degree than perhaps in any other country. The modern Sanūsi brotherhood, with headquarters in the oasis of Kufra and formerly in Jaghbūb, was founded in 1837 by the Algerian Shaykh al-Sanūsi and is clearly distinguishable from the preceding orders in being a congregation-state with political and military as well as religious aims. The leading native fraternity of Egypt is the Aḥmadīyah, after Aḥmad-al-Badawi († 1276), whose centre is at Ṭanṭa. In Turkey one of the strongest orders is the Baktāshi, noted for its connection with the Janissaries. This order, which became firmly established about 1500, encourages celibacy, reveres 'Ali and shows traces of Christian influence in its theology. It seems to represent a sect rather than a Sufi fraternity. Besides inheriting the old religions of Asia Minor the dervish orders of that country

[1] On this see abu-al-Mawāhib al-Shādhili, *Qawānīn Ḥikam al-Ishrāq* (Damascus, 1309); tr. Edward J. Jurji, *Illumination in Islamic Mysticism* (Princeton, 1938).

have preserved traces of shamanism, which the early Turks brought with them from Central Asia.

The Sufi orders represent the only ecclesiastical organization in Islam. The members, commonly called dervishes,[1] live in special quarters, termed *takīyah*, *zāwiyah* or *ribāṭ*, which at the same time serve as social centres, a function which the mosque fails to perform. The fraternity may have, in addition to the masters and neophytes, a third class of affiliated lay members who are subject to the guidance of the superior of the order.

The rosary

Besides introducing a form of monasticism and ritual[2] the Sufis made other contributions to Islam. They were evidently responsible for the diffusion of the rosary (*subḥah*) among Moslems.[3] Today only the puritanical Wahhābis eschew the rosary, regarding it as an innovation (*bid'ah*). Of Hindu origin, this instrument of devotion was probably borrowed by the Sufis from the Eastern Christian churches and not directly from India. During the Crusades the rosary found its way into the Roman Catholic West. The first mention of the rosary in Arabic literature was made by the poet laureate abu-Nuwās († *ca.* 810).[4] The celebrated mystic al-Junayd († 910) of Baghdād used it as a means of attaining a state of ecstasy, and when once a critic remonstrated with him for the use of such an innovation despite his reputation for sanctity, al-Junayd replied: "I will not renounce a path that has led me to God".[5]

The cult of saints

Moreover, Sufism founded and popularized the cult of sainthood. Veneration of saints finds no sanction in the Koran. It sprang up, following the Christian practice, in response to the mystic call and to meet the need of bridging the gap between man and God in Islamic theology. While there is no formal canonization in Islam, popular acclaim based upon the performance of miracles (*karāmāt*) constitutes a saint (*wali*, friend of God). By the twelfth century the original feeling common to both Sunnites and Shī'ites that the invocation of saints was an idolatrous form of worship had been dissipated by a philosophical reconciliation of sainthood with orthodox principles, effected mainly through Sufi influence. When it came to the

[1] Ar. *darwish*, from Pers., commonly explained as poor, needy, a mendicant.

[2] For a criticism by an orthodox Moslem see ibn-al-Jawzi, *Naqd*, pp. 262 *seq.*

[3] Ignaz Goldziher in *Revue de l'histoire des religions*, vol. xxi (1890), pp. 295-300; *Vorlesungen*, p. 164.

[4] *Dīwān*, p. 108, l. 18. Cf. ibn-Qutaybah, *al-Shi'r*, p. 508, l. 2. Qushayri, p. 25.

question of rank among "the friends of Allah", the chivalrous Sufis maintained the principle of complete equality between the sexes.[1] They, for instance, accorded Rābiʻah al-ʻAdawīyah (*ca.* 717–801) of al-Baṣrah, a mystic woman of noble life and lovely character, first place in the list of saints. Since then Rābiʻah has become "the saint par excellence of the Sunnite hagiology". When young she was sold as a slave, but on seeing a radiance round her while she prayed her master freed her. She refused to marry and lived a life of extreme asceticism and other-worldliness. She soon became a revered guide along "the mystic way", inculcating penitence, patience, gratitude, holy fear, voluntary poverty and utter dependence (*tawakkul*) upon God. Asked whether she hated Satan, Rābiʻah replied: "My love for God leaves no room for hating Satan". When in a dream the Prophet asked her whether she loved him, her reply was: "My love for God has so possessed me that no place remains for hating aught or loving any save Him".[2] On another occasion she declared: "I have not served God from fear of God . . or love of Paradise . . . but only for the love of Him and the desire for Him"[3]

An impassioned prayer by one of those lovers of God, al-Suhrawardi, who at the age of thirty-six (A.D. 1191) was executed as a heretic at Aleppo by order of the viceroy al-Malik al-Ẓāhir and his father, Ṣalāḥ-al-Dīn, makes plain the indebtedness of Sufi theosophy to Neo-Platonism as well as to Christianity.[4]

Shīʻah

Another religious movement that took its final form under the ʻAbbāsids and developed offshoots that played decisive rôles in the history of Islam and the caliphate was the Shīʻah. The partisans of ʻAli fared no better under the ʻAbbāsid régime than under the Umayyad, and that in spite of the fact that they had been an important factor in establishing the former at the expense of the latter. The smiles of al-Ma'mūn, who even went so far as to don their colour, green, and proclaim as heir apparent one of their imāms, ʻAli al-Riḍa,[5] proved of no permanent

[1] Abu Nuʻaym († 1038) devotes a section of his voluminous *Ḥilyat al-Awliyā' wa-Ṭabaqāt al-Aṣfiyā'*, vol. ii (Cairo, 1933), pp. 39-79, to women Sufis and saints.

[2] Farīd-al-Dīn ʻAṭṭār, *Tadhkirat al-Awliyā'*, ed. R. A. Nicholson, vol. i (Leyden, 1905), p. 67.

[3] Abu-Ṭālib (al-Makki), *Qūt al-Qulūb* (Cairo, 1932), vol. iii, p. 83. For more on Rābiʻah consult Margaret Smith, *Rābiʻa the Mystic and her Fellow-Saints in Islām* (Cambridge, 1928).

[4] Louis Massignon, *Recueil de textes inédits concernant l'histoire de la mystique en pays d'Islam* (Paris, 1929), pp. 111-12. See below, p. 586.

[5] Yaʻqūbi, vol. ii, pp. 544-5.

avail. Soon came al-Mutawakkil, who in 850 resumed the early practice of persecuting the Shī'ah; he destroyed the tomb of 'Ali at al-Najaf and the more venerated one of al-Ḥusayn at Karbalā',[1] thereby earning the everlasting hatred of all Shī'ites. In 1029 the Caliph al-Qādir drove a Shī'ite leader out of his Baghdād mosque and installed in his place a Sunnite.[2] This general hostility led the Shī'ites to the adoption of the principle of dissimulation (*taqīyah*[3]), i.e. dispensation from the requirements of religion under compulsion or threat of injury. The legitimacy of dissimulation as an ethical principle had already been recognized by some Khārijites,[4] but the Shī'ites made it a fundamental tenet. They contributed to it the further point that when a believer finds himself in a position where his adversaries are in the ascendancy, not only may he profess outwardly the form of the prevailing religion but he must do so as a measure of protection for himself and his co-religionists.[5]

Although a suppressed minority and perpetrators of unsuccessful, though not always unheroic, rebellions against the established order, the non-conformist Shī'ites persisted openly and under cover of *taqīyah* in according their allegiance to whom rightful allegiance (*walāyah*) was due, namely, an imām descended from 'Ali. Unlike the Sunnite caliph the Shī'ite imām had inherited from Muḥammad not only his temporal sovereignty but the prerogative of interpreting the law. In that capacity he was an infallible teacher and to his infallibility (*'iṣmah*)[6] he added the divine gift of impeccability.[7] Contrary to the Sunnite and the Sufi doctrine the Shī'ites maintained that religious certainty could be gained only from the instruction of such an imām divinely protected against error and sin. 'Ali, their first imām, was succeeded by his son al-Ḥasan and then by his other son, al-Ḥusayn,[8] whose line is the more celebrated one. The last nine of the twelve imāms to whom the Twelvers

[1] *Fakhri*, p. 325; Mas'ūdi, vol. vii, pp. 302-3.
[2] Ibn-al-Athīr, vol. ix, p. 278.
[3] Literally "caution", "fear". Koran, 3 : 27.
[4] Shahrastāni, p. 92, l. 15, p. 93, l. 6.
[5] Goldziher, *Vorlesungen*, p. 203.
[6] See above, p. 248. Baghdādi, *Uṣūl*, vol. i, pp. 277-9.
[7] Shahrastāni, pp. 108-9; ibn-Khaldūn, *Muqaddamah*, pp. 164-5.
[8] The numberless descendants of al-Ḥasan and al-Ḥusayn are distinguished from other Moslems by the titles *sharīf* (noble) and *sayyid* (lord) respectively and by the right to wear green turbans. The Sharīfs of Makkah, whose scion was the Sunnite King Fayṣal of al-'Irāq, as well as the Sharīfs of Morocco, represent the line of the eldest son of Fāṭimah.

(*Ithna 'Asharīyah*), the main body of the Shī'ah, swore allegiance, were descendants of al-Ḥusayn. Of these nine, four are said to have met death successively by poison: Ja'far (765) in al-Madīnah, Mūsa[1] (799) in Baghdād, 'Ali al-Riḍa[2] (818) in Ṭūs and Muḥammad al-Jawād (835) in Baghdād. Others fell fighting against the authority of the caliphs or at the hands of executioners. Since the youthful twelfth imām, Muḥammad, "disappeared" (264/878) in the cave of the great mosque at Sāmarra without leaving offspring, he became "the hidden [*mustatir*]" or "the expected [*muntaẓar*] imām".[3] As such he is considered immune from death and in a temporary state of occultation (*ghaybah*). In due time he will appear as the Mahdi (divinely guided one) to restore true Islam, conquer the whole world and usher in a short millennium before the end of all things. Though hidden, this twelfth imām has always been "the master of the time" (*qā'im al-zamān*). In Persia the Twelver Shī'ah was established in 1502 by the Ṣafawids, who claimed descent from the seventh imām, Mūsa al-Kāẓim. Since then the shah has been considered as simply the *locum tenens* of the hidden imām and the *mujtahids* (higher theologians) as his spokesmen and intermediaries with men.

Thus did the imām-mahdi dogma become an essential part of Shī'ite creed. Even today it forms the main line of demarcation between Shī'ite and Sunnite Islam. While the Sunnites do look forward to a future restorer of the faith, they neither emphasize his importance in their eschatology nor call him mahdi.[4]

Ismā'īlites

The Shī'ah soil proved most fertile for the development of heterodoxies. According to a tradition Muḥammad once said, "The Israelites have been divided into seventy-one or -two sects, and so have the Christians, but my community shall be divided into seventy-three".[5] Of these sects many were offshoots from the Shī'ah.

The Twelvers were not the only group among the imāmite

[1] Cf. Ya'qūbi, vol. ii, p. 499.

[2] Ya'qūbi, vol. ii, p. 551; ibn-Khallikān, vol. i, p. 577.

[3] Shahrastāni, p. 128; Baghdādi, ed. Hitti, pp. 60-61; ibn-Ḥazm, vol. iv, p. 138; al-Nawbakhti, *Firaq al-Shī'ah*, ed. Hellmut Ritter (Constantinople, 1931), pp. 84-5. Cf. ibn-Khaldūn, *Muqaddamah*, p. 166. The cave (*sirdāb*) is still shown among the ruins of Sāmarra.

[4] See genealogical tree on next page. The belief in the return of the Mahdi lent itself to imposture and produced many pretenders in all periods of Moslem history.

[5] Ibn-al-Jawzi, *Naqd*, pp. 19-20. Cf. Baghdādi, ed. Hitti, p. 15.

Shī'ah. Another group agreed with the Twelvers as to the succession down to the sixth imām, Ja'far al-Ṣādiq, but at this point diverged, making Ja'far's eldest son, Ismā'īl († 760), in preference to his brother Mūsa, the seventh and last imām. This sect restricted the number of visible imāms to seven and were therefore called Seveners (*Sab'īyah*). Ja'far had designated Ismā'īl as his successor, but having learned of Ismā'īl's intemperance

1. 'Ali, † 661

2. Al-Ḥasan, † 669

3. Al-Ḥusayn, † 680

4. 'Ali Zayn-al-'Ābidīn, † *ca.* 712

Zayd

5. Muḥammad al-Bāqir, † 731

6. Ja'far al-Ṣādiq, † 765

Ismā'īl, † 760

7. Mūsa al-Kāẓim, † 799

8. 'Ali al-Riḍa, † 818

9. Muḥammad al-Jawād, † 835

10. 'Ali al-Hādi, † 868

11. Al-Ḥasan al-'Askari, † 874

12. Muḥammad al-Muntaẓar (al-Mahdi), † 878

Tree showing the Relationship of the Twelve Imāms

changed his decision in favour of his second son, Mūsa. The majority of the Shī'ah acquiesced in the change and continued the imāmate in Mūsa al-Kāẓim, who thus became number seven in the series of the twelve visible imāms. But others, claiming that the imām as an infallible being could not prejudice his case by such a thing as drinking wine, remained loyal to Ismā'īl, who predeceased his father by five years. To these Seveners, also called Ismā'īlites, Ismā'īl became the hidden Mahdi.[1]

In the Ismā'īliyah system, as in the Pythagorean system of old, the number seven assumed sacred importance. The Seveners

[1] Nawbakhti, pp. 57-8; Baghdādi, ed. Hitti, p. 58; ibn-Khaldūn, *Muqaddamah*, pp. 167-8.

"periodicated" all cosmic and historical happenings by this number. In their gnostic cosmogony, partly based on Neo-Platonism, the steps of emanation were seven: (1) God; (2) the universal mind (*'aql*); (3) the universal soul (*nafs*); (4) primeval matter; (5) space; (6) time; (7) the world of earth and man. This world was favoured with seven legislating prophets (sing. *nāṭiq*): Adam, Noah, Abraham, Moses, Jesus (*'Īsa*), Muḥammad and Muḥammad al-Tāmm, son of Ismā'īl. In between each two of these legislating prophets they inserted seven silent ones (sing. *ṣāmit*), of whom the first was the "foundation" (*asās*). The silent prophets included such men as Ishmael, Aaron, Peter and 'Ali. Parallel to them ran another lower hierarchy, arranged in sevens or twelves, of propaganda leaders (sing. *ḥujjah*) and simple missionaries (sing. *dā'i*).[1]

Bāṭinites

The Ismā'īlites organized one of the most subtle and effective means of politico-religious propaganda that the world of Islam ever experienced. From their places of retreat they began to send out missionaries to traverse the Moslem world preaching the doctrine known as *bāṭin*[2] (inner, esoteric). According to the unorganized schools of thought, called Bāṭinites by the orthodox, the Koran should be interpreted allegorically and religious truth could be ascertained by the discovery of an inner meaning of which the outer form (*ẓāhir*) was but a veil intended to keep that truth from the eyes of the uninitiate. Quietly and cautiously the novice was initiated under oath of secrecy in the esoteric doctrines, including such recondite ones as the formation of the universe by emanation from the divine essence, transmigration of souls, the immanence of the Divinity in Ismā'īl and the expectation of his early return (*raj'ah*) as the Mahdi. Initiation is said to have involved seven to nine graded stages[3] which recall modern Freemasonry.

This esoteric system found an able enthusiast in one 'Abdullāh, whose father, Maymūn al-Qaddāḥ, of obscure origin, had practised as an oculist (*qaddāḥ*) in al-Ahwāz before moving to Jerusalem. It was 'Abdullāh who perfected the religio-political system of the Ismā'īlites just delineated. From his headquarters,

[1] Shahrastāni, pp. 145-7; al-Īji, *al-Mawāqif*, vol. viii (Cairo, 1327), pp. 388-9. Consult W. Ivanow, *A Guide to Ismaili Literature* (London, 1933).

[2] Baghdādi, *Uṣūl*, pp. 329-30; Shahrastāni, pp. 147 *seq.*; ibn-al-Jawzi, p. 108.

[3] Initiatory illumination transmitted to the adept by degrees was practised before this time by the Manichaeans and certain Greek schools of thought.

first at al-Baṣrah and later at Salamyah[1] in northern Syria, he and his successors sent secret missionaries who systematically made their starting-point the arousing of scepticism in the would-be follower. They would then direct his attention to the great Mahdi soon to make his public appearance. Taking advantage of the growing enmity between Arab and Persian Moslems, this son of a humble Persian oculist conceived the audacious project of uniting in a secret society, with grades of initiation, both conquered and conquerors, who as free-thinkers would use religion as a scheme to destroy the caliphate and give 'Abdullāh or his descendants the throne—a project as astounding in its conception as it was rapid in its execution and certain in its partial success. For it was this scheme that culminated in the rise of the Fāṭimid dynasty in Tunisia and Egypt.

Qarmaṭians

Before his death, about 874,[2] 'Abdullāh had found a most zealous pupil and proselytizer in Ḥamdān Qarmaṭ,[3] an 'Irāqi peasant who had read in the stars that the Iranians were going to regain the empire of the Arabs.[4] Ḥamdān became the founder of the Bāṭini sect known after him as the Qarmaṭian. In this movement the ancient feud between the native peasantry and the sons of the desert evidently found expression. About 890 the founder built himself, near al-Kūfah, an official residence, Dār al-Hijrah[5] (refuge for emigrants), which became the headquarters of the new movement. Active propaganda among the native masses, especially the so-called Nabataean peasants and artisans, as well as among the Arabs themselves, swelled the number of members in the new sect. Fundamentally the organization was a secret society based on a system of communism. Initiation was necessary for admission. The new community supported itself from a common fund created through contributions which were seemingly voluntary but in reality a series of taxes, each heavier than the preceding. Qarmaṭ even went so far as to prescribe community of wives and property (*ulfah*).[6] In their theology these "Bolsheviks of Islam", as they are called by

[1] See Iṣṭakhri, p. 61; ibn-al-Faqīh, p. 110; Yāqūt, vol. iii, p. 123. The less authentic and modern form is Salamīyah; Maqdisi, p. 190; ibn-Khurdādhbih, pp. 76, 98.

[2] A century earlier according to a note in al-Juwayni, *Ta'rīkh-i-Jahān-Gushā*, ed. Mīrza M. al-Qazwīni, pt. 3 (Leyden, 1937), p. 315.

[3] Etymology of this word doubtful; probably not Arabic (Baghdādi, ed. Hitti, p. 171; *Fihrist*, p. 187, l. 9; Sam'āni, *Ansāb*, fol. 448b) but Aramaic for "secret teacher"; Ṭabari, vol. iii, pp. 2125, 2127; ibn-al-Jawzi, p. 110.

[4] *Fihrist*, p. 188.

[5] Cf. ibn-al-Athīr, vol. viii, p. 136.

[6] For other sects with same views see ibn-Ḥazm, vol. iv, p. 143, ll. 13-14.

some modern writers, used an allegorical catechism based on the Koran and supposedly adapted to all creeds, all races and all castes. They stressed tolerance and equality, organized workers and artisans into guilds (sing. *ṣinf*) and in their ceremonial had the ritual of a guild. The earliest sketch of the organization of Moslem guilds occurs in the eighth epistle of the Ikhwān al-Ṣafā', themselves probably Qarmaṭians. This trade guild movement, in the opinion of Massignon, reached the West and influenced the formation of European guilds and Freemasonry.[1]

The Qarmaṭian movement with its communistic, revolutionary tendencies developed into a most malignant growth in the body politic of Islam. To shed the blood of their opponents, even if Moslem, the Qarmaṭians considered legitimate. Before they were fully organized they had a hand in the servile war of the Zanj (negroes) at al-Baṣrah which between 868 and 883 shook the caliphate to its very foundation. Under the leadership of abu-Sa'īd al-Ḥasan al-Jannābi,[2] originally a missionary of Qarmaṭ,[3] they succeeded in founding (899) an independent state on the western shore of the Persian Gulf with al-Aḥsā'[4] for their capital. Soon this state became at once the bulwark of their power and the terror of the caliphate in Baghdād. From their new headquarters they conducted a series of terrible raids on the neighbouring lands. Al-Jannābi himself subjected al-Yamāmah about 903 and invaded 'Umān. His son and successor, abu-Ṭāhir Sulaymān, laid waste most of lower al-'Irāq and cut the pilgrim routes.[5] His atrocities culminated in 930 in the seizure of Makkah and the carrying off of the Black Stone.[6] After an absence of some twenty years this most sacred relic of Islam was returned (951) to al-Ka'bah by order of the Fāṭimid Caliph al-Manṣūr.[7] Between the tenth and eleventh centuries the followers of Qarmaṭ and al-Jannābi from their headquarters at Salamyah kept Syria and al-'Irāq drenched in blood.[8] Even distant Khurāsān

[1] Art. "Ḳarmaṭians", *Encyclopædia of Islām*.

[2] Jannāb was a town in Fāris near the mouth of a river emptying into the Persian Gulf; Iṣṭakhri, p. 34.

[3] Ibn-Ḥawqal, p. 210.

[4] Modern al-Hufūf. Ibn-al-Athīr, vol. viii, p. 63.

[5] *Ibid.* vol. viii, pp. 124-5, 132-3, 158-9, 232.

[6] Miskawayh, *Tajārib al-Umam*, ed. H. F. Amedroz, vol. i (Oxford, 1920), p. 201; ibn-al-Athīr, vol. viii, pp. 153-4.

[7] Cf. Baghdādi, ed. Hitti, pp. 176-7; ibn-al-Athīr, vol. viii, pp. 153-4.

[8] Ṭabari, vol. iii, pp. 2217 *seq.*; Mas'ūdi, *Tanbīh*. pp. 371-6; Miskawayh, vol. ii, pp. 108-9.

and al-Yaman, because of the Qarmaṭian activity, formed lasting hotbeds of discontent.

The Assassins

The Qarmaṭian state fell but its Isma'īli doctrine passed on to the Fāṭimids of Egypt, from one of whom Druzism sprang, and later to the Neo-Ismā'īlites or Assassins[1] of Alamūt and Syria. The Assassin movement, called the "new propaganda"[2] by its members, was inaugurated by al-Ḥasan ibn-al-Ṣabbāḥ († 1124), probably a Persian from Ṭūs, who claimed descent from the Ḥimyarite kings of South Arabia. The motives were evidently personal ambition and desire for vengeance on the part of the heresiarch. As a young man in al-Rayy,[3] al-Ḥasan received instruction in the Bāṭinite system, and after spending a year and a half in Egypt returned to his native land as a Fāṭimid missionary.[4] Here in 1090 he gained possession of the strong mountain fortress Alamūt, north-west of Qazwīn. Strategically situated on an extension of the Alburz chain, 10,200 feet above sea-level, and on the difficult but shortest road between the shores of the Caspian and the Persian highlands, this "eagle's nest", as the name probably means, gave ibn-al-Ṣabbāḥ and his successors a central stronghold of primary importance. Its possession was the first historical fact in the life of the new order.

From Alamūt the grand master (*dā'i al-du'āh*) with his disciples made surprise raids in various directions which netted other fortresses. In pursuit of their ends they made free and treacherous use of the dagger, reducing assassination to an art. Their secret organization, based on Ismā'īlite antecedents, developed an agnosticism which aimed to emancipate the initiate from the trammels of doctrine, enlightened him as to the superfluity of prophets and encouraged him to believe nothing and dare all. Below the grand master stood the grand priors (sing. *al-dā'i al-kabīr*) each in charge of a particular district. After these came the ordinary propagandists. The lowest degree of the order comprised the *fidā'is*,[5] who stood ready to execute whatever orders the grand master issued. A graphic, though late

[1] From Ar. *ḥashshāshūn*, those addicted to the use of *ḥashīsh*, a stupefying hemp.
[2] *Al-da'wah al-jadīdah*; Shahrastāni, p. 150.
[3] Hence his surname al-Rāzi; ibn-al-Athīr, vol. x, p. 369.
[4] Ibn-al-Athīr, vol. ix, p. 304, vol. x, p. 161.
[5] Variant *fidāwi*, one ready to offer his life for a cause. Cf. ibn-Baṭṭūṭah, vol. i, pp. 166-7.

and second-hand, description of the method by which the master of Alamūt is said to have hypnotized his "self-sacrificing ones" with the use of *ḥashīsh* has come down to us from Marco Polo, who passed in that neighbourhood in 1271 or 1272. After describing in glowing terms the magnificent garden surrounding the elegant pavilions and palaces built by the grand master at Alamūt, Polo proceeds:

Now no man was allowed to enter the Garden save those whom he intended to be his ASHISHIN. There was a fortress at the entrance to the Garden, strong enough to resist all the world, and there was no other way to get in. He kept at his Court a number of the youths of the country, from 12 to 20 years of age, such as had a taste for soldiering. . . . Then he would introduce them into his Garden, some four, or six, or ten at a time, having first made them drink a certain potion which cast them into a deep sleep, and then causing them to be lifted and carried in. So when they awoke they found themselves in the Garden.

When therefore they awoke, and found themselves in a place so charming, they deemed that it was Paradise in very truth. And the ladies and damsels dallied with them to their hearts' content. . . .

So when the Old Man would have any Prince slain, he would say to such a youth: "Go thou and slay So and So; and when thou returnest my Angels shall bear thee into Paradise. And shouldst thou die, natheless even so will I send my Angels to carry thee back into Paradise."[1]

The assassination in 1092 of the illustrious vizir of the Saljūq sultanate, Niẓām-al-Mulk, by a *fidā'i* disguised as a Sufi,[2] was the first of a series of mysterious murders which plunged the Moslem world into terror. When in the same year the Saljūq Sultan Malikshāh bestirred himself and sent a disciplinary force against the fortress, its garrison made a night sortie and repelled the besieging army. Other attempts by caliphs and sultans proved equally futile until finally the Mongolian Hūlāgu, who destroyed the caliphate, seized the fortress in 1256 together with its subsidiary castles in Persia.[3]

As early as the last years of the eleventh century the Assassins had succeeded in setting firm foot in Syria and winning as convert the Saljūq prince of Aleppo, Riḍwān ibn-Tutush († 1113). By

[1] *The Book of Ser Marco Polo, the Venetian*, tr. Henry Yule, 2nd ed. (London, 1875), vol. i, pp. 146-9. Cf. a strikingly similar description of a corresponding ceremony at Maṣyād ascribed to ibn-Khallikān in *Fundgruben des Orients*, vol. iii (Vienna, 1813), ed. and tr. Hammer, pp. 201-6.

[2] Ibn-Khallikān, vol. i, p. 256; see below, p. 478.

[3] Since the Assassin books and records were then destroyed, our information about this strange and spectacular order is derived mainly from hostile sources.

1140 they had captured the hill fortress of Maṣyād[1] and many others in northern Syria, including al-Kahf, al-Qadmūs and al-'Ullayqah.[2] Even Shayzar (modern Sayjar) on the Orontes was temporarily occupied by the Assassins, whom Usāmah[3] calls Ismā'īlites. One of their most famous masters in Syria was Rāshid-al-Dīn Sinān († 1192), who resided at Maṣyād and bore the title *shaykh al-jabal*, translated by the Crusades' chroniclers as "le vieux de la montagne"[4] (the old man of the mountain). It was Rashīd's henchmen who struck awe and terror into the hearts of the Crusaders. After the capture of Maṣyād in 1260 by the Mongols, the Mamlūk Sultan Baybars in 1272 dealt the Syrian Assassins the final blow. Since then the Assassins have been sparsely scattered through northern Syria, Persia, 'Umān, Zanzibar and especially India, where they number about a hundred and fifty thousand and go by the name of Khojas or Mawlas.[5] They all acknowledge as titular head the Āgha Khān of Bombay, who claims descent through the last grand master of Alamūt from Ismā'īl, the seventh imām, receives over a tenth of the revenues of his followers, even in Syria, and spends most of his time as a sportsman between Paris and London.

Nuṣayris

The Nuṣayris of northern Syria, who antedate the Druzes of Lebanon, form another of the surviving Ismā'īlite sects. They are so named after Muḥammad ibn-Nuṣayr, of the end of the ninth century, a partisan of the eleventh 'Alid imām al-Ḥasan al-'Askari († 874).[6] According to Dussaud[7] the followers of ibn-Nuṣayr present a remarkable example of a group passing directly from paganism to Ismā'īlism. This explains the points of marked difference between them and the main body of Ismā'īlites.

The Nuṣayris, in company with other sects of extreme Shī'ites but unlike the Ismā'īlites, consider 'Ali the incarnation

[1] Variants Maṣyāf, Maṣyāth. It still stands on the eastern side of the Nuṣayrīyah Mountain. Ibn-al-Athīr, vol. xi, p. 52; abu-al-Fidā', vol. iii, p. 16.

[2] Ibn-Baṭṭūṭah, vol. i, p. 166.

[3] *Kitāb al-I'tibār*, ed. Hitti, pp. 159-60 = *Arab-Syrian Gentleman*, p. 190.

[4] Cf. William of Tyre, "Historia rerum" in *Recueil des historiens des croisades: historiens occidentaux*, vol. i (Paris, 1844), p. 996.

[5] Other than these the Dāwūdis of Gujarāt in India, who number over a hundred thousand, are likewise Ismā'īlites, but are not followers of the Āgha Khān. On the Dāwūdis see D. Menant in *Revue du monde musulman*, vol. x (1910), pp. 472 *seq*.

[6] The first important references to ibn-Nuṣayr and his followers occur in the manuscripts of Ḥamzah and other Druze polemicists of the early eleventh century.

[7] René Dussaud, *Histoire et religion des Noṣairîs* (Paris, 1900), p. 51.

of the deity.[1] Hence the name 'Alawites given them since the French mandate was established in their territory. Unlike the Druzes and other Moslem sects they possess a liturgy and have adopted a number of Christian festivals, including Christmas and Easter. Some of them bear Christian names such as Matta (Matthew), Yūḥanna (John) and Hīlānah (Helen). In addition to these borrowings from Christian sources their religion, which they practise with even greater secrecy than the Druzes, has retained clear remnants of their former pagan beliefs. Today some three hundred thousand adepts of this system, mostly peasants, inhabit the mountainous region of northern and central Syria and are scattered as far as Turkish Cilicia.

Other Shī'ite heterodoxies

The Nuṣayris, Assassins, Druzes, Qarmaṭians and similar Ismā'īlite sects are considered even by the Shī'ites themselves, that is by the Twelvers, who form the bulk of the Shī'ite group, as extremists (*ghulāh*), mainly because they compromise the divinity of God and disregard the finality of Muḥammad's prophethood.[2] Among the *ghulāh* is a sect which has gone so far as to declare that Gabriel mistook Muḥammad for 'Ali when he called him to his prophetic mission.[3] Of the ultra-Shī'ite sects which had a late development may be mentioned the Takhtajis (woodcutters) of western Anatolia, the 'Ali-Ilāhis ('Ali-deifiers) of Persia and Turkestan, their close of kin the Qizil-bāsh (red-heads) of the east of Anatolia and the Baktāshis of Turkey and Albania.

On the opposite wing stand the Zaydis of al-Yaman, the partisans of Zayd,[4] grandson of al-Ḥusayn, whom they regard as the founder of their sect. Of all the Shī'ite sects this is the nearest akin to the Sunnites and in some respects the most tolerant. Between the *ghulāh* on the one hand and the Zaydis on the other the Twelvers occupy the middle ground of Shī'ism. Contrary to other Shī'ite groups the Zaydis believe in no hidden imām, practise no temporary marriage (*mut'ah*) and allow no dissimulation (*taqīyah*). But they share with all other Shī'ite groups hostility to Sufism. In all, the Shī'ites with their sub-sects do not form more than sixty million people or fourteen per cent. of the body of Islam.[5]

[1] Shahrastāni, pp. 143-5.
[2] For other extremists consult Baghdādi, ed. Hitti, pp. 145 *seq.*; Shahrastāni, pp. 132 *seq.*; ibn-Ḥazm, vol. iv, pp. 140 *seq.*; Ash'ari, *Maqālāt*, vol. i, pp. 5-16.
[3] Baghdādi, p. 157.
[4] Consult the genealogical tree above, p. 442.
[5] Cf. above, p. 249, n. 2.

From Stanley Lane-Poole, "History of Egypt" (Methuen & Co. Ltd.)

DINAR OF AḤMAD IBN-ṬŪLŪN, MIṢR, A.D. 881

CHAPTER XXXI

THE CALIPHATE DISMEMBERED: PETTY DYNASTIES IN THE WEST

1. In Spain

FIVE years after the foundation of the ʿAbbāsid caliphate the youthful ʿAbd-al-Raḥmān, sole distinguished scion of the Umayyads to escape the general massacre which signalized the accession of the new régime, reached Cordova in far-off Spain. A year later, in 756, he established there a brilliant dynasty. The first province was thereby for ever stripped off the ʿAbbāsid empire, still in its infancy. Others were soon to follow.

2. The Idrīsids

In 785 Idrīs ibn-ʿAbdullāh, a great-grandson of al-Ḥasan, participated in one of those recurring ʿAlid revolts in al-Madīnah. The insurrection was suppressed and he fled to Morocco (al-Maghrib),[1] where he succeeded in founding a kingdom bearing his name that lasted for almost two centuries (788–974). The Idrīsids,[2] whose principal capital was Fās (Fez),[3] were the first Shīʿite dynasty in history. They drew their strength from the

[1] Yaʿqūbi, vol. ii, p. 488; ibn-Khaldūn, vol. iv, pp. 12-14; ibn-ʿIdhāri, *Bayān*, vol. i, pp. 72 *seq.*, 217 *seq.*; tr. E. Fagnan, vol. i (Algier, 1901), pp. 96 *seq.*, 303 *seq.*

[2] Consult Stanley Lane-Poole, *The Mohammadan Dynasties* (London, 1893, reproduced 1925), p. 35; E. de Zambaur, *Manuel de généalogie et de chronologie pour l'histoire de l'Islam* (Hanover, 1927), p. 65.

[3] The city was built by Idrīs. Ibn-abi-Zarʿ (al-Fāsi), *Rawḍ al-Qirṭās fi Akhbār Mulūk al-Maghrib*, ed. J. H. Tornberg (Upsala, 1843), p. 15; tr. Tornberg, *Annales regum Mauritaniae* (Upsala, 1845), pp. 21 *seq.*

Berbers, who though Sunnite were ever ready to espouse a schismatic cause. Hemmed in between the Fāṭimids of Egypt and the Umayyads of Spain, their dynasty finally succumbed under the fatal blows of a general of the Caliph al-Ḥakam II (961–76) of Cordova.[1]

3. The Aghlabids

As the Shīʿite Idrīsids were carving for themselves a domain in the western part of North Africa, the Sunnite Aghlabids were doing likewise to the east. Over the territory called Ifrīqiyah (Africa Minor, i.e. mainly Tunisia), a corruption of Latin "Africa", Hārūn al-Rashīd had appointed in 800 Ibrāhīm ibn-al-Aghlab as governor.[2] Ibn-al-Aghlab (800–811) ruled as an independent sovereign, and after the year of his appointment no ʿAbbāsid caliph exercised authority beyond the western frontier of Egypt. The Aghlabids contented themselves with the title *amīr*, but seldom bothered to inscribe the caliph's name on their coinage even as a token of his spiritual suzerainty. From their capital, al-Qayrawān, heir to Carthage, they dominated in their century of power (800–909) the mid-Mediterranean.

Many of Ibrāhīm's successors proved as energetic as he. The dynasty became one of the pivotal points of history in the long conflict between Asia and Europe. With their well-equipped fleet they harried the coasts of Italy, France, Corsica and Sardinia. One of them, Ziyādat-Allāh I (817–38), sent against Byzantine Sicily in 827 an expedition which had been preceded by many piratical raids. This and succeeding expeditions resulted in the complete conquest of the island by 902.[3] Sicily, as we shall see, became an advantageous base for operations against the mainland, particularly Italy. Besides Sicily, Malta and Sardinia were seized, mainly by pirates whose raids extended as far as Rome. At the same time Moslem pirates from Crete were repeatedly raiding the isles of the Aegean Sea and by the middle of the tenth century were harassing the coasts of Greece. Three Kufic inscriptions lately discovered in Athens reveal the existence of an Arab settlement there which may have survived until the early tenth century.[4]

[1] Ibn-abi-Zarʿ, pp. 56-7.

[2] Ibn-al-Athīr, vol. vi, pp. 106 *seq.*; ibn-ʿIdhāri, vol. i, p. 83.

[3] See ibn-al-Athīr, vol. vi, pp. 235 *seq.*; ibn-Khaldūn, vol. iv, pp. 198-204.

[4] D. G. Kampouroglous, "The Saracens in Athens", *Social Science Abstracts*, vol. ii (1930), no. 273; G. Soteriou, "Arabic Remains in Athens in Byzantine Times", *ibid.* no. 2360.

The great Mosque of al-Qayrawān, still standing as a rival to the famous mosques of the East, was begun under this Ziyādat-Allāh and completed by Ibrāhīm II (874–902). The site was that on which the primitive edifice of 'Uqbah, founder of al-Qayrawān, had stood. 'Uqbah's mosque had been adorned by one of his successors with pillars of marble from the ruins of Carthage, which were again utilized in the Aghlabid structure. The square minaret of this mosque, also a relic of the earlier structure of Umayyad days and therefore the oldest surviving in Africa, introduced into north-western Africa the Syrian form which was never displaced by the slighter and more fantastic forms of Persian ancestry and Egyptian development. In the Syrian type stone was used as against brick in the other. Thanks to this mosque, al-Qayrawān became to the Western Moslems the fourth holy city, ranking after Makkah, al-Madīnah and Jerusalem—one of the four gates of Paradise.

It was under the Aghlabids that the final transformation of Ifrīqiyah from an outwardly Latin-speaking, Christianity-professing land to an Arabic-speaking, Islam-professing region took place. Like a house of cards Latin North Africa, which supplied St. Augustine with his cultural environment, collapsed never to rise again. The transformation was perhaps more complete than in any other region thus far reduced by Moslem arms. Such opposition as was raised later came from unsubdued Berber tribes and took the form of schismatic and heretical Moslem sectarianism.

The last Aghlabid was Ziyādat-Allāh III (903–9),[1] who in 909 took to flight before the Fāṭimid advance without offering any resistance.[2] The story of the Fāṭimids, who in 909 succeeded the Aghlabids in North Africa and in 969 displaced the Ikhshīdids in Egypt and southern Syria, belongs to a later chapter. The Ikhshīdids, whose history we shall soon sketch, were preceded by the Ṭūlūnid dynasty.

The Ṭūlūnids

The founder of the short-lived Ṭūlūnid dynasty (*dawlah*, 868–905) in Egypt and Syria was Aḥmad ibn-Ṭūlūn, whose father, a Turk from Farghānah, was sent in 817 by the Sāmānid ruler of Bukhāra as a present to al-Ma'mūn.[3] In 868 Aḥmad went

[1] For other Aghlabids see Lane-Poole, p. 37; Zambaur, pp. 67, 68.

[2] Ibn-'Idhāri, vol. i, pp. 142-6; ibn-Khaldūn, vol. iv, pp. 205-7; ibn-abi-Zar', p. 61.

[3] Ibn-Khaldūn, vol. iii, p. 295, vol. iv, p. 297.

to Egypt as lieutenant to its governor. Here he soon made himself independent.[1] When hard pressed for money by the Zanj rebellion, the Caliph al-Muʿtamid (870–92) demanded but did not receive financial aid from his Egyptian lieutenant. This event was a turning-point in the life of Egypt. It marked the emergence in the Nile valley of an independent state which maintained its sovereignty throughout the Middle Ages. Heretofore Egypt's rich revenues went partly into Baghdād and partly into the pockets of successive governors, who were primarily tax-farmers. Now money remained in the country and was spent in glorifying the reigning house. Down to the time of ibn-Ṭūlūn as many as a hundred different Moslem governors, with an average of about two years and a quarter of incumbency,[2] had succeeded one another in the exploitation of the land. Egypt profited by the Ṭūlūnid régime and entered upon an era of comparative prosperity.

Ibn-Ṭūlūn (868–84) gave his new state a rigid military organization. For the maintenance of authority he depended upon an army of a hundred thousand whose core consisted of a bodyguard of Turkish and negro slaves. From his troops, as well as from his slaves and subjects, he exacted an oath of personal allegiance.[3] When in 877 the governor of Syria died Aḥmad occupied the neighbouring country without much opposition.[4] For the first time since Ptolemaic days Egypt had become a sovereign state, and for the first time since Pharaonic days it ruled Syria. To maintain his hold on Syria Aḥmad developed a naval base at ʿAkka (Acre).[5] For many centuries to come Syria continued to be ruled from the valley of the Nile.

Public works

The Ṭūlūnid régime interested itself in irrigation, the most vital factor in the economic life of the land. Aḥmad improved the Nilometer on the isle of al-Rawḍah, near Cairo. This measuring instrument was first built by an Umayyad governor in 716 superseding the more ancient one of Memphis.[6] The régime was the first since the Arab conquest to make Moslem Egypt famed as a centre of art and as a seat of a splendid court. Al-Qaṭā'iʿ[7] (the wards), the new quarter of al-Fusṭāṭ, the capital,

[1] Yaʿqūbi, vol. ii, pp. 615 *seq.*; Ṭabari, vol. iii, p. 1697.

[2] Cf. lists in Kindi, ed. Guest, pp. 6-212; Suyūṭi, *Ḥusn*, vol. ii, pp. 2-10; de Zambaur, pp. 25-7.

[3] Yaʿqūbi, vol. ii, p. 624.

[4] Ibn-Khaldūn, vol. iv, pp. 300-301; Kindi, pp. 219 *seq.*

[5] Yāqūt, vol. iii, pp. 707-8.

[6] Maqrīzi, ed. Wiet, vol. i, pp. 247-50.

[7] Maqrīzi (Būlāq), vol. i, pp. 313 *seq.*

was adorned with magnificent buildings. One of them was the sixty-thousand-dinar hospital (*bīmāristān*) built by Aḥmad.[1] The mosque that still bears the name of Aḥmad ibn-Ṭūlūn is one of the principal religious monuments of Islam. It shows, especially in its minaret—the oldest in Egypt—the architectural influence of the school of Sāmarra, where Aḥmad had spent his youth. The structure cost 120,000 dinars[2] and is remarkable for the use of brick piers and for the early use of the pointed arch (above, p. 417). About one-seventeenth of the Koran is inscribed in beautiful Kufic characters on the wooden frieze round the inside of the building just below the flat timbered roof.[3]

The palace of Khumārawayh (884–95), Aḥmad's extravagant son[4] and successor, with its "golden hall", whose walls were covered with gold and decorated with bas-reliefs of himself, his wives and his songstresses,[5] was one of the most remarkable Islamic structures. The figures of Khumārawayh and his wives, wearing gold crowns, were life-size and carved in wood. Such representation of living persons is exceedingly rare in Islamic art. The palace stood amidst a garden rich in sweet-smelling flowers planted in beds which were shaped to spell Arabic words, and in exotic trees growing round gilded water tanks.[6] Other outstanding features were an aviary[7] and a zoological garden,[8] but the chief wonder of the palace was a pool of quicksilver in its courtyard. Leather cushions inflated with air were moored on the surface of this pool by silken cords fastened to silver columns; on these the dynast used to lie, rocking agreeably to alleviate insomnia and induce slumber. Traces of the quicksilver were found in later years on the site.[9] Shortly before his violent death Khumārawayh gave his daughter Qatr-al-Nada (dewdrop) in marriage to the Caliph al-Mu'taḍid, settled on her a dowry of a million dirhams and presented her with one thousand mortars of gold and other objects "the like of which

[1] Ibn-Taghri-Birdi, *al-Nujūm al-Zāhirah fi Mulūk Miṣr w-al-Qāhirah*, ed. T. G. J. Juynboll, vol. ii (Leyden, 1855), p. 11; Kindi, p. 216.

[2] Ibn-Khallikān, vol. i, p. 97; ibn-Taghri-Birdi, vol. ii, p. 8.

[3] The best description of this mosque was written about 1420 by Maqrīzi (Būlāq), vol. ii, pp. 265 *seq.*; utilized by Suyūṭi, *Ḥusn*, vol. ii, pp. 152-4.

[4] One of seventeen sons and thirty-three children; ibn-Taghri-Birdi, vol. ii, p. 21; Suyūṭi, *Ḥusn*, vol. ii, p. 11.

[5] Ibn-Taghri-Birdi, vol. ii, pp. 57-8; Maqrīzi, vol. i, pp. 316-17.

[6] Ibn-Taghri-Birdi, vol. ii, p. 56.

[7] *Ibid.* pp. 56-7.

[8] *Ibid.* pp. 60-61.

[9] *Ibid.* pp. 58-9; Maqrīzi, vol. i, p. 317.

had never been given before".[1] On account of his extravagance and luxuries Khumārawayh was held impious by the orthodox. He could, it is claimed, drink four rotls of Egyptian wine at one sitting.[2] It is related that as his body was being lowered into its grave the seven Koran readers appointed to recite the sacred book on the adjacent tomb of his father happened to be chanting: "Seize ye him and drag him into the mid-fire of hell".[3]

The Ṭūlūnid dynasty was the earliest manifestation of a political crystallization in the unruly and heretofore inarticulate Turkish element in the heart of the caliphate. Other and more important Turkish dynasties were soon to follow. The case of Aḥmad ibn-Ṭūlūn was typical of the founders of the many states on the ruins of the caliphate. These states broke off entirely from the central government or remained only nominally dependent upon the caliph in Baghdād. Ahmad served as an example of what could be done in the matter of achieving military and political power at the expense of a bulky and unwieldy caliphate through the strong-handed and confident ambition of a subject soldier and his slave satellites. But the Ṭūlūnid, as well as the Ikhshīdid and most of the other dynasties, had no national basis in the lands over which they ruled and therefore were short-lived. Their weakness consisted in the absence of a strong coherent body of supporters of their own race. The rulers were themselves intruders who were obliged to recruit their bodyguards, which were their armies, from various alien sources. Such a rule can only be maintained by men of outstanding personal influence, and no sooner does the mighty arm of the founder relax or pass away than disintegration sets in. No wonder that we find the state founded by ibn-Ṭūlūn reverting to the ʿAbbāsids under his son and fourth successor, Shaybān (904–5).[4]

[1] Ibn-Khallikān, vol. i, p. 310. Cf. ibn-Khaldūn, vol. iv, pp. 307-8; Ṭabari, vol. iii, pp. 2145-6; ibn-Taghri-Birdi, vol. ii, p. 55.

[2] Tanūkhi, *Jāmiʿ al-Tawārīkh*, ed. D. S. Margoliouth, vol. i (London, 1921), p. 261.

[3] Sūr. 44 : 47.

[4] Kindi, pp. 247-8. Subjoined is a Ṭūlūnid tree:

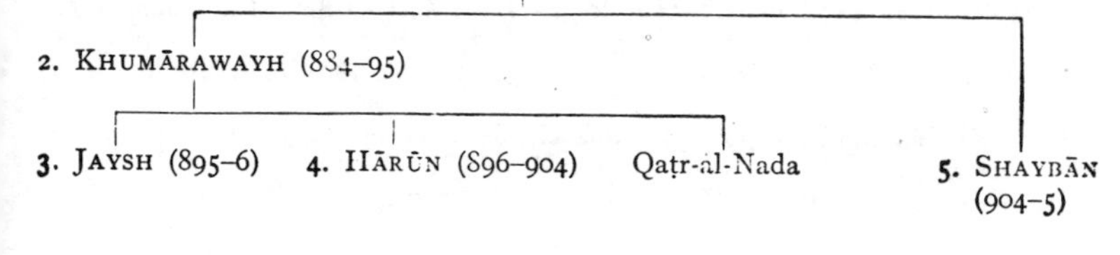

5. The Ikhshīdids

After a brief interval of precarious 'Abbāsid sway in Egypt and Syria, another Turkish dynasty of Farghānah origin,[1] the Ikhshīdid (935–69), was established at al-Fusṭāṭ. The founder, Muḥammad ibn-Ṭughj (935–46), after arranging the disorganized affairs of Egypt,[2] received in 939 from the Caliph al-Rāḍi the old Iranian princely title *ikhshīd*. In the next two years al-Ikhshīd, following the Ṭūlūnid precedent, added Syria-Palestine to his quasi-independent state. In the following year both Makkah and al-Madīnah were incorporated. Henceforth the fate of al-Ḥijāz, a debatable land between east and west, was for several centuries linked with that of Egypt.

A negro eunuch

The two sons who succeeded Muḥammad al-Ikhshīd ruled only in name, the reins of the government being held by the able Abyssinian eunuch abu-al-Misk Kāfūr (musky camphor). Originally purchased by al-Ikhshīd from an oil merchant for the equivalent of about eight pounds, Kāfūr became the sole ruler from 966 to 968.[3] He successfully defended Egypt and Syria against the rising power of another petty dynasty in the north, the Ḥamdānid. His name has been immortalized in the verses first sung in praise of him, later in ridicule, by the greatest poet of his age, al-Mutanabbi',[4] the panegyrist of Kāfūr's adversary, Sayf-al-Dawlah al-Ḥamdāni. The case of this black slave rising from the humblest origin to wield absolute power was the first but not the last in Islamic history. Like other dynasts the Ikhshīdids, and especially their founder, made lavish use of state moneys to curry favour with their subjects. The daily provision for Muḥammad's kitchen included, we are told, a hundred sheep, a hundred lambs, two hundred and fifty geese, five hundred fowls, a thousand pigeons and a hundred jars of sweets. When it was poetically explained to Kāfūr that the recurrent earthquakes of that time were due to Egypt's dancing with joy at his excellences the proud Abyssinian rewarded the would-be seismographer with a thousand dinars. Otherwise the Ikhshīdids made no contribution to the artistic and literary life of their domain and

[1] Ibn-Sa'īd, *al-Mughrib fi Ḥula al-Maghrib*, ed. K. L. Tallqvist (Leyden, 1899), p. 5.

[2] Kindi, p. 288; Miskawayh, vol. i, pp. 332, 366, n.; ibn-Taghri-Birdi, vol. ii, p. 270.

[3] Ibn-Khallikān, vol. ii, pp. 185-9; ibn-Khaldūn, vol. iv, pp. 314-15; ibn-Taghri-Birdi, vol. ii, p. 373.

[4] *Dīwān*, ed. Fr. Dieterici (Berlin, 1861), pp. 623-732; ibn-Sa'īd, pp. 45-6.

no public works have been left by them. The last representative of this dynasty was an eleven-year-old boy, abu-al-Fawāris Aḥmad, who in 969 lost the country to the illustrious Fāṭimid general, Jawhar.[1]

6. The Ḥamdānids

The Ikhshīdids of Egypt had strong rivals in the Shī'ite Ḥamdānids to the north. Originally established in northern Mesopotamia with al-Mawṣil for their capital (929–91), the Ḥamdānids, who were descendants of Ḥamdān ibn-Ḥamdūn[2] of the Taghlib tribe, advanced in 944 into northern Syria and under the leadership of the future Sayf-al-Dawlah (the sword of the dynasty) wrested Aleppo (Ḥalab) and Ḥimṣ from the Ikhshīdid lieutenant in charge. Syria, which never forgot its past glory under the Umayyads, had ever been a hotbed of dissatisfaction and rebellion against the 'Abbāsid régime. Sayf-al-Dawlah (944–67) of Aleppo became the founder of a north Syrian dynasty which lasted until 1003. His second successor, Sa'īd-al-Dawlah (991–1001), however, was a vassal of the Fāṭimids of Egypt. Hard pressed between the Byzantines and the Fāṭimids, the Ḥamdānids[3] in that year gave way in favour of the latter.

Literary efflorescence

Sayf-al-Dawlah owes his fame in Arab annals primarily to his munificent patronage of learning and, in a smaller measure,

[1] Ṭughj
|
1. MUḤAMMAD AL-IKHSHĪD (935–46)
|
2. ABU-AL-QĀSIM UNŪJŪR (946–60) | 3. 'ALI (960–66) | * * 4. ABU-AL-MISK KĀFŪR (966–8)
|
5. AḤMAD (968–9) [son of 3. 'Ali]

The stars indicate a master-slave relationship.

"Unūjūr" is transmitted in several variants. Cf. ibn-Taghri-Birdi, vol. ii, p. 315; Kindi, p. 294; ibn-Khaldūn, vol. iv, p. 314; ibn-al-Athīr, vol. viii, p. 343; Miskawayh, vol. ii, p. 104. See also F. Wüstenfeld, *Die Statthalter von Ägypten zur Zeit der Chalifen*, pt. iv (Göttingen, 1876), p. 37.

[2] Ṭabari, vol. iii, p. 2141.

[3] 1. Sayf-al-Dawlah abu-al-Ḥasan 'Ali (944–67)
|
2. Sa'd-al-Dawlah abu-al-Ma'āli Sharīf (967–91)
|
3. Sa'īd-al-Dawlah abu-al-Faḍā'il Sa'īd (991–1001)
|
4a. Abu-al-Ḥasan 'Ali (1001–3) | 4b. Abu-al-Ma'āli Sharīf (1001–3)

to his taking up the cudgels against the Christian enemies of Islam after those cudgels had been laid down by other Moslem hands. The literary circle of this Ḥamdānid, himself a poet,[1] recalls the days of al-Rashīd and al-Ma'mūn. It included the celebrated philosopher-musician al-Fārābi, whose modest daily needs were met by a pension of four dirhams from the state treasury; the distinguished historian of literature and music, al-Iṣbahāni, who presented to his patron the autograph manuscript of his monumental *Aghāni* and received in reward a thousand pieces of gold; the eloquent court preacher ibn-Nubātah († 984), whose elegant sermons[2] in rhymed prose fired the zeal of his hearers for prosecuting the holy war against Byzantium; and above all the poet laureate al-Mutanabbi' (915–65), whose bombastic and ornate style with its flowery rhetoric and improbable metaphors renders him to the present day the most popular and most widely quoted poet in the Moslem world.[3] An early authority calls his poetry "the height of perfection".[4] Al-Mutanabbi'[5] (prophecy claimant), son of a water-carrier in al-Kūfah, was so named because in his youth he claimed the gift of prophecy among the Bedouins of Syria. His poetical rival in Aleppo was a cousin of Sayf-al-Dawlah, abu-Firās al-Ḥamdāni.[6] Estranged for a time from his Ḥamdānid patron, al-Mutanabbi' sought and received the protection of the Ikhshīdid Kāfūr, in whom he was later disappointed.

As a late product of this ephemeral renaissance in northern Syria we may count the "philosopher of poets and poet of philosophers" abu-al-'Alā' al-Ma'arri (973–1057), who expressed the sceptical and pessimistic sentiments of an age of social decay and political anarchy in Islam. A descendant of the Tanūkh, abu-al-'Alā' was born and died in Ma'arrat al-Nu'mān, whence his surname. His tomb was renovated in 1944 on the occasion of his thousandth anniversary. When four years old he was stricken with

[1] Ibn-Khallikān, vol. ii, pp. 66-8; Tanūkhi, p. 134.

[2] *Khuṭab*, which have appeared in several Cairo and Beirūt editions.

[3] His *Dīwān* was edited by Dieterici and later by Nāṣīf al-Yāziji (Beirūt, 1882). The thousandth anniversary of his death (A.H. 354) was commemorated in 1935 in Syria, Lebanon and other lands.

[4] Ibn-Khallikān, vol. i, p. 63. For an early critical view see Tha'ālibi, *Yatīmah*, vol. i, pp. 78-164.

[5] Properly abu-al-Ṭayyib Aḥmad ibn-Ḥusayn.

[6] *Dīwān*, ed. Nakhlah Qalfāṭ (Beirūt, 1900); tr. in part, Rudolph Dvořák as *Abû Firâs: ein arabischer Dichter und Held* (Leyden, 1895). See also Tha'ālibi, vol. i, pp. 22-62.

smallpox, which cost him his sight, but for which compensation was made by the development of a prodigious memory. In 1009 abu-al-ʿAlā' went to Baghdād, where he spent about a year and seven months and became inoculated with the ideas of Ikhwān al-Ṣafā' as well as with others of Indian origin. On his return home he adopted a vegetarian diet and a life of comparative seclusion. His late works, particularly his *Luzūmīyāt*[1] and *Risālat al-Ghufrān*[2] (treatise on forgiveness) reveal him as one who took reason for his guide and pessimistic scepticism for his philosophy. It was this *Risālah* that is claimed to have exercised a determining influence over Dante in his *Divine Comedy*.[3] His quatrains[4] have been partly done into English. Parallels have repeatedly been drawn between this Syrian poet and the Persian ʿUmar al-Khayyām, who died about sixty years after him and shows decided marks of having been influenced by his predecessor. Al-Mutannabi' and al-Maʿarri close the period of great Arab poetry. Since that day hardly any Arab poet has been able to achieve more than local eminence.

Raids into "the land of the Romans"

After making his position secure in northern Syria, "the sword of the Ḥamdānid dynasty", beginning in 947, conducted annual campaigns into Asia Minor. Until his death twenty years later not a year passed without some engagement with the Greeks.[5] At first fortune smiled on Sayf's efforts. He seized Marʿash among other border towns. But the brilliant leadership of Nicephorus Phocas and John Tzimisces,[6] both future emperors, saved the day for Byzantium. In 961 Nicephorus captured the capital, Aleppo, with the exception of the citadel, put over ten thousand of its youth and all the captives to the sword and destroyed the palace of Sayf-al-Dawlah. But after eight or nine days he retired.[7] After he became emperor (963–9) his troops wrested Cyprus from the Arabs and occupied Cilicia.[8] Thus was the road

[1] *Al-Luzūmīyāt aw Luzūm Ma la Yalzam*, ed. ʿAzīz Zand, 2 vols. (Cairo, 1891, 1895); tr. (in part) Ameen Rihani (New York, 1918).

[2] Ed. Kāmil Kīlāni, 2 pts. (Cairo, 1923); partially translated by R. A. Nicholson in *Journal Royal Asiatic Society* (1900), pp. 637-720; (1902), pp. 75-101, 337-62, 813-47.

[3] Asín, *Islam and the Divine Comedy*, tr. Sunderland.

[4] *Rubāʿīyāt*, stanzas of four lines in which first, second and fourth rhyme; originally a Persian form of composition.

[5] See Yaḥya ibn-Saʿīd al-Anṭāki, "Ta'rīkh", ed. and tr. (Fr.) I. Kratchkovsky and A. Vasiliev in *Patrologia Orientalis*, vol. xviii, pp. 768 *seq.*

[6] "Ibn-Shamshaqīq" of Arab chronicles; ibn-al-Athīr, vol. viii, p. 407; abu-al-Fidā', vol. ii, p. 110, l. 20.

[7] Miskawayh, vol. ii, pp 192-4: Yahya, pp. 786-7

[8] Yāqūt, vol. iii, p. 527.

open again to Syria. In the last year of his reign his army seized Antioch, long coveted as a city of patriarchs, saints and councils and as a religious peer of Byzantium itself. The city remained in Byzantine hands from 969 till 1084. Soon after the occupation of Antioch, Nicephorus' general entered Aleppo and exacted from Sayf's son and successor, Sa'd-al-Dawlah (967–91), a humiliating treaty.[1] The Emperor John Tzimisces (969–76) adopted the policy of consolidating and insuring the conquests in Cilicia and northern Syria, and set for his final goal the freeing of Jerusalem. To this end he started from Antioch on a real crusade, entered Damascus, but did not penetrate far into Palestine. Early in his reign the refractory banu-Ḥabīb of Naṣībīn, cousins of the Ḥamdānids, 12,000 strong, left their homes on account of the high taxes, embraced Christianity and joined the Byzantines in their attacks on Moslem lands.[2] Tzimisces' successor, Basil II (976–1025), though troubled by the Arabs of North Africa, who at this time were in possession of Sicily and many Aegean islands, took the field in person to defend the Syrian possessions now threatened by the Fāṭimids of Egypt. But at the outset of the eleventh century he signed a treaty of peace with the Fāṭimid al-Ḥākim and no further serious collision took place. The efforts of Basil II, preceded by those of Nicephorus and Tzimisces, extended the eastern boundary of the Byzantine empire at the expense of Islam as far as the Euphrates and into the heart of northern Syria.[3] Their reigns covered "the most brilliant period in the history of Byzantine relations with the eastern Muslims".[4]

[1] Yaḥya, pp. 823-4.
[2] Ibn-Ḥawqal, pp. 140-41.
[3] Ibn-al-Athīr, vol. viii, pp. 440-41.
[4] Vasiliev, *Byzantine Empire*, vol. i, p. 381

CHAPTER XXXII

SUNDRY DYNASTIES IN THE EAST

WHILE petty dynasties, mostly of Arab origin, were parcelling out the domains of the caliph in the west, the same process was being carried forward by others, chiefly Turkish or Persian, in the east.

1. The Ṭāhirids

The first to establish a quasi-independent state east of Baghdād was the once trusted general of al-Ma'mūn, Ṭāhir ibn-al-Ḥusayn of Khurāsān, who had victoriously led his master's army against al-Amīn. In this war the one-eyed Ṭāhir is said to have used the sword so effectively with both hands that al-Ma'mūn[1] nicknamed him dhu-al-Yamīnayn (ambidextrous) and a poet described him as the warrior "minus one eye, plus an extra right arm".[2] The descendant of a Persian slave, Ṭāhir was rewarded in 820 by al-Ma'mūn with the governorship of all lands east of Baghdād, with the centre of his power in Khurāsān. Before his death two years later in his capital, Marw, Ṭāhir had omitted mention of the caliph's name in the Friday prayer.[3] Though nominally vassals of the caliph, Ṭāhir's successors extended their dominion as far as the Indian frontier. They moved the seat of government to Naysābūr, where they remained in power till 872,[4] when they were superseded by the Ṣaffārids.

2. The Ṣaffārids

The Ṣaffārid dynasty, which originated in Sijistān and reigned in Persia for forty-one years (867–908), owes its foundation to one Ya'qūb ibn-al-Layth al-Ṣaffār (867–78). Al-Ṣaffār (coppersmith) was a coppersmith by profession and a brigand by avocation. His chivalrous and efficient conduct as head of a band of outlaws attracted the favourable attention of the caliph's governor over Sijistān, who thereupon entrusted him with the

[1] Ṭabari, vol. iii, p. 829; ibn-Khallikān, vol. i, p. 424. Cf. Mas'ūdi, vol. vi, p. 423
[2] Ibn-Khallikān, vol. i, p. 422; ibn-al-Athīr, vol. vi, p. 270.
[3] Ibn-al-Athīr, vol. vi, pp. 255, 270.
[4] Mas'ūdi, vol. viii, p. 42; Ṭabari, vol. iii, p. 1880.

command of his troops.[1] Al-Ṣaffār eventually succeeded his benefactor and added to his domains almost all Persia and the outskirts of India, even threatening Baghdād itself under the Caliph al-Muʻtamid.[2] The Sāmānids fell heir to a large portion of the Ṣaffārid state.[3]

3. The Sāmānids

The Sāmānids of Transoxiana and Persia (874–999) were descended from Sāmān, a Zoroastrian noble of Balkh. The founder of the dynasty was Naṣr ibn-Aḥmad (874–92), a great-grandson of Sāmān, but the one who established its power was Naṣr's brother Ismāʻīl (892–907), who in 900 wrested Khurāsān from the Ṣaffārids.[4] Starting as Moslem sub-governors under the Ṭāhirids, the Sāmānids under Naṣr II ibn-Aḥmad[5] (913–43), fourth in the line, extended their kingdom to its greatest limits, including under their sceptre Sijistān, Karmān, Jurjān, al-Rayy and Ṭabaristān, in addition to Transoxiana and Khurāsān. Though outwardly professing loyalty to the 'Abbāsids, the dynasty was virtually independent. In the eyes of the Baghdād caliph its members were *amīrs* (governors) or even *'āmils* (tax collectors), but within their own territory their authority was undisputed.

It was under the Sāmānids that the final subjugation of Transoxiana to Moslem rule was effected. Their capital, Bukhāra, and their leading city, Samarqand, almost eclipsed Baghdād as centres of learning and art. Not only Arabic but Persian scholarship was protected and fostered. It was to a Sāmānid prince, abu-Ṣāliḥ Manṣūr ibn-Isḥāq of Sijistān, a nephew of the second ruler, that the illustrious al-Rāzi dedicated his book on medicine entitled *al-Manṣūri* in honour of his patron. It was in response to a summons from the Sāmānid ruler Nūḥ II (976–97)[6] that young ibn-Sīna, then living in Bukhāra and still in his teens, was accorded free access to the rich royal library,[7] where he acquired that seemingly inexhaustible fund of knowledge. From this

[1] Ibn-al-Athīr, vol. vii, pp. 124-5; ibn-Khallikān, vol. iii, pp. 350-51; Yaʻqūbi, vol. ii, p. 605; Mustawfi-i-Qazwīni, *Ta'rīkh-i-Guzīda*, ed. E. G. Browne, vol. i (Leyden, 1910), p. 373; tr. (abr.) Browne, vol. ii (Leyden, 1913), p. 72.

[2] Iṣṭakhri, pp. 245-7.

[3] Masʻūdi, vol. viii, pp. 41-5; Ṭabari, vol. iii, pp. 1698-1706, 1880-87.

[4] Ibn-al-Athīr, vol. vii, pp. 192-5, 346-7, vol. viii, pp. 4-6; Iṣfahāni, ed. Gottwaldt, pp. 236-7; Ṭabari, vol. iii, p. 2194; *Tarikh-i-Sistan*, ed. Bahār (Teheran, 1935), p. 256.

[5] Consult Mustawfi-i-Qazwīni, vol. i, pp. 381-3 = vol. ii, p. 74; ibn-al-Athīr, vol. viii, pp. 58-60, 154-6.

[6] Consult ibn-al-Athīr, vol. ix, pp. 69 *seq.*

[7] Ibn-abi-Uṣaybiʻah, vol. ii, p. 4.

epoch modern Persian literature takes its rise. Suffice it to recall that Firdawsi (*ca.* 934–1020) wrote his first poetry in this period and that Bal'ami, the vizir of Manṣūr I [1] (961–76), translated an abridgment of al-Ṭabari's history [2] and thus produced one of the oldest extant prose works in Persian. Ever since the Moslem conquest Persians had used Arabic as the medium of literary expression, but with these writers the brilliant Moslem literature of Persia began its development.

Though one of the most enlightened of the Iranian dynasties, the Sāmānid was not free from those elements which proved fatal to others of the same period. To the usual problems presented by a turbulent military aristocracy and a precarious dynastic succession was now added a new danger, that of the Turkish nomads to the north. Even within the state power was gradually slipping into the hands of Turkish slaves with whom the Sāmānids had filled their court. The Sāmānid territory south of the Oxus was absorbed in 994 by the Ghaznawids, who rose to power under one of these slaves. The territory north of the river was seized by the so-called Īlek (Īlāq) Khāns of Turkestan, who in 992 captured Bukhāra and seven years later gave the *coup de grâce* to the expiring Sāmānid dynasty. Thus for the first but not the last time we note Turanian hordes of Central Asia thrusting themselves to the forefront of Islamic affairs. The struggle between Iranians and Turanians for the mastery of the borderland of Islam in the fourth Moslem century was but a prelude to graver developments. We shall hereafter see these Turks play an increasingly important rôle in world affairs until they finally absorb most of the powers of the caliph of Baghdād, in fact until they establish their own caliphate, the Ottoman, in "Baghdād on the Bosporus".

4. Ghaznawids

Among the Turkish slaves whom the Sāmānids delighted to honour with high governmental posts was one Alptigīn, who started his career as a member of the bodyguard. Soon he rose to the headship of the guard [3] and thence was promoted in 961 to the governorship of Khurāsān. Shortly afterwards, however, he fell out of favour with the new Sāmānid ruler and betook himself to the eastern border of the kingdom. Here in 962 he captured

[1] A flattering description of the internal conditions under him has been left by an eye-witness, ibn-Ḥawqal, pp. 341-2, 344-5.

[2] Mustawfi-i-Qazwīni, vol. i, p. 385 = vol. ii, p. 75.

[3] Ibn-Ḥawqal, pp. 13, 14, refers to him as *Albtakīn, ḥājib ṣāḥib Khurāsān.*

Ghaznah, in Afghanistan, from its native rulers and established an independent realm [1] which developed into the Ghaznawid empire of Afghanistan and Panjāb (962–1186). The real founder of the Ghaznawid dynasty, however, was Subuktigīn (976–97), a slave and son-in-law of Alptigīn. The sixteen Ghaznawids who succeeded him were his lineal descendants. Subuktigīn widened his territory to include Peshāwar in India and also Khurāsān in Persia, which he first held under the Sāmānids.

Maḥmūd of Ghaznah

The most distinguished member of the dynasty was Subuktigīn's son Maḥmūd (999–1030). The location of his capital, Ghaznah, on the crest of a high plateau overlooking the plains of northern India, into which it possessed easy access through the valley of Kābul, gave him an advantageous position for a series of campaigns eastward. Between 1001 and 1024 Maḥmūd conducted no less than seventeen campaigns into India, which resulted in the annexation of the Panjāb, with its centre, Lahore, of Multān and of part of Sind.[2] In the Panjāb Moslem influence was now permanently established. From these raids Maḥmūd returned with fabulously rich spoils from the Hindu temples and won an enviable distinction among his contemporaries as the idol-breaker and champion of orthodox iconoclastic Islam. He was one of the first in Moslem history to receive, and that about 1001, the title *al-ghāzi*, bestowed on him who distinguished himself in war against unbelievers.

Maḥmūd likewise extended the western borders of his domains. Here he wrested the Persian 'Irāq, including al-Rayy and Iṣbahān, from the Shī'ite Buwayhids, who at the time had the caliph under their control. As a Sunnite, Maḥmūd had from the time of his accession acknowledged the nominal suzerainty of the Caliph al-Qādir (991–1031),[3] from whom he later received the title Yamīn-al-Dawlah (the right arm of the state).[4] On their coins he and his immediate successors satisfied themselves with the title *amīr* (governor) or *sayyid* (chief). Though Maḥmūd is credited with being the first in Islam to be designated *sulṭān*,[5] evidence from coins shows that this high designation was first

[1] Mustawfi-i-Qazwīni, vol. i, p. 393 = vol. ii, p. 78.

[2] *Ibid.* vol. i, pp. 395 *seq.*; Bīrūni, *Taḥqīq*, p. 11; M. Nāẓim, *The Life and Times of Sulṭān Maḥmūd of Ghazna* (Cambridge, 1931), pp. 86 *seq.*

[3] See Hilāl al-Ṣābi', *Ta'rīkh al-Wuzarā'* (supplement to Miskawayh, *Tajārib*, vol. iii), ed. Amedroz, pp. 341-5.

[4] Mustawfi-i-Qazwīni, vol. i, p. 395.

[5] Ibn-al-Athīr, vol. ix, p. 92.

officially borne by the Saljūq rulers.[1] At their greatest extent Maḥmūd's dominions, besides northern India in the east and the Persian 'Irāq in the west, included all Khurāsān, Ṭukhāristān with its centre Balkh, part of Transoxiana in the north and Sijistān in the south.[2] He adorned his capital with magnificent buildings,[3] founded and endowed a large academy and made his munificent court the chief resort of poets and men of learning. His assemblage of literary genius included the Arab historian al-'Utbi[4] († 1036), the celebrated scientific and historical author al-Bīrūni and the illustrious Persian poet Firdawsi, the millennial anniversary of whose birth was celebrated in 1934–5 in Asia Europe and America. On dedicating his great epic, the *Shāh-nāmah*, to Maḥmūd and receiving only 60,000 dirhams instead of dinars for its 60,000 verses, Firdawsi denounced his patron in a scathing satire and had to flee for his life.

The rise of the Ghaznawid dynasty represents the first victory of the Turkish element in its struggle against the Iranian element for ultimate mastery in Islam. Yet the Ghaznawid state did not differ radically from the Sāmānid or the Ṣaffārid state. It was loosely held by force of arms, and as soon as the powerful hand wielding the sword relaxed the component parts were certain to fall away. This is what happened after Maḥmūd's death. The provinces of the east gradually separated themselves from the capital in the highlands, thus beginning the series of independent Moslem dynasties of India. In the north and west the Khāns of Turkestan and the Great Saljūqs of Persia parcelled out the Ghaznawid domain. In the centre the hardy Ghūrids of Afghanistan dealt the final blows and in 1186 destroyed the last Ghaznawids in Lahore.

The imperial guard

While the wings of the 'Abbāsid eagle were being clipped at both extremities, a dagger clutched in Perso-Turkish hands was pointed at its heart. Under the domination of the Shī'ite Persian Buwayhids, and after them of the Sunnite Turkish Saljūqs, the caliph had little left except the capital and even there his authority was shadowy. The rise of an unruly imperial guard, followed by a revolt of negro slaves, undermined the central

[1] See below, p. 474.
[2] Hilāl al-Ṣābi', pp. 340, 386.
[3] See S. Flury in *Syria*, vol. vi (1925), pp. 61-90.
[4] His *Kitāb-i-Yamīni*, tr. James Reynolds (London, 1858), originally in Arabic, extols the glorious reign of Maḥmūd.

authority and paved the way for the advent of the Buwayhid régime.

It was the eighth 'Abbāsid caliph, al-Mu'taṣim (833–42), son of Hārūn by a Turkish slave, who first surrounded himself with a bodyguard of Turkish recruits from Transoxiana. The guard numbered four thousand. Originally brought in to counterbalance the influence of the soldiers from Khurāsān, to whom the 'Abbāsids owed the caliphate, the yearly import of Turks became an even greater menace to its integrity. Al-Manṣūr's "city of peace" became a city of turmoil. Facing the danger of a native uprising in Baghdād against the haughty and oppressive conduct of his guard, the caliph in 836 removed his seat of government sixty miles farther up the Tigris to Sāmarra.[1] Originally Assyrian, the name was changed by him to Surra Man Ra'a (pleased is he who sees it) under which name it appears as a mint city on 'Abbāsid coins. It was wittily whispered at the time that what the new name really meant was "he who sees it (with the Turks settled therein) is pleased (with Baghdād well rid of them)".

Sāmarra was beautified by palaces and mosques erected mainly by al-Mu'taṣim and his son al-Mutawakkil (847–61). It remained the capital for fifty-six years (836–92), during the reigns of eight successive caliphs, and its ruins are the most imposing 'Abbāsid monuments extant.[2]

GENEALOGICAL TABLE OF THE 'ABBĀSID CALIPHS AT SĀMARRA

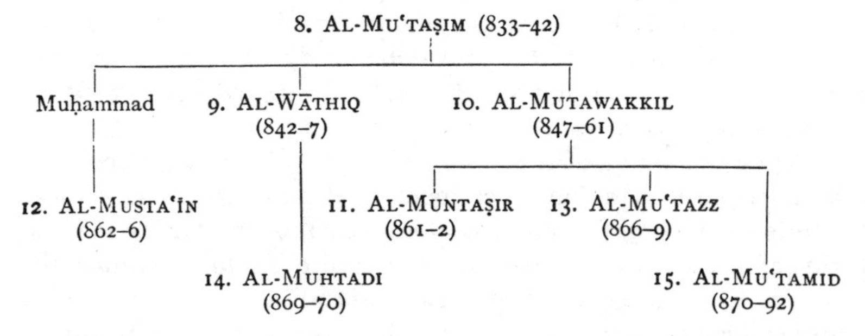

The rise of this body of predominantly Turkish soldiery, which played a part in the caliphate not unlike that of the

[1] Ṭabari, vol. iii, pp. 1179-81; Mas'ūdi, vol. vii, pp. 118 *seq.*; Yāqūt, *Buldān*, vol. iii, pp. 16-17.

[2] Maqdisi, pp. 122-3; Ernst Herzfeld, *Der Wandschmuck der Bauten von Samarra* (Berlin, 1923).

prætorian guard in Rome and the Janissaries in Turkey, marked the beginning of the end of caliphal power. The caliph lived in his new capital almost as their prisoner. The murder of al-Mutawakkil by them in December 861, at the instigation of his son,[1] was the first in a series of events in the course of which the mighty structure of the ʿAbbāsid dynasty—already shaken—stood face to face with imminent collapse. Al-Mutawakkil was the first caliph in the period of decline. After him we find caliphs made and unmade by troops, chiefly Turkish, under generals mostly slaves, striving for mastery. Through their influence over these slaves the women of the court came to play an important political rôle and thus added to the confusion. In the case of the weak and vacillating al-Mustaʿīn (862–6), who eventually fled to Baghdād pursued by his guard after he had been besieged and forced to abdicate, his slave-mother shared with two Turkish generals the supreme power.[2] The mother of his successor al-Muʿtazz (866–9) refused to pay out the 50,000 dinars which might have saved the life of her caliph son, though she kept in a subterranean cellar a cache of 1,000,000 dinars in addition to priceless jewellery.[3] For two centuries the history of the disintegrating caliphate presents a confused picture of nominal rulers ascending the throne with no power and descending to the grave unregretted. Peace and security, if anywhere, were enjoyed only in those outlying provinces where a governor, practically independent, held the reins with an iron hand.

A servile war

One of the most spectacular and sanguinary episodes of the period was the rebellion of the Zanj[4] slaves. These were negroes imported from East Africa and employed in the saltpetre mines on the lower Euphrates. The leader (*ṣāḥib al-Zanj*) was one ʿAli ibn-Muḥammad, a wily pretender, probably of Arab origin. Taking advantage of disturbed conditions in the capital and the uprising of the discontented and wretched miners, he claimed in September 869 that he was an ʿAlid called to their deliverance by visions and occult science. One band of slaves after another rallied under the banner of the new Messiah—"the rogue" and "Allah's enemy" of our main informant, al-Ṭabari.[5] Army after

[1] Ṭabari, vol. iii, pp. 1452-65; abbr. ibn-al-Athīr, vol. vii, pp. 60-64.
[2] Ṭabari, vol. iii, pp. 1512-13, copied by ibn-al-Athīr, vol. vii, pp. 80-81.
[3] Ṭabari, vol. iii, pp. 1718-19.
[4] From Pers. Zang (Ethiopia), whence Zangbār, Ar. Zanjabār, corrupted to Zanzibar.
[5] Vol. iii, pp. 1755, 1786.

army was sent to suppress the strange rebellion, but being on favourable and familiar territory, a patchwork of marshes intersected with canals, the negroes overcame them all and, in accordance with a Khārijite doctrine now adopted by their leader, mercilessly put all prisoners and non-combatants to the sword.[1] During fourteen years (870–83) of the reign of al-Mu'tamid (870–92) this servile war raged. The estimates of those who perished vary, some exceeding half a million. After one engagement the unclaimed heads of Moslems were so numerous that the negroes dumped them into a canal which carried them into al-Baṣrah, where they could be identified by relatives and friends.[2] Al-Baṣrah, Wāsiṭ, al-Ahwāz and al-Ubullah lay desolate. Not until the caliph's brother al-Muwaffaq had taken personal charge of the operations was the backbone of opposition broken. In 883 al-Mukhtārah, the fortress built by the leader, was stormed and he himself slain. "Thus ended one of the bloodiest and most destructive rebellions which the history of Western Asia records."[3] It was in the course of this war that Egypt, one of the first and fairest provinces, fell away from the caliphate under the rule of ibn-Ṭūlūn.

The *amīr al-umarā'* in power

The restoration of Baghdād as capital under al-Mu'taḍid (892–902), after ephemeral Sāmarra had functioned as such for over half a century, changed the scene but not the current of events. The real power continued to slip from caliphal to military hands. The period saw the rise of 'Abdullāh ibn-al-Mu'tazz, who after contesting the caliphate with his second cousin al-Muqtadir had the unique distinction of holding office under the title al-Murtaḍa for one day only (December 17, 908), after which he was deposed and killed. The one-day caliph was more of a poet and belletrist than a politician. Of his many works cited by *al-Fihrist*[4] and ibn-Khallikān[5] only a few have survived.

The twenty-four years of al-Muqtadir's reign (908–32) were marked by the rise and fall of thirteen vizirs, some of whom were put to death.[6] To add to the confusion the caliph's Turkish mother constantly interfered in state affairs. One of these vizirs was ibn-Muqlah, a founder of Arabic calligraphy.[7] Another was

[1] Mas'ūdi, vol. viii, pp. 31, 58-61. [2] Ṭabari, vol. iii, pp. 1785-6.
[3] Nöldeke, *Sketches from Eastern History*, tr. J. S. Black (London, 1892), p. 174.
[4] P. 116. [5] Vol. i, p. 462. [6] *Fakhri*, pp. 360 *seq.*
[7] Miskawayh, vol. i, pp. 185 *seq.*; Ṣābi', *Wuzarā'*, ed. Amedroz, pp. 109, 326, 359-60.

'Ali ibn-'Īsa, who in an age of corruption and oppression under a régime of cruelty and torture stands alone in his integrity and ability. In the two vizirates of 'Ali, which lasted five years, he materially improved the finances of the state by rigid economy and set an example of high efficiency which found no imitators.[1] It was during the caliphate of al-Muqtadir that both the Fāṭimid 'Ubaydullāh (909) in North Africa and the Umayyad 'Abd-al-Raḥmān III (929) in Spain assumed the dignity and insignia of the caliphate, thus creating the unusual phenomenon of three recognized rival caliphs in the Moslem world at the same time. The weak and incapable al-Muqtadir (lit. the mighty [by the help of God]) left the affairs of the state in the hands of his chief of bodyguard Mu'nis al-Muẓaffar,[2] a eunuch on whom he bestowed a newly created title, *amīr al-umarā'* (the commander of the commanders). Mu'nis soon became the real ruler. He dethroned al-Muqtadir and appointed his half-brother al-Qāhir.[3] After a brief restoration al-Muqtadir met his death at the hands of Berber soldiers who carried his head in triumph to their leader, Mu'nis.[4] Al-Qāhir (932–4) fared no better than his predecessor. When deposed the second time he was blinded and was last seen begging for alms in the streets of Baghdād.[5] Two of his successors, al-Muttaqi (940–44) and al-Mustakfi (944–6), followed him through the same process into the realm of darkness—all through the influence of the *amīr al-umarā'*.[6] At one time Baghdād presented the spectacle of three personages who had once held the highest office in Islam but were now deposed, blinded and objects of public charity. The *amīr al-umarā'* of al-Rāḍi (934–40) went so far as to have his name joined with the caliph's in the Friday prayer—a novel procedure in Islamic history.[7] Al-Rāḍi was one of the few caliphs of the period to escape deposition, but he did not escape death at the hands of the soldiery. By the Arab annalists he was considered "the last of the real caliphs", by which they meant the last to deliver the

[1] See Harold Bowen, *The Life and Times of 'Alī Ibn 'Īsà, "the Good Vizier"* (Cambridge, 1928).
[2] "The victorious." Miskawayh, vol. i, p. 76; Ṭabari, vol. iii, p. 2199.
[3] Miskawayh, vol. i, p. 193; ibn-al-Athīr, vol. viii, pp. 147-8.
[4] Ibn-al-Athīr, vol. viii, p. 179.
[5] Miskawayh, vol. i, pp. 291-2; ibn-al-Athīr, vol. viii, pp. 209, 211, 332-3; *Fakhri*, p. 375; Mas'ūdi, vol. viii, pp. 287 *seq.*
[6] Miskawayh, vol. ii, p. 72; Mas'ūdi, vol. viii, p. 409.
[7] Ibn-al-Athīr, vol. viii, p. 241.

Friday oration and conduct certain affairs of state.[1] He was also the last whose poetry has been preserved. With him vanished the last vestiges of power and dignity that were left to his office. The generalissimo, *amīr al-umarā'*, was now well established as the actual ruler of the Moslem state.[2]

5. The Buwayhid dynasty

An even darker chapter in the history of the caliphate was opened in December 945, when the Caliph al-Mustakfi (944-6) received in Baghdād the victorious Aḥmad ibn-Buwayh and made him his *amīr al-umarā'* with the honorific title of Mu'izz-al-Dawlah (he who renders the state mighty). Aḥmad's father, abu-Shujā' Buwayh, claimed descent from the ancient Sāsānid kings, probably, as in most such cases, to bolster up dynastic prestige.[3] He was the chief of a warlike horde consisting mainly of Daylamite highlanders from the mountainous region on the southern shore of the Caspian Sea and had been for some time in the service of the Sāmānids. His three sons, including Aḥmad, gradually worked their way southward, occupying Iṣbahān, then Shīrāz with its province (934) and in the following two years the provinces of al-Ahwāz (present-day Khūzistān) and Karmān. Shīrāz was chosen as capital of the new dynasty. At the advance of Aḥmad into Baghdād (945) the Turkish guard fled, but the lot of the caliph did not improve under the tutelage of his new masters, the Shī'ite Persians. Though his official position was simply that of *amīr al-umarā'*, Mu'izz-al-Dawlah insisted that he be mentioned along with the caliph in the *khuṭbah*. He even had his name stamped on the coinage.[4]

[1] *Fakhri*, p. 380; Tanūkhi, p. 146.

[2] A genealogical table of Baghdād caliphs under the military régime:

- 16. Al-Mu'taḍid (892–902)
  - 17. Al-Muktafi (902–8)
    - 22. Al-Mustakfi (944–6)
  - 18. Al-Muqtadir (908–32)
    - 20. Al-Rāḍi (934–40)
    - 21. Al-Muttaqi (940–44)
  - 19. Al-Qāhir (932–4)

[3] Cf. ibn-Khallikān, vol. i, p. 98; *Fakhri*, p. 376; ibn-al-Athīr, vol. viii, p. 197; Mustawfi-i-Qazwīni, vol. i, pp. 413-14; Friedrich Wilken, *Mirchond's Geschichte der Sultane aus dem Geschlechte Bujeh* (Berlin, 1835), p. 13 (Pers. text), p. 58 (tr.) (extract from Mīrkhwānd, *Rawḍat al-Ṣafā'*).

[4] Miskawayh, vol. ii, p. 158; ibn-al-Athīr, vol. viii, p. 337; Wilken, p. 21 (text), p. 66 (tr.). Cf. Miskawayh, vol. ii, p. 396; ibn-Khallikān, vol. ii, p. 159.

In January 946, the unfortunate al-Mustakfi was blinded and deposed by Mu'izz-al-Dawlah, who chose as the new caliph al-Muṭīʿ (946–74). Shīʿah festivals were now established, particularly the public mourning on the anniversary of al-Ḥusayn's death (tenth of Muḥarram) and the rejoicing on that of the Prophet's alleged appointment of ʿAli as his successor at Ghadīr al-Khumm.[1] The caliphate now passed through the period of its deepest humiliation with the commander of the believers a mere puppet in the hands of a schismatic commander of the commanders. The Buwayhids, however, were not the first in the history of Islam to assume the title of sultan, as is sometimes claimed.[2] They satisfied themselves, according to the testimony of their coins, with *amīr* or *malik* affixed to such honorific surnames as Muʿizz-al-Dawlah, ʿImād-al-Dawlah (prop of the state) and Rukn-al-Dawlah (pillar of the state), appellations which were simultaneously bestowed on the three sons of Buwayh by the caliph. After them similar pompous surnames became the fashion. The dignity of *amīr al-umarā'* was also held by several of Muʿizz' Buwayhid successors, even though it had become nothing more than an honorific fiction.

Throughout their century or so of supremacy (945–1055) the Buwayhids made and unmade caliphs at will. Al-ʿIrāq was governed as a province from the Buwayhid capital, Shīrāz in Fāris. In Baghdād they maintained several magnificent palaces under the collective name *dār al-mamlakah* (the abode of the kingdom).[3] Baghdād was no longer the hub of the Moslem world, for not only Shīrāz but Ghaznah, Cairo and Cordova were now sharing its international pre-eminence.

ʿAḍud-al-Dawlah

The Buwayhid power reached its zenith under ʿAḍud-al-Dawlah (the supporting arm of the state, 949–83), a son of Rukn. ʿAḍud was not only the greatest Buwayhid but also the most illustrious ruler of his time. Under his sceptre he united in 977 the several petty kingdoms that had risen under Buwayhid rulers in Persia and al-ʿIrāq, creating a state that approached in size an empire. ʿAḍud-al-Dawlah married the daughter of the Caliph al-Ṭā'iʿ and had the caliph marry his daughter (980),

[1] A spring between Makkah and al-Madīnah where Shīʿite tradition asserts the Prophet declared, "Whomsoever I am lord of, his lord is ʿAli also". Ibn-Saʿd, vol. v, p. 235; Masʿūdi, *Tanbīh*, pp. 255-6. In memory of this declaration the Shīʿites observed a feast on the 18th of dhu-al-Ḥijjah.

[2] Cf. above, p. 464; below, p. 474.

[3] Khaṭīb, vol. i, pp. 105-7.

hoping thereby to have a descendant of his assume the caliphate.[1] 'Aḍud was the first ruler in Islam to bear the title *shāhanshāh.*[2] Although he kept his court in Shīrāz he beautified Baghdād, repaired canals which had become filled up and erected in several other cities mosques, hospitals and public buildings, as reported by the meritorious historian Miskawayh,[3] 'Aḍud's treasurer.[4] For his charitable enterprises 'Aḍud appropriated funds from his state treasury. One interesting building of his was the shrine (*mashhad*) on the presumed tomb of 'Ali. But the most significant was the famous hospital in Baghdād, al-Bīmāristān al-'Aḍudi, which he completed in 978–9 and endowed with 100,000 dinars. The hospital had a staff of twenty-four physicians who also functioned as a medical faculty.[5] Poets such as al-Mutanabbi' sang 'Aḍud's glory and authors, including the grammarian abu-'Ali al-Fārisi, who wrote for him the *Kitāb al-Īḍāḥ* (book of explanation), dedicated to him their works.[6] In his cultivation of the arts of peace 'Aḍud found an able collaborator in his Christian vizir Naṣr ibn-Hārūn, who with the caliph's authorization erected and repaired churches and monasteries.[7]

The precedent for literary and scientific patronage set by 'Aḍud-al-Dawlah was followed by his son Sharaf-al-Dawlah[8] (983–89). In imitation of al-Ma'mūn, Sharaf constructed one year before his death a famous observatory. Another son of 'Aḍud, his second successor, Bahā'-al-Dawlah[9] (989–1012), who in 991 deposed the Caliph al-Ṭā'i' whose vast wealth he coveted, had an enlightened Persian vizir in the person of Sābūr ibn-Ardashīr. Sābūr built in 993 at Baghdād an academy with a library of 10,000 books,[10] which the Syrian poet al-Ma'arri used when a student in that city. The Ikhwān al-Ṣafā', be it also remembered, flourished under the Buwayhid régime. But the state itself was on

[1] Miskawayh, vol. ii, p. 414; Yāqūt, *Udabā'*, vol. vi, p. 266.

[2] Shortening of *shāhānshāh*, Pers. for king of kings, modelled after the ancient Iranian title of royalty. The Arabic correspondent, *malik al-mulūk*, was perhaps first assumed by 'Aḍud's son Bahā'-al-Dawlah and was especially favoured by the later dynasties of Turkish origin.

[3] Vol. ii, pp. 404-8. See ibn-al-Athīr, vol. ix, p. 16.

[4] Qifṭi, p. 331.

[5] Ibn-abi-Uṣaybi'ah, vol. i, pp. 310, 238, 244; Qifṭi, pp. 235-6, 337-8, 438.

[6] Ibn-Khallikān, vol. ii, p. 159.

[7] Miskawayh, vol. ii, p. 408.

[8] "The honour of the state." Ibn-al-Athīr, vol. ix, pp. 16-17; Rūdhrāwari, *Dhayl* (supplement to Miskawayh, *Tajārib*, vol. iii), ed. Amedroz, pp. 136 *seq.*

[9] "The splendour of the state." Ibn-al-Athīr, vol. ix, pp. 42 *seq.*; Rūdhrāwari, pp. 153 *seq.*

[10] Ibn-al-Athīr, vol. ix, p. 71; ibn-Khallikān, vol. i, p. 356.

its downward course. The wars between Bahā', Sharaf and their third brother, Ṣamṣām-al-Dawlah,[1] the dynastic and family quarrels carried on among their successors and the Buwayhid Shī'ite proclivities, which were deeply resented in Sunnite Baghdād, led to the fall of the dynasty. In 1055 the Saljūq Ṭughril Beg entered Baghdād and put an end to Buwayhid rule. The last of the dynasty in al-'Irāq, al-Malik al-Raḥīm (the merciful king, 1048–55), ended his days in confinement.

The subjoined tree shows the genealogical relationship of the 'Abbāsid caliphs under Buwayhid supremacy (945–1055):

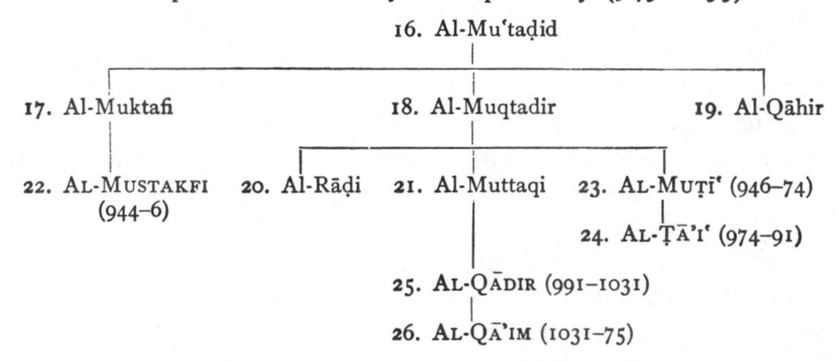

6. The Saljūqs

The advent of the Saljūq Turks ushers in a new and notable era in the history of Islam and the caliphate. At their appearance from the east in the early part of the eleventh century the caliph held but a shadow of his former power and his empire had been almost entirely dismembered. The Umayyads in Spain and the Shī'ite Fāṭimids in Egypt and North Africa were established beyond any hope of displacement from Baghdād. North Syria and upper Mesopotamia, as noted before, were in the hands of turbulent Arab chieftains, some of whom had succeeded in founding dynasties. Persia, Transoxiana and the lands to the east and south were parcelled among Buwayhid and Ghaznawid princes or held by sundry petty dynasts, each waiting for an opportunity to fly at the throat of the other. Political and military anarchy prevailed everywhere. Shī'ite-Sunnite confusion was the order of the day. Islam seemed crushed to the ground.

Into this distracted realm a chieftain named Saljūq had entered about 956 at the head of his clan of Turkoman Ghuzz (or Oghuz). Coming from the Kirghiz steppes of Turkestan,

[1] "The sword of the state." Ibn-al-Athīr, vol. ix, pp. 16-19, 32-5; Rūdhrāwari, pp. 184, 260.

these nomads settled in the region of Bukhāra, where they fervently embraced Sunnite Islam. Slowly but surely Saljūq and after him his sons fought their way through the realms of the Īlek Khāns and Sāmānids.[1] A grandson of Saljūq, Ṭughril,[2] ventured with his brother as far as Khurāsān. In 1037 the two brothers wrested Marw and Naysābūr from Ghaznawid hands. Balkh, Jurjān, Ṭabaristān and Khwārizm, as well as Hamadhān, al-Rayy and Iṣbahān were speedily added. The Buwayhid house tumbled before them. On December 18, 1055, Ṭughril Beg at the head of his wild Turkoman tribes stood at the gate of Baghdād. Al-Basāsīri, the Turkish general and military governor of Baghdād under the last Buwayhids, left the capital[3] and the Caliph al-Qā'im (1031–1075) hastened to receive the Saljūq invader as a deliverer.

Ṭughril in power

After an absence of a year Ṭughril returned to Baghdād and was received with elaborate ceremonies. Wearing the mantle and holding the cane of the Prophet, the caliph took his seat on a platform behind a curtain which was lifted at the approach of the conqueror. Ṭughril sat on an adjoining platform and communicated with the caliph through an interpreter. The conqueror was made regent of the empire and hailed as "king of the East and of the West".[4] His official title was to be *al-sulṭān* (he with authority, sultan).[5] The caliphate now passed under a new and more benevolent tutelage.

Taking advantage of the temporary absence of Ṭughril on an expedition to the north, al-Basāsīri, who had in the meantime espoused the Fāṭimid cause, returned in 1058 at the head of his Daylamite and other troops and reoccupied the capital. The Caliph al-Qā'im was forced to sign a document renouncing his rights and the rights of all other 'Abbāsids in favour of the rival Fāṭimid al-Mustanṣir (1035–94) in Cairo, to whom he now sent

[1] Mustawfi-i-Qazwīni, pp. 434-6, tr. pp. 93-4; Joannes A. Vullers, *Mirchondi historia Seldschukidarum* (Giessen, 1837), pp. 1 *seq.* (ext. from *Rawḍat al-Ṣafā'*).

[2] His father's name was Mīkā'īl, his brother's Dāwūd (David) and his uncle's Mūsa; ibn-al-Athīr, vol. ix, p. 322. Such names, noticeable among early Saljūqs, show Christian, probably Nestorian, influence. See Qazwīni, *Āthār*, p. 394.

[3] Ibn-Khallikān, vol. i, pp. 107-8; ibn-Taghri-Birdi, ed. Popper, vol. ii, pt. 2, p. 225.

[4] Ibn-al-Athīr, vol. ix, p. 436; ibn-Taghri-Birdi, *op. cit.* p. 233; 'Imād-al-Dīn (al-Iṣfahāni), abr. al-Bundāri, *Tawārīkh Āl Saljūq*, ed. M. Th. Houtsma (Leyden, 1899), p. 14.

[5] Al-Rāwandi, *Rāḥat al-Ṣudūr*, ed. Muḥammad Iqbāl (London, 1921), p. 105. Ṭughril was the first Moslem ruler whose coins bore this title. Stanley Lane-Poole, *Catalogue of Oriental Coins in the British Museum*, ed. R. S. Poole, vol. iii (London, 1877), pp. 28-9. With the Saljūqs "sultan" became a regular sovereign title.

the emblems of the caliphate, including the mantle and other sacred relics. Al-Qā'im's turban and a beautiful window from his palace were also sent as trophies to Cairo.[1] On his return, however, Ṭughril reinstated al-Qā'im and made al-Basāsīri pay for his disloyalty with his life (1060). The Daylamite troops were disbanded and the Buwayhid power was for ever crushed.

The reigns of Ṭughril (1037–63), his nephew and successor Alp Arslān (1063–72) and the latter's son Malikshāh (1072–92) cover the most brilliant period of Saljūq ascendancy over the Moslem East. As fresh Turkish tribesmen swelled their armies the Saljūqs extended their conquests in all directions until once more Western Asia was united into one Moslem kingdom and the fading glory of Moslem arms revived. A new race from Central Asia was now pouring its blood into the struggle of Islam for world supremacy. The story of these barbarian infidels, setting their feet on the necks of the followers of the Prophet and at the same time accepting the religion of the conquered and becoming its ardent champions, was not a unique instance in the chequered annals of that religion. Their cousins the Mongols of the thirteenth century, as well as their other kinsmen the Ottoman Turks of the early fourteenth century, repeated the same process. In the darkest hour of political Islam religious Islam has been able to achieve some of its most brilliant victories.

Alp Arslān

In the second year of his reign Alp Arslān (hero-lion) captured Āni, the capital of Christian Armenia, then a Byzantine province.[2] Soon after that he resumed hostilities with the everlasting Byzantine foe. In 1071 Alp won the decisive battle of Manzikart (Malāzkird, Malāsjird), north of Lake Van in Armenia, and took the Emperor Romanus Diogenes prisoner.[3] Saljūq nomadic tribes, the first Moslems to gain a permanent footing in "the land of the Romans", began now to settle in the plateau regions of Asia Minor, which henceforth became part and parcel of *dār al-Islām* (abode of Islam). These Saljūq nomads laid the basis of the Turkification of Asia Minor. It was a cousin of Alp, Sulaymān ibn-Quṭlumish by name, who was later put in charge of this new territory, where he established (1077) the sultanate of the Rūm[4] Saljūqs. Far-off Nicæa (Nīqiyah, Tur. Iznīq) was

[1] See below, p. 622. [2] Ibn-al-Athīr, vol. x, pp. 25 *seq.*

[3] *Ibid.* pp. 44 *seq.*; 'Imād-al-Dīn, pp. 38 *seq.*; Vasiliev, *Byzantine Empire*, vol. i, p. 431.

[4] Ar. *rūm* is the equivalent of "Romans". See above, p. 199.

first made the capital, and it was from that city that Qilij Arslān, son and successor of Sulaymān, was driven by the hordes of the first Crusade. After 1084 Iconium (Qūniyah, Konieh), the richest and most beautiful Byzantine city in Asia Minor, became the Saljūq capital in that land. In the meantime the Saljūq dynasty of Syria (1094–1117), founded by Tutush, son of Alp, in 1094, was contributing its share towards checking the advance of the first Crusade. Aleppo had been held since 1070 by Alp.[1] There he had checked the advance of the Fāṭimid power, from which he also recovered Makkah and al-Madīnah.

Saljūq power at its zenith

The first two Saljūq sultans did not live in Baghdād but exercised their authority through a military resident. Alp never visited or saw the caliph's capital.[2] His seat of government was Iṣbahān; Marw and al-Rayy were seats of his predecessor. It was not until the winter of 1091, shortly before the end of Malikshāh's reign, that the Saljūq seat of government was moved to the capital of the caliphs. The caliph became more than ever a puppet who moved at the will of the sultan, a puppet bedecked in all the regalia of high office and propped on the imperial throne by foreign hands. The name of the sultan was mentioned with that of the caliph in the Friday sermon. In 1087 the Caliph al-Muqtadi (1075–94) married the daughter of Sultan Malikshāh, and when a son was born Malikshāh planned, but unsuccessfully, to combine in his grandson the caliphate and the sultanate on a common throne.[3]

It was Malikshāh (1072–92) under whom Saljūq power reached its meridian. "His domain extended in length from Kāshghar, a town at the extreme end of the land of the Turks, to Jerusalem, and in width from Constantinople to the Caspian Sea."[4] In paying boatmen who once ferried him across the Oxus he issued drafts on his agent in Antioch.[5] But Malikshāh was more than a ruler of an extensive empire. He built roads and mosques, repaired walls, dug canals and spent large sums on the caravanserais dotting the pilgrimage route to Makkah. According to his biographer all the roads of the great empire were safe—safe enough for caravans, even for one or two men, to travel peacefully and without special protection from Transoxiana to Syria.[6]

[1] Ibn-al-Athīr, vol. x, pp. 43-4.
[2] Ibn-Khallikān, vol. ii, p. 443.
[3] *Ibid.* pp. 589-90.
[4] *Ibid.* p. 587.
[5] *Ibid.* p. 589.
[6] *Ibid.* p. 587.

The sanitary measures introduced into Baghdād at this time and credited by ibn-al-Athīr[1] to the Caliph al-Muqtadi were more likely initiated by this Saljūq sultan. These measures included the diversion of the dirty water of the public baths from the Tigris into special cesspools and the allotment of special places for cleaning and curing fish. An anecdote preserved in ibn-Khallikān[2] throws light on Malikshāh's character. On visiting a mosque in Ṭūs the sultan asked his vizir, Niẓām-al-Mulk, who was in his company, what it was that he had prayed for while in the mosque. The latter replied that he had prayed God to grant the sultan victory over his brother, with whom he was then at war. "As for me", remarked Malikshāh, "that was not what I prayed for. I only asked God to give victory to him of the two better fitted to rule the Moslems and more beneficial to his subjects."

An illustrious vizir: Niẓām-al-Mulk

The guiding hand throughout the administration of Alp Arslān and Malikshāh was that of their illustrious Persian vizir, Niẓām-al-Mulk (the organization of the kingdom), one of the ornaments of the political history of Islam. If we are to believe ibn-Khallikān, "for the twenty years covering the reign of Malikshāh, Niẓām-al-Mulk had all the power concentrated in his hand, whilst the sultan had nothing to do but sit on the throne or enjoy the chase."[3]

Although untutored and probably illiterate like his father and grand-uncle, Malikshāh at the suggestion of Niẓām-al-Mulk called in 1074–5 a conference of astronomers at his newly erected observatory and commissioned them to reform the Persian calendar.[4] The result was the remarkable Jalāli calendar (*ta'rīkh*), so styled after Malikshāh, whose full name included Jalāl-al-Dīn (the majesty of religion) abu-al-Fatḥ. This calendar, in the judgment of a modern scholar, is "somewhat more accurate than ours".

Niẓām-al-Mulk was himself a cultured and learned man.[5] From his pen we have one of the most remarkable Moslem treatises on the art of government, the *Siyāsat-nāmah*,[6] which he composed as a result of a competition suggested by Malikshāh.

[1] Vol. x, p. 156. [2] Vol. ii, p. 588. [3] Vol. i, p. 255.

[4] Ibn-al-Athīr, vol. x, pp. 67-8. Site of observatory uncertain, possibly in Iṣbahān, al-Rayy or Naysābūr. See above, p. 377.

[5] Ibn-al-Athīr, vol. x, p. 104; 'Imād-al-Dīn, p. 30.

[6] Ed. Charles Schefer (Paris, 1891), tr. Schefer (Paris, 1893).

The sultan requested his statesmen to give him in written form the benefit of their opinions as to the nature of good government. Among other notable works in Persian produced during this period were those of Nāṣir-i-Khusraw († *ca.* 1074), the celebrated traveller and Ismā'īli propagandist, and of 'Umar al-Khayyām († 1123–4), the great astronomer-poet who enjoyed the patronage of Niẓām and collaborated in the revision of the calendar. But the basis of this Persian vizir's glory is his establishment of the first well-organized academies for higher learning in Islam.[1] Particularly renowned was his Niẓāmīyah, founded 1065–7 at Baghdād. One of its chairs was once adorned by al-Ghazzāli.

Disintegration of the Saljūq realm

The aged Niẓām, as we learned before, was one of the earliest prominent victims of an Ismā'īli Assassin. With his death in 1092 the period of glory that covered the reigns of the first three Saljūqs ended. For a brief but brilliant span these three sultans had brought together most of the far-flung lands that had once formed the Islamic state. But the season of glory that Baghdād and Islam enjoyed under them was only an Indian summer. After the death of Malikshāh civil wars among his sons and subsequent disturbances weakened the central Saljūq authority and led to the break-up of the house. The Saljūq empire, built on a tribal basis by a people nomadic in their habits and form of organization, could be held together only by some dominant personality. The system of military fiefs regularized in 1087 by Niẓām-al-Mulk, according to which grants became and remained hereditary, led to the immediate establishment of semi-independent states. These separate subdivisions attained virtual independence in different parts of the wide kingdom, while the main line, the Great Saljūqs of Persia, maintained a nominal suzerainty down to 1157. One of the chief subdivisions of the family was that of the Persian 'Irāq (1117–94). The Saljūqs of al-Rūm in Iconium were superseded after 1300 by the Ottoman Turks—last great representatives of militant Islam—whose tradition relates their origin to the Ghuzz tribe, to which the Saljūqs also belonged. After penetrating into Europe as far as Vienna (1529) and establishing an empire almost as extensive as that of the Arab caliphs, the Ottoman Turks have since the first World War confined their authority to Asia Minor or Anatolia.

[1] See above, p. 410.

The one permanent contribution of the Saljūq and Ottoman Turks to Islamic religion was a mystic colouring. This is well represented by the several dervish orders which flourished on Turkish soil and maintained ideas of early shamanistic origin with an admixture of indigenous beliefs of Asia Minor and schismatic Christian doctrines. The *futūwah*[1] organizations in which Moslem Arab chivalry sought to express itself took among the Turks a new form, that of the *akhis*. Originally these *akhi* organizations may have been economic guilds. It was in *akhi* hospices that ibn-Baṭṭūṭah[2] was entertained while travelling in Asia Minor.

It may be of interest in this connection to note that the double-headed eagle which originated in the brain of some ancient Sumerian priest and passed on very early to the Babylonians and Hittites was some three thousand years later adopted as an emblem by the Saljūq Turks who settled in Hittiteland (Asia Minor). From the Saljūqs it passed on to Byzantium, whence it reached Austria, Prussia and Russia.

Baghdād unmindful of the Crusades

The Saljūq domination over the caliphate, which began with al-Qā'im in 1055, lasted till 1194 in the reign of al-Nāṣir.[3] Throughout the greater part of this period the Crusades dragged

[1] See below, p. 481.

[2] Vol. ii, pp. 260, 318. *Akhi* is not Ar. for "brother" as ibn-Baṭṭūṭah explained but Tur. for "knightly" or "noble." Consult Franz Taeschner in *Islamica*, vol. iv (1929), pp. 1-47, vol. v, pp. 285-333; J. Deny in *Journal asiatique*, ser. 11, vol. xvi (1920), pp. 182-3.

[3] Caliphs under Saljūq domination:

26. Al-Qā'im (1031–75)
 |
Muḥammad
 |
27. Al-Muqtadi (1075–94)
 |
28. Al-Mustaẓhir (1094–1118)
 |
 ├── 29. Al-Mustarshid (1118–35)
 │ |
 │ 30. Al-Rāshid (1135–6)
 │
 └── 31. Al-Muqtafi (1136–60)
 |
 32. Al-Mustanjid (1160–70)
 |
 33. Al-Mustaḍī' (1170–80)
 |
 34. Al-Nāṣir (1180–1225)

wearily in Syria-Palestine, but neither Saljūqs nor 'Abbāsids interested themselves in the distant affair. To the main body of the Moslem community the Crusades, viewed from headquarters, were but an insignificant episode. When on the fall of Jerusalem (1099) a Moslem delegation arrived in Baghdād to seek aid against the invading Christians tears were shed and kind sympathy was expressed, but no action was taken.[1] The caliph al-Mustaẓhir (1094-1118) referred the delegation to Sultan Barkiyāruq (1094–1104), Malikshāh's second successor and drunkard son,[2] with whom the decline of the sultanate started, and the negotiations ended there. In 1108 a second appeal came, now from Tripoli beset by the Crusaders. The delegation was headed by the chief of the beleaguered city, but its mission was as futile as the preceding one. Three years later, when the Franks captured certain vessels from Egypt carrying goods consigned to merchants in Aleppo, al-Mustaẓhir, on the urgent request of an Aleppine delegation, which smashed the pulpit and interfered with the conduct of prayer in the mosque which the sultan was attending, bestirred himself and sent a handful of troops which, of course, accomplished nothing.[3] Thus did "the commander of the believers" and his Saljūq sultan stand passively by while the most spectacular drama in the history of Christian-Islamic relations was being enacted.

Later, during the caliphate of al-Muqtafi (1136–60), when the Crusades raged furiously, the hard-pressed Moslem leader Zangi[4] made urgent appeals to Baghdād, which in response to popular demand yielded a few thousand recruits. Meanwhile Zangi's warlike son Nūr-al-Dīn and the famous Ṣalāḥ-al-Dīn (Saladin) were turning their arms successfully not only against the Christians but also against the schismatic Fāṭimids in Egypt. By 1171 Ṣalāḥ-al-Dīn had put an end to the Fāṭimid dynasty and, as a loyal Sunnite, substituted the name of the 'Abbāsid caliph al-Mustaḍī' in the *khuṭbah* in Egypt and Syria. Thereby was the nominal supremacy of the 'Abbāsid caliphs once more recognized in these lands.

[1] Ibn-al-Athīr, vol. x, p. 192[4].
[2] Ibn-Khallikān, vol. i, p. 154.
[3] Ibn-al-Athīr, vol. x, pp. 338-9; ibn-al-Qalānisi, *Dhayl*, p. 173.
[4] Founder of the Atābeg dynasty of al-Mawṣil and Syria. The *atābegs* (Tur. *ata*, "father" + *beg*, "prince") were originally guardians or tutors of the young Saljūq princes and finally replaced them in supreme power. Abu-Shāmah, *al-Rawḍatayn fi Akhbār al-Dawlatayn*, vol. i (Cairo, 1287), p. 24.

To the successor of al-Mustaḍī', al-Nāṣir, Ṣalāḥ-al-Dīn sent after the decisive battle of Ḥiṭṭīn (1187) several Frankish prisoners and a part of the booty, including a bronze cross overlaid with gold said to contain some of the wood of the true cross. The caliph buried this cross in Baghdād.[1]

The shahs of Khwārizm

Al-Nāṣir, whose rule from 1180 to 1225 was the longest in 'Abbāsid annals,[2] made a faint and final attempt to restore the caliphate to something like its ancient self. The endless internal broils among the Saljūq princes and the fresh recognition accorded the 'Abbāsid caliphate by the hero Ṣalāḥ-al-Dīn gave al-Nāṣir the semblance of an opportunity. He proceeded to impose his will on the capital, making a display of high living and sponsoring a programme of lavish building. Under his patronage flourished a special order of sworn brotherhood, *futūwah*, a sort of knighthood of chivalry, whose organization he reformed. The brotherhood traced its origin to 'Ali and comprised men of birth and distinction, mostly descendants of the Prophet's son-in-law. Members (*fityān*) were initiated in a special ceremony and wore distinctive garments.[3] Yazīd ibn-Mu'āwiyah was one of the first in Islam to win the title *fata al-'Arab*, the paladin of the Arabs, which at that time had no technical significance.

Al-Nāṣir's attempts, however, were but the flicker of an expiring flame. His first serious mistake was made when he instigated Takash, ruler of Khwārizm (1172–1200) and member of the Turkish dynasty of the Khwārizm Shāhs,[4] to attack the Saljūqs of the Persian 'Irāq,[5] who had succeeded the Great Saljūqs of Persia in ruling Baghdād. The battle between Takash and the Saljūq Sultan Ṭughril (1177–94) was fought in 1194 and

[1] Ibn-al-Athīr, vol. xi, p. 353; abu-Shāmah, vol. ii, pp. 76, 139.

[2] Cf. Mustawfi-i-Qazwīni, vol. i, p. 369. The caliphate of al-Qā'im (1031–75) was the second longest among the 'Abbāsids. The Fāṭimid al-Mustanṣir (1035–94) nominally holds the record in Moslem annals, but as ibn-al-Athīr (vol. xii, p. 286) points out this caliph was only seven years old when he was installed. As for 'Abd-al-Raḥmān III (912–61), of Cordova, he did not proclaim himself caliph until 929.

[3] *Fakhri*, p. 434; ibn-al-Athīr, vol. xii, p. 268; ibn-Jubayr, p. 280. See Hermann Thorning, *Beiträge zur Kenntniss des islamischen Vereinswesens auf Grund von Basṭ Madad et-Taufīq* (Berlin, 1913); H. Ritter in *Der Islam*, vol. x (1920), pp. 244-50.

[4] The founder of this dynasty, destined for over a hundred years to play the leading rôle in the history of Middle Asia, was a slave from Ghaznah who served as cup-bearer for the Saljūq Malikshāh and was appointed by him to the governorship of Khwārizm. Juwayni, pt. 2 (Leyden, 1916), p. 3; ibn-al-Athīr, vol. x, pp. 182-3.

[5] Al-'Irāq al-'Ajami (i.e. Media), so called under the Saljūqs to distinguish it from al-'Irāq al-'Arabi. See above, p. 330, n. 2.

resulted in the defeat of Ṭughril. With him the Saljūq line in al-'Irāq and Kurdistān came to an end. Al-Nāṣir expected the victorious shah to vacate the conquered territory, but Takash schemed differently. After the Saljūq fashion he issued coins bearing his name as sultan and proposed to hold the secular power in Baghdād itself, leaving to the caliph only nominal sovereignty. The dispute continued under his energetic son 'Alā'-al-Dīn Muḥammad (1200–1220). Having reduced (1210) the greater part of Persia, subdued Bukhāra with its sister Samarqand and seized Ghaznah (1214), this Khwārizm Shāh resolved to put an end to the 'Abbāsid caliphate. He planned to install in its place an 'Alid one. In his consternation al-Nāṣir (the defender [of the faith]) is said to have sought in 1216 the aid of a new ally whose star was just rising over the distant east, Chingīz Khān (1155–*ca.* 1227), redoubtable head of pagan Mongolian hordes.[1] Before this appalling swarm of some sixty thousand[2] barbarians, augmented by levies from peoples subjected en route, 'Alā'-al-Dīn had no recourse but flight. His place of refuge was an island in the Caspian Sea, where he died in despair in 1220.[3]

Enter Chingīz Khān

In the meantime the Mongols, riding fleet horses and armed with strange bows, were spreading havoc and destruction wherever they went.[4] Before them the cultural centres of eastern Islam were practically wiped out of existence, leaving bare deserts or shapeless ruins where formerly stately palaces and libraries had lifted their heads. A crimson stream marked their trail. Out of a population of 100,000 Harāt (Herat) was left with 40,000.[5] The mosques of Bukhāra, famed for piety and learning, served as stables for Mongolian horses. Many of the inhabitants of Samarqand and Balkh were either butchered or carried into captivity. Khwārizm was utterly devastated. At the capture of Bukhāra (1220) Chingīz (Genghis) is reported by a late tradition

[1] See W. Barthold, *Turkestan*, 2nd ed., tr. H. A. R. Gibb (Oxford, 1928), pp. 399-400. Chingīz had two Moslems on his staff as he advanced westward. Long before his time Moslem merchants had carried on trade with the nomadic tribes of eastern Mongolia. See above, pp. 343-4.

[2] The estimates, all probably exaggerated, vary from 60,000 to 70,000.

[3] Mustawfi-i-Qazwīni, vol. i, p. 498.

[4] Juwayni, pt. 1, pp. 17 *seq.*; ibn-al-Athīr, vol. xii, pp. 234 *seq.*

[5] Cf. Yāqūt, *Buldān*, vol. iv, p. 958. In 1220, about a year before the disastrous event, Yāqūt visited Harāt, which he described as the largest and richest city he had ever seen.

to have described himself as "the scourge of God sent to men as a punishment for their sins".[1] Ibn-al-Athīr,[2] a contemporary authority, shudders at the narration of these horrors and wishes his mother had not borne him. Even a century later, when ibn-Baṭṭūṭah[3] visited Bukhāra, Samarqand, Balkh and other Transoxianan cities he found them still largely in ruins. As for Baghdād, its turn was soon to come.

Thus did the invincible founder of the largest empire the world has ever seen make his sweep across the realm of Islam. The people he led had by the first half of the thirteenth century shaken every kingdom from China to the Adriatic. Russia was in part overrun and central Europe penetrated as far as eastern Prussia. It was only the death of Chingīz' son and successor in 1241 that saved Western Europe from these Mongolian hordes.[4]

The Caliph al-Nāṣir spent the few remaining years of his long reign, as did his son al-Ẓāhir (1225–6) and grandson al-Mustanṣir (1226–42), in a state of constant alarm. On one occasion these Mongols, or *Tatar* as they are called in the contemporary sources, advanced as far as Sāmarra. This made the terror-stricken population of Baghdād scramble to their defences. But the danger passed for the moment. This was only a lull before the fatal storm.

[1] Juwayni, pt. 1, p. 81. [2] Vol. xii, p. 233. [3] Vol. iii, pp. 25-7, 52, 58-9.

[4] Confused with the Kalmucks, of whose descendants 175,000 were deported to Siberia by the Soviet Union and 600 were found in 1949 in a displaced persons' camp in Western Germany. Of these 250 were permitted two years later to settle on a farm land in New Jersey, where they converted a garage into a Buddhist temple. Cf. below, p. 676, n 1.

CHAPTER XXXIII

THE COLLAPSE OF THE 'ABBĀSID CALIPHATE

IF anything parallels the astounding rapidity with which the sons of the Arabian desert conquered in the first Islamic century most of the civilized world, it is the swift decadence of their descendants' domination between the middle of the third and the middle of the fourth centuries. About 820 more extensive authority was concentrated in the hands of one man, the caliph in Baghdād, than in those of any other living person; by 920 the power of his successor had so diminished that it was hardly felt even in his capital city. By 1258 that city itself lay in ruins. With its fall Arab hegemony was lost for ever and the history of the real caliphate closed.

Among the external factors the barbarian (in this case Mongol or Tartar) onslaughts, though spectacular in themselves, were in reality only contributory to the final downfall. Even the rise, mushroom-like, of the numberless dynasties and quasi-dynasties in the heart of the caliphate and on its periphery was in itself a symptom of the disease rather than the cause of it. As in the analogous case of the Roman Empire of the West, the sick man was already on his deathbed when the burglars burst open the doors and snatched their share of the imperial heritage.

More important than the external factors in bringing about the dissolution of the caliphate were the internal ones. The reader who has followed the preceding chapters with care has doubtless already discerned those factors and noticed their operation throughout several centuries. Many of the original conquests were only nominal. The possibility of decentralization and dismemberment always lurked in the nature of those hasty and incomplete conquests. The method of administration was not conducive to stability and continuity. Exploitation and overtaxation were recognized policies, not the exception but the rule. Lines of cleavage between Arabs and non-Arabs, between Arab Moslems and Neo-Moslems, between Moslems and dhimmis, remained sharply marked. Among the Arabians themselves the old divisive feeling between north and south persisted. Neither the Iranian Persians, nor the Turanian Turks, nor the Hamitic Berbers were ever welded into a homogeneous whole with the Semitic Arabs. No consciousness of kind knit these diverse elements closely together. The sons of Iran were ever mindful of their ancient national glory and never reconciled themselves entirely to the new régime. The Berbers vaguely expressed their tribal feeling and sense of difference by their readiness to embrace any schismatic movement. The people of Syria long expected the rise of a Sufyāni to deliver them from the ʿAbbāsid yoke.[1] Within the fold of religion itself centrifugal forces, no less potent than the political and military, were active, producing Shīʿites, Qarmaṭians, Ismāʿīlites, Assassins and the like. Several of these groupings represented more than religious sects; the Qarmaṭians staggered the eastern part of the empire with their blows, and soon afterward the Fāṭimids seized the west. Islam was no more able to unite its devotees into a corporate whole than was the caliphate to incorporate the lands of the Mediterranean with those of Central Asia into a stable unit.

Then there were the social and moral forces of disintegration. The blood of the conquering element became in course of centuries diluted with that of the conquered, with a subsequent loss of their dominating position and qualities. With the decay of the Arab national life, Arab stamina and morale broke down. Gradually the empire developed into an empire of the conquered. The large harems, made possible by the countless number of eunuchs; the girl and the boy slaves (*ghilmān*), who contributed most to the degradation of womanhood and the degeneration of manhood; the unlimited concubines and the numberless half-brothers and half-sisters in the imperial household with their unavoidable jealousies and intrigues; the luxurious scale of high living with the emphasis on wine and song — all these and other similar forces sapped the vitality of family life and inevitably produced the persistently feeble heirs to the throne. The position of these heirs was rendered still more feeble by their interminable disputes over a right of succession which was never definitely determined.

Nor should the economic factors be ignored or underrated.

[1] Above, p. 286.

The imposition of taxes and the government of the provinces for the benefit of the ruling class discouraged farming and industry. As the rulers grew rich the people grew proportionately poor. Within the states grew statelets whose lords habitually fleeced their serfs. The depletion of man-power by the recurring bloody strife left many a cultivated farm desolate. Inundations in lower Mesopotamia periodically wrought havoc, and famines in various parts of the empire added their quota of disaster. The frequent spread of epidemics—plague, smallpox, malaria and other fevers—before which medieval man stood powerless, decimated the population in large areas. No less than forty major epidemics are recorded in the Arabic annals of the first four centuries after the conquest. National economic decay naturally resulted in the curtailment of intellectual development and in the stifling of creative thought.

Hūlāgu in Baghdād

In 1253 Hūlāgu, a grandson of Chingīz Khān, left Mongolia at the head of a huge army intent upon the destruction of the Assassins and the caliphate. The second wave of Mongol hordes was on. It swept before it all those petty princedoms which were striving to grow on the ruins of the empire of the Khwārizm Shāhs. Hūlāgu sent an invitation to the Caliph al-Mustaʿṣim[1] (1242–58) to join in the campaign against the Ismāʿīli Assassins. The invitation received no response. By 1256 the greater number of the Assassin strongholds, including the "mother convent" Alamūt, had been captured without difficulty and the power of that dreaded order crushed to the ground.[2] Even the babes were ruthlessly slaughtered. In September of the following year, as he was winding his way down the famous Khurāsān highway, the conquering invader sent an ultimatum to the caliph demanding his surrender and the demolition of the outer city wall. The reply was evasive. In January 1258 the mangonels of Hūlāgu were in effective operation against the walls of the capital. Soon a

[1] "He who holds fast" to God. The last caliphs:

34. Al-Nāṣir (1180–1225)
|
35. Al-Ẓāhir (1225–6)
|
36. Al-Mustanṣir (1226–42)
|
37. Al-Mustaʿṣim (1242–58)

[2] Rashīd-al-Dīn, *Jāmiʿ*, ed. and tr. Quatremère, vol. i, pp. 166 *seq.*

breach was effected in one of the towers.[1] The Vizir ibn-al-'Alqami accompanied by the Nestorian catholicos—Hūlāgu had a Christian wife—appeared to ask for terms. But Hūlāgu refused to receive them. Equally ineffective were warnings citing the fate of others who had dared violate "the city of peace" or undo the 'Abbāsid caliphate. Hūlāgu was told that "if the caliph is killed the whole universe is disorganized, the sun hides its face, rain ceases and plants grow no more".[2] But he knew better, thanks to the advice of his astrologers. By the tenth of February his hordes had swarmed into the city and the unfortunate caliph with his three hundred[3] officials and qāḍis rushed to offer an unconditional surrender. Ten days later they were all put to death. The city itself was given over to plunder and flames; the majority of its population, including the family of the caliph, were wiped out of existence. Pestilential odours emitted by corpses strewn unburied in the streets compelled Hūlāgu to withdraw from the town for a few days. Perhaps he intended to retain Baghdād for his residence and, therefore, the devastation was not as thorough as in other towns. The Nestorian patriarch received special favours. Certain schools and mosques were spared or rebuilt. For the first time in its history the Moslem world was left without a caliph whose name could be cited in the Friday prayers.

In 1260 Hūlāgu was threatening northern Syria. Here he captured in addition to Aleppo, where he put to the sword some fifty thousand people, Ḥamāh and Ḥārim. After dispatching a general to the siege of Damascus he felt himself constrained by the death of his brother, the Great Khān, to return to Persia.[4] The army left behind, after subjugating Syria, was destroyed in 1260 at 'Ayn Jālūt (Goliath's spring) near Nazareth by Baybars, the distinguished general of the Egyptian Mamlūk Quṭuz.[5] The whole of Syria was now reoccupied by the Mamlūks and the westward advance of the Mongols was definitely checked.

[1] *Fakhri*, p. 454; Rashīd-al-Dīn, vol. i, pp. 284-5.

[2] *Fakhri*, p. 190; Rashīd-al-Dīn, vol. i, p. 260. *Fakhri*, written in 1301 and dedicated to Fakhr-al-Dīn 'Īsa, governor of al-Mawṣil under the Mongols, contains eye-witness material on the fall of Baghdād.

[3] Three thousand in Rashīd-al-Dīn, vol. i, p. 298.

[4] The Great Khān of Marco Polo was another brother, Qūbīlāy († 1294), the Kubla Khan of Coleridge. It was Qūbīlāy who transferred the capital from Qarāqorum in Mongolia to Peking. Consult Rashīd-al-Dīn, vol. i, p. 128, vol. ii, ed. E. Blochet (Leyden, 1911), pp. 350 *seq.*

[5] Abu-al-Fidā', vol. iii, pp. 209-14; Rashīd-al-Dīn, vol. i, pp. 326-49; Maqrīzi, *Sulūk*, tr. Quatremère as *Sultans mamlouks*, vol. i (pt. 2), pp. 96 *seq.*

Later, Hūlāgu returned and attempted to make an alliance with the Franks for the conquest of Syria but he failed in his purpose.

As founder of the Mongol kingdom of Persia, which extended from the Āmu Darya to the borders of Syria and from the Caucasus Mountains to the Indian Ocean, Hūlāgu was the first to assume the title Īl-Khān.[1] This title was borne by his successors down to the seventh, Ghāzān Maḥmūd (1295–1304), under whom Islam, with Shī'ite proclivities, became the state religion. Under the Īl-Khāns or Hūlāguids Baghdād was reduced to the position of capital of the province called al-'Irāq al-'Arabi. The great Īl-Khān, as Hūlāgu was often entitled, favoured the Christian element among his subjects. In times of peace he delighted to make his home at Marāghah, east of the salt Lake Urmiyah, where many edifices, including the famous library and observatory, were built by him. There Hūlāgu died in 1265 and with him were buried, in accordance with Mongol custom, beautiful young maidens. He and his successors, like the Saljūqs before them, were quick to appreciate and utilize the administrative genius of the Persians and to surround themselves with such cultivated savants as al-Juwayni († 1283) and Rashīd-al-Dīn († 1318), the historians of the period. The seventy-five years of Īl-Khānid rule in Persia were rich in literary achievement.

Hard pressed between the mounted archers of the wild Mongols in the east and the mailed knights of the Crusaders on the west, Islam in the early part of the thirteenth century seemed for ever lost. How different was the situation in the last part of the same century! The last Crusader had by that time been driven into the sea. The seventh of the Īl-Khāns, many of whom had been flirting with Christianity, had finally recognized Islam as the state religion—a dazzling victory for the faith of Muḥammad. Just as in the case of the Saljūqs, the religion of the Moslems had conquered where their arms had failed. Less than half a century after Hūlāgu's merciless attempt at the destruction of Islamic culture, his great-grandson Ghāzān, as a devout Moslem, was consecrating much time and energy to the revivification of that same culture.

[1] Tur. *īl*, "tribe" + Tur. *khān*, "lord" = lord of the tribe, subordinate chief, indicating the feudal homage owed to the Khāqaān (Great Khān) in remote Mongolia, north of the Gobi Desert, later in Peking.

Last champions of Islam

It was not the Mongols, however, who were destined to restore the military glory of Islam and unfurl its banner triumphantly over new and vast territories. This was left to their kinsmen, the Ottoman Turks,[1] the last champions of the religion of Arabia. Their empire under Sulaymān (1520–66) stretched from Baghdād on the Tigris to Budapest on the Danube, and from Aswān, near the first cataract of the Nile, almost to the Strait of Gibraltar. When in January 1516 Sulaymān's father, Salīm, destroyed the Mamlūk army in North Syria,[2] he took among his prisoners a nonentity who under the name al-Mutawakkil represented a line of nominal 'Abbāsid caliphs who for about two and a half centuries had been maintained there as puppets of the Mamlūk sultans. The line was begun in 1261 by an uncle of al-Musta'ṣim, who had evidently escaped the massacre at Baghdād and was installed in Cairo by the fourth Mamlūk ruler, Baybars (1260–1277), with great pomp as caliph under the name al-Mustanṣir.[3] Al-Mustanṣir was soon after killed in a rash attempt on behalf of Baybars to recover Baghdād. He was followed by another scion of the 'Abbāsid house, who in 1262 was installed with similar ceremony. Sultan Salīm carried the Caliph al-Mutawakkil with him to Constantinople but allowed him to return to Cairo, where he died in 1543. With him the shadowy 'Abbāsid caliphate of Egypt may be said to have ended. There is nothing in the contemporary sources to support the claim, often advanced, that the last 'Abbāsid surrendered his title of caliph with all rights and privileges pertaining thereto to the Ottoman conqueror or to his successor in Constantinople.[4]

[1] So called after their eponymous founder, 'Uthmān, born *ca.* 1258.
[2] See below, pp. 677, 705.
[3] Abu-al-Fidā', vol. iii, p. 222. See below, p. 676.
[4] See above, p. 186; below, p. 705.

PART IV

THE ARABS IN EUROPE: SPAIN AND SICILY

CHAPTER XXXIV

CONQUEST OF SPAIN

Gothic kingdom destroyed

THE Moslem campaign in the Iberian Peninsula, the south-western gate of Europe, was, as noted before, the last and most dramatic of the major military operations undertaken by the Arabs. It marked the height of the African-European expansion of the Moslems, just as the conquest of Turkestan marked the apogee of the Asiatic-Egyptian expansion.

In its swiftness of execution and completeness of success this expedition into Spain holds a unique place in medieval military annals. The first reconnaissance was made in July 710, when, with four hundred foot and one hundred horse, all Berbers, Ṭarīf,[1] a client of Mūsa ibn-Nuṣayr, the celebrated governor of North Africa under the Umayyads, landed on the tiny peninsula which is almost the southernmost tip of the European continent. This peninsula, now Tarifa, has since borne his name, Jazīrat (isle of) Ṭarīf.[2] Mūsa, who had held the governorship since about 700, had driven the Byzantines for ever from the territory west of Carthage and had gradually pushed his conquests to the Atlantic, thus acquiring for Islam a *point d'appui* for the invasion of Europe. Encouraged by Ṭarīf's success and by the dynastic trouble in the Visigothic kingdom of Spain and actuated more by the desire for booty than for conquest, Mūsa dispatched in 711 his Berber freedman Ṭāriq ibn-Ziyād into Spain with 7000 men, most of whom were Berbers. Ṭāriq landed near the mighty rock which has since immortalized his name, Jabal (mount of) Ṭāriq (Gibraltar).[3] The ships, so the tradition states, were provided by a certain semi-legendary

[1] Whether he was Arab or Berber is uncertain. Cf. Maqqari (Leyden), vol. i, p. 159; ibn-Khaldūn, vol. iv, p. 117; ibn-'Idhāri, ed. Dozy, vol. ii, p. 6; tr. Fagnan, vol. ii, p. 7; *Akhbār Majmū'ah fi Fatḥ al-Andalus*, ed. Lafuente y Alcántara (Madrid, 1867), p. 6 (text) = p. 20 (tr.).

[2] Mentioned by al-Idrīsi, *Dhikr al-Andalus* (extracts from *Nuzhat al-Mushtāq*), ed. and tr. Don Josef A. Conde (Madrid, 1799), pp. 11, 35, 44.

[3] Idrīsi, p. 36.

Julian,[1] count of Ceuta,[2] where the strait is only thirteen miles wide.

With his forces supplemented, Ṭār'q, at the head of 12,000 men, was met on July 19, 711, by the armies of King Roderick at the mouth of the Barbate River[3] on the shore of the lagoon of the Janda.[4] Roderick had deposed his predecessor, the son of Witiza, and usurped the throne.[5] Though numbering 25,000 men the Visigothic army was utterly routed owing to the treachery of the king's political enemies, headed by Bishop Oppas, a brother of Witiza. What became of Roderick himself remains a mystery. The usual version in both Spanish and Arabic chronicles is that he simply disappeared.

After this decisive victory the march of the Moslems through Spain almost amounted to a promenade. Only towns dominated by Visigothic knighthood offered effective resistance. Ṭāriq, with the bulk of the army, headed by way of Ecija towards Toledo, the capital, sending detachments against neighbouring towns. The strongly fortified Seville in the south was avoided. One column seized Archidona, which struck no blow. Another captured Elvira, which stood close to the spot where Granada now stands and proved an easy prey. A third, consisting of cavalry under Mughīth al-Rūmi (the Roman, Greek), attacked Cordova. After holding out for two months this future capital of the Moslems was delivered to the besiegers through the treachery of a shepherd, we are told, who pointed out a breach in the wall.[6]

[1] Ar. Ulyān, Balādhuri, p. 230 = Hitti, p. 365; Yulyān in *Akhbār*, vol. i, p. 4; ibn-ʻIdhāri, vol. ii, p. 6; Maqqari, vol. i, p. 159; ibn-ʻAbd-al-Ḥakam, ed. Torrey, p. 206; Yūliyān in ibn-al-Athīr, vol. iv, p. 444. According to the reconstruction of Francisco Codera, *Estudios críticos de historia árabe española*, ser. 2 (Saragossa, 1903), p. 47, his real name was Urban or Olban. The story of the violation of his beautiful daughter Florinda by Roderick, which is usually offered in explanation of Julian's co-operation with the Arabs, is purely legendary. In fact the entire story of the conquest has been richly embellished by both Spanish and Arab chroniclers.

[2] Sp., from Ar. Sabtah, originally from L. Septem (seven), its full name being ad Septem Fratres. The city crowned the ancient Abyla, one of the range "Septem Fratres" (seven brothers). Idrīsi, p. 12.

[3] This small river is now called Salado. The Arabs called it Wādi Bakkah (Lakkah), corrupted into Guadiibeca and therefore confused with Guadelete. Cf. Stanley Lane-Poole, with the collaboration of Arthur Gilman, *The Moors in Spain* (New York, 1911), pp. 14, 23.

[4] Referred to in Arabic chronicles simply as al-Buḥayrah (the lake).

[5] Roderick = Ar. Ludhrīq, Lazrīq, Rudhrīq; Witiza = Ghayṭasah, Ghīṭishah, etc. Maqqari, vol. i, pp. 160, 161; ibn-ʻAbd-al-Ḥakam, p. 206; ibn-ʻIdhāri, vol. ii, p. 8; ibn-Khaldūn, vol. iv, p. 117; *Akhbār*, p. 8; Masʻūdi, vol. i, p. 359.

[6] Ibn-ʻIdhāri, vol. ii, pp. 10-11; *Akhbār*, p. 10. Cf. Maqqari, vol. i, pp. 164-5.

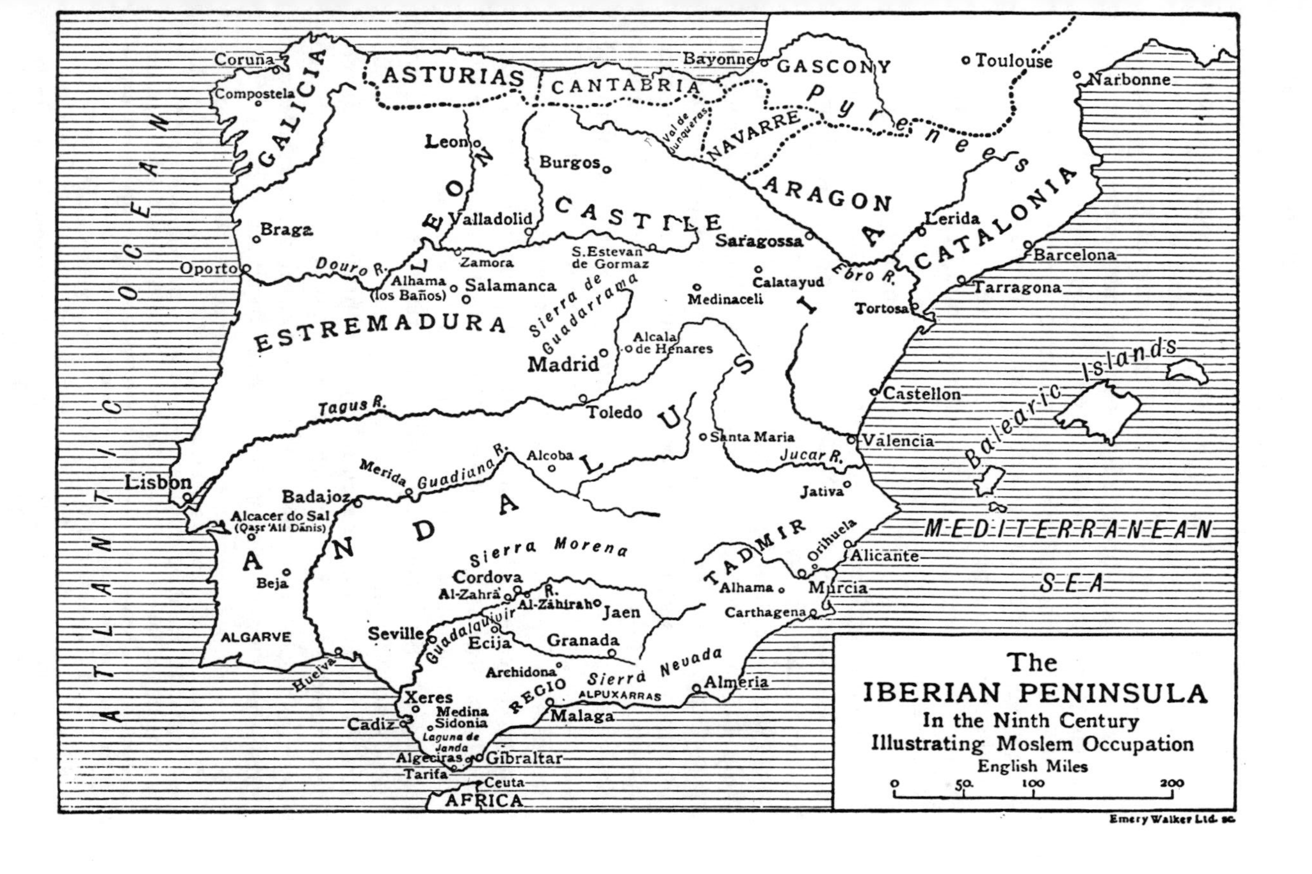

The
IBERIAN PENINSULA
In the Ninth Century
Illustrating Moslem Occupation
English Miles
0 50 100 200
ATLANTIC OCEAN
MEDITERRANEAN SEA
Balearic Islands
GALICIA
ASTURIAS
CANTABRIA
GASCONY
Pyrenees
NAVARRE
Val de Junqueras
ARAGON
CATALONIA
LEON
CASTILE
ESTREMADURA
ANDALUSIA
TADMIR
ALGARVE
REGIO
ALPUXARRAS
AFRICA
Sierra de Guadarrama
Sierra Morena
Sierra Nevada
Douro R.
Tagus R.
Guadiana R.
Guadalquivir R.
Ebro R.
Jucar R.
Coruña
Compostela
Braga
Oporto
Lisbon
Leon
Burgos
Valladolid
Zamora
Alhama (los Baños)
Salamanca
S. Estevan de Gormaz
Saragossa
Medinaceli
Calatayud
Alcala de Henares
Madrid
Toledo
Santa Maria
Alcoba
Merida
Badajoz
Alcacer do Sal (Qasr 'Ali Dānis)
Beja
Bayonne
Toulouse
Narbonne
Lerida
Barcelona
Tarragona
Tortosa
Castellon
Valencia
Jativa
Orihuela
Alicante
Murcia
Alhama
Carthagena
Cordova
Al-Zahrā
Al-Zāhirah
Jaen
Seville
Ecija
Granada
Archidona
Huelva
Xeres
Medina Sidonia
Cadiz
Laguna de Janda
Malaga
Almeria
Algeciras
Gibraltar
Tarifa
Ceuta
Emery Walker Ltd. sc.

Malaga offered no resistance. At Ecija the fiercest battle of the campaign was fought, ending favourably for the invaders. Toledo, the Visigoths' capital, was betrayed by certain Jewish residents. Thus did Ṭāriq, who in the spring of 711 had started as leader of a raid, become by the end of the summer the master of half of Spain. He had destroyed a whole kingdom.

Mūsa crosses the strait

Jealous of the unexpected and phenomenal success of his lieutenant, Mūsa, with 10,000[1] troops, all Arabians and Syrian Arabs, rushed to Spain in June 712. For his objective he chose those towns and strongholds avoided by Ṭāriq, e.g. Medina Sidonia and Carmona. Seville, the largest city and the intellectual centre of Spain and once its Roman capital, held out under siege until the end of June 713. But the most obstinate resistance was met at Mérida. After a year's beleaguerment, however, this city was taken by storm on June 1, 713.[2]

It was in or near Toledo that Mūsa met Ṭāriq. Here, we are told, he whipped his subordinate and put him in chains for refusing to obey orders to halt in the early stage of the campaign.[3] But the conquest went on. Soon Saragossa (Cæsarea Augusta, Cæsaraugusta) in the north was reached and the Moslem troops advanced into the highlands of Aragon, Leon, the Asturias and Galicia. In the autumn of the same year the Caliph al-Walīd in distant Damascus recalled Mūsa, charging him with the same offence for which Mūsa had disciplined his Berber subordinate—acting independently of his superior. As governor of Ifrīqiyah, Mūsa had none but the caliph for his superior

A triumphal procession

Leaving his second son, 'Abd-al-'Azīz, in command of the newly acquired territory, Mūsa slowly made his way overland toward Syria. On his march he was accompanied by his officers, four hundred Visigothic princes, wearing crowns and girdled with gold belts, and followed by an endless retinue of slaves and prisoners of war loaded with enormous treasures of booty.[4] The

[1] Ṭabari, vol. ii, p. 1253. Other sources make the number 18,000.

[2] Ibn-'Idhāri, vol. ii, pp. 15-16; ibn-al-Athīr, vol. iv, p. 447; Maqqari, vol. i, pp. 170-71. Cf. ibn-al-Qūṭīyah, *Ta'rīkh Iftitāḥ al-Andalus* (Madrid, 1868), pp. 9-10; tr. Julián Ribera as *Historia de la conquista de España* (Madrid, 1926), pp. 6-7; tr. O. Houdas as "Histoire de la conquête de l'Andalousie" in *Recueil de textes et de traductions*, etc. (Paris, 1889), vol. i, p. 226.

[3] Ibn-'Abd-al-Ḥakam, p. 210; ibn-'Idhāri, vol. ii, pp. 17-18.

[4] Ibn-'Idhāri, vol. ii, pp. 21-2; ibn-'Abd-al-Ḥakam, pp. 210-11; ibn-al-Qūṭīyah, p. 10; pseudo-ibn-Qutaybah, *Qiṣṣat Fatḥ al-Andalus* (taken from *al-Imāmah w-al-Siyāsah* and issued as supplement to ibn-al-Qūṭīyah), pp. 138, 140 *seq.* See above, p. 235.

triumphal passage of this princely train through northern Africa from west to east forms a favourite theme with Arab historians. Its description brings to mind the picture of the ancient victorious marches of Roman generals. The news of the impressive procession travelled to Damascus faster than the procession itself. On reaching Tiberias Mūsa found orders awaiting him from Sulaymān, brother and heir of the sick al-Walīd, to delay his advent to the capital. The caliph-to-be hoped thereby to have the arrival grace his accession to the throne.[1]

In February 715 Mūsa entered Damascus with his Visigothic princes bedecked in their jewellery and was evidently received with favour by al-Walīd. The official reception, held with great dignity and pomp in the courtyard of the magnificent Umayyad Mosque, is one of the high-water marks in the history of triumphant Islam. For the first time hundreds of Western royalty and thousands of European captives were seen offering homage to the commander of the believers. Mūsa presented the caliph, among other trophies, with the superb table (*mā'idah*) whose workmanship legend assigns to genii in the service of King Solomon. From Jerusalem this unique piece of art, legend asserts, was carried away by the Romans into their capital, whence it was later taken by the Goths. Each Gothic king vied with the preceding one in decorating this table with precious stones. The treasure was kept in the cathedral at Toledo and was captured by Ṭāriq, probably from the bishop who was fleeing with it from the capital. Ṭāriq, so the story goes, had secreted one of its legs when Mūsa seized the table from him in Toledo, and now in the presence of the caliph dramatically produced the missing part as proof of his own exploit.[2]

Mūsa falls from grace

The same fate which befell many another successful Arab general awaited Mūsa. Al-Walīd's successor subjected him to abject humiliation. Besides disciplining him by making him stand until exhausted in the sun, he confiscated his property and deprived him of all authority. The last we hear of the aged con-

[1] Cf. 'Abd-al-Wāḥid al-Marrākushi, *al-Mu'jib fi Talkhīṣ Akhbār al-Maghrib*, 2nd ed., R. Dozy (Leyden, 1881), p. 8; tr. E. Fagnan as *Histoire des Almohades* (Algiers, 1893), p. 10.

[2] Ibn-Khallikān, vol. iii, pp. 26-7; ibn-al-Athīr, vol. iv, pp. 448-9; Maqqari, vol. i, pp. 167, 172; ibn-'Abd-al-Ḥakam, p. 211; *Nabdhah min Akhbār Fatḥ al-Andalus* (ext. *al-Risālah al-Sharīfīyah ila al-Aqṭār al-Andalusīyah* and published as a supplement to ibn-al-Qūṭīyah, Madrid, 1868), pp. 193, 213. See *Arabian Nights*, no. 272.

queror of Africa and Spain is as a beggar in a remote village of al-Ḥijāz, Wādi al-Qura.[1]

The conquest explained

Spain was now a province of the caliphate. The Arabic name it assumed was al-Andalus.[2] Mūsa's immediate successors had only small territories in the north and east of the peninsula to conquer and comparatively few revolts to quell. Within the short space of seven years the conquest of the peninsula, one of the fairest and largest provinces of medieval Europe, was effected. The conquerors were there to stay—for centuries at least.

The reasons for this seemingly unprecedented triumph are not hard to discern even from the above sketchy account. In the first place, the line of national cleavage between the Visigoths (West Goths) who entered Spain in the early part of the fifth century as Teutonic barbarians and the Spanish-Roman population was not yet entirely obliterated. The Goths had to struggle for a long time to displace their predecessors, the Suevi and Vandals, who were likewise invading Germanic hordes. The Visigoths ruled as absolute, often despotic, monarchs. They clung to the Arian form of Christianity until one of them, Recared, in 587 accepted Catholicism, the religion of the natives. As Catholics the people had hated the rule of the heretical Goths. The natives included a considerable class of serfs and slaves, who were naturally dissatisfied with their hard lot. That this enslaved class should have contributed its share to the success of the invasion and co-operated with the invaders is not surprising. Then there was the Jewish element in the population which was estranged from the bulk of the nation through active persecution by the Gothic royalty. Attempts at their forced conversion were consummated by a royal decree issued in 612 enjoining all Jews to be baptized under penalty of banishment and confiscation of property. That explains why several of the conquered towns were left in charge of Jews as the Moslem invaders marched through Spain.

We should, moreover, remember that political disagreements among the royalty and nobility of the Goths themselves, coupled with internal strife, had undermined the state. Toward the end of the sixth century the Gothic nobles had grown into territorial lords. The Moslem invasion coincided with the accession to the

[1] Maqqari, vol. i, p. 180. Cf. ibn-Khallikān, vol. iii, p. 27.

[2] Etymologically this word is connected with the name of the Vandals, who had occupied the land before the Arabs.

throne of a usurper from among the nobility who was readily betrayed by the kinsmen of his deposed predecessor. On the conquest of Toledo, Achila, the deposed son of Witiza, who had naïvely cherished the notion that the Arabs were fighting his battle for him, contented himself with the recovery of his estates in Toledo. Here he continued to live in great pomp. His uncle, Bishop Oppas, was installed over the metropolitan see of the capital. As for Julian, the part he played in the conquest was greatly exaggerated.

Beyond the Pyrenees

The fall of Saragossa removed one of the last barriers between Spain and France. But there remained the Pyrenees. Mūsa never crossed them, though certain Arab chroniclers credit him with the feat and with having even entertained the hope of traversing "the land of the Franks" and joining hands through Constantinople with the caliph in Damascus.[1] Though wild and fantastic, the dream of fighting their way through Europe may have flashed through the brains of the Arab invaders, whose knowledge of the geography of Europe could not have been great. In reality it was Mūsa's third successor, al-Ḥurr ibn-ʻAbd-al-Raḥmān al-Thaqafi,[2] who, in 717 or 718, was the first to cross the range.

Lured by the rich treasures of the convents and churches of France and encouraged by the internal dissension between the chief officers of the Merovingian court and the dukes of Aquitaine (L. Aquitania), al-Ḥurr started the raids which were continued by his successor al-Samḥ ibn-Mālik al-Khawlāni. In 720, under the Caliph ʻUmar II, al-Samḥ seized Septimania, which was a dependency of the defunct Visigothic kingdom, and captured Narbonne (Ar. Arbūnah), which was converted later into a huge citadel with an arsenal and depôts for provisions and arms. But his attempt in the following year at Toulouse, the seat of Duke Eudes of Aquitaine, resulted in failure, thanks to the effective resistance offered. Here al-Samḥ "suffered martyrdom",[3] i.e. fell in battle against non-Moslems. The first great victory by a Germanic prince over Moslems had been won. The subsequent movements of the Arabs beyond the Pyrenees were not successful.

[1] Maqqari, vol. i, p. 175; ibn-Khaldūn, vol. iv, pp. 117-18.
[2] Ibn-ʻIdhāri, vol. ii, pp. 24-5; ibn-al-Athīr, vol. v, p. 373.
[3] Al-Ḍabbi, *Bughyat al-Multamis fi Ta'rīkh Rijāl al-Andalus*, ed. Francisco Codera and Julián Ribera (Madrid, 1884–5), p. 303.

The battle of Tours

The last and greatest expedition northward was led by ʿAbd-al-Raḥmān ibn-ʿAbdullāh al-Ghāfiqi, successor of al-Samḥ as amīr over Spain. ʿAbd-al-Raḥmān advanced through the western Pyrenees, which he crossed in the early spring of 732. Having vanquished Duke Eudes on the banks of the Garonne, he stormed Bordeaux, setting its churches on fire. After burning a basilica outside the walls of Poitiers he pushed northward to the vicinity of Tours. As the resting-place of the body of St. Martin, the apostle of the Gauls, Tours was a sort of religious capital for Gaul. Its votive offerings undoubtedly presented the chief attraction to the invaders.[1]

Here, between Tours and Poitiers, at the junction of the Clain and the Vienne, ʿAbd-al-Raḥmān was met by Charles Martel, mayor of the palace at the Merovingian court, whose aid Eudes had besought. Charles, as the surname Martel (the hammer) which he later won signifies, was valiant and bold. He had subdued many enemies and obliged Eudes, who exercised independent authority in Aquitaine, to acknowledge the nominal sovereignty of the northern Franks. Though not king in name Charles, an illegitimate son of Pepin of Heristal, was king in fact.

For seven days the Arab army under ʿAbd-al-Raḥmān and the Frankish forces under Charles, mostly foot soldiers clad in wolfskins and wearing long matted hair hanging down over their shoulders, stood facing one another anxiously awaiting the moment of joining battle. Light skirmishes dragged on. At last, on an October Saturday of 732, the Arab leader took the initiative in the attack. The Frankish warriors, who in the heat of the fight had formed a hollow square, stood shoulder to shoulder, firm as a wall, inflexible as a block of ice—in the words of a Western historian.[2] The light cavalry of the enemy failed against them. Without giving way they hewed down with their swords all attackers. Among the victims was ʿAbd-al-Raḥmān himself. Darkness at last separated the combatants. At the dawn of day the stillness of the hostile camp caused Charles to suspect a ruse. Spies were sent out to ascertain the facts. Under cover of night the Arabs had quietly deserted their tents and vanished. Charles thus came off victorious.

[1] See Ḍabbi, *Bughyah*, p. 353.
[2] André Duchesne, *Historiae Francorum scriptores*, vol. i (Paris, 1636), p. 786.

Later legends embellished this day of Poitiers or Tours, greatly exaggerating its historic importance. To the Moslems, who, however, have very little to say about it, it has become a *balāṭ al-shuhadā'*,[1] pavement of martyrs. To the Christians it meant the turning-point in the military fortunes of their eternal foe. Gibbon,[2] and after him other historians, would see in Paris and London mosques, where cathedrals now stand, and would hear the Koran instead of the Bible expounded in Oxford and other seats of learning, had the Arabs won the day. To several modern historical writers this battle of Tours is one of the decisive battles in history.[3] In reality it decided nothing. The Arab-Berber wave, already almost a thousand miles from its starting-place in Gibraltar, had reached a natural standstill. It had lost its momentum and spent itself. Internal discord and jealousy between its two component racial elements were beginning to tell on the morale of 'Abd-al-Raḥmān's army. Among the Arabs themselves, as we shall immediately see, there was no unanimity of feeling and purpose. It is true that the Moslems were checked at this point, but their raids continued elsewhere. In 734, for instance, they seized Avignon; nine years later they pillaged Lyons; and not until 759 did they relinquish their hold on Narbonne, the strategic base of their operations. But although this defeat near Tours was not the actual cause of the Arab halt, it does mark the farthest limit of the victorious Moslem arms. One hundred years after the death of the Prophet the domain of his successor in Damascus had become a world-empire extending from China to Gaul.[4]

Civil wars

The strife between the two factions in the Moslem ranks of Spain affords the key to the history of the period between the battle of Tours in 732 and the heroic advent of the Umayyad 'Abd-al-Raḥmān I in 755. It was the same old feud between

[1] *Akhbār*, p. 25; Maqqari, vol. i, p. 146, l. 3. *Balāṭ* is a loan-word through Syriac from Latin or Greek *platea* or *palatium*. The word is common in place-names, especially in Spain (Idrīsi, pp. 32, 59). In this instance the field was referred to as "pavement" because the battle was fought on a paved Roman road. Cf. John 19:13.

[2] *Decline and Fall*, ed. Bury, vol. vi, pp. 15 *seq*. See also Lane-Poole, pp. 29-30.

[3] Edward Creasy, *The Fifteen Decisive Battles of the World*, new ed. (New York, 1918), pp. 159 *seq*.; S. P. Scott, *History of the Moorish Empire in Europe* (Philadelphia, 1904), vol. i, p. 306. Cf. Henry Coppée, *History of the Conquest of Spain by the Arab-Moors* (Boston, 1881), vol. ii, pp. 19 *seq*.

[4] See above, p. 215.

North Arabians, frequently referred to as Muḍarites,[1] and South Arabians or Yamanites. The Yamanites everywhere were inoculated with Shī'ite ideas; the Muḍarites maintained Sunni orthodoxy. At the establishment of the 'Abbāsid dynasty the Yamanites, as 'Alids, naturally sympathized with the new régime; the others remained loyal to the fallen house of banu-Umayyah. The Berbers, who after the Spanish conquest flooded the peninsula from Africa, where many of them had embraced the Khārijite doctrine and espoused its cause against both Umayyads and 'Alids, now constituted a most disturbing factor. They complained that their nationals carried the brunt of the fighting but were nevertheless allotted the arid central plateau, whereas the Arabs appropriated for themselves the most smiling provinces of Andalusia.

Discontent soon led to open revolt. The flame of Berber insurrection which had raged for years (734–42) from Morocco to al-Qayrawān now spread to Spain and threatened the handful of Arab colonists with extermination. In 741 the Caliph Hishām dispatched an army of twenty-seven thousand Syrians to quell the African revolt.[2] The remnant of this army, about one-third of it, crossed the strait under the leadership of Balj ibn-Bishr al-Qushayri. The Syrians turned colonists and, with their ambitions and interests marked by unswerving loyalty to the Umayyad cause, introduced a new problem into an already complicated situation. Balj seized the government and established his men in the capital, Cordova. After that the turbulent Syrians were dispersed. The division of Ḥimṣ was settled in Seville; that of Palestine in Medina Sidonia and Algeciras; that of Damascus in the district of Elvira; and that of Qinnasrīn in the district of Jaen.[3] As an index of the prevailing anarchy in this period suffice it to note that in the short interval between 732 and 755 no less than twenty-three governors succeeded one another in Spain. Under such conditions not much progress could be made into the land of the enemy in the north, though several campaigns

[1] The Muḍar and Rabī'ah, both of North Arab origin, were often included under the collective term Ma'add. See above, p. 280.

[2] *Akhbār*, p. 31. Cf. ibn-al-Qūṭīyah, pp. 14-15; ibn-'Idhāri, vol. i, pp. 41-2, vol. ii, p. 30; Marrākushi, p. 9.

[3] Ibn-al-Qūṭīyah, p. 20; ibn-'Idhāri, vol. ii, p. 33; ibn-Khaldūn, vol. iv, p. 119; ibn-al-Athīr, vol. v, pp. 204-5; ibn-al-Khaṭīb, MS. in R. Dozy, *Recherches sur l'histoire et la littérature de l'Espagne*, 3rd ed. (Paris, 1881), vol. i, app. ii, pp. vii-viii.

were conducted in the course of which certain governors "suffered martyrdom".[1]

The amirate

The government of the peninsula was in the hands of an amīr who ruled almost independently, though nominally under the governor-general of al-Maghrib (i.e. North Africa and Spain) residing in al-Qayrawān. In certain instances the amīr received his appointment from, and held it directly under, the caliph in Damascus. 'Abd-al-'Azīz, son of Mūsa ibn-Nuṣayr and first amīr of al-Andalus, chose Seville (Ishbīliyah) for his seat of government. He married the widow of King Roderick, Egilona, whose name now became umm- (mother of) 'Āṣim. This new Christian wife, according to Arab chroniclers,[2] persuaded her husband to wear a crown, after the usage of Visigothic royalty, and to make the entrance into his audience chamber so low that none could get in without bending in obeisance. She also insisted on having such a low door to her palace chapel that 'Abd-al-'Azīz himself had to bend on entering as if in an act of worship. Rumours centring on these innovations, exaggerated to the point of making of the Moslem amīr a convert to Christianity, reached the Caliph Sulaymān and resulted in the murder of the first governor of Moslem Spain. The tragic event took place near Seville in 716 at the monastery of Santa Rufina, presumably used then as a mosque. The head was dispatched to Damascus, where it was exhibited to 'Abd-al-'Azīz' aged and distressed father.

Three years afterward al-Samḥ ibn-Mālik al-Khawlāni, the fourth in this list of ephemeral amīrs, transferred the seat of government to Cordova[3] (Qurṭubah), destined to become for centuries the brilliant residence of the Western Umayyad dynasty. It was al-Samḥ who rebuilt the bridge in Cordova over the Guadalquivir[4] on the remains of an older Roman structure, made a fresh survey of the land and instituted a new system of taxation. Shortly after al-Samḥ the governorship became a bone of bloody contention between the Muḍarites and Yamanites. The two parties finally hit upon what they considered a brilliant

[1] Ibn-Khaldūn, vol. iv, pp. 118-19; Maqqari, vol. i, pp. 145-6.

[2] *Akhbār*, p. 20; ibn-'Abd-al-Ḥakam, p. 212; ibn-al-Qūṭīyah, p. 11; ibn-al-Athīr, vol. v, p. 14; ibn-'Idhāri, vol. ii, pp. 22-3; Maqqari, vol. i, p. 178. Cf. pseudo-ibn-Quṭaybah, pp. 169 *seq.*

[3] *Nabdhah*, pp. 206-7; ibn-al-Qūṭīyah, pp. 12-13. Cf. ibn-'Idhāri, vol. ii, p. 25; Maqqari, vol. i, p. 190.

[4] From Ar. al-Wādi al-Kabīr, the big valley.

idea: choosing alternately one of their number each year to rule the land.

The first choice of the Muḍarites was Yūsuf ibn-ʿAbd-al-Raḥmān al-Fihri,[1] a descendant of ʿUqbah, the founder of al-Qayrawān. The Caliph Marwān II confirmed (746) the appointment.[2] At the end of the year, however, Yūsuf refused to give turn to the Yamanite candidate and continued to rule for about ten years.[3] Toward the close of 755, as he was in the north busy subduing a revolt, word was received that an Umayyad youth by the name of ʿAbd-al-Raḥmān ibn-Muʿāwiyah had lately landed on the coast south of Granada and was on his way to capture the amīrate. A new and important chapter in the history of Spain was being ushered in.

[1] *Akhbār*, pp. 57 *seq.*; ibn-al-Athīr, vol. v, pp. 286-7.
[2] Cf. pseudo-ibn-Quṭaybah, p. 188.
[3] Ibn-al-Abbār, *al-Ḥullah al-Siyarā'* (*Notices sur quelques manuscrits arabes*), ed. Dozy (Leyden, 1847–51), p. 54; ibn-al-Athīr, vol. v, p. 376.

CHAPTER XXXV

THE UMAYYAD AMĪRATE IN SPAIN

A dramatic escape

WHEN in 750 the 'Abbāsids signalized their accession by a general massacre of the members of the house of Umayyah,[1] one of the very few who escaped was 'Abd-al-Raḥmān ibn-Mu'āwiyah,[2] a grandson of Hishām, the tenth caliph of Damascus. The story of the narrow escape of this twenty-year-old youth and of his five years' wandering in disguise through Palestine, Egypt and North Africa, where more than once he barely escaped the vigilant eyes of 'Abbāsid spies, forms one of the most dramatic episodes in Arabic annals. The flight began from a Bedouin camp on the left bank of the Euphrates where 'Abd-al-Raḥmān had sought refuge. One day the black standards of the 'Abbāsids suddenly appeared close by the camp. With his thirteen-year-old brother, 'Abd-al-Raḥmān dashed into the river. The younger, evidently a poor swimmer, believed the pursuers' promise of amnesty and returned from midstream, only to be slain; the elder kept on and gained the opposite bank.[3]

As he trudged on his way southward 'Abd-al-Raḥmān was joined in Palestine by his faithful and able freedman Badr. In North Africa he barely escaped assassination at the hands of its governor, a relative of Yūsuf al-Fihri. Wandering from tribe to tribe and from town to town, friendless and penniless, the proscribed fugitive finally reached Ceuta (755). His maternal uncles were Berbers from that neighbourhood and offered him refuge. Thence he sent Badr across the strait to negotiate with the Syrian divisions from Damascus and Qinnasrīn which were settled in Elvira and Jaen. Many of the leaders, who were former protégés of the Umayyad house, welcomed the opportunity to rally under the leadership of one who bore a name with which all Syrians conjured. The Syrians won the Yamanites over to their cause,

[1] See above, pp. 285-6, 450

[2] Corrupted by the old Christian chroniclers into Benemaugius.

[3] *Akhbār*, pp. 52-4; ibn-al-Athīr, vol. v, p. 377.

not so much because the latter loved 'Abd-al-Raḥmān as because they hated their titular governor, Yūsuf. A ship was sent to transport the new leader. Tall and lean, with sharp, aquiline features and thin red hair,[1] this scion of the banu-Umayyah, imbued with the spirit of adventure and trained in the best tradition of the house, soon became master of the complicated situation. In vain did the weak-kneed Yūsuf try to satisfy the new pretender with rich gifts and promises, including his daughter's hand. One southern city after another opened its gates without resistance. Archidona,[2] where the Jordan division had established itself, the province of Sidona, in which the Palestine division had settled, and Seville, where dwelt the Arabs of Ḥimṣ, welcomed the prince with open arms.[3]

Cordova captured

As 'Abd-al-Raḥmān with his partisans pushed on toward Cordova, Yūsuf advanced in the direction of Seville. Before the impending battle it was noticed that the prince had no military standard of his own, whereupon the Yamanite chieftain of Seville, abu-al-Ṣabbāḥ al-Yaḥṣubi, improvised a banner by fastening a green turban round the head of a spear.[4] Thus originated, we are told, the standard of the Umayyads in Spain.

The morning of May 14, 756, found the two opposing armies engaged in battle on the banks of the Guadalquivir. Though most of the men on both sides were on horses, which were still scarce in Andalusia, 'Abd-al-Raḥmān, realizing that some of his followers were afraid he might desert, insisted on changing his mount for an old mule belonging to abu-al-Ṣabbāḥ.[5] The issue of the combat was not long in doubt. Yūsuf with his chief general sought safety in flight. Cordova was captured and a general amnesty was declared. 'Abd-al-Raḥmān had no little difficulty in stopping the pillage of the capital and in putting the harem of the defeated governor under his magnanimous protection.

Moslem Spain consolidated and pacified

The mastery of Cordova, however, did not necessarily mean the mastery of Moslem Spain. The fugitive governor continued to foment trouble in the north until he was finally slain near

[1] Ibn-'Idhāri, vol. ii, p. 50; ibn-al-Athīr, vol. vi, p. 76.

[2] The capital of the mountainous province of Regio (Ar. Rayyah); Yāqūt, vol. i, pp. 195, 207.

[3] Ibn-al-Athīr, vol. v, p. 378; ibn-'Idhāri, vol. ii, p. 48; Maqqari, vol. i, p. 212.

[4] *Akhbār*, p. 84. Cf. ibn-al-Qūṭīyah, p. 26.

[5] *Akhbār*, pp. 88-9; ibn-al-Athīr, vol. v, p. 378.

Toledo.[1] This city was not reduced till 764. Yamanite and Shīʿite revolts, fostered by ʿAbbāsid agents, were successive. Berber insurrections took ten years to suppress. The Berbers never forgave their Arab superiors for appropriating to themselves the lion's share of the conquered land. Former staunch supporters of the new amīr now turned enemies and had to be summarily dealt with. The Sevillan sheikh whose banner and mule had led ʿAbd-al-Raḥmān to victory lost his head in an uprising. Badr, ʿAbd-al-Raḥmān's right-hand man, was banished to a frontier town after losing all his property

Enemies within had their confederates without. In 761 the ʿAbbāsid Caliph al-Manṣūr had the temerity to appoint one al-ʿAlā' ibn-Mughīth as governor over Spain. Two years later al-ʿAlā' was decapitated and his head, preserved in salt and camphor and wrapped in a black flag and the diploma of appointment, was forwarded to al-Manṣūr while on a pilgrimage to Makkah.[2] Al-Manṣūr, who on another occasion called ʿAbd-al-Raḥmān "the falcon of Quraysh",[3] now exclaimed, "Thanks be to Allah for having placed the sea between us and such a foe!"[4] ʿAbd-al-Raḥmān is said even to have equipped a fleet to wrest Syria from ʿAbbāsid hands but was forced by domestic problems to stay at home.

A match to Charlemagne

In 777 a formidable confederacy of Arab chiefs in the north-east headed by the governor of Barcelona and a blue-eyed son-in-law of Yūsuf al-Fihri invited Charlemagne, who might have been considered an ally of the ʿAbbāsid caliph[5] and therefore a natural enemy of ʿAbd-al-Raḥmān, to an alliance against the new amīr of Spain. Charlemagne advanced (778) through the north-eastern Spanish marches as far as Saragossa,[6] but had to withdraw when that city closed its gates in his face and domestic enemies threatened his authority at home. On its "dolorous route" of retreat through the defiles of the Pyrenees, the Frankish army was attacked in its rear by Basques and other mountaineers from whom it suffered disastrous loss in men and baggage.[7] Among the leaders who fell was Roland, whose heroic

[1] Ibn-al-Abbār, *Ḥullah*, p. 55.
[2] Ibn-al-Qūṭīyah, p. 33.
[3] Ibn-ʿIdhāri, vol. ii, p. 61; Maqqari, vol. i, p. 213.
[4] Ibn-al-Qūṭīyah, pp. 33-4; Maqqari, vol. i, p. 215.
[5] É. Lévi-Provençal, *Histoire de l'Espagne musulmane*, vol. i (Paris, 1950), p. 121.
[6] *Akhbār*, p. 113.
[7] Éginhard, *Charlemagne*, ed. and tr. Halphen, pp. 29-31; ibn-Khaldūn, vol. iv, pp. 123-4; ibn-al-Athīr, vol. vi, pp. 7-8.

defence has been immortalized in the *Chanson de Roland*, not only a gem of early French literature but one of the most striking epics of medieval times. In effect, 'Abd-al-Raḥmān proved himself the equal of the mightiest sovereign in the West as he had proved himself the equal of the greatest ruler in the East.[1]

An independent amirate

In the process of subduing his multitudinous adversaries 'Abd-al-Raḥmān developed a well-disciplined, highly trained army of 40,000 or more mercenary Berbers, imported from Africa, on whose loyalty he could now depend for the maintenance of his throne. The favour of such a body he knew how to keep by generous pay. In 757 he discontinued the *khuṭbah* hitherto delivered in the name of the 'Abbāsid caliph, but did not assume the caliphal title himself. He and his successors down to 'Abd-al-Raḥmān III contented themselves with the title of amīr, though ruling independently. Under 'Abd-al-Raḥmān I Spain had thus been the first province to shake off the authority of the recognized caliph in Islam.

With his realm consolidated and temporarily pacified, 'Abd-al-Raḥmān turned to the arts of peace, in which he showed himself as great as in the art of war. He beautified the cities of his domain, built an aqueduct for the supply of pure water to the capital, initiated the construction of a wall round it and erected for himself the Munyat[2] al-Ruṣāfah outside Cordova in imitation of the palace built by his ancestor Hishām in north-eastern Syria. To his villa he brought water and introduced exotic plants, such as peaches and pomegranates. To a lonely palm tree in his garden, said to be the first imported from Syria, he addressed some tender verses of his own composition.[3]

Two years before his death in 788 'Abd-al-Raḥmān rebuilt the great Mosque of Cordova[4] as a rival to the two sanctuaries of Islam in Jerusalem and Makkah. Completed and enlarged by his successors, the Mosque of Cordova soon became the Ka'bah of Western Islam. With its forest of stately columns and its spacious outer court this monumental structure, transformed into

[1] Consult Coppée, vol. ii, pp. 167-8.

[2] A loan-word from Gr. (also Coptic) meaning "garden".

[3] Ibn-al-Abbār, *Ḥullah*, p. 34; ibn-al-Athīr, vol. vi, p. 77; Maqqari, vol. ii, p. 37; Nicholson, *Literary History*, p. 418. The first date-palms were introduced by the Phoenicians. The Arabs brought in new varieties which they propagated from offshoots, whereas the earlier culture was based entirely on growing dates from seed.

[4] Ibn-'Idhāri, vol. ii, p. 60, cf. p. 245; Maqqari, vol. i, p. 212.

a Christian cathedral at the reconquest by Ferdinand III in 1236, has survived to the present day under the popular name "La Mezquita" (the mosque). Besides the great mosque the capital could already boast a bridge, over the Guadalquivir, later enlarged to seventeen arches. Nor were the interests of the founder of the Umayyad régime limited to the material welfare of his people. In various ways he diligently strove to fashion into a national mould Arabians, Syrians, Berbers, Numidians, Hispano-Arabs and Goths—a rather hopeless task; and in more than one sense did he initiate that intellectual movement which made Islamic Spain from the ninth to the eleventh centuries one of the two centres of world culture.

The dynasty established by ʿAbd-al-Raḥmān I, styled al-Dākhil (the newcomer) by Arab chroniclers, was to endure for two and three-quarter centuries (756–1031). It reached its height under the eighth amīr, ʿAbd-al-Raḥmān III (912–61), the greatest in the long line and the first to assume the title of caliph (929). In fact the reign of the Caliph ʿAbd-al-Raḥmān marks the zenith of the Arab epoch in the peninsula. Throughout the Umayyad period Cordova continued to be the capital and enjoyed a period of incomparable splendour as the Western rival of Baghdād.

The Umayyad caliphate began to wane after the death of the talented regent al-Ḥājib al-Manṣūr (1002), the "Bismarck of the tenth century" and possibly the greatest statesman and general of Arab Spain, and entirely disappeared in 1031. On its ruins arose sundry petty kingdoms and principalities, many of which were always at daggers drawn with one another and all of which finally succumbed to the growing power of the native Christians, particularly those of the north. With the fall of Granada in 1492 the last vestige of Moslem rule vanished for ever from the peninsula.

Treatment of Christians

The main task of ʿAbd-al-Raḥmān al-Dākhil's successors continued to be the pacification of the land and the solution of the knotty problems arising from the dual character of the population as Christians and Moslems and from the jealousies between old Arab Moslems and newly converted Spanish Moslems. From the beginning the policy followed by the Arab conquerors in the treatment of their subjects in Spain was not fundamentally different from that pursued in other conquered lands.[1] Poll tax (*jizyah*), levied on Christians and Jews only, varied between twelve, twenty-four and forty-eight dirhams a year, according to the economic status of the payer. Women and children, the aged and destitute, as well as monks and people afflicted with chronic diseases, were of course exempt. Land tax (*kharāj*), averaging about twenty per cent. of the yield, was also collected from these dhimmis, but, unlike the poll tax, remained unaffected by the conversion of the taxpayer. Territories acquired by the sword, together with the landed property of the churches and of the lords who fled Spain at the time of the conquest, were confiscated and parcelled out among the conquerors as individuals; but the serfs were left on those lands as cultivators and were required to hand four-fifths of the produce to the new Moslem lords. Out of this confiscated territory, however, one-fifth was appropriated by the state, which exacted from its serfs only one-third of the crops. Certain state lands were later divided into fiefs among Syrians and Arabs imported to quell revolts.

"No bondage in Islam" did not necessarily apply to a slave on becoming Moslem. Christian communities were left unmolested in the exercise of their faith and under their own ecclesiastical laws and native judges, whose jurisdiction, of course, did not include cases involving Moslems and offences against the religion of Islam. In general, therefore, the Moslem occupation of Spain entailed no new unbearable hardships to the natives. "In some respects", declares Dozy,[2] "the Arab conquest was even a benefit to Spain." It broke the power of the privileged group, including the nobility and clergy, ameliorated the condition of the servile class and gave the Christian landowner such rights as the alienation of his property which he was denied under the Visigoths.

Renegades in arms

Nevertheless, Christians flocked to Islam. In mountain and rural regions they maintained the old national pattern and traditional culture, but in the cities they did not. As Neo-Moslems they constituted a social class by themselves, called by the Arabs *Muwalladūn* (sing. *Muwallad*, adopted, affiliated) and by the Spaniards *Muladíes*. In course of time these neophytes became the most discontented body in the population. Their ranks were

[1] See above, pp. 170-71.

[2] *Histoire des Musulmans d'Espagne*, ed. É. Lévi-Provençal (Leyden, 1932), vol. i, p. 278; tr. Francis G. Stokes, *Spanish Islam* (London, 1913), p. 236.

recruited mainly from serfs and freedmen and their descendants who cultivated the soil or toiled as day labourers. Some of them, though professing Islam, were "secret Christians";[1] but they all knew well the clear and inexorable law of apostasy from Islam, which prescribed death. The Moslem Arabs treated all *Muwallads* as inferior, though some of them were of noble descent. By the end of the first century after the conquest these *Muwallads* had become the majority of the population in several cities, where they were the first to take up arms against the established order.

[1] Eulogius, "Memoriale sanctorum", Bk. II, in A. Schottus, *Hispaniæ illustratæ*, vol. iv (Frankfort, 1608), p. 293

CHAPTER XXXVI

CIVIL DISTURBANCES

IN Cordova, the southern suburb, referred to as *al-rabaḍ*,[1] was overwhelmingly populated with such Neo-Moslems, renegades from the Christian point of view. Sections of them were under the influence of students and teachers of theology and law (*faqīhs*), about four thousand of whom flourished in the capital. As long as Hishām I (788–96), the pious and scholarly son[2] and successor of 'Abd-al-Raḥmān, ruled there was no immediate cause for trouble. But the reign of Hishām's successor, al-Ḥakam I (796–822), who was gay and addicted to the chase and wine, changed the situation. Objection was made not only to the levity of al-Ḥakam but also to his bodyguard, composed mainly of negroes and other foreign mercenaries who knew no Arabic.[3] The trouble began in 805 when one day as the amīr was passing in the streets the mob attacked him with stones while the theologians applauded. Seventy-two of the ringleaders who were later found implicated in a conspiracy to depose al-Ḥakam were apprehended and crucified. Uprisings in the renegade quarter followed one another, culminating in a serious outbreak in 814[4] under the leadership of a Berber *faqīh*. Al-Ḥakam was shut up in his palace by the furious mob, but his cavalry finally succeeded in cutting down the insurgents. The suburb was dealt with ruthlessly. Its leaders, to the number of three hundred, were nailed to crosses, head downwards. The whole population was ordered to evacuate Spain in three days and the quarter was levelled to the ground. It was forbidden for anyone to build

[1] Ibn-'Idhāri, vol. ii, pp. 73, 77; ibn-al-Athīr, vol. vi, pp. 209 *seq.*; *'Iqd*, vol. ii, p. 365; ibn-Khaldūn, vol. iv, p. 126.

[2] Ibn-al-Athīr, vol. vi, pp. 101-2; ibn-al-Qūṭīyah, p. 42.

[3] Hence their sobriquet *al-khurs*, the dumb ones; ibn-Khaldūn, vol. iv, p. 127; Maqqari, vol. i, p. 220.

[4] A.H. 202 (817–18) in ibn-'Idhāri, vol. ii, p. 77. Cf. ibn-al-Qūṭīyah, pp 51-2.

there again.[1] Eight thousand families found asylum in Morocco, particularly in Fās (Fez), which Idrīs II, a descendant of 'Ali, was then building as his new capital.[2] Others, comprising fifteen thousand individuals,[3] landed at Alexandria. Here the refugees succeeded in making themselves masters of the town until 827, when they were forced to flee by a general of the Caliph al-Ma'mūn. For a new abode the exiles chose Crete, a part of which still belonged to the Byzantine empire. They reduced the whole island and their leader founded a dynasty which lasted until Crete was reconquered by the Greeks in 961.[4]

The "slaughter of the ditch"

Some Spanish Moslems, it should be noted, were invaluable allies to the Arabs and allowed themselves to be used against their former co-religionists. Such was the case of 'Amrūs ibn-Yūsuf, who in 807 was appointed by al-Ḥakam as governor of Toledo, the proud "royal city"[5] which in the eyes of the conquered natives was politically and ecclesiastically the most important town. Toledo had been restless under Moslem yoke; its renegades and Christians were in a chronic state of revolt. In honour of a visit from the fourteen-year-old crown prince 'Abd-al-Raḥmān, son of al-Ḥakam, 'Amrūs at the suggestion of al-Ḥakam arranged for a banquet to which he invited hundreds of notable Toledans. In the courtyard of his newly erected castle stretched a long ditch, whence had come the clay used in constructing that stronghold. Beside the ditch 'Amrūs now planted an executioner. As each guest entered the courtyard the sword fell upon his neck. The corpses were dumped into the ditch. For several years after this "slaughter of the ditch",[6] turbulent Toledo remained tranquil.[7] But other cities such as

[1] In memory of this sensational episode al-Ḥakam won the sobriquet al-Rabaḍ (the suburban). Ibn-al-Abbār, *Ḥullah*, p. 38.

[2] The quarter where they settled is still called *'idwat al-Andalus*, the bank of the Andalusians.

[3] Ibn-al-Qūṭīyah, p. 51.

[4] Ibn-al-Abbār, *Ḥullah*, pp. 39-40; Maqqari, vol. i, p. 219; Marrākushi, pp. 13-14; Kindi, *Wulāh*, pp. 161-5, 184; Ya'qūbi, vol. ii, p. 561; Yāqūt, vol. i, p. 337. See above, p. 202.

[5] *Urbs regia* in Isidorus Pacensis, "Del chronicon", in *España sagrada: Ṭheatro geographico-historico de la iglesia de España*, ed. Fr. Henrique Florez, vol. viii (Madrid, 1753), p. 297; *madīnat al-mulūk* (the city of kings) in Qazwīni, *Āthār*, p. 366.

[6] *Waq'at al-ḥufrah*, ibn-al-Athīr, vol. vi, p. 135; ibn-Khaldūn, vol. iv, p. 126.

[7] Ibn-al-Qūṭīyah, pp. 45-9; ibn-'Idhāri, vol. ii, pp. 71-2.

Mérida remained in a state of revolt until the reign of ʿAbd-al-Raḥmān II,[1] an energetic artisan of Umayyad Spanish unity and a zealous patron of music and astronomy.

As an amīr ʿAbd-al-Raḥmān II (822–52), later surnamed al-Awsaṭ,[2] was influenced by four personages: a woman, a eunuch, a theologian and a singer. The woman was his favourite wife, Sulṭānah (queen) Ṭarūb, a consummate intriguer. The eunuch was his gifted slave Naṣr, the royal chamberlain, son of a Spaniard and a favourite with the queen.[3] The theologian was none other than the Berber ringleader of the *faqīh*-renegade mutiny of Cordova, Yaḥya ibn-Yaḥya (†849) of the Maṣmūdah tribe, a student of the Imām Mālik ibn-Anas in Baghdād and the man responsible for the introduction of the Māliki rite into al-Andalus.[4] So firmly established did this rite become that the people there were wont to declare: "We know no other works but the Book of Allah and the *Muwaṭṭa*' of Mālik".[5] The singer was a Persian tenor, Ziryāb, who hailed from Baghdād.

Ziryāb[6] was one of those musicians who had graced the court of Hārūn al-Rashīd and his sons, where he had distinguished himself not only as an artist but also as a man of science

[1] Umayyad amīrs of Cordova:

1. ʿAbd-al-Raḥmān I (756–88)
2. Hishām I (788–96)
3. Al-Ḥakam I (796–822)
4. ʿAbd-al-Raḥmān II (822–52)
5. Muḥammad I (852–86)
   - 6. Al-Mundhir (886–8)
   - 7. ʿAbdullāh (888–912)
     - Muḥammad
       - 8. ʿAbd-al-Raḥmān III (912–29, caliph 929–61)

[2] I.e. the middler, for coming between ʿAbd al Raḥmān I and ʿAbd-al-Raḥmān III. Ibn-al-Abbār, *Ḥullah*, p. 61; ibn-Khaldūn, vol. iv, p. 127.

[3] Maqqari, vol. i, pp. 224-5; below, p. 516.

[4] Ibn-Khallikān, vol. iii, p. 173. Cf. ibn-al-Qūṭīyah, p. 34. Mālik, according to ibn-Khallikān, dubbed Yaḥya "the wise man [*ʿāqil*] of al-Andalus", because he remained in his seat listening to the imām's lecture while an elephant was passing along the street and all the other students rushed out to see it.

[5] Maqdisi, p. 236.

[6] Pers. *zar*, "gold" + *āb*, "water"; nickname of abu-al-Ḥasan ʿAli ibn-Nāfiʿ. *ʿIqd*, vol. iii, p. 241, calls Ziryāb a black slave.

and letters. Thereby he aroused the jealousy of his equally renowned teacher, Isḥāq al-Mawṣili, and fled first to north-western Africa. Anxious to make of Cordova a second Baghdād, ʿAbd-al-Raḥmān, who maintained an opulent court and imitated the lavish prodigalities of Hārūn, rode out (822) of his capital in person to welcome the young minstrel.[1] Ziryāb lived with his new patron, from whom he received an emolument of 3000 dinars annually and real estate in Cordova worth 40,000 dinars, on terms of closest intimacy. He soon eclipsed all other musicians in the land. Besides being credited with knowing the words and tunes of 10,000 songs, which like other musicians he believed the jinn had taught him during the night, Ziryāb shone as a poet and as a student of astronomy and geography.[2] What is more important, he proved himself so polished, witty and entertaining that he soon became the most popular figure among the smart set of the time, even an arbiter of fashion. Hitherto hair had been worn long and parted on the forehead, now it was trimmed low on the brow; water had been drunk out of metal vessels, now out of glasses; certain dishes, including asparagus, had been unpopular, now those same dishes became favourites—all because of Ziryāb's example.[3]

Race for martyrdom

Toward the close of ʿAbd-al-Raḥmān's reign the lure of the language, literature, religion and other institutions of the conquerors—including the harem system—had become so strong that a large number of urban Christians had become Arabicized though not actually Islamized. Dazzled by the glamour of Arab civilization and conscious of their own inferiority in art, poetry, philosophy and science, native Christians soon began to ape the Arab way of living. These imitators now became so numerous as to constitute a social class by themselves and acquired the epithet Mozarabs.[4] Spain, be it remembered, was one of the last countries of Europe to be Christianized; some of its country districts were still pagan at the time of the Moslem conquest and its Visigothic Arianism agreed in its Christology with Moslem doctrine. A contemporary Christian writer of Cordova deplores the fact that the Christian laymen shun the works of the Latin Fathers and are "intoxicated with Arab

[1] Cf. ibn-Khaldūn, *Muqaddamah*, p. 357, quoted by Maqqari, vol. i, p. 222.
[2] Maqqari, vol. ii, p. 87; ibn-al-Qūṭīyah, p. 68.
[3] Maqqari, vol. ii, pp. 87–8.
[4] From Ar. *mustaʿrib*, he who adopts the Arabic language and customs.

eloquence".[1] As early as 724 or thereabout John, bishop of Seville, is said to have made an Arabic recension of the Bible for the convenience of Arabicized Christians and the Moors.[2]

As a reaction against this tendency toward Arabicization, a curious movement now started among the Christian zealots of Cordova which resulted in the voluntary martyrdom of several men and women. The leading spirit was an ascetic priest, Eulogius, supported by his wealthy friend, later his biographer, Alvaro.[3] Nothing could have crystallized the sentiment of the movement better than the execution on the feast of Ramaḍān (850) of another Cordovan priest, Perfectus by name, for having reviled Muḥammad and cursed Islam.[4] Headed by the bishop of Cordova the populace lost no time in declaring Perfectus a saint and in attributing miracles to him; for did he not before his decapitation correctly prophesy the immediate death of Naṣr, the eunuch chamberlain in charge of execution? Naṣr, it seems, had entered into a conspiracy with Ṭarūb to poison her royal husband; Ṭarūb's motive was to secure for her own son 'Abdullāh the succession to the throne to the prejudice of Muḥammad (the eldest of 'Abd-al-Raḥmān's forty-five sons), who was born of another wife. 'Abd-al-Raḥmān got wind of the scheme, and when Naṣr brought a phial claiming that it held a wonderful remedy the monarch ordered him to try it first on himself.[5]

Not long after the Perfectus episode a monk named Isaac appeared before the qāḍi on the pretext of wishing to be converted to Islam and began to heap curses on Muḥammad. Like Perfectus he was beheaded and soon became a saint.[6] Now the race began. Clergy and laity went out of their way to blaspheme Islam with the simple intention of receiving the inescapable penalty that they well knew went with such an offence. Eleven thus "suffered martyrdom" in less than two months.

Flora and Eulogius

Instigated by 'Abd-al-Raḥmān, the bishops hesitatingly held a council which, against the protests of Eulogius, forbade Chris-

[1] Alvaro, "Indiculus luminosus", in *España sagrada*, vol. xi, p. 274.

[2] *Primera crónica general, estoria de España que mandó componer Alfonso el Sabio*, ed. Ramón Menéndez Pidal (Madrid, 1906), vol. i, p. 326.

[3] "Vita vel passio Beatissimi Martyris Eulogij", in *España sagrada*, vol. x, pp. 543-63; "Vida y martyrio de S. Eulogio", in *España sagrada*, vol. x. pp. 411 *seq.*

[4] Alvaro, "Indiculus", in *España sagrada*, vol. xi, pp. 225-6.

[5] Ibn-al-Qūṭīyah, pp. 76-7; ibn-Khaldūn, vol. iv, p. 130.

[6] Alvaro, "Indiculus", in *España sagrada*, vol. xi, pp. 237-8.

tians henceforth to aspire to this holy death. But it was all to no avail. At last came the turn of a beautiful young follower of Eulogius, Flora, daughter of a Christian mother and Moslem father. Together with a youthful nun, Mary, who was a sister of one of the previously decapitated monks, Flora had succumbed to the temptation of blaspheming the Prophet and was merely committed to jail by a compassionate qāḍi. Here Eulogius, who had also been cast in jail and had cherished a pure and spotless love for Flora, employed all the persuasive rhetoric at his command to encourage the girl he loved and her companion, as the two wavered in their sacrificial ardour, to go to the scaffold. The virgin would-be martyrs did not recant; they suffered the supreme penalty on November 24, 851.[1] This hysterical desire for self-immolation did not subside until Eulogius himself in 859, then bishop of Cordova, was executed by Muḥammad I (852–86), who had inaugurated a policy of severe repression. The total included some forty-four martyrs.

Provinces in revolt

Other disturbances, not so fantastic though more serious in character, were in store. In the first place, neither Muḥammad nor his two sons and successors, al-Mundhir (886–8) and ʿAbdullāh (888–912), represent the best tradition of tolerance and energy associated with the house of Umayyah. Then there were the usual difficulties attendant on the accession to the throne, which according to Moslem dynastic practice went to the eldest or the ablest in the reigning family. After a rule of less than two years al-Mundhir was poisoned at the instigation of his successor by a lancet used by the surgeon in bleeding him.[2] In the meantime *Muwallad* and Mozarab revolutions were continuing throughout the domain and several states were breaking loose and asserting their independence under Berber or Spanish Moslem rule. Such separatist movements, sponsored by Neo-Moslems who posed as nationalist champions in provinces which in theory were subject to Cordova, continued to engage the attention of the Umayyad amīrs till the beginning of the tenth century.

In the south the mountainous state of Regio,[3] with its capital

[1] *España sagrada*, vol. x, pp. 417-18; Alvaro, "Vita Eulogij", in *ibid.* pp. 547 *seq.*

[2] Ibn-ʿIdhāri, vol. ii, pp. 160-61, 122, vol. i, introduction by Dozy, pp. 44-6. Cf. ibn-al-Qūṭīyah, p. 102; ibn-Khaldūn, vol. iv, p. 132; *Akhbār*, p. 150.

[3] Ar. Rayyah, which ibn-Khaldūn (vol. iv, p. 132, cf. p. 134), among others, makes a town and confuses with Malaga. Malaga was the capital of Regio under the Visigoths and after the reign of ʿAbd-al-Raḥmān III. See Idrīsi, p. 28.

at Archidona, entered in 873 into treaty relations with Muḥammad, who practically recognized its independence subject to a yearly tribute. The natives were mostly Islamized Spaniards. In the northern marches independent Aragon under the banu-Qasi,[1] an old Visigothic family which had embraced Islam, incorporated within itself in the middle of the ninth century Saragossa, Tudela and other important frontier towns.[2] The banu-Qasi were in league with their neighbours to the west, the kings of Leon. Throughout the land around Toledo, a city which was more often in rebellion than in peace, the Berber banu-dhu-al-Nūn, at the head of bands of brigands, carried fire and sword. In Seville, which as the chief centre of Roman culture under the Visigoths had a population mostly descended from Romans and Goths, the banu-Ḥajjāj became all-powerful.[3] These rulers of Seville and its district were descended in the female line from Sarah, granddaughter of Witiza and wife of an Arab. The historian ibn-al-Qūṭīyah (son of the Gothic woman) was also descended from Sarah.[4] In the Galician south-west a daring renegade of Mérida and Badajoz, ʿAbd-al-Raḥmān ibn-Marwān al-Jillīqi[5] by name, founded an independent principality whence, with the aid of Alfonso III, king of Leon and natural ally of all rebels against the Arab government, he spread terror far and wide. At the south-western corner of the peninsula, which is the modern Algarve[6] of Portugal, another renegade established himself as master towards the close of Muḥammad's reign. In the south-east Murcia (Ar. Mursiyah), under another renegade prince, shook off Arab suzerainty. But the most dangerous and implacable of all rebels was one ʿUmar ibn-Ḥafṣūn.

Ibn-Ḥafṣūn

ʿUmar was a Moslem descendant of a Visigothic count. Starting his colourful career about 880 as an organizer of a band of brigands with headquarters in an ancient castle on Mount

[1] Benikazzi in Sebastian, "Chronicon", in *España sagrada*, vol. xiii, p. 487.

[2] Ibn-al-Qūṭīyah, pp. 85, 113-14. Qasi is mistaken for "Mūsa" in ibn-Khaldūn, vol. iv, p. 134, where his descendants are termed "Lub", Lope. Cf. ibn-ʿIdhāri, vol. ii, pp. 175-6.

[3] Ibn-ʿIdhāri, vol. ii, pp. 128 *seq.*; ibn-Khaldūn, vol. iv, p. 136.

[4] Ibn-al-Qūṭīyah, pp. 4-6.

[5] I.e. the Galician. See ibn-ʿIdhāri, vol. ii, pp. 102, 104; ibn-al-Qūṭīyah, pp. 89-90; ibn-al-Athīr, vol. vii, pp. 127-8; Ḍabbi, p. 359; ibn-Khaldūn, vol. iv, p. 131; Yāqūt, *Buldān*, vol. ii, p. 110.

[6] From Ar. *al-gharb*, the west.

Bobastro,[1] 'Umar, after serving temporarily in the royal army at Cordova, rose with the support of the mountaineers of Elvira (Ilbīrah) to a position of leadership in the Spanish south against Moslem rule. His rebellion engaged the attention of three amīrs, Muḥammad, al-Mundhir and 'Abdullāh. To the southern Christians and malcontents 'Umar became the champion of a long-suppressed nationality. To the Arabs, however, he was "the accursed", "the rogue".[2] After many vicissitudes of fortune he succeeded in isolating Cordova and opened negotiations with the 'Abbāsids[3] and the Aghlabid ruler of Africa with a view to receiving an appointment for himself as governor of Spain. Failing in this ambitious plan, he professed about the year 899 the religion of his forbears, which he had long concealed in his heart,[4] adopting Samuel as a baptismal name. Again and again did Samuel shake the Umayyad throne to its very foundation. The authority of the successors of 'Abd-al-Raḥmān I stood jeopardized, sadly in need of a restorer.

[1] Ar. Bubashtar; ibn-al-Qūṭīyah, p. 90; *Akhbār*, p. 150. Cf. ibn-'Idhāri, vol. ii, pp. 108, 120, 204; ibn-al-Athīr, vol. vii, p. 295.
[2] Ibn-'Idhāri, vol. ii, pp. 117, 120, 123. Cf. *'Iqd*, vol. ii, p. 367.
[3] Ibn-Khaldūn, vol. iv, p. 135.
[4] Ibn-'Idhāri, vol. ii, p. 143.

CHAPTER XXXVII

THE UMAYYAD CALIPHATE OF CORDOVA

Caliph 'Abd-al-Raḥmān al-Nāṣir

WHEN 'Abd-al-Raḥmān III succeeded his grandfather, 'Abdullāh, in 912, he was barely twenty-three years of age. 'Abdullāh had instigated one of his own sons to kill the other, 'Abd-al-Raḥmān's father, Muḥammad, on a mere suspicion of disloyalty.[1] Later he connived at the murder of his other son, the fratricide, leaving himself childless. At the accession of 'Abd-al-Raḥmān the vast Moslem state organized by his first namesake had shrunk to Cordova and its environs.

The young amīr proved himself the man of the hour. His were those qualities of resoluteness, daring and candour which characterize leaders of men in all ages. Slowly but surely 'Abd-al-Raḥmān reclaimed the lost provinces, one after the other. With characteristic energy, which he displayed throughout his long reign of half a century (912–61),[2] he extended his conquests on all sides. Ecija was the first to surrender and that on the last day of 912.[3] Elvira followed suit. Jaen offered no resistance. Archidona agreed to pay tribute. Seville opened its gates toward the close of 913. Regio, whose mountain fastnesses had shielded the bold followers of ibn-Ḥafṣūn, was reduced step by step. The redoubtable leader himself remained defiant in his impregnable Bobastro until death came in 917 to put out of the way that formidable enemy of thirty-seven years' standing. Only Toledo remained unsubdued, but in 932 the proud former capital succumbed to famine and siege. The whole land was thus pacified and the state consolidated under the sway of a beneficent absolute ruler.

In the meantime external enemies were threatening. Among these the most dangerous were the Moslem Fāṭimids to the south and the Christian kings of Leon to the north. 'Ubaydullāh al-Mahdi, the founder of the Fāṭimid dynasty in Tunisia in 909, had

[1] Ibn-'Idhāri, vol. i, introduction by Dozy, pp. 47-50; ibn-al-Abbār, *Ḥullah*, p. 91.

[2] Ibn-al-Abbār, *Ḥullah*, p. 99, is right in claiming for 'Abd-al-Raḥmān III the longest reign in Islam down to his time. See above, p. 481, n. 2.

[3] Ibn-'Idhāri, vol. ii, p. 165.

negotiated an alliance with ibn-Ḥafṣūn and sent emissaries and spies across the straits. As they claimed descent from Fāṭimah, daughter of the Prophet and wife of 'Ali, the Fāṭimid caliphs would acknowledge no authority in Islam other than their own. The Cordovan ibn-Masarrah (883–931), the pseudo-Empedoclean philosopher who introduced into the West an esoteric system of writing whose words bore an inner and mysterious meaning which only the initiates could understand, may have been commissioned to establish a Fāṭimid party in Spain through his organized fraternities. Realizing that his position in Spain could not be safe while an enemy flourished in Africa, 'Abd-al-Raḥmān, whose suzerainty was recognized in Morocco as early as 917 or 918, obtained possession of Ceuta in 931 and ultimately secured homage from a great part of the Barbary coast.[1] His enlarged and renovated fleet,[2] second to none in the world of that age, with Almería[3] as chief harbour, disputed with the Fāṭimid navy the supremacy of the western Mediterranean. In 956 a Spanish fleet of seventy ships devastated parts of the African coast in retaliation for a raid made on the Spanish shore by the Sicilian fleet at the command of the Fāṭimid caliph.[4]

While these operations against domestic and foreign foes were in progress 'Abd-al-Raḥmān, whose mother was a Christian slave, was often engaged in the holy war against the Christians of the north who had hitherto never been subdued. Here the land of the Basques[5] occupied the centre, bridging the Pyrenees. To the east lay the still embryonic kingdoms of Navarre and Aragon. To the west stretched those territories which developed into the kingdoms of Castile and Leon. As early as 914 the undaunted

[1] Ibn-Khaldūn, vol. iv, pp. 137-8, quoted in Maqqari, vol. i, p. 227.

[2] The Spanish Moslem fleet had several encounters with the Scandinavian pirates known in England as Northmen (Norsemen), with the Normans of France and with the Danes, to all of whom the Arabs applied the generic term Majūs (fire-worshippers). The first occasion on which the Majūs attempted a landing was in 844, in the reign of 'Abd-al-Raḥmān II, when with their eighty ships they anchored before Lisbon and then occupied Seville. In 858–61, in the reign of Muḥammad I, they attempted several landings on the coasts of the peninsula. Ibn-al-Qūṭīyah, p. 63; ibn-'Idhāri, vol. ii, pp. 89-90, 99; Mas'ūdi, vol. i, p. 364; ibn-al-Athīr, vol. vii, pp. 11-12, 58; Dozy, *Recherches*, vol. ii, pp. 250-371.

[3] From Ar. al-Marīyah (watchtower).

[4] Ibn-Khaldūn, vol. iv, p. 46; tr. de Slane, *Histoire des Berbères et des dynasties musulmanes de l'Afrique septentrionale*, ed. Paul Casanova, vol. ii (Paris, 1927), p. 542.

[5] "Bashkans" of pseudo-ibn-Qutaybah, pp. 121, 132; ibn-al-Athīr, vol. vii, p. 48; ibn-Khaldūn, vol. iv, p. 140.

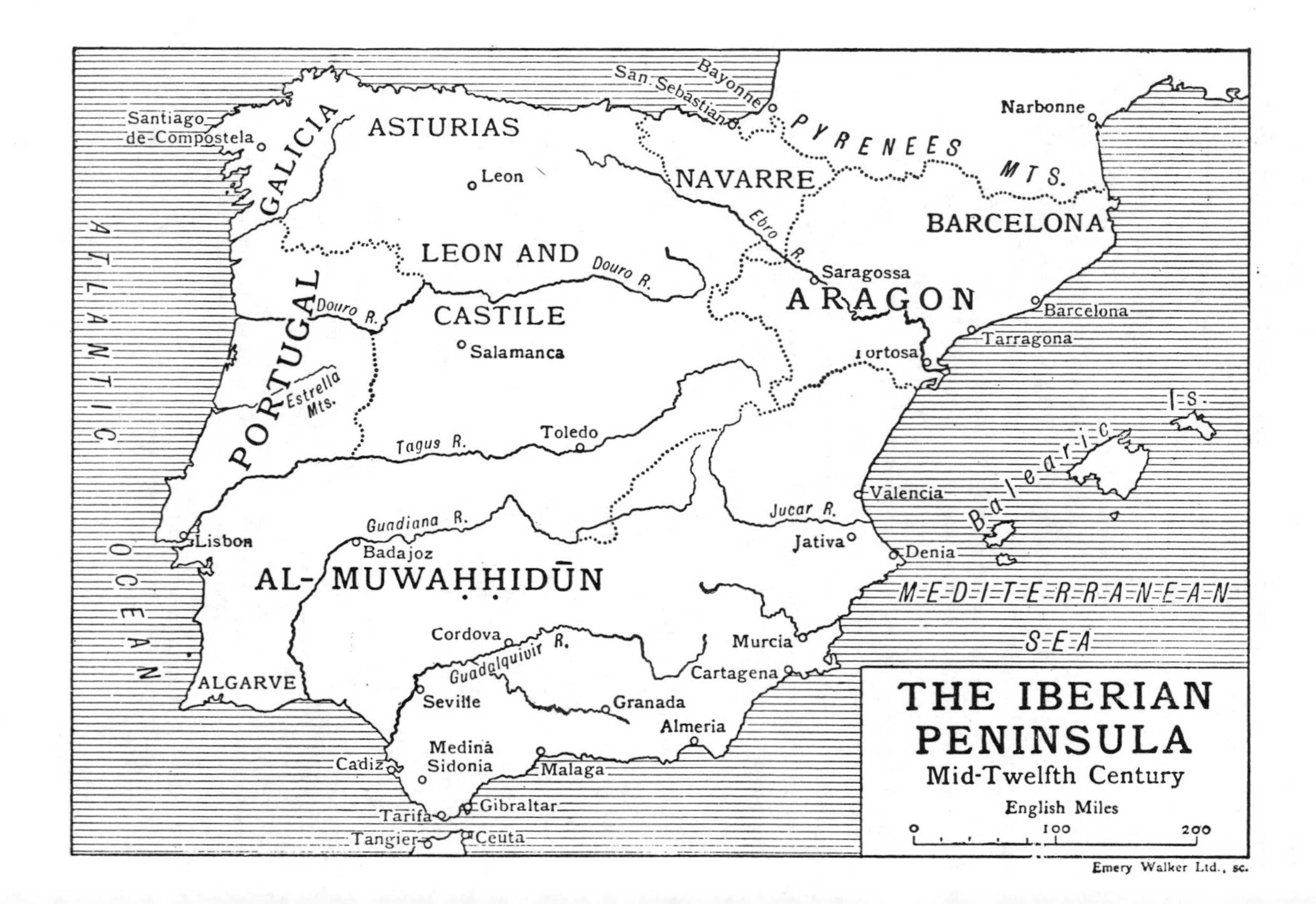
THE IBERIAN PENINSULA
Mid-Twelfth Century
English Miles
0
100
200
ATLANTIC
OCEAN
MEDITERRANEAN
SEA
Balearic Is.
Santiago-de-Compostela
GALICIA
ASTURIAS
Leon
San Sebastian
Bayonne
PYRENEES MTS.
Narbonne
NAVARRE
BARCELONA
LEON AND
CASTILE
Douro R.
Ebro R.
Saragossa
ARAGON
Barcelona
Tarragona
Tortosa
PORTUGAL
Estrella Mts.
Salamanca
Toledo
Tagus R.
Valencia
Jucar R.
Jativa
Denia
Lisbon
Guadiana R.
Badajoz
AL-MUWAHHIDŪN
Cordova
Guadalquivir R.
Murcia
Cartagena
ALGARVE
Seville
Granada
Almeria
Medina Sidonia
Cadiz
Malaga
Tarifa
Gibraltar
Tangier
Ceuta
Emery Walker Ltd., sc.

king of Leon, Ordoño II,[1] taking advantage of the situation in the Moslem kingdom, commenced hostilities by devastating the region to the south. Three years later he succeeded in capturing one of 'Abd-al-Raḥmān's generals and nailing his head beside that of a wild boar to the wall of a frontier fortress, San Esteban de Gormaz,[2] which the Moslem general was besieging. Pillaging forays from these northern enemies were successive. In 920 'Abd-al-Raḥmān took the field in person, razed San Esteban (S. Estevan), demolished a number of other strongholds[3] in that debatable land between Christianity and Islam and at Val de Junqueras (vale of reeds) met the combined forces of Ordoño II and Sancho[4] the Great of Navarre and inflicted on them a severe defeat. After overrunning parts of Navarre and adjacent Christian lands, 'Abd-al-Raḥmān returned triumphantly to his capital. Four years later he penetrated as far north as Pampeluna,[5] capital of Navarre, which he demolished. Its haughty king, the bulwark of Christianity in the east, referred to as "dog" by ibn-'Idhāri,[6] was reduced to impotence for a long time after this. About the same time the other champion of the native cause, Ordoño, died and the civil discord which followed brought a lull in military activity.

The remaining years of 'Abd-al-Raḥmān's long reign were filled with evidences of wise and able administration. One of the first among those was the proclamation that beginning Friday, January 16, 929, the ruling sovereign should be designated in all public prayers and official documents as caliph. For himself he chose the title *al-Khalīfah al-Nāṣir li-Dīn Allāh*, the caliph-defender of the religion of God.[7] It was most appropriate for him who brought Moslem Spain to a higher position than it had ever before enjoyed to assume the rôle of *amīr al-mu'minīn* especially in view of the low level to which the Eastern caliphate had fallen.

[1] "Ardūn" of Mas'ūdi, vol. iii, p. 75; Maqqari, vol. i, p. 233; "Ardhūn" of ibn-'Idhāri, vol. ii, pp. 179, 187.

[2] Or Castro Moros; Ar. Shant Ishtibān, Ashtīn or Qāshtar Mūrush.

[3] Ibn-'Idhāri, vol. ii, p. 183 *seq.* Ibn-'Abd-Rabbihi, poet laureate of 'Abd-al-Raḥmān, speaks of seventy strongholds reduced in one campaign, *'Iqd*, vol. ii, p. 368.

[4] "Shānjah" of ibn-al-Qūṭīyah, p. 114; "Shanjah" of Maqqari, vol. i, p. 233; "Sānjah" of ibn-Khaldūn, vol. iv, p. 141.

[5] "Banbalūnah" in Maqqari, vol. i, p. 234; ibn-'Idhāri, vol. ii, pp. 196, 199.

[6] Vol. ii, p. 200.

[7] *'Iqd*, vol. ii, pp. 368, 369; ibn-'Idhāri vol. ii, pp. 162, 211-12; ibn-Khaldūn, vol. iv, p. 137, copied by Maqqari, vol. i, p. 227

As defender of the faith the Caliph al-Nāṣir felt it his supreme duty to press the holy war against the Christians, who never ceased to cast covetous eyes on their ancestral territory to the south. His campaigns continued until the year 939, in which King Ramiro II of Leon and Queen Regent Tota[1] of Navarre, widow of Sancho the Great, inflicted on him at Alhandega,[2] south of Salamanca, the first serious check his military operations had encountered in twenty-seven years of almost incessant warfare. The caliph's huge army was practically annihilated; he himself barely escaped with his life. This same Tota later appeared at the court of the caliph together with her son, in whose name she was ruling Navarre, and with her grandson Sancho the Fat, ex-king of Leon, seeking medical advice for Sancho and military aid to reinstall him on the throne.[3] The royal guests were received in great state, while the Moslem capital was treated to the grand sight of Christian royalty knocking in supplication at the door of the caliph whose word was law from the mouth of the Ebro to the Atlantic and from the foot of the Pyrenees to Gibraltar. Through the skill of the Jewish court physician and statesman Ḥasdāy ben-Shaprūṭ, Sancho was relieved of his excessive corpulence, which had cost him his crown, and through the caliph's efforts he regained in 960 his lost authority.

Al-Zahrā'

The caliph's court at that time was one of the most glamorous in all Europe. Accredited to it were envoys from the Byzantine emperor as well as from the monarchs of Germany, Italy and France.[4] Its seat, Cordova, with half a million inhabitants, seven hundred mosques[5] and three hundred public baths, yielded in magnificence only to Baghdād and Constantinople. The royal palace, with four hundred rooms and apartments housing thousands of slaves and guards, stood north-west of the town on one of the spurs of the Sierra Morena overlooking the Guadalquivir. 'Abd-al-Raḥmān started its construction in 936 with money left, so the legend goes, by one of his concubines. His first thought was to use the fund for ransoming captives in

[1] "Ṭūṭah" in ibn-Khaldūn, vol. iv, pp. 142-3.

[2] From Ar. *al-khandaq*, the moat. Maqqari, vol. i, pp. 227, 228.

[3] Ibn-Khaldūn, vol. iv, p. 143, quoted in Maqqari, vol. i, p. 235.

[4] Ibn-'Idhāri, vol. ii, p. 229; ibn-Khaldūn, vol. iv, pp. 142-3; Maqqari, vol. i, p. 227.

[5] Three thousand in ibn-'Idhāri, vol. ii, p. 247. Cf. Maqqari, vol. i, p. 355.

Christian hands. Since none were found he acted on the suggestion of his other concubine, al-Zahrā' (she with the bright face), and erected this palatial mansion which he named after her. Marble was brought from Numidia and Carthage; columns as well as basins with golden statues were imported or received as presents from Constantinople; and 10,000 workmen with 1500 beasts of burden laboured on it for a score of years.[1] Enlarged and embellished by al-Nāṣir's two successors, al-Zahrā' became the nucleus of a royal suburb whose remains, partly excavated in and after 1910, can still be seen.

In al-Zahrā' the caliph surrounded himself with a bodyguard of "Slavs" which numbered 3750[2] and headed his standing army of a hundred thousand men.[3] At first applied to slaves and prisoners captured by Germans and others from among the Slavonic tribes and sold to the Arabs, the name Slav[4] was later given to all purchased foreigners: Franks, Galicians, Lombards and the like, who as a rule were secured young and Arabicized. With the aid of these "Janissaries" or "Mamlūks" of Spain the caliph not only kept treason and brigandage in check but reduced the influence of the old Arab aristocracy. Commerce and agriculture consequently flourished and the sources of income for the state were multiplied. The royal revenue amounted to 6,245,000 dinars, a third of which sufficed for the army and a third for public works, while the balance was placed in reserve.[5] Never before was Cordova so prosperous, al-Andalus so rich and the state so triumphant. And all this was achieved through the genius of one man, who, we are told, died at the ripe age of seventy-three leaving a statement that he had known only fourteen days of happiness.[6]

[1] Ibn-'Idhāri, vol. ii, pp. 225, 240, 246-8; ibn-Ḥawqal, p. 77; ibn-Khaldūn, vol. iv, p. 144; Maqqari, vol. i, pp. 344-7; ibn-Khallikān, vol. ii, p. 413.
[2] Ibn-'Idhāri, vol. ii, p. 247.
[3] Mas'ūdi, vol. iii, pp. 74, 78. Mas'ūdi was a contemporary, though distant, author.
[4] Ar. Ṣaqālibah; see above, p. 235
[5] Ibn-'Idhāri, vol. ii, p. 247; ibn-Khallikān, vol. ii, p. 413. Cf. ibn-Ḥawqal, p. 77.
[6] Ibn-'Idhāri, vol. ii, p. 248.

CHAPTER XXXVIII

POLITICAL, ECONOMIC AND EDUCATIONAL INSTITUTIONS

THE reigns of ʿAbd-al-Raḥmān III and his successor al-Ḥakam II (961–76), together with the dictatorship of al-Ḥājib al-Manṣūr (977–1002), mark the apogee of Moslem rule in the West. Neither before nor after this was Moslem Spain able to exercise the same political influence in European and African affairs.

Cordova

In this period the Umayyad capital took its place as the most cultured city in Europe and, with Constantinople and Baghdād, as one of the three cultural centres of the world. With its one hundred and thirteen thousand homes,[1] twenty-one suburbs,[2] seventy libraries and numerous bookshops, mosques and palaces, it acquired international fame and inspired awe and admiration in the hearts of travellers. It enjoyed miles of paved streets illuminated by lights from the bordering houses[3] whereas, "seven hundred years after this time there was not so much as one public lamp in London", and "in Paris, centuries subsequently, whoever stepped over his threshold on a rainy day stepped up to his ankles in mud".[4] When the University of Oxford still looked upon bathing as a heathen custom, generations of Cordovan scientists had been enjoying baths in luxurious establishments. The Arab attitude toward the Nordic barbarians found expression in the words of the learned Toledan judge Ṣāʿid[5] († 1070), who thought that "because the sun does not shed its rays directly over their heads, their climate is cold and atmosphere clouded. Consequently their temperaments have become cold and their humours rude, while their bodies have

[1] Ibn-ʿIdhāri, vol. ii, p. 247. Cf. Maqqari, vol. i, p. 356.

[2] Maqqari, vol. i, pp. 299, 304. Cf. ibn-ʿIdhāri, vol. ii, pp. 247-8.

[3] Maqqari, vol. i, p. 298, ll. 2-3. These lights were evidently fastened to the front doors or corners.

[4] John W. Draper, *A History of the Intellectual Development of Europe*, rev. ed. (London, 1910), vol. ii, p. 31.

[5] *Tabaqāt*, pp. 8-9.

grown large, their complexion light and their hair long. They lack withal sharpness of wit and penetration of intellect, while stupidity and folly prevail among them." Whenever the rulers of Leon, Navarre or Barcelona needed a surgeon, an architect, a master singer or a dressmaker, it was to Cordova that they applied. The fame of the Moslem capital penetrated distant Germany where a Saxon nun styled it "the jewel of the world".[1] Such was the city which housed the Umayyad ruler and his government.

Governmental institutions

The organization of the government in the Western caliphate did not differ radically from that of the Eastern. The caliphal office was hereditary, though army officers and nobles quite often elected him whom they favoured. When there was a *ḥājib* (chamberlain) he stood above the vizirs, who communicated through him with the caliph. Below the vizirs came the *kuttāb* (secretaries), who together with the vizirs formed the *dīwān*. The provinces, which apart from Cordova were six in number, were each ruled by a civil and military governor called *wāli*. Some important cities were also under *wālis*. Justice was administered by the caliph, who as a rule delegated the authority to *qāḍis*, at the head of whom stood the *qāḍi al-quḍāh* in Cordova. Criminal and police cases were heard by a special judge, *ṣāḥib al-shurṭah*. Another special judge in Cordova, *ṣāḥib al-maẓālim*, heard complaints against public officials. The usual sentences involved fine, scourging, imprisonment, mutilation and, in case of blasphemy, heresy and apostasy, death. An interesting officer was the *muḥtasib* (Sp. *almotacén*), who, besides directing the police, acted as overseer of trade and markets, checked weights and measures and intervened in cases of gambling, sex immorality and improper public dress.[2]

Industry

The state depended for its revenue mostly on duties imposed on imports and exports. Spain under the caliphate was one of the wealthiest and most thickly populated lands of Europe. The capital boasted some thirteen thousand weavers and a flourishing leather industry. From Spain the art of tanning and embossing leather was carried to Morocco and from these two lands it was brought to France and England, as the terms cordovan, cordwainer and

[1] Hrotsvitha in *Scriptores rerum Germanicarum; Hrotsvithæ opera*, ed. Paulus de Winterfeld (Berlin, 1902), p. 52, l. 12.

[2] Al-Saqati, *Fi Ādāb al-Ḥisbah*, ed. Colin and Lévi-Provençal (Paris, 1931), pp. 3 *seq.*; Lévi-Provençal, *L'Espagne musulmane au Xième siècle* (Paris, 1932), pp. 79-96.

morocco indicate. Wool and silk were woven not only in Cordova but in Malaga, Almería and other centres.[1] Sericulture, originally a monopoly of the Chinese, was introduced by Moslems into Spain, where it thrived. Almería also produced glassware and brasswork. Paterna in Valencia was the home of pottery. Jaen and Algarve were noted for their mines of gold and silver, Cordova for its iron and lead[2] and Malaga for its rubies. Toledo, like Damascus, was famous all over the world for its swords.[3] The art of inlaying steel and other metals with gold and silver and decorating them with flower patterns, which was introduced from Damascus, flourished in several Spanish and other European centres and left a linguistic heritage in such words as damascene, damaskeen, French *damasquiner* and Italian *damaschino*.

Agriculture

The Spanish Arabs introduced agricultural methods practised in Western Asia. They dug canals,[4] cultivated grapes and introduced, among other plants and fruits, rice,[5] apricots,[6] peaches,[7] pomegranates,[8] oranges,[9] sugar-cane,[10] cotton[11] and saffron.[12] The south-eastern plains of the peninsula, especially favoured by climate and soil, developed important centres of rural and urban activity. Here wheat and other grains as well as olives and sundry fruits[13] were raised by a peasantry who worked the soil on shares with the owners.

This agricultural development was one of the glories of Moslem Spain and one of the Arabs' lasting gifts to the land, for Spanish gardens have preserved to this day a "Moorish" imprint. One

[1] Maqqari, vol. i, pp. 102, 123-4.

[2] Lisān-al-Dīn ibn-al-Khaṭīb, *al-Iḥāṭah fi Akhbār Gharnāṭah* (Cairo, 1319), vol. i, p. 15; *al-Lamḥah al-Badrīyah fi al-Dawlah al-Naṣrīyah*, ed. al-Khaṭīb (Cairo, 1347), p. 13.

[3] For more on industry and metals consult ibn-Ḥawqal, pp. 78-9; Iṣṭakhri, p. 42; Maqqari, vol. i, pp. 90-92, 123.

[4] The Sp. word for canal is *acequia*, from Ar. *al-sāqiyah*.

[5] Sp. *arroz*, from Ar. *al-aruzz*, originally Skr. Cf. below, p. 665.

[6] Sp. *albaricoque* (whence Eng. apricot), from Ar. *al-barqūq*, which came from L. through Gr.

[7] Sp. *albérchigo*, from Ar. *firsiq*, *firsik*, from L., a variety of peaches.

[8] Ar. *rummān*, which has survived in Sp. *romania*, a drink made of pomegranate juice.

[9] See above, p. 351. The Arabs introduced into Europe the bitter, or Seville orange. The sweet, or common orange was introduced later by the Portuguese from India.

[10] Cf. below, p. 667.

[11] Sp. *algodón*, O.Sp. *coton* (whence Eng. cotton), from Ar. *al-quṭn*.

[12] Sp. *azafrán*, Pg. *açafrão*, from Ar. *al-za'farān*.

[13] Ibn-al-Khaṭīb, *Iḥāṭah*, vol. i, pp. 14-15, 27, 37; *Lamḥah*, p. 13; Maqqari, vol. i, pp. 94-6; ibn-Baṭṭūṭah, vol. iv, pp. 366-9.

of the best-known gardens is the Generalife (from Ar. *jannat al-'arīf*, the inspector's paradise), a Naṣrid [1] monument of the late thirteenth century whose villa was one of the outlying buildings of the Alhambra. This garden, "proverbial for its extensive shades, falling waters and soft breeze",[2] was terraced in the form of an amphitheatre and irrigated by streams which, after forming numerous cascades, lost themselves among the flowers, shrubs and trees represented today by a few gigantic cypresses and myrtles.

Trade

The industrial and agricultural products of Moslem Spain were more than sufficient for domestic consumption. Seville, one of the greatest of its river ports, exported cotton, olives and oil; it imported cloth and slaves from Egypt and singing girls from Europe and Asia. The exports of Malaga and Jaen included saffron, figs, marble and sugar. Through Alexandria and Constantinople Spanish products found markets as far away as India and Central Asia. Especially active was the trade with Damascus, Baghdād and Makkah. The international nautical vocabulary of the modern world contains not a few words, for example admiral, arsenal, average,[3] cable, corvette,[4] shallop (sloop),[5] tariff, which testify to the former Arab supremacy on the seas. An interesting echo of brisk maritime activity in the Atlantic, (*baḥr al-ẓulumāt*, classical Mare Tenebrarum, the sea of darkness) is found in an obscure story preserved in al-Idrīsi,[6] who tells of eight "beguiled" cousins who set off from Lisbon on an expedition of exploration which carried them after thirty-five days of sailing west and south to strange islands.[7]

The government maintained a regular postal service. It modelled its coinage on Eastern patterns, with the dinar as the gold unit and the dirham as the silver unit.[8] The copper *fals* [9] of early Islam was likewise current. Arab money was in use in the Christian kingdoms of the north, which for nearly four hundred years had no coinage other than Arabic or French.

The caliph in his glory

The halo that surrounded the court of 'Abd-al-Raḥmān III did not cease to shed its lustre on that of his son and successor

[1] See below, p. 549.
[2] Ibn-al-Khaṭīb, *Lamḥah*, p. 109.
[3] In the sense of duty upon goods. From Ar. *'awārīyah*.
[4] Ar. *ghurāb*, war vessel, through Sp. *corbeta*.
[5] Ar. *jalbah*, boat, through Sp. *chalupa*.
[6] Pp. 51-2.
[7] Perhaps the Canary and Cape Verde Islands.
[8] Ibn-al-Khaṭīb, *Iḥāṭah*, vol. i, p. 37.
[9] From Gr. *phollis*, from L. *follis*.

al-Ḥakam II al-Mustanṣir (961–76), considered by al-Mas'ūdi [1] the most judicious (*aḥkam*) of all men. Early in al-Ḥakam's reign there appeared at the Moslem capital Ordoño the Wicked, seeking reinstatement in the Leonese throne which he had lost through the intervention of 'Abd-al-Raḥmān. The ex-king was escorted to al-Zahrā' by Walīd ibn-Khayzurān, the Christian judge of Cordova, and 'Abdullāh ibn-Qāsim,[2] the metropolitan of Toledo, and instructed by them in the details of proper court etiquette. Dressed in white and wearing a head-gear adorned with jewels, Ordoño, at the head of his nobles, made his way through the serried ranks of Moslem soldiers lining the approaches to the imperial residence. Struck with awe, the Christians began to cross themselves. In the audience chamber sat the caliph on his throne with the members of his household and chief officers on both sides and behind. With abject genuflections the Christian prince advanced, bare-headed, kissed the hand of the commander of the believers, calling himself his slave, implored his aid and retired walking backwards to the door. The same procedure was observed by his noble companions. Walīd acted as interpreter. The caliph promised aid under certain conditions, but the visit proved fruitless.[3]

Educational activity

The real glory of this period, however, lies in fields other than political. Al-Ḥakam was himself a scholar and patronized learning.[4] He granted munificent bounties to scholars and established twenty-seven free schools in the capital.[5] Under him the university of Cordova, founded in the principal mosque by 'Abd-al-Raḥmān III, rose to a place of pre-eminence among the educational institutions of the world. It preceded both al-Azhar of Cairo and the Niẓāmīyah of Baghdād and attracted students, Christian and Moslem, not only from Spain but from other parts of Europe, Africa and Asia. Al-Ḥakam enlarged the mosque which housed the university, conducted water to it in lead pipes and decorated it with mosaics brought by Byzantine artists, spending on it 261,537 dinars and 1½ dirhams.[6] He invited professors from the East to the university and set aside

[1] Vol. i, p. 363.
[2] Note the Moslem form of the names of these two Christian dignitaries.
[3] Ibn-'Idhāri, vol. ii, p. 251; ibn-Khaldūn, vol. iv, p. 145; Maqqari, vol. i, pp. 248, 252-6.
[4] Ibn-al-Athīr, vol. viii, p. 498; ibn-al-Khaṭīb, *Iḥāṭah*, vol. i, p. 305.
[5] Ibn-'Idhāri, vol. ii, p. 256.
[6] *Ibid.* pp. 253, 256-7.

endowments for their salaries. Among its professors were the historian, ibn-al-Qūṭīyah, who taught grammar, and the renowned philologist of Baghdād, abu-ʿAli al-Qāli,[1] whose *Amāli*[2] (dictations) is still studied in Arabic lands. One of the dramatic episodes in the life of al-Qāli was the time he was struck with stage fright while delivering an extemporaneous oration at the pompous reception tendered the Byzantine envoys by the Caliph al-Nāṣir. He could not proceed beyond the introductory praise to Allah and blessing on Muḥammad, whereupon he was immediately replaced by Mundhir ibn-Saʿīd, who "extemporaneously" delivered a most eloquent address, covering two pages and a half in al-Maqqari,[3] all in rhymed prose.

In addition to the university the capital housed a library of first magnitude. Al-Ḥakam was a bibliophile; his agents ransacked the bookshops of Alexandria, Damascus and Baghdād with a view to buying or copying manuscripts. The books thus gathered are said to have numbered 400,000, their titles filling a catalogue of forty-four volumes, in each one of which twenty sheets were devoted to poetical works alone.[4] Al-Ḥakam, probably the best scholar among Moslem caliphs, personally used several of these works; his marginal notes on certain manuscripts rendered them highly prized by later scholars. In order to secure the first copy of the *Aghāni*, which al-Iṣbahāni, a descendant of the Umayyads, was then composing in al-ʿIrāq, al-Ḥakam sent the author a thousand dinars.[5] The general state of culture in Andalusia reached such a high level at this time that the distinguished Dutch scholar Dozy,[6] followed by other scholars, went so far as to declare enthusiastically that "nearly every one could read and write". All this whilst in Christian Europe only the rudiments of learning were known, and that by the few, mostly clergy.

ʿĀmirid dictatorship

Al-Hakam was succeeded by his son Hishām II al-Muʾayyad (976–1009), a boy of twelve. Hishām's mother, a beautiful and able Basque named Ṣubḥ [7] (dawn, aurora), was the real power

[1] Ibn-Khallikān, vol. i, pp. 130-31; Yāqūt, *Udabā'*, vol. ii, pp. 351-4; Samʿāni, fol. 439 b. [2] 2 vols. (Būlāq, 1324). [3] Vol. i, pp. 237-40.

[4] Maqqari, vol. i, pp. 249-50, 256; ibn-Khaldūn, vol. iv, p. 146.

[5] Ibn-Khaldūn, vol. iv, p. 146; Maqqari, vol. i, p. 250.

[6] *Histoire des Musulmans*, ed. Lévi-Provençal, vol. ii, p. 184; Nicholson, *Literary History*, p. 419; Rafael Altamira in *The Cambridge Medieval History*, (New York, 1922), vol. iii, p. 434.

[7] Ibn-ʿIdhāri, vol. ii, p. 268; Maqqari, vol. i, p. 259; Marrākushi, pp. 17, 19.

in state affairs. The Sultanah had a protégé, Muḥammad ibn-abi-ʿĀmir, who started life as a humble professional letter writer and ultimately became virtual ruler of the kingdom. His career provides another illustration of what pluck, talent and ambition could accomplish in a Moslem state. Muḥammad's ancestor, a Yamanite of the Maʿāfir tribe, was one of the few Arabs in Ṭāriq's army of conquest. Under the patronage of the queen, who was said to have been also his mistress, young Muḥammad rose from one office to another in the court, disposing, by clever manipulation or force, of superiors on whose shoulders he climbed until he became royal chamberlain (*ḥājib*) and vizir.[1] In that capacity he dealt a final blow to the Slavonic bodyguard, substituted for it a new unit of loyal Moroccan mercenaries and finally shut up the immature caliph in his palace. In order to set aside al-Zahrāʾ the Ḥājib built for himself in 978 a magnificent residence east of Cordova on a site not yet identified and styled it al-Madīnah al-Zāhirah (the brilliant town).[2] To ingratiate himself with the ulema he burned all books in the library of al-Ḥakam dealing with philosophy and other subjects blacklisted by those theologians. The poets he handled properly through bounteous subsidies. He then had his name mentioned in the Friday prayer and on the coinage, wore robes of gold tissue woven with his name—a privilege of royalty—and after 992 had his seal replace the caliph's on all official documents issued from the chancellery.[3] The only thing he did not do was to overthrow the nominal Umayyad caliph and establish an ʿĀmirid caliphate.

In military affairs ibn-abi-ʿĀmir proved as successful as in peaceful undertakings. He first reformed the army, substituting for the ancient tribal organization the regimental system. The removal of the Fāṭimid seat of power farther east to the newly built Cairo (969) and the internecine conflicts among the petty Christian kingdoms of the north afforded his armies an opportunity to march triumphantly along the north-western African coast as well as in the northern parts of the Iberian Peninsula. His victories led him to assume in 981 the honorific title al-Manṣūr bi-Allāh (rendered victorious through the aid of Allah).

[1] Ibn-ʿIdhāri, vol. ii, pp. 267-9; ibn-Khaldūn, vol. iv, pp. 147-8; ibn-al-Athīr vol. ix, pp. 124-5; ibn-al-Khaṭīb, *Iḥāṭah*, vol. ii, 67-9.

[2] Ibn-ʿIdhāri, vol. ii, pp. 294-7.

[3] Maqqari, vol. i, p. 258.

In the spring and autumn of every year al-Ḥājib al-Manṣūr led his troops as a matter of course against the Christians of Leon, Castile and Catalonia. Here, among other achievements, he captured Zamora in 981, sacked Barcelona in his thirteenth campaign[1] (985) and in 988 razed the city of Leon with its massive walls and high towers, making its kingdom a tributary province. He even ventured into the mountainous passes of Galicia and in 997 demolished the magnificent church of St. Jago (Santiago) de Compostela,[2] a shrine frequented by pilgrims from all of Christian Europe. Subsequent to this last feat his triumphal entry into Cordova was signalized by a multitude of Christian captives bearing on their shoulders the church doors, which were incorporated in the capital's great mosque, together with the church bells, which were utilized as lamps in Moslem edifices. Christians with chains round their ankles were employed by al-Manṣūr in repairing the mosque. Never except under ʻAbd-al-Raḥmān III did the star of Spanish Islam shine with such brilliancy.

Al-Manṣūr's wish to die in the field was realized in 1002 on his way back from a campaign against Castile, the fiftieth of his expeditions.[3] Buried with him in the coffin was the dust which had accumulated on his coat of mail during his numerous campaigns and which he had kept for this purpose.[4] On his tomb at Medinaceli (Madīnat Sālim) was engraved this epitaph:

His story in his relics you may trace,
As tho' he stood before you face to face.
Never will Time bring forth his peer again,
Nor one to guard, like him, the gaps of Spain.[5]

But the pointed comment of the monkish annalist better ex-

[1] Ibn-al-Khaṭīb, *Iḥāṭah*, vol. ii, p. 71; according to others twenty-third campaign,

[2] "Shant Yāqūb" of Arab authors; ibn-ʻIdhāri, vol. ii, pp. 316-19; Maqqari, vol. i, pp. 270-72; Idrīsi, p. 104. Considered by Christians the burial place of the Apostle James, son of Zebedee, who, tradition asserts, introduced Christianity into Spain. The tomb was spared by al-Manṣūr.

[3] Ibn-Khaldūn, vol. iv, p. 148, makes his campaigns fifty-two, quoted fifty-six in Maqqari, vol. i, p. 258, cf. p. 261, l. 17; ibn-al-Khaṭīb, *Iḥāṭah*, vol. ii, p. 69, l. 14; ibn-al-Athīr, vol. viii, p. 498, l. 15; ibn-al-Abbār, *Ḥullah*, p. 149.

[4] Ibn-al-Khaṭīb, *Iḥāṭah*, vol. ii, p. 72; ibn-al-Athīr, vol. ix, p. 125; Marrākushi, p. 26.

[5] Nicholson, *Literary History*, p. 413; ibn-al-Khaṭīb, *Iḥāṭah*, vol. ii, p. 73; ibn-al-Abbār, *Ḥullah*, p. 151. Ar. *thughūr*, rendered "gaps of Spain", means "marches" or "frontier forts".

presses the sentiment of the Christians: "In 1002 died Almanzor, and was buried in hell".[1]

Collapse of Umayyad power

For eighty years after the death of the 'Āmirid dictator the Andalus was torn asunder by Berbers, Arabs, Slavs (*Ṣaqālibah*) and Spaniards, with the prætorian guard playing the same rôle as it did in ancient Rome and decadent Baghdād. His son 'Abd-al-Malik al-Muẓaffar, whom al-Manṣūr had appointed as his successor, thus making the office hereditary, succeeded in maintaining the unity and prestige of the kingdom for six years.[2] In 1008 al-Muẓaffar was poisoned by his brother and successor, 'Abd-al-Raḥmān, surnamed Shanjūl (Sanchuelo, i.e. little Sancho, because his mother was daughter of King Sancho of Navarre), who immediately proclaimed himself heir presumptive to the Umayyad caliphate, a step which aroused the populace and resulted in his execution.[3] For twenty-one years after this, caliph after caliph was set up: one as a puppet of the Cordovans, another of the Slavs and a third of the Berbers. Even the Castilians had a share in unseating one caliph and seating another.[4] The real power was in the hands of the military. The unfortunate Hishām II was dragged out of his thirty years of seclusion but manifested only childish incompetence and was forced to abdicate in 1009 in favour of his second cousin Muḥammad II al-Mahdi.[5] Muḥammad's only claim to distinction

[1] "Chronicon Burgensi" in *España sagrada*, vol. xxiii, p. 308.

[2] Ibn-'Idhāri, ed. E. Lévi-Provençal, vol. iii (Paris, 1930), pp. 3-4, 36-7; Maqqari, vol. i, pp. 276-7.

[3] Ibn 'Idhāri, vol. iii, pp. 43-8, 66-74; ibn-Khaldūn, vol. iv, pp. 148-50; ibn-al-Athīr, vol. viii, p. 499.

[4] Ibn-Khaldūn, vol. iv, pp. 150-51; ibn-al-Abbār, *Ḥullah*, pp. 159-60.

[5] Table showing genealogy of Umayyad caliphs in Cordova:

1. 'Abd-al-Raḥmān III (912 [caliph 929]–61)
- 2. Al-Ḥakam II (961–76)
  - 3. Hishām II (976–1009, 1010–13)
- ('Abd-al-Jabbār)
  - (Hishām)
    - 4. Muḥammad II (1009, 1010)
    - 7. 'Abd-al-Raḥmān V (1023)
- (Sulaymān)
  - (al-Ḥakam)
    - 5. Sulaymān (1009–10, 1013–16)
- ('Abd-al-Malik)
  - (Muḥammad)
    - 6. 'Abd-al-Raḥmān IV (1018)
    - 9. Hishām III (1027-31)
- ('Ubaydullāh)
  - ('Abd-al-Raḥmān)
    - 8. Muḥammad III (1023–5)

was that he held the throne for only a few months, in which he found time to raze the Madīnah al-Zāhirah of the 'Āmirids[1] and have the severed heads of a number of leaders of the northern marches who refused to acknowledge him converted into flower-pots and placed on the banks of the river opposite his palace. His manufacture of wine in his palace won him the sobriquet *nabbādh*, wine-maker.[2] Three of the nine Umayyad caliphs in this period of anarchy held the throne more than once; one of them, Hishām II, was set up and pulled down twice, after which he disappeared in a mysterious way that has never been solved. An impostor bearing close resemblance to him was installed in Seville.[3] One poor wretch, 'Abd-al-Raḥmān V al-Mustaẓhir (1023), the best of the lot and whose vizir was the learned ibn-Ḥazm, hid himself in the bathroom heater, whence he was dragged and butchered before the eyes of his successor, Muḥammad III al-Mustakfi,[4] who two years later was to meet as hard a fate. In 1025 as al-Mustakfi, "whose interest in life centred in sex and stomach",[5] sought flight in the guise of a singing girl wearing a veil, he fell victim, in an obscure village on the frontier, to poison administered by one of his officers.[6] A daughter of this caliph was the poetess Wallādah, whose beauty and talent made her the chief centre of attraction in the court and won her undying fame.

Before coming to its inglorious end the Umayyad caliphate was interrupted by another régime, the Ḥammūdid, which claimed all caliphal privileges. The founder was one 'Ali ibn-Ḥammūd (1016–18), who traced his descent from his namesake the Prophet's son-in-law, but was himself half Berberized. 'Ali had held the governorship of Ceuta and Tangier before proclaiming himself caliph in Cordova. He had also conquered Malaga, where his eight descendants maintained themselves from 1025 to 1057.[7] Two other Ḥammūdid pretenders to the

[1] Nuwayri, ed. Gaspar Remiro, vol. i, p. 74.

[2] Ibn-al-Athīr, vol. viii, p. 500.

[3] See below, p. 538.

[4] Ibn-'Idhāri, vol. iii, pp. 138-9; Nuwayri, vol. i, p. 78; ibn-al-Abbār, *Ḥullah*, p. 164; ibn-Bassām, *al-Dhakhīrah fi Maḥāsin Ahl al-Jazīrah*, pt. 1, vol. i (Cairo, 1939), p. 39.

[5] Ibn-al-Athīr, vol. ix, p. 194.

[6] Ibn-'Idhāri, vol. iii, p. 142; ibn-al-Athīr, vol. ix, p. 194; Marrākushi, p. 40; Nuwayri, vol. i, p. 84.

[7] Marrākushi, pp. 30-37; ibn-'Idhāri, vol iii, pp. 113-17, 119-25; Maqqari, vol. i, pp. 281-2; ibn-Khaldūn, vol. iv, pp. 152-5; ibn-al-Athīr, vol. ix, pp. 188 *seq.* The Ḥammūdids were related to the Idrīsids of Morocco.

caliphate followed, exercising precarious power in Cordova until 1027.[1]

In this year Hishām III al-Mu'tadd recaptured the throne for the Umayyads. But the fifty-four-year-old monarch was no match for the troublous situation. Tired of the endless changes in their government the Cordovans at last decided to take a radical step and abolish the caliphate altogether. Hishām was shut up with his family in a dismal vault attached to the great mosque. Here in total darkness and half frozen in his scanty attire the wretched sovereign, almost suffocating with the foul air, sat for hours trying to warm on his bosom his infant daughter, whom he dearly loved. In the meantime the vizirs were holding a public meeting which proclaimed the abolition of the caliphate for ever and the rule of a council of state under the leadership of one abu-al-Ḥazm ibn-Jahwar. Hishām met the epoch-making announcement by begging for a light and a morsel of bread for his starving child.[2]

[1] Ibn-'Idhāri, vol. iii, pp. 124-35.

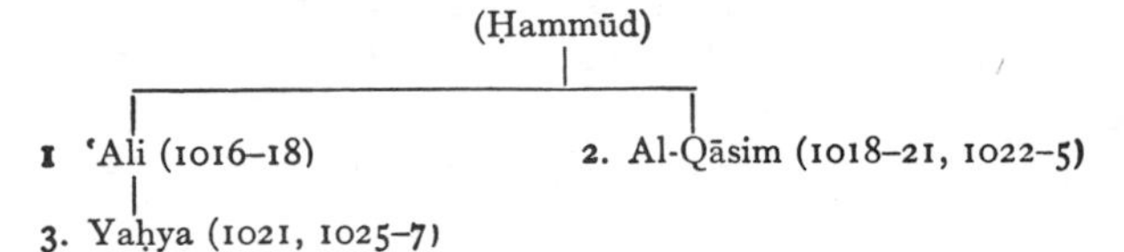

[2] Ibn-'Idhāri, vol. iii, pp. 150-52; Maqqari, vol. i, p. 286; ibn-Khaldūn, vol. iv, pp. 152-3; ibn-al-Athīr, vol. ix, pp. 198-9; Marrākushi, p. 41.

CHAPTER XXXIX

PETTY STATES: FALL OF GRANADA

FROM the ruins of the Umayyad caliphate there emerged an apparently fortuitous conglomeration of petty states which spent themselves in fratricidal quarrels and, after falling in part a prey to two Moroccan Berber dynasties, succumbed one after the other to the rising Christian power of the north. In the first half of the eleventh century no less than twenty such short-lived states arose in as many towns or provinces under chieftains and kinglets called by the Arabs *mulūk al-ṭawā'if* (Sp. *reyes de taifas*, party kings).

In Cordova the Jahwarids headed a sort of republic which was in 1068 absorbed by the banu-'Abbād of Seville.[1] Henceforth primacy among Moslem states lay with Seville, whose fortunes were always closely linked with Cordova's. Granada was the seat of a Zīrid régime, which received its name from its Berber founder ibn-Zīri (1012–19) and was destroyed by the Moroccan Murābiṭs in 1090. This was the only Spanish Moslem town in which a Jew, the Vizir Ismā'īl ibn-Naghzālah[2] († 1055), ever exercised virtually supreme power. At Malaga and in neighbouring districts the Ḥammūdid dynasty,[3] whose founder and his first two successors ruled as caliphs over Cordova too, lasted until 1057. After passing through Zīrid hands Malaga finally came within the orbit of Murābiṭ power.[4] The thronelet of Toledo was occupied by the banu-dhu-al-Nūn (1032 [5]–85), an ancient Berber family which had often been in rebellion, until destroyed by Alfonso VI of Leon and Castile.[6] In Saragossa the banu-Hūd held the sovereignty from 1039 until overpowered

[1] Marrākushi, pp. 50-51.

[2] Naghrālah, Heb. Samuel ben-Nagdela. Ibn-'Idhāri, vol. iii, pp. 261, 264.

[3] The noted geographer al-Sharīf al-Idrīsi was a grandson of Idrīs II (1042–6, 1053–4), the last save one of this line.

[4] Ibn-'Idhāri, vol. iii, pp. 262-6; ibn-Khaldūn, vol. iv, pp. 160-61.

[5] E. Lévi-Provençal, *Inscriptions arabes d'Espagne* (Leyden, 1931), pp. 65-6.

[6] Maqqari, vol. i, p. 288; ibn-Khaldūn, vol. iv, p. 161; ibn-'Idhāri, vol. iii, pp. 276-85; ibn-al-Athīr, vol. ix, p. 203.

by the Christians in 1141.[1] Among these party kings the cultured house of the ʿAbbādids in Seville was undoubtedly the most powerful.[2]

The ʿAbbādids of Seville

The banu-ʿAbbād (1023–91) claimed descent from the ancient Lakhmid kings of al-Ḥīrah. Their Spanish ancestor came as an officer in the Ḥimṣ regiment of the Syrian army shortly after the conquest[3] and the dynasty started in the person of a shrewd qāḍi of Seville who used as his cat's-paw someone who closely resembled the vanished Hishām II.[4] In 1042 the qāḍi's son ʿAbbād succeeded his father as chamberlain to the pretended caliph, the pseudo-Hishām, but lost no time in throwing off the mask and openly reigning under the honorific title al-Muʿtaḍid[5] (he who seeks strength [from Allah]), thus putting an end to the farce perpetrated by his father.

Al-Muʿtamid

Al-Muʿtaḍid was a poet and patron of letters who improvised elegant ditties with his boon companions and enjoyed a harem of nearly eight hundred inmates. But his court was eclipsed by that of his son and successor al-Muʿtamid (he who relies [upon Allah], 1068–91), "the most munificent, the most popular and most powerful of all party kings".[6] Shortly after his accession al-Muʿtamid succeeded in destroying the banu-Jahwar régime and in uniting Cordova to his kingdom. Like many of his contemporaries, however, he was tributary to a Christian monarch, first to Garcia, King of Galicia, and then to his successor, Alfonso VI.[7] Al-Muʿtamid possessed a sensitive and poetical soul. Numerous are the anecdotes told of his life of luxury, his gay parties and his romantic adventures in disguise. He "whose court was the halting-place of sojourners, the rendezvous of poets, the direction toward which all hopes were turned and the haunt of men of excellence"[8] chose as vizir

[1] Ibn-ʿIdhāri, vol. iii, pp. 221-9; ibn-Khaldūn, vol. iv, pp. 163-4; ibn-al-Athīr, vol. ix, p. 204.

[2] For names and dates of rulers in these minor dynasties consult Lane-Poole, *Dynasties*, pp. 23-6; de Zambaur, pp. 53-7; Dozy, *Musulmans*, ed. Lévi-Provençal, vol. iii, pp. 236-41.

[3] See above, p. 502. Seville was often referred to as Ḥimṣ; ibn-Jubayr, pp. 258-9.

[4] Ibn-Khaldūn, vol. iv, p. 156; ibn-al-Athīr, vol. ix, p 201-2; ibn-al-Khaṭīb, *Iḥāṭah*, vol. ii, p. 73.

[5] After the ʿAbbāsid caliph of the same name; Maqqari, vol. i, p. 132.

[6] Ibn-Khallikān, vol. ii, p. 412. Cf. ibn-al-Khaṭīb, *Iḥāṭah*, vol. ii, p. 77.

[7] Ibn-Khallikān, vol. ii, p. 414; ibn-al-Athīr, vol. x, p. 92.

[8] Ibn-Khallikān, vol. ii, p. 412. Cf. the eulogy of al-Fatḥ ibn-Khāqān, *Qalāʾid al-ʿIqyān* (Būlāq, 1283), pp. 4-5.

a poet, ibn-ʿAmmār,[1] and as favourite wife a slave girl of talent and beauty, Iʿtimād. While strolling one evening with ibn-ʿAmmār along the banks of the Guadalquivir, the monarch observed a gentle breeze ruffling the face of the water and improvised this hemistich, challenging his vizir to complete the verse:

> Behold the wind weaving the waves into mail;

Ibn-ʿAmmār hesitated. Meanwhile a young woman who happened to be washing clothes near by instantly supplied the antiphony:

> Oh, were it but frozen—no knight would it fail![2]

That was the youthful Iʿtimād al-Rumaykīyah, the future queen, from whose first name her royal husband is said to have adapted his own[3] and whose every whim and fancy he later tried to satisfy. Impressed on one occasion by the rare spectacle of snowflakes falling in Cordova, Iʿtimād implored al-Muʿtamid for a substitute, and forthwith he ordered the Sierra planted with almonds, whose white flowers bloom in the latter part of winter. Noticing on another day some Bedouin dairy women carrying their jars and walking in the muddy streets with their skirts lifted up, she expressed the wish to imitate their performance; in no time the courtyard of the royal palace was converted into a pool filled with spices and perfumed essences, all moistened with rose-water and made into an aromatic quagmire ready for the delicate feet of Iʿtimād and her pretty attendants.[4]

The last days of al-Muʿtamid were as miserable as his early days were gay. After a lull of several years in which the Christian monarchs of the north had occupied themselves with internal troubles, they were again bestirring themselves against their Moslem neighbours. The kingdoms of Leon and Castile, united under Ferdinand I and his son Alfonso VI, became especially dangerous. Alfonso added to his kingdom Galicia and Navarre, and as Moslem princes vied with the Christian in winning his favour he styled himself "the emperor" like his successor

[1] Marrākushi, pp. 77, 85-90.

[2] Dozy, *Scriptorum Arabum oci de Abbadidis*, vol. ii (Leyden, 1852), pp. 151-2, vol. iii (Leyden, 1863), p. 225.

[3] Ibn-al-Khaṭīb, *Iḥāṭah*, vol. ii, p. 74. Her surname she acquired from her first master, Rumayk.

[4] Dozy, *Scriptorum*, vol. ii, pp. 152-3; Maqqari, vol. i, p. 287.

Alfonso VII, who, in addition to that, claimed to be "king of the men of the two religions". Raids from the north now became regular and reached as far south as Cadiz. In the meantime Rodrigo Díaz de Bivar, "My Cid the Challenger", had established himself with his Castilian followers in Valencia and began to harass the ʿAbbādid domain. As a measure of protection against his suzerain Alfonso VI and the Cid, al-Muʿtamid at this time committed the fatal error of inviting as an ally from Morocco the powerful leader of the Murābiṭs, Yūsuf ibn-Tāshfīn.[1] To his critics who foresaw the danger and warned him of the impossibility of "sheathing two swords in one scabbard", al-Muʿtamid replied that he would rather be a camel-driver in Africa than a swineherd in Castile.[2] These Berber Murābiṭs, in whose veins some negro blood flowed, were now in power from Algiers to Senegal.

Yūsuf accepted the invitation. He marched unopposed through southern Spain, met Alfonso VI at al-Zallāqah,[3] near Badajoz, and with about twenty thousand men inflicted on him, October 23, 1086, a humiliating defeat. The Christian monarch and but three hundred of his horse barely escaped with their lives, leaving enough dead to form a tower of heads which was used as a minaret by the rejoicing Moslems.[4] The Berber chief shipped some forty thousand heads across the straits as a trophy. A wave of enthusiasm spread over Moslem Spain, and the proud ibn-Tāshfīn, who could not understand the flowery eulogies of the Sevillan poets, returned to Africa in accordance with his previous promise. Not long afterwards, however, the Murābiṭ chief, who with his Saharan hordes had tasted enough of the delicacies of civilized Spain to whet their appetites for more and render the barrenness of the desert more distasteful than ever before, came back, but this time as a conqueror rather than ally. In November 1090 he entered Granada; in the following year he took Seville and other leading towns. The whole of Moslem Spain was annexed with the exception of Toledo, which remained in Christian hands, and Saragossa, where the banu-Hūd were

[1] For the letter of invitation see Maqqari, vol. ii, p. 674.

[2] Maqqari, vol. ii, p. 678; Dozy, *Scriptorum*, vol. ii, p. 8; Korʾan 2 : 168.

[3] Sacralias, modern Sagrajas. See Marrākushi, pp. 93-4; ibn-Khaldūn, vol. vi, pp. 186-7; tr. de Slane, *Berbères*, vol. ii, pp. 78-9; ibn-Khallikān, vol. ii, p. 415; ibn-al-Athīr, vol. x, pp. 101-2; ibn-abi-Zarʿ, *Rawḍ al-Qirṭās*, vol. i, pp. 93 *seq*.

[4] Ibn-al-Khaṭīb, *al-Ḥulal al-Mawshīyah fi Dhikr al-Akhbār al-Marrākushīyah* (Tunis, 1329), p. 43, estimates the number of Christian victims at 300,000.

allowed to subsist. Al-Muʿtamid was sent to Morocco, where he lived in chains and utter destitution, sharing his exile with Iʿtimād and his daughters, who spent their time spinning to earn a living.[1] One day the fallen monarch noticed a procession going to the mosque to pray for rain and the old poet in him, still alive, improvised these pathetic lines:

> And forth they went imploring God for rain;
> "My tears," I said, "could serve you for a flood."
> "In truth," they cried, "your tears might well contain
> Sufficiency; but they are dyed with blood." [2]

In 1095 this last of the ʿAbbādids died in Aghmāt. The period of Berber hegemony in Spain had begun.

The Murābiṭs

The Murābiṭs (Almoravides) were originally a religious military brotherhood established in the middle of the eleventh century by a pious Moslem in a *ribāṭ* (whence Murābiṭ),[3] fortified monastery, on an island in the lower Senegal. The first recruits were mainly from the Lamtūnah, a branch of the Ṣanhājah tribe, whose members lived as nomads in the vast wastes of the Sahara and, as their descendants the Ṭawāriq (Touaregs) of south Algeria still do to the present day, wore veils covering the face below the eyes. This strange custom[4] among their men gave rise to the other name *Mulaththamūn* (veil-wearers), sometimes given to the Murābiṭs. Starting with about a thousand warrior "monks", the Murābiṭs forced one tribe after another, including some negro tribes, to accept Islam and in a few years established themselves as masters of all north-western Africa and finally of Spain.[5] Their story serves as another illustration in Islam of what can be produced by the marriage of the sword to religion.[6]

Yūsuf ibn-Tāshfīn (reigned 1061–1106), one of the builders of the Murābiṭ empire, founded in 1062 the city of Marrākush (Morocco, Marrakesh), which became his and his successors' capital.[7] In Spain Seville, instead of Cordova, functioned as a

[1] Ibn-Khallikān, vol. ii, p. 419; ibn-Khāqān, p. 25; ibn-al-Khaṭīb, *Iḥāṭah*, vol. ii, p. 83; Dozy, *Scriptorum*, vol. i, pp. 63-4, vol. ii, p. 151.
[2] Dozy, *Scriptorum*, vol. i, p. 383.
[3] Fr. *marabout* devotee, is a corruption of this word.
[4] Consult ibn-al-Athīr, vol. ix, pp. 428-9; ibn-al-Khaṭīb, *Ḥulal*, p. 10.
[5] The Berber tribe of Dalīm in Morocco claims descent from al-Murābiṭs.
[6] Ibn-abi-Zarʿ, vol. i, pp. 75-87; ibn-Khaldūn, vol. vi, pp. 181-2; ibn-al-Athīr, vol. ix, pp. 425-7.
[7] Ibn abi-Zarʿ, vol. i, pp. 88-9; ibn-Khaldūn, vol. vi, p. 184 = de Slane, vol. ii, p. 73.

subsidiary capital. The Murābiṭ sovereigns reserved for themselves all temporal power and bore the title amīr al-Muslimīn,[1] but in matters spiritual acknowledged the supreme authority of the 'Abbāsid caliph in Baghdād,[2] an authority which had been discarded at the advent of the Umayyad régime. For more than half a century the Murābiṭ power was supreme in north-western Africa and southern Spain. For the first time in history a Berber people was playing a leading rôle on the world's stage.

Coinage

The later Murābiṭ dinar bore the title *amīr al-Muslimīn* on the obverse, with a reference to the 'Abbāsid caliph preceded by the title *imām* on the reverse. King Alfonso VIII of Leon and Castile (1158–1214) imitated it, retaining its Arabic inscription but adapting its legend to the Christian formulas. On it he appeared as *amīr al-Qatūlaqīn* (the commander of the Catholics) and the pope in Rome as the *imām al-bī'ah al-Masīḥīyah* (the leader of the Christian Church). The coin was issued "in the name of the Father, the Son and the Holy Ghost, one only God" in place of the corresponding Moslem formula, and "whosoever believeth and is baptized shall be saved" stood in place of the denunciation of those who refused to accept Islam.

Persecution

Under the Murābiṭs, fresh converts to Islam and heirs to a barbarian legacy not yet dead, an outburst of religious fervour on the part of theological zealots resulted at the beginning of the twelfth century in suffering for many Christians, Jews and even liberal Moslems. Under the devout 'Ali (1106–43), Yūsuf's son and successor, al-Ghazzāli's works were put on the black list or committed to the flames in Spain and al-Maghrib,[3] because of remarks considered derogatory to theologians (*faqīhs*), including those of the Mālikite school of jurisprudence favoured by the Murābiṭs. Al-Ghazzāli, however, had headed the list of Eastern divines who expressed unreservedly their approval of the Andalusian *faqīhs*' legal opinion that Yūsuf ibn-Tāshfīn was absolved from any pledges he had made to the party kings of Moslem Spain and that it was not only his right but his duty to dethrone them.[4] At Lucena, termed by al-Idrīsi[5] a Jewish city, the inhabitants, who were the wealthiest of their co-religionists in the Moslem world, were called upon by the

[1] Ibn-abi-Zar', vol. i, pp. 88, 96 ibn-Khaldūn, vol. vi, p. 188.
[2] Marrākushi, p. 64.
[3] *Ibid.* p. 123; see *Iḥyā'*, vol. i, pp. 28-38.
[4] Ibn-Khaldūn, vol. vi, p. 187.
[5] *Ṣifat al-Maghrib*, ed. Dozy and de Goeje (Leyden, 1866), p. 205.

founder of the Murābiṭ power in Spain to meet out of their pockets the deficit in the public treasury. Under the Umayyads the legal status of the Spanish Jews had greatly improved over that of Visigothic days and their number had increased. During the caliphate of 'Abd-al-Raḥmān III and his son al-Ḥakam, under the influence of whose treasurer Ḥasdāy ben-Shaprūṭ many Jews came from the East, Cordova became the centre of a talmudic school whose foundation marks the beginning of the flowering of Andalusian Jewish culture.[1] The Spanish Jews used the language and dress of the Arabs and followed the same manners.

The would-be Arabs

The Mozarabs, that element in the population of Spain which had assimilated itself in language and ways of living to the conquering Moslems but retained its Christian faith, had assumed by this time large proportions and therefore became the special object of restrictions. In the large cities these Arabicized Christians lived in quarters of their own, kept under the Umayyads their special magistrates[2] and wore no distinctive clothes. Usually they bore double names: one Arabic and familiar, the other Latin or Spanish and more formal. They even practised circumcision and kept harems. Most of the Mozarabs were bilingual, their native tongue being the Romance patois derived from Low Latin and destined to become Spanish. In such cities as Toledo they continued in the use of Arabic as the written language of law and business for two centuries after the Christian conquest by Alfonso VI in 1085.[3] This Alfonso, like several of his successors, stamped his coins with Arabic characters. One of the early kings of Aragon, Peter I († 1104), could write only in Arabic script. Even when writing Latin the Mozarabs used Arabic letters. Not long after the Moslem conquest parts of the Bible were apparently translated into Arabic,[4] and in 946 Isaak Velasquez of Cordova translated Luke and presumably the other three Gospels from Latin.[5]

[1] Ibn-abi-Uṣaybi'ah, vol. ii, p. 50.

[2] The two chief officials were called in Arabic *qūmis* (L. *comes*, Sp. *conde*) and *qāḍi al-Naṣāra* (the judge of the Christians).

[3] For some of their writings consult Angel González Palencia, *Los Mozárabes de Toledo en los siglos XII y XIII*, 4 vols. (Madrid, 1926–30).

[4] See above, p. 516.

[5] Georg Graf, *Die Christlich-arabische Literatur bis zur fränkischen Zeit* (Freiburg in Breisgau, 1905), p. 27.

On a *fatwa* (religious opinion) from his theologians Yūsuf in 1099 ordered a beautiful church, built in the Visigothic age and now possessed by the Mozarabs of Granada, to be levelled to the ground. These same Granadans in 1126 were put to the sword or banished to Morocco because they had entered into communication with a Christian sovereign of the north. Eleven years later a second expulsion of Mozarabs left few of them in Spain.

Racially the line of demarcation between Mozarabs and Moslems in the urban communities was at this time hard to draw. From the beginning, as we have noted before, the real Arabians in the army of conquest and among the colonists were comparatively few, limited to those in command and in high office. The number of women accompanying the army and first immigrants was necessarily small. Disease and fighting decimated the early conquerors and settlers. After the fourth generation the Arabian blood must have become greatly diluted by intermarriage with native women. Concubines, slaves and prisoners of war helped the process of amalgamation, as in other conquered lands. The researches of Ribera[1] have shown that even the Moslems of Spain, the so-called Moors, were overwhelmingly of Spanish blood. In the opinion of this modern Spanish scholar the veins of Hishām II, the third Umayyad caliph, could not have contained more than a thousandth part of Arabian blood.

My Cid the Challenger

It was in the early Murābiṭ period that the most colourful of Mozarabs and at the same time most celebrated of the heroes of Spanish chivalry, Rodrigo Díaz de Bivar, better known as the Cid,[2] carried on his military exploits. A descendant of a noble Castilian family, Rodrigo entered first the service of Alfonso VI but was later (1081) banished by him from the Castilian dominions. He then entered upon a knightly career espousing now the cause of this faction, now that of another and fighting Moslems or co-religionists as the occasion arose. In his behaviour he was almost as much Moslem as Christian. While in the service of the Hūdid dynasty at Saragossa, Rodrigo covered himself with glory and won from his Moslem soldiers the title

[1] Julián Ribera y Terragó, *Disertaciones y opúsculos* (Madrid, 1928), vol. i, pp. 12-35, 109-12.

[2] From Ar. *sayyid*, colloquial *sīd*, lord.

el Cid Campeador.[1] The crowning achievement of My Cid the Challenger was his occupation in 1094 of Valencia, which he held in defiance of the Murābiṭ attacks until his death in 1099. In romance the Cid has lived as the national hero of Spain, the exemplar of its chivalry and its champion against the infidel. Spanish ballads surrounded his name with a saintly aureole of virtue; Philip II († 1598) even presented it to the pope for canonization. The epic *Cantar de mio Cid* woven around the Cid's name in the middle of the twelfth century is one of the grandest and oldest of Spanish poems, one that deeply influenced Spanish thought throughout subsequent ages and contributed powerfully to the establishment of the native language and the consolidation of the national character.

Collapse of the Murābiṭs

The Murābiṭ dynasty in Spain (1090–1147),[2] as was to be expected, was short-lived. It fulfilled the fated cycle of Asiatic and African monarchies with rapidity: a generation of efficient militarism followed by sloth and corruption leading to disintegration and fall. Its rough Berbers, raised on the privations of desert life and suddenly transported to the luxurious regions of Morocco and Andalusia, soon succumbed to the vices of civilization and became enervated, even effeminate. They entered Spain at a time when intellectual pleasures among the Arabs had long since replaced the love of war and thirst for conquest. This gave the African conquerors their opportunity for settling in the land and at the same time proved their undoing, since it gave them contact with a refined civilization for the assimilation of which they were in nowise prepared. In turn they fell an easy prey to their more vigorous kinsmen the Muwaḥḥids. Throughout the twelfth century and well into the first half of the thirteenth Spain

[1] Sp. equivalent of Ar. *mubāriz*, champion. See above, pp. 88, 173. In Ar Campeador was rendered al-Kanbīṭūr; ibn-Bassām, "al-Dhakhīrah", in Dozy, *Recherches*, vol. ii, pp. v, ix; al-Qanbīṭūr, in ibn-ʻIdhāri, vol. iii, pp. 305-6 (supplement). Cf. Maqqari, vol. ii, p. 754.

[2] (Tāshfīn)
|
1. Yūsuf (1090–1106)
|
2. ʻAli (1106–43)
|
- 3. Tāshfīn (1143–6)
  |
  4. Ibrāhīm (1146)
- 5. Isḥāq (1146–7)

was under the successive rule of these two Berber dynasties, whose seat was Morocco.

The Muwaḥḥids

As in the case of the Murābiṭ, the Muwaḥḥid dynasty had its inception in a politico-religious movement founded by a Berber. This was Muḥammad ibn-Tūmart (*ca.* 1078–*ca.* 1130) of the Maṣmūdah tribe.[1] Muḥammad assumed the symbolic title of al-Mahdi[2] and proclaimed himself the prophet sent to restore Islam to its pure and original orthodoxy. He preached among his own and other wild tribes of the Moroccan Atlas the doctrine of *tawḥīd*, the unity of God and the spiritual conception of Him, as a protest against the excessive anthropomorphism then prevalent in Islam. Accordingly his followers were called al-Muwaḥḥidūn.[3] Small, ugly and misshapen, this son of a mosque lamplighter lived the life of an ascetic, and opposed music, drinking and other manifestations of laxity. When a young man, his zeal led him to assault in the streets of Fās (Fez) a sister of the reigning Murābiṭ 'Ali ibn-Yūsuf because she went unveiled.[4]

Founder of the Muwaḥḥid dynasty

In 1130 ibn-Tūmart was succeeded by his friend and general 'Abd-al-Mu'min ibn-'Ali, son of a potter of the Zanātah tribe, who became the caliph-founder of the Muwaḥḥid dynasty, the greatest Morocco ever knew, and of an empire second to none in the annals of Africa. In accordance with the doctrine that theirs was the only community of true believers, these unitarian Moslems now carried fire and sword throughout Morocco and adjacent lands. In 1144–1146 'Abd-al-Mu'min annihilated the Murābiṭ army near Tilimsān (Tlemcen), which he captured together with Fās, Ceuta, Tangier and Aghmāt, and after an eleven-month siege of Marrākush in 1146–1147 he put an end to the Murābiṭ dynasty.[5] The last of the Murābiṭ line, a boy named Isḥāq ibn-'Ali, grandson of the founder of the empire, was executed by the Muwaḥḥid caliph (*amīr al-mu'minīn*) in spite of his childish tears.[6] Marrakesh now became the Muwaḥḥid capital. In 1145 'Abd-al-Mu'min had dispatched into Spain,

[1] Ibn-Khaldūn, vol. vi, p. 225; ibn-al-Athīr, vol. x, p. 400. Cf. Marrākushi, p. 128; ibn-abi-Zar', vol. i, p. 110; ibn-Khallikān, vol. ii, p. 426.

[2] Ibn-al-Khaṭīb, *Ḥulal*, p. 78; *Kitāb Muḥammad ibn-Tūmart*, ed. I. Goldziher (Algiers, 1903), pp. 2-3.

[3] The unitarians, corrupted into Sp. Almohades.

[4] Ibn-Khaldūn, vol. vi, p. 228. Cf. ibn-Khallikān, vol. ii, p. 431.

[5] Marrākushi, pp. 145-6; ibn-Khallikān, vol. i, p. 557; ibn-abi-Dīnār, *al-Mu'nis fi Akhbār Ifrīqiyah wa-Tūnis* (Tunis, 1286), p. 120.

[6] Ibn-al-Athīr, vol. x, pp. 412-13.

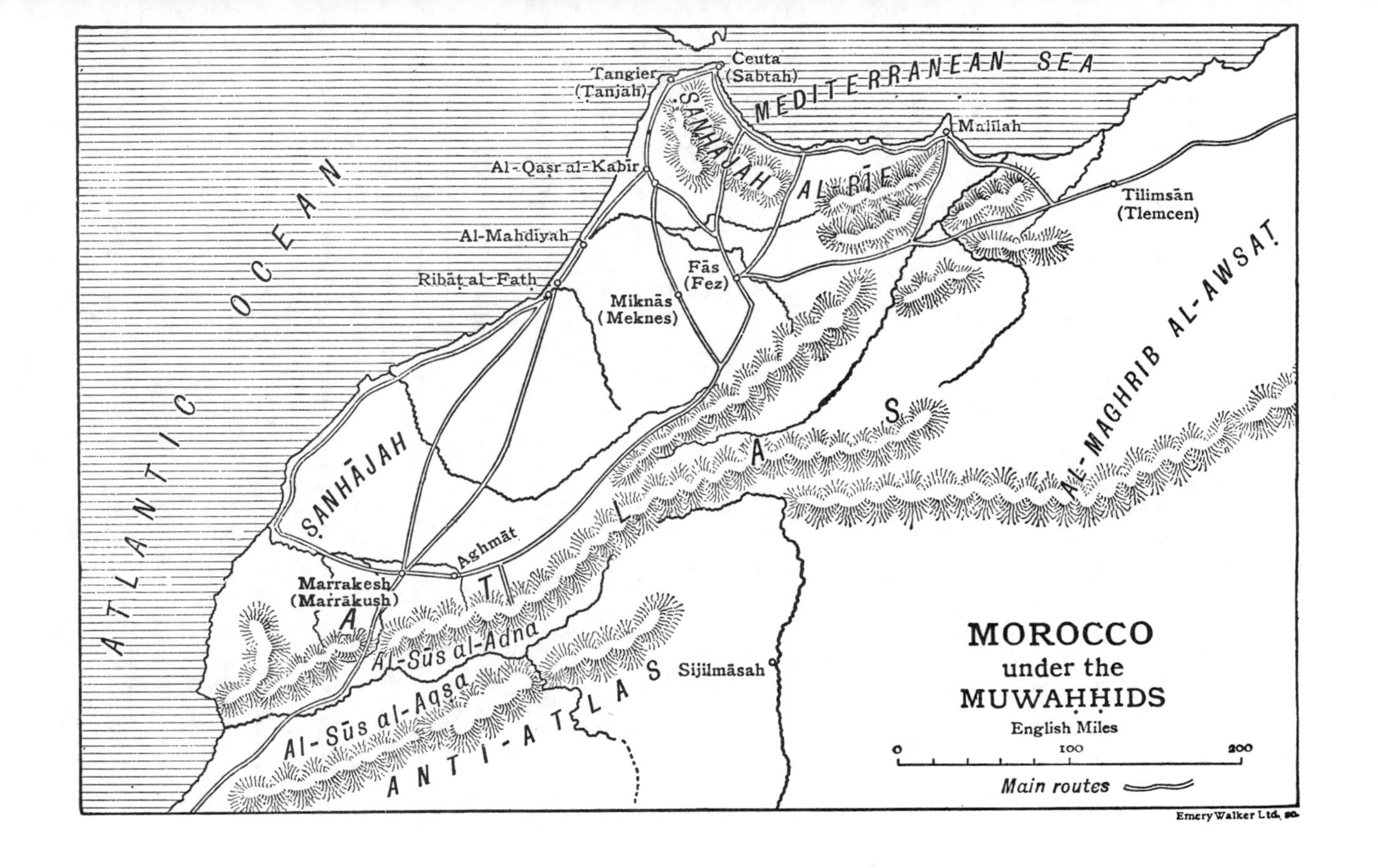
MOROCCO
under the
MUWAHHIDS
English Miles
0
100
200
Main routes
MEDITERRANEAN SEA
ATLANTIC OCEAN
AL-MAGHRIB AL-AWSAT
Ceuta
(Sabtah)
Tangier
(Tanjah)
Malilah
Tilimsān
(Tlemcen)
Al-Qasr al-Kabir
Al-Mahdiyah
Ribāt al-Fath
Fās
(Fez)
Miknās
(Meknes)
SANHĀJAH
AL RĪF
SANHĀJAH
Aghmāt
Marrakesh
(Marrākush)
ATLAS
Al-Sūs al-Adna
Al-Sūs al-Aqsa
ANTI-ATLAS
Sijilmāsah
Emery Walker Ltd. sc.

where political corruption, brigandage and dissatisfaction were rife, an army which in the course of five years reduced the whole Moslem part of the peninsula. The Balearic Isles, attached to the Umayyad amīrate since 903, alone remained for a few more years in the hands of the last representatives of the Murābiṭs.

Master of Morocco and Spain, ʿAbd-al-Muʾmin pushed his conquests in 1152 to Algeria, in 1158 to Tunisia and in 1160 to Tripoli. Thus for the first time in Moslem history the whole coast from the Atlantic to the frontier of Egypt became united with Andalusia as an independent empire. The Murābiṭ empire, on the other hand, had included, besides Spain, only Morocco and part of Algeria. From every pulpit in this immense new empire Friday prayers were read in the name of the Mahdi or his caliph instead of in that of the ʿAbbāsid caliph as heretofore.[1]

Al-Manṣūr

After a long and glorious reign ʿAbd-al-Muʾmin died in 1163. Among the greatest and best known of his successors was his grandson abu-Yūsuf Yaʿqūb al-Manṣūr (1184–99), who, like many other Berber rulers, was the son of a Christian slave.[2] It was to al-Manṣūr's court that Ṣalāḥ-al-Dīn (Saladin) sent with valuable presents an embassy headed by a nephew of Usāmah ibn-Munqidh. Ṣalāḥ-al-Dīn, who recognized the ʿAbbāsid caliph, accredited the embassy to *amīr al-Muslimīn*, instead of *amīr al-muʾminīn*, which at first made al-Manṣūr hesitate to act. Later, however, he is said to have dispatched 180 vessels to assist the Moslems against the Crusaders.[3]

The existing architectural monuments of al-Manṣūr are among the most remarkable in either Morocco or Spain. In Seville, to which the Muwaḥḥids transferred their capital in 1170,[4] his accession was marked by the erection of the tower, now known as the Giralda, in connection with the great mosque. This mosque, begun in 1172 and completed in 1195, is now superseded by the cathedral. In Morocco he built Ribāṭ al-Fatḥ, modelled on Alexandria,[5] and in Marrakesh he built a hospital which his contemporary al-Marrākushi[6] thought had no equal in the world.[7]

[1] For a Muwaḥḥid *khuṭbah* see Marrākushi, pp. 250-51.
[2] Marrākushi, p. 189; ibn-abi-Zarʿ, vol. i, p. 142; ibn-abi-Dīnār, pp. 116-17.
[3] Ibn-Khallikān, vol. iii, p. 381; ibn-Khaldūn, vol. vi, p. 246.
[4] Maqqari, vol. ii, p. 693. [5] Ibn-Khallikān, vol. iii, p. 379. [6] P. 209.
[7] For his other buildings see ibn-abi-Zarʿ, vol. i, pp. 143, 151-2.

The chief anxiety of the Muwaḥḥid caliphs in Spain was the prosecution of the holy war, but they were not particularly successful. The disastrous defeat at Las Navas de Tolosa in 1212 resulted in their expulsion from the peninsula. This battle, called by the Arabs that of al-ʿUqāb (hill), was fought about seventy miles east of Cordova. The Christian army, in which Aragon was represented by its king, Navarre by its king and Portugal by a contingent of Templars and other knights, was led by Alfonso VIII of Castile, whose own forces included French Crusaders. The Caliph Muḥammad al-Nāṣir (1199–1214), son of al-Manṣūr, led the Arab troops, of which only one thousand out of "600,000" escaped.[1] Al-Nāṣir fled to Marrākush, where he died two years later. The overthrow of the Muwaḥḥid régime in Spain was complete. All Moslem Spain lay at the feet of the conquerors. Gradually it was parcelled out among the ever-encroaching Christian sovereigns and local Moslem dynasts. Among the latter the Naṣrids of Granada formed the most conspicuous group and proved the last representative of Moslem authority in the peninsula.

In Morocco al-Nāṣir's successors, nine in number and all descendants of ʿAbd-al-Mu'min,[2] lasted until their capital Marrakesh was captured in 1269 by the semi-nomadic Berber tribe of banu-Marīn, a branch of the Zanātah.[3]

Banu-Naṣr

The founder of the Naṣrid dynasty (1232–1492), which traces its descent to the eminent Khazraj tribe of al-Madīnah, was Muḥammad ibn-Yūsuf ibn-Naṣr, commonly known as ibn-al-Aḥmar. Hence the other name of the family, banu-al-Aḥmar. Ibn-Khaldūn,[4] who resided for a time at Granada and was attached to the court of one of ibn-al-Aḥmar's successors, gives us a detailed account of the career of Muḥammad. After the collapse of the Muwaḥḥid régime, as the Castilians were setting one Moslem chieftain against another and destroying each in turn, Muḥammad entered into alliance with the Christians and contrived to carve for himself a state around Granada which to

[1] Maqqari, vol. ii, p. 696. Cf. Marrākushi, p. 236; ibn-abi-Zarʿ, vol. i, p. 159. A contemporary English chronicler claims that al-Nāṣir received in 1213 from King John, of Magna Charta fame and brother of Cœur de Lion, an embassy offering to hold England under tribute to him and to exchange the Christian faith for Islam.

[2] For lists consult al-Zarkashi, *Ta'rīkh al-Dawlatayn al-Muwaḥḥidīyah w-al-Ḥafṣīyah* (Tunis, 1289); Lane-Poole, *Dynasties*, pp. 47-8; de Zambaur, pp. 73, 74.

[3] Ibn-abi-Zarʿ, vol. i, pp. 174-5, 184.

[4] Vol. iv, pp. 170-72. See also ibn-al-Khaṭīb, *Lamḥah*, pp. 30 *seq.*

a limited extent revived and continued the glories of Seville and for the next two and a half centuries acted as the champion of Islam in its defensive struggle against the rising power of Christianity.

Muḥammad (1232–73) assumed the title of al-Ghālib (the overcomer) and chose Granada for his seat of government. He as well as his successors paid homage and tribute to the Castilian crown. By the Arabs Granada (Gharnāṭah), than which no city in Andalusia was more favoured in site and climate,[1] was likened to Damascus, and in it many Syrians and Jews had settled.[2] Its plain (*marj*), the Vega, fed by abundant streams, presented a rare spectacle of perpetual verdure and beauty, and corresponded to the Ghūṭah of Damascus.[3] At the close of the Naṣrid period it housed about half a million within its walls. Lisān-al-Dīn ibn-al-Khaṭīb († 1374), the hero of al-Maqqari, vizir at the Naṣrid court and literary historian of the dynasty, has left us a number of monographs on the sovereigns and savants of Granada which supply us with interesting details about the capital.

Alhambra

On a hilly terrace on the south-east border of this beautiful city al-Ghālib built on the remains of an earlier Umayyad citadel his world-renowned castle called al-Ḥamrā' (Sp. Alhambra), the red one, from the red stucco used in its construction and not from his personal nickname as formerly supposed. Enlarged and further embellished by three of his successors, the Alhambra became one of the architectural monuments of Spain. Standing sentinel over the surrounding plain, like the Acropolis of Athens, this citadel-palace, with its superb decorations and arabesque mouldings, still excites universal admiration. In it the Naṣrids maintained a court which revived for a time the glory of Moslem Spain in Umayyad and ʿAbbādid days. Their patronage of art and learning attracted many scholars, especially from North Africa. Their encouragement of commerce, notably the silk trade with Italy, rendered Granada the wealthiest city of Spain. Under them the capital became an asylum for Moslems fleeing from Christian attacks as well as heir to Cordova as home of art and science. But these were the last rays of the setting sun of Spanish Islam.

[1] Cf. ibn-al-Khaṭīb, *Iḥāṭah*, vol. i, p. 13.
[2] Maqqari, vol. i, pp. 109, 721. Cf. ibn-Jubayr, pp. 16-17. See above, p. 502.
[3] Ibn-al-Khaṭīb, *Lamḥah*, p. 13; see above, p. 231.

The last days of Granada

The period of Christian reconquest (*reconquista*) started as early as the fall of the Umayyad caliphate in the eleventh century. In fact, Spanish historians consider the battle of Covadonga in 718, in which the Asturian chieftain Pelayo checked Moslem advance, as marking the actual beginning of reconquest. Had the Moslems in the eighth century destroyed the last vestiges of Christian power in the mountainous north, the subsequent story of Spain might have been entirely different. Impeded at first by constant friction among the Christian chiefs of the north, the process of reclamation was greatly accelerated by the final union of Castile and Leon in 1230. By the middle of the thirteenth century the reconquest, with the exception of Granada, was practically completed. Toledo fell in 1085; Cordova followed in 1236 and Seville in 1248.

After the middle of the thirteenth century two major processes were in operation: the Christianizing of Spain and its unification. Christianizing the country was different from reconquering and unifying it. The only part of the peninsula where Islam had struck root was that where the earlier Semitic, Carthaginian, civilization had once flourished. The same was true of Sicily, a fact not without significance. In general the line of cleavage between Islam and Christianity coincided with the ancient line between the Punic and Occidental civilizations. By the thirteenth century many Moslems throughout the land had become subject to the Christians either by conquest or treaty, but had otherwise preserved their laws and religion. Such Moslems were designated Mudejars.[1] Many of the Mudejars were now forgetting their Arabic, adopting exclusively the Romance tongue and becoming more or less assimilated to the Christians.

Progress toward the final unification of Spain was slow but sure. At this time the Christian territory was made up of but two kingdoms, Castile and Aragon. The marriage in 1469 of Ferdinand of Aragon to Isabella of Castile united permanently the crowns of these two kingdoms. This union struck the note of doom for Moslem power in Spain. The Naṣrid sultans, as they were called,[2] were by no means able to cope with the increasing danger. The last of them were involved in dynastic troubles which rendered

[1] From Ar. *mudajjan*, one allowed (by the Christian conquerors) to remain where he is on condition that he pays tribute.

[2] Ibn-Khaldūn, vol. iv, p. 172.

From J. von Pflugk-Harttung, "Weltgeschichte: Orient" (Verlag Ullstein, Berlin)

THE ALHAMBRA AND GRANADA TODAY

their position still more precarious. Of the twenty-one sultans [1] who ruled from 1232 to 1492. six ruled twice and one, Muḥammad VIII al-Mutamassik, ruled thrice (1417–27, 1429–32, 1432–44), giving an average of about nine years for each of the twenty-eight reigns. Final ruin was hastened by the recklessness of the nineteenth sulṭan, 'Ali abu-al-Ḥasan (Sp. Alboacen, 1461–82, 1483–5), who not only refused to pay the customary tribute but commenced hostilities by attacking Castilian territory. In reprisal Ferdinand in 1482 surprised and took al-Ḥammah,[2] which stood at the foot of the Sierra de Alhama and guarded the south-western entrance into the Granadan domain. At this juncture a son of abu-al-Ḥasan, Muḥammad abu-'Abdullāh, instigated by his mother, Fāṭimah,[3] who was jealous of a Spanish[4] Christian concubine to whose children the royal husband was devoted, raised the banner of rebellion against his father. Supported by the garrison, the rebel son seized the Alhambra in 1482 and made himself master of Granada. In the following year this eleventh Muḥammad of the dynasty, whose surname abu-'Abdullāh was corrupted into the Spanish Boabdil, had the temerity to attack the Castilian town of Lucena, where he was beaten and taken captive. Abu-al-Ḥasan then reinstated himself on the Granadan throne and ruled until 1485, when he abdicated in favour of his more able brother Muḥammad XII, nicknamed al-Zaghall (valiant), governor of Malaga.[5] In their prisoner abu-'Abdullāh, Ferdinand and Isabella saw a perfect tool for effecting the ultimate destruction of the ill-fated Moslem kingdom. Supplied with Castilian men and money, abu-'Abdullāh occupied in 1486 part of his uncle's capital and once more plunged the unlucky Granada, which presented the spectacle of having two sultans at the same time, in a destructive civil war. The legend relating to the destruction of the patriotic

[1] For lists consult Lane-Poole, *Dynasties*, pp. 28-9; Zambaur, pp. 58-9.
[2] Ar. for "hot spring", whence Sp. Alhama. Al-Ḥāmmah in Maqqari, vol. ii, p. 801.
[3] Not 'Ā'ishah; L. S. de Lucena in *al-Andalus*, vol. xii (1947), pp. 359 *seq.*
[4] *Rūmīyah* in Maqqari, vol. ii, p. 803.
[5] Genealogical table of the last Naṣrids:

18. Sa'd al-Musta'īn (1445–6, 1453–61)

19. 'Ali abu-al-Ḥasan (1461–82, 1483–5) — 20. Muḥammad XII al-Zaghall (1485–6)

21. Muḥammad XI abu-'Abdullāh (1482–3, 1486–92)

noble family of banu-Sarrāj (Abencerrage) by abu-ʿAbdullāh, at Alhambra, belongs to this period in the mythical history of the last days of Granada.

In the meantime the Castilian army was advancing. One town after another fell before it. Malaga was reduced in the following year and many of its people were sold into slavery. The circle was being narrowed around the doomed capital. Al-Zaghall made a few unsuccessful stands against the army of Ferdinand, but abu-ʿAbdullāh acted as its ally. In his despair al-Zaghall made a final but fruitless appeal to the Moslem sovereigns of Africa, just then busy fighting among themselves. At last he surrendered and retired into Tilimsān,[1] where he passed the remainder of his days in misery and destitution, wearing, we are told, on his mendicant rags, a badge proclaiming, "This is the hapless king of Andalusia". Only the city of Granada now remained in Moslem hands.

No sooner was al-Zaghall thus disposed of than abu-ʿAbdullāh was requested (1490) by his patrons to surrender the city. Under the inspiration of a valiant leader the pusillanimous abu-ʿAbdullāh refused to comply. In the spring of the following year Ferdinand with an army of 10,000 horse again entered the plain of Granada. As in the preceding year he destroyed the crops and orchards and drew the cordon tighter round the last stronghold of Islam in Spain. The siege was pressed into a blockade intended to starve the city into surrender.

When winter advanced with its extreme cold and heavy snow all access from outside was barred, food became scarce, prices soared and misery prevailed. In the meantime the enemy had seized every patch of ground outside the city walls and made it impossible for the besieged to plant or gather any crops. Conditions moved from bad to worse . . . until by the month of Ṣafar [December 1491] the privations of the people had reached their extreme.[2]

Finally the garrison agreed to surrender, if not relieved within a period of two months, on the following terms: The sultan with all his officers and people would take the oath of obedience to the Castilian sovereigns; abu-ʿAbdullāh would receive an estate in al-Basharāt;[3] the Moslems would be left secure in person

[1] Maqqari, vol. ii, p. 810. [2] *Ibid* p. 811.

[3] Sp. Alpujarras. The term, meaning "pastures", included the mountainous foreland south of the Sierra Nevada as far as the Mediterranean.

under their laws and free in the exercise of their religion.[1] The period of grace having expired without any sign of relief from the Turks or Africans, the Castilians entered Granada on January 2, 1492, and "the cross supplanted the crescent" on its towers.[2] The sultan with his queen, richly dressed, left his red fortress and departed in the midst of a gorgeous retinue, never to return. As he rode away he turned to take a last look at his capital, sighed and burst into tears. His mother, hitherto his evil genius, allegedly turned upon him with the words, "Thou dost well to weep like a woman for what thou couldst not defend like a man". The rocky height whence he took his sad farewell look is still known by the name El Último Suspiro del Moro, the last sigh of the Moor.

Abu-ʿAbdullāh made his home first on his allotted estate, but later retired to Fās, where he died in 1533–4 and where his descendants in the year in which al-Maqqari[3] was compiling his history (1627–8) were still objects of charity, "counted among the beggars".

Morisco persecution

Their Catholic Majesties Ferdinand and Isabella failed to abide by the terms of the capitulation. Under the leadership of the queen's confessor Cardinal Ximénez de Cisneros,[4] a campaign of forced conversion was inaugurated in 1499. The cardinal at first tried to withdraw from circulation Arabic books dealing with Islam by burning them. Granada was the scene of a bonfire of Arabic manuscripts. The Inquisition was then instituted and kept busy. All Moslems who remained in the country after the capture of Granada were now called Moriscos,[5] a term applied originally to Spaniards converted into Islam. The Moslem Spaniards spoke a Romance dialect but employed

[1] Cf. *Akhbār al-ʿAṣr fi Inqiḍā' Dawlat bani-Naṣr*, ed. M. J. Müller (Münich, 1863), p. 49.

[2] Legend makes Alhambra in that same year the scene of Christopher Columbus' appeal to Queen Isabella for a subsidy for his maritime adventure, the greatest in history, which resulted in the discovery of America.

[3] Vol. ii, pp. 814-15.

[4] His greatest service was the printing (1502–17) of the Complutensian Polyglot, the first edition of the Bible in the original text with translation.

[5] Sp. for "little Moors". The Romans called Western Africa Mauretania and its inhabitants Mauri (presumably of Phœnician origin meaning "western"), whence Sp. *Moro*, Eng. Moor. The Berbers, therefore, were the Moors proper, but the term was conventionally applied to all Moslems of Spain and north-western Africa. The half-million Moslems of the Philippines are still known by the name Moros, given them by the Spaniards on the discovery of the islands by Magellan in 1521.

the Arabic script.[1] Many, if not most, Moriscos were of course of Spanish descent but all were now "reminded" that their ancestors had been Christians and that they must either submit to baptism or suffer the consequences. The Mudejars were grouped with the Moriscos and many became crypto-Moslems, professing Christianity but secretly practising Islam. Some would come home from their Christian weddings to be married secretly after the Moslem rite; many would adopt a Christian name for public and an Arabic one for private use. As early as 1501 a royal decree was issued that all Moslems in Castile and Leon should either recant or leave Spain, but evidently it was not strictly applied. In 1526 the Moslems of Aragon were confronted with the same alternatives. In 1556 Philip II promulgated a law requiring the remaining Moslems to abandon at once their language, worship, institutions and manner of life. He even ordered the destruction of the Spanish baths as a relic of infidelity. A rising, the second of its kind, started in Granada and spread to the neighbouring mountains, but was put down. The final order of expulsion was signed by Philip III in 1609, resulting in the forcible deportation *en masse* of practically all Moslems on Spanish soil. Some half a million are said to have suffered this fate and landed on the shores of Africa or to have taken ship to more distant lands of Islam. It was mainly from these Moriscos that the ranks of the Moroccan corsairs were recruited. Between the fall of Granada and the first decade of the seventeenth century it is estimated that about three million Moslems were banished or executed. The Moorish problem was for ever solved for Spain, which thus became the conspicuous exception to the rule that wherever Arab civilization was planted there it was permanently fixed. "The Moors were banished; for a while Christian Spain shone, like the moon, with a borrowed light; then came the eclipse, and in that darkness Spain has grovelled ever since."[2]

[1] The literature left by Moriscos is varied and linguistically interesting. It is termed *aljamiado* from Ar. *al-ʿajamīyah*, foreign tongue. A collection of such manuscripts was found under the floor of an old house in Aragon, where they were apparently hidden from the officers of the Inquisition. These are the *Manuscritos árabes y aljamiados de la Biblioteca de la Junta*, ed. J. Ribera and M. Asín (Madrid, 1912). See A. R. Nykl, *A Compendium of Aljamiado Literature* (Paris, 1928).

[2] Lane-Poole, *Moors in Spain*, p. 280.

CHAPTER XL

INTELLECTUAL CONTRIBUTIONS

MOSLEM Spain wrote one of the brightest chapters in the intellectual history of medieval Europe. Between the middle of the eighth and the beginning of the thirteenth centuries, as we have noted before, the Arabic-speaking peoples were the main bearers of the torch of culture and civilization throughout the world. Moreover they were the medium through which ancient science and philosophy were recovered, supplemented and transmitted in such a way as to make possible the renaissance of Western Europe. In all this, Arabic Spain had a large share.

Language and literature

In the purely linguistic sciences, including philology, grammar and lexicography, the Arabs of al-Andalus lagged behind those of al-ʿIrāq. Al-Qāli (901–67), mentioned above as one of the eminent professors of the university of Cordova, was born in Armenia and educated in Baghdād. His chief disciple, Muḥammad ibn-al-Ḥasan al-Zubaydi [1] (928–89), belonged to a family that hailed from Ḥimṣ, but was himself born in Seville. Al-Zubaydi was appointed by al-Ḥakam to supervise the education of his young son Hishām, who later appointed him qāḍi and chief magistrate of Seville. Al-Zubaydi's chief work was a classified list of grammarians and philologists who had flourished up to his time; al-Suyūṭi made extensive use of it in his *Muzhir*. It should be recalled at this point that Hebrew grammar, which was based essentially on Arabic grammar (above, p. 43, n. 1) and to this day uses technical terms which are translations of corresponding Arabic terms, had its birth in Moslem Spain. Ḥayyūj Judah ben-David (Ar. abu-Zakarīyā' Yaḥya ibn-Dāwūd), the father of scientific Hebrew grammar, flourished in Cordova, where he died early in the eleventh century.

In literature the most distinguished author was ibn-ʿAbd-Rabbih (860–940) of Cordova, the laureate of ʿAbd-al-Raḥmān

[1] See Thaʿālibi, *Yatīmah*, vol. i, p. 409; ibn-Khallikān, vol. ii, pp. 338-40.

III.[1] Ibn-'Abd-Rabbih was descended from an enfranchised slave of Hishām I. His title to fame rests on the miscellaneous anthology he composed, *al-'Iqd al-Farīd*[2] (the unique necklace), which after *al-Aghāni* occupies first place among works on the literary history of the Arabs. But the greatest scholar and the most original thinker of Spanish Islam was 'Ali ibn-Ḥazm (994–1064), one of the two or three most fertile minds and most prolific writers of Islam. Ibn-Ḥazm claimed descent from a Persian client, but was in reality the grandson of a Spanish Moslem convert from Christianity. In his youth he adorned the tottering courts of 'Abd-al-Raḥmān al-Mustaẓhir and Hishām al-Mu'tadd[3] in the capacity of vizir, but on the ensuing dissolution of the Umayyad caliphate he retired to a life of seclusion and literary pursuit. Ibn-Khallikān[4] and al-Qifṭi[5] ascribe to him four hundred volumes on history, theology, tradition, logic, poetry and allied subjects. As an exponent of the Ẓāhirite (literalist) school of jurisprudence and theology, long since extinct, he was as tireless as he was vigorous in his literary activity. In his *Ṭawq al-Ḥamāmah*[6] (the dove's necklace), an anthology of love poems, he extols platonic love. The most valuable of his surviving works, however, is *al-Faṣl fi al-Milal w-al-Ahwā' w-al-Niḥal*[7] (the decisive word on sects, heterodoxies and denominations), which entitles him to the honour of being the first scholar in the field of comparative religion. In this work he pointed out difficulties in the biblical narratives which disturbed no other minds till the rise of higher criticism in the sixteenth century.

For the history of literature the period of the party kings, particularly of the 'Abbādids, Murābiṭs and Muwaḥḥids, was one of special importance. The cultural seed sown in the Umayyad age did not come into full fruition until then. The civil wars which closed the Umayyad period and the subsequent rise of new dynasties enabled such centres as Seville, Toledo and Granada to eclipse Cordova. From this last city Arabicized

[1] See Yāqūt, *Udabā'*, vol. ii, pp. 67-72; ibn-Khallikān, vol. i, pp. 56-8.

[2] Several editions, none critical. The one used here is in 3 vols. (Cairo, 1302).

[3] Yāqūt, *Udabā'*, vol. v, p. 87. [4] Vol. ii, p. 22. [5] P. 233.

[6] Ed. D. K. Pétrof (Leyden, 1914); tr. A. R. Nykl, *The Dove's Neck-Ring about Love and Lovers* (Paris, 1931).

[7] No scholarly edition. The one used here is in 5 vols. (Cairo, 1347–8). See Asin, *Abenházam de Córdoba y su historia crítica de las ideas religiosas*, 5 vols. (Madrid, 1927–32).

Christians, Mozarabs, quite conversant with Arabic literature, had communicated many elements of Arabic culture to the other kingdoms of the north and south. In prose the fables, tales and apologues, which began to flourish in Western Europe during the thirteenth century, present unmistakable analogies with earlier Arabic works, themselves of Indo-Persian origin. The delightful fables of *Kalīlah wa-Dimnah* were translated into Spanish for Alfonso the Wise (1252–84) of Castile and Leon, and shortly afterwards into Latin by a baptized Jew. A Persian translation became through French one of the sources of La Fontaine, as acknowledged by him. To the *maqāmah*, written in rhymed prose adorned with all manner of philological curiosity and intended to teach some moral lesson through the adventures of a cavalier-hero, the Spanish picaresque novel bears close affinity. But the most significant contribution of Arabic to the literature of medieval Europe was the influence it exercised by its form, which helped liberate Western imagination from a narrow, rigid discipline circumscribed by convention. The rich fantasy of Spanish literature betrays Arabic models, as does the wit of Cervantes' *Don Quixote*, whose author was once a prisoner in Algiers and jokingly claimed that the book had an Arabic original.

Poetry

Wherever and whenever the Arabic language was used there the passion for poetical composition was intense. Verses countless in number passed from mouth to mouth and were admired by high and low, not so much perhaps for their contents as for their music and exquisite diction. This sheer joy in the beauty and euphony of words, a characteristic of Arabic-speaking peoples, manifested itself on Spanish soil. The first Umayyad sovereign was a poet and so were several of his successors. Among the party kings al-Muʻtamid ibn-ʻAbbād was especially favoured by the Muses. Most of the sovereigns had laureates attached to their courts and took them along on their travels and wars. Seville boasted the largest number of graceful and inspired poets, but the flame had been kindled long before in Cordova and later shone brilliantly at Granada as long as that city remained the bulwark of Islam.

Aside from ibn-ʻAbd-Rabbih, ibn-Ḥazm and ibn-al-Khaṭīb, Spain produced a number of poets whose compositions are still considered standard. Such a one was abu-al-Walīd Aḥmad ibn-

Zaydūn (1003–71), reckoned by some as the greatest poet of al-Andalus. Ibn-Zaydūn belonged to the noble family of Makhzūm, a branch of the Quraysh.[1] He was first a confidential agent to ibn-Jahwar, chief of the Cordovan oligarchy, but later fell from grace, probably on account of his violent love for the poetess Wallādah, daughter of the Caliph al-Mustakfi. After several years in prison and exile he was appointed by al-Muʿtaḍid al-ʿAbbādi to the twofold position of grand vizir and commander of the troops and given the title *dhu-al-wizāratayn*,[2] he of the two vizirates, i.e. that of the sword and that of the pen. It was under his influence that al-Muʿtamid sent an army in 1068 against Cordova and wrested it from Jahwarid hands. In al-Muʿtamid's court, which was temporarily removed to Cordova, ibn-Zaydūn aroused the jealousy of a rival poet and minister, ibn-ʿAmmār, a man of obscure origin who at first led a wandering life singing the praises of anyone who cared to reward him. Ibn-ʿAmmār met his death at the hand of his patron al-Muʿtamid at Seville in 1086.[3] Besides being an accomplished poet ibn-Zaydūn was a distinguished letter writer. One of his most widely read epistles is that in which he denounces ibn-ʿAbdūs, minister of ibn-Jahwar and rival for the hand of Wallādah. Several verses addressed by ibn-Zaydūn[4] to Wallādah depict the glowing beauty of al-Zahrā' with its gardens, and illustrate the deep feeling for nature which is characteristic of Spanish Arabic poetry.

This beautiful and talented Wallādah († 1087), renowned alike for personal charm and literary ability, was the Sappho of Spain, where Arab women seem to have shown special taste and aptitude for poetry and literature. Al-Maqqari[5] devotes a whole section to these women of al-Andalus in whom "eloquence was a second instinct". Wallādah's home at Cordova was the meeting-place of wits, savants and poets.[6]

Among the lesser lights reference may be made to abu-Isḥāq ibn-Khafājah[7] († 1139), who spent his life in a little village south of Valencia without seeking to pay court to the kinglets of his time, and to the young licentious poet of Seville, Muḥammad

[1] Ibn-Khallikān, vol. i, pp. 75-7.
[2] Cf. Marrākushi, p. 74, l. 5.
[3] Marrākushi, p. 89; ibn-Khāqān, pp. 98-9. Cf. ibn-Khallikān, vol. ii, p. 370.
[4] *Dīwān*, ed. Kāmil Kīlāni and ʿAbd-al-Raḥmān Khalīfah (Cairo, 1932), pp. 257-8; tr. in Nicholson, *Literary History*, p. 425.
[5] Vol. ii, pp. 536-639.
[6] Ibn-Bassām, p. 376.
[7] His *Dīwān* published in Cairo, 1286. On his life see ibn-Khāqān, pp. 231-42; ibn-Khallikān, vol. i, pp. 23-4.

ibn-Hāni' (937–73), who addressed several panegyrics to the Fāṭimid Caliph al-Mu'izz.[1] Ibn-Hāni' was considered tainted with the opinions of Greek philosophers.[2]

Muwashshaḥs

Emancipated to a limited degree from the fetters of convention, Spanish Arabic poetry developed new metrical forms and acquired an almost modern sensibility to the beautiful in nature. Through its ballads and love songs it manifested a tenderly romantic feeling which anticipated the attitude of medieval chivalry. By the beginning of the eleventh century a lyric system of *muwashshaḥ*[3] and *zajal* had been developed in the Andalus. Both forms were based on a refrain for the chorus and were undoubtedly sung. Music and song established and maintained everywhere their alliance with poetry.

It was abu-Bakr ibn-Quzmān († 1160), the wandering minstrel of Cordova who travelled from town to town singing the praises of the great, who lifted the *zajal*, till then left entirely to improvisators, to the dignity of a literary form.[4] As for the other variety of folk-song, the *muwashshaḥ*, it was not only developed but invented in Spain, whence it spread into North Africa and the East. Among the noted *muwashshaḥ* composers were abu-al-'Abbās[5] al-Tuṭīli, the blind poet of Tudela who died in his youth, in 1129, after singing the glories of 'Ali, son and successor of Yūsuf ibn-Tāshfīn; Ibrāhīm ibn-Sahl[6] († 1251 or 1260), a Sevillan convert from Judaism whose persistence in the use of wine rendered his Islam suspect; and Muḥammad ibn-Yūsuf abu-Ḥayyān (1256–1344) of Granada, a polyglot of Berber origin who also wrote Persian, Turkish,[7] Coptic and Ethiopic grammars.[8] Of these only the Turkish survived.

It was Arabic poetry in general and this lyric type in particular that aroused native Christian admiration and became one of the

[1] Zāhid 'Ali, *Tabyīn al-Ma'āni fi Sharḥ Dīwān ibn-Hāni'* (Cairo, 1352), pp. 1 *seq.*

[2] Ibn-Khallikān, vol. ii, p. 367; Maqqari, vol. ii, p. 444.

[3] So called by comparison with *wishāḥ*, a double belt ornamented with varicoloured pearls which women wear diagonally round the body from shoulder to hip.

[4] Ibn-Khaldūn, *Muqaddamah*, p. 524. Ibn-Quzmān's poems have been published by A. R. Nykl, *El cancionero* (Madrid, 1933).

[5] Name wrongly given in ibn-Khāqān, p. 273; ibn-Khaldūn, *Muqaddamah*, p. 519.

[6] His *Dīwān*, printed in Beirūt, 1885. On him see Kutubi, *Fawāt*, vol. i, pp. 29-35; Maqqari, vol. ii, pp. 351-4; Soualah Mohammed, *Ibrahim Ibn Sahl* (Algiers, 1914).

[7] *Al-Idrāk li-Lisān al-Atrāk*, ed. Ahmed Caferoğlu (Istanbul, 1930–31); the earliest or second earliest Turkish grammar.

[8] Kutubi, vol. ii, p. 356; Maqqari, vol. i, pp. 823 *seq.* For other poets consult ibn-Khaldūn, *Muqaddamah*, pp. 518-34.

potent factors in assimilation. Two such forms, the *zajal* and the *muwashshaḥ*, developed into the Castilian popular verse form of *villancico*, which was extensively used for Christian hymns, including Christmas carols. The sestet, which in its original form presumably rhymed CDE, CDE, was probably suggested by a form of Arabic *zajal* instanced in the works of the Andalusian poets. Al-Qazwīni[1] († 1283) asserts that at Shilb (Silves) in southern Portugal one would meet even ploughmen capable of improvising verse. This brings to mind the many men in modern Lebanon, *qawwālūn*, who extemporaneously produce such folk-poetry, some of which they still call *zajal* and *muwashshaḥ*.

The emergence of a definite literary scheme of platonic love in Spanish as early as the eighth century marks a distinctive contribution of Arabic poetry. In southern France the first Provençal poets appear full-fledged toward the end of the eleventh century with palpitating love expressed in a wealth of fantastic imagery. The troubadours,[2] who flourished in the twelfth century, imitated their southern contemporaries, the *zajal*-singers. Following the Arabic precedent the cult of the dame suddenly arises in south-western Europe. The *Chanson de Roland*, the noblest monument of early European literature, whose appearance prior to 1080 marks the beginning of a new civilization—that of Western Europe—just as the Homeric poems mark the beginning of historic Greece, owes its existence to a military contact with Moslem Spain.

Education

Primary education was based, as in all Moslem lands, on writing and reading from the Koran and on Arabic grammar and poetry. Though mainly a private concern, education was nevertheless so widely spread that a high percentage of Spanish Moslems could read and write[3]—a situation unknown in Europe of that age. Higher value was placed on the function of the elementary teacher than in other lands of Islam. The position of women in the learned life, as portrayed by such an author as al-Maqqari[4] and verified by the facts of literary history, proves that in Andalusia the maxims prohibiting the teaching of writing to women were but little applied.

Higher education was based on koranic exegesis and theology,

[1] *Āthār*, p. 364. R. Menéndez Pidal in *Bulletin hispanique*, vol. xl (1938), pp. 337 *seq*. A. R. Nykl in *ibid*. vol. xli (1939), pp. 305-15.

[2] This word may have come from Ar. *ṭarab*, music, song; Ribera, *Disertaciones*, vol. ii, p. 141.

[3] Cf. above, p. 531.

[4] See above, p. 560.

philosophy, Arabic grammar, poetry and lexicography, history and geography. Several of the principal towns possessed what might be called universities, chief among which were those of Cordova, Seville, Malaga and Granada. The university of Cordova included among its departments astronomy, mathematics and medicine, in addition to theology and law. Its enrolment must have reached into thousands and its certificate opened the way to the most lucrative posts in the realm. The university of Granada was founded by the seventh Naṣrid, Yūsuf abu-al-Ḥajjāj (1333–54), whose administration was graced by the poet-historian Lisān-al-Dīn ibn-al-Khaṭīb.[1] The building had its gates guarded by stone lions. The curriculum comprised theology, jurisprudence, medicine, chemistry, philosophy and astronomy. Castilian and other foreign students patronized this institution. In it and other universities it was customary to hold occasional public meetings and commemorations in which original poems were recited and orations delivered, usually by members of the faculty. A favourite inscription over collegiate portals ran thus: "The world is supported by four things only: the learning of the wise, the justice of the great, the prayers of the righteous and the valour of the brave".

Side by side with universities libraries flourished. The royal library of Cordova, started by Muḥammad I (852–86) and enlarged by 'Abd-al-Raḥmān III, became the largest and best when al-Ḥakam II added his own collection. A number of persons, including some women, had private collections.

Books

The peculiarities of Moslem life with its lack of political assemblies and theatres, which were characteristic features of Greece and Rome, made books almost the sole means of acquiring knowledge. As a book market Cordova held first place in Spain. This anecdote illustrates the spirit of the time: [2]

When living in Cordova I frequented its book market looking for a book in which I was especially interested. At last a copy of good calligraphy and handsome binding fell into my hands. Full of joy, I began to bid for it but was time after time outbid by another until the price offered far exceeded the proper limit. I then said to the auctioneer: "Show me this rival bidder who has raised the price beyond the worth of the book". Accordingly he took me to a man attired in distinguished

[1] *Lamḥah*, pp. 91, 96. In late years Granada has again become a centre for Arabic studies in Spain.

[2] Maqqari, vol. i, p. 302.

garb. Approaching him I said: "May Allah keep our lord the *faqīh* strong! If you have a special object in acquiring this book I will let it go, for the bidding has already exceeded the limit." His answer was: "I am not a *faqīh*, nor am I aware of the contents of the book. But I have just established a library and made much of it in order to pride myself among the notables of my town. There is still an empty space there which this book will just fill up. Seeing that it was in elegant hand and good cover, I liked it and cared not how much I paid for it. for, thanks to Allah, I am a man of means."

Paper

This accumulation of books in Andalusia would not have been possible but for the local manufacture of writing-paper, one of the most beneficial contributions of Islam to Europe. Without paper, printing from movable type, which was invented in Germany about the middle of the fifteenth century, would not have been successful, and without paper and printing popular education in Europe, on the scale to which it developed, would not have been feasible. From Morocco, into which the manufacture of paper was introduced from the East, the industry passed into Spain in the middle of the twelfth century.[1] Yāqūt[2] mentions Shāṭibah (Játiva) as the centre of the industry in Spain. A philological reminder of this historical fact is English "ream", which is derived through Old French *rayme* from Spanish *resma*, a loan-word from Arabic *rizmah*, a bundle. After Spain the art of paper-making was established in Italy (*ca.* 1268–76), also as a result of Moslem influence, presumably from Sicily. France owed its first paper-mills to Spain, and not to returning Crusaders as claimed by some. From these countries the industry spread throughout Europe. A secretary of 'Abd-al-Raḥmān used to write the official communications in his home and send them to a special office for reproduction—a form of printing (*ṭab'*, perhaps block printing)—whence copies were distributed to the various governmental agents.[3]

After the destruction of Moslem power in Spain less than two thousand volumes survived to be collected by Philip II (1556–98) and his successors from the various Arab libraries. These formed the nucleus of the Escurial library still standing not far from Madrid. In the early part of the seventeenth century the Sharīf Zaydān, sultan of Morocco, fleeing his capital, sent his library aboard a ship whose captain refused to land the books at the

[1] See above, p. 347. [2] Vol. iii, p. 235. [3] Ibn-al-Abbār, *Ḥullah*, p. 137.

proper destination because he had not received full pay in advance. On its way to Marseille the ship fell into the hands of Spanish pirates and its bookish booty, to the number of three or four thousand volumes, was deposited by order of Philip III in the Escurial, which made this library one of the richest in Arabic manuscripts.[1]

Historiography

In Spain Arabic philology, theology, historiography, geography, astronomy and allied sciences had a comparatively late development, since the Moslems there, unlike their co-religionists of Syria and al-ʿIrāq, had but little to learn from the natives. Even after their rise Spanish sciences lagged behind those of the Eastern caliphate. It was mainly in such disciplines as botany, medicine, philosophy and astronomical mathematics that Western Moslems made their greatest mark.

One of the earliest and best known of Andalusian historians was abu-Bakr ibn-ʿUmar, usually known as ibn-al-Qūṭīyah,[2] who was born and flourished at Cordova, where he died in 977. His *Ta'rīkh Iftitāḥ* (variant *Fatḥ*) *al-Andalus*,[3] which we have used in this work, extends from the Moslem conquest to the early part of ʿAbd-al-Raḥmān III's reign. Ibn-al-Qūṭīyah was also a grammarian and his treatise on the conjugation of verbs[4] was the first ever composed on the subject. Another early but more prolific historical writer was abu-Marwān Ḥayyān ibn-Khalaf of Cordova, surnamed ibn-Ḥayyān (987 or 988–1076). Ibn-Ḥayyān's list of works contains no less than fifty titles, one of which, *al-Matīn*, comprised sixty volumes. Unfortunately only one work, *al-Muqtabis fi Ta'rīkh Rijāl al-Andalus*,[5] has survived. The most valuable work on the Muwaḥḥid period was written in 1224 by the Moroccan historian ʿAbd-al-Wāḥid al-Marrākushi,[6] who sojourned in Spain.

Andalusia produced a number of biographers, one of the first among whom was abu-al-Walīd ʿAbdullāh ibn-Muḥammad ibn-al-Faraḍi, who was born in 962 at Cordova, where he studied and

[1] See its catalogue, *Les manuscrits arabes de l'Escurial*, by Hartwig Derenbourg, 2 vols. (Paris, 1884–1903), vol. iii, revised by Lévi-Provençal (Paris, 1928).

[2] See Thaʿālibi, vol. i, pp. 411-12; ibn-Khallikān, vol. ii, pp. 336-8.

[3] (Madrid, 1868); tr. Don Julián Ribera, *Historia de la conquista de España* (Madrid, 1926).

[4] *Kitāb al-Afʿāl*, ed. Ignaz Guidi (Leyden, 1894).

[5] Ed. Melchor M. Antuña, pt. 3 (Paris, 1937).

[6] *Al-Muʿjib fi Talkhīṣ Akhbār al-Maghrib*, ed. R. Dozy, 2nd ed. (Leyden, 1881) tr. E. Fagnan, *Histoire des Almohades* (Algiers, 1893).

taught. When thirty years old he undertook a pilgrimage in the course of which he stopped to study at al-Qayrawān, Cairo, Makkah and al-Madīnah. After his return he was appointed qāḍi of Valencia. During the sack of Cordova by the Berbers in 1013 ibn-al-Faraḍi was murdered in his home; his body was not found till the fourth day afterward and was so decomposed that it was buried without the usual ceremonial washing and wrapping.[1] Only one of ibn-al-Faraḍi's works, *Ta'rīkh 'Ulamā' al-Andalus*,[2] is extant. This collection of biographies of the Arab scholars of Spain was supplemented by ibn-Bashkuwāl, abu-al-Qāsim Khalaf ibn-'Abd-al-Malik, in a volume completed in 1139 under the title *al-Ṣilah fi Ta'rīkh A'immat al-Andalus*.[3] This is one of two surviving works of ibn-Bashkuwāl, who is credited with the composition of some fifty books.[4] Ibn-Bashkuwāl was born at Cordova in 1101 and died there in 1183. His *Ṣilah* was continued by abu-'Abdullāh Muḥammad ibn-al-Abbār (1199–1260) of Valencia under the title *al-Takmilah li-Kitāb al-Ṣilah*.[5] In addition to this work ibn-al-Abbār wrote *al-Ḥullah al-Siyarā'*,[6] a collection of biographies. Another valuable dictionary of learned Spanish Arabs is *Bughyat al-Multamis fi Ta'rīkh Rijāl al-Andalus*, by al-Ḍabbi,[7] abu-Ja'far Aḥmad ibn-Yaḥya († 1203), who flourished in Murcia.

In the history of science we have from the pen of abu-al-Qāsim Ṣā'id ibn-Aḥmad al-Andalusi (1029–70)[8] the *Ṭabaqāt al-Umam*[9] (classification of nations), which was a source of al-Qifṭi, ibn-abi-Uṣaybi'ah and ibn-al-'Ibri. Ṣā'id held the office of qāḍi of Toledo under the banu-dhu-al-Nūn and distinguished himself as historian, mathematician and astronomical observer.

The two names which stand for the highest literary accomplishment and historical comprehension of which Western Islam was

[1] Ibn-Khallikān, vol. i, p. 480; Maqqari, vol. i, p. 546.

[2] Ed. Francisco Codera, 2 vols. (Madrid, 1890–92).

[3] Ed. Codera, 2 vols. (Madrid, 1882–3).

[4] Al-Dhahabi, *Tadhkirat al-Ḥuffāẓ*, 2nd ed., vol. iv (Ḥaydarābād, 1334), p. 129. Cf. ibn-Khallikān, vol. i, pp. 305-6.

[5] One part edited by Codera, 2 vols. (Madrid, 1886–9), another by M. Alarcón and C. A. González Palencia in *Miscelánea de estudios y textos árabes* (Madrid, 1915), pp. 146-690, completed by Alfred Bel and M. Ben Cheneb (Algiers, 1919–20). On ibn-al-Abbār consult Kutubi, vol. ii, pp. 282-4; ibn-Khaldūn, tr. de Slane, vol. ii, pp. 347-50; ibn-Khallikān, vol. i, p. 77.

[6] Edited in part by Dozy (Leyden, 1847–51).

[7] Ed. Codera and Julián Ribera (Madrid, 1884–5).

[8] Ḍabbi, *Bughyah*, p. 311.

[9] Ed. L. Cheikho (Beirūt, 1912).

capable are those of the two friends and officials of the Naṣrid court, ibn-al-Khaṭīb and ibn-Khaldūn.

Lisān-al-Dīn ibn-al-Khaṭīb[1] (1313–74) was descended from an Arab family which had migrated to Spain from Syria. Under the seventh Naṣrid sultan, Yūsuf abu-al-Ḥajjāj (1333–54), and his son Muḥammad V (1354–9, 1362–91), he held the pompous title of *dhu-al-wizāratayn*.[2] In 1371 he fled from Granada because of court intrigues, only to be strangled to death three years later at Fās in revenge for a private grievance. In his death Granada, if not the whole of Arab Spain, lost its last important author, poet and statesman. Of the sixty odd works penned by ibn-al-Khaṭīb, which are chiefly poetical, belletristic, historical, geographical, medicinal and philosophic, about a third have survived. Of these the most important for us is the extensive history of Granada.[3]

ʿAbd-al-Raḥmān ibn-Khaldūn (1332–1406) was born in Tunis of a Spanish Arab family which traced its ancestry to a Ḥaḍramawt tribe. The founder of the family had migrated in the eighth century with Yamanites to Spain; his descendants flourished in Seville until the thirteenth century. ʿAbd-al-Raḥmān himself held a number of high offices in Fās before he fell into disgrace and entered (1362) the service of the sultan of Granada, Muḥammad V. The sultan entrusted him with an important mission of peace to the Castilian court. Two years later, after having aroused the jealousy of his powerful friend ibn-al-Khaṭīb, ibn-Khaldūn returned to al-Maghrib. Here he occupied a number of positions, finally retiring to Qalʿat ibn-Salāmah,[4] where he began work on his history and resided till 1378. In 1382 he set out on a pilgrimage but broke his journey in Cairo to lecture at its mosque al-Azhar. Two years later he was appointed chief Mālikite qāḍi of Cairo by the Mamlūk Sultan al-Ẓāhir Barqūq. In 1401 he accompanied Barqūq's successor al-Nāṣir Faraj to Damascus on his campaign against the dreadful Tamerlane (Tīmūr), who received ibn-Khaldūn as an honoured guest. Thus

[1] Al-Maqqari devotes the second half of his *Nafḥ al-Ṭīb* to the life and works of ibn-al-Khaṭīb. Al-Maqqari was of Tilimsān but compiled this work, which is our principal authority for the whole literary history of Moslem Spain, at Damascus between 1628 and 1630.

[2] See above, p. 560.

[3] *Al-Iḥāṭah fi Akhbār Gharnāṭah*, 2 vols. (Cairo, 1319), an abbreviated edition.

[4] Now called Tawghzūt, east of Tilimsān in northern Algeria.

did this historian play a significant part in the politics of North Africa and Spain, all of which prepared him admirably for the writing of his great work. His comprehensive history, entitled *Kitāb al-ʿIbar wa-Dīwān al-Mubtadaʾ w-al-Khabar fi Ayyām al-ʿArab w-al-ʿAjam w-al-Barbar*[1] (book of instructive examples and register of subject and predicate dealing with the history of the Arabs, Persians and Berbers), is made up of three parts: a *Muqaddamah*[2] (prolegomena), forming volume one; the main body, treating of the Arabs and neighbouring peoples; and the last part,[3] which sketches the history of the Berbers and the Moslem dynasties of North Africa. Unfortunately the critical theories ably propounded in the *Muqaddamah* were not applied to the main part of the work. However, the section treating of the Arab and Berber tribes of the Maghrib will ever remain a valuable guide.

The fame of ibn-Khaldūn rests on his *Muqaddamah*.[4] In it he presented for the first time a theory of historical development which takes due cognizance of the physical facts of climate and geography as well as of the moral and spiritual forces at work. As one who endeavoured to formulate laws of national progress and decay ibn-Khaldūn may be considered the discoverer—as he himself claimed[5]—of the true scope and nature of history or at least the real founder of the science of sociology. No Arab writer, indeed no European, had ever taken a view of history at once so comprehensive and philosophic. By the consensus of critical opinion ibn-Khaldūn was the greatest historical philosopher Islam produced and one of the greatest of all time.

Geography

The best-known geographer of the eleventh century was al-Bakri, a Hispano-Arab, and the most brilliant geographical author and cartographer of the twelfth century, indeed of all medieval time, was al-Idrīsi, a descendant of a royal Spanish Arab family who got his education in Spain.

[1] 7 vols. (Cairo, 1284). At the end of vol. vii, beginning p. 379, is his autobiography, a major source for his life. This was translated by M. G. de Slane, *Journal asiatique*, ser. 4, vol. 3 (1844), pp. 5-60, 187-210, 291-308, 325-53. See Maqqari (Cairo, 1302), vol. iv, pp. 6-17.

[2] Earlier than the Cairo edition is that of M. Quatremère, 3 vols. (Paris, 1858); tr. de Slane, 3 vols. (Paris, 1862–8, ed. Boutboul, Paris, 1934–8).

[3] Tr. de Slane, *Histoire des Berbères et des dynasties musulmanes de l'Afrique septentrionale*, ed. Paul Casanova, 2 vols. (Paris, 1925–7).

[4] Tr. Franz Rosenthal, *Ibn-Khaldūn's Muqaddīmah*, 3 vols. (New York, 1958).

[5] *Muqaddamah*, pp. 4-5.

Abu-'Ubayd 'Abdullāh ibn-'Abd-al-'Azīz al-Bakri,[1] the earliest of the Western Moslem geographers whose works have survived, flourished in Cordova, where he died at an advanced age in 1094. A belletrist, poet and philologist, he won his laurels through his voluminous geography *al-Masālik w-al-Mamālik*[2] (the book of roads and kingdoms), which, like most geographical works of the Middle Ages, was written in the form of an itinerary. The book has survived only in part.

Al-Idrīsi, born at Ceuta in 1100, shed lustre on the reign of Roger II, Norman king of Sicily, and will be treated in that connection.

Travels

After al-Idrīsi Arab geographical literature can claim no great originality and is represented by travellers' narratives, which then become especially numerous. The best known among these travellers was ibn-Jubayr,[3] abu-al-Ḥusayn Muḥammad ibn-Aḥmad, who was born in Valencia in 1145 and educated at Játiva. Between 1183 and 1185 ibn-Jubayr undertook a journey from Granada to Makkah and back, visiting Egypt, al-'Irāq, Syria—parts of which were still in the hands of the Crusaders—and Sicily. He travelled in the East on two further occasions, 1189–1191 and 1217, but on the latter journey he only reached Alexandria, where he died. His *Riḥlah*,[4] the account of his first journey, is one of the most important works of its kind in Arabic literature. Another Hispano-Arab geographer and traveller was abu-Ḥāmid Muḥammad al-Māzini (1080/1–1169/70) of Granada, who visited Russia in 1136. While among the Bulgars in the Volga region he witnessed a commercial activity unreported in any other source, trade in fossil mammoth ivory, which was exported as far as Khwārizm to be made into combs and pyxides.[5]

The travels of ibn-Jubayr and al-Māzini were eclipsed by those of the Moroccan Arab Muḥammad ibn-'Abdullāh ibn-Baṭṭūṭah, the Moslem globe-trotter of the Middle Ages. Ibn-Baṭṭūṭah was born at Ṭanjah (Tangier) in 1304 and died in Marrākush in 1377. In the second quarter of that century he

[1] Consult ibn-Bashkuwāl, vol. i, p. 282; Suyūṭi, *Bughyah*, p. 285.

[2] Edited in part by de Slane (Algiers, 1857).

[3] On him see Maqqari (Leyden), vol. i, pp. 714 *seq.*

[4] Ed. William Wright, 2nd ed. M. J. de Goeje (Leyden, 1907).

[5] "Tuḥfat al-Albāb", ed. Gabriel Ferrand in *Journal asiatique*, vol. ccvii (1925), p. 238.

made four pilgrimages to Makkah in conjunction with which he journeyed all over the Moslem world. Eastward he reached Ceylon, Bengal, the Maldive Islands and China. He also visited Constantinople. His last travels in 1353 took him far into the interior of Africa. His alleged visit to the city of Bulghār, near Kazan and the Volga, seems to be the only serious fabrication in his whole account.[1]

Influence over the West

Arab geographical studies had but a limited influence in the West. They kept alive the ancient doctrine of the sphericity of the earth, without which the discovery of the New World would not have been possible. An exponent of this doctrine was abu-'Ubaydah Muslim al-Balansi (of Valencia), who flourished in the first half of the tenth century.[2] They perpetuated the Hindu idea that the known hemisphere of the world had a centre or "world cupola" or "summit" situated at an equal distance from the four cardinal points. This *arīn* [3] theory found its way into a Latin work published in 1410. From this Columbus acquired the doctrine which made him believe that the earth was shaped in the form of a pear and that on the western hemisphere opposite the *arīn* was a corresponding elevated centre. It was, however, in the realm of astronomical geography and mathematics that a number of new concepts were contributed to Western lore.

Astronomy and mathematics

In Spain astronomical studies were cultivated assiduously after the middle of the tenth century and were regarded with special favour by the rulers of Cordova, Seville and Toledo. Following abu-Ma'shar of Baghdād, most of the Andalusian astronomers believed in astral influence as the cause underlying the chief occurrences between birth and death on this earth. The study of this astral influence, i.e. astrology, necessitated the determining of the location of places throughout the world together with their latitudes and longitudes. Thus did astrology contribute to the study of astronomy. Finally it was through Spanish channels that the Latin West found its Oriental inspiration in astronomy and astrology. The leading Moslem astronomical works were translated in Spain into Latin, and the Alfonsine tables compiled under the ægis of Alfonso X in the thirteenth century were but a development of Arab astronomy.

[1] *Tuḥfat al-Nuẓẓār fi Gharā'ib al-Amṣār wa-'Ajā'ib al-Asfār*, ed. and tr. C. Defrémery and B. R. Sanguinetti, 3rd impression (Paris, 1879–93), vol. ii, pp. 398-9.

[2] Ṣā'id, *Ṭabaqāt*, p. 64. See ibn-Ḥazm, vol. ii, pp. 78-9; above, p. 375.

[3] See above, p. 384.

Spanish Arab astronomers built upon the preceding astronomical and astrological works of their co-religionists in the East. They reproduced the Aristotelian system, as distinguished from the Ptolemaic, and in the name of Aristotle attacked the Ptolemaic representation of the celestial movements. Outstanding among early Hispano-Arabic astronomers were al-Majrīṭi [1] († *ca.* 1007) of Cordova, al-Zarqāli (*ca.* 1029–*ca.* 1087) of Toledo and ibn-Aflaḥ († between 1140 and 1150) of Ṣeville.

Abu-al-Qāsim Maslamah al-Majrīṭi, the earliest Spanish Moslem scientist of any importance, edited and corrected the planetary tables (*zīj*) of al-Khwārizmi,[2] the first tables composed by a Moslem. He converted the basis of these tables from the era of Yazdagird into that of Islam and to some extent replaced the meridian of *arīn* by that of Cordova. In 1126 Adelard of Bath made a Latin version of the tables ascribed to al-Khwārizmi. About fourteen years later another important *zīj*, that of al-Battāni, composed about 900, was rendered into Latin by Plato of Tivoli and long afterwards done directly from Arabic into Spanish under the auspices of Alfonso X († 1284), surnamed the Wise and the Astronomer. Among al-Majrīṭi's honorific titles was *al-ḥāsib*, the mathematician, for he was considered a leader (*imām*) in mathematical knowledge, including mensuration. It was either he or his Cordovan disciple abu-al-Ḥakam 'Amr al-Karmāni [3] († 1066) who introduced into Spain the writings of the Ikhwān al-Ṣafā'.

The so-called Toledan tables were based upon observations and studies made by a number of Spanish Moslem and Jewish astronomers, notable among whom was al-Zarqāli, abu-Isḥāq Ibrāhīm ibn-Yaḥya († *ca.* 1087). These tables comprised geographical information derived from Ptolemy and al-Khwārizmi and were rendered into Latin in the twelfth century by Gerard of Cremona. The works of Raymond of Marseille were likewise largely drawn (1140) from the astronomical canons of al-Zarqāli. Ptolemy's exaggerated estimate of the length of the Mediterranean Sea as 62°, cut by al-Khwārizmi to about 52°, was reduced probably by al-Zarqāli to the approximately correct figure of 42°. Al-Zarqāli was evidently the foremost astronomical

[1] Born in Majrīṭ (Madrid).

[2] Ṣā'id, p. 69, quoted by ibn-abi-Uṣaybi'ah, vol. ii, p. 39. Cf. Qifṭi, p. 326. Ṣā'id, who was himself an astronomer, criticizes al-Majrīṭi.

[3] Ṣā'id, p. 71.

observer of his age.[1] He devised an improved type of astrolabe, called the *ṣafīḥah*,[2] and was the first to prove the motion of the solar apogee with reference to the stars. According to his measurements it amounted to 12·04″, whereas its real value is 11.8″. Copernicus quotes al-Zarqāli (Arzachel) along with al-Battāni in his book *De revolutionibus orbium coelestium*.

In his *Kitāb al-Hay'ah*[3] (book of astronomy), which was also translated by Gerard of Cremona, Jābir ibn-Aflaḥ (Geber filius Afflæ) sharply criticizes Ptolemy and rightly asserts that the lower planets, Mercury and Venus, have no visible parallaxes. This book of ibn-Aflaḥ is otherwise noteworthy for a chapter on spherical and plane trigonometry. About two and a half centuries before ibn-Aflaḥ, al-Battāni had popularized, if not discovered, the first notions of trigonometrical ratios as we use them today. The science of trigonometry, like algebra and analytical geometry, was largely founded by Arabs.

Foremost among the last Spanish astronomers stood Nūr-al-Dīn abu-Isḥāq al-Biṭrūji[4] (Alpetragius, † *ca.* 1204), a pupil of ibn-Ṭufayl. His *Kitāb al-Hay'ah*,[5] on the configuration of the heavenly bodies, is remarkable for its attempt to revive in a modified form the false theory of homocentric spheres. Though considered the exponent of a new astronomy, al-Biṭrūji in reality reproduced the Aristotelian system; his work marks the culmination of the Moslem anti-Ptolemaic movement. By the end of the twelfth century translations had been made from Arabic into Latin of a large number of Aristotle's works on astronomy, physics and meteorology, in which most of Aristotle's thought in geography had also found expression.

Arab astronomers have left on the sky immortal traces of their industry which everyone who reads the names of the stars on an ordinary celestial sphere can readily discern. Not only are most of the star-names in European languages of Arabic origin, such as Acrab (*'aqrab*, scorpion), Algedi (*al-jadi*, the kid), Altair (*al-ṭā'ir*, the flyer), Deneb (*dhanab*, tail), Pherkad (*farqad*, calf),[6] but a number of technical terms, including "azimuth"

[1] Ṣā'id, p. 75. [2] Qifṭi, p. 57. Cf. Khwārizmi, *Mafātīḥ*, pp. 233-4.

[3] Cf. Qifṭi, p. 319, l. 12, p. 393, l. 1; Ḥājji Khalfah, vol. vi, p. 506. Like most other astronomical works this book has survived only in manuscript form.

[4] Of Pedroche, north of Cordova.

[5] Translated into Latin by Michael Scot in 1217 and into Hebrew in 1259.

[6] For more names consult Richard H. Allen, *Star-Names and their Meanings* (New York, 1899); Amīn F. al-Ma'lūf, *al-Mu'jam al-Falaki* (Cairo, 1935).

(*al-sumūt*), "nadir" (*naẓīr*), "zenith" (*al-samt*), are likewise of Arabic etymology and testify to the rich legacy of Islam to Christian Europe. In the mathematical vocabulary of Europe we have another eloquent witness to Arab scientific influence. Other than borrowings, as illustrated by such words as "algebra" and "algorism" cited above, certain Arabic terms were translated into Latin. The algebraic term "surd", a sixteenth-century loan-word from Latin meaning "deaf", is a translation from Arabic *jadhr aṣamm* (deaf root). In trigonometry "sine" (L. *sinus*) is likewise a translation of an Arabic word *jayb* (pocket), which is in turn an adaptation of Sanskrit *jīva*. The English mathematician Robert of Chester, who flourished in the middle of the twelfth century, was the first to use *sinus* as equivalent to Arabic *jayb* in its trigonometrical acceptation.

One of the most interesting mathematical terms borrowed from Arabic is "cipher"[1] or "zero". While the Arabs, as we have learned, did not invent the cipher, they nevertheless introduced it with the Arabic numerals into Europe and taught Westerners the employment of this most convenient convention, thus facilitating the use of arithmetic in everyday life. In the numeral system the cipher is of capital importance. If in a series a unit, a ten or a power of ten is not represented "these little circles" are used "to keep the rows".[2] Without the zero we should have to arrange our figures in a table with columns of units, tens, hundreds, etc., that is, use an abacus.

We have seen earlier that al-Khwārizmi, writing in the first half of the ninth century, was the first exponent of the use of numerals, including the zero, in preference to letters. These numerals he called *Hindi*, indicating their Indian origin. His work on the Hindu method of calculation was translated into Latin by Adelard of Bath in the twelfth century and as *De numero indico* has survived, whereas the Arabic original has been lost. Moreover, the Moslems of Spain had developed as early as the second half of the ninth century numerals slightly different in shape, *ḥurūf al-ghubār* (letters of dust), originally used in conjunction with some kind of sand abacus. Most

[1] Not cognate with "cipher" meaning "code", "monogram", which is derived from Ar. *sifr*, book, originally Aramaic.

[2] Khwārizmi, *Mafātīḥ*, p. 194.

scholars trace the *ghubār* numerals, like the Hindu, back to India; others claim that they were of Roman origin and were known in Spain before the advent of the Arabs.[1] Gerbert, who spent several years in Spain prior to his becoming Pope Silvester II (999–1003), was the first to describe scientifically the *ghubār* numerals, his work appearing about a hundred years after the earliest Arabic manuscripts (874) containing such numerals. The modern European numerals bear closer resemblance to the *ghubār* than to the Hindu figures.

The diffusion of the Arabic numerals in non-Moslem Europe was incredibly slow. Christian arithmeticians throughout the eleventh, twelfth and part of the thirteenth centuries persisted in the use of the antiquated Roman numerals and the abacus or made a compromise and used the new algorisms together with their old system. It was in Italy that the new symbols were first employed for practical purposes. In 1202 Leonardo Fibonacci of Pisa, who was taught by a Moslem master and had travelled in North Africa, published a work which was the main landmark in the introduction of the Arabic numerals. More than that, it marks the beginning of European mathematics. With the old type of numerals, arithmetical progress along certain lines would have been impossible. The zero and Arabic numerals lie behind the science of calculation as we know it today.

Botany and medicine

In the field of natural history,[2] especially botany pure and applied, as in that of astronomy and mathematics, the Western Moslems enriched the world by their researches. They made correct observations on sexual difference between such plants as palms and hemps. They classified plants into those that grow from cuttings, those that grow from seed and those that grow spontaneously, as evidenced by ibn-Sab'īn's answer to one of Emperor Frederick's questions.[3] The Cordova physician al-Ghāfiqi,[4] abu-Ja'far Aḥmad ibn-Muḥammad († 1165), collected plants in Spain and Africa, gave the name of each in Arabic, Latin and Berber, and described them in a way that may be

[1] David E. Smith and Louis C. Karpinski, *The Hindu-Arabic Numerals* (Boston and London, 1911), pp. 65 *seq.*; Solomon Gandz in *Isis*, vol. xvi (1931), pp. 393-424. See ibn-Khaldūn, *Muqaddamah*, p. 4, l. 22.

[2] On the horse and horsemen see ibn-Hudhayl, *Ḥilyat al-Fursān wa-Shi'ār al-Shuj'ān*, ed. Louis Mercier (Paris, 1922); tr. Mercier, *La parure des cavaliers et l'insigne des preux* (Paris, 1924).

[3] See below, p. 587.

[4] Ghāfiq was a town near Cordova.

considered the most precise and accurate in Arabic. His principal work *al-Adwiyah al-Mufradah* (on simples)[1] was not merely quoted but practically appropriated by his later and better-known confrère and countryman, ibn-al-Bayṭār. Towards the end of the twelfth century there flourished at Seville abu-Zakarīyā' Yaḥya ibn-Muḥammad ibn-al-'Awwām, whose treatise on agriculture, *al-Filāḥah*, is not only the most important Islamic, but the outstanding medieval work on the subject. Derived partly from earlier Greek and Arabic sources and partly from the experience of Moslem husbandmen in Spain, this book treats of five hundred and eighty-five plants and explains the cultivation of more than fifty fruit trees. It presents new observations on grafting and the properties of soil and manure and discusses the symptoms of several diseases of trees and vines, suggesting methods of cure. But with all its importance this book was little known to Arab writers; neither ibn-Khallikān, Yāqūt, nor Ḥājji Khalfah knew it and ibn-Khaldūn[2] wrongly considers it a recension of ibn-Waḥshīyah's.[3]

Ibn-al-Bayṭār

The best-known botanist and pharmacist of Spain, in fact of the Moslem world, was 'Abdullāh ibn-Aḥmad ibn-al-Bayṭār, a worthy successor of Dioscorides. Born at Malaga, ibn-al-Bayṭār travelled as a herbalist in Spain and throughout North Africa and later entered the service of the Ayyūbid al-Malik al-Kāmil in Cairo as chief herbalist.[4] From Egypt he made extensive trips throughout Syria and Asia Minor. In 1248 he died in Damascus, leaving two celebrated works dedicated to his patron al-Ṣāliḥ Ayyūb, who, like his predecessor al-Kāmil, used Damascus as his Syrian capital. One of these works, *al-Mughni fi al-Adwiyah al-Mufradah*, is on materia medica; the other, *al-Jāmi' fi al-*

[1] Ibn-abi-Uṣaybi'ah, vol. ii, p. 52. An abridged edition prepared by the famous Christian historian ibn-al-'Ibri has been recently published as *Muntakhab Kitāb Jāmi' al-Mufradāt*, ed. Max Meyerhof and Jūrji Ṣubḥi (Cairo, 1932?), with an English translation. Ibn-al-'Ibri's abridged translation into Syriac has been lost.

[2] *Muqaddamah*, p. 412.

[3] In his *Bibliotheca Arabico-Hispana Escurialensis*, vol. i (Madrid, 1760), pp. 323 *seq.*, the Lebanese scholar Michael Casiri (Ghazīri) was the first to call attention to the complete MS. of ibn-al-'Awwām's work in the Escurial. Casiri's pupil Josef Antonio Banqueri edited it with a Sp. tr., 2 vols. (Madrid, 1802); tr. Clément-Mullet, *Le livre d'agriculture*, 2 vols. in 3 pts. (Paris, 1864–7). Neither the edition nor the translations are satisfactory.

[4] Ibn-abi-Uṣaybi'ah, vol. ii, p. 133; Maqqari, vol. i, p. 934; Kutubi, vol. i, p. 261. Ibn-abi-Uṣaybi'ah was a pupil of ibn-al-Bayṭār and herborized with him in the neighbourhood of Damascus.

Adwiyah al-Mufradah,[1] is a collection of "simple remedies" from the animal, vegetable and mineral worlds, embodying Greek and Arabic data supplemented by the author's own experiments and researches. It stands out as the foremost medieval treatise of its kind. Some 1400 items are considered, of which 300, including about 200 plants, were novelties. The number of authors quoted is about one hundred and fifty, of whom twenty were Greek. Parts of the Latin version of ibn-al-Bayṭār's *Simplicia* were printed as late as 1758 at Cremona.

Medicine

Most of the Spanish Arab physicians were physicians by avocation and something else by vocation. Ibn-Rushd, ibn-Maymūn, ibn-Bājjah and ibn-Ṭufayl were better known as philosophers and will be treated on a later page. Ibn-al-Khaṭīb, whom we have already noted as a stylist and historian, held like many other physicians a vizirial office. In connection with the "black death", which in the middle of the fourteenth century was ravaging Europe and before which Christians stood helpless, considering it an act of God, this Moslem physician of Granada composed a treatise in defence of the theory of contagion, as may be illustrated by the following passage: [2]

> To those who say, "How can we admit the possibility of infection while the religious law denies it?" we reply that the existence of contagion is established by experience, investigation, the evidence of the senses and trustworthy reports. These facts constitute a sound argument. The fact of contagion becomes clear to the investigator who notices how he who establishes contact with the afflicted gets the disease, whereas he who is not in contact remains safe, and how transmission is effected through garments, vessels and earrings.

Al-Zahrāwi

The greatest surgeon of the Arabs, who never produced many surgeons, was abu-al-Qāsim (Abulcasis) Khalaf ibn-'Abbās al-Zahrāwi [3] († *ca.* 1013), court physician of al-Ḥakam II. His claim to distinction rests on *al-Taṣrīf li-Man 'Ajaz 'an al-*

[1] *Al-Jāmi' li-Mufradāt al-Adwiyah w-al-Aghdhiyah*, 4 vols. (Būlāq, 1291); German translation by Joseph v. Sontheimer, 2 vols. (Stuttgart, 1840–42) unsatisfactory; Fr. tr. Lucien Leclerc in *Notices et extraits des manuscrits de la Bibliothèque Nationale*, vol. xxiii (Paris, 1877), pt. i, vol. xxv (1881), pt. i, vol. xxvi (1883), pt. i.

[2] "Muqni'at al-Sā'il 'an al-Maraḍ al-Hā'il", ed. and tr. M. J. Müller, *Sitzungsberichte der königl. bayer. Akademie der Wissenschaften zu München*, vol. ii (Munich, 1863), pp. 6-7, 18-19.

[3] His birthplace al-Zahrā' was the famous suburb of Cordova. He is known to the Latin writers as Abulcasis or Albucasis, a corruption of abu-al-Qāsim.

Ta'ālīf[1] (an aid to him who is not equal to the large treatises), which in its last section sums up the surgical knowledge of his time. The work introduces or emphasizes such new ideas as cauterization of wounds, crushing a stone inside the bladder and the necessity of vivisection and dissection. This surgical part was translated into Latin by Gerard of Cremona and various editions were published at Venice in 1497, at Basel in 1541 and at Oxford in 1778.[2] It held its place for centuries as the manual of surgery in Salerno, Montpellier and other early schools of medicine. It contained illustrations of instruments which influenced other Arab authors and helped lay the foundations of surgery in Europe. A colleague of al-Zahrāwi was Ḥasdāy ben-Shaprūṭ, the Jewish minister and physician who translated into Arabic, with the collaboration of a Byzantine monk Nicholas, the splendid illustrated manuscript of the *Materia medica* of Dioscorides, which had been sent as a diplomatic present to 'Abd-al-Raḥmān III from the Byzantine Emperor Constantine VII.[3]

Ibn-Zuhr

Al-Zahrāwi's rank in the art of surgery was paralleled by that of ibn-Zuhr in the science of medicine. Abu-Marwān 'Abd-al-Malik ibn-abi-al-'Alā', surnamed ibn-Zuhr[4] (L. through Heb. Avenzoar), was the most illustrious member of the greatest medical family of Spain. Ibn-Zuhr was born between 1091 and 1094 in Seville, where he died in 1162 after serving for many years as court physician and vizir to 'Abd-al-Mu'min, founder of the Muwaḥḥid dynasty. His originality he showed by confining himself to authorship in the field of medicine, when his colleagues were spreading themselves over several branches of knowledge. Of the six medical works written by him three are extant. The most valuable is *al-Taysīr fi al-Mudāwāh w-al-Tadbīr*[5] (the facilitation of therapeutics and diet) written at the request of his friend and admirer ibn-Rushd as a counterpart to the latter's *al-Kullīyāt*.[6] The *Taysīr* dealt with more specific topics than the *Kullīyāt*. In his *al-Kullīyāt* ibn-Rushd hails ibn-

[1] *Ta'līf* in ibn-abi-Uṣaybi'ah, vol. ii, p. 52.

[2] The Oxford edition Albucasis, *De chirurgia*, has part of the text with Latin translation by John Channing. The text in its entirety has not yet been published.

[3] Ibn-abi-Uṣaybi'ah, vol. ii, p. 47, where Romanus is credited with the donation.

[4] See ibn-abi-Uṣaybi'ah, vol. ii, pp. 66-7.

[5] The Hebrew translation was rendered into "vulgar language", possibly the Venetian dialect, which was in turn done into Latin in 1280 with the help of a Jew in Venice, where it was repeatedly printed.

[6] Ibn-abi-Uṣaybi'ah, vol. ii, pp. 75-6.

Zuhr as the greatest physician since Galen. At least he was the greatest clinician in Islam after al-Rāzi. Ibn-Zuhr has been often credited with being the first to discuss feeling in bones and to describe the itch mite (*ṣu'ābat al-jarab*); but it has been recently shown that in his discovery of the itch mite he was anticipated by Aḥmad al-Ṭabari (second half of tenth century) in his *al-Mu'ālajah al-Buqrāṭīyah*.[1]

The ibn-Zuhr family produced about six generations of physicians in direct descent. After the above-mentioned abu-Marwān his son, abu-Bakr Muḥammad († 1198–9), was the most distinguished member. His distinction, however, was due more to his control of all branches of Arabic literature than to his medical activity. Several poems, including *muwashshaḥs* of great delicacy of sentiment, are ascribed to him.[2] The Muwaḥḥid abu-Yūsuf Ya'qūb al-Manṣūr appointed him his physician at Marrākush, where he was poisoned by a jealous vizir. The caliph himself preached his funeral sermon. One of the early ibn-Zuhrs, a grandfather and namesake of abu-Marwān 'Abd-al-Malik, had practised medicine not only in Spain but in Baghdād, al-Qayrawān and Cairo.[3] Another Hispano-Arab physician who practised in the East was 'Ubaydullāh ibn-al-Muẓaffar al-Bāhili of Almería (al-Marīyah). Al-Bāhili, a poet as well as physician, entered in 1127 the service of the Saljūq Maḥmūd ibn-Malikshāh in Baghdād and provided him with a field hospital transported on forty camels.[4] He died at Damascus in 1154.

Transmission to Europe

In the first centuries of Moslem domination in Spain, Eastern culture flowed from a higher level into Andalusia, as can be seen from al-Maqqari's[5] list of Spanish savants who journeyed "in quest of learning" to Egypt, Syria, al-'Irāq, Persia and even Transoxiana and China; but in the eleventh and following centuries the course was reversed, as illustrated by ibn-Zuhr and al-Bāhili. Indeed, the current became strong enough in the twelfth century to overflow into Europe. In the transmission of Arab medicine to Europe, north-western Africa and Spain, in particular Toledo, where Gerard of Cremona and Michael Scot

[1] Mohamed Rihab in *Archiv für Geschichte der Medizin*, vol. xix (1927), pp. 123-68.

[2] For specimens consult Maqqari, vol. i, pp. 625-8; ibn-Khallikān, vol. ii, pp. 375-6.

[3] Ṣā'id, p. 84, copied by ibn-abi-Uṣaybi'ah, vol. ii, p. 64; ibn-Khallikān, vol. ii, pp. 376-7.

[4] Maqqari, vol. i, p. 899.

[5] Vol. i, pp. 403-943.

worked, played the leading part. The initiator of this significant movement of acquainting the West with the learning of the Arabs by means of Latin translation was Constantine the African († 1087), who translated the theoretical part of 'Ali ibn-al-'Abbās' *al-Kitāb al-Maliki*.[1] Born in Carthage of obscure origin, Constantine attached himself for some time to the medical school of Salerno, the first medical school of Europe, reputed by legend to have been founded by four masters, a Latin, a Greek, a Jew and a Saracen. To Constantine, to Gerard of Cremona († 1187), translator of al-Zahrāwi's *Taṣrīf*, al-Rāzi's *al-Manṣūri* as well as ibn-Sīna's *al-Qānūn*, and to Faraj ben-Sālim (Fararius, Faragut), the Sicilian Jew, who translated al-Rāzi's *al-Ḥāwi* in 1279 and ibn-Jazlah's *Taqwīm al-Abdān*, medieval Europe was chiefly indebted for its knowledge of Arabic medicine. Thereby were the three main medical traditions, Moslem, Jewish and Christian, at last brought into a position where they could be amalgamated. Through these and similar translations several Arabic technical terms were introduced into European languages. "Julep" (Ar. *julāb*, from Pers. *gulāb*, rose-water), for a medicinal aromatic drink; "rob" (Ar. *rubb*), for a conserve of inspissated fruit juice with honey; and "syrup"[2] (Ar. *sharāb*), a solution of sugar in water made according to an officinal formula and often medicated with some special therapeutic, may serve as an illustration. "Soda", which in medieval Latin meant headache and in the form *sodanum* headache remedy, comes ultimately from Arabic *ṣudā'*, splitting pain in the head. Certain medical terms were translated, as were certain mathematical terms. "Dura mater" and "pia mater" are Latin translations of Arabic *al-umm al-jāfiyah* (the coarse mother) and *al-umm al-raqīqah* (the thin mother) respectively. Among several chemical terms which passed into European languages through Latin from Arabic works ascribed to Jābir ibn-Ḥayyān and other Moslem alchemists, we may note "alcohol",[3] "alembic",[4] "alkali" (*al-qali*), "antimony",[5] "aludel",[6] "realgar"[7] and "tutty".[8]

Philosophy

The crowning achievement of the intellectual class of Arabs

[1] The surgical part was done into Latin by a disciple of Constantine, John the Saracen (1040–1103), a Salernitan physician. See above, p. 367; below, p. 663.

[2] For "sherbet" see above, p. 335.

[3] Ar. *al-kuḥl*, whence Eng. "coal" possibly also comes.

[4] Ar. *al-inbīq*, originally Gr.

[5] Ar. *ithmid*, of Gr. origin.

[6] Ar. *al-uthāl*, vessels.

[7] Ar. *rahj al-ghār*, "the powder of the cave".

[8] Ar. *tūtiyā'*, from Skr.

in Spain was in the realm of philosophic thought. Here they formed the last and strongest link in the chain which transmitted Greek philosophy, as transmuted by them and their Eastern co-religionists, to the Latin West, adding their own contribution, especially in reconciling faith and reason, religion and science. To the Moslem thinkers Aristotle was truth, Plato was truth, the Koran was truth; but truth must be one. Hence arose the necessity of harmonizing the three, and to this task they addressed themselves. The Christian scholastics were faced by the same problem, but their task was rendered more difficult by the accumulation of dogmas and mysteries in their theology. Philosophy as developed by the Greeks and monotheistic religion as evolved by the Hebrew prophets were, as noted above, the richest legacies of the ancient West and of the ancient East. It is to the eternal glory of medieval Moslem thinkers of Baghdād and Andalusia that they reconciled these two currents of thought and passed them on harmonized into Europe. Their contribution was one of first magnitude, considering its effect upon scientific and philosophic thought and upon the theology of later times.

This influx into Western Europe of a body of new ideas, mainly philosophic, marks the beginning of the end of the "Dark Ages" and the dawn of the scholastic period. Kindled by contact with Arab thought and quickened by fresh acquaintance with ancient Greek lore, the interest of Europeans in scholarship and philosophy led them on to an independent and rapidly developing intellectual life of their own, whose fruits we still enjoy.

Ben-Gabīrōl

Among the earliest philosophers of Arabic Spain was Solomon ben-Gabīrōl[1] (Avicebron, Avencebrol), a Jew. Solomon was born at Malaga about 1021 and died in Valencia about 1058. As the first great teacher of Neo-Platonism in the West, ben-Gabīrōl is often referred to as the Jewish Plato. Like ibn-Masarrah[2] before him he was an advocate of the system of philosophy fathered on Empedocles. A thousand years before his time Platonic philosophy had been Orientalized by Philo, the Hellenistic Jewish philosopher of Alexandria, preparatory to its Christianization and Islamization, and now in the form of Greco-

[1] Sulaymān ibn-Yaḥya ibn-Jabīrūl. Cf. Ṣā'id, p. 89.

[2] See Miguel Asín, *Abenmasarra y su escuela. Origenes de la filosofia hispano musulmana* (Madrid, 1914).

Moslem philosophy it was re-Occidentalized by ben-Gabīrōl and restored to Europe. Ben-Gabīrōl's main work was *Yanbū' al-Ḥayāh* (the fount of life).[1] Translated into Latin in 1150 as *Fons vitæ*, it played a part in medieval scholasticism and inspired the Franciscan school.

Ibn-Bājjah

The twelfth was the greatest century in the history of philosophic thought in Moslem Spain. The century opens with abu-Bakr Muḥammad ibn-Yaḥya ibn-Bājjah (Avenpace, Avempace), philosopher, scientist, physician, musician and commentator on Aristotle, who flourished in Granada and Saragossa and died at Fās in 1138. Ibn-Bājjah wrote several treatises on astronomy in which he criticized Ptolemy's assumptions and thus prepared the way for ibn-Ṭufayl and al-Biṭrūji, other treatises on materia medica which were quoted by ibn-al-Bayṭār, and still others on medicine which exerted a powerful influence over ibn-Rushd.[2] But his most important work, the only one extant besides a farewell letter to a friend, is a philosophical treatise entitled *Tadbīr al-Mutawaḥḥid* (*De regimine solitarii*, the régime of the solitary), which has been preserved only in a Hebrew abstract. The aim of this book is to demonstrate how man unaided may attain to union with the Active Intellect, and to teach that the gradual perfection of the human spirit through union with the divine is the object of philosophy. Moslem biographers considered ibn-Bājjah an atheist.[3]

Ibn-Bājjah's philosophic ideas were carried a step further by abu-Bakr[4] Muḥammad ibn-'Abd-al-Malik ibn-Ṭufayl,[5] the Neo-Platonic philosopher who practised medicine at Granada and later became adviser and chief royal physician to the Muwaḥhid abu-Ya'qūb Yūsuf (1163–84)—a combination of functions not unusual in a Moslem state. In 1182 he resigned his position as court physician and was succeeded by his younger philosopher-friend ibn-Rushd, whom he had recommended to the caliph. These two luminaries shed imperishable lustre on the court of the early Muwaḥḥids, a dynasty puritanic in theology but liberal in its patronage of philosophy. Born in the first decade of this

[1] His *Iṣlāḥ al-Akhlāq* has been edited and translated by Stephen S. Wise (New York, 1901).

[2] Ibn-abi-Uṣaybi'ah, vol. ii, p. 63, makes ibn-Rushd (b. 1126) ibn-Bājjah's pupil.

[3] Ibn-Khallikān, vol. ii, p. 372.

[4] Whence his Latinized name Abubacer.

[5] Ibn-al-Ṭufayl in ibn-abi-Uṣaybi'ah, vol. ii, p. 78. Cf. ibn-abi-Zar', vol. i, p. 135; ibn-Khallikān, vol. iii, p. 467.

century, ibn-Ṭufayl died in 1185 in the Muwaḥḥid capital Marrākush, where his second patron the Caliph abu-Yūsuf al-Manṣūr (1184–99) attended the obsequies. His masterpiece was an original philosophic romance entitled *Ḥayy ibn-Yaqẓān* (the living one, son of the vigilant),[1] whose underlying idea was that human capacity unassisted by external agency may attain to the knowledge of the higher world and may find out by degrees its dependence upon a Supreme Being. This story, one of the most delightful and original in the literature of the Middle Ages, was first translated into Latin by Edward Pococke, the younger (1671),[2] and then into most European languages, including Dutch (1672), Russian (1920) and Spanish (1934). Some have sought in it an original of *Robinson Crusoe*. The theory it develops is evolutionary. Ibn-Ṭufayl borrowed his characters' names from ibn-Sīna's short and lifeless tale of the same title, but drew his inspiration from earlier authors beginning with al-Fārābi.

Ibn-Rushd

The greatest Moslem philosopher, judged by his influence especially over the West, was the Hispano-Arab astronomer, physician and Aristotelian commentator abu-al-Walīd Muḥammad ibn-Aḥmad ibn-Rushd (Averroës). Ibn-Rushd was born in Cordova in 1126, and belonged to a distinguished family which had produced several theologians and qāḍis. In 1169–71 he himself was qāḍi of Seville and two years later of Cordova. In 1182 he was called to Marrakesh by abu-Ya'qūb Yūsuf to replace ibn-Ṭufayl as court physician. Yūsuf's son and successor al-Manṣūr banished ibn-Rushd in 1194 on a suspicion of heresy due to his studies in philosophy, but later recalled him to his office in Marrākush, where he died soon afterwards, on December 10, 1198.[3] His remains were later removed to Cordova.

Ibn-Rushd's chief contribution to medicine was an encyclopædic work entitled *al-Kullīyāt*[4] *fi al-Ṭibb* (generalities on medicine), in which the fact is recognized that no one is taken twice with smallpox and the function of the retina is well under-

[1] I.e. the intellect of man derived from the divine intellect.

[2] The translation was published in Oxford together with the Ar. text edited by Edward Pococke, the elder. Several editions of the Ar. text appeared in Cairo and Constantinople in 1299. There is only one critical edition, that of Léon Gauthier (Algiers, 1900; Beirūt, 1936) with a Fr. translation.

[3] Ibn-abi-Uṣaybi'ah, vol. ii, pp. 76-7; ibn-abi-Zar', vol. i, pp. 135-6; ibn-Khallikān, vol. iii, p. 467.

[4] Corrupted into L. *Colliget*, not related etymologically to *colligo*, to collect.

stood. But ibn-Rushd, the physician, was entirely eclipsed by ibn-Rushd, the philosopher and commentator. His chief philosophical work, other than his commentaries, was his *Tahāfut al-Tahāfut*[1] (the incoherence of the incoherence), a reply to al-Ghazzāli's attack on rationalism entitled *Tahāfut al-Falāsifah* (the incoherence of the philosophers[2]). It was this work for which ibn-Rushd was best known, and unfavourably so, in the Moslem world. In the Jewish and Christian worlds, however, he was known primarily as a commentator on Aristotle. A medieval commentator, we should recall, was an author who composed a scientific or philosophic work using some earlier writing as a background and framework. Accordingly ibn-Rushd's commentaries were a series of treatises using in part the titles of Aristotle's works and paraphrasing their contents. As ibn-Rushd knew no Greek he was content to rely on translations made by his predecessors in Baghdād. His chief commentaries on Aristotle were a short *Jāmi'* (summary), an intermediate *Talkhīṣ* (résumé) and a long *Tafsīr* or *Sharḥ* (commentary).[3] Most of ibn-Rushd's commentaries have been preserved in Hebrew translations or in Latin translations from the Hebrew. Only a few have survived in Arabic and even these are generally in Hebrew script.[4]

Last of the great Arabic-writing philosophers, ibn-Rushd produced no progeny in Islam. He belonged more to Christian Europe than to Moslem Asia or Africa. To the West he became "the commentator"[5] as Aristotle was "the teacher". Though using in most instances a Latin translation of a Hebrew rendition of an Arabic commentary upon an Arabic translation of a Syriac translation of a Greek original, the minds of the Christian schoolmen and scholars of medieval Europe were agitated by ibn-Rushd's Aristotle as by no other author. From the end of the twelfth to the end of the sixteenth century Averroism remained the dominant school of thought, and that in spite of the orthodox reaction it created first among the Moslems in Spain, then among the Talmudists and finally among the Christian clergy.

[1] Ed. Maurice Bouyges (Beirūt 1930); tr. S. Van Den Bergh, 2 vols. (Oxford, 1954).

[2] Aristotelian and Neo-Platonic; views stated in his *Maqāṣid al-Falāsifah* (Cairo, 1331).

[3] For a complete list consult Ernest Renan, *Averroès et l'averroïsme*, 2nd ed. (Paris, 1861), pp. 58-79; Sarton, *Introduction*, vol. ii, pp. 356-61.

[4] His *Talkhīṣ Kitāb al-Maqūlāt*, a résumé of Aristotle's *Categories*, has been edited by Maurice Bouyges (Beirūt, 1932).

[5] Or to quote Dante, "Averroìs che il gran comento feo", *Inferno*, canto iv, l. 144.

Ibn-Rushd was a rationalist and claimed the right to submit everything save the revealed dogmas of faith to the judgment of reason, but he was not a free-thinker or unbeliever. His view of creation by God was evolutionary: not a matter of days but of eternity. Earlier Moslem Aristotelians had taken for genuine a number of apocryphal works, including some of Neo-Platonic character; ibn-Rushd's philosophy involved a return to purer and more scientific Aristotelianism. After being purged of objectionable matter by ecclesiastical authorities, his writings became prescribed studies in the University of Paris and other institutions of higher learning. With all its excellences and all the misconceptions collected under its name, the intellectual movement initiated by ibn-Rushd continued to be a living factor in European thought until the birth of modern experimental science.

Ibn-Maymūn

For first place after ibn-Rushd among the philosophers of the age the only candidate is his Jewish contemporary and fellow Cordovan abu-ʿImrān Mūsa ibn-Maymūn (Heb. Mōsheh ben-Maimōn,[1] L. Maimonides), the most famous of the Hebrew physicians and philosophers of the whole Arabic epoch. Ibn-Maymūn was born in Cordova in 1135,[2] but his family left the country as a result of the Muwaḥḥid persecution and settled in Cairo about 1165. The claim of al-Qifṭi[3] and ibn-abi-Uṣaybiʿah[4] that in Spain ibn-Maymūn professed Islam in public but practised Judaism in secret has recently been subjected to sharp criticism. In Cairo he became the court physician of the celebrated Ṣalāḥ-al-Dīn and of his son al-Malik al-ʿAzīz. From 1177 on he held the chief religious office of the Jewish community[5] at Cairo, where he died in 1204. In accordance with his will his body was carried by hand over the route once taken by Moses and buried in Tiberias, where his unpretentious tomb is still visited by throngs of pilgrims. Ailing people among the poor Jews of modern Egypt still seek their cure by spending the night in the underground chamber of the synagogue of Rabbi Mōsheh ben-Maimōn in Cairo.

Ibn-Maymūn distinguished himself as astronomer, theologian, physician and above all as philosopher. His medical science was

[1] Also referred to as *Mōsheh haz-zĕmān*, "the Moses of his time". A popular Jewish saying, "From Moses to Moses there was none like Moses [Maimonides]", expresses the eminent position he has ever held in Jewish estimation.

[2] His eight-hundredth anniversary was observed throughout the civilized world.

[3] Pp. 318-19.

[4] Vol. ii, p. 117.

[5] Ar. *ra's al-millah*, Heb. *nāgīd*.

the standard Galenism of his time derived from al-Rāzi, ibn-Sīna and ibn-Zuhr and enlivened by rational criticism based on personal observation. Ibn-Maymūn improved the method of circumcision, ascribed hemorrhoids to constipation, prescribing for them a light diet predominantly vegetarian, and held advanced ideas on hygiene. His most popular medical work was *al-Fuṣūl fi al-Ṭibb* (aphorisms of medicine). His leading philosophical work bore the title *Dalālat al-Ḥā'irīn*[1] (the guide of the perplexed); in this he tried to reconcile Jewish theology with Moslem Aristotelianism or, in broader terms, faith with reason. Prophetic visions he explained as psychical experiences. To this extent at least he stood as the champion of scientific thought against biblical "fundamentalism" and aroused the anger of conservative theologians, who referred to his book as *Ḍalālah* (misguidance, error). His philosophic ideas resembled those of ibn-Rushd, though developed independently. Like ibn-Rushd he knew no Greek and depended entirely on Arabic translations. The theory of creation which he propounded, but did not share, was the atomistic one as distinguished from the two others held by the Arabic-writing thinkers, namely, the fundamentalist theory, which made God creator of everything, and the philosophical, which was Neo-Platonic and Aristotelian. His works, with one major exception, were written in Arabic, but in Hebrew characters, and were soon translated into Hebrew and later in part into Latin. Their influence, far-reaching in space and time, was exerted mainly over Jews and Christians. Down to the eighteenth century they remained the principal medium through which Jewish thought reached the Gentiles. Modern critics detect traces of that influence in the Dominicans, as attested by the works of Albertus Magnus, in Albertus' rival, Duns Scotus, in Spinoza and even in Kant.

Ibn-'Arabi, the mystic

The ruling mystic of the age was another Hispano-Arab, abu-Bakr Muḥammad ibn-'Ali Muḥyi-al-Dīn ibn-'Arabi,[2] the greatest speculative genius of Islamic Sufism. Ibn-'Arabi was born in Murcia (Mursiyah) in 1165 and flourished mainly in Seville until 1201–2, when he made the holy pilgrimage, after

[1] Edited in Hebrew characters and translated into French by Salomon Munk 3 vols. (Paris, 1856–66).

[2] In the East he is generally known as ibn-'Arabi to distinguish him from his fellow countryman and traditionist abu-Bakr ibn-al-'Arabi. Among his *nisbahs* he bore al-Ḥātimi al-Ṭā'i, implying descent from Ḥātim al-Ṭā'i

which he remained in the East till his death at Damascus in 1240.[1] There his tomb, enshrined in a mosque, is still standing. The twelfth century witnessed in the East the beginnings of a vast organization of Moslem religious life corresponding to the monastic orders in medieval Christendom, and ibn-ʿArabi, who represented the illuministic (*ishrāqi*) or pseudo-Empedoclean, Neo-Platonic and pantheistic school founded by ibn-Masarrah and ben-Gabīrōl, was the man to give this Sufi movement its framework of speculative philosophy. The greatest exponent of this school in the East was al-Suhrawardi († 1191), whose Persian origin and emphasis on the metaphysics of light reveal Manichaean-Zoroastrian influence and whose major work was *Ḥikmat al-Ishrāq* (wisdom of illumination). The illuministic school was so called because, according to its mystical theory, God and the world of spirits should be interpreted as light and our process of cognition as an illumination from above through the intermediary of the spirits of the spheres.[2] To his followers ibn-ʿArabi was *al-shaykh al-akbar*, the grand master. His system is embedded in an enormous mass of writings,[3] of which the most influential are *al-Futūḥāt al-Makkīyah*[4] (the Makkan revelations) and *Fuṣūṣ al-Ḥikam*[5] (the bezels of wise precepts). It is in chapter 167 of the *Futūḥāt*,[6] headed "Kīmiyāʾ al-Saʿādah" (the alchemy of happiness), which contains an esoteric allegory of the ascension of man to heaven, and in another work still unpublished, entitled *al-Isrāʾ ila Maqām al-Asra* (the nocturnal journey toward the station of the Most Magnanimous One), where he develops the theme of the Prophet's ascension to the seventh heaven, that ibn-ʿArabi anticipates Dante.[7]

In jurisprudence ibn-ʿArabi nominally belonged to the Ẓāhiri (literalist) school of his compatriot ibn-Ḥazm; in matters of speculative belief he passed for a *bāṭini* (esoteric);[8] in philosophic theory he was a pantheistic monist, as his doctrine *waḥdat al-wujūd* (the unity of existence) justly proclaims him. His central theme was that things pre-exist as ideas (*aʿyān thābitah*)

[1] Ibn-al-Jawzi, *Mirʾāt al-Zamān*, ed. James R. Jewett (Chicago, 1907), p. 487; Maqqari, vol. i, p. 567; Kutubi, vol. ii, p. 301; al-Shaʿrāni, *al-Yawāqīt w-al-Jawāhir* (Cairo, 1905), p. 8.

[2] Consult Ḥājji Khalfah, vol. iii, pp. 87 *seq.*; Carra de Vaux in *Journal asiatique*, ser. 9, vol. xix (1902), pp. 63-94.

[3] Of the 289 works credited to him Brockelmann, vol. i, pp. 442-8, lists 150 as existing at the present day. [4] 2nd ed., 4 vols. (Būlāq, 1293). [5] (Būlāq, 1252).

[6] Vol. ii, pp. 356-75. [7] See above, p. 114. [8] Maqqari, vol. i, pp. 569 *seq.*

in the knowledge of God, whence they emanate and whither they return. There is no creation *ex nihilo*; the world is merely the outer aspect of God, who is its inner aspect. Between the Essence and its attributes, i.e. God and the universe, there is no real difference. Here Moslem mysticism passes into pantheism. The divine manifests itself in the human, and the perfect man (*al-insān al-kāmil*) is, of course, Muḥammad. Muḥammad is also the *kalimah*, the *logos*, as Jesus was. The true mystic, in the judgment of ibn-ʿArabi, has but one guide, the inner light, and will find God in all religions.[1]

The influence of the illuministic school, whose greatest Spanish representative ibn-ʿArabi was, is manifest not only in Persian and Turkish Sufi circles[2] but in the so-called Augustinian scholastics such as Duns Scotus, Roger Bacon and Raymond Lull.[3] Another Murcian, abu-Muḥammad ʿAbd-al-Ḥaqq ibn-Sabʿīn (*ca.* 1217–69), stood for the same type of thinking and writing as ibn-ʿArabi. His pre-eminence in Sufi circles won him the enviable title Quṭb-al-Dīn (the pole of religion). But he is best known for the answers he wrote, *al-Ajwibah ʿan al-Asʾilah al-Ṣiqillīyah*[4] (answers to the Sicilian questions), to the learned questions on the eternity of matter, the nature and immortality of the soul, the object of theology and the like asked by Frederick II of Hohenstaufen and transmitted by the Muwaḥḥid ʿAbd-al-Wāḥid al-Rashīd (1232–42). Ibn-Sabʿīn, who was then residing at Ceuta, answered at some length in terms of Islamic orthodoxy and offered to set the Christian emperor of Sicily right in a personal interview. In the meantime he refused the reward of money which accompanied the questionnaire. Ibn-Sabʿīn's other leading work is *Asrār al-Ḥikmah al-Mashriqīyah* (the mysteries of illuministic philosophy), still unpublished. He was one of the rare Moslems in history who committed suicide, and that by opening a vein in his wrist while sojourning in Makkah.[5]

[1] Ibn-ʿArabi, *Tarjumān al-Ashwāq*, ed. and tr. Nicholson (London, 1911), pp. 19, 67.

[2] The greatest of the Sufi poets, Jalāl-al-Dīn al-Rūmi, who died some thirty years after ibn-ʿArabi, was linked to the latter through one of ibn-ʿArabi's pupils.

[3] In his *El Islam cristianizado* (Madrid, 1931), Asín develops the thesis that Moslem Sufism as represented by ibn-ʿArabi was consciously or unconsciously an imitation of Christian monastic mysticism.

[4] Still unpublished. See M. Amari, *Biblioteca Arabo-Sicula* (Leipzig, 1855-7), pp. 573-7; in *Journal asiatique*, ser. 5, vol. i (1853), pp. 240-74. See also A. F. Mehren, *loc. cit.* vol. xiv (1879), pp. 341-454.

[5] Kutubi, vol. i, p. 316.

Toledo, centre of translation

In the process of transmitting the treasures of Arabic erudition into the West, Toledo, which maintained its position after the Christian conquest in 1085 as an important centre of Islamic learning, acted as the main channel. Here through the initiative of Archbishop Raymond I (1126–52) arose a regular school for translation. In it a series of translators flourished from about 1135 to 1284. Scholars were attracted from various parts of Europe, including the British Isles, whence hailed Michael Scot and Robert of Chester.[1] In 1145 Robert made the first translation of al-Khwārizmi's algebra; in 1143 he had completed with Hermann the Dalmatian for Peter the Venerable the first Latin translation of the Koran. It was also in Toledo that the first school of Oriental studies in Europe was established, in 1250, by the Order of Preachers with a view to preparing missionaries to Moslems and Jews.

The name of Adelard of Bath, who is said to have visited Spain at this time, is one of the greatest in English science before Roger Bacon. After sojourning in Sicily and Syria Adelard turned into Latin in 1126 the astronomical tables of al-Majrīṭi, which were based on those of al-Khwārizmi and included tables of sines. He translated a number of other mathematical and astronomical treatises and became the first of a long line of English Arabists. The Scotsman Michael Scot († *ca.* 1236), one of the founders of Latin Averroism, studied and worked in Spain before becoming court astrologer to Frederick II of Sicily. In Toledo he translated among several other works al-Biṭrūji's astronomy, *al-Hay'ah*, and Aristotle's *De coelo et mundo* with ibn-Rushd's commentary; in Sicily he translated other Arabic books which he dedicated to Frederick. The most important of these was ibn-Sīna's version of Aristotle's zoology, *Abbreviatio Avicenne de animalibus*. But the most prolific of the Toledan translators was Gerard of Cremona, who before his death in 1187 had rendered into Latin al-Farghāni's version of Ptolemy's *Almagest*, al-Fārābi's commentary on Aristotle, Euclid's *Elements* and various treatises of Aristotle, Galen and Hippocrates—in all seventy-one Arabic works.

As we have seen, Jews, both orthodox and converted, played a major rôle in this work of translation. One of the earliest among them was Abraham ben-Ezra of Toledo († 1167), a distinguished biblical commentator who translated two treatises on astrology

[1] See Charles H. Haskins, *Studies in the History of Mediaeval Science*, 2nd ed. (Cambridge, 1927), ch. i.

by his earlier co-religionist of the East, Māshā'allāh[1] († 815). He also translated al-Bīrūni's commentary on al-Khwārizmi's tables. Ben-Ezra's contemporary, John of Seville (Joannes Hispalensis, often confused with a Mozarab Christian), a baptized Jew, flourished in Toledo about 1135–53 under the patronage of Archbishop Raymond and translated works on arithmetic, astronomy and astrology, medicine and philosophy by al-Farghāni, abu-Ma'shar, al-Kindi, ben-Gabīrōl and al-Ghazzāli. Of these the most important was al-Farghāni's astronomy. John presumably translated from Arabic into the vernacular, Castilian, and an associate put the Castilian into Latin.

By the close of the thirteenth century Arabic science and philosophy had been transmitted to Europe, and Spain's work as an intermediary was done. The intellectual avenue leading from the portals of Toledo through the Pyrenees wound its way through Provence and the Alpine passes[2] into Lorraine, Germany and Central Europe as well as across the Channel into England.[3] Among the cities of southern France deserving mention are Marseille, where Raymond in 1140 drew up planetary tables based on those of Toledo; Toulouse, where Hermann the Dalmatian completed in 1143 al-Majrīṭi's translation of Ptolemy's *Planisphærium*; Narbonne, where Abraham ben-Ezra translated in 1160 al-Bīrūni's commentary on al-Khwārizmi's tables; and Montpellier, which in the thirteenth century became the chief centre of medical and astronomical studies in France. In eastern France Cluny, whose famous abbey housed a number of Spanish monks, was during the twelfth century a significant focus for the diffusion of Arab learning. Its abbot, Peter the Venerable, sponsored (1141–3) the first Latin translation of the Koran, besides various pamphlets directed against Islam. Arabic science, introduced into Lorraine (Lotharingia) in the tenth century, made that region a centre of scientific influence in the following two centuries, Liége, Gorze and Cologne, among other Lotharingian cities, provided the most fertile soil for the germination of Arab learning. From Lorraine it radiated into other parts of Germany and was transported

[1] Mentioned in *Fihrist*, p. 273.

[2] See below, p. 605.

[3] The first book printed in England, *The Dictes and Sayengis of the Philosophres* by William Caxton at Westminster in 1477, was based on *Mukhtār al-Ḥikam wa-Maḥāsin al-Kalim*, by a Syro-Egyptian prince abu-al-Wāfā' Mubashshir ibn-Fātik, fl. 1053 (ed. 'Abd-al-Raḥmān Badawi, Madrid, 1958).

into Norman England by men born or educated in Lorraine. Embassies between German kings in the north and Moslem rulers in Spain were frequent and intellectually fruitful. As early

From Ameer Ali, "A Short History of the Saracens" (*Macmillan & Co., Ltd.*)

PAVILION IN THE COURT OF LIONS, ALHAMBRA, GRANADA

as 953 Otto the Great, king of the Germans, sent as an envoy a Lotharingian monk, John by name, who resided in Cordova for nearly three years, probably learned Arabic and brought back with him scientific manuscripts.[1] Thus did Spanish Arabic learning permeate all Western Europe.

[1] "Vita Johannis abbatis Gorziensis", G. H. Pertz, *Monumenta Germaniæ historica, scriptores rerum Germanicarum*, vol. iv, pp. 337-77.

CHAPTER XLI

ART AND ARCHITECTURE

THE Arabs in Spain carried on almost all the minor and practical arts developed by Moslems in other lands. In metal-work[1] involving decoration, raising patterns in relief or engraving them, inlaying with gold and silver[2] and inscribing characters, the Hispano-Moresque school excelled. One of the earliest specimens is a relic of Hishām II (976–1009) preserved on the high altar of the Cathedral of Gerona in the form of a wooden casket sheathed with silver-gilt plating patterned in *repoussé* with scroll-like foliation. It bears an Arabic inscription stating that it is the work of two craftsmen, Badr and Ṭarīf, and was made for a courtier of al-Ḥakam II (961–76) as a present for the heir apparent, Hishām. In metal-work such as cutlery, sword blades and astrolabes Toledo and Seville[3] were especially noted. Next to damascene blades, toledos had the finest temper and the greatest elasticity. The astrolabe, an astronomical instrument of ancient Greek invention, was perfected by the Moslems and introduced into Europe in the tenth century. Besides its use to determine the hour of prayer and the geographical position of Makkah, the astrolabe was invaluable to mariners for nautical observations and was a necessary adjunct of the astrologer's equipment. In the story told by the tailor in the *Arabian Nights* (no. 29), the glib barber exasperates his customer by trying to find with an astrolabe the precise moment auspicious for shaving. A properly executed astrolabe is a beautiful work of art.

Minor arts

Enamelling found no high favour with Moslem metal-workers, but in the application of coloured glazes to earthenware, Moslems were from an early period past masters. Valencia was the Moslem centre of this industry in the West. The importation of its products laid the foundation of the pottery industry at Poitiers.

Ceramics

[1] Sp. *alhaja*, jewel, is from Ar. *al-ḥājah*.

[2] Generally known as damascening, from European association of the work with Damascus.

[3] Maqqari, vol. i, p. 124.

In the fifteenth century we find imitations of this Moslem pottery produced as far north as Holland. From Spain the industry was meanwhile introduced into Italy. Its influence is noticeable in the later Spanish vessels, with their pseudo-Arabic inscriptions and Christian heraldic devices. In other forms of ceramics, as well as mosaics, especially tile and blue faïence, the Spanish Moslem school distinguished itself. The various kinds of coloured tiles still favourites in Spain and Portugal are a legacy from the Arabs, as the name *azulejo*[1] suggests. In the eyes of modern collectors the Mudejar lustre pottery ranks only below the Chinese. Exquisite pottery was manufactured in Toledo and Cordova as early as the third quarter of the eleventh century, after which Calatayud (Qalʿaṭ Ayyūb),[2] Malaga and above all Manises in Valencia became famous for this ware. In the manufacture and colouring of glass, however, Spain could not compete with Syria.

Textiles

In the development of the sumptuous textile arts which made the Arabic-speaking peoples the leading fabric-makers and silk mercers in the medieval world, the Arabs of Spain had a share;[3] but in carpet-making Spain offered no serious competition to the Eastern, especially Persian, market. Cordova was a centre of the weaving industry. Almería is said to have had four thousand eight hundred looms.[4] Just as al-Mawṣil exported to Italy the fabric known there as *mussolina*, whence our "muslin", and Baghdād supplied the same market with the rich silk cloth bearing the Italianized name *baldacco* and with the silken canopies, "baldachin",[5] suspended over the altars in many Western churches, so did Granada in later times supply the European dress shops with grenadines. Such Oriental silk textiles, with their rich colouring and floral and geometrical designs, were in limited demand for church vestments, for wrapping relics of saints[6] and for aristocratic and royal robes. As the importation of finely wrought stuffs from Moslem lands increased in Europe, Western enterprise saw in this industry a potential source of wealth and began to set up looms in various

[1] Ar. *al-zulayji*. See Maqqari, vol. i, p. 124.

[2] Idrīsi, *Ṣifat al-Maghrib* (Leyden), p. 189.

[3] Ibn-Ḥawqal, p. 79; Iṣṭakhri, p. 44, l. 8; ibn-al-Khaṭīb, *Lamḥah*, p. 13; Maqqari, vol. i, pp. 123-4.

[4] Maqqari, vol. i, p. 102.

[5] See below, p. 668.

[6] See above, pp. 422-3; below, p. 668.

centres of France and Italy. In these early factories some Moslem workmen were undoubtedly at first employed.

As in metal- and glass-work, pottery, architecture and other departments of decorative art, so in textiles we have between the fourteenth and sixteenth centuries numerous examples of European work bearing the stamp of Islamic style. In fact, as early as the twelfth century the adoption of Islamic designs by European weavers became frequent, and from that time on we have numerous illustrations of the use of meaningless imitation of Arabic script merely for decorative purposes. We should also remember that in Spain, and to a greater extent in Sicily, Oriental workmen lingered long after Islam had receded; hence the combination of Christian and Islamic elements in the forms of art and architecture known as Mudejar and the Islamic features in the Sicilian art and architecture of the Norman period. Mudejar workmen excelled in woodwork, pottery and textiles. To this day the Spanish carpenter uses in his trade words that are largely Arabic.

Photo: Casa Moreno

CARVED IVORY CASKET

Made in Cordova, A.D. 964, and now in the Museo Arqueológico, Madrid

In ornament executed in relief the Spanish Arab carvers and modellers followed the same system of design that governed their practice in flat surface decoration and other modes of technical expression. In the tenth century a school of ivory-carvers centred at Cordova and produced many beautiful caskets and boxes made partly or wholly of ivory and decorated with carved, inlaid or painted ornaments. Some of the ornaments represented musical performances and hunting-scenes illustrating the use of animal forms as a decorative motif. Such containers were often used as jewel cases and perfume or sweetmeat boxes. The inscriptions they bear indicate that they were often intended for gifts. One of the finest examples of this work is a cylindrical casket made in A.H. 353 (964), as the inscription round the domed lid reads, for the Caliph al-Ḥakam II as a gift to his wife.

Ivories

The sides are entirely covered with palmettes in addition to peacocks and other birds.

Architecture

All monuments of religious art in Spain have perished with the exception of one of the earliest and grandest, the great Mosque of Cordova. The foundation was laid by 'Abd-al-Raḥ-

Photo: Arexiv Ma

INTERIOR OF THE GREAT MOSQUE OF CORDOVA

mān I in 786 on the site of a Christian church which was originally a Roman temple.[1] The main part of the mosque was completed in 793 by his son Hishām I, who added the square minaret. The Spanish minarets followed the African style, which was of Syrian origin (above, p. 452). Additions to the Cordova mosque were made by Hishām's successors. Twelve hundred and ninety-three columns, a veritable forest, supported its roof. Brass lanterns made from Christian bells[2] illuminated the building. "One chandelier held a thousand lights; the smallest held

[1] See above, pp. 508-9. [2] Cf. above, p. 533.

twelve."[1] For the decoration of the building Byzantine craftsmen were employed, as they may have been employed in the Umayyad mosques of Syria.[2] Eighty thousand gold pieces from the spoils of the Goths were spent on the structure by its founder. Enlargements and repairs were made on it down to al-Ḥājib al-Manṣūr (977–1000). Today it is a cathedral to the Virgin of the Assumption.

Of the secular monuments the Alcázar[3] of Seville and the Alhambra of Granada, with their profuse but graceful decorations, are the most superb remains. Of Madīnat al-Zahrā', now called Córdoba la Vieja, built by 'Abd-al-Raḥmān III and his successors with columns imported from Rome, Constantinople and Carthage, very little has been left to show its former splendour. It is noteworthy that the caliph set up over the gateway a statue of his favourite concubine, whose name the palace bore. He is, moreover, said to have brought for it from Constantinople a fountain decorated with human figures. On the occasion of the Berber revolt of 1010 the Madīnah was sacked and set on fire. About the same time the similarly named villa of al-Manṣūr, al-Madīnah al-Zāhirah, which lay to the east of Cordova, was likewise destroyed by the Berbers and has now entirely disappeared.

The oldest part of the Alcázar of Seville was built by a Toledan architect for the Muwaḥḥid governor in 1199–1200. It was restored in the Moslem style by Mudejar workmen for King Peter the Cruel in 1353 and was used until a few years ago as a royal residence. Among the many Alcázars in Cordova, Toledo and other Spanish towns, this of Seville is the most renowned and the only one surviving. Seville boasts another Muwaḥḥid monument, the Giralda tower, originally the minaret of the great mosque. Erected in 1184, this minaret was decorated with cusped arcading, anticipating later Gothic tracery.

Alhambra

The Hispano-Moslem system of decoration reached its culminating point in the Naṣrid palace Alhambra.[4] This acropolis of Granada, with its excessive decoration in mosaics, stalactites and inscriptions, was conceived and constructed on so extensive and magnificent a scale that it has been accepted as the last

[1] 'Umari, *Masālik al-Abṣār fi Mamālik al-Amṣār*, ed. Aḥmad Zaki, vol. i (Cairo, 1927), p. 212.

[2] Cf. above, pp. 264, 265.

[3] For etymology see above, p. 107, n. 2.

[4] For the best reproductions consult the illustrations in Albert F. Calvert, *The Alhambra*, 2nd ed. (London, 1907).

word in such workmanship. Begun by Muḥammad I al-Ghālib about 1248, its construction was completed by abu-al-Ḥajjāj

From Arnold and Guillaume, "The Legacy of Islam," by courtesy of the Clarendon Press

THE HALL OF THE AMBASSADORS IN THE ALCÁZAR, SEVILLE

With coloured tiles representing Mudejar workmanship

Yūsuf (1333–54) and by his successor Muḥammad V al-Ghani (1354–9). Most of the interior decoration is ascribed by the inscriptions on the walls to abu-al-Ḥajjāj. The most celebrated portion is the Court of Lions. In the centre of this court twelve marble lions stand in a circle, each spouting a jet of water from its mouth. Among the surrounding profusion of decoration these lions, together with the ceiling of the so-called Hall of Justice, are the most important monuments of art. The ceiling depicts scenes painted on leather illustrating tales of chivalry and hunting episodes, besides ten rulers seated on an oval bench. Certain inscriptions embody al-Ghālib's motto, *wa-la ghālib illa Allāh* (but there is no conqueror other than Allah); others, employed for decorative purposes only, are represented as addressing the visitor in their function of ornament.

The arch

The horseshoe form of arch, which became characteristic of Western Moslem architecture, was represented in northern Syria, Ctesiphon and other places even before Islam. The pointed arch, which later became the distinctive feature of Western Gothic architecture, appears first in Islam in the Umayyad Mosque of Damascus and Quṣayr ʿAmrah.[1] The round horseshoe variety was used at the Umayyad Mosque of Damascus. This last type, which in the West became known as the Moorish arch, undoubtedly existed in Spain before the Arab conquest, but it was the Spanish, more particularly the Cordovan Moslems, who realized its structural and decorative possibilities and adopted it generally. Another contribution of Arab Cordova, which was truly original, was the system of vaulting based on intersecting arches and visible intersecting ribs.

These and other architectural features developed at Cordova were carried to Toledo and other centres in the north of the peninsula by Mozarabs. Here by merging of Christian and Moslem traditions arose a definite style characterized by almost regular use of the horseshoe arch and the vault. In the hands of Mudejar workmen this mixed art attained great beauty and perfection and became the Spanish national style. Mudejar work is still to be seen all over the country. The Spanish language has preserved several architectural terms which attest an Arabic origin.[2]

[1] See above, p. 417. Cf. Bell, *Ukhaiḍir*, pp. 5, 9, 12, pl. 7, fig. 1; C. Leonard Woolley, *The Sumerians* (Oxford, 1928), pp. 36-7.

[2] E.g.: *adoquin* (Ar. *kaddān*), paving stone; *alacena* (Ar. *al-khizānah*), cupboard; *albañil*, Pg. *alvanel* (Ar. *al-bannā'*), builder; *alcoba*, Pg. *alcoba* (Ar. *al-qubbah*, whence Eng. alcove), bedroom; *andamio*, Pg. *andaime* (Ar. *al-diʿāmah*), scaffolding;

Music

The corner-stone of Spanish musical art was laid by Ziryāb, a disciple of the Mawṣili school of Baghdād. Ziryāb arrived in 822 in Cordova, where his knowledge of more songs than any other artist, his mastery over the physical sciences, his magnetic personality and his refined manner and ready wit made him the social model.[1] It was at Cordova under the patronage of 'Abd-al-Raḥmān II that Ziryāb, who has also been credited with substituting eagles' talons for wooden plectra, added a fifth string to the lute and opened a school which became the conservatory of Andalusian music. Other schools followed in Seville, Toledo, Valencia and Granada.

After Ziryāb, abu-al-Qāsim 'Abbās ibn-Firnās († 888) is given the largest share of credit for introducing Oriental music into Spain and popularizing it. To his ingenuity is ascribed the discovery of making glass "from stones", as well as the construction in his home of a sort of planetarium where one could see stars, clouds and even lightning. Ibn-Firnās was the first man in Arab history to make a scientific attempt at flight. His flying equipment consisted of a suit of feathers with wings, which, we are told, carried him a long distance in the air. When he alighted, however, he hurt himself because his suit was not provided with a tail.[2] The musical theory and practice introduced by Ziryāb and ibn-Firnās were naturally the Perso-Arabic, but gradually this system gave way to the Greek and Pythagorean theories as works from Greek were translated into Arabic.

In general the Western Moslems proved themselves more addicted to the sweet art than their Eastern co-religionists. By the eleventh century the music of Andalusia had almost paled the fame of Baghdād. At that time Seville under the 'Abbādids, who for a short period also ruled Cordova, became the centre of the music, song and other gaieties which we usually associate with the Moors in the smiling plains of Andalusia. One of the 'Abbādids, al-Mu'tamid (1068–91), was not only a gifted poet but also a singer and performer on the lute. The 'Abbādid capital became famous for its manufacture of musical instru-

azotea, Pg. *açoteia* (Ar. *al-suṭayḥah*), flat roof; *algibe* (Ar. *al-jubb*, the cistern), ogive. On *kaddān* see D. Leopoldo de Eguílaz y Yanguas, *Glosario etimológico de las palabras españolas de origen oriental* (Granada, 1886). Cf. R. Dozy and W. H. Engelmann, *Glossaire des mots espagnols et portugais dérivés de l'arabe*, 2nd ed. (Leyden, 1869); *al-kadhdhān* in ibn-Jubayr, p. 331, l. 18.

[1] See above, p. 514.

[2] Maqqari, vol. ii, p. 254.

ments, in which it developed an export trade. From the Murābiṭ period we have from the pen of the philosopher ibn-Bājjah († 1138), who flourished at Seville and Fās, a treatise on music, now lost, which was as much appreciated in the West as al-Fārābi's work in the East. To another philosopher, ibn-Sab'īn († 1269) of the Muwaḥḥid period, we owe a discussion of related musical notes called *Kitāb al-Adwār al-Mansūb*, of which a solitary copy is preserved in Cairo.[1] In the course of a debate, held in the presence of the third Muwaḥḥid sovereign, al-Manṣūr (1184–99), between ibn-Rushd and abu-Bakr Muḥammad ibn-Zuhr, on the relative excellences of Seville and Cordova, ibn-Rushd, arguing Cordova's case, made this illuminating remark: "I know not what you are talking about, but one thing I do know: When a scholar dies in Seville and his estate wants his books sold, the books are carried to Cordova, where a market is found. But when a musician dies in Cordova his instruments are carried to Seville for sale."[2]

Influence in Europe

As the Christian population accepted the lyric models of the Moslems, Arab songs grew popular throughout the peninsula. Moslem musicians flourished at the courts of the kings of Castile and Aragon. Long after the fall of Granada, Moorish dancers and singers continued to entertain the natives of Spain and Portugal.[3] The recent researches of Ribera[4] tend to show that the popular music of Spain (*musica ficta*), in fact of all south-western Europe, in and after the thirteenth century, like the lyric and historical romance of that region, is to be traced to Anda-lusian and thence through Arabic to Persian, Byzantine and Greek sources. Even as philosophy and mathematics and medicine travelled from Greece and Rome to Byzantium, Persia and Baghdād, then to Spain, and thence to all Europe, so did several phases of musical theory and practice. Many of the instruments shown in the early Spanish miniatures and even some of the performers are of unmistakable Moslem origin.

Some of the early Spanish miniatures show Arab musicians

[1] Aḥmad Taymūr in *al-Hilāl*, vol. xxviii (1919), p. 214.

[2] Maqqari, vol. i, pp. 98, 302.

[3] The Morris dance of England, as the name indicates, is of Moorish origin.

[4] *Historia de la música árabe medieval y su influencia en la española* (Madrid, 1927); *Music in Ancient Arabia and Spain; Being la música de las cantigas*, tr. and abr. Eleanor Hague and Marion Leffingwell (Stanford University, 1929), esp. ch. xii; *Disertaciones*, vol. ii, pp. 3-174.

playing a game of chess.[1] Spanish provides the first description of the game in a European language and that in a work of Alfonso X,[2] king of Castile and Leon from 1252–82 and the greatest apostle of Moslem learning in Christian Spain. Alfonso was the man responsible for that great collection of poetry, *Cantigas de Santa María*, the music of which, according to Ribera, was of Moslem-Andalusian origin. Besides this collection and the astronomical Alfonsine tables, this monarch compiled a code of laws which bears traces of Islamic influence and which has become the basis of Spanish jurisprudence.

Reference has already been made to Arabic poetical influence in the troubadours, who resembled Arab singers not only in sentiment and character but also in the very forms of their minstrelsy. Certain titles which these Provençal singers gave to their songs are but translations from Arabic titles. Adelard of Bath, who studied music at Paris, was probably the translator of al-Khwārizmi's mathematical treatise as *Liber ysagogarum Alchorismi*, which comprised a section on music. This treatise was, therefore, one of the first to introduce Arab music into the Latin world. In Adelard's days, the first half of the twelfth century, the Arabs were already in possession of several ancient Greek treatises on music as well as some most important original works by al-Kindi, al-Fārābi, ibn-Sīna and ibn-Bājjah. Before the end of the century many of these original works had become known in Europe through Latin translations made at Toledo. It is significant that in this same period a new principle appears in Christian European music, the principle that notes have an exact time value or ratio among themselves. The first to give an exposition of this mensural music or measured song was the elusive Franco of Cologne (*ca.* 1190). His notation, called the Franconian notation, is not essentially different from our own. Under the name *īqā'*, rhythm, this same measured music had formed a constituent part of Arab music for at least four centuries prior to Franco's age and was fully described by al-Kindi (fl. *ca.* 870; above, p. 370).

[1] Sp. *ajedrez* (formerly *axedrez*), Pg. *xadrez*, all derived from Ar. *al-shiṭranj*, which is borrowed from Skr. through Pers. See above, p. 339. Playing cards were either of Arab origin or transmitted to Europe by Arabs; Sp. *naipe*, It. *naib*, for playing card, comes from Ar. *nā'ib* (governor) represented on a fifteenth-century pack now in Istanbul. L. A. Mayer, *Bulletin de l'Institut Français d'Archéologie Orientale*, vol. xxxviii (1939), pp. 113 *seq.*

[2] For illustration consult John G. White, *El tratado de ajedrez del Rey d. Alonso el Sabio, del año 1283* (Leipzig, 1913), pl. xliii.

After Franco's time there appeared a treatise ascribed to John of Garland dealing with *ochetus*, i.e. rhythmic mode. The term *ochetus* is probably a transformation of Arabic *īqāʿāt* (pl. of *īqāʿ*).

Mensural music was probably the greatest but certainly not the only contribution the Arabs made in this branch of knowledge. Two of the instruments that have aided most in the progress of the art of music, the lute (Ar. *al-ʿūd*, through Sp. *laúd*) and the rebec (Ar. *rabāb*,[1] through Sp. *rabel*), were introduced into Western Europe by Arabs. The rebec or ribibe, a favourite instrument with Chaucer, may be counted as one of the precursors of our violin. *Rabeca* is still the ordinary word used in Portugal for a violin. Other instruments in the peninsula with names derived from Arabic are the old trumpet *añafil* (Fr. *anafin*, from Ar. *al-nafīr*[2]), the tambourine *pandero* (colloq. Ar. *bandayr*) and the cymbals known as *sonajas* (Ar. pl. *ṣunūj*, sing. *ṣinj*, fr. Pers. *sanj*) round whose edge are "jingles". It was also the Moslems who introduced into Europe the guitar (fr. Ar. *qītārah*,[3] through Sp. *guitarra*, originally Gr.), the horn (Sp. *alboque*, fr. Ar. *al-būq*), the timbal (Sp. *atambal*, fr. Ar. *al-ṭabl*), and the kanoon (fr. Ar. *qānūn*).

[1] See above, p. 426.

[2] Pl. *anfār* (whence perhaps Eng. "fanfare"). This instrument with its name were probably introduced into Europe from Syria during the period of the Crusades, as were the cymbals (*ṣunūj*); Henry G. Farmer, "Oriental Influences on Occidental Military Music," *Islamic Culture*, vol. xv (1941), pp. 235-42. See below, pp. 663-4.

[3] Masculine form *qītār*; see above, p. 427.

CHAPTER XLII

IN SICILY

Conquest

THE Moslem conquest of Sicily (Ar. Siqilliyah) represents the last ripple in the wave that brought the Arabs into North Africa and Spain. The leaders of the expansion into the island and mid-Europe during the ninth century were Aghlabids from al-Qayrawān; but sporadic attempts by Moslem adventurers, soldiers of fortune and pirates had been made much earlier. In fact, the very same year (652) in which the Byzantine navy at Alexandria was crushed and maritime power began to pass into Arab hands witnessed the first attack on Byzantine Sicily, made by a general of Muʿāwiyah.[1] The delights of Syracuse (Saraqūsah, Saraquṣṣah), ravaged in this first attempt, consisted of women, church treasures and other valuable booty which invited repeated returns by Moslem plunderers in the course of the second half of the seventh century. In the eighth, Berber and Arab corsairs from North Africa and Moslem Spain began to harass the islands to the north and east and to cast paralysing fear over the inhabitants of Sicily as well as Corsica and Sardinia. Piracy and privateering, be it remembered, were then considered legitimate means of livelihood by Moslems and Christians alike. But there was no planned policy in these early raids.

The establishment of the powerful Aghlabid state of al-Qayrawān in the first year of the ninth century, however, changed the aspect of the situation. An appeal from a Syracusan rebel for aid against the Byzantine governor in 827 offered a timely pretext for an invasion. Ziyādat-Allāh I (817–38), the third Aghlabid, immediately sent off seventy vessels carrying some ten thousand fighters and seven hundred horses under the leadership of his seventy-year-old qāḍi-vizir, Asad ibn-al-Furāt.[2]

[1] See above, p. 167; Theophanes, p. 348.

[2] Ibn-ʿIdhāri, vol. i, p. 95; Nuwayri, ed. Gaspar, vol. ii, p. 241; Amari, *Biblioteca*, p. 527.

The real conquest began. The African army landed at Mazara [1] and advanced to Syracuse. A plague which spread in the Arab camp carried away Asad and a large number of his fighters.[2]

SICILY AND SOUTHERN ITALY
To illustrate Moslem occupation

Reinforced by fresh troops from Spain, the army captured Palermo (Ar. Balarm, originally a Phoenician colony) in 831,

[1] Ar. Māzar; ibn-al-Athīr, vol. vi, p. 236; Idrīsi, *Min Kitāb Nuzhat al-Mushtāq fi Ikhtirāq al-Āfāq*, ed. M. Amari and C. Schiaparelli (Rome, 1878), p. 32; Amari, *Storia*, ed. Nallino, vol. i, pp. 394 *seq.*

[2] Ibn-'Idhāri, vol. i, p. 96; ibn-Khaldūn, vol. iv, p. 199.

thereby acquiring a vantage point for further conquest and a seat for the new amīrate. About 843 Messina[1] fell. In 878 the strongly fortified Syracuse was taken after nine months' siege and destroyed during the rule of the bloody Aghlabid, Ibrāhīm II (874–902), who towards the close of his reign came in person to Sicily. Here he reduced the district in the neighbourhood of Mount Etna [2] and in 902 destroyed Taormina. Ibrāhīm died and was buried in Sicily. The conquest of the island, which had begun in 827, was now complete. For the next hundred and eighty-nine years Sicily under turbulent Arab chieftains formed in whole or in part a province of the Arab world.

In Italy

Just as Spain was a *point d'appui* for further raids and temporary conquests northward, so was Sicily with regard to Italy. Before his death in 902 Ibrāhīm II had carried the holy war across the straits into the toe of Italy, Calabria,[3] but he was not the first Arab invader to set foot on Italian soil. Shortly after the fall of Palermo, Aghlabid generals had interfered in the quarrels of the rival Lombards of Southern Italy, whose heel and toe were still held by the Byzantine emperor, and when Naples [4] in 837 appealed for Arab aid the Moslem war-cry echoed on the slopes of Vesuvius as it had before on those of its southern sister—"the mountain of fire". About four years later Bari, on the Adriatic, which was to become the main base for the next thirty years, was captured. About the same time the victorious Moslems made an appearance before Venice. In 846 even Rome was threatened by Arab squadrons which landed at Ostia and, unable to penetrate the walls of the Eternal City, sacked the cathedrals of St. Peter beside the Vatican and of St. Paul outside the walls and desecrated the graves of the pontiffs. Three years later another Moslem fleet reached Ostia but was destroyed by the tempestuous sea and the Italian navy. A painting from sketches by Raphael recalls this naval fight and the marvellous rescue of Rome. But the hold of the Moslems over Italy remained so firm that Pope John VIII (872–82) deemed it prudent to pay tribute for two years.[5]

[1] Massīni, Massīnah; Yāqūt, vol. iv, p. 535; ibn-Jubayr, p. 320.

[2] Ar. *jabal al-nār*, the mountain of fire; ibn-al-Athīr, vol. vi, p. 239; Yāqūt, vol. iii, p. 408; Amari, *Biblioteca*, app. 2 (Leipzig, 1887), p. 2.

[3] Qillawriyah in Yāqūt, vol. iv, p. 167; Qallawriyah in ibn-Ḥawqal, pp. 8, 128; see ibn-Khaldūn, vol. iv, pp. 200, 202.

[4] Nābul; ibn-al-Athīr, vol. vii, p. 3; Amari, *Biblioteca*, index; Idrīsi, p. 17.

[5] Amari, *Storia*, ed. Nallino, vol. i, pp. 588-93.

Across the Alps

The Aghlabids did not limit their operations to the Italian coasts. In 869 they captured Malta.[1] From Italy and Spain piratical raids in the tenth century extended through the Alpine passes into mid-Europe. In the Alps are a number of castles and walls which tourists' guides attribute to the invasion of the Saracens. Certain Swiss place-names, such as Gaby and Algaby (*al-jābi*?, tax collector) which appear in Baedeker's *Switzerland*, may possibly be of Arabic origin.[2]

Withdrawal from Italy

The recapture of Bari by the Christians in 871 marks the beginning of the end of the Moslem menace to Italy and Central Europe. In Bari the commanders had gone so far as to declare themselves "sultans" independent of the amīr at Palermo. In 880 the Byzantine Emperor Basil I wrested Taranto (Ṭārant), another important fortress, from Moslem hands and a few years later expelled the last remnants of the Arabs from Calabria. The final stage of the expansion which had begun in distant Arabia two and a half centuries before was thus brought to an end. At the present day numerous "Saracen towers", structures from which the approach of Arab fleets from Sicily or Africa was announced, still contribute to the scenic beauty of the peerless coastline south of Naples.

The Sicilian amīrate

In Sicily the amīr first held his office under the Aghlabids of al-Qayrawān.[3] With the destruction of the Aghlabid dynasty in 909 by the new and more powerful Fāṭimid caliphate, the Sicilian domain became a part of that empire as founded in North Africa by ʿUbaydullāh al-Mahdi. Four years later, however, the Sicilian Moslems under Aḥmad ibn-Qurhub (912–16) asserted their independence and named the ʿAbbāsid Caliph al-Muqtadir, foe of the Fāṭimids, in the Friday prayers.[4] In 917 the Amīr Aḥmad, abandoned by his Berber troops, suffered execution by order of al-Mahdi and Sicily reverted to the Fāṭimid domain. With the island as a base the Fāṭimid fleet carried its plundering raids as far as Genoa, which was sacked in 934 or 935.

The domestic situation in Sicily was far from satisfactory.

[1] Ibn-Khaldūn, vol. iv, p. 201.

[2] Probably the adjective *maur* occurring in the toponomy is a mere synonym for "brown", without reference to Moorish invaders. The inhabitants of the Alpine regions may have become acquainted with such words through the Crusades.

[3] For list consult Zambaur, p. 67; Eduard Sachau, *Ein Verzeichnis Muhammedanischer Dynastien* (Berlin, 1923), p. 26.

[4] Ibn-al-Athīr, vol. viii, pp. 53-4.

The Spanish and African elements in the Moslem population were in constant friction, which was complicated by the eternal feuds arising from the old distinction among the Arabs between South Arabian Yamanites—including Kalbites—and North Arabians. In 948 the third Fāṭimid Caliph al-Manṣūr appointed as governor over Sicily al-Ḥasan ibn-ʿAli ibn-abi-al-Ḥusayn al-Kalbi († 965), who laid the basis of a more or less independent and stable state.[1] Under him and his successors, the Kalbite dynasty, the seeds of Arab culture were afforded an opportunity to germinate in this polyglot isle. It was during the short reign of abu-al-Futūḥ Yūsuf ibn-ʿAbdullāh (989–98), a descendant of al-Ḥasan, that Moslem Sicily reached its height.

The Kalbite amīrs lived in luxurious palaces and maintained enlightened courts in their flourishing city. The Eastern geographer and traveller ibn-Ḥawqal[2] (fl. 943–77), whose description of the capital Palermo is not merely the oldest but the only account by a Moslem eye-witness, found in it over a hundred and fifty butcher shops and the incredible number of three hundred mosques. In the congregational mosques he counted thirty-six rows of worshippers, each with about two hundred men, making over seven thousand in all. He numbered over three hundred public school teachers, who were regarded by the inhabitants as their most pious, excellent and distinguished citizens, and that "in spite of the fact that school teachers are notorious for their mental deficiency and light brains".

Norman conquest

The downfall of the Kalbite régime was brought about by civil wars and Byzantine interference, which paved the way for the Norman conquest of the island. This began with the capture of Messina in 1060 by Count Roger, son of Tancred de Hauteville, culminated in the seizure of Palermo in 1071 and Syracuse in 1085 and ended in 1091. In 1090 Malta was taken by Roger. The Normans, already strong in the possession of a vigorous state on the mainland, were now secure in their newly conquered territory.

Arab-Norman culture

Sicily under the Normans saw the efflorescence of an interesting Christian-Islamic culture. Throughout the Arab period of domination there streamed into the island, already rich in memories of bygone civilizations, Eastern cultural currents which, blending with the precious legacy of Greece and Rome,

[1] Ibn-al-Athīr, vol. viii, p. 354.

[2] Pp. 82-7.

took definite shape under Norman rule and gave the Norman culture its distinctive character. Hitherto the Arabs had been too engrossed in warfare and squabbles to develop the finer arts of peace, but now their genius attained its full fruition in a rich outburst of Arab-Norman art and culture.

Though himself an uncultured Christian, Roger I († 1101) drew from the Moslems the mass of his infantry, patronized Arab learning, surrounded himself with Eastern philosophers, astrologers and physicians and allowed the non-Christians full liberty to follow their rites. The case of the poet ʻAbd-al-Jabbār ibn-Ḥamdīs (*ca.* 1055–1132), who though born in Syracuse retired at the Norman conquest to the Spanish court of al-Muʻtamid, was exceptional.[1] On the whole, Roger maintained the former system of administration and even kept high Moslem officials. His court at Palermo seemed more Oriental than Occidental. For over a century after this Sicily presented the unique spectacle of a Christian kingdom in which some of the highest positions were held by Moslems.

In this century the trade of the country remained to a large extent in the hands of Moslem merchants and the cultivation of the land continued to prosper under Arab husbandmen who, as in Spain, knew how to make the land produce abundantly. Sugar-cane, date-palms, cotton, olives, oranges, mulberries and other plants and fruits were introduced by the Arabs. Sericulture was established by the Normans after 1147. Papyrus, the like of which ibn-Ḥawqal[2] saw nowhere except in Egypt, was now cultivated in greater abundance than ever before. From its fibre, cordage was made for ships. Ibn-Jubayr,[3] who visited the island in 1184, was greatly impressed by its fertility, rich resources and plentiful means of sustenance. He particularly noted grape-vines and other trees cultivated in symmetrical rows.

The earliest extant paper document from Europe is an order in Greek and Arabic issued by the wife of Roger I, presumably in 1109; but it is more reasonable to suppose that the paper of this document was imported by Sicilian Arabs. From the time of King Roger II we have the earliest coin bearing a date in Arabic numerals (1138) and an Arabic inscription.

[1] Ibn-Ḥamdīs later accompanied his Sevillan patron into captivity in Africa. His *Dīwān* was edited by C. Schiaparelli (Rome, 1897); extracts in Amari, *Biblioteca*, pp. 547-73. [2] P. 86. [3] P. 328.

The line of Sicilian Arabophiles started by Roger I culminated in his son and second successor Roger II (1130–54) and in

Photo: Anderson

CAPPELLA PALATINA, PALERMO

Built by Roger II and decorated with medallions bearing Kufic inscriptions

Frederick II. Roger II dressed like a Moslem and his critics called him the "half-heathen king". His robe bore decorative Arabic characters. Even under his grandson William II (1166–89) ibn-

Jubayr[1] saw Christian women of Palermo wearing Moslem costumes. The chapel built by Roger II in his capital had its ceiling covered with Fāṭimid-influenced paintings and Kufic inscriptions. Arab craftsmen were undoubtedly employed in the construction of this and other Sicilian monuments. Several ivory objects, including caskets and croziers now in the Museo Cristiano of the Vatican and other museums, typify Siculo-Arabic craftsmanship of this period.[2] Roger's fleet, which raised Sicily to the position of the leading maritime power in the Mediterranean, was built and commanded by amīrs of whom the greatest was George (Jurji) of Antioch, a Greek formerly in the service of a Moslem prince in al-Mahdīyah, Africa. The highest office in the realm was that of *ammiratus ammiratorum* (*amīr al-umarā'*).

Al-Idrīsi

The chief ornament of Roger II's court was al-Idrīsi, the most distinguished geographer and cartographer of the Middle Ages. Born in Ceuta in 1100 of Hispano-Arab parents, abu-'Abdullāh Muḥammad ibn-Muḥammad al-Idrīsi († 1166) did his life work at Palermo under the patronage of Roger II. His Rogerian treatise (*Kitāb Rujār*) entitled *Nuzhat al-Mushtāq fi Ikhtirāq al-Āfāq*[3] (the recreation of him who yearns to traverse the lands) not only sums up the main features of such preceding works as those of Ptolemy and al-Mas'ūdi but is primarily based upon original reports submitted by observers who had been sent to various lands to secure data. In his critical collation of the material al-Idrīsi shows a remarkable breadth of view and a grasp of such essential facts as the sphericity of the earth. Besides this monumental work al-Idrīsi constructed for his Norman patron a celestial sphere and a disk-shaped map of the world, both in silver.[4]

Frederick II

The second of "the two baptized sultans of Sicily"[5] was Roger II's grandson Frederick II of Hohenstaufen (1215–50), who ruled both Sicily and Germany and, besides holding the title of emperor of the Holy Roman Empire after 1220, became king of Jerusalem by his marriage in 1225 with the heiress,

[1] P. 333.
[2] See Perry B. Cott, *Siculo-Arabic Ivories* (Princeton, 1939).
[3] A synopsis of the text with its seventy-one maps was printed in Rome as early as 1592. It was translated, but inaccurately, into Latin as *Geographia Nubiensis* (Paris, 1619) by two Maronite scholars, Jibrā'īl al-Ṣahyūni (Gabriel Sionita) and Yūḥanna al-Ḥaṣrūni (Joannes Hesronita). Partial editions of the text have been made in Leyden, Madrid, Rome, Bonn, etc. Consult Konrad Miller, *Mappae Arabicae*, vol. vi (Stuttgart, 1927).
[4] Amari, *Biblioteca*, p. 658.
[5] Amari, *Storia*, ed. Nallino, vol. iii, p. 372.

Isabelle of Brienne. The Emperor Frederick therefore was the highest civil authority in Christendom. Three years after his marriage he undertook a Crusade which inoculated him with more Moslem ideas.

In his personal habits and official life Frederick, who kept a harem, was semi-Oriental. In his court flourished philosophers from Syria and Baghdād, with long beards and flowing robes, dancing girls from the Orient and Jews from the East as well as from the West. His interest in the world of Islam he maintained by political and commercial relations, especially with the Ayyūbid sultan of Egypt.[1] From this Sultan al-Kāmil Muḥammad (1218–38), nephew of Ṣalāḥ-al-Dīn, Frederick received for his menagerie, which included camels and accompanied him wherever he went in Europe, a giraffe,[2] the first to appear in medieval Europe. From Egypt he also brought experts to test the incubation of ostrich eggs by the heat of the sun. From another Ayyūbid sultan, al-Ashraf of Damascus, he received in 1232 a wonderful planetarium with figures of the sun and moon marking the hours on their appointed rounds. In return, the emperor sent a white bear and a white peacock which astonished the Damascenes as much as the marvellous beast from Egypt had astonished their Sicilian contemporaries. It was to this Sultan al-Kāmil, among other Moslem rulers, that Frederick propounded, partly for information and partly as a puzzle, those problems of mathematics and philosophy whose solution was successfully undertaken by an Egyptian scholar.[3] The geometrical and astronomical problems, including the squaring of a circle's segment, were solved at al-Mawṣil. The same questionnaire was submitted to ibn-Sab'īn (above, p. 587).

Frederick brought from Syria skilled falconers, watched them train the birds and tried to ascertain by seeling the hawks' eyes whether they could find food by smell. He had his interpreter-astrologer Theodore (Thādhuri), a Jacobite Christian from Antioch,[4] translate an Arabic treatise on falconry. This translation together with another from Persian became the basis of Frederick's work on falconry, the first modern natural history. Theodore also extracted for the emperor a treatise on hygiene from the *Sirr al-Asrār* of the pseudo-Aristotle. As court

[1] Abu-al-Fidā', vol. iii, p. 148. [2] This word is of Arabic origin, *zarāfah*.
[3] Amari, *Biblioteca*, p. 522; cf. p. 514, l. 4. [4] Ibn-al-'Ibri, pp. 477-8.

astrologer Theodore was preceded by Michael Scot, who from 1220 to 1236 represented in Sicily and Italy the learning of Moslem Spain. Scot made for the emperor from Arabic a Latin summary of Aristotle's biological and zoological works, par-

Reproduced by permission of the Bodleian Library, Oxford

AN ARABIC MAP OF THE WORLD
Based on al-Idrīsi

ticularly *De animalibus*, with ibn-Sīna's commentary, which he dedicated to his patron as *Abbreviatio Avicenne*.

This almost modern spirit of investigation, experimentation and research which characterized the court of Frederick marks the beginning of the Italian Renaissance. Italian poetry, letters and music began to blossom under Provençal and Arabic influence.[1] The cultivation of poetry in the vulgar tongue was evidently due to the example of Arabic poets and singers, and the metrics of the early popular poetry of Italy, as represented by the carnival songs and the *ballata*, is fundamentally the same as that of the folk poetry of Andalusia.[2] "Stanza" is evidently a translation of Arabic *bayt*, "house", "strophe". But Frederick's greatest single contribution was the founding of the University of Naples (1224), the first in Europe to be established by a definite charter. In it he deposited a large collection of Arabic manuscripts. The works of Aristotle and ibn-Rushd which he caused to be translated were used in its curriculum; copies of the translations were sent to the Universities of Paris and Bologna. The University of Naples counted among its pupils Thomas Aquinas. In the fourteenth and following centuries Arabic studies were cultivated in several European universities, including Oxford and Paris, but with an entirely different motive: that of preparing Christian missionaries for Moslem lands.

Sicily's place in transmitting thought

The meeting-point of two cultural areas, Sicily was peculiarly adapted to act as a medium for transmitting ancient and medieval lore. Its population comprised a Greek element which used Greek, a Moslem element which spoke Arabic and a body of scholars who knew Latin. All three languages were in current use in the official registers and royal charters as well as among the populace of the many-tongued Palermo. It was in Sicily about 1160 that the first translation of the *Almagest* into Latin was done directly from Greek with the collaboration of a Greek-speaking Sicilian, Eugene of Palermo, surnamed the Amīr. Eugene, who flourished under Roger II and his successor William I, knew Arabic as well as Latin. He made a Latin version from Arabic of the *Optica* ascribed to Ptolemy, the Greek text of which is lost, and helped translate into Greek the Arabic *Kalīlah*. Under William not only translations from Arabic but also from the Greek originals were encouraged.

The Jews of Sicily, like those of Spain, had a significant part in the work of translation. The encyclopædic medical work of al-Rāzi was done into Latin by the Sicilian Jewish physician,

[1] Amari, *Storia*, ed. Nallino, vol. iii, pp. 760 *seq.*; G. A. Cesareo, *Le origini della poesia lirica e la poesia siciliana sotto gli suevi*, 2nd ed. (Milan, 1924), pp. 101, 107.

[2] José M. Millás in *Revista de archives*, vol. xli (1920), pp. 550-64, xlii (1921), pp. 37-59.

Faraj ben-Sālim, in 1279 under the auspices of Charles I of Anjou and was propagated in numerous manuscripts during the succeeding centuries. This was the only major medical work rendered into Latin in Sicily, where the translations dealt mainly with astronomy and mathematics. Though some of the Greek and Arabic books were done again and better in Toledo, nevertheless Sicily's contribution was of prime value.

Via Italy

Since the Norman kings and their successors on the Sicilian throne held not only the island but also Southern Italy, they provided a bridge for the transmission of various elements of Moslem culture into the peninsula and mid-Europe. By the middle of the tenth century traces of Arab learning became clearly noticeable north of the Alps. Dante's ideas of the other world may not have been derived from any particular Arabic text, but they certainly appear to have been of Oriental origin, though drawn by him from the popular lore of Europe. This penetration from the East through various channels is evident in the domain of art as well as in science and literature. The design of Renaissance *campanili*, it would seem, was derived from the square North African, more particularly Egyptian, type of minaret. Long after Sicily and the southern part of the peninsula had reverted to Christian rule Moslem craftsmen and artists continued to flourish, as evidenced by the mosaics and inscriptions of the Palatine Chapel. The renowned weaving-house established by the Moslem rulers in the royal palace at Palermo supplied European royalty with state robes which bore Arabic inscriptions. The first Italian textile workers acquired their technical knowledge and models for designs from Sicily. By the beginning of the thirteenth century silk weaving had already become the principal industry in several Italian towns, which exported fabrics imitating the Sicilian stuffs into various parts of Europe. As in Palermo and Cadiz, so in Venice, Ferrara and Pisa, colonies of Oriental craftsmen taught the natives and collaborated with them. So great was the demand for Oriental fabrics that there was a time when no European could have felt really well-dressed unless he possessed at least one such garment.

During the fifteenth century when opulent Venice was so actively adopting and scattering Moslem fashions in art, books bound in Italian workshops began to assume an Oriental appearance. The peculiarities of Arabic binding, including the flap that folds over to protect the front edges of the volume, appear on Christian books. At the same time new methods of tooling and decorating leather covers were also being learned from Oriental artisans in various Italian towns. Venice, moreover, was the home of another industry, the inlaying of brass with gold,[1] silver or red copper, an art which flourished mainly in al-Mawṣil in the twelfth century.

On the whole, Sicily as a transmitter of Moslem culture might claim for itself a place next in importance to that of Spain and higher than that of Syria in the period of the Crusades.

[1] It. *azzimina*, from Ar. *aʿjami*, Persian, foreign.

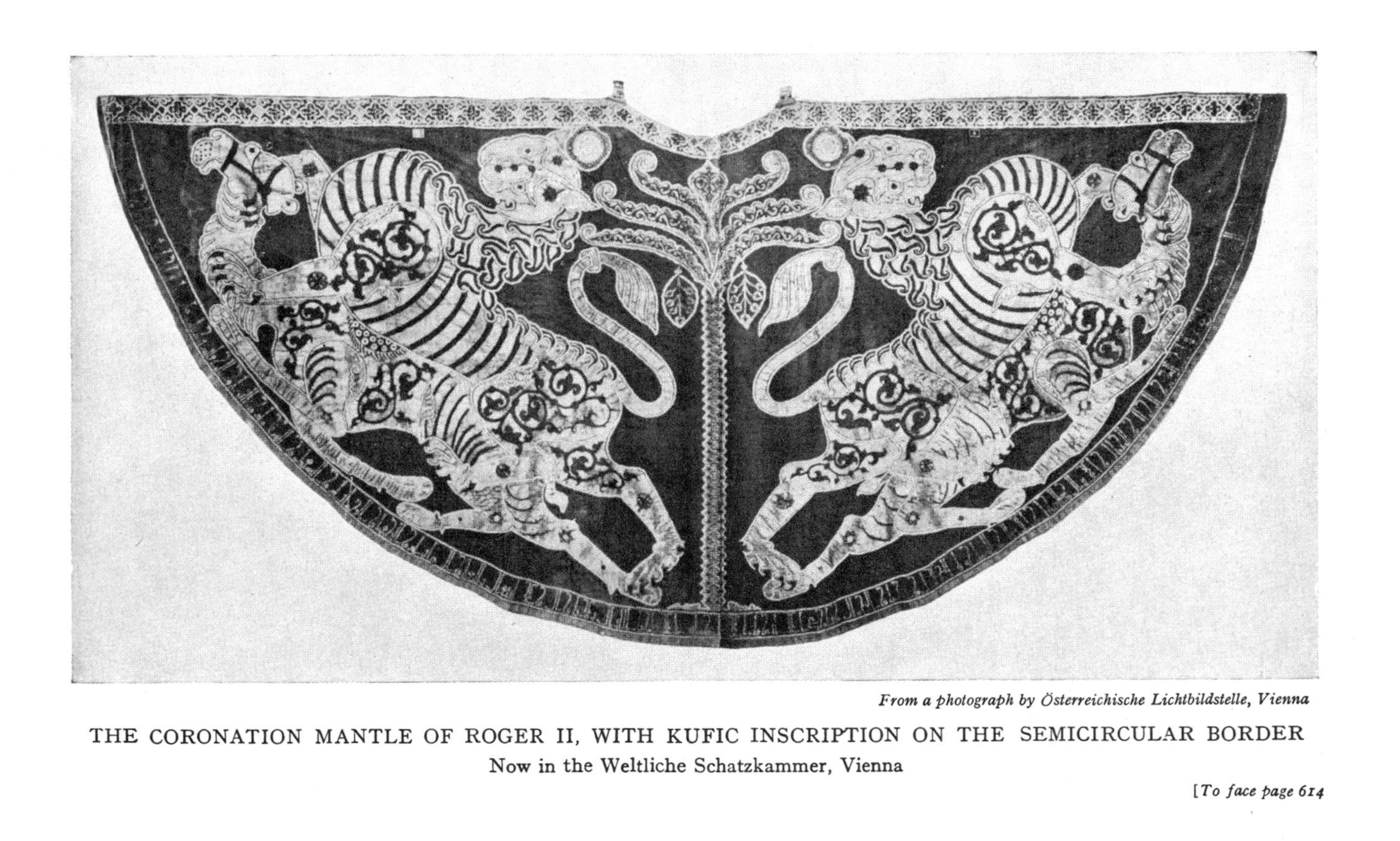

From a photograph by Österreichische Lichtbildstelle, Vienna

THE CORONATION MANTLE OF ROGER II, WITH KUFIC INSCRIPTION ON THE SEMICIRCULAR BORDER

Now in the Weltliche Schatzkammer, Vienna

[*To face page 614*

PART V

THE LAST OF THE MEDIEVAL MOSLEM STATES

CHAPTER XLIII

A SHĪ'ITE CALIPHATE IN EGYPT: THE FĀṬIMIDS

THE Fāṭimid caliphate, the only major Shī'ite one in Islam,[1] established itself in Tunisia in 909 as a deliberate challenge to the religious headship of the Islamic world represented by the 'Abbāsids of Baghdād. The founder was Sa'īd ibn-Ḥusayn, probably a descendant of the second founder of the Ismā'īlite sect,[2] the Persian 'Abdullāh ibn-Maymūn. The spectacular rise of ibn-Maymūn's successor Sa'īd was the culmination of deep-laid, skilfully organized Ismā'īlite propaganda paralleled only by the earlier movement which led to the break-up of the Umayyad caliphate. No small measure of this success was due to the personal efforts of the chief *dā'i* (propagandist), abu-'Abdullāh al-Ḥusayn al-Shī'i, a native of Ṣan'ā' in al-Yaman, who toward the close of the ninth century proclaimed himself precursor of the Mahdi and sowed seeds of sedition among the Berbers of North Africa, especially the Kitāmah (Kutāmah) tribe. His acquaintance with members of this tribe was made in the season of the pilgrimage at Makkah.[3] Ifrīqiyah was then under Aghlabid rule.

Ismā'īlite propaganda

Al-Shī'i's conspicuous success in this distant region gave Sa'īd the signal to leave his Ismā'īlite headquarters at Salamyah and make his way disguised as a merchant into north-western Africa. Thrown into a dungeon in Sijilmāsah by order of the Aghlabid Ziyādat-Allāh (903–9), Sa'īd was rescued by al-Shī'i,[4] who in 909 destroyed the century-old Aghlabid dynasty and drove its last scion Ziyādat-Allāh out of the country. The Aghlabids were the last stronghold of Sunnite Islam in that part of

The enigmatic Sa'īd

[1] For earlier independent 'Alid principalities review the Idrīsids and Ḥammūdids. The Sharīfs of Morocco, whose assumption of sovereignty dates from 1544, trace their lineage through al-Ḥasan to 'Ali and Fāṭimah, but are almost orthodox.

[2] The original founder was the Imām Ismā'īl († 760); above, p. 442.

[3] Ibn-'Idhāri, vol. i, p. 118.

[4] Some wrongly suspect that the real prisoner was slain before the surrender of Sijilmāsah to al-Shī'i.

Africa. Sa'īd was proclaimed ruler under the title of the Imām [1] 'Ubaydullāh al-Mahdi and accepted as a descendant of Fāṭimah through al-Ḥusayn and Ismā'īl. The dynasty he established is often referred to as al-'Ubaydīyah, especially by those who do not believe in his alleged descent.

Moslem historians are divided into two camps on the question of the legitimacy of his Fāṭimid origin. At least eight varying pedigrees were provided for him by his supporters and enemies, some of the latter going so far as to charge that he was the son of a Jew. Notable among the supporters of his legitimacy are ibn-al-Athīr,[2] ibn-Khaldūn [3] and al-Maqrīzi.[4] Among those who suspect or deny the genealogy and regard Sa'īd as an impostor are ibn-Khallikān,[5] ibn-'Idhāri,[6] al-Suyūṭi [7] and ibn-Taghri-Birdi.[8] It is noteworthy, however, that no dispute as to the genuineness of the Fāṭimid descent arose until the year 1011, when the 'Abbāsid Caliph al-Qādir issued in Baghdād a curious manifesto, signed by several Sunni and Shī'ite notables, declaring that his Egyptian rival al-Ḥākim was descended not from Fāṭimah but from Dayṣān the heretic.[9]

The first Fāṭimid

'Ubaydullāh (909–34) established himself first in the Aghlabid residence Raqqādah, a suburb of al-Qayrawān. He proved himself a most capable ruler. Two years after assuming supreme authority he killed his missionary-commander al-Shī'i and soon afterward extended his rule over the whole African territory from the Morocco of the Idrīsids to the confines of Egypt. In 914 he seized Alexandria; two years later he devastated the Delta. To Sicily he sent a new governor from the Kitāmah tribe and with the rebel ibn-Ḥafṣūn in Spain he established friendly relations. Malta, Sardinia,[10] Corsica, the Balearic and other islands felt the power of the fleet which he had inherited from the Aghlabids. About 920 he took up his residence in the new capital al-Mahdīyah,[11] which he founded on the Tunisian coast sixteen miles south-east of al-Qayrawān and named after himself.

[1] As Shī'ites, the Fāṭimids preferred the title imām to caliph.
[2] Vol. viii, pp. 17-20, abridged by abu-al-Fidā', vol. ii, pp. 67-8.
[3] Vol. iv, p. 31.
[4] *Khiṭaṭ* (Būlāq, 1270), vol. i, pp. 348-9.
[5] Vol. i, p. 487.
[6] Vol. i, pp. 150, 157-8.
[7] *Ta'rīkh al-Khulafā'* (Cairo, 1305), p. 214.
[8] Ed. Popper, vol. ii, pt. 2, p. 112.
[9] Text of manifesto preserved in abu-al-Fidā', vol. ii, p. 150.
[10] Finally subjugated in 1003 from Spain.
[11] Yāqūt, *Buldān*, vol. iv, pp. 694-6; Mas'ūdi, *Tanbīh*, p. 334; ibn-Ḥammād, *Akhbār Mulūk bani-'Ubayd*, ed. M. Vonderheyden (Algiers, 1927), pp. 9-10.

The fleet

'Ubaydullāh's successors pursued his policy of aggression and expansion. His son[1] abu-al-Qāsim Muḥammad al-Qā'im (934–946) sent a fleet which in 934 or 935 harried the southern coast of France, took Genoa and coasted along Calabria, carrying off slaves and other booty. All these expeditions, however, led to no permanent conquest. Under al-Qā'im's grandson abu-Tamīm Ma'add al-Mu'izz (952–75) the fleet raided the coasts of Spain, whose caliph was none other than the mighty al-Nāṣir. Three years later (958) the Fāṭimid army advanced westward as far as the Atlantic, whence the commander sent to his caliph live fish in jars. In 969 Egypt was wrested from its Ikhshīdid rulers. Its fleet was strengthened by new units built at Maqs, the predecessor of Būlāq as the port of Cairo.

The commander Jawhar

The hero of these last exploits was Jawhar al-Ṣiqilli (the Sicilian), also called al-Rūmi (the Greek), originally a Christian born in Byzantine territory, probably Sicily, whence he was brought as a slave to al-Qayrawān.[2] Immediately after his victorious entry into the capital al-Fusṭāṭ in 969, Jawhar began to lay out a new quarter which he named al-Qāhirah.[3] This city, modern Cairo, became the capital of the Fāṭimids in 973. After founding the new capital, today the most populous city of Africa, Jawhar in 972 built the great mosque al-Azhar,[4] which was soon afterward made an academy by the Caliph al-'Azīz.

Jawhar thus became the second founder, after al-Shī'i, of the Fāṭimid empire, which now included all North Africa. Western Arabia was inherited from the Ikhshīdids, who had been entrusted by the 'Abbāsids with the guardianship of the Holy City. As soon as Jawhar was established on Egyptian soil he dispatched to neighbouring Syria a lieutenant who in 969 reached and temporarily occupied Damascus.[5] His principal opponents were the Qarmaṭians, who were at this time all-powerful in many sections of Syria.

Fāṭimid power at its height

During the peaceful reign of abu-Manṣūr Nizār al-'Azīz (975–96), the fifth of the dynasty and the first to commence his

[1] His ward, an 'Alid, according to an Ismā'īlite source; Bernard Lewis, *The Origins of Ismā'īlism* (Cambridge, 1940), pp. 51-2.

[2] Ibn-Khallikān, vol. i, pp. 209-13; Maqrīzi, vol. i, pp. 352, 377 *seq.*

[3] "The triumphant", so called after the planet *Qāhir al-Falak* (the triumphant of heaven, Mars), which was in the ascendant; corrupted by Venetians into Cairo.

[4] "The bright (or fair) one", after al-Zahrā', a title of Fāṭimah

[5] Ibn-Khaldūn, vol. iv, p. 48; Maqrīzi, vol. i, p. 378.

reign in Egypt, the Fāṭimid empire reached its zenith. The name of this caliph was cited in the Friday prayers from the Atlantic to the Red Sea and in al-Yaman, Makkah, Damascus, and once even in al-Mawṣil. At least nominally his rule covered that vast area. Under him the Egyptian caliphate not only became the most formidable rival of that of Baghdād but even eclipsed it and appropriated for itself the position of the only great Moslem state in the eastern Mediterranean. Al-'Azīz went so far as to erect a two-million-dinar palace in Cairo to house his 'Abbāsid rivals, whom he hoped to seize after the capture of Baghdād. Like his predecessors he cast covetous eyes on distant Spain, but the proud Cordovan caliph on receiving a sharp note from the Fāṭimid sovereign is said to have sent back the following retort: "Thou ridiculest us because thou hast heard of us. If we had ever heard of thee, we would reply."[1]

Of the Fāṭimid caliphs al-'Azīz was probably the wisest and most beneficent. He lived in luxury, built in Cairo and its environs several new mosques, palaces, bridges and canals and extended to the Christians under him a measure of toleration never enjoyed before. In this attitude he was undoubtedly influenced by his Christian vizir 'Īsa ibn-Nasṭūr and his Russian wife, the mother of his son and heir al-Ḥākim and sister of the two Melkite patriarchs of Alexandria and of Jerusalem.

The decline of the Fāṭimid power began soon after the beneficent reign of al-'Azīz, the first of his house to adopt, following the 'Abbāsid precedent, the fateful policy of importing Turkish as well as negro mercenary troops. The insubordination and constant quarrelling of these troops among themselves and with the Berber bodyguard became one of the chief causes of the final collapse of the kingdom. It was Circassian and Turkish soldiers and slaves who later usurped the supreme authority and established independent dynasties.

A deranged caliph

Al-'Azīz' successor, abu-'Ali Manṣūr al-Ḥākim (996–1021), was only eleven when he came to the throne. His reign was marked with monstrous atrocities. He killed several of his vizirs, demolished a number of Christian churches including that of the Holy Sepulchre (1009), forced Christians and Jews to wear black robes, ride only on donkeys and display when in baths a cross dangling from their necks, if Christians, and a sort of

[1] Ibn-Taghri-Birdi, ed. Popper, vol. ii, pt. 2, p. 2.

yoke with bells, if Jews.[1] Al-Ḥākim was the third caliph in Islam, after al-Mutawakkil and ʿUmar II, to impose such stringent measures on non-Moslems.[2] Otherwise the Fāṭimid régime was remarkably favourable for dhimmis. The edict for the destruction of the Holy Sepulchre was signed by his Christian secretary ibn-ʿAbdūn and the act was one of the contributory causes of the Crusades. Finally this enigmatic, blue-eyed caliph, following the extreme development of Ismāʿīlite doctrine, declared himself the incarnation of the Deity and was so accepted by a newly organized sect, called Druzes, after its first great missionary, a Turk named al-Darazi († 1019).[3] On February 13, 1021, al-Ḥākim was killed on the Muqaṭṭam, probably through a conspiracy headed by his sister Sitt al-Mulūk, whom the caliph had charged with unchastity.

Decadence

After al-Ḥākim immature youths were made caliphs with the real power in the hands of vizirs, who later even assumed the royal title *malik*. Al-Ḥākim's son and successor al-Ẓāhir (1021–1035) was sixteen when he came to the throne. It was this caliph who received permission from Constantine VIII to have his name mentioned in the mosques of the emperor's domain and to have the mosque at Constantinople restored in return for the caliph's permission to have the Church of the Holy Sepulchre rebuilt.[4] Al-Ẓāhir's successor was his eleven-year-old son, Maʿadd al-Mustanṣir (1035–94), whose reign of almost sixty years is the longest in Moslem annals.[5] In the early part of his reign his mother, a Sudanese slave once purchased from a Jew, enjoyed with her vendor most of the power. By this time the Fāṭimid dominions had shrunk to little more than Egypt itself. After 1043 the Fāṭimid possession in Syria, always loosely bound to Egypt, began rapidly to disintegrate. Palestine was often in open revolt. A mighty power advancing from the east, that of the Saljūq Turkomans, was now overshadowing Western Asia. In the meantime the Fāṭimid African provinces were severing their tributary connection and passing into open independence or reverting to their old allegiance to the ʿAbbāsids. The troublesome Arab

[1] Ibn-Khallikān, vol. iii, p. 5; ibn-Ḥammād, p. 54; cf. Yaḥya ibn-Saʿīd, ed. Cheikho *et al.*, p. 187.
[2] For the Shāfiʿite restrictions see Ibshīhi, *Mustaṭraf*, vol. i. p. 100.
[3] For more on this sect consult Hitti, *Origins of Druze People*.
[4] Maqrīzi, vol. i, p. 355. Cf. Yaḥya ibn-Saʿīd, pp. 270-71; above, p. 204.
[5] Ibn-Khallikān, vol. ii, p. 550; see above, p. 481, n. 2.

tribes of the banu-Hilāl and Sulaym, originally of Najd and now of Upper Egypt, were instigated in 1052 to move westward where for years they ravaged Tripoli and Tunisia.[1] Sicily, which for a time acknowledged after the Aghlabid the Fāṭimid sovereignty, was by 1071 mostly subdued by the Normans, who subsequently even overran parts of the African mainland. Arabia alone kept in part faithful to the Shīʿite cause. On the dark horizon the only ray of light was the temporary success at Baghdād of the Turkish general and usurper al-Basāsīri[2] († 1060), through whose domination the Egyptian caliph's name was cited in the Baghdād mosques for forty successive Fridays. Wāsiṭ and al-Baṣrah followed the example of Baghdād. The turban of the ʿAbbāsid Caliph al-Qā'im, who even renounced all his rights to the caliphate in favour of his Fāṭimid rival, the Prophet's mantle and a beautiful window from his palace were brought to Cairo as trophies. The turban and mantle together with the document of renunciation were returned to Baghdād about a century later by Ṣalāḥ-al-Dīn, but the window was used in one palace after another until the Mamlūk Sultan Baybars al-Jāshnakīr added it to the tomb in which he was buried in 1309.

Fall

At home trouble was continually brewing between Turkish, Berber and Sudanese battalions, and state authority was paralysed. Seven years' famine exhausted the economic resources of the country. In 1073 the vacillating caliph summoned the Armenian Badr al-Jamāli, a former slave, from his military governorship of ʿAkka to act as vizir and commander in chief.[3] The new Amīr al-Juyūsh took command with such vigour that he brought order out of apparent chaos and gave the Fāṭimid régime a new lease of life. But the revival was of short duration. Neither Badr's efforts nor those of his son and successor, al-Malik al-Afḍal,[4] who wielded the supreme authority after his father's death in 1094, could check the tide of decline. The remaining years of Fāṭimid rule[5] were marked by continuous struggle between vizirs backed by factions in the army. On the death of al-Mustanṣir, al-Malik al-Afḍal placed on the throne the caliph's

[1] The migratory movements and military exploits of banu-Hilāl provide the historical background of the celebrated epic *Sīrat bani-Hilāl.*

[2] Ibn-Khallikān, vol. i, pp. 107-8.

[3] *Ibid.* vol. iv, p. 64; ibn-al-Athīr, vol. x, pp. 60, 160.

[4] Abu-al-Qāsim Shāhinshāh; ibn-Khallikān, vol. i, pp. 396-7.

[5] For list of Fāṭimid caliphs see genealogical tree on following page.

youngest son under the name al-Musta'li with the expectation of holding him under his influence. After al-Musta'li, his son, a child of five years, was declared caliph by al-Afḍal, who gave him the honorific title al-Āmir (1101–30). When al-Ḥāfiẓ (1130–1149) died his power hardly extended beyond the caliphal palace. His son and successor al-Ẓāfir (1149–54) was then a gay youth and the power was usurped by the Kurdish vizir ibn-al-Sallār, styled al-Malik al-'Ādil. The memoirs of Usāmah,[1] who spent the years between 1144 and 1154 in the Fāṭimid court,

Table of Fāṭimid caliphs:

1. Al-Mahdi (909–34)
2. Al-Qā'im (934–46)
3. Al-Manṣūr (946–52)
4. Al-Mu'izz (952–75)
5. Al-'Azīz (975–96)
6. Al-Ḥākim (996–1021)
7. Al-Ẓāhir (1021–35)
8. Al-Mustanṣir (1035–94)

9. Al-Musta'li (1094–1101) — (Muḥammad)

10. Al-Āmir (1101–30) — 11. Al-Ḥāfiẓ (1130–49)

(Yūsuf) — 12. Al-Ẓāfir (1149–54)

14. Al-'Āḍid (1160–71) — 13. Al-Fā'iz (1154–60)

show that in no court were intrigues, feuds and jealousies more rife. The assassination of ibn-al-Sallār (1153) by his wife's grandson Naṣr ibn-'Abbās, who was later encouraged by the caliph to make an attempt on the life of his father, 'Abbās, ibn-al-Sallār's successor in the vizirate, and finally the secret murder of al-Ẓāfir himself by the young conspirator, form one of the darkest chapters in the history of Egypt. The second day after the caliph had vanished 'Abbās declared the four-year-old son of al-Ẓāfir, al-Fā'iz, caliph (1154–60). The boy caliph died aged eleven and was succeeded by his nine-year-old cousin al-'Āḍid,

[1] Ed. Hitti, pp. 6-33 = *Arab-Syrian Gentleman*, pp. 30-59.

the fourteenth and last in a line which had lasted for over two and a half centuries. The precarious existence of the people, depending as they did for their sustenance on the overflow of the Nile, was in the meantime being rendered more miserable by repeated famines and plagues. The result was heavier taxes and more general extortion to supply the insatiable greed of the caliphs and their soldiery. Matters were complicated by the advent of the Crusaders and the repeated attacks of Amalric, king of Jerusalem, who in 1167 stood at the very gates of Cairo. These conditions were brought to an end by Ṣalāḥ-al-Dīn, who in 1171 dethroned the last Fāṭimid caliph.

CHAPTER XLIV

LIFE IN FĀṬIMID EGYPT

EGYPT was the only land of the once far-flung Fāṭimid domain where the successors of 'Ubaydullāh al-Mahdi impressed the stamp of their cultural characteristics. The precarious relationship that held the several provinces of north-western Africa and Western Asia to Cairo militated against the possibility of leaving in those regions peculiarly Fāṭimid traces. In the cultural history of Egypt the Fāṭimid together with the preceding Ikhshīdid and Ṭūlūnid periods may be described as the Arabo-Persian era as distinct from the Perso-Turkish, which covered the Ayyūbid and Mamlūk periods. The pre-Ṭūlūnid period may be described as purely Arabic. The Ayyūbid dynasty, which supplanted the Fāṭimid, introduced to Africa the spirit and culture of the great Saljūq empire, noticeable in its art and industry and its political and intellectual movements. Under the Fāṭimids, however, it is the influence of Persian culture that is paramount. But the backbone of the populace throughout medieval and modern history was composed of Arabicized Copts. This populace remained under the ultra-Shī'ite régime Sunnite at core, as can be inferred from the facility with which Ṣalāḥ-al-Dīn restored official orthodoxy.

Politically the Fāṭimid period marks a new epoch in the history of the land, which for the first time since Pharaonic days had a completely sovereign power full of vitality and founded on a religious basis. The two preceding dynasties had neither national nor religious footing in the country. Their rise and existence they owed to the military ability of their soldier-founders and to the dilapidated condition of the 'Abbāsid state.

High life

Though the golden age in the history of Fāṭimid Egypt began with al-Mu'izz and culminated with al-'Azīz, yet Egypt in the time of al-Mustanṣir was still the leading country of Islam. The Persian Ismā'īli missionary Nāṣir-i-Khusraw,[1] who visited the

[1] *Sefer Nāmeh*, ed. Schefer, pp. 36-56, tr. pp. 110-62.

country in 1046–49, shortly before the economic and political crash, has left us a description in glowing colours. The caliphal palace housed 30,000 persons, of whom 12,000 were servants and 1000 horse and foot guards. The young caliph, whom Nāṣir saw at a festival riding on a mule, was pleasant looking, clean shaven and dressed simply in a white *quftān* and turban. An attendant carried over the caliph's head a parasol enriched with precious stones. The seven galleys drawn up on the bank of the Nile measured 150 cubits over-all by 60 in beam. The caliph owned in the capital 20,000 houses, mostly of brick, rising to a height of five or six stories, and an equal number of shops, which were let at two to ten dinars a month. The main streets were roofed and lighted by lamps. The shopkeepers sold at fixed prices, and if one cheated he was paraded on a camel through the streets ringing a bell and confessing his fault. Even the shops of jewellers and money-changers were left unlocked. The old al-Fusṭāṭ had seven great mosques; Cairo had eight.[1] The whole country enjoyed a degree of seeming tranquillity and prosperity that made Nāṣir enthusiastically declare: "I could neither limit nor estimate its wealth and nowhere have I seen such prosperity as I saw there".[2]

Of all the Egyptian caliphs al-Mustanṣir was the richest. He inherited millions from his predecessors and lived a life of luxury and ease. He is said to have erected in his palace a Kaʿbah-like pavilion where he used to drink to the accompaniment of stringed music and beautiful singers. Here he declared: "This is indeed more pleasant than staring at a Black Stone, listening to the muezzin's drone and drinking impure water". An inventory of his treasures by al-Maqrīzi [3] includes precious stones, crystal vases, inlaid gold plates, ivory and ebony ink-stands, amber cups, phials of musk, steel mirrors, parasols with gold and silver sticks, chess-boards with gold and silver pawns, jewelled daggers and swords and embroidered fabrics manufactured at Dabīq and Damascus. Exquisite and priceless works of art were dissipated among the Turkish troops. Yet in 1070 this caliph found it necessary to send his daughters and their mother to Baghdād to escape starvation.

[1] Cf. Maqrīzi, vol. ii, p. 264; Yāqūt, vol. iii, p. 901.
[2] P. 53 (text), p. 155 tr.
[3] Vol. i, pp. 414 *seq.* Cf. ibn-Taghri-Birdi, vol. ii, pt. 2, pp. 181-2.

Administration

In its general organization the Fāṭimid state followed the 'Abbāsid, or rather the older Persian prototype. The Egyptian al-Qalqashandi[1] († 1418) has given us in his manual intended for the use of candidates for governmental posts a sketch of the military and administrative systems under the Fāṭimids. The army consisted of three principal ranks: (1) amīrs, who included the highest officers and the sword-bearing escorts of the caliph; (2) officers of the guard, consisting of masters (sing. *ustādh*) and eunuchs; and (3) the different regiments carrying such names as Ḥāfiẓīyah, Juyūshīyah, Sūdānīyah, after some caliph, vizir or nationality. The vizirs were of several classes, of which the highest were "men of the sword", who supervised the army and war-office, and "lords of the door", high chamberlains, whose privilege it was to present foreign envoys. The "men of the pen" included the qāḍī, who was also director of the mint; the inspector of markets (*muḥtasib*), who supervised weights and measures; and the state treasurer, who presided over the *bayt al-māl*. In the lowest rank of the "men of the pen" stood the great body of civil servants, comprising clerks and secretaries in the various departments. The internal administration of the empire is said to have been the creation of al-Mu'izz' and al-'Azīz' vizir Ya'qūb ibn-Killis († 991), a Baghdād Jew who, accepting Islam, began his political career at Kāfūr's court and whose expert administration laid the basis of the economic prosperity of the Nile valley under the early Fāṭimids.[2]

Scientific and literary progress

Ibn-Killis was the first outstanding patron of learning in Fāṭimid Egypt. He established an academy and spent on it a thousand dinars per month. In his time flourished the physician Muḥammad al-Tamīmi, who was born in Jerusalem and moved to Egypt about 970. Before him, under the Ikhshīdids, flourished the historian Muḥammad ibn-Yūsuf al-Kindi,[3] who died at al-Fusṭāṭ in 961. Another historian who died later (1062) in al-Fusṭāṭ was ibn-Salāmah al-Quḍā'i.[4]

Though some of the early Fāṭimid caliphs were men of culture, their period was one unproductive of scientists and writers of special merit. Like other caliphs in Baghdād and Cordova,

[1] *Ṣubḥ*, vol. iii, pp. 480 *seq.*
[2] Ibn-al-Ṣayrafi, *al-Ishārah ila Man Nāla al-Wizārah*, ed. 'Abdullāh Mukhliṣ (Cairo, 1924), pp. 94 *seq.*
[3] Author of *Kitāb al-Wulāh wa-Kitāb al-Quḍāh*, ed. R. Guest (Leyden, 1908–12).
[4] Author of *'Uyūn al-Ma'ārif wa-Funūn Akhbār al-Khalā'if* (unpublished).

al-ʿAzīz was himself a poet and a lover of learning. It was he who made the Azhar Mosque an academy. But most of the learned men at this time not only in law but in history and poetry were members of the *faqīh* class, which included the judges. The heretical character of the dynasty, whose court did not attract orthodox scientists and littérateurs, together with the insecurity of life throughout the latter part of the period, explains the dearth of intellectual activity.

Hall of Science

One of the most remarkable foundations of the Fāṭimids was the Dār al-Ḥikmah or Dār al-ʿIlm (hall of wisdom or of science), established by al-Ḥākim in 1005 for the teaching and propagation of the extreme Shīʿite doctrine. In conjunction with it al-Ḥākim instituted a fund whose income of 257 dinars was to be spent for copying manuscripts, repairing books and general maintenance.[1] The hall was connected with the royal palace and contained a library and rooms for meetings. Its curriculum comprised, in addition to the specifically Islamic subjects, astronomy and medicine. Though closed in 1119 by al-Malik al-Afḍal because of its heretical teaching, the academy survived until the advent of the Ayyūbids.

Astronomy and optics

Al-Ḥākim was personally interested in astrological calculations; he built on al-Muqaṭṭam an observatory to which he often rode before dawn on his grey ass. An informant of the contemporary historian ibn-Ḥammād[2] saw the astrolabe-like copper instrument erected by al-Ḥākim on two towers and measured one of its signs of the zodiac, which was three spans in length.

Al-Ḥākim's court was illumined by ʿAli ibn-Yūnus[3] († 1009), the greatest astronomer Egypt has ever produced, and abu-ʿAli al-Ḥasan (L. Alhazen) ibn-al-Haytham, the principal Moslem physicist and student of optics. The astronomical tables (*zīj*) of ibn-Yūnus, bearing the name of his patron, correct the tables current at his time by original observations made with the armillary sphere and the azimuth circle. Ibn-al-Haytham († *ca.* 1039), who was born in al-Baṣrah about 965, tried to regulate for al-Ḥākim the annual overflow of the Nile, and when he failed he simulated madness and hid himself from the caliph's wrath until the latter's death. No less than a hundred works on mathematics, astronomy, philosophy and medicine are ascribed

[1] Maqrīzi, vol. i, p. 459. [2] P. 50.
[3] Qifṭi, pp. 230-31; ibn-Khallikān, vol. iii, p. 6.

to him.[1] The chief work for which he is noted is that on optics, *Kitāb al-Manāẓir*, of which the original is lost but which was translated in the time of Gerard of Cremona or before and was published in Latin in 1572. It was influential in the development of optics in the Middle Ages. Almost all medieval writers on this subject base their works on Alhazen's *Opticæ thesaurus*; Roger Bacon, Leonardo da Vinci and Johann Kepler show traces of its influence In his work ibn-al-Haytham opposes the theory of Euclid and Ptolemy that the eye sends out visual rays to the object of vision and presents experiments for testing the angles of incidence and reflection. In certain experiments he approaches the theoretical discovery of magnifying lenses which was actually made in Italy three centuries later.

Another important work composed in Egypt in the days of al-Ḥākim is *al-Muntakhab fi 'Ilāj al-'Ayn*[2] (select material on the treatment of the eye) by 'Ammār ibn-'Ali al-Mawṣili. In this the author shows more originality than his contemporary ibn-'Īsa in his *Tadhkirah*, which, however, on account of its completeness became the standard work on ophthalmology. 'Ammār describes a radical operation for soft cataract by suction through a hollow tube of his own invention.

The royal library

In the days of al-Mustanṣir the debacle which resulted in the dissipation of his treasures brought about an even greater loss in the dispersion of the royal library started by al-'Azīz and said to have contained at the time 200,000 books. It treasured 2400 illuminated Korans. Among its rarities were manuscripts in the hand of ibn-Muqlah and other master calligraphers; al-'Azīz had deposited in it an autograph copy of al-Ṭabari's history. In the loot of 1068 a reporter witnessed twenty-five camels carrying away books. Valuable manuscripts were used for lighting the fires in the homes of Turkish officers and exquisite bindings served to mend the shoes of their slaves. Al-Mustanṣir's successors built up new collections. When a century later Ṣalāḥ-al-Dīn made his triumphal entry into the royal palace its library still housed over a hundred thousand volumes, some of which together with other treasures were distributed among his men.[3]

[1] Ibn-abi-Uṣaybi'ah, vol. ii, pp. 91 *seq.*; al-Qifti, pp. 167-8; Muṣṭafa Naẓīf, *ibn-al-Haytham: Buḥūthuhu wa-Kushūfuhu al-Baṣarīyah* (Cairo, 1942), pp. ix-xiv.

[2] Partly preserved in MS. form at the Escurial. Casiri, vol. i, p. 317; tr. J. Hirschberg *et al.*, *Die arabischen Augenärzte nach den Quellen beirbeitet*, vol. ii (Leipzig, 1905).

[3] Maqrīzi, vol. i, pp. 408-9; abu-Shāmah, vol. i, p. 268.

Art and Architecture

Though unfavourable to the cultivation of science and literature, the Fāṭimid era was characterized by works of art and architecture of first importance. The prosperity which the country enjoyed under the first two caliphs in Cairo and later under the two vizirs of Armenian origin, a prosperity worthy of the Pharaonic or Alexandrian age, was reflected in the sphere of art.

The oldest surviving structure is the Azhar Mosque, built by Jawhar in 972. Though it was later restored, its older part, which is the central, has preserved the original form. This part is built of brick after the fashion of the ibn-Ṭūlūn Mosque, has pointed arches and in general betrays Iranian influence. Its minaret is of the heavy square type. The next oldest mosque is that of al-Ḥākim, begun by his father in 990 and completed about 1012. It follows the same plan as al-Azhar and has a cupola of brickwork supported upon an octagonal drum above the prayer niche. Stone was used in al-Ḥākim's Mosque, now in ruins, but since the minaret was not square the craftsmen were probably from northern al-ʿIrāq, rather than Syria. The triumph of stone over brick as a structural material was not effected until the late Fāṭimid age and is illustrated in the façade of the al-Aqmar Mosque, built in 1125. This façade may have been due to some Armenian Christian architect. In al-Aqmar we recognize the first appearance of the later general Islamic feature, the corbelled ("stalactite") niche (*muqarnas*). This pillared mosque and that of al-Ṣāliḥ ibn-Ruzzīk (*ca.* 1160) display the bold designs and austere Kufic inscriptions for which Fāṭimid art is renowned. Such novel features gradually introduced by Fāṭimid architects as the stalactite pendentives and the deep niches in the façade were to undergo further development under the Ayyūbids and Mamlūks. Likewise the treatment of inscriptions on stone or wooden panels foreshadows the glories of the later art. The practice of associating a tomb, usually of the founder, with a mosque began in 1085 with Badr al-Jamāli, whose tomb-mosque on the Muqaṭṭam set the first example.

Of the great gates that testify to the grandeur of Fāṭimid buildings three are extant: Bāb Zawīlah, Bāb al-Naṣr and Bāb al-Futūḥ.[1] These massive gates of Cairo, built by Edessene architects on a Byzantine plan, are among the most enduring relics of Fāṭimid Egypt.

[1] See Maqrīzi, vol. i, pp. 380 *seq.*

Decorative and industrial arts

Among the treasures of the Arab Museum at Cairo are several panels of carved wood dating from the Fāṭimid period and showing living creatures such as deer attacked by monsters, hares seized by eagles and pairs of confronted birds. These motifs suggest borrowing from Sāsānid models. The same affinity is noticeable in Fāṭimid bronzes, most of which were mirrors, ewers or censers. The best-known bronze is the griffin, forty inches high, now in Pisa. The same is true of textiles, samples of which found their way into the West at the time of the Crusades.[1] Weaving was a national art of Coptic Egypt but even then was influenced by Iranian, particularly Sāsānid, models. In Fāṭimid fabrics we find animals in conventionalized and heraldic poses. Among Egyptian cities Dabīq, Dimyāṭ and Tinnīs were noted for their medieval textiles, known after these places as dabīqi, dimyāṭi and tinnīsi. The cloth known in Chaucer's time as fustian came from al-Fusṭāṭ, as the word indicates.

The ceramic art of the Fāṭimids, like their other arts, follows Iranian patterns. Here as in textiles animal motifs are broadly treated. In his inventory of Fāṭimid treasures al-Maqrīzi[2] lists several specimens of ceramic and metallic arts, including Chinese glazed earthenware. This is one of the first recorded appearances of Chinese ware in the Arab East.[3] Nāṣir-i-Khusraw[4] asserts that the Egyptians made earthenware "so fine and diaphanous that one can see one's hand through it".

The earliest-known Islamic bookbindings come from Egypt and may be assigned to the eighth or ninth century. Their decoration and technique have affinity with those of earlier Coptic bindings, from which they were evidently derived. After the development of this Egyptian school tooling and stamping became the most common techniques of Moslem craftsmen working in leather.

[1] See below, p. 668. [2] See above, p. 626.

[3] Cf. Krenkow in *Majallat al-Majma'*, vol. xiii (1935), pp. 386-8, where al-Bīrūni mentions Chinese pottery; *Silsilat al-Tawārīkh*, pp. 35-6; al-Dimashqi, *Nukhbat al-Dahr fi 'Ajā'ib al-Barr w-al-Baḥr*, ed. A. F. Mehren (St. Petersburg, 1866), p. 43, where possibly a reference to porcelain is made. F. Sarre in *Die Keramik von Samarra* (Berlin, 1925), p. 61, records the discovery of ninth-century porcelain at Sāmarra.

[4] Ed. Schefer, p. 52, tr. p. 151.

From Arnold and Guillaume, "The Legacy of Islam", by courtesy of the Clarendon Press

FĀṬIMID CARVED ROCK-CRYSTAL EWER BEARING THE NAME OF THE CALIPH AL-ʿAZĪZ, 10TH CENTURY

Now in the Treasury of St. Mark's, Venice

CHAPTER XLV

MILITARY CONTACTS BETWEEN EAST AND WEST: THE CRUSADES

WHEN at the close of the eleventh century the motley hordes of Christendom made their way into Syria to wrest it from Moslem hands, the country presented the spectacle of division and impotence. It was split up among several local Arab chieftains, while in the north the Saljūq Turks were all-powerful and in the south the schismatic Fāṭimids of Egypt held sway. The population was far from being uniform in composition or even in language. The Druzes in southern Lebanon, the Nuṣayrīyah in their northern mountains and their neighbours the Ismā'īlites, later Assassins, formed three schismatic communities distinct from orthodox Islam. Among the Christian bodies the Maronites of northern Lebanon, who still used Syriac to a considerable extent, constituted the largest minority.

Saljūqs of Syria

With the advent of the nomadic Saljūqs from Central Asia earlier in the eleventh century, their swarming over the western states of the 'Abbāsid caliphate, the establishment of their authority successively in Khurāsān, Persia, al-'Irāq, Armenia and Asia Minor, and their founding (1055) of a sultanate in Baghdād to which the caliphate was subordinate, we have dealt in a foregoing chapter (XXXII). The Saljūqs of Syria, like those of al-Rūm (Asia Minor), formed one of the chief subdivisions of the family, but were not united under one head. Almost every Syrian town of any consequence had at this time its own Saljūq or Arab ruler. Tripoli after 1089 was independent under the Shī'ite banu-'Ammār.[1] Shayzar after 1081 was held by the banu-Munqidh. The Byzantines were time and again capturing and losing towns along the coast and on the northern frontier.

The first Saljūq bands appeared in Syria shortly before 1070. In this year Sultan Alp Arslān made the Arab prince of Aleppo

[1] Consult G. Wiet in *Mémorial Henri Basset* (Paris, 1928), vol. ii, pp. 279-84.

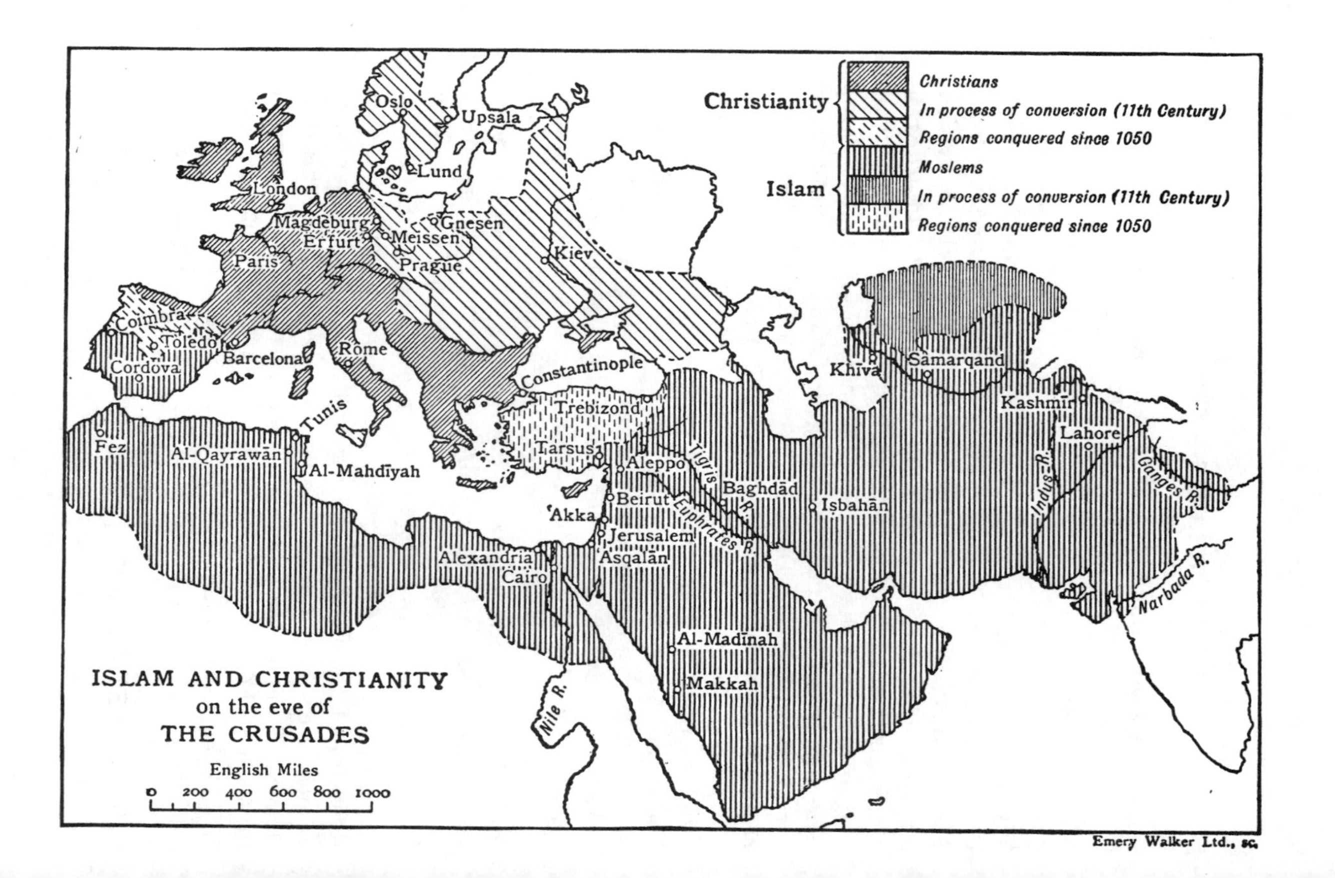
ISLAM AND CHRISTIANITY
on the eve of
THE CRUSADES
English Miles
0 200 400 600 800 1000
Christianity
Christians
In process of conversion (11th Century)
Regions conquered since 1050
Islam
Moslems
In process of conversion (11th Century)
Regions conquered since 1050
Oslo
Upsala
Lund
London
Magdeburg
Erfurt
Meissen
Gnesen
Prague
Kiev
Paris
Coimbra
Toledo
Cordova
Barcelona
Rome
Constantinople
Trebizond
Tarsus
Aleppo
Beirut
'Akka
Jerusalem
Asqalan
Alexandria
Cairo
Tunis
Fez
Al-Qayrawān
Al-Mahdīyah
Tigris R.
Euphrates R.
Baghdād
Işbahān
Khīva
Samarqand
Kashmīr
Lahore
Indus R.
Ganges R.
Narbada R.
Al-Madīnah
Makkah
Nile R.
Emery Walker Ltd., sc.

his vassal and Alp's general Atsiz entered Jerusalem and wrested Palestine from Fāṭimid hands. As Sunnite Moslems the Saljūqs considered it their duty to extirpate the Egyptian heresy. Five years later Atsiz acquired Damascus from the same masters. By 1098, however, Jerusalem had reverted to the Fāṭimids, whose strong fleet had recaptured (1089) all the coast towns, including 'Asqalān (Ascalon), 'Akka (Acre), Tyre (Ṣūr), as far north as Jubayl (Byblos). Alp's son Tutush was the real founder of the Syrian dynasty of Saljūqs. In the spring of 1094 this sultan had established his authority over Aleppo (Ḥalab), al-Ruhā' (Edessa) and al-Mawṣil, in addition to his Khurāsān possessions. But when in the following year he fell in battle, his hard-won Syrian possessions again disintegrated as a result of the rivalry between his two sons Riḍwān and Duqāq and the jealousies of his self-seeking generals. Riḍwān made Aleppo his capital, where he ruled from 1095 to 1113, and Duqāq (1095–1104) chose Damascus.[1] Hostilities between the two brothers, which began in 1096, formed the central event of their reigns.

Complexity of causation and motivation

Viewed in their rightful setting the Crusades appear as the medieval chapter in the long story of interaction between East and West, of which the Trojan and Persian wars of antiquity form the prelude and the imperialistic expansion of modern Western Europe the latest chapter. The geographical fact of difference between East and West acquires its only significance from the competing religious, racial and linguistic differences. More specifically the Crusades represent the reaction of Christian Europe against Moslem Asia, which had been on the offensive since 632 not only in Syria and Asia Minor but in Spain and Sicily also. Among other antecedents we may refer to the migratory and military tendencies of the Teutonic tribes, who had changed the map of Europe since their entrance into the light of history; the destruction in 1009 by al-Ḥākim of the Church of the Holy Sepulchre, the object of pilgrimage for thousands of Europeans and whose keys had been sent (800) to

[1] Saljūqs of Syria, 1094–1117:

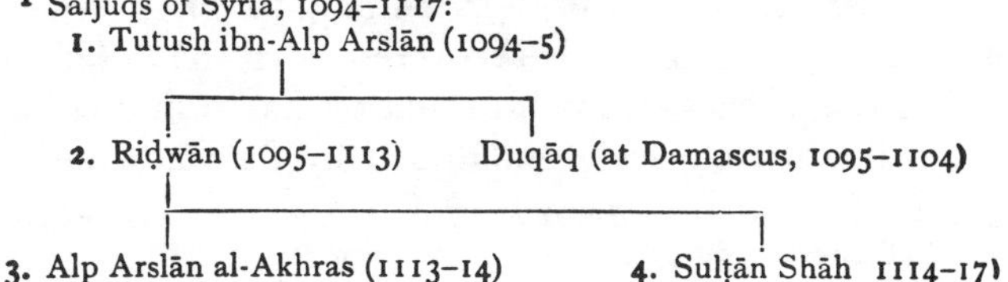

Charlemagne by way of a blessing from the patriarch of Jerusalem,[1] and the hardships to which pilgrims through Moslem Asia Minor were subjected. An immediate cause of the Crusades, however, was the repeated appeal made in 1095 to Pope Urban II by the Emperor Alexius Comnenus, whose Asiatic possessions had been overrun by the Saljūqs as far as the shores of Marmora. These Moslems threatened Constantinople itself. The pope possibly viewed the appeal as affording an opportunity for reuniting the Greek Church and Rome, the final schism between the two having been effected between 1009 and 1054.

When on November 26, 1095, Pope Urban delivered his speech at Clermont in south-eastern France urging the faithful to "enter upon the road to the Holy Sepulchre, wrest it from the wicked race and subject it" to themselves, probably the most effective speech in all history was made. The rallying cry *Deus vult* (God wills [it]) ran through the land and seized high and low with its psychical contagion. By the spring of 1097 a hundred and fifty thousand men, mostly Franks and Normans and partly rabble, had answered the call and met at Constantinople. The first of the Crusades, so called from the cross borne as a badge, was thus launched.

Not all, of course, who took the cross were actuated by spiritual motives. Several of the leaders, including Bohemond, were intent upon acquiring principalities for themselves. The merchants of Pisa, Venice and Genoa had commercial interests. The romantic, the restless and the adventurous, in addition to the devout, found a new rallying-point and many criminals sought penance thereby. To the great masses in France, Lorraine, Italy and Sicily, with their depressed economic and social conditions, taking the cross was a relief rather than a sacrifice.

1. Period of conquest

The customary classification into a definite number of Crusades, seven to nine, is by no means satisfactory. The stream was more or less continuous and the line of demarcation between Crusades not sharply drawn. A more logical division would be into first a period of conquest extending to 1144, when the Atābeg Zangi of al-Mawṣil recovered al-Ruhā'; second, a period of Moslem reaction inaugurated by Zangi and culminating in the brilliant victories of Ṣalāḥ-al-Dīn (Saladin); and third,

[1] Consult Einar Joranson in *American Historical Review*, vol. xxxii (1927), pp. 241-61; A. Kleinclausz in *Syria*, vol. vii (1926), pp 211-33. Cf. above, p. 298.

a period of civil and petty wars in which the Syro-Egyptian Ayyūbids and Egyptian Mamlūks figured, ending in 1291, when the Crusaders lost their last foothold on the Syrian mainland.[1] The period of conquest falls in its entirety before the so-called second Crusade (1147–9) and the third period coincides roughly with the thirteenth century. One of the Crusades of this last period was directed against Constantinople (1202–4), two against Egypt (1218–21) accomplishing nothing, and one even to Tunisia (1270).

The Byzantines recover Asia Minor

The route of the first Crusaders from their rendezvous at Constantinople lay across Asia Minor. This was now the domain of the young Qilij Arslān, Saljūq sultan of Qūniyah (1092–1107). It was in meeting his warriors that Christians measured swords for the first time with Moslems. After a siege of about a month Nicæa, capital of Qilij's father Sulaymān ibn-Quṭlumish, founder of the Saljūq dynasty of al-Rūm, was captured (June 1097). Other than that the only pitched battle the Crusaders fought was that of Dorylæum (Eski-Shahr). Here on July 1[2] they defeated the forces of Qilij. This victorious march restored to Alexius, who had exacted from Raymond of Toulouse and other Crusading leaders an oath of feudal allegiance, the western half of the peninsula and helped to delay the Turkish invasion of Europe for two centuries and a half.

First Latin principality

After crossing the Taurus Mountains and before turning fully southward a detachment of the Crusading army under Baldwin, whose father was count of Boulogne, made a detour into the eastern region occupied by Christian Armenians, where al-Ruhā' was captured early in 1098.[3] Here on Christian territory the first Latin settlement was made and the first Latin state founded. Baldwin became its prince. Other detachments under the Norman Tancred of Southern Italy had turned in the opposite direction to Cilicia, whose population was likewise Armenian with an admixture of Greeks. Here he occupied Tarsus, the birthplace of St. Paul.

[1] See W. B. Stevenson, *The Crusaders in the East* (Cambridge, 1907), p. 17.

[2] *Gesta Francorum et aliorum Hierosolymitanorum*, ed. Heinrich Hagenmeyer (Heidelberg, 1890), p. 197, n. 11, p. 208, n. 62; Fulcher, *Historia Hierosolymitana*, ed. Hagenmeyer (Heidelberg, 1913), p. 192, n. 10. Cf. ibn-al-Qalānisi, ed. Amedroz, p. 134; tr. H. A. R. Gibb, *The Damascus Chronicle of the Crusades* (London, 1932), p. 42.

[3] Matthew of Edessa, *Chronique*, ed. E. Dulaurier (Paris, 1858), p. 218.

Antioch reduced

In the meantime the main body had reached Antioch.[1] The city was under a Saljūq amīr named Yāghi-Siyān[2] appointed by the third Great Saljūq Malikshāh. After a long and arduous siege (October 21, 1097–June 3, 1098) the metropolis of northern Syria fell to the hands of Bohemond through treachery on the part of an Armenian commanding one of the towers. Bohemond was a kinsman of Tancred and the shrewdest of the leaders. The one serious attempt to relieve the city before its fall came from Riḍwān of Aleppo.

No sooner had the besiegers entered the city than they were themselves besieged by Karbūqa,[3] amīr of al-Mawṣil, who had rushed from his capital with reinforcements. Enthused by the discovery of the "holy lance", which had pierced the Saviour's side as He hung upon the cross and had lain buried in a church in Antioch, the Christians by a bold sally raised the siege (June 28), almost annihilating Karbūqa's army. The city was left in charge of Bohemond and became the capital of the second principality acquired. For about a century and three-quarters Antioch remained in Christian hands.

Dissatisfied, Raymond of Toulouse, the wealthiest leader of the Franks, whose men had made the sensational discovery in Antioch, pushed southward. After occupying Ma'arrat al-Nu'mān, famous as the birthplace of abu-al-'Alā', his men left the town (January 13, 1099) after destroying "over 100,000" of its population and committing it to the flames.[4] Count Raymond then occupied Ḥiṣn al-Akrād,[5] commanding the strategic pass between the plains of the Orontes (al-'Āṣi) and the Mediterranean, besieged 'Arqah[6] on the western slope of northern Lebanon and occupied Anṭarṭūs[7] on the coast without resistance. The

[1] Ar. Anṭākīyah, from Gr. Antiochia after Antiochus, father of its founder Seleucus I (300 B.C.). As the place where the disciples were first called Christians (Acts 11 : 26), this city was of special significance.

[2] "Bāghi-Siyān" in ibn-al-Athīr, vol. x, p. 187; abu-al Fidā', vol. ii, p. 220; ibn-Khaldūn, vol. v, p. 20.

[3] Cf. ibn-al-Athīr, vol. x, p. 188; abu-al-Fidā', vol. ii, p. 221. A Turkish adventurer who in 1096 had wrested al-Mawṣil from the Arab banu-'Uqayl and merged it with the Saljūq empire.

[4] Ibn-al-Athīr, vol. x, p. 190, copied by abu-al-Fidā', *loc. cit.* Cf. *Gesta Francorum*, p. 387; Kamāl-al-Dīn, "Muntakhabāt min Ta'rīkh Ḥalab", in *Recueil: orientaux*, vol. iii, pp. 586-7.

[5] Literally "castle of the Kurds", today Qal'at al-Ḥiṣn; Crac des Chevaliers of the Franks. This "Crac" was originally "Crat", a corruption of "Akrād".

[6] Birthplace of Alexander Severus (222–35), of the Syrian dynasty of Roman emperors.

[7] Tortosa of the Latin chronicles, present-day Ṭarṭūs.

Maronite Christians of Lebanon provided him with guides and a limited number of recruits. All these possessions, however, Raymond relinquished and at the urgent appeal of Godfrey of Bouillon, count of Lorraine and Baldwin's brother, joined the army in its march on Jerusalem, the main goal.

Jerusalem captured

On the way southward al-Ramlah was found deserted and became the first Latin possession in Palestine.[1] On June 7, 1099, some forty thousand Crusaders, of whom about twenty thousand were effective troops,[2] stood before the gates of Jerusalem. The Egyptian garrison may be estimated roundly at about one thousand. Hoping the walls would fall as those of Jericho had done, the Crusaders first marched barefoot around the city, blowing their horns. A month's siege proved more effective. On July 15 the besiegers stormed the city and perpetrated an indiscriminate massacre involving all ages and both sexes. "Heaps of heads and hands and feet were to be seen throughout the streets and squares of the city."[3] Another important victory over the Egyptians near ʿAsqalān about a month later rendered the position of the Latins in Jerusalem more secure. But ʿAsqalān remained the base of the Egyptian fleet and the headquarters of a garrison which under the Egyptian vizir al-Malik al-Afḍal continued to harass the enemy.[4] A third Latin state, the most important of all, was thus established. Raymond, rather than a clerical, was reportedly offered the kingship but declined because he was unwilling to wear a crown of gold where the Saviour had worn a crown of thorns.[5] Godfrey,[6] an honest leader and hard fighter, was chosen with the title "baron and defender of the Holy Sepulchre". Many of the Crusaders and pilgrims, considering their vows now fulfilled, sailed back home.

Italian fleets reduce seaports

Godfrey's immediate task was to reduce the coast towns, without which the occupation of the interior would have been pre-

[1] Ibn-al-Qalānisi, p. 136.

[2] Cf. "Annales de Terre Sainte", *Archives de l'orient latin*, vol. ii (Paris, 1884), pt. 2, p. 429; Raimundus de Agiles, "Historia Francorum qui ceperunt Jerusalem", in Migne, *Patrologia Latina*, vol. clv, p. 657.

[3] Agiles, p. 659. Over 70,000 were slaughtered at the Aqṣa Mosque according to ibn-al-Athīr, vol. x, p. 194; 65,000 according to Matthew of Edessa, p. 226.

[4] Ibn-Muyassar, *Akhbār Miṣr*, ed. Henri Massé (Cairo, 1919), pp. 39 *seq.*

[5] Agiles, p. 654.

[6] "Kundufri" in ibn-al-Qalānisi, p. 138; "Kunduhri" in ibn-Taghri-Birdi, ed. Popper, vol. ii, pt. 2, p. 304.

carious and communication with the homeland difficult. The problem was solved with the co-operation of the Italian ships transporting pilgrims, whose commanders saw in the possession of such towns new markets and free ports for their merchandise. In the early part of the next year (1100) the Pisans received special rights in Jaffa (Yāfa). Shortly after, Arsūf, Cæsarea (Qaysārīyah) and 'Akka offered tribute in return for a short period of truce.[1] The Venetian fleet, which in the summer of the year of Godfrey's death was operating against 'Akka, captured Ḥayfa (Haifa) within a month after his death.[2] Ḥayfa's garrison and inhabitants were invited to gather round a cross, as a place of safety, and then mercilessly butchered. The Egyptian fleet, the only Moslem one which could come to the defence of these ports, was ineffective if not inactive throughout.

In the meantime Tancred[3] was penetrating inland to the district around the Jordan. Here Baysān, situated on the route of the armies between the Mediterranean coast and Damascus, formed one of the early acquisitions. Nābulus voluntarily submitted. Tancred took up his residence in Tiberias as Godfrey's vassal. In the following March (1101), however, he relinquished his fief in favour of Antioch, the principality of his uncle Bohemond, who had been taken captive by Gumishtigīn[4] while on an expedition near Mar'ash. In 1103 Bohemond was released on the payment of a ransom.

Baldwin I, king of Jerusalem

On the death of Godfrey[5] his men summoned his brother Baldwin[6] to be his successor. Baldwin came from al-Ruhā' and on Christmas Day 1100 was crowned king at Bethlehem, rather than in Jerusalem, in deference to the clerical party, which aspired to hold Jerusalem as a church domain.

The Latins had in Baldwin a capable, energetic and aggressive leader. During his reign (1100–18) the kingdom extended from al-'Aqabah at the head of the Red Sea to Beirūt. His cousin and successor Baldwin II[7] (1118–31) added a few towns,

[1] Albert of Aix, "Historia Hierosolymitanæ expeditionis", Migne, vol. clxvi, p. 575.

[2] Consult ibn-Khallikān, vol. i, p. 101.

[3] "Ṭankari" in ibn-al-Qalānisi, p. 138; "Dankari" in Usāmah, ed. Hitti, p. 65.

[4] Founder in Sīwās of the Turkoman dynasty of the Dānishmands, which was later absorbed in its greater Saljūq neighbour.

[5] Ibn-al-Qalānisi, p. 138 = Gibb, p. 51.

[6] "Baghdawīn" in ibn-al-Qalānisi, p. 138; ibn-Taghri-Birdi, vol. ii, pt. 2, p. 343; cf. p. 327 ("Bardawīl").

[7] For a genealogy of the royal house of Jerusalem consult René Grousset, *Histoire des croisades*, vol. i (Paris. 1934), p. 686.

chiefly on the Mediterranean. In breadth the kingdom did not reach beyond the Jordan. Beirūt and Sidon were conquered in 1110. The only source from which such cities to the north could hope for aid was Damascus, now under the Atābeg Ṭughtigīn, formerly a slave of the Saljūq Sultan Tutush and the regent over his young son Duqāq.[1] But Ṭughtigīn was for several years in treaty relations with Baldwin. After a short period of truce, Arsūf and Cæsarea capitulated in 1101 to a Genoese fleet, which received one-third of the spoils and had special quarters assigned to it; but Tyre, secure on its peninsula, remained in Moslem possession until 1124 and 'Asqalān until 1153. In the region south of the Dead Sea Baldwin, in 1115, built a formidable fortress, al-Shawbak,[2] commanding the desert road from Damascus to al-Ḥijāz and Egypt.

The third Frankish principality established

In Syria the city of Tripoli (Ṭarābulus, from Gr. Tripolis) was at this time the most frequented port. Count Raymond[3] had his eye on it ever since he had wound his long way southward from Antioch to Jerusalem. After the establishment of the kingdom he returned and began its siege (1101). In order to isolate the town he built two years later a castle[4] on an adjacent hill on the ravine of the abu-'Ali (Qādīsha) River. The hill was named Mons Pelegrinus (pilgrims' hill) and soon became a centre round which grew a Latin quarter. The siege dragged slowly on in spite of reinforcements from the neighbouring Christians and mountaineers.[5] At intervals adjacent towns were reduced by Raymond. With the co-operation of a Genoese fleet of forty galleys he captured Jubayl in 1104, which henceforth marked the southern limit of the county of Tripoli. Raymond died in 1105 in his castle without having attained his goal; beleaguered Tripoli did not fall till July 12, 1109.

Thus was now founded, in addition to the county of al-Ruhā' and the principality of Antioch (which included Cilicia)—both

[1] Following the example of many other atābegs, he usurped the power in 1103 and became the founder of the Būrid dynasty, which lasted till 1154.

[2] Called by the Latins Mons Regalis (Mont Royal, Montréal). According to early chronicles Crac de Montréal refers to its sister to the north-east, Crac des Moabites (al-Karak; Ar. *karak* is from Aram. *karkha*, town, whence Karkh, name of a quarter in Baghdād).

[3] Because he was called Raymond of Saint-Gilles, the Arabs referred to him as Ṣanjīl or ibn-Ṣanjīl.

[4] Repaired later by the Turks, this Qal'at Ṭarābulus has been used until recently as a prison.

[5] Ibn-Khaldūn, vol. v, p. 186.

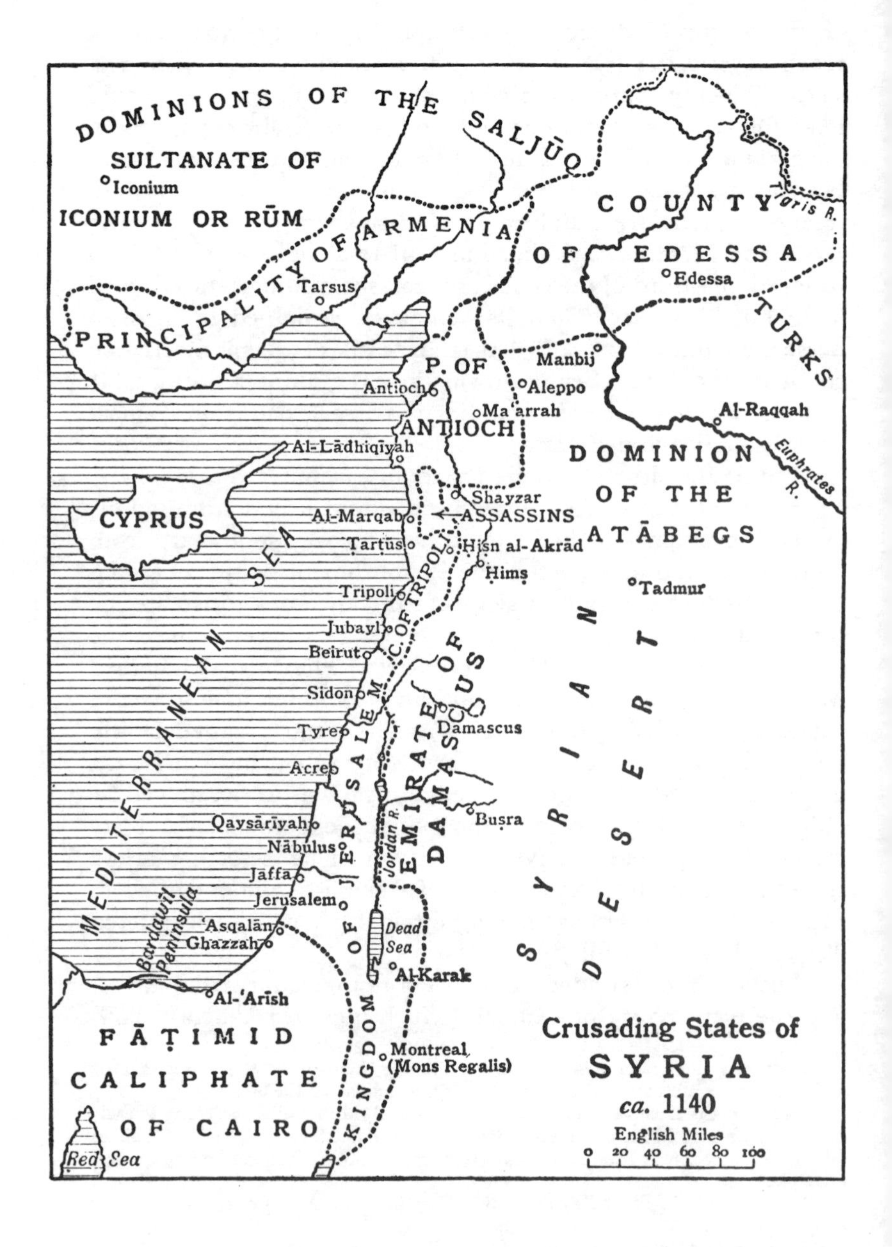

Crusading States of
SYRIA
ca. 1140

held as fiefs of Jerusalem [1]—the county of Tripoli, also under the kingdom of Jerusalem. Al-Ruhā' and Jerusalem were Burgundian princedoms, Antioch was Norman and Tripoli Provençal. These four were the only Latin states ever established on Moslem soil. Their control was confined to the northern part of Syria and to the narrow littoral, a small Christian territory set against a vast and dark background of Islam. Not a town was more than a day's march from the enemy. Even in their states the Latin population was but thinly scattered. Such inland cities as Aleppo, Ḥamāh, Ḥimṣ, Ba'labakk and Damascus were never conquered, though at times they paid tribute. In the year beginning September 1156, Damascus, under Nūr-al-Dīn, paid 8000 dinars.[2]

Social contacts

With the dynastic successions in these Latin states, their squabbles and petty rivalries, we are not concerned. They form a chapter of European rather than of Arab history. But the friendly and peaceful relations developed between the men from the West and the natives should not escape our attention.

It should be remembered in the first place that the Christians came to the Holy Land with the notion that they were far superior to its people, whom they considered idolaters, worshipping Muḥammad as a God. At first contact they were disillusioned. As for the impression they left on the Moslems, Usāmah [3] gave expression to it when he saw in them "animals possessing the virtues of courage and fighting, but nothing else". The forced association between the two peoples in times of peace—which, it should be noted, were of much longer duration than times of war—wrought a radical change in the feelings of both towards each other. Amicable and neighbourly relations were established. The Franks employed trusted native workmen and farmers. The feudal system they introduced was gradually adapted to the local tenure of the land. They had carried with them horses, hawks and dogs, and soon agreements were entered into so that hunting parties might be free from danger of attack. Safe-conducts for travellers and traders were often exchanged and usually honoured by both sides. The Franks discarded their European dress in favour of the more comfortable and more suitable native clothing. They acquired new tastes in food,

[1] I.e. allied states which recognized the primacy of Jerusalem; John L. La Monte, *Feudal Monarchy in the Latin Kingdom of Jerusalem* (Cambridge, 1932), p. 187.
[2] Ibn-al-Qalānisi, p. 336. [3] Ed. Hitti, p. 132 = *Arab-Syrian Gentleman*, p. 161.

especially those varieties involving the generous use of sugar and spices. They preferred Oriental houses, with their spacious open courts and running water. Some intermarried with natives and the half-caste progeny of native mothers were designated as *poulains*.[1] They even in certain instances venerated shrines held equally sacred by Moslems and Jews. In their intermittent quarrels among themselves the Latins often welcomed assistance from the "infidels", and the Moslems often sought alliances with Latins against fellow Moslems.

2. Moslem reaction: The Zangids and Nūrids

The rise of ʻImād-al-Dīn (the pillar of faith) Zangi, the blue-eyed atābeg of al-Mawṣil (1127–46), marks the turning of the tide in favour of Islam. Zangi was the forerunner of a series of counter-Crusading heroes which culminated in Ṣalāḥ-al-Dīn and extended to the Mamlūks of the latter half of the following century. Son of a Turkish slave of Malikshāh, Zangi carved for himself a principality including Aleppo, Ḥarrān and al-Mawṣil, where he founded the Zangid dynasty (1127–1262), easily the greatest among the many established by the atābegs. His were the first hammer-strokes under which the Crusading states were destined to crumble away. The first blow fell on al-Ruhā'. Because of its proximity to Baghdād and its control of the main routes between Mesopotamia and the Mediterranean this city for half a century had been the outer rampart of all Latin states in Syria. After a siege of four weeks Zangi captured it (1144) from Joscelin II.[2] This first of the Crusader states to rise and first to fall was strongly fortified but poorly defended. Its capture meant the removal of the wedge thrust between Moslem Syria and al-ʻIrāq. In Europe it was a signal for what is usually termed the second Crusade (1147–9), led by Conrad III of Germany and Louis VII of France. With an army made up of French and German knights, of Templars[3] and Hospitallers[4] and of troops provided by Jerusalem, Damascus was laid under a futile siege of four days.[5] Nowhere was anything accomplished by this Crusade.

As champion of the Islamic cause Zangi was succeeded in his

[1] "Kids", "young ones", Latinized *Pullani*. Cf. Ar. *fulān*, Mr. So-and-so.

[2] Ibn-al-Athīr, "Ta'rīkh al-Dawlah al-Atābakīyah", in *Recueil: orientaux*, vol. ii, pt. 2, pp. 118 *seq.*

[3] Ar. Dāwīyah, corruption of a Syriac word for "poor", the original name of the order in Latin being Pauperes Commilitones Christi (Poor Knights of Christ).

[4] Or Knights of St. John; Ar. Isbatāriyah (Asbitārīyah).

[5] The clearest account is in the work of ibn-al-Qalānisi, pp. 298-9, who was himself at Damascus and held a high post in the city's government.

Syrian possessions by his son Nūr-al-Dīn (light of the faith) Maḥmūd, who chose Aleppo for his capital. More capable than his father, Nūr was the second to face the Franks on more than equal terms. In 1154 he wrested Damascus, without striking a blow, from a successor of Ṭughtigīn, thereby removing the last barrier between Zangid territory and Jerusalem. Gradually he completed the conquest of the county of al-Ruhā', whose count, Joscelin II, in 1151 had been carried off a prisoner in chains.[1] Nūr also reduced parts of the principality of Antioch, whose young ruler Bohemond III he captured in 1164 together with his ally Raymond III of Tripoli. Both prisoners were later released on payment of ransom, the former after one year of captivity and the latter after nine.

In Palestine, however, the cause of Islam was not so triumphant. Here its bulwark 'Asqalān, which for half a century had resisted the Franks, had fallen (1153) into the hands of Baldwin III of Jerusalem, thus opening the way for the Christians to Egypt.

Enter Saladin

Nūr-al-Dīn had an able lieutenant in one Shīrkūh, who, under orders from his chief and taking advantage of the decrepitude of the Fāṭimid state, managed after several military and diplomatic victories in Egypt to receive in 1169 the vizirate under al-'Āḍid (1160–71), the last of the Fāṭimid caliphs.[2] His predecessor in this high office, Shāwar, had sought and secured against Shīrkūh the aid of Amalric I, brother and successor of Baldwin III. Shortly after his investiture Shīrkūh died and was succeeded by his brother's son, Ṣalāḥ-al-Dīn (rectitude of the faith, Saladin) ibn-Ayyūb.

Al-Malik al-Nāṣir al-Sulṭān Ṣalāḥ-al-Dīn Yūsuf was born in Takrīt on the Tigris in 1138 of Kurdish parentage. In the following year his father Ayyūb (Job) was appointed commander of Ba'labakk by the Atābeg Zangi. Of the youth and early education in Syria of Ṣalāḥ-al-Dīn little is known. Evidently his early interests centred on theological discussion. He did not come into the public eye until 1164, when "in spite of his reluctance"[3] he accompanied his uncle on his first campaign to Egypt. His star then began to rise. The two burning ambitions of his life now

[1] Ibn-al-'Ibri, p. 361; ibn-al-Athīr, vol. xi, p. 101. Cf. Kamāl-al-Dīn, *Zubdat al-Lahab min Ta'rīkh Ḥalab*, tr. E. Blochet (Paris, 1900), p. 25.

[2] Ibn-Khallikān, vol. i, pp. 405-7. Cf. Yāqūt, vol. ii, pp. 246-7.

[3] Abu-Shāmah, vol. i, p. 155; abu-al-Fidā', vol. iii, p. 47.

came to be the substitution of Sunnite for Shī'ite Islam in Egypt and the pressing of the holy war against the Franks. Vizir in 1169, he omitted in 1171 the mention of the name of the Fāṭimid caliph in the Friday prayer, substituting that of the 'Abbāsid caliph al-Mustaḍī'. The momentous change was effected with so little disturbance that not even "two goats locked horns".[1]

For the realization of his other and greater ambition sovereignty over Moslem Syria was a necessary prelude. Here his suzerain Nūr-al-Dīn ruled, and the relations between the two soon became strained. On the death of Nūr in 1174 Ṣalāḥ declared his independence in Egypt and, after a few engagements culminating in the battle of Qurūn (horns of) Ḥamāh, he wrested Syria from the eleven-year-old Ismā'īl, son and successor of Nūr. In the meantime Ṣalāḥ's elder brother Tūrān-Shāh had succeeded in taking possession of al-Yaman. Al-Ḥijāz with its holy cities ordinarily went with Egypt. In May 1175, Ṣalāḥ-al-Dīn at his own request was granted by the 'Abbāsid caliph a diploma of investiture over Egypt, al-Maghrib, Nubia, western Arabia, Palestine and central Syria. The caliph thereby gave away what was in reality not his to give, but what was flattering to him not to refuse. Henceforth Ṣalāḥ considered himself the sole sultan, as his kinsman-historian abu-al-Fidā'[2] expresses it. Ten years later he reduced high Mesopotamia and made its various princes his vassals. Nūr-al-Dīn's dream of first enveloping the Franks and then crushing them between the two millstones of Moslem Syria-Mesopotamia and Egypt was being realized in the career of his more illustrious successor.

In the course of these engagements in northern Syria two attempts were made on the life of Ṣalāḥ-al-Dīn by the Assassins at the instigation of his Moslem enemies. Before this a similar attempt was made on Nūr-al-Dīn and a successful one on the Fātimid al-Āmir (1130). Among the Christians the most distinguished victims of this redoubtable order, which was unusually active in Syria at this time, were Raymond II of Tripoli (*ca.* 1152) and the newly elected king of Jerusalem, Conrad of Montferrat (1192).[3] In 1176 Ṣalāḥ-al-Dīn laid siege to Maṣyād, headquarters of Rāshid-al-Dīn Sinān, the Old Man of the Mountain, but raised it on receiving a promise of immunity against future attacks.

[1] Abu-al-Fidā', vol. iii, p. 53. [2] Vol. iii, p. 60. [3] Ibn-al-Athīr, vol. xii p. 51.

Sinān had made himself independent of Persia. He controlled an efficient secret service and a pigeon-post enabling him to obtain information by what seemed supernatural means. His *fidā'is* (self-sacrificing ones) excelled in the manufacture and use of poisoned knives.[1] It is related that when Henry of Champagne, titular king of Jerusalem, visited him in 1194, the grand master, wanting to impress his guest with the blind obedience he exacted from his henchmen, made a sign to two on top of the castle tower and they immediately leaped off and were dashed to pieces.[2]

Ḥiṭṭīn

With the Assassin threat removed Ṣalāḥ was free to devote his energies to attacks on the Franks. Victory followed victory. On July 1, 1187, he captured Tiberias after a six days' siege. The battle of Ḥiṭṭīn (Ḥaṭṭīn) followed (July 3–4). It began on Friday, the day of prayer and a favourite one with Ṣalāḥ for fighting. This was a sad day for the Frankish army. Numbering about twenty thousand and all but dying of thirst and heat, it fell almost in its entirety into the enemy's hands. The list of distinguished captives was headed by Guy de Lusignan, king of Jerusalem. The chivalrous sultan gave the crestfallen monarch a friendly reception; but his companion Reginald of Châtillon, the disturber of peace, merited a different treatment. Reginald was perhaps the most adventurous and least scrupulous of all the Latin leaders and the most facile in the use of Arabic. Entrusted with the command of al-Karak he more than once had pounced upon peaceful caravans and plundered them as they passed beneath the walls of his castle—and that in violation of treaty relations. He even fitted out a fleet at Aylah and harassed the coasts of the sacred territory of al-Ḥijāz, preying upon its pilgrims. Ṣalāḥ had sworn to slay with his own hand the breaker of truce. And now the time came for the fulfilment of his oath. Taking advantage of a recognized tradition connected with Arab hospitality Reginald secured a drink of water from his captor's tent. But the drink was not offered by Ṣalāḥ and therefore established no guest and host relationship between captive and captor.[3] Reginald paid for his treachery with

[1] Ibn-Baṭṭūṭah, vol. i, pp. 166-7.

[2] Marinus Sanuto, "Liber secretorum" in Bongars, *Gesta Dei per Francos* (Hanau, 1611), vol. ii, p. 201.

[3] See above, p. 25.

his life. All the Templars and Hospitallers were also publicly executed.[1]

The victory of Ḥiṭṭīn sealed the fate of the Frankish cause. After a week's siege Jerusalem, which had lost its garrison at Ḥiṭṭīn, capitulated (October 2, 1187). In the Aqṣa Mosque the muezzin's call replaced the Christian gong, and the golden cross which surmounted the Dome of the Rock was torn down by Ṣalāḥ's men.

The capture of the capital of the Latin kingdom gave Ṣalāḥ-al-Dīn most of the towns of Frankish Syria-Palestine. In a series of brilliantly executed campaigns most of the remaining strongholds were seized. None could offer resistance, for they had all been denuded of their best defenders on the day of Ḥiṭṭīn. Animated with the spirit of holy war which the Crusaders seem now to have lost, the great champion of Islam pushed his conquests north to al-Lādhiqīyah (Laodicea, Latakia), Jabalah and Ṣihyawn, and south to al-Karak and al-Shawbak. All these, as well as Shaqīf Arnūn,[2] Kawkab,[3] Ṣafad and other thorns in the Moslem side, fell before the close of 1189. The Franks came very near being swept out of the land. Only Antioch, Tripoli and Tyre, besides certain smaller towns and castles, remained in their possession.

Siege of 'Akka

The fall of the holy city aroused Europe. Hostilities among its rulers were buried. Frederick Barbarossa, emperor of Germany, Richard I Cœur de Lion, king of England, and Philip Augustus, king of France, took the cross. These three were the most powerful sovereigns of Western Europe, and with them the "third Crusade" (1189–92) began. In point of numbers it was one of the largest. For legend and romance, both Oriental and Occidental, this Crusade, with Ṣalāḥ-al-Dīn and Cœur de Lion as its chief figures, has provided the favourite theme.

Frederick, who was the first to start, took the land route and was drowned while crossing a Cilician river. Most of his followers returned home. En route Richard stopped to capture Cyprus,

[1] Abu-Shāmah, vol. ii, pp. 75 *seq.*, who gives an eye-witness's report; ibn-al-Athīr, vol. xi, pp. 352-5; Ernoul and Bernard le Trésorier, *Chronique*, ed. M. L. de Mas Latrie (Paris, 1871), pp. 172-4.

[2] On the Leontes (al-Līṭāni), the Belfort of Latin chronicles. Its owner had been known as Reginald of Sidon. For etymology see Hitti, *History of Syria, including Lebanon and Palestine* (London, 1950), 602, n. 5.

[3] A newly built Crusading castle north of Baysān by the Jordan. Its full name was Kawkab al-Hawā' (the star of the sky), Belvoir in Latin sources.

Photo: Bonfils

QAL'AT AL-SHAQĪF (BELFORT)

Standing on a precipitous rock 1500 feet above the Līṭāni and commanding the mountain pass from Sidon to Damascus destined to become the last refuge of the Crusaders driven from the mainland.

In the meantime the Latins in the Holy Land had decided on 'Akka as providing the key for the restoration of their lost domain. Against it they marched virtually all their forces, augmented by the remnant of Frederick's army and the contingents of the king of France. King Guy, who had been released by Ṣalāḥ-al-Dīn on pledging his honour never again to bear arms against him, led the attack. Ṣalāḥ arrived the next day to rescue the city and pitched his camp facing the enemy. The struggle was waged by land and sea. The arrival of Richard was hailed with great rejoicing and bonfires. During the progress of the siege many picturesque incidents took place and were recorded by the contemporary Arabic and Latin chroniclers. A Damascene who compounded explosives and burned three of the besiegers' towers refused the reward offered him by Ṣalāḥ in favour of Allah's reward.[1] A flint stone which formed part of three shiploads taken from Sicily by Richard for use in his mangonels and was said to have destroyed thirteen 'Akkans, was saved and shown to Ṣalāḥ as a curiosity. Ṣalāḥ and Richard even exchanged presents, but never met. Carrier-pigeons and swimmers were used for communication between Ṣalāḥ and the beleaguered garrison, which was entirely cut off from the sea. One such swimmer was drowned while attempting to make the passage, and as his body was washed ashore and the 'Akkans obtained the money and letters he carried, Ṣalāḥ's biographer[2] was prompted to remark, "Never before have we heard of a man receiving a trust in his lifetime and delivering it after his death". Richard offered a handsome reward for every stone dislodged from the walls of the city, and the combatants, as well as the women, performed deeds of great valour. The siege, considered one of the major military operations of medieval times, dragged on for two years (August 27, 1189–July 12, 1191). The Franks had the advantage of a fleet and up-to-date siege artillery; the Moslems had the advantage of single command. Ṣalāḥ sought but received no aid from the caliph. Finally the garrison surrendered.

[1] Ibn-Khaldūn, vol. v, p. 321.

[2] Bahā'-al-Dīn ibn-Shaddād, *Sīrat Ṣalāḥ-al-Dīn: Al-Nawādir al-Sulṭānīyah w-al-Maḥāsin al-Yūsufīyah* (Cairo, 1317), p. 120. Cf. tr. as "*Saladin*"; *Or, what Befell Sultan Yûsuf* London, 1897), p. 206.

Two of the conditions of surrender were the release of the garrison on the payment of 200,000 gold pieces and the restoration of the holy cross.[1] When at the end of a month the money was not paid Richard ordered the twenty-seven hundred captives to be slaughtered[2]—an act that stands in conspicuous contrast with Ṣalāḥ's treatment of his prisoners at the capture of Jerusalem. He too had then stipulated for a ransom and several thousand of the poor could not redeem themselves. At the request of his brother, Ṣalāḥ set free a thousand of these poor captives; at the request of the patriarch another batch was released. Then considering that his brother and the patriarch had made their alms and that his own turn had come, Ṣalāḥ freed many of the remaining captives, including numerous women and children, without ransom.

'Akka now takes the place of Jerusalem[3] in leadership and henceforth negotiations for peace between the two combatant parties go on almost without interruption. Richard, who was full of romantic ideas, proposed that his sister should marry Ṣalāḥ's brother, al-Malik al-'Ādil, and that the two should receive Jerusalem as a wedding present, thus ending the strife between Christians and Moslems.[4] On Palm Sunday (May 29, 1192) he knighted with full ceremony al-'Ādil's son, al-Malik al-Kāmil. Peace was finally concluded on November 2, 1192, on the general principle that the coast belonged to the Latins, the interior to the Moslems and that pilgrims to the holy city should not be molested. Ṣalāḥ had only a few months to live and enjoy the fruits of peace. On February 19 of the following year he was taken ill with fever in Damascus and died twelve days later at the age of fifty-five. His tomb close by the Umayyad Mosque is still one of the attractions of the Syrian capital.

Ṣalāḥ-al-Dīn was more than a mere warrior and champion of Sunnite Islam. He patronized scholars, encouraged theological studies, built dykes, dug canals and founded schools and mosques. Among his surviving architectural monuments is the

[1] Abu-Shāmah, vol. ii, p. 188; 'Imād-al-Dīn (al-Iṣfahāni), *al-Fatḥ al-Quṣṣi fi al-Fatḥ al-Qudsi*, ed. C. de Landberg (Leyden, 1888), p. 357; ibn-al-'Ibri, pp. 386-7; abu-al-Fidā', vol. iii, pp. 83-4.

[2] Benedict of Peterborough, ed. W. Stubbs (London, 1867), vol. ii, p. 189; ibn-Shaddād, pp. 164-5.

[3] Ibn-al-'Ibri, p. 413, speaks of the "king of 'Akka".

[4] Cf. abu-al-Fidā', vol. iii, p. 84.

Citadel of Cairo,[1] which he began together with the walls of the city in 1183 and for which he utilized stones from the smaller pyramids. His cabinet included two learned vizirs, al-Qāḍi al-Fāḍil[2] and 'Imād-al-Dīn al-Kātib al-Iṣfahāni,[3] noted for the style and grace of their correspondence. His last private secretary was Bahā'-al-Dīn ibn-Shaddād,[4] who became his biographer. On overthrowing the Fāṭimid caliphate, Ṣalāḥ distributed its accumulated treasures, one of which was an historical seventeen-dirham sapphire as weighed by ibn-al-Athīr[5] in person, among his retainers and troops, keeping nothing for himself. Nor did he touch Nūr-al-Dīn's estate; he left it to the deceased ruler's heir. He himself left on his death forty-seven dirhams and a gold piece.[6] Among the Arabs his name, with Hārūn's and Baybars', heads the list of popular favourites to the present day. In Europe he touched the fancy of English minstrels as well as modern novelists[7] and is still considered a paragon of chivalry.

3. Period of civil and petty wars: The Ayyūbids

The sultanate built by Ṣalāḥ-al-Dīn from the Tigris to the Nile was divided among his various heirs, none of whom inherited his genius. At first his son al-Malik al-Afḍal (the superior king) succeeded to his father's crown at Damascus, al-'Azīz (the mighty) at Cairo, al-Ẓāhir (the victorious) at Aleppo, and Ṣalāḥ's younger brother and confidant al-'Ādil at al-Karak and al-Shawbak. But between 1196 and 1199 al-'Ādil, taking advantage of the discord among his nephews, acquired for himself sovereignty over Egypt and most of Syria. In 1200 he appointed one of his sons governor of Mesopotamia. Al-'Ādil, the Saphadin[8] of Latin chronicles, was the chief agent in the peace negotiations of 1192 and maintained throughout his rule friendly relations with the Crusaders. Small collisions were not lacking, but his general policy was one of peace and the furtherance of commerce with the Frankish colonies. He allowed the Venetians

[1] Qal'at al-Jabal. His inscription can still be read over the old gate.

[2] Ibn-Khallikān, vol. i, pp. 509 *seq.*; Subki, *Ṭabaqāt*, vol. iv, pp. 253-4.

[3] Ibn-Khallikān, vol. ii, pp. 495 *seq.*; Suyūṭi, *Ḥusn*, vol. i, p. 270. His *al-Fatḥ* was drawn upon in the composition of this chapter.

[4] Ibn-Khallikān, vol. iii, pp. 428 *seq.* His *Sīrah* has been extensively used in this chapter.

[5] Vol. xi, p. 242.

[6] Abu-al-Fidā', vol. iii, p. 91.

[7] E.g. Walter Scott in his *Talisman*, Lessing in *Nathan der Weise*. Owing to Salāḥ-al-Dīn's fame a legend grew up to explain the greatness of Thomas Becket on the ground of his descent from a Saracen mother.

[8] From his honorific title Sayf-al-Dīn (the sword of religion). Ibn-Khallikān, vol. ii, p. 446.

to establish special markets with inns[1] at Alexandria and the Pisans to establish consuls there. His name is still borne in Damascus by al-ʿĀdilīyah school, which he partly built.[2]

After al-ʿĀdil's death in 1218 several Ayyūbid branches, all sprung from him, reigned in Egypt, Damascus and Mesopotamia. Other branches, descended from other members of the Ayyūbid family, controlled Ḥimṣ, Ḥamāh and al-Yaman. The Egyptian Ayyūbids were the chief branch and frequently contested with their Damascene kinsmen the sovereignty over Syria. The north Syrian branches were swept away in 1260 by the Tartar avalanche of Hūlāgu, with the exception of the insignificant Ḥamāh branch which continued under the Mamlūks and numbered in its line the historian-king abu-al-Fidā' († 1332), a descendant of Ṣalāḥ-al-Dīn's brother.

The Frankish camp

In the course of these dynastic turmoils not only did Islam lose its power of aggression, but one after another of Ṣalāḥ-al-Dīn's conquests, e.g. Beirūt, Safad, Tiberias, ʿAsqalān and even Jerusalem (1229), reverted to Frankish hands. But the Franks were in no position to take full advantage of the situation. They were themselves in as bad a plight, if not worse. Their colonies depended for their maintenance upon new recruits from Europe which were not forthcoming. Among themselves quarrels between Genoese and Venetians, jealousies between Templars and Hospitallers, personal squabbles among leaders and contests for the empty title of king of Jerusalem—these were the order of the day. In their disputes, as we learned above, one side would often secure aid from Moslems against the other.

Egypt, the centre of interest

The first serious engagements since Ṣalāḥ-al-Dīn's death between Franks and natives took place on Egyptian soil under al-Kāmil (1218–38). Al-Kāmil, the Egyptian successor of his father al-ʿĀdil, was now the leading Ayyūbid figure and nominally received the homage of Syria. His first task was to clear his land of the Crusaders who shortly before his father's death had landed near Dimyāṭ (Damietta) and in the following year had occupied that town. This invasion of Egypt was prompted by the fresh realization by the maritime republics of Italy that the centre of

[1] Ar. *funduq*, from Gr. *pandokeion*; Ar. *bunduq* (hazelnut), from Gr. *pontikos* (adjective, from Pontos); Bunduqīyah, Ar. name of Venice (abu-al-Fidā', *Taqwīm al-Buldān*, ed. Reinaud and de Slane, Paris, 1840, p. 210), from Veneticum.

[2] The names of ibn-Khallikān, al-Subki and others are associated with this school, whose building now houses the Arab Academy of Damascus.

Islamic power had shifted from Syria to Egypt and that only by the conquest of the latter could their ships reach the Red Sea and participate in the opulent commerce of the Indian Ocean. After almost two years of conflict (November 1219–August 1221) al-Kāmil forced the Franks to abandon Dimyāṭ and granted them a free passage.[1]

Like his father, al-Kāmil took a lively interest in irrigation and agriculture and signed several commercial treaties with European countries. He was so favourably disposed toward his Christian subjects that the Coptic church still recognizes him as the most beneficent sovereign it ever had. The year after his accession St. Francis of Assisi visited his court and discussed religion with him. His interest in learning may be illustrated by a personal call he once made to a Cairene subject, 'Umar ibn-al-Fāriḍ (1181–1235), the greatest Sufi poet the Arabs produced, who is said to have refused to receive his royal guest. Formerly a friend of Richard, al-Kāmil now entered into friendly relations with Frederick II, who in 1227 set out on a Crusade. In 1229 an infamous treaty was concluded yielding to Frederick Jerusalem, along with a corridor connecting it with 'Akka, and guaranteeing al-Kāmil Frederick's aid against his enemies, most of whom were Ayyūbids.[2] This was the most singular treaty between a Christian and a Moslem power before Ottoman days. Jerusalem remained in Frankish hands until 1244 when, at the invitation of al-Kāmil's second successor al-Malik al-Ṣāliḥ Najm-al-Dīn Ayyūb (1240–49), a contingent of Khwārizm Turks, previously dislodged from their Central Asian abode by Chingīz Khān, restored the city to Islam.[3]

St. Louis

As he lay on his deathbed al-Ṣāliḥ received the news that Dimyāṭ was again threatened, this time by Louis IX, king of France, and his chevaliers of the "sixth Crusade". The town surrendered (June 6, 1249) without resistance; but as the French army marched on Cairo in a region intersected by canals, while the Nile was at its height, pestilence spread in its ranks, its line of communication was cut off and it was entirely destroyed (April 1250). King Louis, with most of his nobles, was taken prisoner.[4]

[1] Abu-al-Fidā', vol. iii, pp. 135-7; ibn-Khaldūn, vol. v, pp. 349-50; ibn-Khallikān, vol. ii, p. 451, ibn-Iyās, *Badā'i' al-Zuhūr fi Waqā'i' al-Duhūr* (Būlāq, 1311), vol. i, pp. 79-80.

[2] Abu-al-Fidā', vol. iii, p. 148; ibn-al-Athīr, vol. xii, p. 315. [3] See above, p. 482.

[4] Maqrīzi, vol. ii, pp. 236-7; Joinville, *Histoire de Saint Louis*, ed. N. de Wailly (Paris, 1874), pp. 169 *seq.*

In the meantime al-Ṣāliḥ had passed away (November 1249) His daring and energetic widow Shajar-al-Durr (the tree of pearls) kept the news secret for three months until his son and successor Tūrān-Shāh had returned from Mesopotamia.[1] Tūrān failed to make himself agreeable to the slaves (*mamlūks*) of his father and with the connivance of his stepmother was murdered in 1250. Shajar proclaimed herself queen of the Moslems [2] and a six-year-old scion of the Damascene Ayyūbids, al-Ashraf Mūsa, was accorded the nominal dignity of joint sovereignty; but the titular ruler was the Mamlūk Aybak, founder of the Mamlūk dynasty. After a month of captivity Louis and his men were released on the payment of a ransom and the restoration of Dimyāṭ.[3] His work in Syria, where he remained from 1250 to 1254, consisted in the fortifying of such ports as 'Akka, Ḥayfa, Cæsarea and Sidon. In 1270 he led another futile Crusade, now to Tunisia, where he died. Of all the Crusading leaders his, by far, was the purest and noblest character. His "whole life was a prayer, his noble aim was to do God's will".

The Ayyūbids give way to the Mamlūks

Among the Mamlūks it was the fourth, al-Malik al-Ẓāhir Baybars (1260–77), who inaugurated the series of sultans who dealt the final blows to the Crusaders' cause. Baybars had distinguished himself as a general under his predecessor Quṭuz when at 'Ayn Jālūt he inflicted (September 3, 1260) a crushing

The last blows: Baybars

[1] A tree of the Egyptian Ayyūbids, all of whom, excepting al-'Azīz, al-Manṣūr and al-Ashraf, were at least for a time acknowledged by Damascus:

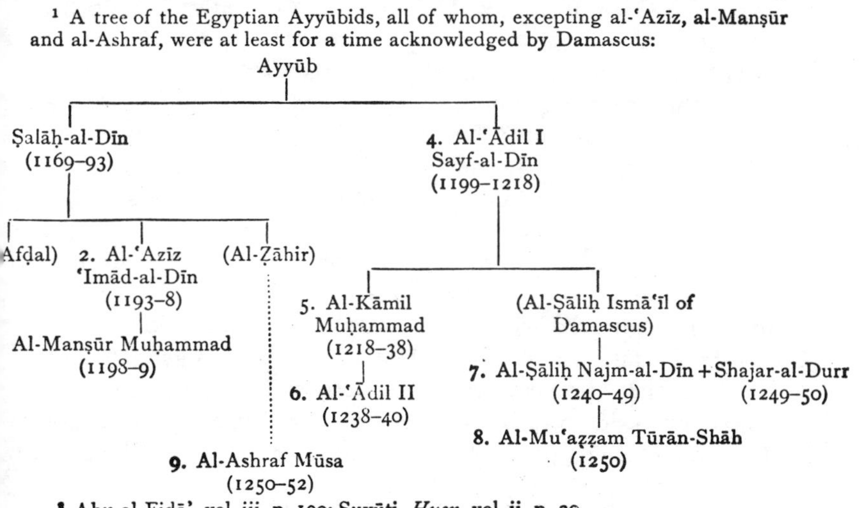

[2] Abu-al-Fidā', vol. iii, p. 190; Suyūṭi, *Ḥusn*, vol. ii, p. 39.

[3] Joinville, pp. 201 *seq.*

defeat on the Tartars. The Mongolian leader was Kitbugha, a Nestorian, whose advance guard had penetrated Palestine down to Ghazzah.[1] This victory is memorable for the history of civilization; if the Mongols had taken Cairo they would have probably destroyed its treasures and manuscripts. Besides averting the danger threatening Syria and Egypt it paved the way for the reunion of the two neighbouring countries, a reunion which lasted under the Mamlūk sceptre until the Ottoman conquest two centuries and a half later.

Baybars' ambition was to be a second Ṣalāḥ-al-Dīn in the holy war against Crusader towns. Especially provoked was he when he found those towns making common cause with the Hūlāguid Īl-Khāns of Persia, now favourably disposed toward the Christian religion. From 1263 to 1271 he conducted almost annual raids against them. One after another of the Latin establishments yielded with little or no resistance. The two military orders which now occupied the leading fortresses of Frankish Syria and formed its bulwark were the ones who received his most devastating blows. But throughout the opposition was so weak that hardly a single battle of importance was fought in the open field.

In 1263 Baybars took al-Karak from an Ayyūbid and demolished the venerated church of Nazareth (al-Nāṣirah). In 1265 he seized Cæsarea, and after a forty-day siege received the surrender of Arsūf from the Hospitallers. On July 23, 1266, the Templar garrison of Ṣafad capitulated on condition that the lives of its two thousand knights be spared. Without delay and in spite of the amnesty granted, the sultan ordered them all executed on a neighbouring hill.[2] The story of the victory of "the Alexander of his age and the pillar of faith" is still engraved on the walls of Ṣafad; and the bridge he built over the Jordan stands to the present day bearing his inscription, with the figure of a lion on either side. In 1268 Jaffa was captured without resistance; Shaqīf Arnūn capitulated after a short siege; and what is more important Antioch, which had maintained amicable relations with the Tartars, surrendered (May 21). Antioch's garrison with others to the number of 16,000 were slaughtered and some 100,000 are said to have been led to captivity, some to be sold in the markets of Egypt. When the plunder was divided, money

[1] Maqrīzi, tr. Quatremère, vol. i (pt. 1), pp. 98, 104.
[2] *Ibid.* (pt. 2), pp. 29-30; abu-al-Fidā', vol. iv, p. 3.

was measured out in cups; an infant fetched twelve dirhams and a young girl five. The city with its citadel and world-renowned churches was given to the flames—a blow from which it has never recovered.[1] On the fall of Antioch a number of minor Latin strongholds in the vicinity were abandoned. In 1271 the formidable Ḥiṣn al-Akrād, the principal retreat of the Hospitallers and probably the most beautiful military monument of the Middle Ages, surrendered after a siege lasting from March 24 to April 8. The adjacent castles of Maṣyād, al-Qadmūs, al-Kahf and al-Khawābi, which belonged to the Assassins who were in alliance with the Hospitallers and often paid tribute to them, were all reduced. The last nest of an order which for years had hatched horror and intrigue was thereby for ever destroyed. Both the Templars of Anṭarṭūs and the Hospitallers of al-Marqab now hastened to make peace.

Qalāwūn

Baybars had a worthy successor in Qalāwūn (1279–90), who was almost as energetic and redoubtable an anti-Crusader. Baybars' truce with the Templars of Anṭarṭūs was renewed (April 15, 1282) for another term of ten years and ten months. A similar treaty was signed (July 18, 1285) with the princess of Tyre who controlled Beirūt.[2] On the battlefield he established his right to the honorific title he bore, al-Malik al-Manṣūr (the victorious king). Al-Marqab,[3] which still looks like a dreadnought crowning a hill near Ṭarṭūs and overlooking the sea, yielded after a siege of thirty-eight days, ending May 25, 1285. The besiegers' arrowheads can still be seen imbedded in its outer walls. Abu-al-Fidā',[4] who was then twelve years old, had his first experience in warfare on this occasion. The citadel's Knights of St. John were conducted under escort to Tripoli. Tripoli, another of the early conquests of the Crusaders and now the largest town in their possession, succumbed in April 1289; the city and its citadel were almost entirely ruined. Abu-al-Fidā'[5] himself was oppressed by the smell of the corpses lying thick on the island outside the port. After Tripoli the stronghold of al-Batrūn to the south was captured. Qalāwūn commemorated his

[1] Ibn-al-'Ibri, p. 500; Maqrīzi, tr. Quatremère, vol. i (pt. 2), pp. 52-4; abu-al-Fidā', vol. iv, pp. 4-5.

[2] Maqrīzi has preserved the texts of both treaties, ed. Quatremère, vol. ii (pt. 3), pp. 172-6, 177-8, tr. pp. 22-31, 212-21.

[3] "The watch tower", Castrum Mergathum, Margat.

[4] Vol. iv, p. 22.

[5] Vol. iv, p. 24.

victories with inscriptions which, like those of Baybars, can still be read on the walls of the citadels he reduced.

'Akka

'Akka was now the only place of military importance left. In the midst of his preparations against it Qalāwūn died and was succeeded by his son al-Ashraf (1290–93), who commenced where his father had left off. After an investment of over a month, in which ninety-two catapults were used against its ramparts, this last bulwark of the Latin Orient was stormed (May 1291). The help received from Cyprus by sea did not save the day. Its Templar defenders, to whom a safe-conduct had been promised, were massacred. The city was plundered, its fortifications were dismantled and houses set on fire.[1]

The fall of 'Akka sealed the fate of the half-dozen towns still retained along the coast, and none resisted the victorious enemy. Tyre was abandoned on May 18, Sidon on July 14. Beirūt capitulated on July 21. Anṭarṭūs was occupied on August 3 and the deserted Templar castle of 'Athlīth (Castrum Peregrinorum, Château Pèlerin) was destroyed about the middle of that month.[2] One of the most dramatic chapters in the history of Syria was closed.[3]

[1] Abu-al-Fidā' (who took part in the siege), vol. iv, pp. 25-6; Maqrīzi, tr. Quatremère, vol. ii (pt. 3), pp. 125-9; *Archives*, vol. ii, pt. 2, p. 460; *Les gestes des Chiprois*, ed. G. Raynaud (Geneva, 1887), p. 256.

[2] See Sanuto in Bongars, vol. ii, pp. 231 *seq.*

[3] Later Crusades were directed against Rhodes, Smyrna, Alexandria and Turkey in Europe, culminating in the Crusade of Nicopolis in 1396. See A. S. Atiya, *The Crusade in the Later Middle Ages* (London, 1938).

From Henri Lavoix, "Monnaies à legendes arabes frappées en Syrie par les Croisés"

A FRANKISH DINAR STRUCK AT 'AKKA IN 1251

Bearing Arabic inscription

CHAPTER XLVI

CULTURAL CONTACTS

BECAUSE of the richness of the Crusades in picturesque and romantic incidents, their historical importance has been somewhat exaggerated. For the Occident they meant much more than for the Orient. Their civilizing influence was artistic, industrial and commercial rather than scientific and literary. In Syria they left in their wake havoc and ruin intensified by the Mamlūk destruction of most of those maritime towns formerly occupied by the Franks. Throughout the Near East they bequeathed a legacy of ill will between Moslems and Christians that has not yet been forgotten.

Nūrid contributions

Notwithstanding its civil and holy wars Syria enjoyed under the Nūrids and Ayyūbids—more particularly under Nūr-al-Dīn and Ṣalāḥ-al-Dīn—the most brilliant period in its Moslem history, with the exception of the Umayyad age. Its capital, Damascus, still bears evidences of the architectural and educational activities of members of these two houses. Not only did Nūr renovate the walls of the city with their towers and gates and erect government buildings which remained in use until recent times, but he established in Damascus the earliest school devoted to the science of tradition,[1] the celebrated hospital bearing his name[2] and the first of those *madrasahs* (academies) which after his time began to flourish in the land. The Nūri hospital, the second in Damascus after that of al-Walīd, functioned later as a school of medicine.[3] The *madrasahs* were in reality collegiate mosques or school-mosques, but they boarded students and followed the type evolved by the Niẓāmīyah. Such collegiate mosques, all of the Shāfiʻi rite, were founded by Nūr in Aleppo, Ḥimṣ, Ḥamāh and Baʻlabakk. His inscriptions on these buildings and on other monuments of his are of special

[1] In this Dār al-Ḥadīth al-Nūrīyah, the contemporary ibn-ʻAsākir (vol. i, p. 222) lectured.

[2] Al-Māristān al-Nūri. Ibn-Jubayr, p. 283; ibn-Khallikān, vol. ii, p. 521.

[3] Cf. ibn-abi-Uṣaybiʻah, vol. ii, p. 192. The building is still standing.

interest for Arabic paleography, since it was about this time that the angular Kufic, in which until then inscriptions were exclusively cut, was replaced by the rounded *naskhi*. An inscription of his on a western tower of the Citadel of Aleppo is still legible. The existing fortifications of this citadel, which is mentioned in Assyrian and Hittite records and is considered a masterpiece of ancient military architecture, owe their restoration to this Syrian sultan. Nūr's tomb in his Damascus academy, al-Nūrīyah, is held in reverence even today. Through this *madrasah* the connection between mausoleum and mosque was established in Syria.[1]

By courtesy of K. A. C. Creswell

THE ANCIENT CITADEL OF ALEPPO
Restored by Nūr-al-Dīn († 1174)

During the Mamlūk period, which in art was a continuation of the Ayyūbid, it became the regular practice for the founder of a collegiate mosque to be buried under a dome (*qubbah*) in the building.

Ṣalāḥ-al-Dīn displayed even more munificent architectural and educational activity than his predecessor. His policy was to combat Shīʿite heresy and pro-Fāṭimid tendencies by means of education. Next to Niẓām-al-Mulk he is reputed to have been the greatest builder of academies in Islam. Under him Damascus became a city of schools. Ibn-Jubayr,[2] who visited it in 1184, refers to its twenty *madrasahs*, two free hospitals and numerous dervish "monasteries". Ṣalāḥ introduced these "monasteries"[3] into Egypt.

[1] Cf. above, p. 630.
[2] Pp. 283-4; above, pp. 408, 412.
[3] Ar. *khānaqāh*, from Pers. *khānagāh*. Suyūṭi, *Ḥusn*, vol. ii, p. 158.

Ayyūbid contributions

"The classical Arab art of the East is represented by the buildings of Damascus and Aleppo dating from the thirteenth century, under the Ayyūbids and their earliest Mameluke successors."[1] The Ayyūbid school of Syrian architecture was continued in Egypt under the Mamlūks and produced some of the most exquisite monuments which Arab art can boast. Its characteristics are strength and solidity. On its durable material of fine stone even the simplest decorative motif assumes infinite grace. But like the Andalusian school it depended for its elegance and beauty upon excessive decoration.

It was Ṣalāḥ-al-Dīn who introduced the *madrasah* type of school into Jerusalem and Egypt.[2] During his reign al-Ḥijāz also saw its first institution of this type. Notable among his Egyptian academies was the one at Cairo bearing his name, al-Ṣalāḥīyah.[3] Ibn-Jubayr[4] found several *madrasahs* in Alexandria. None of these Egyptian institutions have survived, but their architectural influence is manifest. It produced in later years the finest Arab monuments of Egypt, among which the most splendid example is the collegiate mosque of Sultan Ḥasan in Cairo. Its general plan consists of a square central court (*ṣaḥn*) open to the sky, flanked by four walls with four halls or porticos (sing. *līwān*) forming the arms of a cross. Each of these four halls was reserved for instruction in one of the orthodox rites.

Besides schools Ṣalāḥ-al-Dīn maintained in Cairo two hospitals.[5] The edifices were probably planned after the Nūrid hospital in Damascus. Before his time ibn-Ṭūlūn and Kāfūr al-Ikhshīdi had established in Egypt similar free public institutions. Hospital architecture followed also the mosque plan, but has left no traces. Only in military architecture do we have survivals, the Citadel of Cairo being the principal example. This citadel shows that Ṣalāḥ owed a part of his knowledge of fortification to the Norman castles that had by this time sprung up in Palestine. He probably used Christian prisoners in its construction. It was in this citadel that he made his residence, while in Cairo. surrounded by a galaxy of talent which included, besides his

[1] René Grousset, *The Civilizations of the East*, vol. i, *The Near and Middle East*, tr. Catherine A. Phillips (New York, 1931), p. 235; M. van Berchem, *Matériaux pour un corpus inscriptionum Arabicarum*, pt. 2, vol. i (Cairo, 1922), pp. 87 *seq.*

[2] Ibn-Khallikān, vol. iii, p. 521.

[3] Suyūṭi, *Ḥusn*, vol. ii, pp. 157-8.

[4] Pp. 41-2.

[5] Ibn-Jubayr, pp. 51-2.

brilliant vizirs,[1] such men as his distinguished Jewish physician ibn-Maymūn and the versatile, prolific 'Irāqi scholar 'Abd-al-Laṭīf al-Baghdādi (1162–1231), whose short description of Egypt[2] stands out among the important topographical works of the Middle Ages.

In science and philosophy

Despite this manifestation of intellectual and educational activity Islamic culture in the epoch of the Crusades was already decadent in the East. For some time prior to that epoch it had ceased to be a creative force. In philosophy, medicine, music and other disciplines, almost all its great lights had vanished. This partly explains why Syria, which was throughout the twelfth and thirteenth centuries a particular focus of relations between Islam and Western Christianity, proved as a vehicle of Arabic influence very much less important than either Spain, Sicily, North Africa or even the Byzantine empire. Although in Syria Islam acted upon European Christianity by direct impact upon the Crusaders, by the repercussion of that impact upon the West and by a process of infiltration along the routes of commerce, yet the spiritual and intellectual impress it left is barely noticeable. On the other hand, we should recall that the Franks in Syria, besides possessing a lower level of culture than their antagonists, were largely foreign legions quartered in castles and barracks and in close contact with the native tillers of the soil and artisans rather than with the intelligentsia. Then there were the nationalistic and religious prejudices and animosities which thwarted the play of interactive forces. In science and art the Franks had very little to teach the natives. The comparative standing of medical lore in the two camps may be illustrated by the anecdotes cleverly told by Usāmah,[3] who also pokes fun at the Franks' judicial procedure with its trial by duel and by water.

Concrete instances of scientific and philosophic transmission are not entirely lacking. Adelard of Bath, whose translations of Arabic works on astronomy and geometry have already been mentioned, visited Antioch and Tarsus early in the twelfth century. About a century later the first European algebraist, Leonardo Fibonacci, who dedicated a treatise on square num-

[1] See above, p. 652.

[2] *Al-Ifādah w-al-I'tibār fi al-Umūr al-Mushāhadah w-al-Ḥawādith al-Mu'āyanah bi-Arḍ Miṣr*, ed. D. J. White (Tübingen, 1789); tr. into Latin, German and French. Ibn-abi-Uṣaybi'ah, vol. ii, p. 207; Kutubi, vol. ii. p. 10.

[3] Pp. 132 *seq.*= *Arab-Syrian Gentleman*, pp. 162 *seq.*

bers to Frederick II, visited Egypt and Syria. Frederick himself entertained the ambition of reconciling Islam and Christianity and patronized several translators from Arabic. A Pisan, Stephen of Antioch, translated the important medical work of al-Majūsi at Antioch in 1127. This was the only known Arabic work the Franks carried back with them; but since in the twelfth century we find a number of hospices and hospitals, chiefly lazar-houses for leprosy, springing up all over Europe, we may assume that the idea of systematic hospitalization received a stimulus from the Moslem Orient. This Orient was also responsible for the reintroduction into Europe of public baths, an institution which the Romans patronized but the Christians discouraged. It was again in Antioch that Philip of Tripoli found about 1247 a manuscript of the Arabic *Sirr al-Asrār* purporting to have been composed by Aristotle for the guidance of his great pupil, Alexander. Translated by Philip into Latin as *Secretum secretorum*, this pseudo-Aristotelian work, containing the essence of practical wisdom and occult science, became one of the most popular books of the later Middle Ages.

In letters

In literature the influence was more pervasive. The legends of the Holy Grail have elements of undoubted Syrian origin. The Crusaders must have heard stories from the *Kalīlah* and the *Arabian Nights* and carried them back with them. Chaucer's *Squieres Tale* is an *Arabian Nights* story. From oral sources Boccaccio derived the Oriental tales incorporated in his *Decameron*. To the Crusaders we may also ascribe European missionary interest in Arabic and other Islamic languages. Men like Raymond Lull († 1315) were convinced by the failure of the Crusades of the futility of the military method in dealing with the "infidel". Lull, a Catalan, was the first European to promote Oriental studies as an instrument of a pacific Crusade in which persuasion should replace violence. In 1276 he founded at Miramar a college of friars for the study of Arabic; it was probably through his influence that in 1311 the Council of Vienne resolved to create chairs of Arabic and Tartar at the Universities of Paris, Louvain and Salamanca.

In military art

In the realm of warfare the influences, as is to be expected, are more noticeable. The use of the crossbow, the wearing of heavy mail by knight and horse and the use of cotton pads under the armour are of Crusading origin. In Syria the Franks adopted the tabor[1] and the naker[2] for their military bands, which hitherto had been served only by trumpets and horns. They learned from the natives how to train carrier-pigeons[3] to convey military information and borrowed from them the practice of celebrating victory by illuminations and the knightly sport of the tournament (*jarīd*). In fact several features of the chivalry institution developed on the plains of Syria. The growing use of armorial bearings and heraldic devices was due to contact with Moslem knights. The two-headed eagle,[4] the fleur-de-lis[5] and the two keys may be cited as elements of Moslem heraldry of this period. Ṣalāḥ-al-Dīn probably had the eagle as his crest. Most Mamlūks bore names of animals, the corresponding images of which they blazoned on their shields. Mamlūk rulers had different corps, which gave rise to the practice of distinguishing by heraldic designs on shields, banners, badges and coats of arms. Baybars' crest was a lion, like that of ibn-Ṭūlūn before him, and Sultan Barqūq's († 1398) was the falcon. In Europe coats of arms appear in a rudimentary form at the end of the eleventh century; the beginning of English heraldry dates from the early part of the twelfth. Among modern Moslems the star and crescent and the lion and sun form the sole remnant of heraldry. "Azure" (Ar. *lāzaward*) and other terms used in heraldry testify to this connection between the European and Moslem institutions.

Gunpowder

The Crusades also fostered the improvement of siege tactics, including the art of sapping and mining, the employment of mangonels and battering-rams and the application of various combustibles and explosives. Gunpowder was evidently invented in China, where it was used mainly as an incendiary. About 1240 it was introduced by the Mongols into Europe. There the application of its explosive force to the propulsion of missiles, i.e. the invention of fire-arms, was accomplished about a century later. No historian of the Crusades makes an allusion to it. The first European recipe for gunpowder we find appended to a

[1] Fr. *tambour*, from Ar. *ṭunbūr*, from Pers. *ṭumbūr*, a kind of lute.

[2] Fr. *nacaire*, fr. Ar. *naqqārah*, a kettledrum.

[3] Consult Ṣāliḥ ibn-Yaḥya, *Ta'rīkh Bayrūt*, ed. L. Cheikho (Beirūt, 1898), pp. 60-61; al-Ẓāhiri, *Zubdat Kashf al-Mamālik*, ed. P. Ravaisse (Paris, 1894), pp. 116-17. Cf. Suyūṭi, *Ḥusn*, vol. ii, p. 186.

[4] Zangi's coins of Sinjār show this symbol of Sumerian antiquity. Above, p. 479.

[5] L. A. Mayer, *Saracenic Heraldry: A Survey* (Oxford, 1933), pp. 23-4. This, one of the most widely spread elements of decorative art, was known in Assyria. It still figures on the Canadian coat of arms for France.

work written about 1300 by a certain Marc the Greek; Bacon's recipe is apocryphal. Shortly before 1300 Ḥasan al-Rammāḥ (the lancer) Najm-al-Dīn al-Aḥdab, probably a Syrian, composed a treatise entitled *al-Furūsīyah w-al-Manāṣib al-Ḥarbīyah*[1] (horsemanship and military exercises), which mentions saltpetre, a component of powder, and contains pyrotechnic recipes to which those ascribed to Marc bear close resemblance. One of the earliest references to the use of gunpowder is in al-ʿUmari († 1348).[2]

In architecture

The Crusaders took with them from Italy and Normandy a substantial knowledge of military masonry which was partly passed on to the Arabs, as the architecture of the Citadel of Cairo indicates. Castles and churches were their main structures. Most of the castles, including Ḥiṣn al-Akrād, al-Marqab and al-Shaqīf (Belfort), are extant. In Jerusalem parts of the Church of the Holy Sepulchre, "Solomon's Stables" near the Aqṣa Mosque and several of the vaulted bazaars are their work. The Church of the Sepulchre and the Dome of the Rock were deliberately imitated by several churches of the round "temple" type, of which four are found in England and others in France, Spain and Germany. In Beirūt the so-called ʿUmari Mosque was built as the Church of St. John by Baldwin I in 1110. The Crusading arch is generally of the pointed form and the vaulting simple, usually groined. The most beautiful relic of Frankish art in Cairo is a doorway taken from the Christian church of ʿAkka in 1291 and incorporated in the Mosque of al-Nāṣir.[3]

Agriculture and industry

In the realm of agriculture, industry and commerce the Crusades produced much greater results than in the realm of intellect. They explain the popularization in the regions of the Western Mediterranean of such new plants and crops as sesame and carob, millet and rice,[4] lemons and melons, apricots and shallots. "Carob" is Arabic *kharrūb* (originally Assyrian); "lemon" is Arabic *laymūn*, of Indic or Malay origin; and both "shallot" and "scallion", meaning originally the onion of Ascalon, preserve the name of the Palestinian town. For many years apricots were called the plums of Damascus. Also there were other trees and products which were simultaneously diffused

[1] Extracts in Ar. and Fr. tr. by Reinaud and Favé, *Journal asiatique*, ser. 4, vol. xiv (1849), pp. 257-327. See also vol. xii, pp. 193 *seq.*

[2] *Taʿrīf* (Cairo, 1312), p. 208.

[3] See below, p. 681.

[4] Cf. above, p 528. "Sesame", Ar. *simsim*, is derived from Assyrian through Gr.

INTERIOR OF THE CRUSADING CHURCH OF NOTRE DAME AT ANṬARṬŪS (TORTOSA, MODERN ṬARṬŪS)

Photo taken 1929

through Moslem Spain and Sicily, and in certain instances it is not possible to tell whether the bridge was Syria or one of these two other countries.

While in the Orient, the Franks acquired new tastes, especially in perfumes, spices, sweetmeats and other tropical products of Arabia and India with which the marts of Syria were well stocked. These tastes later supported the commerce of Italian and Mediterranean cities. Incense and other fragrant gums of Arabia, the damask rose (*Rosa damascena*) and sweet scents in which Damascus specialized and numerous fragrant volatile oils and attars[1] of Persia became favourites. Alum and aloes figured among the new drugs with which they became acquainted. At the capture of Cæsarea in 1101 the Genoese, we are told, received as their portion of the booty more than sixteen thousand pounds of pepper. Cloves and other aromatic spices together with pepper and similar condiments came into use in the Occident in the twelfth century, and from that time on no banquet was complete without spiced dishes. Ginger (Ar. and Pers. *zanjabīl*, of Skr. origin) was added to the Crusaders' menu in Egypt. More important than all others is sugar (Ar. *sukkar*, ultimately Skr.). Europeans had hitherto used honey for sweetening their foods. On the maritime plain of Syria, where children can still be seen sucking sugar-cane, the Franks became acquainted with this plant which has since played such an important rôle in our domestic economy and medical prescriptions. William of Tyre[2] († *ca.* 1190), who knew Arabic and wrote the most elaborate medieval account of the Crusades (from 1095 to 1184), has left us interesting observations on the sugar plantations of his native town. Sugar was the first luxury introduced into the West and nothing else so delighted the Western palate. With it went soft drinks, waters tinctured by distillation with roses, violets or other flowers, and all varieties of candy and sweetmeats.

Water-wheels

Windmills appear first in Normandy in 1180 and betray Crusading origin.[3] Water-wheels (sing. noria, from Ar. *nā'ūrah*) existed in Europe before this period but the Crusaders took back with them an improved type. This Syrian type may still be seen in Germany near Bayreuth.[4] In Syria it goes back to Roman

[1] See above, p. 351.
[2] "Historia rerum", in *Recueil: occidentaux*, vol. i, p. 559; Jacques de Vitry, "Historia Hierosolimitana", in Bongars, vol. i, p. 1075.
[3] Cf. above, p. 385.
[4] M. Sobernheim, art. "Ḥamā", *Encyclopædia of Islām*.

days, but was presumably improved upon by such native engineers as Qayṣar ibn-Musāfir Ta'āsīf († 1251),[1] an Egyptian, who was in the service of the ruler of Ḥamāh and produced the earliest but one of the Arabic celestial globes extant.[2] As early as the days of Yāqūt[3] († 1229) and abu-al-Fidā'[4] († 1331), Ḥamāh was noted for its water-wheels. These wheels, whose perpetual wailing has lulled to sleep countless generations of Ḥamātites, are still one of the glories of that ancient town.

Not all of the new tastes developed were gastronomic. Especially in the matter of fashions, clothing and home furnishing were new desires and demands created. The custom of wearing beards was then spread. Returning Crusaders introduced into their homes the rugs, carpets and tapestries of which Western and Central Asia had for long made a specialty. Fabrics such as muslin, baldachin, damask,[5] sarcenet or Saracen stuff, atlas (from Ar. *aṭlas*), velvet, silk and satin,[6] came to be more appreciated. Jewels manufactured by Damascene and Cairene Jews, toilet articles and powders became much sought after. Mirrors of glass coated with a metallic film replaced those of polished steel. Camlets (sing. *khamlah*), camel's-hair and fine furs acquired wider vogue. The rosary became familiar.[7] European pilgrims sent home Arab reliquaries for the keeping of Christian relics.[8] With fine clothes and metallic wares went lacquers and dyestuffs, such as indigo, and new colours, such as lilac (fr. Ar. *laylak*, originally Pers.), carmine and crimson (both fr. Ar. *qirmizi*, originally Skr.). Gradually centres appeared in Europe for manufacturing wares, rugs and cloths in imitation of the Oriental products, as at Arras, whose fabrics became highly prized. Stained-glass windows became popular in churches.[9] Benjamin of Tudela,[10] who visited Antioch under the Franks, speaks of its manufacture of glass. Oriental works of art in glass, pottery, gold, silver and enamel served as models for European products.

Trade

The creation of a new European market for Oriental agricul-

[1] See ibn-Khallikān, tr. de Slane, vol. iii, pp. 471-3. Ibn-Baṭṭūṭah, vol. iv, p. 255, refers to water-wheels in Canton, China.

[2] Now in the Museo Nazionale of Naples.

[3] Vol. ii, p. 331.

[4] *Taqwīm*, p. 263.

[5] See above, pp. 346, 592.

[6] From Ar. *zaytūni*, a corruption of Ts'ien-t'ang (modern Hang-chou), a city in south-east China from which this silk originally came.

[7] See above, p. 438.

[8] See above, p. 631.

[9] See above, p. 346.

[10] Tr. Asher, p. 58.

tural products and industrial commodities, together with the necessity of transporting pilgrims and Crusaders, stimulated maritime activity and international trade to an extent unknown since Roman days. Marseille began to rival the Italian city republics as a shipping centre and share in the accruing wealth. The financial needs of the new situation necessitated a larger supply and a more rapid circulation of money. A system of credit notes was thereupon devised. Firms of bankers arose in Genoa and Pisa with branch offices in the Levant. The Templars began to use letters of credit,[1] receive money on deposit and lend at interest. Perhaps the earliest gold coin struck by Latins was the *Byzantinius Saracenatus* minted by Venetians in the Holy Land and bearing Arabic inscriptions. The consular office, primarily commercial rather than diplomatic, now made its appearance. The first consuls in history were Genoese accredited to 'Akka in 1180. They were followed by those sent to Egypt.[2]

Compass

An important invention connected with this maritime activity of the Crusades is the compass. The Chinese were probably the first to discover the directive property of the magnetic needle, but the Moslems, who very early carried on lively trade between the Persian Gulf and Far Eastern waters,[3] were the first to make practical use of that discovery by applying the needle to navigation. This application must have taken place in the eleventh century if not earlier, but for commercial reasons was kept secret. In Europe, Italian sailors were the first to use the compass. The actual use naturally antedates the literary references, of which the first to occur in a Moslem work is in a Persian collection of anecdotes, *Jawāmiʿ al-Ḥikāyāt wa-Lawāmiʿ al-Riwāyāt*,[4] written by Muḥammad al-ʿAwfi about 1230. One story tells how the author as a sailor found his way by means of a fish rubbed with a magnet. The first literary mention in Latin sources belongs to the late twelfth century, thus antedating the Persian reference.

Racial admixture

The number of Franks assimilated by the native Syrians and Palestinians is hard to estimate.[5] Among the modern population

[1] Eng. "check" was borrowed from Ar. *ṣakk* in India in the 18th century.

[2] See above, pp. 652-3.

[3] See above, p. 343.

[4] See Muḥammad Niẓāmu'd-Dīn, *Introduction to the Jawāmiʿ al-Ḥikāyāt* (London, 1929), p. 251. Cf. F. Hirth and W. W. Rockhill, *Chau-Ju-Kua* (St. Petersburg, 1911), pp. 28-9. Cf. S. S. Nadavi in *Islamic Culture*, vol. xvi (1942), p. 404.

[5] See above, pp. 643-4.

of such towns as Ihdin in northern Lebanon, Bethlehem and al-'Arīsh, the sight of men and women with blue eyes and fair hair is quite common. Certain families, mainly Christian Lebanese, such as the Karam, the Faranjīyah (Frankish) and the Ṣalībi (Crusading), have preserved traditions of descent from Frankish ancestry. Among other family names Ṣawāya is said to be derived from Savoie, Duwayhi from de Douai and Bardawīl is undoubtedly Baldwin.[1] The last name also figures in the topography of Palestine and northern Sinai. One Palestinian village, Sinjil, perpetuates the name of Saint-Gilles, and another, al-Raynah, that of Renaud. On the other hand the Druze claim to some connection with a count de Dreux is due to a popular etymology that has no basis in fact.[2]

[1] See above, p. 640, n. 6. [2] Hitti, *Druze People*, p. 15.

British Museum

DINAR OF THE MAMLŪK BAYBARS
Struck 667 (1268/9), showing the lion below his name

CHAPTER XLVII

THE MAMLŪKS, LAST MEDIEVAL DYNASTY OF ARAB WORLD

IN other than Moslem annals the rise and prosperity of such a dynasty as the Mamlūk is hardly conceivable. Even in these annals it is most remarkable, almost unique. The Mamlūks were, as the name indicates,[1] a dynasty of slaves, slaves of varied races and nationalities forming a military oligarchy in an alien land. These slave sultans cleared their Syrian-Egyptian domain of the remnant of the Crusaders. They checked for ever the advance of the redoubtable Mongol hordes of Hūlāgu and of Tīmūr, who might otherwise have changed the entire course of history and culture in Western Asia and Egypt. Because of this check Egypt was spared the devastation that befell Syria and al-ʿIrāq and enjoyed a continuity in culture and political institutions which no other Moslem land outside Arabia enjoyed. For about two and three-quarter centuries (1250-1517) the Mamlūks dominated one of the most turbulent areas of the world, keeping themselves all the while racially distinct. Though on the whole uncultured and bloodthirsty, their keen appreciation of art and architecture would have been a credit to any civilized dynasty and makes Cairo even now one of the beauty spots of the Moslem world. And finally, when they were overthrown in 1517 by the Ottoman Salīm, the last of the local dynasties that had developed on the ruins of the Arab caliphate expired, clearing the way for the establishment of a new and non-Arab caliphate, that of the Ottoman Turks.

Dynasty established

The foundation of Mamlūk power was laid by Shajar-al-Durr, widow of the Ayyūbid al-Ṣāliḥ († 1249) and originally a Turkish or Armenian slave. Formerly a bondmaid and member of the harem of the Caliph al-Mustaʿṣim, Shajar entered the service of al-Ṣāliḥ, by whom she was freed after she had borne him a son. On her assumption of sovereign power her former caliph-master addressed a scathing note to the amīrs of Egypt saying: "If ye have no man to rule you, let us know and we will send you one."[2]

[1] See above, p. 235, n. 1.

[2] Suyūṭī, *Ḥusn*, vol. ii, p. 39. See above, p. 655.

For eighty days the sulṭānah, the only Moslem woman to rule a country in North Africa and Western Asia, continued to function as sole sovereign in the area which had once produced Cleopatra and Zenobia. She struck coins in her own name[1] and had herself mentioned in the Friday prayer. And when the amīrs chose her associate and commander-in-chief (*atābeg al-'askar*), 'Izz-al-Dīn Aybak,[2] for sultan, she married him. In the first years of his reign Aybak was busy crushing the legitimist Ayyūbid party of Syria, deposing the child joint-king al-Ashraf and doing away with his own general who had distinguished himself against Louis IX. In the meantime the queen was not only sharing her consort's power but keeping him in subordination. Finally, on hearing that he was contemplating another marriage, she had him murdered while taking his bath, after a ball game, in the royal palace in the Citadel of Cairo. Immediately after she was herself battered to death with wooden shoes by the slave women of Aybak's first wife and her body was cast from a tower.[3]

Baḥri and Burji Mamlūks

Aybak (1250–57) was the first of the Mamlūk sultans. The series is somewhat arbitrarily divided into two dynasties: Baḥri (1250–1390) and Burji (1382–1517). The Baḥri Mamlūks had their origin in the purchased bodyguard of the Ayyūbid al-Ṣāliḥ,[4] who settled his slaves in barracks on the isle of al-Rawḍah in the Nile.[5] The Baḥris were chiefly Turks and Mongols.[6] In their policy of securing the services of foreign slaves as a bodyguard the Ayyūbids followed the precedent established by the caliphs of Baghdād, with the same eventual results.[7] The bondmen of yesterday became the army commanders of today and the sultans of tomorrow.

The Burjis represent a later importation. Their origin was likewise a bodyguard, but it was founded by the Baḥri Mamlūk Qalāwūn (1279–90). They were mostly Circassian slaves who were quartered in the towers (Ar. sing. *burj*) of the citadel. In all there were twenty-four Baḥri Mamlūks,[8] excluding Shajar-

[1] With the exception of certain coins struck in India and Fāris, hers are the only ones bearing a Moslem woman's name.

[2] He was a Turk, as the name (*ay* moon + *beg* prince) indicates. Maqrīzi, tr. Quatremère, vol. i (pt. 1), p. 1.

[3] *Ibid.* p. 72; *Khiṭaṭ*, vol. ii, p. 237; abu-al-Fidā', vol. iii, p. 201.

[4] Abu-al-Fidā', vol. iii, p. 188; ibn-Khaldūn, vol. v, p. 373.

[5] Colloquially referred to as *Baḥr*, sea.

[6] Ibn-Khaldūn, vol. v, p. 369, and Suyūṭi, *Ḥusn*, vol. ii, p. 80, designate them as the "Turkish dynasty".

[7] See above, p. 466.

[8] For table of Baḥri Mamlūks see p. 673.

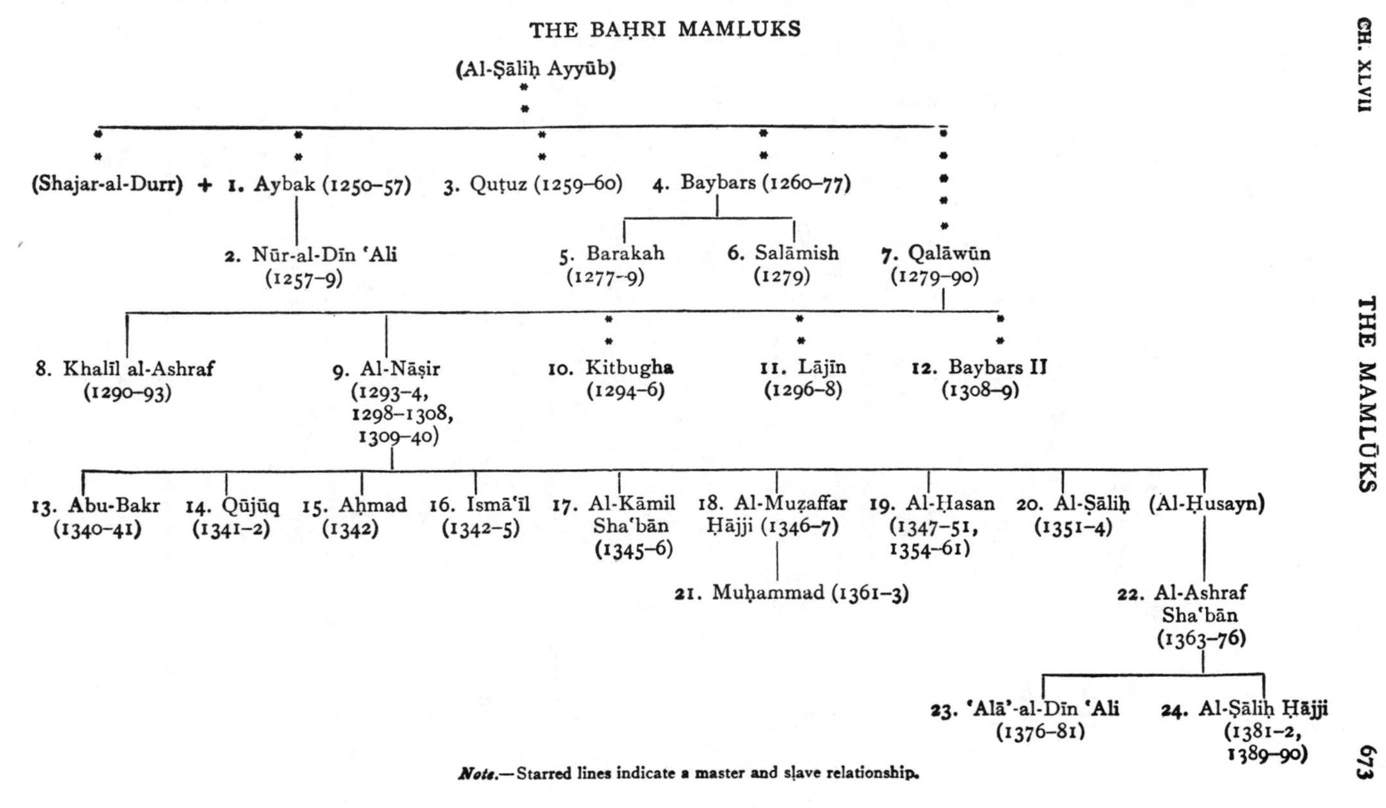

Note.—Starred lines indicate a master and slave relationship.

al-Durr, and twenty-three Burjis. The Burjis recognized no principle of hereditary succession and followed no policy of nepotism. Their throne belonged to him who could capture it or induce the amīrs to elect him to it. In several Baḥri and Burji instances slaves rather than sons of the sultan succeeded him. A large number of the sultans met violent deaths while still young. The average reign of the Mamlūk sultans was less than six years.

Ayyūbids and Tartars repelled

The first task confronting the new dynasty was to consolidate the kingdom and guard its frontiers. Aybak spent most of his time on the battlefield in Syria, Palestine and Egypt. Al-Muẓaffar Sayf-al-Dīn Quṭuz (1259–60), while acting as regent (*nā'ib al-salṭanah*) and before deposing his young protégé, al-Manṣūr 'Ali, Aybak's son, and usurping the throne, repelled an attack from the Ayyūbid sultan of al-Karak. The Syrian Ayyūbids considered themselves the legitimate successors of their Egyptian kinsmen. No sooner had the Ayyūbid invasion of Egypt been repulsed than the Tartar army of Hūlāgu, led by Kitbugha, became a danger. Hūlāgu's envoys[1] to Quṭuz were executed by the latter and the issue was settled at 'Ayn Jālūt (1260). In this battle Baybars led the vanguard and distinguished himself as a general, but Quṭuz took command in person towards the end. The Tartar army was routed, leaving Kitbugha and other leaders dead on the field. Egypt was spared the horrible desolation visited upon its neighbour, which was now occupied by the Mamlūk army. Baybars expected to receive Aleppo as a fief in recognition of his military service, but the sultan disappointed him. On the way homeward through Syria, while hunting with Quṭuz, a fellow-conspirator addressed the sultan and kissed his hand while Baybars stabbed him in the neck with a sword (October 24, 1260).[2] The murdered sultan was succeeded by the murderer. Quṭuz claimed to have been a grand-nephew of a Khwārizm Shāh[3] and is said to have been captured by the Tartars and sold in Damascus, where he was purchased by Aybak.

Baybars

Al-Malik al-Ẓāhir (victorious) Rukn-al-Dīn (pillar of the faith)

[1] The letter they carried is preserved in Maqrīzi, tr. Quatremère, vol. i (pt. 1), pp. 101-2.

[2] Abu-al-Fidā, vol. iii, p. 216; ibn-Khaldūn, vol. v, p. 380. Cf. Maqrīzi, tr. Quatremère, vol. i (pt. 1), p. 113.

[3] Suyūṭi, *Ḥusn*, vol. ii, p. 40. See above, p. 482.

Baybars al-Bunduqdārī[1] (1260–77), the most distinguished of Mamlūk sultans, was originally a Turkoman slave. When young he was sold into Damascus for eight hundred dirhams, but was returned on account of a defect in one of his blue eyes. His last name, meaning belonging to the arbalester (*bunduqdār*), he acquired from the master who owned him in Ḥamāh before he was purchased by the Ayyūbid al-Ṣāliḥ.[2] Al-Ṣāliḥ first appointed him commander of a section of his bodyguard, from which position he worked his way into the highest in the land. Tall, dusky in complexion, commanding in voice, brave and energetic, he possessed the qualities of leadership among men.

Baybars was the first great Mamlūk, the real founder of Mamlūk power. His first laurels he won against the Mongols on the field of 'Ayn Jālūt; but his title to fame rests mainly on his numerous campaigns against the Crusaders.[3] It was these campaigns which broke the backbone of Frankish opposition and made possible the final victories won by his successors Qalāwūn and al-Ashraf. In connection with one of his last expeditions into northern Syria he crushed for ever the power of the Assassins. In the meantime his generals had extended his dominion westward over the Berbers and southward over Nubia,[4] which was now permanently conquered by an Egyptian sultan.

Baybars was more than a military leader. Not only did he organize the army, rebuild the navy and strengthen the fortresses of Syria, but he dug canals, improved harbours and connected Cairo and Damascus by a swift postal service requiring only four days. Relays of horses stood in readiness at each post station. The sultan could play polo in both capitals almost within the same week. Besides the ordinary mail the Mamlūks perfected the pigeon post, whose carriers even under the Fāṭimids had their pedigrees kept in special registers.[5] Baybars fostered public works, beautified mosques and established religious and charitable endowments. Of his architectural monuments[6] both the great mosque (1269) and the school bearing his name have survived. The mosque was turned into a fort by Napoleon and later into a rationing depôt by the British army of occupation. The present Ẓāhirīyah library in Damascus is the structure

[1] "Bendocquedar" of Marco Polo, tr. Yule, 2nd ed., vol. i, p. 22.
[2] Abu-al-Fidā', vol. iv, p. 11; Kutubi, vol. i, p. 109.
[3] See above, pp. 655 *seq.*
[4] Ibn-Khaldūn, vol. v, p. 400.
[5] See above, pp. 323, 664.
[6] Consult Kutubi, vol. i, pp. 113-15.

under the dome of which he was buried. He was the first sultan in Egypt to appoint four qāḍis, representing the four orthodox rites, and organize the Egyptian *maḥmil* on a systematic and permanent basis. His religious orthodoxy and zeal, together with the glory he brought to Islam in the holy war, combined to make his name a rival to that of Hārūn. In legendary history it looms even higher than Ṣalāḥ-al-Dīn's. His romance and that of ʿAntar remain to the present day more popular in the Arab Orient than the *Arabian Nights*.

A feature of Baybars' reign was the many alliances he struck with Mongol and European powers. Soon after he became sultan he allied himself with the chief khān of the Golden Horde[1] or Mongols of Qipchāq (Baybars' birthplace) in the valley of the Volga. Common opposition to the Īl-Khāns of Persia dictated the policy. The Egyptian envoys went through Constantinople, where Michael Palæologus, foe of Latin Christianity, authorized the restoration of the ancient mosque[2] destroyed by the Crusaders during their occupation of that city. Baybars sent, at the emperor's request, a Melkite patriarch to Constantinople for those of that persuasion in its realm. He signed commercial treaties with Charles of Anjou (1264), king of Sicily and brother of Louis IX, as well as with James of Aragon and Alfonso of Seville.

The caliphal episode

A most spectacular event of Baybars' reign was his inauguration of a new series of ʿAbbāsid caliphs who carried the name but none of the authority of the office. The sultan's object was to confer legitimacy upon his crown, give his court an air of primacy in Moslem eyes and check the ʿAlid intrigues which, ever since Fāṭimid days, were especially rife in Egypt. To this end he invited from Damascus in June 1261, an uncle of the last ʿAbbāsid caliph and son of the Caliph al-Ẓāhir who had escaped the Baghdād massacre, and installed him with great pomp and ceremony as the Caliph al-Mustanṣir.[3] The would-be pensioner-caliph was first escorted from Syria in state, with even Jews and Christians carrying aloft the Torah and the Gospel, and the soundness of his genealogy was passed upon by a council of jurists. The sultan in turn received from his puppet caliph a

[1] Eastern Mongols, wrongly identified with the Kalmucks, western Mongols; see above, p. 483, n. 4.

[2] See above, p. 621.

[3] Maqrīzi, tr. Quatremère, vol. i (pt. 1), pp. 146-68; ibn-Khaldūn, vol. v, pp. 382-3; abu-al-Fidā', vol. iii, p. 222; ibn-Iyās, vol. i, pp. 100-101.

diploma of investiture giving him authority over Egypt, Syria, Diyār Bakr, al-Ḥijāz, al-Yaman and the land of the Euphrates. Three months later Baybars rashly set out from Cairo to re-establish his caliph in Baghdād, but after reaching Damascus abandoned him to his fate. Al-Mustanṣir was attacked in the desert by the Mongol governor of Baghdād and was never heard from again.

One year later another scion of the 'Abbāsid house made his way to Cairo and was installed by Baybars as al-Ḥākim. One descendant of al-Ḥākim after another, for two and a half centuries, held the pseudo-caliphate, whose incumbents were satisfied with having their names inscribed on the coinage and mentioned in the Friday prayers in Egypt and Syria. With one exception none of them had his name cited in the Makkah prayers. Their most important duties consisted in administering the religious endowments (*waqf*) and officiating at the ceremony of installing the new sultan. Certain Moslem rulers, including some from India and the Ottoman Bāyazīd I (1394), secured from them diplomas of investiture, which in reality had no significance. In 1412, on the death of the Burji al-Nāṣir, the Caliph al-'Ādil al-Musta'īn declared himself sultan and ruled for a few days, only to be deposed by al-Mu'ayyad Shaykh (1412–21).[1] Certain caliphs were dismissed from office on grounds of disloyalty to the Baḥri 'Ali (1376–81) and to the Burjis Barqūq (1382–98) and Īnāl (1453–60). When in 1517 the Ottoman Sultan Salīm wrested Egypt from the Mamlūks he carried away with him to Constantinople the Caliph al-Mutawakkil, the last of the line.[2]

Qalāwūn and the Mongols

After Baybars the outstanding Mamlūk figure was al-Malik al-Manṣūr Sayf-al-Dīn Qalāwūn (1279–90). Originally, like Baybars, a Turkoman slave from Qipchāq, the youthful Qalāwūn was carried to Egypt, and likewise sold to al-Ṣāliḥ, as his surname al-Ṣāliḥi indicates. His other surname al-Alfi (thousander) suggests the heavy price paid for him, a thousand dinars,[3] and shows that the Mamlūk sultans were not ashamed of their lowly origin. Qalāwūn secured the throne by deposing his ward Salāmish (1279), Baybars' seven-year-old son, who had succeeded his nineteen-year-old brother, the pleasure-loving Barakah (1277–9).

[1] Ibn-Taghri-Birdi, vol. vi, pt. 2, pp. 267-8, 303-21; Suyūṭi, *Ḥusn*, vol. ii, pp. 68-71; ibn-Iyās, vol. i, pp. 357-9.

[2] See above, p. 489, below, p. 705.

[3] Suyūṭi, *Ḥusn*, vol. ii, p. 80; Maqrīzi, tr. Quatremère, vol ii (pt. 3), p. 1.

Qalāwūn was the only Mamlūk in whose line the succession continued to the fourth generation. The last Bahri, al-Sālih Ḥājji, was his great-grandson.

No sooner had Qalāwūn established himself in power than the Mongol Īl-Khāns of Persia began to threaten his Syrian domain. Among these Abāqa (1265–81), who was Hūlāgu's son and successor, and Abāqa's son Arghūn (1284–91), had Christian leanings and entered into negotiations with the pope and other European courts urging a fresh Crusade with a view to driving the Egyptians out of Syria. The scheme did not materialize. Abāqa's army, though superior in number and reinforced by Armenians, Franks and Georgians, was decisively defeated in 1280 at Ḥimṣ.[1] Shortly after this the Mongols adopted Islam. The sultan strengthened the existing amicable relations with the Golden Horde, the Byzantine emperor, the republic of Genoa and the kings of France, Castile and Sicily. Even the ruler of Ceylon dispatched to his court an embassy with a letter which no one in Cairo could read. Little Armenia was ravaged for the help its people had given to the Mongols and the Crusaders' castles were reduced.[2] Tripoli, which was levelled to the ground, was rebuilt a few years later, not on its former site, but several miles from the sea where it now stands on the banks of the abu-ʿAli (Qādīsha). Toward the end of his reign Qalāwūn issued orders excluding his Christian subjects from all government offices.

His hospital

Qalāwūn won distinction in other fields. He renovated on a grand scale the citadels of Aleppo, Baʿlabakk and Damascus. In Cairo he erected a hospital, connected with a school-mosque, and a mausoleum[3] (tomb-"chapel"), which exhibits to the present day its remarkable arabesque tracery and fine marble mosaic. But his hospital (al-Māristān al-Manṣūri), whose remains are among the earliest relics of a Moslem hospital extant, is the most famous of his buildings. The sultan is said to have received the inspiration while lying ill with colic in the Nūri Hospital at Damascus, where he made a vow to establish a similar institution in Cairo in the event of his recovery. The structure, including not only the hospital proper with annexes but also a school and a mosque, was completed in 1284. It comprised special wards for segregat-

[1] Abu-al-Fidā', vol. iv, pp. 15-16; Maqrīzi, tr. Quatremère, vol. ii (pt. 3), pp. 36-40.
[2] See above, p. 657.
[3] Ar. *qubbah*; ibn-Khaldūn, vol. v, p. 403.

ing various diseases, such as fevers, ophthalmia and dysentery, and was provided with laboratories, a dispensary, baths, kitchens and store-rooms. The chief of its medical staff gave instruction in a properly equipped lecture-room. It had an endowment yielding about a million dirhams annually, employed male and female attendants and was open to the sick of both sexes.[1] So closely associated with the curing of infirmities did this sultan thus become that his robe preserved in his mausoleum has since his time been touched by thousands of dumb children, barren wives and diseased people who believed in its healing virtues.

Al-Ashraf

The only exploit of Qalāwūn's son and successor al-Malik al-Ashraf (the most noble) Khalīl (1290–93) was the conquest of ʻAkka in May 1291.[2] Its capture precipitated the fall of the few remaining ports in the possession of the Franks. "A mournful and solitary silence prevailed along the coast which had so long resounded with the WORLD'S DEBATE."[3] In 1302 the Templars who had established a last foothold in the islet of Arwād (Aradus), off the north Syrian coast, were expelled with great slaughter by al-Ashraf's younger brother and successor al-Malik al-Nāṣir Muḥammad.

Mongols repulsed

Al-Nāṣir shares with al-Mutamassik the unique distinction of having ruled thrice: 1293–4, 1298–1308 and 1309–40.[4] He came first to the throne at the age of nine, and his reign is the longest among the Mamlūks and one of the longest in Moslem annals.[5] During his rule the last serious invasions of the Mongols took place under the seventh Īl-Khān Ghāzān Maḥmūd, in whose reign Islam was finally recognized as the state religion of the Īl-Khānate.[6] The Egyptian army, in size about a third of that of the Mongols, was routed (December 23, 1299) east of Ḥimṣ by the invading army, said to have numbered a hundred thousand,[7] reinforced by Armenians and Georgians. The Mongols continued their victorious march and early in 1300 occupied Damascus, which they spared from pillage, but the rest of northern Syria had another sad experience of plunder and rapine. In March of that year they evacuated the Syrian capital without reducing its citadel and the Egyptians reoccupied all the land. Three years later Ghāzān's fresh expedition was checked at

[1] Maqrīzi, *Khiṭaṭ*, vol. ii, pp. 406-7.
[2] See above, p. 658.
[3] Gibbon, *Decline*, ed. Bury, vol. vi, p. 365.
[4] See above, p. 553.
[5] Cf. above, pp. 481, n. 2, 520, n. 2.
[6] See above, p. 488.
[7] Maqrīzi, tr. Quatremère, vol. ii (pt. 4), p. 146.

Marj al-Ṣuffar, south of Damascus.[1] For the fourth time the Mamlūks had beaten the most dangerous enemy Egypt had to contend with since the Moslem conquest. No successor of Ghāzān dared risk another encounter.

Soon after the Mongol evacuation of Damascus al-Nāṣir brought the Druzes of the Lebanon, whose 12,000 bowmen had harassed his army in its retreat a few months before, to a severe reckoning. Other schismatic sects including 'Alids in Kisrawān were also chastised.[2] The Maronites of northern Lebanon were almost crushed. In 1302 and subsequent years he repeatedly devastated the unhappy land of the Armenians.[3] On his Christian and Jewish subjects he re-enforced the outworn restrictions of 'Umar II and al-Mutawakkil.

Al-Nāṣir's long reign is better known for his achievements in the realm of peace rather than war. The sultan himself was short in stature and lame in one foot, but he had a taste for the beautiful and never wearied of luxurious living and lavishing extravagant adornment on his surroundings. On his return to his residence in the citadel from a trip abroad his retinue spread before his mare rugs and costly fabrics for a distance of some four thousand cubits. While on a holy pilgrimage his table was supplied throughout the Arabian desert with fresh vegetables from a travelling garden carried on forty camels.[4] At his son's nuptial feast 18,000 sugar loaves were consumed, 20,000 beasts were slain and 3000 candles shed their light on the royal palace. His far-famed al-Qaṣr al-Ablaq [5] (the palace of varied colours) was built after a model at Damascus. A sportsman, hunter and lover of horses, he kept a proper stud book and did not hesitate to pay 30,000 dinars for a horse he fancied.[6]

Egypt at its cultural height

Nor was al-Nāṣir's extravagance limited to the gratification of his personal tastes. His numerous and beautiful public works, for some ot which forced labour was used, mark his reign as the

[1] Abu-al-Fidā' (vol. iv, p. 50), a personal friend of al-Nāṣir and later restored by him to his ancestors' princedom, saw the invading army pass by his native town Ḥamāh.

[2] Ibn-Yaḥya, pp. 136-7.

[3] Abu-al-Fidā', vol. iv, pp. 48, 53-4, 90-91; ibn-Khaldūn, vol. v, pp. 419-20, 429-30.

[4] Abu-al-Fidā', vol. iv, p. 89.

[5] Maqrīzi, *Khiṭaṭ*, vol. ii, pp. 209-10. Cf. Mas'ūdi, *Tanbīh*, p. 258.

[6] A unique MS. on the horse dedicated to him in gold letters by his secretary al-Ḥusayni is described in Hitti, Faris and 'Abd-al-Malik, *Catalog of Arabic Manuscripts*, no. 1066

climax of Mamlūk culture. He dug a canal, on which a hundred thousand men toiled, connecting Alexandria with the Nile, built (1311) an aqueduct from that river to the Citadel of Cairo, founded throughout his kingdom about thirty mosques, besides a number of dervish "monasteries", public drinking-fountains (sing. *sabīl*), baths and schools. Makkah was especially favoured by his munificence. His own mosque in the citadel he adorned (1318) with materials from the ruined cathedral of ʿAkka. His school, completed in 1304 and named al-Nāṣirīyah after him, is still standing in Cairo. His mosque and school exemplify the finest achievement in Moslem architecture. Minor arts under him were also cultivated to a higher degree of excellence than ever before, as evidenced by the specimens of bronze and brass work, enamelled glass lamps and illuminated Korans preserved in the Arab Museum and National Library of Cairo.

Famine and plague

The heavy expenditure in al-Nāṣir's long reign burdened the people with exorbitant taxes and contributed to the downfall of the dynasty. The sultan took certain economic measures to alleviate the widespread misery. He encouraged trade with Europe and with the East, ordered a new survey of the land, repealed taxes on salt, chickens, sugar-cane, boats, slaves and horses, suppressed wine-drinking and had bakers who charged excessive prices flogged. The effect, however, was only temporary, palliative. After him, civil wars, famine and plague added their share to the wretchedness of the people. The same "black death" which in 1348–9 devastated Europe lingered in Egypt for about seven years and carried away more of its people than any other plague. The total mortality in the capital, according to the exaggerated estimate of ibn-Iyās,[1] reached 900,000. The sultan and all who could fled. Ghazzah is said to have lost 22,000 inhabitants in one month, while the daily average in Aleppo was five hundred.

The downfall of the Baḥris

The twelve descendants of al-Nāṣir who followed him in rapid succession during forty-two years (1340–82) were mere figureheads; their amīrs ruled, deposing or murdering the sultan at pleasure. None of these sultans distinguished himself in any field of endeavour, and the only notable monument is the Mosque of Sultan al-Ḥasan, son of al-Nāṣir, completed in 1362 and considered the most beautiful of those built on a cruciform plan.

[1] Vol. i, p. 191.

The last Baḥri ruler, al-Nāṣir's great-grandson al-Ṣāliḥ Ḥājji ibn-Sha'bān (1381–2, 1389–90) was a child whose reign of two years was first interrupted and later terminated by the Circassian Barqūq, who became the founder of a new line, the Burji dynasty.[1] Barqūq began his career as a slave of the sons of al-Ashraf Sha'bān.[2] Before Barqūq another Circassian, Baybars II (1308–9), a slave of Qalāwūn, was one of the three sultans who interrupted al-Nāṣir's reign, thus presaging the advent of the new régime.

[1] Ibn-Khaldūn, vol. v, p. 472; ibn-Taghri-Birdi, vol. vi, pt. 2, p. 1.
[2] Consult table above, p. 673.

CHAPTER XLVIII

INTELLECTUAL AND ARTISTIC ACTIVITY

MAMLŪK Egypt began its history under proud and triumphant rulers who had cleared Syria of the last vestiges of Frankish dominion and had successfully stood between the Mongols and world power. By the end of the period, however, with its military oligarchy, factions among the dominant caste, debased coinage, high taxation, insecurity of life and property, occasional plague and famine and frequent revolts, both Egypt and its dependency Syria were all but ruined. Especially in the valley of the Nile persistence of outworn ancient superstition and magic, coupled with the triumph of reactionary orthodoxy, hindered scientific advance. Under these conditions no intellectual activity of high order could be expected. In fact the whole Arab world had by the beginning of the thirteenth century lost the intellectual hegemony it had maintained since the eighth.[1] Mental fatigue induced by generations of effort and moral lassitude consequent upon the accumulation of wealth and power were evident everywhere.

Scientific contribution

In science there were only two branches wherein the Arabs after the middle of the thirteenth century maintained their leadership: astronomy-mathematics, including trigonometry, and medicine, particularly ophthalmology. But in the first discipline the contribution was made mainly by Arabic-writing Persian scholars whose centre of activity was the Īl-Khānid observatory and library of Marāghah headed by the illustrious Naṣīr-al-Dīn al-Ṭūsi (1201–74). It is interesting to find the Syrian Jacobite Catholicos abu-al-Faraj ibn-al-ʿIbri[2] (Barhebræus, 1226–86), known as an historian and as the last classical author in Syriac literature, lecturing there on Euclid in 1268 and on Ptolemy in 1272–3.

[1] See Sarton, *Introduction*, vol. ii, especially the introductory chapter. This general decline of Islamic culture marks the end of the Middle Ages; see above, p. 142.

[2] His *Ta'rīkh Mukhtaṣar al-Duwal* was edited by Anṭūn Ṣāliḥāni (Beirut, 1890).

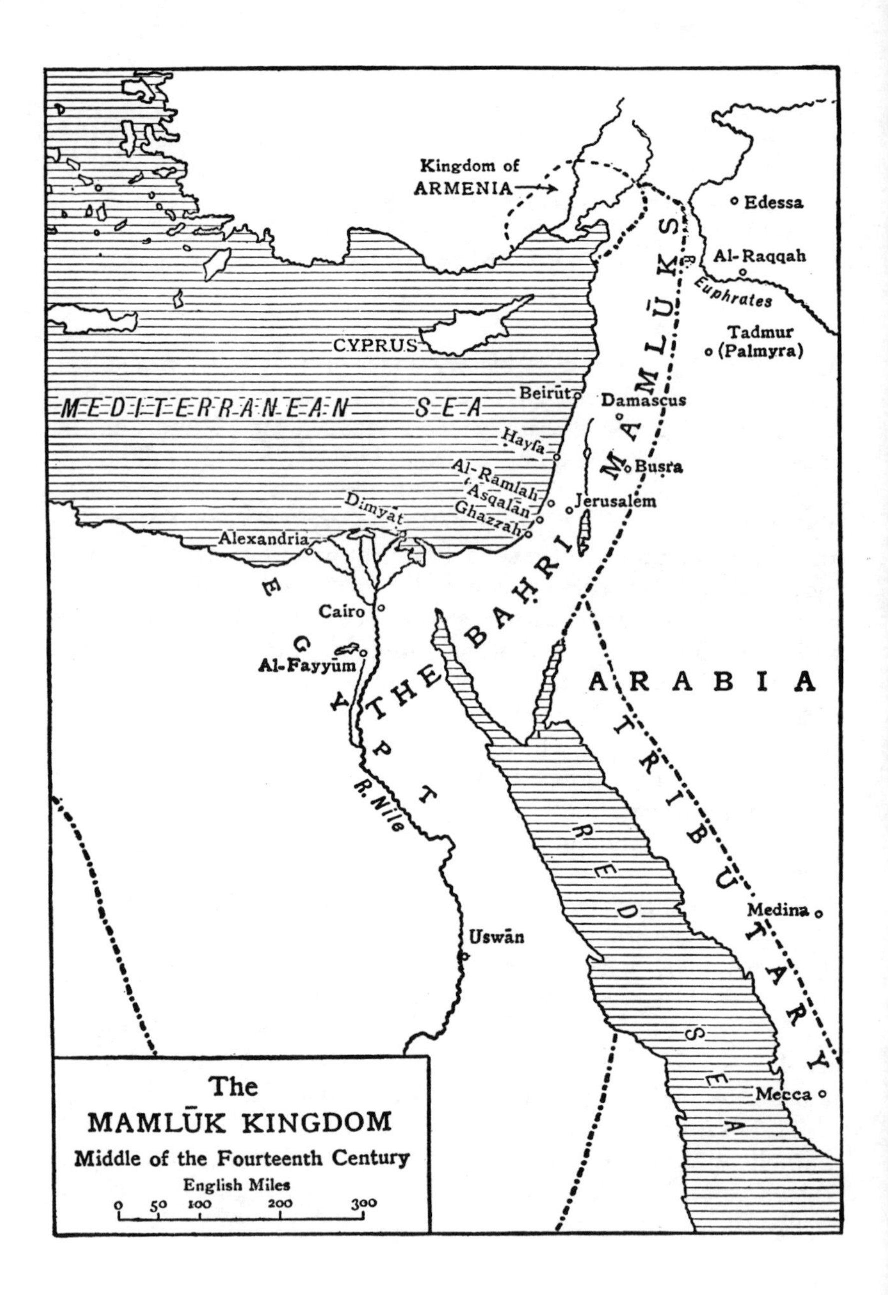
Kingdom of ARMENIA
Edessa
Al-Raqqah
Euphrates
Tadmur (Palmyra)
CYPRUS
MEDITERRANEAN SEA
Beirūt
Damascus
Hayfa
Busra
Al-Ramlah
Asqalān
Ghazzah
Jerusalem
Dimyat
Alexandria
Cairo
Al-Fayyūm
EGYPT
R. Nile
THE BAHRI MAMLŪKS
ARABIA
TRIBUTARY
RED SEA
Medina
Uswān
Mecca
The
MAMLŪK KINGDOM
Middle of the Fourteenth Century
English Miles
0 50 100 200 300

Medicine

The Syro-Egyptian kingdom led in medical science. The elaborate hospital built by Qalāwūn may be taken as an index of Egyptian interest in medicine. Its dean abu-al-Ḥasan ʿAli ibn-al-Nafīs, who studied in Damascus where he later died (1288–9), contributed in his *Sharḥ Tashrīḥ al-Qānūn* a clear conception of the pulmonary circulation of the blood, two and a half centuries before the Spanish Servetus, credited with this discovery.[1] To Qalāwūn's son al-Nāṣir one of the few important Arabic treatises on veterinary medicine known was dedicated under the title *Kāmil al-Ṣināʿatayn: al-Bayṭarah w-al-Zarṭaqah*[2] by his master of the stable, abu-Bakr ibn-al-Mundhir al-Bayṭār († 1340). The Arabic term for veterinary surgeon, *bayṭār*, from Greek *hippiatros*, suggests that although the Arabs since Bedouin days possessed an extensive empirical knowledge of diseases of camels and horses, yet their more systematic knowledge and improved technique must have come from Byzantine sources. Many of the Mamlūks, like Qalāwūn and Barqūq, kept magnificent studs. Several works containing Islamic traditions on horses date from this period, including the *Faḍl al-Khayl* (the excellence of the horse), by ʿAbd-al-Mu'min al-Dimyāṭi († 1306), a lecturer at the Manṣūrīyah academy of Qalāwūn.

Jewish physicians

Egyptian medicine since Ayyūbid days was dominated by Jewish physicians carrying on the glorious tradition of ibn-Maymūn. But among neither Moslem nor Jewish physicians do we find creative activity. The Judeo-Egyptian pharmacist al-Kūhīn (the priest) al-ʿAṭṭār (the druggist) composed in Cairo about 1260 an Arabic treatise on pharmacy, *Minhāj al-Dukkān wa-Dustūr al-Aʿyān* (a manual of officinal drugs and a canon for notables), which has not yet outlived its usefulness in the Moslem East.

The period was especially fertile in works half gynecological, half erotic, of the type we now designate "sex books". Arabic literature, in all ages primarily a male literature, abounds in anecdotes, jokes and remarks which to us today sound obscene. Among the leaders in this field was the Egyptian lapidary al-Tīfāshi, who flourished in the middle of the thirteenth century.

[1] Abdul-Karim Chéhadé, *Ibn an-Nafīs et la découverte de la circulation pulmonaire* (Damascus, 1955).

[2] Or *al-Nāṣiri;* tr. M. Perron, *Le Naçéri: la perfection des deux arts ou traité complet d'hippologie et d'hippiatrie arabes*, 3 vols. (Paris, 1852–60).

We also notice at this time special interest in what al-Rāzi was the first to term *ṭibb rūḥāni* (*ʿilāj nafsāni*, spiritual cure), corresponding to our psycho-therapy. An Egyptian pioneer of this school was a Jewish physician of Ṣalāḥ-al-Dīn, Hibatullāh ibn-Jumayʿ (Jamīʿ), whose principal work bore the title *al-Irshād li-Maṣāliḥ al-Anfās w-al-Ajsād* (instructions in the interest of souls and bodies). Ibn-Jumayʿ, noticing a passing funeral, discovered that the "dead" man was still alive from the fact that his feet were standing straight rather than lying flat.[1]

Diseases of the eye

Ophthalmology, one of the disciplines early developed by the Arabs,[2] was practised on a more scientific basis in Syria and Egypt throughout the twelfth and thirteenth centuries than anywhere else in the world. In the twelfth century the most significant Arabic work on the subject was written by abu-al-Faḍā'il ibn-al-Nāqid († 1188–9),[3] a Judaeo-Egyptian oculist of Cairo, under the title *Mujarrabāt* (tested remedies). But Syria after that took the lead. Here were composed the only two scholarly works of the period: *al-Kāfi fi al-Kuḥl* (the sufficient work on collyrium) by Khalīfah ibn-abi-al-Maḥāsin of Aleppo, who flourished about 1256, and *Nūr al-ʿUyūn wa-Jāmiʿ al-Funūn*[4] (the light of eyes and compendium of arts) by Ṣalāḥ-al-Dīn ibn-Yūsuf, who practised in Ḥamāh about 1296. Khalīfah was so confident of his skill as a surgeon that he did not hesitate to remove a cataract for a one-eyed man. It is noteworthy that the Syrian scholars of the Mamlūk period flourished in inland cities, the coast having been devastated by the Crusades and later by Qalāwūn and his successors, who feared the return of the Franks.

Medical history

The most distinguished historian of medicine the Arab world produced, Muwaffaq-al-Dīn abu-al-ʿAbbās Aḥmad ibn-abi-Uṣaybiʿah (1203–70), flourished at Damascus in the early Mamlūk period. Ibn-abi-Uṣaybiʿah was himself a physician and son of a Damascene oculist. He studied medicine in his birthplace and Cairo, botanized with the celebrated ibn-al-Bayṭār and corresponded with the scientist-physician ʿAbd-al-Laṭīf al-Baghdādi. His masterpiece was his *ʿUyūn al-Anbāʾ fi Ṭabaqāt al-Aṭibbāʾ*[5] (sources of information on the classes of physicians),

[1] Ibn-abi-Uṣaybiʿah, vol. ii, p. 113.
[2] See above, pp. 363-4.
[3] Ibn-abi-Uṣaybiʿah, vol. ii, pp. 115-16.
[4] Ḥājji Khalfah, vol. vi, p. 393.
[5] First edited by "Imru'-al-Qays ibn-al-Ṭaḥḥān" [August Müller], 2 vols. (Cairo, 1882), then republished with additional pages, corrections and index by August Müller, 2 vols. (Königsberg, 1884).

an elaborate collection of some four hundred biographies of Arab and Greek medical men. Since most of these physicians were at the same time philosophers, astronomers, physicists and mathematicians, the work is an invaluable source for the history of Arab science in general. It is almost unique in Arabic literature, the nearest approach to it being al-Qifṭi's *Ikhbār al-'Ulamā' bi-Akhbār al-Ḥukamā'* (acquainting the learned with the story of the philosophers and physicians), which has survived only in a compendium.[1] 'Ali ibn-Yūsuf al-Qifṭi, as the surname indicates, was born in Upper Egypt (1172), but spent a large part of his life in Aleppo, where he acted as vizir to its Ayyūbid rulers until his death in 1248.

Social science: Biography

In the social sciences the main contribution under the Mamlūks was in biography. The foremost biographer Islam produced flourished in Damascus at this time. Shams-al-Dīn (sun of the faith) Aḥmad ibn-Muḥammad ibn-Khallikān, a descendant of Yaḥya ibn-Khālid al-Barmaki, was born in Irbil (Arbela) in 1211. He was educated at Aleppo and Damascus and in 1261 was appointed chief qāḍi of Syria with his headquarters at Damascus. This position he held, with a seven years' interval, until shortly before his death in 1282. His *Wafayāt al-A'yān wa-Anbā' Abnā' al-Zamān* [2] (obituaries of the eminent men and histories of the leading contemporaries) is an accurate and elegant collection of 865 biographies of the most distinguished Moslems in history, the first dictionary of national biography in Arabic. The author took pains to establish the correct spelling of names, fix dates, trace genealogies, verify facts, indicate the main personal traits, sketch the significant events and illustrate by the use of poems and anecdotes. The result is adjudged by some "the best general biography ever written".[3]

History

Not only in biography but in the general field of history the Mamlūk age was moderately rich. Among those often cited in the foregoing pages abu-al-Fidā', ibn-Taghri-Birdi, al-Suyūṭi and al-Maqrīzi were Mamlūk historians. As for the illustrious ibn-Khaldūn († 1406), who held a professorship and judgeship under Sultan Barqūq and headed a delegation under Sultan

[1] Ed. Julius Lippert (Leipzig, 1903).
[2] Several editions. The one used here is in 3 vols. (Cairo, 1299); tr. de Slane, 4 vols. (Paris, 1843–71).
[3] Nicholson, *Literary History*, p. 452.

Faraj to negotiate peace with Tīmūr at Damascus, his antecedents and literary activity connect him with Spain and al-Maghrib. The historian-geographer abu-al-Fidā' (1273–1332), a descendant of a brother of Ṣalāḥ-al-Dīn and governor of Ḥamāh under Sultan al-Nāṣir, epitomized for us in his *Mukhtaṣar Ta'rīkh al-Bashar* [1] (epitome of the history of mankind) the voluminous history of ibn-al-Athīr and continued the narrative to his own time. Abu-al-Maḥāsin ibn-Taghri-Birdi (1411–69) had as his father a high official in the Mamlūk court and as mother a Turkish slave of Barqūq. Ibn-Taghri-Birdi [2] himself had close connections with several of the sultans. His major work is *al-Nujūm al-Zāhirah fi Mulūk Miṣr w-al-Qāhirah* [3] (the brilliant stars regarding the kings of Egypt and Cairo), a history of Egypt from the Arab conquest till 1453. Jalāl-al-Dīn al-Suyūṭi [4] (1445–1505), like ibn-al-Jawzi, ibn-Ḥazm and al-Ṭabari, was one of the most prolific authors of Islam, but his works show no originality. He is unquestionably the outstanding literary figure of the fifteenth century. His pen traversed the whole field of Arab learning: Koran, tradition, law, philosophy, history, philology, rhetoric, etc.[5] Titles of about five hundred and sixty works of his have come down to us. One of these discusses whether the Prophet wore trousers, whether his turban had a point and whether his parents were in heaven or in hell. He was a fine calligrapher and very likely claimed authorship of some manuscripts which he merely copied. His best-known works are *al-Itqān fi 'Ulūm al-Qur'ān*,[6] on koranic exegesis; *al-Muzhir fi 'Ulūm al-Lughah*,[7] a treatise on philology; and *Ḥusn al-Muḥāḍarah fi Akhbār Miṣr w-al-Qāhirah*,[8] a history of Egypt.

The most eminent of Mamlūk historians was beyond doubt Taqi-al-Dīn Aḥmad al-Maqrīzi (1364–1442). Born in Cairo of

[1] The edition used here is in 4 vols. (Constantinople, 1286). His geography is *Taqwīm al-Buldān*, ed. J. T. Reinaud and de Slane (Paris, 1840); tr. Reinaud, 2 vols. (Paris, 1848).

[2] Vol. vi, pt. 2, p. 430, l. 6; p. 552, l. 22; p. 743, l. 19.

[3] Ed. F. G. Juynboll and Matthes, 2 vols. (Leyden, 1855–61), ed. William Popper, 3 vols. (Berkeley, 1909–29).

[4] Born in Asyūṭ (Assiut), Upper Egypt.

[5] Cf. list in his *Naẓm al-'Iqyān fi A'yān al-A'yān*, ed. Hitti (New York, 1927), pp. *kh*, *d*.

[6] Several Cairo editions, none critical.

[7] The edition used here is in 2 vols. (Cairo, 1325).

[8] The edition used here is in 2 vols. (Cairo, 1321).

Ba'labakkan ancestry, al-Maqrīzi held several high offices as deputy qāḍi and as teacher in his native town and in Damascus. His title to fame rests on his *al-Mawā'iẓ w-al-I'tibār fi Dhikr al-Khiṭaṭ w-al-Āthār* [1] (sermons and learning by example on an account of the new settlements and remains) devoted to Egyptian topography, history and antiquities. His contemporary al-Sakhāwi's [2] charge of wholesale plagiarism in the production of this work is well founded; but the fault was common in those days.

Islamics and linguistics

Two Egyptian encyclopædists often quoted in these pages are Aḥmad al-Nuwayri († 1332), author of *Nihāyat al-Arab fi Funūn al-Adab*,[3] and Aḥmad al-Qalqashandi († 1418), whose *Ṣubḥ al-A'sha*,[4] intended as a manual for those who hold secretarial offices in the government, is replete with historical and geographical facts mainly on Egypt and Syria. The remaining authors of this period busied themselves with Islamic studies and linguistics. An exceptional work of major importance is a compendium of theoretical and practical navigation by Aḥmad ibn-Mājid [5] of Najdi ancestry, who, it is claimed, in 1498 piloted Vasco da Gama from Africa to India.

In theology reference should be made to the puritan, conservative Taqi-al-Dīn Aḥmad ibn-Taymīyah[6] (1263–1328), who was born in Ḥarrān and flourished in Damascus. He bowed to no authority other than the Koran, tradition and the practice of the community and lifted his voice high against innovation, saint-worship, vows and pilgrimage to shrines. A follower of ibn-Ḥanbal, his principles were later adopted by the Wahhābis of Najd. Eminent in tradition was ibn-Ḥajar al-'Asqalāni[7] (1372–1449), chief qāḍi of Cairo, who knew the Koran by heart when only nine years old. In poetry perhaps the only name worthy of citation is that of Sharaf-al-Dīn Muḥammad al-Būṣīri[8] (1213–*ca.* 1296), of Berber extraction, who composed the famous ode entitled *al-Burdah* (the Prophet's mantle) in memory of his miraculous cure from a paralytic stroke by a vision of the Prophet

[1] The edition used here is in 2 vols. (Būlāq, 1270).
[2] *Al-Tibr al-Masbūk fi Dhayl al-Sulūk* (Būlāq, 1896), p. 22.
[3] 9 vols. (Cairo, 1923–33), incomplete.
[4] 14 vols. (Cairo, 1913–22).
[5] *Kitāb al-Fawā'id fi Uṣūl al-Baḥr w-al-Qawā'id*, ed. G. Ferrand (Paris, 1921–3).
[6] Of the 500 works ascribed to him some sixty-four survive. Consult Kutubi, vol. i, pp. 48-9.
[7] His *al-Iṣābah fi Tamyīz al-Ṣaḥābah*, 8 vols. (Cairo, 1323–7), was cited above.
[8] Born in Abūṣīr.

casting his mantle over him. No other Arabic ode has attained the popularity of *al-Burdah*. Over ninety commentaries on it have been composed in Arabic, Turkish, Persian and Berber and it has been translated into Persian, Turkish, German, French, English[1] and Italian. Its verses are still recited as charms and the Druzes repeat them to the present day at burials.

Story-telling

We should here recall that the two romances (sing. *sīrah*) of ʿAntar and Baybars, that have not ceased to entertain large audiences in the cafés of the Moslem Orient, took their present form during the Mamlūk period. Likewise the less popular *Alf Laylah*, which through its translations has assumed a place among the immortal pieces of international literature, did not take its final form until this time. Ardent votaries of sports, tournaments, archery, athletics, the chase and horsemanship, the Mamlūks, especially those of the Crusading period, provided the ideal type of hero whose exploits legend never tired of embroidering. The *fāris* who figures in the *Nights* portrays the Mamlūk knight as he flourished in this, rather than in the earlier ʿAbbāsid period. Likewise the folk-manners and customs are drawn from the society which the narrator saw around him in the Cairo of the Mamlūks.

Shadow play

In the late thirteenth century a highly developed specimen of shadow-play literature makes its appearance under the title *Ṭayf al-Khayāl fi Maʿrifat Khayāl al-Ẓill*[2] (phantoms of the imagination on the knowledge of shadow play) by Muḥammad ibn-Dāniyāl al-Khuzāʿi al-Mawṣili († *ca.* 1310). The author was a Moslem physician, possibly of Jewish or Christian origin, who flourished under Baybars, and his production is the only extant specimen of dramatic poetry from medieval Islam. Shadow plays were invented probably in the Far East. The Moslems got them from India or Persia. At the end of the ninth century Arab story-tellers began to introduce national types into their tales and strive for comic effect. By the twelfth century they had developed puppet plays. In Spain a reference to *khayāl al-ẓill* was made in a figure of speech by ibn-Ḥazm in the eleventh century.[3] From Western Asia and Egypt[4] these plays

[1] J. W. Redhouse, "The 'Burdah'", in W. A. Clouston, *Arabian Poetry for English Readers* (Glasgow, 1881), pp. 319-41.

[2] Ed. in part by Georg Jacob, 3 vols. (Erlangen, 1910–12). See Kutubi, vol. ii, p. 237.

[3] *Al-Akhlāq w-al-Siyar*, ed. Maḥmaṣāni (Cairo), p. 28

[4] See ibn Iyās, vol. ii, p. 33.

passed to Constantinople, where the principal character was styled Qaragöz (black-eyed), and thence to the rest of eastern Europe. Some of the material of the Turkish puppet theatre shows evidence of having been borrowed from the *Nights*. The Turkish Qaragöz may have influenced the type of modern actors represented by Charlie Chaplin.

Architecture

The most pleasant surprise of the Mamlūk period, dominated by a régime of blood and iron, is the extraordinary architectural and artistic productiveness of a scale and quality that find no parallel in Egyptian history since Ptolemaic and Pharaonic days. In such mosques, schools and mausoleums erected by Qalāwūn, al-Nāṣir and al-Ḥasan, Moslem architecture reached its most florid expression. In the Burji period the monuments of Barqūq, Qā'it-bāy and al-Ghawri are equally remarkable. Since then no edifice of any importance has made its appearance in Arab lands.

The Mamlūk school of architecture, whose origins go back to Nūrid and Ayyūbid models,[1] received fresh Syro-Mesopotamian influences when in the thirteenth century Egypt became a haven of refuge for Moslem artists and artisans who fled from al-Mawṣil, Baghdād and Damascus before the Mongol invasions. With the ending of the Crusades the obstruction to uninterrupted access to the stone-building territory to the north was removed and brick was abandoned in minaret construction in favour of stone. The cruciform plan of school-mosque structure was developed to its perfection. Domes were constructed that defy rivalry for lightness, beauty of outline and richness of decoration. Striped masonry and decoration (*ablaq*),[2] obtained by using stones of different colours in alternate courses, of Roman or Byzantine origin, became a feature. The period was also noteworthy for the development of the stalactite pendentive as well as for the two other familiar features of Moslem decoration: geometrical arabesques and Kufic lettering. Throughout all the Moslem ages animal forms were less freely used in Egypt and Syria than in Spain and Persia. Happily the finest examples of Mamlūk structures have survived and still form one of the main attractions for tourists and students alike.

Art

Almost all branches of applied art maintained intimate connection with building, especially of the religious type. Extant

[1] See above, pp. 660. [2] Cf. above, p. 680.

specimens of ornate bronze mosque doors, bronze chandeliers in delicate arabesque designs, gold gem-studded Koran-cases, exquisite mosaics in niches and intricate woodwork in pulpits and lecterns testify to their flourishing state.[1] Most of the massive mosque doors are faced with Damascene metal-work. Mosque lamps and coloured windows were made of the finest stained glass with floral designs and Arabic inscriptions. The inner walls of mosques were embellished with the finest decorative glazed tiles. In the minarets of the Mosque of al-Nāṣir in the citadel (1318) are found the earliest Mamlūk examples of faïence architecturally employed. Under the Burjis inlay became especially popular as the doors and pulpits of the Qā'it-bāy's Mosque indicate. In mosaics, ivory carving and enamelling the Copts had been proficient since pre-Islamic times.

Illumination

Among these minor arts none is more individual and characteristic than the illumination of manuscripts, reserved almost exclusively to the "word of Allah". So infinite were the pains taken and such was the skill necessary for the arrangement of colours and the elaboration of decorative elements, that even the best of Korans do not ordinarily have more than two or three pages fully illuminated. Here again the finest collection of illuminated Korans belonged to the Mamlūk sultans and has been recovered by the National Library at Cairo from the various city mosques.

Luxurious living

The delicate refinements of art were not lavished on sacred objects only. Various articles of luxury—cups, bowls, trays, incense burners, testifying to the fidelity of the picture of high life depicted by contemporary chroniclers—have come down to us. Royal princesses bedecked themselves with anklets, ear-rings, necklaces, bracelets and amulets not unlike those still used by modern Egyptians. Mamlūk banquets were followed by entertainments featuring the dancers, jugglers and shadow plays. The court officers included such high personages as master of the household (*ustādār*), armour bearer (*amīr silāḥ*), master of horse (*amīr ākhūr*) and cupbearer (*sāqi khāṣṣ*).[2] Barqūq established between Damascus and Cairo stations to facilitate the transport of ice to Egypt by camel.[3] Of the Burji Mamlūks Jaqmaq (1438–

[1] For illustration consult Gaston Wiet, *Catalogue général du musée arabe du Caire; lampes et bouteilles en verre emaillé* (Cairo, 1929).

[2] *Ṣubḥ*, vol. iv, pp. 18 *seq.*; Maqrīzi, *Khiṭaṭ*, vol. ii, p. 222; Ẓāhiri, pp. 114 *seq.*; Gaudefroy-Demombynes, *La Syrie à l'époque des Mamlouks* (Paris, 1923), pp. L *seq.*

[3] Ẓāhiri, pp. 117-18; 'Umari, pp. 184 *seq.*

1453) expended 3,000,000 dinars in three years on slaves and bounties.[1]

With the Ottoman conquest of Syria and Egypt almost all Mamlūk industrial arts began to decay. A number of architects, craftsmen and carpenters were sent by Sultan Salīm to Constantinople. In one branch only, glazed tile, craftsmanship after the Turkish conquest surpassed anything that had been produced before, as the collection of Damascus tiles in the South Kensington Museum proves. The inlaid trays, bowls, candlesticks, flower-pots and other varieties of brass-work manufactured today in Damascus follow mostly Mamlūk patterns.

[1] Ibn-Taghri-Birdi, vol. vii, p. 246.

CHAPTER XLIX

THE END OF MAMLŪK RULE

UNLIKE the Turkish Baḥris, the Burji Mamlūks were all Circassian with the exception of two: Khushqadam (1461–7) and Timurbugha (1467), who were Greek.[1] The Burjis rejected even more emphatically than the Baḥris the principle of hereditary succession; the sultan was only *primus inter pares* with the real power in the hands of a military oligarchy. Of the twenty-three Burji sultans, whose reigns covered 134 years (1382–1517), nine ruled an aggregate of 124 years. These nine are Barqūq, Faraj, al-Mu'ayyad Shaykh, Barsbāy, Jaqmaq, Īnāl, Khushqadam, Qā'it-bāy and Qānṣawh al-Ghawri.[2] The remaining fourteen were almost all of no consequence, and in one year, 1421, three different sultans were installed. Qā'it-bāy's rule (1468–95) was not only the longest but in some respects the most important and successful.[3]

[1] Ibn-Taghri-Birdi, vol. vii, pp. 685, 842, 847.

[2] His name is thus spelled in a Koran written for him (Moritz, *Palæography*, vol. i, pl. 83); the usual form is Qānṣūh al-Ghūri.

[3] List of Burji Mamlūks:

1.	Al-Ẓāhir Sayf-al-Dīn Barqūq	1382
	(interrupted by the Baḥri Ḥājji, 1389–90)	
2.	Al-Nāṣir Nāṣir-al-Dīn Faraj	1398
3.	Al-Manṣūr ʻIzz-al-Dīn ʻAbd-al-ʻAzīz	1405
	Al-Nāṣir Faraj (again)	1406
4.	The Caliph al-ʻĀdil al-Mustaʻīn	1412
5.	Al-Mu'ayyad Shaykh	1412
6.	Al-Muẓaffar Aḥmad	1421
7.	Al-Ẓāhir Sayf-al-Dīn Ṭaṭar	1421
8.	Al-Ṣāliḥ Nāṣir-al-Dīn Muḥammad	1421
9.	Al-Ashraf Sayf-al-Dīn Barsbāy	1422
10.	Al-ʻAzīz Jamāl-al-Dīn Yūsuf	1438
11.	Al-Ẓāhir Sayf-al-Dīn Jaqmaq	1438
12.	Al-Manṣūr Fakhr-al-Dīn ʻUthmān	1453
13.	Al-Ashraf Sayf-al-Dīn Īnāl	1453
14.	Al-Mu'ayyad Shihāb-al-Dīn Aḥmad	1460
15.	Al-Ẓāhir Sayf-al-Dīn Khushqadam	1461
16.	Al-Ẓāhir Sayf-al-Dīn Yalbāy	1467
17.	Al-Ẓāhir Timurbugha	1467

[*Continued at foot of next page*

Specimens of Burji sulta...

The new régime continued the intrigue, assassination and rapine of its predecessor. In fact it is one of the darkest in Syro-Egyptian annals. Several of the sultans were treacherous and bloodthirsty, some were inefficient or even degenerate, most of them were uncultured. Al-Mu'ayyad Shaykh (1412–21), a drunkard who had been bought by Barqūq from a Circassian dealer, committed some of the worst excesses.[1] Barqūq was the only one of the lot who had a Moslem father.[2] Barsbāy (1422–38), originally enrolled among the slaves of Barqūq, was not familiar with Arabic. He had his two physicians beheaded because they could give him no relief from a fatal malady. Īnāl (1453–60), another slave of Barqūq, could neither read nor write. His contemporary ibn-Taghri-Birdi[3] did not suppose that Īnāl could recite the first sūrah of the Koran without a mistake. His name on the official documents he traced over the writing of a secretary. Nor was he above suspicion in the matter of pæderasty, with which Baybars among other Mamlūks was charged. The *ghilmān* institution of 'Abbāsid notoriety[4] was again flourishing under the Mamlūks. His third successor Yalbāy (1467) was not only illiterate but insane.[5] Qā'it-bāy (1468–95), who was purchased by Barsbāy for fifty dinars and manumitted by Jaqmaq, had the alchemist 'Ali ibn-al-Marshūshi blinded and deprived of his tongue for his failure to turn dross into gold. He levied a burdensome tax on the sale of corn which greatly added to the misery of the masses.

Not only the sultans but the whole oligarchy were more or less corrupt. The numerous Mamlūk amīrs and slaves organized themselves into various factions originating in the bodyguards of Barqūq, Faraj, Shaykh and Barsbāy and were usually at enmity with one another. Each faction was animated solely by the desire of grasping all possible wealth and influence.

Desperate economic situation

The evil economic situation of the kingdom was aggravated by the selfish policy of the sultans. Barsbāy forbade the importa-

18.	Al-Ashraf Sayf-al-Dīn Qā'it-bāy	1468
19.	Al-Nāṣir Muḥammad	1495
20.	Al-Ẓāhir Qānṣawh	1498
21.	Al-Ashraf Jān-balāṭ	1499
22.	Al-Ashraf Qānṣawh al-Ghawri	1500
23.	Al-Ashraf Ṭūmān-bāy	1516–17

[1] Ibn-Taghri-Birdi, vol. vi, pp. 322 *seq.*
[2] Suyūṭi, *Ḥusn*, vol. ii, p. 88.
[3] Vol. vii, p. 559.
[4] See above, pp. 341, 485.
[5] Ibn-Taghri-Birdi, vol. vii, pp. 831, 840, 841.

tion of spices from India, including the much desired pepper, and before the price rose he cornered the existing supply and sold it to his subjects at a great profit. He also monopolized the manufacture of sugar and went so far as to prohibit the planting of sugar-cane for a period in order to realize excessive profits for himself. In his reign another of the periodic plagues visited Egypt and neighbouring countries, and sugar was in special demand as a remedy against the disease. Though not quite as devastating as the "black death", this epidemic is said to have carried away in the capital alone 300,000 victims within three months. Considering the visitation a punishment for the sins of his people, the sultan prohibited females from going outdoors[1] and sought to make atonement by fresh exactions from Christians and Jews. He also deprived non-Moslems of their offices in the government and enforced on them the dress regulations. The same policy against Christians and Jews was pursued by several of his predecessors and by Jaqmaq and Khushqadam.[2] Many of Īnāl's predecessors struck debased silver money and frequently changed the mint value of the precious metals.

Exactions were not limited to non-Moslems. In the absence of a regulated system of taxation, the only way these sultans could raise enough money for their campaigns, extravagant courts and monumental buildings was by extortion from their subjects and from government officials who had enriched themselves at the expense of the public. Marauding Bedouins in the Delta and the desert to the east repeatedly fell on the settled *fallāḥīn* of the narrow agricultural valley and ravaged the land. Locusts, like epidemics, made their periodic visitation. Famine became almost chronic in the land and was intensified in the years of plague and drought caused by low water in the Nile. In the reigns of Faraj and Shaykh starvation was especially widespread. It is estimated that in the course of the Mamlūk period the population of Syria and Egypt was reduced by two-thirds.[3]

Indian trade lost

Towards the end of the period certain international factors began to contribute to the poverty and misery of the land. In 1498 the Portuguese navigator Vasco da Gama found his way round the Cape of Good Hope. This was an event of vital importance in the history of the Syro-Egyptian kingdom. Not only did

[1] Ibn-Taghri-Birdi, vol. vi, p. 760. [2] *Ibid.* vol. vii, pp. 186, 721-2.
[3] Cf. ibn-Taghri-Birdi, vol. vi, pt. 2, p. 273.

attacks from Portuguese and other European fleets become frequent on Moslem ships in the Red Sea and Indian waters but gradually most of the traffic in spices and other tropical products of India and Arabia was diverted from Syrian and Egyptian ports. Thereby one of the main sources of national income was for ever destroyed. The fleet of al-Ghawri had several engagements with Portuguese ships along the coast of Arabia. His threat to the pope, that unless the Portuguese were checked he would destroy the Christian holy places, was of no avail. In 1500 the Portuguese established themselves in Calicut on the west coast of India, and thirteen years later their general, Alfonso d'Albuquerque (from Ar. *abu-al-qurq* [?], sandal maker), bombarded 'Adan (Aden).

Monumental works

The only redeeming feature in this entire period was the erection—as if to atone for the shortcomings of the rulers—of buildings which have stood out to the present day as impressive examples of Moslem architecture. Such were the Mosque and Mausoleum of Barqūq, the Mosque of Qā'it-bāy and the Mosque of al-Ghawri. The memorial Mosque of Qā'it-bāy consists of a mosque proper, a tomb, a fountain and a school. Besides its symphony in two colours, red and white, the dome is decorated with a charming network of conventionalized foliage and rosettes. This and other Mamlūk buildings maintain the traditions of vigour and virile elegance established by the Ayyūbid school of Syria.

The Burjis also continued the earlier practice of applying elaborate arabesque ornament to the minor arts. In these industries, as in architecture, Qā'it-bāy's reign was the richest since the days of al-Nāṣir ibn-Qalāwūn.

Foreign relations

In their foreign relations the Burjis were even less happy than in their domestic affairs. Before the close of the reign of their first sultan the spectre of a new Mongolian invader, Tīmūr, a worthy successor of Hūlāgu and Chingīz, began to loom on the northern horizon. Syria itself was convulsed throughout the whole period by revolts headed by its local governors, some of whom were instigated by the Mongols. Besides Tīmūr another and what proved a more deadly enemy began now to threaten the kingdom, the Ottomans of Anatolia.

Cyprus conquered

The only bright spot in this dark period was the conquest of Cyprus in 1424–1426 by Barsbāy. The object of the Egyptian

From Martin S. Briggs, "Muhammadan Architecture in Egypt and Palestine" (Clarendon Press)

THE MADRASAH OF QĀ'IT-BĀY, CAIRO (EXTERIOR)

expedition to this Mediterranean island was to deprive the corsairs, who had repeatedly ravaged Syrian ports, of a base. The island had been in the hands of Franks, first the Templars and then the house of Lusignan, ever since Richard I occupied it in 1191. It was a powerful ally of the Crusaders and later a permanent menace to the Mamlūk kingdom. In 1270 Baybars made the first attempt to retaliate for the frequent raids by Cypriotes, but his fleet was wrecked off Limassol. Now Barsbāy's formidable forces, after seizing Limassol, advanced to Larnaca and, having defeated the Lusignan army, took King Janus prisoner. Heavily fettered, the king and over a thousand captives were paraded through the streets of Cairo and then brought before the sultan. After kissing the ground[1] at the sultan's feet the king fainted and was borne into the citadel. Ibn-Taghri-Birdi,[2] who later had an interview with the exiled king, gives us an eye-witness's account. Later, through the intervention of the Venetian consul, Janus was returned to his throne on the payment of a ransom of 200,000 dinars and the pledge of a yearly tribute of 20,000. Barsbāy also concluded a treaty of peace with Rhodes, whose Knights of St. John had often collaborated with the Cypriotes in their attacks on the Egyptian coast. Cyprus was the sole acquisition throughout the Burji age, but did not begin to compensate for the many losses suffered.

Tīmūr

Tīmūr Lang, commonly corrupted into Tamerlane, was born in 1336 in Transoxiana. One of his ancestors was vizir to Chingīz' son, but the family claimed descent from Chingīz himself. His satirical biographer ibn-ʿArab-Shāh,[3] however, cites the claim that Tīmūr was the son of a shoemaker and lived at first by brigandage, and that the epithet Lang (lame) he received as a result of a wound inflicted on him while stealing sheep. In 1380 Tīmūr at the head of his Tartar hordes initiated a long series of campaigns which gained for him Afghanistan, Persia, Fāris and Kurdistān. In 1393 he captured Baghdād and in that and the following year overran Mesopotamia. In Takrīt, the birthplace of Ṣalāḥ-al-Dīn, he erected a pyramid with the skulls of his

[1] The custom of kissing the ground before the sultan, established by the Fāṭimid al-Muʿizz, was first abolished by Barsbāy, who substituted for it the kissing of the sultan's hand. Later, however, the old practice was revived with some modification; ibn-Taghri-Birdi, vol. vi, pt. 2, pp. 558-9.

[2] Vol. vi, pt. 2, pp. 612-18, 620.

[3] *ʿAjā'ib al-Maqdūr fi Akhbār Taymūr* (Cairo, 1285), p. 6.

From Martin S. Briggs, "Muhammadan Architecture in Egypt and Palestine" (Clarendon Press)

THE MADRASAH OF QĀ'IT-BĀY, CAIRO (INTERIOR)

victims. In 1395 he invaded the Qipchāq territory and occupied Moscow for over a year. Three years later he ravaged northern India and massacred 80,000 of the inhabitants of Delhi. It was the envoys of Tīmūr whom Barqūq towards the close of his reign ventured to execute, although they came on a friendly mission.

Like a cyclone Tīmūr swept over northern Syria in 1400. For three days Aleppo was given over to plunder. The heads of over twenty thousand of its Moslem inhabitants were built into mounds ten cubits high by twenty in circumference, with all the faces on the outside.[1] The city's priceless schools and mosques of the Nūrid and Ayyūbid ages were destroyed, never to be rebuilt. Ḥamāh, Ḥimṣ and Ba'labakk fell in turn. The advance force of the Egyptian army under Sultan Faraj were routed and Damascus captured (February, 1401). While the city was sacked the fire broke out. The invader—a nominal Moslem with Shī'ite proclivities—extorted a religious opinion from its ulema approving his conduct. Of the Umayyad Mosque nothing was left but the walls.[2] Of the Damascene scholars, skilled labourers and artisans the ablest were carried away by Tīmūr to his capital, Samarqand, there to implant Islamic sciences and to introduce certain industrial arts which have since been lost to the Syrian capital. Ibn-Taghri-Birdi,[3] whose father was chief armour bearer of Faraj, has left us a graphic description of this campaign. Ibn-Khaldūn accompanied Faraj from Cairo and headed the Damascene mission which negotiated peace with Tīmūr. From Damascus the wild conqueror rushed back to Baghdād to avenge the deaths of certain of his officers and dotted the city with a hundred and twenty towers built of the heads of the dead.

During the next two years Tīmūr invaded Asia Minor, crushed the Ottoman army at Ankara (July 21, 1402) and took Sultan Bāyazīd I prisoner. He captured the former capital Brusa and Smyrna. The distinguished captive was kept in chains during the night and made to travel in a litter surrounded by a grille (*qafaṣ*) carried on two horses. The word *qafaṣ*, supported by a misunderstood passage in ibn-'Arab-Shāh,[4] gave rise to the legend that Bāyazīd was shut up in an iron cage. Tīmūr's death

[1] Ibn-Taghri-Birdi, vol. vi, pt. 2, p. 52. [2] *Ibid*. p. 68.

[3] Vol. vi, pt. 2, p. 5, l. 14, pp. 50 *seq*. Cf. Mīrkhwānd, *Ta'rīkh Rawḍat al-Ṣafā'* (Teheran, 1270), Bk. VI. [4] P. 136.

in 1404, in the course of a campaign against China, came as a relief to the Egyptian Mamlūks. His tomb can still be seen in Samarqand.

Tīmūrids

His son and successor, Shāh-Rukh (1404–47), held an angry correspondence with Barsbāy demanding the right, in fulfilment of a vow, of furnishing the Ka'bah with its precious curtain—a privilege maintained by the Mamlūks as the leading sovereigns of Islam. After holding a consultation with his qāḍis of the four rites, Barsbāy deftly replied that Shāh would be absolved of his vow if he would spend the money on the poor of Makkah.[1] Shāh sent another envoy with a courtly robe, commanding that the Mamlūk sultan should receive investiture in it as his vassal, but Barsbāy tore up the robe and had the envoy flogged and ignominiously ducked head downward in a pool. It was a cold day in winter and the scene was witnessed by ibn-Taghri-Birdi.[2] After Shāh the Tīmūrids exhausted themselves in internal struggles which encouraged the rise of the Ṣafawids and the reconstitution of the Ottoman empire.

Ottoman Turks

Reference has been made[3] to the ultimate origin of the Ottoman Turks in Mongolia, their admixture with Iranian tribes in Central Asia and their advent into Asia Minor, where they gradually superseded and absorbed their Saljūq cousins, and in the first years of the fourteenth century established a kingdom destined to supersede the Byzantine empire as well as the Arab caliphate. Bāyazīd I (1389–1402) was the great-grandson of 'Uthmān (1299–1326), the eponymous founder of the dynasty. Under him the Asiatic part of the kingdom, extending from the northern frontier of Syria to the Danube, was almost all lost. In the following ten years, however, it was largely recovered from Europe as a base by Bāyazīd's son Muḥammad I (1402–21). The Ottoman problem began to confront seriously the Egyptian sultans at the time of Muḥammad I's great-grandson, Bāyazīd II (1481–1512), a contemporary of Qā'it-bāy. Rivalry between the two powers found its first expression in repeated conflicts among their vassals on the borders of Asia Minor and Syria. Qā'it-bāy invited fresh trouble in 1481 by harbouring the fugitive Jem, brother of Bāyazīd II and pretender to the throne; and when Jem later was taken to Rome the Mamlūk sultan negotiated with

[1] Ibn-Taghri-Birdi, vol. vi, pt. 2, pp. 722, 725.
[2] Vol. vi, pt. 2, p. 743.
[3] Pp. 475, 478, 489.

the pope with a view to his return to Egypt. But the immediate cause of the final breach was the secret promise of support made by Qānṣawh al-Ghawri to the arch-enemy of the Turks, the Persian Shāh Ismāʻīl (1502–24).

Ṣafawids

Ismāʻīl was the founder of the Ṣafawid dynasty (1502–1736), the most glorious of the native dynasties of Moslem Persia. Its name is derived from the pious Shaykh Ṣafi-al-Dīn (the pure one of the faith), from whom Ismāʻīl was sixth in descent. The family traced its origin to the seventh imām, Mūsa al-Kāẓim, and became ardent in its Shīʻism. Its founder on his accession declared Shīʻism, more particularly the doctrine of the Twelvers, the state religion of Persia, which has ever since remained true to this faith. His collision with the Sunnite Ottoman Salīm I (1512–20), son of Bāyazīd II, took place in August, 1514, at Chāldīrān, north of Lake Urmiyah, where his cavalry gave way before the Janissaries'[1] superior artillery. The Turks then occupied Ismāʻīl's capital Tibrīz, Mesopotamia and part of Armenia (1515).

The decisive battle of Marj Dābiq

In the spring of the following year Qānṣawh proceeded to Aleppo under the pretext of acting as intermediary between the two contestants, but in reality to aid his Persian ally. In order to give his mission a peaceful appearance, he brought in his train his puppet Caliph al-Mutawakkil and the chief qāḍis of his realm. But Salīm would not be deceived; he was kept informed of the intentions of the Mamlūk sultan through a system of spies. When Qānṣawh's envoy arrived at Salīm's camp his beard was shaved—a grave insult—and he was sent back on a mule with a declaration of war. His attendants were put to death. There was no way of averting the impending catastrophe. Though about seventy-five years old, Qānṣawh, once a slave of Qā'it-bāy, was still vigorous. Throughout his reign he had proved himself a man of no mean ability. But he could not depend upon the loyalty of his north Syrian governors, or upon the co-operation of several of his Egyptian amīrs.

The two armies met on August 24, 1516, at Marj Dābiq, a day's journey north of Aleppo. Qānṣawh entrusted the command of the left wing to Khā'ir Bey, the treacherous governor of Aleppo, who at the first charge deserted with his troops. Soon afterward the aged Mamlūk fell from his horse, stricken with

[1] Tur. *yeni-cheri*, new troops, name given to the regular infantry recruited mainly from young captured Christians, and largely responsible for the Ottoman conquests.

apoplexy.[1] The Ottoman victory was complete. The Turkish army was better equipped with the new arms—artillery, muskets and other long-range weapons—which the Mamlūk army, committed to cavalry and comprising Bedouin and Negro contingents, disdained. The Turks had for some time been using powder, but the Syro-Egyptians clung to the antiquated theory that personal valour is the decisive factor in combat. Salīm entered Aleppo in triumph and was welcomed as a deliverer from Mamlūk excesses. The caliph he treated kindly. In the citadel of the city he found immense treasures, estimated in millions of dinars, which the sultan and princes had deposited there. In mid-October he advanced upon Damascus, whose leading men went over to him or fled to Egypt. Syria passed into Ottoman hands, in which it continued for the next four centuries.

Egypt conquered

From Syria the Ottoman conqueror swept south into Egypt. Here Ṭūmān-bāy, a slave of Qānṣawh, had become sultan. The two armies met on January 22, 1517, outside Cairo, where Ṭūmān at first battled valiantly. But the corrupt state of his army, the jealousies among his amīrs, the lack of funds and adequate firearms and the superiority of the Ottoman artillery were sure to tell as the struggle dragged on. Salīm, supported by Bedouin contingents, finally entered and plundered the city, slaughtering all the Mamlūks who fell into his hands. His guns on the right bank of the Nile were brought into action against the remnant of the army. Ṭūmān-bāy fled to a Bedouin chief, but was later betrayed and, strange as it may seem, hanged (April 14) at one of Cairo's main gates.[2] The Mamlūk sultanate was for ever crushed. Cairo, the centre of Eastern Islam since Ṣalāḥ-al-Dīn's time, passed away as an imperial city and became a provincial town. Makkah and al-Madīnah automatically became a part of the Ottoman empire. The Egyptian preachers who led the Friday public services invoked Allah's blessing on Salīm in the following words:

> O Lord! uphold the sultan, son of the sultan, ruler over both lands and the two seas, conqueror of both hosts, monarch of the two ʿIrāqs, minister of the two Holy Cities, the victorious king Salīm Shāh. Grant him, O Lord, Thy precious aid; enable him to win glorious victories, O Ruler of this world and the next, Lord of the universe.[3]

[1] Ibn-Iyās, ed. Paul Kahle *et al.*, vol. v (Istanbul, 1932), pp. 67-9.
[2] *Ibid.* pp. 138 *seq.*, 145 *seq.*
[3] *Ibid.* p. 145.

The Ottoman caliphate

After lingering until the autumn in the valley of the Nile, where he visited the pyramids, Alexandria and other places of interest, the great conqueror returned to Constantinople, the Ottoman capital since 1453, carrying with him the caliph. Charged later with misappropriating trust funds, al-Mutawakkil was held prisoner until allowed to retire to Cairo by Salīm's son and successor, Sulaymān the Magnificent. There he died in 1543. His death closed the last chapter in the history of the mock 'Abbāsid caliphate. Whether, as is alleged without sufficient warrant, he made a transfer of his office to the Ottoman sultan or not,[1] the fact remains that the Turkish ruler in Constantinople gradually absorbed the caliphal privileges and ultimately the title itself. Although some of Salīm's successors styled themselves caliphs and were so addressed, their use of the title was complimentary and unrecognized outside their own territories. The first known diplomatic document which applies the term caliph to the Ottoman sultan and recognizes his religious authority over Moslems outside of Turkey is the Russo-Turkish treaty of Kūchūk Kaynarji, signed in 1774.

The sultan-caliph of Constantinople became the most powerful potentate in Islam, an heir not only to the caliphs of Baghdād but also to the emperors of Byzantium.[2] With the destruction of Mamlūk power and the establishment of the Turks on the Bosporus the focus of Islamic power shifted westward. In fact, by this time the centre of world civilization had moved to the West. The discovery of America and of the Cape of Good Hope transferred the world's trade to new routes, and the entire realm of the eastern Mediterranean began to sink into the background. Herewith the history of the Arab caliphate and the Moslem dynasties that arose in medieval times on the ruins of the Arab empire comes to an end, and the modern history of the Ottoman caliphate-empire begins.

[1] See above, pp. 489, 677.
[2] On the abolition of the Ottoman caliphate see above, pp. 139, 184.

PART VI

OTTOMAN RULE AND INDEPENDENCE

THE FLAG OF THE OTTOMAN EMPIRE

CHAPTER L

THE ARAB LANDS AS TURKISH PROVINCES

FOR about two-thirds of a century after its establishment about 1300 in Anatolia at the expense of the Byzantine empire and on the ruins of the Saljūq kingdom, the Ottoman state was but a frontier amīrate.[1] The state was on a war footing and at times precarious. Its capital, beginning with 1326, was Brusa (Bursa). By 1366 the amīrate had become more stable, gained a firm foothold on the European mainland and developed into a kingdom with Adrianople (Edirne) as capital.[2] The conquest in 1453 of Constantinople by Muḥammad II the Conqueror (1451–81) formally ushered in a new era, that of the empire. The new giant

[1] Genealogical table of the early Ottoman rulers:

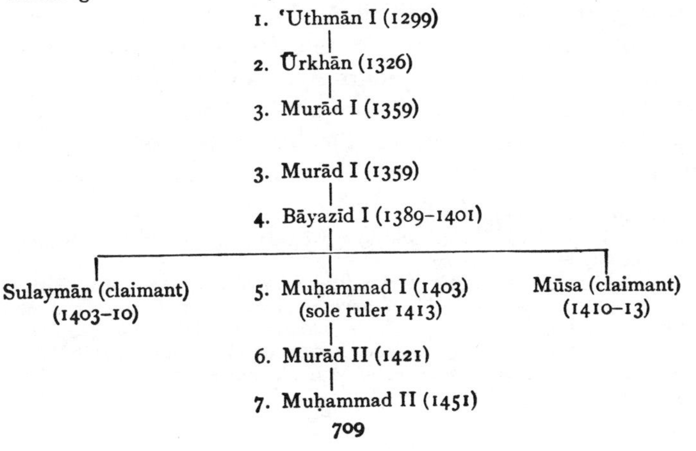

installed himself astride the Bosporus with one foot in Asia and the other in Europe. His expanding domain made him heir not only to Byzantium but also, through the destruction of the Mamlūk power,[1] to the successor states of the Arab caliphate. The inheritance of lands from both East and West had its counterpart in the inheritance of ideas, and the combined heritage is perhaps the most pregnant fact in the history of Ottoman Turkey.

North Africa

Other Arab states, in North Africa, were in the sixteenth century drawn within the orbit of the rising Turkish crescent. Of these Algeria (al-Jazā'ir, roughly Numidia of the Romans) was the first. In 1518, the year after the conquest of Egypt, Khayr-al-Dīn Barbarossa and his brother, two Ottoman corsairs of Greek birth, invaded the land, warded off Spanish encroachments and bestowed it upon the Sublime Porte. In exchange the Porte bestowed upon Khayr-al-Dīn the title of beylerbey (bey of beys).[2] Khayr-al-Dīn inaugurated a military aristocracy with a corps of Janissaries as its backbone. He also organized for the sultan a well-equipped fleet with seasoned crew, recruited mainly from renegade Christians, Italians and Greeks, and ready to implement aggressive imperial policy throughout the Mediterranean. The fleet carried the terror of the Ottoman name westward to the coasts of Spain, as the Janissaries carried it eastward to the banks of the Tigris. A dangerous neighbour was thereby installed west of Tunisia (Africa of the Romans). Taking advantage of a dispute in the native succession to the Tunisian throne, Khayr-al-Dīn temporarily occupied Tunis in 1534; the country, however, was not reduced to a Turkish province till forty years later. The land forces against it were led by Sinān Pasha, a brilliant general of Albanian descent, who in 1568 as governor of Egypt had conducted a campaign against South Arabia which netted al-Yaman to the house of 'Uthmān.[3] Before Sinān a great Turkish admiral of probable Christian origin, Pīri Re'īs, had operated on the southern and eastern coasts of the peninsula, occupied 'Adan

[1] See above, pp. 704-5.

[2] Tur. *bey*, from Turki (East Turkish) *beg*, a title of honour that is still commonly used, especially by Egyptians.

[3] Cf. Joseph von Hammer, *Geschichte des osmanischen Reiches*, vol. iii (Pest, 1828), p. 551; cf. Quṭb-al-Dīn al-Makki, *al-Barq al-Yamāni fi al-Fatḥ al-'Uthmāni*, tr. Silvestre de Sacy in *Notices et extraits des manuscrits de la Bibliothèque Nationale*, vol. iv (Paris, 1791–6), pp. 468 *seq.*; for further on al-Yaman, consult Ḥusayn A. al-'Arshi, *Bulūgh al-Marām fi Sharḥ Misk al-Khitām*, ed. A. M. al-Kirmili (Cairo, 1939), pp. 60-80.

(Aden, 1547) and Masqaṭ (1551) and struck as far as the head of the Persian Gulf. A recently discovered map of his, the so-called Columbus map, shows the Atlantic Ocean and America.[1] First called beys, the governors of Tunisia for over a century after 1705 became known as deys.[2] Even before putting an end to Spanish rule and native dynasties in Tunisia, Sinān Pasha and two other Turkish generals had evicted the Knights of St. John (of Malta) from Tripoli and in 1551 had captured the city. Tripoli (Ṭarābulus al-Gharb) owes its Greek name to three Phoenician-Carthaginian colonies which with the adjoining territory once formed the province of Tripolitania under Rome. In it the Berber element was weakest. Thus did the Barbary [3] states, with the exception of distant mountainous Morocco (al-Maghrib al-Aqṣa, roughly Roman Mauretania), more than half of whose population was of Berber descent, fall within the Ottoman embrace. Generally speaking, the proportion of Berbers in the population increases not only from east to west but also from north to south.

Tripoli, Tunis and Algiers now became seats of provincial governments nominally tributary to the Porte but actually semi-independent, and for a long time each under native or domesticated rulers, many of whom passed on the reins of government to their descendants. All three governments were dominated by military oligarchies. The claims of the Porte were recognized by the annual payment of tribute, which partook more of the nature of a present. Occasionally the states were convulsed by revolts provoked by the extortions of Ottoman agents. From 1711 to 1835 Tripolitania was administered by the Qaramānli house. The deterioration of the Ottoman fleet from the seventeenth century onward loosened the Ottoman grip on the African provinces and gave their governors, whether pashas, beys or deys, the opportunity to practise an even larger measure of local autonomy than their opposite numbers in Egypt and Syria.

Pirate states

The Barbary provinces developed into corsair states. Directed primarily against Christians, piracy partook first of the nature of

[1] Paul Kahle in *The Geographical Review*, vol. xxiii (1933), pp. 621-38; cf. Ḥājji Khalfah, vol. ii, pp. 22-3; consult Pīri Re'īs, *Baḥrīyah*, ed. Paul Kahle, 2 vols. (Berlin, 1926). The Turks had occupied 'Adan once before, 1538.

[2] Tur. *dāy*, maternal uncle.

[3] Land of the Barbarians—a term applied by the Greeks to all peoples living outside the pale of Greek civilization. The Romans applied "Barbary" to the region west of Egypt.

a *jihād*. Like soldiering, it became a profession. The industry was profitable to government and people alike. A fixed duty was levied on the captives and the booty; captives were held for ransom or sold as slaves. For about three centuries the income therefrom was the main source of revenue to the state treasury. Piratical ships took their place at times as units in the Ottoman fleet. Exiles from Moslem Spain [1] swelled the ranks of Mediterranean freebooters whose ravages became the scourge of the sea.[2] The activity reached its height in the first half of the seventeenth century, imperilling the coasts of Italy, France and Spain. In the latter half of that century the naval operations of the British and French compelled respect for their respective flags, but minor powers continued to purchase immunity for their nationals and trade by the payment of annual tribute, an immunity that remained at best precarious. Such was the case with Holland, Denmark and Sweden. Even the United States sought safety in tribute and was in 1783 involved in a war with Algeria, headquarters of the sea robbers. In 1801 the Qaramānli dey of Tripoli insisted on an increase on the $83,000 which the United States had been paying annually since 1796 and a four-year war ensued. In 1815 another hostile naval force from America visited Tripoli. It was these naval engagements with the Barbary states that in part stimulated the development of the American fleet.

The splendour that was Constantinople

Most of the North African conquests were achieved during the reign of Sulaymān I (1520–66), son of the conqueror of Syria and Egypt and the man under whom the Ottoman empire hit the zenith of its might.[3] In Sulaymān's reign the greater part of Hungary was reduced, Vienna was besieged and Rhodes was occupied. The Ottoman sway then extended from Budapest on

[1] See above, p. 556.

[2] For more on this consult Stanley Lane-Poole, *The Story of the Barbary Corsairs* (New York, 1891).

[3]
7. Muḥammad II (1451)
8. Bāyazīd II (1481)
9. Salīm I (1512)
10. Sulaymān I (1520)
11. Salīm II (1566)
12. Murād III (1574)

the Danube to Baghdād on the Tigris and from the Crimea to the first cataract of the Nile. This was the greatest Moslem state of modern times; not only that, but one of the most enduring Moslem states of all time. No less than thirty-six sultans, all in the direct male line of 'Uthmān, reigned from 1300 to 1922.[1]

Sulaymān was known to his people by the honorific title of al-Qānūni (the lawgiver) because of the high esteem in which later generations held the codes which bore his name.[2] He charged Ibrāhīm al-Ḥalabi (of Aleppo, †1549) with the task of compiling

[1]

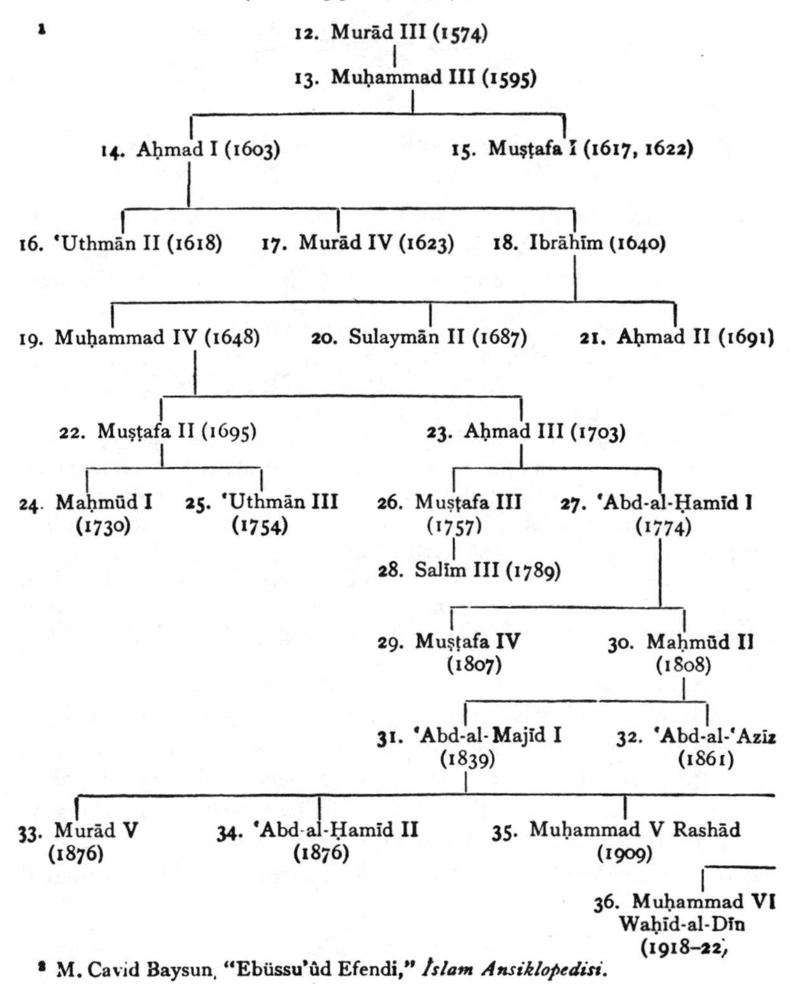

[2] M. Cavid Baysun, "Ebüssu'ûd Efendi," *İslam Ansiklopedisi*.

a book, *Multaqa al-Abḥur* (confluence of the seas), which remained the standard work on Ottoman law until the reforms of the nineteenth century.[1] To Europeans, however, Sulaymān was

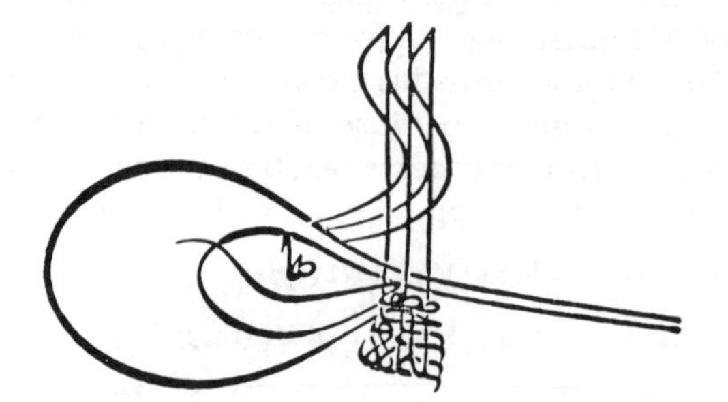

THE *ṬUGHRA*, CALLIGRAPHIC EMBLEM, OF SULAYMĀN THE MAGNIFICENT, BEARING HIS NAME

known as the Magnificent, and magnificent he was. His court was certainly one of the most resplendent in Eurasia. Note the style he used in addressing a letter to Francis I, king of France:

> I who am the Sultan of Sultans, the sovereign of sovereigns, the dispenser of crowns to the monarchs on the face of the earth, the shadow of God on earth, the Sultan and sovereign lord of the White Sea and of the Black Sea, of Rumelia and of Anatolia, of Karamania, of the land of Rum, of Zulkadria, of Diarbekir, of Kurdistan, of Azerbaijan, of Persia, of Damascus, of Aleppo, of Cairo, of Mecca, of Medina, of Jerusalem, of all Arabia, of Yemen, and of many other lands which my noble forefathers and my glorious ancestors (may God light up their tombs!) conquered by the force of their arms and which my August Majesty has made subject to my flaming sword and my victorious blade, I, Sultan Suleiman Khan, son of Sultan Selim Khan, son of Sultan Bayezid Khan: To thee, who art Francis, King of the land of France.[2]

Sulaymān equipped and beautified the capital and other cities with mosques, schools, hospitals, palaces, mausoleums, bridges, aqueducts, caravanserais and public baths, two hundred and thirty-five of which are said to have been built by his chief architect Sinān. Originally a Christian from Anatolia, who perhaps found his way into Constantinople with the usual levy of youth,[3] Sinān developed into the most energetic and distinguished

[1] See Hitti, *History of Syria*, p. 664.
[2] Roger B. Merriman, *Suleiman the Magnificent* (Cambridge, 1944), p. 130.
[3] See above, p. 703, n. 1.

architect that Turkey produced. His masterpiece was the magnificent mosque named Sulaymānīyah, in commemoration of his master's name, and designed to eclipse Santa Sophia. Its majestic dome exceeds that of the Justinian cathedral by about sixteen feet. The *miḥrāb* and rear wall are ornamented with exquisite tile in the Persian style. While the limelight illumined the city on the Bosporus, the once glamorous Madīnah. Damascus, Baghdād, Cairo—former capitals of mighty empires and brilliant seats of culture—were functioning as residences for provincial governors and armed garrisons from Constantinople, the city before whose walls had stood on four historic occasions threatening Arab armies from Damascus and Baghdād.[1]

Ottoman culture

Turkish culture in its entirety was a striking blend of diverse and disparate elements. From the Persians, with whom the Turks had contacts even before migrating to Western Asia, came artistic motifs, belletristic patterns and such political ideas as the exaltation of the monarch. Among possible bequests from Central Asian nomadism, mention may be made of a predisposition to war and conquest and a hospitable assimilative tendency.[2] The Byzantines, chiefly by way of the Saljūqs of Rūm, provided certain military and governmental institutions. But, above all, the Arabs were the teachers of the Turks, in the same sense as the Greeks were the teachers of the Romans. From the Arabs the Turks acquired their sciences, their religion—with its socio-economic principles and sacred law—and an alphabetic system of writing that lingered till 1928. While still in Central Asia the Turks had but little written literature and, for that, Syriac script, introduced by Christian Syrians,[3] was used. With the adoption of Islam and the Arabic characters thousands of religious, scientific, legal and literary terms were borrowed from Arabic and Persian, and many of them are still embedded in Turkish despite recent nationalistic attempts at linguistic purge. In three fields the Ottomans made original contributions of major significance: statesmanship, architecture, and poetry.

The imperial set-up

The empire of the Ottomans, like those of the Romans and 'Abbāsids before it, was essentially military and dynastic in

[1] See above, pp. 299-300.
[2] Albert H. Lybyer, *The Government of the Ottoman Empire in the Time of Sulciman the Magnificent* (Cambridge, 1913), p. 18.
[3] See Hitti, *History of Syria*, pp. 518-19.

character and in organization. The main objective sought was not so much the welfare of its subjects as the welfare of the state personified by the sultan-caliph. The subjects were a conglomeration of nationalities—Arabians, Syrians, ʿIrāqis, Egyptians, Berbers, Kurds, Armenians, Slavs, Greeks, Albanians—with diverse creeds, languages and ways of life, held together by the sword of ʿUthmān. Even the peasant Turks—as distinct from the ruling class, members of which preferred to call themselves *ʿUthmānli*, Osmanli, Ottoman—could be included among the subject peoples. The Turks themselves were, and remained, a dominant minority group in their vast domain and made no attempt at colonization in the Arab lands. But they kept their blood fresh by marrying non-Moslem women and by admitting to full citizenship any subject who accepted Islam, adopted the Turkish tongue and joined their court. The regular levy of boys, as long as it lasted, enabled them to press into their military and civil service and to assimilate the flower of the male youth of the subject non-Moslem communities. Some of the best talent of the conquered people was sucked and funnelled into the capital, there to be Islamized, Turkicized and utilized to the glory and advancement of the imperial state. Circassians, Greeks, Albanians, Slavs, Italians and even Armenians rose to the highest offices in the empire including the grand vizirate.

Inherent elements of weakness

A state organized primarily for warfare rather than for the welfare of its people and covering a far-flung unwieldy area with under-developed means of communication and a heterogeneous population among whom the line of cleavage was clearly marked between Moslems and Christians—even between Moslem Turks and Moslem Arabs and between one Christian sect and another—had the seeds of decay embedded in its basic structure. Once it was confronted with a world in which nationalism was triumphing, its condition became aggravated. The persistence and elaboration of the millet[1] system whereby each religious community enjoyed a considerable measure of home rule—which was the classic way by which Islam tried to solve its minority problem—the centralization of supreme authority (at least in theory) in the hands of one man—the sultan-caliph—and the ambiguity in the line of succession added to the inherent weaknesses in the imperial

[1] See below, p. 727.

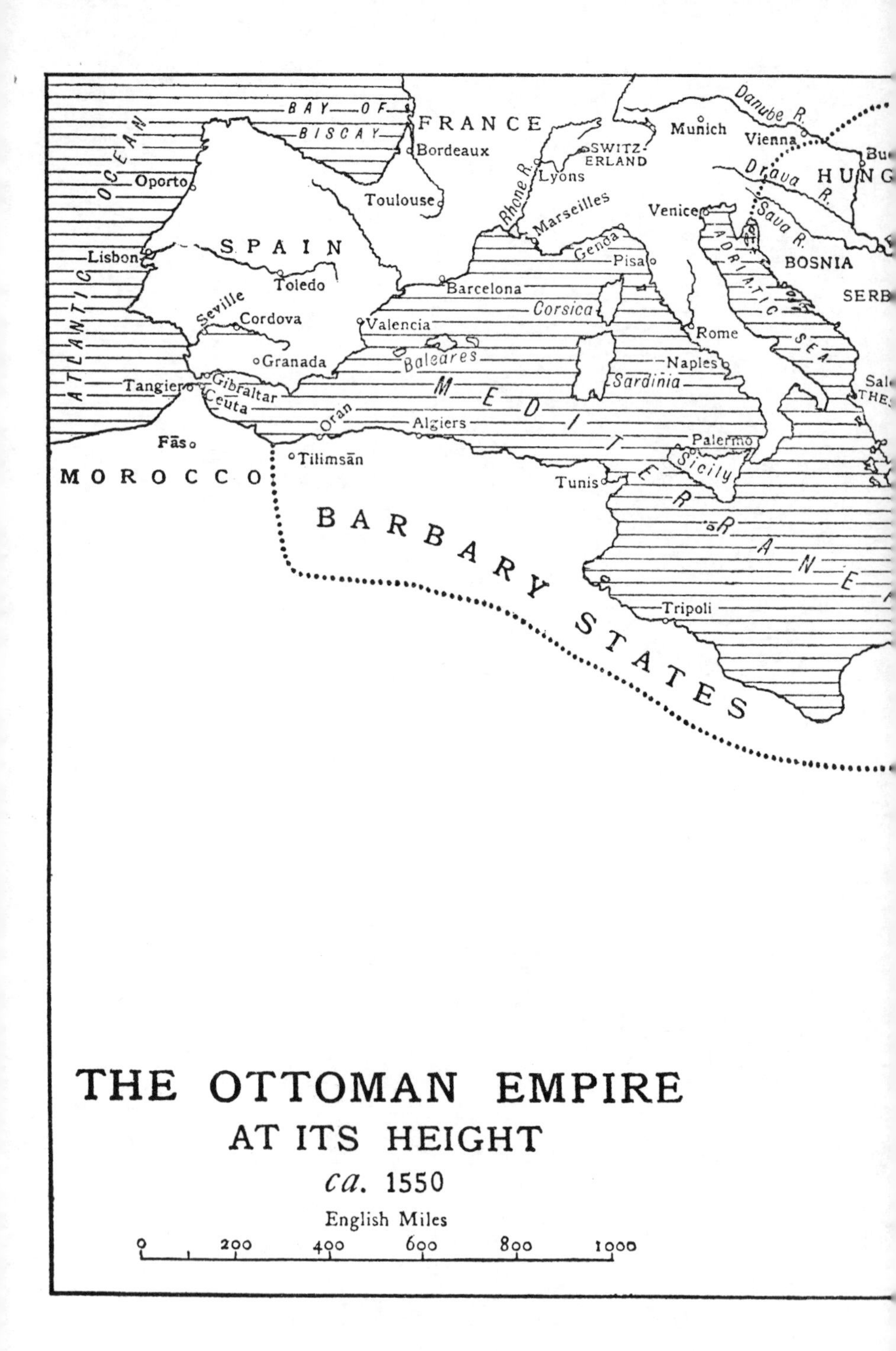

BAY OF BISCAY
ATLANTIC OCEAN
FRANCE
Bordeaux
Toulouse
Oporto
Lisbon
SPAIN
Toledo
Seville
Cordova
Granada
Valencia
Barcelona
Tangier
Gibraltar
Ceuta
Fās
MOROCCO
Tilimsān
Oran
Algiers
Rhone R.
Lyons
Marseilles
SWITZERLAND
Munich
Danube R.
Vienna
Drava R.
Sava R.
Venice
Genoa
Pisa
Corsica
Sardinia
Baleares
Rome
Naples
ADRIATIC SEA
BOSNIA
Palermo
Sicily
Tunis
MEDITERRANEAN
BARBARY STATES
Tripoli
THE OTTOMAN EMPIRE
AT ITS HEIGHT
ca. 1550
English Miles
0
200
400
600
800
1000

[*Between pages 716 and 717*

set-up. The wonder is that disintegration did not set in much earlier than it did.

Shortly after the death of Sulaymān the empire started on its downward course, a course that was both long and tortuous. The failure of the second attempt on Vienna in 1683 may be considered as marking the beginning of the end; Turkey's expansion in Europe made no further progress. After that the problem for the Turks became how to hold what they already got rather than to get more; the rôle of the armed forces was no more one of offence but of defence. To the internal forces of corruption and decay were added external forces in the eighteenth century when France, England, Austria and eventually Russia started their quest for "spheres of influence" and began to cast covetous eyes on some possession of the "sick man" of Europe. Mutual jealousies, however, among the competing powers and lack of concerted action gave the patient more than one lease on life.

The loss of North African states

Of the Arab lands those of North Africa were the first to be lost to the Ottoman empire. Those lands constitute a block by themselves. Proximity to South Europe, distance from the centre and heart of Islam in Western Asia, the weakness of their Islamic tradition and the high proportion of Berber and European blood made them from the outset pursue a course of their own.

Algeria was the first of the Arab states to be detached from the empire. This was done in 1830, when French troops landed on its shores ostensibly in reprisal for piratical activity and to avenge an insult offered by the ruling dey Ḥusayn to the French consul. Eighteen years later the country was declared French territory with its littoral as an integral part of France. When American troops landed there in November 1942, Laval protested, invoking the decree of 1848 and maintaining that Algeria was a natural prolongation of France.[1] Like any other *département*, it sent representatives to the French parliament. An eight-year-old bloody conflict between French troops and Algerian nationalists ended in 1962 with a peace treaty leading to Algeria's independence.

The eastward expansion of imperial France resulted in 1881 in the occupation of Tunisia, where the same policy was pursued to a hardly less extent. As in Algeria French replaced Arabic as the literary language of the natives. Though its status was

[1] *The New York Times*, November 21, 1942.

that of a protectorate, Tunisia was a French possession in all but name. A French resident-general, installed beside the native bey, controlled all the public services. Its proximity to Egypt, however, has kept the national Moslem tradition in it comparatively strong. In Tunisia as in Algeria thousands of French colonists have been domiciled. The Tunisian situation is complicated by the large number and size of Italian colonies. Both countries admittedly enjoyed a higher measure of security and public health and greater facilities for communication under the French. Tunisia was accorded internal autonomy in 1955 and full independence in 1956. Both Tunisia and Algeria are now republics.

Tripolitania, being mostly arid desert with a string of oases along the littoral, was the last Turkish outpost in the Barbary states. As a sequel to the Turko-Italian war of 1911–12 Tripolitania was wrested from Ottoman hands, made a colony, and, together with Cyrenaica, incorporated in 1934 into Libia Italiana. In the course of the second World War the Italian troops, assisted by Germans, were expelled from Libya by British, French and native forces. The country was declared in 1951 an independent sovereign kingdom.

In 1901 the French conquest of Morocco, once the seat of two mighty Arab-Berber empires but never a part of the Ottoman empire,[1] began; the French zone was fully acquired between 1907 and 1912. Meantime Spain was busy acquiring her share in the territory just across from its coast. In 1956 both France and Spain renounced their protectorates in favour of the sultan, now king. Thus did the entire "white Africa" (generally separated from black Africa by the Sahara), which in the eighty-two years following 1830 lay in the hands of the three Latin states of South Europe, liberate itself after the second World War. Until then it had remained relatively unaffected by nationalistic stirrings.

[1] As noted above, p. 711.

CHAPTER LI

EGYPT AND THE ARAB CRESCENT

GEOGRAPHICALLY a part of Africa, Egypt has been throughout the ages historically and culturally a part of Western Asia. With greater Syria and al-'Irāq it forms one Arab block, distinct from the North African block, on one hand, and from the Arabian block (peninsula), on the other.

Mamlūks remain in control

Other than appointing an Ottoman pasha to act as viceroy over Egypt and leaving an army of occupation consisting of some five thousand Janissaries, Sultan Salīm made few radical changes in the administration of Egypt. His choice for viceroy fell upon the traitorous Khā'ir Bey, Turkish governor of Aleppo who had betrayed his Mamlūk master.[1] Salīm spent a few days in Cairo enjoying himself and returned to his capital with a shadow play [2] for the entertainment of his son Sulaymān, the crown prince.[3] The twelve sanjāqs [4] into which Egypt was then divided remained under the old Mamlūks. Each Mamlūk bey surrounded himself with a coterie of slave warriors who did his bidding and upheld his authority. Mamlūk blood was kept fresh by the importation of slaves mainly from the Caucasus. As in the preceding régime, Mamlūks collected taxes and levied troops, but now they acknowledged Ottoman suzerainty through the payment of annual tribute.

It was not long before the Ottoman pasha sent from Constantinople ceased to exercise any real control over local affairs. His ignorance of the colloquial and of the local scene was a decided handicap. His tenure of office was at best of short duration. In the two hundred and eighty years of direct Turkish rule over Egypt no less than a hundred such pashas succeeded one another.[5] The frequent change in personnel weakened the hold over the army which tended to become unruly and un-

[1] See above, p. 703. [2] Cf. above, p. 690.

[3] Ibn-Iyās, vol. v, p. 188.

[4] Tur. *sanjāq* (Ar. *sanjaq*), a translation of Ar. *liwā'*, banner.

[5] Cf. list in Zambaur, pp. 166-8.

disciplined. Beginning with the seventeenth century, mutinies became common. Conflicts between pashas and beys became a recurring theme in the political history of the land, with the pasha getting his chance when mutual jealousies and the struggle for supremacy among the beys themselves reached an acute stage. As the central authority in Constantinople pursued its downward course, respect for its viceroys decreased throughout the empire.

Under the dual form of control the native sank deeper in the abyss of misery and poverty. By pasha and Mamlūk the cultivator of the soil was relentlessly exploited and driven into a state of abjectness unparalleled except perhaps in the preceding era. Corruption and bribery prevailed. Insecurity, famine and pestilence added their quota of misery. One pestilence, that of 1619, is said to have carried away more than a third of a million people; another, that of 1643, left two hundred and thirty villages desolate.[1] A contemporary chronicler al-Isḥāqi [2] states that while the 1619 plague raged, most of the shops of Cairo were closed, with the exception of those which dealt in shrouds and which remained open day and night. The population of the land, which under the Romans reached some eight millions, had by the end of the eighteenth century dwindled into one-third its former size.

'Ali Bey declared sultan

The rising Mamlūk power reached its zenith in 1769 when 'Ali Bey, reportedly son of a Christian priest from the Caucasus, who as a boy had fallen into the hands of brigands and been sold into slavery, acquired enough strength to expel the Ottoman pasha and declare himself independent of the Porte. With the army which the sultan, then engaged in a critical struggle against Russia, had ordered him to amass, 'Ali Bey now proceeded to conquer Arabia and Syria for himself. His lieutenant and son-in-law, abu-al-Dhahab,[3] entered Makkah victoriously in July 1770.[4] Its sharīf was replaced by a claimant who in turn bestowed upon 'Ali the pompous title of "sultan of Egypt and ruler of the two seas" (the Mediterranean and Red). The *sharīfate* or government of Makkah was always held by a descendant of the Prophet.[5] 'Ali not only assumed the title but also the prerogatives that

[1] Cf. Jurji Zaydān, *Ta'rīkh Miṣr al-Ḥadīth*, 3rd ed. (Cairo, 1925), vol. ii, pp. 31, 39-40.

[2] *Akhbār al-Uwal fi Man Taṣarrafa fi Miṣr min al-Duwal* (Cairo, 1296), p. 258.

[3] "Father of gold", so called because he gave nothing but gold pieces as bakshish.

[4] Al-Jabarti, *'Ajā'ib al-Āthār fi al-Tarājim w-al-Akhbār* (Cairo, 1322), vol. i, pp. 422, 353.

[5] See above, p. 440, n. 8.

pertain thereunto, including the striking of coins and the mention of his name in the public worship. In 1771 abu-al-Dhahab at the

British Museum

COIN OF 'ALI BEY

Silver (*yigirmīlik*, 20 paras), dated 1183 (1769), struck at Miṣr (Cairo)

head of about thirty thousand men marched against Syria and captured several of its cities, headed by Damascus.[1] In the flush of victory he betrayed his master, entered into secret negotiations with the Porte and turned his troops against Egypt. 'Ali fled (April 1772) to his Palestinian ally and fellow-rebel, Ẓāhir al-'Umar,[2] in 'Akka. There he received ammunition and a reinforcement of 3000 Albanians from Russian warships anchored in the harbour and returned to fight for his lost throne. Wounded in battle, he died shortly after that (1773), either as a result of the wound or by poison. Abu-al-Dhahab, his former slave, thereupon combined in his person the title of *shaykh al-balad* (head of the community), a title which had hitherto distinguished the leading Mamlūk, and that of pasha, which he received with his investiture from the Porte. The next highest Mamlūk office after the *shaykh al-balad's* was that of *amīr al-ḥajj*, held by the official in charge of the annual holy pilgrimage. The rise of 'Ali Bey, ephemeral as it was, exposed the vulnerability of the Ottoman position; the installation of abu-al-Dhahab conceded the right of a Mamlūk to become Ottoman viceroy.

Napoleon Bonaparte

The fight among the leading Mamlūks for the government of Egypt continued until, unexpectedly and as if from nowhere, a strange, mighty invader landed in Alexandria (July 1798), Napoleon Bonaparte. His professed purpose was to punish the Mamlūks, whom he accused in the Arabic proclamation he issued on landing, of being not as good Moslems as he and his

[1] Jabarti, vol. i, p. 367.

[2] See below, pp. 731-2.

fellow-Frenchmen were, and to restore the authority of the Porte.[1] His real purpose was to strike a fatal blow at the British Empire by intercepting her communication with the East and thus make a bid for world dominion. The destruction of the French fleet at Abūqīr Bay (Aboukir, August 1, 1798), the check of the ill-fated expedition at ʿAkka (1799)[2] and the defeat in the battle of Alexandria (March 21, 1801) frustrated the Napoleonic ambitions in the East and forced the evacuation of the French troops from Egypt. The land hitherto playing a minor rôle in world events—as a source of tribute for Turkey and a base of operation for maintaining Ottoman dominion over Syria and Arabia—was suddenly drawn into the vortex of international politics as the gateway to India and the rest of the extreme Orient.[3] The Napoleonic expedition turned Europe's eyes to the somewhat forgotten land route to India and set in motion a chain reaction which made the Near East the storm centre of European intrigue and diplomacy.

Muḥammad ʿAli: founder of modern Egypt

In the Turkish army that helped to drive Napoleon out of the land was a young officer born in Macedonia named Muḥammad ʿAli. The Porte made him pasha in 1805 and he made himself the new master of the valley of the Nile, in nominal subordination to the Porte. The history of Egypt for the first half of the nineteenth century is virtually the story of this one man. Founder of the dynasty that was until 1952 still ruling, Muḥammad ʿAli has been rightly called the father of his country—at least in its modern phase. The initiative, energy and vision he displayed and exercised find no parallel among any of his Moslem contemporaries. In peace and in war he stood supreme. By confiscating all land holdings in the hands of private individuals among his subjects he became sole proprietor of the country; by creating a monopoly of the chief products of the land he made himself its only manufacturer and contractor. This was the first attempt at nationalization in the Arab world. In pursuit of his economic policy he excavated canals, promoted scientific agri-

[1] Copy of proclamation in Jabarti, vol. iii, pp. 4-5; it begins Moslemwise with the formula: In the name of God, the Merciful, the Compassionate; summarized in al-Sharqāwi, *Tuḥfat al-Nāẓirīn fi man Waliya Miṣr min al-Walāt w-al-Salāṭīn* (Cairo, 1286), p. 55; English translation in *Copies of the Original Letters from the Army of General Bonaparte in Egypt, Intercepted by the Fleet under the Command of Admiral Lord Nelson*, 11th ed., vol. i (London, 1798), pp. 235-7.

[2] See below, p. 733.

[3] On the cultural effects, see below, p. 745.

culture and introduced the cultivation of cotton from India and the Sudan (1821–2). Himself an illiterate man, he yet patronized learning, started a ministry of education, created a council of education and founded the first school of engineering in his realm

MUḤAMMAD 'ALI, FOUNDER OF MODERN EGYPT

(1816) and the first school of medicine.[1] Professors and physicians he brought mostly from France. He invited missions—military and educational—to train his people, and sent native missions—

[1] Founded in 1827 this school is today included in Fu'ād I University; Roderic D. Matthews and Matta Akrawi, *Education in Arab Countries of the Near East* (Washington, 1949), p. 80.

military and educational—to study in Europe. Records show that between 1813 and 1849 (the year of his death)[1] three hundred and eleven Egyptian students were sent to Italy, France, England and Austria at an expense to the state of £E273,360.[2] In Paris a special house was maintained for the benefit of these students. The preferred subjects of study were military and naval, engineering, medicine, pharmacy, arts and crafts. Since then the French language has enjoyed a favoured place in the Egyptian curriculum; the French schools in Egypt have even today a higher attendance of students than any other foreign institutions.[3]

A French colonel, Sève, who professed Islam under the name of Sulaymān Pasha, reorganized and modernized the Egyptian army and took part in the invasion of Syria. His name is commemorated in one of Cairo's principal streets and his descendants married into the 'Alid family. Another Frenchman, a naval engineer, constructed the Egyptian navy. The first military venture was in 1811 against Wahhābi Arabia, a war that was not ended till 1818. In honour of the departure of the first troops, some 10,000, under his sixteen-year-old son Ṭūsūn, the viceroy held a reception in the Cairo Citadel to which the Mamlūks were, of course, invited among the honoured guests. The coffee drinking over, the Mamlūks filed out through a narrow passage toward the main gate and were then and there abruptly assailed and slaughtered. Of the four hundred and seventy, very few escaped. The slaughter on the hill was a signal for an indiscriminate one for the rest of them throughout the land. Their properties were confiscated. The almost six-hundred-year-old Mamlūk problem in Egypt was for ever solved.

The second series of military campaigns carried the Egyptian flag triumphantly in 1820 into the eastern Sudan (al-Nūbah). The conquest was continued by Muḥammad 'Ali's successors and bequeathed a problem with which the Egyptians and British are still grappling. In the third venture the Egyptian army and navy collaborated with the forces of the Porte against the Greeks in their struggle for independence. Maḥmūd II (1808-39), celebrated for his bold reforms and the extermination of the Janissary corps,

[1] The centennial of his death was commemorated by founding a university in Asyūṭ bearing his name.

[2] 'Umar Ṭūsūn, *al-Ba'athāt al-'Ilmīyah* (Alexandria, 1934), p. 414.

[3] Matthews and Akrawi, p. 116.

was then the ruling sultan. The Turko-Egyptian fleet was destroyed at Navarino (October 20, 1827) by a combined Anglo-French-Russian fleet. Of the seven hundred and eighty-two vessels only twenty-nine remained afloat. The Porte had promised his Egyptian viceroy the government of Syria and the Morea in consideration of his support, and when the promise was not ful-

The American Numismatic Society

COIN OF MAḤMŪD II

Gold (one-half *sikkah*, sequin), dated in the twenty-fifth year of his reign, 1247 (1831–2), struck at Miṣr (Cairo)

The American Numismatic Society

COIN OF MAḤMŪD II

Copper (five paras), dated in the thirty-first year of his reign, 1253 (1837), struck at Miṣr (Cairo)

filled, Muḥammad ʻAli commissioned his son and "mailed arm", Ibrāhīm, in 1831 to conquer Syria. Ibrāhīm had led the successful 1816 to 1818 campaigns against the Wahhābis and the unsuccessful expedition against the Greeks. This was indeed the last and greatest military enterprise of Muḥammad ʻAli's reign. After occupying Syria for ten years and coming near giving the *coup de grâce* to the entire Ottoman empire, Muḥammad ʻAli at the behest of the European powers had to withdraw his troops to Egyptian soil.[1] Those powers were determined to keep the empire intact, for their own benefit. They considered the rise of a youthful, vigorous state as something endangering their influence and lines of communication in the East. A firman issued February 13, 1841,

[1] See below, pp. 733-7.

made the pashalik of Egypt hereditary in Muḥammad 'Ali's family; [1] another of the same date invested him with the government of the Sudan.[2] The dream of an Egyptian-Asiatic empire thereby came to an inglorious ending.

Syria

The conquest of Syria by Salim I [3] (1516) resulted in no major internal changes in the administration or population of the land. The administrative divisions assumed a new name *walāyah*. That of Damascus, enlarged by the addition of Jerusalem, Ṣafad and Ghazzah, was put under Jān-Birdi al-Ghazāli, the treacherous governor of Damascus, who like Khā'ir Bey had betrayed his Mamlūk master al-Ghawri at the decisive battle of Dābiq.[4] This made al-Ghazāli virtual viceroy of Syria.[5] Not satisfied with that, he, on the death of Salīm (1520), proclaimed himself an independent sovereign under the title al-Malik al-Ashraf (most noble monarch), struck coins in his name and invited his Aleppo counterpart, Khā'ir Bey, to do likewise. But Sulaymān was quick to act. His Janissaries demolished a large part of the Syrian capital and its environs, meted out a punishment to the populace reminiscent of Tīmūr's days[6] and laid the basis for the association between Janissaries and terror which still haunts Syrian memory.

Provincial administration

Turkish pashas now followed one another in rapid succession; in the first hundred and eighty years (1517–1697) no less than a hundred and thirty-three of them in Damascus[7]—much worse

[1] Genealogical tree of the royal Egyptian family:

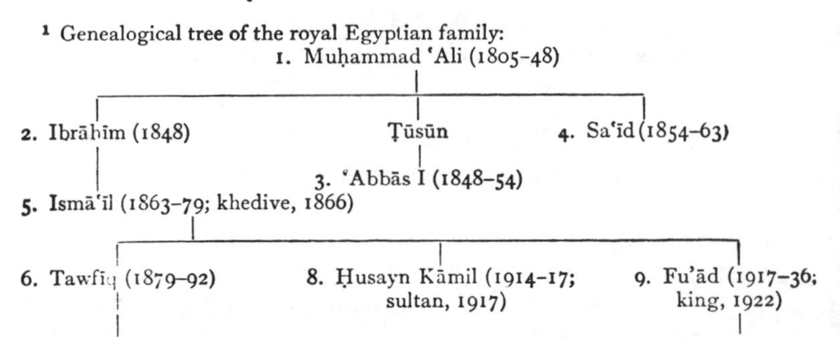

[2] For the Arabic texts consult Zaydān, *Ta'rīkh Miṣr*, vol. ii, pp. 172-5; for French translations consult Édouard Driault, *L'Égypte et l'Europe: la crise orientale de 1839–1841*, vol. iv (Rome, 1933), pp. 275-82. [3] See above, p. 703.

[4] See above, p. 703; ibn-Iyās, vol. v, pp. 156, 157; Sa'd-al-Dīn, *Tāj al-Tawārīkh*, vol. ii (Constantinople, 1280), pp. 364-5.

[5] Ottoman authorities revived the old name *Sūrīyah*; Ar. *al-Sha'm* fell into disuse; see above, pp. 57-8. [6] Ibn-Iyās, vol. v, pp. 363, 371, 376-8, 418-19.

[7] Lammens, vol. ii, p. 62.

than the Egyptian record.[1] Aleppo saw the faces of nine different wālis in the period of three years. Most of these officials had practically bought their appointments and looked upon their office as a means of replenishing their financial resources and glorifying their own selves. At times, even over its imperial officials, the Porte exercised but loose control. The subjects were rayahs,[2] flocks to be shepherded, fleeced and milked. As rayahs they were classified into those religious groups called millets[3] which made of the Syrians a congeries of small self-contained nationalities. Even Europeans residing in the land were treated as millets, subject to the laws of their own religious heads and enjoying other privileges granted by capitulations. The Venetians were the first to be granted capitulations. In 1521 Sulaymān

The American Numismatic Society

COIN OF SULAYMĀN I

Gold (*altūn*), dated 926 (1520), struck at Ḥalab (Aleppo)

signed a treaty with them set up in thirty chapters.[4] Fourteen years later the French received theirs and the English in 1580. Weak attempts at ameliorating the condition of the subjects in the empire were made by three bold reformers among the sultans, Salīm III (1789–1807), Maḥmūd II (1808–39) and ʿAbd-al-Majīd I[5] (1839–61), but the practical results were nil. No effective implementation was provided for the *tanẓīmāt*, reform regulations, which aimed at removing disabilities under which the rayahs laboured, abolishing the farming out of taxes and guaranteeing the lives, property and honour of all subjects—irrespective of creed or race—who were declared equal before the law. Equally ineffective were the Young Turks' reforms in 1908.

Economic decline

Ottoman maladministration could not be held entirely responsible for the steady decline in Syrian economy. The discovery in 1498 of the sea route from Europe to India around the Cape of

[1] See above, p. 719.
[2] From Ar. *raʿāyah*, herds.
[3] From Ar. *millah*, religion, nationality.
[4] Late Lat. *capitula*, whence "capitulation".
[5] So numbered to distinguish him from the Caliph ʿAbd-al-Majīd (1922-4).

Good Hope diverted the course of international trade from the Arab East and substituted the Portuguese for the Arabians and Syrians as the middlemen. The Arab lands were thus commercially by-passed. The discovery of the New World in 1492 shifted the centre of gravity in world affairs westward and relegated the Mediterranean, hitherto in name as well as in deed the middle sea, to a side position. That sea had to wait three and a half more centuries before it could regain its position as the great highway of international trade—thanks to the opening of the Suez Canal in 1869 by a successor of Muḥammad ʻAli, Ismāʻīl.[1] In the depopulated Palestine of the eighteenth century the revenue from pilgrims constituted the main item. By the middle of that century the once fertile, sufficiently irrigated plains between Aleppo and the Euphrates had become what they are today, a desert.[2] By the end of that century the entire population of Syria had estimatedly shrunk to about a million and a half, of whom perhaps less than a couple of hundred thousand lived in Palestine.[3] Jerusalem in the early nineteenth century had an estimated population of 12,000; in the mid-nineteenth Damascus had 150,000, Beirūt 15,000 and Aleppo 77,000.[4]

As Syrian merchants developed overland trade in the first century under Ottoman rule, Aleppo came to be the terminus of the route connecting with al-ʻIrāq and ultimately Persia and India. Several European colonies grew in Aleppo, first among which was the Venetian. The French colony capitalized on the capitulations granted Francis I by Sulaymān in 1535 and on the treaty signed in 1740 by Maḥmūd I and Louis XV, putting all Christian visitors to the Ottoman empire under French protection.[5] Soon French settlements (factories) were spread into other Syrian towns. English merchants followed the French. They all tried to meet the Western demand for Eastern luxuries and products promoted in the Crusading period. All foreigners, being considered by Moslems as inferior to them, had in the early period to wear native dress and thus reduce the chances of personal insult or harm. In the wake of European businessmen came European missionaries, teachers, travellers, explorers. The

[1] See below, p. 750.

[2] Christina P. Grant, *The Syrian Desert* (New York, 1938), p. 161, n. 1.

[3] Cf. Alfred Bonné, *The Economic Development of the Near East* (New York, 1945), p. 10.

[4] Bonné, p. 11

[5] F. Charles-Roux, *France et chrétiens d'orient* (Paris, [1939]), pp. 68-77.

Christian missionary activity, mostly Jesuit, Capuchin and Lazarist, resulted in the seventeenth and eighteenth centuries in the founding of Uniat churches—Syrian (using Syriac in the ritual) and Greek (using Greek). The enlightened and liberal régime of a Lebanese prince, Fakhr-al-Dīn al-Maʿni II (1590-1635), opened the door wide to Western cultural influences.

Fakhr-al-Dīn, enlightened amīr of Lebanon

This prince was named after his grandfather Fakhr-al-Dīn I (†1544), who, when the battle raged at Dābiq between Turk and Mamlūk for the mastery of Syria, advised his people to stay on the fence and then leap to the winning side as soon as that was determined. When Salīm emerged victorious, Fakhr-al-Dīn presented himself with his coterie of Lebanese leaders, kissed the ground before the conqueror and delivered such an impassionately eloquent oration [1] that the sultan confirmed him and his fellow-amīrs and shaykhs in their Lebanese fiefs, allowing them the same autonomous privileges enjoyed under the preceding régime and imposing on them a comparatively light tribute. The Turks realized at the outset that Lebanon with its hardy mountaineers of Druzes and Maronites was entitled to a different treatment from Syria. The Turkish wāli in Damascus normally acted as liaison between the Porte and the Lebanese feudal lords, who on the whole acted independently in internal affairs, transmitted their fiefs to their progeny, exacted taxes and duties and rendered no military service to the sultan.

Under Fakhr-al-Dīn II the power of the house of Maʿn, originally an Arab tribe, reached its apogee. The most energetic and fascinating figure in the history of Ottoman Lebanon if not of all Syria, this diminutive man, from "whose pocket should an egg fall it wouldn't break", cherished a threefold ambition: creating a greater Lebanon, severing all relations between it and the Porte and setting it on the road of progress—and he came near realizing his dream. From the Porte he received the sanjāqs of Beirūt and Sidon, from his neighbours to the north he wrested Tripoli, Baʿlabakk and al-Biqāʿ, from his neighbours to the south he received the homage of Ṣafad, Tiberias and Nazareth. He then began to look beyond the seas. In 1608 he signed with Ferdinand, the Medici grand duke of Tuscany, a treaty containing

[1] Quoted in Ḥaydar, 561; Isṭifān al-Duwayhi, *Taʾrīkh al-Ṭāʾifah al-Mārūnīyah*, ed. Rashīd K. al-Shartūni (Beirūt, 1890), p. 152; Ṭannūs al-Shidyāq, *Taʾrīkh al-Aʿyān fi Jabal Lubnān* (Beirūt, 1859), p. 251; see Hitti, *History of Syria*, pp. 665-6.

a secret military article clearly directed against the Porte.[1] A Turkish army from Damascus succeeded in chasing him out of the land, and he, with his family and suite, had to seek haven in Florence, capital of his Italian ally. After a sojourn of five years in Europe (1613–18) he returned to his hereditary domain more determined than ever to enlarge and modernize it. In 1624 the

From Giovanni Mariti, "Istoria di Faccardino grand-emir dei Drusi" (Livorno, 1787)

FAKHR-AL-DĪN AL-MAʿNI II, AMĪR OF LEBANON 1590–1635

Porte recognized him as the lord of *ʿArabistān*, from Aleppo to the frontiers of Egypt. He imported from Italy architects, engineers and agricultural experts and encouraged improved methods of tilling the soil among his farmer subjects.[2] One of his projects was draining the swampy part of al-Biqāʿ. More than that, he welcomed Christian missionaries, mainly French Catholic, who now established centres in Beirūt, Sidon, Tripoli, Aleppo, Damascus and even in Lebanese villages. Professing Islam before the

[1] For this and other treaties consult P. Paolo Carali (Qara'li), *Fakhr ad-Dīn II e la corte di Toscana* (Rome, 1936–8), vol. i, pp. 146 *seq.*; vol. ii, pp. 159 *seq.*; G. Mariti, *Istoria di Faccardino grand-emir dei Drusi* (Livorno, 1787), pp. 74 *seq.*

[2] Carali, vol. ii, pp. 52 *seq.*

Ottoman authorities, Druzism before his people, Fakhr manifested such sympathetic interest in Christianity that he was reported to have been baptized.[1] In his amīrate Druzes and Christians lived in harmony. His sympathy with Christianity turned once more the suspicious eye of the Porte towards him. Again an army from Damascus marched against him. After offering some resistance he fled to a cave in the mountain near Jazzīn, where he was discovered and led in chains to Constantinople in February 1635.[2] There he was beheaded, with his sons, who accompanied him, and his corpse was exhibited for three days in front of a mosque. The independent greater Lebanon which he envisaged and for which he laboured was attempted again by another amīr, Bashīr al-Shihābi (1788–1840), but was not fully realized until 1943. The Shihābs, who in 1697 succeeded the Ma'ns, trace their pedigree to one of the noblest Arabian tribes, the Quraysh. The founder of the Lebanese ruling family was the son-in-law of the last Ma'nid ruler.

The 'Aẓms in Syria

Syrian local governors did not begin to assert themselves until the eighteenth century. First among these was Ismā'īl Pasha al-'Aẓm, a Damascene who in 1724 was made wāli over his home town. More distinguished than Ismā'īl was his son and successor, whose palaces in Ḥamāh and Damascus are still among the show places of those cities. Other members of the 'Aẓm family were appointed over Sidon and Tripoli, but, unlike the Lebanese amīrs, remained loyal to the Porte, despite maltreatment from those quarters. Ismā'īl was jailed before his death and As'ad was treacherously killed (1757) in the bath by orders from Constantinople.[3]

Palestine has its dictators

As the Ottoman empire throughout the eighteenth century speedily declined in authority, dignity and prestige, the number of local chieftains who sought or achieved independence progressively increased. Palestine, like Lebanon and Egypt, was the scene of the activity of such men, one of the most colourful among whom was al-Shaykh Ẓāhir al-[Āl] 'Umar. A Bedouin whose father was installed by the Shihābi governor of Lebanon as shaykh over the Ṣafad district, young Ẓāhir made his political

[1] Carali, vol. ii, pp. 640 *seq.*
[2] Duwayhi, pp. 204-5; Shidyāq, pp. 330-35; Carali, vol. ii, pp. 340-56.
[3] Muḥammad Kurd-'Ali, *Khiṭaṭ al-Sha'm*, vol. ii (Damascus, 1925), pp. 289, 290-91; Ḥaydar al-Shihābi, *Ta'rīkh*, ed. Na' 'ūm Mughabghab (Cairo, 1900), p. 769.

debut about 1737 by adding Tiberais to his shaykhdom.[1] Other cities submitted to him, and by 1750 the usurper had established his seat in 'Akka. This city, which had been in partial ruin since Crusading days, was fortified and developed into an important trade centre. Its new lord ruled with an iron hand. He stamped out brigandage and lawlessness, encouraged the raising of wheat and the industry of silk and cotton and treated with toleration his Christian subjects. In the words of his biographer: [2] "Even a woman could travel around carrying gold in her hand with no fear of being molested".

Feeling secure in his dictatorial seat Ẓāhir entered into alliance with 'Ali Bey of Egypt. With the co-operation of Russian ships then manœuvring in the eastern Mediterranean, Russia at that time being embroiled in a bitter struggle with Turkey, he occupied in 1772 Sidon [3] at the foot of Lebanon. Three years later the Shihābi amīr of Lebanon allied himself with the wāli of Damascus and with a contingent from Constantinople attacked Ẓāhir in his capital. In the course of the siege Ẓāhir was killed by one of his men hired to do it. In the Syrian army that had tried to defend Sidon was a petty officer, named Aḥmad al-Jazzār, who then succeeded Ẓāhir and played an even more dramatic rôle.

Originally a Christian from Bosnia, the boy, later to be called Aḥmad, committed a sex crime, fled to Constantinople, sold himself to a Jewish slave dealer and landed in the possession of 'Ali Bey in Cairo. The distinguished service he rendered as executioner to his master earned him the epithet *al-jazzār*, the butcher. From Egypt al-Jazzār fled to Syria and, in recognition of his performance in Sidon against Ẓāhir, was made governor of the city.[4] Gradually he extended his authority northward into Lebanon and southward into Palestine, where he succeeded Ẓāhir in 'Akka. Here he surrounded himself with a cavalry corps of Bosnians and Albanians and an infantry corps of Maghribis, fortified the city by forced labour and constructed a small fleet in its harbour. In 1780 the Porte deemed it expedient to bestow on its vassal the wilāyah of Damascus, making him virtually the viceroy of Syria

[1] Volney, *Voyage en Syrie et en Égypte*, 2nd ed. (Paris, 1787), vol. ii, p. 85; Shidyāq, p. 360; Ḥaydar, p. 801; Mikhā'īl N. al-Ṣabbāgh (al-'Akkāwi), *Ta'rīkh al-Shaykh Ẓāhir al-'Umar al-Zaydāni*, ed. Qusṭanṭīn al-Bāsha (Ḥarīṣa), pp. 31-3.

[2] Ṣabbāgh, p. 50.

[3] Ṣabbāgh, p. 115; Shidyāq, p. 389.

[4] Ḥaydar, pp. 811, 827.

and the arbiter of Lebanon. Though acknowledging the nominal authority of the Porte, he put Sultan Salīm III's messenger to death with impunity. It was this Aḥmad Pasha al-Jazzār who, with the aid of an English fleet under Sir Sidney Smith, successfully withstood and repelled Napoleon's onslaught on 'Akka.[1] A usurper and dictator, al-Jazzār was ruthless in the treatment of enemies and suspects. He had a reputation to uphold associated with his name and uphold it he did. A native chronicler [2] reports how al-Jazzār on one occasion had all thirty-seven of his harem, on a suspicion of infidelity on the part of certain ones among them, dragged to a burning pyre by his eunuchs. His name still lives throughout the land as a synonym of terror and cruelty. In 1804 a career unmarred by failure or defeat came to an end through natural death—an unusual phenomenon.

Bashīr al-Shihābi

The lord of Lebanon in the days of al-Jazzār was the Amīr Bashīr II (1788–1840), who on the occasion of Napoleon's invasion had failed to rush aid to the lord of 'Akka and had thereby incurred his disfavour. Bashīr had then to withdraw to Cyprus on a British ship. In 1821 he fled to Egypt, after having reattached al-Biqā' to Lebanon and got involved in disputes with the wālis of Damascus and Tripoli. While in Egypt he struck up a friendship with its viceroy Muḥammad 'Ali. When Egyptian troops in 1831 under Ibrāhīm invaded Syria,[3] they found in Bashīr and his men a ready ally. Lebanese assisted Egyptian troops in storming 'Akka, which Ibrāhīm besieged after occupying Jaffa and Jerusalem. Druzes stood before the walls of Damascus, when it surrendered. With the routing of the Turkish army at Ḥimṣ, the way was open to Asia Minor. The pass in the Taurus had to be in places widened to enable the Egyptian artillery to go through. With the victory at Konieh (Qūniyah, 1832) the road was clear to Constantinople. The Egyptian camp was at last pitched at Kutahiah (Kūtāhiyah), almost within sight of the Bosphorus. This aroused Russia. Suspicious of her, England as well as France, the latter of which had up to this time encouraged Muḥammad 'Ali in his expansive ambitions, were forced to act—all in behalf of the sultan. Thus was the Egyptian ambition frustrated.

[1] See above, p. 722.

[2] Mīkhā'īl Mushāqah, *Mashhad al-'Ayān bi-Ḥawādith Sūrīya wa-Lubnān*, ed. Mulḥim K. 'Abduh and Andarāwus H. Shakhāshīri (Cairo, 1908), p. 54.

[3] See above, p. 725.

Ibrāhīm first wooed the favour of his Syrian subjects, especially the Christians among them, by establishing security and justice and introducing social reforms. Hitherto no Christian in such a city as Damascus could appear in public riding on a horse or wearing a white, red or green turban. No Christian could hold a responsible position in government. All these disabilities were now removed. But later, acting on instructions from his father, Ibrāhīm raised the taxes to about three times of what they had been, established a state monopoly over silk and other native products—following the Egyptian precedent [1]—and worst of all insisted on disarmament and conscription. Nothing could have outraged the Syrians, particularly the Lebanese, more than that last measure. The uprising which started in Palestine in 1834 spread into all other parts of Syria. In the manifesto issued June 8, 1840, the Lebanese rebels listed disarmament and conscription first among their grievances.[2] Lebanon was at that time accorded a privileged treatment under its friendly amīr. From its forests Muḥammad ʿAli hoped to rebuild his navy, almost annihilated at Navarino.[3] Traces of Egyptian exploitation of coal at Qarnāyil and iron at Marjaba, in the district of al-Matn, are still noticeable. Tempted by these uprisings Sultan Maḥmūd dared again in 1839 to send an army which was crushed at Nizzīb (Nezib, north Syria), putting the empire once more at the feet of its vassal. But again the powers intervened and forced Muḥammad ʿAli on November 22, 1840, to evacuate Syria. Ibrāhīm started on his way back from Damascus December 29 via Ghazzah. Bashīr was carried on a British ship to Malta.[4] On the international level the Syro-Egyptian episode resulted in strengthening British interest in the East at French expense.

Autonomy of Lebanon internationally recognized

The Ottoman authorities were now convinced that the only way to bring Lebanon under their direct control was to stir up strife between Maronites and Druzes, among whom the general

[1] See above, p. 722. The first modern silk factory was established in a Lebanese village, Batātir, by a Frenchman in 1841.

[2] Asad J. Rustum, *al-Uṣūl al-ʿArabīyah li-Taʾrīkh Sūrīyah fi ʿAhd Muḥammad ʿAli*, vol. ii (Beirūt, 1933), pp. 101-3; do., *The Royal Archives of Egypt and the Disturbances in Palestine 1934* (Beirūt, 1938), pp. 47-51; Sulaymān abu-ʿIzz-al-Dīn, *Ibrāhīm Bāsha fi Sūrīya* (Beirūt, 1929), pp. 313 *seq.*

[3] Asad J. Rustum, *The Royal Archives of Egypt and the Origins of the Egyptian Expedition to Syria* (Beirūt, 1936), pp. 63-6. See above, p. 725.

[4] Shidyāq, p. 620; Mushāqah, pp. 132-4; al-Jamʿīyah al-Malakīyah al-Jughrāfīyah, *Dhitra al-Baṭal al-Fātiḥ Ibrāhīm Bāsha* (Cairo, 1948), pp. 372 *seq.*

alignment under Bashīr as under Fakhr-al-Dīn had followed party rather than sectarian lines; Lebanon's intermittent intestine warfare has up till now been feudal rather than religious. The Turks were no novices in the application of the maxim—old as Rome—of "divide and rule". Then this was the time in which they were launching a new policy, that of centralization, in the control of the provinces. The masses among both Christians and Druzes—particularly Christians—were in a state of unrest, cherishing discontent toward their feudal aristocracy. North Lebanese peasants, urged by their Maronite clergy, rose in 1858 against their local lords and planned to divide up their large estates among themselves. Bashīr, one of the strongest governors Lebanon ever had, had maintained high standards of public safety and equity, opened new roads and encouraged Western cultural and educational influences, but his namesake and successor was of different stuff.[1]

Civil disturbances between Druzes and Maronites, which under Turkish stimulation began in 1841, culminated in the massacre of 1860, a year which will remain infamous for all time in the annals of the land. 'Abd-al-Majīd I was then sultan. In

The American Numismatic Society

COIN OF 'ABD-AL-MAJĪD I

Silver (10 *ghurūsh*, piastres), dated 1255 (1839), struck at Miṣr (Cairo)

this massacre eleven thousand Christians, mostly Maronites, are estimated to have perished and a hundred and fifty villages burned. Lebanese peasants still date local events in their history from this *sanat al-ḥarakah* (the year of the strife).[2] The massacre

[1] Following the Egyptian example, Bashīr I and his sons doffed the turbans in favour of the Maghribi fez (*ṭarbūsh*), short with thick tassel, still worn by some of the old generation in Lebanon and Syria. Cf. Ḥaydar, pp. 1035-6.

[2] See Hitti, *History of Syria*, pp. 694-5.

invited European intervention and the occupation of Lebanon by French troops. Consequently the mountain received in 1861 a statute, revised three years later, in which it was allowed an autonomy under a Christian governor-general (*mutaṣarrif*) appointed, for a renewable term of five years, with the approval of the signatory powers. All the governors were Catholics. The new Mutaṣarrifīyat Jabal Lubnān, had no Turkish garrison, paid no tribute to Constantinople and its citizens rendered no military service. The name of its first mutaṣarrif, Dāwūd Pasha (1861–8), has been borne by a college for boys in ʿAbayh, founded in 1862 and supported as a Druze institution from the waqf.

Under its mutaṣarrif and its elected administrative council Lebanon prospered as no other neighbouring province prospered; it was regarded as "the most useful example of autonomy applied to a Turkish province".[1] In it "public security and standards of social and political life advanced to a point not nearly reached by any other province of the Ottoman Empire".[2] The increase in its population found an outlet through emigration to Egypt, the Americas and Australia, where descendants of Lebanese colonists still flourish. Lebanon's autonomy continued until the first World War, when it was destroyed by the Turks. To autonomous Lebanon, Western teachers, preachers, physicians and merchants were drawn as to no other land of the Near East. The fact that its population was preponderantly Christian rendered it more hospitable to European and American ideas and practices. More than in the days of Bashīr and Fakhr it became the window through which the Arab quadrangle looked westward into the outside world.

Al-ʿIrāq

The Ottoman career of the valley of the Euphrates, which began in 1534, paralleled that of the valley of the Nile. Turkish pashas and local lords and Mamlūks struggled for ascendancy, while the masses suffered from corruption, insecurity and miscarriage of justice. Here as elsewhere the authority of the provincial governors began to weaken at the end of the sixteenth century, after the brief noontide of the empire had passed. The historical theme revolved on personalities and intrigues in Baghdād, the most important of the three walāyahs into which

[1] William Miller, *The Ottoman Empire, 1801–1927* (Cambridge, 1936), p. 306.

[2] *Syria and Palestine* (handbook under the direction of the historical section of the Foreign Office) (London, 1920), p. 37.

the country was divided, the other two being al-Baṣrah and al-Mawṣil (Mosul). The land of ancient renown under Hammurabi and Nebuchadnezzar and of medieval splendour under Hārūn and al-Ma'mūn faded under the Ottomans to a degree of unprecedented and perhaps unparalleled obscurity.

The distinctive features of the 'Irāqi situation stemmed from the preponderance of the Shī'ite element in its population, difficulty of communication with headquarters in Constantinople, proximity to Shī'ite Persia and cleavage between town and tribe. Now, as in Byzantine days, the possession of the country was disputed between Constantinople and Persia. As the seat of the holiest shrines of the Shī'ah—those of al-Ḥusayn in Karbalā', of 'Ali in al-Najaf and of the seventh and ninth imāms in al-Kāẓimayn—al-'Irāq was a stronghold of Shī'ism, many of whose adherents looked upon Sunnite caliphs, like the Ottoman sultans, as usurpers. Meanwhile they considered the Persians as friends and allies. The Shī'ah cause constituted a strong bond between al-'Irāq and Persia. Throughout the sixteenth century Turkey and Persia were in a state of passive if not active hostility. In 1508 Shāh Ismā'īl occupied and held Baghdād till after Salīm's victory.[1] In November 1623 Shāh 'Abbās occupied Baghdād again, thanks to the betrayal by a Janissary rebel. For fifteen years al-'Irāq remained a province of the Ṣafawid kingdom. Turkish interest, aside from tribute, centred in the use of the country as a base against the eastern shores of the Arabian peninsula, which, however, the Turks were never able to hold firmly. The Turko-Persian wars adversely affected the economy of the land and interfered with pilgrimage to the Shī'ite shrines—an important source of national income. The rise of the English East India Company in the early seventeenth century placed al-'Irāq in a strategic position on the overland route between East and West. By the end of that century the British had won the race for maritime trade supremacy over their Portuguese and Dutch rivals in the Persian Gulf. The discovery of oil in 'Irāqi soil enhanced the strategic importance of the country. The oil concession was obtained by the 'Irāq Petroleum Company in 1925 for a period of seventy-five years.

Bedouins by their raids, undiscipline and lawlessness were a perennial source of trouble. Turkish communications between

[1] See above, p. 703.

the federal capital and the provincial capital lay at the mercy of wanderers from the desert and tribesmen from the hills. About the mid-eighteenth century several Bedouin tribes of the lower Euphrates who had banded themselves into a federation, al-Muntafiq, brought recurring headaches not only to the pashas of Baghdād but also to the local Mamlūks and townspeople.

The Mamlūks, whose government was one of autonomous vassalage rather than viceroyalty, were mostly imported Circassian (Cherkes) slaves, the first of whom, Sulaymān Agha [1] (later Pasha) abu-Layla, rose to power in 1747. The last Mamlūk was Dāwūd (†1830), who was enlightened enough to build schools in Baghdād. For over eighty years the land was in the grip of a Mamlūk oligarchy. After the Crimean War (1853–6) Constantinople endeavoured to assert its authority more pronouncedly and planted a strong garrison in Baghdād. It sent in 1869 one of its most progressive and liberal statesmen, Midḥat Pasha, as wāli. Midḥat tried to check lawlessness, settle the Bedouins as peasants, improve irrigation and introduce a system of land registration. So honest was this Turkish official that he had reportedly to sell his watch to meet his travelling expenses back to Constantinople.[2] His brief administration stands out as the only bright spot in an otherwise dark picture. He won further laurels by writing the first constitution of his land,[3] abolished in 1877 by ʿAbd-al-Ḥamīd.

Arabia

The Arabian peninsula stands as a block by itself, distinct from the North African and the Egyptian-Fertile Crescent blocks. As the cradle of Islam, Arabia has a halo of sacredness around it and holds a unique place in the hearts and minds of believers throughout the world. Its sacred association, geographic isolation and underdeveloped communications stamped it with a medieval feature which it still maintains. Especially isolated and insulated against Western ideas and influences have been al-Ḥijāz and al-Yaman, the most self-contained parts of the Near East.

Though it never formed an integral part of the scene of the activity of the Prophet, al-Yaman, nevertheless, has been equally as self-contained as al-Ḥijāz, if not more. Its people are followers of Zayd, grandson of al-Ḥusayn, who was killed about 740 in an

[1] Originally a Turki word meaning elder brother. *agha* was used by Ottoman Turks first for *master, lord*, and later as a title for any army officer up to the grade of captain.

[2] Stephen H. Longrigg, *Four Centuries of Modern Iraq* (Oxford, 1925), p. 300.

[3] See Hitti, *History of Syria*, p. 670

uprising against the Umayyads. Though an offshoot of the Shīʻah the Zaydis (Zuyūd) do not emphasize Shīʻite tenets and come close to being Sunnites. One of them, Qāsim by name, succeeded in 1633 in expelling the Turkish wāli and establishing a native imāmate which endured with many vicissitudes till 1871. Beginning with 1849, however, the country was again administered as a Turkish walāyah until the rise of the Imām Yaḥya in 1904. In the following year the imām occupied Ṣanʻā', later to become his capital, but the autonomy of his state was not recognized by the Porte until 1911. In fact the Turks did not entirely withdraw from the country until the last year of the first World War. Yaḥya fell victim to a palace conspiracy in February 1948. A recent visitor to al-Yaman, himself a Moslem from Damascus and accompanied by a special guard from the imām, came near being attacked by natives at Ma'rib simply because he looked *gharīb*, foreign.[1] A Lebanese American writer, Ameen Rihani, met in the early 1920s theologians in al-Yaman who would put dark glasses on their eyes to avert defilement by the sight of a Christian.

Aside from the fully independent Suʻūdi Arabia and al-Yaman, the peninsula prior to 1960 consisted politically of the Aden colony and Aden protectorate, the sultanate of Masqaṭ (Muscat) and ʻUmān, the trucial shaykhdoms, and the autonomous shaykhdoms of Qaṭar and al-Baḥrayn, all dependent in varying degrees on Great Britain, and under her protection. Another Persian Gulf shaykhdom, al-Kuwayt, was declared by the British autonomous in 1914 and an independent amirate in 1961. This oil-rich country is perhaps the most affluent in the world in per capita income terms. ʻUmān and the south-eastern coast of Arabia came early under Portuguese, and later British, influence and, unlike al-Ḥijāz, Najd and al-Yaman, were never brought under Turkish control.[2] For nearly a century and a half its sultanate, nominally independent with its seat at Masqaṭ, had maintained close ties with the British government, ties that were reaffirmed in a treaty signed as late as 1939. From the south-eastern end of the peninsula of Qaṭar to a distance of three hundred and sixty miles south-eastward, the coast of the Gulf, formerly known as the Pirate Coast, belongs to the trucial shaykhs. After a period of hostility with the East India Company

[1] Nazīh M. al-ʻAẓm, *Riḥlah fi Bilād al-ʻArab al-Saʻīdah* (Cairo, 1937?), p. 20.
[2] Royal Institute of International Affairs, *The Middle East* (London, 1950), pp. 110-13. Cf. above, pp. 710-11.

these shaykhs signed (1820) with the British government a general treaty prescribing peace and abstention from piracy and slave trade. Qaṭar's relation to the British government was similar to that of the shaykhdoms to its south and was regulated by a treaty signed in 1916. Al-Baḥrayn's status is practically the same. To the island's world-famous but declining pearl-fishing industry was added in 1932 a much more remunerative industry —that of oil.

In 1968 the British government announced plans to withdraw in three years all military forces in the Persian Gulf. Representatives of al-Baḥrayn, Qaṭar and the seven trucial states then began planning the creation of a federation of Arabian amirates.

The Aden (ʿAdan) protectorate extended eastward from the Aden colony and included Laḥaj, Ḥaḍramawt, Mahrah and Suquṭra (Socotra). Until the mid-eighteenth century the region was under the imām of Ṣanʿā'. Aden, the seaport-fortress and capital, was acquired in 1839. In 1967 the entire area became independent and formed the Republic of Southern Yaman.

Wahhābis The modern history of Arabia does not begin till the rise of the Muwaḥḥidūn (unitarians) in the mid-eighteenth century. This was a puritan revival inaugurated by a Najdi from al-ʿUyaynah named Muḥammad ibn-ʿAbd-al-Wahhāb (†1792). After travelling in al-Ḥijāz, al-ʿIrāq and Syria, ibn-ʿAbd-al-Wahhāb returned home impressed with the idea that Islam, as practised by his contemporaries, had deviated widely from the orthodox practice and theory as prescribed by the Prophet and the Koran, and he himself determined to purge it and restore it to its primitive strictness. His inspiration he obviously drew from ibn-Ḥanbal as interpreted by ibn-Taymīyah.[1] The new prophet found in Muḥammad ibn-Suʿūd (†1765), who was then a petty chief in Central Arabia, an ally and son-in-law. This was another case of marriage between religion and the sword, resulting in the speedy spread of religion and of the authority of ibn-Suʿūd throughout Central and Eastern Arabia. The followers of ibn-ʿAbd-al-Wahhāb were called Wahhābis by their opponents. In their zeal to rid Islam of its cult of saints and other innovations (sing. *bidʿah*) they sacked Karbalā' in 1801, captured Makkah in 1803 and al-Madīnah the following year, destroyed venerated tombs and purged these cities of all

[1] See above, p. 689.

that savoured of idolatry.[1] In the following year they invaded Syria and al-ʿIrāq and extended their domain from Palmyra to ʿUmān, the largest in the peninsula since the Prophet's days. Their success was interpreted as a token of displeasure on the part of God with the innovations of Salīm III.[2] Alarmed, the Porte requested Muḥammad ʿAli to conduct the series of campaigns which ended in 1818 with the destruction of the Wahhābi power and the razing of their capital al-Dirʿīyah to the ground.[3] Wahhābi tenets, however, continued to spread, and their influence was felt from Sumatra in the east to Nigeria in the west.

Ibn-Suʿūd

Except for a short period of restoration beginning in 1833, the movement remained in a state of eclipse until resuscitated by its present head ʿAbd-al-ʿAzīz ibn-Suʿūd, the restorer of the Wahhābi state and Wahhābi dynasty. Starting his career as an exile in al-Kuwayt, ʿAbd-al-ʿAzīz in the first quarter of the twentieth century carved for himself a kingdom, at the expense of the ibn-Rashīd family in Ḥā'il and the Sharīf Ḥusayn family in Makkah, extending from the Persian Gulf to the Red Sea. Ḥusayn had, at the instigation of the British, declared himself "king of the Arabs" in 1916, and in 1924 he assumed the title of "caliph of the Moslems".[4] ʿAbd-al-ʿAzīz put an end to the Rashīd dynasty in 1921, occupied Makkah in 1924, al-Madīnah and Juddah in 1925, and in 1932 created the Suʿūdi Arabian kingdom with himself at its head.[5] Ibn-Suʿūd declared tribal raids illegal, regulated fees for the transport of pilgrims, established a high standard of public safety, introduced the radio, wireless telegraphy, telephone and motor-car to certain localities and tried, but not very successfully, to establish his nomadic subjects as *Ikhwān* (brethren) in agricultural settlements.[6] More than the holy pilgrimage, the Arabian American Oil Company, which received its first concession in 1933, has become the greatest source of income to both government and people. Its contribution to the modernization of Arabia is still progressing.

Intellectual activity

No intellectual work of high order could be expected under the

[1] ʿUthmān ibn-Bishr, *ʿUnwān al-Majd fi Ta'rīkh Najd* (Makkah, 1349), vol. i, pp. 121-3; Musil, *Northern Neǧd*, pp. 261-7.

[2] See above, p. 727.

[3] See above, p. 727; ibn-Bishr, vol. i, pp. 155-207.

[4] For his uprising against the Turks, see Amīn Saʿīd, *al-Thawrah al-ʿArabīyah al-Kubra*, vol. i (Cairo, 193–?), pp. 120 *seq.*

[5] For details, consult H. St. J. B. Philby, *Arabia* (London, 1930), pp. 160 *seq.*

[6] K. S. Twitchell, *Saudi Arabia* (Princeton, 1947), pp. 121 *seq.*

political and concomitant social and economic conditions that prevailed in Arab states under Ottoman rule. But the source of evil went deeper. The Islamic creative spark had faded away centuries before the advent of the Turks.[1] The complete victory of scholastic theology beginning with the thirteenth century, the ascendancy of the orthodox and the mystics in the spiritual realm, the decay of the scientific spirit and the prevalence of uncritical reverence for the past and adherence to tradition militated against scholarly investigation and productivity. The fetters which bound Arab intellect did not begin to loosen until the early nineteenth century under the impact of the West.[2]

The writers of the period were by and large commentators, compilers and abridgers. Literary formalism and intellectual rigidity characterized their works. Among the Arabic-writing Turks the name of Ḥājji Khalfah († 1657) stands supreme. Called by the Turks Kātib Chelebi (young scribe), this Constantinopolitan started his career as a military clerk in the army operating in Baghdād and Damascus. His *Kashf al-Ẓunūn ʿan al-Asāmi w-al-Funūn* [3] (removing of doubts relating to titles and sciences) is one of the greatest and most valuable bibliographic and encyclopædic treatises in the Arabic language

The literary activity in Egypt was exemplified in ʿAbd-al-Wahhāb al-Shaʿrāni († 1565), a mystic whose works embraced not only Sufism but also koranic and linguistic sciences. Al-Shaʿrāni conversed with angels and prophets,[4] was tried for impiety by conservative theologians and left a long list of works,[5] some of which became popular despite their lack of originality. In his *al-Ṭabaqāt al-Kubra* [6] (the great classes) the lives of the most famous mystics are sketched.[7] Egypt was the scene of the scholarly activity of a noted lexicographer, al-Sayyid Murtaḍa al-Zabīdi, who was born in 1732 in north-west India. While pensioned by the government, al-Zabīdi produced in Cairo a voluminous commentary on al-Fīrūzābādi's monumental *al-*

[1] See above, p. 683. [2] See below, pp. 745 *seq.*

[3] Ed. and tr. Gustav Flügel, 7 vols. (Leipzig and London, 1835–58).

[4] *Al-Anwār al-Qudsīyah fi Bayān Ādāb al-ʿUbūdīyah*, on margin of his *al-Ṭabaqāt al-Kubra* (Cairo, 1935), vol. i, pp. 2 *seq.*

[5] For this, consult Brockelmann, *Geschichte*, vol. ii, pp. 336-8.

[6] 2 vols. (Cairo, 1925).

[7] For Sufism as the dominant feature of Islam in Ottoman Egypt consult Tawfīq al-Ṭawīl, *al-Taṣawwuf fi Miṣr ibbān al-ʿAṣr al-ʿUthmāni* (Cairo, 1946), pp. 6-51, 200-232.

Qāmūs[1] entitled *Tāj al-'Arūs* (the bride's tiara).[2] He also wrote a massive commentary on al-Ghazzāli's *Iḥyā'*. Al-Zabīdi was a victim of the plague of 1791. Of the Egyptian chroniclers used in the composition of this chapter the most important is 'Abd-al-Raḥmān ibn-Ḥasan al-Jabarti († 1822), whose ancestors had come to Cairo from Jabart in Abyssinia. Al-Jabarti held the chair of astronomy in al-Azhar and was appointed by Napoleon member of the grand council (*dīwān*), through which the French invader hoped to rule the country. That al-Jabarti was murdered on his way home on orders from Muḥammad 'Ali, of whom the historian was critical, has no basis in fact. His *'Ajā'ib al-Āthār fi al-Tarājim w-al-Akhbār*[3] (the marvels of relics concerning biographies and news) is partly a chronicle and partly a necrology.

Of the Lebanese chroniclers cited in this chapter three were Maronites. Iṣṭifān al-Duwayhi[4] († 1704) was educated in the seminary established by Pope Gregory XIII in 1584 in Rome for training Maronite students for clerical careers. Al-Duwayhi rose to the highest office in his church, the patriarchate. Al-Amīr Ḥaydar[5] († 1835) was a member of the aristocratic Shihāb family, which provided Lebanon with many of its feudal governors. Ṭannūs al-Shidyāq[6] († 1859) was born near Beirūt and held a judgeship under the Shihābi amīrs. But the most distinguished Maronite—in fact, Lebanese—scholar of the age was undoubtedly Yūsuf Sim'ān al-Sim'āni (Assemani, 1687–1768), another product of the seminary in Rome. It was mainly through the efforts of this erudite Lebanese that Oriental studies, especially as they relate to Christian sects, were somewhat popularized in the West. His work at the Vatican Library resulted in the addition of a large number of Oriental manuscripts to the collection now considered one of the richest in the world. Al-Sam'āni's masterpiece *Bibliotheca Orientalis*[7] embodies his researches on these manuscripts in Syriac, Arabic, Hebrew, Persian, Turkish, Ethiopic and Armenian, and is still a major source of information on the churches of the East.

[1] Originally meaning ocean, this word has become synonymous with dictionary.
[2] 10 vols., Cairo, 1307.
[3] The edition used here is in 4 vols. (Cairo, 1322).
[4] *Ta'rīkh al-Ṭā'ifah al-Mārūnīyah*, ed. Rashīd K. al-Shārtūni (Beirūt, 1890).
[5] *Ta'rīkh*, ed. Na' 'ūm Mughabghab (Cairo, 1900).
[6] *Akhbār al-A'yān fi Jabal Lubnān* (Beirūt, 1859).
[7] 4 vols. (Rome, 1719-28).

In Syria two authors may be considered as typifying the literary spirit of the age, al-Muḥibbi and al-Nābulusi. Both were Damascenes and wrote prolifically. Muḥammad al-Muḥibbi († 1699) received his education at Constantinople and was for a time assistant judge in Makkah and professor in his native city. His principal work [1] is a collection of twelve hundred and ninety biographies of celebrities who died in the eleventh Moslem century (1591–1688). 'Abd-al-Ghani al-Nābulusi († 1731), whose family, as the name indicates, was originally Palestinian, was a Sufi and traveller. He produced a large number of works, most of which remain unpublished.[2] Mysticism lay at the centre of his interest, but his travel reports, though emphasizing holy shrines and legends connected with them, constitute his main contribution to knowledge.

[1] *Khulāṣat al-Athar fi A'yān al-Qarn al-Ḥādi-'Ashar*, 4 vols. (Cairo, 1284).
[2] One of his last works to be published deals with tradition, *Dhakhā'ir al-Mawārīth fi al-Dalālah 'ala Mawāḍi' al-Ḥadīth*, 4 vols. (Cairo, 1934).

CHAPTER LII

THE CHANGING SCENE: IMPACT OF THE WEST

NAPOLEON'S descent on Egypt was epoch making in more than one way. It marked the beginning of the break with the past Along with his other equipment the French invader brought to Cairo an Arabic press which he had plundered from the Vatican. This press was the first of its kind in the valley of the Nile. It developed into the renowned Maṭba'at Būlāq, still the official printing institution of the government. The French conqueror used it for issuing a propaganda sheet in Arabic. He moreover inaugurated a sort of *académie littéraire* with a library. Until that time the people of the Arab world were generally leading a self-contained, traditional, conventional life, achieving no progress and unmindful of the progress of the world outside. Change did not interest them. This abrupt contact with the West gave them the first knock that helped to awaken them from their medieval slumber. It kindled the intellectual spark that was to set a corner of the Moslem world on fire.

Cultural penetration: Egypt

Recognizing the possibilities of this preliminary cultural contact, Muḥammad 'Ali started the process of inviting French and other European officers to train his army. He went beyond that and sent student missions to be trained in Europe.[1] In this he followed the precedent established by the Ottoman Turks. In both cases the point of departure was the military. But language, a prerequisite for military training, once acquired, holds the key for unlocking an entire treasure house of thought—in this case Western thought with its nationalistic, democratic, scientific, secular and other explosive ideas. The founder of modern Egypt proceeded to establish on the soil of his own land schools not only for military science but for medicine, pharmacy, engineering and agriculture. Unfortunately, however, of the multitude of educational institutions then founded by Muḥammad 'Ali only a few survived his death. His grandson 'Abbās (1848–54) dismissed

[1] See above, pp. 723-4.

all foreign advisers and abolished all foreign schools as well as most other institutions of European character; his successor Saʿīd (1854–63) was equally opposed to Western ways. Nor did many of the institutions founded by Ismāʿīl (1863–79) live long. Ismāʿīl, who employed American officers in his military academy, was the first to establish schools for girls in Egypt. His sympathetic attitude toward the West found expression in the alleged declaration that Egypt was part and parcel of Europe. These schools were not adequately equipped or effectively implemented, had no special endowments, no continuous supply of trained scholars from whom to choose the staff, and could count on no uninterrupted output of text-books in Arabic, the language of instruction. One institution, however, founded by Ismāʿīl achieved permanency, the national library, which he started with a few books from palaces and mosques and now contains half a million volumes. The Royal Geographical Society of Egypt, also founded by him, celebrated its seventy-fifth anniversary in 1950 to 1951.

During Ismāʿīl's reign an American college was founded at Asyūṭ (1865) and is still in operation. The American College for Girls at Cairo began as a primary school in 1861. Seven years earlier the American United Presbyterian Mission had launched its work in Egypt.

Syria and Lebanon

The decade of Egyptian occupation of Syria (1831–40)[1] was epoch making in the cultural history of that land. Ibrāhīm undermined the powers of local lords (sing. *muqāṭiʿji*), enforced regular taxation, and compelled recognition of the rights of non-Moslems to hold office in the local government.[2] Unlike earlier proclamations by sultans,[3] his proclamation in 1839 of equality before the law of members of all religious denominations was immediately implemented and put into effect. Against the Moslems of Damascus and Ṣafad who objected to the changed status of their dhimmi fellow-citizens, he did not hesitate to use force. Four years before the issuance of his proclamation the British consul had to be closely guarded as he entered Damascus riding; the year following the issuance he could go where he pleased unattended.[4]

The evidence of a new liberal policy and of public security attracted Europeans as never before. The Jesuits, whose order had been suspended by the pope in 1773, returned in force.[5]

[1] See above, p. 725. [2] See above, p. 734. [3] See above, p. 727.
[4] *Syria and Palestine*, p. 27. [5] Cf. above, pp. 730-31.

Protestant missionaries—British and American—established a firm foothold on Lebanese soil. In 1838 the native Protestant Church of Syria was founded. In the same year an American archaeologist, Edward Robinson, made an exploratory tour of Palestine, the first in a chain of events that ultimately resulted in unearthing, interpreting and publicizing the region's priceless treasures of the past. Three years before that the American mission press was moved from Malta to Beirūt. The Imprimerie Catholique of the Jesuits was founded in 1853 on the other side of the town. These two are still the outstanding Arabic presses of Western Asia. Translations of the Bible into modern Arabic were issued by both establishments. Syria had its first Arabic press before this time, in 1702 at Aleppo, to which it was introduced by Christians. Moslem conservatism as it relates to the treatment of the word of God may have retarded the admission of the printing industry; even today the Koran may be handwritten or lithographed but not printed. The origin of the Aleppine press, the first of its kind in the East, is still shrouded in mystery. Very likely it stemmed from some European antecedent. The earliest Arabic press in Europe made its appearance in Fano, Italy, evidently under papal aegis. From its output there has survived a book of prayer dated 1514. Lebanon had, in one of its monasteries, Qazḥayya, a Syriac press which may have been introduced from Rome by one of those Maronite scholars who studied there.[1] From this press we have copies of the Psalms not only in the Syriac language but also in Arabic printed in Syriac characters.[2] Syriac, it should be remembered, was still spoken in North Lebanon as late as the end of the seventeenth century.[3]

American educational enterprise crowned its efforts in 1866 by the establishment of the Syrian Protestant College, now the American University of Beirūt. Jesuit educational activity, which had its start in the early seventeenth century,[4] culminated in the founding in 1881 of the Université Saint-Joseph in Beirūt. These two universities have maintained their educational leadership in that part of the world.

Earlier than the American University came the American

[1] See above, p. 743.

[2] *Garshūni*; see Hitti, *History of Syria*, p. 546. Consult Louis Cheikho, "Ta'rīkh Fann al-Ṭibā'ah fi al-Mashriq", *al-Mashriq*, vol. iii (1900), pp. 251-7, 355-62.

[3] Cf. d'Arvieux, *Mémoires* (Paris, 1735), vol. ii, p. 407; above, p. 361.

[4] See above, p. 730.

School for Girls in Beirūt (1830), which has continued to the present day. The Lazarist mission, inaugurated in Damascus as early as 1755, started about two decades later a school for boys, the oldest modern school still in existence in that city. These schools preceded any modernized government schools and served as models for later institutions, whether public or private. Until the present day the study of foreign languages is emphasized, even in native schools, and either French or English is often the medium of instruction on the higher and professional levels. The personnel enjoyed special privileges, including protection by virtue of the capitulations

Native schools, presses, newspapers, magazines and literary societies, following Western patterns, soon began to make their appearance Egypt witnessed its first Arabic paper in 1828, when Muḥammad 'Ali founded *al-Waqā'i' al-Miṣrīyah* (Egyptian events), still the official organ of the government. Syria had its first newspaper in 1858, when Khalīl al-Khūri founded in Beirūt *Ḥadīqat al-Akhbār* (orchard of news). Twelve years later Buṭrus al-Bustāni (1819–83), who headed a native school and collaborated with American missionaries, started in Beirūt a political, scientific and literary fortnightly, *al-Jinān* (gardens), one of many periodicals founded by him. The motto he chose for his new publication, "Patriotism is an article of faith", gave the formula a new meaning in the Arabic language. In 1876 al-Bustāni began publication of an Arabic encyclopaedia (*Dā'irat al-Ma'ārif*) of which he himself completed the first six volumes.[1] The writings of this Christian scholar, which also included a dictionary and several text-books in mathematics and grammar, prepared the way for arousing national consciousness and starting the Arab national movement Lebanon has achieved the highest rate of literacy among Arab states largely through the efforts of foreign and private institutions of learning rather than through publicly supported schools.[2] Even today the highest type of education is conducted in American and French institutions. Lebanon as well as other Arab lands proved hospitable to this cultural migration from the West chiefly because their two civilizations, while differing in certain important respects, still

[1] For more on him consult Jurji Zaydān, *Tarājim Mashāhīr al-Sharq fi al-Qarn al-Tāsi'-'Ashar* (Cairo, 1903), vol. ii, pp. 24-31.

[2] Matthews and Akrawi, p. 407.

belong to the same main stream. Both European and Near Eastern civilizations share in a common heritage of Judaeo-Christian and Greco-Roman traditions. Social and commercial contacts were maintained, with varying degrees of closeness, from the earliest of days. In fact, up to the fourteenth century, the early Mamlūk era, distinction between East and West was more artificial than real. It was not until the sixteenth century, the dawn of the Ottoman age, that the paths of the two began seriously to diverge, the West exploiting the scientific method with its adjunct of experimentation and developing technical knowledge with the resultant greater control over physical nature, while the East remained unmindful of all that. By the end of the eighteenth century the divergence had reached its limit and the two cultures began to come together again.[1]

In this process of cultural cross-fertilization al-ʿIrāq had no significant share. Catholic missionaries had been admitted to Baghdād and al-Baṣrah as early as the seventeenth century but had left no dent on its Moslem society. Of the ʿIrāqis hardly any but officers and functionaries trained in Constantinople were exposed to modern ideas, and those were of a special brand. But the country was wide open to commercial penetration. As the British consolidated their position in the Persian Gulf, commercial infiltration led eventually to political penetration and the country was drawn into the orbit of world affairs.

Political penetration

Ibrāhīm's invasion of Syria and Napoleon's invasion of Egypt produced in a sense the same results: they closed the ancient order of decentralized authority in both lands and ushered in a new era of centralized dependence. More than that, they threw these lands into the cockpit of foreign imperial machinations. The expansionist trends of the Great Powers began to clash there as nowhere else. Especially keen was the rivalry between England and France, each endeavouring to obtain for herself a preponderating influence in Egyptian and Syrian affairs for the same reason: securing the fullest measure of advantage for her trade with India and the Far East. Many of the wars of the nineteenth century may be traced to some origin in the Near East. The Crimean War (1854–6) had as one of its causes conflicting claims on the part of France and Russia for the protection of the holy places in Palestine.

[1] Sarton, *Introduction*, vol. iii, pp. 21-2.

The opening of the Suez Canal in 1869 enhanced the strategic importance of these lands and accelerated their re-entry upon the scene of world trade and world affairs. The canal soon became an integral part of the life-line of international communication and compensated for the loss sustained through the discovery of the route around the Cape of Good Hope.[1] The digging of the canal, a hundred miles long, cost about £20,000,000, most of which was raised by public subscription in Europe, chiefly in France. The khedivial shares were 176,602 at £20 each, which in 1875 were purchased by the British government.

The British occupy Egypt

In Egypt the extravagance of Ismā'īl, in whose reign the canal was opened, led to state bankruptcy and eventually to European intervention. In consideration of Ismā'īl's generous offer to double Egypt's tribute, the Porte bestowed upon him (1866 and 1873) the right of primogeniture for his family and the title of khedive,[2] which amounted almost to an acknowledgment of sovereignty. In 1879 a dual control by England and France was established over the land, and the khedive was deposed. Meantime the grievances of the army, which was officered mostly by Circassians, and of the peasantry, which suffered under heavy taxation, conscription and a system of *corvée* by which the government could force any able-bodied male to work for little or no pay on public projects often of doubtful utility, found a champion in an army officer, Aḥmad 'Arābi, who was himself of peasant stock.[3] The insurrection was brought to a sudden end by the British victory at al-Tall al-Kabīr (Tell el-Kebir) on September 13, 1882, and the banishment of 'Arābi.[4] The occasion provided the British with a chance to occupy the land which, however, remained under nominal Turkish suzerainty until shortly after the outbreak of the first World War, when England declared a protectorate over Egypt. The Khedive 'Abbās Ḥilmi was then deported and his uncle Ḥusayn Kāmil, with the title of sultan, succeeded.[5] Fu'ād, who in 1917 followed his brother Ḥusayn, was proclaimed *malik* (king) in February 1922, at which time the protectorate

[1] See above, pp. 727-8.

[2] Per. *khadīw*, lord, ruler. For the Arabic text of the firman consult Zaydān, *Ta'rīkh Miṣr*, vol. ii, pp. 206-8.

[3] For more on him consult Zaydān, *Tarājim*, vol. i, pp. 229-52.

[4] For a defence of the 'Arābi case by an Englishman, consult Wilfrid S. Blunt, *Secret History of the English Occupation of Egypt* (New York, 1922), pp. 323-63.

[5] Consult table above, p. 726, n. 1.

was terminated, Egypt was declared independent and a constitution was promulgated. This concession by England was not made without struggle on the part of the natives. The nationalist leader, Sa'd Zaghlūl, was a follower of 'Arābi and, like him, the son of a peasant, but more capable and more highly educated. In 1919 this fiery lawyer, a pupil of Jamāl-al-Dīn al-Afghāni and a former editor of *al-Waqā'i' al-Miṣrīyah* under Muḥammad 'Abduh,[1] sought permission from the British to leave the country with a delegation (*wafd*) to plead its cause before the Peace Conference in Paris and in London but was rebuffed and sent to Malta, an act which immediately made a national hero of him. His and his party's efforts were crowned with success when, in 1936, an Anglo-Egyptian treaty was signed stipulating the withdrawal of the British troops of occupation to the Canal zone, the relinquishing of British responsibility for the life and property of foreigners in favour of the Egyptian government and the rendition of reciprocal aid against enemies involving the use of ports, aerodromes and means of communication.

A bloodless military coup in 1952 dethroned Fu'ād's son, King Fārūq (Farouk), abolished the monarchy and led, in 1954, to a republic headed by Colonel Jamāl 'Abd-al-Nāṣir (Nasser), whose bold stand against Israeli, British and French invaders in 1956 raised him to the rank of a Pan-Arab hero. He has since introduced political and economic reforms of the socialistic type.

French and British mandates

In the Arab Crescent political intervention took the form of mandates, with the British established in Palestine and al-'Irāq, and the French in Syria and Lebanon subsequent to the first World War. France's interest rested on economic considerations, a policy of prestige as a counterbalance to British influence and *amitié traditionnelle* going back to Crusading days [2] and sanctioned by the capitulations granted by Sulaymān the Magnificent to Francis I.[3] It was French troops who, in 1860, were landed, with the consent of the great powers, on the Lebanese shore as a measure of security against further massacre.[4]

The administration of these mandates, termed class A, fell short of the ideal set in the covenant of the League of Nations that the well-being of the mandated peoples formed "a sacred trust of civilization" and that the chief concern of the mandatory power

[1] See below, pp. 753-5.
[2] See above, p. 594.
[3] Cf. above, p. 728.
[4] See above, pp. 735-6.

was to provide such advice and assistance as might be necessary to achieve their full independence. Especially provoking were the grievances felt by the Syrians who charged French officials with employing the same colonial methods as in North Africa, use of the native government as a façade, failure to take cognizance of the rising national spirit, discouragement of the use of Arabic, depreciating the native currency by tying it to the franc, playing one party or sect against another and resorting to repressive measures involving espionage, imprisonment and exile.[1] Dividing the country into several *états* for administrative purposes and ceding the sanjāq of Alexandretta to Turkey on the eve of the second World War were other major complaints. Any benefits that might have accrued to the mandated territories by way of maintaining law and order, improving communications, widening areas of cultivation, extending facilities of education and setting up the framework of a modern government and modernized society were not enough to stem the tide of rising discontent. Rebellion broke out in Jabal al-Durūz in July 1925. It soon spread to Damascus and neighbouring towns. The reaction thus set off did not cease until the last French troops were expelled in 1945 from Syrian soil. That was two years after Lebanon, which had started with amicable relations with the French mandate, had succeeded in freeing itself from it and proclaiming itself a republic.

Al-'Irāq had even earlier begun to pursue a hostile course against the British mandate. The rebellion of 1920, which started among the tribes on the lower Euphrates and in the holy cities of al-Najaf and Karbalā',[2] led the British to substitute indirect for direct rule. Fayṣal, second son of King Ḥusayn,[3] was crowned in August 1921 constitutional king over al-'Irāq after occupying the improvised Syrian throne from March 8 to July 25, 1920. Several treaties followed, in one of the most important of which, that of

[1] George Antonius, *Arab Awakening* (Philadelphia, 1939), pp. 372-6; Albert H. Hourani, *Syria and Lebanon* (Oxford, 1946), pp. 176-8.

[2] Philip W. Ireland, *'Irāq: A Study in Political Development* (New York, 1938), pp. 266-76.

[3]

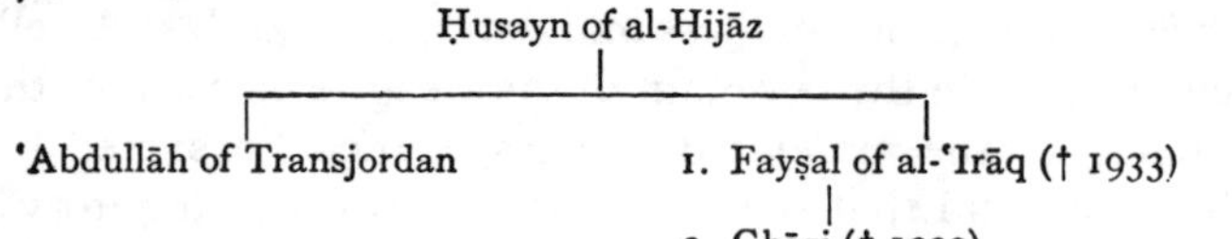

December 1927, Britain recognized al-'Irāq as independent and entered into a twenty-five-year alliance with it. The treaty of June 1930 was decisive: Britain renounced its mandatory rights and recognized the full sovereignty of al-'Irāq.[1] Credit for this achievement should be given to the statesmanship of King Fayṣal I (1921–33), whose régime, however, became discredited under his second successor. In a military coup in 1958 Fayṣal II (1939–58) was slaughtered with his regent uncle and prime minister, and a socialist republic was established.

An Egyptian reformer

The Arab peoples at this time presented a seeming paradox: resisting with one arm European advances while with the other receiving and adopting European ideas and techniques. The new acquisitions from Europe were utilized in the fight against Europeans. Of the numberless novel ideas imported from the West, nationalism and political democracy were undoubtedly the most powerful. The espousal of nationalism encouraged the principle of self-determination and both led to the struggle for independence from foreign rule. Meantime the new ideology from the West, with its stress on secular and material values and the importance it attaches to ethnic limitations and geographic boundaries, ran counter to the most cherished traditions of Islam, with its concepts of religious universality, political theocracy and exclusive sovereignty. Pan-Islam rather than Pan-Arabism would be the ideal toward which Moslems should strive. The conflict was on internal as well as external levels. In Egypt of the late nineteenth century the intellectual climate was rendered congenial for the reception and growth of the new concepts mainly through the writings and speeches of the liberal reformer Muḥammad 'Abduh (1849–1905), who rose to the highest religious position of his land, that of mufti. Muḥammad 'Abduh had for teacher Jamāl-al-Dīn al-Afghāni (1839–97), the first chief agent in the inception of modernism in Islam.[2] Born in Afghanistan, Jamāl-al-Dīn sojourned in India, Makkah and Constantinople before taking up his residence in Egypt, where he identified himself with the movement which culminated in the 'Arābi uprising[3]

[1] Ireland, pp. 409-18; for Arabic text of the treaty consult 'Abd-al-Razzāq al-Ḥasani, *Ta'rīkh al-'Irāq al-Siyāsi* (Baghdād, 1948), vol. ii, pp. 197-204.

[2] On modernism in Islam consult H. A. R. Gibb, *Modern Trends in Islam* (Chicago, 1945), pp. 39 *seq.*

[3] See above, p. 750. For more on Jamāl-al-Dīn consult Charles C. Adams, *Islam and Modernism in Egypt* (London, 1933), pp. 4 *seq.*; Zaydān, *Tarājim*, vol. ii, pp 5[illegible] 60.

Muḥammad ʿAbduh was exiled to Syria for complicity in this uprising. The decadent condition of Islam weighed heavily on his heart and mind. He followed ibn-Taymīyah[1] in the condemnation of superstitions and accretions that had contaminated the faith. His prescription embraced intellectual and political revivification of religion together with political unification under one supreme head The man who had studied and taught at al-Azhar and

MUḤAMMAD ʿABDUH, MODERN EGYPTIAN REFORMER

edited with Jamāl-al-Dīn an Arabic paper in Paris, maintained that basically there was no conflict between Islam and science. He interpreted certain koranic passages rationally and recognized the insufficiency of Islamic scholasticism.[2] While Jamāl-al-Dīn advocated political revolution, Muḥammad ʿAbduh advocated religious awakening to bring about reform. More than any other modern writers, these two contributed to the breaking of the scholastic shell which had encased Islam since medieval times. While neither achieved fully what he set out to do, yet both left an intellectual progeny which counted in its membership Qāsim Amīn († 1908), the first to attack vehemently polygamy, divorce

[1] See above, p. 689.

[2] For more on him consult Muḥammad Rashīd Riḍa, *Ta'rīkh al-Ustādh al-Imām al-Shaykh Muḥammad ʿAbduh*, 3 vols. (Cairo, 1324); Adams, pp. 106-10.

and the use of the veil[1] and Muḥammad Rashīd Riḍa († 1935), born in al-Qalamūn, North Lebanon, who went to Egypt in 1897, edited Muḥammad 'Abduh's works,[2] wrote his biography and carried on in the magazine *al-Manār* his tradition. Reconstructing Arab society on a democratic political basis and reconciling Islam and the modern world remain the greatest tasks confronting the contemporary generation.

Nationalism

Arab nationalism started from a wide base—the thesis that all Arabic-speaking peoples were one nation. It began as a purely intellectual movement having for pioneers mostly Syrian intellectuals, more specifically Christian Lebanese, educated at the American University of Beirūt and operating in Egypt.[3] Its early manifestations in the 1870s were revived interest in the Arabic classics and research in Islamic history. A consciousness of the past glory of the Moslem empire and of the brilliant cultural achievements of the Arabs suggested a future possibility. Political awakening came in the wake of intellectual awakening. Political passivity gave way to political activity; for once in centuries change became a desideratum. Everywhere the movement fed upon resistance to Western imperialism.

Before long this nascent Pan-Arab movement was confronted with varied local problems. In Egypt the main hurdle was British occupation. Opposition to British rule began to absorb Egyptian interest. Then and there Egyptian nationalism was born, parting company with Arab nationalism and developing provincial aspects. Egypt for the Egyptians became the battle cry of the new order. With the further fragmentation of the Arab East, consequent upon the first World War, Arab nationalism suffered further fragmentation. In Syria it concentrated its force against the imposition of the French mandate. Lebanon, which was first favourably disposed toward the French mandate, became in the second World War equally bitter. Likewise in Palestine hostility to the British mandate and to its adjunct, political Zionism—which has since eventuated in the birth of Israel—generated a local type of national feeling. Even tiny Transjordan, which was amputated by the British in February 1921 from South Syria and

[1] His *Taḥrīr al-Mar'ah* (emancipation of woman) (Cairo, 1316) was translated by O. Rescher into German (Stuttgart, 1928).

[2] Chief among which was *Tafsīr al-Qur'ān al-Ḥakīm*, 8 vols. (Cairo, 1346).

[3] Antonius, pp. 79-86.

made a new state under the Amīr ʿAbdullāh, developed a measure of nationhood of its own. Its creation was meant to appease ʿAbdullāh, who had resented the dethronement of his brother Fayṣal, and to act as buffer against the Bedouins. The amīr became, in 1946, king of Transjordan and in 1949 head of the Hāshimite Kingdom of Jordan (*al-Mamlakah al-Urdunnīyah al-Hāshimīyah*). A pronounced ʿIrāqi nationalism was born in the 1920s largely as a reaction against British imperialism.

As nationalism struggled against foreign powers, political democracy contended with native feudalism. Liberty had internal as well as external opponents. Throughout the Arab East feudalism continued to be a dominant social feature with political complications. The system centred on chiefs who held power by virtue of descent and the accumulation of extensive land property. It was at first supported by a vassalage not of birth so much as by appointment, a hierarchy of *muqāṭiʿji's*,[1] as called in Lebanon and Syria, to whom taxes were farmed out and who exercised even penal powers. As these vassals acquired wealth, their office became hereditary, too. The institution and functioning of a democratic form of government against such a background was not an easy task. The search for a new political structure has not yet ended. Politically, no less than socially and economically, the entire Arab East is still in a state of transition.

Trend toward union

If the first World War severed the Arab components of the Ottoman empire and set them on the way to full or semi-nationhood, the second World War, combined with the threat of political Zionism, which was viewed by Arabs everywhere as an intrusive movement, contributed to bringing those parts closer together. Common interest and the rising feeling of solidarity found expression in the pact of the League of Arab States, signed in Cairo, March 1945. The pact indicates a firm intention to promote co-operation among member states in matters relating to education, trade and communication. It provides for consultation in case of aggression against any member state and forbids the use of force in settlement of disputes among them. To the membership of the League, consisting of Egypt, Syria, Lebanon, al-ʿIrāq, Transjordan, Suʿūdi Arabia and al-Yaman, were added the newly declared independent states of Morocco, Tunisia,

[1] See above, p. 746.

Libya, Sudan, al-Kuwayt and Algeria. A bloodless military coup in 1961 broke off the weak three-year-old chain connecting Syria with Egypt and forming the United Arab Republic. Al-Yaman, which had related itself loosely to the union, soon followed suit, and in the autumn of 1962 experienced another one of those military coups current in the Near East, aiming at replacing the imamate-kingdom by a republic with socialist leanings. The record in such coups is held by Syria, which in twenty years ending February 1966 experienced no less than thirteen coups—some unsuccessful. Of all the Arab republics of the area, Lebanon has been the most stable.

Originators of the third monotheistic religion, beneficiaries of the other two, co-sharers with the West of the Greco-Roman cultural tradition, holders aloft of the torch of enlightenment throughout medieval times, generous contributors to European renaissance, the Arabic-speaking peoples have taken their place among the awakened, forward-marching independent nations of the modern world. With their rich heritage and unmatched natural resource of oil, they should be able to make a significant contribution to the material and spiritual progress of mankind.

INDEX

Titles of books, as well as Arabic words and technical terms occurring in the text, in italics.
Initial letters of book-titles and of certain Oriental nouns capitalized.
Main references indicated in heavy type.
In pronouncing Arabic names the accent generally falls on the long vowel bearing the macron (-); the ' stands for a glottal stop; the ' for a deep guttural that has no correspondent in English; such dotted letters as *ṣ* and *ṭ* are emphatically sounded; *aw* and *ay* are diphthongs.
Of the prefixes listed below, al- means the; abu-, father of; ibn-, son of; dhu-, possessor of; umm-, mother of; 'Abd-, slave (servant) of.

THE END